PRAISE FOR

CITY OF DREAMS

"Mr. Anbinder has provided a valuable service by crafting a single volume that focuses solely on New York as a gateway, a haven and a crucible that forged the fates of millions of immigrants who in turn shaped the destiny of our nation."
— *Wall Street Journal*

"*City of Dreams* is a rich, rewarding history of New York's master narrative: the expansive story of the city's immigrant past and present. It's a necessary book for any reader — New Yorker or not — curious to know the astonishing sweep of transforming migrations that have made the city the polyglot extravaganza that it is."
— Philip Roth

"At last! A history of New York's immigrant experience from Peter Minuit right up to the present day, meticulously researched and wonderfully well written. *City of Dreams* will captivate readers and historians alike."
— Kevin Baker, author of *The Big Crowd*

"Enlightening, impressive, and thorough, *City of Dreams* is a monumental endeavor: a great resource that fills in many historical blanks, and a riveting saga with something for everyone. And in these times of so much divisiveness and xenophobia, a necessary book, too. Tyler Anbinder reminds us that the dreams that brought my Dominican family to Nueva York are the very bedrock and foundation of this country."
— Julia Alvarez, author of *How the García Girls Lost Their Accents*

"Like the city of New York itself, Tyler Anbinder's *City of Dreams* is a marvel — a work of astonishing breadth and depth that weaves many threads into a compelling whole. Anbinder's vibrant narrative stretches from the Dutch of New Amsterdam to the Fujianese of Sunset Park, from the draft riots to the Crown Heights riot, depicting waves of immigrants who have overcome persistent nativism to transform the city, the nation, and themselves."
— T. J. Stiles, author of the Pulitzer Prize–winning biographies *Custer's Trials* and *The First Tycoon*

"A tale of tragedy and triumph that comes with political teeth . . . Anbinder is a master at taking a history with which many readers will be familiar — tenement houses, temperance societies, slums — and making it new, strange, and heartbreakingly vivid. The stories of individuals, including those of the entrepreneurial Steinway brothers and the tragic poet Pasquale D'Angelo, are undeniably compelling, but it's Anbinder's stunning image of New York as a true city of immigrants that captures the imagination."

— *Publishers Weekly*, starred review

"This thoroughgoing work offers a host of immigrant sagas that were integral to the creation of the New York City cauldron . . . [Anbinder] impressively conveys the sense of a city truly forged by the people who were determined to live and work there . . . An endlessly fascinating kaleidoscope of American history. A fantastic historical resource."

— *Kirkus Reviews*, starred review

"Full of fascinating, rock-solid history and provides compelling texture behind the larger trends . . . Balanced and excellent."

— *Booklist*, starred review

CITY OF DREAMS

CITY OF DREAMS

*The 400-Year Epic History
of Immigrant New York*

Tyler Anbinder

Mariner Books
Houghton Mifflin Harcourt
BOSTON   NEW YORK

First Mariner Books edition 2017
Copyright © 2016 by Tyler Anbinder

For information about permission to reproduce selections from this book, write to
trade.permissions@hmhco.com or to Permissions, Houghton Mifflin Harcourt
Publishing Company, 3 Park Avenue, 19th Floor, New York, New York 10016.

www.hmhco.com

Library of Congress Cataloging-in-Publication Data is available.
ISBN 978-0-544-10465-5
ISBN 978-1-328-74551-4 (pbk.)

Book design by Chloe Foster

Printed in the United States of America
DOC 10 9 8 7 6 5 4 3 2 1

The author wishes to thank Guernica Editions for permission
to reprint Pascal D'Angelo's poem "Omnis Sum."

An earlier version of chapter 10 previously appeared in Daniel Peart and
Adam I. P. Smith, *Practicing Democracy: Popular Politics in the United States from
the Constitution to the Civil War* (Charlottesville, 2015), and is reproduced here
in revised form with permission of the University of Virginia Press.

To Lisa, Maya, and Celia, with all my love

CONTENTS

MAPS

PROLOGUE

AS MIDNIGHT DREW NEAR on New Year's Eve 1891, New Yorkers thronged lower Broadway. Its watering holes had been packed for hours, with revelers throwing back shots of whiskey, hot toddies, and eggnog as they prepared to brave the cold for the traditional outdoor countdown. It seemed as if every city resident, young and old, man and woman, native and newcomer, was out in the streets blowing a "fish horn," the favorite New Year's noisemaker of the era. In the final minutes before midnight, thousands surged out of the bars, brownstones, and tenements of lower Manhattan toward two traditional spots where New Yorkers had been celebrating this occasion for generations.

The largest crowd squeezed into City Hall Park, the nine-acre triangle of land that lies just east of Broadway and south of Chambers Street. "Flags floated over the City Hall," wrote a *New York Times* reporter who was there that night, and "small boys festooned the bare limbs of the trees; calcium lights shed a glare upon the crowd, and people pushed and jostled and tooted horns and gave each other good greeting." When the hands of the City Hall clock both reached twelve, a band positioned on the front steps struck up "Hail, Columbia." "Momentarily the fish-horn orchestra was dumb," noted the *Times* correspondent, as the crowd paid its respects to what was then considered the American "national song." (Only in 1931, by which point "Hail, Columbia" had fallen out of favor, did Congress designate "The Star-Spangled Banner" as the United States' first "national anthem.") The moment the band concluded the patriotic tune, the crowd "burst forth with redoubled fury. Men shouted, the band played, the elevated and bridge locomotives shrieked their welcome, and red lights were burned."

Barely a half mile to the south, thousands more gathered around Trinity Church, at the corner of Broadway and Wall Street, to partake of another New

The *Nevada,* the ship that carried Annie Moore and
her brothers to New York in December 1891.

York tradition — hearing Trinity's famous bells "ring in" the New Year. Yet "the horn-blowing of the multitude" around the church was so deafening that "it was impossible to hear even the sounding of the hour of 12 by the 'Great Tom,' the mammoth of the chime of bells." On a normal night Great Tom could be heard as far away as Long Island and New Jersey. But on this occasion, the bell master's selection of "peals, triplets, roulades, carols, and the like" was completely drowned out by the din of the jubilant, drunken, raucous revelers.[1]

At the stroke of midnight a mile farther south, seventeen-year-old Annie Moore was probably in her bunk in the aft starboard steerage compartment of the S.S. *Nevada,* which lay at anchor in New York Harbor off the southern tip of Manhattan. Somewhere close by were Annie's younger brothers, fifteen-year-old Anthony and twelve-year-old Philip. The three Moores, all natives of the city of Cork, were coming to New York to join their parents, Matthew and Julia, and their older siblings, twenty-one-year-old Mary and nineteen-year-old Cornelius, who had ventured to America four years earlier and were living in lower Manhattan at 32 Monroe Street, a few blocks from the waterfront, just north of the Brooklyn Bridge.[2]

The *Nevada* was no luxury liner. It was an exceedingly low and narrow vessel, 346 feet long but only 43 feet wide at its broadest point, with one short exhaust funnel amidships and a mast fore and aft just in case the engines gave out. The ship had been plying the route from Liverpool to New York via Queenstown, County Cork, since 1869, just as steamships had begun to outnumber sailing ships on transatlantic crossings. The *Nevada* certainly was a sturdy ship; when it collided with the *Romano* in 1884, it was the other vessel that sank to the bottom of the Atlantic. But by 1891 it had clearly seen better days. The ship's steerage compartments had once overflowed with English, Irish, and Scandinavian immigrants, sometimes a thousand or more on a single voyage. On this journey, however, it held only 127 passengers, most of them impoverished Russian Jews fleeing discrimination and persecution in tsarist Russia. It took the *Nevada* eleven days to chug its way from Ireland to New York, while other ships could make the voyage in six. In 1891 the *Nevada* was a ship for those who could afford no better. Five years later, its owners would sell it for scrap.[3]

The *Nevada* had arrived in New York Harbor too late on the thirty-first for its passengers to be processed by immigration officials, so Annie and her shipmates were forced to spend New Year's Eve aboard the steamer. The twenty or so first- and second-class passengers, with private or semiprivate cabins, probably celebrated the occasion slurping New York's famous oysters and sipping champagne with the captain in the ship's elegant (albeit dated) dining salon. The remaining 107 passengers would have been confined either to the small portion of deck where they were allowed to take fresh air or to their fetid, airless steerage quarters in the bowels of the ship.[4]

For the immigrants on the *Nevada* who, like Annie, would be reuniting in New York with parents, spouses, and other loved ones after years of separation, this last night of waiting, just yards from their destination, must have been excruciating. Add to this anticipation the excitement of New Year's Eve and the din of the celebrations all around them in Manhattan, Brooklyn, and New Jersey, and we can assume that Annie, Anthony, and Philip probably got very little sleep.[5]

Another person who had reason to sleep restlessly that night was Colonel John B. Weber. The forty-nine-year-old Buffalo native had always brimmed with ambition. Enlisting in the Union army as a private at age eighteen, he achieved the rank of colonel two days before his twenty-first birthday, making him the youngest colonel, North or South, in the entire Civil War. Nor was he lacking in idealism, for the command he chose upon his promotion was one many other Union officers refused — the supervision of a regiment of African American troops drawn from the emancipated slaves of Louisiana. Weber, who as an infantryman had survived some of the bloodiest fighting of the war at Malvern Hill outside Richmond, saw little combat with his black troops, who were stationed in Texas, far from the main theaters of war. At the conclusion of the conflict, Weber entered politics back in Buffalo, serving two terms in Congress. After he lost his bid for a third term in 1888, a political patron secured

Weber an appointment as the first federal superintendent of immigration for the port of New York.[6]

Weber's new post was created in the spring of 1890, a moment when responsibility for the processing of immigrants was in flux. In the first two centuries after New York City was founded, immigrants underwent no inspection whatsoever. They did not need passports or any other documents to gain entry into or establish residence in the British colonies or the young United States. Around the time of the American Revolution, doctors began boarding immigrant ships a few miles from the city to inspect the passengers for signs of smallpox, yellow fever, typhus, and (beginning in the nineteenth century) cholera. Sick immigrants, or in some cases everyone on board, would be quarantined on Staten Island, five miles south of Manhattan, until they were either no longer contagious or dead. But other than this fairly cursory medical inspection, immigrants had to meet no requirements of any kind; they simply walked off their ships and onto the streets of New York to begin their new lives in America.

In 1855 New York's commissioners of emigration, whose main jobs to this point had been to run the quarantine and oversee the care of indigent immigrants, decided to create an immigrant reception station at the southern tip of Manhattan in Castle Garden, a cavernous indoor arena built within the surviving walls of a post-Revolutionary fortification known as Castle Clinton. They did so not out of a desire to better inspect the newcomers and thereby protect Americans from them. Rather, the Castle Garden immigration center was founded to protect the immigrants from *Americans*. Each arriving ship would be met at the docks by a swarm of "immigrant runners," men who would besiege the dazed and bewildered newcomers, grab their luggage, and lead them to boardinghouses whose owners typically gouged them, then held their luggage hostage if the newcomers refused to pay. The commissioners of emigration could not regulate the runners at a hundred different docks all over town, so they made Castle Garden into an immigration depot, hoping that if all the runners had to congregate in a single place, the police could better supervise them and the immigrants could be warned to resist their lures and promises.

By 1890, however, Castle Garden was no longer large enough to hold the thousands of immigrants who arrived in New York each day. In this era, each transatlantic vessel might hold a thousand passengers or more, and while on average five ships arrived per day, it was not unheard of for ten ships to enter the harbor in a twenty-four-hour period, especially during immigration's "high season" from April to June. Many immigrants remained in Castle Garden overnight or longer, waiting to be met by loved ones and stretching the facility's capacity to the breaking point.

The need to replace Castle Garden increased as the United States began to modify its open-door policy. In 1875 the first immigration restrictions in American history banned the landing of convicts, prostitutes, and Chinese "contract laborers" (those who signed labor agreements before they arrived in the United States and could ascertain the prevailing wages). Seven years later, "idiots," the insane, those likely to become a "public charge," all contract laborers, and all Chinese laborers were added to the list of illegal immigrants. By the time Annie Moore arrived in New York, Congress had also barred paupers, polygamists, and those with "loathsome" or "dangerous contagious diseases" as well. As the restrictions multiplied, federal authorities began to doubt that the state's immigration inspectors were up to the task. Every worker at Castle Garden, from the commissioners of emigration right down to the baggage handlers, had received his job as a favor to some politico. Furthermore, the board of commissioners that ran Castle Garden had become dysfunctional by the late 1880s as a result of feuding within its ranks.[7]

And so it was in April 1890 that Weber, a resident of Buffalo who admitted that he knew nothing about immigrants, took control of immigration policy enforcement at the American port that received more of the newcomers than all the others combined. Immediately he began the search for a new location for the inspection of immigrants, and a month later Ellis Island, then serving as the navy's New York gunpowder storage facility, was selected. It took only eighteen months to triple the size of the island with landfill and construct the proper facilities. Weber soon announced that the Ellis Island immigrant inspection station would open on January 1, 1892. While construction progressed, Weber spent several months crisscrossing eastern Europe to investigate the "immigration problem" at the behest of President Benjamin Harrison.[8]

Just after dawn on New Year's Day, Weber boarded a small ferry at the southern end of Manhattan. Skies were cloudy, the temperature was in the low thirties, and the wind, though light on shore, blew briskly over the water. The launch arrived at Ellis Island around 8:00 a.m., at which point Weber began to scrutinize the hulking new facility one last time to insure that that the inspectors, translators, railroad ticket agents, baggage handlers, commissary workers, doctors, and nurses knew their assignments. The mammoth main building, three stories of Georgia pine measuring 400 feet long and 165 feet wide, with turrets at each corner, could easily accommodate as many as fifteen thousand immigrants per day, Weber assured the press. Around 10:30, when the colonel was satisfied that all the employees as well as invited dignitaries and newspaper reporters were ready, he ordered the flags to be dipped three times, the prearranged signal that the transport carrying the first boatload of immigrants should proceed to Ellis Island.[9]

An hour or so earlier, a ferry festooned in red, white, and blue bunting had

The original Ellis Island immigration depot. After fire destroyed this wooden structure in 1897, it was replaced by the iconic brick reception buildings that we associate with Ellis Island today.

tied up alongside the *Nevada*. Annie and the other steerage passengers clambered aboard while sailors brought the immigrants' trunks, bags, and bundles onto the ferry. The reason why their transport was so festively decorated soon spread among the passengers: of the three immigrant ships that had spent the night anchored in New York Harbor, theirs had been chosen to be the first processed at New York's new immigrant landing station.

Had the "ladies" and "gentlemen" who occupied the *Nevada*'s first- and second-class cabins been aboard the ferry, Weber undoubtedly would have granted them the honor of disembarking first. But immigration officials had already processed the "cabin passengers" on board the *Nevada*. Once the small ferry with Annie and the other steerage passengers cast off, a pilot steered the *Nevada* up the Hudson to Pier 38, just south of Houston Street on the west side of Manhattan, where these travelers could disembark at their leisure. Only steerage passengers ever set foot on Ellis Island.[10]

Exactly how seventeen-year-old Annie Moore, whom the *Times* described as "a little rosy-cheeked Irish girl," came to be at the front of the line waiting to descend the gangplank onto Ellis Island is not clear. According to one newspaper account, an Italian at the head of the queue gave Annie his place when he saw her in tears, seemingly overcome by the emotions of the moment. In contrast, a reporter for Joseph Pulitzer's *World* (not a paper renowned for high journalistic standards) wrote that "a big German with a shawl rolled thirty or forty times around his neck had one foot on the gang plank. He was about to earn fame as the first foreigner to set foot on Ellis Island" when one Mike Tierney (appar-

ently a sailor on the ferry) shouted "Ladies first!" while simultaneously pulling the German back and pushing young Annie forward. Most press accounts
mention indecision at the top of the gangplank, suggesting that the identity of
the first immigrant to land was one detail that Weber did not dictate.[11]

In any event, "little" Annie walked down the ramp first. Weber and other
dignitaries immediately hustled her and her brothers inside the vast wooden
edifice to a tall lectern-like desk, where an official recorded her name, age, occupation, last place of residence, and intended destination in the United States,
which she listed as her parents' home on Monroe Street. Colonel Weber then
made a short speech welcoming her to the United States and handed her a glis-
tening $10 gold coin. Father Callahan of the Mission of Our Lady of the Holy
Rosary (an organization that provided assistance to young female Catholic immigrants) then blessed her and gave her a silver coin, "while another bystander
supplemented the gift with a five dollar gold piece." With her brothers in tow,
Annie then "hurried along to the local waiting-room, where she found her parents, and in less than half an hour from the time she landed she was on her way
to the city to spend the rest of New Year's Day."[12]

Over the next sixty-two years, 15 million immigrants followed in Annie
Moore's footsteps through the inspection rooms of Ellis Island to begin their
new lives in America. Annie was quickly forgotten.

Her name did not appear again in the columns of the *Times* until 1965, when
she was mentioned in a story on a presidential proclamation declaring the abandoned, crumbling Ellis Island complex a "national shrine" and part of the Statue
of Liberty National Monument. Twelve years later, in an article on "the ghosts
of Ellis Island," *Times* reporter Francis X. Clines invoked Annie's name once
again. "If she is still alive, she is 100 years old," he noted. "If she is dead, there
is regret none of us can hear her colleen's story of what happened after Ellis Island."[13]

Regret that stories such as Moore's seemed lost to history had grown more
widespread at the time Clines toured the remains of Ellis Island, where, as he
reported in his story, plans were already under way to restore the facility and
turn it into a museum of the American immigration experience. The impetus to create such a museum gained momentum from the phenomenal success
of Alex Haley's *Roots* (1976), a book describing the author's efforts to trace his
family history back to Africa, which attracted huge audiences both in print and
as a television miniseries. Equally important was the "white ethnic revival" of
the same period. Ever since World War I, Americans had been encouraged to
downplay their ethnic heritage and think of themselves as "100 percent American." But that imperative waned in the 1970s, perhaps owing to a thaw in the

Cold War, and Americans once again began to more visibly take pride in their ethnic backgrounds and immigrant origins. The opening of the Ellis Island Museum in 1990 was the culmination of these larger trends.[14]

The organizers of the Ellis Island restoration and museum put out a call for the descendants of Annie Moore to come forward. It was answered by Margaret O'Connell Middleton, a seventy-two-year-old resident of Tucson, who reported that her mother, Annie Moore, had moved, after her arrival at Ellis Island, to Hill County, Texas. There she married a descendant of the famed Irish nationalist Daniel O'Connell and started a family. Annie and her children relocated to New Mexico after her husband died, Middleton reported, but on returning to Texas to visit a sick brother in 1923, Moore was run down and killed by a Fort Worth streetcar.[15]

At a ceremony in 1988 marking the kickoff of fund-raising for a family history center in the restored Ellis Island complex, Mrs. Middleton presented a $10 bill to the restoration committee in honor of the $10 gold piece Colonel Weber had given Annie almost one hundred years earlier. Middleton's family members were also on hand in Cobh (as the Irish had renamed Queenstown) in February 1993, when a bronze statue of Annie and her brothers was unveiled near the spot where they had boarded the *Nevada,* and at Ellis Island a few months later when a statue of Annie was dedicated there. Soon, the story of how Annie Moore had sought opportunity in the West, like so many immigrants before her, filled American history textbooks.[16]

Annie Moore and her brothers commemorated in a statue that sits by the docks at Cobh (formerly Queenstown), ten miles southeast of the city of Cork. Large ships taking passengers from Cork to North America departed from Queenstown rather than from Cork itself.

In the fall of 1993, I took my students from the University of Wyoming on a tour of immigration history sites in New York City. On our visit to Ellis Island, we stopped at the new statue of Annie and I told the students the story of her Irish roots and tragic death in Texas. I continued to visit Ellis Island and Annie's statue regularly with my students even after I moved to take a teaching position in Washington, D.C.

One evening in 2004, after many class trips and many lectures to my students about Annie Moore, I was having dinner in Washington with the family of my twelve-year-old son's best friend. His parents, Jackie Judd (a former ABC News correspondent) and Michael Shulman, an investment adviser, asked me about my work. I mentioned my book project on the history of immigrant life in New York City.

Shulman asked if I knew who the first immigrant was to land on Ellis Island.

"Annie Moore, of course," I said.

"Do you know what happened to her?"

"She was killed by a streetcar in Texas," I replied.

"No," he said. "That's what the history books say, but it's not true. The real Annie Moore was my great-aunt. She never left New York City."

I was a bit incredulous, but he impressed me with his certitude. He was confident that the truth would eventually come out.

It did not take long. Several years before that dinner, a genealogist named Megan Smolenyak, working on a historical documentary about immigration to be aired on PBS, had decided to check Margaret O'Connell Middleton's story as part of her research on Annie Moore. The genealogist was shocked to discover that while Middleton's mother was indeed named Annie Moore, census records indicated that she had been born in Illinois, not Cork. Census documents are often inaccurate, but every kind of original source the genealogist could find indicated that Middleton's mother was Illinois-born and could not possibly be the Ellis Island Annie. Smolenyak tried to use those same census records to find out what had happened to the immigrant Annie Moore, but she did not succeed before the documentary was completed. As a result, the story of Annie Moore was left out, and Smolenyak moved on to other assignments.

Her failure to track down the "real" Annie gnawed at Smolenyak, as it would any good genealogist. In the summer of 2006 she offered a $1,000 reward to the online genealogical community for anyone who could discover the fate of the Ellis Island Annie and her descendants.

Young women who later marry are a genealogist's nightmare, because if one does not know their married name, they can be lost forever. So the researchers who took up the challenge focused their attention on Annie's brothers. In a couple of weeks, followers of Smolenyak's blog found evidence that a Philip Moore who had lived in Brooklyn in the mid-twentieth century was the Philip who had accompanied Annie on the *Nevada*. Other records showed that this Philip had a daughter, Anna, who married a man named Shulman, and that among their children was a son named Michael. After several false starts, Smolenyak dialed the phone number of the Michael Shulman with whom I had had dinner. "As soon as I said 'Annie Moore,' he knew instantly: 'That's us,'" she said, describing the call. "I think they're very happy to be found." Just six weeks after Smolenyak posted the challenge on her blog, the mystery of what had happened to the real Annie Moore had been solved.[17]

The real Annie's story after she left Ellis Island was a bit less dramatic than that of Texas Annie but no less interesting, and was far more revealing about the typical life of an Ellis Island immigrant. Like the preponderance of those processed at Ellis Island, Annie settled in New York, and like many, she stayed there her entire life. Also like thousands of scared and misinformed newcomers, Annie lied during her brief Ellis Island interview. She told officials that it was her fifteenth birthday; in fact, "little Annie" was seventeen and a half.

Annie, Anthony, and Philip moved in with their parents and probably their older brother and sister in a tiny apartment in a five-story sliver of a building on Monroe Street. Annie's father was likely at that point a laborer on the docks, the occupation the census recorded for him eight years later in 1900. Money must have been tight, for soon the family had moved out of the somewhat respectable Seventh Ward and into the adjoining Fourth Ward, the most run-down waterfront district on the East River, full of brothels, sailors' boarding-houses, squalid tenements, and rowdy saloons.

It was probably the move to the Fourth Ward that led Annie to meet her future husband, Augustus Joseph Schayer, known to his friends and family as "Gus." Schayer's father, Simon, was a German immigrant from Baden who owned a bakery at 5 Batavia Street, a couple of blocks from where the Moores lived. Simon's claim to fame was that he had invented the macaroon — or to be precise, the modern, filled version. This was apparently no idle boast. He patented his creation in 1885.

It was impossible for an immigrant entrepreneur in the Fourth Ward to protect a patent, and as a result, Simon never did parlay his confectionery innovation into riches. This fact, of course, had a significant impact on Simon's children and their opportunities. His son Gus married Annie in 1895, when he was nineteen and she was twenty, but theirs was never a secure or comfortable life. Annie bore eleven children over the next twenty years, only five of whom survived to adulthood. Infant mortality was common in those days, especially in neighborhoods like the Fourth Ward waterfront, but losing more than half one's children was uncommon even for that era. The maladies listed on the death certificates of her offspring convey not merely their causes of death but a sense of the pain Annie must have felt as each tiny life faded away — "exhaustion w/tubercular pneumonia," "diphtheria and broncho-pneumonia," "haemophilia, . . . bleeding from mouth continuously," "enterocolitis for 24 days," "chronic valvular disease," and perhaps saddest of all "m[a]rasmus," a condition in which an infant cannot put on weight and starves to death. These ailments accompanied a life of poverty in dilapidated tenements with poor ventilation, terrible sanitation, and inadequate medical care. Annie's mother was always nearby to help (Annie and Gus never lived more than three or four blocks from their parents), but even so, the unrelenting march of disease and death must have been hard for Annie to bear.[18]

When Annie's brother Anthony died at age twenty-one in the Bronx, he was initially buried in the city's potter's field, the resting place for those who could not afford a burial plot. Annie's father, Matthew, succumbed to cirrhosis of the liver in 1907 at age fifty-five in the House of Relief, the ward for the indigent in New York Hospital. In January 1909, when Annie's fifty-four-year-old mother, Julia, became ill with chills and fever, Annie and Gus sent her to the city alms-house for medical care. She recovered, but a decade later, suffering from "senile psychosis" (what today we would call Alzheimer's disease), she was again brought by her family to an institution for the poor, the state hospital on Wards Island, where she spent the last seven years of her life until she died, at age seventy, in 1927.[19]

Even so, Annie and Gus were not the poorest of the poor. Gus's income from work as a salesman at the Fulton Street Market must have been decent, at least some of the time. They managed to buy a family plot at Calvary Cemetery in Brooklyn, where they buried their children, albeit without headstones. They could also afford to purchase the occasional family photo. We know that Annie was not lacking for food, either; by her forties she was quite obese. That excess weight must have contributed to her death from heart failure at age forty-nine, in 1924. According to family lore, when she

Annie Moore at about age thirty with one of her eleven children. Only five survived to adulthood.

passed away, her casket was too big to be carried down the narrow staircase and had to be taken out a window instead.[20]

It is a shame that Annie did not survive into her sixties to enjoy some of the good luck that finally came her family's way. In 1938 Gus inherited $3,000 from a mysterious benefactress named Anna Kientsch. At the time, that sum would have conveyed the "economic status" of a $200,000 bequest today. But Gus does not seem to have spent much of his inheritance on himself. He continued to live in the old neighborhood at 90 Oliver Street, in the same tenement where he and Annie had raised their kids.[21]

It is also a shame that Annie did not live long enough to see her clan turn into an almost archetypal New York immigrant family, intermarrying with other transplants from around the globe. Annie's marriage to a German American was considered a mixed marriage in its day, especially since Gus's father, Simon, was probably Jewish. Today, the descendants of Annie and her brothers include representatives from all the other leading New York City immigrant groups—Italians, eastern European Jews, Chinese, and Dominicans. Annie and her brothers, the first immigrants to pass through Ellis Island, truly became prototypical New Yorkers, with lives and families inextricably linked to the New York immigrant experience.

One last mystery surrounds the story of Annie Moore. Colonel Weber, it turns out, did not preside over Ellis Island for very long. When Benjamin Harrison lost his reelection bid to Grover Cleveland eleven months after Ellis Island opened, Weber was forced to make way for an appointee of the new administration. A century later, when the Ellis Island Museum opened, Weber's descendants donated to its archives a few dozen photos dating from his brief tenure as immigration commissioner. Shulman and Smolenyak are convinced that one of them, depicting a girl and two younger boys set apart from a crowd of immigrants, is a photo of Annie and her brothers at Ellis Island on January 1, 1892.

Archivists at Ellis Island insist that this photo cannot be the Moores. It is, they contend, a photo of immigrants at the "Barge Office," a facility at the eastern edge of Battery Park used to process immigrants from the time Castle Garden closed in 1890 until Ellis Island opened in 1892. But Smolenyak notes that the unusual support beams in the background of the photo precisely match those used in the original Ellis Island building. She has offered a $1,000 reward, as yet unclaimed, to anyone who can prove that this photo does not depict the famous trio. Shulman says that the girl in the picture is the spitting image of his mother, while I was struck by the uncanny resemblance that the older boy in the photo bears to Shulman's twin sons, Anthony and Philip. It is hard to imag-

Some of Annie Moore's descendants are convinced that she and her brothers Anthony and Philip are the subjects of this photo, which was donated to the Ellis Island archives by the family of Colonel John B. Weber, the first superintendent of immigration at Ellis Island.

ine, however, that the younger boy in this photograph could be twelve, Philip Moore's true age, even accounting for malnutrition in Ireland. Yet the ship's first officer thought that Philip was only nine and that Annie was thirteen, and the *Times* referred to her as "little" Annie. If Shulman and Smolenyak are ever proved right, then someday this photo may become one of the iconic images of American history.[22]

The story of Annie Moore is a microcosm of the New York — and American — immigrant saga. Families are separated and sometimes reunited. Unrealistic expectations clash with harsh reality. There are tragic deaths and miraculous tales of survival and success. Loved ones are lost, and sometimes found. There are lies and heartache. "Hating one another, loving one another, agreeing and disagreeing in a hundred different languages, a hundred different dialects, a hundred different religions. Crowding one another, and fusing against their wills slowly with one another," is how one immigrant described the New York experience a century ago, a characterization that has pretty much held true for four hundred years.[23]

More than anything else, the immigrants come with dreams — dreams that hunger might become a thing of the past, dreams that restrictions and discrimination might be replaced by rights, and dreams that poverty might be traded for security and opportunity, if not for oneself, then at least for one's children or grandchildren. These dreams characterized the New York immigrant story from the arrival of the city's first Dutch settlers through the heyday of Five Points, the Lower East Side, and Little Italy. Those same dreams dominate the lives of New York's newest immigrants, whether they are Chinese or Guyanese, Jamaican or Dominican, Mexican or Ghanaian. The story of immigrant New York is truly a story of dreams.

City of Dreams attempts to tell the story of New York's immigrants from the founding of the city nearly four hundred years ago to the present day. In order to do justice to the immigrants' compelling life stories yet still cover the entirety of the city's colorful history, I have chosen to focus the narrative on the largest immigrant groups of each era. *City of Dreams* therefore pays particular attention to the Dutch, the English, and the Scots in the pre-Revolutionary years, Irish and German immigrants in the nineteenth century, Italians and eastern European Jews in the early twentieth century, and immigrants from China and the Caribbean in the late twentieth and early twenty-first centuries. As a result, some very visible immigrant groups, such as Greeks and Indians, that never ranked among the most populous foreign-born populations in the city are not addressed to the extent that some readers might hope or expect. I also decided to concentrate on the eras in which immigration to New York was heaviest and on events that were especially important in shaping the city's history and Americans' perceptions of its immigrants. As a result, I allot much more space to the 1770s, 1860s, and 1910s than I do to the early part of the nineteenth century or the middle of the twentieth.

I also devote fewer chapters to recent immigration than I do to earlier large influxes of newcomers. As a historian, I especially value the perspective that hindsight offers, and we are still too close to the most recent immigration to be able to determine which trends and events are defining and which will soon be forgotten. There is also very little existing historical literature on the most recent immigrants for me to rely upon to write their story. Few of their scrapbooks, diaries, and photos have made their way from their grandchildren's attics to archives and historical societies. Social scientists are studying today's immigrants, but their data-heavy, theoretically oriented publications lack the compelling personal narratives that make New York's immigration history so rich and rewarding. I was able to use press coverage to supply some of their stories, but in the end I decided that journalism could take me only so far. Otherwise, *City of Dreams* would have just as many chapters on today's newcomers as it does on those of the great waves of immigration of the past. But I am comforted in the knowledge that a generation from now, historians will be able to document the sagas of New York's newest immigrants with the nuance and detail that their stories so richly deserve.

CITY OF DREAMS

1

SETTLEMENT

PETER MINUIT WAS FURIOUS. It was springtime, 1632, and he had a colony to run, which he directed from a spot — Manhattan Island — that he had personally chosen and bought from the *wilden*, or Indians, known to the Dutch as the Canarsie. He should have been there now organizing fur-trading expeditions up the great river that Henry Hudson had discovered only a few years earlier, directing the planting of a new crop, policing the port of New Amsterdam for smugglers, adjudicating disputes between quarreling settlers, and writing letters trying to induce more Europeans to immigrate to the fledgling colony — *his* colony.

But instead, the forty-three-year-old Minuit was under arrest, in Plymouth, England, of all places, charged with theft of property from England's King Charles. The five thousand beaver pelts in the hold of his ship *Unity* rightfully belonged to Charles, insisted his captors, because Minuit's settlement sat on a continent that Italian explorer Giovanni Caboto had claimed for England in the sixteenth century. Besides, the person who "discovered" Manhattan, Hudson, was himself an Englishman, further confirming England's sovereignty over the territory. Never mind that Hudson's voyages in his ship, *Half Moon*, were sponsored by Dutch merchants.

Minuit, of course, contended that New Amsterdam was Dutch. If an Italian in the employ of England could claim territory for the English, then an Englishman hired by the Dutch could surely claim it for the Netherlands. But the English would not listen to reason. They retorted that even if Hudson had claimed Manhattan for the Dutch, that claim was null and void because Manhattan lay in the northern portion of the English colony of Virginia, established several years *before* Hudson's voyage to North America. The Dutch minister to the Court of St. James's understood that Minuit and his ship were merely pawns in a much larger North American chess game. England could not afford to ruin its amicable relationship with the Netherlands over animal pelts when both nations faced a much more menacing threat from Spain. Yet while the Dutch minister worked confidently but patiently over the course of a month to negotiate the release of the vessel and its passengers, Minuit remained under lock and key in Plymouth. His prospects for regaining the directorship of the colony of New Netherland — already in doubt before he had set sail — diminished with each passing day.[1]

Minuit's journey from obscurity to international incident had been a circuitous one. He had been born in about 1589 in Wesel, a town in the Rhine River valley in the western German duchy of Kleve near the Dutch border. Minuit's parents were Walloons, French-speaking members of the Dutch Reformed Church who originated in the predominantly Catholic region that is now southern Belgium. This district belonged, in theory, to the Netherlands, but Spain had occupied it for more than fifty years. Wallonia had become less tolerant of Protestants under the Spanish Inquisition, and approximately 150,000 Walloons fled the resulting persecution and settled in England, Holland, and the far western German states such as Kleve.[2]

Young Minuit overflowed with ambition. In 1613 he married Gerdruudt Raets, daughter of the mayor of Kleve's capital. Soon they moved to the prosperous central Dutch city of Utrecht, where Minuit learned diamond cutting. Yet the gem trade did not satisfy him. He yearned for something more exciting, more lucrative. Learning that some Walloons had volunteered to serve as the first immigrants to a Dutch colony in North America, Minuit asked to make the journey too. He did not, however, want to commit to living in the wilderness for six years, like the expedition's typical colonists. Nor did he desire employment with the Geoctroyeerde West Indische Compagnie (Dutch West India Company, henceforth WIC), the group financing the expedition. Minuit merely wished to serve as an expedition volunteer who would aid the organizers of the colonization effort in exchange for the opportunity to scout out North American trading opportunities. Having found only thirty or so Walloons initially willing to settle in New Netherland, the WIC agreed to take Minuit too. After all, if Indians attacked or a fire broke out, another able-bodied soul would be welcome, no matter his ulterior motives.[3]

It appears that Minuit arrived in New Amsterdam with the colony's provisional director, Willem Verhulst, in the spring of 1625, about nine months after those thirty original Walloons had begun the arduous work of constructing a colony from scratch in the wilderness thousands of miles from home. The instructions given to Verhulst by the WIC refer to Minuit as a "volunteer" who would explore trading opportunities with the Indians near Fort Orange, modern-day Albany. Three months later, when the WIC sent further directives to Verhulst, it named Minuit to the colony's governing council. Minuit returned to Europe in 1625, but he apparently relished his elevated status in the fledgling colony and arranged to go back there, leaving Holland and his family in January 1626 and arriving in New Amsterdam, most likely via a Dutch possession in the Caribbean, on the fourth of May.[4]

Minuit must have been shocked by what he found upon disembarking in New York Harbor that second time. The very colonists Verhulst was supposed to direct had placed him under arrest. Precisely why the settlers turned on Verhulst is not clear. Some claimed he had misappropriated funds, others that he had cheated the Indians, putting the colonists at risk of attack. Indians had recently ransacked Fort Orange, and the immigrants may have blamed Verhulst. One gets the sense that the colonists simply found him insufferable. So, "on account of the bad conduct of Verhulst," wrote one immigrant in 1626, the colony's council voted upon Minuit's return to make him their new director.[5]

Minuit believed that Verhulst's approach to operating the colony had been completely misguided. Following WIC instructions, Verhulst had divided his tiny contingent of colonists among far-flung settlements that stretched from Cape May to Trenton on what the Dutch called the South River (what we call the Delaware), from New Amsterdam to Albany on what the Dutch labeled the North River (the Hudson), and even farther north and east up the waterway the Dutch called the Fresh River (the Connecticut). The WIC had envisaged the South River settlements as the most important, but Minuit correctly foresaw New Amsterdam as the key trading hub, and reallocated most of the company's resources there. Minuit also decided, probably for defensive purposes, to concentrate most of the WIC's settlers in one place, so he ordered the bulk of the colonists stationed in other places to relocate to New Amsterdam. Finally, while Verhulst had followed WIC orders and made one of New York Harbor's smaller islands, Nut Island (now Governors Island), the headquarters of WIC operations at the mouth of the Hudson, Minuit countermanded that directive, too, and moved the settlement to the much larger island the natives called Mannahatta.[6]

Unlike Nut Island, Mannahatta was inhabited by Indians, so the move there raised the question of how the *wilden* would react. If land that the Dutch wanted to occupy was "inhabited by some Indians," wrote the WIC leadership, "these should not be driven away by force or threats, but should be persuaded by kind words or otherwise by giving them something, to let us live amongst them." WIC instructions dictated that such transactions should be codified in a contract, signed by the Indians "in their manner, since such contracts upon other occasions may be very useful to the Company."[7]

Thus originated the famous transaction popularly known as the "purchase" of Manhattan Island. It is likely that despite the language barrier, both the Indians and the Dutch initially understood it as a long-term agreement to share the island, because for decades afterward Indians continued to live on Manhattan Island and the Dutch made no efforts to evict them. Nonetheless, when the Dutch government's representative in the WIC's governing body wrote from Amsterdam to his superiors in The Hague to describe the arrival of a ship from New Amsterdam, he stated that the settlers "have purchased the Island Manhattes from the Indians for the value of 60 guilders." Minuit did not pay cash but instead gave the Indians "trade goods" — axes, kettles, awls, "duffel cloth," and the like. The idea that the Indians bartered Manhattan for beads is a myth, though it is possible that *wampum,* the Indians' currency made of strung precious seashells, was part of the transaction. The WIC must have been pleased with the deal, for while the company had instructed Verhulst to find a piece of arable land at least two thousand acres in size, Minuit had won the right to settle an island ten times larger. Yet the best feature of Manhattan, Minuit recognized, was its location. Manhattan stood at the mouth of the Hudson and several other rivers, an early twentieth-century historian noted, "like a great natural pier ready to receive the commerce of the world."[8]

Minuit worked to solidify the Dutch presence on Manhattan Island. At the southernmost tip, which was perfectly positioned to catch the breeze coming off the harbor, Minuit oversaw the construction of two windmills: one for grinding grain, the other for sawing lumber. These would dominate the southern Manhattan skyline for decades. Minuit also strove to improve the other major structure in the young settlement — the fort. The colonists had skimped on the defensive structure, substituting sod walls for stone, so Minuit ordered it rebuilt. The immigrants, seeing that New Amsterdam would be a more important outpost than originally envisioned, soon began, in the words of their first pastor, Jonas Michaëlius, "to build sturdy new houses in place of the huts and hovels in which up until now they have not so much lived as lodged." It seemed that New Amsterdam finally had a leader who could make the settlement a success.[9]

But while New Amsterdam continued to expand under Minuit, it did not turn a profit for the WIC. The immigrants sent thousands of beaver pelts back to Amsterdam each year, but the proceeds did not bring in enough to compensate the company for the cost of maintaining fortified settlements, paying the dozens of employees living in the colony, subsidizing the shipping of food and people to North America, and transporting furs back to Europe. Minuit argued that the colony would become more profitable if the WIC invested more in it by financing the emigration of additional colonists, but company officials claimed they could find few Dutchmen willing to risk their lives in the wilds of North America.

The directors started to lose faith in Minuit, in part because of the red ink, and in part because Michaëlius had begun to undermine him by sending reports critical of Minuit's conduct back to company headquarters. Minuit might seem energetic and capable on the surface, wrote the minister, but in fact he was "a slippery man, who under the treacherous mark of honesty is a compound of all iniquity and wickedness." He could deceive WIC officials because "he is accustomed to the lies, of which he is full, and to the imprecations and most awful execrations." Furthermore, although Minuit was a married man, wrote Michaëlius, "he is not free from fornication . . . and deems no one worthy of his favor and protection, who is not of the same kidney as he is." Minuit denied the charges, insisting that Michaëlius was the liar, but the WIC directors, not knowing whom to believe and realizing that such a feud could not be allowed to continue, recalled them both at the end of 1631 for an investigation. Together, the two men, along with other leaders of the colony, boarded the ironically named *Unity,* filled with the year's bounty of furs and timber, and sailed for Amsterdam.[10]

Winter was not the ideal time of year to cross the Atlantic. Passengers struggled to stay warm on the windswept wooden vessel, icebergs were a constant menace, and while hurricane season might be over, winter storms at sea were nearly as brutal. The *Unity* had made it almost all the way across the Atlantic when just such a storm struck. Rather than risk losing his ship, the captain decided to seek shelter in the southwest English port of Plymouth. Minuit expected the Dutch ship to be welcomed by the English; after all, the two Protestant nations were allies against their powerful common enemy, Catholic Spain. But when the English learned that the *Unity* had sailed from "a certain island named Manathans" in North America, authorities in Plymouth arrested Minuit and Michaëlius, insisting that the *Unity's* hold contained *English* property taken from *English* territory without permission. Minuit must have told his captors that the goods originated in territory he had purchased from the Indians, but the English contended that the natives had no right to sell land that already belonged to England.[11]

After they had remained in English custody in Plymouth for more than a month, the Dutch envoy to England finally negotiated the release of the men, their ship, and their cargo. England and the Netherlands could not afford a prolonged diplomatic crisis. But the English had made their point: they laid claim to *all* of North America, including New Amsterdam, which even Michaëlius recognized would eventually be "the key and principal stronghold of the country."[12]

When Minuit finally reached WIC headquarters on the third of May, 1632, the tulips were fading as rapidly as his prospects for reclaiming the director-ship of New Netherland. After a perfunctory hearing, the company officials dismissed Minuit, citing as the cause, of all things, his failure to induce more Dutchmen to settle in New Amsterdam. Minuit could only console himself with the knowledge that they had fired Michaëlius too. But Minuit would have at least a modicum of revenge. After several years of underemployment, he agreed to lead a Swedish expedition aimed at seizing part of New Netherland in the name of Christina, Sweden's eleven-year-old queen. Minuit, with two ships and fewer than one hundred men, planned to take control of the South River, which he knew would be lightly guarded because he himself had ordered the transfer to New Amsterdam of most of the Dutch colonists previously sta-tioned there. Minuit's plan succeeded. In the spring of 1638 the colony of New Sweden, encompassing the Delaware River valley as far north as the future cit-ies of Trenton and Philadelphia, was born. It would remain a thorn in the side of the Dutch and English for nearly twenty years. Yet once again Minuit did not get a chance to enjoy the fruits of his labor. Ever on the lookout for the deal of a lifetime, he died in a Caribbean hurricane in August 1638. He had sailed there hoping to buy tobacco that he could resell at a steep markup in Europe, whose inhabitants had developed an insatiable demand for North America's "vile weed."[13]

It might seem surprising that the Dutchmen who formed the WIC would risk so much hard-earned money on a highly risky fur-trading venture thousands of miles from home on a continent that Europeans barely knew and in terri-tory over which the Dutch had, at best, a tenuous hold. After all, the Dutch merchants on whose behalf Minuit operated could have contented themselves with the wealth they already had. The early seventeenth century was the Neth-erlands' "Golden Age," one that gave birth to Rembrandt and Vermeer, the mi-croscope, and one of the wealthiest societies the world had ever known. "In this country there is no-one who cannot live with ease according to his rank," Venetian ambassador Girolamo Trevisano reported enviously to his govern-ment. "Nobody begs, and those who want to give alms, would not know to whom." Dutch prosperity resulted in part from the fact that Dutch merchants (like those who started the West India Company) dominated many of Europe's most important trade routes. Before refrigeration, salt for food preservation was a highly prized commodity, and the Dutch in this period played the lead-ing role in Europe's lucrative salt trade. In an era when the European diet was dominated by bland boiled foods, spices were likewise exceedingly valuable, far more so than today. Dutch merchants virtually monopolized the era's spice trade with Asia. As a result, the Dutch enjoyed the highest standard of living in Europe.[14]

It was the desire to preserve their status as the merchant princes of the Continent that accidentally led the Dutch to found New Amsterdam. When Columbus "discovered" America in 1492, he had been seeking not a new continent but rather a more direct route to the spice dealers of Asia. More than a century later, Englishmen, Frenchmen, Portuguese, and Spaniards, all hoping to break the Dutch stranglehold on this commerce with Asia, still sought a shortcut to the mercantile centers of "the Orient" that would allow them to circumvent Dutch middlemen. If one of them found it, the lucrative Dutch spice trade might quickly collapse. So the Dutch decided that they had to find the new route first.

Pecuniary interests were not their sole motivation. By the time the Dutch founded New Amsterdam, they had been fighting for their independence from Spain for sixty years. Spain still occupied some Dutch-speaking provinces in what would eventually become Belgium. Spain's ouster could only be financed with profits from the spice trade. Thus, the very survival of the Dutch nation was at stake in this battle to preserve the Dutch trading advantage with Asia.[15]

The leaders of the Dutch Republic were not thrilled when Hudson failed to find a shorter route to Asia. But when Dutch fur dealers learned that Hudson had discovered a wilderness full of "skins and peltries" from beavers, otters, foxes, and other animals, they were elated. The Dutch fur industry had long been dependent on the French colony in what is now Quebec for their raw materials. They could not wait to exploit Hudson's discoveries to secure animal pelts without the markups imposed by French middlemen. These Dutch fur merchants secured permission from the Dutch government to trade in the area Hudson had explored and immediately began sending ships there.[16]

The fur traders did not attempt to settle Manhattan or any other part of what they called New Netherland. Typically, they sailed inland looking for Indians with furs to barter, loaded their ships with the Indians' pelts, and then returned immediately to Europe. The Dutch government eventually decided that it wanted more from New Netherland than animal skins, for while it was not yet clear what else North America could offer the Dutch, the fact that their rivals Spain, France, and England were all establishing more permanent outposts on the continent suggested that perhaps they ought to do the same. So when the Dutch fur traders' patent to do business in New Netherland expired in 1618, the Dutch government declined to renew it. Instead, it created the West India Company, modeled on the wildly successful Dutch East India Company which monopolized the spice trade in Asia. The new company's investors would be the only Dutch merchants permitted to buy and sell goods in North America,

South America, and on the west coast of Africa. Its employees would have near total authority to govern, administer justice, and make treaties with natives in territories where it operated.[17]

The WIC made its first forays into colonization in the winter of 1623–24. Initially, Manhattan and its immediate environs were not a priority for the company. Instead, the WIC gambled the bulk of its start-up capital on an audacious attempt to invade and occupy the Brazilian port of São Salvador de Bahia and thereby gain control of southeast Brazil's sugar trade. The company assembled a squadron of twenty-six warships carrying 3,300 men for the invasion, to this day the largest-ever privately financed invasion flotilla.[18]

At the end of January 1624, as the WIC squadron was hurtling toward Brazil, the company dispatched a single sailing vessel (aptly named *New Netherland*) to North America to set up the company's trading outpost there. The ship was commanded by Cornelis Mey, a seasoned Dutch captain who had made several previous trips to North America. Whereas European ships that had come to this part of North America in the past had carried only sailors or others suited for the business of exploration, the *New Netherland* was the first vessel to bring *immigrants,* people who planned to live in this fledgling colony on a long-term basis.

WIC leaders instructed Mey to set up his base of operations on the southernmost of the rivers Hudson had explored, the modern-day Delaware. Company officials chose this location in the belief that the climate in what is now southern New Jersey would be similar to that in Spain's tropical settlement in Florida. Mey installed an outpost on the north bank of the Delaware Bay (the town there now, Cape May, is named for him) and then set out to fulfill his orders to revive the fur trade on the river now known as the Hudson. When Mey arrived at the mouth of the Hudson, he found a French ship already in the harbor. Its captain told Mey that he intended to plant the French flag there and claim it for France. But Mey, with his "yacht of two guns," chased the Frenchmen off the Hudson. It was the last time that France would try to intrude on the Dutch possession.[19]

Having disposed of the French threat, Mey did not establish a stronghold at the mouth of the Hudson, as one might expect. The key to the fur trade, Mey and the WIC believed, lay one hundred miles up the North River, where plentiful pelts awaited Dutch traders. Mey therefore shipped most of his colonists up the river to establish a fortress and settlement on the site of present-day Albany. Others were sent to what is now the Connecticut River, with only a handful of settlers left in New York Harbor on Nut Island. Those settlers used Manhattan Island, a few hundred yards across the bay, to pasture their cattle. It was Minuit, two years later, who had the good sense to put the cattle on Nut

Island and the people on Manhattan, launching its history as a magnet for immigrants.[20]

Manhattan seemed to hold an almost limitless bounty for these settlers. "We were much gratified on arriving in this country," one wrote in 1624. "We found beautiful rivers, bubbling fountains flowing down into the valleys; basins of running waters in the flatlands, agreeable fruits in the woods, such as strawberries, pigeon berries, walnuts, and also . . . wild grapes." Another noted that "there grows an abundance of chestnuts, plums, hazelnuts, large walnuts of several sorts," and blueberries. The nut trees would feed the settlers, the firs and pines would bring a handsome profit in Europe as timber and ships' masts, and the acorns from the tall oaks would fatten their pigs. Until their livestock were established, the colonists could feast on abundant deer, waterfowl, and seafood. "There is considerable fish in the rivers," the immigrants reported. They thought the abundance of shellfish especially impressive, and particularly enjoyed the mussels, clams, and oysters, "fine for stewing and frying. As each one fills a big spoon, they make a good bite." Other than missing the beef and pork to which they were accustomed, the earliest Europeans to settle in New York Harbor concluded that "whatever we desire in the paradise of Holland, is here to be found."[21]

The immigrants also liked Manhattan because of something the island did not have in abundance: Indians. In contrast to the situation farther up the river, where Native Americans were plentiful, in New Amsterdam one could come and go "without fear of the naked natives of the country." According to accounts written in the 1620s, only two to three hundred Indians lived on Manhattan Island, "under different chiefs, whom they call *Sackimas*." The men "in general are rather tall, well proportioned in their limbs, and of an orange color, like the Brazilians." Another early Dutch observer described the natives as "tolerably stout" with "black hair, with a long lock, which they braid and let hang on one side of the head. The hair is shorn on the top of the head like a cock's-comb . . . Their clothing is a coat of beaver-skins over the body, with the fur inside in winter, and outside in summer; they have, also, sometimes a bear's hide, or a coat of the skins of wild cats." Nonetheless, in comparison to Europeans, the Indians seemed "almost naked." Quaint as the natives might have appeared, early settlers insisted that they had to be avoided whenever possible. "Their disposition is bad. They are very revengeful; resembling the Italians," wrote one early immigrant. "They are very much addicted to promiscuous intercourse," claimed another. Worst of all, wrote Michaëlius in 1628, they are "devilish men," "strangers to all decency," "thievish and treacherous," experts in "sorcery and wicked arts" — in short, "entirely savage and wild."[22]

· · ·

The primary lure for the Walloon refugees and other early settlers in New Amsterdam was the prospect of acquiring land. The WIC promised them homesteads in America if they completed a six-year stint working for the company. If they got the same terms as typical Dutch indentured servants, they would have received free passage to America, room and board (though those first Walloons would have had to *build* the rooms themselves), plus a small annual salary until they had fulfilled their contracts, which ranged from three to six years. Having first crack at Manhattan real estate might seem like a great deal for the settlers, but the odds were stacked heavily against their ever getting that property. Fewer than half the initial settlers in Virginia survived as long as *one* year, much less six. Many other colonists would surely have tired of the hardships and danger and fled back across the Atlantic before their contracts had been fulfilled. But for those who were willing to stick it out and lucky enough to survive, such ventures offered those of low social rank a rare opportunity to acquire land and enjoy the upward mobility that they imagined would accompany it.[23]

The WIC's directors in Amsterdam observed that "as people here encourage each other with the prospect of becoming mighty lords" in New Netherland, interest in settling the colony grew. Rising from rags to riches in New Amsterdam would typically entail indenturing oneself, as the Walloons had done, as a laborer, farmhand, carpenter, or "maidservant." Under an indenture agreement, teenagers typically had to agree to work for their "master" for six years; those in their twenties and thirties (more sought after for their experience and maturity) could typically negotiate a three-year indenture. Over the course of the forty years that the Dutch controlled New Netherland, about six thousand Dutch men and women and about three hundred French-speaking Walloons migrated to the colony, some 55 percent of them as indentured servants.[24]

Immigrants considered indentured servitude in New Amsterdam less onerous than in English North America. In Virginia and New England, an indentured servant received no wage other than room and board, while the Dutch earned cash wages (ranging from 30 to 40 guilders per year for teenagers to 120 guilders for older servants). Unlike the Dutch system, English custom allowed a master to sell the remainder of a labor contract to someone else, something servants particularly dreaded because one might be transferred from a kind master in a populous town to a cruel one living in dangerous isolation on the frontier. Yet no matter the terms, indentured servitude involved plenty of hard work. The journeyman shoemakers, for example, whom Coenraet ten Eijck brought to New Amsterdam to help with his shoemaking business agreed in their indenture contracts to work from 5:00 a.m. to 9:00 p.m. and were expected to produce ten pairs of shoes per week.[25]

The penalties for failing to fulfill these agreements were harsh. In 1639 Jonas Bronck (namesake of the Bronx) brought maidservant Clara Matthijs to New Amsterdam, where she promised to work five years for room and board plus forty guilders per year. After three months, however, Clara found a mate and asked to be released from service. Bronck sued Clara's fiancé and won an award of one hundred guilders in damages to compensate for both the cost of her transportation to America and the trouble of finding another servant. Even if mistreatment by a master led the courts to annul a servant's contract, the servant often had to reimburse the employer for the cost of the voyage to New Netherland.[26]

Upward mobility was not the foremost thought on the minds of every immigrant to New Amsterdam. In 1660 Boudewijn van Nieuwlandt fled to New Amsterdam rather than marry his pregnant fiancée, Maria Besems. The determined fiancée, however, followed him to New Netherland. There she convinced authorities that Boudewijn should post a bond to discourage him from fleeing again, and soon thereafter she gave birth to the baby, whom she named Boudewijn junior. But Boudewijn senior could not be induced to raise his child with Maria. Before year's end, he slipped out of New Amsterdam with a new paramour on a ship headed for Virginia. Jannetje Blockx, in contrast, fought with her fiancé because he *refused* to immigrate to New Amsterdam, where her sister lived. When her fiancé would not budge, Jannetje called off the wedding.[27]

Many others, employed by the WIC, came to New Amsterdam not planning to be immigrants at all, but for one reason or another decided to stay—especially soldiers and sailors. The WIC typically had one hundred or more soldiers, mostly non-Dutch mercenaries, stationed in New Amsterdam at any given time, and many chose to make the town their home when their tour of duty ended. One was Jacob Leisler, a native of Frankfurt. Sent to New Amsterdam as a soldier in about 1660, he eventually became one of the city's most prominent merchants. A sailor employed by the WIC, Abraham Willemsz van Amsterdam, left the company's employ when he married New Amsterdam resident Aechtje Jans van Norden in 1647. He became a carpenter, albeit a hot-tempered one. In November 1649 he was mortally wounded in a duel.[28]

Another sailor, Govert Loockermans, became a clerk for the WIC after his ship arrived in New Amsterdam in 1633. Soon he married into the prominent Dutch Verbrugge trading family, but his in-laws forced Govert to remain in New Amsterdam and oversee family business there even though his wife had fled the hardships of the fledgling colony and returned to Holland. When Govert asked why he could not move back home as well, his employers told him to remember his humble roots. "There is many a good man," they wrote, "who, to gain further advancement, is absent from his wife for two, three, or even more years." Govert's wife eventually sailed back to America, and by 1642 he had purchased his own ship with another New Amsterdam merchant and begun to trade independently, transacting business with Indians up the Hudson as well as with English colonists in Virginia and New England. He eventually bought land in Maryland and on Long Island and died one of the wealthiest men in New Netherland.[29]

The sea voyage that took these pioneering colonists to New Amsterdam was longer, more difficult, and, for those who paid for themselves or their servants, more expensive than that of any subsequent generation of New York immigrants. For a variety of reasons, many Dutch ships sailing to New Amsterdam did not take a direct route across the Atlantic but sailed southwest from Amsterdam in order to stop first at Curaçao or St. Maarten. As a result, immigrants often spent two to three claustrophobic, seasick months aboard these small wooden vessels before reaching New Netherland.

The voyage was expensive because the WIC, which monopolized transatlantic shipping in and out of New Netherland, charged passengers by the day rather than a fixed rate. If the wind shifted or simply became calm, it could add weeks to the journey. Each ship had one or two private cabins, for which the fare was one guilder per day. Immigrants who wanted to spend a little less

The sailing ships most commonly used by the WIC to transport immigrants to New Amsterdam were "pinnaces" such as that pictured here.

could share space in another cabin known as the "hut," which cost twelve stivers per night. (There were twenty stivers to the guilder.) Most passengers, however, including all indentured servants, would reside "between decks" (the term "steerage" would not become standard for this space until the nineteenth century), for which the WIC charged eight stivers per day. It's no wonder that most of New Amsterdam's early settlers were shipped there at someone else's expense. Only in the 1650s, in an effort to stimulate immigration, would the WIC institute a fixed fare to New Amsterdam.[30]

"The long crossing," observed Barbara and Henri van der Zee, two authorities on Dutch New York, "was an ordeal in summer and hell in winter . . . [The immigrants] cooked, ate, slept, and were seasick in one wretched crowd." Passengers had to provide their own food and water. Cabin passengers could afford to bring ample fare. John Winthrop, governor of the Massachusetts Bay Colony, founded a few years after New Amsterdam, advised that for the transatlantic journey his wife should pack a "store of fresh provisions, meale, egges put in salt or grounde malt, butter, peas and fruits . . . a large frying panne, a small stewinge panne, and a case to boyle pudding." The majority of immigrants would not have had such an ample and varied diet aboard ship. Although employers supplied an indentured servant's food, stingy masters could not be counted on to provide a generous amount of sustenance, especially if the trip took longer than average. Stores of food might initially seem ample, but much of it would rot or become infested with worms or bugs over the course of the voyage.

Even humble Dutch citizens were accustomed to a rich, nourishing, and varied diet (a common complaint among Dutch servants of this era was that their masters too often fed them salmon!), so two or three months of malnourishment, with almost no protein at all, made immigrants especially susceptible to illness and death. Passengers threw up frequently from seasickness, and the cramped below-deck areas that the passengers shared quickly became suffused with vomit. Adjusting to a strange new diet, many immigrants developed diarrhea, which was difficult to contain within tempest-tossed chamber pots. As a result, bacteria-laden feces, mixed with vomit, soon ran in small rivers around the feet of the third-class passengers. Although the Dutch were not accustomed to roomy homes, the transatlantic voyage forced them into much closer contact with far more people for longer periods of time than ever before. Viruses spread quickly, as did body lice, which transmitted additional deadly bacteria to the passengers through the bugs' own feces (the source of typhus, commonly known as "ship fever"). Measures that might have forestalled these threats — such as bathing or even hand washing — were not customary to begin with, and out of the question on a vessel where every drop of fresh water was precious.

On ships of this era, boiling vinegar was commonly sprinkled in the passenger quarters in an attempt to disinfect these putrid compartments, but such efforts could not hold back the tidal wave of filth, germs, and vermin. Burials at sea were a sad rite of passage for any immigrant voyage. Losing 10 percent of the passengers and crew on a single seventeenth-century transatlantic crossing was common. Twenty or even 30 percent was not an unusual toll. Knowing this, and not trusting the ship's doctor (who typically moonlighted as a barber), passengers often traveled with their own medical remedies. But as the Van der Zees note, these "syrups, balsams, unguents, suppositories, pills, and quack remedies" could not forestall the march of death aboard each immigrant ship.[31]

Once the decision was made to move New Amsterdam's infant settlement from Nut Island to Manhattan, the settlers had to decide where on the larger island to place their dwellings. Willem Verhulst, Minuit's predecessor, had been instructed by the WIC to build on whatever part of the island was best suited for a fort, "keeping in mind that the fittest place is where the river is narrow, where it cannot be fired upon from higher ground, where large ships cannot come too close, where there is a distant view unobstructed by trees or hills, where it is possible to have water in the moat, and where there is no sand, but clay or other firm earth." It was apparently Minuit who chose to locate the settlement at the southeast end of the island. This spot, about where the Museum of the American Indian sits today at the foot of Broadway, did not meet all of the WIC's specifications, but it did command unobstructed views of the harbor and both the Hudson and East rivers.[32]

Upon arrival, the settlers set to work simultaneously building homes for themselves and a fort that could be used as shelter in case of attack by either Indian or European foes. They initially constructed houses in dugout style, excavating the sides of hills, so that some of the structure's walls would be made of dirt and they would need as little wood as possible. The roofs were fashioned from tree bark or thatch made from reeds. These "huts and hovels," as the colony's first minister, Michaëlius, described them in 1628, sat on what are now Stone, Bridge, and Pearl streets in lower Manhattan.

As for the fort, the WIC's ambitious plans called for a five-sided structure whose walls would measure 1,050 feet in length and be surrounded by a moat fifty-four feet wide and eight feet deep. The company envisioned that the settlers would build more permanent houses inside the fortress once they had completed it, but since the fortress never became as large or substantial as the company hoped, the settlers never relocated their homes. With the arrival of more carpenters in the year or two after the initial colonization of Manhattan, the dugout homes gave way to wooden structures. Eventually some would be

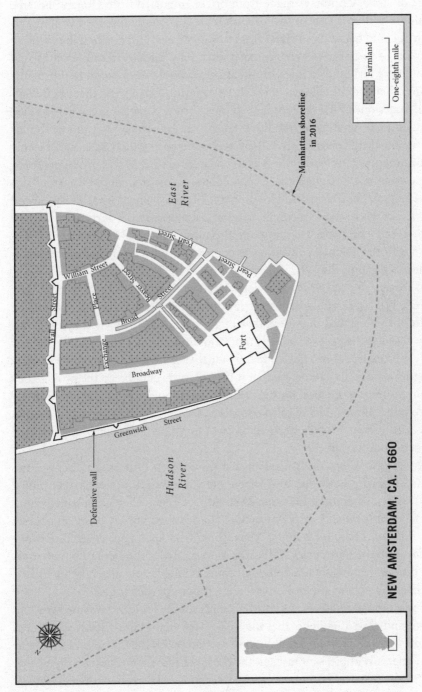

NEW AMSTERDAM, CA. 1660

Note: Street names are the modern names of roads that existed in 1660.

made of stone. Chimneys made from bricks imported from Holland became common. Within a year or two of Minuit's taking command, the fledgling settlement could boast about thirty homes situated east and north of the fort.[33]

While at first almost every colonist must have pitched in to help construct the colony's earliest dwellings, eventually they would have begun to pursue the callings that had brought them to North America. "Men work there as in Holland," states one of the earliest descriptions of New Amsterdam, which divided the adult male inhabitants into three categories: "one trades . . . ; another builds houses, the third farms." This offhand account is surprisingly accurate; the only significant group of workers it fails to consider are the WIC's own employees. These eventually included dozens of soldiers, sailors to man the company's local watercraft, a director and vice director, a finance officer, a secretary, several clerks, a cargo overseer, a foreman, a barber, a minister, a surgeon, a schoolteacher, and a midwife. The company also ultimately hired a "slave master," because with the colonists unwilling to contribute much effort toward the completion of the fort, the WIC imported slaves to finish the job.[34]

In 1625, a year after Mey first deposited Dutch colonists in New York Harbor, the WIC ordered the settlers to lay out six farms on Manhattan Island just north of the fort and the initial dwelling houses — farms owned by the company. Because the pace of land clearance and the amount of food grown did not meet WIC expectations, the company in 1629 began granting farmland directly to settlers, correctly predicting that if the colonists could reap the profits, they would produce more food for the colony. The colonists' propensity to grow tobacco rather than foodstuffs also contributed to the constant scarcity of food in New Amsterdam. The fledgling colony was for many years dependent on food imports from Europe.[35]

On one occasion, the WIC sent a shipload each of horses and cows, and a third carrying both pigs and sheep. Yet the ravenous colonists consumed the livestock faster than the animals could reproduce, then complained about shortages of meat and dairy products. "There are no horses, cows, or laborers to be obtained here for money," Michaëlius wrote in August 1628. "Every one is short in these particulars and wants more . . . [R]efreshment of butter, milk, etc., cannot be here obtained; though some is indeed sold at a very high price, for those who bring it in or bespeak it are jealous of each other."[36]

The shortage of laborers that Michaëlius mentioned in the same breath as horses and cows highlights that the well-to-do viewed these lowly workers as mindless suppliers of brute strength who, along with the slaves, undertook the most onerous, unpleasant tasks in the colony. Laborers were especially vital to the building trades. Without an adequate supply of laborers, craftsmen such as carpenters, masons, and roofers could not work efficiently, because they would have to do more of the digging, hauling, preparing, and cleanup that they preferred to delegate to unskilled co-workers.[37]

Trade was the third main source of employment in early New Amsterdam. Even the very earliest Manhattanites had an entrepreneurial bent. Then as now, food and alcohol were mainstays of the city's small-business economy. Butchers slaughtered and dressed any animal brought to them. Bakers were important as well, so much so that the WIC regulated bread prices.

The making and sale of alcohol seem to have been the most popular and lucrative food service vocations. Beer was far and away the favorite drink of early New Yorkers. It was considered such an important staple that even prisoners in the colony's jail received beer each day — with double rations in summertime. Brewers became a significant element of the city's elite. Families whose names would remain etched for centuries in New York life, such as the Kips, the Beeckmans, and the Van Cortlands, all first became prominent as Manhattan brewers. Oloff Stevensz van Cortland, for example, was one of the many soldiers sent to New Amsterdam who decided to stay permanently. He got work as a brewer when his tour of duty ended and eventually started his own brewery and became one of the city's wealthiest residents. Taverns to market the town's beers were omnipresent. City officials complained in 1648 that liquor sellers accounted for nearly one in four retail establishments.[38]

The business that attracted even more New Yorkers than alcohol was the beaver trade. Early Manhattanites were obsessed with the fur markets. In theory the WIC monopolized the trade in pelts, and the role of New Amsterdamers was merely to facilitate that commerce by supplying the traders who sailed up the Hudson and bought furs from Native Americans, outfitting the ships that carried the furs back to the Netherlands, and guarding the Hudson from encroachments by other nations. But in reality, Manhattanites illicitly traded furs to one another and to smugglers. Officials grumbled that ships sailing from New Amsterdam carried so many black market furs (in packages sent by the inhabitants to family in Europe) that there was hardly room for legal cargo. New Amsterdamers made little effort to hide their illegal fur trading. One WIC official reported that he was approached by "the wife of Wolfert Gerritsz [who] came to me with two otters, for which I offered her three guilders, ten stuivers. She refused this and asked for five guilders, whereupon I let her go, this being too much." Mrs. Gerritsz did not accept the offer because she knew she had other options. Sure enough, the wife of Jacob Laurissz, overhearing their haggling, "went to her and offered her five guilders." To prevent the skins from entering the black market, the official then gave Mrs. Gerritsz five guilders. Every

Manhattanite, whether of high or low station, hoped to supplement his or her income by moonlighting as a fur trader.[39]

The beaver trade defined early New Amsterdam. The town shipped about ten thousand beaver skins per year in the 1620s and 1630s and thirty to forty thousand in the 1640s and 1650s. The skins were especially valued for their pelts, the layer below the fur that was used to make the felt that lined expensive gentlemen's hats in the seventeenth century. (All those large black hats in Rembrandt's paintings of Dutch businessmen were lined with felt made from beaver pelts; so were nineteenth-century top hats.) Beaver skins were considered a form of legal tender in New Netherland, as acceptable for the payment of debts as gold coins. To this day, the beaver remains on the official seal of the City of New York.[40]

One of the biggest problems early New Amsterdamers faced was getting the WIC to pay attention to them. The company generated far greater profits from the slave trade in Africa and its sugar plantations in Brazil. The arrival of a new director did occasionally bring a spate of "reforms" and "improvements" to the colony. Such was the case when Minuit's successor, Wouter van Twiller, arrived in 1633. He directed workers (primarily slaves) to begin expanding and strengthening the fort (replacing sod walls with stone), to complete the moat, and to increase the size of the fort so the entire population could hide there in case of attack. Van Twiller also authorized New Amsterdamers to start work on the town's first wharf and a new warehouse. But the WIC often lost interest in such undertakings before they could be completed. When hostilities with the Indians broke out in the Connecticut River valley, Van Twiller drafted most of the construction workers into the military and ordered them to sail to Connecticut. The wharf and warehouse plans were scrapped, while the fort was completed with less expensive building materials. By 1636 it was again beginning to crumble, and the WIC fired Van Twiller soon thereafter.[41]

In 1638 the struggles of New Netherland began to attract the attention of the Dutch government. Fearing that the English would seize the entire colony, Dutch leaders threatened to take it from the WIC if the company did not improve its fortifications and make it more attractive to settlers who could help defend the colony in case of attack. With this threat looming over it, the WIC took action. Beginning in 1639, the company drastically cut the cost that immigrants paid to get to the colony; it offered two hundred acres of land free to any man who brought five family members or servants with him to the colony; it rescinded its monopoly on shipping goods to and from New Netherland; it allowed the colonists to appoint a council of twelve men to advise the colony's director so that colonists would have a say in how they were governed; and, perhaps most important of all, it gave up its monopoly on the fur trade, allowing anyone to buy and sell furs (and any other goods) in the colony.[42]

As Russell Shorto has noted, the effect of these changes "was electric. Small-scale entrepreneurs in Amsterdam who were willing to brave the hazards of the ocean voyage now had, in Manhattan, a hub to exploit — a base around which the circle of Atlantic trade could turn." The lifting of commercial restrictions "gave rise, within the space of a few years, to an intensively active merchant class — people who wanted to buy, sell, grow, spend. Convinced now that there was a future here, they began putting down roots."[43]

For the WIC, however, these changes made New Netherland even more unprofitable, and the company made it clear to the colony's new director, Willem Kieft, that he had better find new revenue streams if he hoped to keep his job. So Kieft decided to impose a tax on the one group that seemed, from the European perspective, to derive a variety of benefits from the WIC presence in New Netherland without contributing anything in return: the Indians. Relations with the various tribes that inhabited New Netherland, which had been relatively good to this point, deteriorated rapidly after Kieft demanded tribute.[44]

When the Indians refused to pay taxes to the Dutch, Kieft launched attacks on their villages. The colonists, who generally opposed what became known as Kieft's War because they recognized how ill-conceived it was, sent letters of protest back to Amsterdam complaining of both the policy and the manner in which Kieft's soldiers carried it out. "Infants were torn from their mother's breasts," complained one immigrant, David de Vries, concerning a raid that took place in February 1643 north of Manhattan, "and hacked to pieces in the presence of their parents, and the pieces thrown into the fire and in the water, and other sucklings, being bound to small boards, were cut, stuck, and pierced, and miserably massacred in a manner to move a heart of stone. Some were thrown into the river, and when the fathers and mothers endeavored to save them, the soldiers would not let them come on land but made both parents and children drown." Others managed to escape into the winter woods, but the next morning, "those who had fled the onslaught and concealed themselves, were murdered in cold blood when they came out to beg a piece of bread, and to be permitted to warm themselves." These colonists called Kieft's War "a disgrace to our nation" and to "the Prince of Orange, who has always endeavoured in his wars to spill as little blood as possible."[45]

Kieft's policy could succeed only if the various tribes of New Netherland continued to view one another more warily than they did the Dutch. But Kieft's War brought about an unprecedented unification of the Hudson River valley tribes, who now combined forces to counterattack the tiny Dutch settlements, often with weapons they had bought from the Dutch themselves. "All the men whom they could surprise on the farmlands they killed," reported de Vries of the Indian assaults, "but we have never heard that they ever permitted women or children to be killed. They burned all the houses, farms, barns, grain, haystacks, and destroyed everything they could get hold of." These raids took place not only in Manhattan but also on Long Island, in the Hudson River valley, and in what is now New Jersey and Westchester.[46]

In his zeal to blame Kieft for all the troubles, de Vries understated the ferocity of the Indians' counterattacks, as the Indians often did not spare women and children either, and sometimes the women and children whose lives the Indians did spare were taken as captives and adopted into the Indian tribes, never to be seen again. During the Indian counterattack, New Amsterdam's residents huddled in their fort in hastily built straw huts, cursing Kieft and his reckless Indian policy and taunting him for remaining safely in the fortress rather than leading a counteroffensive against the *wilden*.

One of the victims of Kieft's War was an Englishwoman named Anne Hutchinson. Hutchinson was a determined woman, *very* determined, and deeply religious, too. She and her husband, William, were devout Puritans, Protestants who believed that the Church of England needed purification because it retained too many trappings of Catholicism. Puritans wanted less money spent on elaborate church decoration and priestly vestments, less interference in local practices by distant bishops, and more direct participation by laypeople in church services. They also insisted that only true believers touched by God (whom they called "saints") should be admitted to church membership, in contrast to the Church of England practice of embracing even doubters and sinners. Finally, Puritans sought to replace the traditional mass with a simpler service in which the sermon — an analysis of a Bible passage by the minister — was the featured event.[47]

While Puritans agreed about these basic principles, they clashed over how to carry them out. A minority of Puritans thought that the Church of England could never reform itself and wanted no further relations with it. They fled England because disavowing the state church was a crime punishable by death. These self-styled "Pilgrims" settled first in Holland and later, in 1620, established the Plymouth Colony in what is now southeastern Massachusetts. The majority of Puritans, however, did not want to disavow the Church of England but instead sought to reform it from within. When it became clear in the late 1620s that King Charles was making the church *more* rather than less Catholic, many of these Puritans decided to leave England too. In 1629 they created their own North American settlement, the Massachusetts Bay Colony, just up the coast from the Pilgrims. There the Puritans could remain nominal members of the Church of England while instituting their reforms far from meddling bishops. They hoped that their "city upon a hill," Boston, would set an example that other Englishmen would one day emulate, eventually allowing the Puritans to return triumphantly to a better, purified England.

Anne Hutchinson found the concept of the city upon a hill absolutely thrilling. When her favorite minister, John Cotton, moved to Boston in 1633, Anne became determined to settle there too. There was only one problem. Most immigrants who risked life and limb on a perilous, potentially months-long ocean journey to a wild, untamed continent were young men and women. Anne, in contrast, was in her early forties (almost a senior citizen in those days) and had ten children, with an eleventh on the way. But once Anne had made up her mind, nothing could stop her. She first sent her eldest son, Edward, to Boston to pave the family's way, and in 1634 Anne and her husband, with their ten other children in tow, crossed the Atlantic on the *Griffin* and settled in Boston.

Even within the Massachusetts Bay Colony, the Puritans argued over the doctrinal changes they might institute. Most Puritans believed that a person's elevated worldly status — one's popularity, one's health, and especially one's wealth — was an indicator of divine approbation. Anne could easily have adopted this view, as she lived in one of the finest homes in Boston, was a popular midwife, and hosted a weekly Bible study group that drew large crowds. But Hutchinson was convinced that because God had predetermined everything in one's life even before birth, one's standing in the earthly world was no evidence of saintly status in God's eyes. Hutchinson boldly espoused this view at her Bible study meetings.

Puritan leaders found Hutchinson's arguments alarming and threatening, because Puritans relied heavily on worldly standing to determine church membership. Only Cotton, among all the ministers in Massachusetts, endorsed her views. After failing to persuade her to recant, the colony's leaders charged her with heresy. She would not back down, and during her trial she made even more radical claims. When asked how she knew that she was right and the other Puritan leaders were wrong, she stated that God, speaking through the Holy Spirit, had told her so. In 1638 the court excommunicated her and, to insure that she could not spread her "heresies" to others, banished her from Massachusetts.[48]

Hutchinson and her family moved initially to Rhode Island at the invitation of Roger Williams, another Puritan Dissenter whom the Massachusetts Puritans had expelled. Anne's husband, William, became a government official there. But she soon persuaded him to quit that job. She had come to believe that all civil government was illegitimate in God's eyes. William died sometime in 1641, and in the following year, Anne decided to truly practice what she preached. Packing up seven children, a son-in-law, and a half-dozen or so servants, she moved the family to a place where she believed she would not have to answer to any government — a forest homestead about fifteen miles north of the New Amsterdam settlement, in what is now the northeast portion of the Bronx, which she had purchased from an Englishman. She hired another local Englishman to build her family a home on the property near Split Rock, a granite geological oddity that still sits today just a few feet south of Interstate 95, only a few yards east of where that highway passes over the Hutchinson River Parkway.[49]

The Indians involved in Kieft's War who knew about Hutchinson's new home probably did not care that she was English rather than Dutch. In the summer of 1643, they killed every adult inhabitant, including Anne, her son-in-law, her servants, and all but one of her children. According to legend, only after the killing spree ended did the attackers find Hutchinson's red-haired ten-year-old daughter, Susanna, cowering in the Split Rock crevice. They took her prisoner and only released her several years later, after the Dutch and the various Indian chiefs ratified a peace treaty at Fort Amsterdam in 1645. A year later, Massachusetts governor John Winthrop reported that Susanna was living in Boston. She later moved to Rhode Island and there bore eleven children of her own. Her mother, stubborn and independent to the end, was one of the very first Americans to take a stand in defense of freedom of conscience.[50]

Kieft's disastrous war on the Indians convinced WIC leaders that they had once again chosen the wrong man to operate their struggling settlement. They needed a proven leader with a track record of success in running a profitable colony. He needed to be diplomatic enough to maintain peace with the Indians, yet strong enough to squelch the never-ending flow of complaints that New Amsterdam's colonists kept sending to the Dutch government, much to the embarrassment of the WIC. The man they chose, in 1647, was the company's peg-legged governor of Curaçao, thirty-seven-year-old Peter Stuyvesant.

Stuyvesant was born in about 1610 in the cold, windswept northern Dutch province of Friesland. His father was a minister of local prominence, and Peter grew up in a comfortable home. He attended the local college, probably with the goal of following his father into the ministry, but around 1630, midway through his studies, the university expelled him, apparently because he was caught sleeping with the daughter of his boardinghouse keeper. Seeing that Peter was not cut out for the ministry, his father sent him to Amsterdam to learn a profession. The Reverend Stuyvesant probably had some connections with

Friesland's representatives on the WIC's board of directors, because Peter soon landed an entry-level job as a clerk at company headquarters in Amsterdam.[51]

After Peter served five years as a WIC clerk in Amsterdam, his father used his influence to get him a promotion. The company made him its supply officer on Fernando de Noronha, an idyllic but lonely seven-square-mile islet that lies 225 miles east of the Brazilian coast. Soon they transferred him to a similar position in the far more important Brazilian coastal trading stronghold of Pernambuco and in 1638 to the same position in Curaçao, where the WIC stationed its officer in charge of all Caribbean operations. When that station chief died, the WIC gave his job to Stuyvesant.[52]

Stuyvesant was tough, and loyal to the company. On WIC orders, he led a doomed attack on the Spanish fort at Puerto Rico, losing his leg in the process. After a two-year recuperation period, during which he married his nurse, Stuyvesant was rewarded with a significant promotion. The WIC made him director general of Curaçao, Bonaire, Aruba, and all of New Netherland, with a base of operations in New Amsterdam. Sailing at the head of a flotilla of four ships, Stuyvesant left Holland on Christmas Day 1646 and, after stopping first in the Caribbean, arrived in New Amsterdam to replace Kieft on May 11, 1647.[53]

The WIC told Stuyvesant that past problems in New Amsterdam had originated with "the slackness of the late Director and the neglect of duty by the preacher," so he immediately set about trying to restore order and respect for authority. Learning that drunken knife fights were a common occurrence, he announced that he would henceforth punish the participants in such brawls with six months in jail on a bread and water diet, eighteen months if anyone was stabbed. He also banned the sale of alcohol after 9:00 p.m. When he caught sailors employed by the WIC on shore without permission, he sentenced them "to be chained for three consecutive months to a wheelbarrow or a handbarrow and put to the hardest labor, strictly on bread and water." Stuyvesant also warned the settlers against appealing these harsh fines or punishments to the WIC directors in Amsterdam, as they had in the past. "Should any one do so, I would have him made a foot shorter, pack the pieces off to Holland and let him appeal in that way."[54]

Stuyvesant was also appalled at the lack of respect that New Amsterdam's residents paid to the observance of the Sabbath. He therefore announced that those caught on Sundays sowing, mowing, plowing, hunting, fishing, woodcutting, or working in iron or tin would be fined. Those found engaging in more frivolous activities on "God's Day" would pay double the fine imposed for industrious pursuits. The list of these prohibited pastimes conveys a sense of how New Amsterdamers typically amused themselves: playing bocce, bowling, and tennis, racing boats or wagons, dancing, and playing games associated with gambling such as cards and backgammon. Stuyvesant also banned the sale of alcohol on Sundays before 2:00 p.m., though determined tipplers knew behind which closed doors they might quietly obtain a beer during the prohibited hours.[55]

Drinking continued to be the most popular leisure activity in New Amsterdam. Taverns were everywhere, and boardinghouse keepers served alcohol to their tenants as well. Many of New Amsterdam's court cases involved drunken flirtations that, in the eyes of at least one participant, had gone too far. Englishman Thomas Beech flew into a rage at a tavern when his wife, Nanne, fondled "at the front of the breeches" of the men who were present. Another fight started when a wife found her husband in a taproom "with another man's wife . . . touching her breasts and putting his mouth on them." Groping and fondling in a public setting did not seem to warrant punishment in the eyes of the Dutch, unless the illicit relationship was fully consummated. Adulterers caught *in flagrante* were publicly flogged and sometimes banished from the colony. It was far safer for men to patronize one of New Amsterdam's prostitutes, who accepted payment in cash or beaver pelts.[56]

Besides attempting to bring some semblance of propriety to New Amsterdam, Stuyvesant also sought to wring more revenue from its inhabitants. He cracked down on smugglers who sent furs to New England or Virginia to avoid the WIC's export duties. Stuyvesant also instituted infrastructure projects that he paid for not out of WIC coffers but through a tax on alcohol. These improvements included restorating the crumbling fort, building the town's first pier, and constructing a school and a church. (Services to this point had been held in one of the mills.)[57]

Stuyvesant undoubtedly believed that the prosperity that New Amsterdam soon enjoyed resulted from his "firm hand." But the boom resulted from factors largely beyond his control. It originated in part from the treaty Kieft had negotiated with a dozen or so Indian tribes to end his ill-conceived war. With peace secured, pelts once again began flowing down the Hudson, and immigrants once again began arriving from all across Europe. The economic upsurge also had its origins in another peace treaty, signed in Munster in 1648, ending eighty years of hostilities between the Dutch and Spain. No longer fearing that their ships and cargo might be seized as part of the ongoing warfare, merchants from Holland and elsewhere were more willing to trade with New Netherland.

The Dutch government also stimulated immigration to New Netherland. In 1650 it ordered Dutch captains with space on their ships to transport immigrants to New Amsterdam free of charge. The government required the WIC to give such immigrants free land upon arrival, exempted their crops from taxes, and mandated that no restrictions be put on their right to trade. This policy would be expanded to cover more groups in 1656. The new immigrants included merchants or aspiring merchants hoping to supply other immigrants with rooms to rent, food to eat, and beer to drink. Others were tradesmen or aspiring tradesmen who hoped to provide colonists with furniture, tools, and clothing.

Stuyvesant did not like this change in policy. These new immigrants, accustomed to rights and privileges in the Netherlands, expected them in New Amsterdam, too, even if it was not in the best interests of the WIC to grant them. It would be far better, Stuyvesant insisted, if the WIC would instead recruit common "farmers and farmhands, foreigners and refugees, who are used to labor and poverty." He was overruled. "Formerly New Netherland was never spoken of," the directors wrote to Stuyvesant, "and now heaven and earth seem to be stirred up by it and every one tries to be the first in selecting the best pieces [of land] there." These new arrivals settled all over the colony (present-day Brooklyn and Queens were especially popular), so this influx raised the population of New Amsterdam to only about eight hundred. But since the number of inhabitants had sunk to two hundred during Kieft's War, the immigration boomlet, modest as it might have been, was a welcome relief to skittish WIC investors.[58]

A final stimulus to immigration mandated by the Dutch government was the requirement, announced in 1652, that the WIC relinquish its absolute authority over the residents of New Amsterdam by creating a municipal government and offering immigrants the opportunity to attain "burgher" status. In his first years in New Amsterdam, Stuyvesant delighted in boasting that he and the WIC were "absolute and general lords and masters of this province." But this "haughty" manner and Stuyvesant's autocratic tendencies infuriated the town's growing ranks of substantial merchants, who would have enjoyed far more rights and privileges in the Dutch Republic. Fearing that these businessmen might flee the colony and drain it of valuable capital, the Dutch government ordered the WIC to institute a representative government more like that found in Amsterdam and other Dutch cities.

While Stuyvesant would remain the colony's chief executive, his actions would now be subject to review by judicial and legislative bodies. Only "great burghers," residents who paid a substantial sum to the town coffers in order to have a say in political affairs, could hold these offices. But "small burghers," in return for payment of a lesser fee, enjoyed enhanced trading privileges and due process rights. Although they could not serve in the main ruling bodies, they did qualify to hold minor municipal offices. Those who did not have the neces-

New Amsterdam as it appeared in about 1650. Other than the mill, the tallest building in town was the church, and the second tallest was the governor's house to the left of the church.

sary twenty guilders could pay in installments. Servants and sailors could not become small burghers until they had completed their service obligations. People of color were ineligible.

The ease with which one could become a member of the body politic in New Amsterdam soon became a significant incentive for dreamers from all over Europe to move to the little Dutch colony in America. By 1657, the town had two thousand residents crowded into about three hundred houses.[59]

One characteristic for which New Amsterdam became renowned in this period was the unprecedented diversity of its population. "On the island of Manhate . . . the Director General told me that there were men of eighteen different languages," marveled one French visitor. A Dutchman complained that the city was becoming a "Babel of confusion." By this time, in addition to the Dutch, there were Irishmen and Italians, Poles and Portuguese, Spaniards and Swedes, as well as Africans, Danes, Frenchmen, Germans, Jews (considered a race of their own), Norwegians, and Walloons. Intermarriage between these groups was common.[60]

But the largest "foreign" group in the city by far was the English, a fact that increasingly concerned both Stuyvesant and the WIC. While some English immigrants came directly from Europe, most had lived first in Virginia or Massachusetts. Many from those two colonies were former indentured servants whose terms had expired or who had run away. Others were religious Dissenters who chafed under the Puritan demand for conformity. Some of these Dissenters made New Amsterdam their home, but the majority chose to live on western Long Island in the growing villages of Breukelen, Midwout (now Midwood or Flatbush), Boswyck (Bushwick), Gravesande (Gravesend), Vlissingen

(Flushing), and Rustdorp (Jamaica). These immigrants chose New Netherland over the English colonies, according to one resident, "both to enjoy freedom of conscience and . . . because many more commodities were easier to be obtained here than there." Meanwhile, the English population of New Amsterdam became so large that the town had its own English quarter southeast of the fort.[61]

Though the Dutch may have offered their settlers more religious freedom than found in other colonies, their concept of "freedom of conscience" does not seem very free by modern standards. The Dutch believed that one should be free to *think* whatever one chose, but they did not believe that one should necessarily be able to express nonconformist views in public. Take the case of New Amsterdam's Jews. The first documented Jewish immigrant in New York, businessman Jacob Barsimon, appears to have caused relatively little controversy when he arrived in August 1654. One or two other Jews may have preceded him. But earlier in that same year, the Portuguese reclaimed northeastern Brazil from the Dutch, confiscated the property of Dutch colonists there, and gave them three months to clear out. Among those forced to flee were Portuguese Jewish traders whom the Dutch had brought to Brazil because their ability to speak Portuguese made them particularly valuable colonists. In the summer of 1654, twenty-three of these Jews boarded a ship in the Brazilian port of Recife and sailed to New Amsterdam, where they landed in September.[62]

Stuyvesant and his fellow New Amsterdamers were horrified by the prospect of a significant, permanent population of Jews in the colony. The governor immediately asked the WIC for permission to expel them, or as he put it in his letter, "to require them in a friendly way to depart." He justified his request on the grounds that (1) other residents of the town found the Jews "very repugnant"; (2) their "customary usury and deceitful trading with the Christians" would disrupt the colony's commerce; (3) "owing to their present indigence," the colony might have to support them in the coming winter; and (4) such a "deceitful race — such hateful enemies and blasphemers of the name of Christ" — should "not be allowed further to infect and trouble this new colony."

New Amsterdam's Dutch Reformed minister Johannes Megapolensis wholeheartedly agreed with Stuyvesant. Jews, he complained, "have no other God than the Mammon of unrighteousness, and no other aim than to get possession of Christian property, and to overcome all other merchants by drawing all trade towards themselves." Furthermore, the minister insisted, Jews would make the colony *too diverse*. "We have here Papists, Mennonites and Lutherans among the Dutch; also many Puritans or Independents, and many Atheists and various other servants of Baal among the English," he wrote in March 1655.

"It would create a still greater confusion, if the obstinate and immovable Jews came to settle here." Allowing them to stay would only encourage more Jews to immigrate.[63]

The WIC directors denied these requests to expel the Jews, though not for particularly high-minded reasons. Under normal circumstances, the directors would have "gladly . . . carried out your wish," they told Stuyvesant, so that New Netherland would "not be infected any more by any Jewish nation, as we foresee from this the same difficulties which you anticipate." But given the losses "sustained by the Jews in the taking of Brazil" by the Portuguese, and also because of "the large sums of money for which they are still indebted to the Company," the WIC in April 1655 directed Stuyvesant to permit the Jews "to live and remain there, provided the poor among them shall not become a burden to the Company or the community, but be supported by their own nation." The WIC was motivated in part by lobbying from the Jews of Amsterdam, in part by "reason and fairness," and in part by a desire to be repaid the money the Recife Jews owed the company, something more likely to happen if Stuyvesant allowed them to work and trade in New Amsterdam.[64]

Stuyvesant allowed the Jews to stay, but he and other New Amsterdamers never passed up an opportunity to make these newcomers feel unwelcome, hoping that such treatment might persuade them to self-deport. Initially, Jews in New Amsterdam could not own real estate, conduct trade with other parts of New Netherland, or open shops. City officials barred Jewish men from taking their turn standing guard with the citizens' militia and then forced the Jews to pay a tax because they did not stand guard. The town council required them to pay other taxes at higher rates than Christians. They could not become burghers, either. And Stuyvesant told them that under no circumstances could they build a synagogue for their "abominable religion." If they did not like these restrictions, he told Jewish community leaders, they could leave.[65]

Stuyvesant's unabashed discrimination did not please WIC leaders once they found out about it, in part because it discouraged immigration, and in part because the company's Jewish investors and trading partners voiced their disapproval. "We wish . . . that you had obeyed our orders," the directors scolded, "which you must always execute punctually and with more respect." As a result, New Amsterdam's Jews soon received permission to trade throughout New Netherland, to become butchers and bakers (Asser Levy became the town's first kosher butcher), to establish their own cemetery, and to become small burghers. Despite Stuyvesant's efforts, the Jewish community began to prosper and slowly grow.[66]

Stuyvesant took a similarly hard line against some Christian groups, such as the colony's Lutherans. The WIC was happy to have German Lutherans settle in New Amsterdam, but Stuyvesant steadfastly refused to allow them to hire a minister or to worship in public. This was the policy in the Netherlands, too. Only informal religious observances in private homes were permitted, but since the tiny homes of New Amsterdam's Lutherans could hardly fit a dozen people in a single room, this policy was, in effect, a ban on services altogether. If the colony granted Lutherans the right to hire a minister and worship publicly, Megapolensis and another Dutch minister warned in 1653, the colony "would become a receptacle for all sorts of heretics and fanatics."[67]

Like the Jews, the Lutherans did not meekly accept Stuyvesant's restrictions. The WIC, they complained, had led them to believe that public worship would be tolerated in New Amsterdam, as it was in old Amsterdam, with the "winking of the eye." Yet when the Lutherans in 1656 held public services in defiance of Stuyvesant, their leaders were arrested and jailed. "We would have been better pleased, if you had not . . . committed them to prison," Stuyvesant's exasperated employers wrote to him in June, "for it has always been our intention," in order to encourage as much immigration as possible, "to treat them quietly and leniently."

Just at this time, international diplomacy appeared to aid the Lutheran cause. In 1655, at about the time he was sparring with New Amsterdam's Lutherans, Stuyvesant managed to wrest New Sweden, the portion of New Netherland on the banks of the Delaware which Minuit had taken from the Dutch a quarter century earlier, back from the Swedes. In the treaty that accompanied the transfer, the Dutch promised to allow a Lutheran minister in New Netherland. Yet when that minister, Joannes Goetwater, arrived in New Amsterdam in 1657, Stuyvesant would not let him preach. The treaty, Stuyvesant insisted, said only that the Lutherans could send a minister, not that he could build a church or preach. Stuyvesant then banned Goetwater from New Amsterdam in spite of the treaty, and tried to deport him from New Netherland altogether. To avoid expulsion, the determined clergyman went into hiding on Long Island, hoping that Lutheran appeals to WIC officials in Holland would force Stuyvesant to reverse course. But Stuyvesant prevailed. In 1659 Goetwater conceded defeat and returned to Europe. As long as the Dutch ruled New Amsterdam, Lutherans' "freedom of conscience" would not include the right to a minister or public worship.[68]

Stuyvesant's treatment of Lutherans seems lenient in comparison to that of another Christian group, the Society of Friends, or Quakers. Like Anne Hutchinson, Quakers believed that God could speak directly to them. But the Quakers' theology seemed even more threatening than Hutchinson's because they believed that they did not need a minister to direct their services. Instead, members could speak when they felt moved by God to do so. This disdain for authority figures frightened Stuyvesant as much as the group's theological beliefs.

When a small shipload of English Quakers arrived in New Amsterdam in the summer of 1657, Stuyvesant let them know they were not welcome. The vessel left the next day for Rhode Island — "the latrine of New England," scoffed Megapolensis. But the Quakers had left a few of their followers in Manhattan, and two of them, Dorothy Waugh and Mary Weatherhead, "one about twenty, and the other about twenty-eight," immediately began to proselytize. According to Megapolensis, the women would "quake and go into a frenzy," warning that "the day of judgment" was at hand. "Our people not knowing what was the matter, ran to and fro, while one cried 'Fire' and another something else." The sheriff dragged Waugh and Weatherhead to jail, where they "continued to cry out and pray according to their manner." Stuyvesant had them deported.[69]

Stuyvesant soon discovered that the other Quakers had not gone to Rhode Island but instead had merely sailed around the bend of the East River and disembarked on the east bank in the Dutch settlement of Vlissingen, modern-day Flushing in the New York City borough of Queens, where they too began to proselytize. When one, Robert Hodgson, was caught in the fall of 1657, the New Amsterdam court sentenced him "to work at the wheelbarrow for two years with the Negroes." When Hodgson refused to leave his cell to carry out his sentence, he was "whipped on the back in public" and deported. Stuyvesant made sure he was conveyed all the way to Rhode Island. He then banned the residents of Flushing from harboring Quakers.[70]

But Flushing's inhabitants, mostly English, decided to protest Stuyvesant's harsh treatment of the Quakers. They wrote a "remonstrance," signed in December 1657 by thirty-one community members, including many of Flushing's leaders, in which they reminded Stuyvesant that in most of its colonies, the Netherlands offered "love[,] peace and libertie," even "to Jewes[,] Turkes and Egiptians." Surely a Christian group deserved the same rights, and ought to be left alone to enjoy religious freedom. Today the Flushing Remonstrance, as it came to be known, is considered the first public expression of a desire for the freedom of religion written on American soil, and is considered an important precedent for the Constitution's Bill of Rights.[71]

Stuyvesant's response to the Flushing Remonstrance was as swift as it was emphatic. He ordered the signers arrested and jailed. He offered them a choice of two punishments: pay a fine and recant, or be banished for life from New Netherland. Stuyvesant probably thought he was being lenient; in Massachusetts the Puritans executed four Quakers for proselytizing, cut off the ears of three more, branded one, whipped forty, and imprisoned sixty-four. Yet the WIC again reprimanded Stuyvesant for his actions. "We doubt very much, whether we can proceed against them rigorously without diminishing the population and stopping immigration," the directors wrote, "which must be favored at a so tender stage of the country's existence." Therefore "shut your eyes" and do "not force people's consciences, but allow every one to have his own belief, as long as he behaves quietly and legally, gives no offence to his neighbors and does not oppose the government." Yet with three thousand miles of ocean between himself and his employers, and the knowledge that he was a more effective governor of New Netherland than any of his predecessors, Stuyvesant felt free to ignore his employers and let the punishments stand. In the end, most of the Flushing protesters recanted.[72]

Another group that persisted in New Amsterdam despite discrimination was its free black population. Most free people of color had come to New Amsterdam as slaves, but the Dutch seem to have granted freedom to their slaves a bit more often than did the English to the north and south. Typically these slaves had to buy their freedom. Philip Ringo freed Manuel de Spanjaard in 1649 on the condition that the freedman pay Ringo one hundred guilders each year for three years. In 1644 the eleven survivors from among the first slaves brought to New Amsterdam, who had labored for the WIC for eighteen years, petitioned Governor Kieft for their freedom. He granted it, and gave each a few acres of land north of the main Manhattan settlement, on the condition that each year at harvest time they pay the WIC thirty *schepels* (about twenty-two bushels) of corn and one fat pig. Kieft would not, however, emancipate their three children. By 1664, about seventy-five New Amsterdam slaves had negotiated their freedom through such agreements.[73]

Free people of color clearly had a lower status than most whites in New Amsterdam. Governor Van Twiller declared in 1638 that the Dutch must refrain from "adulterous intercourse with heathens, blacks, or other persons." Authorities sentenced a sailor who had deserted his ship and his bride to have his head shaved, "his ears bored, and to work two years with the negroes." Yet freed slaves in some senses had a higher status than religious pariahs such as Jews. Unlike Jews, they were never banned from standing guard or owning real estate, and did not pay higher taxes than other citizens. Yet African Americans could not become burghers, a right eventually granted to Jews. In the earliest years of North American colonization, therefore, racial and religious difference each carried liabilities, but in the case of African Americans and Jews, these could often be overcome.[74]

A case in point is the New Amsterdam slave Manuel Gerrit, better known as "Manuel the Giant" or "Big Manuel." In 1641 authorities accused him and seven other slaves of murdering Jan Premero. The slaves admitted to being involved in the fight that led to Premero's death, but each vehemently insisted that he had not struck the fatal blow. Executing all of them would have cost the WIC too many of its slaves, so the magistrates decided that the accused should draw lots to determine who would hang, thus letting "God designate the culprit." God chose Big Manuel.[75]

A week later, Big Manuel stood on a ladder at a makeshift gallows as the executioner slipped "two good ropes" around his neck. Many of the town's residents gathered to witness the gruesome spectacle. Yet when the fateful moment arrived and the executioner pushed Big Manuel off the ladder, both ropes broke and he fell to the ground unharmed. Interpreting the result as a sign from God, the crowd demanded that the punishment be rescinded. Town officials agreed. Big Manuel eventually won his freedom from bondage too, probably in the same manner as did other slaves. Like those other former bondsmen, he soon acquired farmland on the east side of Manhattan near what is now the Bowery. More than forty African American men and women owned land in this vicinity in the years when the Dutch ran New York.[76]

The number of African Americans living in New Amsterdam began to increase dramatically in the mid-1650s, but not in a manner that free blacks such as Big Manuel would have found heartening. The Dutch loss of Brazil in 1654 meant that the WIC could no longer sell the slaves it had taken from Africa to sugar planters in Brazil. They disposed of some of their human cargo in the Caribbean, but calculating that their profits would be higher in North America, where laborers were scarce, WIC leaders decided to bring most of their newly captured African slaves to New Amsterdam. So while previously small consignments of a dozen or fewer slaves might occasionally appear when a ship arrived in town, now three hundred or more might be brought ashore on a single day, several times a year. Slave traders took most of these bondsmen to English settlements for resale, but some remained in New Amsterdam. By 1664 the town's enslaved population had mushroomed to about three hundred, constituting some 15 to 20 percent of New Amsterdam's inhabitants.[77]

If the increasing importance of the slave trade to the New Amsterdam economy troubled Stuyvesant, he never indicated so in writing. What did worry the governor was that with each passing year, Dutch slave traders found English customers for their bondsmen closer and closer to the city. While the Dutch population of New Netherland increased by the hundreds over the course of the 1640s and early 1650s, the English population in the area surrounding New Amsterdam grew by the thousands. Contented Dutchmen in these years enjoyed prosperity at home and saw little reason to emigrate. England, in contrast, was convulsed by a long and bloody civil war beginning in 1642. The conflict inspired thousands to flee to the relative safety of North America.

In the end, the initial Dutch decision to encourage English immigrants to settle in New Netherland cost the WIC dearly. The Dutch claimed ownership of not only Manhattan Island and the Hudson River valley but the Connecticut River valley and Long Island as well, though as Minuit discovered in Plymouth, the English contested all these claims. The settlement of thousands of English immigrants in Connecticut and on Long Island in the 1640s undermined the sovereignty of the Dutch in their possessions. Recognizing that the demographic trends favored them, the English in 1650 forced Stuyvesant, in the Treaty of Hartford, to cede to England all of Connecticut and the eastern three-quarters of Long Island.

When Oliver Cromwell took control of England in 1653, he was not content merely to consolidate his hold on power at home. Like King Charles before him, Cromwell coveted the remaining portions of New Netherland, and organized a flotilla to capture it during the Anglo-Dutch War, which broke out around the time he seized the reins of government. "New Netherland is in great danger and imminently exposed to invasion," exclaimed the Dutch government in alarm, as Cromwell's intentions became clear. Recognizing the threat, the WIC's directors ordered Stuyvesant to garrison the fort in preparation for the looming attack. But the very day in June of 1654 when the English invasion force was to leave Boston, news reached Massachusetts that a peace treaty between the two nations had been signed. The Dutch in New Amsterdam breathed a huge sigh of relief.[78]

Although the immediate threat had passed, the English did not give up on their ambition to absorb New Netherland into their own North American colonies. To that end, a group of English settlers in 1654 bought from Indians much of modern-day Westchester County and the Bronx (northeast of Manhattan) to block potential Dutch expansion in that direction. The English government also launched a public relations campaign, reiterating the argument that Dutch land claims in North America were invalid. Cromwell in 1657 even sent a letter to English settlers in western Long Island encouraging them to revolt against the Dutch.[79]

Stuyvesant tried to persuade the English to leave New Netherland alone. He poured on the flattery when New England officials visited Manhattan and

Peter Stuyvesant, around 1660.

he also negotiated a trade agreement with Virginia. But the English government forced the Virginians to annul that treaty, and Connecticut governor John
Winthrop Jr. devoted most of his visit to Manhattan to reconnoitering Dutch
defenses. Cromwell died in 1658, and after King Charles II took back the throne
in 1660, England's determination to take Manhattan intensified. The English
intended to use Manhattan as the centerpiece of their plan to control all of
coastal North America.[80]

Finally, in 1664, just as Stuyvesant had perhaps begun to believe that his efforts had persuaded the English to turn their attention elsewhere, the long-
dreaded warships arrived in the harbor, anchoring there in menacing silence.
When Stuyvesant could stand the suspense no longer, he sent a message to the
visitors asking what they wanted. The reply, from squadron leader Sir Richard Nicolls, came the next morning: "In his Majesties name, I do demand the
town, scituate upon the island commonly knowne by the name of Manhatoes
with all the forts there unto belonging, to be rendered unto his Majesties obedience, and protection into my hands." Nicolls did not wish to spill "Christian
blood," he wrote, but if Stuyvesant did not surrender, the Dutchman would experience "the miseryes of a war." Stuyvesant wanted to fight, but when even his
own son Balthasar signed a petition begging his father to surrender, he saw that
his people did not have the resolve necessary to defeat a foe of superior size and
strength. On September 6, 1664, Stuyvesant capitulated, and New Amsterdam
officially became New York.[81]

Stuyvesant did manage to negotiate unusually favorable terms for the Dutch
men and women who chose to remain in New York—what the king's brother,
the Duke of York (later King James II, and New York's namesake), characterized as "immunities and privileges beyond what other parts of my territory doe
enjoy." The Articles of Capitulation guaranteed the Dutch religious freedom
and unrestricted trade (unlike in other English colonies, which had to import
and export all goods through England). In fact, the agreement promised that
the political leaders of the colony would "continue as now they are," as long
as they swore an oath of allegiance to the king of England, and that in future
"the towne of Manhatans shall choose deputyes, and those deputyes shall have
free voices in all publique affaires." This was especially ironic, since Stuyvesant
had worked so hard to prevent the colonists from gaining these rights when he
ruled them. But their willingness to grant these privileges reflected the fact that
the English wanted the Dutch to stay. They liked Manhattan's mixture of traders from across the globe and wanted those traders to serve as the linchpins for
England's expanding Atlantic empire.[82]

Those traders included Asser Levy, the kosher butcher. By the time the English took over New York, Levy had diversified into real estate (both in Man-

hattan and near Albany) and the fur trade. His account books, which survive to this day in the Netherlands, document the wide and multifaceted trade that helped early New Yorkers thrive. Big Manuel continued to enjoy his freedom, farming on land in what is now New York City's East Village. He may have moved to New Jersey. But given how rapidly the English expanded slavery after 1664 — the proportion of New York City residents who owned slaves quadrupled during the first forty years of English rule — his golden years must have felt a bit precarious.[83]

Perhaps the most interesting case of a Dutchman who chose to live out his final years in Manhattan was Peter Stuyvesant himself. He returned to Holland in about 1665, when the Dutch lost sovereignty over New Amsterdam, but he must have missed Manhattan. After three years of feeling out of place in the Netherlands, he petitioned the Dutch government for permission to return to his New York farm, which had remained his property under the terms of the Articles of Capitulation. He spent the last four years of his life there on his *bouwery,* or farm, dutifully attending services each Sunday at the chapel he built there, dedicated to Saint Mark. The church, rebuilt in about 1800, still stands today in the same location, now East 10th Street at Second Avenue, known as St. Mark's Church-in-the-Bowery. Stuyvesant was laid to rest there after his death in 1672, at about age sixty-two.[84]

Stuyvesant could have spent his final years in Holland, away from the daily reminders of the ignominious end to his tenure as governor of New Netherland. He had plenty of money and was a man of status in the Netherlands, a patriot who had sacrificed a limb in service to the nation. But as with so many others who would venture to New York, his years there changed him. When he went back to his homeland, it no longer felt like home. Though the term had barely been coined, he understood that he had become an "American." This was the only place he could now imagine living and dying. And he had laid the groundwork for the millions who would follow in his footsteps and eventually feel the same way.

2

REBELLION

IN THE SEVENTEENTH CENTURY, wealthy and powerful New Yorkers, like wealthy and powerful New Yorkers today, jumped at any chance to escape the city's summertime heat, humidity, and foul smells. Such was the case in August 1673, when the man who presided over the town, Governor Francis Lovelace, decided to take a sailing excursion to Connecticut, on "official business," of course, and since England was at war and he needed protection, he took the bulk of the soldiers who usually guarded the city with him.

Lovelace probably felt that he could leave New York lightly guarded because that war, between the English and French on one side and the Dutch on the other, was going very well for England. In 1672 France had invaded the Netherlands from the south and east and quickly occupied significant portions of Dutch territory. Meanwhile, the English began a blockade of the Dutch coast. England's King Charles II envisioned making parts of Holland, the central and most populous portion of the Netherlands, into English territory. With three of the Netherlands' seven states in enemy hands and the rest in danger of being overrun, Dutch military commanders turned to drastic measures, ordering dikes opened so that the invaders would be halted by the resulting floods. When winter came and the floodwaters froze, French troops tried to advance, but were repulsed by Dutch soldiers on skates. With their nation half-occupied and most of their crops destroyed by self-inflicted floods, the Dutch appeared to be in no position to threaten an English colony thousands of miles away.

But Lovelace miscalculated badly. The Dutch had decided that the best defense might be an audacious offense. Despite their desperate domestic situation, Dutch leaders sent much of their most feared fighting force, their navy, across the Atlantic in hopes of drawing the enemy away from the Netherlands. The commander of one squadron, Admiral Cornelis Evertsen Jr., had been instructed to target French and English possessions in the Americas and "to capture and ruin everything possible." In the summer of 1673, Evertsen decided to attack New York, arriving there with eight ships in early August. Expecting a fight, the Dutch commanders, after lying at anchor for days in the lower harbor, were shocked that New York authorities did not even inquire about their intentions. Finally, a party of Dutch farmers from Long Island rowed out to the fleet and informed Evertsen that Governor Lovelace was away, that most of the town's soldiers were absent as well, and that the city's fort was in disrepair. The farmers complained "about the hard rule of the English" and predicted that most New Yorkers — three-quarters of whom were Dutch — would welcome Evertsen if he recaptured the city for the Netherlands.[1]

That night, Dutch saboteurs spiked the guns ringing New York Harbor. The next morning, August 9, six hundred Dutch marines landed on the banks of the Hudson near where Trinity Church now stands and captured the fort and the town, cheered on by "demonstrations of joy" from Dutch New Yorkers. One English soldier died in the fighting; a couple of Dutchmen were wounded. Evertsen renamed the city New Orange (after the Dutch prince William of Orange), and when Lovelace returned to town three days later, Evertsen deported him.[2]

The Duke of York was mortified that his namesake colony, the cornerstone of his plan for a North American mercantile empire, had been left so recklessly undefended. The loss of New York demonstrated that while it might be easy to acquire territory, it was far harder to make the conquered populace into

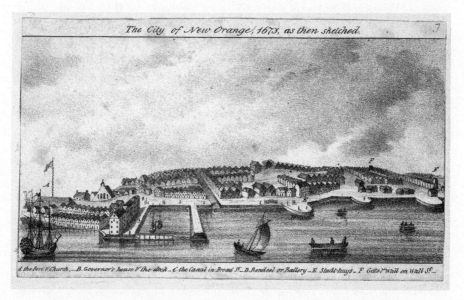

New York City as it appeared in 1673, when it briefly became "New Orange."

loyal citizens. This turn of events led the English to regret the duke's decision, reached a decade earlier, to leave New Amsterdam's ruling Dutch elite largely in place after England acquired the town and to avoid any concerted effort to re-populate New York with Englishmen. They would not make this mistake again.

Lovelace must have breathed a sigh of relief when, in February 1674, just six months after the Dutch took New York, they agreed to give it back as part of the Treaty of Westminster, in which all sides consented to a return to the status quo ante. Some Dutch New Yorkers, especially those who had actively helped overthrow the English or gloated publicly to their English neighbors after the Dutch reestablished control, bristled at how little effort Dutch leaders made to keep the city. These Dutch New Yorkers hurled "curses and execrations" at the Dutch government and demanded a chance to "slay the English doggs." Some, fearing retaliation, decided to move to another Dutch possession or to Holland itself before the city was officially handed back to the English on November 10.

The speedy return of New York to England did not make the Duke of York any less angry at Lovelace for having lost it. The duke decided to make an ex-ample of him, one that would cause every court retainer to think long and hard before leaving any royal possession lightly guarded. The duke had Lovelace ar-rested, confiscated his property, and in January 1675, months after New York had returned to English control, had Lovelace jailed in the notorious Tower of London. Spending an English winter shivering in the Tower was not salubrious for the health of a fifty-three-year-old accustomed to the finer things in life. By April, Lovelace was so sick that authorities let him go — and by the end of the year he was dead.[3]

Some of the duke's advisers suggested that he should relocate his Dutch subjects to Albany, where they would pose far less of a security threat. Others called for the total expulsion of the Dutch from the province. Instead, the duke sent to New York a new, younger governor, Sir Edmund Andros, who had ex-tensive military experience and close connections with the royal family, and was fluent in Dutch. The duke instructed Andros to reestablish friendly rela-tionships with the province's Dutch elite — the merchants, ministers, and land-owners who dominated the city's economic and political affairs. But the English also decided to actively stimulate immigration and thereby make New York a more English city.[4]

At first glance, changing the ethnic composition of New York might not have struck the English as difficult. The city had had only about 1,500 white inhab-itants (5 percent of them English) when Stuyvesant surrendered it in 1664. Just a dozen years later, the proportion of Englishmen had climbed to 28 percent.

Yet with Boston, Philadelphia, and other English-dominated cities in North America thriving, Andros had trouble persuading Englishmen to immigrate to New York, which still felt very Dutch. "Our chiefest unhappyness here," observed a newly arrived English military officer in 1692, "is too great a mixture of nations." Even when English men and women did come to New York, they did not remain there very long. "Not knowing the knack of trading here to differ from most places," explained an English New Yorker, "they meet with discouragements and stay not to become wiser." Even thirty-five years after Stuyvesant surrendered the town to the English, the city "seemed rather like a conquered foreign province held by the terrour of a garrison," not "an English colony, possessed and settled by people of our own Nation." New York City had grown to nearly five thousand inhabitants by 1700, but the English constituted only 30 percent of that population, only fractionally higher than in 1677, and most of these English New Yorkers were relative newcomers. The most prominent Dutch families, meanwhile, further entrenched themselves in the economic and political aristocracy of the city.[5]

One of the reasons why New York stayed so Dutch is that Dutch immigrants continued to move to the city even after it fell into English hands. Most of these Dutch newcomers did not migrate to New York directly from the Netherlands but relocated there after first settling in other parts of North America. In the late 1680s and early 1690s, for example, Dutch Americans abandoned Albany by the hundreds as warfare with the Indians made life on the frontier perilous. Most of these refugees settled in New York City. Other Dutch immigrants arrived in New York after first living in the lower Hudson River valley or East Jersey. The few who did immigrate to New York directly from the Netherlands after 1664 typically came to join Dutch family members already living there.[6]

The vast majority of the New Yorkers whom the English referred to as "Dutch" were not actually natives of the Netherlands; by 1695 nearly 90 percent had been born in America. Yet these Dutch Americans went to great lengths to retain their language and customs, even decades after the English takeover, so much so that Englishmen could not easily distinguish these second- and third-generation New Yorkers from Dutch immigrants. Years after New Amsterdam became New York, Dutch inhabitants of the city continued to build their houses in what one contemporary called "the Dutch manner, with the gable ends toward the street." Dutch New Yorkers dressed differently from their English neighbors, too. The Dutch, wrote a Bostonian visiting New York in 1704, wear "French muches wch are like a capp and a head band in one, leaving their ears bare, which are sett out wth jewells of a large size and many in number. And their fingers hoop't with rings, some with large stones in them of many coullers as were their pendants in their ears, which you should see very old women wear as well as young." In winter months, English New Yorkers gawked at Dutch men and women "flying upon their skates from place to place," with huge loads "upon their heads and backs," on canals they had built before the English takeover.[7]

The trait whose persistence most amazed other New Yorkers was the devotion of the Dutch to their ancestral language. In 1699, thirty-five years after the English takeover of the city, the New York governor, Richard Coote, the first Earl of Bellomont, lamented that the typical Dutch resident of the city was "very ignorant, and can neither speak nor write proper English." The Dutch merchant elite, whose members dominated city government, did not find it necessary to learn much English either. Bellomont noted how ironic it was that three of the four candidates put forward for the office of alderman by the city's so-called English party, Johannes van Kipp, Rip van Dam, and Jacobs van Courtlandt, could "scarce speak English." Even the children and grandchildren of these Dutch New Yorkers sometimes knew little English. The city would not create public schools until the nineteenth century, so Dutch parents in this era educated their offspring in Dutch-language schools run by the Dutch Reformed Church, exacerbating the cultural isolation of Dutch New Yorkers from the rest of the population. This linguistic segregation was perpetuated by social isolation as well. Ninety-nine percent of Dutch men in New York who married in the late seventeenth and early eighteenth centuries chose Dutch women as mates, guaranteeing that another generation of New York–born children would be raised speaking a language other than English.[8]

The dangers of having an English colony that seemed so Dutch and whose inhabitants felt so little loyalty to England became apparent in the chaotic years of Leisler's Rebellion. The crisis, which lasted from 1689 to 1691, grew out of tensions in England stemming from the news that members of the English royal family had converted to Roman Catholicism. Many residents of England's North American possessions, like Anne Hutchinson, had moved to the colonies because they believed that the Church of England retained too many remnants of Catholicism. Even though few Puritans lived in New York City, its populace still harbored intense anti-Catholic sentiment. The Dutch, after all, resented recent invasions of their territory by the Catholic powers France and Spain, while most of the city's French and German immigrants were Protestants who had come to America fleeing Catholic persecution in their homelands.

During the period when Oliver Cromwell ruled England, the surviving members of the royal family lived in France and often attended Catholic services there. When Cromwell died and the English restored the Stuarts to the throne, those members of the royal family seemed even more sympathetic to Catholicism than they had been before they fled England. In 1683 King Charles II appointed an Irish Catholic, Thomas Dongan, as governor of New York. Dongan brought several Jesuit priests with him to New York City, and as soon as they arrived, they celebrated mass in the fort, the first Catholic service ever held in the city. Dongan appointed Catholics to key positions in his administration and also allowed the Jesuits to open a Catholic school. None of this could have pleased the Dutch, German, and French Protestants who dominated New York's populace. In England it was widely believed that Charles was a secret Catholic, in sentiment if not in fact, a theory seemingly confirmed by his deathbed conversion to Roman Catholicism in 1685.[9]

Because Charles died with no legitimate heirs, he was succeeded by his fifty-two-year-old brother, James, the Duke of York, after whom New York had been named twenty-one years earlier. James *had* secretly become a Catholic in the 1660s. His conversion became public in the early 1670s, when, in taking an honorific naval title, he refused to obey a parliamentary act that (in an effort to ferret out closet Catholics in government) required officeholders to repudiate transubstantiation and other Roman Catholic doctrines when they took their oath of office. English Protestants at first seemed willing to tolerate King James's Catholicism because his only surviving children, two daughters from his first marriage, had been raised as Protestants. The older, Mary, had been married (against her will at age fifteen) to her Protestant first cousin, the Dutch prince William of Orange, in an effort to reassure Englishmen who feared that James would establish a Catholic dynasty. It appeared that William and Mary and their Protestant children would succeed James and once again make England a Protestant nation.

Yet James's ascension to the throne in 1685 may have inspired him to devote more effort than he had previously to siring a male heir. In 1688, more than a decade after her last known pregnancy, James's second wife, a thirty-year-old Italian Catholic known as Mary of Modena, shocked nearly all of England by bearing him a son. This Catholic infant would become first in line for the throne if he survived. Unwilling to take such a risk, a group of Protestant noblemen asked Prince William in the Netherlands to invade England, depose James, and serve as co-monarch with his wife, Mary. William and his invasion force landed at Torbay in southwest England in November 1688, at which point James's supporters began abandoning him in droves. The king withdrew his crumbling army from the field after only a single skirmish with William's forces

and fled to France in December. Parliament quickly arranged for the coronation of William and Mary, and the "Glorious Revolution," so called because it
had transpired almost bloodlessly, was now complete.[10]

As word of these events started to trickle across the Atlantic, New York's
rulers initially tried to suppress the news, because they had been appointed
to their positions by James or his surrogates. When definitive proof of James's
ouster reached Manhattan in the early spring of 1689, New Yorkers wondered
why the ships that conveyed the news did not also carry orders to replace his
"papist" appointees with new ones loyal to William, Mary, and Protestantism.
New Yorkers who supported the Glorious Revolution demanded that city officials declare their allegiance to the new monarchs, and when those leaders
equivocated, wild rumors began to circulate about their motivations. Some
imagined that Dongan was leading an effort to make New York part of Catholic New France (modern-day Quebec). Three French warships were rumored
to be approaching New York for that very purpose. The city's leading English
official, Lieutenant Governor Francis Nicholson, slipped out of town and returned to England rather than face the crisis. Other city leaders went into hiding on Long Island or in New Jersey. The man who eventually filled this power
vacuum was an ambitious German immigrant named Jacob Leisler.[11]

Leisler was born in Frankfurt in 1640. His father, a minister whose church
catered to Frankfurt's French Protestants, was prominent in western European
Calvinist circles and had diplomatic experience as well. After his father's death
in 1653, Leisler attended a Protestant military academy, and by age eighteen he
had moved to Amsterdam. There he went to work for Cornelis Melyn, who had
once been a prominent resident of New Amsterdam but had returned to the
Netherlands after a protracted feud with Peter Stuyvesant. Nonetheless, Melyn
remained a major shareholder in the West India Company, and it was probably
through his influence that the WIC appointed the twenty-year-old Leisler as
captain of a company of WIC soldiers that left the Netherlands for Manhattan
in April 1660.[12]

Leisler's ambition and drive were impressive even by New York standards.
By age twenty-two he had established himself as a fur and tobacco merchant. A
year later he married an older woman, widow Elsie Tymens, whose stepfather,
merchant Govert Loockermans, was probably the city's wealthiest inhabitant.
Taking advantage of his new mercantile connections, Leisler came to dominate
the city's tobacco trade with the Chesapeake, though like most merchants he
tended to buy and sell whatever he thought might bring a profit. He exported
furs, salt, grain, fish, whale oil, and horses, while importing sugar, spices, cloth,
and "trade goods" to exchange with the Indians for furs. He even dabbled in indentured servants and slaves. Like any good businessman, he invested his prof-

its in a diversified portfolio, buying whole or partial shares in a number of ships as well as real estate in Manhattan, Westchester, Long Island, Albany, New Jersey, and Europe. Later he and his brothers, who lived in Basel, would branch out into banking as well. By 1676, he was the third-wealthiest resident of New York City.[13]

Leisler was also a deeply religious man, a "strict" and "ultraorthodox" Calvinist. While more and more Christians were coming to believe that humans could exert some influence over whether or not they ultimately achieved salvation, Leisler and other orthodox Calvinists thought that such ideas were heresy. So when New York's Anglican and Dutch Reformed ministers urged passive obedience to the will of the province's Catholic ruler, Leisler left New York's Dutch Church rather than endorse such notions. He instead joined New York's more militantly anti-Catholic French Reformed Church. When King Louis XIV revoked the Edict of Nantes in 1685, once again making Protestantism illegal in France, it convinced men and women like Leisler that passive obedience to Catholic monarchs was naïve and dangerous. Leisler henceforth devoted a large part of his fortune to active opposition to Catholicism. Leisler paid the immigration expenses of destitute French Protestants (known as Huguenots) and purchased 6,100 acres of land just north of New York City in what is now Westchester County for the resettlement of Huguenot refugees. The center of Protestantism in France was the city of La Rochelle, so Leisler named their American refuge New Rochelle. Another four hundred or so Huguenots settled in New York City itself; they made up about 10 percent of its population by 1689.[14]

In that year, when the Glorious Revolution prompted fears that a French Catholic invasion of New York was imminent and that the city's troops, led by officers appointed by James II, could not be trusted to repulse such an attack, New Yorkers who supported William and Mary decided to call up their own militia units to defend the city, as they put it in a letter to the king and queen, "against all your Majesties ennemies whatsoever until such time [as] your Majesty's royall will shall be further known." This movement to immediately replace the city's governing officials appealed especially to New Yorkers who felt that they had little voice in community affairs, a group that included those Dutch merchants who resented English rule, zealous Protestants who disliked Anglican acceptance of a Catholic monarch, and New Yorkers of modest means (in particular those of Dutch descent) who believed that they lacked a real voice in government. All these groups admired Leisler, and they asked him to lead their movement. He declined initially, but after the militiamen overran the fort and disarmed the "papists therein," he agreed on June 2 to command the militia until William and Mary could choose replacements for

King James's military appointees who, as Leisler put it in a letter to William and Mary, "under the aparance of the functions of the Protestant religion, remain still affected to the Papist."[15]

When word of William and Mary's coronation reached New York a day later, their ardent supporters created a "Committee of Safety" to protect what Leisler called the "Protestant power that now raigns in England." The committee members put Leisler in charge of the fort. In mid-August they expanded his military command to include the entire province. They had chosen Leisler, wrote members Samuel Edsall and Peter Delanoy to the new king in August, because he was "a true Protestant Germanian, an old stander [trained military officer] & merchant," and "a man of fervent zeale for the protestant religion." Soon thereafter, a letter arrived from King William addressed to Nicholson "and in his absence, to such as for the time being take care for preserving the peace and administering the lawes in our said Province of New York in America." It asked Nicholson to retain his position and carry out the laws with the assistance of the province's "principal freeholders and inhabitants." Since Nicholson had been missing for two months, and the mayor was still nowhere to be found, the Committee of Safety declared Nicholson's office of lieutenant governor vacant and assigned his position and responsibilities to Leisler.[16]

Leisler set to work in the summer of 1689 organizing a new provincial government. He appointed military officers, law enforcement officials, tax collectors, and justices of the peace. He even oversaw the election of a mayor, a position won by Delanoy, the first popularly elected chief magistrate the city had ever had (or would have again until 1834). Leisler seems to have honestly believed that he was merely keeping the province out of the hands of "Popish doggs & divells" until William and Mary finally found the time to appoint a new government. But some of Leisler's followers seem to have had other motives. Many were ordinary workingmen and artisans who chafed at being excluded from office under the old regime and wanted a more egalitarian form of government. Others were Dutch New Yorkers who resented English rule or Huguenots who had escaped one Catholic king only to feel threatened by another. And still others were anti-Catholic zealots convinced that James and his minions had sought "to damn the English nation," including its American territories, "to Popery and slavery."[17]

Yet while Leisler was winning over the hearts and minds of most New Yorkers, his enemies were winning the propaganda war at court back in England. Nicholson returned there and informed government leaders that Leisler was the leader of a revolutionary mob that had overthrown royal authority, slyly omitting Leisler's stated justification for taking command. Anti-Leisler New Yorkers — English officeholders as well as the Dutch grandees they had appointed to office — also flooded the court with misinformation. One typical missive depicted Leisler and his followers as "a rable" unfit "to bear the meanest offices among us." Another, from "men of quality," denounced his "drunken crue" as "most abject comon people." Leisler, they said, was the leader of a plot to put the Dutch back in command of New York. Only when it was too late did Leisler realize that the lobbyists he had sent to England were incompetents who, in the understated words of one historian, "made a very poor impression at court." Leisler apparently had no idea that what he considered a heroic intervention on behalf of William and Mary might be misconstrued in London as a radical, revolutionary plot against them.[18]

In January 1691, after Leisler had run New York for nearly eighteen months, three shiploads of English soldiers commanded by Major Richard Ingoldsby arrived in the harbor and demanded that Leisler turn the city over to them. When the troops could not produce a royal commission documenting their authority (a fourth ship carrying their leader, Colonel Henry Sloughter, had run aground off Bermuda), the officious Leisler refused to capitulate. The city was once again thrown into chaos as Ingoldsby appointed a new town council and gathered English militiamen from the city and surrounding areas to augment his military force. Leisler refused to dissolve his own legislative bodies, declaring the major and all his confederates "enemies to God."

With his popular support deteriorating as New Yorkers started to realize that Ingoldsby probably did represent William and Mary, Leisler in March retreated into the fort with his remaining adherents. On March 17, Leisler ordered his troops to fire on the English forces surrounding them; several died and more were wounded. Two days later, Sloughter arrived in New York bearing his commission. When he offered amnesty to everyone in the fort but Leisler and his ringleaders, Leisler's four hundred remaining followers laid down their arms and surrendered. On March 20, Ingoldsby took Leisler and his inner circle into custody, charging them with murder, treason, and riot.[19]

Reflecting the belief that Leisler's Rebellion had been a Dutch plot, Sloughter ordered that an all-English jury try the accused. In a further break with precedent, testimony could be given only in English, despite complaints from some of the Dutch defendants that such a rule prevented them from adequately participating in their own defense. Edsall and his son-in-law Delanoy convinced the jurors of their innocence. The court found the remaining dozen or so defendants guilty and sentenced them to be "hanged by the neck and being alive their bodys be cutt downe to the Earth, that their bowells be taken out and they being alive burnt before their faces that their heads shall be struck off and their bodyes cutt in four parts and which shall be desposed of as their Majties shall assigne."[20]

Sloughter eventually granted bail to most of the Leislerians, meaning that they could go free but that any future misbehavior might result in the revocation of their bail and their immediate execution. This ploy allowed Sloughter to look merciful while guaranteeing that the Leislerian leaders would henceforth remain politically inactive. When New Yorkers a few years later elected one of them to office anyway, a successor of Sloughter's nullified the results.

There were two men to whom Sloughter showed no mercy: Leisler and his right-hand man, Leisler's son-in-law Jacob Milborne. On May 17, 1691, the date set for their execution, Leisler briefly addressed the huge crowd assembled to witness his hanging. Leisler was humble yet unrepentant, insisting that what he had done "was for King William & Queen Mary, for the defence of the protestant religion & the good of the country." The executioner then swiftly hanged and beheaded the two men, an especially gruesome spectacle because hanging alone did not kill Milborne. Afterward, according to stories New Yorkers passed down for generations, "the crowd cut off pieces of [Leisler's] garments as precious relics, also his hair was divided, out of great veneration, as for a martyr."[21]

Why had William and Mary turned their backs on such an ardent supporter as Jacob Leisler? The monarchs probably knew nothing about him. Even the king's letter to Nicholson was ghostwritten. They left the running of the colonies to Tory parliamentary leaders who had appointed Nicholson and his subordinates and saw any challenge to their placemen as defiance of their own authority. When Parliament swung from the Tories to the Whigs in the mid-1690s, the new leaders declared Leisler and Milborne patriots and overturned their convictions. Supporters disinterred their bodies from their graves on Leisler's old farm just southeast of modern-day City Hall, and in 1698, with pomp, fanfare, and spectators attending from as far away as Pennsylvania, reburied them in a place of honor at the city's Dutch Reformed Church graveyard on Garden Street (now Exchange Place between Broad and William). Yet ever wary of celebrating anyone who questions authority, New York's leaders have never erected a monument commemorating Leisler or his "rebellion." Only in New Rochelle, whose residents never doubted the purity of his motives, is there a statue honoring him.[22]

3

ANGLICIZATION

AT THE BEGINNING of the seventeenth century, the English embarked on a bold plan to make their new colony of Ireland less Catholic and less Irish by sending thousands of Protestant Scots and Englishmen to settle there. After Leisler's Rebellion, in which Dutch, French, and German New Yorkers appeared to question English sovereignty over the city, authorities decided that they needed to Anglicize New York's institutions and population as well. In 1691, just months after they put Leisler to death, colonial officials implemented a Judiciary Act that eradicated the remnants of New York's Dutch-based legal codes and replaced them with a system predicated on English common law. The Judiciary Act also created new courts which derived their authority from the crown and whose officers had more powers than their predecessors. A few years later, the English mandated that the colony switch to the English system of weights and measures from the Dutch system, which had persisted as the standard in New York City for more than thirty years after the English conquest. Beginning around 1700, English authorities also suppressed the city's Dutch-language school system, which had allowed Dutch New Yorkers to raise children who spoke little English.

Construction of a grand new building for New York's Anglican church also began. Thirty years after the English takeover of New Amsterdam, the Church of England had no building of its own. Anglican ministers held services in the city's Dutch Reformed Church when the Dutch were not using it. In the aftermath of Leisler's Rebellion, New York Anglicans purchased land on the lower west side of Manhattan. Trinity Church, completed in 1698, towered far above every other building in the city until it was destroyed during the American Revolution.[1]

The main thing the English did to Anglicize New York, however, was the same thing they had done with Ireland decades earlier: get more English men

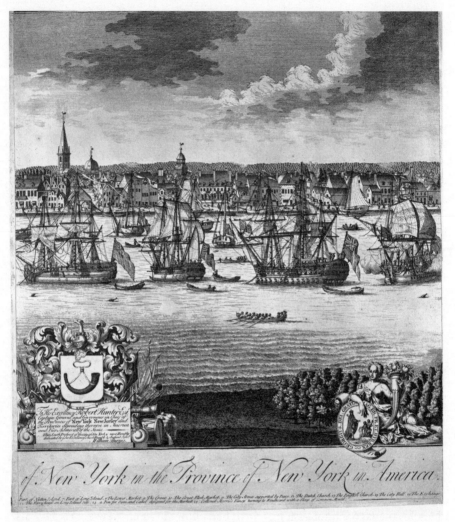

Detail of a view of New York from 1719 focusing on the portion of the city north of Wall Street. On the left is Trinity Church, by far the tallest structure in the city.

and women to immigrate. After the Glorious Revolution, increasing numbers of English immigrants came to New York, and these newcomers were more likely than previous English immigrants to settle there permanently. Few of these new New Yorkers were religious refugees. As historian Joyce Goodfriend has noted, the English influx in the early eighteenth century "was essentially an opportunistic migration of individuals who sought to improve their economic position and consequently their status in society." Most were single young adults who came to New York without other family members.

Many of these immigrants needed to indenture themselves in order to afford passage to America. John Chasy from Somerset began working off his debt in 1718 through a seven-year indenture to a New York tanner. In return for her passage, Hester Crudge from Plymouth pledged in 1726 to work for five years for New York "victualler" James Murphy. He had to provide "sufficient meat, drink, apparel, lodging and washing" for her, and at the end of her five-year term "give her . . . a gown and petticoat & a good garlix shift" made of linen. Servants who fled town before finishing their terms of service were a perennial problem for New York employers. In 1730 a brewer advertised for information concerning the whereabouts of Henry Pincher, a runaway "servant man . . . about 26 years of age . . . by trade a house carpenter, a mason and a pump maker." Even though Pincher was a native of England's "West Country," the ad said, he "speaks pretty good English."[2]

While some immigrants financed their passage to America through an indenture, New York actually stood out in this period for its relative *lack* of indentured servants. An indentured servant was a big and relatively risky investment for employers. They had to pay the servant's ship fare up front, and if the servant died or ran away, employers would have nothing to show for their investment.

In most parts of America, immigrants came overwhelmingly from the lowest socioeconomic strata of English society, but that was not the case in New York. Many English merchants sent sons or junior partners to New York to personally oversee their operations in the thriving colony. Trading conditions could change virtually overnight as a result of a tropical storm, a foreign threat, or hints of a bad harvest, so it paid for England's hundreds of substantial import-export concerns to have trusted employees in New York to make the snap decisions that could turn a sudden catastrophe into a cash windfall. The remaining English immigrants coming to New York were much more likely to be skilled artisans than were those going to Virginia, Maryland, or rural portions of Pennsylvania and New York. Artisans had the means to pay their own way, in the hope that New York's large merchant population would provide a robust market for their goods and services.[3]

Another characteristic of New York's English immigrants in this era is that a surprising number of them — perhaps nearly half — came from London. In the first half of the eighteenth century, Londoners had heard more about North America than Englishmen in the countryside. Londoners were also more likely to know someone who had immigrated to New York, know when the next ship for America would be leaving if they hoped to join their friends or associates, and know where to find people who could finance the journey if they could not do so on their own. Even the shorter trip from their residence to the immigrant ship made Londoners more likely than other Englishmen to emigrate in this period, as they would need to spend fewer days unemployed and away from home before the voyage to America began. Immigrants from all over England lived in eighteenth-century New York, but Londoners dominated.[4]

As part of their Anglicization effort, New York's leaders also encouraged the emigration of more Scots to New York. The Acts of Union of 1706 and 1707, which more firmly bound Scotland to England under a single kingdom known as Great Britain, brought about political and economic upheaval in Scotland that persuaded many of its inhabitants to emigrate. Most Scots who settled in New York before 1760 were Lowlanders from southeast Scotland. Some had bought shares of "proprietary lands" in New Jersey before their arrival. King James had granted this property to royal favorites, who then sold their rights to consortiums of well-connected investors who tried to create Scottish settlements in New Jersey. The investment consortiums sold shares in their communities to ambitious individual Scots. When these communities struggled, their residents often moved to New York City.

As was the case with New York's English immigrants, merchants constituted a disproportionate share of the Scottish arrivals. One did not need to be a merchant before coming to America, however, to become one in the New World. David Vilant, a Scot who initially came to America to settle on a share of proprietary land he had bought in New Jersey, had by 1695 moved to New York City, where he worked initially as a schoolteacher. By 1707 he had joined the city's large merchant community.

The increasing Scottish presence in New York manifested itself in a number of ways. Scottish accents became less of a novelty in the city's markets and taverns. Scots established a Presbyterian church, the city's first, on Wall Street in 1717. The city's Scots had previously gone to Dutch or French churches, though they found those so foreign they often gave up churchgoing altogether. Three Scotsmen — Robert Hunter, William Burnet, and John Montgomerie — even held the governorship of New York for twenty of the twenty-two years from 1710 to 1731. As one historian has noted, "a majority of the colonial elite" that gathered around these governors "were Scots-born," and "most were of obscure origin and would have remained unknown if they had stayed in Great Britain." The significance of New York's Scottish immigrants was further confirmed in 1744, when they set up a mutual aid society to distribute charity to "their indigent countrymen in these parts." In 1756, Scots reorganized these efforts under the auspices of the St. Andrew's Society, which operates to this day.[5]

Immigration to New York from Ireland also increased markedly in the early 1700s. Depressed prices for Irish linens and woolens, and high rents charged by absentee English landlords, drove many Irish men and women to leave for America. Irish Presbyterians, primarily the descendants of immigrants from Scotland, suffered discrimination at the hands of Ireland's Anglican rulers, so they, too, often departed for New York.

The bulk of the Irish immigrants, reported Governor Hunter in 1720, came "from the North of Ireland." Ulster, the northeast portion of Ireland, directly across the Irish Sea from Scotland, was home to many of these dissatisfied "Scots Irish." Most were Protestants — Presbyterians in particular — but Catholics made up about a quarter of the total. Irish Catholics began to leave Ireland for the same reasons as the Irish Protestants — hoping they would find greater religious freedom and economic opportunity in New York.[6]

New Yorkers did not welcome the Irish Catholics with open arms. Commenting on a shipload of Irish soldiers who arrived in New York in 1700 after a twelve-week transatlantic journey, New York's Irish-born Protestant governor Lord Bellomont complained that "the recruits that came from Ireland are a parcel of the vilest fellows that ever wore the King's livery, the very scum of the army in Ireland," including many "papists."[7]

The city's residents were also wary of Irish immigrants because they were poor. Writing in 1726, twenty-year-old Ben Franklin found appalling "the miserable circumstances of the passengers" on board an Irish immigrant ship headed for New York from Dublin. He wondered how the more well-to-do passengers could live for weeks "confined and stifled up with such a lousy, stinking rabble." Irish immigrants were much more likely to be indentured than immigrants from elsewhere. "You can emigrate for nothing, boys," declared an old Irish ballad, so rather than "toil and starve like slaves," they should "trust [themselves] across the waves, / And emigrate for nothing." But coming to America as an indentured servant when most other immigrants had ceased to do so carried a stigma. An ad in the New-York Gazette from 1729 seeking places for fifty Irish indentured servants from Dublin insisted that they not originate in the lowest strata of Irish society. "Most of the men are handy-crafts," stated the notice, meaning they were artisans trained "as weavers, taylors, coopers [barrel makers], blacksmiths, cordwainers [shoemakers], felt-makers, brasiers [brass founders], brewers, butchers and the rest are farmers and labourers." In another ad offering the services of Irish indentured servants, a ship captain felt obliged to state that "master and mate make oath that none of them are convicted criminals but that they are persons that freely and voluntarily engaged themselves by indentures, to serve a certain time for their passage."[8]

Even though most Irish New Yorkers in the early eighteenth century were Protestants of English or Scottish ancestry, they still seemed socially and culturally distinct from other New Yorkers. In part this was because Irish was the primary language of many, even those from Ulster. And like most immigrant groups, the Irish tended to socialize among themselves. In 1716 a French Huguenot with Irish kin recorded in his journal that when he visited New York, he "went to the tavern and was there with the Irish club until ten." Even as the Irish immigrant community in New York grew larger and more heterogeneous in the decade or two before the American Revolution, Irish origins would remain a stigma that these immigrants would have to fight to overcome.[9]

The British islands of the Caribbean were another source of immigrants who helped Anglicize New York. Some of these immigrants had been born in England and immigrated to the West Indies, as these islands were then known, before deciding to relocate to New York. Others were the children or grandchildren of Caribbean immigrants who decided that greater opportunities awaited them on the North American mainland. In both cases, the choice of New York as a new home was probably inspired by the close commercial ties between the Caribbean Islands and New York City.

The dream of James II to make New York the mainland hub of an English Caribbean empire largely came true in the early 1700s. While most ships leaving Dutch New Amsterdam carried goods bound ultimately for Europe, English New Yorkers sent most of their exports to the Caribbean. New York became the main source of supplies for the inhabitants of Barbados, Jamaica, and other English islands. Some of the immigrants from the English Caribbean were men of substance who had failed in their attempts to become sugar barons and were now seeking a fresh start in New York. Others were experienced Caribbean merchants who had traded with New York for years and now sought the more wide-ranging business opportunities available on the mainland. And still others were men and women of modest means who had heard that New York offered ambitious newcomers many paths to upward mobility.[10]

As the British worked to Anglicize New York, they ironically allowed it to become more religiously diverse as well. In his last years on the throne, James had pressed for more religious freedom in England, in part so his own Catholic faith would be less maligned. As a result, New York's leaders were much more tolerant of religious minorities than New Amsterdam's rulers had been. On the eve of the Glorious Revolution, Governor Dongan catalogued New York's religious diversity without the sense of alarm that had characterized similar reports from his Dutch predecessors. The city, he wrote, was home to a Church of England congregation, a "Dutch Calvinist" congregation, a "French Calvinist" congregation, and a "Dutch Lutheran" congregation. There were only a "few Roman Catholicks," but an "abundance of Quakers," as well as "Sabbatarians;

Antisabbatarians; some Anabaptists[;] some independents; some Jews; in short of all sorts of opinions there are some."[11]

Parliament refused, during the reign of James II, to comply with the king's request to make religious toleration the law of the land. Once he had gone into exile in France, however, and the monarchy was back in the hands of Protestants, Parliament did approve in 1689 an Act of Toleration that guaranteed the right of public worship to everyone *except* Catholics. New York's provincial assembly enacted a similar measure in 1691, and provincial governors were subsequently instructed to "permit a Liberty of Conscience to all Persons (except Papists) so they be contented with a quiet and peaceable enjoyment of the same." New Yorkers, who already lived in one of the most religiously diverse places in the world, could now practice their religions more freely. The city became even more religiously diverse with the arrival of the Scotch Presbyterians, German Lutherans, and German Jews who immigrated in ever larger numbers after 1700.[12]

Of course, eighteenth-century New York City was no idyll of toleration. Jews were sometimes mocked and taunted on the streets; even their funeral processions were not safe from molestation. Jews were also barred from voting and serving in the government, though New Yorkers often ignored these laws, allowing Jews to vote for and hold municipal offices. Christians could face persecution as well. In 1707 Lord Cornbury, the province's governor and a zealous proponent of quickly Anglicizing the colony, ordered the arrest of Presbyterian leader Francis Makemie for preaching without a license. Cornbury insisted that the full protections of the English Acts of Toleration did not apply in the colonies. The courts ruled otherwise, but only after Makemie had spent three months in jail. Presbyterians finally opened their first New York church in 1716. Cornbury also claimed the right to fill ministerial vacancies in the province's Dutch Reformed Church — with *Anglican* clerics! British officials eventually countermanded these appointments as well. Lord Cornbury was exceptional in his zeal to circumscribe religious freedom, but every governor after 1689 took pains to enforce the "except Papists" clause of the toleration laws. New Yorkers banned Catholic priests from the province altogether; any found there after 1700 faced imprisonment for life.[13]

While many considered the diversity of beliefs to be the most notable feature of New York's religious landscape, other observers found New York more remarkable for its citizens' lack of religious devotion. A visitor from Boston in 1697 was shocked to discover that New Yorkers "seeme not very strict in keepeing the Sabbath." He found women "shelling peas at they[r] doors[,] children playing at they[r] usuall games in the streetes & ye taverns filled." John Miller, an Anglican minister who arrived in New York in 1695, also considered its citizens' lack of piety alarming. The city, he reported to his bishop, was a sink of "irreligion, drunkenness, cursing and swearing, fornication and adultery, thieving, and other evils." Rather than settle down and marry, Miller reported, New Yorkers of both sexes were "wandering libertines" for whom "ante-nuptial fornication" was "not looked upon as any scandal or sin at all." Women often did not marry "till a great belly" obliged them to wed their lover. A Virginian visiting the city a few years earlier did not find New Yorkers' lack of religious rectitude as shocking as Miller, but he nonetheless considered it noteworthy that the residents "seem not concerned what religion their neighbor is of, or whether hee hath any or none."[14]

Aside from groups like the Huguenots, few immigrants in this period came to New York mainly for religious freedom. After all, the religions New Yorkers practiced did not enjoy a higher status or more protections there than in any other part of the British Empire. Instead, it was economic opportunity that still attracted most prospective immigrants to New York. "Read this Letter," Irish immigrant James Murray wrote in 1737 to his former minister in County Tyrone, "and tell aw [all] the poor folk of your place, that God has open'd a door for their deliverance; for [t]here is ne [no] scant of breed [bread] here." People in New York earn as much in one year, Murray boasted, as they make in three years doing the same work in northern Ireland. "I had but sma [small] learning when I left ye, and now wad ye think it, I hea [have] 20 pund a year for being a clark." The "trades are ow [all] gud here" too, Murray reported. "A wabster [weaver] gets 12 pence a yeard, a labourer gets 4 shillings and 5 pence a day, [and] a lass gets 4 shillings and 6 pence a week for spinning on the wee wheel," he wrote, revealing the persistence of Scottish dialect among the Irish of Scotch descent. Murray recommended, however, that immigrants bring to America all the clothing and tools they would need, for while artisans' wages were high in New York, so too was the price of their products. But overall, Murray concluded, "the young foke in Ereland are aw [all] but a pack of couards" if they refuse to come to America, "for I will tell ye in short, this is a bonny country."[15]

As Murray noted, one of the attractions of New York was the high pay it offered even to unskilled workers. The pay "rate of laborers runs high in this country," complained New York governor Benjamin Fletcher in 1696, a sentiment employers reiterated throughout the colonial period. Another factor luring immigrants to New York, as Murray recognized, was the occupational mobility it offered. "Every man of industry and integrity has it in his power to live well," wrote one New Yorker in 1757, "and many are the instances of persons, who came here distressed by their poverty, who now enjoy easy and plentiful fortunes." Murray, for example, who was a poor writer, could nonetheless become a clerk in his new home. The shortage of skilled workers in the city meant that employers were more likely to share trade secrets with their hired hands in order to keep up with demand for their products, making it easier for indentured servants to follow a "handycraft" when their term expired. And we have seen how immigrants from almost any walk of life could enter the ranks of the merchant class with the right combination of ambition, contacts, and good luck, though that was undoubtedly becoming more difficult as the eighteenth century progressed and the amount of capital needed to compete with New York's merchant princes grew steadily higher.[16]

By 1730, the majority of male New Yorkers were tradesmen, while the bulk of the remainder were merchants, shopkeepers, and lower-status white-collar workers such as clerks, schoolteachers, government functionaries, and the like. Only a very small number were unskilled day laborers. Back in their European homelands, in contrast, day laborers made up a large portion of the population. The ability to ascend beyond the ranks of the unskilled attracted many immigrants to New York.[17]

Precisely how high one might climb depended to a significant degree on an immigrant's birthplace, because already by the late 1600s, well-defined ethnic niches had developed in New York's workshops and on its waterfront. In both 1695 and 1730, attorneys, tavern keepers, food purveyors, mariners, and ship carpenters were overwhelmingly British. House carpenters, by contrast, remained predominantly Dutch, as did the ranks of the city's shoemakers, bakers, and metalworkers, even in 1730, when Dutch Americans no longer constituted a majority of the city's population. French immigrants and Jews (of both German and Iberian origin) were overrepresented in only one area of the city's economy: its merchant ranks.[18]

A New Yorker's ethnicity influenced not just what occupation he followed but also to some extent where in the city he or she lived. In the early 1700s, Dutch New Yorkers concentrated in the North Ward just above Wall Street and in the South Ward, especially on Pearl Street. In that same period, the English predominated in the East Ward and the Dock Ward, especially on Queen and Dock streets near the East River. The location of religious institutions sometimes contributed to these patterns. French immigrants congregated near their Protestant church on Marketfield Street, a large number of Dutch lived near the Dutch Reformed Church on Garden Street, and many Jews settled in the South and Dock wards near the city's first synagogue, which opened on Mill Street in 1730.[19]

By that date, despite the continuing presence of non-English residential enclaves and occupational clusters, the city was largely Anglicized. New Yorkers of Dutch descent, for example, no longer constituted the majority by 1720, and by the mid-1730s, much of the city's population could trace its ancestry to the British Isles. Dutch New Yorkers also wielded less political power. Their representation on the Board of Aldermen, their last bastion of power, had declined precipitously by the 1730s. Perhaps most dramatic was the near disappearance of the Dutch language from the life of the city. "As late as 20 years ago," wrote a German minister in 1749, "most everything was still Dutch." But since then, "everything seems to have turned to English." Dutch New Yorkers also recognized the change. "All affairs are transacted in English and that language prevails generally amongst us," reported a wistful Dutch New Yorker in the 1740s. A few years later, another lamented that "the Dutch tongue is . . . almost entirely become useless. It is scarce necessary in an office, business, condition, or employment." Some of the city's "elderly people" still spoke Dutch, and Dutch Reformed services were still conducted in that language, but otherwise Dutch New Yorkers "were succumbing to the English language."[20]

With the arrival of so many immigrants from Great Britain, the population of New York in the eighteenth century grew more rapidly than it had under the Dutch. From about 5,000 inhabitants in 1700, the city grew to 7,500 inhabitants in the 1720s, 10,000 around 1740, 15,000 around 1760, and 22,000 in 1771, the year of the last census before the Revolution. We know the colonies experienced a huge influx of immigrants from Great Britain after that census, because rumors that the authorities would ban further British emigration to the thirteen colonies as punishment for their inhabitants' resistance to parliamentary taxation brought an unprecedented influx. The population of the city probably stood at about 25,000 by the fall of 1775, when the Revolutionary War effectively closed the port of New York.[21]

This impressive rate of growth took place despite occasional outbreaks of epidemic disease. One of the most dreaded of these maladies was yellow fever, a virus spread by mosquitoes that causes fevers, vomiting, and organ failure. The degeneration of the liver brings on jaundice and, consequently, a yellowing of the skin that gives the disease its name. Yellow fever is a tropical malady, but mosquitoes carrying the virus occasionally made their way to New York on ships originating in the Caribbean. In 1702 an outbreak of yellow fever killed 570 New Yorkers, more than 10 percent of the city's population. Many hundreds more fell ill but managed to survive. Those who could afford to do so relocated out of town until the scourge had passed.[22]

More common than yellow fever, and just as deadly, were measles and smallpox. Though measles is not usually fatal, children are especially vulnerable to it. Smallpox, by contrast, is a more gruesome viral malady in which the body becomes covered with pustules that ooze a thick yellow fluid. Fever and vomiting commonly accompany the pox. The disease can be spread either through the air or through contact with pus from another sufferer. Though both measles and smallpox claimed victims throughout the colonial period, New York suffered a particularly severe outbreak of both in 1731. "There never was so great a mortality here since I came to this place as now," wrote one immigrant about the epidemic that year. "Theres no day but what theres numbers of buryings." In particular, "many children dye," reported another New Yorker, "and the country people are afraid to come to town which makes markets thin, provisions dear, and deadens all trade, and it goes very hard with the poor." At least 549 New Yorkers, 6 percent of the population, died of the two diseases in this outbreak. Such epidemics were common throughout the British Empire, so while they might delay potential immigrants from coming to New York, they did not deter them.[23]

The growth of the city's population necessitated an expansion of its size. Until about 1700, settlement had been constrained by the defensive wall that ran

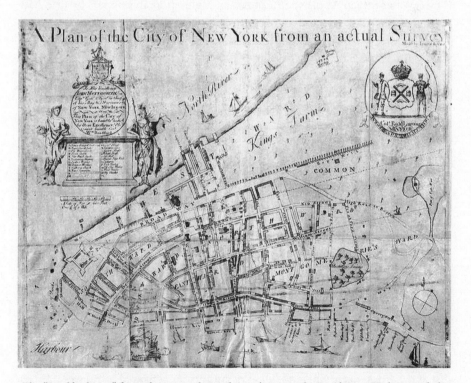

The "Bradford Map" from about 1731 shows the city's six wards. Dutch New Yorkers tended to live in those that ran down the center of the island, while the wards along the East River held larger numbers of English immigrants.

along the north side of Wall Street from the Hudson to the East River. With the removal of the barrier, the city expanded rapidly northward. A detailed map of the city published around 1731 by printer William Bradford shows streets laid out and houses built as far north as modern-day City Hall, with almost all the new construction concentrated on the east side of Manhattan. The expansion came as a relief to immigrants, who, even in this era, found rents in the city shocking. "I have eight in family and know not yet where to fix them," wrote a newly arrived colonial official around 1700. "Houses are so scarce and dear."[24]

Though it was not difficult to find property to develop on the northern fringes of town, New Yorkers then, as now, wished they could instead add more land to the city's most desirable neighborhoods. City fathers came up with an answer: auction off the rights to expand the landmass of Manhattan by dumping landfill at the water's edge along the East River. Thus, while in Peter Stuyvesant's day the banks of the East River lapped up to the edge of Pearl Street (then known as Dock or Queen Street), Bradford's map shows that by 1730, the southeast edge of the island had been expanded one block farther east to what is now Water Street. At the southern end of Manhattan, developers by 1730 had expanded Manhattan by two blocks to what is now Front Street. Over the next century, developers expanded lower Manhattan farther still, so that one had to walk three entire blocks (six hundred feet) from the original East River shoreline at Pearl Street to the new waterfront at South Street. On the west side of lower Manhattan, two entire blocks were added to the island's landmass. When Hurricane Sandy hit New York City in 2012, the river reclaimed every bit of its old territory. A map of the storm's high-water mark eerily (and almost identically) matches the river's original boundaries.[25]

Bradford, whose map documenting the expansion of Manhattan's shoreline is one of the gems of the city's cartographic treasury, took as much interest in politics as he did in printing. He had been born to Quaker parents in Leicestershire, England, in 1663. Bradford's father was also a printer, but, following the custom of the day, he apprenticed his son to another printer, Andrew Sowle (the foremost Quaker printer in London), rather than teach William the trade himself. Bradford must have impressed his master, for Sowle allowed his daughter Elizabeth to marry him. Perhaps feeling that business prospects for Quakers in England were constrained before the Glorious Revolution and the Acts of Toleration, Sowle arranged for the couple to emigrate to William Penn's new Quaker sanctuary of Pennsylvania, where they arrived in 1685.

Bradford discovered that printing Quaker tracts in Pennsylvania could be just as hazardous as in England. Quaker authorities censured him several times and jailed him for four months in 1692 when he printed the writings of a controversial Society of Friends leader. Fed up with Pennsylvania's quarrelsome

THE RELATIONSHIP BETWEEN THE EXPANSION OF MANHATTAN ISLAND
AND THE FLOODING RESULTING FROM HURRICANE SANDY, 2012

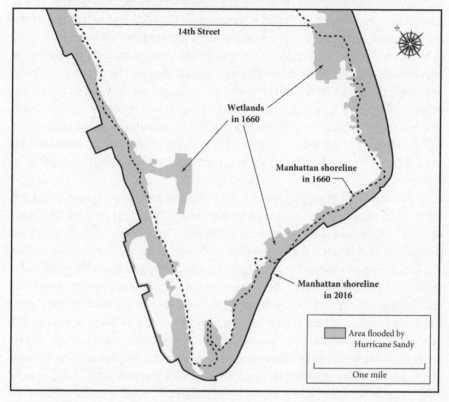

Quakers, Bradford accepted an offer to become the official printer of the province of New York. In the spring of 1693, he moved his family to New York City,
where he quit the Friends and, like many newcomers looking to get ahead,
joined Trinity Church.

Bradford built himself a booming business in New York. He printed the first
published records of American legislative proceedings, produced New York's
first paper money, and issued the first American edition of the Church of England's Book of Common Prayer. In 1725 he established New York City's first
newspaper, the weekly *Gazette,* which, along with miscellaneous news items,
carried government advertisements notifying the public of judicial proceedings and new laws. Bradford understood that his livelihood depended in large
part on the government printing that made up such a huge portion of his business. Even a piece of ephemera like his map of the city was aimed at maintaining that patronage. Bradford appears to have originally intended it as a gift for

the province's new governor, John Montgomerie, whose favor Bradford would need to curry if he hoped to maintain his contracts.[26]

Bradford employed a staff of journeyman printers and apprentices. In exchange for free room, board, and instruction in the "arts and mysteries" of the printer's craft, an apprentice promised to work for Bradford without pay for five years, sometimes even longer. In Europe, guilds strictly limited the number of apprentices who could be trained to prevent an oversupply of competitors in any single trade, but American cities did not have guilds, and that fact explains, in part, why there was so much upward occupational mobility in New York. When Bradford, who lived almost to age ninety, looked back on his long career and the dozens of apprentices he had trained, there was one he undoubtedly wished he had turned away: a thirteen-year-old German refugee named John Peter Zenger.

While the English primarily encouraged British immigrants, they could not resist, from time to time, helping other travelers to New York, especially if they, like the Huguenots, were persecuted European Protestants. In the early 1700s the most famous such refugees were the "Palatine" Germans. Members of either the Lutheran or Reformed (Calvinist) Church, they came from the small rural region of Pfalz on the west side of the Rhine River midway between Frankfurt and Strasbourg. In 1688–89 and again in the early 1700s, French armies overran Pfalz, implementing a scorched-earth policy that left "such a desolation," according to one of Louis XIV's own military commanders, that the king's ministers feared it would sully his reputation for posterity. Famine, epidemics, and economic calamity resulted for the region's surviving residents. After several years of such hardship, thousands of these Germans fled, and many were drawn to England by rumors that the British would give them free land. Eager to act once again as a sanctuary for oppressed Protestants but not wanting the Palatines to settle in England, Parliament enacted a special law naturalizing the Germans and sent 2,500 of them to New York.[27]

The Palatine Germans arrived in New York Harbor in the summer of 1710 malnourished, sick with typhus, and eager to settle on the farms promised to them. New Yorkers, wanting as little interaction as possible with the sickly newcomers, quarantined them on Nut Island until they could be shipped up the Hudson. Several hundred died in quarantine before they ever set foot on the American mainland. Most of the rest were transported northward into the interior of the colony, but forty or so boys found apprenticeships in the city. One was Zenger, who parted ways with his mother and two younger siblings (his father had died during the sea voyage) and moved in with the owner of the city's only printing shop, William Bradford.

In a perverse way, it was probably good for Zenger that his father died when he did. Had he not, Zenger would have been shipped up the Hudson, where the Palatine Germans were not given farms as they had been promised but were instead put to work making pine tar, noxious labor that other Americans refused to do. When the Palatines tried to leave, they were forcibly detained and told that the price for their passage to America was seven years of servitude boiling pine tar. Only after two years of protests and litigation were the Germans able to vacate the pine tar camps. By that point Zenger had learned English, a new and valuable trade, and, from observing Bradford, how to parlay political connections into a thriving business.[28]

As soon as his apprenticeship ended in 1718, Zenger struck out on his own, moving first to Philadelphia and then to Chestertown, the capital of Maryland, where he hoped to emulate Bradford by establishing relationships that would enable him to become the colony's official printer. He failed to do so, and his young wife, Mary, died, leaving the widower to care for their young son, John junior. Perhaps hoping that his mother or sister might help care for the youngster, Zenger returned to New York, where he remarried in 1723 and went back to work for Bradford in 1725, the year the *Gazette* first appeared. One short year later, Zenger had set up shop for himself, in direct competition with Bradford; they had the only two print shops in town. Still, Zenger had trouble drumming up business. He did manage to become the printer of choice for New Yorkers wishing to publish Dutch-language pamphlets, tracts, or books, but by this point there was rarely more than one or two of those produced per year.

The political world did eventually bring Zenger more business — a lot more — though in a manner that neither he nor Bradford could have anticipated. When Governor Montgomerie died suddenly in 1731, the British sent as his replacement William Cosby, an Irish-born Protestant military officer who had married his way into the English aristocracy and then brazenly used those connections to enrich himself. New Yorkers understood, as their Supreme Court chief justice wrote in 1729, that their governors "do not come here to take the air" but "either to repair a shattered fortune" or to acquire one for the first time. But even by those standards, Cosby was a particularly shameless spoilsman. At a posting in Minorca, Cosby confiscated, on trumped-up charges, a shipload of snuff from a Portuguese merchant and then sold it for his own profit. Cosby was sued for this crime in London, and a court there ruled against him. The huge judgment nearly bankrupted him. Barely solvent, Cosby lobbied his wife's first cousin, Thomas Pelham-Holles, the Duke of Newcastle and one of King George II's chief foreign policy advisers, for a colonial appointment. Newcastle first gave Cosby a minor sinecure in the Caribbean, but as he was about to take up the post, Cosby heard about Montgomerie's death and demanded the governorship of New York instead. Newcastle acquiesced, and Cosby arrived in Manhattan in August 1732.

Upon taking office, Cosby immediately made clear his intentions to sup at the public trough. When the provincial assembly awarded him a welcome "present" of £750, Cosby deemed it insufficient and browbeat the legislators into giving him more. Cosby then demanded that his predecessor, interim governor Rip van Dam, give Cosby half the salary Van Dam had collected while holding that position. When Van Dam refused, Cosby sued him and ordered that the provincial Supreme Court decide the case rather than a jury. When the court's chief justice, Lewis Morris, dismissed Cosby's suit in April 1733, Cosby retaliated by firing Morris.[29]

Even before Morris's dismissal, Cosby had managed to offend the vast majority of New Yorkers. "No man was ever so universally hated as he is," insisted Morris. Those nursing grievances against the governor included not only Morris and his political supporters but also those who feared corruption by a despotic governor with nearly unlimited powers; wealthy New York landowners outside of the mercantile elite who believed that Cosby turned too often to merchants for advice and appointments; and most New Yorkers of modest means, who cherished political rights they had gained under Governor Montgomerie and feared losing them under Cosby's authoritarian and arbitrary rule. When these groups, led by Morris, Van Dam, and attorneys James Alexander (an immigrant from Scotland) and William Smith (who had come to New York as a teenager from Buckinghamshire), sought an outlet through which to publicize their complaints against Cosby, they knew they could not go to Bradford, whose livelihood demanded loyalty to the governor. They turned to the only other printer in town, John Peter Zenger.[30]

Morris, Van Dam, Alexander, and Smith flooded Zenger with work printing broadsides, tracts, satirical poems, and political cartoons publicizing Cosby's misdeeds and advocating that the city's voters punish the governor's cronies at the polls. In November 1733 the group started to publish its own newspaper, the *New-York Weekly Journal*. Sometimes the *Journal* reprinted essays from the English press on the threats to liberty that could arise from the abuse of power. In other cases the paper directly attacked Cosby for turning "the laws themselves" into "a dead letter" through the exercise of "arbitrary power," flouting the law, and corrupting the judicial system of New York. The columns of the paper even contained fake advertisements lampooning the governor and his lackeys. Alexander was the driving force behind the paper, but the only name that appeared on the masthead was that of its printer, Zenger.[31]

The Morrisites advocated a slew of political reforms already in place in Philadelphia and Boston: making fewer government positions appointive; holding more frequent elections to make officeholders more accountable to the people; using a secret ballot to prevent electoral intimidation; and safeguarding judges from gubernatorial coercion. Only in this manner, insisted an allegorical essayist sympathetic to the Morrisites, could honest workingmen such as "Shuttle" the weaver, "Plane" the carpenter, "Drive" the cartman, "Mortar" the mason, and "Tar" the sailor protect their "rights and liberties" from "Gripe" the merchant, "Squeeze" the shopkeeper, and attorneys "Spintext and Quible." When the next major election was held, in September 1734, Morris and his informal opposition party won control of the city's Common Council.[32]

Cosby had tried to silence the *Journal* just weeks after it began publication, asking a grand jury to charge Zenger with "seditious libel" for the abuse the governor suffered at the hands of its parodists. The jurors, however, refused to indict him. After the 1734 elections, Cosby renewed his efforts. When a new grand jury also declined to charge Zenger, Cosby bypassed normal judicial process and instructed the man he had handpicked as Morris's successor as chief justice of the Supreme Court, James De Lancey, to order the editor's arrest for seditious libel. A proclamation signed by Cosby charged that the *Journal* contained "scandalous, virulent, false and seditious" attacks on the governor and, implicitly, on King George II as well. Cosby also directed four issues of the *Journal* "to be burned by the hands of the common hangman or whipper near the pillory in this city." De Lancey set bail so high that Zenger remained in jail until his trial started, nearly nine months later. During that period, Zenger's wife, employees, and friends continued to publish the *Journal*. His jailhouse letters were the featured content of each issue, and the public was so absorbed by the case that circulation reached an all-time high.[33]

Cosby and his henchmen tried every trick in the book to secure the guilty verdict they sought. The clerk of the court attempted to pack the jury with Cosby supporters, though Zenger's allies discovered the ruse and foiled it. When Alexander and Smith filed a pretrial motion challenging De Lancey's authority to charge Zenger, De Lancey disbarred them and designated as Zenger's new defense counsel a Cosby supporter with minimal courtroom experience. The printer's partisans insisted that he not rely solely on this court-appointed attorney. Knowing that a New York lawyer might be reluctant to take the case, Alexander traveled to Pennsylvania, where he persuaded one of that colony's best trial attorneys, Andrew Hamilton, to take it on.[34]

The celebrated trial of John Peter Zenger, at City Hall on Wall Street, was begun and completed on a single day, August 4, 1735. The prosecution commenced by calling witnesses to prove that Zenger had printed the newspaper issues in question. Hamilton stunned the court by agreeing to stipulate that

Zenger had indeed published the offending pieces. This was a risky strategy, because under the law of that era, seditious libel was defined as the dissemination of *any* information, even the truth, that might bring the government into disrepute. With Hamilton's admission, the prosecutor was so certain of conviction that he immediately rested his case, on the presumption that since "Mr. Hamilton has confessed the printing and publishing [of] these libels, I think the jury must find a verdict for the king."[35]

"Not so," retorted Hamilton. He took the floor and argued that the jury had the right to determine both the facts of the case and the meaning of the libel law, and could decide that even though Zenger did print the issues of the *Journal* in question, doing so might not constitute seditious libel if the newspaper's accusations were true. De Lancey informed Hamilton and the jury that Zenger's attorney was mistaken, but Hamilton would not be deterred, insisting that the twelve jurors had "a right beyond all dispute, to determine both the law and the fact." In an impassioned speech on the theme of justice and liberty lasting several hours, Hamilton told the jurors that no matter what the court might instruct them, "if there is no falsehood in Mr. Zenger's papers," they should find him innocent: "It is your right to do so."

Hamilton concluded by reminding the jurors of the huge stakes involved in the Zenger case. "The question before the court and you, gentlemen of the jury, is not of small or private concern; it is not the cause of a poor printer, nor of New York alone, which you are now trying: no! It may, in its consequence, affect every freeman that lives under a British government on the main of America. It is the best cause: it is the cause of liberty!" If the jurors did the right thing, Hamilton promised that "every man who prefers freedom to a life of slavery will bless and honor you, as men who have baffled the attempt of tyranny." Furthermore, he told them, they will have "laid a noble foundation for securing to ourselves, our posterity, and our neighbors, that, to which nature and the laws of our country have given us a right — the liberty — both of exposing and opposing arbitrary power . . . by speaking and writing truth." With those stirring words, Hamilton rested his case.

De Lancey and the prosecutor instructed the jurors to ignore Hamilton's hyperbole and "leave to the court" the question of what constituted libel. The jurors should merely rule on whether or not Zenger "was guilty of printing and publishing the libels" described in the charges. Nonetheless, after deliberating for only a few minutes, the jurors returned to the courtroom and pronounced Zenger not guilty. "There were three huzzas in the hall, which was crowded with people" when the verdict was announced, and the next day Zenger was set free.[36]

The Zenger case is one of the landmarks of American legal history, though not because it set any precedent; it was not a judicial opinion that later jurists could cite. Instead, the Zenger trial was important for two main reasons. First, Hamilton's argument on Zenger's behalf is widely seen as the ideological precedent for the notion of freedom of the press that Americans would enshrine fifty years later in the Bill of Rights. Second, the case helped to crystallize Americans' growing unhappiness with their servile colonial status and the arbitrary rule that often came with it. According to Gouverneur Morris, a signer of the Constitution and grandson of Lewis Morris, "The trial of Zenger, in 1735, was the germ of American freedom — the morning star of that liberty which subsequently revolutionized America." Generations of scholars have come to the same conclusion.[37]

New Yorkers valued their "liberty," but they did not believe that all should share in it equally. In September 1737, for example, the very same William Smith who had represented Zenger appeared once again before a New York judge, this time in support of the disenfranchisement of the city's Jews. Successfully arguing that it was an insult to "the honor of Christianity" to allow Jews to exercise "the civil rights of citizenship," Smith (according to his son) "so pathetically described the bloody tragedy at Mount Calvary" that a member of the jury hearing the case "cried out with agony and in tears, beseeching him to desist . . . Many others wept; and the unfortunate Israelites were content to lose their votes, could they escape with their lives; for some . . . were so inflamed by this oratory, that but for the interposition of their demagogues, . . . the whole tribe . . . would have been massacred that very day."[38]

Attorney Smith also played a central role in an even greater miscarriage of justice against other New York minority groups four years later. In March and early April of 1741, a number of suspicious fires broke out in the city. The first completely destroyed the residence of Lieutenant Governor George Clarke inside Fort George (as the English had rechristened the fortress at the southern tip of Manhattan). Week after week, New Yorkers discovered more unusual fires, though none caused nearly as much damage as the first. The climax came with four blazes on a single day, April 6. Eyewitnesses saw a slave fleeing the scene of one, and suddenly it all seemed to make sense. Cries of "The Negroes are rising!" rang throughout the city. Authorities quickly uncovered a conspiracy among a small group of slaves to secure their freedom by burning the city to the ground. Some of these bondsmen had specific grievances. One had set fire to Clarke's home because the lieutenant governor would not let the bondsman spend occasional nights there with his wife, one of Clarke's slaves. Another complaint involved restrictions that city authorities had put in place after foiling a previous suspected slave uprising in 1712; these included a ban on African

Americans gathering in groups larger than three. This constraint clearly infuriated the slave Ben, who grumbled to one of his compatriots that they "could not so much as take a walk after church-out, but the constables took them up; therefore in order to be free, they must set the houses on fire, and kill the white people."[39]

As news of the first arrests spread across the city, prosecutors became convinced that this "master-piece of villainy" could not be the work of a handful of ignorant slaves. Suspicion immediately fell upon the city's Catholics. England was yet again at war with Spain in 1741, so New Yorkers imagined that their dozens of Spanish-speaking slaves, assisted by white Catholics, might be sowing mayhem to facilitate a Spanish invasion (not a completely far-fetched idea, given that a year later, Spain *would* invade Georgia as part of this conflict, though without internal assistance from American Catholics). At their trials, the African American arsonists repeatedly pointed to their grievances as slaves as the justification for their actions, but prosecutor Smith insisted that "the late fires in this city, and the murderous design against its inhabitants, are the effects of a Spanish and popish plot." New York's Irish Catholic population was especially suspect in prosecutors' eyes. A vastly disproportionate number of the whites arrested for aiding and abetting the black conspirators had Irish surnames, such as Connolly, Corker, Fagan, Kelly, Kerry, Murphy, and Ryan.[40]

In the end, New Yorkers meted out most of the punishment to slaves. Thirteen were burned at the stake, another seventeen were hanged, and about eighty more were banished to the Caribbean. Among the white suspects, all either avowed or suspected Catholics, four were hanged and seven were pardoned on the condition that they leave the province. One of those executed, English-born John Hughson, seems to have had a relationship with the core black conspirators, though whether he plotted with them (as the prosecution insisted) or was merely the fence for their stolen goods is not clear. The guilt of Hughson's wife and daughter — both also hanged — seems even more dubious. The conviction of the fourth, Latin teacher John Ury, rested largely on the erroneous suspicion that he was a priest, illegally smuggled into the city by Catholics to spread "their hocus pocus, bloody religion." Because none of the slaves implicated Ury in the arson plot, Smith had to devote the bulk of his closing arguments in Ury's trial to the "barbarous," "savage," and "monstrous" traits of Catholicism.[41]

By July 1741, after thirty-four gruesome executions had taken place for fires that had resulted in not one fatality, some observers began to fear that New Yorkers had gone too far — that while a few slaves had undoubtedly committed arson, there had not been a wide-ranging interracial conspiracy involving one hundred people or more. The court had relied far too heavily on witnesses who were told — sometimes while they stood on the executioner's scaffold or pyre —

that they might be pardoned if only they would name more names. The "horrible executions," wrote an anonymous critic from Massachusetts, "[put] me in mind of our New England witchcraft in the year 1692 which if I dont mistake New York justly reproached us for, & mockt at our credulity."[42]

If New Yorkers had overreacted to the fires of 1741, it may have been because they wanted their actions to speak even louder than their words. The very men who had urged the Zenger jurors to ignore the law and acquit the German printer so New Yorkers could enjoy "liberty" rather than "a life of slavery" sought to impress upon the city's bondsmen that there could be no life for them other than slavery. In succeeding decades, many New Yorkers (including thousands who had only recently arrived in the city) would begin clamoring for more "rights" and "liberty" as they started to question their subordinate status in the British Empire. Other immigrants would urge their fellow New Yorkers to acquiesce to royal authority. Part of this struggle would involve whether Americans should retain the limited definition of "liberty" advocated by William Smith, or instead apply their lofty rhetoric to all Americans — black as well as white, Catholic as well as Protestant, and newcomer as well as native-born.

4

AMERICANIZATION

HAD THE REVOLUTIONARY WAR turned out differently, or had he chosen to support the other side, Cadwallader Colden of New York might be as well known to Americans today as his rival Benjamin Franklin. Franklin, who was born in Boston in 1706, moved to New York as a teenager to find work as a printer. Unable to land a job, he relocated to Philadelphia, where he went on to fame and fortune. Colden, born in Ireland in 1689 to Scottish parents, grew up in Scotland and graduated from the University of Edinburgh in 1705. He then studied medicine in London, but lacking the means to establish a medical practice in England, he immigrated in 1710 to Philadelphia, where his aunt had already settled. Several years later a fellow Scot, New York governor Robert Hunter, persuaded Colden to make Manhattan his home, promising him government appointments so that he would not have to rely solely on the unpredictable income from his medical practice. Colden, his Scotch-born wife, Alice, and their toddler, Alexander, moved in 1718 to New York City, where the couple had eight more children. Hunter, true to his word, secured Colden a variety of patronage appointments, culminating in 1720 with his appointment as surveyor of the entire colony.[1]

Like Franklin, Colden was also a true Renaissance man. He dabbled in the mechanical arts and is credited by some with inventing the important printing process known as stereotyping. Colden was a historian as well, publishing in 1727 his pathbreaking *History of the Five Indian Nations,* the first attempt to write in English the history of Native Americans. Colden was also an innovative public health scientist, surveying the location of New York City residents who got sick during summer fever outbreaks in the 1740s in an attempt to determine the cause of the contagions. He found Newtonian physics just as fascinating as medicine, and when Sir Isaac died without having determined the causes of the gravitational properties he had observed, Colden published his own theories on the subject. Colden's most important scientific contributions came in botany, a nascent yet vitally important field in an era when most people derived their livelihood from agriculture. In this area Colden collaborated with his daughter Jane, whose botany notebooks are deemed important enough to be preserved at the British Museum. Contemporaries called Colden a "genius," but today's historians of science do not hold him in such high regard because he typically published his theories without first doing the experimentation necessary to test them. Nonetheless, it is not much of an exaggeration to assert, as one scholar has, that "next to Franklin," Colden in his day "was the most eminent scientist and philosopher in America." He was the first New Yorker with a truly international reputation.[2]

Also like Franklin, Colden owned slaves for most of his life, and Colden's letters reveal that he was not a particularly sympathetic master. Just before leaving Philadelphia, he shipped two of his slaves, a thirty-three-year-old woman and her child, to Barbados for sale. He told the trader to whom he consigned them that he had decided to sell them in the West Indies because the bondswoman was sullen and insolent and because of "the custome of the country that will not allow us to [discipline] our Negroes as you doe in Barbados when they displeas you." He also wanted to separate her from "several other of her children which I value & I know if she should stay in this country she would spoil them." He asked the trader to exchange the woman and child for "the best & whitest Muscavado sugar you can get[.] It is for my own use & therefor doe not mind the price & the rest in good rum."[3]

Another similarity between Colden and Franklin was their love of politics. Soon after he moved to New York, Colden landed an appointment on the governor's council, the small board of prominent citizens that offered advice on pending policy decisions to the colony's chief magistrate. (With the more overbearing governors, the council did little more than rubber-stamp their edicts.) That Colden managed to remain on the council for fifty-five years, far longer than any other New Yorker, reflects both how highly he was regarded by the colonial elite and how adept he was at winning the respect of his fellow citizens as well as a lengthy succession of royal governors, no matter in what direction the constantly shifting political winds might blow.

Yet Colden was no sycophant, trimming his sails to maintain good relations with whoever the monarch might send to govern New York. In the 1730s Colden was one of the leaders of the political faction opposed to Governor William Cosby, the rapacious spoilsman who prosecuted John Peter Zenger. Colden wrote many of the attacks on Cosby in Zenger's New-York Weekly Jour-

Cadwallader and Alice Colden, ca. 1750. In the decades before the American Revolution, Colden was New York's best-known resident, famed for his scientific writings and his political clout.

nal that resulted in the printer's trial for libel. Colden was also one of the most prominent opponents of Governor James De Lancey, who ruled New York for most of the 1750s.[4]

When De Lancey died of a heart attack in 1760, Colden, as the longest-serving member of the governor's council, became acting governor of New York. In the following year, King George III appointed Colden lieutenant governor, a post he would hold for nearly fifteen years. But because New York had a veritable revolving door of governors in the 1760s and 1770s, Colden found himself time and again thrust into the role of acting governor of the colony — from 1760 to 1761, 1763 to 1765, 1769 to 1770, and 1774 to 1775. It was in this position that Colden's reputation was transformed from that of an irascible but otherwise harmless know-it-all to one of the city's most despised leaders.[5]

The story of immigrant life in New York during the Revolutionary decades is harder to reconstruct than one might imagine. The records that have been preserved, the reminiscences that contemporaries recorded, and the histories scholars have written focus overwhelmingly on the causes and consequences of the breach with Great Britain rather than the experiences of the immigrants who moved to Manhattan in these years. The lives of common New Yorkers are particularly hard to reconstruct for this era. So for this period, I focus on the stories of a handful of immigrants on either side of the Revolutionary struggle whose experiences are well documented. Cadwallader Colden, for example, an immigrant who remained loyal to the king and the empire, was vilified and despised as a result. Alexander McDougall, in contrast, risked the small fortune he had made in New York for the cause of American independence. Somewhere in between these extremes, there were thousands of other New Yorkers, like Irish immigrant Waddell Cunningham, who did not really care which side prevailed as long as they could continue to turn a profit. Their stories and the others recounted in this chapter and the next may not be typical, but they exemplify the saga of New York's immigrants in the Revolutionary era.

Colden's fall from grace actually began in the summer of 1763 near the corner of Wall and Water streets when Cunningham, brandishing a sword, attacked another businessman armed with a horsewhip. We know very little about the man with the whip, Thomas Forsey, other than that in late December 1762, he and his brother purchased some wholesale goods from the Charleston firm of Torrans, Greg, and Poag on credit, with a promise to pay within thirty days. When the Forsey brothers did not forward their payment in thirty, sixty, or even ninety days, the South Carolinians asked Cunningham to collect it for them.[6]

Cunningham's story is well known. He was born about ten miles west of Belfast in 1729. Both his father's family and his mother's, the Waddells, had well-established roots in farming, linen production, and overseas trade in the region surrounding Belfast. About the time Cunningham turned twenty-one, the family sent him to New York to assist a kinsman with his annual importation of North American flaxseed, a vital trade good for northern Ireland. Irish farmers planted the seeds each spring, and then in the fall extracted the long fibers found inside the flax plant's tall stems and sold them to weavers, who spun them into Irish linen. Cunningham liked the energy and competitiveness of the New York merchants he met on his trip and decided to make the city his home. By 1752 he had set up his own import-export operation there.[7]

Young Cunningham's rapid rise as a New York merchant resulted in part from what one biographer has termed "competitive pricing, careful management of debt," and "ties to men of power and influence." Cunningham also took on a sagacious partner twelve years his senior, Thomas Greg of Belfast, who skillfully directed the firm's European operations. But the real source of Cunningham's success — by age thirty-five he was one of the wealthiest men in New York and the leader of its Irish merchant community — resulted from his daring as a privateer and smuggler during the French and Indian War that began in the mid-1750s. Privateering was, in essence, government-endorsed piracy against a nation's wartime enemy. Cunningham invested in at least ten privateering expeditions, and when these ships captured French vessels in the Caribbean, Cunningham shared in the huge profits.

Yet it was smuggling, rather than piracy, at which Cunningham truly excelled. He was one of the most brazen participants in the "Dutch trade," a euphemism for evading import duties levied in New York Harbor by landing goods from the Netherlands, Copenhagen, and Hamburg on Long Island or at some small Connecticut port supervised by compliant customs officers, even though these taxes helped pay for the war that brought Cunningham his privateering windfall. When these imports arrived in Manhattan via smaller coastal vessels, it was clear that the cargo had been smuggled, but Cunningham also paid bribes in New York so customs officials there would look the other way. "I am on such a footing with the officers here," bragged Cunningham in a letter to Greg in Belfast, "that if any person can have favours, I will."

Cunningham also traded directly with the enemy, selling to French settlements in the Caribbean the very goods his privateers had seized days or weeks earlier. When customs officials began to crack down on Cunningham's smuggling, he gathered a mob to harass and intimidate the man suspected of inform-

Merchant Waddell Cunningham, ca. 1786, twenty-three years after his run-in with Thomas Forsey.

ing on him. He was arrested and briefly jailed in 1759 for these activities, but he relied on his influential connections to shield him from serious punishment. By 1763, in only slightly more than a decade in New York, the young bachelor had amassed a fortune that included part-ownership of ships and trading companies, real estate in Manhattan and on the American frontier, and a sugar planation stocked with slaves on the island of Dominica. He had also acquired a reputation as someone not to be crossed. "I would shudder," wrote one acquaintance, "if WC's interest, ambition, and therefore inclination and abilities were [ever] combined against me."[8]

Thomas Forsey was either ignorant of these facts or foolish enough to ignore them. When Cunningham began hounding Forsey for payment of his debt, Forsey complained to Torrans, Greg (the brother of Cunningham's own Belfast partner), and Poag that Cunningham was not behaving like a gentleman. Cunningham was furious when he learned what Forsey had written about him and demanded that Forsey immediately retract the insult to his honor. Forsey refused, even after Cunningham (according to Forsey) vowed to horsewhip him should he not comply. Cunningham claimed that the first threat of horsewhipping had come from Forsey, and that it was this threat that led Cunningham to take his sword with him in late July to the Merchants' Coffee House.

Pedestrians at the corner of Wall and Water streets were stunned when, a little after noon on Thursday July 29, 1763, Forsey, carrying a horsewhip, came bursting out of the coffeehouse, chased by a sword-wielding Waddell Cunningham. After a scuffle, Cunningham's blade sliced what Forsey later claimed was an eight-inch-deep gash in his upper chest near his shoulder. Cunningham fled and hid, but was later arrested. He remained in jail for about two weeks, until it was certain that Forsey would not die, at which point New York prosecutors granted Cunningham bail and charged him with assault. Rejecting Cunningham's claims of self-defense, a jury in January 1764 found him guilty. His sentence: a fine of £30. Not satisfied with that punishment, Forsey filed a civil suit against Cunningham seeking £5,000 in damages for physical suffering and lost income, and that case was tried on October 25, 1764. The following day, a jury awarded Forsey £1,500, a small fortune for a New Yorker in that era.[9]

Cunningham was not present when the jury announced its huge judgment. In the summer of 1764, faced with Forsey's lawsuit as well as several smuggling indictments, Cunningham had left his trading company in the hands of junior partners and sailed for Belfast, where he got married and lived out the remaining thirty-three years of his life. His move did not relieve him of his obligation to pay Forsey, but Cunningham thought that friends in high places could shield him from having to hand over the massive award. Cunningham's ace in the hole, he believed, was a letter from King George III pardoning him for the attack on Forsey. Even if Forsey should die from his wounds, the letter stated, Cunningham should go free. Cunningham believed that the king's pardon should apply to the civil judgment as well and demanded that his attorneys appeal the fine on that basis. When his own lawyers told him that the king's pardon had no bearing on a civil penalty rendered by a jury in America, the Irishman hired new counsel to pursue the appeal. New York's highest court ruled unanimously against Cunningham, finding that to allow an appeal in the absence of procedural errors would threaten the sanctity of jury verdicts. Undaunted, Cunningham's representatives appealed the judges' ruling to the acting governor, Cadwallader Colden.

Colden could simply have followed the advice of both the high court and his attorney general, who urged him to endorse the justices' decision and reject Cunningham's appeal. After all, Colden had been one of the most zealous and prominent supporters of Zenger, whose landmark acquittal relied on the premise that juries were the ultimate determiners of guilt or innocence. But Colden now occupied the gubernatorial office and answered to the king. Fretting that "the King's authority" and "prerogative" might be threatened if his subjects believed they had the power, even through juries, to contravene the monarch's wishes, Colden in the winter of 1764–65 allowed Cunningham's appeal to go forward to the king's Privy Council in England.

Colden's decision brought forth howls of indignation from all strata of New York society. "People are extremely incensed," wrote one council member. "The old body [Colden] was allways dislik'd enough, but now they would preferr Beelzebub himself to him." An article in the *New-York Gazette* in February 1765 called Colden's "wicked" and "vindictive" attempt "to deprive his most loyal and affectionate subjects of all the benefits of a trial by their peers" the most "momentous affair that ever engaged our attention, since the existence of this province." That summer, the Privy Council ordered Cunningham's petition to be heard by Colden and his council acting as a court of appeals, but in protest the members of the colony's Supreme Court refused to hand over documents related to the case. An unprecedented standoff between New Yorkers and Great Britain was under way.[10]

Before the *Forsey* case could be resolved, it was overshadowed by a far more wide-reaching attack on Americans' rights — the Stamp Act. Parliament had approved this law in March 1765 in an effort to recoup the costs of stationing troops in America in the wake of the French and Indian War, and to force Americans like Cunningham who profited from it to pay a larger share of the cost. Beginning on the first of November, all legal documents, newspapers, and other printed materials sold in the American colonies, as well as playing cards and dice, would be taxed, and those who issued or sold such items would have to prove they had paid the tax by attaching a government-issued stamp (much like a modern-day postage stamp) to these items. Perhaps because they expected the colonists to object, British officials placed an age-old Latin inscription on the stamps that means "Shame to him who thinks badly of it."

New Yorkers did object to the Stamp Act, not only because it imposed a hated tax, but also because it required that legal cases related to its enforcement be tried in admiralty courts, in which military officers rather than juries would determine a defendant's guilt or innocence. Americans considered this provision an egregious infringement upon their rights, arguing that those accused of tax evasion in England were never tried by military tribunals. According to the Stamp Act Congress that met in New York City to protest the hated law, "two privileges essential to freedom, and which all Englishmen have ever considered as their best birthrights," were "that of being free from all taxes but such as they have consented to in person, or by their representatives, and of trial by their peers."[11]

Many Americans vowed to block the Stamp Act's implementation. New Yorkers initiated a movement to boycott English goods, hoping to pressure the British to repeal the act, and the idea caught on in other colonies. Some decided to take more direct action. Protesters threatening violence induced the Boston stamp distributor to resign rather than face the mob's wrath. His Maryland counterpart fled for his life to New York City with only the clothes on his back. When New Yorkers discovered his presence in September and vowed to attack his lodging house and "destroy him," he fled to Colden for protection. Colden later spirited him away to his farm in Flushing, across the East River, to hide him from potential assailants. New York's own stamp distributor, James McEvers, fearing "my house would have been pillag'd" and "my person abused" by the recently formed Sons of Liberty, quit before the province's allotment of stamps even arrived in North America. Stamp Act opponents knew that if they could prevent the distribution of the stamps, the tax could not be collected.[12]

New Yorkers vented most of their anger over the Stamp Act at Colden. Not only had he harbored Maryland's stamp distributor and sworn a special oath promising to enforce the law, but also he had ordered that Fort George's guns be turned toward the town itself so the fort could be defended against the mobs that had vowed to seize the sheets of stamps, which Colden had taken into the fortress for safekeeping. On October 31, the day before the law would go into effect, "a mob in 3 squads went through the streets crying 'Liberty,'" breaking "some thousands of windows," and telling suspected supporters of the Stamp Act that they would "pull down their houses."

"Every man is wild with politics," reported Robert Livingston at the height of the crisis. On November 1, mobs appeared in several parts of the city, some carrying effigies of Colden. One group intent on staging particularly elaborate street theater erected a mobile gallows so its members could wheel the effigy of the villain (with a devil whispering instructions in his ear) all around town and publicize his fate at the end of a noose should he enforce the statute. After nightfall, the various anti-tax groups combined into a vast throng of several thousand who, carrying candles and torches, moved menacingly toward the fort and its occupant Colden, the "chief murderer of their rights and privileges." The crowd spared the fort but stormed Colden's carriage house, carrying off a coach and two sleighs. These were piled high, along with some torn-up fencing and the street theater props, "to which setting fire, it soon kindled to a great flame, and reduced the coach, gallows, man, devil, and all to ashes." The mob then ransacked the home of Major Thomas James, head of the fort's military force, before tolling the town's church bells and declaring their work done for the night.[13]

The crowd that had menaced the fort left a note at the gate demanding that Colden "this night solemnly make [an] oath before a magistrate" swearing not to enforce the Stamp Act. The mob promised him a violent death if he did not comply. In subsequent days the threats continued, forcing Colden and his family to seek refuge on a naval vessel in the harbor. Colden believed that New Yorkers must respect the law, no matter how much they disagreed with it, but both his council and his main military adviser, General Thomas Gage, advised him to surrender the stamps and repudiate the act rather than precipitate a bloody "civil war." Finally, on the evening of November 5, Colden acquiesced, delivering the stamps to the mayor and the city government and promising not to enforce the act in his remaining days as acting governor. New Yorkers of every political persuasion breathed a sigh of relief as all sides stood down.

When the new governor, Sir Henry Moore, arrived a day later, he too took no steps to enforce the Stamp Act, perhaps because he knew that plans were in the works to repeal it. A few months later, word reached New York that Parliament had revoked the odious statute. Americans relished their victory.[14]

It was, in fact, a double victory. The new governor also announced that he had received new Privy Council instructions concerning the appellate law at issue in *Forsey v. Cunningham*. Reversing course, the council members declared that the defendant could not appeal the jury verdict. Cunningham was forced to pay the huge judgment against him. Trial by jury had been vindicated.

Poor Colden, who had bent over backwards to protect the prerogatives of the king and had defended the despised Stamp Act longer than any other colonial official in the province, was rewarded for his loyalty with a reprimand from London. His "want of firmness" in dealing with the mobs displeased the king and his ministers. Adding injury to insult, the assembly refused to pay him for his last months in office, citing as justification (among other things) his inept handling of the Stamp Act.

To make matters worse, Franklin, the one man who could challenge Colden for the title of America's greatest scientist, had emerged from the Stamp Act controversy as a hero. On February 3, 1766, Franklin appeared before the House of Commons in London urging the act's repeal. His testimony was so witty, persuasive, and sensible that he not only cemented his position as the best-known American in the world but became the most admired as well. Disgusted, Colden moved across the East River to his farm in Flushing, where he immersed himself in his botany and other scientific projects, happy to leave to others the thankless job of governing New York at the dawn of the Revolutionary crisis.[15]

Political animal that he was, Colden could not resist observing with resentment the relatively favorable reception afforded his successor. Noting the new governor's conciliatory attitude toward New Yorkers, even those who had recently led the mobs and encouraged obstruction of the law, Colden groused that Moore "has yielded every thing in order to quiet the minds of the people." And yet, he wrote in 1766, the city's residents have continued "as much insulting [the] government as ever. The only difference is, [their insults] are not directly personally against him, as they were against me."[16]

The relationship between New Yorkers and their imperial government remained somewhat tense throughout the duration of the 1760s. Before long, the two sides began butting heads again, this time over whether or not the colonists should have to finance the lodging of British troops in America. The British argued that since the soldiers protected the Americans from the French and the Indians, the colonists should shoulder the burden. Americans insisted that their own militia units were adequate to these tasks, and that the British government had really stationed troops in the colonies to intimidate the colonists into accepting Parliament's unfair taxes. New York's assembly repeatedly refused to pay for the quartering of soldiers (legislatures in Massachusetts and South Carolina demurred as well), and Moore, finally reaching the limits of his patience, dissolved New York's legislature as punishment.[17]

Yet most New Yorkers were more concerned with the terrible recession that had plagued the city since the Stamp Act crisis than with the quartering issue. After all, the city's economic fortunes rose and fell with trade, and if trade was suppressed, then all New Yorkers suffered. "What a dismal prospect is before us!" wrote "A Tradesman" to the *New-York Journal* in the late fall of 1767. "A long winter, and no work; many unprovided with fire-wood, or money to

buy it; house-rent, and taxes high; our neighbors daily breaking, their furniture at vendue" at every corner. The city's perennial shortage of hard currency
became even more pronounced. "Never was a country so embarrassed as this,"
remarked a recently arrived English immigrant in 1767. "Our paper curr[ency]
allmost exhausted: all the gold and silver sent home, & trade quite dead, the difficulty to live here is inconceivable." For years, New York business leaders and
their representatives in the assembly had been begging the British to allow the
province to issue paper money, but colonial regulations forbade them to do so.
Moore was certainly not going to bend the currency rules for an assembly that
would not appropriate a farthing for the soldiers who protected the province.

In September 1769, just as the standoff between New Yorkers and their
elected assembly on the one side and the governor and the British government
on the other was nearing the boiling point, the fifty-six-year-old Moore suddenly died after a sixteen-day struggle with "mortification of the bowels." His
interim replacement? Eighty-one-year-old Cadwallader Colden, of course. "He
fairly lives himself into office," sniffed one New Yorker as Colden returned to
town to resume the governorship yet again.[18]

Colden believed he could use his new term as acting governor to repair the
damage to his reputation. He conferred with the leaders of the assembly and, he
said, "had assurances from them of their disposition to make my administration easy to me." His plan was to negotiate a grand bargain with the legislature
that would end the impasse over quartering soldiers and simultaneously give
New Yorkers something that would endear him to them. First, in exchange for
guaranteeing to pay him his salary, Colden promised ample patronage (government jobs and contracts that ambitious politicians dole out as rewards to their
most important followers) to the leaders of the De Lancey faction, which controlled the assembly. Then, even though it contravened colonial policy, Colden
agreed to sign a bill authorizing the printing of £120,000 in paper money for
the province. In return, the legislature would appropriate £2,000 (half of which
could come from the new paper money) to supply British soldiers stationed in
the province. This last measure passed the assembly by just a single vote on December 15, 1769.[19]

Colden thought that if he persuaded the assembly to appropriate funds for
the quartering of soldiers while the governors of Massachusetts and South Carolina had failed to do so, colonial officials in London would consider him a
hero. Instead, the secretary of state, the Earl of Hillsborough, castigated Colden
for signing the currency bill without authorization from the Privy Council.
"Your conduct on this occasion," chided Hillsborough, "has justly incurred His
Majesty's displeasure, which I am commanded to signify to you."[20]

The reaction to the bills in New York surprised Colden even more. New

Yorkers were delighted to have the currency bill enacted, but not as a quid pro quo for the quartering of British troops. The extent of their unhappiness became clear when New Yorkers left their homes to go to church on Sunday morning December 17. On fences and walls all around town were posted broadsides addressed "To the Betrayed Inhabitants of the City and Colony of New York," protesting in scandalously frank terms the assembly's decision to fund the British soldiers. The author, knowing that his screed might land him in jail, or even on the gallows, merely signed his work "A SON OF LIBERTY."[21]

Realizing that even those he hired to post his missive would be liable to arrest, the author of the broadside disseminated it utilizing an old ploy of European radicals that involved a strongman, a boy, and a large crate. Up and down the city's streets under cover of darkness, the strongman carried the crate, which contained the youngster, the posters, some glue, and a brush. Every so often the strongman would lean the box against a wall or fence as if to rest. At that point, the boy would slide open a panel, paste the broadside to the surface facing him, and shut the panel when he was done. The process was repeated all around town until the posting of the handbills was complete.[22]

Outraged at the impudence of the broadside's author, Colden ordered a manhunt to track him down, offering a £100 reward for information leading to his arrest. A journeyman printer from Cork could not resist this life-changing sum and informed authorities that his employer, James Parker, had printed the posters. Parker, thrown in jail and threatened with a long prison term, was granted immunity in exchange for naming the author, a Scottish immigrant who to this point had played no known role in leading the opposition to Great Britain's American policy. His name was Alexander McDougall.[23]

McDougall's life story is another of the rags-to-riches tales that seem so common in early New York history. He was born in 1732 on the rocky, windswept island of Islay, which sits fifteen miles off the Atlantic coast of Scotland, about sixty miles due west of Glasgow. Islay's nearly 250 square miles were home to only a few thousand people. By the early 1700s, they would have heard about the wonders of America and its increasing Scottish immigrant population, but most of the adult inhabitants with families or aged parents could not indenture themselves and leave their kin unsupported, making it financially impossible for them to move to the American colonies.

So it must have seemed like a gift from heaven when an ambitious and seemingly well-to-do ex–military officer, Captain Lauchlan Campbell, returned to his native Islay in 1737 and announced that he would transport to America, free of charge for those who could not pay, anyone who would help him settle thirty thousand acres on the northern frontier of New York. The colony's leaders, he explained, had announced their intention to give such tracts in "Mohocks

Country" (about fifty miles north of Albany) to those who would establish settlements with enough inhabitants to create a defensive buffer against the Native
Americans. McDougall's parents, Ranald and Elizabeth, were among the first to
accept Campbell's offer. In July they piled their family—five-year-old "Alick,"
his older brother John, his younger sister Mary, and their half sister Eleanor—
onto a ship chartered by Campbell.[24]

Things started to go badly as soon as the colonists arrived in New York. First,
they found out that they could not immediately go to the land they intended to
settle. Campbell asked the immigrants to wait for him in New York City while
he went back to Scotland for more settlers. After he returned, they learned that
they would not receive grants of land on the frontier as they had been led to
believe. Even after years of backbreaking toil to clear the dense forests to create
farms, they would merely be Campbell's tenants. The outraged Scots, Colden
recalled, "met together in companies in the streets, and . . . loudly exclaimed
against it, saying, they had left Scotland to free themselves from the vassal-
age they were under to their lords there, and they would not become vassals to
Laughlin Campbel in America." Seeing that Campbell did not have the settlers
needed to populate the territory, the assembly refused to grant him the land.
His prospective settlers were left to fend for themselves.[25]

Ranald McDougall was forced to indenture himself to a New York City farm
owner, Gerard Beekman, in order to repay Campbell for the expense of transporting him and his family to America. Beekman put McDougall to work selling the milk from his Manhattan farm, and Alick often accompanied his father
on his rounds, carrying pails of milk on his shoulders. Ranald eventually completed his indenture and bought his own dairy, but Alick had no interest in following his father into that business. After a short stint as a tailor's apprentice,
Alick at age fourteen went to sea as a common sailor. He worked his way up
the nautical ranks in this hard and dangerous line of work, visiting Islay in 1751
with the apparent intention of finding a bride. A few months later he married a
distant cousin, Nancy McDougall. They returned to New York and quickly had
three children, John, Ranald, and Elizabeth.[26]

In Manhattan, McDougall was able to land jobs commanding the vessels
that merchants used to move their goods up and down the East Coast and into
the Caribbean. McDougall must have conveyed both competence and confidence to his employers, because at age twenty-five he was put in command of
a sizable eight-gun sloop, the *Tyger*, with a crew of sixty-two at the young captain's command. His mission: to engage in privateering against French shipping
as part of the French and Indian War. He spent most of the war in the Caribbean, fearlessly capturing several French ships and the cargoes of many more
vessels, French and otherwise. Having made himself and his backers substan-

tial profits, McDougall in 1759 was given command of an even larger ship, the twelve-gun *General Barrington*. McDougall's family begged him to come home before his luck ran out (for "the sake of our dear babies, our grandchildren," wrote his father-in-law). But McDougall was determined to make even more, and by the end of 1762 his privateering proceeds enabled him to return to New York with a small fortune and become a merchant.[27]

McDougall would not fully enjoy his newfound wealth for long. In February 1763 Nancy died of smallpox. Alick, who had spent little time with his children for nearly a decade, became their sole caretaker. At least he had the means to spoil them, for he had invested his privateering proceeds well. He had rental income from three thousand acres of land near Albany and from urban rental properties in Wilmington, North Carolina. He owned a share of a Caribbean sugar plantation and acted as an agent for several St. Croix planters, taking a commission for selling their sugar and molasses in New York. Like many New York merchants, he also made money lending funds to other businessmen. Finally, also like most New York merchants, McDougall invested in slaves, typically renting them out to others rather than using them himself. In November 1767 he noted matter-of-factly in his ledger of expenditures that he had bought "a Negro wench called Beth" for £40.

McDougall's net worth came nowhere close to that of Waddell Cunningham or the city's merchant elite. Nor could money buy McDougall standing in the city's already snobbish elite social circles. He was mocked for dressing garishly, lacking refinement, talking too much despite a terrible stutter, and for referring too often to his Scotch eccentricities and his humble origins as "the milk mon's son." Admirers, however, found him friendly, humorous, and sincere, even while admitting that he seemed to dwell a bit too much on "his national peculiarities."[28]

Before December 1769, McDougall was not very well known beyond the city's Presbyterian circles. He was a middling merchant of no great renown, with little apparent interest in politics. In the voluminous published record of the Stamp Act controversy in New York, his name never appears. As a result, most

Alexander McDougall in 1786. His rise from milkman's son to wealthy merchant exemplified the opportunities for advancement that attracted so many immigrants to New York.

New Yorkers were shocked when they learned that it was the affable McDougall who had written the broadside, which to that point was the most incendiary anti-British document ever published in the city.[29]

McDougall's outrage flowed like a torrent from his pen on the night of December 15 as he raced to finish his polemic so copies of the broadside could be posted on Sunday. "The minions of tyranny and despotism in the mother country and the colonies are indefatigable in laying every snare that their malevolent and corrupt hearts can suggest, to enslave a free people," McDougall wrote. New Yorkers have "been striving under many disadvantages for three years past, to preserve their freedom, which to an Englishman is as dear as his life." Referring to the boycott of British goods that New Yorkers had organized to protest British infringements on their rights, McDougall insisted that merchants "have nobly and cheerfully sacrificed their private interest to the public good, rather than . . . promote the designs of the enemies of our happy constitution." Given these facts, McDougall wrote, "it might justly be expected" that the assembly "would not be so hardy, nor be so lost to all sense of duty to their constituents, (especially after the laudable example of the colonies of Massachusetts Bay and South Carolina before them) as to betray the trust committed to them . . . And what makes the Assembly's granting this money the more grievous, is, that it goes to the support of troops kept here not to protect but to enslave us."

No one connected with the British policy escaped McDougall's vitriol. He called one of New York's leading military officers "domineering and inhuman." The British Parliament was "tyrannical." Colden was greedy and self-serving. McDougall aimed his most stinging accusations at the members of the assembly who had passed the despised quartering measure, calling them "pusillanimous," "abominable," "repugnant" purveyors of a "ridiculous farce . . . by which the liberties of the people are betrayed." McDougall ended his rant with a call to action: "Is this a state to be rested in, when our all is at a stake? No, my countrymen, rouse!" Radicals in England, he noted, "rather than be enslaved, contend for their right[s] with k——g, lords and commons." Americans must do the same and thereby thwart "the designs of tyrants."[30]

McDougall's broadside, and another he published on the morning of the eighteenth, called on New Yorkers to demonstrate their outrage at the assembly's decision to fund the quartering of soldiers by attending a public meeting at the Liberty Pole in "the Fields," the town common located just north of present-day City Hall. The Sons of Liberty had provocatively erected this symbol of their commitment to safeguarding Americans' rights in the Fields even though (or perhaps *because*) the barracks that held many of the city's British troops were also located there. At the meeting, more than one thousand New Yorkers turned out to denounce the assembly's treachery.

New Yorkers also began to treat soldiers with increasing disdain in the wake of McDougall's harangues. Troops were harassed in the streets, pelted with stones and rotten eggs, and were fired from the part-time jobs they had taken in New York to supplement their meager pay. Fed up with such treatment, drunken soldiers on Saturday night, January 13, 1770, tried to cut down the Liberty Pole, which was protected at its base by a web of iron rings (because British troops had destroyed three previous liberty poles), but were repulsed by angry New Yorkers. The redcoats made a second attack on the "Liberty Tree" on Monday night, but an alderman intervened. The soldiers were determined, however, to destroy this symbol of American insolence. On Tuesday night, working quietly and soberly as the city slept, they bored a hole in the pole, filled it with explosives, and blasted it to the ground.[31]

The next day, Wednesday the seventeenth of January, three thousand New Yorkers gathered in the Fields at the site of the destroyed Liberty Pole to mourn its loss and plan a response. How many of these demonstrators, or members of other Revolutionary throngs that gathered in New York from 1765 to 1776, were immigrants? It is impossible to say with any certainty. One might imagine that those born in America would have been more likely to support the cause of American "rights" and "liberty" than those who had only recently left the British Isles. Within the leadership of the Sons of Liberty, a majority of those whose birthplace can be identified were born in the thirteen colonies. But many were immigrants like McDougall. Sailors were particularly numerous in the mobs that roamed the streets, carrying effigies and intimidating opponents of the cause of "liberty," and most of these seamen were immigrants.

We also know that men on both sides of the colonial conflict believed that "Dissenters" (sometimes called "independents"), those who did not belong to the Church of England, were more likely to join the American cause than were Anglicans. Opponents of Parliament in New York "consist chiefly of Dissenters, who are very numerous," reported Colden to his superiors in England. "The most active among them are independents from New England," Colden observed, but a large minority were Scotch Presbyterians who had no great love for England and resented the perks and privileges granted in America to the Church of England and its members. In a letter to McDougall, Benjamin Franklin agreed with Colden's assessment that Dissenters formed the core of the Americans' supporters, but added that Irish immigrants were also particularly sympathetic to the American cause. All these groups were especially likely to favor "shaking off the yoke of dependency [on] their mother country."[32]

Those three thousand New Yorkers, natives of New York and New England, Ireland and Scotland, and even the Caribbean and London, met en masse to draft a petition asking that the city demolish the soldiers' barracks in the Fields, even as furious redcoats, many carrying their weapons, looked on with barely concealed rage. On Friday the nineteenth, the soldiers of the Sixteenth Foot Regiment posted their own broadside, mocking the Sons of Liberty for acting as if "their freedom depended in a piece of wood." When some Liberty Boys came upon a couple of soldiers posting these handbills, the Boys captured two of the soldiers and hauled them off to City Hall (then located at the corner of Wall and Nassau streets, where Federal Hall stands today), apparently expecting the mayor to arrest them or at least have them disciplined by their officers. Other soldiers gathered to try to free their captured comrades. Sons of Liberty, armed with clubs and makeshift weapons, simultaneously converged on City Hall to prevent the redcoats' release.

The mayor ordered the troops to return to their barracks, but the crowd pursued and managed to surround them about six blocks away at the crest of the hill at the corner of John and William streets. New Yorkers called this area Golden Hill. In an earlier era the hill had given off a golden glow when viewed from the East River waterfront because of the grain that farmers had once planted there. But the soldiers scarcely thought of their situation in glowing terms. Surrounded and frightened, they decided to cut their way through the mob with their bayonets, while the Liberty Boys and their supporters fought back as best they could with the improvised weapons at their disposal. "Much blood was spilt," wrote a New Yorker a few days later, describing the chaos to an acquaintance in London. "One sailor got run through the body, who since died: one man got his skull cut in a most cruel manner." A fisherman lost a finger, and others suffered stab wounds. Several soldiers were injured badly enough that they had to be carried back to their headquarters by the retreating troops. The following day, soldiers again clashed with the townsmen, "the chiefest part being sailors with clubs to revenge the death of their brother, which they did with courage, and made [the troops] all run to their barracks. What will be the end of this God knows!" Although the Battle of Golden Hill is hardly remembered today, it marked the first bloodshed between British soldiers and dissatisfied colonists in the struggle that would eventually become the American Revolution. Only seven weeks later would British troops with similar grievances kill five men in what became known as the Boston Massacre.[33]

The hunt for the author of the broadside intensified after the battle. On February 7, 1770, the day the journeyman printer came forward, the Sons of Liberty unveiled their new Liberty Pole, nearly eighty feet high, built on privately owned land adjacent to the Fields after the city council denied them permission to erect another one on the common. Two days later, McDougall was arrested.

The unrepentant agitator was brought before the colony's chief justice, Daniel Horsmanden. "You have brought yourself into a pretty scrape," he told McDougall. "May it please your honor," McDougall replied, "that must be judged by my peers." The judge informed him, as McDougall later recalled, "that there was full proof that I was the author" of the scurrilous broadside, "which he called a false, vile, and scandalous libel. I replied again, 'This must also be tried by my peers.'" Told by the judge that he must post bail or await trial in jail, McDougall defiantly declared, "Sir, I will give no bail."[34]

McDougall correctly calculated that even though he could easily afford the bond set by the judge, he would do far more service to the colonial cause if he stayed in prison and became a living martyr to liberty. McDougall's supporters saw their hero as an American John Wilkes, the English radical who had been imprisoned for seditious libel in 1763 for criticizing, in issue number 45 of his newspaper *The North Briton*, a speech by King George III. Wilkes did not spend long in jail, but he was idolized by those Britons, in both Europe and America, who believed in unfettered freedom of speech. To insure that the parallels to Wilkes's case were not lost on New Yorkers, McDougall's supporters threw him a celebratory dinner on the forty-fifth day of the year, February 14. The feast made news throughout the colonies. A Boston newspaper recounted that "forty-five gentlemen, real enemies to internal taxation . . . and cordial friends of American liberty," marched in procession to McDougall's cell at the city jail, where they "dined with him on forty-five pounds of beef steaks, cut from a bullock of forty-five months old." On another occasion, McDougall's confinement was brightened by a visit from what the press described as forty-five "virgins," who serenaded McDougall with forty-five songs.[35]

At the end of April, a grand jury indicted McDougall for propagating a "wicked, false, seditious, scandalous, malicious, and infamous libel." Informed that he would likely not be tried until the end of the year, McDougall's friends persuaded him to post the £1,000 bail. He returned home after nearly three months in jail, escorted by six hundred raucous supporters. Before long, the legal case against him fell apart. The Sons of Liberty so tormented the journeyman who had led the authorities to McDougall that the printer left the colonies altogether, while his employer Parker, another potential witness against McDougall, died that summer. With no living witnesses able to link McDougall to the broadside, prosecutors withdrew the indictment. But the assembly, not satisfied that McDougall should escape punishment for insulting the honor of its leading members, demanded in December that he appear before them to answer questions. When he refused to incriminate himself, he was jailed for contempt.[36]

This time no fanfare accompanied McDougall's jail term. He wrote letters for publication in the press, but they attracted little attention. Not until the assembly concluded its session, on March 4, 1771, was McDougall quietly freed. There were several reasons why McDougall's second stint in jail did not capture the public's imagination: McDougall had begun to appear to be an attention seeker. The novelty of his efforts to draw parallels to the Wilkes case could hold the public's attention for only so long. The quarrel with the legislature also struck New Yorkers as more of a partisan struggle between the faction led by the De Lanceys (McDougall's enemies) and the one headed by the Livingstons and Clintons (McDougall's allies) rather than as a fight for liberty between Americans and their colonial rulers.

But perhaps the most important reason was that after the Battle of Golden Hill, both Americans and the British decided to step back from the brink of war. Parliament had indicated its desire to improve relations with the colonies in 1770 by repealing almost all of the taxes it had imposed on the Americans three years earlier. New Yorkers, for their part, were eager to resume normal trade with England after years of boycotts and the severe economic hardship that accompanied them. Having struggled to get by for several years, New Yorkers wanted to make money again. They hoped that their demonstrations of resolve had, once and for all, persuaded the British Parliament not to impose internal taxes on the colonies without their consent.[37]

5

REVOLUTION

THE PEACE AND PROSPERITY of the early 1770s brought a flood of immigrants into Britain's North American colonies. With the English and the Americans no longer on the brink of war, Europeans whose plans to relocate to New York had been put on hold during the Stamp Act crisis rushed to take advantage of the job opportunities and upward mobility for which America had become famous. But the goodwill between Americans and the British government came to an abrupt end in the spring of 1773 with Parliament's passage of the Tea Act, an attempt to get Americans to accept a tax on British tea if the price of the tea itself was drastically reduced. The bill's sponsor, Lord North, predicted that Americans would cheerfully pay the tax on legally imported tea now that it would be so cheap, but his forecast was one of the worst in all of British history.

"A new flame is apparently kindling in America," wrote one New Yorker prophetically after word of the Tea Act reached New York. "We shall repeat all the confusions of 1765 & 1766." As the textbooks tell it, the Revolution originated in Boston with its Tea Party. But New York's Sons of Liberty, revived again under immigrant Alexander McDougall, might easily have become the more famous firebrands if not for the fickle hand of fate. North Atlantic squalls battered the *Nancy*, the tea ship bound for New York, blowing it so far off course that the captain decided to land in Antigua to take on additional supplies before continuing the journey to Manhattan. When the *Nancy* finally departed for New York with six hundred cases of tea, it was engulfed by an even more violent storm. The mizzenmast was torn clear off, the mainmast was severely damaged, and the ship was thrown completely over on its side.[1]

The governor of New York, William Tryon, initially vowed to land the tea, even if it had to be done at bayonet point, though he promised not to allow it to be sold until the colonists had a chance to air their grievances in London.

McDougall and the other Sons of Liberty pledged that under no circumstances would they allow the tea to come ashore, even if New York's streets had to run red with blood. But as day after nervous day went by without the arrival of the *Nancy,* Tryon literally worried himself sick over the impending clash. Unable to stand the suspense any longer, the governor announced in March 1774 that he was going back to London for rest and recuperation, handing responsibility for whatever might occur to his lieutenant governor, Cadwallader Colden.[2]

The *Nancy,* meanwhile, had been repaired and resumed its star-crossed voyage in late March. When it arrived off Sandy Hook, New Jersey, on April 18, 1774, Captain Benjamin Lockyer dropped anchor in order to pick up a pilot to guide it into New York Harbor. But the pilots, having heard the threats of the Sons of Liberty, refused to take the ship to Manhattan. Learning of its arrival, the Sons sent a delegation, including McDougall, to warn Lockyer that harm would come to both him and his beleaguered vessel should he try to land his cargo of tea. While Lockyer considered his options, New Yorkers proved that their threats were more than idle bluster. A ship captain named James Chambers, believing that he could make a windfall profit if he could smuggle some tea into the city, tried to slip into the port with eighteen crates hidden among other cargo. On April 22, when New Yorkers discovered Chambers's deceit, they stormed his ship and dumped his tea into the East River, more than five months after Boston's better-known "Tea Party." So had it not been for the storms and the extended stay in Antigua, this New York tea party might have come first. Colden, having learned that sticking his neck out to defend British authority got him nothing but burnt effigies and official rebuke, did nothing to stop the mob. The crowd next tried to hunt down Chambers to punish him for his duplicity, but he had escaped to the *Nancy,* which Lockyer wisely sailed back to England with both Chambers and the tea.[3]

It is amazing that even after the Tea Act crisis began, with the American colonies in political chaos and their continued place in the British Empire highly uncertain, immigrants nonetheless continued pouring into New York. Immigration from Ireland and Scotland peaked, in fact, in the very years that led to the Revolutionary War. The opportunities for upward mobility and religious freedom in America were so alluring that even the prospect of war with Great Britain did not deter these emigrants. Americans' household income was, on average, 56 percent higher than in England, and the gap was even greater with Scotland and Ireland. Sensing that the chance to immigrate to America might be cut off by the Revolutionary crisis, Britons did everything possible to make their way to the colonies before it was too late. Sailors on the *Nancy,* for example, built themselves a raft so they could jump ship and remain in New York. Even after redcoats and Minutemen had begun shooting at each other in Massachusetts at the battles of Lexington, Concord, and Bunker Hill, Scottish Highlanders packed onto ships, trying to make it to America before they lost the opportunity. Having often risked everything to relocate, these new arrivals were especially determined to protect American independence, which they saw as a key to their future economic prosperity. As a result, New York City filled with new immigrants in the two decades before the war, and the town's population nearly doubled, from 13,000 in 1756 to about 25,000 in 1776.[4]

One such immigrant was an eighteen-year-old orphan from St. Croix named Alexander who arrived in New York in 1773. That young Alex had made it to New York at all was something of a miracle, for his childhood story was one that even Dickens and Alger would have dismissed as too far-fetched to be believed. It began even before Alex's birth, when Rachel, his mother, abandoned her husband and their child, Peter. This act of audacity and independence made her persona non grata wherever she went. Yet Rachel was a resilient woman. She soon took up with the ne'er-do-well fourth son of a minor Scottish nobleman, but because of the way her marriage had ended, this later relationship did not elevate her status. Quite the contrary, she was now branded "indecent," "shameless," a "whore."

The Scotsman's reputation was hardly better. Having failed to distinguish himself in Scotland, he fled to the West Indies, hoping to strike it rich in the Caribbean as a sugar planter. He failed in this pursuit as well, though in the meantime he and Rachel had two sons, James junior and then Alex. James senior had to support his family working as a clerk and debt collector for his brothers and their associates, successful Glasgow merchants with financial interests in the Caribbean. But sometime around Alex's tenth birthday in 1765, James abandoned Rachel and their boys and left St. Croix, never to see them again. Looking for the easy way out one more time, he moved to the tiny Caribbean island of Bequia, a place so inhospitable that the British government, desperate to get any white men to settle there, awarded him twenty-five acres of mountainous jungle in return for his promise to live on the island for a year. It was an ideal place to hide from life's disappointments.[5]

Now the boys' prospects seemed truly bleak. Even before their father abandoned them, the youngsters, as the bastard children of a woman of questionable morals, had been precluded from attending school or church with the offspring of respectable couples, foreclosing to them the usual avenues of upward mobility in the exceedingly proper society of the British West Indies. Determined nonetheless that her sons should succeed, Rachel hired an elderly widowed "Jewess" to tutor them. Two years later, Rachel suddenly fell ill with a high fever. She spent days writhing in bed, sweat drenching her sheets, and soon passed away.

The boys were now essentially orphans, for the news that their mother had died inexplicably failed to induce James senior to return for them. They at least seemed to be on somewhat secure financial footing. Rachel had inherited three slaves after James senior left her, and she rented the bondsmen out to local planters, using the income to supplement the meager profits from the grocery she had opened after James disappeared. Now Alex and his brother could use that rental income to support themselves.

Or so they thought. As soon as Rachel died, in swooped the husband *she* had abandoned. He argued in court that Rachel's slaves were now rightfully the property of *their* son, Peter, rather than of her illegitimate "whore-children." The court agreed, awarding the slaves to Peter and leaving Alex and James junior homeless and destitute. The judge ordered the brothers to join the household of their first cousin, also named Peter.

Moving in with cousin Peter in no way improved the boys' status. Not only did their cousin live openly and scandalously with an African American woman (a major transgression in a slave society), but also his emotional instability was such that his own brother considered him insane. This living arrangement cemented the boys' status as social pariahs. Perhaps it was a blessing for the boys that eighteen months after James junior and Alex moved in with him, Peter committed suicide (supposedly stabbing himself to death in his own bed). An uncle then took custody of the boys, but less than a month later, he died as well.

At this point the brothers parted ways. Since his mother's death, Alex had been working as a clerk in the St. Croix offices of a prominent New York import-export house, Beekman and Cruger. When Alex's uncle died, the fourteen-year-old went to live with the family of another merchant, Thomas Stevens, whose fifteen-year-old son, Edward, looked remarkably like Alex. This set tongues in Christiansted wagging yet again. Perhaps Alex's mother had been even more licentious than people had realized. Perhaps this was why James senior had abandoned the boys and refused to care for them even after Rachel died.[6]

In any event, Beekman and Cruger did not seem bothered by Alex's checkered past, perhaps because he came highly recommended by Stevens. Besides, the boy proved that he had a knack for business. When Cruger and his partner left St. Croix for months at a time, they put young Alex in charge of the company's entire island operation, which included running a wharf and a warehouse, negotiating the sale of imported goods with merchants, and collecting debts. Alex proved himself worthy of that trust. When flour that the company had imported from Philadelphia turned out to be spoiled, Alex sold it at a deep discount rather than discard it altogether. When a shipment of superior flour arrived and bakers besieged Alex with orders, the sixteen-year-old on his own authority raised the price above the usual rate. "Believe me Sir," he reported proudly to Nicholas Cruger of this decision, "I dun as hard as is proper."[7]

Young Alex had interests other than debits and credits in the company ledger books. He had literary ambitions, too, and persuaded the island's main newspaper, the *Royal Danish-American Gazette,* to publish his poetry occasionally. Several of his poems had already appeared in its columns by August 1772, when a terrible hurricane, the worst in local memory, devastated St. Croix. The storm reached its peak on Monday evening the thirty-first, with gale-force winds howling almost all night. When the sun rose the next morning, the residents of Christiansted were astounded by the extent of the destruction. The ships in the harbor had been torn from their moorings and strewn across the city's streets as haphazardly as toys a child might leave after losing interest in them. At least thirty people had been killed. (The *Gazette* listed only the thirty white victims, but given that slaves outnumbered whites by ten to one on St. Croix, the death toll must have been in the hundreds.)

Once the storm had passed, Alex's thoughts turned to his father, with whom he still occasionally corresponded. Feeling compelled to let him know that he had survived the storm unscathed, Alex wrote him a long, effusive letter describing the devastation and the emotions that it aroused in him. According to the editors of the *Gazette,* a copy of Alex's letter "fell by accident into the hands of a gentleman, who, being pleased with it himself, shewed it to others to whom it gave equal satisfaction, and who all agreed that it might not prove unentertaining to the publick." On October 3 the letter appeared in the columns of the *Gazette,* credited to "a youth of this island":

> Good God! What horror and destruction . . . It seemed as if a total dissolution of nature was taking place. The roaring of the sea and wind — fiery meteors flying about in the air — the prodigious glare of almost perpetual lightning — the crash of falling houses — and the ear-piercing shrieks of the distressed, were sufficient to strike astonishment into angels . . .
>
> Where now, oh! vile worm, is all thy boasted fortitude and resolution? What is become of thy arrogance and self-sufficiency? — Why dost thou tremble and stand aghast? How humble — how helpless — how contemptible you now appear . . . Oh, impotent presumptuous fool! how darest thou offend that omnipotence, whose nod alone were sufficient to quell the de-

struction that hovers over thee, or crush thee into atoms? . . . Death comes rushing on in triumph veiled in a mantle of ten-fold darkness. His unrelenting scythe, pointed and ready for the stroke.[8]

Despite the purple prose, St. Croix's governor and other prominent residents considered the epistle a literary masterpiece and demanded to know what "youth" could write so movingly. When the island's leaders learned that the author was a seventeen-year-old orphaned clerk, without a day of organized schooling to his name, they immediately began soliciting funds to send him to the mainland to attend college so that his raw intellectual talents could be properly cultivated. Alex jumped at the opportunity to leave Christiansted. In the spring of 1773, he boarded a ship bound for Boston. Yet fate tossed one last obstacle in Alex's path. During his voyage northward, his ship caught fire. The crew and passengers probably worked together bailing seawater to extinguish the smoky blaze. They successfully doused the flames, and the ship eventually limped into Boston Harbor.[9]

At first, Alex considered attending the College of New Jersey at Princeton, where, in an interview with the president, he asked if he could graduate ahead of schedule by working at his own pace rather than being tied to a particular graduating class. Informed that he would need four full years to graduate, Alex instead chose to settle in New York and attend King's College (soon renamed Columbia), a less prestigious school, but one willing to accommodate a "chronically impatient" and unabashedly ambitious young man like Alexander Hamilton.[10]

According to his friends' later accounts, Hamilton had sympathized with the American cause even before moving to New York City, and it did not take him long to find other Manhattanites who shared his point of view. He joined the Sons of Liberty and befriended McDougall, who took an immediate liking to Hamilton and lent him books necessary for his studies. When it appeared that New Yorkers might send moderates to the Continental Congress, McDougall organized and chaired a meeting in the Fields on July 6, 1774, to demand that the colonists take a more belligerent stance toward the British Parliament. It was here that the nineteen-year-old Hamilton gave his first public political speech. He urged that Americans unite against the Coercive Acts (which closed Boston Harbor in retaliation for the Boston Tea Party) with a renewed boycott of British goods. Otherwise, he predicted, "fraud, power, and the most odious oppression will rise triumphant over right, justice, social happiness, and freedom."[11]

No one knew who Hamilton was when he gave this speech, nor did he get public credit five months later, when he anonymously published a thirty-five-page pamphlet defending the Continental Congress. Two months later, in February 1775, he came out with an eighty-page tract espousing the American cause, in which he argued that Parliament had overstepped its authority both in taxing the American colonies and in punishing the colonists when they refused to pay those taxes. When one of Hamilton's pro-British critics cited legal precedent for Parliament's policy, Hamilton replied that "the sacred rights of mankind are not to be rummaged for, among old parchments, or musty records. They are written, as with a sun beam, in the whole *volume* of human nature, by the hand of the divinity itself; and can never be erased or obscured by mortal power."[12]

While the Continental Congress tried to negotiate a peaceful resolution to the crisis with the British government, redcoats in Massachusetts marched west from Boston to confiscate the Americans' caches of weapons and ammunition. The colonists' attempt to stop the British raid resulted in the battles of Lexington and Concord in April 1775. When news of these skirmishes reached New York four days later, all hopes of reconciliation evaporated. "The most violent proposals," unthinkable just a few months earlier, wrote a correspondent for the *London Chronicle*, are "meeting with universal approbation! The whole city is arming." The Sons of Liberty took control of the Custom House, seized the city's supply of guns, and closed the port to prevent it from being used to supply the British army in Massachusetts. The American Revolution in New York had begun.[13]

New York's patriots initially thought they could retain control of the city against an anticipated British invasion. In the summer of 1775, the Continental Congress put McDougall, who had no military experience but was a proven leader of men, in charge of the city's military forces. McDougall used his new authority to help his favorite patriots gain the most prestigious assignments. Hamilton, for example, turned down a position most college students would have coveted, aide-de-camp to a brigadier general, in order to become captain of an artillery company. This position gave him both an independent command and the chance he sought to lead men into battle.[14]

Realizing that the British would attempt to capture New York, General George Washington in early 1776 sent his most experienced subordinate, Major General Charles Lee, to assess New York's preparedness for the inevitable invasion. Lee, born in Cheshire, England, in 1732, had first come to America as a British officer in the French and Indian War, during which he earned a reputation for eccentricity by marrying the daughter of a Mohawk Indian chief. Another manifestation of what Lee himself called his "distemper of . . . mind" was his fanatical devotion to his dogs. He never went anywhere without six or more of his faithful hounds. Lee also loved war. Rather than take the usual colonial assignments in Ireland or North America, he traversed Europe in the 1760s as a mercenary, commanding units for the Portuguese against Spain and for Poland and Russia against the Ottoman Empire. Perhaps sensing that the American clash with Parliament might lead to military conflict, Lee immigrated to North America in 1773, expressing sympathy for the American cause and calling King George III "despicable," "stupid," and a "dolt." Lee had expected the Continental Congress to make *him* the head of the American armies, and resented that the post was offered to Washington, who had far less military experience.[15]

After several months in Manhattan, Lee decided that his motley crew of untested citizen soldiers could not prevent Britain's well-trained and experienced military from capturing the city, especially if the British devoted significant naval resources to such an attack. The Americans could not allow the British to take New York without a fight, but the best outcome they could hope for, Lee argued, would be to inflict heavy casualties on the British forces before conceding the city. When the British began amassing troops and ships in the lower harbor in the summer of 1776 in an attempt to awe the Americans into submission, the accuracy of Lee's prediction soon became evident. "I could not believe my eyes," wrote one New Yorker when first gazing upon the hundreds of British ships and tens of thousands of troops amassed in the harbor. "I do declare that I thought all London was in afloat."[16]

New Yorkers began to flee the city en masse. "New York is deserted by its old inhabitants," wrote one of the remaining New Yorkers in April to another who had returned to England, "and filled [instead] with soldiers from New England, Philadelphia, Jersey, &c." By the time the British launched their invasion, which began with an assault on Brooklyn on August 22, Manhattan contained only 5,000 inhabitants, down from 25,000 a year earlier. The Revolution also brought immigration to a halt. Any ship bound for America was likely to be boarded by British troops and its able-bodied male passengers forced into the British army or Royal Navy.[17]

Hamilton, McDougall, and Washington fought bravely to hinder the invaders, but over the course of the next several weeks they wisely retreated, first to Manhattan, then north to Westchester, and finally west to New Jersey, rather than risk losing Washington's entire army at the very onset of the Revolutionary struggle. Washington, told that Hamilton was too brilliant to be left in an artillery regiment, made him one of his key staff members, treating him like the son he never had. For much of the war, Washington's army would control the portion of New Jersey just across the Hudson from Manhattan and Westchester County, but it would take seven years to rid New York City of its British occupiers. Colden, who must have been pleased to hear that his radical enemies had beaten a hasty retreat, passed away in Flushing at age eighty-seven on September 20, 1776, just five days after the British began to occupy Manhattan.[18]

To what extent did New York's immigrants follow McDougall and Hamilton into the Continental Army? It is impossible to say with any certainty. Unlike in later wars, in which Americans would carefully document the birthplaces of their citizen soldiers, record keeping was poor in the Revolutionary military, and even when such muster rolls were kept, birthplace was considered irrelevant. But we do know that immigrants played a key role on the American side. A loyalist (as those who remained loyal to Great Britain were called) appearing before Parliament in 1779 testified that three-quarters of the American soldiers were immigrants. A British officer who helped invade New York agreed, asserting that "the chief strength of the rebel army at present consists of natives of Europe, particularly Irishmen: — many of their regiments are composed principally of these men." Another British official in New York reported that "great numbers of emigrants, particularly Irish, are in the rebel army, some by choice and many for mere subsistence." Scotch Presbyterians like McDougall and Hamilton also made up a significant portion of the Continental Army. Most of the Irish who enlisted on the American side were also Protestants. Noting the preponderance of Dissenters among the American troops, especially among their officers, a Hessian officer fighting for the British insisted that the conflict should not be called "an American rebellion," because it was really "nothing more nor less than an Irish-Scotch Presbyterian rebellion." The rebel army, he observed, also contained Germans as well as "many Englishmen, Irishmen, Scotchmen, Frenchmen and others."[19]

With the British occupation of New York City complete, "Tories," or loyalists, began to return to the city. In November they issued a "Declaration of Dependence," pledging their allegiance to Great Britain and asking in return that the city not be punished for the indiscretions of the departed Revolutionaries. Although some loyalists were immigrants (the first signer of the Declaration of Dependence was Irish-born merchant Hugh Wallace), newcomers were not particularly prominent within their ranks. The best-known New York City Tories were second-, third-, or fourth-generation Americans — members of what one might call the city's ruling class. These included the Crugers, for whom Hamilton had worked in St. Croix, as well as the Phillipses, the De Lanceys, the Coldens, the Bayards, and the Van Schaacks. Members of the Church of England also disproportionately dominated the Tory ranks. These loyalist leaders imagined themselves to be members of the British aristocracy, and could not easily give up that exalted status. Other New York City Tories felt a strong devotion to England, while still others were businessmen who perceived that the

The New York City fire that began on September 21, 1776, rendered a quarter of the city's buildings uninhabitable. The area between Broadway and the Hudson River south of what is now Chambers Street suffered the most damage.

war presented them with unique opportunities to turn a quick profit if they swore loyalty to the crown and remained in the city, especially if their pro-Revolutionary competitors had fled. Some, like the printer and newspaper publisher Hugh Gaine (an Irish immigrant), had businesses they could not easily move.[20]

On September 21, just days after the British took New York, a horrific fire consumed a huge swath of the city, reducing the southwest quarter of the town to a smoldering ash heap. It would take several decades for the city to fully rebuild. The British suspected that saboteurs had set the blaze, and immediately arrested dozens of alleged spies. One of those taken into custody was Haym Salomon. Born in Poland in about 1740, Salomon was one of those immigrants who made it to New York just before the American Revolution began. He left the city in the patriot exodus during the summer of 1776, and may have worked provisioning Washington's army for several months, but returned to the city at about the time the British occupied Manhattan. The British put him in the same jail where McDougall had been imprisoned.[21]

Some of those arrested at this time were shown very little mercy. Nathan Hale, lamenting that he had but one life to give for his country, was one of several prisoners executed in New York immediately after the fire. Others rotted for months or years in the city's many makeshift prisons, first on land (nearly every Dissenting church in the city was seized by the British and made into a detention center), and when those were filled, on water as well, in Wallabout Bay, Brooklyn. That was where the British anchored their infamous prison ships, "floating hells" on which thousands died of malnutrition or contagious disease. The British often dumped the dead prisoners, sewn into blankets, into the harbor; hundreds, perhaps thousands of others were buried in shallow mass graves on the Brooklyn shoreline. For years after the Revolution, after particularly violent storms, Brooklynites would find their beaches, as one resident recalled, "covered as thick with skulls as a cornfield ordinarily appears to be in Autumn with pumpkins."[22]

Salomon was lucky not to suffer that fate. Hearing that his prisoners included a Jew who spoke German and had experience provisioning troops, a Hessian general paroled Salomon on the condition that he take an oath of loyalty to Great Britain and become a sutler for the German mercenaries. Salomon agreed and was allowed to trade on his own account as well, turning a tidy profit. He even bought a slave. Salomon became a model loyalist, and in July 1777 he laid down additional roots in the community by marrying fifteen-year-old Rachel Franks. A year later they had their first child, a son named Ezekiel.[23]

At just about the time Salomon got married, printer James Rivington returned to New York. Rivington, an English immigrant and editor of *Rivington's New York Gazetteer*, was the city's best-known publisher and bookseller on the eve of the war. He had come to New York in about 1760 to escape huge debts he had run up in England gambling on horse racing. He had printed Hamilton's two anti-British pamphlets in 1775 but had angered the Sons of Liberty by also publishing British propaganda. Pro-American mobs twice attacked his offices on the eve of the Revolution. A Massachusetts newspaper called Rivington a "Judas," and even Hamilton, who deplored the attack on Rivington's press, admitted that he found the editor "detestable . . . in every respect." Rivington fled the city after a second attack on his press but reappeared in September 1777, having secured an appointment as the king's official New York printer. He resumed publication of his newspaper, now called the *Royal Gazette*, filling it with anti-Revolutionary vitriol. To those who supported the Revolution, he was one of the most hated men in New York.[24]

But appearances could sometimes be deceiving. Salomon, for example, continued to promote the American cause while working for the Hessians, recruiting defectors among the German soldiers and helping American prisoners escape, sometimes slipping them money so they could bribe their jailers. When he came to believe that the British had finally discovered his treachery, he fled to Philadelphia. There he managed to become a specialist in brokering "bills of exchange," the monetary instruments governments used to buy goods and services when they had no cash on hand. Salomon's job was to find Americans willing to trade gold, silver, or American currency for French and Spanish bills of exchange. The more bills he sold, the more he made in commissions. Salomon's renown for brokering foreign bills of exchange became so widespread that Robert Morris, the man assigned by the Continental Congress to finance the fledgling American government and military, hired Salomon in June 1781 to broker the American government's own bills of exchange. Salomon's ability to market the government's debt that summer, even as the Americans teetered on the brink of insolvency, played a key role in keeping the American army in the field long enough to defeat the British. That fall, Washington earned a decisive victory over Lord Cornwallis at Yorktown. It was there that Hamilton, after five years on Washington's staff, was granted his oft-expressed wish to return to a field command, leading three infantry battalions in an assault on Yorktown that captured a key British defensive position and helped precipitate the British surrender.[25]

After Yorktown, it appeared that an American victory was inevitable, as the patriots had pushed the British out of almost every part of the thirteen colonies except New York City. Tories fled the city by the thousands over the course of 1782 and 1783. The city's population, which had swelled to 33,000 during the war, now plummeted, just as it had in 1776. Many of the loyalists hated to go and accused the British government of abandoning them. Members of the city's first families, whose wealth consisted mostly of real estate they could not take with them, were especially bitter. "God d—m them, I thought it would come to this," raged loyalist William Bayard. "What is to become of me, sir. I am totally ruined." On November 25, 1783, British troops finally evacuated New York City, having over the preceding months taken about thirty thousand inhabitants of the city and vicinity to England or Canada. As soon as the British lowered their flags and departed, George Washington and the American army, which had already taken upper Manhattan weeks earlier, came marching into town.[26]

When supporters of the Revolution returned to New York, they were shocked to find that Rivington had not fled with the other loyalists. In fact, soon after Washington arrived in the city, he paid a visit to Rivington's offices accompanied by two of his officers, who were amazed that the general wanted to see such an infamous Tory. The officers were even more astonished when Washington, on the pretext of examining a list of agricultural treatises, went into a back room with Rivington. The curious soldiers listened closely through the slightly open door and, as Martha Washington's grandson later retold the story, "heard the chinking of two heavy purses of gold" being placed upon Rivington's table by the general. It turned out that Rivington had also been a spy for the American side, smuggling out intelligence to Washington by sewing documents into the bindings of books. Rivington had even helped the Americans obtain the British fleet's signals, which were passed on to the French navy in time for the decisive engagement at Yorktown. But the public either did not know about Rivington's work for the Americans or believed that he had engaged in espionage out of opportunism rather than devotion to the American cause. A month after Washington's visit, Rivington was beaten by a mob and forced to shutter his newspaper for good. A gambler to the end, Rivington tried to recoup his losses through risky investments in the India trade. He lost £20,000 that he did not have and spent the last five years of his life in a New York debtor's prison, where he died in 1802.[27]

Some loyalists, who either stayed in New York or, more often, returned after initially fleeing, did not suffer such a dire fate. Rivington's fellow printer and publisher Hugh Gaine, initially arrested for supporting the enemy, eventually reestablished his business and was awarded many printing contracts by the state; he even produced the state's first paper money. But few regained their former status and wealth. Colden's sons and daughters fought a losing battle to have some of their property restored. One of his sons, David, managed to regain permission to live in the United States and settled on his father's old farm in Ulster County. David's son eventually became a well-regarded American politician and lawyer. But David's brother Cadwallader junior, a more active Tory, was banished for life.[28]

Those who had supported the Revolution, of course, did much better. Salomon became a wealthy financier and philanthropist in Philadelphia before his death in 1785. McDougall was elected to the New York State Senate after the war, an office he held until his death in 1786. He also served from 1784 until his death as the first president of the Bank of New York, the first bank founded in the newly established United States.

The moving force behind the Bank of New York was Hamilton, who had continued his meteoric rise from immigrant orphan to wunderkind of the new nation. After Yorktown, with the war clearly over and only the treaty negotiations remaining, Hamilton resigned from the army and, with New York City still occupied, went to Albany to become a lawyer. The established route into that profession involved reading law for two or three years under the tutelage of an established attorney and working uncompensated in that lawyer's office in exchange for the legal education one received. Hamilton, far too impatient to follow that path, began in January 1782 to read the necessary legal tomes on his own; nine months later he was admitted to the bar. That same year, New Yorkers chose Hamilton to represent them in the congress set up under the Articles of Confederation. When the government established under the Articles proved unworkable, the Constitution written to replace it was ratified thanks in no

This portrait miniature of Alexander Hamilton, painted by Charles Willson Peale ca. 1780, is the earliest surviving likeness of New York's most famous Founding Father.

small part to Hamilton's eloquent defense of its principles in *The Federalist Papers*. In the first federal election held under the Constitution, George Washington was elected president, and he reserved the post of secretary of the treasury for his young, ambitious protégé.[29]

With the end of the Revolution and the establishment of a new government, immigration to New York would now resume. Initially, the newcomers trickled in at only a fraction of the former pace. Great Britain was still at war with France and Spain, and wages and crop prices in the British Isles rose dramatically as a result, persuading many to stay at home rather than assume the risks associated with relocation to the fledgling republic. The British considered it a crime to desert one's country in wartime and made every effort to prevent their citizens from emigrating. Even if one managed to slip aboard a vessel headed for America, British sailors continued to board such ships and force any suspected British citizens found on board to join the Royal Navy. In such circumstances, few residents of Great Britain (still the primary source of potential American immigrants) chose to venture to the new United States. Only with Napoleon's defeat in 1815 at Waterloo in present-day Belgium would that warfare come to an end and immigrants once again stream unimpeded into New York, beginning the "century of immigration" that would dramatically reshape New York City and the flow of migrants around the world.

6

REPUBLIC

IN 1835, as New York was being transformed by unprecedented immigration from Ireland and the German states, a group of gentlemen nostalgic for old New York founded the St. Nicholas Society. One of the moving forces behind the new group was Washington Irving, who chose the name to poke fun at immigrant organizations such as the St. Andrew's Society, which catered to Scots, and the Shamrock Society, formed by the Irish. Membership in the new group, which was by invitation only (and remains so to this day), was limited to those who could prove that they were descended from someone who had lived in New York before 1785. Among its founding members were Astors and Aspinwalls, Bayards and Bleeckers, Coldens and Crosbys, Delafields and DePeysters, Hamiltons and Jays, Ludlows and Lorillards, Rhinelanders and Roosevelts. Some Jews with deep roots in the city were also invited to join.[1]

The highlight of the St. Nicholas Society's calendar was its annual dinner, and in 1848 the club asked one of its more erudite charter members, Judge William Alexander Duer, to provide the after-dinner remarks. Following a childhood spent in New York City, Duer had lived in Philadelphia and New Orleans before moving to upstate New York, where he was active in politics and held his judgeship. In 1829 he returned to Manhattan to become president of Columbia College. During his thirteen-year tenure there he published one of the nineteenth century's most widely respected guides to constitutional law. The nostalgic members of the St. Nicholas Society asked that Duer deliver a lecture describing what New York City had been like "in the early days of our Republic."[2]

Duer began his address by recounting the afternoon sixty-five years earlier, in November 1783, when, as a young boy, he first set foot on Manhattan Island. His most vivid memory was "the *Burnt District*," the huge swath of the city that fire had destroyed in September 1776. "No visible attempts had been

From his arrival in New York as a small boy in 1783 to his death seventy-five years later, Judge William Alexander Duer saw New York grow from a small town of 20,000 inhabitants to a teeming metropolis of 800,000.

made since the fire to remove the ruins," Duer observed, "and as the edifices destroyed were chiefly of brick, the skeletons of the remaining walls cast their grim shadows upon the pavement, imparting an unearthly aspect to the street." Virtually every building on the west side of Broadway south of what is now Chambers Street lay in ruins, as did almost every structure between Broadway and Broad Street from the East River to within one block of Wall Street. Only as Duer and his family, walking north from the Battery up Broadway, reached the "ghastly" remains of Trinity Church and turned right off of the main thoroughfare did they seem, "at last, to have entered a city of the living."[3]

Duer, a small child at the time, obviously had no role in choosing the newly liberated city as his home. His father, also named William, was one of the thousands of people who began pouring into New York after the British evacuated. Many, like the Duers, were returning refugees who had previously lived in the city. Born to wealth in Devonshire in 1743 and educated at Eton, the elder William Duer became the aide-de-camp to a senior British army officer in India

NEW YORK UNDER BRITISH OCCUPATION, 1776–1783

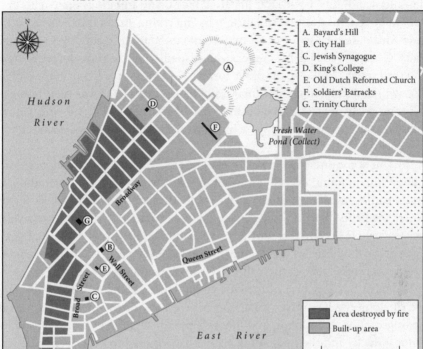

A. Bayard's Hill
B. City Hall
C. Jewish Synagogue
D. King's College
E. Old Dutch Reformed Church
F. Soldiers' Barracks
G. Trinity Church

Hudson
River

Fresh Water
Pond (Collect)

Broadway

Queen Street

Wall Street

Broad Street

East   River

Area destroyed by fire
Built-up area

One-quarter mile

once he finished his education. He returned to England just after the death of his father, who bequeathed William a substantial estate, including a large sugar plantation with slaves on the Caribbean island of Dominica. Duer could have left the management of the distant agricultural enterprise to others, as was typical of the English elite, but determined to wring more profit from the venture, Duer moved to Dominica to run it himself. Like many Caribbean Britons, Duer ordered most of his supplies from New York, and while on a trip there to buy lumber in 1768, he decided to relocate and become a merchant and real estate speculator.

The baby-faced Duer was particularly adroit at ingratiating himself with the rich and powerful, and by 1776 he had been selected to serve in the Continental Congress in Philadelphia. There he earned the respect of Alexander Hamilton and Robert and Gouverneur Morris for his work managing the finances of the fledgling republic. It was during these years, spent mostly in Philadelphia and upstate New York, that Duer became, as his biographer put it, "quite adept at turning the public posts he filled — and he filled many — to his own profit." He used his connections and those of his highly placed friends to secure contracts to supply the Spanish navy with lumber, the French army with food, and the American military with war matériel. Like many ambitious men of his era, Duer improved his position still further by "marrying up." In 1779 he wed Catherine Alexander, daughter of an important confidant of George Washington, Major General William Alexander, who helped Duer close his lucrative deal with the French. Unlike many of the former New Yorkers arriving in the city in 1783, who had suffered terrible financial setbacks during the war years because of lost property or interrupted business, Duer returned — with his wife, young namesake, and servants in tow — a much wealthier man than he had left it.[4]

As the Duers continued their walk through New York to their rented mansion, young William found everything about the city strange and new. Even though streets had been laid out almost as far north as modern-day Chambers Street (where the British had built a defensive palisade stretching from river to river), very few people lived in that northern extremity, and none of the thoroughfares north of the modern-day 9/11 Memorial had yet been paved with cobblestones. Significant rainfall turned these dirt roads into quagmires of mud and manure.

The most bustling part of the city, young Duer observed, was a mile-long stretch along the East River waterfront where forty or so wharves welcomed the brigs, schooners, sloops, and other ships entering the harbor. The southernmost docks and their adjoining warehouses catered to "the river trade" up the Hudson as far as Albany. From those wharves northward to just past Wall Street, noted Duer, were the piers that catered to "foreign commerce." These welcomed vessels from London, Liverpool, Glasgow, and Bristol, as well as Canada, but even more from Caribbean and Bahamian islands such as Jamaica, St. John, St. Thomas, St. Martin, Hispaniola, Curaçao, and Turks Island. Farther north still, stretching to about where the Brooklyn Bridge now sits, were the docks and warehouses devoted to trade with other American states and "our neighbors from Long Island," who supplied Manhattanites with "substantial freights of oysters, clams, and fine white sand." Beyond these piers, at the very northern extremity of the developed East River waterfront, lay New York's shipyards. They had sat virtually dormant during the Revolution, but would soon spring back to life now that peace had returned.[5]

What little industry New York could boast in 1783, Duer recalled, was located on the shores of the Fresh Water Pond, or "Collect," a small lake (about seven hundred feet across) located two blocks east of Broadway and a block south of modern-day Canal Street. "Its southern and eastern banks," Duer remembered, "were lined with furnaces, potteries, breweries, tanneries, ropewalks, and other manufactories; all drawing their supplies of water from the pond." Adjacent to the lake was the "Tea-water Pump," which took water from the same underground spring that supplied the Collect. In 1783, Duer marveled, that single pump supplied drinking water for virtually the entire city. Casks mounted on carts were used to transport it to every part of town.

Duer also recollected that in the 1780s, tall hills and sunken valleys could still be found in lower Manhattan. A high ridge, Duer informed his younger listeners, had run up much of the west side of Manhattan until it was leveled in the early nineteenth century to make the streets leading from the Hudson to the center of town less steep. And he wistfully remembered the tallest and most prominent peak in old New York, Bayard's Hill, which rose from the Collect's western shore "to the height of one hundred feet, and nothing can exceed in brilliancy and animation the prospect it presented on a fine winter day, when the icy surface was alive with skaters darting in every direction . . . while the hill side was covered with spectators, rising as in an amphitheatre, tier above tier." According to Duer, one of the biggest mistakes ever made by city leaders was their decision to level Bayard's Hill and use the earth excavated from it to fill the Collect. Duer found this decision especially galling because the Irish immigrant enclave known as Five Points, which had replaced his childhood idyll, was in his eyes a repugnant, vice-infested slum.[6]

More than one hundred feet high, Bayard's Hill had tiered slopes that provided an amphitheater-like view of the Collect Pond. The hill was eventually leveled to allow Broadway to be extended northward.

From the day Duer arrived in New York at the end of the Revolution in 1783 to the time he gave his address to his fellow patricians of the St. Nicholas Society in 1848, immigration completely transformed New York. The founders of the St. Nicholas Society, steeped in the city's history, knew that it had taken until 1820, two hundred years after New Amsterdam's founding, for the population of Manhattan to reach 100,000. Beginning in 1825, however, the city would add 100,000 residents *per decade.* By 1845, the city contained 371,000 residents, a number once unimaginable to those, like Duer, who had settled in the fire-damaged, war-weary town of about 20,000 in 1783.[7]

The peace treaty that ended the war opened the immigrant floodgates. In particular, 1784 saw a huge migration across the Atlantic as thousands who had waited years to go to America, often to join family members already there, were finally able to make the journey. Some of the best-known immigrants of this era arrived in New York in the immediate postwar years. A thirty-nine-year-old Scotsman named Archibald Gracie, for example, landed in New York City in 1784 after having spent most of the war clerking for an import-export merchant in Liverpool. In Manhattan, Gracie became a successful businessman and an associate (in both business and politics) of Alexander Hamilton. Perhaps seeking to escape the noise and congestion of the growing city, Gracie built a mansion for his family several miles north of town at Hell Gate, the place where Long Island comes closest to Manhattan Island (modern-day East 88th Street near East End Avenue). In the twentieth century, the city acquired the home and made it the official residence of New York's mayors.[8]

Another Scotsman who came to New York in 1784 was fourteen-year-old Duncan Fife. Along with his parents, three brothers, and two sisters, Fife initially settled in Albany, but by 1792 he had moved to New York City, where he likely served an apprenticeship as a cabinetmaker. A year later in a ceremony at the First Presbyterian Church on Wall Street, Fife married Rachel Louzada, a New York–born Jew whose brother was also a cabinetmaker. They raised their seven children as Presbyterians, though Rachel herself did not convert until nearly fifty years later.

In 1794 Fife changed the spelling of his name to Phyfe and launched his career as a furniture maker to well-to-do New Yorkers. Phyfe's insistence on employing only a handful of trusted craftsmen and using nothing but the finest mahogany and rosewood soon brought him a large clientele of discriminating customers in New York, Philadelphia, the South, and the Caribbean. "Mr. Phyfe is so much the United States rage," lamented New Yorker Sarah Huger in 1816, "that it is with great difficulty now, that one can procure an audience even of a few moments" with him. Customers typically waited half a year or longer for their furniture. Despite Phyfe's enormous success, recalled his nephew, he remained throughout his life "a very plain man, always working and always smoking a short pipe." Like many driven entrepreneurs, "he was very strict in his habits, and all the members of the family had to be in bed by 9 o'clock." Though he could have afforded to relocate to a more fashionable neighborhood, especially after he turned the business over to his sons and retired, Phyfe lived in the same house across from his workshop on Fulton Street, near the corner of Church (a block east of the 9/11 Memorial), from 1795 until his death in August 1854.[9]

Scots were not the only Europeans to rush to New York as soon as the British had evacuated the city. Many Germans immigrated as well, including John Jacob Astor, who became the best-known German New Yorker of this era. The fifth child of a butcher named Jacob Astor, Johann Jacob Astor was born in July 1763 in Walldorf, a town in the independent German state of Pfalz, which is now part of Baden-Württemberg. Astor's mother, Maria Magdalena, died when Johann Jacob was just nine months old, but his father soon remarried and had six more children.[10]

Whether or not stories of a "cruel stepmother" and "drunken father" are true, Jacob's older children seem to have been particularly anxious to get away from home and Walldorf as quickly as possible. Johann Jacob's eldest brother, Georg Peter, moved to London when Johann Jacob was a boy and became a musical instrument maker. Johann Heinrich moved to New York at the start of the American Revolution (some said he had arrived with the Hessian troops hired by George III) and became a butcher and sutler. Johann Melchior moved to the German countryside and became a farmer. All this before Johann Jacob had even turned fourteen. At that age his schooling ended, and he became an assistant in his father's butcher shop.

But Johann Jacob also yearned to get away. As soon as he turned sixteen, in 1779, he traveled to London, moved in with his brother Georg, and Anglicized his name to John. We don't know what John Jacob did in London — perhaps his brother got him a job making musical instruments — but we do know that four years later, as soon as the peace treaty ending the Revolutionary War was signed in September 1783, John Jacob made plans to join Johann Heinrich, now known as Henry, in New York. Late autumn was not an ideal time to embark on a transatlantic voyage. Hurricanes and frigid weather could make the trip miserable, even deadly. But John Jacob Astor apparently wanted to get to America before the anticipated rush of immigrants the following spring. So in

John Jacob Astor became a veritable "money-making machine" after his arrival in New York in the 1780s. He made one fortune in the fur trade and another investing in Manhattan real estate, and still ranks as one of the wealthiest Americans of all time.

late November, carrying seven flutes and sheet music he planned to sell in the United States, he boarded the *North Carolina* bound for Baltimore, from where he would travel north to join his brother in New York.[11]

Astor's voyage did not go as planned. The North American winter of 1783–84 was unusually cold, and as Astor's ship sailed into the Chesapeake Bay, it became trapped in ice just a day's sail from Baltimore's harbor. The captain waited for the cold snap to break, but week after week passed without relief. Soon brave and impatient passengers began walking across the ice to shore, but Astor was not that courageous. After spending two months icebound (and four months overall on the small vessel), he finally reached Baltimore in late March. Three weeks later he joined his brother in New York.[12]

In Astor's first weeks in New York, he worked as a "baker's boy," hawking the baked goods of another German immigrant from Walldorf. He also seems to have worked as a peddler, selling pins and needles, cheap jewelry, and other trinkets. Soon he took employment with a New York City fur dealer as a "beater," cleaning the newly acquired pelts to make them ready for retail sale. In 1785 Astor married Sarah Todd, the niece of an acquaintance from England, in one of the city's German Reformed churches. The newlyweds moved in with Sarah's widowed mother, and using Sarah's dowry and her mother's house, Astor opened a music shop. He advertised that the store sold "an elegant assortment of musical instruments, such as piano fortes, spinnets, piano-forte guitars, guitars, the best of violins, German flutes, clarinets, hautboys [oboes], fifes, . . . and every other article in the musical line, which he will dispose of on very low terms for cash."[13]

But Astor had far grander ambitions, primarily involving New York's oldest trade — the fur business. By April 1788, Astor had added to his usual music store advertisement the news that "he also buys and sells for cash all kinds of furs," including "beaver, beaver coating; raccoon skins, raccoon blankets, and spring musk rat skins; which he sells by large or small quantities." Being a diehard believer in eliminating the middleman whenever possible, Astor left Sarah in charge of the music shop and trekked into the wilds of northern and western New York State, seeking out Indian fur traders from whom he could make purchases. He was also an obsessive cost cutter, cleaning the furs himself when he could have easily hired others to do that menial job for him. He even ventured into Canada, though it was illegal for Canadians to sell furs directly to Americans. By 1788, the twenty-five-year-old Astor, a humble peddler just a few years earlier, was able to broker deals in Montreal for thousands of dollars' worth of furs and finance their shipment to New York and Europe.[14]

One of Astor's defining traits as a businessman was his belief in diversification. Knowing that the fur market in the United States or Europe could crash at any moment, he began selling his pelts (as well as ginseng) in China, and reinvesting the proceeds in Chinese tea, silks, and cloth, which he imported back to North America. Not wanting to become overly reliant on suppliers in the Northeast and Quebec, he tried to establish a fur-trading outpost in Oregon. And while some of the most famous businessmen of his era often gambled everything for the chance at a huge payout, Astor was renowned for his caution and prudence. "Tho desirious to make some business I am equally so to avoid risks," he wrote to one of his agents in 1813. "Some I know must be run, but let [them] be as little as possible." The elder William Duer, in contrast, lost his entire fortune and spent the last seven years of his life in debtor's prison after failing in 1792 in an audacious attempt to corner the New York market for government bonds.[15]

One way Astor hedged his risk was to plow much of his fur-trading profits into real estate. In terms of sheer acreage, the bulk of his property purchases were in fur-hunting grounds in upstate New York and Canada. But it was his huge investment in Manhattan real estate that transformed him from a wealthy merchant into one of the richest Americans ever. He made his first New York City land purchases in 1789 and added steadily to his portfolio after that. Foreseeing that Manhattan's population would expand faster than most New Yorkers imagined, he bought large swaths of farmland from Greenwich Village all the way up to modern-day midtown Manhattan. Some of these he and his children later sold to developers as new neighborhoods were laid out over the once bucolic fields. The majority he retained, collecting each year in rents what would have been the fortune of a lifetime to almost any other American. In 1819, when he turned the day-to-day operations of his business empire over to a son and other partners and left for an extended tour of Europe, he was the single largest property owner in the city and the wealthiest man in America. He was, as the *New York Herald* put it after his death in 1848, "a self-invented money-making machine." At its peak, his fortune, when translated into current dollars, was the third largest in American history, nearly 50 percent larger than that of Microsoft founder Bill Gates.[16]

Along with Scots and Germans, the English also began to immigrate to America after 1783, though in lower numbers than previously, owing to the lingering English hostility toward the United States. One such immigrant was William Colgate. He came to America from Kent in 1795 at age twelve with his siblings, mother Sarah, and father Robert, who had been threatened with prison for his outspoken criticism of King George III. After stints living in rural Maryland and Virginia, the family moved in 1800 to Baltimore, where Colgate and his father became business partners with a soap maker. Though Robert tired of city life and returned to farming, William soon set up his own soap- and candle-making business. In 1803 he moved to New York City and took a job with a New York company in that same trade, but in 1806 he quit and opened his own soap business, William Colgate & Company.

In those days, manufactured soap was considered a luxury only the wealthy could afford. Most New Yorkers either used no soap at all or made their own by boiling fat drippings from their kitchens with potash, which contained high concentrations of lye. Homemade soap, however, was greasy, foul smelling, and extremely abrasive. Colgate's stroke of genius was to recognize that if he could significantly lower the price, the unwashed masses would gladly pay a few cents for a less abrasive manufactured soap. Colgate slowly but surely built up his business, even delivering purchases to his retail customers, something unheard of in those days. By 1817 Colgate soap dominated the New York market. A decade later he came up with the idea of scented soap, and this innovation drove sales higher still. By the 1840s, his Manhattan factory was boiling twenty tons of soap at a time to keep up with demand. Colgate soap became one of the first nationally known American brands. A devout Baptist, Colgate spent much of his fortune distributing free Bibles in dozens of languages all across the world. He also financed the creation of the university that bears his name.[17]

The largest group of newcomers in this era came from Ireland. "The young men of Ireland who wish to be free and happy should leave it and come here as soon as possible," wrote one satisfied immigrant, for "there is no place in the world where a man meets so rich a reward for good conduct and industry as in America." Since the Revolution, however, the background of the typical Irish immigrant had changed. Immigrants of means, like Waddell Cunningham, became the exception rather than the rule. One Irish customs officer reported in 1793 that emigrant ships contained "no people of real property" but only "the lower order of tradesmen . . . besides numbers of no occupation that went as servants." They were, he concluded, "almost entirely of a very inferior class."[18]

Irish immigration to New York increased in part because Irish Catholics now looked more favorably upon the United States than they had when it was a British colony. By going to war with and defeating their English oppressors, Americans had taken on a new, exalted status in Irish Catholic eyes. Furthermore, the Revolution's egalitarian ethos led to the repeal of restrictions that had previously prevented Catholics from opening their own church in New York. After the British evacuation, Catholics bought a plot of land at the corner of Barclay and Church streets and opened the city's first Catholic house of worship in November 1786.[19]

Sectarian violence in Ireland escalated in the 1790s. "We remain here," wrote a Catholic woman in County Wexford to her son in New York in 1800, "but do not know how long it may be a place of residence, as the country is much disturbed by some unknown people who are rioting and burning every night. Our chapples are burning and tearing down." She promised to join her son "if we don't get some change for the better," because "if we don't get some relief the Catholics cannot live here." Many headed for New York.[20]

The city's appeal grew still further as many of Ireland's most prominent freedom fighters went into exile there. The most famous of these was a Protestant, Thomas Addis Emmet. The son of a physician from Limerick, Emmet was born in 1764 in County Cork in the south of Ireland. He graduated from Trinity College, Dublin, in 1782 and then went to medical school in Edinburgh. Yet as soon as Emmet finished his residency in London in 1787, he decided to become an attorney. He completed his legal studies in 1790 and then returned to Ireland, where he was quickly admitted to the bar. In 1791 he married Jane Patten, the daughter of a Presbyterian minister.

Naturally gifted at the art of persuasion, Emmet quickly established a thriving law practice in Dublin. He also became active in Irish politics. A child of the Enlightenment, Emmet believed in universal manhood suffrage at a time when only those with significant real estate holdings could vote; he supported separation of church and state at a time when Catholics in Ireland faced legally sanctioned discrimination; and he advocated self-government for Ireland at a time when the English, having recently lost thirteen valuable colonies in North America, made it a crime to promote independence for Ireland. In 1792 he joined the Society of United Irishmen, an organization made up of both Protestants and Catholics who sought autonomy for the Irish people.

In the same year, England went to war with France. Knowing that the British opposed every facet of the United Irishmen's agenda, the group asked the French to invade Ireland and free it from English rule. Word of their treasonous collusion eventually leaked out, and Emmet, as one of the group's most prominent leaders, became known to the British as "the most dangerous man in Ireland." Authorities arrested Emmet and the organization's other Dublin leaders in the spring of 1798. Undaunted, the United Irishmen launched attacks against British rule across Ireland that summer. A small French invasion force even landed on Ireland's west coast to aid the uprising in County Mayo. The British military suppressed each revolt, capturing and executing several thousand of the Irish freedom fighters who participated.

At this point, Emmet and the other Dublin leaders offered the authorities a plea deal: they would reveal the inner workings of the United Irishmen (without disclosing any specific names) and describe their attempts to win foreign support if, in return, their lives were spared and they were allowed to go into exile in a country not at war with Great Britain. The British, eager to have evidence that would help justify the mass executions they had carried out, accepted the offer. Emmet and the other incarcerated leaders of the United Irishmen were expected to immigrate to the United States.[21]

But here the story took an unexpected turn. Just seven years after the ratification of the Constitution, politics in the new American republic had become bitterly polarized. During George Washington's first term as president, his secretary of the treasury, Alexander Hamilton, had won congressional approval for a program that would allow the federal government to play an active role in the young nation's economy by establishing a national bank and creating federal subsidies for manufacturers. Those who supported this expanded federal role in the nation's economic development became known as Federalists. The program's opponents, led by Vice President Thomas Jefferson, called themselves Republicans. The two factions (they were not really parties in the modern sense) also fought over foreign policy. Republicans, carrying on Americans' Revolutionary legacy of anti-British sentiment, sought to ally the new nation with England's enemy France. The Federalists, however, found the radicalism of the French Revolution alarming, and preferred to make good relations with Great Britain the nation's priority. As a result, most Irish immigrants supported the Republicans.

By 1798, the Republicans' popularity was increasing so rapidly that Federalists anticipated a calamity in the upcoming elections unless they took some drastic action. Claiming that they had to prevent "hordes of wild Irishmen," as one Federalist congressman put it, from immigrating to the United States, Federalists pushed through Congress a series of bold and brazenly partisan bills that became known collectively as the Alien and Sedition Acts. The Sedition Act infamously made it a crime to write anything "false" or "malicious" about Congress or the president or to bring them into "contempt" or "disrepute." Zealous Federalists jailed nearly a dozen Republican editors under this provision, including one of New York City's Irish-born newspapermen, John Burk, who fled to Virginia and lived under an assumed name rather than face deportation. While Burk was prosecuted under the Sedition Act for his scurrilous statements about President Adams, he was also subject to prosecution under the terms of the Act Concerning Aliens, which gave the president the power to deport immigrants he deemed "dangerous." Finally, the statute known as the Naturalization Act lengthened from five to fourteen years the period immigrants had to wait until they could become citizens and vote. This measure was clearly aimed at reducing the support "wild Irishmen" could give to Jefferson and the Republicans. The Alien and Sedition Acts are today remembered as terrible extremes of partisanship, but they also marked the first, but by no means the last, case of anti-immigrant fever to infect American politics.[22]

One of the Federalist advocates of this all-out attack on Republicans and their immigrant supporters was the American minister to the Court of St. James's, New Yorker Rufus King. When the British in 1798 informed King of their deal with Emmet and the United Irishmen, King told the English that the United States would not accept the "malcontents." As a result, Emmet and his co-conspirators spent an additional four years in prison. In 1802 the Treaty of Amiens between Britain and France ended the war and mandated the release of the Irishmen, who were considered French collaborators. Emmet went to France to try to secure Napoleon's support for the cause of Irish independence, but when the French leader made it clear that Ireland was not one of his top priorities, Emmet decided that he could do no more for the Irish cause in Eu-

Thomas Addis Emmet, leader of an outlawed organization that united Protestants and Catholics seeking independence for Ireland, spent several years in British prisons before immigrating to New York in 1804.

rope. In 1804 he immigrated to New York City with his wife and children. A year later Emmet was joined there by another leader of the United Irishmen, Dr. William MacNeven. A third, lawyer William Sampson, moved to New York in 1806. Several others had preceded them.[23]

Famous immigrants like these Irish revolutionaries had an easier time making new lives for themselves in New York than did the typical immigrant. Emmet quickly became a highly sought-after lawyer and was eventually elected the attorney general of New York. One of his clients in private practice was steamboat developer Robert Fulton, who consulted with the jurist when competitors challenged the validity of the New York law granting him and partner Robert Livingston a thirty-year monopoly on operation of a ferry from New York to New Jersey. Emmet told Fulton that the law that protected his ferry monopoly was unconstitutional, but Fulton and Livingston hired him anyway, and he argued the case, known as *Gibbons v. Ogden,* before the U.S. Supreme Court in

1824. As Emmet had predicted, the court ruled against Fulton's licensee, Aaron
Ogden. Sampson also became a prominent attorney, while MacNeven was appointed a professor of obstetrics and chemistry by New York's College of Physicians and Surgeons. He later served as alderman of New York's heavily Irish
Fourteenth Ward.[24]

Many of the Irish who fled to America in this period had more difficulty
finding work at their old occupations. Bernard M'Kenna, a Catholic schoolteacher who left County Tyrone when two of his kinsmen were arrested for
their support of the independence movement, could not find employment as a
schoolmaster when he arrived in New York City in 1797. He had to tramp thirty
miles east into the wilds of Long Island before he could secure a teaching job.
Even in this rural district, his employers deemed him deficient in grammar,
math, and geography, and not until M'Kenna improved his preparation in these
subjects was he able to land a decent teaching job.

M'Kenna did not have an easy life. His wife, Phoebe, died, leaving Bernard
to care for their two daughters, a three-year-old and a fourteen-month-old.
Fearing M'Kenna might try to convert children to Catholicism, the Long Islanders fired him from his teaching job, so he moved back to New York City
with his daughters and found work at a Catholic school there.

In a letter to his parish priest back in Ireland, M'Kenna characterized his
first decade in America as "disastrous." Yet his "severe trials" did not tarnish
his love for his adopted home. The United States, he wrote in 1811, was "a land
of peace and plenty, . . . the garden spot of the world; a happy asylum for the
banished children of oppression." Despite his "troubles," he had no shortage of
work in New York City and was paid so much better than he had been in Ireland that he had, he boasted, "procured a handsome fortune for each of my
children."[25]

Despite the rave reviews these political refugees gave to their adopted homeland, not many Irish men and women could immediately follow their countrymen to the United States. Not long after Emmet and MacNeven arrived in New
York, Britain and France plunged back into war. That made it difficult for aspiring immigrants to find ships to take them to the United States. Even if they
could secure passage, any able-bodied male found on a ship in the Atlantic still
faced impressment into the British navy. When the United States entered the
conflict by declaring war on Great Britain in 1812, immigration virtually ceased.
"Many is the time I wished I had gone to your country ten years ago," lamented
one Irishman, who regretted that he had not immigrated to "the richest country in the world in every respect" when he had had the chance.[26]

New York continued to grow rapidly nonetheless because other Americans
— New Englanders in particular — were moving there by the thousands. Phila-

delphia and New York had had the same number of inhabitants at the end of the American Revolution, but by 1820, New York's population of 124,000 was twice that of Philadelphia and three times that of Boston. New Yorkers estimated at this time that somewhere between one-fifth and one-quarter of the population had been born abroad, and that half the immigrants were Irish.[27]

Once the war ended in 1815, immigration rebounded. A minister reported in 1822 that the Irish remained the city's dominant immigrant group, followed (in descending order) by Scots, Germans, English, French, Dutch, and Jews. He even found contingents of "Swedes, Danes, Italians, Portuguese, Spaniards, and West-Indians." Author James Fenimore Cooper marveled that "the city of New-York is composed of inhabitants from all the countries of christendom," while a German immigrant found it amazing that New Yorkers conducted business not only in English but also German, French, Spanish, and Italian. By 1830, New York had four times as many immigrants as Philadelphia and five times as many as Boston.[28]

While some of the Irish settling in New York in this period sailed there directly from Ireland, most had to travel in the wrong direction, to Liverpool, in order to get to New York. But beginning in 1819, the voyage to the United States for most of the Irish became even more circuitous. Legislation enacted in Great Britain that year allowed British ships headed for Canada to cram three times as many passengers into their holds as those sailing to the United States. This law, and one passed in the United States that same year which increased the amount of food a ship had to provide for each passenger, made the fare to New York twice as high as that to Canada. As a result, most Irish emigrants bound for the United States after 1819 took one ship from Ireland to Liverpool, took a second from there to Canada, and after working in Canada for a while to earn money for food and transportation, finally made their way to the United States.[29]

The American immigration legislation enacted in 1819 mandated, for the first time, that the government count the number of immigrants landing on its shores by requiring ship captains to submit manifests containing the names, ages, occupations, and geographic origins of the passengers they carried. Because most officials interpreted the law's vague language on origin to mean "country of last residence," the Irish immigrants coming to the United States via Canada were counted as Canadian rather than Irish (if they were counted at all, since many traveled by foot or train and were therefore not recorded). The official American immigration figures for Irish immigrants from 1820 to 1847 (when Canadians passed legislation that drove the fare to Canada up to American levels) thus record only a fraction of the true influx.[30]

What the official figures do tell us is that the flow of emigrants from Ireland rose sixfold from the early 1820s to the early 1830s. This increase resulted in part from the growing desperation of poor Irish peasants who found it more and more difficult to feed and clothe themselves and their children. These impoverished souls had once been unable to emigrate, but the use of "chain migration" had begun to make the move to the United States possible. Chain migration was a strategy in which a family scrimped and saved to send one family member (typically a young man) to the United States. He would work as many jobs and spend as little as he could (by boarding in another immigrant's home, wearing the same clothes day in and day out, and so on) so that he could save enough to bring the next member of the family over as soon as possible. When that brother or sister arrived, the two of them would repeat the process, combining their savings until they were able to pay the fare of a third sibling. This procedure would be repeated until all family members who wanted to immigrate had done so. Through chain migration, unskilled laborers and servants, once a tiny fraction of the Irish newcomers, became just as numerous as the skilled craftsmen, merchants, and professionals who had previously dominated.[31]

New York's Irish-born men of "rank and property" greeted the unprecedented influx of uneducated, unskilled Irish immigrants with pride but also trepidation. They worried that the recent arrivals might sully the good reputation that they themselves had worked so hard to achieve. They also believed that less affluent Irish immigrants were coming to America wholly ignorant of the hard work involved in succeeding in the United States. Merchant John Caldwell, another United Irishman who fled to New York, lamented of his fellow Irishmen that "we are too apt when we approach these shores . . . to expect [to find] the dollars on the sea shore[,] the apple pyes hopping down the chimnie & the little birds perching on your shoulders crying 'come who'll eat me.'" Too many Irish immigrants, he fretted, were "idle & dissolute" rather than "industrious & well conducted."[32]

Caldwell, Emmet, MacNeven, and others took a number of steps to help the new Irish immigrants become respectable and independent. They set up an Irish Emigrant Society to assist in their adjustment to American life; Emmet served as its first president. Believing that New York could not handle unlimited numbers of Irish immigrants, the society petitioned Congress to set aside federal land in Illinois for the exclusive settlement of Irish newcomers. When that effort failed, they established a "labor office" in New York to direct immigrants to canal and other construction jobs around the country so that unscrupulous labor brokers could not take advantage of them. Emmet and MacNeven even wrote a guidebook for Irish immigrants, offering advice on adjusting to life in the United States. Among their tips: don't drink very cold water when

you are hot; don't be tempted to drunkenness by cheap American alcohol; and
don't try to eat as much meat as the Americans.[33]

On the surface, the message Emmet and MacNeven were conveying was
clear: We have assimilated and helped the Irish become more accepted by
Americans than they once were. Don't embarrass us and spoil all our hard
work. But privately, even Emmet struggled to balance the yearning to fit in with
the desire to retain some kind of Irish identity for himself and his children. In
a letter written in 1818 to his daughter Jane Erin Emmet, who was born in Scotland while he was imprisoned there, he blamed her stance in a disagreement
they were having on her "Scotch partialities," an assertion she found insulting.
"Perhaps it was," he admitted, attempting to mend fences. His fear that Scotland had shaped her character might have stemmed, he suggested, from "my
wish to have you entirely Irish (except so far as you ought to be American) . . . I
meant to make you Irish, in spite of your birth place, when I gave you the name
of Erin[.] I meant to give you the feeling which little John Bradstreet once expressed with infantile naiveté to a gentleman who asked where he was born — 'I
was born in America Sir; but I am to be brought up an Irishman.'" Americans
today, both foreign- and native-born, struggle just as mightily with how immigrants should balance these competing forces.[34]

One institution that simultaneously promoted native pride and assimilation was the immigrant newspaper. The very first, it seems, was *The Shamrock*,
which was begun in 1810 but went out of business before year's end. Other papers aimed at the Irish soon followed, but the first truly successful one was *The
Truth Teller*, established in 1825. *The Truth Teller* was not actually published by
Irish immigrants (one of the proprietors was born in England and the other in
Scotland), and it often reads more like a religious tract than a newspaper, but
it gained a place in the hearts of the Irish Catholic community in New York
and elsewhere for its anti-English, anti-Protestant zeal. The editors' canny decision to run missing persons advertisements, placed mostly by Irish immigrants
looking for lost relatives, was also instrumental in its success. An arriving immigrant might place an ad seeking information about a brother who had emigrated before him but now could not be found. A wife might advertise for the
whereabouts of a spouse who had left town to work on a canal but had not been
heard from in months. *The Truth Teller* circulated wherever there were Irish
Americans. Despite the immigrants' oft-repeated hosannas to the freedom and
opportunity that the United States offered, *The Truth Teller*'s missing persons
ads show just how precarious their lives could be.[35]

The Irish were by no means the only New York immigrant group to publish
newspapers in this period. *El Redactor Espagnol*, aimed at Spanish-speaking
New Yorkers, began publication in 1827. So too did *The Albion*, aimed at Eng-

lish immigrants, and published continuously until 1863. French New Yorkers got their own paper, the *Courrier des États-Unis,* in 1828. It was funded in large part by Napoleon's older brother Joseph Bonaparte, the onetime king of Spain, who immigrated to the United States when his family fell from power and settled in Bordentown, New Jersey. Welsh immigrants started a Welsh-language periodical, the *Cymro America,* in 1832. And in 1834 German immigrants established the *New Yorker Staats-Zeitung,* a newspaper still published today.

Along with their ethnic newspapers, immigrants in the years after the War of 1812 created distinctive ethnic neighborhoods as well. Workers in the late eighteenth and early nineteenth centuries had often resided with their employers, so New York's earlier neighborhoods were much more heterogeneous than one might expect. The two-and-a-half-story home of a New York–born shoemaker, for example, might house his retail space in the front on the ground floor, his family behind the shop, his workshop and storerooms on the second floor, and

This photograph of Five Points depicts the typical two-and-a-half-story buildings that landlords converted into the city's first tenements after 1815. Directly behind the cart at the right is the five-cornered intersection of Anthony, Orange, and Cross streets (now Worth, Baxter, and Mosco) that gave Five Points its name.

his apprentices and journeymen shoemakers (some or all of whom might be immigrants) on the top floor.

But as New York became increasingly crowded with immigrants as well as migrants from other states, landlords like Astor found that they could reap greater profits by subdividing those two-and-a-half-story houses into five or more apartments rather than leasing the whole building to a single renter. Some landowners tore down these smaller houses and built four-, five-, or even six-story brick buildings so they could cram as many tenants as possible onto each standard twenty-five-by-one-hundred-foot New York lot. Most property owners, however, merely converted their existing frame buildings into multi-family dwellings. Because both the frame two-and-a-half-story houses and the taller brick buildings held so many unrelated tenants, they became known as "tenant houses," and by the 1840s as "tenement houses." Areas dominated by such housing became New York's first distinctly residential districts, and some of these became the city's first immigrant neighborhoods.[36]

The first and best known of these immigrant neighborhoods was Five Points. This area, half a mile northeast of City Hall, had once been the site of William Duer's beloved Collect Pond. But by 1810, as Duer later lamented, the industries that lined the pond's shores had so polluted it that city officials decided to fill it in while simultaneously leveling Bayard's Hill so that more streets could be laid out to facilitate the traffic flow to and from downtown. Because an underground spring had supplied the Collect's water, the ground under the new streets and the houses built on them remained damp and unsettled, causing buildings to tilt and shift dramatically just a few years after construction. Basements in the area were perpetually dank and seemed to flood during even the lightest rain or snowfall. Most medical maladies of the day were attributed to dampness and "vapours," so New Yorkers who could afford to do so avoided such housing. As a result, Five Points quickly became the least desirable of neighborhoods.

The two poorest groups of New Yorkers — Irish Catholic immigrants and African Americans — quickly came to dominate Five Points. The race mixing that went on in the neighborhood's raucous saloons and dance halls, and the drunken brawls that the two groups engaged in by day and by night, made the neighborhood especially notorious. By 1830, Five Points was also home to a preponderance of the city's bordellos.[37]

Native-born New Yorkers might have tolerated the "debauchery" of Five Points had its vices not threatened to spill out into their own neighborhoods. "Something ought to be done," complained a letter writer to the editor of the *New York Evening Post* in 1826, about this "disgusting and pernicious" district. Its "filthy state and 'villanous smells'" were an embarrassment to the city. The

With prostitutes perched in the windows, pigs running amok, the races mixing indiscriminately, and brawls everywhere, this George Catlin painting of Five Points from about 1827 conveys what made this Irish immigrant neighborhood so notorious.

situation had not improved by 1834, when a reporter for the *Sun* visited Five
Points. "In the afternoon of each day," he wrote, "when drunkenness is at its
height, the most disgusting objects, of both sexes, are exhibited to the eyes of
the examiner. Indecency, squalid poverty, intemperance and crime, riot and
revel in continued orgies, and sober humanity is shocked and horrified, at the
loathsome spectacles incessantly presented." The journalist concluded that
"if ever wretchedness was exhibited in a more perfect garb, if ever destitution
and degradation were more complete, if ever immorality and licentiousness
were presented in more disgusting forms, we confess we have never yet beheld
them."[38]

As George Catlin's painting of Five Points from around 1827 reveals, pigs
wandered freely in these years (not merely in Five Points but all over New York).
The city's residents had kept pigs ever since colonial days, and their owners
were not about to pay to feed them when they could roam the streets and find
all the food they needed in New York's gutters and trash heaps. Besides, as the
city's population exploded, pigs helped with garbage collection. In those days,
property owners were responsible for disposing of their own waste. (City employees occasionally swept the streets but did not begin hauling trash away un-

til 1895.) Yet as tenements with absentee landlords proliferated, property owners rarely paid to have the garbage removed, except in July and August, when
the stench became truly unbearable. The swine were supposedly very loyal and
would return each night from their travels about the city to sleep either in their
owners' backyards or sometimes even in the tenements with them.

After the War of 1812, some New Yorkers began to demand that pigs no
longer be allowed to roam the streets. A resident of Second Avenue complained
that the swine in his neighborhood were "extremely ferocious and dangerous
to children." But when the city council passed an ordinance banning pigs from
foraging freely beginning in 1818, the outcry of opposition was so great that
the law was rescinded before it could go into effect. Many who opposed such
bans were Irish immigrants who had earned a bit of extra cash for their families by raising piglets in Ireland and wanted to continue the custom in America. When the city council did finally outlaw the practice for good in the early
1830s, the decision was met with outrage among many in the city's Irish American community. Irish immigrants (and other New Yorkers) flouted the law in
large numbers. As late as 1842, the *Tribune* estimated that ten thousand pigs
still roamed the city's streets, and they remained a problem north of 42nd Street
on the eve of the Civil War.[39]

Pigs and all, Five Points was not really as terrible a neighborhood as sensa-
tion-seeking journalists led New Yorkers to believe. Inebriates and prostitutes
were unusually visible there, and criminals did find it a good place to hide from
the police, but drunks and crooks were far outnumbered by hardworking, law-
abiding immigrants. They scrimped and saved in order to support aged parents back in Ireland and to bring more kinsmen to America. They also sought
to accumulate nest eggs that could be used either to start a business or to support the family should one of its breadwinners succumb to any of the numerous contagious diseases such as cholera and measles that spread like wildfire
through New York's crowded tenements.[40]

Nonetheless, New Yorkers became increasingly intolerant toward Irish immigrants in these years, in part because of their unprecedented numbers. "In
some quarters," wrote a visitor to the city, "one might suppose that a slice of
Cork or of Dublin had been transferred to America — houses, people, dirt and
all." Many natives believed that the Irish were not appropriately deferential to
their native-born employers. Any attempt to reprimand an Irish employee, it
was said, would be met with "We're all aqual here!" and a threat to quit. Irish
"servant girls," in particular, were notorious for resigning on the slightest provocation. As a result, many employers would not hire them. Some even tried to
insert "No Irish need apply" into their help-wanted ads. Relatively few notices
with this infamous proviso actually made it into print (in part because most

publishers refused to run them), but the dozens that did appear in the press convinced New York's Irish immigrants that many employers would not hire them no matter their qualifications.[41]

The trait that especially unsettled native-born New Yorkers was Irishmen's purported propensity for violence and mayhem, for as the city's Irish population increased, so too did the number of riots that broke out. That so many of them took place in Five Points seemed to confirm, in the minds of alarmed natives, that the Irish were the source of the problem. But in a number of these disturbances in early nineteenth-century New York, the immigrants were actually the *targets* of crowd violence rather than the perpetrators. In other cases, the Irish could justifiably claim to have been provoked, such as when they attacked a band of New Yorkers parading a noosed effigy of "Paddy" through the streets in 1802.

A bigger street fight broke out on July 12, 1824, when Irish Catholics disrupted a demonstration by Irish and English "Orangemen" celebrating the anniversary of the Battle of the Boyne, fought near Drogheda, Ireland, in 1690. This was the clash in which the Protestant-backed forces of King William III of England (formerly Prince William of Orange) triumphed over those of his rival in the English Civil War, his deposed father-in-law, King James II, a Catholic. When police arrested thirty-three Irish Catholics but not a single Orangeman, Irish Catholic immigrants called the prosecutions a clear sign of prejudice. Emmet won acquittals for all thirty-three, reciting the long history of anti-Irish sentiment in England and America in order to convince the jury that the arrests had been unjustifiably one-sided.[42]

By the mid-1830s, clashes between natives and Irish immigrants in New York became much more common, and much more violent. During the three-day municipal elections held in April 1834, hundreds of Whigs vowing to "*keep those damned Irishmen in order*" fought pitched battles of "the most unrelenting barbarity" with the immigrants (most of whom were Democrats) in and around Five Points. Although no one was killed, the three days of bloodshed were unprecedented in the history of New York City. "The extent and violence of the disturbance went well beyond any riot of the eighteenth century and far exceeded any previous political tumult in New York," writes historian Paul Gilje. "Never before had an election pushed the city so near the brink. Never before had there been such anarchy."[43]

A year later, in June 1835, another huge riot between natives and immigrants broke out in Five Points. The violence this time originated with the news that some of the city's Irish immigrants planned to form a militia unit. The United States in this period had no standing army of any significance, and instead relied on volunteer militia units to defend the nation and at times quell domestic disturbances. By this point, two decades since the country's last war, militia companies had become more like social clubs, in which picnics and drinking took precedence over drilling and target practice. Because Irish immigrants tended to socialize with one another and probably felt unwelcome in units consisting primarily or exclusively of natives, it was inevitable that they would seek to form militia units of their own.

Yet some New York newspapers vehemently objected to the possibility that Irish immigrants might organize into armed units. "No greater insult was ever offered the American people than the arrangements now being made for raising in this city an *Irish* regiment to be called the '*O'Connell Guards*,'" insisted the *Courier and Enquirer*. "Such a corps would soon attempt to enforce with the bayonet what too many of the misguided and ignorant of the foreign voters already boast of — the complete subjection of the *Native* Citizens to their dictation." On Sunday evening the twenty-first of June, a gang of nativists incited by the *Courier*'s diatribes came to Five Points spoiling for a fight, and a fight was what they got. "Ireland and America were the battle cry of the contending parties," reported the *Sun,* "and both sides found plenty of zealous friends. Bloody noses, bunged eyes, cracked craniums, and barked knuckles soon became the distinguishing marks of scores of combatants." The fighting recommenced the next day, and spread beyond Five Points to the more prosperous Irish enclave in the Fourteenth Ward to the north. There, on the twenty-second, Irish immigrants formed a defensive perimeter around St. Patrick's Cathedral on Mott Street, certain that the nativist mobs would attack. None ever did, but by the time the fighting ended on the twenty-second, two immigrants lay dead, making it the most lethal riot in all of New York's history to that point.[44]

This unprecedented hostility toward immigrants had political manifestations as well. A few weeks later, anti-Catholic New Yorkers formed a new political party called the Native American Democratic Association (NADA). The group condemned the appointment of immigrants to political office, the immigration of paupers and criminals to the United States, and efforts by the Catholic Church to influence American political affairs. Irish Catholic immigrants, complained one of the movement's supporters, might become American citizens yet still "clan together as a separate interest and retain their foreign appellation." In New York City's fall elections of 1835, the NADA captured 39 percent of the vote, although its ticket benefited from the fact that the Whigs decided not to nominate candidates. Buoyed by this success, the NADA's most prominent member, artist and inventor Samuel F. B. Morse, ran as the NADA nominee for mayor in 1836. Morse was a well-known Democrat, so Whigs refused to endorse him, and he captured only 6 percent of the vote, at which point the

NEW YORK'S LARGEST IMMIGRANT ENCLAVES, 1845

NADA quickly faded into obscurity. Yet it was an ominous sign of things to come.[45]

Nativist resentment increased as the number of Irish immigrants settling in New York skyrocketed. Twice as many Irish settled in the United States in 1834 as in any previous year, and immigration in 1835 was almost as high. Three times as many Irish settled in the United States from 1835 to 1844 as in the previous decade. The characteristics of the typical Irish immigrant changed markedly, too. A majority now hailed from the south and west of Ireland rather than from the north, so Catholics outnumbered Protestants. Manhattan's Irish population, already majority Catholic, became overwhelmingly so by 1845. Immigration from other parts of Europe rose as well, but Ireland sent more immigrants to the United States in these years than all the other nations of Europe combined. With so many immigrants settling in New York, the city's foreign-born residents, who had consistently accounted for 20 to 25 percent of the city's population since 1815, jumped to 36 percent of the total by 1845.[46]

By 1845, New York had become a major metropolis, thanks in large part to immigration. The circular building connected to the mainland by a walkway, Castle Garden, would become the city's immigrant processing facility in 1855.

Immigrant neighborhoods began to multiply as a result of the unprecedented influx. The district along the East River waterfront in the Fourth Ward (especially Water, Cherry, Madison, Catharine, and Oliver streets) now became nearly as Irish as Five Points; by 1845 a majority of the ward's inhabitants were immigrants. Corlears Hook, an East River enclave at the very northern end of the developed waterfront in the easternmost portion of what is now the Lower East Side, also became heavily Irish. The Fourteenth Ward had by this point become the residence of choice for the city's more prosperous Irish Americans. Its major residential streets (such as Mulberry, Mott, and Elizabeth) were lined with newer, roomier tenements whose inhabitants included many more successful tradesmen and business owners than were found in the residences of Five Points. The city's German immigrants, now overtaking the English and Scots as the second-largest immigrant group in the city, also created their own enclaves in this period. Germans concentrated east of the Bowery on the present-day Lower East Side, especially in the Eleventh Ward in what is now Alphabet City (Avenues B, C, and D and the numbered streets that ran between them).

Few cities had ever grown so big so fast. By 1845, New York was home to 70,000 Irish immigrants, 65,000 immigrants born elsewhere, and 236,000 American-born residents. In fact, from the day young William Duer first set foot on Manhattan Island in November 1783 to 1845, the city's population had grown by 50 percent per decade for six consecutive decades. Few New Yorkers, with the possible exception of John Jacob Astor, could imagine it continuing to grow at that pace.[47]

Yet within the holds of the very ships that carried the Irish and Germans to America lay the seeds of a catastrophe that would make this flood of immigrants seem minute. The vessels that brought newcomers to the United States returned to Europe crammed full of American exports. Among those goods in late 1844 were sacks of American-grown seed potatoes, tiny tubers with at least one "eye," just enough to sprout a full plant if buried underground. These would be sold throughout Great Britain and especially Ireland, whose poorest inhabitants ate potatoes for every meal, day after monotonous day.

The hundreds of thousands of Irish men and women who planted these seed potatoes in the spring of 1845 were unaware that they were infested with a fungus originating in the Peruvian guano used to fertilize American fields. The fungus had escaped notice in the United States because it did not thrive in the continent's hot, dry summers. But Ireland, cool and damp all year round, provided a perfect breeding ground. Through airborne spores, the fungus spread throughout Ireland and over the sea to Scotland, England, and the German states, utterly destroying potato crops wherever it went. The failure of the potato crop in Ireland in 1845, 1846, 1847, 1848, and 1849, and the famine that followed, caused an exodus of unprecedented proportions, one of the largest, most sudden outpourings of people from one continent to another in all of human history.

The blight hit continental Europe as well, but it did not have such a devastating impact there because its residents were not as dependent on the potato. Food shortages did occur, and the resulting increases in commodity prices played a role in fomenting the revolutionary uprisings led by Germans, Austrians, Hungarians, Italians, Danes, Swiss, and Frenchmen in 1848. Chafing under the autocratic rule of authoritarian regimes, these revolutionaries often took inspiration from the American Revolution and the United States' democratic form of government. Yet every single one of these revolts was violently suppressed, and in the counterrevolutionary crackdowns that followed over the next few years, European soldiers killed tens of thousands of their own countrymen. Hundreds of thousands more fled their homelands, which meant unprecedented numbers of continental European immigrants began arriving in New York in the same years as the Irish famine victims. By 1855, New York's immigrants outnumbered the native-born. Two-thirds of the city's adults were foreign-born. In 1860, with a population of 813,000, New York would become the fourth most populous city on the planet. Of all the world's great metropolises, New York was the only one whose stature could be attributed primarily to immigration.

7

FAMINE

WHEN THE POTATO BLIGHT struck in the summer of 1845, it dealt a devastating blow to several million Irish men and women whose diets consisted primarily or entirely of potatoes. That first year, the blight destroyed only 30 to 40 percent of the crop, and while it caused great hardship, government, church, and family assistance kept actual starvation rare. Yet all Ireland waited anxiously for the 1846 harvest, knowing that unless it was a success, those teetering on the brink of catastrophe would soon begin to starve.

From planting in the spring of 1846 to midsummer, as the stalks grew and blossomed, Ireland's potatoes seemed perfectly healthy. Father Theobald Mathew, traveling by coach from Cork to Dublin in the last week of July, found the potato plants blooming "in all the luxuriance of an abundant harvest." But just below the moist surface, the fungus was thriving. Traveling over the same roads a week later, Mathew saw "one wide waste of putrifying vegetation." Just as heartbreaking as the desolated fields were "the wretched people," already overwhelmed with hunger, "wringing their hands and wailing bitterly the destruction that had left them foodless." The same scenes played out across Ireland. The fungus destroyed 90 percent of the island's potato crop.[1]

By autumn, people all over Ireland began to starve or die of starvation-related diseases. When a landlord went to investigate conditions on his estate in west Cork near Skibbereen, he discovered "six famished and ghastly skeletons, to all appearance dead . . . I approached with horror, and found by a low moaning they were alive . . . in a few minutes I was surrounded by at least two hundred of such phantoms," pleading for food. "Their demoniac yells are still ringing in my ears, and their horrible images are fixed upon my brain." Conditions were just as bad farther north in Meath and Galway, where Irish freedom fighter John Mitchel "saw sights that will never wholly leave the eyes that

Skeletal victims dressed in tatters, such as these residents of County Cork, became a common sight across Ireland in the famine years.

beheld them: — cowering wretches, almost naked in the savage weather, prowl-
ing in turnip-fields, and endeavoring to grub up roots."[2]

By late 1846 and early 1847, the Irish were exhibiting the classic symptoms of
starvation, including bloated bellies (because bodily fluids typically confined to
blood vessels escape when the body is deprived of protein and other nutrients
for extended periods) and bloody diarrhea (from disintegrating, malnourished
intestines). Death became omnipresent. In the southwest, in the village of Kenmare, the local priest recorded in his diary in early 1847 that there was "noth-

ing more usual than to find four or five bodies in the street every morning." In the northwest, in County Sligo, a relief official reported from a rural parish that "it is no exaggeration to affirm that . . . the people are dying from starvation by dozens daily."[3]

The death toll would not have been so horrific had the English government, which controlled Ireland, not handled the crisis with such coldhearted ineptitude. The administration of Prime Minister Lord John Russell maintained that much of the crisis was the fault of the Irish themselves for seeking handouts rather than sufficiently exerting themselves. Public works projects were created to employ some of the indigent, but the sufferers were so debilitated from hunger, and given so little food in exchange for their labor (out of fear that they would come to prefer this work to their usual employment), that thousands died even while participating in them. Most of England believed that "Irish property must pay for Irish poverty," meaning that wealthy Irish landlords ought to foot the bill for famine relief. This became the justification for cutting back on assistance that might have saved hundreds of thousands of lives. From 1846 to 1851, about 1.1 million Irish men, women, and children died as a result of the famine.[4]

Record numbers fled Ireland — to the United States if they could raise the money needed for the fare, or to Canada if they could not afford the more expensive ticket to New York. Those who were hardest hit could not emigrate, for in addition to the fare, one needed to supply most of one's own food for the four-to-six-week transatlantic journey. The only way that the truly destitute could make the crossing to America was through the assistance of others. As many as 50,000 had their fares paid by their landlords, who were motivated primarily by the fact that it was cheaper to pay for their tenants to emigrate than it was to support them in local poorhouses. Perhaps another 25,000 had their fares subsidized by religious or charitable organizations. But such programs accounted for no more than 5 percent of the total famine emigration.[5]

The vast majority of Ireland's destitute inhabitants could make it to North America only with the financial support of family members who had immigrated before them, and victims of the famine did everything in their power to induce these relatives to send such assistance. "Pen cannot dictate the poverty of this country, at present," wrote two residents of County Sligo in one such plea. "Pity our hard case, and do not leave us on the number of the starving poor . . . [I]f you knew what hunger we and our fellow-countrymen are suffering, if you were ever so much distressed, you would take us out of this poverty Isle . . . Don't let us die with the hunger."[6]

Thousands of Irish Americans answered such calls, sending money and ship tickets to help loved ones escape the famine. In 1847, known to the Irish as "Black '47" for the incredible suffering that befell their nation in that year, American immigration from Ireland tripled over pre-famine levels, and these figures exclude the tens of thousands who landed in Canada before continuing southward to the United States. Referring to it as "the hungry invasion," the *Times* of London called the Irish exodus of 1847 "one of the most marvellous events in the annals of human migration. The miserable circumstances under which the majority left their homes, . . . the thousands of miles over which the dreary pilgrimage was protracted, the fearful casualties of the voyage by shipwreck, by famine, and by fever, constituted a fact which we believe to be entirely without precedent." It was, the *Times* recognized, "a movement which has already exceeded all human experience."[7]

Yet 1847, it turned out, was only the tip of the iceberg, as those who made it to America in 1846 and 1847 paid for additional loved ones to immigrate in subsequent years. "Our fine country is abandoned by all the population," wrote a woman in County Meath in 1850. "The few that remain [are] in great need [because] there is no person to employ them . . . I think [we] will see you in America before long." Remittances made such emigration possible. In County Galway, one newspaper reported in 1851, "each mail . . . brings letters containing money, and giving glowing pictures of the prosperity that awaits the emigrant in the new world." The lucky recipients immediately booked passage "to what they call the land of liberty and plenty." By 1851, annual Irish immigration to the United States had reached *five times* the pre-famine level, and it continued nearly as high through 1854. By the end of the 1850s, 2.1 million Irish men, women, and children — out of Ireland's pre-famine population of 8 million — had fled their country. Of that total, 1.5 million emigrated to the United States, and 950,000 of them landed in New York.[8]

Conditions on board the sailing ships that took these immigrants to America were notoriously dreadful. Often these vessels were referred to as "coffin ships" because the shipboard death rates reached unprecedented levels. But in recounting the stories of the Irish passage to North America in the famine years, writers sometimes confused myth and legend with fact. One unscrupulous author even went so far as to copy passages from a late nineteenth-century work of fiction about the famine emigration and present it as a long-lost famine "diary." The book, with its lurid descriptions of suffering aboard a coffin ship, was a best seller in Ireland until the fraud was exposed.[9]

The typical Irish emigrant in the famine years would have walked to Cork, Dublin, Belfast, or some other Irish port and taken a steamship from there to Liverpool, the European port of departure for 76 percent of the famine Irish sailing to the United States. The steamship journey from Ireland to Liverpool was an ordeal in itself.* Poor Irish emigrants could not afford tickets that granted them access to the interior of the vessel, so they typically spent the entire overnight crossing of the Irish Sea (fourteen hours from Dublin, thirty from Cork) outside on the deck without even benches to sit on. As a parliamentary committee noted in 1854, "all that time the cattle and live stock" transported on those steamers "are protected, while the deck-passengers . . . are left without shelter or accommodation of any kind on the bare deck." Buffeted by fierce winds and doused by the persistent sea spray and frequent rainstorms, the emigrants arrived in Liverpool "positively prostrated," shivering and soaked to the bone, "as wet as if they had been dipped in the sea," according to a Cork shipping official. "The manner in which passengers are conveyed from Irish to English ports," he told a parliamentary committee in 1854, was "disgraceful, dangerous, and inhuman." To add insult to injury, as the dazed emigrants disembarked from the steamers, they would have had to pass through a gauntlet of "runners," employees of ticket brokers and boardinghouse keepers who used every scam imaginable to induce the Irish to purchase their employers' services at inflated prices.[10]

If the emigrants were lucky, they had bought or been sent a ticket to New York aboard a packet liner, a sailing ship that ran on a regular schedule. If so, they could have timed their trip to Liverpool so as to leave as short a layover there as possible, since Liverpool's emigrant boardinghouses were notoriously seedy and expensive. One proprietor was prosecuted for lodging ninety-two emigrants in a house licensed to hold nineteen. Many Irish emigrants slept on the streets rather than pay for such places. The vast majority, however, would not have traveled on packets but would have bought tickets on the cheaper unscheduled ships, which never seemed to depart as soon as the ticket agent promised. These vessels cast off at the whim of the owner, typically when sufficient cargo, human or otherwise, had been found to make the voyage profitable. Emigrants sometimes had to wait weeks for their ship to finally leave Liverpool — stressful days during which their meager savings might be exhausted in paying for food and lodging.[11]

The emigrants usually arrived in Liverpool in the spring. Not only was the

* While the emigrants could take steamships from Ireland to Liverpool, sailing ships were really their only option for the longer leg of their journey to North America. Steamships made the transatlantic crossing in only ten to fourteen days in the famine years, but they were prohibitively expensive for famine emigrants. Steamships did not begin carrying a significant percentage of immigrants to the United States until the very end of the 1850s, after the famine immigration had subsided.

THE DEPARTURE.

Emigrant ships like this one leaving the Liverpool docks in 1850 carried far more passengers during the Irish famine years than they ever had before.

weather on the transatlantic journey best at that time of year, but also they were most likely to find work immediately after their voyage if they arrived in mid-to-late springtime, when employers did the bulk of their annual hiring. Even in 1847, when the Irish were literally fleeing for their lives, 46 percent of the emigrants left Liverpool in April, May, or June. Knowing they would probably land in New York with little money and no food, they did everything within their power to time their arrival to coincide with the season when their employment prospects would be brightest.[12]

As the ship floated away from the Liverpool docks and headed down the river Mersey toward the Atlantic, the famine immigrants were less likely to feel a sense of regret at leaving Ireland than had previous generations. Nonetheless, many were overcome with sadness at the idea that they would likely never see home again. Others were "quaking with fear, . . . some crying, some cursing" the spouse who had talked them into emigrating. Some even demanded to be brought back to the Liverpool docks. Before long, seasickness would set in, and within hours of departure, rivers of vomit might be flowing back and forth across the floor of the steerage quarters if these passengers were not permitted to retch over the side of the vessel. Emigrant guidebooks offered many seasickness remedies, which ranged from taking cayenne pepper to wearing woolen socks.[13]

Once the passengers' seasickness subsided, they soon became overwhelmed by the tedium of the voyage. The time necessary to make the 3,043-mile journey from Liverpool to New York could vary tremendously, depending on the type of vessel, the cargo, prevailing winds, and storms. The trip typically took about five weeks, though six weeks was common and seven weeks was not unheard of. The fastest sailing vessel of the period that regularly carried immigrants, the *Yorkshire*, took twenty-nine days on average to make the crossing. This means that even the speediest immigrant ship traversed the Atlantic at just four miles per hour, and the typical ship did so at a snail-like three miles per hour. No wonder boredom was such a common complaint.[14]

Immigrants protested even more about the food served on board their vessels, both the quality and the quantity, than they did about the tedium of the voyage. Before 1803, ships were not required to provide their passengers with any food whatsoever. Immigrants were expected to bring their own. Any food that a passenger did receive was the result of negotiation with the shipping company at the time the ticket was purchased. But as immigrants became poorer, no longer able to afford the large cache of supplies that previous generations had brought with them, some began arriving in North America at death's door, having eaten only what they could beg from other passengers. In 1803 Parliament passed its first so-called Passengers Act, requiring ships leaving British ports to provide enough food for each passenger to insure that no one would starve to death while crossing the Atlantic. The law mandated that emigrants receive per day at least one gallon of water; one and a half pounds of bread, biscuit, or oatmeal; half a pound of meat; and a half pint of molasses. As the emigrants became even more impoverished, Parliament amended the law in 1835. But rather than increase the allowance now that fewer immigrants could afford to bring substantial supplies of food with them, the lawmakers actually *reduced* the water ration to three quarts, cut the bread or biscuit ration to one pound daily, and eliminated the meat and molasses altogether. Flour, potatoes, and rice were later added as acceptable substitutes for bread and biscuit.[15]

Not only did the emigrants not get much food, but what they got was awful. The "ship bread" and "biscuit" were typically months old and rock hard. The voyagers needed to soak them in their precious ration of water to make them edible. Sometimes even that did not help. Often these foodstuffs became infested with maggots or otherwise spoiled. In 1848 on a ship headed for New York, Irish emigrant Henry Johnson received his weekly ration as two pounds of "meal" (probably cornmeal) and five pounds of "biscuit," but the latter was so foul that even the pigs on the ship would not eat it. He had brought provisions from Ireland to supplement the ship's allowance, but when he opened his trunk after a week at sea, he found it "alive with maggots and was obliged to throw it overboard." He tried to beg food from others, "but it was every man for himself." As a result, he recalled, "for the remainder of the passage I got a right good starving." His voyage from Liverpool to New York took nearly eight weeks.[16]

Even preparing the food that *was* edible could be an ordeal. Rice, oatmeal, and potatoes required large quantities of water to be cooked, so immigrants who used some of their daily water ration to prepare them might satiate their hunger pangs only to find themselves overwhelmed by thirst. Some tried cooking with seawater, but they usually deemed the results inedible. Even those who had enough fresh water for cooking often found it impossible to gain access to the limited number of cooking stations. The ship's cook would boil an immigrant's rice or oatmeal in exchange for a bribe, but few could afford this expense, and instead took their chances at the public "galley." The meek, weak, sick, and elderly, admitted a British investigative committee, could rarely muscle their way to the cookstoves, and were the ones most likely to suffer from hunger on an immigrant voyage. Only beginning on October 1, 1852, did Par-

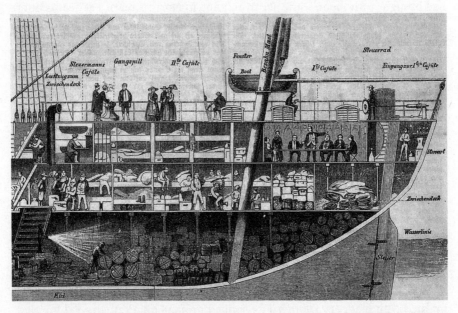

This cutaway view of a sailing ship in the emigrant trade provides an unusually clear view of the passenger quarters. "Cabin passengers," those who paid a premium in exchange for less crowded conditions, are berthed on the first level below deck, steerage passengers are crammed into the middle level, and freight fills the lowest level.

liament require ships leaving Great Britain to serve immigrants their allowance of food already cooked.[17]

To make matters worse, the ship's crew often shortchanged the passengers when doling out their meager food allowance. Vere Foster devoted himself to famine relief after witnessing how the blight devastated the tenants living on his family's estate in County Louth. On a fact-finding voyage on a fairly typical immigrant sailing ship in 1850, a year after Parliament had increased the minimum food allowance by 50 percent (and added molasses and tea to the required fare), Foster discovered that the common complaint that crews withheld food from the immigrants was true. Passengers on the *Washington* got less than half the promised allotment of oatmeal, biscuit, tea, and molasses, and only 60 percent of the stipulated rice. Foster thought that the complaint of a gentleman might put things right, but the captain vowed to declare him a pirate and throw him in irons if he persisted in interfering. "By Jesus Christ I'll rope's end you," he and his crew threatened when any passenger persisted in demanding the proper ration.[18]

Conditions in the "steerage" compartments, where all but a handful of immigrants were berthed, were even more dreadful than their shipboard diet. The first level below the ship's deck was divided into cabins. "Cabin passengers" from Liverpool to New York might pay £5 instead of £4 in return for larger food allowances and better-ventilated, roomier accommodations, with only two persons per bunk and four to twelve passengers per cabin. Some ships even offered more luxurious accommodations, with meals served in a dining "saloon" and sleeping quarters that were not shared with strangers.[19]

Descending a level farther, one reached the steerage compartments, so called because ships were once steered from that part of the vessel. Situated far below deck, the steerage compartments were pitch-black unless lit by candles (which the crew frowned upon) or dim lamps. The steerage quarters were huge, typically the width of the entire ship and half its length, with the berths placed along the walls. Whereas cabin passengers slept two to a bed, in steerage four adult passengers were shoehorned into each six-by-six-foot bunk, giving each adult eighteen inches of bed space. Those aged thirteen or younger got nine inches. The bunks were placed one right next to the other, with no dividers of any kind, for one hundred feet or more, so that the effect was of two long slabs of humanity, one on top of the other, on each side of the ship. On larger ships, a one-hundred-foot-long steerage cabin might hold three hundred passengers or more (depending on how many were children), and there were typically two such compartments, one in the bow and the other in the stern. The empty space between the rows of bunks lining either wall could be used to eat or congregate, though that space could barely hold all the passengers during crowded

EMIGRATION VESSEL.—BETWEEN DECKS.

No image can adequately convey the overcrowding, the putrid stench, and the pitch-black darkness of the steerage compartments of famine era sailing ships. This attempt was made by a sketch artist from the *Illustrated London News* in 1851.

spring and early summer voyages. "Pigs are taken care of . . . much better than the emigrants," admitted a British official summing up the passengers' crowded plight. "Somebody has an interest in [the pigs'] lives, but nobody seems to care about the poor emigrants."[20]

Emigrants found steerage travel mortifying not merely because their berths were so crowded but because they often had to share them with total strangers. The emigrants typically got to choose their own berths, but if a family of three claimed one of the four-person bunks, a stranger would have to squeeze in with them. Unmarried women would undoubtedly have sought to bunk with other women, but if they were among the last to arrive, or if they managed to fill only three of the four places in a bunk, a strange man might join them. If women wanted to change their clothes or use a chamber pot (which they tended to prefer to the vile privies on deck), they had to do so in front of complete strangers, male and female. "There is," as one official admitted, "no privacy whatever."[21]

Parliament did eventually try to mitigate these conditions. Beginning in 1852, when most of the famine emigration was over, a new Passengers Act required unmarried men age fourteen and older to be housed in a separate steerage compartment at the front of the ship. The statute also reduced from four to two the number of unrelated passengers who could be placed in the same bunk, and banned shipping companies from putting men and women above the age of fourteen in the same berth unless they were married. But while this law meant that single women no longer had to disrobe in front of single men, they were still subject to the wandering eyes of the ship's married male passen-

Even when steerage passengers were not locked into their compartments, it was
difficult for them to find good places to ride out an Atlantic storm, something this
image from 1881 clearly illustrates.

gers. Not until after the Civil War would regulations mandate that single men,
single women, and families each have their own separate steerage quarters.[22]

Nearly every transatlantic crossing involved at least one terrifying
storm. During a violent gale, wrote Irish emigrant Thomas Reilly, his vessel
"screech[ed] with every stroke of the waves, every bolt in her quaked, every
timber writhed, the smallest nail had a cry of its own." The huge waves struck
at the ship's "bows and sides with the force and noise of a thousand sledge
hammers upon so many anvils." During these storms, the crew battened down
the hatches and locked the steerage passengers inside their teeming, pitch-
black compartments, though when conditions became especially dire, the sailors might release some of the men in order to have them assist with pumping
out the seawater that sometimes flooded the ship's lower compartments. The
women and children remained below, praying earnestly and loudly until the
emergency had passed.[23]

Incredible as it may sound, steerage was not the worst place to be in a storm.
In order to transport even more immigrants than could be berthed in steerage,
some enterprising ship owners placed crude huts on the main deck near the
privies. At first glance, these accommodations might seem superior to steerage,

but inspectors found them to be the worst of all because of exposure to the elements, especially the wind. During a storm, these cabins were pummeled by seawater as well.

Emigrant John Ryan from Limerick was placed in one of these huts along with eight members of the Fitzgerald family and five other single passengers aboard the *E.Z.*, a ship that carried thousands of famine emigrants to New York. He initially thought his accommodations were "not bad at all." But Ryan soon discovered that the wind and spray were so constant and the hut so crudely built that while his shipmates in steerage were dry, he spent the day in water up to his knees. When a storm hit about two weeks into his crossing, Ryan — fed up with being so wet — decided to ride it out in another part of the ship. It was a wise decision, because as the storm intensified, his hut was torn from the deck and "washed overboard, . . . people and all." No trace of the hut or its thirteen inhabitants was ever found.[24]

Immigrants also dreaded steerage because of the deadly diseases that spread among those forced to spend most of the journey in its suffocating confines. The vomit that seasick passengers began heaving up nearly from the moment their ship began its journey was rarely cleared away from the steerage compartments. No one, least of all the ship's crew, was willing to clean up that mess. Furthermore, in the rough waters of the North Atlantic, the contents of the passengers' chamber pots would spill onto the steerage cabin floor. There it mixed with the vomit and the seawater that leaked (or in some cases poured) into the compartment during storms, creating, as one official who inspected these ships would later recall, "the foulest stench that can be conceived of."[25]

The prevalence of feces in the vile muck that swirled around the steerage passengers' feet increased as many became sick and confined themselves to their berths. The terrible shipboard diet of spoiled, rock-hard, undercooked food caused severe digestive ailments, of which diarrhea and dysentery were the most common. The propensity of the sick to stay in bed explains why those who boarded ships early chose the top steerage bunks so they would not have to worry about vomit or diarrhea dripping down on them from a sick passenger above.

Contagious diseases spread quickly in these close quarters. The most prevalent was typhus, known as "ship fever." Body lice, which reproduced exponentially in the sardine-can crowding of the steerage cabins, carried this bacterial infection in their own feces. Scratching at the lice caused tiny abrasions in the skin through which the feces entered and infected their human hosts. Those suffering from typhus endured severe headaches, high fevers, chills, and nausea. They had neither the strength nor the desire to leave their beds. Immigration officials were undoubtedly referring to these lice when they complained that they found the steerage cabin's "filthy beds teeming with abominations."

Even in the days before antibiotics, three in four typhus sufferers managed to recover on their own, though their fever and other symptoms lasted for several weeks. Some were debilitated for months. The unlucky ones developed delirium and gangrene and would eventually succumb to kidney or cardiac failure. Because it took ten days from infection for the first symptoms to emerge, and then several weeks after that until death occurred, most of these fatalities took place not at sea but in hospitals and tenements in the United States and Canada. "In this country . . . there is thousands of people dieing" from "the tipes [typhus] fevir," one Irish immigrant wrote from Canada to her parents back in Ireland. Because of the particular overcrowding on the vessels with cheap fares headed to Canada, mortality from typhus was much more common there than in New York, where the annual death toll from the disease was likely to be in the hundreds rather than the thousands. Famine immigrants to Canada were three times more likely to die on or immediately after the voyage than those who were able to afford passage on a ship sailing directly to New York.[26]

Immigrants sailing across the Atlantic feared cholera even more than typhus, for while it was a relatively rare disease, those who contracted it usually did not survive. The cholera bacteria typically entered the body when the victim ingested water or food contaminated with the feces of someone already infected with the ailment. Symptoms included acute vomiting, severe abdominal cramps, high fever, and "rice water" diarrhea, in which the "rice" was actually pieces of the victim's colon flaking away as the bacteria destroyed the digestive system. What made cholera particularly terrifying was that someone who seemed perfectly healthy one moment might become incapacitated with fever a few hours later and die the following day. The cholera bacteria sloshed around in the liquid filth of many a steerage cabin during the famine migration, especially in 1849 and 1853, and while it killed fewer immigrants than typhus, it spread to others in the cities where the famine immigrants settled. More than one thousand inhabitants of the Irish neighborhoods of New York perished during the cholera epidemic of 1849.[27]

In the years immediately before the famine, four or five passengers on average would die during the voyage of the typical five-hundred-passenger immigrant vessel headed for New York (a mortality rate of 0.9 death per one hundred passengers). During the famine years, the death rate on board immigrant vessels landing at New York doubled to eight deaths per five-hundred-passenger ship. The mortality rate peaked in 1849, the year of the worst cholera outbreak, at fifteen fatalities per five hundred passengers. An equal number probably died after disembarking from diseases (especially typhus) contracted during the journey. Whether the higher death rate during the famine years was the result of deteriorating conditions on board or the pre-voyage debilitation of famine victims is hard to determine. This 3 percent mortality rate for ships arriving in New York is frighteningly high, but perhaps not enough to justify calling them "coffin ships."[28]

Immigrant ships bound for Canada, however, did sometimes arrive in North America with dozens of dead passengers. In the years before 1848, when the fare to Canada was half that to the United States, and relatively few famine victims already had relatives in the States who could pay for their tickets, the most destitute, desperate Irish emigrants would almost always book passage to Canada. These famine immigrants, the ones already suffering from severe malnutrition and unable to afford food to supplement the ship's allowance, were the ones most likely to succumb to the common shipboard ailments. The death toll was also far higher on ships headed to Canada because conditions on these British vessels, many of which were not designed for the transportation of immigrants, were far worse, in terms of both crowding and cleanliness. "The Black Hole of Calcutta was a mercy compared to the holds of these vessels," complained the Montreal Board of Health.* In the most extreme cases — fewer than a dozen — these ships would arrive in St. John, New Brunswick, or Quebec City with 15, 20, or even 30 percent of their passengers already dead, and just as many severely ill. "Coffin ship" is not too strong a term to describe these vessels.[29]

Canadians compounded these problems by quarantining both the sick and their family members in tents on Grosse Isle, an island in the middle of the St. Lawrence River, thirty-five miles east of Quebec City. In September 1847 the *Times* of London characterized the Grosse Isle facilities as "ridiculously insufficient," owing to both lack of care and the subfreezing temperatures of the Canadian autumn. At least five thousand immigrants died on Grosse Isle that year. Many might have survived had they been treated in real hospitals, as sick immigrants were in New York. According to some estimates, 30 percent of the famine Irish who secured passage to Canada in "Black '47" died either during the crossing or soon after arrival.[30]

Many Britons recognized that their treatment of the Irish was nothing less than, as the *Times* of London put it, a "national inhumanity," one that would be "an eternal scandal to the British name." Yet only about 10 percent of New

---

* The Black Hole of Calcutta was an infamous dungeon in Fort William, one of the city's British-built fortifications. In 1756, Indians captured the fortress and forced so many British prisoners into the tiny, windowless dungeon that more than one hundred were crushed to death or asphyxiated.

York's famine Irish immigrants came to the city via Canada. As a result, few of New York's Irish-born inhabitants were forced to endure the infamous "coffin ships."[31]

While the terrible journeys would remain forever seared in their memory, the immigrants' first sighting of land, and of New York Harbor in particular, was also something they would never forget. "Early in the afternoon, the exciting cry of 'Land!' 'Land!' 'Land!' ran through the ship like wild fire," recalled English immigrant William Smith, whose ship from Liverpool limped into New York Harbor in 1848 after a voyage of nearly eight weeks. "The effect it had upon the passengers, baffles all description. Some fell upon their knees and thanked God for his mercy to them, some wept for joy, others capered about, exhibiting extravagant demonstrations of joy." A German immigrant whose ship dropped anchor in New York Harbor at night under a moonlit sky called her first view of the city "enchanting, unforgettable."[32]

Before immigrants were allowed to disembark, however, they had to pass a

ATTACK ON THE QUARANTINE ESTABLISHMENT, ON SEPTEMBER 1, 1858.

Staten Islanders hated having the immigrant quarantine hospital in their midst. When state officials delayed acting on their promise to move the facility, angry residents took matters into their own hands in 1858 and burned it to the ground.

medical inspection. "Each passenger's name was called over, and every one had to pass in review" before a doctor sent from the immigrant quarantine hospital on Staten Island, recalled one English steerage passenger. Those deemed fit were allowed to continue on to Manhattan, while those suffering from typhus or other diseases had to go to Staten Island to recuperate. The immigrants forced to convalesce on Staten Island considered the experience hellish, ignorant of how much worse their fate would have been in the same situation in Canada. "'Is it their object to kill or cure the patients?' was a question I asked myself more than once during my stay there," wrote Smith, who had contracted typhus, after his experience in the quarantine hospital in 1848. "From the moment I entered the hospital to the time of leaving it, I saw no kind feelings, no generous actions." Smith was one of 3,944 immigrants sent to the quarantine hospital in 1848, out of 189,176 immigrants landing that year. Before they could finish their journey, about two out of every one hundred immigrants arriving in New York in the early famine years (the late 1840s) had to convalesce on Staten Island. In the 1850s, only about one in one hundred was required to do so.[33]

For those who managed to avoid the quarantine hospital, there was one more challenge to face before or upon landing. "People may think that if they get safe through Liverpool they are all right," wrote Michael Hogan to his aunt Catherine in County Carlow in 1851, "but I can assure you that there is greater robberies done in New York on emigrants than there is in Liverpool." Hogan was referring to the "runners," those "scoundrels of the very lowest calibre" who pocketed a commission if they could entice the dazed and confused immigrants to buy a railroad or steamship ticket from their employer. Runners also worked for boardinghouse keepers, preying on immigrants desperate for a good night's sleep before they looked for their own place to live, hunted down their friends and relatives in the city, or continued on by boat or train to their final destination.[34]

Through much of the famine era, runners could board the immigrant ships even before they landed and sell train or boat tickets at double or triple the actual fare to unsuspecting newcomers. "It is not uncommon, after the vessel is cleared from quarantine, for eight or ten boat loads of runners to surround it," testified a physician in 1847. "They are desperate men, and can be kept off only by an armed force." Even if the immigrants refused to do business with them, the runners might make off with an immigrant's luggage and hold it hostage until the newcomer paid a "handling fee." Runners were often immigrants themselves. "We find the German preying upon the German — the Irish upon the Irish — the English upon the English," reported an investigative committee, though the report admitted that many native-born Americans were also

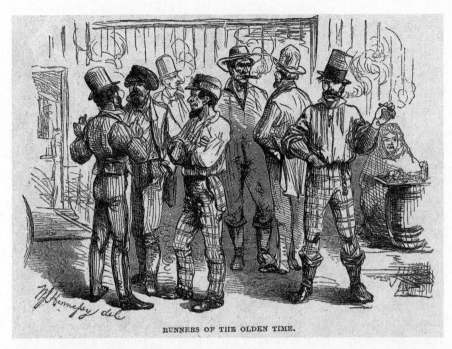

RUNNERS OF THE OLDEN TIME.

"Runners" did everything in their power to swindle the arriving immigrants. New York's first immigrant depot, opened at Castle Garden in 1855, was created largely to allow government officials to have access to the immigrants before the runners.

engaged in this "nefarious business." The New York legislature attempted to rein in the runners by licensing them, but the law was completely ineffectual. The threat posed by the runners became internationally known. Guidebooks warned against their "extortionate charges" and urged immigrants to walk right past them, no matter what they might say. But many an exhausted, disoriented immigrant fell prey to their lures and snares.[35]

Knowing how susceptible the immigrants were to the runners, New Yorkers set up aid societies to give the new arrivals a ready alternative to the scammers. While organizations aimed at assisting those from foreign lands had long existed in New York, these had been intended primarily to aid foreign-born residents after they settled in the city. But by the 1840s, tens of thousands of immigrants were passing through town annually on their way to other cities and states. They too needed protection from swindlers and help getting their bearings before heading to their final destinations. To this end, a British Protective Emigrant Society was established in 1844 on Rector Street, joining the already existing Irish Emigrant Society on Chambers Street. These groups also had satellite offices adjacent to the East River piers of the busiest transatlantic shipping lines. The society's goal was to protect British immigrants "from fraud and imposition" and help them find employment, either in New York or elsewhere. In its first six years of operation, the protective society found jobs for 3,400 of 4,100 immigrants who sought them, and offered advice to 66,000 more. The Germans, French, Italians, and Dutch soon created their own aid organizations. Polish and German Jews ran separate societies to aid their respective communities.[36]

One of the reasons why immigrants were so susceptible to runners was that prior to 1855, there was no single place where all immigrants landed. On any given day, especially during the height of the immigration season in the late spring and early summer, a ship from the Black Ball Line might tie up at Pier 23, north of Fulton Street, while a vessel from the Black Star Line docked at the foot of Dover Street, and yet a third, from the Dramatic Line, landed its immigrants at Pier 14, just south of Wall Street. Runners would be on hand to greet the immigrants at all these locations, while the emigrant aid societies rarely had that kind of manpower.[37]

Realizing that the landing of immigrants could no longer remain wholly unregulated, in 1855 the commissioners of emigration of the State of New York opened a landing depot in Castle Garden at the southern end of Manhattan. Castle Garden was a beloved theater founded in 1824 within the walls of a former military fortress known as Castle Clinton, which sat on a little artificial is-

PASSING
THE INSPECTING PHYSICIAN

The medical examination of immigrants at Castle Garden was a cursory affair compared to the more thorough inspections that would take place at Ellis Island beginning in 1892.

land two hundred feet southwest of Manhattan's southern tip. As recently as 1850–1851, it had played host to such noted performers as the Swedish soprano Jenny Lind and the exotic dancer Lola Montez. But with New Yorkers of means moving ever farther uptown, Castle Garden now sat empty most nights, and in 1855 the commissioners leased it and converted it into an immigration depot.[38]

When the Castle Garden Emigrant Depot opened on August 1, immigrants for the first time underwent a standardized series of screening and processing steps before they were free to begin their lives in the United States. Barges towed by steamboats carried the passengers and their baggage from their ships moored in the harbor to the new facility. As the immigrants disembarked and entered the building, a physician would inspect them and pull out of line for further examination any who appeared sick. (This was in addition to the shipboard inspection done by a doctor from the quarantine hospital, so not many failed this second test.) The healthy immigrants then passed to the center of the cavernous hall to the huge registration desk, where clerks recorded their name, age, occupation, the number of accompanying family members, the name of the ship that brought them to New York, their destination, and the amount of money they had with them.[39]

"Next, the emigrant is shown to the baths," reported the *Times*. With a deep trough of fresh running water, plenty of soap, tubs behind a screen, and "coarse

Immigrants lingering inside Castle Garden before venturing out to begin their new lives in America.

roller towels, . . . every facility is granted the new comer, whatever may be his condition on entering it, to leave Castle Garden personally clean." After washing, the immigrants returned to the pier to claim their luggage. If they planned to stay in the city, they could either take the baggage with them or leave it there out of the reach of the runners, who congregated just outside the depot, and claim it once they had found a place to live or located their friends or relatives already living in Manhattan. Before long, the commissioners would add currency and labor exchanges to the Castle Garden facility. The food offered for sale to the immigrants, initially just bread and cheese, later became more varied and substantial as well.[40]

Unlike modern travelers who try to make it out of airports to their final destinations as rapidly as possible, the newly arrived immigrants did not leave Castle Garden as quickly as they might have. Even after they had completed their processing, hundreds upon hundreds of them lingered in clusters all around the cavernous hall — some in the seats that remained from the building's theatrical past, others on the floor around the tall central fountain. "The children were rollicking about it — sailing their paper boats, and full of unrestrained glee," reported the *Times* during Castle Garden's first days as an immigrant depot. "The women sat in groups, talking in some of those crooked old-country languages . . . , some knitting, some cutting and eating slices of rye German bread and cheese, some patching and fixing up the wardrobes of their family." The immigrants found safety and comfort in the vast, sturdy rotunda, such a contrast to the rolling ships in which they had spent their previous five or six weeks. As long as they stayed inside Castle Garden, their European languages, accents, habits, and clothing would remain the rule rather than the exception and find acceptance rather than ridicule. In Castle Garden they could spend a few precious hours, sometimes even a day or two, decompressing from their harrowing ocean voyage and preparing for the challenges that lay ahead in creating the brand-new lives they had long dreamed of starting in New York.[41]

8

IRISH METROPOLIS

THE FAMINE IRISH were the most impoverished immigrants ever to arrive in the United States and the least prepared for life in New York. Only 12 percent had a trade; only 2 percent had been merchants or professionals. The rest would have to start life in America in the lowest-paying, most menial, least secure jobs. Many of the famine Irish, especially those from west Cork, Kerry, and Galway, would not have known much more English than a German or French immigrant.[1]

Before the famine, New York's Irish immigrants lived primarily in a smattering of neighborhoods in lower Manhattan. But by the end of the famine immigration, there was virtually no part of the city that did not have a large Irish presence. Irish-born adults outnumbered native-born adults in fifteen of the city's twenty-two wards in 1860. Furthermore, the wards in which the Irish had merely congregated in 1845 were *dominated* by them ten years later. Irish immigrants constituted an overwhelming majority of the adult population in the First Ward at the southern tip of Manhattan (which the *Herald* called "the thirty-third county of Ireland"), the Fourth Ward (the heart of the East River waterfront), and the Sixth Ward (home to Five Points), and made up almost as large a proportion of the population in the Seventh.[2]

They did not settle haphazardly. Those from counties Kerry and Sligo, for example, concentrated in Five Points in the pre–Civil War years. Another Kerry enclave existed in the First Ward along Washington Street. Natives of Limerick, in contrast, congregated along the East River in the Fourth Ward. Immigrants from Cavan and Tyrone, in Ireland's north Midlands, frowned on all of those lower Manhattan Irish enclaves and instead tended to live in the Seventh, Thirteenth, and Eighteenth wards. Emigrants from Cork were especially numerous near Corlears Hook in the Seventh Ward, but Cork was so large and populous

THE NATIVITY OF ADULT NEW YORKERS BY WARD, 1860

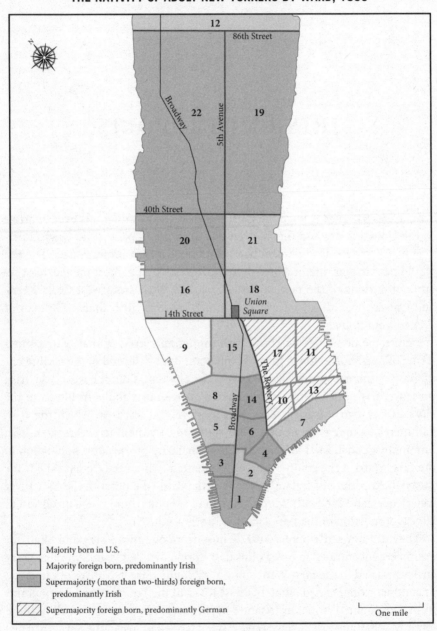

Source: Manuscript population returns, New York County, 1860 census.

and emigration from that county was so huge that "Corkies" outnumbered the contingents from other Irish counties in almost every ward.[3]

Like the generation that arrived before them, many of the famine Irish lived in two-and-a-half-story wooden tenements. These "tenant houses" — "so old and rotten that they seem ready to tumble together into a vast rubbish-heap" — were considered the city's worst. Many apartments in these buildings consisted of a single room, which often had to provide cooking, eating, bathing, and sleeping quarters for an entire family. If the apartment had a bedroom, it was typically windowless, and the resulting lack of air circulation created an "atmosphere productive of the most offensive and malignant diseases."[4]

New York's wooden tenements were especially miserable in winter. Wind often whistled through gaping holes in the buildings' walls, while windows did not close properly and were frequently missing whole panes of glass. These structures were "open to the wind and the storm" and "exposed to all the rigors of inclement weather, and to every possible cause of wretchedness and suffering," complained the *Courier and Enquirer* in 1847. Visitors commonly found snow drifting in the entranceways, halls, and sometimes even in the apartments themselves. These buildings — "worn out, . . . disgustingly filthy, and unhealthy beyond description" — were the most notorious tenements in the famine era.[5]

By the end of the famine migration, brick tenements outnumbered those made of wood by a ratio of about three to two in lower Manhattan neighborhoods such as Five Points and by an even wider margin in the more recently developed wards farther uptown. These brick tenements tended to be fairly uniform on Manhattan's identical twenty-five-by-one-hundred-foot lots. The dwelling typically measured twenty-five feet wide by fifty feet deep and generally stood three, four, or (especially after 1845) five stories high. Each floor above the entrance level contained four two-room apartments, while the front half of the ground floor was devoted to retail space. Each apartment's main room, which at various points in the day had to serve as the kitchen, living room, dining room, and a bedroom, usually measured about twelve feet square and typically had two windows on one wall, facing either the street or the backyard. The apartment's other room — the "sleeping closet" — was aptly named. It was windowless and, at eight by ten feet, hardly bigger than a modern walk-in closet. The entire apartment covered just 225 square feet.

If a family of five inhabited one of these apartments, the parents would spend the night in the sleeping closet while the children slept in the main room on straw or rags that sat in the corner during the day but were brought out at night and covered with a sheet to make a bed. Five persons was the average household size in Five Points and the First and Fourth wards. But 46 percent of Five

Taken in 1875, this photograph of tenements on Baxter Street just north of Worth dramatically illustrates the differences between frame and brick dwellings. Although it appears that the two-story buildings at the center of the image have sunk into the ground, in fact the level of the street was raised after they were built, probably at the time sewer lines were laid.

Points apartments housed six or more people, and one in six accommodated eight or more.[6]

Tenements were so crowded in part because many immigrants took in boarders or lodgers to help cover the rent. (Lodgers received only a place to sleep; boarders got breakfast and supper, too.) In 1855, 28 percent of Five Points families had lodgers or boarders; the proportion would have been about the same in the Fourth Ward and a bit lower in less impoverished neighborhoods. In the rear building at 51 Mulberry Street in Five Points, for example, Patrick Hogan and his wife, Mary, took in one boarder; the Fox family rented space to two lodgers; the Shieldses, McCormacks, Mullins, and McManuses had three lodgers each; the Kavans and Conways four lodgers each; the Hanlans eight lodgers and a boarder; and widow Mary Sullivan one lodger. These were more boarders and lodgers than one found in the typical tenement. Most families

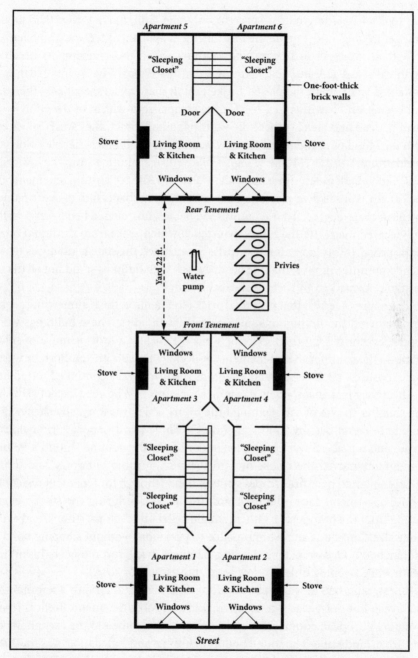

These floor plans represent the typical front and rear brick tenements built in New York in the era of the Irish famine emigration. The smaller floor plan is the design for a rear tenement that would sit off the street in the yard behind the bigger one.

that took in boarders rented space to only one. Still, having even that single stranger in one's midst made the tiny tenement apartment feel even smaller.[7]

With so much crowding and no running water, these tenements became terribly dirty. A city inspector reported that the typical Five Points tenement contained walls "with the plaster broken off in many places, exposing the lath and beams, and leaving openings for the escape from within of the effluvia of vermin, dead and alive." Where the walls remained intact, they were "smeared with the blood of unmentionable insects, and dirt of all indescribable colours." Another investigation found "sluggish yellow drops pending from the low ceilings, and a dank green slime upon the walls." A reporter visiting tenements in the Fourth Ward likewise encountered "dirt in every shape, filth of every name, smells in every degree, from . . . unwashed babies, unchanged beds, damp walls and decayed matter, to the full-blown stench which arose from the liquid ooze of the privy." It was "a matter of surprise," concluded the state legislature's tenement committee in 1856, that the occupants of such buildings "did not all die of pestilence generated by their unspeakable filth."[8]

The oppressive heat that pervaded brick tenements in the summertime probably bothered the immigrants just as much as the dirt. These buildings were supported entirely by their exterior walls — typically a foot or more of solid brick. In the summer these tenements, especially those with southern or western exposures, became veritable ovens, as the brick walls continued to radiate the heat they had absorbed by day long after sunset. "The very idea of refreshing slumber in one of the seething little ovens which must usually shelter not one, but several persons, and sometimes a whole family, appears ridiculous," wrote one reporter investigating tenement life in the summer months. Many immigrants moved their beds next to their living room windows, and those lucky enough to have fire escapes slept on them (though for tenement residents whose apartments faced the backyard, this meant enduring the stench emanating from the outhouses). Others sought relief on rooftops, stoops, and even sidewalks, "until it is almost impossible to pass along without stepping upon a human body." Occasionally, a sleeping tenement dweller would fall to his or her death while sleeping on a window ledge, fire escape, or roof.[9]

Immigrants had to worry about stifling tenement heat for only a few months each year, but noise was a constant annoyance. Most tenement dwellers came from the European countryside and were not accustomed to the cacophony of the urban landscape. The sound pollution immigrants hated most was that created by other immigrants — living above, below, and next to them. The thin interior walls in both wooden and brick buildings blocked very few sounds. With wooden floors and minimal carpeting, virtually no movement from above

392 [August 12, 1882.]   FRANK LESLIE'S ILLUSTRATED NEWSPAPER.   [August 12, 1882. 393

NEW YORK CITY.—THE RECENT "HEATED TERM" AND ITS EFFECT UPON THE POPULATION OF THE TENEMENT DISTRICTS.—A NIGHT SCENE ON THE EAST SIDE.
FROM A SKETCH BY A STAFF ARTIST.—SEE PAGE 394.

Tenement dwellers sleeping on rooftops, windowsills, and wooden storefront canopies to escape the heat inside their brick tenements.

could escape the attention of those below. Children shouting, spouses fighting, and babies wailing all contributed to the din, often making sleep impossible.[10]

Noise was such a problem in part because of how many immigrants every landlord tried to squeeze onto a twenty-five-by-one-hundred-foot lot. Each one typically held one twenty-five-by-fifty-foot building, while the back half of the lot held privies, pumps, sheds, and clotheslines. But many landlords, hoping to extract as much rent as possible from their property, built a second brick tenement — twenty-five feet wide, twenty-five feet deep, and four or five stories tall, with two apartments per floor — in the yard behind the front tenement. The *only* windows in these rear tenements faced the outhouses, which would become severely overtaxed by the additional residents in the second tenement. "These tumbling and squalid rookeries," concluded an investigative committee, were "the most repulsive features of the tenant-house system."[11]

With so much demand for inexpensive housing, some enterprising immigrants rented previously uninhabited tenement basements and converted them into lodging houses. The overcrowding in these "filthy, damp and dismal" establishments was truly awful. A friend of minister Samuel Prime saw subterranean lodging houses in Five Points with rooms "as thickly covered with bodies as a field of battle could be with the slain." In many of these establishments, lodgers slept on two-tiered bunks, often consisting of canvas stretched between two wooden rails. "Without air, without light, filled with damp vapor from the mildewed walls, and with vermin in ratio to the dirtiness of the inhabitants," commented the *Tribune,* "they are the most repulsive holes that ever a human being was forced to sleep in. There is not a farmer's hog-pen in the country, that is not immeasurably ahead of them in point of health — often in point of cleanliness."[12]

Before the famine immigration, few of the city's notorious tenements lay outside Five Points. But with the Irish now flooding all across Manhattan Island, nearly every part of town soon had its own infamously crowded and filthy buildings. In the Eighth Ward sat six "infected receptacles" known as "Rotten Row" on Laurens Street (now West Broadway) between Grand and Broome. A few blocks closer to the Hudson was "Soap Fat Alley" at 42 Hamersley Street (now the west end of West Houston Street). Just north of Soap Fat Alley in the Ninth Ward was another teeming tenement complex, Smith's Court, at 16 Downing Street, whose front and rear buildings in 1856 housed seventy-four families, "all in a filthy condition."[13]

Perhaps the most infamous tenement outside Five Points in the famine era was the Fourth Ward's Gotham Court. Occupying both 36 and 38 Cherry Street, Gotham Court was undoubtedly the biggest tenement in Civil War–era New York, measuring five stories high, 34 feet wide, and a staggering 240 feet deep. Whereas the typical brick tenement had four apartments per floor, Gotham Court had twenty-four. Twelve could be entered only from the alley on the east side of the building and the others only from the alley on the west side. Ironically, when the huge tenement was constructed in 1850, observers called it "praiseworthy" and "well worthy of imitation." A few years later, however, it had become clear that trying to cram so many impoverished immigrants into so small a space had been misguided. Gotham Court, reported the *Times* in 1857, was "in a very filthy condition." It housed as many as eight hundred inhabitants in its 120 two-room apartments, almost all "wretched-looking Irish people" with "scores of haggard, hungry-eyed, half-nude children."[14]

One reason Gotham Court teemed with so many immigrants was that, unlike most tenements, it had no backyard. The builder placed the pumps and privies on the cellar level under the alleyways and positioned grates on the surface above the privies in an attempt to provide ventilation. Nonetheless, the odor emanating from the alleys was "most sickening." Inside was no better. The hallways were "filled with a fetid vapor, so thick that you can see it." Even in the years immediately after the Civil War, when tenement conditions generally im-

proved and the building was far less crowded, the death rate of Gotham Court's inhabitants was thirteen times greater than that in the city's less crowded upper wards. "Divill a bit of sickness is iver here," an elderly Irish resident told a reporter. Thirty percent of babies born to Gotham Court mothers, reported the *Times* in 1872, died before their first birthday.[15]

With the proliferation of five-story brick tenements and rear tenements, the taking in of boarders, and the spread of basement lodging houses, New York's Irish neighborhoods became, by the conclusion of the famine emigration in the mid-1850s, the most crowded plots of land on the planet. The most densely populated was Five Points, with 198,000 inhabitants per square mile. Close behind was the residential portion of the Fourth Ward around Water, Cherry, and Oak streets, bursting at the seams with 192,000 per square mile. Even with

The tenement on the right, Gotham Court, was the city's largest in 1860 and its most notorious. It stood near the East River waterfront on Cherry Street, a half block east of where the Brooklyn Bridge first touches the Manhattan mainland.

the advent of high-rise buildings, no part of New York is as densely populated today as were these neighborhoods in the 1850s. In fact, only a few places in the contemporary world (the Mong Kok section of Hong Kong and the slums of Mumbai, Dhaka, and Nairobi) surpass the crowding of these antebellum New York neighborhoods.[16]

Most famine immigrants arrived in the United States without any occupational training and had to take the lowest-paying jobs New York had to offer, almost all of which required long hours of backbreaking labor. Even by 1860, when some had had the chance to acquire training in a trade and move up the occupational ladder, 46 percent of male Irish immigrants still did work that required no training or experience whatsoever. Some worked as longshoremen, loading and unloading barrels and crates from the hundreds of ships that arrived in and departed from New York Harbor each week. Others worked as cartmen, coachmen, or porters.

EMPLOYMENT OF NEW YORK MEN BY OCCUPATIONAL CATEGORY AND BIRTHPLACE, 1860[17]

	IRISH-BORN MEN	AMERICAN-BORN MEN
Professionals	0.1%	4%
Business owners	5%	14%
Clerks/Lower-status white collar	6%	25%
Skilled manual workers	38%	33%
Unskilled workers	46%	15%
Other/Difficult to classify	5%	9%

Source: Integrated Public Use Microdata Series (IPUMS), "1% sample of the 1860 U.S. Census."

The vast majority of the unskilled toiled as day laborers, and the building industry provided most of a laborer's employment in New York. Pretty much anything done on a construction site today by a backhoe, bulldozer, steam shovel, or construction crane was done in the antebellum era by Irish day laborers. They dug foundations, carried heavy hods full of bricks and mortar to masons, hoisted lumber and beams to the carpenters, and hauled away debris. Municipal projects also employed many laborers, especially the digging of sewer lines and the paving of streets with cobblestones. Laborers' work was frequently very dangerous. "How often do we see such paragraphs in the paper," complained one immigrant, "as an Irishman drowned — an Irishman crushed by a beam — an Irishman suffocated in a pit — an Irishman blown to atoms by a steam engine — ten, twenty Irishmen buried alive . . . and other like casualties and perils to which honest Pat is constantly exposed, in the hard toils for his daily bread."[18]

As hazardous as a laborer's work might be, his greatest fear was probably not death but unemployment. Some might secure a long-term commitment from the foreman at a single construction site, but others had to search for a new position each and every morning. And on days too wet or cold to work (almost the entire New York construction industry shut down in midwinter), even the steadily employed laborer did not get paid. Sudden sickness or a job-related injury could also throw one out of work at any time. Even in perfect health, noted the *Tribune,* only "an energetic and lucky man . . . can make more than two hundred and fifty days' work as an out-door laborer in the course of a year, while the larger number will not average two hundred." Laborers had to fall back on summer savings to get by during the lean winter months. As an Irish journalist observed, "A month's idleness, or a fortnight's sickness, and what misery!" The majority of Irish immigrants who arrived in New York as laborers remained laborers for the rest of their lives. Many may not even have minded, reasoning that their circumstances were far better than they had been in Ireland. They may also have enjoyed working in a field dominated by the Irish. In 1855, 98 percent of the city's laborers were immigrants, and 88 percent of those immigrants were Irish-born.[19]

Those who did manual labor, both skilled and unskilled, generally worked six days a week for ten hours each day from 7:00 a.m. to 6:00 p.m., with a one-hour "dinner" break at noon. While the long workday was nothing new to New York's immigrants, they were startled by the productivity Americans expected from their employees. "'Hurry up' is a phrase in the mouth of every person in the United States," noted an English immigrant. German bricklayers found that while laying 1,000 to 1,200 bricks was an acceptable day's work in their native land, contractors demanded 1,500 in New York. When English visitor John White told a New York Irish American that he should be happy earning "three times the Irish wages," the laborer complained that "he did six times the Irish work."[20]

We associate New York's famine Irishmen with menial day labor, as did contemporary New Yorkers. Yet 54 percent of male Irish immigrants held jobs farther up the occupational hierarchy. If a laborer hoped to secure a position that paid better or was more secure, there were a number of strategies he might employ. One was to learn a building trade from co-workers on construction sites, a possibility because, as a German immigrant reported gleefully to family back in Europe, "you don't have to pay to learn a trade in America." That may be how John Tucker, a famine immigrant from Limerick who worked as a laborer during his first five years in the city, managed to become a stonecutter by 1857. Others learned crafts unrelated to their previous work. Laborer James Carson, who emigrated from County Tyrone in 1850, became a blacksmith; laborer Michael Coghlan from County Limerick became a bookbinder; and laborer Francis Campbell from County Mayo became a chair maker. Once one family member managed to acquire a trade, he could teach it to his siblings and eventually to his children.[21]

A plurality of Irish-born artisans labored in the building industry — as carpenters, plasterers, painters, bricklayers, masons, plumbers, and gas fitters. Many Irish immigrants also toiled in the clothing industry as tailors and shoemakers. Some of the most lucrative trades, however, seemed to have glass ceilings that only the exceptional Irish immigrant could break through. Relatively few found work as butchers or bakers, for example. Nor did the Irish often get jobs in high-end carpentry specialties such as shipbuilding and cabinet, furniture, or coach making. Such barriers cost them dearly. Tailors and shoemakers made little more than a dollar a day, and a carpenter could also command only $7.50 to $8 a week, whereas a baker earned $9 to $10, a cabinetmaker $10, and a ship carpenter $12 to $15 per week.[22]

If an immigrant wanted to earn significantly more money, his best chance to do so was to move out of manual labor altogether. If he could read and write well, the famine immigrant might transition into an office job. Hugh Hughes from Armagh worked four years as a laborer after his arrival in 1850 before he landed a job as a clerk. Maurice Ahern, after emigrating in 1848 from County Cork, toiled for more than a decade as a porter before he, too, became a clerical worker around 1860.[23]

The most common path up the socioeconomic ladder was entrepreneurship. Immigrants who wanted to open their own businesses often started out as peddlers because the start-up costs were so low. Peddlers were a ubiquitous sight in antebellum New York, hawking anything that would bring a profit, but especially items that the immigrant housewife (who did not stray far from home) might need: buttons, thread, cheap jewelry, used clothes, and food. "The Emerald Isle furnishes a large quota to the ranks of these street-merchants," noted *Scribner's Monthly*. Irish immigrants were especially known for peddling seafood, crying, "Fresh sha-a-d!" or "My clams I want to sell to-day; the best of clams from Rock-away." Irishmen from Donegal were especially drawn to peddling; one-fifth of New York's Irish peddlers were natives of that single Irish county. But Germans were even more ubiquitous than the Irish among the ranks of New York's peddlers (outnumbering the Irish by about three to one).

Jews, who made up only a small fraction of the city's German immigrants in this period, constituted a majority of New York's German-born peddlers.[24]

Some peddlers became well known all over town. In 1842, Englishman Henry Smith immigrated to New York from London, where he had worked in a textile factory. He brought with him £6 his friends had collected as a parting gift, for, as he later explained, "it is customary in England, when a workman leaves home and friends, for his shopmates to get up a subscription, or 'petition,' as it is called, for his benefit, as a token of their esteem and confidence, and as a kind of memento to cheer him on his way." Upon his arrival in New York, Smith peddled spools of cotton he had brought with him from his old workplace. He soon became a peddler of razor strops, the strips of leather used to hone straight razors. His sales pitch, often delivered on the steps of the Stock Exchange or in front of a swank hotel, was a masterpiece of showmanship that made him one of the city's best-known characters. He made a small fortune as a peddler, lost it all in the Panic of 1857, was shot in the leg at the Battle of Gettysburg, and after the war returned to New York and peddling.[25]

Irish immigrant peddlers could also do quite well. Hugh Torpey, who emigrated from Mitchelstown, Cork, to New York in 1847, hawked "port-monnaie," small pocketbooks and wallets. By 1864 he had accumulated in his account at the Emigrant Savings Bank more than $2,000, equivalent to $50,000 today. Most would have earned more moderate sums, while some failed altogether at peddling. Laborers Patrick Healy from County Galway and James Higgins from County Tyrone both tried peddling in the early 1850s but were back at day labor just two years later.[26]

For every Irish immigrant who worked as a peddler, there were several who managed to save enough to open their own brick-and-mortar businesses. Irish immigrants could be found in almost every conceivable commercial enterprise, wholesaling hay and hosiery, lemons and linen, paper and potatoes, milk and morocco leather. The Irish became especially associated with the junk trade, a line of work they could enter without having to rent a storefront. James Deasey of the Seventh Ward and County Cork, Patrick Sullivan from Kerry and the Fourth Ward, and John Harrington from Kerry and Five Points all moved from day labor to the junk trade during the 1850s.[27]

The businesses Irish immigrants owned more than any others were groceries. Grocers carried virtually everything a tenement dweller might need — food, fuel, soap, candles, crockery, pipes, and tobacco. Irish grocers knew they had to stock their shelves with cheap goods in order to appeal to their frugal customers, yet their shops did not lack variety. Even in Five Points, the cornucopia of products for sale at a neighborhood grocery store was quite impressive. In Crown's Grocery at 150 Anthony Street (now Worth), reported one journalist,

> piles of cabbages, potatoes, squashes, egg-plants, tomatoes, turnips, eggs, dried apples, chestnuts and beans rise like miniature mountains round you. At the left hand as you enter is a row of little boxes, containing anthracite and charcoal, nails, plug-tobacco, &c. &c. which are dealt out in any quantity, from a bushel or a dollar to a cent's-worth. On a shelf near by is a pile of fire-wood, seven sticks for sixpence, or a cent apiece, and kindling-wood three sticks for two cents. Along the walls are ranged upright casks containing lamp-oil, molasses, rum, whisky, brandy, and all sorts of cordials, (carefully manufactured in the back room, where a kettle and furnace, with all the necessary instruments of spiritual devilment, are provided for the purpose.) The cross-beams that support the ceiling are thickly hung with hams, tongues, sausages, strings of onions, and other light and airy articles, and at every step you tumble over a butter-firkin or a meal-bin. Across one end of the room runs a "long, low, black" counter, armed at either end with bottles of poisoned fire-water, doled out at three cents a glass . . . while the shelves behind are filled with an uncatalogueable jumble of candles, all-spice, crackers, sugar and tea, pickles, ginger, mustard, and other kitchen necessaries. In the opposite corner is a shorter counter filled with three-cent pies, mince, apple, pumpkin and custard — all kept smoking hot — where you can get a cup of coffee with plenty of milk and sugar, for the same price, and buy a hat-full of "Americans with Spanish wrappers" [cigars] for a penny.

Irish groceries may have been renowned for their variety, but those glasses of "fire-water" made them notorious. Women in the United States rarely drank in public, but that did not stop some Irish immigrant housewives from stopping at the bar of their local grocery for a glass of gin or brandy. As a result, natives saw Irish groceries as one of the most objectionable features of New York's Irish enclaves.[28]

While a grocery could be very profitable, the American dream of most Irish immigrants was to become a saloonkeeper. In contrast to crowded groceries, saloons were typically long, narrow open spaces with a bar running down one long wall and an empty floor beside it. They contained no barstools or seating of any kind, primarily because there was no space for them. Unlike the palatial watering holes one might find on Broadway, the typical saloon in an immigrant neighborhood was the same size as a tenement apartment — twelve feet wide and at most twenty-two feet deep. Those that were particularly successful might break through to the back half of the tenement, but even then, that extra space usually remained separate — a back room that local labor, fraternal, and political organizations could use for meetings. Unlike the grocery, the saloon was an exclusively male domain. Anyone could open a saloon in an Irish neighborhood, but most were run by Irish Americans, for as one journalist noted, Irish immigrants preferred patronizing "the bar-keeper whose name has in it a flavour of the shamrock."[29]

With "scarcely room enough to turn around" inside their tenements, one immigrant noted, the saloon was a place where men could escape their cramped domestic life for a bit of camaraderie with their friends and neighbors. At the local saloon, observed charity pioneer Charles Loring Brace, the immigrant "can find jolly companions, a lighted and warmed room, a newspaper, and, above all, a draught which . . . can change poverty into riches, and drive care and labor and the thought of all his burdens and annoyances far away . . . His glass is the magic transmuter of care to cheerfulness, of penury to plenty, of a low, ignorant, worried life, to an existence for the moment buoyant, contented, and hopeful."[30]

The saloonkeeper won most of his respect because of his palpable power among his fellow immigrants. He "was a social force in the community," re-

THE VOTING-PLACE, NO. 488 PEARL STREET, IN THE SIXTH WARD, NEW YORK CITY.

The circular pieces of paper hung high on the wall of this Five Points saloon are targets, indicating that a neighborhood militia company held its meetings here. The man behind the bar is probably the proprietor, Irish immigrant Richard Barry. In 1860 and 1861 he served as alderman for the Sixth Ward, the pinnacle of success for most saloonkeepers.

membered minister Charles Stelzle, a child of German immigrants who grew up in New York.

> Often he secured work for both the workingman and his children . . . As a young apprentice, when I was arrested, . . . the first man to whom my friends turned was the saloon-keeper on the block. And he furnished bail gladly. He was doing it all the time. He had close affiliation with the dominant political party; he was instrumental in getting the young men of the neighborhood onto the police force and into the fire department, the most coveted jobs in the city among my young workmen friends. He loaned money . . . [and] no questions were asked as to whether or not the recipient was deserving.

The Nation agreed, reporting that "the liquor-dealer is [the immigrants'] guide, philosopher, and creditor. He sees them more frequently and familiarly than anybody else, and is more trusted by them than anybody else, and is the person through whom the news and meaning of what passes in the upper regions of city politics reach them."[31]

Given saloonkeepers' power and largesse, immigrants deferred to them in virtually every arena, and the liquor business thus became a natural stepping-stone into politics. Almost every Irish American political leader in New York in the antebellum period had at some point been a saloonkeeper. Matthew Breen recalled that in the Civil War era, if you had business to transact with your alderman, you went to his saloon, "as it was the Alderman's *only* place of business." A saloon was a virtual precondition for candidacy, as saloonkeepers built up the network of support necessary for a successful candidacy by treating customers and supporting other saloonkeepers in their campaigns for office until they had garnered enough political capital to make a run themselves. Irish immigrants operated more than a thousand saloons in New York by the eve of the Civil War, more than all other New Yorkers combined. Any Irish immigrant looking to escape manual labor, earn a substantial income, win the respect and admiration of his neighbors, and wield political clout would do whatever it took to open a saloon. Even some who arrived penniless at the height of the famine managed to do so.[32]

Irish immigrant women were much more likely to work for pay than other female immigrants or native-born women. Thirty-five percent of female Irish-born New Yorkers aged sixteen and older reported working for pay, while among native-born women and those from the rest of Europe, only one in six was employed. Poverty was undoubtedly the reason why Irish-born women worked in greater numbers than other female New Yorkers. Furthermore, many Irish women came to America on their own expressly to raise money to support indigent parents or finance the emigration of other family members, a practice that was less common among other European immigrant groups in this period.[33]

Nearly two-thirds of all employed Irish women worked as domestic servants. Irish-born women dominated domestic service almost as thoroughly as their menfolk did day labor: Irish immigrants held 70 percent of domestic service jobs in 1860 even though they accounted for only 39 percent of the city's adult female population.[34]

EMPLOYMENT OF IMMIGRANT WOMEN IN NEW YORK, 1860

	IRISH-BORN WOMEN	OTHER IMMIGRANTS
Percentage of population employed	35%	18%

OCCUPATIONS OF EMPLOYED WOMEN[35]

	IRISH-BORN WOMEN	OTHER IMMIGRANTS
Household servant	63%	43%
Needle trades	17%	38%
Washing	7%	3%
Business owner	4%	2%
Nurse	3%	2%
Other/Difficult to categorize	7%	11%

Source: Integrated Public Use Microdata Series (IPUMS), "1% sample of the 1860 U.S. Census." Percentages may not equal 100 due to rounding.

One of the most difficult aspects of domestic service for an immigrant was finding that first job without references (though some, anticipating this need, brought letters of recommendation from Ireland). Many New Yorkers preferred not to hire the Irish. An 1853 advertisement in the *New York Sun* read: "WOMAN WANTED — To do general housework; she must be clean, neat, and industrious, and above all good tempered and willing. English, Scotch, Welsh, German, or any country or color will answer except Irish." A help-wanted notice in the *Herald* two days later likewise specified "any country or color except Irish." The *Irish-American* — voice of the New York Irish community in this era — condemned such prejudice, vowing to "kill this anti-Irish-servant-maid

Many Irish immigrants found work as domestic servants through placement agencies such as these photographed in New York in the late nineteenth century.

crusade" and hiring a lawyer to sue the advertisers and newspapers involved. While the *Irish-American*'s campaign did halt the appearance of specifically anti-Irish advertisements, employers simply modified their ads. About one in ten continued to specify "Protestants" or "Americans" (though ads seeking male employees were remarkably free of such overt discrimination). While the *Irish-American* might boast by 1857 that "No Irish need apply" provisos had virtually disappeared, thinly veiled prejudice against hiring Irish Catholics, especially as domestic servants, continued to be a staple of New York life.[36]

Once an Irish immigrant secured a position as a domestic, her workday was grueling. Typically living with her employer, she was expected to rise each morning well before the family to light the fires and prepare breakfast from scratch. She then spent the rest of the day cooking meals (again, doing everything from scratch), cleaning the dishes and the rest of the house, scrubbing the floors on hands and knees, washing and ironing the clothes (in an era when clothes had to be washed by hand and heavy irons had to be heated over a stove), and caring for children. Her typical workday did not end until well after the family had gone to bed. Some domestics slept in quarters far nicer than they could have afforded in Five Points or some other Irish enclave, but many were "thrust into noxious dark bed-rooms or unventilated garrets and lofts." All this for as little as $4 to $8 per month (plus room and board).[37]

Domestic service also involved a heavy psychological toll. "The relationship between the servant girl and her employer, is nearly the same as that of master and slave," wrote a southern visitor to New York. "The duties expected and exacted are precisely the same. The respect, and obedience, and humility required, are also nearly the same." As under slavery, a male employer might try to force himself on his young female servants, knowing that he was unlikely to face any consequences unless his wife found out. In some ways the domestic was in an even worse position than a slave, because the employer had no obligation to care for a sick servant and might simply fire her when she was unfit to work.

Servants also had very little free time. Because most of them lived with their employers, they were on duty nearly every waking moment. The typical servant got every other Sunday off, reported the *Tribune*, alternating with the cook, chambermaid, or laundress "so that the house shall never be 'left alone.'" But if she worked for a middle-class family and was the only employee, she might get only one Sunday off a month, especially if she lacked experience or references, or had a child who might distract her from her work. Even if a servant had two days off per month, this meant that she had virtually no social life whatsoever, making the young Irish woman's already difficult task of finding a mate (in a city where Irish-born women outnumbered men by three to two) exceedingly difficult.[38]

There were some advantages to domestic service. Domestics ate well (often the same food they cooked for their employers) and lived rent-free in safer, cleaner neighborhoods than other immigrants. Furthermore, with middle-class New Yorkers so utterly dependent on their servants, in some ways Irish domestics had more leverage over their employers than perhaps any other immigrants. "Whenever one thinks she is imposed upon, the invariable plan is to threaten to leave the situation at once," noted the *Tribune*, "instead, as in other kinds of employment, of being fearful of losing it." This power could translate into better pay, more time off, and other benefits.[39]

With room and board covered, the domestic could also send virtually all her income to relatives back in Ireland to support elderly parents or finance the emigration of other family members. "The great ambition of the Irish girl is to send 'something' to her people as soon as possible after she has landed in America," observed a visiting Irish journalist in 1868.

> Loving a bit of finery dearly, she will resolutely shut her eyes to the attractions of some enticing article of dress, to prove to the loved ones at home that she has not forgotten them; and she will risk the danger of insufficient clothing, or boots not proof against rain or snow, rather than diminish the amount of the little hoard to which she is weekly adding, and which she intends as a delightful surprise to parents who possibly did not altogether approve of her hazardous enterprise. To send money to her people, she will deny herself innocent enjoyments, womanly indulgences, and the gratifications of legitimate vanity.

Of the $120 million (according to one estimate) that Irish Americans remitted to Ireland from 1845 to 1865, a large portion came from the savings of domestic servants.[40]

That figure came from an Irish journalist, John Francis Maguire, who sought to dramatize the sacrifices of his countrymen. A more conservative estimate, made by the British government, was that Irish emigrants sent $57 million to Ireland from 1848 to 1860. Even that smaller figure equates to a staggering $1.67 billion in 2015 dollars. Maguire's figure, which covers two decades rather than thirteen years, equates to $3.5 billion.[41]

The second most common occupation for Irish immigrant women in the antebellum era was needlework. A few needleworkers had relatively high-paying jobs as dressmakers or milliners to wealthy New Yorkers, while others sewed part-time, supplementing the incomes of husbands, fathers, or brothers. Most needleworkers, however, supported either themselves or whole families doing piecework — barely eking out a living sewing collars or hems for a penny apiece, working eighteen- or twenty-hour days yet earning only a few dollars a week. New York's needlewomen, reported the *Times,* inevitably led lives of "misery, degradation, and wretchedness."

The vast majority of women who sewed for a living did so because they had children to care for and thus could not work as domestics. Knowing this, employers exploited needleworkers terribly, often refusing to pay for work completed on the grounds that it was subpar or late. But since the employer owned the shirt and the collar the needlewoman had stitched together, he took them from the seamstresses, who suspected that he sold these "ruined" shirts anyway, pocketing the extra money. "No serf in the middle ages," concluded the *Tribune,* "was ever more helplessly under the absolute control of his superior lord as are the needle women to the employers." In the 1850s, "the wretchedness of needlewomen" became something of a *cause célèbre* in New York. Newspaper exposés documented their pitiable lives, reformers held meeting to organize relief for them, and charitable organizations chronicled their struggles to support themselves and their families. Approximately 70 percent of these needlewomen were immigrants.[42]

The next most common avocation for Irish immigrant women in the Civil War era was taking in washing. The city was full of single men who could afford to pay someone else to do their laundry. The advent of the commercial laundry was still decades away, so immigrant women filled the void. Some women took in washing on a casual basis, from men who lived in their tenements. Others were ambitious businesswomen who ran small washing empires, farming out the work to other immigrants and keeping the bulk of the profits for themselves.

That seems to have been the case with Mary Mulvey, who emigrated from Dublin to New York in 1846 at age thirty-five with her husband, Charles, and four daughters aged ten or less. A year later Charles disappeared, probably while out of town looking for work, and was never seen again. Needing to support herself and her children, Mary began working as a "washer and ironer." In 1851 she opened an account at the Emigrant Savings Bank with an initial deposit of $200. Somehow, Mary saved an additional $2,000 (equivalent to about $57,000 today) by January 1857 and nearly $1,000 more by the eve of the Civil War. Perhaps her children helped her save. (We know two became teachers, but only one was old enough to have been so employed by 1857.) Perhaps she inherited the money. Perhaps her brother, who lived around the corner, contributed to his sister's account, though as a tailor he was not in a high-income occupation either. More likely she was very frugal or a very smart businesswoman — probably both. These accomplishments are all the more impressive because Mary Mulvey was illiterate. Like 63 percent of the Emigrant Bank's female Irish-born depositors and 21 percent of its male Irish customers, she could not even write her own name. Washerwomen did not typically accumulate nearly this much cash, but their median savings at the Emigrant Bank, about $200 (a little more than $5,000 in today's dollars), was twice as high as that of needlewomen.[43]

There were undoubtedly a lot more employed women than the historical records indicate. Even in the Irish immigrant community there was a stigma attached to married women working for pay, so women often lied about their employment. Kerry native Catherine (Kate) Sullivan of Five Points, for example, described herself as a homemaker married to husband Sandy, a laborer, when she opened an account at the Emigrant Bank in 1860. Nor did she report an occupation to the census taker who visited her later that year. Yet a few months earlier, a reporter and sketch artist for the *New York Illustrated News* had visited "Mrs. Sandy Sullivan's Genteel Lodging House" in the basement of 35 Baxter Street. Kate was undoubtedly the one who ran the place, keeping it clean, feeding the inhabitants if they paid for food as well as a bed, and washing the sheets each Thursday. Another reporter who toured the "damp and filthy cellar" in the summer of 1859 found "wretched beds," "fetid odors," and floors and walls "damp with pestiferous exhalations." But Sandy, "with much loquacity," assured the visitors that the beds were "clane and dacent sure" and that, for six cents per night, "the place was quite sweet." In the summer of 1860, the Sullivans' boardinghouse lodged a seventy-one-year-old Irish paperhanger, his thirty-five-year-old daughter, five Irish-born domestic servants, and a baby.[44]

Children would also help immigrant families make ends meet, although most did not typically earn a wage. Five Points was famous for its adolescent bootblacks, newsboys, and girls peddling hot corn in summertime, but these waifs were typically orphans living on their own or with adoptive parents, or children who helped keep their family afloat after their father died. Thousands of children in immigrant neighborhoods did, however, supplement their fam-

ily income in informal ways. The most common was to scavenge for coal, looking for chunks of the shiny black rocks on the street near coal yards or by the
docks, where it was transferred from barges to wagons. Owen Kildare knew not
to come home until he had met his daily coal quota, thus reducing the amount
of money his stepparents had to spend on fuel. Other children collected scrap
wood, which could be burned in the family stove or sold for kindling. Still others prowled the streets looking for (or stealing) scrap metal, glass, or anything
that could be sold to the city's many Irish junk dealers.[45]

Given these struggles, scholars tend to paint a "gloomy picture of Irish-
American deprivation," arguing that the famine Irish did not thrive in New
York, but instead lived a life "of poverty and hardship." There is certainly much
evidence to support this interpretation. "It is a well established fact," reported
one Irish American, "that the average length of life of the emigrant after landing here is six years; and many insist it is much less." In a similar vein, a New
York Irish newspaper complained in 1859 that most of the famine immigrants
were still "a mere floating population" who lacked real economic security and
were despised by native-born Americans.[46]

Yet there is more evidence to support the argument that the Irish viewed
their move to New York in mostly positive terms. Despite the terrible conditions and high mortality rates in certain tenements, the death rate for immigrants in New York City was no higher than for the native-born population.
In the year ending on June 1, 1855, when immigrants made up 51 percent of
the city's population, the foreign-born accounted for 50 percent of New York's
deaths. The famine Irish believed that they were healthier in New York than
they had been in Ireland, and attributed this improvement in large part to their
American diet. Even laborers in New York "can eat good beef, and pork, and
butter, and eggs, and bread — not so at home in the old country," remarked an
immigrant from County Carlow living in Five Points, even though "an Irish laborer had to work harder there than here."

There were other benefits, ones that could not be measured in bank balances
but were nonetheless palpable and important to the immigrants. "Here we have
a free government, just laws, and a Constitution which guarantees equal rights
and privelages to all," a far cry from the "tyrany and persecution at home,"
wrote Peter Welsh to his father-in-law in Ireland. "And those who posses the
abilitys can raise themselves to positions of honor and emolument. Here Irishmen and their decendents have a claim, a stake in the nation and an interest in
its prosperity . . . It is the best and most liberal government in the world . . . It is
impossible to estimate the amount of distress and misery that has been warded
off" by those Irish men and women who chose to immigrate to America.[47]

Other immigrants shared Welsh's point of view. Comparing his old life in Ireland to his new one in New York as he proudly sent his parents $20 (the equivalent of about $500 today) just months after arriving from County Sligo, Pat McGowan wondered why he had waited so long to emigrate. Despite living in decrepit Five Points, Eliza Quinn felt the same way. The United States, she reported to her family back in Ireland, "is the best country in the world."[48]

9

KLEINDEUTSCHLAND

THE IRISH FAMINE MIGRATION was front-page news on both sides of the Atlantic. To this day we tend to associate immigration in the years immediately before the Civil War with the famine and the Irish. But in the three years with the highest levels of immigration before the Civil War, 1852 through 1854, German immigrants actually outnumbered the Irish. In fact, in no three-year period during the famine migration did the Irish influx surpass the German immigration of those three years. In 1854, when a record 400,000 newcomers landed in the United States, 177,000 Germans arrived in New York Harbor, more than ever came from Ireland to New York in any single year.*

While Irish immigration grew steadily over the course of the nineteenth century, German immigration mushroomed seemingly overnight. In the 1820s, fewer than 1,000 Germans per year immigrated to the United States, a tenth of the Irish total. By the decade before the Irish famine, German immigration had become more substantial, averaging 15,000 per year to all American ports — but that was still half the tally from Ireland, whose population was a quarter that of the German states. During the early years of the Irish famine, German immigration grew substantially, averaging 60,000 per year up to 1851. But whereas Irish emigration tailed off after that year, the German exodus suddenly doubled, to more than 140,000 in 1852 and 1853, and then increased another 25 percent in 1854. Seventy-nine percent of those German immigrants landed in New York.[1]

---

* There was no single country called "Germany" in this period, but rather about three dozen German-speaking kingdoms, principalities, and duchies. Austria was considered a German state before it was, in effect, excluded from Bismarck's unification efforts that led to the creation of the German Empire in 1871.

Unlike the Irish, who often could not afford to continue their journey past their port of arrival, Germans typically had the resources to move beyond the eastern seaboard if they chose to do so. Many of them settled in the "German Triangle" bounded by the cities of Cincinnati, Milwaukee, and St. Louis. Germans dominated the immigrant populations of those cities by 1860, and outnumbered the Irish in Chicago, too. Buffalo was another German-dominated city. The first ancestor in my family tree to immigrate to America, my great-great-grandfather Moritz Weil, left the town of Ihringen in Baden's Rhine River valley sometime in the mid-1840s and made it to Buffalo by 1847, when the twenty-year-old peddler helped found the city's first Jewish burial society. But despite the large numbers of Germans in Buffalo and the Midwest, no other American city had even half as many German immigrants as New York. The city had 120,000 German-born residents in 1860, accounting for 23 percent of the city's adult population. By that date, only Berlin and Vienna contained more Germans than New York.[2]

Historians have long debated why German emigration spiked so dramatically. The most famous German immigrants of the period — such as Carl Schurz and Franz Sigel — were leaders of the failed revolutions of 1848, uprisings that attempted to overthrow the monarchs of the various German states and replace them with republican governments. Early historians consequently focused on politics as the main cause of the growing German emigration. Yet the peak immigration came years after the revolutionary fighting had ended, so later scholars have emphasized economic motivations, including the potato blight, which affected food supplies all over western Europe. German grain prices rose by 250 to 300 percent in those years, and the price of potatoes rose by more than 400 percent; hunger riots were widespread.

Like the Irish, Germans in the eighteenth and early nineteenth centuries subdivided their land among their sons over so many generations that each plot eventually became insufficient to support a family. Germans who had once supplemented their incomes through seasonal textile work found that the Industrial Revolution reduced or altogether eliminated those additional earnings. Economic conditions became particularly dire in southwestern German states such as Baden, Württemberg, Bavaria, and the portion of the southern Rhine River valley that by this point belonged to Prussia. Bankruptcies in the region reached record levels in the early 1850s, just as emigration peaked. It was exceedingly difficult for Germans in economically depressed areas to move to other German states where work was more readily available, as these small nations imposed restrictions on emigration. Even moving within a state could be impossible. In Mecklenburg, for example, a man could not move from his birthplace to a different part of the state without the permission of the governor. He could not marry unless he owned a house. Feeling trapped, many Germans escaped to America.[3]

Yet it is extremely difficult to untangle economics from politics. Frederick Bultman, an apprentice locksmith in Hanover, later recalled that he had decided to immigrate to the United States at age thirteen in 1852, on the day he went to the town hall to deliver his father's tax payment. Remembering the gilded royal coach he had seen earlier in his youth, he realized that such aristocratic ostentation was possible only because of the taxes his father struggled mightily to pay. He vowed that day that he would escape to the United States, where there was no king. "When their patience finally breaks," a German socialist explained, "they move to America."[4]

Furthermore, some German emigration in the 1850s was a delayed reaction to the revolutions of 1848. Many Germans held out hope that their failed efforts in that fateful year would bear fruit a few years later. Some sought temporary refuge in France or England while they waited for the revolutionary tide to turn in their favor, while those not sought by the authorities bided their time at home. But in 1851 the French began to expel German radicals, and in December a reactionary monarchist, Napoleon III, seized Paris in a coup, eliminating the possibility that a more democratic regime in France might indirectly help advance the republican cause in the German states. "In the summer of 1852 the future lay before us in a gloomy cloud," recalled German radical Carl Schurz, explaining why he chose to immigrate to the United States at that time. Arriving in New York "with the buoyant hopefulness of young hearts, we saluted the New World." Thousands of other Germans did the same.[5]

The German immigration to America was drawn primarily from southern and western Germany, with about three-quarters originating in Bavaria, Württemberg, Baden, the Hessian states, and the Prussian Rhineland. Most of the rest came from Prussia in what is now northeast Germany. New York's Germans came from the same places, but the contingents of Bavarians and Hessians in the city were especially large (25 percent bigger than in other major American cities), while the Prussian portion of the population was comparatively small (25 percent smaller than in other U.S. cities with large German populations).[6]

Whereas the Irish lived in virtually every part of Manhattan by 1855, German immigrants concentrated in a portion of New York that became known as "Kleindeutschland." "Our neighborhood rightly bears the name 'Little Germany,'" wrote one German New Yorker. "It is a small German town in the middle of a big city." Kleindeutschland comprised the area that later generations

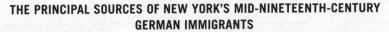

THE PRINCIPAL SOURCES OF NEW YORK'S MID-NINETEENTH-CENTURY GERMAN IMMIGRANTS

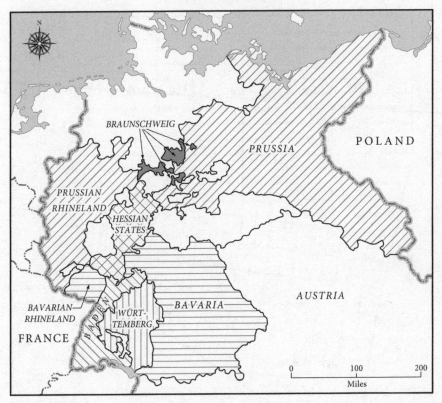

would call the Lower East Side. It was bounded by the Bowery to the west, Division Street and the east end of Grand Street to the south, and the East River to the east. The northern boundary varied as the enclave grew, but by the end of the Civil War it reached almost as far north as 14th Street. In 1860, about half the Germans in New York lived in the four wards that made up Kleindeutschland. The four most heavily Irish wards in the city, in contrast, held only 25 percent of the city's Irish immigrants.[7]

"What multitudes from Germany are in our midst," marveled the *Times* as Kleindeutschland filled with these immigrants. Little Germany had several main commercial arteries. "As one passes along the Bowery," observed one German immigrant, "almost everything is German." Grand Street, Second Avenue, and Avenue B were also important commercial thoroughfares for German immigrants, while Avenue A, like the Bowery, was renowned for its beer

NEW YORK'S KLEINDEUTSCHLAND, 1860

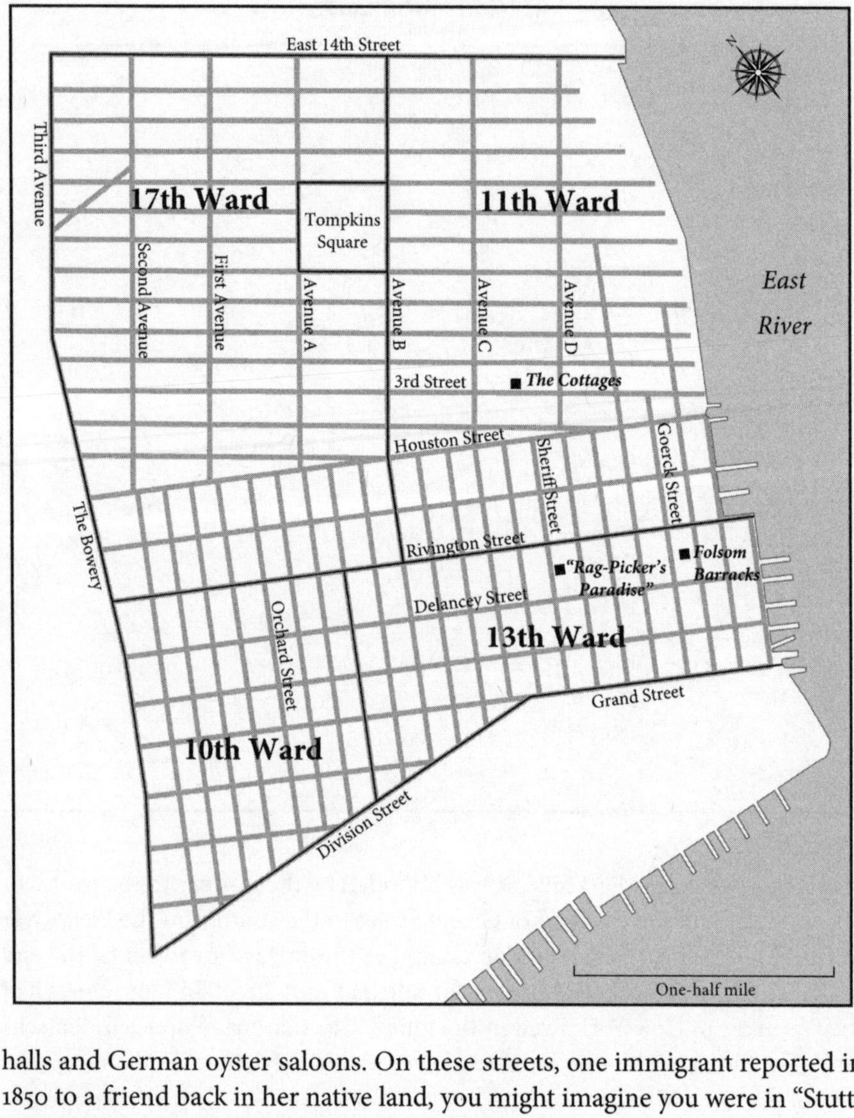

East 14th Street

Third Avenue

17th Ward

Tompkins Square

11th Ward

Second Avenue

First Avenue

Avenue A

Avenue B

Avenue C

Avenue D

East River

3rd Street   ■ *The Cottages*

Houston Street

Sheriff Street

Goerck Street

The Bowery

Rivington Street

■ *"Rag-Picker's Paradise"*   ■ *Folsom Barracks*

Delancey Street

Orchard Street

13th Ward

Grand Street

10th Ward

Division Street

One-half mile

halls and German oyster saloons. On these streets, one immigrant reported in 1850 to a friend back in her native land, you might imagine you were in "Stuttgart, that's how many Germans you can see here."[8]

Like the Irish, the Germans did not settle haphazardly within their enclave. "The Brandenburgers and Plattdeutschen [north Germans] seem . . . little inclined to be among the Süddeutschen [south Germans]," a journalist reported. Other observers noted antagonisms within the north and south German communities too. Hessians concentrated in the southeast part of Little Germany in the Thirteenth Ward, while the Prussians congregated heavily in the Tenth

Ward, the southwest part of Kleindeutschland near the Bowery. Bavarians tended to settle anywhere in Little Germany *except* the Prussian Tenth Ward. Those from Baden and Württemberg did not concentrate in any particular locale before the Civil War, but would do so later on.[9]

These German enclaves were less decrepit-looking than the city's most notorious Irish districts. The buildings were newer and better maintained, and the streets were typically less filthy. The inhabitants of Kleindeutschland also had a bit more room in their tenement apartments. Many of their dwellings, especially in the recently built northern portion of Little Germany, had three rooms rather than the two typically found in the Irish Fourth and Sixth wards. But the older, southeast portion of Little Germany contained just as many decaying wooden tenements as Five Points.[10]

Over the course of the mid-1850s, tenement conditions in the older portions of the district became nearly as frightful as those in the city's worst Irish neighborhoods. In the Tenth Ward, whose center was the intersection of Grand and Orchard streets, the state tenement committee in 1856 found buildings in a "filthy condition, without ventilation, and destitute of the accommodations necessary for the use of civilized beings." Worse still were the eastern portions of the Eleventh and Thirteenth wards near the East River. There, an inspection tour uncovered tenement complexes such as the "Folsom Barracks" in an alley that ran from Goerck Street to Mangin between Delancey and Rivington, and "The Cottages" on 3rd Street between Avenues C and D. These tenements were "most wretched and filthy — alike disgraceful to the owners of the property and the city that tolerates such nuisances." It was startling, wrote the committee, that "the occupants did not all die of pestilence generated by their unspeakable filth and dissolute habits of living." In one apartment a "disgusting spectacle was presented. The side walls were frightfully decorated with traces of blood and mutilated remains, which plainly showed that a deadly and unremitting warfare had been carried on against bed-bugs, and those of the largest and most voracious type." The "poor German who occupied this apartment looked pale and attenuated, as if his vitality had been sucked out by these insatiate creatures, or his strength totally spent in giving them battle."[11]

In some portions of Little Germany, especially in the northeastern Eleventh Ward, the tenements sat among noxious industries that did not operate in the neighborhoods where most Irish immigrants lived. One Jewish immigrant remembered that when he moved to Kleindeutschland in 1863, his tenement on Sherriff Street "was just opposite a slaughter house. All day long we could see the animals being driven into the slaughter-pens and could hear the turmoil and the cries of the animals. The neighborhood was filled with the penetrating, sickening odor." A brewery sat behind his tenement, spewing pungently yeasty fumes that mixed with the stench of the slaughterhouse. Even after he moved, he recalled, "the suffering of the animals and the nauseating odor made it physically impossible for me to eat meat for many months."[12]

Frequently the most filthy and dilapidated tenements in Little Germany were occupied by "ragpickers," scavengers who collected discarded rags to sell to papermakers and unwanted bones to peddle to fat renderers and soap makers. The "most horrible stench," odors "beyond description," sometimes infused these buildings as a result of the ragpickers' trade. In the notorious rear tenements at 88 and 90 Sheriff Street known as "Rag-Picker's Paradise," for example, inspectors found that "in the yard, and on the stoops and in the entries, were bags and baskets of bones and calves' heads, with the flesh still clinging to them, and emitting a stench bad enough in itself, but absolutely refreshing compared to the other prevailing smells of the place."[13]

Even where ragpickers did not predominate, the crowding in some parts of Little Germany by the mid-1850s had become nearly as bad as that in Five Points and the Fourth Ward. "The families were innumerable, and the number of the children somewhat beyond compute," wrote a *Times* reporter who visited Kleindeutschland in the summer of 1856. A third of Little Germany's families took in lodgers in these years, exacerbating the district's overcrowding. By 1860, the Thirteenth Ward, in the southeast portion of Kleindeutschland, had a population density of 183,000 residents per square mile, making it almost as crowded as the city's most teeming Irish enclaves, while the Tenth and Eleventh wards had 166,000 and 156,000 inhabitants per square mile, respectively. They would become more crowded still in the coming decades as landlords replaced the district's remaining smaller, older tenements with five- and six-story brick buildings.[14]

In contrast to New York's Irish immigrant population, in which women outnumbered men, German-born men in New York outnumbered German women, making up 56 percent of the population in 1850 and 54 percent in 1860 (the decline coming as male immigrants brought other family members to New York). German Jews also made up a disproportionate number of New York's German immigrants in this period. We do not know the precise number, but about 30,000 of New York's 120,000 German-born residents in 1860 were Jewish.[15]

German-born men dominated the artisanal trades in New York in the decade before the Civil War. German immigrant artisans outnumbered both Irish and American-born by wide margins even though those other groups made up a much larger percentage of the population. Nearly 60 percent of male German immigrants worked in skilled trades in 1860, the highest proportion of any immigrant group in the city. German men controlled fields such as cabinet and furniture making, woodcarving, and gilding. A majority of the city's shoemakers, tailors, locksmiths, bakers, brewers, and cigar makers were also German. In contrast, German workers made up only a tiny fraction of New York's menial day labor force, a contrast to the workforce in cities such as Chicago, Cincinnati, Milwaukee, and St. Louis, where there were thousands of German day laborers.[16]

The single most popular occupation among German immigrants was tailoring: about one-fifth of all German artisans worked in this field. Tailors were not paid much, barely more than day laborers, but the immigrant tailors seem to have been pleased with their pay compared to what they had received in their homeland. Nickolaus Heck and his wife, Angela, came to the United States in 1854 from the tiny village of Irrel in the part of the Prussian Rhineland in western Germany known for its Riesling wines. The Hecks had planned to settle in the American interior, but upon their arrival after a harrowing two-month journey, Angela wrote, a "man told us that if you were a tailor you should stay in New York," so they did, while the villagers they had accompanied boarded trains for the Midwest. The Hecks did not regret their decision. "We had hardly been here for fifteen minutes," she added, "when they came running to us with cards looking for tailors."

Six weeks later, Angela proudly reported to her relatives that Nickolaus "earns a dollar every day" making men's jackets. "I always help him with the sewing." Journeyman tailors such as Heck typically needed the assistance of a spouse to complete the tasks given them by garment contractors. Accustomed to backbreaking toil in the Mosel vineyards, Angela was happy to be helping Nickolaus with his needlework. "There aren't any women at home who have such a good life and it gets better every day," she gushed. "The worst bread that they eat here is better than the finest cake at home." She also found it comforting to live in Kleindeutschland, where "we are among nothing but good people who are all Catholic and German." Concluding her letter, she wrote, "I only wish that everyone who has to stay at home and lead a life of poverty could live like we do. Young people who have learned a trade have more here than someone at home who has a fortune . . . Give my best to Anna Bisdorf and Elisabeth Mutsch too and tell them they should burn up their grape baskets and get themselves some tailors, even if they are windbags," so they could move to America too.[17]

Tailoring could be especially lucrative for those who were able to make the move from sewing to selling. When Levi Strauss arrived in New York from Bavaria in 1847, he initially worked for his older brothers Jonas and Louis in their wholesale clothing business. As thousands of young, unmarried men from New

York and all over the nation began streaming into California in 1849 in hopes of striking it rich in the Gold Rush, Levi sensed an opportunity. He moved to San Francisco in 1853, and by 1860 had become one of the city's merchant princes, wholesaling tents, clothing, and other "dry goods" to purveyors from Nevada all the way to Hawaii. He bought most of his merchandise from his brothers, who hired other New York immigrants to manufacture most of the goods that Levi sold. A few years after the Civil War, a Nevada tailor came to Strauss with the idea for a more rugged pair of overalls made of durable denim cloth with metal rivets to fasten the pockets. The pair patented the innovation, and Levi Strauss blue jeans were born.[18]

Germans also dominated cigar making in New York. Cigar makers were highly sought after because, as visitors to New York frequently noted, everyone in the city seemed to smoke. The best description of the work life of a cigar maker in this period comes from an English-born immigrant. Samuel Gomperts, the London-born son of Dutch Jews, immigrated to New York with his parents in 1863 at age thirteen, by which point he had already been working three years as a cigar maker. The Gompertses managed to immigrate to America only because Solomon Gomperts's English trade union offered to subsidize the move. Their resettlement in New York was further facilitated by Sam's uncle and other Jewish cigar makers from London who had already immigrated.[19]

As soon as they arrived in New York in July 1863, the Gomperts family settled among the city's German Jews in Kleindeutschland. Solomon and thirteen-year-old Sam immediately went to work in a nearby cigar-making shop. The keys to the trade, Gomperts later recalled, were to hide the less attractive tobacco leaves inside the cigar "and to use both hands so as to make a perfectly shaped and rolled product. These things a good cigarmaker learned to do more or less mechanically, which left us free to think, talk, listen, or sing." Detesting boredom, the cigar makers "chose someone to read to us who was a particularly good reader, and in payment the rest of us gave him sufficient of our cigars so he was not the loser. The reading was always followed by discussion, so we learned to know each other pretty thoroughly . . . The fellowship that grew between congenial shopmates was something that lasted a lifetime."

One of the most popular songs for Solomon and Sam Gomperts and their co-workers to sing as they rolled cigars while they were still in England was "To the West," which recounted the desire of so many Europeans to immigrate to America:

> *To the west, to the west, to the land of the free*
> *Where the mighty Missouri rolls down to the sea;*
> *Where a man is a man if he's willing to toil,*

And the humblest may gather the fruits of the soil.
Where children are blessings and he who hath most
Has aid for his fortune and riches to boast.
Where the young may exult and the aged may rest,
Away, far away, to the land of the west.
Away! Far away, let us hope for the best
And build up a home in the land of the west.

Sam never forgot the words to that song. Andrew Carnegie, too, mentioned it as the inspiration for his family's immigration to America. By the 1870s, Gomperts decided to make his name less Jewish and Dutch by changing it to Gompers. He would go on to make that name one of the most famous in the annals of the American labor movement.[20]

Another line of work favored by German immigrants was the grocery business. German immigrants made up only 25 percent of New York's male workforce in 1860, but they owned over half of the city's grocery stores. Even in an overwhelmingly Irish neighborhood like Five Points, German grocers outnumbered their Irish counterparts. North Germans were especially active in the grocery trade. Immigrants from Hanover, who constituted only 12 percent of the city's German population, owned about two-thirds of New York's German groceries in 1860. Frederick Bultman, the teenager who had rebelled at having to pay taxes to finance the gilded coach of Hanover's royal family, worked in his cousin's Five Points grocery when he first arrived in New York in 1852. He described their customers as "the toughest, hardest looking men I had ever seen."[21]

Other Germans had the wherewithal to start more substantial and lucrative businesses. Many became brewers, operating neighborhood microbreweries in an era when they were the norm. Occupying the position that saloonkeepers held in the Irish community, the city's German "brewer princes" financed many of Kleindeutschland's social, cultural, and charitable institutions.[22]

Some Germans, such as Heinrich Steinweg, made fortunes in other entrepreneurial endeavors. Born in 1797 in the small north-central German duchy of Braunschweig, Heinrich spent his youth deep in the forest, where his father was a charcoal maker. Having lost his mother as a small child, Heinrich was orphaned at age fifteen when his father was struck by lightning in his charcoal-making grounds in the Harz Mountains. The orphan joined the army and soon found himself in the thick of the Napoleonic Wars. In the army he apparently developed an interest in music — he supposedly earned a commendation for bugling under fire — and after his discharge at age twenty-one returned to Braunschweig, where he learned to make organs and pianos.

In 1825 Steinweg married Julianne Thiemer, the daughter of a glove maker, with whom he had nine children. Heinrich was able to afford such a large family because he had become a very successful piano maker. He won a prize for his craftsmanship in 1836 and even sold a piano to the Duke of Braunschweig for three thousand marks, remarkable achievements for a man who could not even write his own name. Nonetheless, by the 1840s Heinrich had begun contemplating a move to America. He could sell only so many pianos in Braunschweig, and trade barriers between the various German states made it nearly impossible to expand his business at home. The United States' reputation as a land of unlimited opportunity was already widespread: another German who had begun as a musical instrument maker, John Jacob Astor, was by that point the richest man in America.[23]

When the revolutions of 1848 demanding democracy and freedom of speech broke out, Heinrich's second-eldest son, nineteen-year-old Karl Gottlieb, became a supporter. As the tide turned against the revolutionaries, Heinrich and Julianne decided to smuggle Karl abroad and move the family to America. As a first step, Karl was sent to Switzerland, then to Paris and London, and finally to New York, where he arrived in June 1849. Although Karl was well educated and could have found white-collar work of some kind, Heinrich asked him to seek employment in one of the city's piano-making shops so that he might appraise the state of that business in the city. He immediately found a job at one of the city's biggest piano works, Bacon & Raven, on Grand Street, just east of Broadway.[24]

The rest of the family (all except Heinrich and Julianne's eldest son) emigrated a year later. They had enough money to travel by steamship, albeit in the steerage section of the vessel. They may even have brought a servant with them. Upon arrival, Heinrich and his sons also went to work in New York's thriving piano-manufacturing industry. Twenty-year-old Heinrich junior got a job building keyboards for $7 a week for piano maker James Pirsson on Leonard Street near Five Points. Fifteen-year-old Wilhelm found a position a few blocks away making soundboards for William Nunns at 88 Walker Street, and Karl began working there as well. Even Heinrich senior took a lowly job as a soundboard maker for a German piano manufacturer, Ferdinand Leuchte, for $6 per week. They lived at 199 Hester Street in a brick tenement on a mostly German block in a predominantly Irish neighborhood just north of Five Points. The tenement is still there today.

Their life was not easy. "I cannot advise you to come here if you are able . . . to make a living in Germany," Karl wrote to his eldest brother, still in Braunschweig. "People here have to work harder than abroad." Karl injured himself badly moving a piano and told his brother that he would have returned to Braunschweig to recuperate (New York doctors charged exorbitant fees, he complained) but for his fear of getting "into trouble in Germany because of the military." To make matters worse, Nunns eventually went bankrupt, and Karl lost several hundred dollars in back pay. Luckily, the Steinwegs had ample savings to fall back on. Finally, after several years spent gathering intelligence on the competition, the family members Anglicized their names and, in 1853, "Henry," "Charles," and "William" opened Steinway & Sons, piano manufacturers. Initially they rented space at 85 Varick Street. They sold eleven pianos that first year, made entirely by members of the family. With those profits they bought the Nunns piano workshop and hired their first five employees. Masters of both craftsmanship and self-promotion, the Steinways were so success-

Wilhelm Steinweg arrived in New York in 1850, rechristened himself William Steinway, and then helped lead the family piano-manufacturing business to world renown.

ful that by 1861, they had built a huge new factory filling half a city block, on Fourth Avenue (now Park) between 52nd and 53rd streets. A decade later, when they would begin constructing an entire "factory village" in Astoria, Queens, their pianos had become famous the world over.[25]

The Steinway women — mother Julianne and daughters Doretta, Wilhelmina, and Anna — did not have to work, though Doretta, an accomplished pianist, sometimes prowled the showroom floor, demonstrating the capabilities of the pianos and offering free lessons if doing so would close a sale. But for most of the one in six German-born women who worked for a living, the popular line of employment was domestic service. "On the same day I arrived in New Jork, I went into service for a German family," Anna Maria Klinger wrote to her parents and siblings back in Württemberg in 1849. The employment opportunities for German domestics were far more limited than for most of the Irish, however, for as Klinger explained, "if you can't speak or understand English you can't ask for so much pay." Only German American families would hire these women, who as a result sometimes earned even less than Irish-born domestics. Klinger's first job as a domestic, working for a German American pharmacist, paid only $4 per month, plus room and board. But, she reported, "I am content with my wages for now, compared to Germany . . . I hope that things will get better, for it's always like that, no one really likes it at first, and especially if you are so lonely and forlorn in a foreign land like I am, [with] no friends or relatives around."[26]

Germans who had worked as servants before emigrating found that domestic service in the United States was far better than in their native land. In Germany, restrictive laws made it almost impossible for servants to quit a bad job. They were even liable to corporal punishment. In contrast, wrote one German servant in New York, "here one is respected as a human being."

Another factor that inspired German women to emigrate was that doing so greatly improved their marriage prospects. Servants in Germany were not paid well enough to amass a dowry. In America, not only did servants earn more, but also a dowry was wholly unnecessary. "Here the girl does not need anything," wrote one servant concerning dowries. "If the boy has a little something they get along." Furthermore, meddling parents could not prevent marriages in the United States as they could in the German states. Emile Dupré from Braunschweig, for example, wanted to marry a woman whose father did not approve of the match. "If we lived in Europe, he might be able to keep me from marrying his daughter," Dupré wrote to his mother back in Braunschweig, "but here in the land of freedom, parents can't block marriages." A German emigration guide promised that "industrious, settled girls, who are comely of body can be sure to receive marriage offers in the first year" in America.[27]

Such was the case for Anna Maria Klinger. About a year after she arrived in New York, she quit working as a domestic and married stonecutter Franz Schano, who had come to America after deserting the Bavarian army. He had trouble finding work in his trade (perhaps because it was dominated by the Irish) and decided instead to become a woodcarver, a very German vocation in New York. While Franz was learning his new line of work, Anna Maria helped make ends meet by taking in laundry, which, after domestic service and needlework, was the third most common paid vocation for German women. "You probably never thought I would be a washerwoman, but in America you needn't be ashamed if you work," she wrote in 1851. Besides, in America "you don't have to soak things in lye," because "soap is cheap." Anna Maria also liked that "they don't carry the water on their heads here." The work hours were better in America too: "You start in the morning when it gets light and stop when it's nighttime." This was a hard life, but she and Franz managed to support themselves and finance the immigration of five of Anna Maria's siblings.[28]

The social life of immigrant men revolved around their saloons, but since no respectable unmarried woman would set foot in a tavern, men looking for a mate might promenade up the Bowery hoping to meet groups of "g'hals" out on the town. Immigrant women would not have been able spend a night out without a chaperone in their homeland, but the city's thousands of young immigrant women who worked as domestic servants had left those restrictions behind them when they set sail for America.

All working-class New Yorkers, and Germans in particular by the mid-1850s, went to the Bowery for a good time, especially on Saturday nights after they had just been paid. Young men with their dates, as well as large single-sex groups of journeymen and factory girls, cruised up and down the famous street simply to see and be seen. According to Walt Whitman, the Bowery presented "the most heterogeneous melange of any street in the city: stores of all kinds and people of all kinds are to be met with every forty rods." In contrast to Broadway, wrote journalist Junius Browne, with its fashionable shops and well-heeled patrons, the Bowery was "the Cheapside of New-York; the place of the People; the resort of mechanics and the laboring classes; the home and the haunt of a great social democracy . . . You may be the President, or a Major-General, or be Governor, or be Mayor, and you will be jostled and crowded off the sidewalk just the same." To a visiting South Carolinian, the Bowery looked "like a vast holiday fair two miles long."[29]

By the eve of the Civil War, the Bowery had become the particular haunt of German immigrants. It was home to the city's most famous beer halls, the Atlantic Garden and the Volks Garden, which faced each other just south of Canal Street. The Atlantic was the better known of the two, boasting several bars, a shooting gallery, billiard tables, bowling alleys, and an orchestra. One New Yorker remembered its "dense clouds of tobacco-smoke, and hurry of waiters, and banging of glasses, and calling for beer." Even if one had neither the money nor the inclination to patronize these famous watering holes, there was plenty to see, do, and buy out on the sidewalks. Street vendors thronged the boulevard, peddling oysters, hot yams, freshly roasted peanuts, hot corn in season, and pears baked in pans filled with syrup.[30]

Despite the lively social scene on the Bowery, immigrants in this era were much more likely to meet future mates either in their tenements or through introductions made by kin or friends from the same part of Ireland or the German states. In Five Points, for example, more than a quarter of all marriages taking place in the neighborhood's Roman Catholic church involved people who lived at the same address. More than half of all the Irish weddings involved immigrants born in the same Irish county. Germans exhibited the same traits, with three-quarters of Bavarians marrying Bavarians and two-thirds of Prussians marrying Prussians. At age seventeen, Samuel Gompers married a Jewish co-worker, Sophia Julian, a tobacco "stripper girl" also born in London.[31]

German New Yorkers were obsessive organizers, creating a mind-boggling number of *Vereine,* or recreational societies. Almost any shared characteristic could result in the creation of a *Verein.* Some were for immigrants from the same German state or city; others provided camaraderie for followers of the same trade; still others were based on political or artistic organizing principles. Singing societies were especially numerous. There was even a German bald-headed men's *Verein.*

The most important *Vereine* in Kleindeutschland were the *Turnvereine,* or gymnastics unions. *Turnvereine* had begun in the Napoleonic era as nationalistic societies aimed at making Germans more physically fit so they would be prepared to repulse French invasions. By mid-century, the "Turner" movement had become associated with republicanism and "free thought," and its members were especially active in the revolutions of 1848. Turners were as vigorous in their debates on German politics as they were in the gymnastic displays they put on at Kleindeutschland civic events. But the *Turnverein* members also knew how to have a good time, as evidenced by their annual picnic excursion. "We never saw the like before!" reported the *Times* concerning their 1855 extravaganza, attended by thirty thousand immigrants. "Such a pouring down of *lager bier,* such swarms of Germans, such extravagantly jolly times, we should not have expected to see if we had planned a year's travel . . . in Germany." The Irish had their Ancient Order of Hibernians and other benevolent societies, but in the Civil War era these never inspired the same communal devotion as the German *Vereine.*[32]

The unprecedented number of Irish and German immigrants who settled in New York in the late 1840s and early 1850s changed New York from a city with many immigrants to a metropolis defined by them. As noted, New York in 1855 contained more immigrants than native-born inhabitants (322,000 of 630,000 residents). By 1860, after immigration had slackened and the newcomers began having large numbers of children, the immigrant portion of the population fell back to 47 percent, even as the total population climbed to 814,000. The population of New York had more than doubled in only fifteen years. In 1845, New York did not even rank as one of the twenty most populous cities in the world, yet by 1860, only London, Paris, and Beijing were bigger.[33]

"New York has had a most extraordinary rise," marveled an English tourist. "There is no city in the world composed of so many different nations." An Irish visitor concurred, calling New Yorkers a "heterogeneous mass." The city's extraordinary growth had come about not merely because of record immigration, but also because so many of the immigrants made the decision to settle on Manhattan Island. And as the 1850s progressed, more and more immigrants were choosing to make New York their new home. By 1860, 52 percent of immigrants landing at Castle Garden reported that they planned to stay in New York State, and about 70 percent of them settled in New York City.[34]

Remarkably, relatively few New Yorkers complained as whole sectors of the workforce came to be dominated by the foreign-born. In the realm of politics, however, the famine era immigrants provoked far more hostility. By 1860, 69 percent of the city's voting-age inhabitants were foreign-born. "New York . . . is much more of a foreign than an American city," complained the *Evening Express,* whose editor, Erastus Brooks, represented the anti-immigrant Know Nothing Party in the New York State Senate. Previous generations of immigrants had been willing to defer to natives in most areas of politics, but now immigrants began to demand a larger role in the political life of the city, a fact that infuriated Know Nothings like Brooks. The resulting fight between natives and newcomers for control of the city's parties and political institutions would take nearly twenty years to be decided. By the time that battle was concluded, party "bosses" had taken over municipal politics and would rule the city, with only a few interruptions, for the next hundred years.[35]

TOP TEN SOURCES OF NEW YORK'S IMMIGRANTS, 1860

Ireland	203,740
German states	119,984
England	27,082
Scotland	9,208
France	8,074
Canada	3,899
Switzerland	1,771
Poland	1,586
Italy	1,464
West Indies	1,202
Total foreign-born	**383,717**
Total population	**813,669**

Source: *Population of the United States in 1860* (Washington, D.C., 1864), 609. Includes Manhattan plus Blackwell's, Randall's, and other harbor islands.

10

POLITICS

NEW YORK'S IRISH IMMIGRANTS were the first to become a major voting bloc in city politics. Yet in the first decades of the nineteenth century, the Irish tended to defer to the city's prominent native-born citizens in political affairs. Well-known merchants and manufacturers held the most important elective offices, even ward-level posts. With the adoption of universal white male suffrage in the 1820s, however, this deference began to wane. The election of the uneducated and uncultured Andrew Jackson as president in 1828 and his raucous inauguration the following year reflected the changed political landscape at the national level. New York's election riots of 1834 marked the turning point in this transformation in the city, as Irish immigrants began to seize power over their local affairs. First in Five Points, and then in other districts where the Irish were numerous, Irish Americans began to demand a greater voice in determining how and by whom they were governed.[1]

Irish New Yorkers voted overwhelmingly for Democrats like Jackson. By the eve of the Civil War, non-Democratic candidates had trouble garnering even 15 percent of the vote in heavily Irish districts. Opposition to laws that would restrict the sale of alcohol drew many Irish immigrants to the Democratic fold. So too did the party's renown as a friend of Catholic immigrants and a foe of nativism, a reputation that originated with its opposition to the Alien and Sedition Acts in 1798.

But substantive issues were rarely discussed during political contests in antebellum New York's Irish neighborhoods. Platforms and policy statements are conspicuously absent from local political campaigns. Instead, the outcome of electoral battles in New York's Irish enclaves usually turned on (1) the personal popularity of Democratic factional leaders; (2) the ability of those leaders to deliver patronage to their followers; and (3) the leaders' skill at using violence and intimidation at primary meetings and on election day to secure power and maintain it thereafter.

Just because the New York Irish were Democrats did not mean that Democrats welcomed them into their ranks, a fact exemplified by events that took place in the spring of 1842. Until that year, public schools in New York City were run by a Protestant organization, the Public School Society. Its curriculum featured readings from the Protestant King James Bible, the singing of Protestant hymns, and textbooks that — according to Catholics — presented "the grossest caricatures of the Catholic religion, blaspheming its mysteries, and ridiculing its authority." As immigration increased their numbers, New York Catholics complained bitterly about the overtly Protestant curriculum. Some Irish Catholics asked that religion be removed altogether from the schools. But a majority, following the lead of Roman Catholic leaders, asked the state to "split the school fund," diverting some tax revenue to Catholic schools to counter the Protestant influence of the Public School Society.[2]

The New York legislature, attempting to mollify these Catholics without losing the support of Protestants, passed the Maclay Act, which created a new city-run public school system while leaving the Public School Society and its schools intact. The new system's policies on Bible reading and other contentious issues would be set by school boards popularly elected in each New York City ward. Neither side was satisfied with the Maclay Act. New York's Roman Catholic leaders such as Bishop John Hughes, an immigrant from County Tyrone, Ireland, believed that the city's Catholics (who constituted a majority of the voters in at most one or two wards) would not receive fair treatment from the new boards, while Protestants perceived *any* changes to the prevailing system as capitulation to Catholic demands.[3]

One of these perturbed Protestants was poet Walt Whitman, then the young editor of a Democratic newspaper called the *Aurora*. Whitman condemned the Maclay Act as a "statute for the fostering and teaching of Catholic superstition" and insisted that New York Democrats should not submit to the ultimatums of Catholic leaders: "Shall these dregs of foreign filth — refuse of convents — scullions from Austrian monasteries — be permitted thus to dictate what Tammany *must* do?"* If Democrats yield to "the foreign riffraff . . . in this case, . . . there will be no end to their demands and their insolence." The best way to teach the

---

* By this point, the Democratic Party in New York City had become synonymous with the Saint Tammany Society, a fraternal order whose membership included most of the party's leading members, and whose headquarters, Tammany Hall, hosted meetings of the powerful general committee that ran the city's Democratic Party.

newcomers to respect American institutions, Whitman argued, was to resist Catholic educational demands.[4]

These Democratic divisions manifested themselves in the New York City municipal elections of 1842, which began just two days after passage of the Maclay Act. The Sixth Ward, with its particularly high concentration of Irish Catholic immigrant voters, was especially on edge. In the race for alderman, William Shaler captured the "regular" Democratic nomination, though a second Democratic ticket, headed by former alderman Jim Ferris, entered the fray as well. It was not unusual to find two Democratic candidates vying in a Sixth Ward aldermanic race. But as the *Herald* pointed out, "all this quarrel arose out of the School question also. For Con Donohue [Donoho], the former Collector of the ward, was turned out by the Common Council for the part he took in the School Question . . . When the nominations were made, Donohue was sacrificed and thrown overboard; on this his Irish friends rallied, made a new ticket, with Ferris at the head, to run it against Shaler, who had become very unpopular by his crusade against the little boys for crying Sunday newspapers." The entry into the contest of a third Democratic candidate, Shivers Parker, whom the *Herald* described as "the Bishop Hughes candidate" (meaning that he probably favored using a portion of the city's school funds to finance Catholic schools), further complicated matters, raising the real possibility that the Whig nomi-

New Yorkers casting ballots on election day in 1860. Voters were required to bring their own ballots; they usually picked them up at booths set up by each party outside polling places. Voters then went inside and deposited their ballots in the ballot "boxes," typically glass bowls set within wooden frames like the ones on the table in this illustration.

nee, earthenware manufacturer Clarkson Crolius Jr., might win the alderman's post.[5]

On election day in the Sixth Ward, each faction attempted to prevent the supporters of the others from casting their ballots. "The fight was bloody and horrible in the extreme," reported the *Herald*. Men were "so beaten about the head that they could not be recognized as human beings." A detachment of policemen, led by the mayor himself, arrived to quell the violence, but as soon as they left, nativist thugs invaded the Sixth Ward. Their goal, noted Whitman approvingly, was to rebuke "the outrageous insolence of [the ward's] foreign rowdies." Choosing their targets carefully, the rioters attacked Donoho's Orange Street grocery "and injured it considerably." Then they moved uptown to Hughes's home, where rioters broke windows, doors, and furniture before the authorities dispersed them. "Had it been the reverend hypocrite's head" that had been smashed, snarled Whitman, "instead of his windows, we could hardly find it in our soul to be sorrowful." The divisions among Sixth Ward Democrats allowed Crolius to carry the race for alderman, giving the Whigs a one-vote majority on that board. Though a Democrat, Whitman rejoiced at his own party's defeat in the contest to control the Board of Aldermen, asserting that it would teach Tammany to resist Catholic demands.[6]

The "School Question" continued to simmer for the next couple of years. The ire that native-born Americans felt as immigrants criticized the school system led to the formation of the anti-immigrant American Republican Party, which, in alliance with the Whigs, elected publisher James Harper mayor of New York in 1844. But with tens of thousands of immigrants arriving in the city annually, neither major party was willing to endorse the nativist agenda on a permanent basis. While the Whig dalliance with the nativists further cemented immigrants' ties to the Democrats, the Irish remained convinced that they would have to continue to battle within the Democratic Party to insure that their views were taken seriously and that Irish Americans won a fair share of the offices.[7]

Who were these candidates for whom Irish New Yorkers fought so fiercely? Until about 1840, wealthy merchants and manufacturers such as Crolius had held most elective offices, even in wards with many immigrants. In some parts of the city, this remained the case into the 1850s. But by 1840, Irish immigrants had begun to develop a different kind of political elite, made up of saloonkeepers, firefighters, and policemen.

The political power of these three groups resulted from their particular ability to influence voters. We have already witnessed the political power of saloonkeepers. The second route to political prominence ran through the volunteer fire department. In antebellum New York, a well-drilled fire company was just as likely to turn out in force to support a particular electoral slate as to extinguish a fire. The renowned toughs of the Irish American fire companies were often the ones who determined the outcome of primary meetings or general elections in an era when the ability to fight one's way to the ballot box or prevent one's opponents from doing so was often crucial to the outcome of elections in immigrant enclaves. Most companies admitted at least a few members to their exclusive ranks specifically for their fighting skills. Many of New York's antebellum politicians first came to prominence as foremen of the city's fire companies, and although they typically lacked the social graces necessary to make a run for citywide office, they might nonetheless rise as high as alderman or a police court judgeship. The first New Yorker to attain citywide office after having initiated his political career leading a fire company was "Boss" William M. Tweed. Though he was not an immigrant, Tweed's ultimate success, and that of Tammany Hall, the Democratic organization he eventually led, would be inextricably tied to his ability to win immigrant votes for Tammany.[8]

Another path to political power ran through the police department. It was almost impossible to get a position on the police force unless one had demonstrated loyalty to the party in power in previous campaign efforts. In return for such a high-paying and secure job (about $12 per week in the mid-1850s), the officer was expected not only to continue laboring for the party at election time, but also to contribute a portion of his salary (typically 2 percent) to party coffers and use his influence to assist party members who might run afoul of the law. Proving one's loyalty in this manner enabled many an Irish policeman to rise out of the ranks to both party leadership and elective office.[9]

An Irish New Yorker could sometimes claw his way to political power without first working in the police or fire department or owning a saloon. He might promise a Tammany precinct captain that he would deliver the votes of a couple of large tenements or of the district's immigrants from a certain Irish county. Or he might bring his gang to intimidate the leader's opponents at a primary meeting. Whether he offered voters or fighters, this political aspirant would expect something in return. While some asked for money, the more politically ambitious sought patronage — jobs with the local, state, or federal government — either for themselves or for their allies. Patronage was one of the keys to increasing political clout, especially for those who could not count on the support of a fire company or saloon customers. The aspiring politician who could deliver jobs to his supporters was in the best position to increase his influence. This was especially the case in Irish neighborhoods, whose residents found it so hard to land a steady job.[10]

However an Irish New Yorker had risen to prominence in his home district, it took additional work to parlay that prominence into a nomination. The leaders of each Democratic faction drew up a slate of candidates in advance of the primary (or "caucus") meeting. In heavily Irish neighborhoods, Democrats so outnumbered their opponents that the party always consisted of at least two factions and sometimes more. Each faction's leaders chose nominees for all the offices up for grabs (from alderman to constable to school board member) and candidates to represent the ward at nominating conventions for city, state, and federal posts. The faction leaders then prepared to present their tickets at the ward primary meeting, which typically took place about a month before election day.[11]

The convention's first vote, to select the meeting's chairman, was the most important. The faction whose candidate was chosen to preside would control the remainder of the proceedings and could, with official sanction, use its fighters to "maintain order," the typical excuse given for expelling the weaker faction's strongmen from the building. "Once," recalled New York politico Florence "Florry" Kernan, "when John Emmons was the candidate [for Sixth Ward alderman], nothing gave him the victory but the fact that Bill Scally [a noted pugilist], with Con Donoho and his men, arrived just in the nick of time to save the chairman from going out of the window, and the secretary following him; but their timely arrival changed the complexion of things, and sent the opposition chairman and officers out through the same window." Candidates could not sit idly by while hired bullies did the fighting for them. Those nominees who did not "take a hand along with their friends in battling for their cause" at the primary meetings would be derided as cowards. As a result, "knowing politicians" in Irish wards "never went well dressed to a caucus meeting," wrote Kernan. Nominations were "only won by black eyes, torn coats, and dilapidated hats."[12]

Women, who did not have the right to vote in New York until 1917, theoretically had little reason to take an interest in such battles. The world of politics lay outside of what was considered a woman's sphere of family and home. Yet when a female immigrant knew that her family's livelihood depended on political victories, she might find ways to make a difference. If her husband's job as a street sweeper or in the police department required staying in the good graces of the local saloonkeeper, she might flirt with him if she passed him on the street, or lobby the ward heeler's own spouse on her husband's behalf. The wives of political leaders had their own role to play as well. Kernan recalled that the wife of Five Points grocer Con Donoho was particular adept at influencing the outcome of neighborhood political contests:

When Con was away on business, his good woman, Mrs. Donoho, stood behind the counter to attend to all customers; and an able helpmate was she to just such a rising man and politician as Con gave promise to be. Should Mrs. Conlan, or Mrs. Mulrooney, or the wife of any other good voter of the old Sixth [Ward], come for her groceries, or with a milk-pitcher for a drop of good gin, or a herring to broil for the good man's twelve o'clock dinner, she would avail herself of the opportunity to have a bit of talk with her concerning how her James, Patrick, or Peter would vote on the approaching aldermanic election . . . and heaven help the customer if she talked up in favor of John Foote on the split,* or hinted that her man believed in Bill Nealus. If she did, the smallest herring or potatoes to be found in the barrel would be dealt out with a jerk, and a wink with it, that said when she had sense, and wanted to see her old man with a broom in his hand [as a city-employed street sweeper] and ten shillings a day, work or no work, and pay from Con's own hand on Saturday nights, she had only to make her husband send the Nealuses to the devil, and hurrah for Felix O'Niel! In this way, Mrs. Con Donoho made many a convert to the banner of her liege lord, the bold Con Donoho.[13]

When the day of the general election finally arrived, the scenes of intimidation found in the Democratic primary often repeated themselves at each polling station. Sometimes fighting broke out between the factions that had battled at the caucus meeting. More often, fighters in immigrant neighborhoods patrolled the polls to suppress the Whig or Republican vote. They did so less to insure a victory in the local races, in which the Democrats rarely had to fear defeat, than to suppress the citywide or statewide vote of those other parties. Doing so might tip the balance in one of those contests toward the Democrats.[14]

In contrast to New York's Irish immigrants, who jumped quickly and enthusiastically into the city's political frays, German immigrants seemed politically apathetic. The German newcomer "cares . . . little who governs and what is done over him," commented the *Times* in a typical assessment. In the early 1850s one finds very few German Americans playing a prominent role in New York City politics. Even in Kleindeutschland, Irish surnames always far outnumbered German ones on ballots in the Civil War era, even in races for minor ward-level offices. Until the mid-1850s, no more than one German surname appeared on any party's Little Germany ballot, and the nominations the Germans

---

* If someone ran for office "on the split," it meant that he had lost his bid for the regular Democratic nomination but decided to stay in the race as an "independent" candidate. Doing so "split" the party's vote and, in Five Points and other Democratic strongholds, created the possibility that the candidate of the Whig or Republican Party might carry the election.

did get were always for the lowliest positions, such as constable or election inspector.[15]

New York's Germans did, however, maintain distinct organizations within each party, something the Irish never did. In the month or so before any given election, newspapers brimmed with announcements of meetings of German Democrats, Whigs, or Republicans. As election day drew near, these gatherings inevitably concluded with torchlight parades designed both to rally support for the party's ticket and to increase the visibility of German immigrants on the New York political scene.[16]

Like the Irish, German New Yorkers voted overwhelmingly Democratic and did so for many of the same reasons. Even immigrants who had not yet arrived in New York when Harper was elected mayor in 1844 would have been reminded by other Democrats that the nativist publisher's victory had been made possible by the Whigs' tacit endorsement of Harper through the withdrawal of their own candidate. Germans also perceived the Whigs as the party most inclined to restrict or ban the sale of alcohol, something they adamantly opposed.

German political apathy ended rather abruptly in 1854, when nativism, prohibitionism, and a third issue, slavery, simultaneously erupted in controversy. In the first months of the year, the New York legislature began to consider a bill, sponsored by Whig Myron Clark, that would have banned the sale of alcohol in the state. (Such statutes, modeled after one enacted in Maine in 1851, were known in that era as "Maine Laws.") The bill passed both houses of the New York legislature in the first days of spring, but Democrat Horatio Seymour vetoed the measure. Temperance advocates vowed to continue fighting to enact a Maine Law. When New York Whigs nominated Clark for governor, New York's Germans vowed to make his defeat their highest priority.[17]

In the very months when the liquor prohibition bill was wending its way through the legislature in Albany, an equally controversial bill, one that would *repeal* a different kind of prohibition, was under consideration in Congress. That legislation, proposed by Illinois Democrat Stephen A. Douglas and eventually known as the Kansas-Nebraska Act, would end the ban on slavery, in place since 1820, in most of the land acquired in the Louisiana Purchase. Under Senator Douglas's proposal, the settlers in each territory would vote on whether or not to allow slavery. Passage of the Kansas-Nebraska Act in May of 1854 brought German anti-slavery activists to the forefront of Kleindeutschland's political stage.[18]

Just when the Maine Law and the Kansas-Nebraska Act were roiling New York politics, a new anti-immigrant political organization, the Know Nothing Party, burst onto the political scene, creating a third reason for German New Yorkers to become more politically active. Its peculiar name resulted from its origin as a secret fraternal order; when asked about the group, members were required to feign ignorance. With so many New Yorkers saying "I know nothing" when reporters asked about a surprise electoral ticket that appeared unexpectedly at polling places all over New York City on election day in November 1853, the *Tribune* dubbed the new organization the "Know Nothing Party." The name stuck, even though members preferred to call their organization the "American Party."

The Know Nothings were far more popular and powerful than either Morse's Native American Democratic Association of the 1830s or Harper's American Republican Party of the 1840s. Although the previous nativist parties had managed to elect a mayor in New York and a couple of congressmen in Pennsylvania, the Know Nothings in 1854 and 1855 elected eight governors, more than one hundred congressmen, and thousands of state legislators and local officials. The Know Nothings were especially popular in New England. Massachusetts voters elected more than four hundred Know Nothings to the state legislature in 1854, while the remaining parties combined — Whigs, Democrats, and Republicans — elected just three.[19]

Several factors contributed to this sudden success. First, the Know Nothings' popularity peaked in 1854, the very year when immigration to the United States reached an all-time high. The Know Nothings also benefited from the renewed efforts made by Catholic leaders in 1853 and 1854 to win state aid for Catholic schools, something most Protestants continued to vehemently oppose. Know Nothings in the North also drew support by endorsing temperance legislation and opposing the Kansas-Nebraska Act.

In New York City, where immigrants made up two-thirds of the adult population and neither the temperance nor the anti-slavery movement was particularly popular, Know Nothing recruiters focused on other issues. First, they charged that Ireland and the German states were dumping their paupers onto America's shores in order to shift the burden of supporting them to New York City's taxpayers. "Our Alms Houses are filled with foreigners," complained the *Express,* the Know Nothings' leading New York newspaper, while "our citizens have their pockets drained to clothe and feed" them. Even the Republican *Tribune,* no friend of the Know Nothing movement, agreed that New York was becoming "a Botany Bay* for German paupers."[20]

The Know Nothings' claims that German governments were shipping thousands of their mendicants to the United States as a cost-saving measure, once thought to be the product of overwrought nativist imaginations, were actually

---

* Botany Bay was the notorious penal colony in Australia where England sent its undesirables.

not so far-fetched. Virtually all the German states instituted secret programs in
the 1840s or early 1850s to transport criminals and paupers to the United States
and Canada. The German state of Hanover actually halted its program of state-
subsidized emigration of undesirables in reaction to Know Nothing protests.[21]

New York Know Nothings also condemned Catholic immigrants for interfering with America's public schools — both by trying to siphon off tax dollars for Catholic schools and by demanding that the Bible no longer be read
in school (a part of the curriculum Protestants considered essential but Catholics opposed). Furthermore, while later generations of nativists would condemn immigrants for their radicalism, Know Nothings complained of Catholic newcomers' reactionary tendencies, claiming that Catholic opposition had
doomed the efforts to overthrow the monarchies of Europe in 1848 and replace
them with republics. Many immigrants agreed with this critique of the Catholic Church. "If the 'Roman Catholic press' would confine itself to religious matters," asserted the editors of the New York *Irish-American,* "and not intermed-
dle with the school question, not apologise for and excuse and shield European
despotisms, not sneer at and ridicule radicalism and republicanism, . . . we,
most certainly, should have no *Know-Nothingism.*"[22]

Know Nothings also complained that immigrants had brought unaccept-
able levels of violence to the city's political life. The increase in "election riots"
was directly attributable to the rise of "our foreign population," charged the *Express.* "Government is a science, which an Irishman, who cannot read, or a German, who knows not our language, and customs, and traditions, cannot learn
in a single day." Even many non–Know Nothings found merit in this argument.
"Our immigrant population is deplorably clannish, misguided, and prone to
violence," lamented the *Tribune.* "We never saw a party of Americans-born approach a peaceable poll with weapons in their hands; we *have* seen Irish bands
of two or three hundred, armed with heavy clubs, traversing the streets on election day and clearly provoking a fight." Know Nothings promised to restore vir-
tue and fairness to American politics.[23]

The final facet of the Know Nothing worldview was that the United States
could not absorb and assimilate all the immigrants seeking to settle within its
borders. "This vast influx of aliens to our shores has been going on in regularly
increasing ratio[s] for the period of half a century," argued the *New York Mirror,* "until our land groans under the weight of ignorance, superstition and pestilent dogmas which they have infused into our population . . . When we consider that this immense mass of alien citizens are under the control of a vicious
priesthood — that they are wedded to the worst forms of superstition and vice
— that their feelings are diametrically averse to the Protestant institutions of

this country, . . . how manifest is it that the papacy is acquiring a dangerous ascendancy in the United States?"[24]

In response to the charge that they were bigots, New York's Know Nothings pointed to their benign attitude toward the city's Jews. "The Jews let us alone, — and we all let them alone," boasted the editors of the *Express.* "However repugnant their religion may be, — their religion is Republican, and consistent with the peace, prosperity, and existence of a Commonwealth." The city's Catholic voters, in contrast, could not vote their consciences but, according to Know Nothings, had to cast ballots exactly as their priests and bishops commanded.[25]

Know Nothings in immigrant-dominated cities like Philadelphia and New York promoted themselves not as anti-immigrant but as anti-Catholic. Protestant immigrants, in fact, often harbored more intense anti-Catholic sentiment than the Know Nothings. Wherever there is anti-Catholic street preaching "or an attack on [a] Catholic church or convent," complained *The Citizen,* a New York Irish Catholic periodical, you can "be sure that certain faithful *Irish* Calvinists are foremost" among the instigators. The president of the city's predominantly Irish Catholic Cartmen's Society likewise noted at the height of the Know Nothing movement that "a loud outcry has been raised against adopted citizens . . . And who raised this cry? Why, foreigners themselves — Englishmen, brutal Britishers, and North of Ireland weavers, butchers and ruffians." These men could not join Know Nothing lodges, but many of them supposedly voted the Know Nothing ticket anyway.[26]

The Know Nothings proposed three main remedies for the problems they associated with immigration: (1) Protestants must resist Catholic demands to make changes to the American school system; (2) immigrants should be required to wait twenty-one years, rather than five, until they could become citizens and vote; and (3) immigrants and Catholics should be banned from elective and appointive political offices. Outside New York City, Know Nothings endorsed prohibiting the sale of liquor as well.[27]

Of the three issues — temperance, slavery, and nativism — that rocked the political landscape in 1854, temperance seems to have been the one that motivated German voters most. The Maine Law was omnipresent in both the German press and the mainstream media's reporting on German political activity. "GERMANS! — The pride of your fatherland, lager bier, is imperiled," cried the *Herald* as it implored them to vote the Democratic ticket on November 7, 1854. "Next they'll want your pipes." Addressing a crowd from atop a barrel that same day, a German grocer warned that the Whigs wanted "to meddles mit te croceries and mit te lager bier places. I shall say you mush not vote to dem. I shall say eef you shall vote for dem my pizeness shall pe all proke smash to pieces." Nevertheless, Clark won the governorship, prompting German New Yorkers to fear that the enactment of a prohibitory law was imminent. Germans denounced "the dark aims hidden under these pretended moral movements" and vowed to resist such legislation, "peaceably if we can, forcibly if we must."[28]

Such sentiments reflected more than the simple desire of Germans to drink. Immigrants organized much of their political activity in their saloons and beer halls. Prohibition would strike at their political power, not just their drinking habits. Most immigrant political leaders could afford to run for office only because of the income generated from the sale of alcohol. Germans agreed with the Herald's assertion that "the Know Nothing Order is the sign of the first movement against these . . . grog shop politicians." Thus, the German grocer speaking from atop a barrel predicted that "eef dem mans [the prohibitionists] pe made pig den all der Toichmans shall pe made so smaller as notings mitout lager bier." The Germans' social lives, economic well-being, and political clout would all suffer if "dey shall pe all dry up like ter Yankees."[29]

Those New Yorkers who hoped to pry German Americans away from the grip of the Democratic Party thought that the Kansas-Nebraska Act might make such a realignment possible. For while Seymour's veto had killed New York's Maine Law in April 1854, Congress had enacted the Kansas-Nebraska bill and President Franklin Pierce had signed it into law a month later. Yet New York's German community was bitterly divided over the issue. When German Democrats called a meeting in February to demonstrate support for the bill, the gathering did not go according to plan. Half of the two thousand Germans in attendance refused to endorse as meeting chairman a German American who supported the pro-slavery legislation. The anti–Kansas-Nebraska nominee for chairman could not secure a majority vote from the audience either. According to the Herald, the shouts of those in attendance, "louder than the revelry among the imps of Pandemonium, prevented a decision in favor of any one." Pleas for "compromise and conciliation" fell on deaf ears. A German priest attempted to calm the crowd, but "he was received with cries of 'Down with Catholicism.' 'Down with the Pope.' 'Down with him.'"[30]

When brewer Erhard Richter, the leader of the meeting's anti-slavery contingent, tried to address the audience from the speakers' platform, "a rush was made for it" by the pro-slavery Germans, reported the Herald, "and it was upset and smashed into pieces and Richter laid sprawling upon the heads of the crowd." At this point, according to the Herald's account, there "began a general fight. Men were tossed over heads, trampled under foot, and pulled and pummelled in every quarter." Some of the combatants attempted to raise a make-shift standard declaring, in German, "No Slaves," but that merely enraged the pro-slavery forces. "The fight then became terrific; some seized pieces of broken table, knocked men over the head and brought blood from several." After two hours of this mayhem, the conclave dissolved without ever having come to order. Such scenes were common at primary meetings in Irish wards, but this kind of bloodshed was unprecedented at German immigrant political gatherings.[31]

The anti–Kansas-Nebraska movement brought the city's "Forty-eighters" (leaders of the failed German revolutions of 1848 who had fled to the United States to avoid arrest) into New York politics for the first time. On the third of March, the German opponents of the Kansas-Nebraska bill held their own meeting, and again the hall was packed with several thousand immigrants. "Lager bier," reported the *Herald,* "flowed in abundance, and the majority of the sons of the 'Faderland' appeared to show their contempt for all prohibitory liquor laws" by consuming "copious draughts of that refreshing beverage."

After the assemblage elected Richter chair of the meeting, German "Turners" marched into the hall, led by Colonel Franz Sigel, who had helped lead the failed revolution in Baden in 1848 and was now a New York schoolteacher. The Turners were accompanied by their band "playing the 'Marseillaise,' and bearing the red republican flag. They were received with a tremendous outburst of enthusiasm." Next came another group "bearing the tri-colored revolutionary flag of Germany, which also obtained its share of applause. Then came several banners, one inscribed 'No Slavery,' another, 'No Maine Liquor Law,' and a third was a caricature intended as a lampoon on the editor of the *Staats Zeitung* [the leading German-language newspaper in New York], who made himself obnoxious to a portion of the Germans by his support of Mr. Douglas's bill." According to the *Herald,* these ex-revolutionaries denounced the Kansas-Nebraska bill "in the most unmeasured language, and every opprobrious epithet in the vocabulary was heaped upon it most unsparingly."[32]

Tammany Hall made sure to stage a German pro–Kansas-Nebraska Act rally a few weeks later that drew an even larger crowd than the anti–Kansas-Nebraska meeting. Nevertheless, fearing that German defections might cost them in the 1854 elections, Democrats for the first time in years put German Americans on their citywide tickets. "The German Democrats," as the *Times* later put it, were no longer willing "to quietly give their votes and get none of the spoils." Though the Germans were nominated for relatively insignificant posts, the fact that they received any citywide nominations at all indicated that their votes were now considered both important and potentially up for grabs.[33]

Given the Whigs' past support for nativism and temperance, their leaders understood why few German immigrants would vote for their candidates. Yet with the demise of the Whig Party and the rise of the new Republican Party, which put limiting the spread of slavery above all other issues, Republicans hoped to win a large portion of the New York German vote. German Republicans organized sizable rallies in the city for the 1856 Republican presidential nominee, John C. Frémont. At these gatherings, the heroes of '48 would address New York's German immigrants in their native tongue, exhorting them to be faithful to the republican cause in Germany by joining the Republican Party in the United States. Frederick Hecker, who in 1848 along with Sigel had led the failed attempt to overthrow the government of Baden, told a New York audience that the "honor of the German name and of the German nation, and the hatred of aristocratic arrogance and tyranny, make it the sacred and imperative duty of every German to enter the lists against Slavery and the Slaveocracy." Another exile argued, "We have not come here to this country in order to go hand-in-hand with those who stand in the same category with our aristocrats at home." The *Times*, a Republican paper, confidently predicted that "the majority of the Germans in New-York were now with the Republicans."[34]

But election day proved that the *Times'* assessment had been wildly overoptimistic. In no part of Kleindeutschland did Frémont come close to defeating Democrat James Buchanan. Republicans tried to sugarcoat the results, defying mathematical logic by insisting that "in several of the strong German Wards of this City probably full *one-third* of the Germans voted with the Republicans." The estimate made by a German paper that only six thousand New York Germans had cast Republican ballots was probably closer to the mark.[35]

Why did the anti-slavery movement fail to motivate German New Yorkers to switch parties? Germans seem to have believed that the Republican Party was just as tainted with nativism and prohibitionism as the Whig Party had been. The many instances in which Republicans cooperated with northern Know Nothings, they argued, made it impossible to cast a vote for free soil without also tacitly endorsing Know Nothingism. "If you Americans will but present to the Germans a truly free party — free in every respect [i.e., not tainted with nativism] — you will be sure to command their votes, and you might count upon their best aid in forming such a party," commented one German American. Other Germans cited the liquor issue as decisive: because many upstate Republicans had pledged to enact alcohol restrictions, German immigrants would not vote for their New York City brethren. German Republicans asked their countrymen at least to support Republicans for national offices that did not involve enforcement of the liquor laws, but such pleas went unheeded.[36]

Germans' association of the Republican Party with liquor restriction seemed to be confirmed after the Republicans won New York's statewide races in 1856. Although support for outright prohibition had faded, the new Republican-con-

The Bowery Boy Riot of July 1857 was sparked by Five Pointers' unhappiness with the state legislature's decision to disband the city police force and replace it with a state-run unit that hired far fewer
immigrants.

trolled legislature enacted a law in 1857 that closed New York's saloons and beer
gardens on Sundays and imposed steep licensing fees on all establishments that
sold alcohol. Fearing that New York City's police would not implement the statutes, the legislature disbanded the entire city police force and replaced it with a
state-run unit from which immigrants were largely excluded and whose ranks
were filled with former Know Nothings. (The Know Nothing Party had almost
entirely disintegrated by the end of 1856.)[37]

New York's immigrants greeted the unwelcome legislation, which went into
effect on July 1, 1857, with a series of unprecedented riots. Five Pointers attacked
the new policemen on the Fourth of July when the officers attempted to break
up drunken fights. The neighborhood's gangs joined in the melee that ensued,
and the fighting soon devolved into a turf war between rival Irish gangs. What
had begun as a shower of brickbats aimed from tenement rooftops devolved
into a gunfight from behind huge street barricades. When the "Bowery Boy
Riot" finally subsided at dusk, twelve New Yorkers, almost all Irish immigrants,
lay dead.[38]

A week later, the city's German community also made good on its vow to
resist the temperance legislation. When the new policemen came to Kleindeutschland on July 12 to enforce the Sunday closing law, Germans in the Seventeenth Ward pelted them with stones. When the officers called in reinforcements, the violence escalated, and immigrant Johann Müller was shot dead
by one of the inexperienced patrolmen. "This is what we can expect now," ex-

claimed one outraged German immigrant. "We shall be shot down like dogs; when our husbands go out in the morning, we do not know [if] they will ever come back again."

News of Müller's death enraged the residents of Kleindeutschland, and they battled the police for much of the following day until the militia was called in to quell the crowds. "It would seem that the City of New York was singled out as a target by the dastard Legislature for obnoxious laws that would make Berlin or Munich swim in blood," charged one immigrant. "Great God! What did we come here for if such things can be in this land of the brave and home of the free?" German immigrants blamed the rioting on an overreaching Republican Party whose "farmer" legislators in Albany were seen as meddling in the city's affairs. "Shall we submit tamely and quietly to this tyranny?" asked a speaker in German at a protest meeting held on the fourteenth. *"Nein!"* was the crowd's emphatic response. Republicans' attempts in the same legislative session to extend the waiting period before immigrants could vote reinforced the notion that Republicans were nativists as well as prohibitionists, and helped the Democrats maintain their grip on the vast majority of the German voters in the city.[39]

As for slavery, the city's Irish, Catholic, and Democratic press consistently argued that both abolitionism, and even the more moderate movement to prevent the spread of slavery to additional American territory, threatened the survival of the nation. "We are totally opposed to Abolitionism in every shape; — not because we desire to perpetuate slavery, but to preserve the Union," announced the *Irish-American* in 1853. "That slavery is inconsistent with the Declaration of Independence and our Republican Constitution we will not affect to deny," its editors admitted four years later. But they argued that Americans had been "forced to accept the 'institution' of slavery" as one of the compromises that created the nation, and that those pledges could not subsequently be broken.[40]

Some New York Democrats argued that slavery was beneficial to blacks and whites alike. The *Day Book,* a Democratic paper aligned with Mayor Fernando Wood, who was especially popular among the city's immigrants, asserted that "'slavery,' or negro subordination to the will and guidance of the superior white man, is a law of nature, a fixed truth, an eternal necessity, an ordinance of the Almighty, in conflict with which the efforts of human power sink into absolute and unspeakable insignificance." Free blacks such as those in New York had been better off as slaves, argued the newspaper's editors, because while they were now still subordinate to whites, they were no longer guaranteed the subsistence of food, clothing, and shelter that plantation owners provided. Most

Irish immigrants believed that abolitionists ought to focus their attention on the 6 million white slaves of the British in Ireland before interceding on behalf of the 3 million black slaves in the United States.[41]

Although immigrants tried to stay out of the slavery debate for as long as possible, by the mid-1850s it was unavoidable. The editors of the New York *Irish-American,* a nonpartisan journal that focused its political coverage on Ireland and rarely discussed American elections, felt compelled to admit in early 1858 that whether to allow slavery in Kansas, and Douglas's role in the congressional fight over that issue, dominated "thought, talk, and writing, North and South . . . Few sounds are uttered without these all-absorbing names being heard." This was the case even in New York's immigrant enclaves, because nominations for office and even many patronage appointments had begun to depend on whether one supported Douglas (who opposed the "Lecompton Constitution," which would allow slavery in Kansas) or President James Buchanan (who advocated approval of the Lecompton document).[42]

By this point, immigrant New Yorkers, and especially the Irish, began to demand not only patronage but prestigious elective offices as well. In 1858, when the Irish insisted that they be given two of the dozen or so positions on the citywide ticket, native-born and German immigrant Democrats complained that such a ticket "would be entirely 'too Irish.'" But the Irish prevailed, electing John Kelly and John Clancy (both the children of Irish immigrants) as sheriff and city clerk, respectively. A German immigrant running on the Republican ticket won election as an almshouse governor in that same year, not because he drew more Germans than usual to the Republican ticket, but because the nomination of a popular Irish immigrant, James Lynch, on an insurgent Democratic ticket split the Democratic vote, allowing the Republican to win this race. Henceforth, Irish and German Americans would receive larger shares of the citywide nominations.[43]

Just weeks after the contests of 1858 had been decided, New Yorkers began discussing the upcoming presidential election of 1860, knowing that a Republican victory might bring about southern secession. This possibility became a cause for alarm even in immigrant enclaves that had once paid relatively little attention to national issues and contests. In early 1859, Clancy could be found at his favorite Five Points saloon, the Ivy Green, regaling the tavern's patrons with his enthusiasm for the candidacy of Douglas, "the Little Giant" from Illinois. Douglas had just won reelection to the U.S. Senate over Republican Abraham Lincoln, a name few New York immigrants would have recognized before that contest.[44]

When Douglas and Lincoln became the Democratic and Republican nominees for president in 1860, few New York City immigrants were inclined to support "Honest Abe." The city's leading Catholic newspaper, the *Freeman's Journal,* though nominally nonpartisan, took the unusual step of condemning Lincoln's candidacy. "It is not the business of the political power to settle moral questions," the *Journal* argued in explaining its stance. Only when a majority of Americans North and South could be brought by "moral suasion" to oppose slavery would it be appropriate for politicians to interfere with the institution. Democrats also used other arguments to woo immigrant voters, including a circular in German aimed at tailors (and reprinted in English in the *Herald*), warning that "if Lincoln is elected to-day, the bread will be taken out of the mouths of your children. The trade with the South will be entirely destroyed, and that is the mainstay of your occupation . . . Vote to maintain yourselves and your children, and let the negro take care of himself." An editorial in the *Herald* directed at "IRISH AND GERMAN LABORERS" likewise predicted that "if Lincoln is elected to-day you will have to compete with the labor of four million emancipated negroes . . . The North will be flooded with free negroes, and the labor of the white man will be depreciated and degraded . . . Go to the polls, every man of you, and cast your votes against Lincoln and abolitionism. Vote early." The *Daily News* appealed to the immigrants' fears of nativism in calling on them to reject the Republicans, who had tried to close the Germans' beer

 coln rally passing "Newspaper Row" (now Park Row) opposite City Hall Park a few
 eks before the 1860 presidential election.

halls and treated Irishmen like "barbarians . . . Help us crush them," implored the *News*, "as they have sought and will seek again to crush you."[45]

Lincoln managed to poll a respectable 40 percent of the vote in the most heavily German ward in the city, but that was a smaller proportion of votes than the district had given to the hopeless candidacy of Whig presidential nominee Winfield Scott in 1852. In the Irish Fourth and Sixth wards, Lincoln could muster only 13 percent of the vote. He won the election with very little support from New York's immigrants.[46]

This election had an even bigger impact on New York's immigrants than the usual patronage turnover. By March 4, 1861, the day Lincoln took the oath of office on the steps of the Capitol, seven southern slave states had seceded from the Union and formed a new nation, the Confederate States of America. A month later, after South Carolinians attacked Fort Sumter, four more states joined the Confederacy.

New York and the nascent Confederate nation could hardly have been more different. More immigrants lived in the ten square miles of Manhattan below 42nd Street than lived in the entire 770,400 square miles of the Confederacy. Yet politically, the Confederates and New York's immigrants seemed, on the surface at least, very much alike, as both had overwhelmingly rejected Abraham Lincoln's candidacy for president. Confederate leaders such as Robert E. Lee were certain that sympathy for the southern cause and disdain for Republicans in places like New York would enable the South to win its independence. But Confederates miscalculated. Most New York immigrants may have hated the Republican Party, but they loved their adopted homeland and did not want to see it break apart. New York and its immigrants would play a key role in maintaining the Union whose freedoms and opportunities they so dearly cherished.

11

WAR

FELIX BRANNIGAN OUGHT to be remembered for something else. The Irish immigrant, who arrived in the United States at age seventeen in 1855, must have been the kind of man others looked up to, because upon enlisting in Company A of New York's Seventy-fourth Infantry Regiment on July 18, 1861, he was immediately made a corporal rather than a lowly private. Eleven months later, he became a sergeant. Brannigan fought bravely in the Peninsula Campaign southeast of Richmond in the spring and summer of 1862, at Chancellorsville north of Richmond in May 1863, and at Gettysburg in July of that same year. For his valor at Chancellorsville, Congress awarded Brannigan the Medal of Honor, a decoration bestowed on only 1,522 of the Union's 2 million soldiers.[1]

Brannigan is remembered not for his bravery, however, but instead for two sentences in a letter he wrote to his sister in the summer of 1862. Brannigan reiterated the claims of his commander, General George B. McClellan, who insisted that his men would not have needed to retreat after almost reaching the Confederate capital in the first summer days of 1862 but for Lincoln's last-moment decision to keep part of McClellan's army in Washington to safeguard the capital. Echoing McClellan, Brannigan told his sister that he and his comrades were outnumbered three to one, when in fact McClellan's army was almost twice as large as that of Confederate commander Robert E. Lee. Brannigan contended that there would have been enough men both to protect Washington and to take Richmond if northerners would only volunteer in sufficient numbers. "It makes even a foreigners blood boil to look at the apathy" in the North, Brannigan fumed. He could not understand why so many northerners were unwilling to defend "a country which is looked upon by the oppressed of all nations as a haven of liberty."

Many in Congress thought that the answer to the perceived manpower shortage was to allow African Americans (both free blacks and runaway slaves) to fight for the Union, but Brannigan would not countenance that idea. He was willing to "let the niggers be sent here to use the pick and shovel" to dig entrenchments "in the broiling sun as we are now doing," he said, because that would free up white men to "take up a soldiers tool — the gun and bayonet." Such menial labor was the only African American war effort that Brannigan would sanction. "We don't want to fight side and side by the nigger," he insisted. "We think we are too superior a race for that."[2]

These last two sentences are quoted in dozens of history books because they perfectly fit our preconception of the Irish immigrant's role in the Civil War.[3] The Irish may have fought for the Union, but they never embraced the egalitarian wartime goals that Lincoln and the Republican Party eventually advocated. The limits of Irish immigrants' support for the war effort became especially clear in the event most closely associated with New York's role in the war — the New York City draft riots of July 1863. During four days and three nights, some bordering on total anarchy, mobs of New Yorkers dominated by Irish immigrants went on a rampage against prominent Republicans and the city's African American populace. The rioters killed about a dozen black New Yorkers, set dozens of fires, and fought pitched battles against the police, local militia units, and national guardsmen. By the end of the rioting, more than one hundred New Yorkers lay dead. The draft riots are still, to this day, the deadliest episode of civil unrest in all of American history.[4]

Yet Brannigan's story, it turns out, is far more complicated than historians have realized. Three days before Brannigan wrote his oft-quoted letter, the president told several cabinet members of his intention to issue the Emancipation Proclamation, which, in addition to freeing slaves, would for the first time allow African Americans to enlist in the military. Nearly 200,000 answered the call when the proclamation went into effect on January 1, 1863, fighting in units commanded by white officers. While many whites refused to lead these regiments, one who accepted such an assignment was Felix Brannigan. In December 1864, Brannigan became second lieutenant of the Thirty-second Infantry Regiment of U.S. Colored Troops, stationed at Hilton Head, South Carolina. Four months later he was promoted to first lieutenant of the 103rd U.S. Colored Infantry Regiment, which occupied Savannah from the beginning of 1865 until April 1866.

After the war, Brannigan moved to Washington, where he clerked in the Treasury Department. He was living in New York City when he became a U.S. citizen in 1868. But soon he was back in Washington, attending law school at Columbian College, now George Washington University. When he completed his legal studies in 1871, Brannigan landed a plum job as a federal prosecutor, a position he could not have secured had he not become a Republican.[5] The attorney general made Brannigan the assistant U.S. attorney in Jackson, Missis-sippi, where, among other things, he was responsible for prosecuting Klansmen who attempted to intimidate African American voters. When Brannigan's boss resigned two years later, President Ulysses S. Grant promoted the Irish immi-grant to the office's top post, making him United States attorney for the south-ern district of Mississippi, where prosecution of crimes against freedmen con-tinued to be a major part of his responsibilities.[6]

As Brannigan's career demonstrates, the Civil War changed many Ameri-cans. Abraham Lincoln, who at the beginning of the war in 1861 had allowed his military commanders to return runaway slaves to their southern owners, had by the summer of 1862 embraced the cause of emancipation, though he continued to worry that blacks and whites would not be able to live together peaceably in postwar America. Brannigan had changed as well. In the summer of 1862, he was an enlisted man condemning "those legislators who have made the 'nigger' the all-important question." By the end of 1864, he was an officer leading ex-slaves back into the South as occupiers, and a few years later he was a dedicated Republican. Brannigan, who was a New Yorker for only a short pe-riod of time, is clearly not a "typical" Irish immigrant. But his story does show that the draft riots were merely a part of the immigrants' Civil War experiences, a dramatic but not necessarily defining episode in a very large and complicated drama.[7]

The typical New York immigrant was far less invested in the sectional con-flict than other Americans. Newcomers to the United States focused far more on their financial goals than on political debates in Congress, especially those concerning an institution like slavery that did not seem to impact their daily lives. Immigrants looked on incredulously, therefore, as southern states began seceding in December 1860, wondering how Americans could jeopardize their wealth and prosperity over a fraternal squabble.

Immigrants such as Julius and Lisette Wesslau from Prussia felt the need to explain the crisis to Julius's parents:

For a long time now there's been a big fight about slavery: in the South, where it is too hot for the white race of men to work, for centuries now people have been buying black Negroes, and they grow cotton so exten-sively on their plantations that they now constitute the world market in cotton. In the northern states slavery is seen as unjust, and they abolished it more than 50 years ago, and they don't want it to spread to the new, un-settled territories in America . . . For many years the presidents were of the southern party, but this fall the candidate of the northern states won. Now the southern states are claiming that their property and their lives are in danger, and they have cut themselves off from the Union.

For immigrants focused on economic advancement and long-term financial security, a civil war could prove catastrophic to all they had worked so hard to achieve. Julius Wesslau and his older brother Karl, for example, had started out as journeymen cabinetmakers when they arrived in New York in 1850. By 1853 they had managed to open their own furniture-making business, and in 1860 they were selling their bureaus, desks, and chairs to customers all across the United States. The possible breakup of the Union threatened them on a very personal level. Even in December 1860, when only a single state had seceded, customers from all over the South had begun repudiating their debts to the Wesslaus. "Our main business was with the South, and up to now we've lost about 600 dollars, and we may lose most of another 1,500 dollars, and we've let half of our workers go, and if things don't get better soon we'll have to send more away," Julius and Lisette wrote at the end of December. "Business all over the country has collapsed. The South always bought its industrial goods from the North, and we can't continue to exist without them."

Perhaps as a result, the Wesslaus had little sympathy for Lincoln or the Republican Party. "The North would have been well advised to stay out of things that are none of its business," they wrote disgustedly. "Everyone in business hopes things will be settled, but now the ball has started to roll, and no one knows what will happen. It would be a real shame, though, if a country like this, which has no equal in the world in terms of wealth and riches, should be destroyed because of the willfulness of its politicians." The Wesslaus' laid-off German workers, and other German immigrants whose livelihoods depended directly or indirectly on trade with the South, undoubtedly agreed.[8]

Many observers believed that New York's Irish immigrants sympathized even more strongly with southern secessionists than did the city's disgruntled Germans. Southern nationalist Charles C. Spencer of Alabama, who visited New York in December, reported to a Charleston newspaper: "I hear many expressions of sympathy for us in this City, and in case of an attempt to coerce us, I believe we can safely rely upon much material aid from here, and especially from the Irish. They hate the nigger as they do the devil, and will fight to sustain our rights, if it finally comes to that."

Just days after Spencer wrote these observations, James E. Kerrigan, one of the city's best-known Irish American politicians and congressman-elect for the district that included the most heavily Irish portions of New York City, published an advertisement in the *New York Herald*. In it he announced his intention to form "a military organization to protect . . . the constitutional rights of

the citizens of the country, in the event of a revolution." Most observers interpreted the ad as a thinly veiled attempt to recruit New Yorkers to fight for the
Confederacy in case the secession crisis resulted in civil war. The New York
correspondent of the *Charleston Mercury*, who claimed to know Kerrigan well,
reported that Kerrigan's unit "will be pro-slavery in principle and will take
prompt action in case of secession to take New York out of the Union."[9]

Yet many of New York's Irish immigrants objected to being stereotyped as
pro-southern zealots. One wrote to the *Times* that most Irish Americans "are
opposed to 'secession,' 'rebellion,' or any other movement having in view the
destruction of the Union . . . Whatever may be their opinion of Slavery, or the
wrongs of the South, they will not countenance a destruction of the Government, which has naturalized, enfranchised, and protected them."[10]

On April 12, 1861, seeking to destroy any possibility of a compromise that
might forestall their independence, southern nationalists in Charleston began
bombarding Fort Sumter. After thirty-three hours of shelling, Sumter's commander, Major Robert Anderson, surrendered to his former West Point student, Confederate general Pierre Beauregard. The Civil War had begun.

"The city seems to have gone suddenly wild and crazy," attorney George
Templeton Strong scrawled in his diary as news of the surrender reached Manhattan. In response, thousands of New Yorkers, even those who had been reluctant to "coerce" southerners back into the Union, now enthusiastically answered Lincoln's call for 75,000 troops to suppress the rebellion. "New York
looks like an army camp," grocer Emile Dupré from Braunschweig wrote to his
parents. "There are armed men everywhere, everyone carries a revolver, and
we're living in an absolute torrent of commotion. Heaven knows how it will
all turn out. Both sides are deadly serious." Furthermore, "business is terrible,"
fretted Dupré. "Only guns and more guns are in demand."[11]

Many New York immigrants leaped at the chance to answer the president's
call. Some did so by volunteering for regiments being raised by their favorite
politicians. Kerrigan organized the Twenty-fifth New York Infantry Regiment
after the post-Sumter groundswell of support for the Union made it impossible
for him to deliver his unit to the Confederacy (if indeed that had ever been his
intention). Tammany Hall, the city's leading Democratic organization, created
the Forty-second New York Infantry Regiment, while its rival Mozart Hall, under the control of Mayor Fernando Wood, organized and outfitted the Fortieth
New York. To entice Irish immigrants, organizers of the Tammany Regiment
made one of that community's most respected figures, famed Irish nationalist
Michael Doheny, a lieutenant colonel.[12]

The most common way for New York immigrants to join the war effort
was through "ethnic regiments," units established by and for the city's foreign-

born residents. The most famous of these was the Sixty-ninth New York Infantry Regiment, a bastion of the city's Irish American community from before the Civil War until after World War I. The commander of the Sixty-ninth on the eve of Lincoln's election was Colonel Michael Corcoran. Son of an Irish military officer, Corcoran was born in 1827 in comfortable circumstances in County Sligo. After serving for a year in the Royal Irish Constabulary in Donegal, Corcoran became a supporter of the Irish efforts to overthrow English rule which peaked in 1848. With the failure of these uprisings, Corcoran sailed in 1849 for New York. There he became a clerk, boarding in the home of an Irish-born saloonkeeper, who lived above his bar at 42 Prince Street, facing the south side of the original St. Patrick's Cathedral on Mott Street. Corcoran soon married the saloonkeeper's niece Elizabeth, and by 1855 he had taken over the saloon, known as Hibernia Hall.[13]

After his arrival in New York, Corcoran enlisted as a private in the Sixty-ninth, which in peacetime functioned as a large Irish American militia company (akin to today's National Guard). The Sixty-ninth was the most prominent of the many ethnic militia units whose proliferation filled nativists with such dread during the Know Nothings' heyday. With a "winning smile," "unbounded" generosity, and "a kind word and friendly salute for all," Corcoran quickly rose through the ranks over the course of the 1850s, first to sergeant, then lieutenant, and then captain. When the regiment's commanding officer resigned in the summer of 1859, the men unanimously elected Corcoran their new leader.[14]

Corcoran earned the undying admiration of Irish Americans across the nation a year later when the Prince of Wales arrived in New York just weeks before the election of 1860 for a tour of the United States. The commander of the state militia ordered the city's military companies to parade in celebration of the prince's arrival, but Corcoran would not allow the Sixty-ninth to take part in any effort to honor the oppressors of Ireland. Native-born New Yorkers were aghast at this act of impertinence, and the state's militia commanders initiated court-martial proceedings against their stubborn subordinate. Yet Corcoran's decision made him a hero to Irishmen on both sides of the Atlantic. With this single act of defiance on the eve of the war, Corcoran instantly became the most idolized figure in New York's Irish American community.[15]

Corcoran's legal team was still presenting his defense at the court-martial when news of the shelling of Fort Sumter reached New York. Realizing that he could not afford to have New York's most popular Irish American military leader under arrest at such a moment, Governor Edwin Morgan, a Republican, quashed the indictment and restored Corcoran to his command. The result was just what the governor had envisioned: "The rush of volunteers to the ranks

Colonel Michael Corcoran and his officers posing at Fort Corcoran, built by
the men of the Sixty-ninth and named in his honor, in what is now Arlington, Virginia. Corcoran is at the far left.

of the 69th, for the past few days, has been tremendous," reported the city's
leading Irish American newspaper after Corcoran's reinstatement. So intense
was the desire of Irish Americans to serve in this unit that Corcoran brought
nearly 1,500 men to the capital in late April, making the Sixty-ninth the largest regiment to answer Lincoln's initial call for troops. Among the recruits was
Thomas Francis Meagher, one of the most famous leaders of the failed Irish
uprising against British rule in 1848. Corcoran made Meagher a captain and
gave him command of a company of about one hundred troops. Realizing that
Corcoran's unit could hold no more men, city judge John H. McCunn, an immigrant from Londonderry and an aspiring Tammany politico, quit the Sixty-
ninth and raised a second Irish regiment, the Thirty-seventh New York. Organizers of ethnic regiments told immigrants that, as Corcoran put it, "they
should go with their own countrymen [rather] than have their services unap-
preciated, and their national identity lost among strangers."[16]

In the days after the bombardment of Sumter, the city's Germans raised infantry units of their own: the Seventh Regiment (known as the Steuben Guard),
the Eighth (the First German Rifles), the Twentieth (the Turner Regiment),
the Twenty-ninth (the First German Infantry), and the Forty-first (the DeKalb
Regiment).[17] The commanders of these units were typically veterans of the antigovernment forces that had fought in the German revolutions of 1848. The
Eighth Regiment, for example, was initially led by Colonel Louis Blenker, a

wine dealer from Worms who had served as a colonel in the revolutionary militia that temporarily overthrew the Grand Duke of Baden. When Prussian and Bavarian troops arrived to repulse the rebels, Blenker fled to Switzerland and then New York. He spent part of the 1850s farming in Rockland County, New York, but had become a shopkeeper in New York City by the eve of the war. Blenker chose as his lieutenant colonel Julius Stahel, a Hungarian who had served as an officer in the Austrian army until 1848, when he joined the revolutionaries attempting to free Hungary from Austrian rule. When that effort failed, he moved first to Prussia, then to England, and then in 1858 to New York, where he worked as a newspaper writer and editor until the attack on Fort Sumter. One of Blenker's captains was Gustav Struve, among Baden's most famous and radical revolutionary leaders. After fleeing Baden, Struve lived in Switzerland and London before settling on Staten Island and becoming an ardent Republican.[18]

The organizers of the other German regiments had military backgrounds similar to those of Blenker and Stahel. Max Weber, who raised the Twentieth Regiment, was a lieutenant in the army of the Grand Duke of Baden before defecting to the revolutionary forces in 1848. Like Blenker, he fled to New York, and by 1855 had become proprietor of the Hotel Konstanz, just east of City Hall, which he ran until the outbreak of the war. Leopold von Gilsa, commander of the Forty-first Regiment, had served as a major in the Prussian army before coming to the United States. In New York he at times supported himself singing and playing the piano in the Bowery's many beer halls. Adolph von Steinwehr, leader of the Twenty-ninth Regiment, had attended a military academy in his native Braunschweig and served as an officer in its army before immigrating to the United States in 1847. Only one of New York's German regimental commanders had not received his military training in Europe: Colonel John E. Bendix arrived in America in his teens in the 1830s and worked as a pattern maker for the manufacture of machine parts. Like Corcoran, he rose through the ranks of the state's volunteer militia and held the rank of lieutenant colonel by the time Sumter was attacked.[19]

After the assault on Fort Sumter, members of nearly every immigrant community in the city volunteered. Scotch-born stonecutter Alexander Campbell enlisted in the Scotch American Seventy-ninth New York "Highlanders" Regiment (though his brother James, who had settled in Charleston, volunteered for the Confederate military). Many New York immigrants joined the Thirty-ninth New York Infantry Regiment, probably the most diverse military unit to fight in the Civil War. It included soldiers from Argentina, Armenia, Austria, Belgium, Bohemia, Canada, Chile, Cuba, Denmark, England, France, the Ger-

Born in Hungary, Julius Stahel helped organize New York's predominantly German Eighth Regiment. Rising from lieutenant colonel to the rank of major general, he won the Congressional Medal of Honor for his gallantry at the Battle of Piedmont in northwestern Virginia in 1864.

man states, Greece, Grenada, Holland, Hungary, Ireland, Italy, Malta, Nicaragua, Norway, Poland, Portugal, Russia, Scotland, Spain, Sweden, and Switzerland.[20]

The man who organized the Thirty-ninth, Colonel Frederick D'Utassy, seemed perfectly suited to the task of managing this polyglot unit. D'Utassy was a Hungarian Jew who had served as a lieutenant in the Austrian army before defecting to the Hungarian revolutionary forces in 1848. Like so many of the other failed revolutionaries, he floated around Europe for several years, but eventually he relocated to Canada. The faculty of Dalhousie University in Nova Scotia, impressed with D'Utassy's command of English, French, German, Hungarian, Italian, and Spanish, made him a professor of foreign languages. But he left Canada for New York City in 1860, settling there with his wife, son, mother, sister, and two brothers.

To fill his regiment, D'Utassy joined forces with New York's Italian revolutionary refugee community. Several of his officers, veterans of Giuseppe Garibaldi's revolutionary army of 1848, had fled to the United States and remained in America even after Garibaldi, who lived on Staten Island from 1850 to 1851, returned to fight in Italy. Other leaders of the Thirty-ninth, according to the *Tribune*, had held "important commands" in the revolutionary armies in France, Hungary, and the German states, while the enlisted men could rally around "the revolutionary battle-cries of many a hard-fought struggle against tyranny in Europe."[21]

New Yorkers gave these units huge, festive send-offs, like "many Fourth of Julys rolled into one," reported one newspaper. Northerners expected that amassing such impressive forces would persuade the South to abandon its dreams of independence. If not, then surely one small battle would bring the crisis to a close. Southerners viewed the conflict in much the same way. Scoffing at the idea that secession would result in a long and deadly civil war, former U.S. sen-

ator James Chesnut of South Carolina promised that he would drink
all the blood spilled as a result of the
creation of the Confederacy. Northerners were so certain of a quick
resolution to the standoff that they
asked the men who volunteered to
commit to only three months of
military service.[22]

In mid-July, with the three-month
enlistments about to end and no indication that the Confederacy would
back down, Union forces moved
twenty-five miles west from Washington to attack the Confederate
army camped just south and west of
the Bull Run stream near Manassas,
Virginia. When the Union army,
led by General Irvin McDowell, attacked Beauregard's troops on the
morning of July twenty-first, many
of New York's ethnic regiments
played key roles. The engagement
went well for the North at first, as

Befitting its appeal to "friends of liberty" from
all over Europe, the Garibaldi Guard sought
recruits in Italian, Hungarian, French, and
German. Immigrants from more than two
dozen nations served in its ranks.

the Union troops pushed the Confederates back from their defensive positions
on the south bank of the stream. "Victory! victory! We have done it," declared
McDowell's chief of staff around 12:30. Others, just arriving on the scene, lamented that the war was over and they had missed their chance for glory.[23]

But by 2:00, from their vantage point on Matthews Hill, the Union forces
could see thousands of Confederate reinforcements amassing to the south on
Henry House Hill. Fearing that these fresh and increasingly numerous troops
would mount a counterattack, McDowell ordered Colonel William T. Sherman's brigade to strike at them first. When Sherman's Wisconsin regiment
failed to dislodge the Confederates, led by General Thomas Jackson (whose
tenacity defending this spot earned him the nickname "Stonewall"), Sherman
sent the Scotch Americans of the Seventy-ninth New York forward toward Jackson's men. "Up we rushed," wrote one of the officers, American-born Lieutenant William Thompson Lusk, through what another soldier called a "hurricane
of iron." "Tall men were mowed down about me," Lusk recalled. "Wounded

men begged their comrades to press on." When an American flag began wav-
ing at the top of the hill, the officers of the Seventy-ninth ordered their men to
hold their fire, thinking that another Union regiment had taken the hill. Private Campbell, the stonecutter, thought that "we had them entirely licked." But
it turned out to be a Confederate trick. "As we lowered our arms, and were
about to rally where the banner floated," a soldier recounted, "we were met by
a terrible raking fire," which "decimated the regiment in an instant." Twenty-six
were killed, including their colonel, James Cameron, brother of U.S. Secretary
of War Simon Cameron. Eighteen more were injured. Another fifty were captured, while the remainder of the stunned and demoralized Highlanders beat a
hasty retreat.[24]

Sherman then ordered his last regiment, Corcoran's Sixty-ninth, to assault
the Confederate position. "It was a brave sight," wrote a reporter from the
World, "that rush of the Sixty-ninth into the death struggle!" The Irishmen,
many stripped to the waist in the July heat, took the hill under what Captain
James Kelly called "a continuous fire of musketry and artillery," dislodging the
Confederate forces with a combination of gunfire and bayonets and capturing
the southerners' artillery. "The most conspicuous man in the field," according to a Sixth Ward saloonkeeper who served in the Sixty-ninth, was Meagher,
"riding on a white horse, with his hat off, and going into the battle most enthusiastically." When at one point the regimental flag was captured by the Confederates, Meagher seized the unit's green Irish flag and "went to the front, leading
the men to the charge" that recaptured the regimental colors.[25]

But the Confederates gathered reinforcements and counterattacked, driving
the Irishmen back off the hill. Under Corcoran's direction, the Sixty-ninth regrouped and charged the hill twice more, yet the combination of muskets and
artillery — the latter firing grapeshot directly into the oncoming Irishmen —
was too much to overcome, and after the third charge the regiment retreated
chaotically. Sensing the panic setting in on the Union side, the Confederates
expanded their counterattack, eventually sending the entire northern army
back toward Washington in what McDowell described as "a confused mob, entirely demoralized."[26]

"I runn right into the woods," Campbell wrote of the retreat to his wife without the slightest hint of embarrassment. Leaving the road because they feared
being caught by pursuing Confederate cavalrymen, Campbell and a comrade
took to the fields, "running as fast as we could." It was only when he was utterly
exhausted that he heard horsemen approaching from behind. "I was not able
to go anny farther so I lay down and gave up all hop[e]s." But even though he
thought he was in plain sight, the horsemen passed him by. Campbell got back
up and did not stop again until he had walked and run the entire twenty-five

GALLANT CHARGE OF THE SIXTY-NINTH REGIMENT, NEW YORK STATE MILITIA, UPON A REBEL BATTERY AT THE BATTLE OF BULL RUN.—[See Page 503.]

Members of the predominantly Irish Sixty-ninth Regiment, some stripped to the waist in the summer heat, attacking the Confederates on Henry House Hill at the Battle of Bull Run, July 21, 1861.

miles back to his camp in Arlington, Virginia, just across the Potomac from Washington.[27]

Corcoran, meanwhile, was wounded and captured, along with two other officers and ninety-two of his enlisted men. It was during the retreat that the German regiments of Blenker, von Steinwehr, and von Gilsa, plus the Garibaldi Guard, finally saw action protecting the flanks and rear of the fleeing soldiers, "the great majority" of whom were doing so "in wild confusion," Blenker reported. The Germans received praise for remaining calm and professional while conditions became increasingly chaotic all around them. They suffered minimal casualties. But the soldiers who had charged Henry House Hill had not been so lucky. Thirty-eight of Corcoran's comrades were killed or mortally wounded at Bull Run. No regiments on the Union side, and only one on the Confederate, suffered more total losses (killed, wounded, and captured) in that battle than the Seventy-ninth and Sixty-ninth.[28]

It was now painfully clear that the war would not end with a single grand battle: "3 days ago I still thought it might be possible to defeat the slaveholder party within 6 months," lamented Julius Wesslau after news of the defeat reached

New York, "but losing this battle makes that very doubtful. There was great commotion here in the city, and everyone was very disheartened." The loss also inspired more New York immigrants to enlist. In the aftermath of Bull Run, German New Yorkers created the Forty-fifth, Forty-sixth, Fifty-second, Fifty-fourth, and Fifty-eighth New York regiments. Nickolaus Heck, whose wife had advised her friends to burn their grape baskets and find tailors to marry in America, joined the Fifty-second. The Fifty-eighth was actually a Polish-German unit, led by Colonel Wlodzimierz Bonawentura Krzyzanowski, a nobleman who fled to America around 1848 to escape prosecution for taking part in the failed Polish uprising against Prussia. French immigrants also formed regiments after Bull Run, the Fifty-third and Fifty-fifth.[29]

More Irish immigrants joined the army after Bull Run as well, creating the Irish Sixty-third and Eighty-eighth New York Infantry regiments, though the famed Sixty-ninth was still Irish New Yorkers' preferred option. These three regiments (along with some Irish units from Pennsylvania and Massachusetts) became known as the "Irish Brigade." In the absence of prisoner of war Corcoran, command of the brigade was given to Meagher, who was promoted to brigadier general. The Confederates offered Corcoran his freedom if he would promise not to return to the army, but he refused those terms, and when word reached New York, it only increased his stature.

Some Irish immigrants decided to join units tied to their political rather than ethnic identities. Many, for example, enlisted in the "mainly Irish" Excelsior Brigade, organized by another ambitious New York Democrat, former congressman Dan Sickles. He had become famous in 1859 for killing his wife's lover and then managing to win an acquittal on the resulting murder charges by pleading temporary insanity (the first successful use of this defense in American legal history). Felix Brannigan enrolled in the Excelsior Brigade soon after the bombardment of Fort Sumter, but the unit did not fill up and get deployed until after Bull Run. Other New York immigrants joined already existing units at this point, replacing the dead, wounded, sick, and those who had deserted.[30]

Why did so many Irish immigrants enlist given that, as an Irish-born officer of the Sixty-ninth observed, these were "men who have always stood by the South" in politics? According to the officer, lawyer Joseph Tully, part of the answer lay in the fact that Irish immigrants' "regard for the South is far from equalling their love for the Union." Irish immigrants were eager for the opportunity to "demonstrate their devotion to the Union."[31]

Irish Americans also saw military service as a means to counteract anti-Irish prejudice and perhaps finally earn the respect of native-born Americans. This was the view of Charles Halpine, a native of County Meath who arrived in the United States in 1851 and, after a stint at a Catholic newspaper, became an associate editor at the *Times* in 1855. He enlisted in the Sixty-ninth immediately after Fort Sumter and observed that his comrades believed that by volunteering, they were "earning a title, which hereafter no foul tongue or niggard heart would dare dispute, to the full equality and fraternity of an American citizen." The Irish were "now proud peers of the proudest and brave brothers of the best." Meagher believed this too. After the Sixty-ninth Regiment's gallant performance at Bull Run, Meagher proclaimed that "know nothingism is dead!" From that point onward, "the Irish soldier . . . shall proudly stand by the side of the native born."[32]

A third rationale for Irish enlistment, one mentioned again and again by members of the Civil War's Irish military units, was the belief that the martial skills they gained fighting the Confederacy would aid them in eventually overthrowing British rule in Ireland. Meagher told an audience in New York that "if only one in ten of us come back when this war is over, the military experience gained by that *one* will be of more service in a fight for Ireland's freedom than would that of the entire ten as they are now." One of Meagher's enlisted men agreed, calling the war "a school of instruction for Irishmen" in the battle for Ireland's liberation. Even an Irish-born Confederate took pleasure in the fact that so many Irish immigrants were enlisting in the Sixty-ninth New York because, he wrote, "I imagine the men who faced Beauregard's artillery and rifles until Bull Run ran red, will not be likely to shrink on the day (when will it dawn, that white day?) that they will have the comparatively light task of whipping their weight of red-coats" in Ireland.[33]

One Irish volunteer, Peter Welsh, told by his wife in New York that her father did not understand why he would risk his life participating in a fight between northern Republicans and southern slaveholders, admitted in a letter to him that many Irish immigrants saw things the same way. But Welsh insisted that Irish immigrants had as much at stake in the war as native-born Americans: "Would to God that every man in the loyal states felt truly and unselfishly how great an interest he has in the supression of this hellish rebellion . . . How many thousands have been rescued from the jaws of the poorhouse and from distress and privation by the savings of the industrious sons and more particularly by the daughters of Irland who have emigrated here? It is impossible to estimate the amount of distress and misery that has been warded off from the down trodden and tyrant crushed people of any of the poorer districts of Irland by this means." As a result, "when we are fighting for America we are fighting in the interest of Irland, striking a double blow, cutting with a two edged sword . . . Destroy this republic and her hopes are blasted."[34]

The pressure on able-bodied young men, Irish or otherwise, to enlist after Bull Run must have been overwhelming. Before that battle, Alexander Dupré, ne'er-do-well younger brother of German grocer Emile Dupré, ridiculed the "stupid people who sign up" for the army. But by August he had relented and enlisted in a German artillery regiment. Architect Robert Sneden, a Canadian immigrant, likewise enrolled in the Mozart Regiment after Bull Run.[35]

These new recruits and their officers rarely had military experience and therefore required extensive training. At the end of September, after several weeks of drilling, one half of Sneden's regiment fought the other half in a mock battle, firing "blank cartridges" to make the exercise as realistic as possible. The results verged on comical. The artillerymen could fire their "howitzer gun" rapidly, but it often toppled over from the recoil. At another point, they mistakenly shot into the distance the rammer they used to load the ammunition. The infantrymen were hardly better. They discharged their guns too close to the "enemy," so that "many were burnt and singed by the wads." Several inadvertently fired their iron ramrods at their colonel. Others badly injured themselves trying to leap over fences and other obstacles. For these and other mishaps, many members of the regiment had to be carted away on makeshift stretchers. In the end, Sneden lamented, the exercise "resulted in filling up the hospital with as many wounded and maimed men as if there had been a big skirmish with the enemy."[36]

Embarrassing spectacles such as these weighed on the mind of General George McClellan, who after Bull Run had replaced McDowell as head of the main Union army in the east, known as the Army of the Potomac. Despite pleas from Lincoln for a renewed offensive against the Confederacy before the end of the year, McClellan decided that the northern forces, now numbering several hundred thousand after the rush of summer recruits, could not effectively attack the Confederacy before the spring of 1862. When spring finally came, McClellan put in motion a complicated plan to capture the Confederate capital of Richmond by sailing his army down the Potomac and landing it at Hampton Roads, at the end of the peninsula formed by the York and James rivers. From there, the army would move northwest, past historic Jamestown, Yorktown, and Williamsburg, and attack Richmond from the southeast, rather than from the north as the Confederates would expect. Lincoln thought that McClellan should focus his energy on destroying the Confederacy's army rather than capturing its capital. Others pointed out that by the time McClellan could move his huge army to the Peninsula, the Confederates would have been able to reposition themselves. McClellan's plan might also leave his soldiers trapped on the peninsula, just as Lord Cornwallis had been trapped by George Washington on this very same peninsula eighty years earlier. In the end, however, Lincoln deferred to his general in chief.[37]

Most of New York City's post–Bull Run recruits saw their first real action in this "Peninsula Campaign." Brannigan's baptism in blood took place at the Battle of Williamsburg, on May 5, 1862, a relatively unimportant clash that merits just two sentences in James McPherson's authoritative nine-hundred-page history of the war, *Battle Cry of Freedom.* Yet to Brannigan, the battle was "horrible" beyond imagination. "The reality surpasses any description of a battle I ever heard of," he wrote to his sister afterward. "The field is literally covered with our dead."[38]

While Bannigan's commander, Brigadier General Joseph Hooker, characterized the Battle of Williamsburg as "one of gigantic proportions," subsequent Civil War clashes would soon dwarf this encounter as McClellan's forces inched their way closer to Richmond. Sneden's unit first saw combat on the last day of May at the Battle of Fair Oaks, six miles southeast of the Confederate capital. The Union suffered twice as many casualties there (a total of five thousand killed, wounded, or captured) as at Williamsburg. Sneden, however, did not have to take part in any infantry charges. He had been given far safer duty thanks to his skills as a draftsman, talents highly prized because both armies were woefully lacking in maps. At a moment's notice, Sneden could copy the maps the army possessed or captured or create new ones if the Union had none. So while Sneden remained a private, he spent much of his time in relative safety with McClellan's generals.[39]

With Union forces so close to Richmond, but McClellan determined not to attack in haste, it fell to the new Confederate commander, General Robert E. Lee, who had taken control of the southern troops in Virginia after Fair Oaks, to initiate the climax of the Peninsula Campaign. Lee decided that destroying McClellan's army on the outskirts of Richmond might end the entire war, so he adopted a bold offensive strategy, risking nearly all by attacking McClellan's army on seven consecutive days from June 25 to July 1 in what became known as the Seven Days Battle.

Brannigan's regiment, decimated at Williamsburg, was held in reserve throughout the Seven Days Battle, but the Tammany Regiment and Sneden's Mozart unit saw action at several of these engagements. At Savage Station on June 29, the fifth day of the Seven Days Battle, Sneden reported that "the heat was terrible . . . Not a breath of air was felt." The soldiers sweltered in the hot sun all day until finally, around 5:00 p.m., the Confederates attacked, sending "showers of shells into our lines. Two burst very close to where [the generals] were standing, covering them with dust and earth. Our batteries now vigorously replied, . . . and for an hour the crash and concussion of air was so great that I could hardly keep my feet."

Soon the artillery duel slackened, but "a series of prolonged yells from the Rebels was now heard, and two strong lines . . . soon came rushing to the charge. The setting sun glisten[ed] on their bayonets, as they came on in beautiful order of battle, with piercing yells and confidence. Our lines stood firm as a rock, 5,000 muskets were simultaneously pointed and discharged with a terrific crash! To [this] the enemy replied by double the number, when all in front was hid in smoke."

After a pause that seemed like an eternity, the Confederates who had not been mowed down by the northerners' first musket volley emerged from that smoke, hurtling themselves forward toward the Union lines. Again "there was a terrific crash of musketry" from the Union side, "while the artillery fire was redoubled." By this point,

> the storm of lead was continuous and deadly on the approaching lines of the Rebels. They bravely rushed up, however, to within twenty feet of our artillery, when bushels of grape[shot] and canister [artillery balls even smaller than grapeshot] from the cannon laid them low in rows. Large gaps were made in their alignments and whole companies tumbled to the ground at once. The ranks in their rear still came on stumbling over those already fallen, yelling and firing as they came . . . Beaten back by the storm of lead and iron, the enemy hesitated, wavered, and fell back a short ways to the railroad, while fresh regiments of Rebels came up behind . . . Again our lines poured in a terrible crushing fire from 10,000 muskets, and again the enemy fell back in disorder and dismay.

The Union lines had bent but not broken.[40]

For five consecutive days, Lee had sent his troops to attack well-entrenched or positioned Union forces. Every day the Confederates suffered horrible casualties, far greater than those they inflicted on McClellan's much larger army. But McClellan, convinced that he would lose each battle before it even began, ordered a retreat at the end of every day. In fact, rather than direct his troops as the battle progressed like a typical general, McClellan spent each day miles to the rear, choosing the place to which his men would retreat after the anticipated defeat. Lee came to the conclusion that the northern army must be on the verge of imminent collapse. What else could explain why the northerners kept falling back, even after inflicting far more casualties than they suffered? So although his supply of battle-ready troops was perilously small after another failed attack the day after Savage Station, Lee decided on the morning of July 1 to make one final attempt to destroy the Union army with an all-out attack. The northerners were waiting for the Confederates in the best defensive position McClellan had chosen all week, a high plateau known as Malvern Hill.

After being held in reserve for most of the Peninsula Campaign, some of New York's best-known ethnic regiments took part in this climactic clash of the Seven Days Battle, in particular the German Seventh, the French Fifty-fifth, and those that composed the Irish Brigade. Sneden, from his perch with the generals, was also there to witness the Confederate assault. At first the northern troops responded to the onrushing southerners with artillery only. "The whole side of Malvern Hill seemed a vast sheet of fire," Sneden wrote that night in his diary. "The bursting shells could be seen dealing destruction on all sides to the yelling assailants." But as thousands upon thousands of Confederates climbed the hill and got within range of the infantry, the well-positioned Union ground troops

> opened on them with terrible effects . . . Several times our infantry with-held their fire until the Rebel column, which rushed through the storm of canister and grape, [came] close up to the artillery. Our men then poured a single crashing volley of musketry and charged the enemy with the bayonet with cheers. [We] thus captured many prisoners and colors and drove the remainder in confusion from the field. These would rally under cover of the woods and charge again, but only to be met with the same murderous volleys of shot, shell, and bullets, leaving piles of dead and dying on the plateau along our front. Hundreds of poor maimed wretches were continually crawling on hands and knees across the open [field], many of whom were killed before they regained shelter in the woods.

As a result of Lee's poorly worded orders, even more Confederates rushed into the slaughter than he had intended. "The battlefield at the foot of the slopes," Sneden reported when it was all over at dusk, "presented a shocking sight of dead, dying, and mangled corpses, while the numerous dead and wounded horses were crawling and kicking in death agony among them." Contemplating the results of the ill-advised assault, one of Lee's disgusted officers charged that Malvern Hill "was not war, it was murder."[41]

Despite driving back Lee's forces, this time for good, the Union troops found little reason to celebrate afterward. That night McClellan ordered yet another retreat, this time to a landing on the James River, where he would begin evacuating his men back to Washington. "This order produced great dissatisfaction and excitement in the ranks," Sneden reported, "but more so from the general officers, who . . . were loud in their protestations against the order. [They] denounced McClellan for a coward or traitor!" Even enlisted men knew that when an enemy with an army half as large as your own suffers three times as many casualties (nine thousand versus three thousand) in a day's fighting, the proper course of action is to attack the weakened opponent, not retreat.

Furthermore, the northern victory had come at a terrible price. Only three hundred were killed, but 2,700 were wounded or missing. Many of the

Sneden's depiction of the clash at Malvern Hill, fifteen miles
southeast of Richmond, July 1, 1862.

wounded, "disfigured beyond recognition," suffered severe injuries that would
require amputations. Of the missing, most were injured men the northerners
had to leave on the battlefield because of McClellan's order to retreat. A disproportionate number of "the dying and the dead" abandoned as a result of Mc-
Clellan's order were members of the Sixty-ninth. It suffered the third most fatalities out of the more than ninety Union regiments that participated in the
climactic clash of the Seven Days Battle at Malvern Hill.[42]

When the Peninsula Campaign ended in July 1862, a year after Bull Run, it provided another sudden plunge in what, on the home front, had been a roller-
coaster year for New Yorkers, both emotionally and economically. In the first
half of 1861, many sectors of the city's economy ground nearly to a halt as southern orders evaporated and even northerners drastically cut spending as they
waited for the secession crisis to play out. "Business here is very bad," wrote
cabinetmaker Julius Wesslau to his parents in Prussia soon after Bull Run.
"There's nothing to do. Even though more than thirty thousand men have left
the city to go to war, there are as many people here as there are stars in the sky,"
and these unemployed or underemployed workers "are suffering badly. What a
disaster." Some of Wesslau's acquaintances decided to return to their German
homelands.[43]

Economic prospects were no better for New York's Irish. The construction sector, which employed a disproportionate number of them, came to a standstill as political and military uncertainty prompted real estate developers to cut back drastically on their building plans. With thousands leaving the city to fight and immigration at record low levels, Manhattan's usually brisk market for rental properties slackened. A sharp reduction in American imports in the first half of 1861, combined with the collapse of trade with the South, meant that there was far less work than usual for the city's Irish dockworkers and cartmen as well. "From the largest merchant to the apple woman," noted the *Daily News*, "an observer can plainly see an extra tightness on the money bag" of most New Yorkers.[44]

The defeat at Bull Run, however, actually helped revive the New York economy. Seeing now that the war would surely not end with one battle, the federal government began placing huge orders for uniforms, weapons, equipment, and food. New York's garment manufacturers, already the nation's leading producer of clothing before the war, secured huge contracts for uniforms. The shipyards also sprang back to life as the navy commissioned new ships and, more frequently, contracted to have existing vessels retrofitted for military use. The city's thousands of immigrant machinists were suddenly in high demand to help keep up the pace of production in every war-related field.

The economic vitality of the city quickly spread even to fields not directly related to the war. Western farmers who had once shipped their grain and cattle to market down the Mississippi River now moved those goods eastward by rail to New York City. New York brokers sold some of this agricultural surplus to the military and shipped much of the rest to Europe, which had endured poor harvests in 1860 and 1861. Wherever these goods might go, New York's Irish cartmen, stevedores, and laborers benefited from the new flow of agricultural products in and out of New York.

All New Yorkers noticed the upturn in the economy. "Business in Neu York has improved a lot," reported Julius Wesslau to his parents in May 1862. "We now have enough work to keep 24 men busy." By 1863, business was absolutely booming. "Things here in the north are in a great state of prosperity," observed the vice president of the Chamber of Commerce, mining magnate William Dodge, in March 1863. "The large amount expended by the government has given activity to everything and but for the daily news from the War in the papers and the crowds of soldiers you see about the streets you would have no idea of war. Our streets are crowded, hotels full, the railroads, and manufacturers of all kinds except cotton were never doing so well and business generally is active." Even New Yorkers of modest means saw some relief. The New York Association for Improving the Condition of the Poor reported in 1865 that "there was less suffering from indigence in this city" during the four years of the war "than in any preceding four years in our history."[45]

Not everyone shared equally in this wartime prosperity. Those who fared worst were the soldiers' families, for while the troops earned salaries, they were paid irregularly. New York's immigrants mobilized to relieve the hardships of parents, spouses, and children dependent on the departed soldiers. On August 29, 1861, the Irish community held a "monster festival" in Jones' Wood, parkland that stretched from present-day Third Avenue to the East River from 65th Street northward to 75th Street. Sixty thousand New Yorkers, predominantly Irish Americans, paid the twenty-five cents admission to picnic, dance, and hear speeches from prominent Irish Americans, including a description of the Battle of Bull Run from Meagher himself. Proceeds were distributed to the families of the Sixty-ninth Regiment. Similar fund-raisers were held later in the war for the Irish and members of the city's other immigrant communities. The city government aided soldiers' families as well.[46]

Despite such charity, the soldiers' dependents could not always make ends meet. When the city's food and fuel assistance program for soldiers' families was temporarily curtailed in December 1861, two hundred women gathered in Tompkins Square Park in Kleindeutschland to protest. "You have got me men into the souldiers," one complained, "and now you have to kepe us from starving."[47]

Sometimes the strain on the home front could be as much emotional as economic. "My dear wife I am troubled a goodeal about you," wrote Irish Brigade member Peter Welsh in July 1863 to his "lonesome" wife, Margaret, in New York. "I can see from your letters that you are teribly fretted . . . You are wearing yourself away and destroying your health by this constant fretting and worrying." But Margaret Welsh worried for good reason. Ten months later Peter was shot at the Battle of Spotsylvania Courthouse in Virginia. He wrote to Margaret in New York three days later, telling her it was nothing to worry about, just a "flesh wound." But unforeseen complications developed and two weeks later he was dead. The couple had no children, and Margaret never remarried.[48]

Jane Campbell fretted too. When her husband, Scottish-born stonecutter Alexander Campbell, departed New York with the Seventy-ninth Regiment in the spring of 1861, he left twenty-year-old Jane alone to care for their two boys, Alexander junior and Johnny, both under the age of two. She wrote to him often, begging him to get a furlough so he could visit them and help settle their debts. But Alexander counseled patience because his unit was constantly engaged. On June 16, 1862, Campbell as regimental color bearer led his unit's unsuccessful assault on a Confederate fortress on the southern outskirts of Charleston known as the Battle of Secessionville. "It was a verry severe fight," Alexander reported to Jane afterward; a "terrible slaughter" for the Union side, according to one of the Confederates present. What made the battle even more extraordinary for Campbell was that his brother James (who had settled in Charleston shortly after his arrival in the United States) was one of the Confederates inside the fort who were trying to kill him, a fact neither of them knew until the battle was over. "I hope that you and I will never again meet face to face bitter enemies in the battle field," James wrote to Alexander in a letter sent across the lines. "But if such should be the case you have but to discharge your deauty to your caus for I can assure you I will strive to discharge my deauty to my country & my cause." Even for immigrants, the Civil War could pit father against son and brother against brother.[49]

Jane Campbell continued to prod Alexander to come home, but despite the heavy casualties his unit had taken, the ban on leaves for the able-bodied remained in place. "Theres no such thing as getting a furlough," he wrote a few weeks after Secessionville, by which point he had been away for more than a year. "They wont listen to it. I tried . . . They only give fourloughs to them that has been wounded and wont be fit for duty for sometime."

A few weeks later, however, Alex finally found a way to make it home to Jane. On the first of September, Campbell was shot in the calf at the Battle of Chantilly, a clash in northern Virginia that followed the Second Battle of Bull Run. Although the bullet passed through his leg, Campbell insisted that he was "only slightly wounded" and that the injury "won't amount to much." Nonetheless, the wound earned Campbell a four-month recuperation furlough at Bellevue Hospital in New York, enabling him to see his young boys and wife often.[50]

Perhaps a bit too often. In March 1863, two months after Campbell rejoined his unit in Virginia outside Fredericksburg, an apparently distraught Jane wrote to tell her husband that she was pregnant. (Her letters do not survive, so we must infer her state of mind from Alex's responses to her.) She could not bear the thought of caring for two toddlers plus a baby on her own and warned Alex that she was considering an abortion. He tried to dissuade her. "It's a very dangerious operation to tryphle with," he argued. "I was just reading of an instance where a young girl got a Dr to take a baby away and it resulted in her Death. But you have read enough about such things yourself." Besides, he reminded her, "you said you would like a little girl." Finally, as a last resort, he tried to shift the blame. "You will just have to take better care the nixt time," he wrote, though "you I suppose will put all the blame on me."[51]

Luckily, Alex was not present to hear his wife's reaction to his claim that the pregnancy was all her fault. He was also lucky in another sense. The wound he had dismissed so cavalierly in September would not heal properly. Even after several months back with his unit, he could not get his boot on without excruciating pain. So while his comrades had to serve until their three-year enlistments expired in April 1864, Alex Campbell secured a medical discharge in May 1863, returned to New York and his work as a stonecutter, and was there in October when Jane gave birth to their third son.[52]

Campbell's luck eventually ran out. All three of his sons died in a three-week period at the end of 1865, undoubtedly from one of the childhood diseases so prevalent in that era. Perhaps hoping that a change of scenery might ease the pain, Jane and Alex moved a few months later to central Connecticut, whose bountiful quarries (the source of the brownstone that dominated New York's postwar townhouse building boom) provided endless work for stonecutters. A few years later, Alex opened his own stone yard with several of his brothers-in-law, two of whom had also served in the Seventy-ninth. By the mid-1870s, Alex had become the business's sole proprietor. He was soon one of the most prominent stone dealers in Middletown, providing the materials for the prosperous city's finest homes and cemetery monuments. In Connecticut, Alex and Jane had three more children, a son followed by two daughters, all of whom lived to adulthood. In 1906 Jane and Alex moved back to Manhattan to a home in Harlem on West 128th Street. Alex died there in 1909 at the age of seventy-one.[53]

In the summer of 1862, after Second Bull Run, Lee moved north into Union territory for the first time. On September 17, McClellan responded by attacking the Confederate army with uncharacteristic vigor at Antietam Creek near the town of Sharpsburg, just north of the Potomac River in western Maryland. With both sides fighting as if the outcome of the entire war depended on the result, Antietam became the single deadliest day in the entire war.[54]

The bloodiest spot at Antietam was a cornfield split by a sunken road just east of Sharpsburg at the center of each side's lines. One of the first northern commanders to arrive in this area was New York's Max Weber, now a brigadier general and commander of troops from Delaware, Maryland, and New York. When Weber's men crested the small rise on the northeast side of the sunken road, they saw thousands of Confederate troops, row upon row, lying prone, shoulder to shoulder, interspersed among the ripe corn. If either side hoped to push the other back, it would require a suicidal dash down the unplanted hill to the roadbed and up the other side, all within easy range of even the poorest marksman. Nonetheless, following orders, Weber sent his troops, led by the soldiers from Delaware, down the exposed slope. They were cut to pieces, and Weber was badly wounded in the arm.

Hard as it may be to believe, over the next several hours a dozen or so other units made the same suicidal dash along a half-mile-long stretch of sunken road, including the four regiments of the Irish Brigade. After attempting to soften up the Confederate line with five or six volleys from his infantry's muskets, Meagher commanded his men to charge the seemingly impregnable line. "Relying on the impetuosity and recklessness of Irish soldiers in a charge," Meagher reported afterward, he "felt confident that . . . the rebel column would give way and be dispersed." Yet the Confederate line held, while the small ravine that contained the sunken road filled with Irish bodies.

The Confederates, ordered by Lee to destroy McClellan's army and end the war once and for all, counterattacked many times across the same bloody lane, piling southern corpses atop the northern ones already there. Back and forth the two sides went for several hours until the Confederates, their lines dangerously thin, finally fell back to the outskirts of Sharpsburg. Back at the sunken road, where northerners began tending to the wounded and burying their dead, the scene was more gruesome than anything else even the grizzled veterans of the Sixty-ninth had yet witnessed. Many of the injured begged "to be shot dead rather than endure the pain of their wounds," reported one eyewitness. "It was certainly the most awful sight that ever I witnessed and may God forbid I shall ever witness another of the same sort." A Confederate regiment from Texas lost 83 percent of its men to death or injury, the highest casualty rate for any unit in any battle in the entire war. New York's Sixty-ninth and Sixty-third regiments, both part of the Irish Brigade, lost 60 percent of their men, among the very highest casualty rates on the Union side.[55]

The casualties at Antietam utterly shocked Manhattanites. A German New Yorker visiting the military hospitals in Alexandria, Virginia, a few weeks after the battle found "20,000 wounded soldiers lying there; one man without legs, the next without hands, yet another without ears and so on." After eighteen months of war, "there's no end in sight," complained Angela Heck, whose husband's German regiment had fought at Antietam that same month. The Wesslaus likewise lamented after Antietam that each battle produced "thousands of cripples."[56]

Support for the war effort in the Irish Catholic community began to wane. Responding after Antietam to a comment in a Republican newspaper that the Irish Brigade was not bringing in as many new recruits as it once had, an Irish American asked: why were Republicans "singling out Irishmen to fight the battles of America? Is it not rather a stigma on this party that it should be forced to call upon foreigners, and especially upon Irishmen, whom they have always denounced as inferior to 'niggers,'" to do the most dangerous fighting? Other New Yorkers expressed similar sentiments. "The Irish believe the abolitionists

With thousands upon thousands of wounded soldiers filling Union medical
facilities such as the Armory Square Hospital in Washington, depicted here,
many immigrants in New York began to doubt the Lincoln administration's
handling of the war.

hate both Irish and Catholic and want to kill them off," wrote Maria Lydig Daly,
a prominent Catholic New Yorker, in her diary. "The abolitionists always, the
Irish say, put them in front of the battle."[57]

This feeling that Irish units were suffering disproportionate losses intensified a few months later with the disastrous Union defeat at Fredericksburg,
Virginia. After McClellan refused to attack Lee's battered forces as they fled
from Antietam, Lincoln put one of McClellan's subordinates, General Am-
brose Burnside, in charge of the Army of the Potomac and directed him to
pursue a more aggressive strategy. Yet Burnside, who received the promotion
despite telling Lincoln that he did not feel competent to command an entire
army, adopted an *overly* aggressive plan. Failing to surprise Lee by crossing
the Rappahannock River at Fredericksburg on December 13, Burnside attacked
the Confederates there anyway across an open field on the slope of a large hill
known as Marye's Heights.

The result was one of the most appalling Union defeats in the entire war. Yet
again the Irish Brigade was at the center of the ill-fated attacking force, charging six times into Lee's impregnable line. "The place into which Meagher's bri-

gade was sent was simply a slaughter-pen," wrote the brigade's chaplain, Father William Corby. "It was not a battle," agreed one of the brigade's officers, "it was a wholesale slaughter of human beings." While New York's German Seventh Regiment suffered the largest number of casualties of any single unit in the battle, the Irish Sixty-ninth lost a far greater proportion—54 percent of its engaged troops killed or wounded. The three New York regiments of the Irish Brigade, initially 3,500 strong, could now, as a result of losses at Bull Run, the Peninsula, Antietam, and Fredericksburg, muster only 150 healthy soldiers. Walking through the brigade's camp after Fredericksburg, wrote one of the enlisted men, "you feel as if you were going through a grave yard alone; all is dark, and lonesome, and sorrow hangs as a shroud over us all."[58]

Some in New York's Catholic community blamed the appalling casualty rates on the Irish Brigade's leader. Daly characterized Meagher as "reckless" for endangering the lives of his soldiers with one frontal assault on the enemy after another—far more, it seemed, than any other unit. Yet other Irish New Yorkers defended Meagher, insisting that he was merely following orders. Had he disobeyed them, he would have "disgraced himself and his race for all future time." What we know for sure is that of the six hundred or so Union regiments that fought in the war, only three suffered casualty rates of 50 percent or more at *two different battles*. One of them was New York's Irish Sixty-ninth. As a result, lamented an Irish Brigade officer, "it will be a sad, sad Christmas by many an Irish hearth-stone in New York."[59]

12

UPRISING

NEW YORKERS' SUPPORT for the war effort slackened in the fall of 1862 not only because of the increasingly appalling death toll, but also because of Lincoln's announcement, five days after Antietam, of his plan to issue the Emancipation Proclamation. On September 22 the president declared that if the insurrection in the South did not cease by the end of the year, then on January 1, 1863, he would use his powers as commander in chief to confiscate the slaves of citizens living in areas still under rebellion. Doing so would deprive southerners of the slave labor that helped perpetuate the insurrection by giving slaves an added incentive to escape to the North. The proclamation might also persuade foreign powers not to recognize the Confederacy because to do so now could be seen as an endorsement of slavery.

It is difficult to gauge precisely the reaction of New York's immigrants to the Emancipation Proclamation. Little of their private correspondence survives, and the subject rarely comes up in the immigrant letters that are extant. We do know that immigrant soldiers, having seen slavery firsthand while fighting in the Confederacy, were more likely to support emancipation than their countrymen back home in New York. "I had read about the blacks, but I'd never been able to imagine how slaves were treated," wrote Private Alphons Richter of New York's German Fifty-sixth Regiment in his diary in September 1862, "but now I've had unbelievably horrible experience with it." A German brick maker, by contrast, complained after the proclamation was announced, "I don't want to fire another shot for the negroes and I wish that all the abolitionists were in hell," though sensing that the tides of public opinion were shifting, he told his wife to "keep quiet about what I've just written."[1]

Irish soldiers also held conflicting views about the proclamation. Peter Welsh of the Irish Brigade wrote to his wife in New York that in his unit "there is disatisfaction and loud denunciation" of the decree. But he had personally concluded that "if slavery is in the way of a proper administration of the laws and the integrity and perpetuety of this nation then I say away with both slaves and slavery. Sweep both from the land forever rather than the freedom and prosperity of a great na[t]ion such as this should be destroyed." That did not imply any sympathy for the slaves themselves. "The feeling against nigars is intensly strong in this army," wrote Welsh in early 1863, and "especialy strong in the Irish regiments."[2]

On the home front, reaction to Lincoln's announcement broke down primarily on partisan lines, with New York's Democrats mostly opposing emancipation while Republicans endorsed it. The city's most widely read German newspaper, allied with the Democrats, condemned the president's proclamation, complaining that it was unconstitutional and would prolong the war, causing "terrible, endless bloodshed." The response from Horace Greeley's newspaper, the *Tribune* — "GOD BLESS ABRAHAM LINCOLN" — summed up the Republican reaction. The city's more conservative Republican paper, the *Times,* was more circumspect but equally supportive.[3]

New York's Irish immigrants had from the very beginning of the war attempted to use their political influence to prevent the conflict from becoming a fight to end slavery. "We Catholics and a vast majority of our brave troops have not the slightest idea of carrying on a war that costs so much in blood and treasure just to gratify a clique of abolitionists in the North," warned the city's Irish-born Catholic leader, Archbishop John Hughes, in an article published in 1861. He denounced, "in the name of all Catholics, the 'Idea' of making this war subservient to the philanthropic nonsense of abolitionism." There would "be time enough to regulate this unhappy question of slavery when the war shall have terminated." The New York *Irish-American,* whose editors actively avoided religion and partisan politics and were far less conservative than Hughes, nonetheless agreed with him, predicting that "the first inkling of a design to convert this war into a mere Abolition crusade, not for the restoration of our glorious Union, ... will cause the withdrawal of the public confidence" on the part of Irish Americans. Because it would divert the government's attention from restoring the Union, the paper's editors characterized Lincoln's emancipation plan as "treason."[4]

Immigrant New Yorkers, especially the Irish, seemed confident that their viewpoint would prevail. After all, wrote another priest, "the North could not be so crazy as to attempt the emancipation of nearly four millions of slaves at once. Where would they go, or what would be done with them? What would become of the community upon which they would be let loose? Habitually, naturally lazy, they would substitute theft and crime for labor."[5]

When Lincoln announced his emancipation plan, the reaction from New

York's immigrants was relatively muted. But once it took effect on January 1, 1863, the floodgates of vitriol opened wide. The editors of the *Irish-American*, who had supported the war from day one and had hesitated to criticize the president, now let loose a torrent of hostility toward the abolition movement and its supporters. The same men who advocated abolition, they wrote, had once been America's leading nativists, whose political organization, the Know Nothing Party, had tried to block the naturalization of every Irish American immigrant, "persecuted him for his religious opinions, debarred him from offices of public trust and emolument, and by every means at its disposal tried to keep him in the position of a hewer of wood and drawer of water." As both nativists and abolitionists, they

> libelled his character before the whole world, fastening upon him the odium of furnishing the bulk of the crime and wickedness of the community. Even when the rebellion broke out, and the presence of a foe and the imminence of the public danger might be supposed to crush out such miserable bigotry, in view of the unselfish patriotism everywhere exhibited by Irish-Americans, the glorious generosity of the hour only brought into stronger relief the irredeemable malignity of this Abolition hate for our race, which was still more strongly exhibited in the unjust and partial discrimination of State officials against Irish-born officers and Irish military organizations, — aye, even down to the distribution of the relief afforded to the destitute families of the men who were risking their lives upon the battle-fields of the Republic.

The "primary cause" of the war and all the death and suffering that had come of it, insisted the *Irish-American*, was the "Abolition agitation" of the "Nigger propagandists . . . We have not words to express the loathing and contempt we feel for the besotted fanatics."[6]

Historians often mistakenly assume that these anxieties originated in the fear that emancipated slaves might move north to take Irish jobs, or that emancipation in the South would somehow enable the African Americans who already lived in New York to do so. Nearly every history of Civil War New York, for example, repeats the story that in June of 1863, "some 3,000 striking longshoremen, most of whom were Irish, were forced to watch as black men, under police protection, took their jobs on the docks."[7] But this tale is apocryphal, repeated over and over since the first historian mistakenly published it in 1910. White soldiers, not African Americans, temporarily replaced the strikers in question. In fact, there were barely three thousand black men *in all of New York City* in June 1863, and most of them knew better than to try to take a white man's job. The strikers, who were demanding $2 per nine-hour day (employers were offering $1.50) plus fifty cents per hour overtime, eventually got employers to agree to $2 per day and twenty-five cents per hour overtime, at which point the strike petered out.[8]

In fact, immigrants were far more of a threat to African Americans' livelihoods than the other way around. "Every hour sees the black man elbowed out of employment by some newly arrived emigrant, whose hunger and whose color are thought to give him a better title to the place," Frederick Douglass complained in 1853. Nine years later, Brooklyn minister and abolitionist Henry Ward Beecher found that the only careers "free blacks" were truly free to pursue were as waiters and barbers, and "they were being driven from that as fast as possible." New York's poorest Irish American workers might have felt economically vulnerable in 1863 as the war dragged on, but not primarily from the fear that blacks would take their jobs.[9]

Also contributing to the Irish immigrants' negative view of emancipation was the perception that it threatened their tenuous social status in the United States. When supporters of the Emancipation Proclamation pointed out that the measure would reduce white military casualties by allowing African Americans to take the place of white soldiers, the editors of an antiwar and antiemancipation weekly, the *Day Book,* declared that fact wholly irrelevant. Granting blacks the right to serve in the army was even more objectionable than the continued slaughter of whites, insisted the editors, because "equality as a soldier means equality at the ballot-box, equality everywhere." As a result of the proclamation, poor whites would be "degraded to a level with negroes."[10]

An Irish immigrant might not have much money, might find it impossible to secure work outside the most menial fields, and might be subject to slurs against his religion and "race," but at least he could take comfort in the fact that African Americans occupied an even lower rung on the American socioeconomic ladder than he did. In the eyes of many Irish Americans, the Emancipation Proclamation jeopardized that hierarchy. It threatened the Democratic principle, famously espoused in 1857 by Chief Justice Roger Taney in the *Dred Scott* decision, and echoed by Stephen A. Douglas a year later in the Lincoln-Douglas debates, that blacks had "no rights which the white man was bound to respect." The heartfelt conviction among New York's Irish immigrants that granting rights to African Americans decreased the value of those same rights for whites was something New York's Republicans never understood.[11]

After the usual winter hiatus, during which the Emancipation Proclamation became the law of the land, fighting in the east resumed, with Felix Brannigan's old brigade commander, General Joseph Hooker, replacing Burnside as head of the entire Army of the Potomac. Hooker, displaying none of the self-doubt that tormented Burnside, hatched a daring plan to march his army back south across the Rappahannock to attack Lee. While a portion of Hooker's forces would feign an attack on the Confederates at Fredericksburg, where Lee's army was still entrenched, the bulk of Hooker's men would cross the river farther north and launch a surprise attack on Lee's rear. Nearly all the major New York immigrant regiments would take part in Hooker's bold offensive. "May God have mercy on General Lee," Hooker declared, "for I will have none."[12]

On May 1, 1863, Hooker put his plan in motion. But when his troops first encountered resistance, Hooker, in the words of one New York immigrant officer, "completely lost his head," exhibiting the same hesitancy that had plagued McClellan at the Peninsula. Rather than attack the Confederates as planned, Hooker retreated to the safety of his defenses in the hamlet of Chancellorsville, eight miles west of Fredericksburg. Again sensing his opponent's psychological weakness, Lee mounted a daring counteroffensive. Confident that Hooker would not attack, Lee dangerously divided his already outnumbered force and on May 2, in plain sight of the Union soldiers, sent thirty thousand men under the command of Stonewall Jackson on a westward march to attack Hooker's rear. Convinced that Lee was retreating, Hooker did not adequately prepare the predominantly German American Eleventh Corps at the far western end of his line for Jackson's attack late that afternoon, which came through a dense and scrub-covered forest known as the Wilderness. The Germans, including six of New York City's German regiments, and brigades led by von Gilsa, von Steinwehr, and Krzyzanowski (all now generals), retreated chaotically. Rather than accept responsibility for his inept handling of the battle, Hooker and his officers told the press that the debacle stemmed from the Germans' lack of bravery and discipline. For decades afterward, German Americans would seethe at the mere mention of Chancellorsville, a symbol of the deep-seated prejudice Germans faced in both the army and the press. Meanwhile, a division that included Felix Brannigan's heavily Irish Excelsior Brigade from New York filled the gap left by the Germans and stopped Jackson's advance at dusk.[13]

As darkness enveloped the forest battlefield, the commander of Brannigan's division, General Hiram Berry, craved more information. In daylight, the forest and its undergrowth were so thick that men could barely see twenty yards ahead of themselves. In the dark of night, even with a full moon, they were totally blind, clueless as to the size of the force they faced and whether Jackson's men were nearby or had pulled back after Berry's troops had repulsed them. Unable to stand the uncertainty, Berry ordered the commander of the Excelsior Brigade, General Joseph Revere, to find volunteers to sneak past the Confederate pickets (the army's advance guard) to within sight of Jackson's camp and under cover of darkness ascertain the strength and position of the Confederate force. Revere rode down the line formed by his brigade and, stopping at the Seventy-fourth New York Infantry Regiment, asked the most senior officer he could find, Captain Francis Tyler, to choose trustworthy men who could be asked to volunteer for the perilous assignment.

Tyler went immediately to Company A and "called for FELIX BRANNIGAN, who had been with me all during the war, and whom I knew from long experience to be a cool, courageous, intelligent soldier. I told him what I wanted, gave him my ideas as to how to get out of the lines and what to do, and suggested the other men whom he should take along." Brannigan rounded up Sergeant Gottlieb Luty, a twenty-one-year-old Swiss-born machinist from Pittsburgh who had arrived in America as a small child; Sergeant Major Eugene Philip Jacobson, a twenty-one-year-old Polish-born Jew from Rockland County, New York; and Private Joseph Gion, a thirty-seven-year-old "glass flattener" from the French province of Lorraine who had a thick German accent and was also from the Pittsburgh area. The four men split into two groups—Brannigan and Luty in one, Gion and Jacobson in the other—and crept westward into the night toward the Confederate line.[14]

Several hundred yards away, Stonewall Jackson was just as anxious as Berry to know what lay beyond the trees in front of his troops. Jackson decided to take a look for himself, riding on horseback with a guide and members of his staff down the plank road that led toward the Union lines. "It was always Old Jack's way to lead like this from up front," one historian has noted, "to see the battlefield for himself rather than rely on others." But with shots from the pickets of both armies occasionally ringing out and ricocheting wildly off the trees, Jackson's officers feared for their commander's life. "General, don't you think this is the wrong place for you?" asked one of his aides. "The danger is all over," replied Stonewall curtly. "The enemy is routed."[15]

Meanwhile, Brannigan and Luty crept forward to the very same road. Luty later recalled, "We heard horses coming down the plank-road" and decided "to drop and await developments. They came down to within fifteen yards of us." All of a sudden, "firing commenced," directed at the horsemen, which "appeared to come from all sides at the same time . . . I think probably it was Gen. Jackson and staff, as we heard them say the general was shot just after the firing ceased." Brannigan and Luty may have witnessed the mortal wounding of Stonewall Jackson, probably the single most costly casualty to befall the Confederacy in the entire war. It is even conceivable that their presence in the woods had helped precipitate the attack, with the sound of their movements setting the Confederate pickets on edge and causing them to shoot recklessly into the darkness and kill Lee's most valuable subordinate.[16]

Thinking this news was enough to satisfy Berry, Brannigan and Luty turned back, but disoriented amidst the thickets and dense canopy of trees, they instead stumbled deeper behind enemy lines. The Confederates they soon encountered "were terribly excited about General Jackson being shot. All was confusion." Brannigan and Luty again attempted to retreat and this time succeeded in clawing their way back to Union lines, a task made all the more difficult because the federal forces had begun an attack on the Confederate position, firing bullets, grapeshot, and canister into the very woods that Brannigan and Luty had to re-cross to return to their unit. Finally, around 3:00 a.m., they made it back safely to camp. Gion didn't reappear until just before dawn, hours after Jacobson.[17]

All four — the Irishman, the Pole, the Swiss, and the French German — received the Congressional Medal of Honor for their valor. Yet the information the volunteers had obtained did not do the Union side much good. Over the next four days, Lee's troops drove Hooker's back across the Rappahannock, killing, wounding, or capturing seventeen thousand Union soldiers over the course of the battle and leaving the North more demoralized than ever. The Irish Brigade lost 20 percent of its men at Chancellorsville, reducing the size of the unit that had once boasted 3,500 troops to only 400, too few even for a regiment. Unable to recruit many more Irish immigrants in New York, Boston, or Philadelphia, Meagher resigned in disgust.[18]

With the defeat at Chancellorsville and the casualties that came with it, Lincoln felt he had no choice but to implement the military draft that Congress had authorized in March. This would be the first time the United States had ever resorted to compulsory military service, and Lincoln knew it would be unpopular in many parts of the North. Three provisions of the draft seemed particularly unfair to New York's immigrants. First, while the draft law specifically exempted non-citizens from the draft, the Lincoln administration announced that immigrants who had begun the naturalization process by declaring their intention to become citizens (a prerequisite to naturalization) could be drafted. These immigrants could not vote — yet they would have to serve. Second, because many of New York City's congressional districts contained far fewer native-born men than immigrant men, federal officials set the number of men to be drafted from New York County at about twice the level for New York's rural counties. Provost marshals claimed, correctly, that once the exempt immigrant draftees were winnowed out, the city's congressional districts would end up with no more conscripted soldiers than the state's rural ones. But many city Democrats argued that if the city's congressional districts had fewer draft-eligible residents, they *should* supply fewer soldiers to the army than other areas. These higher quotas were a public relations nightmare for the Lincoln administration as they made the city's residents feel that they were being forced to do a disproportionate share of the fighting, while those in the heavily Republican rural parts of the state could more easily avoid military service.

According to the conscription law, drafted men had to enlist in the military unless they failed the physical examination or were found to be exempt for other reasons. (These included being the sole support of elderly or infirm parents, the father or sole support of motherless children, a felon, or an immigrant who had not yet become a citizen or declared the intent to become one.) If a draftee did not qualify for any of these exemptions, he could hire a substitute to take his place in the army (a centuries-old custom in Europe) or purchase, for $300, a "commutation," which excused him from service for that draft.[19]

This "$300 clause" was the third part of conscription that many New Yorkers, and immigrants in particular, found repugnant. They believed that "the draft was an unfair one," wrote a reporter from the *Herald*, paraphrasing their sentiments, "inasmuch as the rich could avoid it by paying $300, while the poor man, who was without 'the greenbacks,' was compelled to go to the war." Republicans countered that commutation was intended not to shield the rich from service but to create a ceiling on the price of substitutes, thereby making the hiring of a substitute feasible for more Americans. "Without the money provision," wrote Lincoln, "competition among the more wealthy might, and probably would, raise the price of substitutes above three hundred dollars, thus leaving the man who could raise only three hundred dollars no escape from personal service ... The money provision enlarges the class of exempts from actual service simply by admitting poorer men into it. How then can this money provision be a wrong to the poor man?" Some immigrants agreed. "No conscription could be fairer than the one which is about to be enforced," wrote a member of the Irish Brigade to his wife in New York. "It would be impossible to frame it to satisfy every one." Subsequent events proved Lincoln right. When the $300 clause was eliminated in 1864, the price of substitutes doubled and the proportion of drafted men who could afford to buy their way out of the army fell by 50 percent.[20]

The commutation provision might have been good policy, but it was terrible politics, one of the rare instances in which Lincoln was completely tone-deaf to the political impact of his party's policies. From the perspective of poor New York immigrants, the $300 clause meant that both the wealthy *and* the middle class could afford to buy their way out of the army while they could not. Those who were less well-off resented having to choose between keeping their life or their life's savings. The commutation provision also angered many immigrants because it suppressed the price that they might *charge* wealthier New Yorkers to take their places as substitutes on the battlefield.

To immigrants who saw the United States as a land of freedom, the draft also seemed wholly un-American. "If I was unwilling to be treated like a piece of government property in Prussia, I am just as unwilling to do so here," wrote Julius Wesslau, describing his opposition to the draft when it was first proposed. "At any rate there'll be a riot when they try it here in New York." Wesslau's prediction was spot-on. Only after the New York City draft riots had produced four unprecedented days of murder and mayhem did Lincoln fully appreciate how the urban poor viewed emancipation, the draft, and the $300 provision.[21]

Sensing ahead of time that there might be trouble, officials began the draft for New York City in just a single far-flung ward, the Twenty-second, which covered the west side of Manhattan from 40th to 86th Street. On Saturday July 11, provost marshals drew about half of the 2,500 names they needed from their spinning wooden drum and announced that they would complete the draft on Monday. In the interim, however, as anti-conscription New Yorkers scanned the lists of the drafted in the Sunday papers and imagined seeing their own names or those of loved ones appearing there in the near future, they became determined to stop the draft by any means necessary.

Early on Monday morning, workingmen in the Twenty-second Ward streamed out of their tenements as usual. But rather than settle in at their shops and construction sites, they insisted that their employers close down for the day so that the workers could proceed en masse to the site of the ward draft office to protest the conscription. Walking uptown along the west side avenues, the ever-growing throng, carrying makeshift "No Draft" signs, invaded each work site it passed and added still more supporters to its ranks. "A large number of workmen's wives, &c. began also to assemble along the various avenues," reported the *Herald,* "and, if anything, were more excited than the men, who were armed with sticks, stones, adzes, axes, saws, and some with even old swords."[22]

Around 10:00 a.m., when the mob, perhaps one thousand strong, reached the site of the draft, 677 Third Avenue (at the northeast corner of 46th Street), the drawing of names had just resumed. The crowd launched a shower of stones at the windows, shattering them to pieces. The rioters then rushed the building, attacking the draft officers, dragging out and destroying the draft records with "savage yells," and, overcome by "devilish rage and fury," burning the building (and three adjacent ones) to the ground. When Superintendent of Police John A. Kennedy arrived on the scene, the sixty-year-old officer was beaten to within an inch of his life. The mob then proceeded a mile southwest to 1188–1190 Broadway (between 28th and 29th streets), where the draft for that district had been scheduled to begin that morning. Hearing of the rioters' approach, the provost marshal canceled the draft and abandoned the premises, but later in the day a mob returned and burned it as well as ten surrounding buildings to the ground. They also tore up several rail lines and cut telegraph wires that led north out of the city, apparently in an attempt to prevent city leaders from calling in police reinforcements from upstate.[23]

By that point, residents of lower Manhattan who sympathized with the uptown draft protesters were venturing northward either to observe the excitement or to join in the rioting. By afternoon, violent mobs could be found in nearly every part of town. Having halted the draft, the rioters now focused their attention on two kinds of targets: Republicans and the city's African American population. One mob numbering four to five thousand stormed a four-story wire factory at the northeast corner of Second Avenue and 21st Street that had been converted into a munitions plant by its principal owners, the city's Republican mayor George Opdyke and his son-in-law George Farlee. Forty policemen and fifteen employees, armed with breech-loading rifles, killed five attackers in an attempt to repulse them. Eventually the attackers captured the "armory" and burned it down, though not before the employees managed to move the munitions to another factory up the block. Rioters with similar incendiary intentions twice rushed the offices and printing plant of the *New York Tribune,* the city's best-known pro-emancipation newspaper, located on the east side of City Hall Park on what is now Park Row. Both attacks, one at 8:00 p.m. and the other at 11:00, were beaten back by the police.[24]

The most savage violence of the day was aimed at the city's African American community. Crowds in the most heavily Irish parts of the city, the Fourth and Sixth wards, "showed particular spite against the negroes," reported the *Evening Post,* and those who fell into the mob's hands were mercilessly beaten. Rioters attacked every black enclave in the two wards, on Baxter, Pell, Park, Leonard, and Little Water streets in the Sixth and on Dover and Roosevelt streets in the Fourth. In the latter ward, the mob chased three black men into a small tenement, where they fled to the pitched roof. Rather than chase them, the rioters set fire to the top floor of the house, knowing it would spread to the roof as well. When the police arrived, the three victims were hanging from "the side of the building, clinging to the gable-end." Before the police could find ladders, recounted a reporter, the men, "becoming exhausted, . . . successively fell to the ground — one of them, whom the fire had reached, with his clothes in flames. Each one was badly injured." Miraculously, they all survived. That evening a huge mob, after giving the inhabitants two hours' notice, looted and then burned to the ground the huge five-hundred-bed Colored Orphan Asylum at

Rioters looted the Colored Orphan Asylum on Fifth Avenue at 43rd Street and then set it on fire.

the northwest corner of Fifth Avenue and 43rd Street. One rioter, Irish-born Jane Berry, was killed when a bureau thrown from an upper-story window by one of the looters fell on her head.[25]

Most heinous of all were the lynchings. The first occurred Monday evening on the west side of town just north of Houston Street. There, a small crowd led by Irish-born bricklayer John Nicholson attacked three African Americans headed home from work on Varick Street. Two fled, but the third escaped only by drawing a pistol, shooting Nicholson, and running toward the Hudson River via Clarkson Street. The enraged crowd, pursuing the shooter, came upon another black man, William Jones, whose wife had sent him out to buy a loaf of bread. Shouting "Kill the Nigger!" the mob seized Jones, lynched him from a tree on Clarkson Street that shaded the cemetery of St. John's Episcopal Church, and then lit a fire beneath him that charred his lifeless and mutilated body beyond recognition.[26]

In the early hours of Tuesday morning, the city's military leaders contemplated declaring martial law but were talked out of it by prominent Democrats and Mayor Opdyke. They argued that transferring law enforcement responsibilities from civilian to military authority would only enrage the rioters, who might calm down now that they had had the chance to air their grievances. When Tuesday dawned, however, the rioters were, as the *Times* put it, "still infuriate, still insatiate." Now even more of the city seemed to be engulfed in anarchy. Additional railroad tracks were pulled up in the East 80s. More telegraph lines were cut on both the east and west sides of Manhattan. The mayor's man-

The lynching of William Jones on Clarkson Street on Monday July 13, 1863, was the first of nearly a dozen grotesque murders that took place during the four days of rioting.

sion at 79 Fifth Avenue was trashed, as was that of the city's Republican post-master. A mob in Harlem destroyed several buildings and damaged the Ma-combs Dam Bridge, one of only two connecting Manhattan to the mainland. On the west side, they torched the ferry house and dock at West 42nd Street and attacked the homes of African Americans on West 35th Street.

Downtown in the Fourth Ward, hundreds of rioters looted the already fa-mous clothing emporium of the three Brooks brothers, Daniel, Elisha, and John, at 116–118 Cherry Street, near the East River. The mob apparently tar-geted the clothing retailer because it was a large supplier of uniforms to the army — shoddy ones under government contract to the enlisted men and ex-pensive custom-made ones for many of New York's best-known officers. These were just some of the most notable of the hundreds of attacks on life and prop-erty that took place in virtually every part of the city on that terrible Tuesday. Well-dressed New Yorkers who ventured out into "the disturbed districts" were likely to be attacked "with the shout, 'There goes a $300 man!'" To one fright-ened immigrant, Marie Wesslau, "it looked like the world was coming to an end."[27]

The city's militia units, which had remained in their barracks and forts on Monday, were ordered out on Tuesday to clear the streets and restore order, and their violent clashes with the rioters caused the death toll to soar. In Klein-deutschland, which had remained relatively peaceful on Monday, several thou-sand rioters gathered on Pitt Street near Broome and Delancey, apparently to protest the fact that an employer had refused to shut down operations and allow his men to join the demonstrations. When 130 members of the Ninth U.S. Infantry Regiment arrived on the scene and their commander, Lieutenant Thomas Wood, ordered the mob to disperse, the rioters responded with a hail of bricks, stones, and clubs. The commander then ordered his troops to fire; they did, killing and wounding more than thirty rioters. If the names of the dead are any indication, even these rioters in Kleindeutschland were predominantly Irish. Many still refused to give ground, so the infantrymen charged with their bayonets, finally scattering the crowd. When the troops spotted another mob a few blocks south at the corner of Division and Grand streets who also refused orders to disperse, the soldiers made another bayonet charge and scattered those rioters as well.[28]

Ironically, a military commander who sought to avoid firing on civilians that Tuesday met with the most gruesome fate of any white victim of the mob. Colonel Henry O'Brien, an Irish immigrant, had been sent that morning with about 150 men to the corner of 34th Street and Second Avenue, his own neighborhood, to reinforce the police, who had been engaged there for nearly an hour in brutal hand-to-hand combat with a large mob. O'Brien had only a couple of months' military experience serving under Corcoran as a captain, but had been sent to New York and promoted to colonel in light of his promise to enlist enough men to reconstitute the disbanded Eleventh New York Infantry Regiment. As the highest-ranking soldier present, O'Brien assumed command of all the troops and equipment at the scene, including two small artillery pieces. In order to disperse the huge throng still occupying the avenue while minimizing casualties, O'Brien ordered his artillerists to fire blanks at the crowd, while directing the infantry to load real ammunition but to aim over the heads of the rioters. After they fired, the mob scattered, but several rioters fell dead and wounded in the streets and the surrounding buildings. It is unclear whether live ammunition had ricocheted off the tenements or the soldiers did not aim properly. The *Herald* reported that O'Brien shot and killed a woman and child with his own pistol, but this seems to have been an unfounded rumor.[29]

O'Brien's actions enraged the residents of the neighborhood. Finding the colonel inside a drugstore back at 34th and Second that afternoon, Irish-born marble cutter Thomas Kealy grabbed O'Brien from behind while another rioter pistol-whipped the officer. They dragged O'Brien out into the street, where Kealy pounded the prostrate soldier in the face with a paving stone. The crowd then hanged O'Brien from a lamppost but, apparently feeling that the colonel had not suffered enough, they cut him down, still alive, and pummeled him further. "Nature shudders at the appalling scenes which here took place," wrote the *Herald*'s reporter, who estimated that three hundred different rioters took turns kicking, stabbing, and clubbing O'Brien, while others shoved their clubs down the unconscious man's throat. "The body was mutilated in such a manner that it was utterly impossible to recognize it. The head was nearly one mass of gore, while the clothes were also saturated with the crimson fluid of life." Remarkably, O'Brien was still alive, occasionally twitching or moving his lips. When he would try to lift his head, one of the rioters would stomp it back to the ground. The mob dragged O'Brien into the nearby yard of his own house, "and there the most revolting atrocities were perpetrated." When the druggist tried to give him some water, the mob trashed his store. By late afternoon, when it was certain that O'Brien had finally expired, the crowd allowed a priest to take his body to Bellevue Hospital in a wheelbarrow.[30]

Meanwhile, rioters in other parts of town on Tuesday afternoon had begun erecting barricades "after the Parisian fashion" to impede the movement of troops and to provide a defensive position from which to fight them. They constructed several barricades on First Avenue between 11th and 14th streets and a whole network of them on Eighth and Ninth avenues between 35th and 43rd streets. While fighting between authorities and rioters took place in both these areas, the biggest confrontation of the day occurred back on Second Avenue at 22nd Street at the Union Steam Works, where on Monday the employees of Opdyke's "armory" had hidden their guns and ammunition. Word that four thousand rifles were still in the neighborhood brought a huge, "very wild" crowd to the site around 11:30 a.m., as the rioters realized that only weapons such as these could enable them to fend off the well-armed military. Through much of the afternoon, the rioters and police engaged in hand-to-hand combat, first outside the premises and then floor by floor inside. Once the police regained control of the plant's interior (several rioters jumped to their deaths

THE DRAFT RIOTS IN NEW YORK.—THE BATTLE IN SECOND AVENUE.

Troops firing at the rioters on Second Avenue in front of the Union Steam Works on Tuesday July 14, 1863.

from upper-story windows in an attempt to evade arrest), an imposing line of policemen and soldiers cleared Second Avenue of the still menacing mob by firing musket volleys into the huge throng. The troops killed about a dozen and wounded many more before the rioters finally dispersed. "A scene, which defies all powers of description then followed," reported the *Times*. "Pools of blood" were everywhere, and "as the dead and wounded were borne from the place, the wild howlings of the bereaved were truly sad to hear."[31]

African Americans continued to bear the brunt of the rioters' wrath. According to the *Herald,* the heavily Irish Fourth Ward continued to be the scene "of more destruction of negro residences than any other." Almost every frame tenement housing blacks there (mostly on Roosevelt and Catharine streets) had been gutted by Tuesday night. Many had been torn literally to pieces and the remains carted away for the rioters to use as firewood in their homes.

Meanwhile, in the Fifth Ward on the west side, a small-time Democratic politico and grocer named William Cruise, who had arrived in New York from King's County, Ireland, in 1852, decided that riots provided just the opportunity he needed to purify his neighborhood for the white race. First, he led a gang of neighborhood toughs in an attack against a white prostitute who lived across the street from him on Thomas Street just east of West Broadway, and who catered to black clients. She fired her revolver at Cruise and chased him away. Cruise then directed his followers one block north and west to the Worth Street home of an interracial couple, William and Ann Derrickson. "He's the big nigger we want," cried Cruise. "We'll hang him to the lamp-post." When Cruise and his gang burst into the Derricksons' apartment, William had already escaped out the back window, thinking the rioters would spare his white wife and their eight-year-old son, Alfred. But Cruise and his accomplices viciously set upon the dark-skinned boy, beating him with a cart rung and other cudgels. "For God's sake," screamed his mother, "kill me and save my boy." That's exactly what the rioters did. By the end of Tuesday, the *Herald* estimated, 150 African Americans had been attacked all over the city.[32]

The most Irish district in the city, Five Points, remained relatively quiet, not because the African American population there was left unmolested, but because, as the *Herald* pointed out, "the blacks are now all gone, and there is no cause for disturbance left." This black flight was a citywide phenomenon. The *Herald* noted that most of the city's ten thousand or so African American residents had fled to Long Island or New Jersey. But even flight could be dangerous. Realizing that he might be attacked if found on the streets, Jeremiah Robinson had dressed in women's clothes in an attempt to evade the mob as he tried to make his way from his Fourth Ward home to an East River ferry. But rioters spied his beard beneath his cape and hood and set upon him viciously, "and the atrocities they perpetrated are so revolting," wrote journalist David Barnes, "that they are unfit for publication." Hundreds more African Americans, primarily women and children, sought shelter in the city's police stations. "We are overrun with Negroes," complained the patrolmen, but the commissioner of police had told them to turn no one away.[33]

The onslaught against African Americans reached its height on Wednesday the fifteenth, when rioters lynched three black men and drowned or bludgeoned to death at least three more. At 6:30 a.m. a mob on 32nd Street near Seventh Avenue chased African American shoemaker James Costello, who lived nearby at 97 West 33rd Street. Costello managed to shoot one of the attackers with his pistol before he was seized by the throng, beaten, kicked, stoned, and finally lynched on a nearby tree. Later that morning, despite torrential rain, rioters led by Irish-born laborer James Cassidy went house to house through the neighborhood in search of any remaining African Americans. "All you damned niggers get out of here in five minutes," shouted Cassidy when he found any, "or we will burn down the house over your heads . . . Don't never show your face in this street again."

Disabled coachman Abraham Franklin did not heed these warnings. Early that afternoon a mob found him hiding with his sister Henrietta in a house at the corner of Seventh Avenue and West 27th Street. The crowd beat Henrietta and lynched her brother from a lamppost on 28th Street. Helping the predominantly Irish rioters hoist Franklin to his death was a Jewish immigrant from England, tailor Mark Silva. A passing company of troops cut Franklin down, but the mob strung him back up after the militiamen had passed on. According to one eyewitness, a "demon in human form" approached the lifeless body, pulled out a knife, and asked, "Who wants some Nigger meat?" "I, I, I," replied the crowd, as the knife wielder cut off Franklin's fingers and toes and tossed them to the crowd. Later, sixteen-year-old Irish-born butcher Patrick Butler dragged Franklin's body down the street by the genitals. Rioters lynched a third African American that same day in the West 30s between Sixth and Seventh avenues. Even neighborhoods with few blacks and relatively little rioting saw brutal attacks on African Americans that day.[34]

There were not enough troops in the city on Wednesday to allow the authorities to maintain order; the militiamen might disperse the rioters in one place, but the mob would simply reorganize a few blocks away. Again and again rioters defied the authorities' threats to open fire, daring troops to shoot. These showdowns eventually led to the most deadly episodes of the four days of rioting. Wednesday morning, facing hundreds of protesters who refused to obey orders to clear the streets, a twenty-three-year-old artillerist, Lieutenant Benjamin Ryer, ordered his fifty-man platoon to fire two musket volleys into the crowd on Seventh Avenue near 32nd Street. Around 4:00 that afternoon, a crowd of about five thousand thronged that same west side neighborhood and re-lynched the men whom the troops had cut down that morning. Colonel Thaddeus Mott, a thirty-one-year-old artillery officer under McClellan who now ran the local operations of the Fourteenth New York Cavalry Regiment, arrived on the scene on horseback and cut down one of the lynch mob's victims with his saber. Considering any tampering with their victims a provocation, the crowd rushed Mott and his troops. Half mounted and half on foot, they responded by charging at the rioters with bayonets and sabers. The mob drew back but then regrouped and still would not disperse despite warnings that they would be fired upon if they did not do so. Mott then ordered the soldiers to let loose several thunderous volleys of canister from his two artillery pieces, which finally cleared the streets.

Simultaneously, on 42nd Street between Ninth and Eleventh avenues, a mob of two thousand had gathered. Ryer was dispatched to the scene with fifty soldiers, who were pelted with stones, brickbats, and gunfire from the surrounding tenements. The crowd ignored Ryer's warning that the troops would fire if the rioters did not begin clearing the street in one minute. His men had to fire five musket volleys, at twenty- to thirty-second intervals (the time it took to reload), to finally disperse the mob, and two more volleys when the rioters reorganized and pursued the departing troops. Ryer estimated that fifty rioters had been killed, undoubtedly an overestimate but one that gives a sense of how many bodies lay strewn on the streets after the encounter. The *Times* reporter at the scene found "the women and children filling the air with their cries and lamentations, while the men who were happily spared from the dreadful fate of their friends and companions sat mournful and sullen."[35]

The military did not always get the better of the rioters, in part because there were not enough soldiers to respond to every outbreak of violence. Around 6:00 p.m., authorities learned that a huge throng had gathered on First Avenue near 18th and 19th streets. With the most experienced troops still stationed on the west side, the two hundred militiamen sent to First Avenue were primarily New Yorkers who had volunteered to help put down the riots but had little or no military experience. Hearing that troops were approaching, "the mob seemed to swell into vast dimensions," wrote one eyewitness a few years later. "Hundreds hurried out on the house-tops, tore up brickbats, and hurled them with savage howls at the approaching soldiers. Shots were fired from secret ambushes, and soldiers fell before they had fired."

Despite firing each of their two artillery pieces at least ten times, these inexperienced troops made little headway in dispersing the crowd, and within min-

Rioters behind a makeshift barricade exchanged gunfire with the military on First Avenue on Wednesday July 15.

utes, ten of the militiamen lay dead or badly wounded in the street. The soldiers retreated, leaving their dead and wounded behind and almost losing their artillery pieces to the mob. One of the severely injured soldiers was their commander, thirty-three-year-old Colonel Edward Jardine, who had survived both Antietam and Fredericksburg unscathed but suffered a gaping bullet wound to his thigh on First Avenue. He might have endured the same fate as O'Brien but for the kindness of neighborhood residents who took in the wounded officer and hid him from the vengeful crowd that went door-to-door searching for him. Around 11:00 p.m. the militiamen returned to retrieve their fallen comrades, firing several more rounds from their artillery pieces before retreating once again after midnight.[36]

Had it not been for the appearance of additional military forces from Pennsylvania and Maryland late Wednesday night and early Thursday morning, it is hard to know whether the exhausted policemen and local militia units could have, on their own, subdued the rioters. Their hatred of the draft, Republicans, and African Americans seemed no less fervid on Wednesday night than it had been on Monday morning. The units that arrived on Wednesday and Thursday — the Seventh, Sixty-fifth, Seventy-fourth, and 152nd New York — were National Guard regiments, not, as legend has it, battle-hardened veterans straight from the fields of Gettysburg.[37] They had traveled to New York from places like Baltimore and Frederick, Maryland, and Carlisle and Harrisburg, Pennsylvania, where they had been assigned as a rear guard in the event that

Lee defeated the Army of the Potomac at Gettysburg. These troops were actually better equipped to handle the draft rioters than the veterans of Gettysburg because as guardsmen they had been specially trained to smother civil unrest.[38]

The additional troops who arrived overnight (raising the city's total to six thousand) certainly seemed to have the desired effect. "Law and order appear to be getting the upper hand again," wrote attorney Joseph Choate on Thursday. The *Times* agreed that the riot was apparently "subsiding." But the fighting was far from over. Around 1:00 p.m. Thursday afternoon, a mob attacked a contingent of several dozen state militiamen on First Avenue at about 22nd Street. The troops fired both their muskets and artillery pieces to clear the boulevard so they could make their way north to the corner of 28th Street, where they were to guard a foundry that produced war munitions. The soldiers took up positions inside the building and were immediately surrounded by a mob that may have numbered as many as four thousand. After a standoff that lasted all afternoon, the rioters attacked the building, but the well-positioned militiamen quickly drove them off with a fusillade of gunfire.[39]

The final significant clash of the riots took place near Gramercy Park soon after the standoff at the foundry had concluded. Cavalry troops patrolling the neighborhood were ambushed on 22nd Street between Second and Third avenues by snipers hiding in and on top of the buildings that lined the street. After initially retreating, the soldiers returned around 6:00 p.m. with reinforcements — about two hundred troops and policemen — and stormed the houses from which rioters appeared to be firing. A mob in the streets attacked the troops, but the soldiers drove the rioters to Second Avenue and then north to 31st Street, where the mob made a stand, firing at the soldiers from the street and from windows and rooftops. The military responded with artillery fire and by going house to house to root out the remaining snipers. "Some of them fought like incarnate fiends, and would not surrender," reported one of the soldiers. "All such were shot on the spot." By dusk these rioters had been subdued, arrested, or dispersed. Disgruntled rioters took a few more potshots at passing troops or policemen that evening from windows and rooftops, but by midnight even that type of resistance to the rule of law had ended. After nearly ninety hours of anarchy, the New York City draft riots were finally over.[40]

The "saturnalia of pillage and violence" that had rocked New York for four days left a staggering trail of death and destruction. We will never know exactly how many people were killed. One hundred and five deaths can be documented — ten soldiers and policemen, another ten or so bystanders, eleven African Americans, and about seventy-five rioters. Newspaper reporters and other contemporaries often insisted that many more had died. A few years later, Police Superintendent Kennedy put the death toll at 1,155, insisting that the rec-

ord number of "sunstroke" deaths in the summer of 1863 were actually the result of head wounds suffered by rioters beaten back by the police with their
truncheons. But even if the death toll was greater than 105, it was certainly
much, much closer to that figure than to Kennedy's unsubstantiated one. Reporters seeing twenty rioters lying on the ground in pools of blood after a musket volley from soldiers assumed that all the gunshot victims were dead or dying. But three-quarters of Union Civil War soldiers who were shot survived
their wounds, and a similar proportion of rioters probably did as well.[41]

Yet the impact of the riots went far beyond the death toll. One hundred sev-
enty-eight policemen and soldiers were wounded, and more than one hundred
of those injuries were serious. We know of 128 wounded rioters, but surely that
number represents only a fraction of the total, as many would have sought care
on their own rather than go to a hospital and face arrest for having been injured
as part of a lawbreaking mob. If rioters survived gunshot wounds at about the
same rate as Civil War soldiers, then there should have been about 250 rioters with bullet wounds, and hundreds more with concussions and contusions
caused by blows from police billy clubs.[42]

There was also the physical toll on the city itself. Dozens of fires had been
set, hundreds of homes invaded and ransacked, and hundreds of businesses
looted, from Harlem to the Battery. We will never know the true number of
such attacks, because as lawyer George Templeton Strong noted in his diary
when it was all over, "not half the history of this memorable week has been
written. I could put down pages of incidents that the newspapers have omitted,
any one of which would in ordinary times be the town's talk." These crimes, if
tallied, would certainly number in the thousands.[43]

The riots had a long-lasting psychological impact on the city. Anti-Irish and
anti-Catholic prejudice, whose death Meagher had celebrated in 1861, came
roaring back in a matter of days as a result of "the atrocities, the murders, the
arson, the pillage." Placards calling for a revival of the Know Nothing Party appeared all over the city. *Harper's Weekly* predicted that many employers would
now refuse to hire the Irish. Strong found the "feeling against Irishmen" to be
"more bitter and proscriptive" than at any point in his forty-three-year lifetime.
"No wonder. The atrocities those Celtic devils perpetrated can hardly be paral-
leled in the history of human crime and cruelty." Strong himself was swept up
in the anti-Irish animus, confiding to his diary that if he could have his way, he
would have "war made on [the] Irish scum as in 1688." It would take years for
this anti-Irish bigotry to subside.[44]

Irish New Yorkers tried to defend themselves. Only a tiny fraction of the
200,000 Irish-born New Yorkers played any role in the rioting, argued the
Irish-American. An entire people should not be condemned for the crimes of a

few. Privately, however, Irish immigrants were more likely to accept that their community deserved at least some of the scorn that other New Yorkers were heaping upon them. "I am very sorry that the Irish men of New York took so large a part in them disgracefull riots," wrote Sergeant Peter Welsh to his wife in New York. "God help the Irish[.] They are to easily led into such snares which gives their enemys an oppertunity to malighn and abuse them." Welsh told his wife that "the originaters of those riots should be hung like dogs[.] I hope the authorutys will use canister freely[.] It will bring the bloody cutthroats to their censes."[45]

What, in the end, had inspired these rioters to commit, over four days, what one German immigrant called "every atrocity imaginable"? The mobs were clearly inspired in part by class grievances. Yet political resentments seem to have been even more important; after all, the rioters attacked only those wealthy New Yorkers who supported abolition and the war. And racial bigotry clearly played an equal if not even larger role in motivating the mobs.[46]

In part, the rioters were responding to a belief that Republicans cared more about black slaves than white Irishmen. "Fernando Wood told us to burn the Colored Asylum, and we think it is right," proclaimed one rioter. "Why should [the orphans of] niggers live in the Fifth avenue," while the orphans of poor "white folks have to go to the Island," a reference to the neglected state-run asylum on what is now Roosevelt Island, where the city also warehoused convicts and the insane. Catholic Maria Daly confided to her diary that she hoped the riots "will give the Negroes a lesson, for since the war commenced, they have been so insolent as to be unbearable. I cannot endure free blacks. They are immoral, with all their piety." While Daly was not an immigrant herself, her views undoubtedly reflected those of many immigrant rioters who, through acts of grotesque violence, sought to intimidate African Americans into once again becoming servile and deferential, or drive them from the city altogether.[47]

Ultimately, the specific grievance that drove most of the rioters into the streets was not emancipation but the hated $300 commutation clause of the draft law. "You will, no doubt, be hard on us rioters tomorrow morning," wrote one of them to the *Times* in a letter written on Tuesday the fourteenth and published the next day,

> but that 300-dollar law has made us nobodies, vagabonds and cast-outs of society, for whom nobody cares when we must go to war and be shot down. We are the poor rabble, and the rich rabble is our enemy by this law. Therefore we will give our enemy battle right here, and ask no quarter. Although we got hard fists, and are dirty without, we have soft hearts, and have clean

consciences within, and that's the reason we love our wives and children more than the rich, because we got not much besides them and we will not go and leave them at home for to starve. Until that draft law is repealed, I for one am willing to knock down more such rum-hole politicians as KENNEDY. Why don't they let the nigger kill the slave-driving race and take possession of the South, as it belongs to them.

The writer signed himself "A POOR MAN, BUT A MAN FOR ALL THAT."[48]

Just a couple of weeks after order had been restored, the authorities resumed the draft, lest it appear that mob law would trump civil law. When the city conscription was completed in late July and August, it became apparent that immigrants' fears of being forced en masse into the army were largely unfounded. The overwhelming majority of drafted immigrants successfully claimed exemptions, on the basis of either medical ailments or their status as non-citizens. (In an era when there was no central repository of naturalization records, and any court could conduct naturalization proceedings, it was virtually impossible to prove that any given immigrant was a citizen.) Almost all of the remaining immigrant draftees evaded service simply by not showing up at the draft office after their names were chosen. As one German reported, most merely "move to another address so they can't be found." But a few left the city altogether. "I was drafted and was supposed to go to war," Heinrich Müller confided in a letter to his parents near Hamburg, "but to keep my wife and children from misery, I ran away and went deep into the countryside, and they didn't get me." Others, like grocer Emile Dupré, had the wherewithal to purchase the services of substitutes.[49]

In the end, only a tiny number of immigrants were obliged to enter the military as a result of the conscription. In Five Points, for example, home to thousands of draft-age men, only a single draftee, a twenty-seven-year-old laborer named Hugh Boyle, was compelled to join the army under the 1863 draft. In the Fourth Ward, the second most Irish ward in the city, not a single draftee had to join the army. Other than Boyle, all the draftees in these two wards received exemptions, failed to report, hired substitutes, or paid the $300 commutation fee. Some of the substitute fees may have been financed by the city government, which in reaction to the draft riots and the perception that a disproportionate number of city residents were being conscripted, allocated $2 million for the hiring of substitutes for municipal workers and other New Yorkers who could not raise the money themselves and had dependents who relied on them for support. Even in northern cities that did not allocate funds to pay substitutes, the results were similar. In all of Boston, for example, only three Irish immi-

Thousands of immigrants came to New York in the last years of the war expressly to enlist in the army and collect the huge bounties offered by the federal and state governments. This image shows recruiters attempting to enlist immigrants into the military just outside the immigration reception station at Castle Garden.

grants had to join the army as a result of the 1863 draft. In cities from New Haven to Harrisburg and Scranton, not a single Irish immigrant was forced into service.[50]

Many of New York's immigrants did join the army at this time, but not because they had to. Thousands of foreign-born Americans jumped at the chance to become substitutes, because between the fee paid by the draftee and the bounties paid by local, state, and federal authorities, a substitute could sometimes make as much as $700 (nearly two years' wages for a day laborer) in a single day by joining the army. Some decided to emigrate from Europe in the middle of the war expressly for this purpose. James Murphy of County Clare asked the American consul in Dublin if the United States government would pay his way to New York, "as I have a great wish to join the northern army . . . I would suffer death for North America and the gallant Corcoran."[51]

Another European enticed to emigrate by a war bonus was a seventeen-year-old Hungarian Jew named Joseph Pulitzer, who accepted free passage to Boston from a Hamburg recruiter in August 1864 in exchange for the promise of a $100 enlistment payment. When Pulitzer and several of his shipmates discovered that the enrollment bounty was actually $300, and that the recruiter was pocketing two-thirds of that sum, they decided to seek a better deal. The army placed the new recruits on Deer Island in Boston Harbor, but before they could be enrolled, Pulitzer and his comrades swam ashore and made their way to New York. They headed to City Hall Park, where officials from all over the country had set up tents from which to recruit immigrant substitutes to fill their state and local enrollment quotas. Telling the recruiter he was twenty years old, though he was still just seventeen, Pulitzer agreed to serve as a substitute for a twenty-two-year-old farmer from upstate New York in exchange for a $200 substitution fee plus the enrollment bonuses that all enlistees received. Claiming (with much exaggeration) to be an accomplished equestrian, Pulitzer was assigned to a predominantly German and Hungarian company in one of General Philip Sheridan's cavalry divisions in Virginia's Shenandoah Valley. He served with that unit from September 1864 until the end of the war.[52]

Immigration also picked up mid-war because labor shortages (and to some extent inflation) had sent wages to unheard-of levels, enticing hundreds of thousands of Europeans to emigrate. "These are golden times for craftsmen, workers and soldiers," reported Karl Wesslau to his family in Prussia. Wages in the summer of 1863 were "twice as high as last year, a good cabinetmaker can earn 2½ dollars a day, a laborer 1½ dollars, instead of ¾ of a dollar before." Wages remained high in the first half of 1864, resulting in an influx of immigrants three times higher than in the first year of the war.

For some immigrants, of course, wartime inflation was disastrous. Those with significant savings like Wesslau saw "the value of their wealth just melt away." But overall, immigrants of modest means who stayed out of the army fared well during the war years.[53]

For those immigrants who joined the military, the risks sometimes far outweighed the rewards. Take the case of Robert Sneden, the Canadian-born architect turned army mapmaker. In November 1863 his regiment left him behind to finish a map as the rest of the troops evacuated their position at Brandy Station, Virginia, sixty miles southwest of Washington. Sneden was supposed to catch up with his unit the next day. But before he could do so, he was captured by Mosby's Rangers, a semiautonomous battalion of Virginia cavalrymen who patrolled northern Virginia and harassed Union soldiers and sympathizers. Though he did not put up a struggle, Sneden was pistol-whipped by his captors before being personally interrogated by twenty-nine-year-old Major John Mosby.

That beating was nothing compared to the ordeal Sneden would soon suffer. In his first months as a prisoner of war, Sneden nearly died of typhoid fever in Pemberton Prison, a converted tobacco warehouse in Richmond. His reward for recovering was a transfer to the notorious Andersonville prison camp, 120

Sneden's depiction of the Andersonville prisoner of war camp, sketched while he was held there. He added watercolor details after the war.

miles south of Atlanta, where exposure and grossly inadequate rations turned the camp into what Sneden called, without exaggeration, a "hell on earth." Because the Confederacy vowed to enslave rather than imprison any of the Union's African American soldiers it captured, the Lincoln administration had halted POW exchanges, meaning that Sneden might have to endure these conditions for months, even years. "Not a hope left for exchange," he wrote in his diary in March 1864. "Every one is despondent . . . Hunger gnaws at our vitals day and night." His teeth began to fall out that summer as Sneden became one of the camp's 35,000 emaciated walking skeletons.[54]

As Sneden's health deteriorated further over the summer of 1864, the war seemed to have reached a stalemate. After impressive victories in 1863 over Confederate forces at Vicksburg, Mississippi, in July and at Chattanooga, Tennessee, in November, General Ulysses S. Grant was transferred east by Lincoln in order to take charge of the Army of the Potomac's fight against Lee. Northerners were full of optimism as Grant began his Overland Campaign against Lee's Army of Northern Virginia in the spring of 1864, hoping that the relentlessness that had made Grant so successful in the west would enable him to defeat Lee and end the war. Grant initially made quick progress, driving Lee back toward and beyond Richmond, albeit at a terrible cost in dead and wounded. But his offensive stalled in June outside Petersburg, twenty-five miles south of the Confederate capital, with the Confederates so well entrenched that frontal assault seemed suicidal. As Grant's army settled in for a siege, suddenly the war appeared to be no closer to its conclusion than it had six months earlier.

With the competing armies at a stalemate, the North turned its attention to the upcoming presidential election. New York, which had given its electoral votes to Lincoln in 1860 but chosen a Democrat as governor in 1862, would be a key battleground state. Believing that Americans in general, and New Yorkers in particular, would not reelect Lincoln if they fully understood the implications of his emancipation policy, an Irish immigrant Democrat in New York City decided to take matters into his own hands. In doing so, he perpetrated one of the most elaborate and far-reaching political hoaxes of the nineteenth century and changed the vocabulary Americans used to talk about race.

The instigator of this ruse, David Goodman Croly, was by no means a typical New York Irish immigrant. Born in Clonakilty, County Cork, on the southwest coast of Ireland in November 1829, Croly moved with his family to New York at age five. His father was a silversmith, and young David apprenticed in that trade and worked at it for several years after finishing his training. But "conscious that he was out of place as a mechanic," as a biographer later put it, Croly decided to become a journalist. At age twenty-four he enrolled in a one-year program at New York University, and after graduation he landed a job as a reporter for the New York *Evening Post*. He must have been an impressive young man, because before long he moved to the *Herald*, which placed him in charge of its "City Intelligence" column. Soon afterward, on Valentine's Day 1856, he married Jane Cunningham, an English immigrant (and daughter of a Unitarian minister) who had also come to America as a child. She had moved to New York City from upstate in 1855 to start her own career in journalism, quite a daring endeavor at a time when not a single woman writer was employed by any of the dozens of newspapers and magazines then published in the city.[55]

Most men with a job such as David Croly's would have discouraged their wives from working for pay outside the home, especially after their first child, Mary, was born in May 1860. But David Croly prided himself on being open-minded, a visionary, a modern thinker. Besides, the "volcanic force" of Jane's personality, as her brother characterized it, combined with what a colleague called her "magnetism and charm of a rare nature," meant that she would not be stopped, baby or no baby. In 1859 she had secured her first steady newspaper job, writing a weekly women's column for the *New York Sunday Times* (wholly unaffiliated with the famous daily of that name) under the pen name "Jenny June." By the fall of 1864, Jenny June was famous across the United States, regularly quoted in newspapers nationwide even though her true identity was still shrouded in secrecy.

David Croly, meanwhile, had become city editor of the *New York World* on the eve of the war and in 1862 its managing editor. In these years the paper established itself as the city's (and perhaps the nation's) leading Democratic publication. Croly's meteoric ascent in New York's journalistic circles was due in part to the fact that, like his wife, Croly was an unabashed workaholic. He even tried to control the subject matter of his dreams so he could continue to work in his sleep and awaken with an even longer list of potential stories for his editors to assign. Whether in his dreams or his waking hours, at the end of 1863 Croly came up with one of his most audacious ideas yet.[56]

Thinking ahead to the presidential election of 1864 and how the Democrats might best exploit white Americans' unease with the Emancipation Proclamation, Croly decided to write (with the help of a *World* colleague) a lengthy pamphlet, designed to look like the work of an abolitionist or a Republican, which would endorse racial equality so radically that it would drive white voters into the Democratic fold. To attract the public's attention, Croly chose to invent an entirely new word to describe the terrible fate Americans would suffer if Lincoln was given four more years in the White House. He plastered the new word across the cover of his seventy-two-page publication in huge block letters: MISCEGENATION.

Pretending to be a believer in total equality between the races, Croly wrote about how happy he was that as a result of emancipation, whites and blacks would soon begin to intermarry in huge numbers. The offspring of these interracial couples would blur the boundaries between the races through a process he approvingly termed "miscegenation" (a word he coined, he wrote, by combining the Latin words for "mixed" and "race"). The children born as a result of miscegenation would themselves indiscriminately marry blacks and whites and have more mixed-race children, and before long, predicted the authors with feigned enthusiasm, there would be no whites or racial boundaries left in the United States. "It is the duty of anti-slavery men everywhere to advocate miscegenation . . . In the millenial future, the most perfect and highest type of manhood will not be white or black, but brown."[57]

Croly sent *Miscegenation* anonymously to prominent abolitionists and Republicans, asking that they comment on its ideas in the hope that he could publish their positive responses and thereby embarrass Republicans on the eve of the election. While quite a few abolitionists did take the bait, Republican officeholders were too smart or suspicious to fall for the trap. But Democratic politicians and newspapers, including the *World,* quoted extensively from *Miscegenation* itself as evidence of the Republicans' secret agenda for ending the separation of the races and ultimately destroying the "white race" altogether. The pamphlet even became the subject of a debate on the floor of Congress and drew the attention of the European press. Confederates cited it as proof that they had been right to secede. Croly had succeeded in shaping the campaign of 1864 to a greater extent than he could ever have imagined possible.[58]

Yet Croly could not alter the outcome of the race. Lincoln carried New York and won even more states in 1864 than he had four years earlier. The residents of New York City had not grown any more fond of Lincoln since 1860; his support there fell from 35 percent in 1860 to 33 percent in 1864. Lincoln won less than 10 percent of the vote in the city's most Irish neighborhood, Five Points, and his tally fell significantly in the most heavily German wards. None of that mattered, however, as he easily carried the state and the presidency. The hoax was exposed immediately after the campaign, but Croly's part in it came to light only after his death in 1889.[59]

Croly could not pry enough votes away from the Republicans to win New York for the Democrats in part because most of those who had joined the army, immigrants included, felt that a repudiation of Lincoln would send the wrong message to the Confederacy. They feared that a Democratic president, who might be willing to end the war short of total victory and full restoration of the Union, would squander their sacrifices. Immigrant August Horstmann aptly summed up the reasons why so many Americans — native-born and immigrant alike — voted to reelect Lincoln even though they might have misgivings about the conduct of the war or the Emancipation Proclamation. Writing to his parents, who had expressed shock that their son had reenlisted when his three-year commitment to the army expired in the summer of 1864, he replied: "You rebuke me for having signed up for another three years? Dear parents! Men of principle do not put up with 3 long years of the greatest hardships imaginable — without receiving some kind of reward, being able to see either the successful or unsuccessful outcome of their efforts. He who fights for ideals and principles cannot stop halfway! . . . Believe me, this war will be fought to the end, the rebellion will be defeated, slavery abolished, [and] equal rights established in *all America*."

Irish soldiers were less likely to express their support for Lincoln and the war in such terms, but they too wanted the war to be fought to its conclusion to insure that the Union remained whole. The Democratic platform of 1864, in contrast, called for "a cessation of hostilities" and a negotiated settlement. Lincoln's determination to see the war through to its end won him many votes and secured his reelection.[60]

Another factor that led to Lincoln's easy victory was the success of General William T. Sherman's invasion of northern Georgia in the summer of 1864, which ended in the capture of Atlanta in September. Sherman's campaign may also have saved Sneden's life. More than a quarter of the 45,000 prisoners who entered Andersonville's wooden stockade walls perished there. As Atlanta fell, however, and it appeared possible that Sherman would move south from there toward Andersonville, the Confederates decided to move many of the camp's prisoners. Sneden was one of the lucky ones transferred out, in his case to Savannah, where his rations increased exponentially. In December, with Sherman now approaching the Georgia coast on his march to the sea, Sneden's captors moved him again, this time to South Carolina. When the two sides agreed to resume POW swaps, Sneden was finally exchanged. By Christmas he was in Baltimore, and the next day he returned to New York. Sneden carried the war's scars — both physical and psychological — with him for the rest of his life. So too did New York's thousands of other immigrant veterans.[61]

Sherman, too, moved north from Savannah, entering South Carolina on the first of February. His army wreaked havoc and left a wide swath of destruction in its wake as it advanced toward a reunion with Grant in southern Virginia. As word of Sherman's exploits reached Lee's troops in Petersburg and Richmond, they deserted by the thousands in order to return home to protect their families. Lee abandoned his Petersburg trenches on April 2, and after a week spent trying to fight his way to safety in western Virginia, he surrendered at Appomattox Courthouse, eighty-five miles west of Richmond, on April 9, 1865. After four long years, 600,000 deaths, and nearly as many wounded, the Civil War was finally over.

New Yorkers began celebrating the news from Virginia as soon as Richmond fell, and these celebrations reached their peak with Lee's surrender. "Every day was like a holiday during the first half of April," wrote Julius Wesslau. But, he recalled, "the rejoicing came to a sudden end on Good Friday, when the president was murdered by a rebel conspiracy. I can't begin to describe what a shattering effect this had here." With Lincoln's assassination, neither North nor South could feel good about the end of the war, perhaps a fitting ending for such a horrific, deadly conflict that had left so many Americans dead, so many more gruesomely injured, and still more with permanent psychological wounds. When Lincoln's body arrived in New York on the twenty-fifth and his funeral cortege processed up Broadway, it seemed as if the entire city had turned out to pay its last respects, even though relatively few New Yorkers, and very few of New York's immigrants, had voted for him. "Everyone was most deeply moved, and in the procession and in the entire city, with all its good and evil men, there was nothing but solemn silence," wrote Wesslau, who himself had been no fan of Lincoln's. "The rebellion is now over, but anyone who experienced it here will never forget it."[62]

13

TRANSITION

IN THE WRITING of American history, the Civil War usually marks a turning point. The war brought about the United States' transition from slavery to freedom. It was the catalyst for the economic shift away from agriculture and toward industrialization. Before the war, the country's population was concentrated in the East; henceforth, the most dynamic demographic growth would take place in the West. Prior to the war, many Americans saw themselves as part of a collection of political entities they called "these United States," but afterwards they perceived the country as a more unified nation they called "the United States."[1]

In terms of immigration history, however, the Civil War was not a turning point, either for New York or for the United States as a whole. On the eve of the war, 81 percent of the immigrants arriving at the port of New York came from just two places: Ireland and the German states. That figure was virtually unchanged in 1865, when the war ended.

Over the ensuing decades, however, a slow but steady transition took place. The Irish and German proportion of the immigrants arriving in New York dropped to 53 percent in 1875, 43 percent in 1885, and just 22 percent in 1895. The decline in Irish immigration was particularly steep, falling from 55 percent of total New York arrivals in 1850 to only 30 percent in 1870, 20 percent in 1880, and just 12 percent in 1890. Instead, immigrants from other parts of Europe, particularly Italians and east European Jews, began to outnumber the Germans and the Irish. Immigrants from China and the Caribbean began to settle in New York as well.[2]

The immigrants on the S.S. *Nevada,* the first ship processed at Ellis Island when it became the port's immigration station in 1892, exemplified this evolution. The most famous passenger on the *Nevada,* Irish-born Annie Moore, garnered all the press coverage as the first immigrant registered at the new facility.

Moore's shipmates included seven other Irish immigrants, twelve from England, fourteen from Sweden, and fourteen from other parts of western Europe. But southern and eastern European immigrants (primarily Italians and Russian Jews) outnumbered those from western Europe on the *Nevada* by two to one. And while the northwestern European immigrants on board the *Nevada* planned to scatter all across the United States, almost all of the Jews and Italians told officials at Ellis Island that they intended to make New York City their new home. Slowly but surely, the changes exemplified by the passengers on the *Nevada* would transform New York's immigrant communities, the city, and the entire nation.[3]

The one revolution in the immigrant experience that did coincide with the Civil War involved the means by which immigrants traveled to America. Sailing ships had slowly and perilously carried several million immigrants to the port of New York in the 240 years since Henry Hudson first claimed Manhattan for the Dutch in 1609. But by 1850, machinists had improved steam engine safety and reliability to such an extent that huge steam-powered vessels could now cross the Atlantic four times faster than those sailing ships. And because immigrants arriving by steamship spent so much less time in steerage, the voyage became much safer. While one out of every one hundred steerage passengers died in the typical transatlantic crossing by sail in the immediate pre–Civil War years, only one per one thousand perished on steamship voyages. In 1856, the first year port officials identified modes of transportation, steamship passengers made up fewer than 4 percent of the total. But as competition drove down the price, more and more immigrants chose steamships. In 1861, nearly one in three immigrants came to America on a steamship. By the war's end in 1865, steamship passengers for the first time were a majority, and by 1870, steamships carried more than 90 percent of all immigrants. Never again would the voyage to America be the most terrifying portion of the immigrant experience.[4]

Another change in the lives of New York's immigrants in the immediate postwar years was the advent of the political "machine" developed by the city's leading Democratic organization, Tammany Hall. Fascinated by the potential of mechanization to revolutionize their lives, Americans in the Civil War years began to describe as a "machine" any entity that worked so ceaselessly and efficiently as to seem unstoppable. That politicians were already notorious for their "machinations" made the comparison of powerful political organizations to machines seem even more apt. By 1850, the term "machine politics" had entered the American lexicon, and by the late 1850s, New Yorkers commonly complained about the "wireworkers now running the Tammany machine."[5]

In the immediate postwar years, it was not perfectly clear who directed New York's Democratic machinery. The face of the city's Democratic Party was Mayor John T. Hoffman, who was elected to that post in 1865 and held it until he became governor in 1869. But even before Hoffman moved to Albany, insiders and eventually the whole city came to realize that the true wizard behind the curtains of Tammany Hall was a man named William M. Tweed.

Contrary to popular belief, Tweed was not an immigrant but was born in 1823 in New York City, where his father and grandfather had also been born. Growing up on the east side in the Seventh Ward, Tweed held a variety of jobs in his teens, but as a young adult took a position as a bookkeeper in a neighborhood brush- and bellows-making shop in which his father owned a stake. In 1844 Tweed married Mary Jane Skaden, the daughter of the majority shareholder. A year later the couple had the first of their ten children, eight of whom survived to adulthood. By 1855, Tweed and his brother were concentrating their efforts on the family chair business, which had retail outlets on Cherry and Pearl streets and a workshop on Ridge. Yet Tweed does not appear to have been a very good businessman; sales were so poor that he declared bankruptcy in 1861.[6]

Although Tweed struggled with his personal finances, he was a natural at politics. Affable and garrulous, Tweed excelled at the backroom bargaining and deal cutting necessary to win nominations for himself and his friends. He rose to power not by holding positions such as the mayoralty, which would have placed him in the public spotlight, but instead through leadership positions in the Democratic Party or through relatively minor government posts to which he was often appointed rather than elected. These included a seat on the board of supervisors beginning in 1858, the chairmanship of the New York City Democratic Committee in 1861, head of the general committee of Tammany Hall in 1863, election as "grand sachem" of the Tam-

"Boss" William Tweed, leader of the New York City Democratic Party after the Civil War, became the personification of Gilded Age political corruption.

many Society that same year, appointment as deputy street commissioner, also in 1863, and later commissioner of public works.[7]

By 1863, Tweed could have had virtually any Democratic nomination he chose. He undoubtedly selected the street department because it gave him control over the appointment of the several thousand city workers who paved, repaired, and cleaned the city's ever-expanding network of thoroughfares. Tweed vastly increased that workforce to insure patronage for every deserving Democrat. Meanwhile, Tweed's positions in Tammany Hall — he was the first to hold so many top posts simultaneously — gave him unprecedented power over Democratic electoral nominations, such that the vast majority of active Democrats in the city owed their offices and political futures to him. Furthermore, through his posts in the street department and on the board of supervisors, Tweed and his close ally Peter Sweeny were never very far from the spigots through which the city's budget monies flowed.

Tweed's power in the mid-1860s was never absolute and was often tenuous. Other Democrats struggled to displace him, and for a while, immediately after the war, they succeeded. But by 1867 or 1868, the "Hoffman, Sweeny and Tweed Ring" was firmly in control of Tammany Hall, "extending itself and encircling within it all the [elected and appointed] offices in the city." In 1870 the press began to refer to him as "Boss Tweed."[8]

New Yorkers might not have objected to Tweed's rise within Tammany Hall had it not coincided with a huge increase in city expenditures. After the unprecedented taxes levied to pay for the Civil War, New Yorkers of means wanted the city budget scaled back to prewar levels. But under Tweed and his allies, New York's municipal budget continued to grow for several years after the war. That increase coincided with the creation and growth of Tweed's personal fortune.

By 1870 it was hardly a secret how the recently bankrupt Tweed had become a multimillionaire despite the tiny salaries he earned as a deputy street commissioner and a supervisor. Tweed and his cronies became masters of "pay to play" decades before that term was even coined. If a real estate developer wanted a street paved or improved to make his property more valuable, he had to compensate Tweed. If a business sought an edge in securing a city contract, it had to pay the "Boss." "He thrives on percentages of pilfering, grows rich on the distributed dividends of rascality," complained the *New York World,* a Democratic paper, in 1870. "His extortions are as boundless in their sum as in their ingenuity." The *Times* agreed, calling Tweed "the prime mover in the audacious faction which are now trying hard to ruin this City, and are making their own fortunes in the process . . . We look upon Mr. TWEED as the incarnation of all the vice in the City Government."[9]

How did Tweed and his "Ring" maintain power despite such vitriolic opposition? In part through electoral fraud. One infamous case involved Judge John McCunn, the Irish immigrant who had organized the Thirty-seventh New York Infantry Regiment in the spring of 1861 and served as its colonel. Soon after arriving in Washington, McCunn was court-martialed for having refused to show his pass while he was away from camp drinking at the bar in the Willard Hotel. Facing this embarrassment, plus charges from his own subordinates that he was an incompetent officer, McCunn resigned. Back in New York, he resumed his place in the municipal judiciary, but in 1863 Tweed decided to elevate the loyal magistrate to a more powerful position on the state Superior Court. The *Times* found the nomination astounding, calling McCunn "probably the worst man that ever offered himself as a candidate for a judgeship in any civilized country." When the preliminary returns were announced on election night, McCunn came up a few hundred votes shy of victory. But Tweed and Tammany were not about to let that stop them. Their henchmen in Five Points were directed to "recount" the ballots, and sure enough the Five Points poll workers found that they had "transposed" a few numerals in the preliminary returns. The new, fraudulent results gave McCunn a narrow victory. He would later repay Tweed by using his new judgeship to help the Ring maintain its power.[10]

Changing already announced election results was dangerous, so Tweed came to rely on two other methods to produce the polling place tallies that he sought. Sometimes, as Tweed later admitted once he was finally arrested, Tammany's operatives would alter the results after counting the ballots but before announcing them to the press. In other cases they would not even bother counting the votes and instead turn in completely fictitious tallies. When Republicans and reform-minded Democrats demanded to observe the vote counting, Tammany tried bribing or threatening the inspectors.[11]

Bribes were also risky, so the Tweed Ring began to rely on other methods to steal elections. First, they hired hundreds, and sometimes thousands, of New Yorkers as "repeaters," men paid to vote multiple times in a given election. In 1868 Alderman Edward Cuddy, an Irish-born ward heeler, directed the registration and voting of repeat-

An Irish immigrant, Judge John McCunn was one of the key judicial allies of the Tweed Ring.

"THAT'S WHAT'S THE MATTER."

Boss Tweed. "As long as I count the Votes, what are you going to do about it? say?"

"Boss" Tweed's manipulation of the electoral system for the benefit of Tammany Hall's candidates was notorious.

ers from his Bowery saloon. State senator Mike Norton, an Irish immigrant from County Roscommon, had his brother Peter direct the repeaters operating in his west side district farther uptown.[12]

Norton epitomized the immigrants who could rise to prominence through the ranks of the Tweed Ring. Norton's impoverished family sent him to work at a New York crockery factory for three years beginning at age eight and then at a sugar refinery, where he worked until he was sixteen. After a year at sea as a mess boy on one of the first transatlantic steamers, Norton trained to be a cooper, but by age nineteen was working instead as a cartman. He must have been politically active even as a teen, for at age twenty-two he had secured a highly coveted position as a patrolman in the police department. In May 1861 he joined James Kerrigan's rowdy Twenty-fifth New York Infantry Regiment and was immediately elected a captain. Norton left the army to take care of his younger siblings after his father died and his mother became severely ill. Back in New York, he ran unsuccessfully for alderman in 1862 but did capture a seat on that board in 1864 and was reelected in 1866. In 1867, a month shy of his thirtieth birthday, he captured a seat in the state senate, the same year Tweed first won election to that body. Norton "makes no pretensions to speech-making," noted one biographer, "and is a man of few words." But he was "stout, muscular and powerfully built," the most important qualifications for office in the rough-and-tumble world of Tammany politics. He was also a shrewd political operator, outmaneuvering a number of far more experienced rivals for the state senate nomination. Once in Albany, Norton could expect to grow rich, selling his votes to the highest corporate and political bidders at the dawn of the Gilded Age. Like many allies of the Tweed Ring, Norton was admitted to the New York State bar without a single day spent studying the law, enabling him to hold a civil court judgeship after leaving the state legislature.[13]

A final Tammany method of manufacturing votes was to manufacture citizens, and here McCunn played the leading role. Political parties had for years offered to pay the naturalization fees of immigrants on the eve of important elections so that the grateful new voters might cast ballots for their benefactors. In 1868, desperate to elect Hoffman governor, Tweed cranked up Tammany's "Naturalization-mill" to unprecedented levels. McCunn alone naturalized 27,897 immigrants in 1868. To save time, McCunn did not even admit the immigrants to his courtroom, but had their witnesses file through "in a long train," in which each one quickly swore that the immigrant in question had been in the United States five years and was of good character. When even this proved too slow, McCunn allowed one apparently very well known New Yorker

The chaotic scene in Judge John McCunn's courtroom as he rushed through the naturalization of immigrants on the eve of the 1869 elections.

named Patrick Goff to attest to the qualifications of 2,162 different immigrants, more than a thousand of them in one frenzied three-day marathon. Once word of his naturalization irregularities made it into the press, McCunn scaled them back, but other Tammany judges picked up the slack. And those who needed additional naturalization certificates to facilitate repeat voting could purchase them illegally from Benjamin Rosenberg, a Bavarian-born Jewish immigrant who managed Tammany's naturalization headquarters on Centre Street.[14]

Even when these frauds became common knowledge, many New Yorkers, and immigrants in particular, remained remarkably loyal to Tweed and Tammany. This was ironic because early in his political career, Tweed had been an avowed nativist. In the New York mayoral race of 1844 he supported James Harper, candidate of the nativist American Republican Party, which called for a ban on the appointment of immigrants to political office. Tweed remained active in the nativist movement throughout the 1840s, serving in 1848 and 1849 as president of his ward's nativist fraternal society, the Order of United Americans.

Nativists rarely became members of the Democratic Party, an organization that, in big northern cities like New York, relied heavily on immigrants for its success. But Tweed was, above all, a practical politician. With tens of thousands of immigrants settling in New York every year, and an overwhelming majority of them becoming Democrats, he could see that there was no future for an aspiring New York officeholder in any other party.[15]

New York's immigrants apparently forgave Tweed for his nativist past, if they knew about it at all, because under his leadership Tammany consistently addressed the issues that immigrants considered most important. After the draft riots, Tweed led a successful effort to have the city pay for substitutes for all drafted New Yorkers with dependents who could not afford to purchase a commutation with their own savings. In 1868 Tweed also secured tens of thousands of dollars in state funding for the city's Catholic schools, something the city's Irish immigrants had sought for decades. Tweed's vastly expanded municipal workforce pleased immigrants too, creating thousands of new jobs constructing and repairing roads, parks, and buildings, jobs that were far more steady and reliable than Irish immigrants could typically find. For those who still could not secure employment, or were unable to work because of illness or disability, Tweed set up his own network of relief organizations (the Tweed Poor Relief Association and the Tweed Benevolent Association) to alleviate their hardships. Tweed was one of the first American politicians to link his name so publicly to efforts to help the poor.[16]

Even though the leaders of the Tweed Ring were predominantly American-born, native New Yorkers blamed immigrants — and the Irish in particular—for both the Ring's crimes and its ability to maintain control of the city government. "Our rulers are partly American scoundrels and partly Celtic scoundrels," wrote attorney George Templeton Strong in his diary in 1868. "The Celts are predominant, however, and we submit to the rod and the sceptre of Maguires and O'Tooles and O'Shanes." As a result, Strong believed, New York was "governed by lower and baser blackguard scum than any city in Western Christendom, or in the world." At the height of the Ring's power in 1871, Strong continued to bemoan living under "the direct rule of 30,000 beastly Celtic bog-trotters."[17]

Immigrants may have helped perpetuate the reign of the Tweed Ring, but they also played nearly all the important roles in the drama that led to its eventual downfall. Crusading prosecutors, rival politicians, or muckraking journalists might have taken the lead in the crusade against Tweed, but in the end they assumed only supporting roles. Instead, the unlikely star was, of all things, an artist, a German immigrant from the Rhine River valley named Thomas Nast.

Nast was born in 1840 in the southwest German city of Landau. Deviating from the typical pattern of "chain migration," Nast's father, Joseph, a trombonist, sent the rest of his family ahead to New York in 1846 while he remained behind, first to complete his commitment as a musician in the Bavarian army, and then to work as a crewman on transatlantic sailing ships. The family eventually settled in Kleindeutschland, where young Thomas attended public schools until he faltered in his studies and his parents transferred him to a private German academy.[18]

Nast's lackluster academic work was primarily the result of indifference. Thomas loved to draw and could seemingly set his mind to nothing else, so his parents eventually allowed him to attend art school. At age fourteen, while still a pupil at one of the city's many small art academies, the ambitious Nast was already advertising himself as an "artist" with a studio on Broadway. When commissions failed to pour in, he bundled up a portfolio of his best work and took it to the city's only illustrated periodical, *Frank Leslie's Illustrated Newspaper,* where the fifteen-year-old was granted an audience with Frank Leslie himself.

Leslie, born Henry Carter in Ipswich, England, in 1821, had immigrated to the United States in 1848, two years after Nast. As a teen, the Englishman taught himself engraving, and kept at it even after his disapproving parents sent him to London to learn to be a merchant like his uncle, the owner of a glove-making business. Carter's work was eventually accepted for publication in the *Illustrated London News,* the world's first illustrated newsweekly, but Carter signed his contributions "Frank Leslie" to keep his artistic activities hidden from his parents. Sometime in his twenties, Leslie left the family glove-making business to work full-time for the *News,* eventually becoming its superintendent of engraving. Brimming with ambition, however, Leslie quit his enviable position and in 1848 immigrated to Brooklyn with his wife and three sons. After several false starts, he settled on the formula for *Frank Leslie's Illustrated Newspaper,* which first hit newsstands in 1855. During the Civil War, when Americans craved images from the battlefields, *Frank Leslie's* became a huge success.[19]

Later in life, when Nast recalled in caricature that first interview with Leslie, the German depicted Leslie as an aged spats-and-gold-watch-wearing giant of New York publishing, towering over an exceedingly short and rotund aspiring artist. When they first met, however, Leslie was only thirty-five and still years away from becoming a press tycoon. Yet the image is pure Nast; he sacrifices factual detail in order to make his point as clearly, dramatically, humorously, and memorably as possible.

Nast got the job, starting at $4 a week, eventually working his way up to $7. But with Leslie's newspaper struggling in the years before the Civil War, Nast lost his position and had to take freelance work. He lampooned police corruption in *Harper's Weekly* in 1859. In 1860 he covered both a bare-knuckle prizefight in England and Giuseppe Garibaldi's invasion of Italy for the *New York Illustrated News,* a short-lived competitor to *Leslie's* and *Harper's.* He returned to New York just as Lincoln passed through town on the way to his inauguration, and the *News* eventually assigned Nast to cover the Civil War.

Nast's depiction of the meeting in 1856 at which he, at age fifteen, asked Frank Leslie for a job.

Leslie immediately grasped that the war was a godsend to the illustrated press. Because Nast had proven his ability to get close to the action in Italy, Leslie wooed him back in early 1862 by offering him the unprecedented sum (for an artist) of $50 a week. Yet after several months, the fickle publisher decided that he could not afford Nast and summarily fired him.[20]

That dismissal turned out to be just the break Nast needed. He soon landed back at *Harper's Weekly,* where his work over the next decade would bring him fame and fortune. Fletcher Harper (son of James Harper, the nativist elected mayor in 1844) let Nast choose his own as-

Nast's image of a soldier and his wife thinking of each other on Christmas Eve in 1862 helped Nast solidify his position as the most popular artist at *Harper's Weekly*.

signments, and the artist soon proved that he had a unique gift for touching the hearts of *Harper's* readers. At the end of 1862, Nast portrayed a homesick soldier in camp on one page and his family in the North on the opposite page, each thinking of the other on Christmas Eve, separated by a row of soldiers' graves. One battle-hardened Union colonel reported that the image reduced him to tears. "It was only a picture," he wrote, "but I couldn't help it." At the end of the war, when General Ulysses S. Grant was asked who "he regarded as the most notable individual developed by the war," he answered, "I think Thomas Nast."[21]

In these very same years, Nast used the pages of *Harper's* to create the modern American image of Santa Claus. The issue that contained the drawing of the soldier and his family on Christmas Eve also included, on its cover, "Santa Claus in Camp," depicting a white-bearded Santa distributing gifts from home to the troops. Nast later portrayed Santa presiding over a workshop at the North Pole and with a ledger book recording which children had been naughty and which had been nice. Nast did not invent these aspects of the Santa tradition, but he made them indelible in Americans' minds.[22]

What made *Harper's* the perfect home for Nast was not the magazine's sentimentality but its politics. While *Leslie's* was scrupulously nonpartisan, *Harper's* was proudly Republican, and Nast flourished in an environment where he could take a stand, drawing editorial cartoons that starkly contrasted right and wrong, good and evil. After the war, the evil that Nast focused on first was the reactionary platform of the national Democratic Party. Nast's masterpiece in this regard, "This Is a White Man's Government" from 1868, takes its name from a phrase Democrats had been repeating since the end of the war to justify denying political rights to African Americans. Nast's drawing asked why an Irish Five Pointer who had burned an orphan asylum and lynched unoffending blacks during the draft riots was more deserving of the vote than an African American veteran who had risked his life to keep the Union together. Why did an unrepentant Confederate like General Nathan Bedford Forrest, the self-proclaimed founder of the Ku Klux Klan, portrayed at the center of Nast's composition, have political rights but not a black Union soldier? The third pillar of the Democratic Party portrayed in the cartoon, Fifth Avenue "capital," is personified by one of the nation's best-known German immigrants, New York financier August Belmont, chair of the Democratic National Committee. It did not bother Nast that he was presenting a fellow German immigrant in such an unflattering light. Nast was on the right side — the Republican side — and Belmont was not. Everything else was irrelevant.[23]

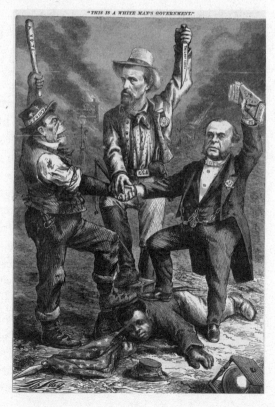

In "This Is a White Man's Government," produced for the 1868 presidential election, Nast conveys the idea that the only Americans who support Democratic candidate Horatio Seymour are riotous Five Pointers, ex-Confederates, and Fifth Avenue tycoons like August Belmont, who are united in their opposition to granting African Americans, even those who fought in the Civil War, the right to vote.

"This Is a White Man's Government" was part of *Harper's* successful campaign to elect Grant president in 1868. With the general in the White House and Republicans firmly in control of Congress, Nast began to direct his vitriol at Tweed and the Democrats who dominated New York City's government. Initially, Nast focused his fire on native-born politicos such as Tweed, Hoffman, Sweeny, and Hoffman's successor as mayor, A. Oakey Hall. Irish immigrants were portrayed as "slaves" of Tammany, lured to the polls with whiskey and the worst jobs the city had to offer.[24]

Irish immigrants became a more consistent target for Nast in the early 1870s after a pair of deadly riots involving Irish Catholics rocked the city. The first, on July 12, 1870, grew out of an attack on, of all things, a picnic. The outing was organized by several New York lodges of the Orange Order, a Protestant fraternal organization founded in northern Ireland in the late eighteenth century to celebrate the victories in Ireland of the armies of Prince William of Orange over Irish Catholic forces. The "Orangemen" organized their picnic on July 12 to celebrate the 180th anniversary of the Battle of the Boyne, one of the climactic battles that secured English control of Ireland.

Orangemen took particular pleasure processing through the streets of Ireland on the twelfth of July singing century-old anti-Catholic songs. Irish Catholics found these demonstrations humiliating and purposefully provocative, and the resulting fights in Ireland between Orangemen and Catholics on Boyne Day eventually led the English to ban Orange Order processions in Great Britain.[25]

After the Civil War, New York's Protestant Irish immigrants had paraded from their lodges to picnic grounds without incident until 1869, when fights between Orangemen and Irish Catholics had broken out both downtown on the Bowery and uptown on the Boulevard (as Broadway above 59th Street was then known) near 115th. A year later the Orangemen decided to organize an elaborate five-mile march from Cooper Square (at East 6th Street and the Bowery) to Elm Park, which ran from 91st to 92nd Street midway between Ninth and Tenth avenues in what was then the outskirts of the developed portion of the city. At the park, the Orangemen and their families would enjoy a picnic lunch and could dance in the pavilion or test their marksmanship in the shooting gallery. They would also hear speeches from the order's leaders recalling the heroic exploits of the Protestant armies at the Boyne River 180 years earlier.[26]

When the parade stepped off from in front of Cooper Union, the procession included all the usual trappings of a Boyne Day celebration. The participants wore orange sashes and ribbons and carried banners reading "Boyne," "Aughrim," and "Derry," the most significant Protestant victories in the Williamite War. According to the *Tribune*, these were "names odious to [Catholic] Irishmen, who can only see in them the humiliation of their race and the overthrow of their nationality." Accompanied by a marching band, the parade's participants sang their favorite sectarian tunes such as "The Boyne Water" and "Croppies, Lie Down," whose title refers to a pejorative nickname Irish Protestants gave Catholics, alluding to the cropped hair worn by members of certain Catholic religious orders. The song's chorus was sure to enrage any Irish Catholics who might come within earshot:

> Oh, Croppies, ye'd better be quiet and still
> Ye shan't have your liberty, do what ye will
> As long as salt water is found in the deep
> Our foot on the neck of the Croppie we'll keep.[27]

As the procession moved up the Boulevard, it passed several hundred Irish Catholic municipal employees laboring on improvements to the wide thoroughfare. After the parade had gone by, a rumor spread among the workers that the Orangemen had fired shots at a Catholic church as they passed it. White with rage, reported the *Tribune,* "the whole body of Boulevard men, as if by common consent and preconcerted action, quitted work, and, each carrying whatever tools he was working with, they went in a body toward Elm Park."[28]

When several hundred of the incensed road workers arrived at the park, they began heaving rocks and stones over the fence at the two thousand to three thousand Orangemen and their family members gathered there. While the women and children ran for cover at the other end of the park, the Orangemen hurled whatever projectiles they could find back at the rioters. Both sides eventually drew revolvers, reported the *Times,* though the Orangemen seem to have had many more of these than the Catholics. "Pistol-shots were exchanged in rapid succession; men fell bleeding and wounded; Irish yells rent the air." The gunplay caused a stampede of picnickers out of the park toward Ninth and Tenth avenues.[29]

The Catholics were not content merely to break up the Orange celebrations. They pursued the Irish Protestants to the avenues east and west, where the picnickers had jammed themselves into streetcars. "Stones and pistol bullets were fired through the windows into cars literally packed with men, women, and children," wrote the *Tribune*'s reporter, "and the fire was liberally returned from the inside." By 4:00 p.m. the "war of mutual extermination" comprised several battlefronts from Tenth Avenue to the east side of Central Park and from 94th Street to 82nd. "Men ran about in all directions, some armed with picks, shovels, bludgeons, but the greater part carrying huge cobble stones which they hurled at one another with demonic ferocity." Only at nightfall did the fighting finally end.[30]

When the coroner announced the riot's toll, it became clear that the Orangemen had meted out just as much punishment as they had received, if not more. Of the eight dead rioters, only two were Orangemen; the rest were apparently Irish Catholics. Dozens more were badly injured. Teamster Thomas Murray, who was approached on the Upper West Side by a "tall, well-dressed man" shouting, "You're one of them, you Papal son of a b----; I'll fix you," was shot in the face. Miraculously, he survived. The press found it "incomprehensible" that more New Yorkers did not die in the mayhem.[31]

As one might imagine, reaction to the riot broke down along religious lines. Most native-born New Yorkers, like Strong, blamed the bloodshed on "base and brutal Celts, such as those who burned orphan asylums and got up a Negro massacre in July, 1863 . . . Execrable Celtic *canaille!* The gorilla is their superior in muscle and hardly their inferior in moral sense." An Irish Protestant argued that signs with mottoes such as "Down With Popery" were a necessary response to New York's Irish Catholics, who through their prior actions had shown that their own mottoes were "down with freedom and liberty! down with free schools and the Bible! down with science and progress! down with intelligence and enlightenment! down and to death with heretics, and all who refuse to believe the Pope infallible! down with independence and free speech!"[32]

It was difficult for Irish Catholics to defend themselves from such assaults when it seemed indisputable that they had instigated the bloodshed. Instead, they tried to explain why the sight of Orangemen parading through the streets awakened such traumatic memories and triggered such a violent response. "Americans forget how these men [the Orangemen] treated us when they had the power," wrote one Irish Catholic to the editor of the *Herald*. They burned our churches, he said, "and forced us to say mass in the ditches, and they would do so again . . . if they got the upper hand in this city." Taunts concerning these past humiliations and outrages in Ireland could not go unanswered, another Irish Catholic told the *Herald*. Otherwise, the Orangemen would "get the American Know Nothings to join them in committing the same outrages upon us here, and that's why we are determined to put an end to them before they get strong enough to be as bad as they were in Ireland."[33]

These arguments won little sympathy from Protestant New Yorkers such as Nast, who began to focus more and more of his cartoons on the Catholic menace. He portrayed the pope covetously eyeing the United States as his next home as the Italian unification movement threatened his sovereignty in Rome. He depicted American Catholic leaders attempting to blur or erase the separation between church and state, aided and abetted by simian Irish American thugs. Nast's anti-Catholicism was all the more remarkable because he had been baptized a Catholic at birth, though as an adult he married a devout American-born Episcopalian. Whatever its source, Nast's anti-Catholicism became more vituperative after the 1870 Orange riot.[34]

As July 12, 1871, approached, New Yorkers began to fear that worse civil unrest would take place if Orangemen again celebrated Boyne Day. Irish Catholics demanded that New York authorities follow the British lead and ban parades marking the anniversary. Orangemen and their many American-born sympathizers, however, insisted on the group's right to parade and peaceably express its views. With "the low Irish Catholics having been allowed to have their parade" on St. Patrick's Day, one New Yorker wrote to the *Times*, "the decent Irish should also have theirs."[35]

On July 10, Police Superintendent James Kelso, having consulted with Tweed, Hall, Sweeny, and other Tammany leaders, announced that in order to preserve the public peace, the Orangemen would not be accorded the privilege of parading in the streets. "Has it come to this," complained one outraged Protestant to the *Tribune*, "that as the 'Irish Catholics' have sold the most bad whisky, made the most drunkards, created the most riots, committed the most murders, polled the most votes with the least number of voters, and now hold the most offices and receive the greatest amount of the public money, they are now to dictate who shall and who shall not enjoy the liberty of American citizens?" Despite calls to defy the ban, the leader of the Orangemen announced that he would comply with Kelso's order.[36]

The Tammany chieftains who had pressured Kelso to prohibit the parade had apparently not consulted with their former compatriot, Governor Hoffman. Angling for the 1872 Democratic presidential nomination, Hoffman calculated that any association with the Tweed Ring's capitulation to Irish Catholic "dictation" might irreparably damage his chances. At the eleventh hour (literally so — 11:00 p.m. on the night before Boyne Day) he countermanded Kelso's parade ban. In order to prevent the predicted bloodshed, Hoffman hastily ordered six regiments of the state militia to report at 7:00 the following morning to protect the Orangemen and their parade. Feeling betrayed, many Irish Catholics vowed that the Orangemen would not march in peace.[37]

The result was disastrous. By 2:30 p.m., when the Orangemen emerged from their headquarters at the northwest corner of Eighth Avenue and West 29th Street, they found thousands of Irish Catholic New Yorkers thronging the parade route. Some merely sought to witness the spectacle; it was not unheard of in those days for New Yorkers to rent hotel rooms for the express purpose of securing ringside seats for a good riot. But others took up positions on the sidewalks or in the windows of the tenements along Eighth Avenue armed with rocks, bricks, pistols, and a "dogged determination" to put a stop to what they considered an affront to their religion and their persecuted Irish forebears. The one hundred or so marchers, nearly all carrying pistols under their coats, could only inch their way down Eighth Avenue, for they were closely surrounded by one thousand policemen, who themselves were flanked by several thousand militiamen — one regiment at the front, a second to the left of the Orangemen, a third to the right, while a fourth and fifth brought up the rear. One of the militiamen at the front of the parade, in the Seventh Regiment, was Thomas Nast.[38]

As the marchers crept down Eighth Avenue, onlookers began pelting them with rocks, bottles, and bricks, some from the sidewalks but especially from the windows and rooftops of the surrounding buildings. Pistol shots occasionally rang out, including several fired by "two Irish girls, dressed in white," positioned in a tenement window between 24th and 25th streets. Militiamen started firing at these snipers and rock throwers, while the police used their truncheons to beat back the crowd. Finally, at the corner of West 24th Street, the members of the Eighty-fourth Regiment, increasingly fearing for their lives, panicked and fired a volley into the crowd on the east side of Eighth Avenue. Members of the other militia units then began firing as well, also directing their fire at the east side of Eighth Avenue between 24th and 25th streets. According to a reporter for the *Sun,* the shooting was "indiscriminate, reckless, pointed at no one in particular," and lasted "several minutes" (though each soldier could fire only one bullet at a time before having to reload). As screams, shrieks, and curses rent the air, the crowd tried to flee east, but was impeded by those on the cross streets who had been pressing toward the avenue for hours to catch a glimpse of the parade. Once the onlookers did finally escape, an eerie silence fell over the scene. Then, reported the *Times,* in one of the most egregious acts of bad taste in all of New York's history, the bands struck up "a lively tripping quickstep" and the Orangemen marched away, "leaving [their] dead still on the street," in order to complete their parade to Cooper Union as planned.[39]

The scene they left behind was truly shocking. "The street literally ran with blood," reported the *Sun.* According to the *Times,* "strong men looked on aghast with horror. Women wept and children moaned at the spectacle. It was a panorama of blood, a vista of gore, an arena of agony." To pass from 24th to 25th Street, wrote the *Sun*'s correspondent, "you had to pick your way among the corpses." The *Herald*'s reporter found a half-dozen bodies on the stairs leading to a basement barbershop. The steps were "smeared and slippery with human blood and brains," he noted, "while the landing beneath was covered two inches deep with clotted gore, pieces of brain and the half digested contents of a human stomach and intestines. Floating in this horrid puddle was an old

Militiamen firing into the crowd on Eighth Avenue at West 25th Street in the
climactic moment of the Orange riot of 1871.

low-crowned felt hat, such as laborers wear." In all, two policemen, three militiamen, and sixty-two civilians were killed in what the *Irish World* dubbed "the
slaughter in Eighth Avenue."⁴⁰

To the mainstream New York press, which viewed the carnage in the context of the draft riots of 1863, the outcome was an emphatic victory over chaos
and mob rule. "Excelsior! Law Triumphs — Order Reigns," trumpeted the *Herald.* The *Times* called the result "a noble vindication of the might of the popular
will and of the justice which lives in the unperverted instincts of a free people."
Brushing aside the frightful death toll and the soldiers' failure to warn the rioters to disperse before firing, as was typical in cases of urban unrest, the *Tribune*
argued that this "unfortunate blunder . . . had the one happy effect of cowing
and crushing the rioters. It is probable that this one hasty error saved the city
from greater bloodshed at a later hour." The title of a *Harper's Weekly* cartoon
allegorically depicting the suppression of the riot succinctly summed up native-born New Yorkers' opinion of the outcome: "Bravo! Bravo!"⁴¹

Irish Catholic immigrants viewed the outcome of the riot completely differently. "We demand justice," cried the *Irish-American.* A shower of rocks and
even bricks did not justify over sixty fatalities. "Murder has been done by wholesale, *and the murderers must be traced and punished.*" Much of the blame, argued the *Irish-American,* lay with nativists like those at *Harper's Weekly,* whose
stereotyping of the Irish (most notably by Nast) made it possible for troops to

fire indiscriminately as if Irish lives did not matter, as if the Irish were animals rather than human beings. "Though oppressed, our people are *not* low; though wronged we are *not* guilty — though pictured with gorilla faces, and mishapen forms by base bigots, we are *men, Irishmen,* having *free* souls and spirit sufficient to work for freedom for our own loved land."[42]

The riots did, however, lead both Irish immigrants and native-born New Yorkers to one shared conclusion: that they could no longer live under the thumb of Tweed and his henchmen. The Irish were furious that Tammany's leaders were doing nothing to punish those responsible for the carnage on Eighth Avenue. "*Not one man,* of all those we have put into office by our votes and influence, appears to have the pluck to come forward and demand that there shall be a full and fair investigation," complained the *Irish-American.* "Has our value at the ballot-box, here, been forgotten?"[43]

Native-born New Yorkers, in contrast, saw the riots as a direct result of the Tweed Ring's venality. "These frightful scenes will not cease," declared the *Tribune,* "until that corrupt party which depends for its existence upon the votes of the ignorant and vicious loses its tyrannical control of our public life." The *Times* went even further, calling the Irish "dupes" of Tammany Hall, whose leaders had "shamefully corrupted" the immigrants and systematically inflamed Irish Catholics' "worst passions" to maintain the Ring's grip on power and access to plunder. The *Times* implored the Irish to free themselves from their Tweed Ring overlords. "The ax is already laid to the root of the tree," proclaimed the *Times,* "and it needs but a persistent series of strong and well-directed blows to send it home."[44]

In a sense, that is exactly what transpired, though historians have typically not recognized it. Instead, they have argued that the Orange riots "stoked the nativist reform crusade . . . led by wealthy merchants and lawyers, most of whom were Protestants," which eventually toppled Tweed and his Ring. While there is some truth to this characterization, immigrants in fact played the largest role in the destruction of the Tweed Ring. Nast, of course, was both an immigrant and a reformer, and he had been one of the first to begin the campaign for Tweed's ouster. Nast's crusade against the Ring intensified after the Orange riot of 1870, but at that point he still devoted more attention to other issues, such as his opposition to the exclusion of Chinese immigrants from the United States and Pope Pius IX's claims of infallibility.[45]

In the aftermath of the 1871 riot, however, the Tweed Ring became virtually Nast's only subject, as week after week he pilloried the Boss, his cronies, and his "simian" supporters in devastating, ingenious caricatures. Nast portrayed Tweed and his henchmen as vultures bloated from devouring the carcasses of the city's taxpayers; Tweed and his cronies drinking champagne while New Yorkers were left with an empty city treasury; Tweed and other Ring leaders kneeling in supplication before their Irish Catholic masters; and Tammany's leaders standing in a circle, each pointing his finger at someone else in answer to the question "Who Stole the People's Money?" The whole nation looked forward each week to discovering how Nast might next skewer Tweed and his compatriots. *Harper's* acknowledged Nast's celebrity status that August by publishing a full-page portrait of the artist, accompanied by a glowing biographical sketch of the man now famous for "his part in the good fight against every species of meanness and wrong."[46]

What made Nast's work all the more powerful was that Irish immigrants once associated with Tammany were beginning to come forward to offer hard evidence of Tweed's corruption. Just days before the riot, Matthew J. O'Rourke, a forty-year-old famine immigrant and off-and-on journalist who had worked as a bookkeeper in the office of the county auditor, leaked to the *Times* figures proving that the city was grossly overpaying for the rental of armories. The overages, said O'Rourke, went into the bank accounts of the Ring's leaders. The *Times'* London-born editor-in-chief, thirty-five-year-old Louis Jennings, realized that these frauds were just the tip of the iceberg, but could not yet find proof of the larger-scale thievery in which the Tweed Ring leaders were clearly engaged.[47]

Jennings's big break came when he acquired an even better source, former alderman and county sheriff James O'Brien. O'Brien had arrived in New York as a thirteen-year-old from County Westmeath in 1852 and worked as a stonecutter before entering politics. In 1870, believing he had not received his fair share of the Ring's riches, he submitted an invoice for $350,000 in "expenses" (approximately $6.5 million in today's dollars) that he claimed he was owed from his term as sheriff. When Comptroller Richard B. Connolly, the one Irishborn member of Tweed's inner circle, rejected O'Brien's request as excessive even by Ring standards, O'Brien resorted to blackmail. Unless Connolly paid his claim, O'Brien threatened, he would release to the public copies of account books documenting the enormous kickbacks Tweed's inner circle was receiving from the decade-long construction of the new county courthouse behind City Hall (a monument to corruption that still stands and is popularly known as the "Tweed Courthouse"). Taking O'Brien's threats seriously, Tweed entered into negotiations with him through an intermediary, the city's Scotch-born county auditor, James Watson. But when Watson died in January 1871 from injuries suffered when his horse-drawn sleigh crashed in Harlem, and no subsequent intermediary came forward to continue the negotiations, the ex-sheriff decided to make good on his threats. On the sweltering evening of July 18, he personally

At the top, two of Nast's most ingenious depictions of Tweed. Top left, Manhattan Island literally under Tweed's thumb; top right, Tweed as the personification of greed and graft. At the bottom, two of Nast's simian caricatures of Irish immigrants. Bottom left, the Irish as slaves to Tammany in 1870; bottom right, Tammany leaders kneeling in submission to the city's Irish Catholic immigrants as part of Nast's commentary on the Orange riots of 1871.

delivered a copy of the courthouse construction expense ledgers to Jennings at the Park Row headquarters of the *Times*.[48]

It took several days for Jennings and his staff of City Hall reporters, headed by a twenty-eight-year-old Scotch-born immigrant named John Foord, but now including O'Rourke as well, to make sense of the dozens of pages of figures. In the meantime, in desperation, the Ring tried to silence the *Times* by purchasing it through acquisition of the shares controlled by the widow of its former owner, Henry Raymond. But publisher George Jones managed to broker a deal in which former governor Edwin Morgan, a banker, merchant, and active Republican, acquired those shares instead. Tammany even resorted to strong-arm tactics. "I was arrested two or three times a day as the fight grew brisk," Jennings later recalled, but wealthy Republicans always posted Jennings's bail so he could return immediately to work.[49]

The Ring's leaders apparently went to even greater lengths to stop Nast. Through intermediaries, Tweed's associates offered Nast $100,000 if he would take a sabbatical from *Harper's* to pursue artistic study in Europe. Nast negotiated the bid up to a whopping $500,000 (nearly $10 million today) before rejecting it.* "I made up my mind not long ago to put some of those fellows behind the bars," Nast supposedly exclaimed, "*and I'm going to put them there.*"[50]

When the *Times* began printing excerpts from O'Brien's ledgers on Saturday, July 22, 1871, it was a journalistic bombshell just as momentous as its publication of the Pentagon Papers exactly one hundred years later. The unrelenting headlines — "The Master Thief," "The Secret Accounts," "Proofs of Tweed's Guilt" — marked the beginning of the Tweed Ring's demise. In late October the state filed a civil suit against Tweed to recover funds stolen in connection with the county courthouse kickback scheme. Other indictments followed over the course of 1872. His first trial, in January 1873, resulted in a hung jury, but at his retrial in November a jury convicted Tweed on more than two hundred counts of financial impropriety, and he was sentenced to twelve years in prison. In June 1875 the New York State Court of Appeals ruled that Tweed's sentence exceeded the maximum allowed for his crimes and ordered him released. Prosecutors immediately re-arrested Tweed on other pending charges and returned him to jail to await trial, but in January he escaped, first to Florida and then to Cuba, where he boarded a ship headed for Spain. Alerted to his impending arrival, Spanish officials distributed copies of a Nast caricature of Tweed to facilitate his apprehension. Captured on September 6, 1876, he was returned to New York, where in his absence he had been found liable for more than $6.5 million

---

* Most accounts of this episode begin with Tweed justifying the attempt to bribe Nast by saying, "My constituents don't know how to read, but they can't help seeing them damned pictures." Yet this remark is certainly apocryphal. It originally appeared without quotation marks in a laudatory profile of Nast. See "Thomas Nast," *Harper's Weekly* (August 26, 1871): 803.

in damages in a civil suit. Unable to pay, Tweed returned to jail, where he died in 1878.[51]

Historians tend to focus on prosecutor Samuel Tilden as the protagonist in Tweed's downfall. Indeed, Tilden rode notoriety from the case to the governorship of New York and to within a single electoral vote of the White House in 1876. Others primarily credit the revelations published in the *Times*. Yet contemporaries saw Nast's role as equally or even more important. "To Mr. Nast it is hardly possible to award too much praise," insisted *The Nation*. He "brought the rascalities of the Ring home to hundreds of thousands who never would have looked at the figures and printed denunciations." The *Evening Post* agreed, stating that "Mr. Nast has been the most important single missionary in the great work; and it is due to his telling work, more than to any other cause," that the Ring's corruption was exposed. The *Hartford Courant* presciently predicted that in one hundred years, Tweed would be better remembered than any other member of the Ring, "and he will not owe it to his own vices even, but to Thomas Nast."[52]

Scholars also tend to see the fall of the Tweed Ring as part of a "nativist reform crusade" against the immigrant-backed political machine of Tammany Hall, and it is certainly true that many native-born New Yorkers perceived the battle against the Ring in that light. Most immigrants in New York did vote for the Ring's leaders in their heyday, yet Nast was far from Tweed's only key immigrant opponent. Two German-born Democrats, August Belmont and Oswald Ottendorfer (editor of the most popular German-language newspaper in the city), broke with Tweed long before most other members of Tammany were willing to do so, helping to seal his fate. And as Tammany became divided between pro- and anti-Tweed factions in the wake of the *Times*' revelations, the split took place for the most part along ethnic fault lines. In a cartoon titled "A House Divided Against Itself Shall Not Stand," one of Nast's colleagues at *Harper's Weekly* depicted the edifice of Tammany Hall literally breaking in two, with one half labeled "American Democrat" and the other labeled "Irish Democrat." It is not coincidental that after several years of internal struggle, the man who emerged as the new ruler of Tammany Hall was the city's first Irish Catholic political boss, "Honest John" Kelly, who had been born in New York City to immigrant parents in 1822. The Tweed scandal revealed the Democratic Party's ethnic divide, a split that had remained largely invisible to the public for many years.[53]

One of the reasons why these ethnic cleavages within the Democratic Party are not well documented in the history books is that they were not well understood by contemporary Republicans, to whom Tammany and the Irish were synonymous. Democrats nominated two candidates for mayor in 1872. Tam-

"A House Divided against Itself shall not Stand."

In "A House Divided Against Itself Shall Not Stand," *Harper's* acknowledged
that the growing divisions within Tammany Hall were, to a large extent, a re-
flection of the animosity between "American" and "Irish" Democrats.

many as usual chose a native-born candidate, Abraham Lawrence, while reform Democrats chose O'Brien, who now made no effort to hide his role in
bringing down Tweed. With the Democratic vote split, however, the Republican candidate, William Havemeyer, won with just 39 percent. The rule of the
Irish "is over," exulted the *Times*. "The ignorant, unthinking, bigoted hordes
which Tammany brought up to its support year after year are hopelessly scattered. Americans — truly so-called — are now determined to have some share
in the government of this City, and will no longer leave it to be tyrannized
over by our esteemed friends from the Emerald Isle. This is going to be an
American City once more — not simply a larger kind of Dublin. The iron rod
of our 'oppressed' friend is broken." The *Times*' bigoted evaluation indicates just
how completely native-born New Yorkers associated Irish immigrants with the
Tweed Ring's misdeeds.[54]

This anti-Irish sentiment pervaded the new Havemeyer administration.

Irish immigrants protested that even though they made up a plurality of the adult male population, they were now "almost entirely" excluded from the municipal workforce. Alderman Robert McCafferty complained that the council Havemeyer utilized to fill patronage positions was "intensely American," by which he meant anti-Irish and anti-Catholic. Havemeyer, however, was unapologetic. "I don't wonder that some of the Irish feel uneasy at the present outlook of things," he replied. "They have been accustomed to fill nearly all the offices in the city, to draw large pay and do very little work." German immigrants, according to the German American mayor, "don't apply for political positions in such numbers as the Irish. Generally the Germans have something better to do than fill political offices."[55]

One of the most prevalent means for Americans to vent their anti-Irish and anti-Catholic sentiment in the 1870s was the "School Question." As they had in the 1850s, American Catholics again pressed for state aid for their parochial schools. When Tweed had secured aid for New York City's Catholic schools in 1868, it was in secret in the state budget, and large numbers of New Yorkers howled when they learned of it. Some Catholics gladly sent their children to New York's public schools, but priests and devout Catholics condemned them as engines of Protestant proselytization. "We all know how impossible it is for a Catholic to frequent the public schools," wrote one, "without imbibing from its books and teachers a kind of shame for the faith in which he was born." North America's Catholic bishops codified this view in 1884 in a pastoral letter. Summarizing its contents, one Catholic commentator called parochial schools "institutions of paramount necessity, as the public school system is controlled absolutely by Protestants, conducted on Protestant principles, and made an instrument for debauching the faith of Catholic children."[56]

Devout Protestants viewed the School Question differently. Writing in *Harper's Weekly*, Eugene Lawrence argued that Catholic leaders "for twenty years waged a ceaseless war against the cause of education" in the United States for the express purpose of keeping their followers "ignorant" and obedient. The "succession of riots and disorders" that had plagued New York from 1863 to 1871 and the concurrent rise of an unprecedentedly corrupt set of city leaders, wrote Lawrence, both resulted from the growth of the city's "ignorant multitude to whom the priests have refused the education of freemen." Public funding for parochial schools had to be resisted, said Lawrence, because public schools provided "the surest bulwark against the rising flood of European ignorance and barbarism." The Catholic demand that the Bible be banished from the classroom also had to be fought, Protestants argued, because the Bible was the basis of all morality. Furthermore, if the state created publicly funded schools for every religious sect, the United States would become hopelessly divided and weakened, while pushing all children into a single public school system would create a stronger, more united, more *American* populace.[57]

In September 1871, at the height of the Tweed scandal, Nast tackled the School Question in one of his masterpieces, "The American River Ganges." At first glance, the print seems to depict crocodiles emerging from a river to threaten a schoolteacher (with a Bible at his breast) and his pupils, who cower behind him and pray for their lives. The creatures emerging from the water, though, are actually Catholic bishops, and what appear at first glance to be crocodile heads are really their miters. Up above the riverbank, Boss Tweed approvingly observes the Catholic invasion, while his Irish American henchmen lead other schoolteachers to a gallows set up next to a public school that lies in ruins. No work better encapsulates both Nast's genius and the bitter divisions engendered in the 1870s by the School Question, which the *Tribune* dubbed "The Irrepressible Conflict."[58]

More moderate voices existed on both sides of the school debate. Some native-born Americans admitted that public schools ought to be made less overtly Protestant, while some Catholics, such as New York's Father Edward McGlynn, conceded that the shift to popularly elected school boards in each ward and the

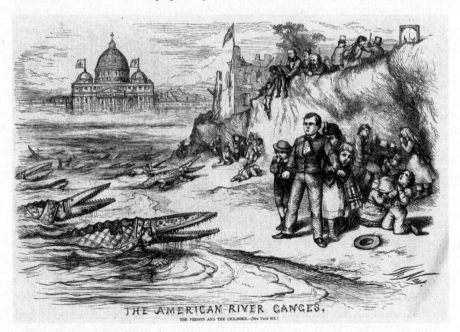

THE AMERICAN RIVER GANGES.

THE PRIESTS AND THE CHILDREN.—[See Page 912.]

In Nast's masterpiece "The American River Ganges," what at first glance appear to be crocodiles threatening a teacher and his pupils are actually Catholic prelates invading the United States in the hopes of imposing Catholic religious doctrine on all Americans through the destruction of the public schools.

consequent hiring of Catholic teachers had made the public schools accept-able. But as is so often the case, the moderates tended to get drowned out in the press by the extremists. In December 1875 both President Grant and Speaker of the U.S. House of Representatives James G. Blaine announced their support for a constitutional amendment prohibiting federal, state, and local governments from subsidizing parochial schools. In the following year, as many states be-gan adding such bans to their state constitutions, the School Question finally started to fade from public discourse.[59]

Anti-Catholic sentiment in general began to diminish slowly in the late 1870s and 1880s. In 1880 New Yorkers for the first time elected as mayor an Irish Catholic immigrant, William R. Grace. Though Grace had arrived in New York at the start of the famine migration in 1846, he was not your typical fam-ine immigrant. A particularly headstrong and adventurous child, Grace left his comfortable home (his family owned large tracts of farmland and quarries as well) and at age fourteen sailed alone for New York even after his father had for-bidden him to do so. He worked in New York as a printer's devil and a cobbler's helper before taking work on a ship headed for Cuba. From there he returned to Ireland.

Grace left Ireland again in 1851, this time headed for Peru, where he became a junior clerk for a merchant in Callao, the port serving Lima. The firm he worked for specialized in supplying food and other necessities to the hundreds of ships that anchored in the Pacific off the Peruvian coast, filling their holds with guano, the bird droppings that were prized as fertilizer in Europe and the United States. Ingenious and hardworking, Grace moved up quickly in the busi-ness, especially after he suggested stationing a ship full of supplies at the guano islands themselves. This earned his company a fortune because it saved each American or European ship captain the one-hundred-mile trip north to Callao before he headed back south for the return voyage home around Cape Horn. Grace eventually bought out his partners and lived for several years aboard his company's supply ship next to the reeking guano fields. In those fetid waters he even courted his future wife, Elizabeth, whom he met while selling supplies to her father, a sea captain from Maine.

In 1865 Grace, now a rich man, left his brother in charge of their thriving Peruvian business and relocated with his wife and two daughters to New York. There he managed to multiply his fortune many times, transporting everything from sewing needles to locomotives to the American entrepreneurs building the railroads of Peru. He subsequently started his own shipping line, which soon dominated the trade between New York and the west coast of South America, and made an additional fortune as the main arms supplier to the Peruvian government in its war with Chile, which began in 1879. He later expanded his interests to include major mining, chemical, construction, sugar, rubber, and cotton interests in Brazil, Chile, Costa Rica, and Ecuador. W. R. Grace and Co., headquartered until recently on West 42nd Street across from the New York Public Library, is today considered one of the first American multinational corporations.[60]

Grace had no political experience whatsoever when he was asked to run for mayor in 1880. Kelly, not wanting to repeat the increasingly familiar scenario in which a split between Tammany and anti-Tammany Democrats brought about the election of a Republican, agreed to select a "reform" candidate so both factions could support the same man. Kelly picked Grace, perhaps because Kelly thought he could control the mayoralty of the political neophyte. The campaign was filled with what Irish New Yorkers considered "bigotry and intolerance." A speech by a leading Methodist clergyman, reprinted on the front page of the *Times,* charged that a Catholic mayor would have to follow "the dictates of his spiritual and ecclesiastical master, the Pope," and would therefore have no choice but to destroy the public schools. Grace nonetheless won the race, although by a much smaller margin than other candidates on the Democratic ticket: Grace won by fewer than 3,000 votes, while Winfield Scott Hancock, the Democratic presidential nominee, carried the city by 41,000 (out of about 200,000 votes cast).[61]

In office, Grace refused to follow Kelly's orders and became one of the city's most reform-minded nineteenth-century mayors. He removed the street de-

Even after the election of the city's first Irish Catholic immigrant mayor, the pictorial press continued to occasionally depict the Irish as simian, something that deeply offended New York's Irish immigrants.

A REFUTATION OF DARWINISM.

DENNIS (*at the Zoo*). "Tim, there's thim that sez we was all iv us the loike iv that onct; sure I don't belave it."

partment from the control of the Tammany-dominated police commissioners, resulting in the cleanest streets most New Yorkers could remember. He also spearheaded an investigation into corruption among the police commission-ers. When Grace left office, having declined to run for reelection in 1882, even many of his most vociferous foes from the 1880 campaign admitted that he had been an excellent and unusually effective mayor.[62]

One of the reasons these Irish immigrant politicians were able to win so many elections is that Irish immigration did not end when the Great Famine sub-sided in the 1850s. Tens of thousands of Irish-born men and women continued to settle in New York in the 1870s, 1880s, and 1890s. While most of these immi-grants came to New York expecting to find work in construction or domestic service, by the end of the nineteenth century, some Irishmen began moving to New York to pursue another kind of vocation — athlete. In the Civil War era, Ireland's best bare-knuckle boxers would immigrate to the United States be-cause they could earn far more for prizefights in America than they could in Great Britain. Ireland still produced its fair share of fighters at the turn of the twentieth century, but the most prominent Irish athletes to move to the United States at that time were track and field stars, and in particular a group of burly Irish immigrants known as the "Irish Whales" who dominated international track and field's weight-throwing events for a generation.

The Irish Whales got their name not from their girth, exactly, but from the incredible amounts of food they ate before and after their contests. A waiter on a ship taking them across the Atlantic to one of their competitions became ex-hausted bringing tray after tray of food to the athletes. "They're not men," he moaned to a reporter. "They're whales." Forever after the press referred to them as the Irish Whales.

Their training menus do boggle the mind, though they also show that the association of protein with muscle is nothing new. For breakfast, hammer thrower Simon Gillis ate a dozen boiled eggs, including the shells — "eggs with the fur on," he called them. Anticipating how hungry they would be after a competition in Baltimore, he and two other Whales placed an advance order, asking a restaurant to have twenty-seven dozen oysters and six T-bone steaks ready at 5:00 p.m. When the three athletes arrived, they were taken to a table set for thirty-three and asked if they wanted to wait for the remaining guests. The staff looked on in amazement as the three men devoured the entire ban-quet table of food.[63]

It was during the Olympics that Americans most closely followed the ex-ploits of the Irish Whales. Martin Sheridan from County Mayo, whom the *Times* aptly called "one of the greatest athletes this country has ever known,"

Matt McGrath was one of the "Irish Whales," Irish immigrants living in New York who dominated the throwing events at the early Olympic Games.

won a gold medal in the discus at the 1904 St. Louis Olympics and three medals (including two gold) at the 1908 London Games. John Flanagan from Limerick won gold for the United States in the hammer throw at the 1900 Games in Paris and the 1904 and 1908 Olympics as well. Matt McGrath, from Tipperary, won the hammer throw gold in 1912 at Stockholm. Pat McDonald from County Clare captured gold in 1912 in the shot put and at the 1920 Antwerp Games in the fifty-six-pound-weight throw, a rarely held event at which the Irish particularly excelled. (Pat Ryan, another Whale, took the silver.)[64]

Most of the Whales competed for the Irish-American Athletic Club, whose state-of-the-art training facility was in Sunnyside, Queens.* The club lured its Irish-born athletes to America in part by promising to secure them jobs with the police department which would give them time to train and flexible work hours so they could travel to far-flung competitions. Every Whale worked for the city's police force. They were usually assigned to traffic detail so they would not risk injury arresting the city's well-armed criminals.[65]

The typical Irish immigrant's employment options were far more limited, even in the last decades of the nineteenth century. In 1860, 46 percent of New York's adult male Irish immigrants worked in low-paying unskilled occupations such as day laborer. In 1880 the figure was essentially unchanged, at 47 percent, and in 1900 it had actually inched up to 51 percent. The proportion of Irish immi-

---

* One did not have to be Irish to compete for the Irish-American Athletic Club. One of the most acclaimed I-AAC athletes was Myer Prinstein, a Polish Jew who had immigrated to New York as a boy. He won gold in the triple jump at the Paris Olympics in 1900 and in both that event and the long jump at the St. Louis Games in 1904. Abel Kiviat, the son of Jewish immigrants from Bialystok who grew up on Staten Island, was also an I-AAC athlete. He held the world record in the 1,500 meters for several years and at that distance at the 1912 Olympics came in an excruciatingly close second to Englishman Arnold Jackson, an Oxford undergraduate, in what was hailed at the time as "the greatest race ever run." The result was so close that the winner had to be determined from a photograph of the finish, the first "photo finish" in Olympic history.

grants who owned their own businesses also remained basically the same over that forty-year period, rising from 5 percent to 6 percent.

But by other measurements, Irish immigrants' job prospects had begun to brighten just a bit. In both 1860 and 1880, only one in one thousand male Irish immigrants worked in the professions — doctor, lawyer, clergyman, and so on. — but by 1900 this proportion had grown to seven in one thousand. The percentage of Irish immigrants in lower-status "white-collar" work (mostly clerks, but also teachers, salesmen, conductors, foremen, and agents) rose from 6 percent in 1860 to 11 percent in 1900.[66]

The employment of German immigrants changed as well in late nineteenth-century New York, though with some significant variations compared to that of the Irish. New York's male German immigrants were also more likely to work in low-paid unskilled occupations in 1900 than in 1860 — the figure rose from 11 percent to 19 percent — probably because the German immigration of the late nineteenth century came primarily from urban areas of Germany's industrializing north, in contrast to the predominantly southern German artisanal immigration of the late antebellum years. The proportion of Germans who ran their own businesses was hardly higher in 1900 than it had been in 1860. Nor did German immigrants make significant gains in either the professions or lower-status white-collar work in these decades, perhaps because of the language barrier. These figures suggest that no matter how much the status of Irish or German Americans might have changed in the public consciousness, most immigrants still could not break into New York's higher-paying occupations. Only rarely could the foreign-born crack the city's glass employment ceiling.[67]

The story was much the same for Irish and German immigrant women. Sixty-three percent of employed Irish immigrant women worked as household servants in 1860, and that figure climbed to 69 percent in 1880 and 73 percent in 1900. The rate at which Irish-born women owned their own businesses or worked as nurses held steady at 3 percent each throughout this forty-year period, as did the proportion who worked as teachers — rising from 0.3 percent in 1860 to a still minuscule 0.5 percent in 1900. Although half of employed German immigrants worked as domestics, a significantly higher proportion of Germans held jobs as teachers, business owners, and clerks than did Irish immigrants. Still, the employment opportunities for female immigrants, no matter where they were born, were far more circumscribed than those of white native-born women.[68]

Most immigrants accepted these limitations because they had been motivated to move to America in large part in the belief that by doing so, they would give their children better opportunities than they themselves enjoyed, and an analysis of the jobs held by the American-born children of New York's immigrants indicates that such beliefs were not unrealistic. Yet even in the late nineteenth century, the native-born children of Irish and German immigrants did not hold jobs that brought the same status or income as did those held by the children of white native-born New Yorkers. The American-born sons of immigrants in 1900 were only a third as likely to enter the professions as were the sons of native-born Americans. About half the U.S.-born sons of white U.S.-born parents in New York had some kind of "white-collar" job (ranging from clerk or salesman all the way up to doctor, lawyer, or business owner), but only 36 percent of the U.S.-born sons of German immigrants held such jobs, and only 28 percent of the U.S.-born sons of Irish immigrants had white-collar employment. Both class and ethnicity probably played some role in keeping the children of Irish and German immigrants out of white-collar work.

The employment pattern of the American-born daughters of immigrants more closely matched that of New York women of native stock. About the same proportion of each group held jobs as office workers, clerks, and servants. The U.S.-born daughters of immigrants were more likely than those of native stock to work in the needle trades, but these women were primarily dressmakers and did not, for the most part, work in the garment-trade sweatshops that Jewish and Italian immigrants were coming to dominate. One of the highest-status jobs that a woman could have in this period was schoolteacher, and the children of immigrants found it much harder to land such work. The American-born daughters of Irish immigrants were only half as likely to work as teachers as were children of native-born New Yorkers. Nonetheless, these second-generation Americans knew that their own children would have even better employment opportunities than they had.[69]

A few examples dramatically illustrate this point. Mary Bergen, the New York–born daughter of a famine immigrant blacksmith, married real estate broker John W. McGuire, also the American-born child of Irish immigrants. Mary and John's daughter Susan married John J. Pulleyn, who worked his way up from dry goods clerk all the way to the presidency of the Emigrant Savings Bank.[70] Joseph Kingsley arrived in New York from Dublin in 1852 and settled in Five Points, where he became a tailor. His son Joseph junior, born in New York, chose a low-status white-collar job as a railway station agent in Baltimore. His son, Joseph III, started out as a station agent also — but advanced to become president of the Norfolk Southern Railroad. Such cases were the exception rather than the rule, of course, but immigrants knew that with talent and luck, their children and grandchildren at least had the *chance* to achieve significant success in America.[71]

There was one more reason for Irish and German immigrants to be optimistic about their prospects. Employers might have once hesitated to hire an Irish immigrant because of his religion, or a German immigrant because he might secretly belong to a labor union. But with immigrants from southern and eastern Europe, like those who traveled on the *Nevada* with Annie Moore, now settling in New York by the thousands, native-born Americans suddenly found Irish and German immigrants desirable compared to these swarthy newcomers. It was not just their complexion or, in the case of the Jews, their religion that made natives fearful. Jewish immigrants seemed especially drawn to socialism, a movement that appeared far more threatening to Americans than your run-of-the-mill trade union. And according to some alarmist accounts, Italian immigrant ranks overflowed with stiletto-wielding criminals and bomb-throwing anarchists. In 1900 there were twice as many Irish and German immigrants living in New York as there were Italians and eastern European Jews. By 1920, however, this ratio had been reversed. Emigrants from the Caribbean and Asia were now clamoring to settle in New York as well. For centuries overwhelmingly northern European, New York was fast becoming the destination for far-flung peoples whose ancestors had never considered emigration possible. In a few short decades, they would totally remake the City of Dreams.

14

LIBERTY

THE STATUE OF LIBERTY is America's, and the world's, quintessential symbol of immigrant hope. But it did not start out that way.

The statue and its illuminated torch were initially conceived not as a welcoming beacon to Europe's emigrants but as a memorial to the emancipation of American slaves during the Civil War. The idea for the bronze colossus originated in the 1860s with Édouard René de Laboulaye, a prominent French legal scholar. Laboulaye, like most French intellectuals of his day, adored the United States (how things change!). It was not American culture that he admired but rather the American Constitution, with its republican form of government and freedoms guaranteed in a written Bill of Rights. Laboulaye and his circle were thrilled when the destruction of slavery became part of the North's wartime agenda, as they had always believed that slavery was inconsistent with the United States' republican ideals.

When Robert E. Lee surrendered at Appomattox Courthouse and the slaves' freedom became irreversible, Laboulaye established the French Emancipation Committee, which raised funds to assist the freedmen with their transition out of bondage. Living in Paris, a city full of grandiose monuments to heroic military accomplishments, Laboulaye hoped that Americans would erect a colossal memorial to their historic act of liberation. If it should ever be built, Laboulaye and his friends decided, it ought to be a joint Franco-American effort, because the French too prized liberty above all else.[1]

For a decade, Laboulaye's idea languished. No one in the United States seemed interested, while Laboulaye and his associates (among them the statue's eventual designer, sculptor Frédéric Bartholdi) were distracted and disheartened by the suppression of their political views under Napoleon III. But they revived their plan in the mid-1870s once their autocratic ruler had been deposed, promising to design, construct, and pay for the colossal statue, and asking only that Americans provide a suitable pedestal and location. As the sculptor entered New York Harbor on a visit to the United States to promote his idea, the ship passed tiny Bedloe's Island, recently ceded by New York to the federal government for military purposes. The Frenchman eventually decided that the statue should be placed there, so that every ship passenger arriving at the United States' busiest port would see it. In 1877 both President Ulysses S. Grant and his successor, Rutherford B. Hayes, authorized the erection of the monument on the island.[2]

Yet the United States was a profoundly different place in 1877 than in 1865. Tired of sectional strife and still staggering from the worst depression in the nation's history (one that saw the unemployment rate surpass 25 percent in cities of the Northeast and Midwest), white Americans did not want to be reminded of issues that had so recently divided them. Other states could not be motivated to contribute to a project that would grace the harbor of a rival, while New Yorkers believed that in tough economic times, they could not spare the funds necessary to build the one-hundred-foot-tall pedestal that the colossus required. Believing that the statue would cost ten times what the French had budgeted and would therefore never be built, the *Times* scoffed at the idea of the state or federal government allocating $100,000 for the enormous granite base. "It would unquestionably be impolitic to look a gift-statue in the mouth," pronounced the *Times* glibly, but given how unlikely it was that the French would ever complete the project, the paper advised against "any such expenditure for bronze females in the present state of our finances . . . Unless the Frenchmen change their minds and pay for the statue themselves, we shall have to do without it."[3]

By this point, few Americans were aware of the original relationship between the proposed statue and the Civil War. American boosters now promoted the monument as a commemoration of the one hundredth anniversary of American independence and the "ancient alliance of the French and American people" that had helped the thirteen colonies liberate themselves from Great Britain. But vestiges of the project's anti-slavery origins were still evident. The leaders of the pedestal fund-raising committee, established in 1877 — William Evarts, Edwin D. Morgan, William Cullen Bryant, Parke Godwin, and nineteen-year-old Theodore Roosevelt — were all Republicans. Democrats, never enthusiastic supporters of emancipation or civil rights for the freedmen, tended to oppose the project but justified their opposition on economic grounds.[4]

The pedestal committee members tried every imaginable strategy. They published memorials in the New York press. They arranged benefit performances of popular plays. They persuaded wealthy New Yorkers to exhibit their art collections and charged the public for admission. They arranged for Bar-

The hand and torch of the yet-to-be-completed Statue of Liberty on display in Philadelphia in 1876.

tholdi to send the statue's torch to the United States to be displayed as a means of conveying to Americans the magnitude of the project. They even held an auction in December 1883 for which they solicited artwork and literary manuscripts. These would be assembled in a leather-bound, velvet-lined portfolio that would include twenty-five watercolors and sketches, letters from President Chester A. Arthur, Mark Twain, Henry James, and Bret Harte, and two original poems.[5]

One of the writers asked to submit a poem was thirty-four-year-old Emma Lazarus. She was born into what the *Times* characterized as "one of the best-known and oldest Hebrew families" in the city. Her father, Moses Lazarus, amassed a fortune as a sugar refiner by taking on a Louisiana sugar planter as his partner and thereby significantly reducing the cost of his raw materials. Moses spent most of his time in New York but summered in a Newport mansion by the sea. Emma could count among her good friends not only other wealthy Jews but also members of the well-connected Gilder and Schuyler families. Her parents socialized with Astors, Belmonts, and Vanderbilts. Emma's modest literary renown at this point resulted from the poetry and magazine articles (primarily on Jewish topics) that she occasionally published in *Lippincott's*, *The Century*, *Scribner's*, and *The American Hebrew*. Prominent writers also respected Lazarus and her work; Ralph Waldo Emerson and Henry James corresponded with her regularly.[6]

Despite her wealthy upbringing, Emma had a strong social conscience. If they had been asked to choose one word to describe her, "serious" is what most of her friends and literary acquaintances would have chosen. "One never failed to bring away from a talk with her an impulse to higher things, more serious endeavor, less of satisfaction with the mere touch-and-go relations with the world of every day," recalled one, the writer Constance Cary Harrison. The problems of the world, Harrison noted, seemed to "weigh strangely heavy upon the mind of a woman so young."[7]

The anti-Semitic pogroms that broke out in Russia after the assassination of Tsar Alexander II in March 1881 profoundly disturbed Lazarus. With eastern European Jews suddenly arriving in New York in large numbers, she volunteered to assist the refugees, working at the employment bureau of the Hebrew Emigrant Aid Society, helping to establish the Hebrew Technical Institute to provide vocational training for the newcomers, and demanding improvements in living conditions at the Jewish paupers' "refuge" on Wards Island in the East River. A *Times* article describing a visit to the island, probably written by Lazarus herself, notes how excited the immigrants were "to breathe in America the air of freedom . . . Every American must feel a thrill of pride and gratitude in the thought that his country is the refuge of the oppressed, . . . and however wretched be the material offered to him from the refuse of other nations, he accepts it with generous hospitality."[8]

With anti-Semitism still rife in the United States, Lazarus believed that the best hope for Europe's Jews lay in Palestine. She was the first American Jew of note to call for the creation of a Jewish state there. More than a dozen years before Theodor Herzl is credited with "founding" the Zionist movement, Lazarus visited England early in 1883 to enlist the support of Britain's most wealthy and influential Jews, who might bankroll the project and push for the British government to support it. She was able to make little headway there, however. For the time being, the United States would be the best destination for eastern Europe's Jewish refugees.[9]

Soon after returning home, Lazarus was contacted by Harrison, another of the city's well-known female writers. A native of Mississippi, Harrison was the Confederacy's Betsy Ross, having sewn (along with her sisters) the first Confederate battle flag, the famous "Stars and Bars," while her husband, Burton, served as Jefferson Davis's private secretary in Richmond. Relocating to New York after the war, she became a successful novelist, contributing many pieces to *Scribner's* and *The Century,* and thereby becoming acquainted with Lazarus.[10]

Harrison was one of the literary socialites responsible for assembling the portfolio to be auctioned off at the December 1883 pedestal fund benefit. (One wonders what Laboulaye would have thought of this unrepentant Confederate soliciting contributions for his project, but the Frenchman had died a few months earlier.) When Harrison approached Lazarus about contributing a poem, the southerner recalled four years later, Lazarus "was at first inclined to rebel against writing anything 'to order,'" condemning the whole enterprise with "the summer-lightning of her sarcasm." Besides, Lazarus said, any poem she might attempt on such short notice, without proper inspiration, would "assuredly be flat."

But Harrison refused to take no for an answer. She suggested that for motivation, Lazarus "think of that Goddess standing on her pedestal down yonder in the bay, and holding her torch out to those Russian refugees of yours you are so fond of visiting at Ward's Island." Harrison saw instantly that her remark had struck a nerve. The poet's "dark eyes deepened — her cheek flushed — the time for merriment was passed — she said not a word more, then." A few days later, Lazarus delivered a handwritten sonnet titled "The New Colossus."[11]

That fourteen-line poem gave a new meaning and purpose to the figure of Liberty, which had remained abstract and remote in Americans' minds, especially since Laboulaye's abolitionist message had long since been forgotten. While Bartholdi's personification of Liberty might appear on the surface to be quiet and dignified, her "silent lips," according to Lazarus, were actually crying out to Europe's tyrants:

> Give me your tired, your poor,
> Your huddled masses yearning to breathe free,
> The wretched refuse of your teeming shore.
> Send these, the homeless, tempest-tost to me,
> I lift my lamp beside the golden door!

Like every other moneymaking scheme the pedestal fund-raising committee dreamed up, the portfolio auction was a disappointment. It brought in $1,500 (about $30,000 in today's dollars), only half the amount the committee had expected. The portfolio quickly disappeared inside a New York mansion, and Lazarus's sonnet, which organizers had read at the auction, was immediately forgotten.[12]

The project's supporters, doubting that they could ever pay for the monumental pedestal with private donations, turned their hopes once more to the government. But they again encountered partisan obstacles. When the Republican-controlled New York legislature in 1884 allocated $50,000 for the pedestal, Democratic governor Grover Cleveland vetoed the bill. A year later, congressional Republicans proposed an expenditure of $100,000 for the base, but Democrats in the Senate blocked the measure. With the pedestal committee's treasury depleted, construction of the base was now suspended. Bartholdi's colossal work of art, which he called Liberty Enlightening the World, gathered dust in more than two hundred crates in a European warehouse. The French people who had paid to have it cast became increasingly bitter, while civic leaders in Boston and Philadelphia promised to build a splendid pedestal immediately if the statue was sent to them.[13]

Poet Emma Lazarus was the first person to link the Statue of Liberty to the American immigration experience. It might never have been placed in New York Harbor but for the fundraising efforts of Joseph Pulitzer.

Just when it seemed certain that New York would lose the statue, Joseph Pulitzer initiated a one-man crusade to fund the completion of the project. Pulitzer had come to America in 1864 at age seventeen to enlist in the Union army. After the war, still just eighteen years old, Pulitzer moved to St. Louis. He worked a series of odd jobs while simultaneously ingratiating himself with the city's German intellectuals, reading and playing chess with them at the St. Louis Mercantile Library. One of these acquaintances eventually hired Pulitzer as a cub reporter for one of the city's German-language newspapers. Brimming with ambition, he also studied law and won election to the Missouri legislature in 1869 at age twenty-two. Pulitzer was eventually able to buy two struggling St. Louis newspapers, the *Post* and the *Dispatch*. He combined them and made them hugely profitable. Most immigrants would have been content to rule over a lucrative Midwest publishing empire and enjoy local political power and prestige. But Pulitzer's outsized ambition was not sated. In 1883 he moved to New York and bought one of the city's struggling dailies, the *New York World*.[14]

Pulitzer attracted readers by launching crusades — against monopolies, corruption, and the greed and misdeeds of the wealthy. In March 1885 he decided to make Bartholdi's statue one of the *World*'s crusades. Correctly foreseeing that the statue would become a beloved landmark that would evoke "more sentiment than we can now dream of," Pulitzer argued that it would be "an irre-vocable disgrace to New York City and the American Republic to have France send us this splendid gift without having provided even so much as a landing-place for it . . . Let us not wait for the millionaires to give this money," Pulitzer insisted. "It is not a gift from the millionaires of France to the millionaires of America, but a gift of the whole people of France to the whole people of Amer-ica." Pulitzer announced that what the high-society fund-raisers had not been able to accomplish in a decade, he and the readers of the *World* would accom-plish in a matter of months. "The *World* is the people's paper," he intoned, "and it now appeals to the people to come forward and raise this money."[15]

Pulitzer's journalistic instincts proved impeccable once again. Donations poured in. The notes humble New Yorkers sent with their pennies, dimes, and quarters were gems of popular patriotism, just what readers of the jingoistic *World* adored. Circulation soared. Organizers ordered work on the pedestal to resume. It was nearly complete when the statue — still in pieces — arrived in New York Harbor, amid much pomp and excitement, in June 1885. On Tuesday morning August 11, Pulitzer announced that the one-hundred-thousandth dol-lar had arrived at the offices of the *World* on the previous day.[16]

Lazarus was not in New York during the climax of Pulitzer's pedestal cam-paign. Just months after she wrote "The New Colossus" late in 1883, she began to feel occasionally weak and debilitated. Soon the symptoms became chronic. When she sailed for Europe in 1885, two years after her previous visit, she said that she felt twenty years older.

Lazarus was no hypochondriac. She had cancer, lymphoma, which was grad-ually sapping her immune system. Over the next two years she slowly withered; eventually she was bedridden. While still in Europe the following summer, sensing that she would never recover, Lazarus decided that she could at least try to shape her literary legacy. Into a notebook she copied by hand all of her favorite compositions, putting them in the order in which she wanted them to be published upon her death. On the very first page, in the place of honor, she put "The New Colossus." In November 1887, just after returning to New York from Europe, Lazarus succumbed to the cancer. She was only thirty-eight.[17]

None of her obituaries mentioned "The New Colossus." When Emma's sis-ters, who controlled her literary estate, brought out a two-volume set of her collected works in 1888, they defied her instructions concerning her proudest achievement. They buried "The New Colossus" on page 202.[18]

Meanwhile, the Statue of Liberty had been assembled. It was dedicated amidst extraordinary pomp and ceremony on October 28, 1886. None of the speeches by President Grover Cleveland or any of the other dignitaries in atten-

Immigrants admiring the Statue of Liberty as their steamship arrives in New York Harbor. Just eight months after its unveiling, newcomers viewed the colossal statue as a symbol of the very reasons why they had immigrated, even if native-born Americans did not yet associate the monument with immigration.

dance mentioned immigrants or immigration. Native-born Americans could barely perceive how the sight of the statue would unleash a torrent of pent-up emotions in immigrants — most of whom had been praying that they might live to one day see its welcoming outstretched arms.[19]

It was completely appropriate that a Jewish New Yorker, inspired by the plight of indigent Russian Jewish immigrants, had written the words that would come to define the Statue of Liberty. In 1865, the year Laboulaye conceived the statue, Irish immigrants arriving in the United States outnumbered Russians by 162 to 1, but by 1883, when Lazarus wrote "The New Colossus," Russian immigration (consisting almost entirely of Jews) had increased fifty-fold. When Bartholdi's monument was unveiled in 1887, the immigrant ships steaming past her up-lifted torch carried three Russian Jews for every five Irish immigrants. In 1892, the year Ellis Island opened, Russian immigrants outnumbered the Irish for the first time.

East European Jews were not the only immigrant group drawn to New York by what one immigrant called "the far-flung clarion call of American liberty and her promise of equal opportunity." Scandinavian immigration grew tremendously in the 1880s, as did the influx from Austria-Hungary, then encompassing a large swath of central Europe stretching from Lake Constance, near Zurich, all the way to what is now eastern Romania and western Ukraine. Several thousand Chinese immigrants also moved to New York in these years, creating the city's first Chinatown.[20]

But the largest group of new immigrants, larger even than the Russian Jews, came from Italy. In 1895 Italians outnumbered all other groups arriving in the United States, surpassing even the Germans, who had held the top spot on the annual arrivals list for forty consecutive years. Italians outnumbered all other immigrants for seventeen of the twenty years leading up to World War I. (Russian immigrants ranked first in the remaining three years.) By 1900, Italian and Russian immigrants disembarking at the port of New York outnumbered Irish and German immigrants four to one. That margin grew to nearly seven to one in 1910, and nine to one in 1914. New York's immigrant population, which had been dominated by Irish and German newcomers for generations, became predominantly Italian and Jewish by the start of the war. Yet more of the arriving eastern European Jewish immigrants stayed in New York than did their Italian counterparts, so New York City ended up with more Jews than Italians. At the end of World War I, New York's population of 5.6 million included 2 million immigrants. Of that total, about 200,000 were Irish, 200,000 were Germans, 400,000 were Italians, and 600,000 were east European Jews. One-quarter of the nation's Italian immigrants and about one-third of its east European Jewish immigrants lived in New York City in 1920. By that point it was said that 50 percent of all Jews living in the United States, and 10 percent of all Jews in the world, called New York City their home.[21]

Like New York's Irish immigrants, eastern European Jews came to America fleeing both economic hardship and oppression. This discrimination related mainly to where Russian Jews could live and what occupations they could follow. Muscovites in the late eighteenth century had begun complaining that too many Jews were living and working in their midst. The tsars and their ministers promulgated a series of laws from the 1790s to the 1830s that banned Jews from residing in the interior regions of Russia, stipulating that they must instead settle in the Russian Empire's western borderlands — the area that roughly comprises modern-day Lithuania, Belarus, Moldova, and Ukraine. This confinement zone was not a cramped space. Its nearly 5 million Jewish inhabitants lived alongside 37 million non-Jews in an area twice the size of contemporary France that stretched from the Baltic to the Black Sea. But within that area, Jews could not farm or even live in rural villages, a prohibition that effectively banned them from inhabiting most of the area in which they were confined.

In einer polnischen Judenstadt

A Jewish neighborhood in a Polish shtetl, the small to medium-sized towns in which most east European Jews lived in the late nineteenth century.

The Russian term for the territory where they were forced to live literally translates as the "boundary of settlement," but in English it became known as the Pale of Settlement.[22]

Within the Pale, most Jews lived in shtetls. Notwithstanding the modern popular imagination, a shtetl was not a village but a small or medium-sized town of five thousand to fifty thousand inhabitants. In some shtetls Jews made up as much as 80 percent of the population, but more often they accounted for only about 40 to 50 percent. The typical shtetl was big enough to have its own synagogue, Jewish cemetery, Jewish schools, and Jewish community associations, but small enough to allow most Jews to know one another, either personally or by reputation. In a shtetl, Jews usually lived in Jewish neighborhoods and earned their livelihoods in the Jewish segment of the town's overall economy. As a result, they followed almost every occupation at every income level, ranging from prosperous merchants to day laborers barely making ends meet.[23]

What made life in the Pale and its shtetls so demoralizing were the constant indignities and ever-increasing list of constraints placed on Jews, especially after the promulgation in 1882 of the "May Laws." These placed quotas on the number of Jewish doctors who could serve in the military and on the number of Jewish students who could enroll in high schools and universities. Jews' ability to obtain mortgages was restricted. Jews were later banned from holding political office, voting, or working for railroads and steamship companies. The authorities even forbade Jews to change or conceal their names so that non-Jews would not mistakenly patronize their businesses. Soon they were also banned from selling liquor, an ironic and especially damaging restriction because several generations earlier, Jewish families had been allowed to migrate to eastern Europe on the *condition* that they agree to sell liquor (and pass on a portion of the income to the state). The government insisted that these restrictions were necessary to protect Russians from Jewish exploitation.[24]

Life for Jews in the Pale became especially intolerable in the early 1880s when they became the targets of widespread organized violence known as pogroms. While rioting in nineteenth-century New York was especially common in the sweltering summer months, Russian pogroms most often began around the simultaneous springtime celebrations of Easter and Passover. The Christian holiday gave clerics the opportunity to recount the role of Jews in the death of Jesus, while the concurrent Jewish celebration of Passover offered Russian anti-Semites the chance to once again propagate the "blood libel," the legend that Jews use the blood of secretly murdered Christian children as an ingredient in their Passover matzos.

On April 27, 1881,* just a few days after Russians had finished celebrating Easter, the first systematic assaults on Jews and Jewish property began. Over the course of the next several months, Russians attacked Jews in at least 250 different communities, almost all of them in modern-day Ukraine. One of the first, on April 29, occurred in the shtetl of Golta (now known as Pervomais'k), located midway between Kiev and Odessa and just twenty miles east-south-east of the shtetl of Holoskov (now usually transliterated as Holoskove), the home of my great-grandfather Froim Leib Anbinder, then seven years old. The attackers in these pogroms generally targeted Jewish property rather than the Jews themselves. Nonetheless, rioters killed many men, raped dozens of women, and ruthlessly beat thousands. Tens of thousands more were terrorized, as their homes and businesses were looted and their meager possessions stolen or destroyed. Even in places where no pogroms took place, Jews feared for their lives. "It is as if we were besieged," a Jew in Odessa wrote in his diary. "The courtyard is bolted shut . . . We sleep in our clothes . . . for fear that rob-

---

* Russians still used the Julian calendar, but for the sake of consistency, I have rendered all dates according to the Gregorian calendar in use in New York at this time. In the nineteenth century, the Julian calendar was twelve days behind the Gregorian calendar, so while New Yorkers identified the date when the pogroms began as April 27, Russians considered it April 15.

bers will fall upon us and so that we can then quickly take the little children . . . and flee wherever the wind will carry us."[25]

In April 1882 the pogroms resumed. One of the most notorious took place in Balta, a shtetl of about twenty thousand inhabitants (half of them Jewish) located forty miles west-southwest of Holoskov. "What I saw defies description," wrote a Russian journalist who toured Balta's scenes of destruction after the mobs had dispersed. On one of the town's main streets, nothing remained of one grand building but

> heaps of debris of furniture, household utensils, and merchandise. I move on to a second building, then a third — the picture is the same everywhere! I go to other streets and find the same picture of devastation. It took me seven hours by the clock, walking and riding in my carriage, to traverse the most important parts of a town — in which, in one word, everything that had belonged to Jews had been demolished, destroyed, sacked . . . Nothing remained standing other than the carcasses [of buildings], the walls and the roofs . . . The entire Jewish population of Balta at this moment lacks clothing, furniture, beds, household utensils, crockery. The sacked homes are without windows, doors, and often without stoves.

Victims at the time and historians ever since have assumed that the Russian government orchestrated the attacks, but Russian archival records indicate that Tsar Alexander III and his ministers objected to any inflaming of popular passions, even when those passions were directed at Jews. Local officials, however, seem to have put little effort into suppressing most of the attacks. "I am very anxious to leave Russia," wrote one Jew in his diary in the wake of the rampages of 1882. "Do I not rise daily with the fear lest the hungry mob attack me and rob me of my possessions and destroy everything that I have acquired with the sweat of my brow? Do I not pray that my sisters may escape the clutches of drunkards lest they be raped? Do I not pray that my parents be not killed trying to defend their children and that my brothers and sisters do not die of hunger and thirst?"[26]

The tsar's leftist opponents could be just as anti-Semitic as the government reactionaries who tacitly condoned the anti-Jewish violence. "Who takes the land, the woods, the taverns from out of your hands? The Jews," read one socialist broadside. "Wherever you look, wherever you go — the Jews are everywhere. The Jew curses you, cheats you, drinks your blood." It was not always like this, insisted the author, but by creating the Pale, the tsars had caused Ukraine to become overrun with Jews. "You have begun to rebel against the Jews," the author wrote, referring to the pogroms of 1881. "You have done well.

Soon the revolt will be taken up across all of Russia against the tsar, the [land-lords], the Jews."[27]

Russian immigration to the United States tripled in 1882 in the wake of the pogroms, and it was the influx of refugees that attracted the attention of Emma Lazarus and many other New Yorkers. Nonetheless, for every 2 Russian Jews who decided to emigrate in 1881–82, another 998 remained in Russia. Many of the Jews who stayed came to the conclusion that they were no longer safe in their shtetls, so after 1882 there was a massive movement of Jews into the region's major cities. Odessa, which had only 200 Jews in 1800, had 139,000 by 1900. The Jewish population of Bialystok in what is now Poland grew more than tenfold over that same time span, and Warsaw's mushroomed from 9,000 to 219,000. In the early years of the twentieth century, the urban influx accelerated even further. Kiev's Jewish population expanded from 32,000 in 1897 to 81,000 fifteen years later, while that of Lodz, now the third-largest city in Poland, grew from 99,000 to 167,000 in the same fifteen-year period.[28]

But Russia's cities did not welcome the influx of Jews. In 1891, for example, the Russian government expelled all twenty thousand Jewish inhabitants from Moscow. They had previously been exempted from the requirement to live in

Newly arrived Jewish immigrants from Russia leaving Castle Garden in 1882 during the first big wave of east European Jewish immigration to New York.

the Pale because as merchants or artisans whose trades were in high demand, they had been deemed "useful" Jews. Some of the banished Jews clearly chose to emigrate, as did others who thought their turn might come next. A "mighty wave" of emigration swept through Russia and Poland in 1891 and 1892, recalled Mary Antin, who left Poland at that time. Immigration from Russia to the United States increased more than 125 percent from 1890 to 1892, reaching 82,000 in the latter year. One of these immigrants was my mother's maternal grandfather, Barnet Gutkin, a furrier who emigrated from Odessa to New York late in 1891. For every immigrant who was forced from his home, however, there were many more who were motivated by economic aspirations or long-standing grievances, and merely considered the new round of restrictions the last straw.[29]

Living conditions for Jews in the fast-growing cities of Poland and the Pale were far worse than they had been in the shtetls. An English member of Parliament visiting Vilna (in modern-day Lithuania) at the beginning of the twentieth century found "the miserable dens and cellars" in which the Jews lived truly shocking. "The walls of the houses were blistered and rotting, as if poisoned by the pestilent atmosphere within ... During my walks through the ghetto I was surrounded by a crowd of gaunt, curious, anxious faces — sad, careworn, hungry-looking people." In Lodz the situation was no better. "The Jews are crowded together in the *Balout* quarter where the atmosphere is almost unbreathable," reported one eyewitness in 1897. "Their misery is indescribable." The situation had not improved a few years later when the same English M.P. toured the Jewish ghetto of Lodz. "The people had the appearance of half-starved consumptives," he reported. "It would need the pen of a Zola to do justice to them ... I have never seen human beings living under more awful conditions."[30]

Meanwhile, the circumstances of the majority of east European Jews who remained in the shtetls were deteriorating as well, as the exodus to the cities siphoned off their customers and made earning a living increasingly difficult. Perhaps worst of all, these Jews saw no possibility of future improvement for themselves or their children. "The Russian peasant, poor as he may be, is the proprietor of a small piece of land," wrote one Lithuanian Jewish émigré of his former neighbors. "And his condition is not hopeless — one feels that sooner or later it will improve. But Jewish poverty is utterly without a cure; the Jew has no available means for improving his condition, which will remain abject as long as he lives among alien peoples."[31]

Jews were encouraged to emigrate by letters that earlier Russian and Polish Jewish immigrants sent to friends and relatives in the Pale. "It is a beautiful country, the land of freedom," wrote back one immigrant to the shtetl of Eishyshok in what is now southeast Lithuania. "Wherever [a Jew] wants to move he can go, whatever he wants to accomplish he can attain." Such letters convinced Jews still in the Pale that the United States was far more "civilized" than eastern Europe, "and offers the most guarantees of individual freedom, freedom of conscience, and security of all property." Furthermore, they had learned, America "endows every one of her inhabitants with both civil and political rights." At home, Russian Jews enjoyed neither.[32]

By 1890, so many residents of the Pale had received such "America letters," or had friends or neighbors who had, that east European Jews became obsessed with the prospect of immigrating to the United States. "All my relatives and all our neighbors — in fact, everybody who was anybody — had either gone or was going to New York," recalled Marcus Eli Ravage of the days before he emigrated from Romania in about 1900. Mary Antin, who came to the United States at age eleven in 1894, three years after her father, likewise remembered that on the eve of her departure, "'America' was in everybody's mouth. Business men talked of it over their accounts; the market women made up their quarrels that they might discuss it from stall to stall; people who had relatives in the famous land went around reading their letters for the enlightenment of less fortunate folks; the one letter-carrier [in her hometown in what is now Belarus] informed the public how many letters arrived from America, and who were the recipients; children played at emigrating."[33]

Like the Irish before them, east European Jews often employed "chain migration," first sending one family member to New York to establish a foothold and find steady work before mailing steamship tickets back to loved ones so their families could be reunited. This was what my mother's father's family had done. Isidor Munstuk, my great-great-grandfather, immigrated to New York at around age twenty-nine from Plotzk, Poland. Upon arrival in about 1871, he found work as a barber on Hester Street in what would later be known as the Lower East Side. Only after about five years did he manage to bring his wife, Bertha, and his children Rachel, Sarah, and Jacob (my great-grandfather) over to join him.[34]

In 1900, Russian Jewish immigration set a new record, and it continued to climb from there. Jewish immigration spiked still higher in 1903, when Russia was once again wracked by pogroms. This outbreak of anti-Jewish violence was much more deadly than previous waves and lasted four years. "At our door four Jews were hanged, and I saw that with my own eyes," recalled Marsha Farbman, who fled to America in 1904. "The Gentiles were running and yelling, 'Beat the Jews, Kill them!'"[35]

One of the most notorious and deadly of these pogroms began on Easter Sunday, April 19, 1903, in Kishinev, a city of about 150,000 located one hundred

Grausam hingeschlachtete jüdische Kinder in Jekaterinoslaw.

Child victims of the Ekaterinoslav pogrom of 1905. Such violence
prompted many Jews to leave for America.

miles northwest of Odessa in what is now Moldova but was then the portion of
the Pale known as Bessarabia. Wielding crowbars, clubs, axes, and occasionally
pistols, thousands of marauding townsmen joined peasants from surrounding
villages in a three-day rampage in which they killed about fifty Jews and injured
five hundred (out of a Jewish population of about fifty thousand). The rioters
destroyed Jewish homes and property throughout the city, leaving ten thousand homeless. The pogrom sparked international outrage, especially when the
Russian ambassador to the United States told the press that the Jews themselves were "responsible for the troubles." Many Jews from Bessarabia had immigrated to New York before the renewal of violence in 1903. One of my pa-
ternal great-grandfathers, Mendel Dandishensky, from the shtetl of Briceni in
northern Bessarabia, arrived in New York in 1896, and his wife, Liba, joined
him a year later. But the Kishinev pogrom and the official response to it persuaded even more east European Jews from Bessarabia and all over the Pale to
flee to America in 1903 and 1904.[36]

In 1905, socialist revolutionaries gained increasingly large followings across
Russia. They organized general strikes in many cities and attempted to seize
and collectivize the landholdings of Russia's aristocracy, with the ultimate goal
of driving the tsar from power. This wave of uprisings became known as the
Russian Revolution of 1905. Many Russians who supported the tsar blamed
Jewish socialists for the revolutionary tumult. As a result, the number of anti-
Jewish rampages multiplied, including one that resulted in one hundred deaths
in Kiev in July of that year.

Meanwhile, other opponents of the Russian government, best described as
"reformers," pursued a more moderate strategy. They sought to reduce the au-

thority of the Russian aristocracy without overthrowing it, to create a constitutional monarchy that would allow a less powerful tsar to retain his title, and to grant civil and political rights to all Russians. Influenced by both radicals and reformers, Russian workers organized a nationwide general strike in October in which millions participated. Russia's rulers became increasingly panicked. If the strike lasted very long, it might cripple the Russian economy and create further discontent. At the end of October, the Russian ruler and his ministers acceded to many of the reformers' demands in the hopes that doing so would undercut the radicals and prevent a true revolution. Among the concessions that the government made in this "October Manifesto" was the granting of political and civil rights to all Russians, including the heretofore disenfranchised Jews.[37]

Jews could not celebrate for long. The new law prompted a vicious popular backlash against the Jews by anti-Semites who objected to granting them equal rights. In the weeks after the tsar signed the October Manifesto, rightwing mobs shouting "Death to the rebels. Death to the Jews" formed in almost all the major cities of the Pale and Poland and in hundreds of shtetls as well, instigating six hundred pogroms, the deadliest yet. Russians killed approximately 2,500 Jews in November and December 1905 and injured many thousands more. In Odessa, where the deadliest pogrom took place, estimates put the fatalities as high as eight hundred and the number of injured at five thousand. Pogroms also broke out again in the shtetls of Balta and Golta near the home of my Anbinder ancestors in southern Ukraine. These pogroms caused another huge spike in the emigration of east European Jews. The number of Russians arriving annually in the United States rose steadily from 107,000 in 1902, before the violence erupted, to 259,000 in 1907.[38]

Pogroms alone, however, do not explain why so many Jews immigrated to the United States in these decades. Thousands emigrated from portions of the Pale such as Lithuania that experienced relatively few pogroms. Thousands of Jews also left Romania and Galicia (now the southern part of Poland) in the Austro-Hungarian Empire, where anti-Jewish violence was also relatively rare. In fact, a higher proportion of the Jewish population emigrated from Lithuania and Galicia than from violence-ridden Ukraine. "The small town felt narrow to me, and I wanted to go somewhere else," recalled Aaron Domnitz, who emigrated from what is now Belarus, in an autobiographical sketch. "The mood in town in general was to emigrate . . . There was no friction with non-Jews."[39]

Hunger, political oppression, and a lack of economic opportunity drove most of these immigrants to the United States, just as these same factors had pushed the Irish and the Germans to America before them. One tailor, who left for America at the height of these pogroms, did not even mention anti-

Jewish violence when recounting his decision to leave the Pale: "Those days everybody's dream in the old country was to go to America. We heard people were free and we heard about better living . . . I figured, I have a trade, I have a chance more or less to see the world. I was young." A Jewish immigrant from Poland also did not mention pogroms when explaining why he decided to emigrate. "I want to go to a country where everyone is equal, where the rich also work, and work is no disgrace," his daughter recalled hearing him say. "I want to go to America, where a Jew does not have to take off his hat and wait outside to see a Pole . . . I want to go to a country where I can work hard and make a living for my wife and children and be equal to everyone."[40]

Some Jews emigrated to escape the gender conventions that constrained them in the Old World. Emma Goldman left St. Petersburg for New York in large part because her father, she later recounted, "had tried desperately to marry me off at the age of fifteen. I had protested, begging to be permitted to continue my studies. In his frenzy he threw my French grammar into the fire, shouting: 'Girls do not have to learn much! All a Jewish daughter needs to know is how to prepare *gefüllte* fish, cut noodles fine, and give the man plenty of children.'" Young Emma was incensed. "I wanted to study, to know life, to travel. Besides, I never would marry for anything but love, I stoutly maintained. It was really to escape my father's plans for me that I had insisted on going to America." At age sixteen, the headstrong Goldman sailed for America accompanied by her older half sister Helena.[41]

Yet the sharp rise in emigration corresponding to each new wave of pogroms is unmistakable, and clearly these played some role in the decision of many Jews to immigrate to the United States. Furthermore, one did not have to experience pogroms firsthand to be frightened. A Jew might choose to emigrate out of fear that her shtetl could be next. "The accounts in the newspaper were terrifying," one east European Jewish memoirist wrote, vividly recalling the day when news of a Bialystok pogrom reached his town. "Yosele translated into Yiddish the report of the atrocities committed against babies, about old men who had been hacked to death with axes, and about pregnant women whose bellies had been slit open. The people in the [synagogue] were left pale and shaken." Many would have resolved to emigrate before the violence could spread to their shtetl. And for those who did live in the centers of violence, the reason for emigrating was simple: "Pogroms, pogroms without end," wrote Bertha Fox, who came from Skvira, near Kiev. "That is why I left the old country."[42]

East European Jewish immigration fell off a bit after the four-year wave of pogroms ended in late 1906 (and perhaps in part because of the American Fi-

A photo of my great-grandmother Beyle Anbinder (seated left) and her five children, taken some time before they were able to leave Ukraine and join Froim Leib Anbinder in New York. My grandfather Tulea is in the center, standing.

nancial Panic of 1907 as well), but then the emigration from Russia rose once more. My great-grandfather Froim Leib Anbinder left Holoskov in this period, arriving in New York on April 2, 1910. Immigration to the United States from Russia hit an all-time high of 291,000 in 1913 as Russian Jews joined hundreds of thousands of other Europeans rushing to emigrate before military tensions in Europe could spiral out of control and make such a move impossible. From that first pogrom in 1881 to the end of 1914, a few months after World War I had begun, about 2.1 million east European Jews (one-third of the total) immigrated to the United States. Of that number, 1.6 million came from Russia (including the portion of Poland that Russia controlled), 400,000 from the Austro-Hungarian Empire (including lands such as Galicia that are now in southern Poland), and 80,000 from Romania. Demographers estimate that approximately three-quarters of those Jews who immigrated to the United States initially made New York City their new home.[43]

Once the war started in 1914, Froim Leib, who had not yet managed to accumulate enough money to bring his wife, four daughters, and son over to join him, must have been wracked by guilt. With U-boats sinking transatlan-

tic steamers like the *Lusitania,* now was not the time to cross the ocean, especially once the United States entered the war in 1917. The outbreak of the Russian Revolution that same year made it even more difficult for the remaining
Anbinders to emigrate. Every couple of years, Froim Leib's wife, Beyle, would
mail him a photograph of herself and the children so he could see how they had
grown (or perhaps to make sure he would not think about abandoning them).
There must have been times when Froim Leib wondered if he had done the
right thing, and if he would ever see his wife and children again.

Italy had no pogroms. But it had crushing poverty, and America beckoned.
More than 4 million Italians moved to the United States from 1880 to 1914.
But while Jews invariably bade good riddance to Russia, many Italians initially
thought of themselves as temporary migrants, not immigrants. Not until the
end of World War I would the bulk of the Italians living in New York commit
to making the United States their permanent home.

For most Italians who immigrated, it was a feeling of despair on behalf of
themselves and their children, and the apparent impossibility of ever owning
their own land to farm, that played the key role in their decision. "In Italy it was
work and work hard with no hope of any future," recalled Leonard Covello long
after he immigrated. "A few years of schooling and then work for the rest of
one's life — no prospect of ever going beyond the fifth grade or ever becoming
other than what one started out to be." Most Italians in the nineteenth century
did agricultural labor, but at the time of Italian unification in 1871, fewer than 10
percent of Italian farmers owned the fields they cultivated. Italy's landed gentry,
the *signori,* controlled most farmland, especially in southern Italy (the portion
of the country known as the *mezzogiorno*), and as the Italian peninsula's population skyrocketed over the course of the nineteenth century, the land barons
raised rents to unprecedented levels. "Every bit of cultivable soil is owned by
those fortunate few who lord over us," complained Pascal D'Angelo, who lived
in the mountains of the Abruzzi region east of Rome and whose family began
immigrating to the United States in 1910. Those who did manage to scrape together enough money for a down payment on a small farm often had to sell
the property at a loss after the first poor harvest in order to satisfy creditors or
tax collectors. The influx of cheap imported grain from the United States and
Russia in the 1870s and 1880s and a tariff war with France in the 1890s made it
especially hard for Italian farmers — both landowners and renters — to make a
profit.[44]

Italian peasant farmers often lived in squalid conditions. "The life of the
men, the beasts and the land seemed fixed in an inflexible circle, hemmed in

by the position of the mountains and the passage of time, as if condemned by nature to life imprisonment," wrote the Italian novelist Ignazio Silone, who was also from Abruzzi. The farmers lived in "huts" that were "irregular, unformed, blackened by time and worn down by wind, rain, and fire, with their roofs poorly covered by all sorts of tiles and scrap lumber. Most of these hovels have only one opening, which serves as door, window, and chimney," and most had dirt floors, too. Inside these dingy one-room cabins, "the men, the women and children, and their goats, chicken, pigs and donkeys live, sleep, eat and reproduce, sometimes all in the same corner." Nonfiction writers conveyed similar accounts, albeit in less melodramatic prose, of "huts" without windows or chimneys, peasants sleeping with their animals, "sanitary conditions . . . abominable," and no hope for improvement. In Italy, an American journalist concluded in 1909, "poverty, — or rather misery, abject and hopeless, — is a chronic phenomenon."[45]

By this point, many Italian men found that thievery was the only way to break out of this cycle of destitution. Thousands of southern Italians became brigands, members of criminal gangs who waylaid well-to-do travelers on remote mountain roads. But for those not suited to a life of crime, another option seemed more attractive. "I can be a thief or I can emigrate," one Italian confessed to his priest when explaining his decision to leave Italy. A blacksmith came to the same conclusion: "When I found that the only way I could prevent my family from starving was to turn to stealing, I decided it was time to leave." He emigrated in 1906.[46]

One might imagine that the unification of Italy in 1871 would have ameliorated some of these problems in southern Italy, but in fact the situation got worse rather than better. The sense of paternalism the *signori* felt for their peasant workers disappeared after unification because the elite now believed that the state was ultimately responsible for the welfare of its poorest residents. The ambitions of the new national government also led to higher taxes; some peasants previously considered too poor to pay government levies were now taxed for the first time. They considered the new system unfair inasmuch as it taxed mules, considered a necessity even for indigent farmers, but not cows, which in the south only wealthy farmers could usually afford. "It is progressive taxation topsy-turvy," observed Pasquale Villari, a Neapolitan who taught history at the University of Florence. "The less a man has, the more he pays." Poor Italians in the *mezzogiorno* found the regressive tax policy especially galling because the new national government, even with all that income, seemed incapable of addressing the problems such as chronic disease that ravaged southern Italy. Thousands there contracted malaria each year, and 55,000 died in the *mezzogiorno* during a cholera outbreak that lasted from 1884 to 1887.[47]

One of the reasons why poor Italians felt so hopeless about their future was their lack of political power. In the first decade after unification, only 2 percent of Italians were eligible to vote, and from 1882 to 1912, just 7 percent qualified to participate in elections. Only in 1912 did the Italian parliament grant all men age thirty and over the right to vote; men in their twenties could not vote until 1918. Women could not cast ballots until 1945. Excluded from the polity, and feeling that they lacked a real future in Italy, many Italians saw the United States as the next best option. "No, I will not stay vegetating here, I thought. The world is big, there's America, and New York is a vast metropolis," Adolfo Rossi remembered thinking when, at age twenty-two, he decided to emigrate in the summer of 1879. A native of the Veneto region of northeast Italy, Rossi first found employment in New York as an apprentice eyeglass maker; a year later he was making gelato at the Metropolitan Concert Hall, a precursor to the Metropolitan Opera House. Rossi eventually landed a position with one of the city's Italian-language newspapers and later wrote guidebooks for aspiring Italian emigrants.[48]

The United States was not initially the favored destination of Italian migrants. In the late nineteenth century, more chose to move to other parts of Europe than to relocate across the Atlantic. And of those who did decide to cross the sea, more initially settled in Argentina than in the United States. In 1890 Buenos Aires had four times as many Italian-born residents as did New York. The northern Italians who moved to Argentina believed they could more quickly ascend to the middle class in South America than in the United States.[49]

Nineteen hundred was the first year in which Italians immigrating to the United States outnumbered those headed to South America. Northern Italians leaving Europe continued to prefer Argentina or Brazil, while central and southern Italians, who in the twentieth century began to outnumber northerners as emigrants, overwhelmingly chose the United States. "All people talked was, 'America, America, America,'" an immigrant from Calabria recalled years later in an interview. The southern Italians had trouble imagining that they could reach the middle class anywhere, and the day labor and construction jobs they hoped to land paid better in New York than in Buenos Aires. The letters sent back to Italy by the earliest immigrants also induced many Italians to venture to the United States.[50]

Unlike the east European Jews, who rarely returned to visit Russia or Poland, many Italians went back to Italy in the winter, when American construction work dried up, especially if they were doing well in America. These return migrants were always men; unlike the Irish, Italians never sent a female family member to America first. The stylish clothes and worldly sophistication of the returning "Americani" mesmerized their former neighbors. "But the great change is that he has money—more money than ever before, more money than [any of] his old neighbors have," remembered one Italian of his first en-counter with a returning "Americano." "He is an advertisement that there is prosperity for the stranger in America." Shortly thereafter, this awestruck vil-lager boarded a ship for New York.[51]

Many of these returning "Americani" stayed permanently in Italy. For some, their whole goal in traveling to New York had been to save enough money to put a down payment on a piece of farmland back in Italy, pay off a family debt, purchase a business, or build better housing for their parents. These Italians became known as "birds of passage" because, like migratory birds, they spent part of the year in one part of the world and the remainder in another. Fare wars among the steamship companies drove ticket prices to unprecedentedly low levels, making it feasible for them to cross the Atlantic twice a year. Tens of thousands of Italians made the migratory voyage to the United States each spring to find construction work, then returned to Italy the following winter. In the heaviest years of return migration (1903 and 1904), two Italians went back to Italy in the winter for every three who had arrived the previous spring, though the more typical ratio was two returnees to every five immigrants.[52]

Yet many Italians who planned to be birds of passage eventually became im-migrants. Pascal D'Angelo and his father, Angelo, for example, left Abruzzi for New York in 1910, intending to stay only long enough to pay off the loan sharks to whom the family was indebted. Yet Pascal never returned home. Some re-

Italian emigrants near Lake Como in northern Italy heading for an emigration office as they began their journey to America.

mained in New York because they had not managed to save much money and were ashamed to show their faces back in their hometowns. "It is not as you believe that here in America money is found on the ground," wrote another native of Abruzzi to his parents in Italy. Others decided to settle permanently in the United States after World War I devastated the Italian economy. Still others found that they liked life in America more than they had expected. And some decided to stay only after the United States began imposing immigration restrictions in 1921. These migrants chose to become permanent American residents so their children would not have to suffer through the same "abysmal misery" in Italy that they had endured.[53]

As time passed, a new reason to remain permanently in the United States developed: there was not much left in the *mezzogiorno* to go back to. In the early years of the twentieth century, many southern Italian villages became virtual ghost towns as the majority of men moved to America, eventually sending for their families or returning to Italy just long enough to choose brides and bring them back to the United States. When the first Italian prime minister to tour the *mezzogiorno* arrived in the Basilicata region in 1902, the mayor of Moliterno greeted him by saying, "I salute you in the name of my 8,000 fellow villagers, of whom 3,000 have emigrated to America and 5,000 are preparing to join them." The town of San Demetrio in Calabria lost so many men to emigration that no one was left to light its streetlamps at night. Visiting another southern Italian town, an American reporter found "nowhere the vibrant toil of young men; nowhere the cheerful sound of intense, hopeful, human activity. The village is dead." The inhabitants who remained, "aimlessly filling a weird, fatal silence, seem like denizens of an accursed land. Their only thought is America."[54]

Natural disasters accelerated the immigration from southern Italy still further. A parasite spread throughout southern Italian vineyards in 1890, destroying the grapevines and consequently the livelihoods of many residents. The eruption of Mount Vesuvius and the earthquakes that accompanied it in April 1906 killed approximately two thousand Italians, persuading many from the region surrounding Naples to make the trip to America. An even more important stimulus was the horrific earthquake and tidal wave that struck the Straits of Messina on December 28, 1908. Approximately 150,000 Italians died in that cataclysm of tremors, fires, and flooding. (The earthquake and fire in San Francisco two years earlier, in contrast, had claimed three thousand lives.) Only 2 percent of the buildings in Messina, in northeast Sicily, were left intact after the quake. On the other side of the straits, Reggio Calabria, the capital city of Calabria, was equally devastated. Thousands of charred corpses could be seen floating in the straits in the days after the quake.

These natural disasters prompted even more southern Italians to depart their seemingly accursed homeland for the United States, leaving in their wake, according to an Italian parliamentary inquiry in 1910, "abandoned houses, orchards transformed into thorny thickets," and villages as empty as if they "had been stricken by the plague." An Italian member of parliament from Basilicata expressed the prevailing sentiment this way: "Oh God," he wrote, please "never let the United States choose to close its doors to the surging flood of our wretched countrymen!"[55]

Natural disasters are dramatic, but the recurring subtheme in the Italian emigrants' tales of woe was hunger. While starvation in Italy might be rare, a British report noted in 1901, "there is a terrible permanent lack of food." A few years later, an American journalist found that emigration "from the Peninsula is only too plainly an emigration of hunger." This privation was not soon forgotten. When the mayor of a Sicilian town was asked in the 1970s where an American might find documents describing why the city's residents had emigrated in the early twentieth century, he replied that a trip to the archives was unnecessary: "You want to know why people left? Hunger, that's why."[56]

Huge numbers of Italians emigrated from every region of Italy, but while northerners continued to emigrate primarily within Europe, 90 percent of southern Italian emigrants relocated to the Americas, and 70 percent of them settled in the United States. From 1880 to 1914, 375,000 Italians emigrated from remote and sparsely populated Basilicata to the United States; 420,000 from Calabria, the "toe" of the Italian "boot"; 425,000 from the Campania region surrounding Naples; 530,000 from Abruzzi e Molise; and 960,000 from Sicily.[57]

For those who came to the United States in the late nineteenth and early twentieth centuries, the journey from their homeland to New York was far different from that of the Irish and Germans a half century earlier. Jews traveled on huge ocean liners that now took a week rather than a month to cross the Atlantic (a bit longer for those sailing direct from Italy). Deaths among the passengers, common in the 1850s, were rare by 1900. But psychologically, the weeklong journey was just as traumatic and indelible in the mind as the much longer, more perilous passage had been for their predecessors in the age of sail. The journey is "a kind of hell," reported a guidebook for Jewish immigrants published in 1891 by an author who had made the journey himself, one "that cleanses a man of his sins before coming to the land of Columbus."[58]

The memorable portions of the immigrants' journeys to America began even before they left their hometown. For many, a hearty, festive farewell meal or going-away party would be held on the night before the date of departure.

The following morning, an entourage of dozens or even hundreds of family members, neighbors, acquaintances, or merely curious onlookers would accompany the emigrant to the train station, sometimes a journey of many miles.

Few emigrants forgot the moment when the train began approaching the station, for tears would start to flow in abundance. Since it was the younger generation that typically emigrated, most mothers and grandmothers expected that they would never see their offspring again. "The scene at the station was one of undescribable confusion, lamentation and exclamation," recounted D'Angelo of his departure from Introdacqua in the Abruzzi region in 1910. "Everything was obscured by a mist of tears." Marcus Ravage's Romanian Jewish mother at first "seemed calm and resigned" to his departure, but when his train approached the station, "she lost control of her feelings. As she embraced me for the last time," he wrote, "her sobs became violent and father had to separate us. There was a despair in her way of clinging to me which I could not then understand. I understand it now. I never saw her again."

The wailing as the emigrant departed was very much like the heartfelt sobbing one found at a funeral, and with good reason. "A person gone to America," Ravage recalled, "was exactly like a person dead," and the procession to the station very much like a funeral, with the train station replacing the cemetery. "The whole community turned out, and marched in slow time to the station, and wept loudly and copiously, and remembered the unfortunates in its prayer on the next Saturday," or the next Sunday in the case of the Italians, whose memoirs recount similar scenes.[59]

For Italians, the trip to the port of embarkation was relatively simple from this point onward, albeit full of new sights and sounds at every turn. Most had never ridden on a train or visited a big city. Those from the interior had usually never seen the sea or ocean before, even if they lived only ten or twenty miles inland. Italians could at least take comfort in the fact that they traveled with passports — the Italian government demanded it as a condition of emigration — giving them some sense of security as they approached the port where they would board the ship that would take them to the United States.[60]

For Russian Jews, by contrast, it was illegal to emigrate. Many carried no passport, and others bought fakes. In truth, neither the Russian authorities nor the security services of the nations Jews would pass through en route to their ports of embarkation in western Europe had much interest in stopping them. But because one could never be sure, and emigrants were occasionally arrested and jailed, the Jews' journeys to reach a steamship were fraught and stressful. Russian Jews would take a train as far west as they could and then transfer to a hired horse and cart for the trip to either the Austro-Hungarian border (for those from the southern part of the Pale) or the German border (for those from the Pale's northern regions). Approaching the border, they would leave the cart and travel by foot, usually at night to avoid detection. Typically they were led by professional immigrant smugglers — sometimes peasants and sometimes other Jews — who (then as still today) charged outrageous sums to help the immigrants avoid the supposedly omnipresent border guards.

The more the emigrants could be made to fear that capture was imminent, the more their guides could extort from them. They were often subject to interminable layovers in rural cabins until the smugglers had extracted every possible bit of cash from them. "We waited a long time in the hut before we realized we were being held for more money," recalled Abraham Cahan, who later went on to edit New York's most widely read Yiddish newspaper. "Having paid, we moved on. We made a strange group going across fields and meadows in the night, halted suddenly every few minutes by the tall peasant holding up his finger and pausing to listen for God-knows-what disaster."[61]

Having made it across the border, some Jewish immigrants would regroup and decompress in towns such as Brody in Austria-Hungary (now western Ukraine), where they might receive advice from the Jewish community about the best way to proceed to a port city. Others, like Mary Antin, did not dare tarry and instead pressed immediately onward.

In a great lonely field opposite a solitary wooden house within a large yard, our train pulled up at last, and a conductor . . . hurried us into the one large room . . . Here a great many men and women, dressed in white, received us . . . This was another scene of bewildering confusion, parents losing their children, and little ones crying; baggage being thrown together in one corner of the yard, heedless of contents, which suffered in consequence; those white-clad Germans shouting commands always accompanied with "Quick! Quick!"; the confused passengers obeying all orders like meek children, only questioning now and then what was going to be done with them . . . A man came to inspect us, as if to ascertain our full value; strange looking people driving us about like dumb animals, helpless and unresisting; children we could not see, crying in a way that suggested terrible things; ourselves driven into a little room where a great kettle was boiling on a little stove; our clothes taken off, our bodies rubbed with a slippery substance that might be any bad thing; a shower of warm water let down on us without warning; again driven to another little room where we sit, wrapped in woollen blankets till . . . we . . . hear the women's orders to dress ourselves . . . "Quick, quick, or you'll miss the train!" Oh, so we really won't be murdered! . . . Thank God!

Some immigrants would have been warned by the America letters from those who had made the journey before them to expect this delousing by the German railway officials. For others it would have been a sudden, bewildering shock.[62]

At this point, most of these east European Jews boarded trains heading for Vienna, Frankfurt, or Berlin, where they would transfer to yet another train, this time headed for the port of Hamburg or Bremen, though some sailed via Amsterdam, Rotterdam, Antwerp, or even Trieste or Fiume. Those with the least money might take a ship to England so that they could sail from Liverpool, where the transatlantic fare was about 25 percent cheaper. Froim Leib Anbinder was one of the Jews who trekked there to board his vessel and save a few precious dollars. Italians initially would have sailed to America almost exclusively from just two ports, Genoa and Naples. Only in the years immediately before World War I did ships begin to carry immigrants regularly from Palermo to New York as well.[63]

The array of bewildering and frightening experiences did not end once the immigrants arrived at the port. In the 1880s and early 1890s these would have been experiences very similar to those faced by the Irish immigrants in Liverpool fifty years earlier. In Naples and Bremen alike, "porters" who promised to carry luggage ran off with it instead; agents peddled tickets with fares too low to be true, because they were not real tickets at all, or they were the wrong tickets; quayside boardinghouse keepers tried to fleece the immigrants of what little money they had left.

Beginning in 1892, when Ellis Island opened and the immigrants faced a more rigorous medical inspection upon arrival, a whole new array of traps were set at the European ports of departure. Self-described dentists made the rounds of immigrant boardinghouses, insisting that if an aching tooth was not removed before departure, it would surely cause the immigrant to be rejected at Ellis Island. Others peddled smallpox vaccination certificates to those who could be fooled into believing that such a document would relieve them of the requirement either to show a welt on the arm as proof of vaccination or to be vaccinated on board the ship prior to arrival in New York. A guidebook for Italian emigrants succinctly summed up the situation by giving travelers the following advice: never, ever trust anyone who approached them or showed the least interest in them, no matter what story they might tell, offer they might make, or product they might sell.[64]

The American Immigration Act of 1891, part of the movement for the more thorough examination of arriving immigrants that led to the creation of the Ellis Island immigration station, required steamship companies to pay for the feeding and transportation home of any immigrant turned away by inspectors.

The Immigration Act of 1907 went further, and made the shipping companies liable to a stiff fine for each rejected immigrant. As immigration skyrocketed and the potential liability of the steamship companies multiplied, the shipping lines began instituting their own medical inspections to weed out those who might be turned back at Ellis Island. First, the German shippers got German railway companies to inspect and disinfect Jews as they crossed into Germany from Russia, Poland, or Austria-Hungary. (These were the white-robed Germans who deloused Mary Antin immediately before she first boarded a German train.) To further prevent sick passengers from sailing for America, the German steamship companies started requiring that steerage passengers undergo a two-week quarantine to make sure they would not spread or contract any ailments during the sea voyage. Italy, fearing that its own citizens might become stigmatized if they were rejected at Ellis Island more often than others, introduced its own state-run health inspections in 1901. Italian emigration officials asked the emigrants headed for the United States the same questions they would face at Ellis Island and advised them to alter their responses if they gave ones that were likely to cause problems. On top of all this, Congress directed American consuls to initiate their own inspections of emigrants to insure that those likely to be rejected at Ellis Island never made it that far. As a result of such examinations, 4 percent of those attempting to emigrate from the port of Naples to the United States were turned back in 1907, and 5.5 percent were turned away in Bremen that same year.[65]

Once the immigrants passed through that gauntlet of examinations and made it on board their ship, all but the most well-to-do were ushered down into the bowels of the vessel to the steerage compartments. In some ways, steerage in the early twentieth century was a far cry from steerage during the age of sail. Floors and bunks were now made of metal instead of hard-to-clean wood. There were toilets and sinks with running water, luxurious conveniences beyond the wildest dreams of the famine Irish. There was even electric lighting, though not much of it.

Yet the essence of steerage — the crowding, the indignities, and above all the pandemonium — had not changed at all. "Steerage was a horror; to this day I can feel the smell, the nausea, the crowding," recalled one Jewish immigrant. "We were huddled together in the steerage literally like cattle," recounted another. Congressional investigators agreed that despite decades of reform efforts, steerage was still "disgusting and demoralizing," its inhabitants overwhelmed by "filth and stench." In order to learn about conditions firsthand, a congressional commission sent Anna Herkner to cross the Atlantic in disguise.

"During these twelve days in the steerage," she testified, "I lived in a disorder and in surroundings that offended every sense . . . Everything was dirty, sticky, and disagreeable to the touch. Every impression was offensive." There might be toilets, but they were "filthy" and no one could figure out how to use them, and as a result, human waste was everywhere, though it did not wash around the feet of the passengers in the bunkrooms the way it had in the famine era.[66]

Seasickness was one of the most vivid memories of steerage passengers in the early twentieth century. "Nine days on the boat . . . Nine days I was sick. Nine days I don't eat nothing," recounted Rosa Vartone, who moved to New York from Calabria in 1928. "Hundreds of people had vomiting fits, throwing up even their mother's milk," a Jewish immigrant likewise recalled. "As all were crossing the ocean for the first time, they thought their end had come. The confusion of cries became unbearable . . . I wanted to escape from that inferno, but no sooner had I thrust my head forward from the lower bunk I lay on than some one above me vomited straight upon my head. I wiped the vomit away, dragged myself onto the deck, leaned against the railing and vomited my share into the sea, then lay down half-dead upon the deck."[67]

One aspect of steerage that is rarely commented upon in immigrant recollections from this era is how particularly offensive it was for women. From the moment they got up in the morning to the moment they went to bed at night, women were pawed, groped, and propositioned, primarily by the ship's crew, but also by male passengers. "The atmosphere was one of general lawlessness and total disrespect for women," reported Herkner. Sailors addressed the female steerage passengers in the most "revolting, . . . vile . . . indecent" language imaginable. "Not one young woman in the steerage escaped attack," Herkner testified. "The screams of the women defending themselves" below decks rent the air all day and half the night.[68]

For Jews, another part of the steerage experience that was particularly difficult was the lack of food. Unlike in the famine era, when ship passengers had to provide almost all their own sustenance, food was relatively plentiful on the ocean liners of the twentieth century, even in steerage. But women traveling alone often found that other greedy passengers grabbed all the food before they could get any. Also, the food that was offered wasn't kosher, and for the majority of the Jewish passengers this was a problem. "We could not eat the food of the ship, since it was not kosher," recalled one immigrant from Minsk who traveled to America with his mother and sister. "We only asked for hot water into which my mother used to put a little brandy and sugar to give it a taste" and supplemented it with bread his mother had brought with her. But their voyage was an unusually long one (two weeks), and when their bread began to run out, they decided they must ask the steward for some of the ship's bread. "But the kind he gave us was unbearably soggy," so they went hungry until they reached New York. Many other Jewish immigrants remembered grappling with this same dilemma. Even those who were willing to eat the ship's food found it "miserable."[69]

A final aspect of the voyage that most immigrants would recall, even decades later, was "the much-dreaded vaccination muster. Many and loud were the objections raised to the enactment of this law," wrote one of the numerous journalists who crossed the ocean in steerage in these years in order to provide a firsthand account. When the occupants of "No. 1 steerage lined up with bared arms for the doctor's inspection, a more sullen lot of men I never saw. Those who had no marks, or whose marks were not sufficiently distinct, were vaccinated again. One man, an Irishman, made a stir by refusing to be operated upon, and insisting that the scar of a knife stab was a vaccination mark. When told that he could not enter America as he was, he submitted to the process." Authorities eventually required emigrants to receive their vaccinations before boarding their transatlantic vessels.[70]

Steerage conditions gradually improved in the first decades of the twentieth century. The same Italian law of 1901 that mandated the inspection of emigrants also required that more and better food be served aboard ship. Furthermore, many vessels built after 1900 were outfitted with the "new steerage," a vastly improved arrangement for the shipboard housing of immigrants in which even those paying the lowest fare slept in rooms that held no more than eight berths (accurately depicted in Leonardo DiCaprio's small steerage room in *Titanic*) rather than in cavernous spaces accommodating one hundred or more passengers. Those lucky enough to travel in the new steerage rarely had the usual complaints, other than the ever-present seasickness. But for every ship that could boast the new steerage, there were dozens more that continued to ply the Atlantic offering only the older variety. Ships making the voyage from Italy to the United States rarely provided the updated steerage accommodations.[71]

The part of the voyage that immigrants seemed to remember most vividly, to judge from how frequently it was referred to in interviews and memoirs, was the sight of the Statue of Liberty as they entered New York Harbor. "The Statue of Liberty rising out of the ocean so free and majestic, thrilled me! An entrance never to be forgotten," wrote a Danish milliner, Anna Walther, of her arrival in New York. Goldie Stone, a Russian Jew, called her sighting of the Statue of Liberty from the deck of her ship "a thrill, somehow different from any other I have ever known, or hope to know." Larry Edelman, who arrived from Poland at age ten, agreed: "That was the biggest thrill, to see that statue there." To him it represented "freedom from want." Lilly Daché, the French-born hatmaker and designer, remembered that even though the statue was "all shadowy and mysterious in the fog," she felt sure as she gazed upon its face that it was conveying "a special promise for me."[72]

It is hard to know whether these reactions resulted from the symbolic meaning the statue had for the immigrants or merely the fact that seeing it meant that they had safely completed their journey to America. Slovenian immigrant Louis Adamic, for example, recalled the "garlicky crowd on the steerage deck . . . pushing toward the rails, straining and stretching to catch a glimpse of the new country, of the city; lifting their children, even their infants, to give them a view of the Statue of Liberty; women weeping for joy, men falling on their knees in thanksgiving, and children screaming, wailing, dancing." Given that immigrants arriving in New York before the statue existed recalled similar scenes of shipboard rejoicing as they entered New York Harbor, no doubt much of the outpouring of emotion felt at this moment was not a reaction to the sight of the statue.[73]

Yet for many immigrants in this era, the Statue of Liberty itself clearly held profound meaning, and symbolized the very reasons why they had chosen to risk so much, leave behind everything they had ever known, and make the perilous journey to America. Almost fifty years later, Emma Goldman could vividly recall the day when she and her half sister, "our eyes filled with tears," entered New York Harbor. "Everybody was on deck. Helena and I stood pressed to each other, enraptured by the sight of the harbour and the Statue of Liberty suddenly emerging from the mist. Ah, there she was, the symbol of hope, of freedom, of opportunity! She held her torch high to light the way to the free country, the asylum for the oppressed of all lands. We, too, Helena and I, would find a place in the generous heart of America."[74]

The "generous heart of America" welcomed more than 17 million immigrants to the United States from the day the Statue of Liberty was dedicated in 1886 to the beginning of World War I, twenty-eight years later—a movement of people without precedent in human history. And for nearly all of them, the term "liberty" perfectly encapsulated the reasons they had come to America. Liberty from hunger, liberty from fear, liberty from violence, liberty to pursue any occupation, liberty to live where they chose, and political liberty—these were the motives that had driven this extraordinary mass of humanity to the United States.

While newcomers immediately recognized the relationship between the message conveyed by the Statue of Liberty and their own immigration experiences, it took native-born Americans nearly twenty years to acknowledge the connection. They did so in 1903, when they placed a bronze tablet just inside the entrance to the statue's pedestal bearing Emma Lazarus's transcendent sonnet. The poem's sentiments have spoken to millions of aspiring immigrants ever since.[75]

15

ELLIS ISLAND

IMMIGRANTS ABOARD THEIR transatlantic steamships often responded with tears or shouts of joy when they first spotted the Statue of Liberty, but as their steamers chugged past the bronze marvel, a more foreboding sight came into view. "There's Ellis Island," Russian immigrant Kyra Goritzina remembered one of the passengers on her ship exclaiming as it approached the city. "'Ellis Island!' I echoed, and my heart sank. 'This dreadful, unavoidable Ellis Island!'" Italian immigrants often referred to Ellis Island as *l'Isola dell Lagrime*, the "Island of Tears."[1]

The island that endless boatfuls of tourists now visit to rediscover their immigrant roots was for their ancestors a terrifying gauntlet of physical and oral examinations. Before the immigration station opened there, the inspection of immigrants at Castle Garden had been relatively perfunctory. Doctors might send sick arrivals to quarantine on Staten Island, but once recovered, they could enter the city and begin new lives. Yet from 1875 to 1917, Congress created an increasingly long list of conditions that might bar a potential immigrant from entering the United States. Medical problems, political beliefs, even one's occupation or employment status could cause inspectors to turn an immigrant away. The officials at Ellis Island could even reject an immigrant who had been living in New York for years if he had not yet become a citizen and had left the United States temporarily to visit his homeland. The immigrants viewed their arrival at Ellis Island, in the words of a journalist who made the crossing in steerage with them, as "the nearest earthly likeness to the final Day of Judgment, when we have to prove our fitness to enter Heaven."[2]

The first restrictive immigration legislation, the Page Act of 1875, is known primarily as the law that banned the landing of Chinese "cooly" laborers — indentured workers not free to keep the fruits of their labor. The act also banned prostitutes and those still serving sentences for "felonious crimes" (an attempt by Congress to prevent foreign nations from emptying out their prisons by paroling their convicted felons in exchange for the promise to emigrate).

In 1882 Congress enacted additional restrictions. The most infamous was the so-called Chinese Exclusion Act, which "suspended" for ten years the admission of Chinese laborers to the United States. Because aspiring Chinese immigrants tried to evade the law by claiming to be students, merchants, or the adult children of already established Chinese American businessmen, this statute resulted in the creation of a significant immigrant inspection regime meant to ferret out such deceit. But because nearly all Chinese immigrants landed on the West Coast, this statute had little impact on the inspectors at Castle Garden.

More important for Castle Garden was another statute enacted in 1882. It barred the landing of convicts (except those guilty of political offenses), lunatics, "idiots," and "any person unable to take care of himself or herself without becoming a public charge." In 1885 Congress expanded the list of banned immigrants to include those who had accepted a job in America before actually arriving in the United States. Labor unions had pushed for this "contract labor" law because they feared that if immigrants were allowed to sign labor contracts before reaching America's shores, the newcomers would accept wages lower than the prevailing American pay rate. Union leaders insisted that immigrant contract laborers drove down the wages of those already living in the United States.[3]

During the 1880s, as immigration reached record levels, many Americans became convinced (not wholly inaccurately) that the government's screeners at Castle Garden were political hacks "unfit for their work." The requirement for obtaining and keeping their jobs was party loyalty, not competence. A Treasury Department investigation also found that the state board that ran Castle Garden allowed politically connected food and transportation concession holders to fleece the immigrants. Castle Garden was "a delusion to the public and a snare to the immigrant," testified an employee of an immigrant aid society at a Treasury Department hearing on the matter. Congress then ordered its own inquiries, which concluded that "large numbers of persons not lawfully entitled to land in the United States are annually received at this port." The "method and system now followed" to identify and return barred immigrants, the congressmen concluded, "was a perfect farce."[4]

Another complaint about Castle Garden was that its employees gave free rein to "immigrant runners," even though the immigration station there had been created expressly to protect the immigrants from these swindlers. A federal official sent to reform Castle Garden's operations recalled that as soon as immigration officers released a shipload of immigrants from the facility, the runners would sprint "towards the affrighted aliens, calling out their respective boarding houses, pulling and hauling the poor dazed creatures this way and that, frequently quarreling among themselves over some confused, bewildered victim. After herding them in groups they were finally marched off to their temporary quarters where they could be plucked at leisure."

Boardinghouse runners were not the only waiting predators. Con artists might pretend to come from the same part of Italy or the Pale as the immigrants in order to cheat them out of their precious savings. "Thieves, blackmailers, and agents of bawdy-houses made their harvest on many a hapless immigrant," in particular women traveling alone, reported a Catholic priest in 1899. The Catholic Church set up a mission directly across the street from Castle Garden in an attempt to protect single women from "these scheming wretches" who might trick female immigrants into a life of crime or prostitution.[5]

Federal authorities came to the conclusion that conditions at Castle Garden were irreparable. In the spring of 1890 they canceled the contract under which they paid New York State employees to process the immigrants and took over the job themselves. Treasury Department officials temporarily moved the immigration station to the west end of the Battery to a building known as the Barge Office while they searched for a better permanent location. Seeking a site that would be beyond the reach of the runners and that would isolate the newcomers from the rest of the American population until they had been deemed eligible to enter the country, the authorities decided to place the new immigration station on an island in the harbor. They chose Ellis Island.[6]

Ellis Island sits one mile west-southwest of the southern tip of Manhattan, much closer to New Jersey than to New York. Dutch settlers had referred to it as Little Oyster Island because it sat amidst a huge oyster reef. (The nearby island on which the Statue of Liberty would later sit was known as "Great Oyster Island.") In the eighteenth century, a New Yorker named Samuel Ellis bought the island, which is how it got its modern name. The Ellis family later sold the property to the State of New York for use as part of the harbor's defenses. A few years later, in the first decade of the nineteenth century, the state decided that defense against foreign invaders was a federal responsibility and transferred ownership to the federal government. For the next several decades, the island was best known as the place where those convicted of federal capital offenses such as piracy were executed. From mid-century on, the military used it as a munitions depot.[7]

As construction progressed on the immigration station for Ellis Island, Congress decided to give even more duties to the inspectors who would work there. The Immigration Act of 1891 added paupers, polygamists, and anyone ever convicted of a felony or a "misdemeanor involving moral turpitude" to the list of those banned from entering the United States. (Previously, a felon who had finished serving his or her term of punishment was acceptable.) Perhaps most important, the new law also banned "persons suffering from a loathsome or a dangerous contagious disease." Before that, a sick person could receive medical treatment and enter the country once cured. Now these would-be immigrants would be returned to their country of origin. The law mandated thorough medical inspections to weed out the sick and infirm, formal hearings for those deemed ineligible to enter the United States, and the provision of housing, food, and other care for immigrants—at the government's expense—while they waited for those hearings (and any appeals) to take place. Congress designated the secretary of the treasury as the final arbiter of all appeals regarding an immigrant's eligibility to enter the country. Finally, the new act gave the government one year from arrival to deport any immigrant who entered the country in violation of these laws, so that if new evidence of ineligibility came to light after the newcomer left Ellis Island, or if the immigrant became a "public charge" within a year of arrival, he or she could still be deported.[8]

When seventeen-year-old Annie Moore stepped ashore on January 1, 1892, as the first of 12 million immigrants who would eventually be processed at Ellis Island, she did not enter the iconic brick and limestone building that we associate with the island today. The Fifty-first Congress, known as the "Billion Dollar Congress" for its spendthrift ways, was uncharacteristically tightfisted when it came to appropriating money for the Ellis Island immigration station. The Treasury Department officials in charge of the project decided that, given their limited budget, they would sacrifice impressive design and superior building materials in favor of square footage. As a result, the *Tribune* reported, the new immigration station, "though of gigantic proportions," was "little more than a big business shed." The station's main building, constructed with 4 million board feet of Georgia pine and measuring 404 feet long, 154 feet wide, and three stories high, could accommodate twice as many inspectors as Castle Garden. The immigrants would store their baggage, buy food and train tickets, and undergo medical inspections on the first floor and then proceed to the second floor for questioning and registration by immigration inspectors. But the press predicted that with thousands of people passing through the wooden structure each day, it could not possibly last very long.[9]

How right they were. Shortly after midnight on June 15, 1897, a huge fire destroyed the massive wooden building and virtually everything else on Ellis Island. "The fire ate its way ravenously through every part of the big structure," reported the *Times,* but miraculously, no one was killed or even injured in the enormous blaze. This was because the commissioner of the station was so certain it was a firetrap that he directed that a ferry, with full steam up, be stationed at the docks all night, every night, so the immigrants detained there and the employees who supervised them could escape in just such an emergency.[10]

The most tragic loss resulting from the fire was the destruction of the registry books listing every immigrant who had landed in New York since the opening of Castle Garden in 1855. These huge leather-bound volumes had been sitting safely in Albany for decades, but Ellis Island officials demanded that they be transferred to them so that if arriving foreign-born passengers claimed that they already resided in the United States, the registers could be consulted to verify their stories. The loss of these registers, which were significantly more detailed than the passenger manifests provided by the crews of the ships the immigrants sailed on, is a tragedy for anyone trying to trace the stories of immigrant ancestors who arrived in New York in the latter half of the nineteenth century.[11]

After the fire, immigrants were initially processed on the piers of Manhattan and then once again at the Barge Office on the Battery until the Ellis Island facilities could be rebuilt. This time, Congress appropriated sufficient funds to build a more impressive and durable structure. The legislators also allocated money to increase the size of the island to seventeen acres so that additional buildings could be constructed. The Treasury Department quickly organized an architectural competition for the new buildings, and the winners were a pair of young architects, William Boring and Edward Lippincott Tilton, who had trained at McKim, Mead & White but had few finished buildings to their credit when they snagged the Ellis Island commission. The main building they designed was almost precisely the same size as the one it replaced and was laid out almost identically, with baggage, food, and transfers being handled on the first floor, inspections and registration on the second floor, and administrative offices and a gallery overlooking the inspection area on the third level, capped with towers at each corner of the structure. The exterior, with its mixture of classical and French and Italian motifs, exemplifies the Beaux-Arts style, named for the art school in Paris where both Boring and Tilton had studied architecture. The building set just the right tone — governmental but not grandiose, serious but not somber. The architects won gold medals for their design at both the Universal Exposition in Paris in 1900 and the Pan-American Exposition in Buffalo in 1901. The inspection of immigrants in the new station began on December 17, 1900.[12]

For nearly every immigrant, the inspection process was an anxiety-laden

After the original wooden inspection station on Ellis Island burned down in 1897, it was replaced by the iconic brick and limestone building that still stands there today.

experience. For some, like Kyra Goritzina, it was downright terrifying. More often than not, the steamship passengers would not go to Ellis Island immediately upon entering the harbor but would have to remain overnight aboard their ship before the immigration station was ready to process them. This last night, spent so close to America and yet so far, given the uncertain reception that awaited, was incredibly stressful, creating a ship full of insomniacs. According to a journalist who traveled in steerage to report on the experience, "nobody had slept the night before" their arrival at Ellis Island.[13]

Even before they could set foot on shore, the immigrants had to undergo a health inspection so that no one with a potentially lethal contagious disease could spread it at the immigration station. A physician from the Marine Hospital Service (later renamed the Public Health Service) would climb a ladder from a launch to board the immigrants' ocean liner and search for any signs of cholera, typhus, or other deadly diseases. Sometimes these medical inspections took place in the middle of the night so that the passengers could land at Ellis Island first thing the next morning. Those found to have these illnesses were sent to the quarantine hospital on Staten Island. In such cases, the whole shipload of passengers would have to wait several days in the harbor so that those who might have been infected but were not yet exhibiting symptoms could be identified and quarantined. For many immigrants, this exam was their third medical inspection — the first having been administered by the railway that carried them across Europe, and the second by the steamship company at the port.

Before the immigrants could leave the ship, the crew would gather them on deck, call out their names from the ship manifest, and, when each one stepped forward, pin a large piece of paper to the person's clothing with a letter and a number on it. Tags with the same letters and numbers would be pasted onto every piece of luggage the immigrants carried. The letter on the tag allowed officials on Ellis Island to identify the ship on which the immigrants and their baggage had traveled, while the number corresponded to each passenger's place on that ship's manifest. Finally, dockworkers or sailors herded the arrivals, carrying all their worldly possessions, onto barges or ferries that would take them to Ellis Island. "In the work of hustling the immigrants aboard the barges," one journalist observed, "the dock men displayed great unnecessary roughness, sometimes shoving them violently, prodding them with sticks, etc."[14]

If the processing of immigrants began to back up, they might have to wait, standing on the barges (or sitting on their luggage) for hours until the lines inside the immigration station subsided. "Waiting, waiting, waiting, without food and without water; or, if there was water, we could not get to it on account of the crush of people," wrote journalist Broughton Brandenburg, describing his experience with a boatload of Italian immigrants. "Children cried, mothers strove to hush them, the musically inclined sang or played, and then the sun went down while we waited and still waited." Sometimes the inspectors' workday would end before all the immigrants could be processed and they would be brought back to their ship to spend another night. But more often than not, the inspectors would work overtime until everyone transported to Ellis Island that day had been processed. In Brandenburg's account in mid-October 1903, only well after sunset did the barge hands drag out the gangplank and lower the restraining ropes, at which point "the weary hundreds, shouldering their baggage yet once again, poured out of the barge on to the wharf" at Ellis Island.[15]

On a typical day it could take anywhere from two to five hours from the time the immigrants left their ship to the completion of their processing, but given the anxiety and the interminable waiting, it seemed much longer. "The day I spent on Ellis Island was an eternity," recalled Louis Adamic of his inspection there in December 1913. "Rumors were current among immigrants of several nationalities that some of us would be refused admittance into the United States and sent back to Europe. For several hours I was in a cold sweat on this account, although, so far as I knew, all my papers were in order."[16]

Once landed on Ellis Island, the immigrants left their luggage outside the main building and headed inside for inspection, which began with the medical examination. The exam was performed not by one doctor but in assembly-line fashion by more than a dozen officials stationed at various points along the line that led to the Registry Room on the second floor.* First, the immigrants had to produce a medical certificate indicating that they had received a smallpox vaccination before boarding their ship. Next, they filed past inspectors who looked for signs of physical ailments that might prevent the immigrant from finding work in America. Dr. Alfred Reed, who examined immigrants at Ellis Island for many years, explained that as each immigrant approached each physician, he or she would study "the gait, attitude, presence of flat feet, lameness, stiffness at ankle, knee, or hip, malformations of the body, observes the neck for goitre, muscular development, scars, enlarged glands, texture of skin, and finally as the immigrant comes up face to face, the examiner notes abnormalities of the features, eruptions, scars, paralysis, expression, etc." Poor posture might indicate a bad back. A limp could be a sign of a permanent deformity of the lower extremities. Holding one's head at an odd angle might be evidence of a neck ailment.

Even as the immigrant passed this inspector, the examination continued, as the view from the side offered the doctor a glimpse of the ears, scalp, side of neck, and hands, which might be examined for signs of paralysis or deformity. "If anything about the individual seems suspicious," Reed reported, "he is asked several questions." This was one of the ways the examiners fulfilled the requirement to screen for "lunatics" and "idiots." "Often simple questions in addition and multiplication are propounded," recounted another Ellis Island physician, Dr. Eugene Mullan. "Should the immigrant appear stupid and inattentive to such an extent that mental defect is suspected," said Mullan, the immigrant would receive a more thorough mental examination from a different physician in another part of the building. Unlike the inspectors in the Registry Room, who were hired for their facility with languages, the doctors were rarely fluent in the immigrants' native tongues, and would instead memorize the questions they typically asked in the most common immigrant languages.

---

* Ellis Island officials constantly tweaked the immigrant inspection process. Early on, for example, immigrants carried their baggage with them as they were examined; later the newcomers left their bags on the ground floor. In some years there was an inspector whose sole job was to look for scalp fungus; at other points that task was combined with others. For more than a decade, the medical inspectors were stationed at various points along the line that stretched to the Registry Room and did some of their examinations in that room itself; closer to World War I, however, only those who had passed the medical inspections were admitted to the Registry Room. My description of Ellis Island procedures does not attempt to recount those that were in place at any one moment, but instead relies on the most detailed accounts provided by the inspectors who worked there and the immigrants who underwent the inspections to convey the experience most immigrants would have had.

Often they could not understand the answers, but this fact did not concern them. Rather, they used the speed and tone of the answer, as well as the facial expression of the immigrant, as the main criteria by which to discern a potential mental defect.

Because the doctors who looked for signs of such ailments had to keep the line moving as quickly as possible, they did not pull aside those suspected of having these conditions. Instead they would mark the immigrants' clothing on the right shoulder with chalk so that the individual could be pulled out of the line later on for a more comprehensive examination before reaching the Registry Room. Scrawling a "B" on an immigrant's shoulder indicated a suspected back problem; "F" stood for face, "Ft" feet, "G" goiter, "K" hernia, "L" lameness, "N" neck, "S" senility, "Sc" scalp, "X" mental illness (a circled "X" meant acute mental problems). Some suspected ailments, such as "hand," "measles," "nails," "skin," "temperature," and "vision," would be written out in full on the immigrant's clothing.[17]

Soon the immigrants reached a second doctor. "This examiner is known in service parlance as 'the eye man,'" Mullan reported. He stood with his back to a window so that he could use the natural light to examine the immigrants' eyes. First he looked directly into each eye for signs of opaque corneas or other common eye diseases. Then, using either his thumb and forefinger or a buttonhook-like medical instrument, the doctor would pull the immigrant's lower eyelid away from the face to look for signs of conjunctivitis or trachoma, a bacterial infection of the eye whose telltale symptom was roughening of the inner eyelid. In the days before antibiotics, trachoma was considered one of the "loathsome" diseases that rendered an immigrant ineligible to enter the United States.

Because of the desire to process the immigrants as quickly as possible, Ellis Island eye doctors did not typically bother to wash their hands or clean their instruments between the examination of successive immigrants. Perhaps the physicians believed that steerage passengers were already so dirty that they did not deserve anything better. Even laymen understood that the physicians might be infecting healthy immigrants through their lax practices. "I was struck by the way in which the doctors made the [trachoma] examinations with dirty hands and with no pretense to clean the instruments," complained President Theodore Roosevelt to his secretary of commerce and labor, Victor Metcalf, after touring Ellis Island in 1906. "It would seem to me that these examinations as conducted would themselves be a fruitful source of carrying infection from diseased to healthy people."[18]

Nearly 80 percent of the immigrants denied entry to the United States for

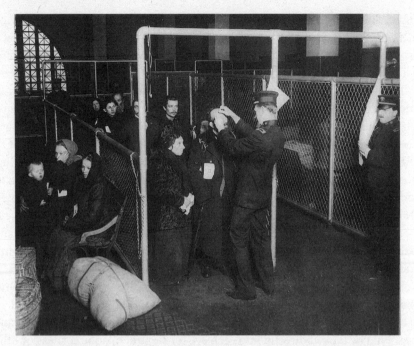

Inspectors at Ellis Island pulling back eyelids to check for
trachoma and other eye diseases.

medical reasons suffered from trachoma. "When they learned their fate, they
were stunned," recalled Fiorello La Guardia, who worked as an interpreter at
Ellis Island before he entered politics. "They had never felt ill. They had never
heard the word trachoma. They could see all right." Worst of all, La Guardia
wrote, were the cases in which a family had sold virtually everything it owned
to come to America, only to find that one member of the family had the disease. "Sometimes, if it was a young child who suffered from trachoma, one of
the parents had to return to the native country with the rejected member of the
family," an especially grim prospect because often "they had no homes to return
to." But because of the potential for trachoma to spread, especially from child
to child during play, inspectors considered its discovery a cause for mandatory
exclusion. Only in 1919 did Congress pass a law requiring trachoma examinations at ports of embarkation.[19]

The 15 to 20 percent of immigrants who received a chalk mark in these initial inspections were led to the examination rooms of the Public Health Service. Those whose suspected ailment was physical — the vast majority — were
segregated by sex, with the men going to one room and the women to another.
Here, again, an assembly line of examinations took place. "The line of male

immigrants approached the first medical officer with their trousers open," recounted the British ambassador, Aukland Geddes, after a tour of this part of the immigration station in 1922. "The doctor examined their external genitals for signs of venereal infection. Next he examined the inguinal canals for hernia. The doctor wore rubber gloves. I saw him 'do' nine or ten men. His gloves were not cleansed between cases." At other stations within the room these immigrants had their heart and lungs examined, their scalp and eyes checked, and so forth. Laboratory specimens were taken for analysis if necessary.[20]

Women, often with their children in tow, went through a similar procedure in their examination room. They had to strip to the waist, and until 1913 this was done in front of male doctors, which the female immigrants found mortifying. Even once female doctors became the exclusive examiners of female immigrants, most of the women considered the process excruciating. The exam "was so embarrassing for me," recalled an Austrian immigrant years later. "I wasn't even twenty-one, very bashful, and there were these big kids [both male and female] running around, but you had to do it." Some of these children recognized how humiliating the process was for their parents. "My mother had never, ever undressed in front of us," Enid Jones from Wales remembered of her experience as a ten-year-old in the female examination room. "In those days nobody ever would. She was so embarrassed."[21]

Those immigrants whom inspectors had marked with an "X" were sent to the "mental room." It held two desks where doctors sat and benches to accommodate more than one hundred waiting immigrants. Here the newcomers underwent an interview and were asked to count and do simple addition. Beginning in the mid-1910s, those suspected of mental retardation also had to pass the Knox Cube Test. This was one of many tests developed by Ellis Island physician Howard Knox to measure intelligence without requiring any oral communication with the immigrant, who might speak only an obscure language or dialect. In this test, an examiner moved a black cube in a certain pattern over four differently colored cubes attached to a board on the desk. The immigrant then had to move the black cube across the colored cubes in the same order as the inspector had.

Eighty percent of the immigrants sent to the "mental room" immediately satisfied the doctors that they were not suffering from a mental "defect," and were either returned to the line snaking toward the Registry Room or asked to undergo a physical exam if the doctors believed that the symptoms that had originally been flagged as mental might instead reflect a physical ailment. The remainder would be held for a day or more to undergo a thorough battery of mental testing. Of the group kept overnight, doctors would eventually declare about 10 percent (1 percent of those originally marked with an "X") "feebleminded" or "insane" (a group that in this era also included epileptics). All in all, Ellis Island officials turned away about one in every ten thousand immigrants owing to mental "defects" from 1892 through 1909 and one in every 750 from 1910 until the end of World War I.[22]

The dramatic increase in the number of immigrants classified as mentally ill was due partly to the fact that Congress in the first decade of the twentieth century expanded the list of criteria that inspectors could use to turn away immigrants. In 1903 Congress added epileptics, beggars, anarchists, and importers of prostitutes to the list of undesirables. In addition, the length of time immigration officials were given to deport such newcomers after their initial admission to the country increased to two years, and the "head tax" assessed per immigrant was doubled to $2. In 1907 Congress further expanded the definition of mental "defects" beyond idiocy and lunacy to include "imbeciles" and "feebleminded" persons ("idiot" was the term used for someone with severe mental retardation, an "imbecile" was someone with moderate mental handicaps, and a "feebleminded" person had mild mental impairments), thus increasing the number of immigrants liable to be barred from entry. The new law also banned the immigration of unaccompanied minors. With other prohibitions added by these two laws, there were now twenty separate reasons for an immigrant to be rejected at Ellis Island. Furthermore, the 1907 statute doubled the head tax yet again, to $4. Supporters expressly suggested that this higher landing fee (which immigrants paid when purchasing their steamship ticket) would prevent poor immigrants from entering the United States, thereby reducing immigration overall. The new law also increased to three years the period during which immigration officials could deport immigrants who became public charges or were subsequently found to be unqualified for entry. Some in Congress attempted to go even further by proposing that immigrants be required to show Ellis Island inspectors that they had $25 (the equivalent of about $650 today) in order to enter the country. Families of two or more would have to produce twice that amount. But this provision was stripped from the bill before it became law.[23]

The impact of these new laws would depend on the guidance immigration inspectors received concerning how to interpret and enforce the statutes. Early in his presidency (1901–1909), Theodore Roosevelt had expressed the fear that Americans were committing "race suicide" by admitting so many southern and eastern European immigrants of "low moral tendency" while native-born Americans were having fewer and fewer children. In his first State of the Union message, in 1901, Roosevelt called for both an "educational test" for immigrants as well as "economic tests" to exclude those "who are below a certain standard of economic fitness." Of course, newcomers from southern and eastern Europe would be the ones most likely to fail these tests. But by the fall of 1903, after complaints from the immigrant press, the president had begun to reconsider, and by the middle of his second term in office, Roosevelt had changed his tone entirely. "We must treat with justice and good will all immigrants who come here under the law," the president wrote in his State of the Union message in December 1906.* "Whether they are Catholic or Protestant, Jew or Gentile; whether they come from England or Germany, Russia, Japan, or Italy, matters nothing."[24]

Roosevelt's evolving attitude toward the "new immigration" from southern and eastern Europe was exemplified by his selection in 1906 of Oscar Straus, a Jewish immigrant from New York, as his secretary of commerce and labor, the department that had taken over the administration of immigration law from the Treasury Department. Straus, the youngest of five children, was born in 1850 in what is now southwest Germany. When he was four and a half years old, he, his mother, and siblings immigrated to the United States to join Straus's father, who had arrived two years earlier. They settled in a small town in west-central Georgia, where they became merchants. After the Civil War they relocated to New York City, where, according to the *Times*, Oscar's father, Lazarus, became one of the most successful importers of "china, pottery, glassware, clocks, and bronzes . . . in the world." Unlike his older brothers Nathan and Isidor, who entered the family business, Oscar went to college, receiving from Columbia both his undergraduate degree in 1871 and a law diploma two years later. Straus became a successful commercial litigator, specializing in railway cases, until he left his legal practice in 1881 to join the family business. The company later branched out into retailing, acquiring a struggling New York department store called R. H. Macy & Co. and turning it into one of the city's most successful. The Straus family also bought one of Brooklyn's leading department stores, Abraham & Weschler, and renamed it Abraham & Straus. Macy's and Abraham & Straus would become two of the region's leading retailers for much of the twentieth century.[25]

Roosevelt must have seen Straus as something of an intellectual soul mate. Both men were active in the progressive wings of their New York City political organizations (Straus as a Democrat and Roosevelt as a Republican). Both were voracious readers of history, amassing two of the largest private libraries

---

* From 1802 to 1912, presidents delivered the State of the Union message to Congress in writing, not in person in a speech. It was not until Woodrow Wilson became president in 1913 that the nation's chief executives again began to give their reports on the state of the union to the legislators in person.

in the city specializing in that subject. Both were prolific writers, with Roosevelt publishing on subjects as varied as history and natural science, while Straus focused on American politics, religion, and law. Straus was not a political neophyte when he joined the cabinet, having represented the United States as minister to the Ottoman Empire from 1887 to 1889. In selecting a Democrat for the cabinet, Roosevelt may have sought to portray himself as a man above party. But in placing a Jew in the cabinet for the first time in American history, and putting him in charge of the administration's immigration policy, no less, Roosevelt clearly hoped to signal that he no longer shared Americans' increasing unease at the record numbers of southern and eastern Europeans coming to the United States. The appointment was also meant as a rebuke to Russia in the wake of the continuing stream of anti-Jewish pogroms. "I want to show Russia and some other countries," Roosevelt said when he told Straus of his intention to nominate him, "what we think of the Jews in this country."[26]

Straus clearly sympathized with the immigrants threatened with debarment and did everything in his power to blunt the impact of the stricter 1907 immigration law.* When inspectors denied entry to one son of an Irish family of seven because he had been certified as feebleminded, and the mother considered going back to Ireland with him so the rest could enter the United States, Straus overruled his Ellis Island inspectors and allowed the entire family to remain. When the medical staff declared fifty-nine-year-old Russian immigrant Chena Rog unfit (due to trachoma) to join her five adult children and three dozen grandchildren in Reading, Pennsylvania, Straus overturned the decision on appeal. And when the station's commissioner denied entry to Schimen Coblenz, a forty-two-year-old butcher from Lithuania, because his psoriasis (a "loathsome" disease) might prevent him from finding work in his trade and therefore lead him to become a public charge, Straus again countermanded the debarment order on the grounds that psoriasis was not communicable. Exclusions clearly troubled Straus, so much so that he gave the head of the Ellis Island immigration station several hundred dollars of his own money (the equivalent of several thousand today) to be doled out anonymously to immigrants whose rejection he could not prevent. Under Roosevelt's administration, the percentage of immigrants turned away at Ellis Island changed very little in the two years after the new 1907 immigration law.[27]

Things did change, however, when William Howard Taft became president

---

* In order to emphasize the fact that an immigrant at Ellis Island had not yet entered the United States in a legal sense, immigration officials called the process of returning rejected immigrants to their homelands "debarment" (because the newcomers had been "barred" from the country) rather than "deportation," a term that refers to expulsion from a nation after a person has been granted permission to enter.

in 1909. Roosevelt had handpicked the Ohioan as his successor because he thought Taft shared his progressive outlook. But Taft turned out to be more conservative than Roosevelt in a number of areas, including immigration policy. Taft's choice to head the Ellis Island immigration station was William Williams, a forty-six-year-old native of New London, Connecticut, who had an undergraduate degree from Yale and a law degree from Harvard. Williams had spent nearly three years as head of the Ellis Island immigration station under Roosevelt, from 1902 to 1905, but had resigned when the president made it clear he was displeased with Williams's management of his subordinates. As Roosevelt put it, Williams "found it difficult to get on with men of inferior education and social status."[28]

When Williams took charge again at the end of May 1909, he immediately announced that the more welcoming attitude toward immigrants that had previously characterized the administration of Ellis Island would not continue. "We are receiving too many low-grade immigrants," Williams told the press. He vowed to enforce the existing immigration laws far more strictly than his predecessor and weed out the "unintelligent," immigrants "of low vitality," and those whose lack of savings indicated that they did not possess the intellect or work ethic necessary to succeed in the United States. "We owe our present civilization and standing amongst nations chiefly to people of a type widely different from that of those now coming here in such numbers," Williams argued. He promised to use every means at his disposal to keep as many of these "undesirables" out of the country as possible.[29]

Williams accomplished his goal in three ways. First, he instructed his inspectors to flag and debar not merely those immigrants who seemed "likely to become a public charge" immediately but also those who might be unable to support themselves ten or fifteen years in the future.

Secretary of Commerce and Labor Oscar Straus, the first Jewish cabinet officer in U.S. history, was sympathetic to the plight of immigrants deemed inadmissible by Ellis Island's medical officers and overturned many of their debarment decisions.

Second, he decided unilaterally to institute the "economic test" that Congress had rejected two years earlier, deeming any adult immigrants who did not arrive with $25 (above and beyond the price of the rail ticket to their final destination) as, by definition, likely to become a public charge and thus subject to debarment. Third, Williams told his inspectors that even if they could not find anything physically wrong with an immigrant, they could still reject the newcomer for "poor physique." According to this line of reasoning, immigrants who were thin and pale would find it difficult to satisfy American employers and, if they had no specialized occupational training, were likely to become public charges. As a result of these policy changes, the rejection rate at Ellis Island increased by nearly 150 percent, from fewer than one immigrant out of every one hundred before Williams took over to nearly two out of every one hundred in his first full fiscal year in office.[30]

REJECTION RATE FOR IMMIGRANTS SEEKING ADMISSION TO THE UNITED STATES AT ELLIS ISLAND FOR THE TWELVE-MONTH PERIOD ENDING JUNE 30 OF THE YEAR INDICATED

	1907	1908	1909	1910	1911	1912	1913	1914	1915
Immigrants debarred	6,752	4,643	4,361	14,771	12,917	8,294	10,720	16,588	2,674
Total seeking admission	1,011,508	590,613	584,978	800,865	799,011	613,445	903,373	894,640	181,090
Percent rejected	0.67	0.79	0.75	1.84	1.62	1.35	1.19	1.85	1.48

Source: *Annual Report of the Commissioner General of Immigration for the Fiscal Year Ended June 30* (1907): 49; (1909): 15; (1911): 12; (1912): 66; (1913): 38; (1915): 57, 126.

Immigrants reacted with outrage to what they interpreted as Williams's arbitrary and prejudiced reinterpretation of the immigration laws. A Russian Jewish immigrant being held at the Ellis Island detention center sent a letter to the editor of the *Forward*, a Yiddish newspaper in New York, calling Williams's $25 rule "nonsense" and an "outrage." Another wrote directly to Williams in broken English: "You don't realize what you are doing. You kill people without a knife. Does money make you a person? A person who has a mind and hands and has not $25 cash is not a person? Has he to be killed? . . . If you would have conscious in you would not do such things." Eastern European Jews especially resented the poor physique rule, which they perceived — not wholly inaccurately

— to be directed at them. The number of Jews barred for this reason "has been constantly increasing," charged a Jewish attorney, Max Kohler, in 1911, "because of ever newer misconstructions of the law furtively forced upon inspectors at Ellis Island" by Williams. The *Forward* dubbed Williams "the Haman* of Ellis Island."[31]

Predictably, many Americans applauded Williams's increased scrutiny of incoming immigrants. "What a stench in the nostrils of true Americans are the dirty Jew lawyers who rush to the 'defense' of their kin whom you would exclude," wrote Orville Victor, a New Jerseyan "of early colonial ancestry," to Williams. "More power to you, and success to your efforts to keep out the dirty scum of European fields, bogs and warrens." Williams must have found such letters gratifying. "I have enforced the laws," he solemnly told the *Times* when explaining the increase in debarments. "Why shouldn't I? That is what I am here for."[32]

Victor's reference to "dirty Jew lawyers" representing their kinsmen at Ellis Island reflects the fact that immigrants did not face the appeals process alone. Some, especially those who already had family in the United States, hired lawyers to contest the doctors' diagnoses or inspectors' interpretations of the law. Fiorello La Guardia, who studied law at night while working as an interpreter on Ellis Island, built his fledgling legal practice representing immigrants denied entry to the United States for $10 per case.[33]

Most immigrants, however, could not afford a private attorney, and were instead assisted in their appeals by lawyers employed by the immigrant aid societies that proliferated in the years after the Ellis Island immigration station opened. Just as the English, Scots, Irish, and Germans each had their own immigrant aid organizations working to assist antebellum immigrants at Castle Garden, now the Jews, Italians, and other European groups created them too. By the beginning of World War I, immigrants could get assistance from the Belgian Bureau, the Czech Relief Association, the Danish Aid Society, the Hebrew Sheltering and Immigrant Aid Society, the Home for Scandinavian Immigrants, the Hungarian Relief Society, the Irish Emigrant Society, the Lutheran Emigrants House, the Lutheran Immigrant Society, the Netherland Benevolent Society, the Norwegian Evangelical Emigrant Mission and Emigrant Home, the Polish National Alliance, the Russian Orthodox Christian Immigrant Society, the Saint Raphael's Italian Emigrant Society, Saint Raphael's Society for the Protection of German Catholic Immigrants, Saint Raphael's Spanish Emigrant So-

---

* As described in the Book of Esther in the Hebrew Bible, Haman was a Persian ruler whose plan to kill all the Jews of Persia was foiled by Queen Esther.

ciety, the Slavonic Immigrant Society, the Society for Italian Immigrants (not Catholic affiliated), the Spanish Home for Immigrants (also non-Catholic), the Swedish Lutheran Immigrant Home, the Swiss Benevolent Society, and the Syrian Mount Lebanon Relief Society. The Salvation Army, the Red Cross, and the Travelers Aid Society also assisted immigrants at Ellis Island. All these groups helped the newcomers find lost luggage, family members, temporary lodging, and work, made sure they were not cheated by railroad ticket agents, and, in the case of immigrants not immediately admitted to the country, offered free legal counsel as well.[34]

The Hebrew Sheltering and Immigrant Aid Society (known universally as HIAS) became the largest and most visible immigrant aid organization at Ellis Island. A Yiddish-language guidebook for Jewish immigrants urged the newcomers to take advantage of the services offered by HIAS, whose doors were open twenty-four hours a day at 229–231 East Broadway on the Lower East Side. "Accommodations are provided for men, women and children . . . There are excellent baths, always at the free disposition of guests. A physician and a nurse are in attendance. The kitchen supplies excellent Kosher cooking." For those who did not know landsmen who could assist them, the HIAS employment bureau would help the immigrants find jobs, either in New York or outside the city. All of their services were provided free of charge.[35]

Perhaps the most important work HIAS did was to assist immigrants who could not leave Ellis Island because inspectors had declared them ineligible to enter the country. HIAS employees did everything in their power to overturn unfavorable rulings by the station's inspectors. HIAS workers explained the immigrants' rights in the appeal process, helped the detainees round up witnesses to testify in their defense, supplied attorneys to argue cases before the appeals panels, and even wrote letters to the secretary of commerce and labor in an effort to get unfavorable appeals decisions overturned. About half of all debarment orders at Ellis Island were overturned on appeal, but three-quarters of those handled by HIAS were reversed. No wonder Victor resented the work of the HIAS lawyers.[36]

Once the immigrants had satisfied Ellis Island's medical officials that they were healthy enough to enter the United States, the newcomers ascended a tall flight of stairs to the center of the station's Registry Room, known as the Great Hall. The Registry Room was an imposing space, 189 feet long and 102 feet wide with a 60-foot-high vaulted ceiling. Here the immigrants would wind their way through iron railings toward immigration inspectors waiting at imposing wooden desks on raised platforms along the northwest wall. In order to make

Immigrants climbing the stairs to the Registry Room at Ellis Island in 1908.

the hall easy to clean even as several thousand immigrants passed through it each day, the entire room — floors, walls, and ceiling — was lined with tile. The reverberating din from the hundreds of chatting immigrants waiting in line was positively deafening.

The 90 percent of immigrants who either made it through the medical inspection without getting a chalk mark on their clothing, or were quickly cleared after a brief additional medical inspection, entered the Registry Room with the other passengers from their ship. If the vessel had arrived from Naples, all the immigrants might be placed in a single line and processed by a single Italian-speaking inspector, who would use the ship manifest to tally each immigrant and record additional information required by law. The passengers from vessels bringing immigrants from a variety of nations (like the *Nevada,* which carried Annie Moore) might be divided into several lines, with the Italians in one, the east European Jews in another, the Scandinavians in a third, and so

The Registry Room at Ellis Island, where immigrants who had passed the physical examination waited to be questioned and processed. Each of the pens pictured here was designed to hold thirty immigrants, the same number that fit on a manifest page.

forth, depending on the linguistic abilities of the inspectors on duty that day. If the Yiddish-speaking inspector got the manifest first, the Italians would not be called for examination until all the east European Jews from their ship had been processed. Then the Italian-speaking inspector would receive the manifest and begin examining the Italians. That process would repeat itself until all the immigrants from each ship had been examined. Typically, no matter how many languages they spoke, the immigrants from one ship would wait on the north side of the Registry Room, while the newcomers from a second ship would be simultaneously accommodated on the south side.[37]

With so many people crammed together on benches waiting to be examined, the Registry Room became very hot in the late spring, when immigration was at its peak. The heat was exacerbated by the fact that the immigrants wore their best clothes in order to impress the inspectors. Women wore elaborate dresses and men (even those in steerage) landed wearing jackets and ties. An Irish immigrant who arrived at Ellis Island in late summer remembered that it was "hot as a pistol and I'm wearing my long johns and a heavy Irish tweed suit . . . I'm dying with the heat. I never experienced such heat . . . I just wanted to get the hell out of there." Owing both to the heat and to their nervousness about the impending examination, those waiting to be examined perspired profusely.

Immigrants answering questions posed by the inspectors in the Ellis Island Registry Room. In 1911, the iron pens in the Registry Room had been removed and replaced with long rows of wooden benches.

As a result, the Registry Room did not smell much better than the steerage compartments the immigrants had just left.[38]

When the newcomers' names were finally called, they stepped forward — palms sweaty, mouth dry — for what they knew might be the most important interrogation of their lives. Like most of the immigrants, Louis Adamic vividly remembered his, which took place on New Year's Eve 1913:

> The examiner sat bureaucratically — very much in the manner of officials in the Old Country — behind a great desk, which stood upon a high platform. On the wall above him was a picture of George Washington. Beneath it was an American flag. The official spoke a bewildering mixture of many Slavic languages. He had a stern voice and a sour visage. I had difficulty understanding some of his questions. At a small table, piled with papers, not far from the examiner's desk, was a clerk who called out our names, which, it seemed, were written on the long sheets of paper before him. When my turn came, toward dusk, I was asked the usual questions. When and where was I born? My nationality? Religion? Was I a legitimate child?

What were the names of my parents? Was I an imbecile? Was I a prostitute? . . . Was I an ex-convict? A criminal? Why had I come to the United
States? I was questioned as to the state of my finances and I produced the
required twenty-five dollars. What did I expect to do in the United States?
I replied that I hoped to get a job. What kind of a job? I didn't know; any
kind of job.[39]

Like most immigrants, Adamic had probably been coached on how to answer that last question. Many newcomers had jobs waiting for them when they
arrived, but admitting this was grounds for debarment. So immigrants learned
to say simply that they planned to find a job but had neither received nor accepted any offers before their arrival. Doing so seemed so counterintuitive —
didn't it increase the risk of becoming a public charge? — that every day, four or
five immigrants answered this question incorrectly (though perhaps truthfully)
and were barred from entering the country.[40]

Beginning in 1917, one additional test was added to the Registry Room examination: a literacy test. Congressmen had been pushing since the 1890s to
ban immigrants who could not read. In the words of Senator William Dillingham of Vermont, one of the test's most vociferous advocates, the point was to
reduce the "menace to American institutions from immigrants from southern
and eastern Europe." President Grover Cleveland had vetoed a bill containing
such a literacy test in his last days in office in 1897. Taft rejected one in 1913. Wilson did the same in both 1915 and 1917, but in the latter year Congress overrode
his veto, and the literacy test became law. The new statute required male immigrants over the age of sixteen to be able to read a passage of up to forty words
in any language or dialect of their choosing. Ellis Island inspectors would administer the test to women only if they were not traveling with or joining an
already admitted male family member. Men over age fifty-five reuniting with
family were also exempted from the literacy test, as were those who could prove
they were fleeing religious persecution.[41]

It is difficult to measure the impact of the literacy test. Before its imposition, upwards of 200,000 immigrants per year admitted that they were illiterate
when asked, but once the law took effect, fewer than 2,000 per year were turned
away at Ellis Island for failing it. To opponents of the law, this fact showed that
immigrants were not nearly as unintelligent as restrictionists claimed, but supporters of the literacy restriction asserted that illiterates no longer tried to immigrate or were turned away by steamship companies before they could board
U.S.-bound vessels.[42]

The immigration inspectors in the Registry Room who guarded what H. G.

Wells aptly called "the gate of America" had enormous control over the fate of each immigrant. Decades later, newcomers recalled with gratitude the officer who had waved them past even though they had only $22 instead of the required $25, or who did not ask to see their money at all, or who had suggested that an immigrant rethink his answer when, out of nervousness or ignorance, he gave a reply that might get him turned away.[43]

One thing the inspectors could not do, despite decades of handed-down family stories to the contrary, was change the immigrants' surnames. Thousands of Americans believe that their last name differs from those on their ancestors' immigration manifests because the inspectors at Ellis Island altered their family name. Yet there is absolutely no evidence that such name changing took place in the Registry Room or anyplace else on Ellis Island. Several factors may explain this widespread misconception. Some immigrants, embarrassed to admit to their children or grandchildren that they themselves changed their surname to something "more American" in order to fit in, may have invented tales of mandated Ellis Island name changes to hide the truth. Others, speaking no English when they arrived at the immigration station, might have mistaken the officers' awful mispronunciations of their transliterated or misspelled name on ship manifests to be their new American name. Still others might have assumed that the identification tag pinned to their clothing, which listed but often misspelled the immigrants' surnames, was an official immigration document that contained their new American name. In fact, immigrants did not leave Ellis Island with any official paperwork whatsoever. Only Chinese immigrants had to possess proof of their legal entry into the United States. The newly admitted immigrant was free to use any name he or she desired.[44]

One reason why the inspectors could not change immigrants' names is that they did not have the time. On average, they could spare only one minute for the inspection of each family. Given how many questions they were required to ask, there was no opportunity to assign new names. In fact, after hours of waiting in line, the interrogation in the Registry Room was over so quickly that immigrants hardly felt like celebrating when the inspectors waved them through. It all seemed so anticlimactic.

Once the immigrants passed beyond the Registry Room desks, they faced a staircase divided by two railings into three sections, leading back down to the building's first floor. These were known as "the Stairs of Separation." The right-hand section led to the railroad room, where immigrants continuing on from New York by rail would be met by railroad employees who led them to ferries bound for railroad stations either in New Jersey (where trains headed south and west generally originated) or in New York (for those bound for New England). The stairs on the left were for those immigrants who were free to leave the station and were staying in New York City; ferries dropped them at the Barge Office on the western edge of the Battery at the southern tip of Manhattan. The central section of the staircase led to waiting rooms. Married women and children not transferring to trains were not allowed to leave Ellis Island unless accompanied by an adult male. These immigrants waited in the detention area to be picked up by family members or friends.[45]

Waiting in the detention room could be just as nerve-wracking as the voyage to America or the Ellis Island inspection process. Wives worried that their husbands might no longer find them attractive after years surrounded by fashionable American women. The Red Cross actually distributed American clothes to newly arrived female immigrants specifically so that husbands would not be disappointed when they claimed their wives. Children feared that they would not recognize parents they had not seen for years. Marie Jastrow, who arrived at Ellis Island as a child with her mother in 1907, remembered that as they waited for her father to arrive, "a million catastrophic possibilities assaulted our imaginations. 'Where is Papa?' 'Was there an accident?' 'Has he forgotten that we were coming?' 'Is he coming at all?' These fantasies took their toll. My mother's eyes filled, and I panicked. 'Where is my Papa? Where is my Papa?'" When loved ones finally did arrive, the reunions were often more awkward than joyous. Young children cried in fear when embraced by fathers they did not remember. Wives stared at their husbands, wondering why they looked so old and careworn. But for most, the awkwardness eventually dissipated and the exhausted and relieved immigrants boarded the ferry for the mile-long trip across the harbor to New York.[46]

When the immigrants headed for New York City landed in lower Manhattan, their senses were bombarded with strange new sights, sounds, and smells. "I could hardly believe my eyes, it was so wonderful at first," recounted an Italian immigrant of his initial impression of New York. "I was bewildered," Russian immigrant Morris Shapiro told an interviewer of his arrival in 1923, "at the sight of trains running overhead, under my very feet, trolleys clanging, thousands upon thousands of taxis tearing around corners, and millions of people rushing and pushing through the screaming noise day in and day out. To me this city appeared as a tremendous overstuffed roar, where people just burst with a desire to live." The city blazed with light even at night, an amazing phenomenon to immigrants from the countryside. The noise was deafening. People moved so fast. The air smelled bad. Where was the sky? Where were the stars? As a German immigrant who arrived in 1910 recalled, "It was just overwhelming."[47]

But eventually, after a few hours or a few days, the enormity of what they had just been through would sink in, and the immigrants would realize that after years of planning, saving, convincing, organizing, and arranging, and after weeks or months of travel by foot, cart, train, and ship, their long-held dream had finally become a reality: "I was in America!"[48]

16

THE LOWER EAST SIDE

IN THE EARLY 1920s, journalist Konrad Bercovici published a series of articles in *Harper's Monthly* on the immigrant "quarters" of New York. One piece profiled the small but well-known Lebanese and Syrian enclave on Washington and Greenwich streets south of where the World Trade Center later sat. Another took readers on a guided tour of the neighborhood around St. Mark's Place where, despite their ancient feuds, Serbs, Croats, Montenegrins, and Bulgarians all concentrated. Bercovici identified two dozen ethnic enclaves in the city: African (meaning African Americans from the Caribbean), Armenian, Bulgarian, Chinese, Croatian, Czech, French, German, "Gipsy," Greek, Hungarian, Italian, Jewish, Macedonian, Montenegrin, Polish, Romanian, Russian, Scandinavian, Scotch, Serb, Slovak, Slovene, and Spanish. Bercovici, an immigrant from Romania who had lived in Paris and Montreal before settling in New York, found the city's mixture of peoples intoxicating. New York, he concluded, is "not a city, but a world."

There was an apparent rationale to how all these people spread themselves out across the city. As Bercovici noted in 1924:

A map of Europe superposed upon the map of New York would prove that the different foreign sections of the city live in the same proximity to one another as in Europe: the Spanish near the French, the French near the Germans, the Germans near the Austrians, the Russians and the Rumanians near the Hungarians, and the Greeks behind the Italians. People of western Europe live in the western side of the city. People of eastern Europe live in the eastern side of the city. Northerners live in the northern part of the city and southerners in the southern part. Those who have lived on the other side near the sea or a river have the tendency here to live as near the sea or the river as possible.[1]

SELECT MANHATTAN IMMIGRANT ENCLAVES, 1900

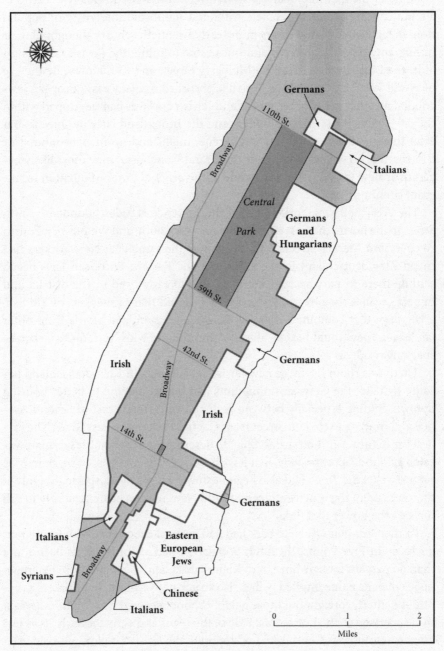

All of these observations were accurate.

Some of these ethnic quarters were tiny. A few were not really enclaves at all, but concentrations of retailers without a significant foreign-born population. In fact, when New Yorkers in the early twentieth century thought of their immigrant "colonies," three major ones came to mind: the Jewish Lower East Side, the Little Italy centered on Mulberry Street, and Chinatown. By the eve of World War I, however, New York had absorbed so many east European Jews and Italians that many other Italian and Jewish enclaves had developed within the city—first in Harlem, Brooklyn, and the Bronx, and later in Queens. But even though Italian or Jewish immigrants might end up in Bensonhurst or Brownsville, on Arthur Avenue or the Grand Concourse, they most likely began their new lives in America in one of the original lower Manhattan immigrant communities.

The area that New Yorkers called the Lower East Side (bounded by 14th Street to the north, the East River to the east and south, and the Bowery, Fourth Avenue, and Market Street to the west) was the same area New Yorkers had called Kleindeutschland in the Civil War era. Eastern European Jews began settling there in part because German Jews already lived in the district and in part because the newcomers probably believed that as speakers of Yiddish, a language that combined Hebrew, German, Russian, and words from other languages, they would best be able to communicate with New York's German-speaking residents.

There was room for these new Jewish immigrants in Kleindeutschland because by 1880, the German immigrants had begun moving to better housing uptown, settling especially between 50th and 59th streets east of Second Avenue and from 72nd to 96th Street from Central Park to the East River. The earliest use of the term "Lower East Side" to describe the area that the Germans vacated is found, appropriately, in a Jewish weekly, *The Jewish Messenger*, in May 1880. By 1888 the *Times* had also begun using the term, albeit sparingly. Only at the very end of the nineteenth century did New Yorkers begin regularly to call the area the Lower East Side.[2]

By then, residents of New York had had years of experience with immigrant enclaves. In Five Points, the adult population had at some points been more than 90 percent foreign-born, and Kleindeutschland—always more heterogeneous than its name implied—had also struck native-born New Yorkers as exotic and utterly foreign. But those neighborhoods seemed downright *American* in comparison to the Lower East Side of the 1890s and early 1900s. It "is as unknown a country as Central Africa," reported the *Herald* in 1892, "a world in itself, . . . one of the most foreign quarters to be found in any city in the world." Jacob Riis, a Danish immigrant, was even more blunt about what he discovered

THE CENTRAL AND SOUTHERN PORTIONS OF THE
LOWER EAST SIDE, 1910

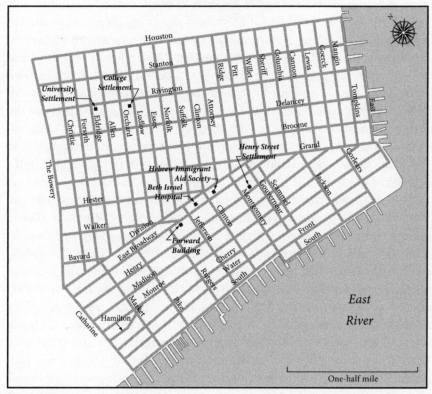

when he crossed to the east side of the Bowery around the same time: "There is no mistaking it: we are in Jewtown."[3]

Comprising more than 250 square blocks, the Lower East Side was far too big to be called a neighborhood; it was really a series of neighborhoods. Contemporaries believed that the Lower East Side's Jews chose where in the district to settle on the basis of their European origins. "The different groups form separate colonies, the boundaries of which are easily distinguishable," wrote immigrant–turned–social worker David Blaustein. "The Hungarians occupy the territory between Avenue B and the East River almost to the exclusion of all other Jews; the Galicians [southern Poles] are found east of Suffolk street; the Roumanians in the territory enclosed by Houston street, Suffolk street, Grand street and the Bowery, and the Russians south of Grand street as far as Monroe street." Scholars have made the same assertions ever since.[4]

Yet New York's Jews did not really organize themselves so uniformly. There were only enough Romanian Jews in New York to allow them to dominate a

couple of blocks, not the thirty-five Blaustein described. And while it is true
that Hungarians did congregate in the northeast portion of the Lower East Side
(north of Broome Street and east of Attorney as of 1900), they constituted only
about half the inhabitants of each block, and that many only if we include in
their numbers the Polish Jews from areas controlled by the Austro-Hungarian
Empire. By contrast, Blaustein's contention that Russian-born Jews dominated
the southernmost portion of the Lower East Side is accurate. South of Division Street in the old Seventh Ward near the waterfront, most of East Broadway, Cherry, Monroe, Madison, and Henry streets, as well as the roads that ran
south to the waterfront such as Pike, Rutgers, Jefferson, Clinton, Montgomery, Gouverneur, Scammel, and Jackson, were populated almost exclusively by
Russian Jews. They also accounted for three-quarters of the population in the
Tenth Ward south of Grand between the Bowery and Norfolk Street. Even so,
more Russian Jews actually lived in the remainder of the Lower East Side than
within the portion designated by Blaustein as their "colony." Most of the Lower
East Side was a heterogeneous mixture of Jews from all over eastern Europe.[5]

Whether they were from Pinsk or Minsk, Plotzk or Polotsk, the Jews of the
Lower East Side had one characteristic that distinguished them from nearly all
the other "new" immigrant groups arriving in New York at the same time: their
community contained many women and children. In 1920, 48 percent of the
foreign-born Jewish population in New York was female. In contrast, women
accounted for 41 percent of Slavic immigrants, 35 percent of Italian immigrants,
and only 21 percent of Greek immigrants. For children, the contrast was even
greater. Children under the age of fourteen made up one-quarter of the Jewish
immigration in this period but only one-ninth of the immigration from other
sources.[6]

Jewish migration was a family affair. As a result, the Lower East Side became
extraordinarily crowded. "The supreme sensation of the East Side is the sensation of its astounding populousness," wrote an English visitor in 1912. "The architecture seemed to sweat humanity at every window and door." In comparison to these heaving tenement blocks, a "crowded . . . uptown thoroughfare . . .
is an uninhabited desert!" Abraham Cahan found the Lower East Side so teeming with humanity that daily life there was a veritable "battle for breath . . . It is
one of the most densely populated spots on the face of the earth — a seething
human sea fed by streams, streamlets, and rills of immigration flowing from all
the Yiddish-speaking centres of Europe."[7]

By 1895, fifteen years before the Lower East Side reached its peak population, the portion just south of Houston Street between Clinton and Columbia already housed more than eight hundred inhabitants per acre, making
it the most densely populated place on earth. The district to the southwest

The "astounding populousness" of the Lower East Side:
Hester Street looking west from Norfolk Street, 1898.

(bounded by the Bowery on the west, Rivington to the north, Norfolk to the east, and Division to the south) housed 626 inhabitants per acre, increasing to 728 by 1905. But because the Lower East Side contained some uninhabited lots dedicated to commercial activity, the population density of the area's residential blocks was actually much higher. In 1900, more than one hundred Lower East Side blocks held over 750 persons per acre — and nearly fifty held more than 900 per acre. The most crowded zones were the twenty or so square blocks from Henry Street to Cherry between Catharine and Jackson, dominated by Russian Jews, and the sixty or so square blocks between Delancey and Houston from the Bowery to the East River, populated by a mixture of east European Jews. Thirty blocks in these two zones contained more than one thousand inhabitants per acre. The most densely populated of these as of 1900, bounded by Delancey, Goerck, Rivington, and Mangin, housed 1,756 per acre.

Not every block was so crowded. The population density of the entire Lower East Side in 1910 was about 625 persons per acre. Even so, that meant that the Lower East Side's 1.35 square miles had more inhabitants in 1900 than the 444,000 square miles of Wyoming, Nevada, Arizona, and New Mexico combined. Put in modern perspective, the Lower East Side of 1910 was more than three times as densely populated as New York's most crowded neighborhood today (Manhattan's Upper East Side), even though the predominant five-story tenements of 1910 were only a fraction of the height of today's residential tow-

A family of seven in a two-room barracks-style tenement apartment, ca. 1910. The front room (in which the family is posed) served as kitchen, dining room, living room, and at night as the bedroom for the kids. The parents would have slept in the back room, the "sleeping closet." The window between the kitchen and the sleeping closet was not original but would have been added around 1879 after a new law mandated that every inhabited room have a window.

ers. None of the most congested neighborhoods in the world today — in Dhaka, Nairobi, and Mumbai — are as densely populated as were the most crowded neighborhoods of the Lower East Side in the decade before World War I.[8]

The tenements those immigrants inhabited were not primarily the same structures that the district's German and Irish immigrants had called home back in the 1850s and 1860s. In those days, New York's immigrants had lived primarily in two types of tenements — two- to three-story wooden buildings that had been converted from single-family dwellings, and four- to five-story brick buildings that usually measured twenty-five by fifty feet and had four two-room apartments per floor.

By the time Italians and east European Jews began arriving in large numbers at the end of the nineteenth century, the wooden tenements had almost all disappeared. Although several thousand of the city's antebellum brick tenements, sometimes referred to as "barracks," were still in use in 1900, two new tenement designs were now favored by developers. The first increased the footprint of the barracks-style tenement to cover 80 or 90 percent of the lot. These buildings struck New Yorkers as the epitome of landlord greed, as they contained more dark, windowless interior rooms than any previous design.

The overcrowding and lack of ventilation made life inside barracks tenements truly miserable. In 1894 Pulitzer hired investigative journalist Nellie Bly to spend a weekend in one such tenement on the Lower East Side. Bly found conditions in the building, at 223 East 2nd Street between Avenues B and C, nearly identical to those chronicled by reporters in Five Points forty years earlier — dangerous pitch-black hallways and stairwells, unbearable noise, "vile stench," and stifling heat. "Oh, the smell of it!" Bly exclaimed upon opening the door of her third-floor apartment. "It seemed to me that more than a million kinds of smell rushed out to embrace me in strong, if unseen, arms." A good portion of the stench came from the tenement inhabitants themselves. Lower East Siders bathed just a few times a year because only 8 percent of them had bathtubs. Bly also discovered that with 3,500 people living on her block, there was no escaping "the constant sound of voices which rose in one unbroken buzz from the street," all day and all night. That noise, plus the endless cacophony of crying babies, stairwell traffic, and other loud sounds produced inside her own building, made it impossible for Bly to sleep for more than a few minutes at a time.[9]

New immigrants moved around the Lower East Side a lot, each year seeking a slightly better apartment or a marginally more affordable rent. In the first eight years that he appears in the New York City directory, for example, my great-great-grandfather Isidor Munstuk lived in the rear barracks-style tenement at 103 Hester Street, then at 115 Delancey, 25 Orchard, 144 East Broadway, 407 Grand, 165 Clinton, and 385 Grand.[10]

While lot-sized barracks-style tenements may have been the worst dwellings in New York, there were at most several hundred of them in Manhattan in 1900. By far the most common type of new tenement built after the Civil War was the "dumbbell tenement," typically referred to as the "double-decker." It was created in response to complaints about the lack of light and fresh air in the inner rooms of the barracks-style buildings. In December 1878 a building trades magazine called *The Plumber and Sanitary Engineer* announced a $500 reward for the best new design for a tenement on a twenty-five-by-one-hundred-foot lot that would provide fresh air and light to every room. The magazine received more than two hundred entries and displayed them all in an exhibit that accompanied the contest. The magazine's jury selected as the winner architect James E. Ware's "dumbbell" design.

Ware's winning entry, which called for a building that was as wide as the lot in the front and the back but narrower in the middle, vaguely resembled a weightlifter's dumbbell. The narrow part of the tenement, set back eighteen

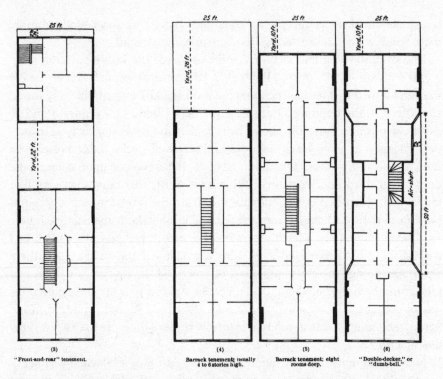

(3)   (4)   (5)   (6)
"Front-and-rear" tenement.   Barrack tenement; usually   Barrack tenement; eight   "Double-decker," or
                                      4 to 6 stories high.   rooms deep.   "dumb-bell."

The evolution of the New York tenement: On the left at the bottom, the typical twenty-five-
by-fifty-foot brick tenement and above it a twenty-five-by-twenty-five-foot rear tenement.
These were the typical tenements built in the years before the Civil War. In the middle, two
"barracks-style" tenements with three and four rooms per apartment, but very dark interior
rooms. On the far right, the "dumbbell" or "double-decker" tenement with four-room apartments in the front of the building and three-room apartments in the rear. Most dumbbell
tenements had three-room apartments front and rear, leaving more room in the backyard
for the outhouses and hydrants.

inches to three feet from the property line, had windows that admitted a bit of
light and air into interior rooms via an airshaft. If a barracks-style tenement sat
next door, however, these airshaft windows would face the solid brick wall of
the neighboring building. The press dubbed these buildings "double-deckers,"
because the floor plan looked like one house stacked upon another.[11]

Observers recognized that the dumbbell design was only a modest improvement. Referring to Ware's plan as well as those of the runners-up, the *Times* lamented that "if the prize plans are the best offered — which we can hardly believe — they simply demonstrate that the problem is insoluble . . . If one of our
crowded wards were built up after any one of these three prize designs, the evils
of our present tenement-house system would be increased ten-fold." Nonethe-

less, Ware's floor plan became the standard Manhattan tenement design in the last twenty years of the nineteenth century. Thousands of them, "great prison-like structures of brick, with narrow doors and windows, cramped passages and steep rickety stairs," were built throughout the city. As a congressional commit-tee noted in 1901, it was New York's "Hebrew district," the Lower East Side, that was "preeminently the region of the double-decker."[12]

Though one might imagine that the bigger three-room apartments in the double-deckers would have held more immigrants than the Lower East Side's remaining two-room barracks apartments, that was not always the case. Rel-atively well-to-do immigrants who could afford more space often leased the larger apartments, even if they did not have very big families. The oldest build-ings with the smallest, cheapest apartments thus often had the most inhabi-tants. Journalist Jacob Riis reported that a two-room apartment on Essex Street was once found to house twenty inhabitants — a mother and father, their twelve children, and six boarders.[13]

Some dumbbell tenements were incredibly crowded. In 1900, one of my pa-ternal great-grandfathers, mattress stuffer Mendel Dandishensky (who, after his arrival in 1896, "Americanized" his name to Max Dandeshane), lived in a narrow, towering six-story dumbbell tenement at 538 East 6th Street along with his wife, Liba ("Lizzie"), three children (they would eventually have four more), Liba's sister Victoria, Max's brother Froim, and a boarder. The eight of them shared an apartment smaller than the family room of the house I live in today.[14]

As the *Times* had predicted, dumbbell tenements did not alleviate any of the problems they were designed to solve. "The greatest evil is the lack of light and air," lamented one tenement resident. Rear rooms in the dumbbell buildings might receive a bit more light than those in barracks-style buildings, but "the airshaft is so narrow," she complained, often measuring just eighteen inches across, that the benefit to the residents below the top floor was negligible.[15]

In fact, the airshafts exacerbated two other problems — noise and stench — that had long plagued tenement dwellers. The shafts acted as echo chambers that amplified the sounds of screaming babies, boisterous children, and quar-reling adults. In the barracks-style tenement, inhabitants could hear noise from apartments above, below, and next to their own, but with the advent of the air-shaft, sounds from half the apartments in the building (and half the apartments in the tenement next door if it had an adjoining airshaft) were transported loudly and clearly into every other flat. "The noise hurts me," lamented one New York tenement dweller. "It comes down the airshaft so that sometimes I can't sleep." The racket from the airshafts combined with the unending din em-anating day and night from the streets prompted those inside the tenements to

There is no photograph that can do justice to the dumbbell tenement airshaft. Jacob Riis's photo of a tin bathtub hanging under a window inside an airshaft gives some sense of its narrow dimensions, as does this photo of a tenement rooftop with children.

yell in order to be heard. "It becomes habitual for us to raise our voices," as one Lower East Side resident put it, raising the decibel level still further and making life for those living in tenements even more miserable.

Airshafts also worsened the "vile stench" that often permeated the Lower East Side's tenements. A woman who lived at the bottom of a five-story tenement reported that her upstairs neighbors constantly "throw out garbage and dirty papers and the insides of chickens, and other unmentionable filth" into the airshaft. "Unmentionable filth" undoubtedly referred to the contents of chamber pots or dirty diapers which some tenants tossed out their windows rather than allowing them to accumulate inside their own apartments. "Because of the refuse thrown down in the airshaft," testified another tenement dweller, Henry Moscowitz of 95 Forsyth Street, "the stench is so vile and the air is so foul that the occupants do not employ the windows as a means of getting air." Between the noise and the smell, nearly all tenement dwellers kept their airshaft windows closed.[16]

As a result, dumbbell tenements remained just as torturously hot in summertime as the old barracks-style buildings. With huge brick edifices soaking up the summer sun and more than a hundred perspiring, sweltering residents inhabiting each one, charity workers found "tenement districts" like the Lower East Side and Little Italy "ten times hotter" than middle-class neighborhoods just a few blocks away. This helps to explain why the thoroughfares in immigrant neighborhoods were thronged day and night, as inhabitants tried to spend as little time as possible in their torrid apartments. As they had in the Civil War years, thousands of immigrants slept on their rooftops in the summer and thousands more spent the night on fire escapes. In order to fit as many family members on the fire escapes as possible, some ingenious residents used iron pins to fasten planks to the exterior walls of their tenement buildings, creating outdoor bunk beds, an arrangement copied, according to the *Tribune*, "from the upper Bronx to the Armenian quarter, near the Battery."[17]

In the early twentieth century, city officials began to allow New Yorkers to sleep in parks during heat emergencies. And on one Saturday night in 1915, twenty thousand city residents slept on the beach at Coney Island rather than endure another night in their sweltering apartments. Nonetheless, many tenement dwellers, especially the sick and elderly, succumbed to heat prostration and dehydration during heat waves. In July 1901, eighty-seven New Yorkers perished as temperatures reached ninety-eight degrees. Two years later, forty-four New Yorkers died over two days when temperatures hit the mid-nineties. With so many more people per acre, and so many more brick tenements per block, heat-related deaths became much more common in the early twentieth century than they had been in the Civil War era.[18]

Dumbbell tenements were also more prone to fatal fires than the barracks-style buildings. "It started in the basement of the building and ran swiftly up the airshaft," newspapers reported with alarming frequency, in this case describing an unusually deadly fire that killed eighteen tenement residents in 1903. "The airshaft again played the leading part," began the description of another blaze, this one in 1891. Deadly tenement fires, a relative rarity in the antebellum years, became a weekly occurrence by 1900. Press accounts of these blazes were often heartrending, as in the one at 137 Orchard Street in 1893 that took the life of twenty-two-year-old tinsmith Morris Cohen, his twenty-year-old wife, Sophia, and their three-month-old daughter Esther. Sophia was found dead of smoke inhalation on the floor of her fifth-story apartment, with her lifeless baby "closely pressed to her heart."[19]

Sometimes the airshaft actually offered tenement dwellers a means of escape from dumbbell blazes. In cases where the flames were confined to the interior of the building, the inhabitants of one double-decker could climb to safety out their airshaft windows and into those of the building next door. This was one of the rare occasions when having a neighbor's windows just inches away seemed a blessing rather than a curse.[20]

Despite this one benefit, the New York State legislature's tenement committee called "the 'double-decker' . . . the one hopeless form of tenement-house construction" because it "can not be well ventilated; it can not be well lighted; it is not safe in case of fire." The immigrants heartily agreed. When one was asked in 1900 by a member of the state tenement commission how she would like to see tenements changed, she "exclaimed without a moment's hesitation and very emphatically: 'No airshafts!'"[21]

In 1901 the New York state legislature banned the construction of new dumbbell tenements, requiring residential buildings to occupy a smaller portion of each lot and creating setback rules that mandated far more space between exterior windows and adjacent buildings. But because a building constructed according to these new rules on Manhattan's predominant twenty-five-by-one-hundred-foot lots could house far fewer families than existing tenements, landlords chose to keep their old but lucrative buildings rather than replace them. The new law thus had so little impact on the Lower East Side that by 1916, fifteen years after it went into effect, 92 percent of the neighborhood's tenements were still either dumbbell buildings or the even more crowded and dilapidated barracks-style structures. In that year, in fact, the Lower East Side still had three barracks-style tenements for every dumbbell tenement. Today, nearly all these tenements are still standing — and inhabited, but by far, far fewer people.[22]

Irish and Italian men tended to leave their tenement neighborhoods six days a week to go to work, but tens of thousands of Jews were employed *inside* neighborhood tenements, contributing to the Lower East Side's unprecedented overcrowding. "The homes of the Hebrew quarter are its workshops also," wrote Riis in 1890. "You are made fully aware of it before you have travelled the length of a single block in any of these East Side streets, by the whir of a thousand sewing-machines, worked at high pressure from earliest dawn till mind and muscle give out together."

This was hardly an exaggeration. New York's Jewish immigrants flocked to the garment industry just as Irish immigrants had taken to day labor and domestic service. As the *Herald* noted, "the most familiar sound in these streets is the click of the sewing machine; the most familiar sight men, women and children staggering along under the weight of huge packs of half-finished clothing." Because this work was so often done at home, Riis noted, "every member of the family, from the youngest to the oldest, bears a hand, shut in the qualmy rooms, where meals are cooked and clothing washed and dried besides, the livelong day. It is not unusual to find a dozen persons — men, women, and children — at work in a single small room." By 1900, 90 percent of jobs in New York's garment industry were held by Jews.[23]

Several factors contributed to this Jewish dominance. Restrictions placed

Jacob Riis titled this photo "Knee-Pants at Forty-Five Cents a Dozen — A Ludlow Street Sweater's Shop."

on Jews in the Pale of Settlement had forced them out of agricultural work and into the large towns and cities of Russia and Poland, where they had adopted urban trades such as tailoring. Then, when the first east European Jews arrived in New York in the late nineteenth century, they found that the German Jews already living on the Lower East Side dominated the clothing industry there and were more willing to employ them than were other New Yorkers. They also liked working with other Jews. "Even a greenhorn feels at home in a tailor shop," one immigrant wrote, recollecting his first days in New York. "I felt a bit surer of the work and that people would treat me like a human being." Finally, the new immigrants also gravitated to this work because the industry's predominantly Jewish employers were more likely than others to allow them to observe the Jewish Sabbath by working Sundays rather than Saturdays.[24]

It would be a mistake, however, to assume that most Jewish immigrants came to New York with experience making clothing for a living. Only one-third of New York's Jewish immigrants could find work in the same occupation they had followed in the Pale. Aaron Domnitz, for example, had been a teacher in the shtetl of Slutsk near Minsk. "My plan was to learn a trade, work and be

independent," he recalled years later in an autobiographical sketch. He tried to
get an apprenticeship with a plumber, but without a landsman or relative willing to train him, "the trade was completely closed to outsiders who wanted to
get in." He tried large metal factories, anything "as long as it wasn't tailoring,"
but the work was either too difficult or too boring and low paid. Finally, he later
recalled, "I got tired of constantly changing jobs and looking for work. I felt the
need to have stable employment with a more or less secure income." His friends
and relatives told him "that it was now time to settle down and do what everyone else did — become a tailor. I became a tailor."[25]

Facing such unexpected obstacles, many newly arrived immigrants became
depressed, wondering why they had moved so far from everything that was
familiar and comforting and come to a world that was so different, so difficult, so expensive — so *foreign*. Morris Raphael Cohen could not believe the
"intensity and hurry" that Americans demanded, a sharp contrast to the "lei-
surely" pace of work and life in Minsk. Marcus Ravage recalled, "With every
day that passed I became more and more overwhelmed." In these first, doubt-
filled weeks, the newcomers missed almost everything they had left behind.
"I am overcome with longing," wrote one immigrant, "not only for my Jewish
world, which I have lost, but also for Russia." They had traded the fresh air of
Russia for the "gray, stone world of tall tenements, where even on the loveli-
est spring day there was not a blade of grass . . . The sun, gray and depressed;
the men and women clustered around the pushcarts; the gray walls of the tenements — all looks sad." Some were so wracked with despair that they wrote
letters to their homeland warning others there not to make the same mistake
they had. "For God's sake, do not come here," wrote one new immigrant to a
Yiddish newspaper in Poland. All Americans care about is "money and money
and again money." Abraham Cahan expressed similar sentiments in a letter to
a Russian newspaper. "Curse you, emigration," he cried. "How many lives have
you broken, how many brave and mighty have you rubbed out like dust!" But
most of the immigrants managed to fight through such despondency. "I promised myself that I would never set eyes on Warsaw again," one Polish Jew reminded himself in those demoralizing first months in New York, "and I'll keep
my word."[26]

Whether or not my great-grandfather Froim Leib Anbinder battled such
doubts, he must have found the lack of employment options demoralizing. In
his shtetl in Ukraine, he had probably worked at the family inn; he told the inspectors at Ellis Island that he had been a "merchant." Now, without the capital to start his own business in New York, and needing to earn and save money
to bring his wife and five children to America, he took work as a lowly presser,
ironing the clothes that other garment workers had sewn to make them ready

for the wholesaler who had ordered them. Pressers were not paid as well as cutters or those who operated sewing machines. It was also taxing labor, requiring one to stand all day, Riis observed, over "a big red-hot stove to keep the pressing irons ready for use," even in the heat of summer inside sweltering tenements.[27]

Like most Jewish newcomers, Froim Leib probably found his first job in New York through a "landsman," someone from his hometown of Holoskov. "We knew which landsman was looking for a new place and who could take someone in to work," Domnitz recollected. "Nearly everyone had a greenhorn [new immigrant] guest or expected to get one soon. They were always occupied with looking for work for new arrivals ... To take someone into your shop was considered the greatest good deed, almost the only good deed" that immigrants could perform for the even more recent arrivals. The newcomers would eventually look for something better than that initial menial job, and they would again turn to landsmen for leads and advice. The importance of landsmen in the lives of the Jewish immigrants was reflected in the fact that New York's Jews created more than one thousand *landsmanschaften* — "hometown associations" — which pooled dues money to provide assistance to the sick and unemployed and sometimes even covered burial costs when the immigrants passed away.[28]

But even before the search for a job began, an immigrant's family or landsmen already living in New York would insist on taking the newcomer to buy new clothes. "You think you can walk around like that, looking as green as grass?" Louis Waldman's sister Anna asked the Ukrainian immigrant rhetorically upon his arrival from Ellis Island at the family's Orchard Street apartment in 1909. "Why, no one, not even a peddler, will give you a job!" Domnitz recalled with relish the times he took newcomers to buy their first American clothing. "Going to the stores with the greenhorn on Canal Street was a joyful procedure," he wrote. "Everything had to be American. Clothes from home were defective, even if they were of good quality and well sewn." Having completed the transformation, the greenhorn was often taken to a photographer's studio so that his or her picture could be sent to relatives still in Europe.[29]

Immediately after ceremonially purchasing their first set of American clothes, the new immigrants had to find jobs, for as they quickly discovered, in America, even more so than in the Pale, "work, mean, hard, endless work, is the order of the Jew's life." When we think of the garment work that Froim Leib and his landsmen did on the Lower East Side, what invariably comes to mind is the "sweatshop," a large workplace in which employers compelled dozens of immigrants to toil long hours in unhealthy conditions for meager pay. But the original sweatshops were housed in tiny tenement apartments. Only after New York banned tenement workshops in 1892 did clothing contractors begin moving their employees to the commercial workspaces we associate with sweatshop labor. Even after 1900, thousands of immigrants continued to do garment work illicitly in their tiny tenement homes.[30]

The "sweating" system out of which the sweatshop developed had its origins in the long-standing practice whereby clothing manufacturers farmed out tasks to the poorest and most desperate workers, those least likely to complain about the starvation wages. In mid-nineteenth-century New York, these needleworkers were typically widowed women with children or Irish and German Jewish immigrants. As the Irish became more prosperous, and the number of east European Jews in New York grew exponentially, Jewish immigrants came to dominate the manufacturing end of the garment industry.[31]

Here's how the sweating system worked. A large clothing retailer — the Sears, Roebuck catalogue company, for example — might solicit bids from wholesalers for ten thousand pairs of boys' knickers, known as "knee pants." The lowest-bidding wholesaler would then seek bids from among the thousands of New York clothing contractors, and might allot one thousand pairs each to the ten lowest bidders. These contractors would then subcontract the work to the family-operated garment shops like the one Riis photographed on Ludlow Street, whose proprietor had agreed to make knee pants for forty-five cents per dozen. The wholesaler provided the cloth to the contractors, who passed it down to the garment shop proprietors.

This garment worker, photographed by Lewis Hine around 1908, appears to be carrying finished clothing from her workplace back to a contractor.

In the typical tenement garment workshop, the proprietor would break the production of the knee pants into separate tasks, doing the most highly skilled work (cutting the cloth and operating the sewing machine to assemble the pants) himself while hiring employees to do the rest. After the cloth was cut, a "baster" pinned the various pieces together so that the sewing machine operator could focus solely on stitching the pieces of cloth into one article of clothing. Depending on the complexity of the task required of the baster, he or she might get ten to twelve cents per dozen pairs of knee pants. After being sewn together, the pants went to the buttonhole maker, typically a young apprentice, who earned eight to ten cents per hundred buttonholes sewn. The "finisher," usually a woman in her teens or twenties earning perhaps ten cents per dozen, then put the finishing touches (such as sewing buttons) on the pants by hand. Finally, the knee pants went to the presser, who might get paid eight cents per dozen pairs of pants pressed.

Many contractors managed to squeeze two such teams of workers into a single twelve-by-twelve-foot tenement room. When they could not quite fit, the workers might spill out into the hallways, and "when the weather permits," inspectors reported, it was not uncommon to see "the fire-escapes occupied by from two to four busy workmen." For more complicated garments, such as men's coats, two or three basters and finishers might be employed, each with different tasks. The contractor's children might be put to work at any of these jobs once old enough to learn them. Even before that, they might pull loose threads from the finished garments, bring materials to the workers, and sweep up the ever-growing piles of scraps and dust. The crowding of workers in these tenement garment shops created especially trying conditions for young, unmarried women. "Keep your hands off, please," was the first English phrase that Rose Cohen, a twelve-year-old baster in a Monroe Street tenement garment shop, learned from an older female co-worker who used it to fend off advances from her boss.[32]

With buildings groaning under the weight of both their residents and those who showed up to work in them each day, the Lower East Side's tenements quickly became run-down and dilapidated. A *Times* reporter visiting a tenement full of garment workers at the corner of Orchard and Broome streets in 1894 found that "the stairs were worn and splintered. The plaster was cracked and unspeakably foul. A few barrels of refuse of various kinds occupied the landing." The apartments in which garment work was done were littered with fabric scraps, coarsely torn strips of cloth, and bits of thread, often piled inches high on the floor. Yet neighboring apartments could be quite clean if no garment work was performed in them.[33]

The system of bidding out garment work to tenement workers became

known as the "sweating" system because all the participants in the manufacturing process — the retailer, the wholesaler, the contractor, and the subcon-
tractor — "sweated" their profits out of those one level below them by compelling the subordinates to work incredibly long hours at a breakneck pace in
order to make any money at all. To complete enough pieces each day to pay the
rent, feed their families, and put some money aside for steamship tickets for
loved ones waiting to be brought to America, garment workers took no breaks
despite being hunched over their tables all day. They ate lunch at their work-
benches and toiled late into the night. "There is no recognized [maximum] of
working hours in most of these shops," noted an inspectors' report, "the limit
being a matter of endurance, and sometimes ninety hours a week are worked."
According to the *Tribune,* some employers demanded 108 hours of work per
week from female garment workers. Each person in the chain referred to his or
her boss as the "sweater," and the work done by those at the bottom of the hierarchy was known as "sweated labor." All these terms — "sweating," "sweater,"
and "sweated labor" — were widely used before the Civil War.[34]

The word "sweatshop," however, only entered the American lexicon in the
1890s, because it wasn't until 1892, when New York State banned the manufacture of clothing in tenements, that this work moved into commercial loft
spaces, both on the Lower East Side and farther uptown. Even in these new
locations, manufacturers continued to compel garment workers to toil long
hours for pennies per garment sewn, and thus the "sweatshop" was born. Yet
the law allowed small-scale manufacturing to continue in tenements as long as
only immediate family members were employed and the workshop applied for
and received a permit. In 1901, twenty thousand New Yorkers had permits for
tenement work, and thousands of other garment workers took work home with
the connivance of sweatshop owners. The sweating system trapped the city's
Jews in what the *Herald* called a form of "servitude worse than that of Egypt"
under the Pharaohs.[35]

One of the most difficult aspects of the Lower East Side garment industry
was its seasonality. Then as now, people bought most of their clothing in the
spring and fall, so while garment workers had steady employment in summer
and winter, and were inundated with orders at the end of each of those seasons,
they often found themselves underemployed or wholly unemployed the rest of
the year. Those pennies per garment that they earned had to feed and house
them and their families not just in the weeks they were working but also in the
many weeks they were not. And during economic slowdowns, their situation
became truly dire.

One year into the depression that began in the fall of 1893, a *Times* reporter
found the Lower East Side full of "attenuated creatures, clad in old, faded,

A sweatshop at 30 Suffolk Street, photographed in 1908 by Lewis Hine.

greasy, often tattered clothing ... All of them only too plainly suffer from a perpetual insufficiency of food," with the result that their "cheeks are pinched and pale and hollow." They looked "like a group of figures from a life-size picture of a famine."[36]

Immigrant garment workers were also notorious for their poor health. They "fill the air with incessant coughing," noted a *Times* reporter in 1894. Some suffered from tuberculosis (known in those days as "consumption"), a bacterial infection of the lungs that spread especially easily in the close confines of tenement workshops and sweatshops. The Lower East Side's tenements, according to one charitable organization, "are known to be hotbeds of the disease, the very walls reeking with it." But despite the popular stereotype of the time that portrayed them as more prone to tuberculosis than other New Yorkers, Jews actually contracted the disease at a much *lower* rate than other city residents. What most of the Lower East Side's chronic coughers had actually contracted was bronchitis or asthma from years of working in poorly ventilated garment shops whose air was filled with soot, tiny shreds of fabric, and what one garment worker recalled as "millions of specks of dust."[37]

Despite public perceptions to the contrary, the majority of New York's employed male east European Jewish immigrants were not garment workers. In 1900, only 38 percent of them made clothing, though the figure rose to 44 percent on the Lower East Side.[38]

Jewish immigrant women, however, had fewer employment options than men, so nearly two-thirds of employed female east European Jewish immigrants living on the Lower East Side in 1900 were garment workers. Another 9 percent were employed as domestic servants. The remaining women were divided evenly among business owners (5 percent, mostly shopkeepers), office workers (5 percent), skilled workers (5 percent, mostly cigar makers), and non–garment factory workers (5 percent). Only 2 percent worked as teachers or nurses. Young east European Jewish women labored outside the home much more often in New York than they had in Europe, in part because they could do so without endangering their marriage prospects. "The girl has lots of time. America is not Poland," immigrant Sophie Ruskay remembered being told. "Here a girl is not considered an old maid until she is at least twenty."[39]

There were thousands of Lower East Side women who earned money for their families by taking charge of boarders — making up their beds each day, cooking their food, and doing their laundry. According to a congressional report published in 1911, 48 percent of New York's Russian Jewish immigrant households rented space to at least one lodger; 30 percent of Jews from other parts of eastern Europe did so. Taking in boarders was, according to one historian, "by far the most important economic activity for Jewish immigrant wives."[40]

Jewish immigrants who worked in the garment business did not typically do so for their entire adult lives. "The Jew considers the industry as a stepping stone to something higher," wrote economist Jesse Pope in an exhaustively detailed study of the garment trade published in 1905. "Every year large numbers desert the clothing industry to go into such occupations as small shopkeepers, insurance agents, and clerks." My grandfather Tulea Anbinder was a prime example. Arriving in New York at age thirteen in 1921, he finished school and then went to work in the garment industry. By 1940, however, he had become a dentist. Others did not leave the garment industry but worked their way up to better positions within it. Tulea's father, Froim Leib, for example, was still a presser in 1925, fifteen years after his arrival in America, but by 1930 he had managed to become a garment contractor, employing Tulea and his sisters Florence, Rae, and Sonia as sewing machine operators in the family business making baby clothes.[41]

For east European Jewish men looking to move out of the garment industry, there was virtually no occupational field that was off limits. About one-fifth of them in 1900 worked in what might be called a "skilled trade" outside the garment industry. As Domnitz had discovered, breaking into the most lucrative building and metal crafts was difficult, and as a result, most skilled Jewish workers were cigar makers, butchers, bakers, or painters (the least well-paid job in the building industry). Eight percent worked at what might be termed "unskilled" jobs requiring little previous training, such as day laborer, porter, and janitor, and another 8 percent worked in lower-status white-collar jobs as clerks or salesmen. In 1900, only 1 percent worked in the "professions" as a doctor, lawyer, dentist, or rabbi.

The single most popular vocation for east European Jews in New York outside the garment industry was retailing. In 1900, about one in six male east European Jewish immigrants was a merchant of some kind — about two-thirds as storekeepers and the remainder as street peddlers. Many of the shopkeepers had started out as peddlers. Peddling was attractive to devout Jews who balked at entering the garment industry, where the sweating system might force them to work on the Sabbath. Others tried peddling out of desperation, while still others did so because it allowed them to remain connected to the occupation they had followed in eastern Europe.[42]

Minnie Goldstein, for example, who immigrated to New York from Warsaw as a child, recalled that when her father failed in his attempts to resume work as a shoemaker after his arrival in New York, he began peddling baby shoes manufactured in the United States. "He took a wooden box, bought some baby shoes, took up position on Hester Street, and sold the shoes at a profit of five or ten cents a pair . . . Before very long the women of Hester Street found out that my father would sell them a pair of shoes for thirty cents, while they had to pay fifty cents in a store for the same pair" elsewhere. Goldstein eventually made enough money as a peddler to rent a storefront on Hester Street from which he sold both children's and adult shoes.[43]

Others peddled their wares door-to-door. If a Jewish immigrant "straight off the boat" tried to peddle in non-Jewish neighborhoods, he would have to memorize the English names of the goods he hoped to sell. "Suspenders, collah buttons, 'lastic, matches, henkeches — please, lady, buy," he might plead to the skeptical housewives he encountered uptown. If they had a question or a comment, he could do little but repeat the line he had committed to memory.[44]

Isaac Benequit began peddling to escape the drudgery of sewing shirtsleeves in a sweatshop. On the advice of a landsman, he began selling straw baskets on Saturdays outside the Washington Market, a wholesale emporium at the northwest corner of Chambers and Greenwich streets, where shoppers often struggled to carry all their purchases. He earned more peddling on Saturdays alone than he had been making in an entire week doing garment work. "In seven weeks I saved up sixty-five dollars apart from what I paid my mother every week for food," he wrote in a memoir. What did he do with his profits? "I borrowed a few more dollars from my mother — and became the 'boss' of a shirt factory." But Benequit found himself torn between idealism and profit, and closed his business at one point so he could join a garment workers' union and lead strikes. Later he became president of a paper manufacturing company and spent the last decade of his business career investing in real estate. The conflict in his own mind between the benefits of capital and the rights of labor clearly troubled him to his dying day. On his deathbed he felt compelled to assure his friends and family, "My soul is with the labor movement."[45]

Jewish peddlers who took to the road to sell in the countryside carried all their wares — typically eighty pounds on their backs and a forty-pound "balancer" on their chests. But those who remained in New York City usually displayed their wares on a rented pushcart. Many of the Lower East Side's streets became almost impassable because of the dozens of pushcarts set up on the district's busiest blocks. The city's "army of pushcart men, twenty-five thousand strong," reported a journalist in 1906, "turns whole blocks of the East Side Jewry into a bazaar, with high-piled carts lining the curb." Jewish pushcart peddlers worked primarily in Jewish enclaves, but on weekends often ventured into Irish and Italian neighborhoods as well.[46]

"Every conceivable thing is for sale" from the Lower East Side's pushcarts, observed the New York State Bureau of Labor Statistics in 1900. Harry Roskolenko likewise remembered that "everything in the cosmos was on a pushcart for somebody at some sort of price," as long as that price was "cheap." On a visit to Hester Street in the late 1880s, Riis found "bandannas and tin cups at two cents, peaches at a cent a quart, 'damaged' eggs for a song, hats for a quarter, and spectacles, warranted to suit the eye . . . for thirty-five cents . . . Old coats are hawked for fifty cents, 'as good as new,' and 'pants' . . . at anything that can be got."[47]

The scene at a pushcart market on a Friday afternoon was both colorful and chaotic. "There seems to be no order," observed a Romanian immigrant:

> The push-cart venders call out their wares in a Babel of tongues, in the singsong of the Talmud and the wailing of the prayer of the Day of Atonement. Bearded men and mustached men, blond men and high-cheekboned men, with their wives, stout and thick, and their daughters, bob-haired and trim, stand behind the glare of the burning white light of the acetylene lamps, yelling, talking, calling, and singing while dealing and bargaining with the customers pressing around them. One is carried along by the wave of humanity pressing homeward and from all sides. If one wants to buy something at a push-cart one holds on to it as if firm ground in an attempt to get to the shore had suddenly been struck.

Lower East Side pushcart peddlers had to adapt their trade to the modest means of their customers. According to the state labor bureau, "the yolk or the

Pushcart peddlers two rows deep on Hester Street in 1898.

white of an egg, or a chicken leg or wing, or an ounce of tea, coffee, or butter, is not an uncommon purchase." The most successful pushcart peddlers were those who, as Roskolenko put it, used both "moral and economic cunning" to wring profits from even the smallest transactions.[48]

Even more than garment workers, pushcart peddlers saw their vocation as a starting point on their way to something more respectable, stable, and re-munerative. "The pushcart is a means to an end," a journalist observed in 1905 in an article about these street peddlers. "He is a pushcart man only until by means of his cart he can step to something higher." Indeed, a comparison of the occupations of New York's east European Jewish immigrants in 1900 and 1920 indicates that most peddlers succeeded in achieving "something higher." In that twenty-year period, the proportion of Jewish immigrants working as ped-dlers dropped by nearly 75 percent. The percentage toiling in garment sweat-shops fell by more than a quarter. Meanwhile, the proportion of business own-ers increased by more than a third and the percentage of men working as office clerks, as salesmen, or in managerial jobs nearly doubled. The proportion of professionals doubled too, albeit to only 2 percent of the whole.[49]

The occupational opportunities for east European Jewish immigrant women also changed from 1900 to 1920. In 1920 a smaller proportion of Jewish immi-grant women were employed outside the home, and of those who reported be-ing employed, the percentage working in the garment industry had fallen to 45 percent from 59 percent. The percentage of teachers and nurses had doubled, albeit only to 4 percent. The biggest change by far was the move of female Jewish immigrants into office jobs. Only one in twenty had done such work in 1900, but by 1920 the figure was nearly one in three, mostly as typists, copyists, stenographers, and bookkeepers. With the increasing availability of respectable office work, the proportion of Jewish women working as household servants, which most immigrants regarded as degrading labor, plummeted by over 60 percent.[50]

As Jewish immigrants found better jobs, they could afford to move to better neighborhoods. In 1892, 75 percent of the Jews in what would become the five boroughs of New York City lived on the Lower East Side.* By 1916, only 25 percent did so. For those who left the East Side but remained in Manhattan, the most popular destination was central Harlem. Harlem's residents were not initially happy to see the new immigrants moving into the neighborhood. One Jewish immigrant recalled rental properties there displaying signs that read "Keine Juden, und keine Hunde" — "No Jews and no dogs." Nonetheless, the immigrants began finding apartments, among them my maternal great-grandfather Jacob Munstuk (a printer) and his wife, Matie, who lived at 66 West 118th Street in 1905. His father, Isidor, moved at around the same time to 319 West 116th Street. By 1910, about 100,000 Jews lived in Harlem.[51]

Another popular destination for Lower East Side Jews was the Bronx. For those without much money, Mott Haven, the southernmost neighborhood in the Bronx, was a popular choice. By 1910, Jacob and Matie Munstuk had moved from Harlem to Mott Haven, where they opened a "dry goods emporium" at 174 Willis Avenue. The store apparently did not flourish, because by 1920, Jacob had returned to the printer's trade and relocated back to Manhattan, to Washington Heights, a popular locale for German immigrants. (Though born in Plotzk, now part of Poland, Jacob told census takers that he was German-born, which was technically true since at the time of his birth Plotzk was controlled by Prussia.) Other Jewish immigrants moved to the neighborhoods on either side of Crotona Park in the central portion of the Bronx. That's where my

---

* Up until 1874, New York City comprised only Manhattan Island and the small islands surrounding it. In that year the city expanded its boundaries by annexing the portion of Westchester County west of the Bronx River and south of the northern tip of Manhattan Island. In 1895 the remaining townships in what became Bronx County were also added to the jurisdiction of New York City. And in 1898 New York annexed Brooklyn (Kings County), the western portion of Queens County (the remainder became Nassau County), and Staten Island (Richmond County). Together with New York County (Manhattan), these five counties became known as the five "boroughs" of New York.

mother's maternal grandfather, furrier Barnet Gutkin from Odessa, had settled by 1912, first at 456 East 175th Street and then by 1915 at 1815 Crotona Avenue.[52]

But for those who had really succeeded, or wanted to look as if they had, the place to settle in the Bronx was the Grand Concourse, a wide boulevard that opened in 1909 and ran up the west side of the Bronx from West 138th Street to Van Cortland Park. The Grand Concourse was "the culminating point of any-one's aspirations," recalled Ruth Gay, who moved with her immigrant parents to an apartment a few blocks from the famous boulevard when she was a young child. Moving to the Bronx was something one did not just for oneself but for one's children. When a regular Jewish customer of a Lower East Side public li-brary told the librarian he was moving to the Bronx and the librarian asked why, he said, "Vell, I haf a daughter to marry." In the Bronx, one could hope that one's children would meet and marry more well-to-do Jewish immigrants or their children.[53]

An even more popular destination than the Bronx was Brooklyn. As early as the 1880s, central and east European Jews had begun settling in the German neighborhood of Williamsburg. But the destination that drew the most Lower East Siders was Brownsville. "Only yesterday," reported the *Forward* in 1903, "everybody laughed when you mentioned Brownsville. But today business is booming." Those who got in early had the last laugh: lots that had sold for $200 in 1899 brought $5,000 to $10,000 five years later, as demand for housing in Brownsville far outstripped supply. One of the attractions of the neighborhood, which still contained hundreds of empty lots when Jews began moving there, was that it seemed to offer a much less stressful lifestyle than the Lower East Side. "Jews could live as in the old country, without any rush or excessive wor-ries," enthused one contemporary observer. "Brownsville will never have ten-ements," agreed the *Forward*. "The houses are three stories, apartments have four or five rooms, with a bathtub and other conveniences."

My great-grandfather Max Dandeshane was one of the Manhattan Jews at-tracted to Brownsville. By 1910 he had escaped his teeming dumbbell tenement on the Lower East Side and could be found living at 550 Rockaway Avenue with his wife and six daughters. Their Brownsville apartment building housed about the same number of families and tenants as had his tenement on East 6th Street, but the Brooklyn apartment was twice as large, and there was lots of open space nearby in which children could play.[54]

The new Jewish residents brought many of their Manhattan customs to Brooklyn. While the neighborhood's main shopping street, Pitkin Avenue, remained relatively upscale, Belmont Avenue became the new Hester Street, jammed with pushcarts on Thursdays and Fridays as Jewish residents stocked up on food and cleaning supplies in preparation for the Sabbath. Many Brooklynites resented these changes. Brownsville had "very much deteriorated by the settling of a low class of Hebrews," complained the *Brooklyn Daily Eagle*, which especially objected to Jews opening small shops or doing garment work in buildings that had once been strictly residential. Nonetheless, the influx of Jews continued unabated. By 1920, 80 percent of Brownsville's 100,000 residents were Jewish immigrants and their children.[55]

With real estate prices skyrocketing in Brownsville, Jews seeking more reasonably priced housing left the neighborhood for even more far-flung portions of Brooklyn. Many moved farther east, to East New York, or southeast to the New Lots district. The Dandeshanes joined this migration, relocating to 311 Hinsdale Street in East New York by 1920. Max, who had been working in a garment factory in 1910, was back at mattress stuffing by this point. Never very well-off, he, his wife, and six daughters rented the basement apartment of the two-story house that remains there today. (The owner, with a wife and six children of his own, occupied the rest of the house.) A few years after the Dandeshanes arrived in East New York, the Anbinders moved there too, to 636 Miller Avenue, just half a mile east of the Dandeshanes. They managed to purchase the house by 1930, though they rented the basement to tenants to help make it affordable. Later on, as Jewish immigrants such as the Anbinders and the Dandeshanes continued to improve their socioeconomic status, they would begin to relocate to more affluent parts of Brooklyn, such as Midwood and Flatbush.[56]

Whether they were affluent or just scraping by, living in a spacious apartment on the Grand Concourse or in a tiny two-room tenement apartment on the Lower East Side, food played a central role in the lives of Jewish immigrants. At no time of the week was this more evident than in their efforts, no matter what their budgets, to make their Friday night Sabbath meal special. "Everything was so tasty, it melted in one's mouth," recalled Louis Lozowick, an American painter who was born in Ukraine and came to the United States in 1906, of his Friday night meals in America. "Chicken noodle soup, chopped liver with onions and chicken fat, roast chicken, and compote of carrots and prunes . . . And last, the crowning glory of a Sabbath meal, the *kugel* made of noodles or potatoes filled with raisins and other goodies."[57]

When a family's financial situation became truly dire, of course, even the Friday night menu underwent changes. Samuel Golden recalled "periodic unemployment seasons, during which my father earned no money." In those dark days, "the food we ate underwent a complete change. Tastier dishes disappeared and the menu eventually consisted almost entirely of bread, butter, herring and potatoes."[58]

Another Jewish staple during hard times was the pickle. "Pickles are [a] favorite food in Jewtown," reported Jacob Riis in 1890, noting that many destitute Jewish newcomers subsisted on bread and pickles alone. Immigrants told Riis that they relied on pickles because they "are filling, and keep the children from crying with hunger." In fact, a pickle sandwich was a typical Lower East Side lunch for those who were unemployed or scrimping and saving to bring family members to America.[59]

As Jewish immigrants became more financially stable, they began to partake of the American custom of eating out, which the *Forward* reported "is spreading every day, especially in New York." To meet this demand, the iconic New York Jewish "deli" was born. In their delis, Jews could enjoy smoked fish, borscht, matzo ball soup, corned beef and pastrami sandwiches on rye, and cream soda or Cel-Ray tonic. Some of these foods, like corned beef, had been served in New York for generations. Others, like pastrami, a beef brisket that is brined, then covered in a dry rub of salt and spices before being smoked and later steamed, only arrived in New York with the east European Jews. One of its most famous purveyors, Katz's Deli, has been operating on the block of Ludlow Street that intersects with Houston for more than 125 years.[60]

For many Jews, delis became hubs for socializing, fulfilling the same role in their community that the saloon did for Irish New Yorkers. "It was as if we had entered into our rightful heritage," recalled Alfred Kazin of the feeling he got as a boy when he crossed the threshold into his local Jewish deli. Yet for most Jews in this era, who were still hoping to move to a better neighborhood or put away a nest egg for the future, the deli was at most a once-a-week treat. In Kazin's family, deli fare "was food that only on Saturday nights could be eaten with a good conscience."[61]

Because those who strictly followed Jewish dietary laws would not eat meat and dairy products at the same meal, Jewish New Yorkers also opened "dairy restaurants." The most famous was Ratner's, first on Pitt Street, but after 1918 at 138 Delancey. There, diners could enjoy cheese blintzes, kreplach (dumplings), and Ratner's famous gefilte fish. The restaurant's borscht, potato soup, and kasha varnishkes (buckwheat groats with noodles) were also Lower East Side favorites. For dessert there was cheesecake, or one could opt for the ultimate Jewish comfort food, sour cream with bananas. In its heyday, Ratner's served 2,500 customers a day.[62]

By 1920, about 1.6 million Jews (both immigrants and native-born) lived in New York, around three-quarters of them in Brooklyn and the Bronx. Yet until their dying day, the city's east European Jewish immigrants considered their years on the Lower East Side their formative American experience. After passing through Ellis Island and finding a home and a job with the help of landsmen, the typical Jewish immigrant would rarely (if ever) have ventured west of the Bowery or north of 14th Street. Almost all of them, men and women, boys and girls, would have done at least some garment work, either at home, in a neighbor's tenement apartment, or in a sweatshop. They could go months, even years, without having to speak a word of English, because at work, in the market, and in their tenements, almost everyone spoke Yiddish, and those who did not spoke Russian or Polish. Even after several years in New York, an excursion to Midtown or Central Park would have been both frightening (especially for women) and exotic, like a trip to a foreign country. Some immigrants called such an outing going "to America."[63]

Just across the Bowery there was another enclave, Little Italy, whose inhabitants went through many of the same experiences as the newcomers on the Lower East Side. The Italians lived in overcrowded, dilapidated tenements. They depended on *paesani*, other immigrants from the same parts of Italy, for help finding housing and work. They could go years in America without speaking more than a few words of English. And most of them would eventually move out of their initial lower Manhattan neighborhood to cleaner, healthier, roomier housing in the city's outer boroughs. Yet Little Italy, like the Lower East Side, was its own entire world.

17

LITTLE ITALYS

WHEN PASQUALE D'ANGELO arrived in New York in April 1910 from Introdacqua, a mountainous village eighty miles east of Rome in the Abruzzi region
of central Italy, he discovered that life in America as a day laborer would not
be as easy as he had imagined. "Everywhere was toil — endless, continuous toil,
in the flooding blaze of the sun, or in the slashing rain — toil." D'Angelo, along
with his father, Angelo, and seven other townsmen, were met at the Battery by
an Italian labor contractor (*padrone* in Italian) from the same part of Italy. He
had jobs waiting for them building roads 125 miles north of New York City. Although it was illegal to enter the United States with a job already arranged, back
then, as today, day laborers had no trouble finding contractors who were willing to flout the law.

D'Angelo initially liked his new life. He was only sixteen, with a strong back
and plenty of experience doing hard work in the fields surrounding Introdacqua. But when the contractor ran out of jobs for D'Angelo and his "gang," their
prospects worsened. New bosses were cruel, the pay was miserable, and the
work was often very dangerous. Two of D'Angelo's co-workers were crushed
to death by a falling derrick on a railroad construction site. Over the course
of about two years, D'Angelo and his surviving co-workers found employment
in Spring Valley, Tappan, Poughkeepsie, Staatsburg, and Glens Falls along the
Hudson, Utica and Oneonta in central New York, White Lake in the Catskills,
and Otter Lake in the Adirondacks, as well as in Westwood and Ramsey, New
Jersey, Falling Waters, West Virginia, Williamsport, Maryland, "and many
other places . . . , always as a pick and shovel man."

When a job ended and a new one could not be found nearby, D'Angelo and
his compatriots often returned to New York's Mulberry Street, headquarters of
dozens of Italian *padroni*. In Five Points, D'Angelo and his friends would rent
spots in one of the overcrowded boardinghouses on Bayard Street, enjoy a brief

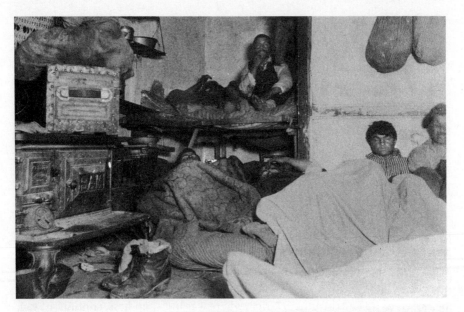

When Pasquale D'Angelo and the other members of his day labor gang could not find work
in the countryside, they would travel to New York to look for work. While staying in the city,
they would rent space in cheap Bayard Street boardinghouses like this one photographed by
Jacob Riis around 1890.

respite from work, and weigh various opportunities, often in some far-flung
southern or western location. "Going to a distant job is a gamble," D'Angelo
later noted. "A man may pay a large part of his scanty savings for fare. And
when he gets there he may find living conditions impossible and the foreman
too overbearing. Perhaps he will be fired at the end of the week. Where will he
be then?" Sometimes a contractor went bankrupt, and D'Angelo might then
lose weeks of back pay.[1]

Some of the immigrants could not stand these hardships. D'Angelo's father,
concluding that he was no better off in America than he had been in Introdacqua and that he would never save enough to bring his wife and remaining children to America, decided to return to Italy. Two other members of D'Angelo's
original work gang also went back. But Pasquale was determined to succeed in
America. His life became a bit easier when, at the end of 1915, after five years of
itinerant labor, he found steady work doing track maintenance just across the
Hudson from New York in the Erie Railroad rail yard in North Bergen, New
Jersey. The pay was so miserable — just $1.13 a day — that D'Angelo lived in an
unused boxcar on a siding rather than squander most of his wages on rent.

The work that winter was just as hard as any he had yet encountered.
D'Angelo was "liable to be called out at any hour — usually in the middle of

the night," if there was "a wreck or other trouble . . . In spite of rain, snow, sleet and icy wind, we had to work until the wreckage was removed and the damaged tracks repaired." It was dangerous work, too, "with the heavy ties and rails on our shoulders and the slippery ice under our feet." Yet a fall was the least of D'Angelo's worries. "All around was noise and confusion; trains piling on trains — cars creeping smoothly at you in the darkness, bells, toots." Two of his predominantly Italian and Polish co-workers were crushed by the wheels of a locomotive. Several more died under an avalanche of coal in the yard's "coal dumps." Another "suffocated in the steam house."[2]

Meanwhile, as World War I entered its third year, East Coast ports became increasingly frenetic supplying Europe with war matériel. To fill a labor shortage in the rail yard, the Erie brought Mexican immigrants from Texas to New Jersey, and a couple of them moved into D'Angelo's already crowded boxcar. One of the Mexicans spent hours each week reading a Spanish-language newspaper sent by mail from Texas. "I had gotten to think of a newspaper as something to start a fire with or to wrap objects in," D'Angelo later wrote, but now he decided to start reading again and also to learn English. At first he studied American newspapers, decoding words from their context or enlisting the aid of co-workers. "When I did learn a word and had discovered its meaning," he recalled, "I would write it in big letters on the mouldy walls of the box car."

Once he had command of basic English vocabulary, D'Angelo bought a secondhand dictionary for a quarter and began obsessively memorizing its contents. Word of the "queer Italian laborer" with the phenomenal English vocabulary soon spread throughout the rail complex. The American-born brakemen and office clerks would try to embarrass D'Angelo by challenging him to define obscure words, "but their efforts and mental ambushes were all useless." Soon these "high school lads" left him alone. By this point he had become a regular visitor to the nearby Edgewater Public Library, where he fell in love with the work of the Romantic poets Percy Shelley and John Keats. He also decided that his true destiny was to write. At first, he tried his hand at sketch comedy, hoping to sell his work to a vaudeville producer. But poetry seemed a far nobler calling, and sometime in 1919, feeling an insatiable urge "to cry out my hopes and dreams to this lovely unheeding world," D'Angelo burned the piles of comedy manuscripts that he had drafted, quit his job with the railroad, and moved to Brooklyn, determined to become a poet.

D'Angelo rented an unheated one-room apartment in "the slums along the Brooklyn waterfront," probably the neighborhood now known as Gowanus. "I wrote continuously for several weeks. It seemed to be a great relief to have all my time free for my beloved poetry." He began submitting his work to magazines, newspapers, and literary journals, but in every case his submissions were quickly returned, accompanied by pre-printed rejection slips. "Now I realized that I was merely a small drop in the sad whirlpool of literary aspirants . . . I was one, only one of the millions of literary beggars who clog the halls of literature, who stand like a sluggish crowd in the way of anyone wishing to forge ahead." He went back to day labor, finding a job "in a wild, insane shipyard" in Gowanus.

"But the Enchantress would not let me free." Abandoning poetry was "soul-torture. It was hard for me to combat the spell of beauty. It was hard for me to think that I could never succeed." Deciding that he had a better chance of being published if he personally delivered his poems to the city's literary editors, D'Angelo quit his waterfront job toward the end of the summer of 1920 and once again devoted himself entirely to poetry. He moved to an even less expensive apartment, "the cheapest hole that I could find in the slums of Brooklyn. It was a small room which had previously been a chicken coop and wood shack . . . The entrance to it was through a toilet which served ten families" as well as "unwelcome strangers and dirty passers-by." The toilet would often clog and overflow, causing its contents to run beneath his door "and stand in malodorous pools under my bug-infested bed." He cut his food budget, too, now buying only stale bread the bakeries would otherwise throw away and rotten bananas that vendors sold at a steep discount and assumed he was feeding to a pet.

Meanwhile, at his local branch of the Brooklyn Public Library, D'Angelo made a list of the names and addresses of every one of the two hundred or so newspapers and magazines published in the city. He vowed "to pay personal visits to all of them" until one agreed to publish his poems. "It took courage to continue writing in those months, but I kept it up. I forced myself to believe in eventual success." He devoted all of 1921 to this task — introducing himself as "Pascal" rather than Pasquale D'Angelo because he wanted to sound more assimilated — yet every editor he met rejected his work. His financial situation became so dire that he could no longer afford even stale bread and rotten bananas. Some nights he shivered so badly from the cold that he would walk three miles to the warm Flatbush Avenue depot of the Long Island Railroad because he knew he could stay there all night.[3]

Then, in January 1922, all of D'Angelo's hard work and perseverance suddenly paid off. Carl Van Doren, a professor of literature at Columbia University who also judged The Nation's annual poetry contest, later recalled that when he first read the impassioned plea that D'Angelo sent to accompany his submission, "it drowned the loud noises of Vesey Street" in lower Manhattan, where The Nation had its headquarters. "It seemed to me to widen the walls of my cramped office . . . Some incalculable chance had put the soul of a poet in the body of an Italian boy whose parents could not read or write and who came

At left, "Pascal" D'Angelo in 1922 at age twenty-eight, when literary critic Carl Van Doren discovered him. Publicity photos for the publication of *Son of Italy,* like the one from 1925 in which he is wielding a pickaxe, emphasized his humble beginnings.

into no heritage but the family tradition of hopeless labor." Van Doren did not award the prize to D'Angelo, but he arranged a meeting with the poet and wrote a short profile of him in *The Nation* in which he recounted D'Angelo's life story, accompanied by two of the young man's poems.[4]

The recognition from Van Doren was the break D'Angelo had long hoped for. Within days, Henry Seidel Canby, editor of the *New York Evening Post*'s literary review, published two more of D'Angelo's poems. *The Bookman* soon ran several others, *The Century Magazine* printed two more, and *The Nation* published another toward the end of the year. Several were included in *The Best Poems of 1922*. "The literary world began to take me up as a great curiosity and I was literally feasted, welcomed and stared at." Letters of congratulation poured in from across America. Those he found most gratifying "were the tributes of my fellow workers who recognized that at last, one of them had risen from the ditches and quicksands of toil to speak his heart to the upper world." Sweeter still to D'Angelo was the happiness of his parents, "who realized that after all I had not really gone astray, but had sought and attained a goal far from the deep-worn groove of peasant drudgery."[5]

Van Doren urged D'Angelo to turn some biographical fragments the poet had shared with him into a full-length autobiography. When Macmillan published *Son of Italy* at the end of 1924, with an introduction by the Columbia don, D'Angelo received even more publicity, as newspapers nationwide told the extraordinary story of his improbable rise from day laborer to literary sensation. "There's something very clean and strong and elemental about Pascal, something like the rough brown earth on whose bosom he was born," gushed an interviewer from the *Brooklyn Daily Eagle.* "He seems well on the way up the ladder of literary fame," observed the *Boston Herald.* "Young D'Angelo may never become one of our great poets, but after the miracles that his life has known thus far, almost anything in his future seems possible."[6]

Once D'Angelo burst on the literary scene and admirers heard about his "unspeakably shabby" living situation, they offered him improved housing, free of charge, so he could properly concentrate on his art. Others proposed to pay his way through college, and still others sent him checks so that he might live and eat better. Yet he rejected these offers and refused to cash the checks. "If people want to help me, let them pay more for good poetry," he insisted, referring to the nation's publishers. Given that he made only $5 or at most $10 for each published poem, he continued to live in an unheated room (albeit now in a far less shabby Brooklyn neighborhood, Prospect Heights) and subsist on stale bread and bananas. "He neglects his body's needs," concluded one interviewer, "while feeding those of his heart and mind."[7]

Given D'Angelo's experiences, it should come as no surprise that his poems are dark and bleak. Words like "torment," "darkness," "emptiness," "blackness," and "anguish" predominate:

> On the Calvary of thought I knelt, in torment of silence.
> The stars were like sparks struck from the busy forge of
>   vengeful night.
> The sky was like a woman in fury
> Disheveling her tresses of darkness over me.
> It seemed as if the whole universe were accusing me
> Of the anguish of Deity.[8]

Perhaps it was inevitable that those terms characterized the short and tragic remainder of his life. Within a few months of the publication of his memoir, D'Angelo disappeared completely from the New York literary scene. It is not clear whether he stopped sending his poetry to publishers or his submissions were rejected. At the time his autobiography appeared, he told an interviewer that he planned to begin work on several novels. Perhaps he became one in a long line of New Yorkers to suffer writer's block. We do know that short of cash, he was eventually forced to move back to Gowanus to what the *Herald Tribune* characterized as an "incredibly bare and cold shanty" at 98 16th Street. He stopped answering letters from his relatives, including a brother in New Jersey and a cousin in Philadelphia. They wondered if "the strain and deprivations of his struggling years had affected his mind." Indeed, his landlady reported that "he sometimes acted strangely." Among other oddities, he decided that despite his desperate circumstances, he had to teach himself Chinese. The onset of the Great Depression must have made things even more difficult. With Americans by the millions canceling their magazine subscriptions, editors had even less money to spend on poetry. Nonetheless, D'Angelo assured his landlady at the beginning of 1932 that some of his latest work would be published very soon.

This was obviously wishful thinking. By that point D'Angelo had pawned his typewriter and could not even afford paper. He continued to write, however, scrawling his poems in the margins of old newspapers, on the backs of calendars, and eventually on the walls of his apartment. He began suffering from severe stomachaches, but given his mental and financial condition that winter, he probably waited too long to seek medical care. By the time he made it to Kings County Hospital, it was too late. He died there on Sunday night March 13, 1932, at age thirty-eight, of acute appendicitis.[9]

Few outside Brooklyn took note of D'Angelo's death, but one journalist did: a young midwestern wire service editorial writer named Bruce Catton. Decades later he would become one of America's best-known authors for his books on the American Civil War. Catton found D'Angelo's death poignantly meaningful. In a piece titled "Why Poets Starve," which ran in several newspapers across the nation, the thirty-two-year-old Catton described the circumstances of D'Angelo's death and lamented that the zeal and commitment it took to devote one's life to poetry seemed incompatible with earning a decent income or even maintaining one's sanity. "So they go along," Catton observed, "writing poems, starving in chilly attics, and generally stubbing their toes over obstacles the rest of us never even see. They make the world brighter for the rest of us — but they pay for it with their hearts' blood." At least D'Angelo left us with *Son of Italy,* a work that Van Doren aptly called one of the "precious documents" of American literature.[10]

Pascal D'Angelo may not seem like the typical Italian immigrant, but in most ways he really was. Like the vast majority of Italian newcomers, he arrived in New York in the period between the turn of the twentieth century and the beginning of World War I. Like most, he spent many of his early years in America toiling on labor gangs at dangerous work in the countryside. Like the typical Italian immigrant, he eventually managed to free himself from dependence on unscrupulous labor contractors and find steady employment on his own through his network of *paesani* (immigrants from the same part of Italy). Finally, like most first-generation Italian Americans, he aspired to move beyond the "drudgery" of menial day labor, all the while recognizing that he might never succeed.

• • •

D'Angelo was one of several hundred thousand Italians who moved to New York in the late nineteenth and early twentieth centuries. The Italian-born population of New York, like that of its eastern European Jews, began to rise meteorically toward the end of the nineteenth century. From 12,000 Italian immigrants in 1880, the city's Italian-born community grew to 40,000 in 1890 and 145,000 in 1900, when the city's boundaries had expanded to include Brooklyn, Queens, and Staten Island. At the turn of the century, New York City was home to 30 percent of all Italian immigrants living in the United States.

The Italian rate of immigration grew even faster in the next decade and a half, so that by 1910 there were 340,000 Italian immigrants residing in New York's five boroughs and 390,000 in 1920. That last figure would have been far higher but for World War I, which almost completely cut off the flow of immigration from Europe. The Italian influx resumed briefly after the war until Congress enacted laws in 1921 and 1924 severely restricting the number of southern and eastern Europeans who could enter the United States. As a result, the Italian-born population of the city peaked just before the Great Depression. When it was next carefully measured, in 1930, the city had 440,250 Italian-born inhabitants, 25 percent of the nation's total.[11]

The first Italians to arrive in New York settled primarily in Five Points at the very southern ends of Baxter and Mulberry streets. But a larger Italian "colony" (the term New Yorkers of this era used to describe immigrant enclaves) soon developed along Macdougal, Sullivan, and Thompson streets just north and south of Houston Street in what New Yorkers now refer to as the West Village and SoHo. By 1890, an even more populous Italian enclave developed in East Harlem, running from Second Avenue to the East River and 109th to 115th streets. As Italian immigration increased, these Little Italys expanded their boundaries to accommodate the additional newcomers. The two lower Manhattan Italian colonies became contiguous, creating a huge swath of territory dominated by Italian Americans that covered central Manhattan from Five Points all the way up to Washington Square, including all of SoHo and the West Village. Uptown, the Little Italy of Harlem came to encompass everything east of Third Avenue from 104th to 119th Street.[12]

The housing occupied by these immigrants was very similar to that found on the Lower East Side. Some blocks primarily contained barracks-style tenements — especially in Five Points, where the housing stock was the oldest. On other streets, dumbbell tenements predominated, while on still others there was a fairly even mix of the two.

Yet a few things distinguished these Italian enclaves from one another. The tenements in Five Points were by far the most dilapidated; in 1890 journalist Jacob Riis called them "ramshackle structures . . . with every kind of abomination." The most infamous portion of the enclave was "Mulberry Bend," the block bounded by Mulberry, Bayard, Baxter, and Park (now Mosco) streets. In 1888 *Frank Leslie's* called Mulberry Bend "a seat of iniquity, poverty and dirt. It is one of the danger-spots of the town." A few months later, another journalist stated that "the most vicious, ignorant and degraded of all the immigrants who come to our shores are the Italian inhabitants of Mulberry Bend and the surrounding region of tenements." Riis called Mulberry Bend "a vast human pigsty."[13]

Was Mulberry Bend really that bad? Riis admitted that the Bend was "ordinary enough to look at from the street," but behind those brick walls, he insisted, lay three acres "built over with rotten structures that harbored the very dregs of humanity . . . Every foot of it reeked with incest and murder. Bandits' Roost, Bottle Alley, were names synonymous with robbery and red-handed outrage." Others argued that the press exaggerated the Bend's true conditions. Journalist Charlotte Adams found that while some apartments on Baxter Street were "neglected and squalid; others were clean and picturesque, with bright patchwork counterpanes on the beds, rows of gay plates on shelves against the walls, mantels and shelves fringed with colored paper, red and blue prints of the saints against the white plaster, and a big nosegay of lilacs on the dresser among the earthen pots."[14]

One aspect of Mulberry Bend that *was* truly awful was the death rate, especially for children. Youngsters living in the Bend's cramped, dirty tenements became especially susceptible to such contagious deadly diseases as tuberculosis, measles, and diphtheria. At 61 Mulberry Street, eight children under the age of five died in 1882. Next door at 59½ Mulberry, eleven small children perished that same year. Of the nine children under age five who lived in that building at the start of 1888, only four were still alive at the end of the year. These were extreme cases, yet the overall death rate in Mulberry Bend was about 50 percent higher than the citywide average, and for children under age five it was about three times the citywide rate.[15]

Riis's iconic photograph of "Bandit's Roost," an alleyway in Mulberry Bend, helped insure that the Bend's infamy would live on for centuries. In Riis's image, the pavement is damp and dotted with puddles. Overflowing garbage barrels are visible on the left, while clotheslines heavy with the day's wash filter the afternoon sunlight. Tall buildings, the rear tenements of 57 and 59 Mulberry Street, loom on either side. The people in the photo add to the sense of foreboding. In the right foreground stands a neatly dressed young man in a bowler hat who would have been recognized by contemporaries as a menacing gang member. Just behind him is an older bearded figure holding a double-barreled shotgun. Leaning out a window above these two toughs is one of Riis's omni-

Jacob Riis's photograph of Bandit's Roost (an alleyway between 57 and 59 Mulberry Street) helped establish Mulberry Bend's reputation as one of the most decrepit and dangerous blocks of tenements ever inhabited by New York immigrants.

present "old hags." Stairs leading to the alley's numerous "stale beer dives" are visible as well. Riis clearly went to great lengths to pose this variety of Mulberry Bend residents for a single photo. Nonetheless, his image of Bandit's Roost created a sense of menace and dread that is nearly as palpable today as it was in 1888 when the Danish immigrant first exhibited it.[16]

The overwhelming majority of reporting on Italian immigrants' tenements focused on Mulberry Bend and its vicinity, even though only a small minority of the city's Italian immigrants lived there. We have far fewer descriptions of the tenements in New York's other Italian enclaves. We do know that the Italians' West Village and SoHo housing, built originally for middle-class native-born New Yorkers or relatively well-to-do Irish immigrants, should have been better than that near Mulberry Bend, especially as one moved north toward Washington Square, since these tenements tended to be newer and less run-down.

By contrast, the Italian enclave around Houston Street was within the city's light manufacturing district. On many of these blocks, especially in the western portion of the neighborhood, tenements alternated with large commercial loft spaces. In the late twentieth century, apartments on these blocks became highly prized because of the lofts' high ceilings and spacious floor plans. But in the earliest decades of the century, the factories located in these lofts created noise and air pollution that made life for the neighborhood's residents especially uncomfortable, in particular for those immigrants who had come to New York from the bucolic Italian countryside. Asked if she liked New York, one Italian immigrant said: "Not much, not much. Good money, good people, but my country — my country — good air, much air, nice air down Italy." In New York, there was "good money, but no good air."[17]

Another disadvantage of the SoHo–West Village enclave was the terrible overcrowding. Rather than take in a boarder or two as the Irish had done to help make ends meet, Italians tended to share their apartments with an entire second family. In the district's typical three-room apartments, one family might occupy one room while the boarding family slept in the second. The third room — the kitchen — would be used by both. In some three- and four-room apartments, three families might share the space. Riis found a tenement on Elizabeth Street in which forty-three families inhabited sixteen apartments. Settlement house worker Lillian Betts estimated that fifty-six Italian families lived in the twenty-eight apartments in the large SoHo tenement she called home.[18]

Because there are so few contemporary descriptions, one of our best sources for understanding conditions in these tenements is the pathbreaking documentary photography of Lewis Hine. Trained as a sociologist before he decided to pursue a career as a photographer, the Wisconsin native brought a social scientist's sensibility to his work. Beginning in 1908, when he became the staff photographer for the National Child Labor Committee, Hine photographed conditions in hundreds of New York tenement apartments, including many in the Italian enclave between Canal Street and Washington Square. "High up on the top floor of a rickety tenement" at 214 Elizabeth Street, for example, Hine found an Italian-born mother and her two children living in one "tiny" room where they spent their days and evenings "finishing garments." They barely had room to work, squeezed in between the stove, the dresser, and the bed. Hine likewise found the Ceru family inhabiting a "dirty attic" in the rear tenement

Lewis Hine's photo of Italian immigrants in their one-room apartment at 214 Elizabeth Street finishing garments while crammed between their stove, dresser, and bed epitomizes the overcrowded conditions in which many of them lived.

at 143 Thompson Street in similar circumstances. A note he wrote on a caption to one photo could have been applied to almost any of them: "Photograph very inadequately represents congestion."[19]

Census reports substantiated Hine's observations. They show that portions of this Italian enclave were just as crowded as the most congested sections of the Lower East Side. In 1905 the Italian-dominated block bounded by Houston, Mott, Prince, and Elizabeth streets housed 1,107 people per acre, while the one bounded by Jones, Cornelia, West 4th, and Bleecker held 975 inhabitants per acre. The most crowded Italian block in the city, however, was that immediately north of Mulberry Bend: in 1905 it housed 1,125 inhabitants per acre. Only eleven blocks in Manhattan, all on the Lower East Side, crammed more residents into each acre.[20]

New York's third Italian enclave, in East Harlem, was initially far less congested than the others. In 1900, many lots in the area were still vacant. By 1910, however, the neighborhood overflowed with tenements, built in part with Italian immigrant labor. Barracks-style tenements with windowless bedrooms predominated here. In the worst parts of the neighborhood, wrote a reporter from the *Times*, "the streets are dirty and littered with refuse and decayed fruits and vegetables thrown from windows and discarded by vendors, while the houses are foul smelling and unfit for habitation." Although the streets and common areas might be dirty or dilapidated, through painstaking effort tenement homemakers often kept the grime of the outside world at bay. A social worker visiting a four-room apartment in East Harlem admitted that despite the work the inhabitants did inside the flat processing feathers, the apartment was "clean as a pin." Still, when assessing the tenement house problem in New York, most observers concluded that "the Italian quarters are the worst."[21]

Even though Italian Harlem's tenements had been built relatively recently, developers did not provide tenants with the modern amenities that had become standard in other parts of town. As late as 1935, 67 percent of tenants in the most heavily Italian portion of East Harlem had no access to a tub or shower, and 83 percent of residents still got their only heat from their kitchen stoves; 55 percent still had to go outside to relieve themselves. The "unforgettable toilets" in the tenement yards were insufficient in number and poorly maintained, prompting the immigrants to complain of the "urine-draft of air that moves up the stairs" of their buildings.[22]

Even those East Harlem Italians who had the luxury of indoor toilets and running water in the hallway found their tenements depressing and demoralizing. Leonard Covello, who emigrated as a boy with his parents from Basilicata and eventually became a prominent New York City educator, described his first American home in his memoirs:

This photograph of First Avenue, the main thoroughfare of Harlem's Little Italy, was taken near the corner of East 115th Street early in the twentieth century. The two huge gas storage tanks of the Consolidated Gas Company, visible in the distance, sat between 110th and 111th streets and stretched from First Avenue toward Second.

The sunlight and fresh air of our mountain home in Lucania were replaced by four walls and people over and under and on all sides of us, until it seemed that humanity from all corners of the world had congregated in this section of New York City known as East Harlem. The cobbled streets. The endless, monotonous rows of tenement buildings that shut out the sky . . . The smell of the river at ebb tide. The moaning of fog horns. The clanging of bells and the screeching of sirens as a fire broke out somewhere in the neighborhood. Dank hallways.

His parents were homesick for Italy.[23]

Running water, something that had been unattainable for most of these immigrants back in Italy, was to many Italians insufficient compensation for the crowding, heat, noise, and stench of tenement living. Edward Corsi, who also immigrated as a child and later went on to become commissioner of immigration at Ellis Island, recalled in his autobiography that his wistful mother "spent her days, and the waking hours of the nights, sitting at that one outside window staring up at the little patch of sky above the tenements. She was never happy here and, though she tried, could not adjust herself to the poverty and despair in which we had to live."[24]

Covello's and Corsi's mothers, like many of the immigrants in these Italian neighborhoods, led a fairly isolated existence. Children, older men, and married women rarely left their enclaves. A social worker in the first years of the twentieth century found many Italian immigrants "who had never crossed to the east side of the Bowery, never seen Broadway, nor had ever been north of Houston street." When she arrived in New York, Marie Concistre later remembered: "I did not see any reason for learning English. I didn't need it. Everywhere I lived, or worked, or fooled around there were only Italians . . . I had to learn some Sicilian, though." The rest of the city seemed so exotic to these immigrants that, having ventured a few blocks outside the confines of their neighborhood, upon their return they would tell their friends, "I have been down to America today."[25]

Like the Irish, Germans, and east European Jews, Italian immigrants did not settle haphazardly across the city or even within the Italian enclaves themselves. "In this country immigrants of the same town stick together like a swarm of bees from the same hive," D'Angelo wrote in his memoir. One's Italian region of birth seemed especially consequential. "The Sicilians are strongly fortified in Elizabeth Street," reported the *Times* in 1910. "A colony of Neapolitans and Calabrians are in Mulberry Street, and Genoese are around Five Points. The northern Italians are not found there, their nearest colony being in the neighborhood of Bleecker Street, west of Broadway."[26]

Such segregation, however, was far from absolute. The vast majority of New York's Italian immigrants came from just two of Italy's regions — Sicily and Campania (the district containing Naples). Like the Irish from Cork and the Jews from Russia, the Italians from these two regions were so numerous that they lived in every Italian enclave and on every block. There were undoubtedly concentrations of Italians from certain regions or even certain towns on certain blocks, but not to the extent imagined by contemporaries.[27]

The defining feature of life for New York's Italian immigrants was work, that "endless, continuous toil" recounted by D'Angelo. Upon arrival in the city, the prototypical Italian immigrant found employment, as D'Angelo had, as a day laborer. Already by the mid-1890s, Italians accounted for three-quarters of all New York construction workers and 90 percent of the day laborers employed by the city. New York's Italian laborers worked primarily on construction sites or public works projects. Italian immigrants, for example, provided most of the pick and shovel work necessary to excavate the city's subway tunnels. They also

Italian day laborers on Sixth Avenue, photographed in 1910 by Lewis Hine.

became the predominant source of longshoremen on the docks in Manhattan, Brooklyn, and Staten Island. Italian laborers did the same backbreaking and dangerous hauling and excavating that the Irish had once dominated. "We can't get along without the Italians," commented one police officer in 1895. "We want somebody to do the dirty work; the Irish are not doing it any longer."[28]

Like D'Angelo, most new arrivals found employment through a labor broker known as a *padrone*. The *padroni* were notorious for charging exorbitant fees, often amounting to one or even two weeks' pay. The broker would deduct this fee from a worker's first pay envelopes, meaning that a newcomer might not receive a dime in wages for quite some time, or be given only enough to buy food to keep him alive until he could pay off his debt. *Padroni* were infamous for firing workers without cause in order to generate a new round of fees. Some *padroni* actually supervised their charges at the work site. A more established broker, however, would hire foremen to manage his laborers in the field so that he could oversee the recruitment of more workers, typically from an office on Mulberry Street. As *Harper's Weekly* commented in 1890, "The moment an Italian arrives in New York — that is, one of humble means and without friends in the city — he wends his way to Mulberry Street" to the office of a *padrone* to look for his first American job.[29]

A *padrone* might also force an Italian laborer into debt by taking him to some far-off work site and then telling him he could not leave until he paid off the transportation costs, which could be quite substantial. One such laborer told the anarchist journalist Saverio Merlino his harrowing tale:

> We started from New York on November 3, 1891, under the guidance of two bosses. We had been told we should go to Connecticut to work on a railroad and earn one dollar and seventy-five cents per day. We were taken, instead, to South Carolina . . . to the "Tom Tom" sulphate mines [near Charleston]. The railroad fare was eight dollars and eighty-five cents; this sum, as well as the price of our tools, nearly three dollars, we owed the bosses. We were received by an armed guard, which kept constant watch over us, accompanying us every morning from the barracks to the mines and at night again from the work to our shanty . . . Part of our pay went toward the extinction of our debt; the rest was spent for as much food as we could get at the "pluck-me" store. We got only so much as would keep us from starvation. Things cost us more than twice or three times their regular price. Our daily fare was coffee and bread for breakfast, rice with lard or soup at dinner-time, and cheese or sausage for supper. Yet we were not able to pay off our debt; so after a while we were given only bread, and with this only to sustain us we had to go through our daily work. By and by we became exhausted, and some of us got sick. Then we decided to try, at the risk of our lives, to escape. Some of us ran away, eluding the guards. After a run of an hour I was exhausted and decided to stay for the night in the woods. We were, however, soon surprised by the appearance of the bosses and two guards. They thrust guns in our faces and ordered us to return to work or they would shoot us down. We answered that we would rather die than resume our former life in the mine . . . We went before a judge, who was sitting in a bar-room. The judge asked if there was any written contract, and when he heard that there wasn't, said he would let us go free. But the bosses, the policemen, and the judge then held a short consultation, and the result was that the bosses paid some money (I believe it was forty-five dollars), the policemen put the manacles on our wrists, and we were marched off. At last, on April 1, we were all dismissed on account of the hot weather. [Sulfate mining was such hard work it was done only in the cooler half of the year.] My comrades took the train for New York. I had only one dollar, and with this, not knowing either the country or the language, I had to walk to New York. After forty-two days I arrived in the city utterly exhausted.

Although they were aware of the pitfalls of traveling to a distant work site and thereby incurring a debt, as winter approached and jobs became scarce in and around New York, many Italian laborers felt they had no choice but to take the risk.[30]

Many Italian immigrants who had spent the warmer months of the year working in labor gangs all around the United States would spend the winter in one of New York City's Italian enclaves. "They come in from the country, the railroad and other work having stopped," reported a labor journal in 1884. "Some of them find odd jobs, but the majority live on their scanty earnings — a piece of bread and an onion for breakfast, about the same for dinner, and maccaroni for supper." During the winter, Italian immigrants from the South and West "fill up the streets of New York," wrote an Italian immigrant in 1899, "where the young polish shoes and the adults are engaged in work refused by workers of other nationalities — emptying garbage from barges into the sea, cleaning sewage — or they go around with a sack on their shoulders rummaging for bones" to sell to fat renderers or soap makers. New York's Italian neighborhoods burst at the seams each winter as permanent residents made room in their apartments for out-of-work friends and relatives, while commercial boardinghouses filled to overflowing with the temporary winter residents.[31]

Some Italian day laborers opted to forgo such conditions and instead spend the winter back in Italy, where food and lodging were much less expensive. Italians were the first major New York immigrant group (but by no means the last) to engage in a seasonal "return migration." The U.S. government began tallying the phenomenon in the decade before World War I, and found that the number of Italians leaving the United States each autumn was sometimes almost as high as the number who had arrived earlier that year. Many men who left New York for Italy as winter approached would return the following spring with an Italian bride.[32]

Even though more Italians worked as day laborers than in any other occupation, they never constituted a majority of the Italian immigrant workforce in New York City. In 1900, about one in three employed Italian-born male adults was a laborer or longshoreman (a job with essentially the same requirements and pay as day labor but done on the waterfront); by 1920, the proportion had fallen to around one in five. Still, in the latter year there were roughly 40,000 Italian-born laborers residing in New York out of an Italian male workforce of about 180,000.

While the remaining Italian immigrant men worked in hundreds of different occupations, they tended to concentrate in a handful of fields. Italians, for example, came to dominate the barber's trade in New York. There were about ten thousand Italian barbers in the city in 1920, accounting for two-thirds of New York's total. Next most numerous were tailors; some nine thousand Italian immigrants worked at this trade in 1920. But given the huge scale of the gar-

ment industry, Italians made up only 20 percent of the city's male needleworkers. Italians also dominated shoemaking, with the city's six thousand Italian
shoemakers in 1920 constituting about half that workforce.[33]

Italian immigrants were also especially drawn to retailing. They were ten
times more likely than native-born New Yorkers to work in the streets as peddlers, and twice as likely to operate brick-and-mortar retail shops. Italian retailers specialized in food sales. Many were grocers, and an even larger number sold just fruits and vegetables. "The fruit trade is in the hands of Italians in
all its branches," reported *Harper's New Monthly Magazine* in 1881, "from the
Broadway shop with its inclined plane of glowing color, to the stand at a street
corner." Even the poorest Italian immigrants had impeccably high standards
when it came to produce, and Italian greengrocers did not disappoint their
demanding customers. "What strikes one first is the beauty and variety of the
vegetables and fruits sold there in what is supposed to be one of the poorest
quarters," observed Hungarian immigrant journalist Konrad Bercovici at the
outdoor produce market on Mulberry Street. "Peaches with blooms on, and the

The produce market on Mulberry Street,
looking north toward Canal, photographed in about 1900.

softest and the most luscious plums, the largest apples and most beautiful pears, the cleanest salads, are sorted and handled in the most expert and delicate way." Much of this produce, Bercovici noted, including "the most unusual vegetable leaves and roots," was grown in and around New York by Italian-born farmers expressly for fussy Italian immigrants.[34]

While Italian men worked in dozens of different occupations, Italian women concentrated overwhelmingly in just two: garment work and home manufacturing. About two-thirds of Italian immigrant women employed outside the home in 1920 worked in garment factories. Italian women initially had trouble breaking into this business. Some gave Jewish-sounding names to prospective employers in order to snag a position. Augusta Solamoni, for example, introduced herself as Gussie Solomon when she applied for garment factory work. Filomena Macari did not have to lie about her ethnicity to get her first garment industry job, but as one of her descendants later recalled, her employer advised her "not to tell anyone she was Italian because everyone in the shop was Jewish and they didn't want other groups there." Jews feared (with some justification) that employers had begun hiring Italians expressly to drive down the garment workers' already pitiful wages. But once the two groups came to know each other, and especially once they had walked off the job on strike together, Italian and Jewish women learned to work with each other harmoniously.[35]

Italian women found conditions in New York's garment sweatshops as brutal as did their Jewish co-workers. "I was so unhappy to stay there all day," recalled Agnes Santucci years later. "The forelady used to be back and forth, back and forth, look this way, look the other way. Do your work, do your work." According to Grace Grimaldi, "you couldn't talk . . . You couldn't even go to the bathroom. We were treated like slaves." Her employers, the Scher brothers, "used to pick people from the boat and use them for slavery. But people had to earn. So when you want to earn your own, you take anything."[36]

The Italian proportion of workers in the garment industry grew steadily in the first decades of the twentieth century. East European Jewish women outnumbered Italians five to two in the New York garment industry labor force in 1900, but by only three to two in 1920, when about 22,000 Italian-born women worked in the field. As one Lower East Sider put it, "Amid garlic and wine and Yiddish and Italian the garment industry work force became a huge sausage."[37]

It is much harder to pin down the number of Italian immigrant women who did "home work." In 1892, New York State made it illegal to do work inside tenement apartments without a license, and either because they feared they would be turned down or because they did not want to be subject to the accompanying inspections, few Italian home workers applied for one. In 1902, the

New York City Bureau of Vital Statistics estimated the number of New Yorkers working for pay at home to be somewhere between 25,000 and 30,000. At that point, even though they made up only 11 percent of the city's immigrant population, Italians did about 60 percent of the city's home work.[38]

The variety of work done at home was nearly endless. Italian women folded boxes, shelled nuts, made and packaged chocolate cigarettes, plaited hat straw, pinned buttons to cards, manufactured children's toys, rolled the paper that would later be stuffed with tobacco to make cigarettes, and assembled purses and handbags. They even "willowed" ostrich plumes, a term that describes the process by which ostrich feathers were made more fluffy and attractive by using thread to tie the hundreds of fronds on each plume into groups of three. Nonetheless, about 80 percent of Italian home workers in New York did one of just two things — garment finishing or artificial flower making. Home work also varied somewhat by neighborhood. In lower Manhattan east of Broadway, garment work predominated because the Italians in that enclave lived near the garment factories. In the West Village, artificial flower making was more common. In Harlem, feather pluming was the home work most widely available in the decade before World War I, when ostrich feathers became all the rage. "Everybody," said an immigrant there, "all a people, they willow the plumes."[39]

The Bureau of Vital Statistics estimated that six-sevenths of all New York home work involved garment finishing. Even after a coat or pair of pants had been sewn by machine in a sweatshop, it usually required "finishing," whether pulling loose threads, sewing on buttons, or making small repairs. It could also involve adding ribbons, embroidery, or lacework to women's clothing, sewing beads on shoes or slippers, or making garters.

Home work was controversial because the immigrants who engaged in it almost always used their children to assist with the work. Youngsters who went to school all day might work until eight, nine, or ten at night helping their mothers complete their tasks on time. If a deadline was particularly tight, as was often the case in the fast-moving and seasonal world of fashion, children might be kept home from school so they could work all day. One young girl named Giovanna, for example, awoke each morning at five o'clock so she could help her mother with her home work task for four hours before leaving for school. When she got home, she went right back to work. "I have no time to play. I must work my feathers. At 10 o'clock I go to bed."[40]

Apart from garment finishing, the most prevalent line of home employment was artificial flower making. In an era before fresh flowers were available year round, there was a huge demand for artificial flowers that middle- and upper-class Americans could display in their homes when fresh blooms were not available. Most of these flowers were assembled by Italian immigrants and their

The Malatesta family making artificial flowers in their Sullivan Street tenement apartment in the West Village around 1908.

children. Immigrants picked up the machine-made stems, leaves, and petals from the manufacturer or wholesaler, brought them back to their tenement, and gathered the kids around the kitchen table to assist in assembling them. For each gross of 144 flowers the family managed to complete, they might receive as much as eight or as little as three and one-half cents. Despite the miserly pay, "so general is the custom of home work in this district [the Italian enclave in Manhattan below 14th Street] that as one mounts the stairs in any one of these houses one finds on every floor, and in almost every apartment, families of flower-makers."[41]

One such family was the Malatestas from Genoa. In about 1908, Hine found the whole family, father Angelo, mother Agostina, fourteen-year-old Frank, eleven-year-old John, and four-year-old Lizzie, around their kitchen table at 122 Sullivan Street making flowers. Mr. Malatesta helped because he was too sick to work at day labor. Even little Lizzie was not too young to work; she separated the petals, which often came from the manufacturer stuck together. They earned six cents per gross, and working late into the night could assemble ten to twelve gross per day. Somehow the Malatestas survived on that pittance. Most families used the money from flower making to supplement the income of the household's main breadwinner. Three blocks from the Malatestas, for example, Hine found a Mrs. Mortaria and her four children — aged three to fourteen — working on flowers until 10:00 p.m., even though Mr. Mortaria was steadily employed as a soap maker earning $3 per day.[42]

While Italian girls would typically work only inside the home, boys could be

Although most of New York's newsboys in the decades before World War I were Italians, the boys depicted in this photograph are Greek immigrants (or the American-born children of immigrants). Greek immigrants would become particularly visible New Yorkers in the mid-twentieth century through the restaurant industry, yet in only one census year — 1960 — have Greeks made it onto the list of the city's top-ten immigrant groups.

sent out to earn money on the streets. By the 1890s, Italian American boys constituted the overwhelming majority of both newsboys and bootblacks. Thousands of Italian boys roamed the streets hawking one of the city's dozen daily papers. Some got up before dawn to begin selling one of the morning broadsheets, went to school or took a midday nap, and then went back to work selling one of the evening papers. In 1894 a survey found that fully 98 percent of the city's shoeshine boys were Italian Americans. The proportion hawking newspapers could not have been much lower.[43]

One of the reasons why Italian immigrants put so many of their family members to work was to be able to send remittances to loved ones back in Italy. Some did so in order to pay the living expenses of aged or impoverished parents or to help them settle their debts. Others hoped to pay the transatlantic passage of siblings, spouses, and parents. Still others wired donations to the

Roman Catholic churches they had once attended in Italy and to which they still felt a deep attachment. Remittances might be earmarked for the construction of a new family home, either for parents or in some cases for the immigrants themselves, who planned to return to Italy and live in the new home once they had earned enough money in America to finance its completion. Whatever their motivation, the amount of money the immigrants sent to Italy was truly staggering. From 1906 to 1914, Italian immigrants transferred an average of about 846 million lire per year to Italy (equal to about $161 million at the time, and about $4 billion per year in 2015).[44]

That struggling Italian immigrants would send some of their precious savings to support churches thousands of miles away in Italy reflects how important a role the Roman Catholic Church played in their lives. Yet Italian Americans found it difficult to reestablish their religious practices in the United States, more so than other immigrant groups of the period. East European Jews might object to the "Reform" or "Conservative" Judaism practiced by the German Jews who arrived before them, but they could easily start their own congregations in order to maintain the precise liturgical practices they had grown accustomed to in their particular portion of the Pale. When Polish Jews began arriving in the city in the post–Civil War years and did not like the services in German American synagogues, they created their own. When the Russians followed and objected to Polish practices, they organized still more synagogues. There was no centralized Jewish authority to prevent them from doing so. It also took very little money to start a congregation. Like-minded Jews would often pool their resources to rent a tenement apartment in which to operate their new synagogue. By 1900, hundreds of these tenement synagogues dotted the Lower East Side. Not until these congregations had been operating in the city for many years, and included members who had been in New York long enough to accumulate substantial savings, did they begin to construct free-standing synagogue buildings.[45]

The Roman Catholic Church, in contrast, insisted that its adherents attend services at the existing churches in the parishes in which they settled. Rather than being pleased with the huge new infusion of Italian Catholics into its churches, the Irish American leadership of the Catholic Church in New York expressed disdain for these new parishioners. "Ignorance of their religion and a depth of vice little known to us yet, are their prominent characteristics," wrote one American bishop to another about the Italian newcomers. They did not know the Apostles' Creed or the other basic "elementary truths of religion, such as the Trinity, the Incarnation, and the Redemption." Italians instead focused their religious energies on what the Irish considered frivolities, such as "pilgrimages, shrines, miraculous pictures and images," and feasts in honor of their hometown patron saints. "Nowhere among other Catholic groups in our midst," the prelates complained, "is there such crass and listless ignorance of the faith as among the Italian immigrants."[46]

The parish priests who worked directly with the Italians might have been expected to develop familiarity and sympathy for the newcomers, but this was often not the case. In fact, most New York parish priests banned the Italian immigrants from attending mass with the rest of the congregation, requiring the Italians (and *only* the Italians) to celebrate mass in their church basements. Even at the Church of Our Lady of Mount Carmel in East Harlem, where more than 90 percent of the parishioners were Italian, the newcomers were forced into an overcrowded basement chapel while a tiny handful of Irish and German Americans celebrated mass in the three-quarters-empty main sanctuary. Archbishop Michael Corrigan justified the subterranean exile on the grounds that "these poor Italians are not extraordinarily clean, so the [other parishioners] don't want them in the upper church, otherwise they will go elsewhere, and then farewell to the income" they contributed each week to the collection plate. Responding to the charge that the Italians must have found their banishment insulting, an Irish American lay church leader insisted that "the Italians as a body are not humiliated by humiliation."[47]

In fact, the Italians did find such treatment humiliating. They complained bitterly to the city's small contingent of Italian-born priests, who primarily served as assistants to the Irish American pastors who ran most of the city's parishes. The Italian priests wrote letters to Rome complaining of the ill-treatment their countrymen received at the hands of the Irish and asking the Vatican to intervene.

Rather than accept second-class status at their local parish churches, some Italians celebrated mass at the Church of St. Anthony of Padua on Sullivan Street, just south of Houston. The city's Irish Catholic leaders had authorized the Franciscan order to set up this parish in 1866 specifically to minister to the needs of Italian immigrants. Vatican officials wrote to New York's Catholic leaders suggesting that more such "national parishes" be created for the Italians, but the church's Irish American leaders balked. They insisted that New York was so heterogeneous that if they established national parishes for the Italians, they would have to do so for the Germans, the Hungarians, the French, and so forth, until the Catholic Church would no longer be "catholic" at all.

Yet with the city's Italian-born population increasing exponentially, Catholic leaders eventually came to the conclusion that they had to make some accommodations. They reluctantly lifted the ban on street processions for the Italians' patron saints. In 1891 they created new Italian parishes, such as the Church of Our Lady of Loreto, established in a tenement storefront on Elizabeth Street near Houston; the Church of the Most Precious Blood on Baxter Street; and in 1892 the Church of Our Lady of Pompei (its original spelling) on Bleecker Street, just east of Sixth Avenue. Beginning in 1901, Catholic leaders went a step further and transferred a few existing parishes, such as the Church of the Transfiguration on Mott Street, to Italian control. Yet at the most important church to New York's Italian Catholics, Our Lady of Mount Carmel in East Harlem, they were required to attend mass in the basement until 1919.[48]

While Italians fought for equal treatment in the Catholic churches of New York, another kind of fight was going on within the Italian community itself. This was a struggle between the Italian immigrants and their children. As was the case with immigrant groups before and since, the Italian immigrants' children — teenagers in particular — desperately wanted to fit in with their "American" peers. Italian American teenagers, however, believed that their parents' Old World manners and customs made such efforts all but impossible.

Some of these intra-family battles involved the kinds of things that parents and children of all backgrounds fight about — such as clothes, friends, and dating. Others were unique to the immigrants and their children. "Lunch at elementary school was a difficult problem for me," one of Leonard Covello's high school students recounted. Week after week, year after year, New York's public school teachers told their Italian students that the diet their parents fed them was unhealthy and reflected their parents' backward customs. As a result, this student, like thousands of others, sought desperately to avoid eating the embarrassing lunch his mother had packed for him. "My mother gave me each day an Italian sandwich, that is half a loaf of French bread filled with fried peppers and onions, or with one half dipped into oil and some minced garlic on it. Such a sandwich would certainly ruin my reputation; I could not take it to school." In order to evade this fate, the student "either stole some money from home" or took it from what he earned shining shoes on Saturdays and Sundays. "With this money I would buy the same stuff that non-Italian boys were eating."

Such battles eventually found their way into the Italians' homes as well. The young Italian Americans who refused to eat traditional Italian foods at school soon worked up the nerve to demand "American" food for breakfast and dinner, too. They might also refuse to speak Italian or try to assimilate in other ways that infuriated their parents. When mothers and fathers objected, their children retorted that their parents simply did not understand. Covello recalled that when he was a teenager, his mother found such backtalk exasperating: "I don't understand. I don't understand. What is there to understand? Now that you have become Americanized you understand everything and I understand nothing." Raising teenagers is trying under any circumstances, but even more so for immigrants whose children could cite their better understanding of American norms and values and the authority of their teachers to justify their rebelliousness. After the umpteenth fight with their children over such issues, many immigrant parents must have wished they had never moved to America.[49]

Some Italian immigrants did, in fact, choose to return permanently to Italy. It is impossible to ascertain how many, but the returnees were numerous enough that government officials and the press commented on their political, economic, and even cultural impact on Italy. There were certainly thousands who made the same decision as Pascal D'Angelo's father and Leonard Covello's mother and moved back to Italy.[50]

A much more common response to dissatisfaction with life in their Manhattan neighborhoods was to move to the city's outer boroughs. In 1910, 59 percent of New York's Italian immigrants lived in Manhattan. By 1920, that number had fallen to 47 percent, and in 1930 it had plummeted to just 27 percent. The primary destination for them, as it was for the Jews, was Brooklyn. In 1930, 193,000 Italian immigrants lived in Brooklyn versus only 118,000 in Manhattan. By that point, 68,000 Italians had settled in the Bronx, 50,000 in Queens, and 11,000 on Staten Island. Italian immigrants were especially populous in the waterfront neighborhoods of Brooklyn such as Gowanus, Gravesend, Red Hook, Sunset Park, and Williamsburg, but they could also be found in large numbers in Bensonhurst, Borough Park, Dyker Heights, and the eastern edge of Bedford-Stuyvesant. In Queens, the Italian neighborhood of choice was Corona, while in the Bronx, Italians concentrated immediately south of Fordham University in the streets that radiated out from Arthur Avenue. In these far-flung neighborhoods, Italians made it a priority to find houses whose backyards could be transformed into gardens. The immigrants' subsequent harvests of tomatoes, zucchini, and other vegetables made life in New York much more tolerable. Thousands of others left the city for more distant American locales. The Malatestas photographed by Hine making flowers, for example, moved to Bridgeport, Connecticut, and became greengrocers.[51]

Many Italian immigrants began to feel far more at home in America once they left the congestion of their overcrowded Manhattan tenements for the relative fresh air and breathing space of Brooklyn and the Bronx. But that was small comfort for the 225,000 who still lived in Manhattan in 1910, working in the borough's sweltering sweatshops and residing in its teeming tenements. From 1890 to 1914, reformers, both immigrant and native-born, started movements aimed at ameliorating the problems that had driven many immigrants from Manhattan in the first place. Their successes, and even their setbacks, changed the lives of thousands of immigrants and also the way native-born New Yorkers perceived their foreign-born neighbors.

18

REFORM

IF NEW YORKERS recognize the name Jacob Riis today, it is probably because they have been to Jacob Riis Park, a beach in the Rockaways, a part of Queens most commonly reached by crossing a causeway from southeast Brooklyn. Or they may know the Jacob Riis Houses, a nineteen-building public housing complex that covers the northeast corner of the Lower East Side between 6th and 13th streets from Avenue D to the East River.

But 125 years ago, Jacob Riis was a household name. First as a newly arrived immigrant from Denmark, and then fifteen years later as a crime reporter for the *New York Tribune*, Riis became intimately familiar with the dreadful conditions that the newest New Yorkers faced both at work and in their tenement homes in Five Points, in Hell's Kitchen, in the tenements near the East River under the Brooklyn Bridge in the old Fourth Ward, and on the Lower East Side. Riis was not content merely to chronicle conditions in these neighborhoods. He wanted to inspire Americans to fix them. When his writings did not succeed, he almost single-handedly invented photojournalism in the hope that the camera could move people to act when the pen alone could not. His masterpiece, *How the Other Half Lives*, is widely considered one of a handful of "books that changed history." It helped inaugurate a flurry of urban reform movements that defined the Progressive Era, the period from about 1900 to 1917 when politicians from all parties generally agreed that something had to be done to ameliorate the living and working conditions of the poorest Americans, many of whom were immigrants.[1]

In June 1870, when twenty-one-year-old Jacob Riis arrived in New York, he seemed an unlikely candidate to revolutionize journalism. Trained as a carpenter, Riis had left the small town of Ribe, Denmark, not because of poverty or persecution but on account of a broken heart. When the object of his affection, sixteen-year-old Elisabeth Gortz, rejected his offer of marriage at her home, Riis "kissed her hands and went out," he recalled years later, "my eyes brimming over with tears, feeling that there was nothing in all the wide world for me any more, and that the farther I went from her the better. So it was settled that I should go to America."

Unlike some immigrants, who read guidebooks and prepared thoroughly for their new lives in the United States, the heartbroken Riis arrived in New York friendless and totally unprepared. Believing that America was wild and dangerous, Riis spent half his life savings on the largest pistol he could find, which he wore strapped to his waist as he strode up Broadway. A policeman, "seeing that I was very green," suggested that Riis leave it at home. Unable to find work in New York, Riis visited the employment office at Castle Garden and signed on for a job at a new ironworks in western Pennsylvania, where he used his carpenter's skills to construct huts for the company's employees.[2]

At this point in his life, Riis never stuck with one employer for very long, spending the summer working at a variety of jobs in Pennsylvania, New Jersey, New York City, and its northern suburbs. He remained obsessed with Elisabeth. Several times he quit good jobs and depleted his meager savings to return to New York, where he made several fruitless attempts to join the French military because he thought Elisabeth might fall for a man in uniform.

Riis soon learned how foolish he had been to squander his nest egg while the immigrants all around him were saving in anticipation of unemployment in New York's seasonal labor market. "Homeless and penniless, I joined the great army of tramps," Riis later recalled, "wandering about the streets in the daytime with the one aim of somehow stilling the hunger that gnawed at my vitals, and fighting at night with vagrant curs or outcasts as miserable as myself for the protection of some sheltering ash-bin or doorway . . . It was under such auspices that I made the acquaintance of Mulberry Bend, the Five Points, and the rest of the slum, with which there was in the years to come to be a reckoning."[3]

He spent weeks in Five Points, sleeping in the doorways or alleys of the district's worst dwellings, sometimes relocating to a stoop in Chatham Square when Five Points' "utter nastiness" was too much to bear, and subsisting on "meat-bones and rolls" that a sympathetic French cook at Delmonico's would slip him out a rear kitchen window. After contemplating suicide as winter temperatures dipped below freezing, Riis instead decided to seek shelter at a police station house. But the officers evicted him from his cell for fighting, killed the dog he had adopted, and put Riis on a ferry to Jersey City. He vowed he would never return to New York. Elisabeth, meanwhile, had become engaged to a Danish cavalry officer.

Doing odd jobs in exchange for meals, Riis managed to survive the winter of 1870–71. Once spring came, the peripatetic Dane continued to move from one position to another in Pennsylvania and western New York. He made cradles, felled trees, repaired steamboats, and harvested ice. He worked as a courier, a trapper, a house carpenter, and a farm laborer. He stacked boards in a lumberyard, made bedsteads, planed doors, laid track with a railroad construction crew, and worked in a Buffalo shipyard. All in a single year. "Only the Lord knows what is in store for me," he wrote in his diary on New Year's Eve 1871. "Please God, let it not be something terrible."[4]

The following year he worked as a door-to-door salesman. Tiring of the nomadic life, however, Riis broke his vow and returned to New York to enroll in telegraphy school. But he ran out of money before he could finish.

All this time Riis dreamed of being a newspaper reporter. His motivation may have originated with his father, who had once published a small weekly paper in Ribe. He saw the life of a reporter as far more dignified and honorable than the others he had pursued. So when he was forced to quit telegraphy school, he applied for a job as the "city editor" at a neighborhood newspaper just across the East River from New York in Long Island City. Amazingly, Riis got the position, never pausing to wonder how he managed to land it despite his complete lack of experience. After two weeks on the job, he got his answer: his employer was penniless. Recognizing that he would never be paid, Riis quit in disgust.

By this point, the autumn of 1873, a terrible depression had brought business to a virtual standstill, and steady employment was nearly impossible to find. Riis sold books door-to-door on commission, but often went hungry, until one day at the end of the year he happened upon the principal from his telegraphy school. Perhaps remembering Riis's career goal, the man told him of an opening for a reporter at the New York News Association, a wire service. With the clips from his two-week stint in Long Island City and a reference from the principal, Riis was hired. He never went hungry again.[5]

Five months later, Riis left the wire service to take a position with the *South Brooklyn News,* a local Democratic organ. In fact, he was the paper's only employee. After the politicians who owned the newspaper captured the fall elections of 1874, they decided to close their money-losing venture. Riis, inspired by the news that Elisabeth's dashing fiancé had died, induced the politicos to sell the paper to him, for $75 down and the remaining $575 when he could raise it. Riis toiled unceasingly to make the paper a success, and his pluck, enthusiasm, boundless energy, and ambition soon began to pay dividends. In half a year he had repaid his entire debt, delivering the final installment on the fifth of June, 1875, Elisabeth's birthday.

Now free to speak his mind, Riis began to lambaste the very politicians who had given him his big break. After suffering nearly a year of withering criticism, the ward heelers decided that they had better buy back the paper. Recognizing their desperation, Riis held out until the pols agreed to pay five times his purchase price. His pockets bulging with his newfound wealth (the equivalent of $65,000 today), Riis boarded the next steamer to Hamburg and from there went directly to Ribe, where, despite her parents' continuing objections, Elisabeth agreed to marry him.[6]

Back in New York, Riis eventually landed a job at the *Tribune*, though given his lack of serious journalistic credentials,

Jacob and Elisabeth Riis photographed in about 1876, not long after they were married.

he got stuck with the worst assignments the prestigious paper had to offer. Eventually he worked his way up to the graveyard shift covering crime at police headquarters on Mulberry Street. Each day at dawn when his shift ended, Riis would walk the length of Mulberry Street southward toward the East River to catch the ferry back home to Brooklyn. He could have taken a train to the docks, but he preferred to walk and see "the slum when off its guard." Riis knew Five Points and Mulberry Bend well from his days and nights as a homeless immigrant. Now he made Mulberry Bend his special cause, accompanying the police there to capture murderers and tagging along with health inspectors as they hunted for the source of epidemics. He became intimately familiar with Bottle Alley, Bandit's Roost, and the reputation of every tenement in the neighborhood.

Riis began to make shocking slum conditions a theme of his reporting. Most journalists attributed the persistence of immigrant "slums" to the "ignorant" and "backward" newcomers who inhabited them, but Riis assigned some of the blame to the tenement buildings themselves and the greedy landlords who refused to provide adequate light, ventilation, or maintenance. As early as 1880, he would drag powerful New Yorkers sympathetic to his cause downtown to see Gotham Court on Cherry Street and Bandit's Roost on Mulberry Bend, hoping that they would use their influence to bring attention to the tenement problem.[7]

Riis was not above prejudice; greedy Jews, lazy Italians, and crafty Chinese fill his writings. He was convinced, however, that tenements actually bred many of the social ills that Americans blamed on immigrants. Exorbitant rents drove tenement dwellers to take in too many boarders, and the resulting overcrowding led to epidemics. Poor ventilation exacerbated the spread of illness. Constant sickness made it impossible for the tenement dwellers to keep steady jobs. Unlike most Americans, Riis knew from his own experience that most impoverished immigrants were not too lazy to work.[8]

But what could Riis do to improve their lot? "It was upon my midnight trips with the sanitary police that the wish kept cropping up in me that there were some way of putting before the people what I saw there . . . We used to go in the small hours of the morning into the worst tenements to count noses and see if the law against overcrowding was violated, and the sights I saw there gripped my heart until I felt that I must tell of them, or burst, or turn anarchist, or something." He considered publishing drawings, but *Harper's Weekly* and *Frank Leslie's* had printed these for years to little effect. Riis continued to write about the tenements, "but it seemed to make no impression."[9]

In 1887, however, Riis had his "eureka" moment when he read about the invention of flash photography. He excitedly contacted Dr. John T. Nagle, head of the Health Department's Bureau of Vital Statistics and an avid amateur photographer. A few weeks later, Riis, Nagle, and a couple of other photography buffs were using flash photography to document the filth and overcrowding in New York's most notorious tenements. "I had at last," Riis wrote, "an ally in the fight with the Bend."

A police escort initially accompanied Riis's photographic "raiding party" into the tenements, but as he later recalled, "they were hardly needed. It is not too much to say that our party carried terror wherever it went." That was because in order to create the flash of light to illuminate his subjects, Riis and his friends would burst open the door of a tenement apartment, point a pistol at the inhabitants, and pull the trigger. The muzzle flash from the blank cartridge would illuminate the room for the camera. Soon Riis bought his own camera and — using a frying pan for the flash powder instead of a revolver — started taking the photos himself.[10]

Riis put some of his pictures to practical use immediately. He submitted his photo of men crammed into bunks in a Bayard Street apartment, for example, to help secure a judgment against the lessee before the city's Board of Health. But his sights were set much higher. "For more than a year," he later wrote, "I had knocked at the doors of the various magazine editors with my pictures, proposing to tell them how the other half lived, but no one wanted to know." When *Harper's* offered to take the photos but insisted on hiring "a man who could write" to tell their story, Riis stormed out of the office. Yet Riis was nothing if not persistent. Rejected by the press, he found an increasingly receptive audience in church groups, delivering lectures to them about life in the "slums" and illustrating his talks with slides made from his photographs.[11]

Riis's persistence and penchant for self-promotion paid off. An editor at *Scribner's* who attended one of Riis's church lectures soon approached him about converting it into an illustrated article. "How the Other Half Lives" appeared in the December 1889 issue of *Scribner's Magazine,* illustrated mostly with drawings based on Riis's photos, but also with nine "halftones," a relatively new process for reproducing photographs in print media. Although some of the halftones look more like drawings than photographs, others, including an image of homeless children sleeping on the streets and another of children praying at the Five Points House of Industry, are quite vivid and moving.[12]

The *Scribner's* article is a landmark in the history of photojournalism. Never before had photographs played such a central role in the telling of a news story. The photos really *were* the story. Ever since, journalists have used photographs not merely to add color or variety to news reporting but to document their allegations. Given the notoriety that the article attracted, *Scribner's* asked Riis to expand his essay into a book. He wrote the entire manuscript in just a few months, working late at night after his family had gone to bed. "I had had it in me so long that it burst out at last with a rush," he recalled. In November 1890, *How the Other Half Lives* appeared.[13]

In twenty-five short chapters, Riis surveyed the variety of tenement evils that had frustrated reformers for decades. His thesis, reiterated for years in his police reporting, was that the tenements themselves were the source of the slum problem, incubating disease and crime and perpetuating poverty. He blamed the situation in part on the landlords, who charged exorbitant rents, did little to maintain their buildings, and refused to build better ones. He also blamed the city's political bosses, who did not want to anger powerful property owners by insisting on effective enforcement of the existing laws. But Riis also charged that the immigrants were themselves an obstacle to reform, taking in too many boarders, allowing filth to accumulate in tenement yards, and failing to demand better housing. "This is true particularly of the poorest" immigrants, he argued. "They are shiftless, destructive, and stupid; in a word, they are what the tenements have made them. It is a dreary old truth that those who would fight for the poor must fight the poor to do it."[14]

Riis did not demand new laws, insisting that "the law has done what it could." The main obstacle to tenement reform, he believed, was an apathetic public. "The law needs a much stronger and readier backing of a thoroughly enlightened public sentiment to make it as effective as it might be made," he declared. Noting that a landlord would always try to avoid spending money to improve a property, Riis argued that "nothing short of the strongest pressure will avail to convince him that these individual rights are to be surrendered for the clear benefit of the whole." Wretched tenements threatened not merely impoverished immigrants, Riis concluded, but every American through the crime, disease, and political unrest that the newcomers might spread if conditions were not immediately improved.[15]

How the Other Half Lives quickly became a sensation. Reviewers called it "thrilling," "harrowing," "startling," "a book of immense, shuddering interest," and "a saddening, terrifying book." Many commentators noted the importance of Riis's photos. "His book is literally a photograph," wrote one, while another praised Riis for looking at the tenements "with the unerring eye of the 'Kodak.' His own camera, not the imagination of a draughtsman, has furnished the illustrations."[16]

No human being, stated the Chicago Tribune, could read How the Other Half Lives "without an instant and unappeasable desire to do something." Soon after its publication, a thirty-two-year-old civil service commissioner named Theodore Roosevelt stopped by Riis's office at police headquarters hoping to meet the author. Finding Riis away from his desk, Roosevelt left his card, scribbling a note on the back saying that he had read Riis's book and had "come to help." Riis enlisted other powerful allies too, such as attorney-financiers Robert de Forest and Robert Fulton Cutting, editor Richard Watson Gilder, and social and religious reformer Felix Adler.[17]

The changes Riis and his allies sought came exceedingly slowly — tenement owners had enormous political clout and used every bit of it to resist renovating their lucrative properties — but change eventually did come. Thanks to Riis's efforts, the block of decrepit tenements known as Mulberry Bend was condemned by the city, torn down in 1895, and replaced by Mulberry Bend Park, which opened in 1897. Riis also helped to enact a requirement that all schools have playgrounds and spearheaded the construction of "recreation piers," where children could play when school was not in session. He advocated these ideas out of a belief that their realization would reduce both childhood illness and juvenile delinquency. By 1900, the city had opened five of these massive waterfront recreation facilities.[18]

Eventually, Riis and his supporters made progress in their efforts to reshape tenement conditions. Roosevelt, who had become governor of New York in 1899, appointed a tenement commission in 1900 that included Riis and his allies de Forest, Gilder, and Adler. Acting on the commission's recommendations, the state legislature passed the Tenement House Act of 1901, a landmark of Progressive Era legislation. The law banned the construction of dumbbell tenements by increasing the minimum width of an airshaft in new buildings from eighteen inches to six feet for the typical five-story tenement, making it impossible to use the dumbbell floor plan on the standard twenty-five-by-one-hundred-foot Manhattan lot. The law also required that in new buildings, every room (other than bathrooms) have windows opening to the outside and have ceilings at least nine feet in height, and that all buildings have running water and toilets inside every apartment.

The 1901 tenement statute also required significant changes for existing buildings. All outhouses in which sewage collected in vaults directly below rather than draining straight into the sewer system had to be removed. Toilets for existing tenements could still be located outside, but each one now had to be enclosed in its own cubicle. Tenements also now had to have at least one toilet for every two families. The new law required landlords to install running water on every floor of existing buildings as well. Finally, as amended in 1903, the act mandated that landlords provide more air and light to the city's 364,000 windowless bedrooms by giving them a new window either to the outside or to an adjoining room that had an exterior window. (The law as originally enacted required a window to the outside in every room, but lobbyists for the city's landlords convinced the legislature that this modification was too costly.) The city would enforce these codes through the creation of a city Tenement House Department, whose inspectors and magistrates would prosecute violations of the new code.[19]

On the surface, the impact of the 1901 Tenement House Act may seem negligible. Landlords with properties in Manhattan decided to keep their old buildings rather than build new ones that, in order to comply with the new law, would have to contain fewer apartments. Consequently, at the end of 1915, dumbbell and the even older barracks-style tenements outnumbered "new law" tenements that followed the new codes by a ratio of seven to one; the ratio on the Lower East Side and in Five Points was ten to one. But the Tenement Act of 1901 did help insure that the relatively underdeveloped outer boroughs would not become blighted with such buildings. By the beginning of 1916, the outer boroughs had only two "old law" tenements to every "new law" tenement, and with the post–Word War I building boom, the healthier, less crowded new-style tenements soon outnumbered the old-style death traps. Now, immigrants could be sure to have better housing to move to once they could afford to leave Manhattan.[20]

Riis, meanwhile, through his writings and lectures, kept advocating for further tenement reform (in particular for those "old law" buildings), more parks in tenement districts, and better schools and play opportunities for children. Today he is generally acknowledged as the first muckraking journalist of the Progressive Era and the first documentary photographer. When Riis died of heart disease in 1914, Roosevelt called him "the ideal American citizen."[21]

While Riis and other progressives worked to improve the homes in which New York's immigrants lived, another set of reformers simultaneously tried through the "settlement movement" to better immigrants' lives by bringing medical and social services to them in those very tenements. Since the 1850s, well-to-do New Yorkers had attempted to relieve suffering in their city through charitable organizations set up in the newcomers' neighborhoods. The Five Points Mission and the Five Points House of Industry, for example, had distributed food, fuel, and used clothes to the indigent and offered vocational training as well. But these groups were suspect in the eyes of the immigrants because their charity came with religious strings attached. Volunteers at the Five Points Mission worked relentlessly to convert their clients to Methodism, while the House of Industry made attendance at its Sunday school a condition for receiving assistance. Five Points' Irish Catholic community leaders condemned both institutions and urged Catholic immigrants not to accept charity from them.[22]

The first settlement houses provided some of the same services as these older institutions, but they did not offer religious programs. Most of the settlement employees were university-trained women who saw their work as a vocation, not a charitable diversion. Furthermore, the settlement house workers believed that the only way to earn the trust of their clients and truly understand their needs was to live in the immigrants' own neighborhoods. "The idea of this work is to have a group of college educated women live in a house in the very locality of the people who are to be reached," reported the *Times*, "becoming a part of their social life and learning all that is possible of the civic life of the neighborhood."

Settlement founders were motivated by a healthy dose of idealism as well as a disgust for the excesses of the Gilded Age. Settlements "are trying to overcome the materialism of the times, under which the rich are stifled in luxury and the poor are stunted in want," explained Vida Scudder, a professor of literature at Wellesley College and a founder of Boston's Denison House, one of the nation's first settlement houses. "We are really living in a stratified society, in which each class is by itself, and is ignorant of the lives of every other class. It is only by making it possible to pass from class to class, and thus by obliterating class distinctions, that we can reach a true democracy."[23]

New York's first settlement, the Neighborhood Guild, began operating in 1886 in a rented basement on the Lower East Side. In 1889 it became affiliated

with Columbia University, was renamed the University Settlement, and in 1898
moved into a five-story home at 184 Eldridge Street. The city's second settlement, the College Settlement, was opened by graduates of Smith College in
1889 at 95 Rivington Street. By 1903, three dozen settlement houses had been
established in Manhattan, with the majority located on the Lower East Side and
in Hell's Kitchen (on the western edge of what is now midtown Manhattan),
Yorkville (on the eastern edge of Manhattan from East 72nd to 89th Street), and
East Harlem. By 1920, New York had sixty-four settlements, including thirteen
in the outer boroughs.[24]

The Henry Street Settlement, founded in 1895 by Lillian Wald, became the
city's best known. Wald, the daughter of a Polish Jewish father from Warsaw
and a German Jewish mother, was born in Cincinnati in 1864. In 1878 Wald's father, Max, a grocer turned optician, moved the family to Rochester. The Walds
were worldly, cultured, comfortable, and secular. Lillian later recalled a childhood filled with Shakespeare and Mozart, and she took a pre-collegiate curriculum while attending Miss Cruttenden's English-French Boarding and Day
School for Young Ladies and Little Girls as a day student.[25]

Wald, however, never did go to college. She held several jobs but found them
unsatisfying. Nor did she want to marry. At age twenty-five, she decided that
nursing was her true calling, but rather than enter Rochester's nursing school,
she insisted on distancing herself from her family by pursuing her degree in
New York City. Life in Rochester "does not satisfy me now," she wrote in 1889 in
her application to the New York Hospital School of Nursing. "I feel the need of
serious, definite work," something she thought she could not achieve under the
constraints of her familial and "social ties" in Rochester.[26]

After finishing nursing school in 1891, Wald took a job at an institution for
orphaned and abandoned children in upper Manhattan. Finding this work depressing, she quit after a year and entered medical school at New York's Woman's Medical College. About six months into her program, Wald volunteered
to teach a weekly course on home nursing to immigrant women on Henry
Street in the southeast portion of the Lower East Side. One day, while she was
instructing the women on how to make a bed properly, a girl came into the
classroom crying, saying that her mother, who usually attended the sessions,
was very sick. Wald immediately dismissed class and followed the child to her
mother. Twenty years later, Wald vividly recalled that March day in 1893 in her
memoir:

> The child led me over broken roadways, — there was no asphalt, although
> its use was well established in other parts of the city, — over dirty mattresses
> and heaps of refuse, ... between tall, reeking houses whose laden fire-

escapes, useless for their appointed purpose, bulged with household goods of every description. The rain added to the dismal appearance of the streets and to the discomfort of the crowds which thronged them, intensifying the odors which assailed me from every side. Through Hester and Division streets we went to the end of Ludlow; past odorous fish-stands . . . ; past evil-smelling, uncovered garbage-cans; and . . . past [trucks and pushcarts that made some streets nearly impassable] . . . The child led me on through a tenement hallway, across a court[yard] where open and unscreened closets [toilets] were promiscuously used by [both] men and women, up into a rear tenement, by slimy steps whose accumulated dirt was augmented that day by the mud of the streets, and finally into the sickroom.

In the windowless room, Wald found her student in a bed caked with dried blood. The immigrant had given birth two days earlier and had hemorrhaged during the difficult delivery. The baby, too, was covered in dried blood. Her disabled husband was not able to offer significant assistance, and the family could not afford a doctor or midwife. Wald cleaned the mother and her newborn and replaced the soiled bedsheets with the ones she had been using for

demonstration purposes in her class. She examined both mother and child and found, miraculously, that neither needed additional medical treatment. "At the end of my ministrations," Wald recollected, both the mother and her husband "kissed my hands" in gratitude.[27]

Horrified by what she had seen, Wald decided that very day to make alleviating such conditions her life's work. "That morning's experience was a baptism of fire," she wrote, an "awakening." Her use of Christian terminology could not have been totally coincidental. She had never belonged to a synagogue, and members of her father's family in Rochester had converted to Christianity and married gentiles. Throughout her life, Wald considered her stereotypically Semitic features — dark hair, dark eyes, and

Lillian Wald's 1891 yearbook photo from the New York Hospital Training School for Nurses.

swarthy complexion — an embarrassment. She placed a Christmas tree in her settlement house even though the vast majority of its clients were Jewish. Like many children of immigrants, Wald wanted desperately to fit in and be accepted as an American.[28]

Wald quit medical school so that she could immediately begin devoting the rest of her life to relieving the suffering of the Lower East Side's eastern European Jews. She decided that she would open a settlement focused on providing medical care and hygiene training to immigrants. A friend from nursing school, Mary Brewster, agreed to join her in the endeavor. They initially called it the Nurses' Settlement.

Wald secured support from German Jewish immigrants Jacob Schiff (a banker at Kuhn, Loeb & Co.) and Fanny Kuhn, who was sister to one of Schiff's banking partners and wife to another. They agreed to pay the two nurses $15 per week and cover the rent on their sixth-floor tenement apartment at 27 Jefferson Street. After several years, Wald informed their benefactors that the line of immigrants queuing up at their apartment door before dawn each day made it impossible for the nurses to do their daily rounds, and that they really needed a work space in which to house their operations. Schiff bought them the building at 265 Henry Street, next door to the school where Wald had taught that original hygiene class. They moved into their Henry Street headquarters in 1895. The Henry Street Settlement operates there to this day.[29]

The work was exhausting and not for the faint of heart. "Today Miss Brewster and I have seen enough sorrow and poverty and illness to fill a world with sadness," Wald wrote to Schiff in 1893. The nurses found that the *Herald*'s observation, made a year earlier, that on the Lower East Side children "die like flies" was hardly an exaggeration. In one instance in 1893, Brewster sat up all night with Lily Klein, a youngster suffering from pneumonia, but the girl died the next day. "Little coffins are stacked mountain high on the deck of the charity commission boat when it makes semi-weekly trips to the cemetery," Wald reported to Schiff.[30]

Wald was especially skilled at persuading wealthy New Yorkers to bankroll the growth of her settlement. In 1898 the settlement had eleven full-time staff members, nine of them nurses. By 1900, fifteen nurses; in 1906, twenty-seven nurses; and in 1913, ninety-two nurses making tens of thousands of house calls per year. By that point the Henry Street Settlement had taken over six additional neighboring buildings, and Wald herself had long since given up making tenement house calls. Instead, she supervised the staff, cultivated donors, and publicized her organization's work.[31]

Wald needed all that additional space because she was now offering much more than a visiting nurse service. Early on, she had let tenement dwellers

Nurses who went door-to-door in immigrant neighborhoods often crossed from one building to the next by way of the rooftops in order to reduce the number of dark stairways they had to climb.

bathe at the settlement because they had no access to bathtubs in their dwellings. When she learned that students could not find the peace and quiet necessary to study in their tenements, she provided study halls and tutors. Children could also join the settlement's athletic clubs or simply play in its huge playground, which Wald had constructed in the combined backyards of her Henry Street properties. When school was out, youngsters could attend the settlement's summer camps or go on "fresh air" retreats, weeklong stays at a home or farm in the countryside sponsored by the Henry Street organization. Adults could take classes in the arts and "citizenship," attend lectures and dances, or even obtain vocational training.

Wald urged the city to do even more. Given that she could accommodate only a fraction of the tenement dwellers who sought to bathe at the settlement, Wald successfully lobbied the city to build public baths (which, to the modern eye, look like large enclosed swimming pools in photos). The first one opened in 1901. Wald also persuaded city officials to establish a "public nursing" corps to provide services like hers throughout the five boroughs, and to put a nurse in every public school, an innovation that eventually became the norm throughout the United States.[32]

Wald was a progressive in every sense of the word. She vigorously supported women's suffrage, helped women organize labor unions, and championed the movement to restrict child labor. She even hosted the first New York meeting of the National Association for the Advancement of Colored People at the Henry Street Settlement. Only her peace activism during World War I seemed to reduce, albeit slightly, New Yorkers' enthusiasm for her and her work.[33]

One of the goals of Lower East Side settlement houses like Wald's was to disabuse Americans of the idea that east European Jews were genetically doomed to be gaunt and weak. To this end, the settlements organized sports programs of all kinds for the immigrant community. Yet there was one game the city's Jewish immigrants quickly embraced above and beyond all others: basketball.

Despite a total lack of experience with the game, Jews through the settlement leagues became basketball whizzes of national renown. "It is a well established fact that in basketball, the Jew has no superior," proclaimed *The American Hebrew* in 1908. This was no idle boast. Of the six players on the University Settlement's 1907 squad, two went on to decades-long professional basketball careers. By 1917, *The American Hebrew* could claim that basketball had changed the perception "of the Jew in this country from a shrunken, wizened creature afraid of its own shadow into a being unafraid, buoyant and erect . . . Two generations ago he cowered timidly in the ghettoes of the dark countries; now he leaps toward the light like a young god of the sun."[34]

Gentiles found the Jewish aptitude for basketball amazing, given the preponderant stereotypes, but they nonetheless managed to explain it without having to revise their preconceptions. Basketball "appeal[s] to the temperament of the Jews," commented the *Daily News*, because of its "premium on an alert, scheming mind . . . flashy trickiness, artful dodging and general smart aleckness." The assessment of *The American Hebrew* was actually not so different. Basketball demands "a good deal of quick thinking [and] lightning like rapidity of movement and endurance," the newspaper argued. "It does not call for brutality and brute strength and that is why the Jews excel in it."[35]

Basketball of that era was vastly different from the contemporary sport. With no shot clock or tall players, basketball games in the early twentieth century rarely saw teams score more than twenty or thirty points. But the sheer physicality of the sport provided plenty of excitement. In those days, inbounds possession was given to the team whose player reached the out-of-bounds ball first; not surprisingly, this rule led to violent melees whenever the ball went astray. The solution was, in its own way, no less violent: a wire or rope "cage" encircling the court. "You could play tick-tack-toe on everybody after a game because the cage marked you up," recalled Joel "Shikey" Gotthoffer, a son of Jewish immigrants who was a star in the American Basketball League in the 1930s. "Sometimes you were bleeding and sometimes not. You were like a gladiator, and if you didn't get rid of the ball, you could get killed."[36]

Today's major college basketball programs find their stars at elite private schools that groom their athletes for big-time athletics. In the early twentieth century, knowledgeable basketball scouts sought their star recruits in the New York settlement house basketball league. Wanting to stay close to home, the most sought-after players usually chose to play for City College, which was as much a basketball powerhouse in that era as the universities of Kentucky and North Carolina are today. The Lower East Side relished each City College victory over the team's more prestigious opponents. "The high standards of our curriculum could not have done, in years, what the glorious triumph of the varsity basketball team over Yale accomplished in one short evening," exclaimed the City College student newspaper after the "lavender quintet" defeated Yale, 20–15, in 1911. Five years later, another victory over Yale prompted *The American Hebrew* to call the outcome "a striking example of real American democracy." The team's "immigrant boys" were "the red-blooded aristocrats of America's future." This was precisely the lesson that settlement house workers hoped the wider world would draw from Jews' athletic triumphs.[37]

The success of the Henry Street, University, and College settlements spawned many imitators, and although those first settlements had scrupulously avoided discussions of religion, by 1920 about half the city's settlement houses were church-affiliated. Their employees considered it their duty to attempt to convert their clients. "The last time we went, Miss Peters, after the sewing, started to talk religion to us, as if we didn't have any ourselves," recalled a Jewish immigrant taking a sewing class with a friend at one of these settlements. "She told us that Jesus loved us and wanted to save us. Amy and I wanted to stuff our ears . . . Wild horses couldn't drag me there again!" When Dr. Jane Robbins, one of the founders of the College Settlement, was walking on the Lower East Side with three small Russian Jewish boys in her organization's earliest days, an older boy standing with some friends at an intersection called out: "Don't go with her! Don't go with her! She is going to make you Irish!" In 1908 an Orthodox Jewish leader likewise asserted that "the vast majority of the Jewish children who come under the influence of the settlements become agnostics, atheists, infidels, and Anarchists."[38]

Wald, however, became one of the most beloved and respected reformers in New York because she learned to be neither judgmental nor preachy. (Riis, in contrast, was both.) When Wald died in 1940, the *Times* remarked that "the mere list of the ideas that came out of 265 Henry Street . . . would fill several columns" in the newspaper's pages. Perhaps her greatest accomplishment was to serve, as her friend and fellow reformer Josephine Goldmark put it, as "the great interpreter of one social class to another, of the newcomer and the alien to the native-born, of people of different racial backgrounds to one another, of the underprivileged to the overprivileged."[39]

Although Wald believed that most sick immigrants were better off treated at home, some became so ill that they required hospitalization. Yet immigrants were often deathly afraid of admitting themselves or family members to New York's major hospitals. Many feared the expense. Others thought that because doctors and nurses could not speak their language, they might be misdiagnosed. Orthodox Jews worried that they might starve to death in the hospital because they would be unable to eat its non-kosher food. Furthermore, even though the city's two main hospitals were public, Catholic and Jewish immigrants were subjected to proselytization efforts by Protestant religious groups that were given free rein in their wards.

As a result, New York's immigrants founded their own hospitals as soon as they were able to do so. The first, Saint Vincent's, opened in 1849 to cater to the city's huge new population of Catholic immigrants. Sister Mary Angela Hughes, sister of Bishop John Hughes of New York and mother superior of the Sisters of Charity, organized and operated the institution. By the early twentieth century, New York could boast eight Catholic hospitals.[40]

Nuns (more formally "women religious") played a key role in the establishment of almost all of New York's Catholic hospitals. Columbus Hospital, for example, which opened on East 20th Street in 1892 to cater to the city's Italian immigrants, was the brainchild of Mother Frances Xavier Cabrini. Born Francesca Cabrini in a town just southeast of Milan in 1850, she was a small, frail, sickly child. When she applied to become a nun with a local religious order at age twenty, she was rejected on the grounds that she was too weak for their rigorous life of work and self-sacrifice. Cabrini taught for a while instead, but in 1880 she founded her own religious order, the Missionary Sisters of the Sacred Heart of Jesus. Cabrini established seven homes for orphans and foundlings in her order's first five years, a level of accomplishment that brought her work to the attention of church leaders in Rome. Yet Cabrini, not satisfied with her life in Italy, yearned to do missionary work for the church overseas. When she asked for permission to work in China, she was directed to go to America instead to work with Italian immigrants, whose needs, in the opinion of Vatican officials, were being ignored by Irish American Catholic leaders. Cabrini arrived in New York on March 31, 1889.

Cabrini brought the same energy and determination to her American work that she had exhibited in Italy. Initially she focused on establishing orphanages and schools for Italian American children. She also organized catechism classes for adult immigrants who, in the minds of Cabrini and Archbishop Michael Corrigan, were woefully ignorant of the Catholic liturgy. She then opened Columbus Hospital, raising the funds herself from prominent Italian Americans when Corrigan declined to assist her. Not satisfied with helping only the New York Italian community, she soon left to replicate her work in other American cities with significant Italian populations. She became an American citizen in 1909, and by the time of her death in 1917, she had established more than sixty orphanages, schools, hospitals, and other Catholic institutions all over the United States. She was canonized in 1946, the first American immigrant to be so honored.[41]

New York's first Jewish hospital, Mount Sinai, which opened in 1855, was run by assimilated German Jews and did not offer kosher meals. Eastern European Jews were thus elated to celebrate the founding of Beth Israel Hospital in 1891 at 196 East Broadway, one of the main thoroughfares of the Lower East Side. Not only did it serve kosher food, but also both its nurses and doctors spoke Yiddish. Other notable Jewish hospitals included Montefiore on East 84th Street at York Avenue (1884), Lebanon Hospital in the south Bronx (1893), and Brooklyn's Jewish Hospital (1906). Meanwhile, Catholics had added St. Francis Hospital (1865) in Kleindeutschland aimed at German Catholics, St. Peter's and St. Catherine's hospitals in Brooklyn (1864 and 1893), and St. John's Hospital in Long Island City (1891). Over the years, other immigrant groups had established medical facilities independent of religious organizations. These included the German Hospital (now Lenox Hill) on East 77th Street (1861), the French Hospital on West 34th Street (1881), and the Italian Hospital on East 83rd Street (1905).[42]

Many immigrants believed that the efforts at improving their lives led by Riis, Wald, and Cabrini would not have been necessary had the newcomers received better pay from their employers. Hoping to win higher wages and healthier working conditions, immigrants arriving in New York in the late nineteenth and early twentieth centuries joined labor unions in huge numbers. The Jewish and Italian immigrants' affinity for organizing labor unions eventually helped reshape both the newcomers' lives and the perceptions of the immigrants held by native-born Americans.

Previous generations of immigrants had tried to create labor unions in New York, but their efforts met with little success. Courts in the mid-nineteenth century viewed strikes as illegal restraints of trade, and those who led them were imprisoned. As a result, while New Yorkers organized unions for shoemakers, laborers, cigar makers, and a whole host of other trades, they were mostly ineffectual. Union advocates were divided between moderates, who focused on winning improvements in wages, hours, and working conditions, and radicals, who saw the labor movement as a means to achieving wholesale changes in the relationship between labor and capital.

The best known of the moderates was Samuel Gompers. As a leader of the city's cigar makers' union, Gompers helped introduce a new way of organizing workers. Recognizing that earlier unions had charged very minimal dues and failed in part because they lacked financial clout, Gompers and fellow immigrant Adolph Strasser decided in the 1870s that the cigar makers' union would charge much higher membership fees. Those increased dues would go not only toward sick relief, unemployment compensation, and travel money to help out-of-work union members search for jobs, but also to create a sizable strike fund. The organization could thus sustain hundreds of members should a lengthy strike be deemed necessary to win a better labor contract. Knowing the size of the union's strike fund, employers took their threats of work stoppages seriously, and as a result, cigar makers remained relatively highly paid during the 1880s even as their industry became more mechanized.[43]

In the belief that reformers might aid his work, Gompers in 1883 lobbied intensively and successfully in the state capital for a bill banning the manufacture of cigars in tenement apartments, which was unhealthy for both the cigar makers and their families. In 1884, however, the state's highest court, by a unanimous vote, declared the law unconstitutional on the grounds that denying citizens the right to work in their own homes at lawful occupations contravened the Constitution's ban on taking property without due process. Theodore Roosevelt found the ruling appalling. He remembered it years later as one of the defining events of his conversion to progressivism and "one of the most serious setbacks which the cause of industrial and social progress and reform ever received."[44]

The ruling also inspired Gompers to redouble his unionization efforts, as he realized that government could not be relied on to improve the conditions faced by his members. In 1886 he and his allies created the American Federation of Labor (AFL), a confederation of unions from around the nation. "Gompers was indefatigable," notes one biographer, "answering letters, traveling incessantly, and giving speeches to organize workers and to alter the public's impression of the labor movement." Gompers was also a careful leader, using strikes only as a last resort, and only when the union had the leverage and funds to win a protracted battle. As a result, the AFL grew steadily, from a few thousand members at its founding to 250,000 in 1893, and 1.7 million in 1904. Gompers served as AFL president for thirty-nine of the organization's first forty years.[45]

Despite the AFL's success, workers seemed at best to be barely scraping by while employers got exponentially richer during the height of the Gilded Age. Many of New York's immigrants, especially its east European Jews, were persuaded to seek more radical change and embraced the burgeoning social-ist movement. The best-known socialist in late nineteenth-century New York was Johann Most, already a celebrity radical when he immigrated to New York in 1882. As a socialist, Most believed that significant property such as mines, forests, railroads, and major industries should be owned by all citizens, who should share in the profits they created. In the decade before coming to Amer-ica, Most had represented the socialist cause in the German Reichstag, but the derision he faced in the legislature convinced him that socialist goals could not be achieved through political means. Speeches, pamphlets, and other tra-ditional forms of propaganda would not sufficiently arouse the masses. Most instead advocated "propaganda of the deed," acts of anarchist violence against the state, or the plutocrats it protected, as the best and only path to inspire the proletarian uprisings he sought.

After serving a term in a German prison for espousing these views, Most settled in London, where he became editor of *Freiheit* (Freedom), the organ of Germany's expatriate socialists. In its columns Most continued to espouse the idea that only dramatic acts of violence against the capitalist order could attract adherents to the cause. The British authorities were hardly more toler-ant of Most than the Germans, and he was jailed in 1881 for celebrating the as-sassination of Tsar Alexander II. When released a year later, Most left for New York, hoping that in the United States he would enjoy the freedom of speech necessary to foment revolution back in Europe. He quickly became the most famous socialist in the city, as a saloonkeeper (every prominent German anar-chist seems to have had his own beer hall), public speaker, and editor of *Frei-heit*, which he continued to publish in New York.[46]

One of the immigrants Most drew to the anarchist movement was Emma Goldman. Upon arriving in the United States from Russia in 1885, she had moved to Rochester, reluctantly married a man she did not love, and taken dreary work there in a garment sweatshop. Like Wald, Goldman yearned to leave her family behind and make a name for herself in New York City. Inspired by Most's fiery editorials, Goldman left her husband and moved to New York to join the anarchist cause. She arrived on August 15, 1889, with a few dollars, a sewing machine, the address of an aunt, the address of an anarchist medical student she had heard lecture in New Haven, and the address of *Freiheit*.

Sensing that the aunt did not want her to stay, Goldman found the medical student on the Lower East Side. He immediately introduced her to his anar-chist comrades, one of whom, Alexander Berkman, offered to take her to hear Most speak that very night. Goldman could hardly believe her good fortune but was shocked when she first laid eyes on the famous firebrand. "My first impression of him was one of revulsion," she later recalled. "His face was twisted out of form by an apparent dislocation of the left jaw." But as he began to lecture, "as if by magic, his disfigurement disappeared, his lack of physical distinction was forgotten. He seemed transformed into some primitive power, radiating hatred and love, strength and inspiration. The rapid current of his speech, the music of his voice, and his sparkling wit, all combined to produce an effect almost overwhelming. He stirred me to my depths."[47]

With her blond hair, blue eyes, and fiery rhetoric, Emma Goldman quickly became one of the anarchist movement's most popular public speakers.

Most, at forty-six twice as old as Goldman, was even more taken with the blond-haired, blue-eyed young radical than she was with him. Sensing her potential as a lecturer, he tutored her on public speaking and then sent her out on a lecture tour. Meanwhile, she had moved in with Berkman and his cousin Modest "Fedya" Aronstam. True to her anarchist beliefs, which, as she proudly recalled in her memoirs, included a rejection of bourgeois institutions such as marriage or the right of a man to "possess" a woman in any way, she slept with both of them (and, for a while, with Most, too), though that did not prevent her from becoming jealous when they slept with other women. Goldman believed that "binding people for life was wrong. The constant proximity in the same house, the same room, the same bed," she said, "revolted me. 'If ever I love a man again,'" she told Berkman, "'I will give myself to him without being bound by the rabbi or the law, . . . and when that love dies, I will leave without permission.'" Goldman could take lovers in part because she did not have to worry about becoming pregnant, as a medical condition had left her infertile. Later she would become one of the nation's most famous advocates of "free love." She was also an ardent supporter of the movement to make birth control available to all women.[48]

Toiling eighteen hours a day as garment workers to support themselves, Goldman, Berkman, and Aronstam had little time or energy for revolutionary struggle. Despairing of ever having the opportunity to foment an uprising of the masses, they left New York and eventually opened an ice cream shop in Worcester, Massachusetts, in 1892. But they still yearned to inspire a revolution.

They decided that they could do so by focusing their attention on one of the most hated industrialists in America, Henry Clay Frick. Earlier that year, when steelworkers at a plant in Homestead, Pennsylvania, owned by Andrew Carnegie but run by Frick had formed a union, Frick declared he would never negotiate with any of its members. The workers then called a strike. Goldman and Berkman decided to go to Homestead and seek anarchist recruits among the strikers. Before they could arrive, a gun battle broke out on July 6 between the strikers and the heavily armed Pinkerton guards hired by Frick to protect the replacement workers. Seven strikers were killed and dozens injured.

Hearing the news, Berkman decided they should change plans and assassinate Frick—the ultimate act of propaganda by deed. On July 23, armed with a pistol and a dagger, Berkman barged into Frick's large wood-paneled Pittsburgh office and fired at his head from about twenty-five feet away. The shot glanced off the industrialist's neck and he fell to the floor. "Murder! Help!" Frick cried from beneath his desk. As Berkman approached the prostrate Frick and tried to fire a second time, one of Frick's associates struck the anarchist's arm, causing his shot to ricochet wide of the mark. While grappling with the associate, Berkman managed to get close enough to the cowering magnate for a third shot, but the gun would not fire. Finally, a carpenter who had been working in the outer office rushed in and struck Berkman in the back of the head with a hammer. Berkman made one last lunge at Frick with his dagger, managing a few cuts to Frick's leg before being dragged away. Berkman was quickly convicted of attempted murder and sentenced to twenty-two years in prison. The public, which had initially sympathized with the strikers after the Pinkerton battle, now turned decidedly against them, enabling Frick and Carnegie to crush the union.[49]

Goldman felt terrible that Berkman was languishing in prison while she had got off scot-free, but she was determined to use that freedom and her skill as an orator to advance the cause. In the summer of 1893, when a financial panic led to massive unemployment, Goldman implored a huge crowd in Union Square not to accept the situation meekly. "Men and women," she shouted in German, "do you not realize that the State is the worst enemy you have? It is a machine that crushes you in order to sustain the ruling class, your masters . . . Wake up . . . Become daring enough to demand your rights . . . Demonstrate before the palaces of the rich; demand work. If they do not give you work, demand bread. If they deny you both, take bread. It is your sacred right!" For uttering these words, Goldman was arrested, tried for incitement to riot, and sentenced

to a year in prison. By this point, she had displaced Most as the best-known anarchist in America.*

By the time of her release, Goldman was a media sensation. A horde of reporters waited to greet her at the prison gates on Blackwell's (now Roosevelt)
Island, and that same night a thousand supporters cheered her at a welcome-
home rally at the Thalia Theatre on the Bowery. "The crowd was made up of
various nationalities," reported the *Times,* including a few Germans, but primarily "Italians, Russian Jews, Hungarians, Frenchmen, Cubans, and Spaniards. If there were any native Americans there they were so few as not to be
noticeable." Goldman was the incarnation of the radical threat many Americans believed to be the result of loosely regulated immigration.[50]

From time to time, Goldman and Gompers wondered why exploited workers would not follow their lead. Conversely, workers sometimes wondered why
union leaders would not take more decisive action on their behalf. Such was
the case in 1909, when New York's "shirtwaist" sewers decided to strike. The
shirtwaist was the fashion sensation of the early twentieth century. Initially it
consisted of a tailored shirt and was worn with a separate skirt. The skirt, which
stopped at the top of the ankles, made moving around much easier than the
floor-length dresses that women of all classes had dressed in to that point. And
because it could be worn without a corset or bustle, the skirt worn with the
shirtwaist was much more comfortable than other socially acceptable options.
Soon the shirtwaist and skirt were combined into a dress, known simply as a
"waist." They remained fashionable for decades. All the iconic women of early
television, such as Donna Reed and Lucille Ball — and their modern imitators
on shows like *Mad Men* — wore shirtwaist dresses.[51]

Jewish and Italian immigrant women in New York manufactured most of
America's shirtwaists. Employers paid them even less than the pittance that
male garment workers made, justifying these starvation wages on the grounds
that women's earnings merely supplemented the income of a male family member. In the summer and fall of 1909, the shirtwaist sewers in a number of shops
struck for better pay, but with limited success. The unit of the International
Ladies' Garment Workers' Union (ILGWU) that organized many of these

---

* The story of Most's descendants reminds us that even if certain immigrants came to the
United States as radicals, their children typically turned out to be ordinary Americans. Johann
Most's son John became a dentist in the Bronx. The dentist's son "Johnny" Most eventually
moved to Boston and became one of the city's most beloved citizens in his thirty-five years as
the radio play-by-play announcer for the Boston Celtics.

workers, the Ladies' Waist-Makers' Union, pressed for a general strike of all shirtwaist workers to force shops to pay a minimum wage and to put caps on overtime, but the ILGWU leadership refused to endorse a work stoppage, fearing the union could not sustain thousands of workers through what might be a protracted walkout.

By late fall, the rank and file had lost all patience with both employers and the union's leaders. At a mass meeting of three thousand shirtwaist workers at Cooper Union on Monday evening, November 22, 1909, workers heard equivocal speeches from Gompers and other leaders. Before another speaker could take the podium, a twenty-three-year-old member of the Waist-Makers' executive committee named Clara Lemlich, who had arrived in New York six years earlier from Ukraine, forced her way to the dais to address the crowd. "I am a working girl, one of those striking against intolerable conditions," Lemlich declared in Yiddish. "I am tired of listening to speakers who talk in generalities. What we are here for is to decide whether or not to strike. I offer a resolution that a general strike be declared — now." The crowd went wild. By acclamation the strike was approved. The meeting's chairman then administered the strikers' oath: "If I turn traitor to the cause I now pledge, may this hand wither from the arm I now raise." The next day, nearly twenty thousand shirtwaist workers went out on a strike that became known as the Uprising of the 20,000 (even

Although Jewish immigrants were initially reluctant to work with Italians in New York's garment industry, the two groups eventually became allies in the movement for better wages and working conditions in the city's sweatshops.

though the number who walked out eventually topped thirty thousand). It was the first great strike by women in American history.[52]

The strikers, estimated to be 70 percent Jewish immigrants and 30 percent Italian, demanded a 20 percent raise for piecework and a 15 percent raise for those paid a set weekly wage, a fifty-two-hour workweek for wage workers, extra pay for work done on legal holidays, and no more than two hours' overtime per day for wage earners. Employers agreed to most of these terms fairly quickly, but they refused to recognize the union, even though they had consented to negotiate with its leaders. The strikers were willing to endure hunger and jail in an effort to win recognition for their labor organization. "It is the most astonishing strike I ever knew," commented one shirtwaist factory owner. "The wage demands mean nothing."

Police showed little sympathy for the strikers. Some were convicted of disorderly conduct merely for calling the replacement workers who crossed their picket lines "scabs." But the majority of those arrested, often quite brutally, had attempted to use force to stop the strikebreakers from entering their workplaces. In the end, after a five-month walkout, the smaller manufacturers (the majority of the employers) tacitly recognized the union, while the very largest held firm and refused to do so. The strikers also failed to win approval of "closed shops," in which employers could hire only union members. But Lemlich and the waist makers took comfort in the fact that their union, which had had only a few hundred paid members before the strike, now had more than twenty thousand.[53]

Strikes continued to roil the New York garment industry in the years leading up to World War I. With Gompers calling their working conditions "a blot on civilization," 75,000 cloak makers went on strike in the summer of 1910 in what the *Times* called "the city's biggest labor war" ever. The cloak makers managed to assemble an even more powerful lineup of outside advocates than the shirtwaist workers. It included Schiff and one of the nation's most prominent attorneys, Louis Brandeis of Boston. With such allies prodding the manufacturers, the union's lead negotiator, Meyer London, a Jewish immigrant from Lithuania, was able to win more concessions for the cloak makers than the shirtwaist makers had been able to secure. The cloak manufacturers agreed to a "limited" closed shop — limited in the sense that while employers committed to hiring only union workers, they would not promise to hire a particular worker recommended by the union. The manufacturers also agreed to the union's demands on hours, wages, and working conditions. In return, the workers agreed to a "protocol of peace" that would allow a committee of union and employer representatives to settle workplace complaints, eliminating the constant small-scale work stoppages that had plagued this portion of the garment industry in the past.[54]

Perhaps if the shirtwaist workers had also been able to win recognition of their union, the worst accidental workplace disaster in all of New York City history might never have taken place. But the Triangle Waist Company, with 850 employees, was one of the large manufacturers whose owners had refused to yield an inch in the Uprising of the 20,000. Its operators had to return to work on the company's terms or seek employment elsewhere.

The Triangle Company was located a block east of Washington Square Park on the top three floors of the ten-story Asch Building, which occupied the northwest corner of Washington Place and Greene Street. When it was built in 1900, the building was considered a huge step forward for the garment industry. Unlike the fetid Lower East Side tenement sweatshops, the Asch Building offered nearly ten thousand square feet per floor of brightly lit workspace and twelve-foot ceilings. Perhaps most important, the building was "fireproof."

Tragically, its contents were not, a fact ignored by those who constructed and occupied the structure. When the building's plans were submitted to the city for approval, officials suggested that the architect add a third emergency stairwell. He never did. They recommended that the fire escape extend to the ground rather than end six feet above a skylight. It was never altered. A fire prevention expert told the Triangle owners that they ought to hold fire drills, but none was ever scheduled. He also advised the firm to stop locking the doors to one of its two stairwells, but the company's managers, convinced that unlocking them would lead to rampant theft by the employees, ignored this advice as well.

None of these failures might have mattered had rag dealer Louis Levy shown up a few days earlier to make his periodic collection of garment scraps. Six times a year Levy would cart off Triangle's "cutaways," the shreds and strips of fabric left over after each piece of cloth needed to make a shirtwaist had been cut and sewn. Levy paid Triangle about seven cents per pound for the fabric scraps, which he then resold to papermakers. On Saturday March 25, 1911, it had been ten weeks since Levy's last visit to Triangle. Well over a ton of fabric scraps sat in the Triangle Waist Company's eighth-floor factory space that day at 4:45 p.m., when the managers finished handing out the week's pay envelopes and rang the quitting bell.

Suddenly, someone noticed smoke and flames shooting out from under one of the sixty-foot-long cutting tables, where the bulk of the fabric scraps lay. A carelessly tossed match or cigarette butt was probably responsible. The workers tried to pour buckets of water on the blaze, but the cutting tables' tops and sides (which reached almost to the floor in order to hold in the cuttings) prevented the water from reaching the rapidly spreading blaze. The workers on the eighth floor fled for their lives, taking the elevator, the fire escape (whose location was unknown to most of the workers, as it was hidden behind metal shutters), or in most cases squeezing their way single file down the narrow spiral staircases.[55]

With several thousand pounds of highly combustible fuel lying on the floor, the fire soon became an inferno. It spread via the airshaft to the company's ninth-floor workspace, where about 250 workers, almost all women, had just shut down their sewing machines and put on their coats. A few made it down one stairwell before it became engulfed in flames. The door to the other stairway was locked. Workers tried in vain for several minutes to break the lock but finally gave up. Meanwhile, the small number of workers on the tenth floor, where the pressing, packing, and executive offices were located, fled up the stairs to the roof, where they were able to climb to the roof of the New York University building next door via ladders put in place by students and faculty who had seen the blaze from their classroom windows.[56]

Back on the ninth floor, the flames were now spreading quickly from the rear of the building toward the windows that faced Washington Place and Greene Street. About three dozen women managed to squeeze out the window onto the narrow fire escape, yet because it ended in midair high above a glass skylight, the women were stranded there. Not designed to hold so many people for so long, it came loose from the side of the building and began to dangle precariously. Several other workers managed to throw themselves onto the top of the elevator as it sat two floors below. Once it descended for good, several more escaped to safety by shinnying down the elevator cables before the shaft filled with flames. Ida Nelson, perhaps the most enterprising of the trapped workers, escaped by wrapping herself in a cocoon of shirtwaist fabric, then dashing up two flights of stairs through the fire to the roof, peeling off the burning layers of the cotton-linen weave as she went.

Within minutes after the fire had been discovered, it became impossible for ninth-floor workers to escape. No more of them could fit onto the fire escape; one stairwell was locked; the other was engulfed in roaring flames; and the raging inferno was now rapidly spreading toward the remaining workers huddled in the southeast corner of the building. As the fire approached them, and with every other means of escape exhausted, many climbed outside onto the window ledges and prepared to jump. Onlookers shouted up that they should wait. The fire department was arriving and would extend their ladders to them. But when the firemen raised the ladders — the longest the department had — they reached only to the sixth floor, thirty feet below the trapped workers.

By this point, flames were shooting out the ninth-floor windows and dozens of workers had climbed out onto the ledge to escape them. The huge floor-to-ceiling windows, designed to let in as much light as possible, left no room to

The scene outside the Asch Building as the Triangle Waist Company fire was extinguished. By the time this photo was taken, more than 140 workers, all but 10 of them immigrants, had perished in the blaze.

hide from the flames, and the hair and clothing of the stranded workers soon began to catch fire. One seamstress, her clothes aflame, tried to jump to the ladder thirty feet below but missed and "hit the sidewalk like a flaming comet." The firemen next took out their "life nets," but these too were not designed for use from such heights. A few jumpers managed to hit them, but the force of their falls tore the nets from the hands of even the burliest firefighters.[57]

About eighty of the Triangle workers on the ninth floor, seeing no alternative, cowered in the southeast corner of the building by the windows or in the southwest corner in a coatroom next to the locked stairwell. They died inside the factory from burns and asphyxiation. Nineteen workers leaped into the elevator shaft, hoping somehow to survive their fall onto the top of the elevator car on the first floor. All of them perished as well.

Another forty or so, out on the ledges, refusing certain death inside, decided to jump. Some leaped alone, the women's long hair trailing high above them as they fell. Others jumped holding hands or locking arms with sisters or friends.

Bodies of Triangle Waist Company workers who jumped from the ninth floor when all other means of escape from the fire were exhausted. The bystanders are probably looking at other trapped workers standing on the building's ledge. More than forty workers jumped to their death.

Many threw their pay envelopes to the ground first, not wanting a week's pay to go to waste. Still others, not able to bring themselves to take the final step, asked friends to push them.

No matter how they did it, the result was the same. "Thud — dead! Thud — dead! Thud — dead!" wrote the one journalist who was present as the workers jumped. "They hit the pavement just like hail," reported a fireman who witnessed the horror. "We could hear the thuds faster than we could see the bodies fall." As if the scene were not gruesome enough, the very last employee to jump was impaled on an iron hook that protruded from the Asch Building six stories above the ground. The burning body hung there for about a minute before it finally fell to the pavement.

There were still about two dozen women stranded on the fire escape in the airshaft, out of sight of the crowds gawking at the fire from the street. A few women tried to jump down but crashed through the skylight underneath and perished. Some had the presence of mind to use the fire escape to reenter the building on the sixth floor and take the stairs down to safety. But the iron shutters on the exterior of the building blocked most of the other workers from doing so too. They held on for dear life, hoping to be rescued. But the roaring flames so heated the top of the fire escape that it began to twist and groan under the weight of the women. It finally snapped and partially crashed to the ground, killing everyone who had been desperately clinging to it.[58]

Amazingly, the fire died out quickly once the fabric and tissue paper on the floors of the factory had been consumed. The fire department had the blaze under control in just eighteen minutes and it was completely out in thirty. The building was indeed fireproof. The only part of it that burned was the wood trim of the windows. It still stands today, at 23–29 Washington Place, now part of New York University.

One hundred forty-six workers lay dead. All but fifteen of the victims were women. All but ten were immigrants. Just over one hundred were east European Jews; forty were Italian Americans. The sole immigrant who was not Jewish or Italian, Daisy Lopez Fitze, was born in Jamaica. The immigrant victims had lived in the United States, on average, for five years. A seventeen-year-old victim, Sarah Brenman, had arrived from Russia just six weeks before the fire. One of Triangle's owners was an immigrant too: Max Blanck had come to the United States from Russia at age twenty-one in about 1891.[59]

Daisy Lopez Fitze, a twenty-six-year-old immigrant from Jamaica, was the only immigrant victim of the fire who was not of Italian or east European Jewish origin. Several thousand West Indian immigrants settled in New York in the first decades of the twentieth century.

The fire's unprecedented toll horrified New Yorkers. The *Times* called it an "appalling disaster, . . . a calamity to put the whole town in a sorrowful mood." Even the city coroner, Herman Holtzhauser, who thought himself inured to such tragedies from years of work with the dead, was found outside the Asch Building "sobbing like a child," overcome by the enormity of the senseless slaughter.

On the Lower East Side and in the city's Italian neighborhoods, of course, the pain was far greater.

"Yesterday was one of the most horrific days in the history of the Jewish quarter," reported the Yiddish-language *Forward*. "Our entire immigrant population moves about in a daze of horror and pain." A Jewish immigrant writing an autobiographical sketch years later vividly remembered how the loss of life had devastated him even though no immediate family members had perished. "For half a year I was unable to enjoy the taste of food," he recalled. "Through those days and nights, I had no rest neither in the shop nor at home," because in his mind's eye, he said, "I saw their forms living and dead."[60]

From almost the moment the fire was extinguished, New Yorkers demanded that someone be held accountable for the deaths. On April 11 a grand jury indicted Blanck and Isaac Harris, the Triangle Waist Company's co-owners, for manslaughter on the grounds that their locking the ninth-floor stairway was the principal cause of their employees' deaths. "I think the mute testimony of the fastened lock left no question as to the guilt of the partners," District Attorney Charles Whitman told the court in explaining the grand jury's decision.[61]

As the trial commenced on December 4, New Yorkers found it hard to imagine that Harris and Blanck could win an acquittal, given the graphic testimony of the fire's survivors that the ninth-floor emergency stairwell door was routinely locked to prevent theft. Yet the owners' attorney insisted that if the door was locked, it was done by the factory's managers without the owners' knowledge or approval. Other witnesses, survivors who still worked for Triangle, insisted that the stairway doors were not routinely locked. The judge instructed the jury members that if they were not sure the owners had ordered the doors to be locked, they should not convict them. As a result, after less than two hours of deliberations, the jury found Harris and Blanck not guilty on all counts. The *Tribune* called the verdict "one of those disheartening failures of justice which are all too common in this country . . . The monstrous conclusion of the law is that the slaughter was no one's fault . . . This conclusion is revolting to the moral sense of the community."[62]

Disgusted with the verdict, the victims' families instituted civil proceedings against Blanck and Harris for negligence leading to the deaths of their loved ones. But the owners' lawyer managed to drag the cases out for years, apparently hoping that the victims' families would run out of patience and money for legal fees. "The claimants have been tired out," observed the *World* in 1914. In the end, only twenty-three families appear to have received compensation. They settled their cases with Triangle's insurance company, receiving a mere $75 per victim.[63]

The Triangle fire quickly led to the enactment of long-overdue workplace safety laws, which served as models for the rest of the nation. The state established a Factory Investigation Committee with a large staff, including Lemlich and many other union activists, which took testimony and conducted investigations. Over the next several years, the New York legislature enacted nearly twenty laws based on the committee's recommendations, including a workmen's compensation law (one of the first in the nation), a statute requiring automatic fire sprinklers and fire drills in tall buildings, and tougher regulations involving fire escapes, fire and factory inspection, exit stairwells, and exit doors. A reorganized and revitalized state department of labor and its factory inspection division would enforce all these rules.

But industry pushed back, winning modifications to or exemptions from a number of these laws and intimidating the factory inspectors. Exemplifying this fact was Blanck's arrest in 1913 for locking the emergency exit doors at the new Triangle garment factory at 79 Fifth Avenue. His punishment: a fine of $20, the minimum allowed under the law. The judge, who believed that the inspector who had cited Blanck was overzealous, apologized at sentencing for having to punish him at all. Never again was there another calamity on the scale of the Triangle disaster, but a factory fire in Williamsburg, Brooklyn, that killed twelve workers in 1915 gave proof that immigrants still often toiled in very dangerous conditions.[64]

Italians and east European Jews had not been political bystanders before the Triangle fire, but just as the famine Irish had initially deferred to native-born New Yorkers when they first arrived in the city, Jews and Italians had at first deferred to the Irish. "The Irish are natural leaders," argued Tammany boss George Olvany. "They have the ability to handle men. Even the Jewish districts have Irish leaders. The Jews want to be ruled by them." The political leaders of the city's Jewish and Italian districts had names like Walsh, Foley, Sullivan, Kelly, O'Brien, and Murphy throughout the years leading up to the Triangle fire.[65]

New immigrants did, however, sometimes rise to neighborhood prominence within the city's major political organizations. One of the Lower East Side's first Jewish politicos was Charles "Silver Dollar" Smith, who had emigrated from the German states as a small child and had changed his surname from Solomon to facilitate his entry into politics. Smith earned his nickname when he opened the Silver Dollar, a saloon at 64 Essex Street where Smith installed a marble-paved floor embedded with hundreds of silver dollars. The lights and mirrors had silver dollars in them as well. Smith insisted that he made back his investment in just three days from gawkers who "wanted to see how this fool had wasted his money." Smith served three terms on the Board of Aldermen and five in the New York State Assembly.[66]

The power of "ward heelers" like Smith depended on their ability to provide work for their constituents. Tammany leaders supplied "labor tickets" to their subordinates, which entitled the bearer to a job as a day laborer on a municipal construction project. When one of the city's early Italian power brokers, attorney Michael Rofrano, lost the power to dole out jobs after a falling-out with Tammany leader Thomas Foley, Rofrano made an alliance with the reformist mayor John Purroy Mitchel, who in 1914 appointed Rofrano deputy street commissioner, a position once held by "Boss" Tweed. That gave Rofrano control of six thousand city jobs. The willingness to use violence was still in these years a prerequisite for gaining and maintaining ward-level political power such as that wielded by Rofrano. Both he and Smith spent a good deal of time in court defending themselves from charges ranging from voter intimidation and felonious assault to (in the case of Rofrano) arranging the murder of a political foe. Rofrano spent eight months in hiding rather than face that charge, but after he finally turned himself in, a jury acquitted him.[67]

Just as the Irish had to fight to win positions of power within Tammany until the fall of "Boss" Tweed, Jews and Italians struggled in vain to wrest top party positions from the Irish, especially in the Democratic Party. Political leaders tried to placate the new immigrants by nominating ethnic figureheads for relatively unimportant positions or ones they knew they could not win. Republicans, for example, nominated a Jew, Edwin Einstein, for mayor in 1892. He lost by a nearly two-to-one margin to the Irish-born Democratic nominee, Thomas Gilroy. A few years later, in 1895, Einstein quit the Union League Club because that bastion of the city's Republican establishment was no longer admitting Jews. On the Democratic side, Henry Goldfogle, like Einstein a native-born Jew, represented the Lower East Side in Congress from 1901 to 1915. Goldfogle, however, never wielded significant power within the party, and never seemed to care much about the issues that mattered to residents of the Lower East Side. The *Forward* called Goldfogle "the Tammany politician who serves the rich."[68]

Lower East Side reformers and labor activists managed to displace Tammany flunkies like Goldfogle only by working outside the mainstream parties. On the Lower East Side, the Socialist Party decided to pin its hopes on the hero of the cloak makers' strike of 1910, labor lawyer Meyer London. London had arrived in New York from Russia in 1891 at about age twenty, learned English quickly, and graduated from New York University's law school in 1898. A year later he married Anna Rosenson, a dentist who had arrived in America from Russia two years before him. They had only one child, an extremely small family for the Lower East Side. "It is bad to be a poor man, but to be a poor man's wife is a calamity," London told a reporter when asked why they had but one child. "The wife should choose the number of her children."

London earned his first Socialist Party nomination for elective office even before finishing law school. And in 1910, a few months after he gained fame for representing striking cloak makers, London secured the party's nomination for Congress for the district that represented most of the Lower East Side. London "spoke with fiery force," recalled Russian immigrant Harry Roskolenko years later, "and we loved his socialist language. Meyer was Samson, George Washington, [and] Zane Grey" all rolled up into one heroic figure, as far as Roskolenko was concerned.[69]

That "socialist language" included demands for government assistance to the unemployed and a limit on what landlords could charge for rent. The latter was a stopgap measure until the socialists could achieve their goal of having the government build and operate its own worker housing so dwellings could be rented at cost rather than at the rates charged by greedy landlords. "Private ownership of land," London declared on the campaign trail, "is as absurd as private ownership of the air."[70]

Socialists also called for a government program of workers' insurance so those injured on the job would not have to fight for compensation from employers' parsimonious insurance companies, and for a system of government-run old-age pensions. "The amount of the pension, while small," wrote two of the city's socialist leaders, "at least is sufficient to take the edge off the fearful poverty and hopelessness of old age of members of the working class." Such a plan would also cover those rendered permanently unable to work through accident, injury, or illness. Socialists called as well for the elimination of child labor in the state's factories and on its farms.[71]

Of course, socialists knew that they had no hopes of enacting these plans in the short term. But they correctly predicted that by airing their ideas and simultaneously demonstrating their strength at the polls, they might shift the national conversation about issues of social justice and persuade the mainstream parties to adopt some of their ideas. They also believed that if any place in the United States was likely to elect a socialist to Congress, it was the Lower East Side, "where the victims of capitalism struggle and suffer."

In his first bid for Congress, in 1910, London polled 33 percent of the vote, nearly twice the proportion captured by the Republican nominee, but still came in second to Goldfogle. Two years later, London probably had the support of *more* voters than Goldfogle, but Tammany leaders used blatant polling place intimidation and vote-counting fraud to deny him the victory.[72]

The election of 1914, when London again challenged Goldfogle, was the first in New York State in which voters could cast their ballots in privacy in a voting booth and the first in which the government provided the ballots. Up to that point, a voter had obtained the ballot of his favored political organization at a booth outside the polls. London defeated Goldfogle in 1914, winning 49 percent of the vote in the three-way race. He was the first successful Socialist Party candidate in New York City, and only the second ever elected to Congress. "The eyes of the nation," a Washington paper predicted, "will watch his every act."[73]

"I don't expect to make many laws," London acknowledged to the press days after winning his seat in Congress. "I'm too small a minority." But he planned to use his office as a bully pulpit from which to "preach the gospel" of socialism, focusing in particular on the creation of a system of unemployment insurance. He also intended to push for nationalization of the nation's mines and railroads and for a ban on child labor.[74]

In the weeks before London was elected, however, war had broken out in Europe. Americans initially thought they could remain neutral and therefore isolate themselves from the martial "madness" that was gripping Europe, but the war, and the possibility of American involvement in the conflict, soon came to dominate debate in Washington. Because the United States was home to millions of recent arrivals from the very nations now at arms, Americans began to wonder if their welcoming policy toward immigrants ought to continue. The immigrants already in the United States (especially radicals like London and Goldman) began to appear much more threatening to native-born Americans than they had just a few months earlier.[75]

In fact, the war triggered a series of events that would eventually convince Americans that their centuries-old policy of accepting almost unlimited numbers of European immigrants ought to come to an end. At the beginning of 1914, most Americans looked at socialists like London as harmless gadflies. (Anarchists like Goldman were another matter.) By the time the war ended in 1919, Americans perceived these same immigrant radicals as a "red menace." Within a few years, congressmen representing fearful Americans would enact the harshest restrictions ever imposed on immigration, reducing the flow of newcomers to a trickle, leaving only a tiny handful of slots available for Italians, east European Jews, and other immigrants from southern and eastern Europe, and none at all for those from Asia and Africa. These restrictions would profoundly alter both the immigrant experience in New York and the course of American immigration history.

TOP TEN SOURCES OF NEW YORK'S IMMIGRANTS, 1910

Russia	484,193
Italy	340,770
Germany	278,137
Ireland	252,672
Austria	190,246
England	78,483
Hungary	76,627
Sweden	34,952
Romania	33,586
Canada	27,180
Total foreign-born	**1,944,357**
Total population	**4,766,883**

Source: *Thirteenth Census of the United States Taken in the Year 1910,* vol. 1, *Population, 1910* (Washington, D.C., 1913), 856–57.

Note: Because Poland was being occupied by Austria-Hungary, Germany, and Russia in 1910, the Census Bureau apportioned New York's Polish-born population among those three nations in its 1910 tally.

19

RESTRICTION

IN JANUARY 1913, *Popular Science Monthly* published an article called "Going Through Ellis Island" by Dr. Alfred C. Reed, a member of the United States Public Health Service medical team that inspected newcomers at the immigration station. Many such articles appeared in the popular press, typically describing the huge variety and number of immigrants arriving each year at Ellis Island, while reassuring the public that the thorough, scientific system of inspection taking place there insured that only healthy, "desirable" immigrants gained admission.

Reed's article was different. The "character" of American immigration "has changed markedly in the past thirty years," Reed warned pessimistically. "Previous to 1883, western and northern Europe sent a stalwart stock, 95 per cent. of all who came. They sought new homes and were settlers. Scandinavians, Danes, Dutch, Germans, French, Swiss and the English islanders, they were the best of Europe's blood. They were industrious, patriotic and far-sighted. They were productive and constructive workers. Where nothing had been, they planted, and mined, and built, and toiled with their hands, while yet finding time to educate their children and train them to love the new mother-country and appreciate the blessings she furnished."[1]

But now, Reed insisted, all that had changed. Beginning in the 1890s, "the immigrant tide has flowed more and more from eastern and southern Europe. The others still come, but they are far outnumbered by the Jews, Slavs, the Balkan and Austrian races, and those from the Mediterranean countries. In contrast with the earlier immigration, these peoples are less inclined to transplant their homes and affections. They come to make what they can in a few years of arduous unremitting labor, and then return to their homes to spend it in comparative comfort and ease." Unlike their predecessors, who, according to Reed, immediately put down roots and assimilated, the new immigrants "tend to form a floating population. They do not amalgamate." They had come to America merely "for what they can get."

In order to protect the United States from the "deteriorating character" of the southern and eastern European newcomers, Reed argued, an end to America's centuries-old tradition of virtually unrestricted immigration was now "justifiable and necessary. No one can stand at Ellis Island . . . without becoming a firm believer in restriction and admission of only the best." By "the best," Reed did not mean the smartest or the strongest; he meant northern and western Europeans. "Restriction is vitally necessary if our truly American ideals and institutions are to persist, and if our inherited stock of good American manhood is not to be depreciated."[2]

Reed may have been a good doctor, but he was a poor student of American immigration history. The "old" immigrants had not assimilated any more thoroughly or quickly than the "new" ones. The Germans and Scandinavians had concentrated in homogeneous urban and rural enclaves, continued to speak their native tongues, and did not have much contact with outsiders unless their work required it. The Irish, too, had seemed utterly foreign and unassimilable to most native-born Americans when they arrived in the famine era. Whether thinking about foreign policy or an upcoming boxing match, they found it almost impossible to put "American interests" above Irish ones. The children of these immigrants were the first in their families to "amalgamate" in the manner Reed desired. They were no different in this regard from the Italians: the adult immigrants clung steadfastly to their language, food, and culture, while their children were determined to be utterly "American." The famine Irish had been just as much physical wrecks upon arrival in America as Italians and Jews seemed to be fifty years later.

Nonetheless, Americans in the first quarter of the twentieth century became convinced that Reed was right — that the new immigrants were demonstrably inferior to those from previous generations and that the new wave of immigration, if left unchecked, would dilute the nation's Anglo-Saxon bloodlines and leave the United States a poorer, weaker, less "American" nation. World War I, and the threat of a massive influx of refugees after it was over, fed these fears, leading Congress to enact a series of successively harsher immigration restrictions, culminating in the National Origins Act of 1924, which reduced by nearly 95 percent the number of immigrants who could enter the United States from southern and eastern Europe — the very places where most of New York's immigrants originated.

In the two decades before World War I, more immigrants came to the United States from Italy than from any other single nation, and the reaction of Americans to the Italian newcomers epitomizes the feelings that eventually led Congress to enact its restrictions. One complaint about the Italians had been leveled against each new wave of immigrants for centuries: it was said that unlike previous newcomers, this latest group was altogether *too* foreign ever to become true Americans. A letter writer to the *Times,* for example, complained that when Jacob Riis looked at New York's Italian enclaves for his books and articles, he did so through "rose-colored" glasses:

> Instead of humor I found — dirt; instead of picturesqueness — squalor and a reprehensible neglect of the commonest laws of decency. Beer and tobacco, garlic and filth, quarrel and stiletto, noise and noxious odors alternate and fill up the gamut of these people's lives, to the disgust and weariness of soul of all near-by people who have a fractional claim to respectability and culture. Is there no redress when one of them has spat upon your coat or cape from a second-story window while you were passing by? Can they not be compelled to clothe their children in the warm weather with at least a ribbon? . . . What can be done to stop the advance of this octopus of sensuality and filth? A single family of these Italians being allowed in a new street lowers the tone and acts as a wedge through which hundreds, yea, thousands, of his countrymen and countrywomen bring their frowsiness and garlic, beer and rotten tobacco.[3]

According to restrictionists, the Italians' uncivilized behavior stemmed from genetic inferiority. Southern Italians were members of "the long-head, dark, Mediterranean race, with no small infusion of Greek, Saracen, and African blood in the Calabrians and Sicilians," wrote Edward Alsworth Ross, a professor of sociology at the University of Wisconsin at Madison, in 1914. Those from Naples, he continued, "show a distressing frequency of low foreheads, open mouths, weak chins, poor features, skew faces, small or knobby crania, and backless heads." In short, they could not help their illiteracy, poverty, and disease, these Americans argued. Italians were genetically deficient.

Another problem with the Italian newcomers, according to their detractors, was that they did not assimilate or become citizens to the same extent as previous generations of immigrants. "The Southern Italians remain nearly as aloof as did the Cantonese who built the Central Pacific Railway," Ross contended. He argued that Italian immigrants who live in a remote labor camp "or a box-car, or herd on some 'Dago flat,' are not really in America" at all. That this segregation was the choice of the immigrant rather than something forced upon him by American society was evident, said these naysayers, in the Italians' low naturalization rates. South Italian immigrants who had lived in the United States from five to nine years as of 1911 were only half as likely to have become American citizens as Germans who had arrived in the same period. Irish immigrants were nearly four times as likely as Italians to have become citizens. The Italians were true "Birds of Passage" whose lack of interest in assimilating or becoming citizens rendered them permanently foreign and therefore undesirable.[4]

Perhaps the most undesirable of the traits attributed to the Italians was their supposed propensity toward violence. "The knife with which [the Italian] cuts his bread he also uses to lop off another 'dago's' finger or ear," complained lawyer James Appleton Morgan in another article in *Popular Science Monthly,* this one called "What Shall We Do with the 'Dago'?" According to Morgan, the Italian man did not even restrict his violence to other men: "His women follow him like dogs, expect no better treatment than dogs, and would not have the slightest idea how to conduct themselves without a succession of blows and kicks . . . When a woman is seriously hurt, she simply keeps out of sight somewhere till she is well enough for the kicking and striking to begin over again." Mercurial and hot-blooded, Italians were said to draw stilettos and switchblades at the slightest provocation. Even journalist George Kibbe Turner, a progressive, could not resist hyping "the notorious tendency of the low-class Italian to violence and murder."[5]

Much of the violence associated with Italian immigrants was ascribed to various criminal organizations supposedly imported from Italy: the Camorra from Naples, the 'Ndrangheta from Calabria, and especially the "Black Hand" from Sicily. At the height of the hysteria over the presumed importation of organized crime to America, from 1907 to 1909, the *New York Times* mentioned the Black Hand in more than six hundred articles. Italian Americans insisted that the panic was all "arrant nonsense." There might be Italian American criminals, and even small Italian American criminal gangs, but even as it touted the alleged threat posed by the Black Hand, the *Times* admitted in 1908 that "there is no regular organization of these criminals outside the columns of the yellow press."[6]

The defenders of Italian Americans unwittingly provided additional ammunition to the restrictionists. Gino Speranza, a New York attorney and son of Italian immigrants, admitted that the Black Hand existed but claimed that it was "a sort of Tammany Hall in its worst form and dealing with its own problems in its own way. It is largely confined to Palermo and does not assassinate except in extreme cases." Most murders in New York involving Italians, Speranza insisted, resulted from personal vendettas rather than organized crime. Neither of these observations was likely to reassure nervous Americans.[7]

The killing of the man charged with stamping out Italian crime in the city, Lieutenant Joseph Petrosino of the New York Police Department, added sensational fuel to the immigration-restriction fire. Petrosino, who was born in Padula, an inland village one hundred miles southeast of Naples, arrived in New York at age eleven in 1872 with his fifty-five-year-old father, a tailor. They settled on Mulberry Bend, and young Joe worked after school selling newspapers and shining shoes. When he finished his education, he worked for a butcher, at an Italian bank, and with an Italian labor gang employed by a railroad contractor. Because Petrosino could speak both Italian and English fluently, he was able to land a job on the Hudson River docks directing Italian laborers in the loading of the garbage scows that hauled away the city's refuse. In that work he impressed a neighborhood police captain, who suggested that Petrosino apply to join the force. In 1894 he managed to secure one of these coveted positions.

Petrosino rose slowly through the ranks, apparently because of prejudice he faced in the predominantly Irish American police force. "In those days," a biographer wrote in 1914, "advancement came only through 'pull,'" typically from a political officeholder or some patron in Tammany Hall. Lacking these, Petrosino was given a lowly assignment: patrolling Battery Park to protect immigrants arriving from Ellis Island from the "runners" who tried to swindle ignorant newcomers. He was also sent on loan to the Paterson, New Jersey, police to infiltrate the city's anarchist organizations. It took Petrosino eleven years to get his first promotion, but four years later he received a second and joined the Detective Bureau. As the number of crimes involving Italian criminal gangs increased, Petrosino proved himself indispensable at solving them, and he was eventually put in charge of the Detective Bureau's new "Italian Squad."[8]

"The idea that there is a big criminal club in this city called the 'Black Hand' is all a myth," Petrosino told the *Times* in 1908. "It has grown out of the custom of the newspapers of calling every crime committed by an Italian a 'Black Hand' outrage." But Petrosino *did* believe that lax immigration laws had permitted the United States to become "the dumping ground for all the criminals and banditti of Italy." He proposed that "a special bureau of inspectors" obtain from the Italian government a list of Italian felons, because "with the aid of this the inspectors could prevent a great many of these men from ever entering the country," stopping them either at the Italian ports or at Ellis Island. When no one followed up on his suggestion, Petrosino proposed traveling to Italy himself to obtain copies of the criminal records of Italian immigrants he had already arrested in New York so the convicts could be deported for having lied at Ellis Island about their felonious past.[9]

Arguing that Petrosino had become too valuable to be allowed to leave the city, Police Commissioner Theodore Bingham tried to persuade him to send a subordinate to Italy, but the detective insisted on going, even after the attempt to make the trip in secrecy was foiled by the *Herald* in February 1909, just days before his departure. After consulting with Italian organized crime experts in

THE FOOL PIED PIPER.

Rats labeled MURDERER, ASSASSIN, THIEF, and BLACK HAND stream out of Europe's sewers and follow Uncle Sam toward the Statue of Liberty and America's shores as a result of "lax immigration" laws in this *Puck* cartoon from 1909.

Rome, Petrosino headed south to Sicily. He had spent only a day or two in Palermo collecting information on New York's Sicilian criminals before he was lured by a potential informant to a midnight rendezvous at the Piazza Marina, where Petrosino was shot and killed.

Petrosino was the first American police officer killed abroad in the line of duty. No one was ever arrested for his murder. While his story is largely forgotten in the United States, except within the New York City Police Department, it is better known in Italy, where as recently as 2014 an Italian organized crime suspect in Palermo was caught on a wiretap bragging that his great-uncle was the one who had gunned down the famous American detective. Petrosino's murder seemed to contradict his own insistence that organized crime was a figment of Americans' overwrought imagination. In 1914 the *Herald* ran an eight-part series on Petrosino's fight against the Black Hand based on his own investigative diaries (which were displayed at the Museum of the New York Police Department in 2009 after being discovered in a Brooklyn attic). In them, Petrosino frequently referred to "the mafia" and the attempts of Sicilian immigrants to bring it to New York. So despite his efforts to persuade the public that the Mafia was a myth, his life and death left Americans convinced that it was both very real and very dangerous.[10]

Native-born New Yorkers considered Jewish immigrants just as likely to be

criminals as Italians. Just a few months before Petrosino was gunned down in
Palermo, Bingham published an article in the *North American Review* in which
he asserted that Jews, who constituted about a quarter of New York City's population, committed about half of its crime. "They are burglars, firebugs, pick-
pockets and highway robbers," Bingham charged, though "pocket-picking is
the one to which they seem to take most naturally." New York's Jews responded
swiftly and emphatically. They produced statistics showing that fewer than 20
percent of New York's convicted criminals were Jews, figures corroborated by
modern historians. Bingham eventually retracted his claims, insisting that he
had used data provided by a subordinate without checking their accuracy. A
congressional report published in 1911 likewise found that "immigrants are less
prone to commit crime than are native Americans," something still the case today. Nonetheless, the belief that the new immigrants were predisposed to crime
— violent crime in the case of the Italians — was a constant refrain of restrictionists.[11]

The new immigrants' reputation for criminality was enhanced by the fact that
natives associated them with far-left political movements that, in some cases,
preached violence as a valid response to workers' grievances. Although only a
few thousand immigrants out of millions joined the anarchist ranks, these radical socialists constantly made headlines and disproportionately shaped Americans' views of the southern and eastern European newcomers. There was no
denying the anarchists' proclivity to violence. Alexander Berkman, of course,
had shot and wounded steel magnate Henry Clay Frick in 1892. Six years later,
an Italian anarchist assassinated Empress Elisabeth of Austria, while in 1900, an
Italian immigrant anarchist from Paterson, New Jersey, shot and killed Italy's
King Umberto I. Another anarchist, Ohioan Leon Czolgosz, assassinated President William McKinley in 1901. Czolgosz was not an immigrant, but his Polish
Catholic surname indicated that he too could not trace his origins to "the best
of Europe's blood." On the eve of World War I, New York's anarchists — predominantly Jewish and Italian immigrants — continued to organize public rallies and threaten leading industrialists with death. When a bomb intended for
John D. Rockefeller Jr. detonated prematurely in an anarchist's tenement apartment at 1626 Lexington Avenue in Harlem in July 1914, killing four immigrant
radicals, injuring dozens of the building's residents, and destroying the top two
floors of the six-story building, the association between the new immigrants
and anarchist violence became stronger still.[12]

With the start of Word War I a month later, native-born Americans became
even more suspicious of the immigrants in their midst. At this point, to the
relief of most Americans, the United States did not enter the war, which pit-

ted the "Central Powers" (Germany, Austria-Hungary, and the Ottoman Empire) against the "Allies" (Great Britain, France, and Russia). President Woodrow Wilson declared that in order to stay out of the conflict, the United States "must be neutral in fact as well as in name during these days that are to try men's souls." Wilson's insistence on neutrality resulted not merely from a desire to keep the nation out of war. Millions of immigrants were associated with either side of the conflict, and if all expressions of sympathy for one side or the other could not be repressed, Wilson feared that "our mixed populations would wage war on each other."[13]

These fears were not unfounded. As word of the European declarations of war reached New York in August 1914, nearly two thousand German immigrants took to the streets to show their support for the Central Powers, marching four abreast up Broadway while singing "The Watch on the Rhine" and other German martial airs. Many of these immigrants were reservists in the German army who hoped to return to the Fatherland to fulfill their military obligations. Should a group of them happen to cross paths with a contingent of French or English New Yorkers, it was hard to imagine how bloodshed could be avoided.[14]

Outside of these three groups, however, it was not easy to determine which side New York's immigrants might take. Irish Americans, many still citizens of Great Britain, hated the English and hoped that their defeat would cause the breakup of the British Empire and bring about independence for Ireland. Russia was fighting on the side of the British and the French, but New York's Russian Jewish immigrants had been oppressed under the tsar and could not bring themselves to support a war that might consolidate his shaky hold on power. Emperor Franz Josef of Austria-Hungary, in contrast, was adored on the Lower East Side for being a friend of the Jews. The British, however, had offered more support than any other Europeans for a Jewish homeland in Palestine, so they too were considered allies of the Jews. Italy declared itself neutral at the outset of the war. So of all the city's major immigrant populations, only the position of the German immigrants was unambiguous.[15]

One of the underpinnings of Wilson's neutrality policy became known as "anti-hyphenism," the idea that for the United States to avoid an internal struggle between its immigrant communities over the issues being contested in Europe, newcomers needed to immediately cease considering themselves "Irish-Americans" or "Italian-Americans" and instead think of themselves solely as Americans. "Some Americans need hyphens in their names because only part of them have come over," said Wilson, "but when the whole man has come over, heart and thought and all, the hyphen drops of its own weight out of his name." Despite his calls for complete neutrality, Wilson made little effort to hide his

Only about four thousand Chinese immigrants lived in New York during World War I, and because they were barred from becoming citizens, their loyalty to the United States was particularly suspect in the eyes of many Americans. Perhaps in order to dispel such suspicions and prove that they were not "hyphenated Americans," these Chinese immigrants agreed to dress in patriotic garb for this parade in 1918 to promote the sale of Liberty Bonds to help fund the war.

sympathy for the Allies, and the fact that the United States sold munitions to them but not to the Central Powers galled many Irish and German New Yorkers. Many of these immigrants saw the "anti-hyphen wave" as a thinly veiled cover for a revival of Know Nothingism.[16]

Some immigrants were willing to buck the tide of hyperpatriotism and assert that there was nothing wrong with having affection for two countries. "I glory, as an American, in my hyphen," insisted Irish-born Percy Andreae, a Chicagoan whose views mirrored those of many New Yorkers. According to Andreae, it was the dual allegiance of the founding fathers that had made the American Revolution possible. A German-born New Yorker, attorney Theodore Sutro, likewise proudly celebrated "my dual relation to the country of my birth and to this, the country of my citizenship and unqualified devotion." Yet such admissions, even when accompanied by absolute declarations of loyalty to the United States, were not considered sufficiently patriotic in the midst of the anti-hyphen crusade. Immigrants could not concede *any* feelings for their native land if they wanted to avoid suspicion or rebuke, especially if their native land was Germany or Ireland.[17]

Before the war, of course, elected officials had highlighted and even appealed to the immigrants' dual loyalties. "The politicians, both Democratic and Republican, have taught it to us," one confused voter told the socialist newspaper *The Call* in August 1914. Politicians, he said, "get to us by way of the hyphen," appealing for the immigrants' votes by promising that they would be the greatest "friend to Italy" or "champion of the Irish cause" if elected. These very same politicians were now condemning the dual sympathies that they had implicitly endorsed just months earlier.[18]

The presidential campaign of 1916 exemplified this sea change. Many observers anticipated that the Democrat Wilson's tacit support for the Allies would cost him the votes of millions of German and Irish Americans, typically loyal adherents of the Democratic Party. But when the German-American Alliance endorsed Wilson's Republican challenger, Charles Evans Hughes, the New Yorker all but repudiated the endorsement. "My attitude is one of undiluted Americanism," Hughes defensively told the press upon hearing of the Alliance's decision, "and anybody who supports me is supporting an out-and-out American and an out-and-out American policy and absolutely nothing else."

Wilson was not about to let Hughes position himself as the only superpatriot in the race. When in October the president received a telegram from an Irish American from upstate New York named Jeremiah O'Leary condemning Wilson's "pro-British policies," Wilson replied with the most memorable zinger of the campaign. "I would feel deeply mortified to have you or anybody like you vote for me," Wilson replied to O'Leary. "Since you have access to many disloyal Americans and I have not, I will ask you to convey this message to them." On election day, many observers ascribed Wilson's loss of New York State, which he had won four years earlier, to a falloff in support from New York's German and Irish Americans. But the president still won reelection comfortably.[19]

The growing anti-immigrant feeling in the city and the nation during the campaign might have become even stronger had Americans known the true source of a series of huge explosions that jolted New Yorkers out of their beds at 2:00 a.m. on Sunday July 30, 1916. The blasts took place on Black Tom Island, now part of the mainland but at the time a small islet just off the New Jersey shoreline that lay two and a half miles west-southwest of the lower tip of Manhattan. Black Tom Island was connected to Jersey City by a railroad bridge and was the place where trains from the nation's munitions factories deposited hundreds of boxcars brimming with military ordnance for loading onto ships that would transport it to the Allies in Europe.

At first, no one understood the source of the explosions, which shattered most of the windows in lower Manhattan as well as many uptown and in Brooklyn. "Women became hysterical . . . Police whistles were blown frantically," reported the *Times,* as every policeman, finding his beat covered in broken glass, assumed that the blast had taken place within his jurisdiction. Only after an hour or so of chaos could enough New Yorkers see the black plume of smoke emanating from the Jersey side of the Hudson, below the Battery, and realize that the explosions had taken place miles away.[20]

Evidence suggests that a German agent operating out of a Manhattan safe house organized this brazen act of sabotage. To carry out the plot, the agent recruited Kurt Jahnke, a German immigrant who had become an American citizen and served in the U.S. Marine Corps in the Philippines, as well as a Slovak immigrant named Michael Kristoff, a former employee at Black Tom. They were assisted by a German spy known as Lothar Witzke who posed as an immigrant. Bribing guards to gain access to the facility, the three men lit small fires and then escaped. When the flames reached the munitions, the resulting explosions were probably the strongest ever to rock New York. Amazingly, only seven people were killed. Among the dead was a baby thrown from its crib in Jersey City. The explosions were heard and felt as far away as Philadelphia. The blasts were initially blamed on carelessness by the companies that ran the rail yard and docks; prosecutors indicted their officers for manslaughter. Only after the war was the spy ring uncovered. (In 1939 the United States–German Mixed Claims Commission ruled that the German government owed the Lehigh Valley Railroad and the Black Tom installation's insurers $21 million in damages. Adolf Hitler refused to abide by the decision, but after World War II the West German government agreed to pay the award in installments. Only in 1979 did

Some of the destruction on Black Tom Island in New York Harbor caused by German saboteurs, several of them immigrants, in July 1916.

it make the final payment.) Had it been revealed sooner, the city's immigrants would undoubtedly have come in for severe censure — and not only the Germans. It turned out that the same German operative who directed the Black Tom sabotage was also bribing Irish American longshoremen to orchestrate slowdowns and strikes on the waterfront in Brooklyn in order to impede the delivery of munitions to the Allies.[21]

With accumulating grievances against Germany — in particular its resumption of unrestricted submarine warfare at the beginning of February 1917 and its offer to support a Mexican invasion of the American Southwest, revealed in the infamous intercepted Zimmermann telegram later that same month — Wilson asked Congress to declare war on Germany and institute a draft to fill the army's ranks. Congress overwhelmingly supported the president, with more than 450 members voting in favor of war and only 56 against. One of the dissenters was the Lower East Side's socialist congressman, Meyer London. "Modern wars are at the bottom sanguinary struggles for the commercial advantages of the possessing classes," asserted another New York Socialist Party leader, immigrant labor lawyer Morris Hillquit, in explaining the socialists' opposition to American entry into the conflict. "They are disastrous to the cause of the workers, their struggles and aspirations, their rights and liberties." German Americans and Irish Americans were the other New Yorkers most likely to oppose the declaration of war.[22]

Once the United States officially entered the conflict, suspicion of immigrants grew even more intense. In the declaration of war promulgated by Wilson after Congress granted its approval, the president designated male German immigrants aged fourteen and up who were not American citizens as "alien enemies." Wilson barred them from possessing a weapon, flying an aircraft, operating a two-way radio, or coming within one-half mile of any American military installation, vessel, or munitions plant. Alien enemies were also not allowed to "write, print, or publish any attack or threat against the Government" or its policies. Realizing that non-Germans might engage in the same activities as German provocateurs, Congress in June 1917 passed the Espionage Act, which made it a crime for *anyone* to promote the success of the nation's enemies during times of war, or to cause or attempt to cause insubordination, disloyalty, or refusal of duty. The reach of this legislation was extended in 1918 with passage of the Sedition Act, which explicitly made publishing, speaking, or even drawing cartoons opposed to the war punishable by imprisonment. Officials announced that so much as complaining that "the government is controlled by Wall Street, or munition manufacturers or any other special interests" was grounds for arrest, as was any statement criticizing "our allies."[23]

· · ·

At the start of the war, the city's quarter of a million German immigrants worried security experts and the public. Everything German became suspect in the eyes of "100 percent Americans." The Metropolitan Opera announced that it would no longer perform the works of Richard Wagner because, as the American Defense Society put it, German music was "one of the most dangerous forms of German propaganda." The city stopped teaching German in its elementary schools and drastically reduced its German-language offerings in high schools. School officials even debated no longer calling the first year of elementary school "kindergarten."

To German immigrants, it seemed as if every passerby was casting suspicious eyes on them. "You couldn't walk the street with a German paper under your arm," recalled New Yorker Helen Wagner. "You'd be abused from one end of the block to the other." Before America's entry into the war, it had been just as common to hear German spoken on Manhattan's Upper East Side as it was to hear Yiddish on the sidewalks of the Lower East Side or Italian on Mulberry Street. But once the United States declared war, Wagner noted, "we kept speaking German at home, but we avoided it on the street."[24]

German New Yorkers were sometimes subjected to merciless beatings or public humiliations. Mobs dragged several German immigrants out of their homes and forced them to kiss the Stars and Stripes, sing "The Star-Spangled Banner," or perform other ritual demonstrations of American loyalty. Roving gangs of superpatriots broke up public meetings of socialists and Irish nationalists, too. Mob actions of this sort were much more common and violent in the Midwest — a German American suspected of disloyalty was lynched in Collinsville, Illinois — but many of New York's German immigrants lived in fear nonetheless.[25]

As a result, many German New Yorkers attempted to hide their ethnic background, and businesses that catered to German immigrants tried to distance themselves from associations with the Fatherland. The German Savings Bank of Manhattan renamed itself the Central Savings Bank, while the bank of the same name in Brooklyn became the Lincoln Savings Bank. The Germania Life Insurance Company was rechristened the Guardian Life Insurance Company. The German Hospital and Dispensary, which just a few years earlier had dedicated its new Kaiser Wilhelm Pavilion, was renamed Lenox Hill Hospital. Most of these changes took place in 1918, once the United States had entered the war and over 1 million Americans had joined the fighting.[26]

Many of those indicted in New York for seditious activities were socialists. Most, like Max Eastman, John Reed, and Scott Nearing, were American-born, but several were east European Jews. The best known, Emma Goldman and Alexander Berkman, were arrested on the very day the Espionage Act took effect, for discouraging enlistment in the armed forces in *Mother Earth* (an anarchist magazine owned by Goldman) and *The Blast* (the journal run by Berkman). They were convicted a month later and sentenced to two years in prison. Both were required to do nine hours of garment work per day in their prisons' sweatshops, Goldman in Jefferson City, Missouri, and Berkman in Atlanta.[27]

Despite the efforts of Goldman and Berkman to foment opposition to the draft, conscription was implemented in June and July 1917 with far less dissent than had greeted the Civil War draft fifty-four years earlier. The widespread acceptance of conscription resulted in part from the fact that the World War I law authorizing it did not offer draftees the opportunity to provide substitutes or pay a commutation fee. Every draftee who passed the physical exam had to serve. It also helped that the government needed to enlist a much smaller proportion of New Yorkers than it had during the Civil War.

Most of New York's draftees served in the army's Seventy-seventh Division, known as the "Melting Pot Division." Though its men supposedly spoke forty-two languages, and even included several Chinese Americans, it was dominated, one Jewish veteran jokingly recalled years later, by "the Jews and the wops and the *dirty* Irish cops." In all, the city sent 38,000 troops to the front lines in France, a large proportion of whom were immigrants.[28]

The Seventy-seventh reached France in the waning days of the war in June 1918 and made it to the front lines in August. Nonetheless, the fighting the New Yorkers did experience was intense and deadly. They were strafed by aircraft, pummeled by heavy artillery, sprayed with machine-gun fire, immolated by flamethrowers, and subjected to numerous mustard gas attacks. By the time the war ended in November, about 2,500 of the New Yorkers in the Seventy-seventh had been killed and 7,500 wounded. Overall, 7,300 residents of New York City died in the war. Among the dead was Goldman's nephew, Lieutenant David Hochstein, a twenty-six-year-old virtuoso violinist who had been declared exempt from service but felt guilty and enlisted anyway.[29]

The Seventy-seventh's most famous engagement was in the Argonne Forest, where nearly a thousand New Yorkers became detached from the main Allied force and were surrounded by German troops, who demanded that the Americans surrender or face certain death. The Americans refused, expecting that the rest of their division would soon come to their rescue. Division commanders, however, did not know the whereabouts of the "Lost Battalion." Two days, three days, four days went by without food or water, and still no rescue effort materialized. Under near constant bombardment from both the Germans and the Americans (who did not realize they were aiming their artillery at their own men), the 650 New Yorkers suffered a casualty rate that surpassed 65 percent. "We can hear the moaning of your wounded," read a message the Germans sent across the lines, written by an immigrant from Spokane who had returned to Germany to fight for the Fatherland. "In the name of humanity, why not surrender?"[30]

But the Americans refused to give in. "Do you remember how hard it used to be for me to go without food for twenty-four hours on Yom Kippur?" Irving Liner from Brownsville reminded his immigrant parents in a letter he wrote a few weeks later. "Well, I had to go without food for five days, and it didn't affect me in the least." The Americans' strategy for breaking the siege was to send out "runners," whose mission was to race across the no-man's-land between the two sides, then somehow make their way through the German lines and out the other side to division headquarters a few miles away. After four days, three dozen men had volunteered for this suicide duty. Each one was shot or captured.

Nonetheless, on the fifth morning of the siege, October 6, one more volunteer stepped forward: twenty-six-year-old barber Abraham Krotoshinsky from Plotsk, who had immigrated to New York in 1912. "I started out at daybreak," Krotoshinsky later recalled, and immediately came under heavy fire. "I ran across an open space, down a valley and up a valley into some bushes. I remember crawling, lying under bushes, digging myself into holes. Somehow or other — I don't know how to this day — I found myself at nightfall in German trenches." When some German soldiers came upon him, he played dead. One even stepped on his fingers to make sure Krotoshinsky wasn't alive, "but I kept myself from making any outcry," he said. When they had passed on (the Germans could not keep their trenches fully manned by this point in the war), Krotoshinsky crawled out of the trench and into a deserted one closer to the American lines. From there he could hear American voices, but even in uniform, he could not simply race to his fellows in arms without fear of being shot. He began shouting "Hello! Hello!" in his thick Yiddish accent, and finally persuaded a scouting party to come out and meet him. They took him in, and a few hours later Krotoshinsky himself led the first rescue squad back to the Lost Battalion. The war ended a few months later, in November 1918. For his heroism, Krotoshinsky was awarded the Distinguished Service Cross. The *Times* later called him "New York's greatest hero of World War I."[31]

Because of the valor of soldiers like Krotoshinsky, many of their non-immigrant comrades left the army with more positive feelings toward the southern and eastern European immigrants than they had harbored when they entered. "We have about every nationality you can think of in my company," wrote a soldier in the Seventy-seventh, Charles Minder (a native-born New Yorker), to his German-born mother. "The last six months of my life in the army, living and suffering with these fellows, has done more for me to get rid of race-prejudice than anything else could have done." Minder was not referring to prejudice against African Americans. From the content of this letter, it is clear that the race Minder was speaking of in particular was the Jewish "race."[32]

Back in the city, however, Jewish political activity made the eastern European immigrants seem even more radical and distinct from the American mainstream. In the November 1917 elections, the first held after the United States entered the war, the Socialist Party was the only political organization to campaign for peace. With many New Yorkers still ambivalent about risking American lives in the deadly conflict, socialist candidates garnered more votes than they ever had before. Their mayoral candidate, Hillquit (born Moishe Hillkowitz in Riga, Latvia), captured 22 percent of the vote, to this day the highest proportion ever won by a socialist candidate in a New York citywide contest.

In the legislative races, New York socialists captured ten seats in the state assembly (another record), all in predominantly Jewish immigrant districts. Swiss-born August Claessens was elected in central Harlem, while Elmer Rosenberg (from Hungary), William Karlin (Kiev), and Louis Waldman (also Ukraine) represented the Lower East Side. William Feigenbaum (Antwerp), Joseph Whitehorn (Romania), and Abraham Shiplacoff (Ukraine) won races in Brooklyn, while Samuel Orr (born Shmul Orkoski in Poland), Charles Garfinkel (Ukraine), and Benjamin Gitlow (the American-born son of Russian immigrants) were elected in the Bronx. Most of the immigrant legislators had arrived in New York as children or in their teens, and nearly all of them were either labor lawyers with degrees from Columbia and New York University or union organizers. Besides speaking out against the war, the socialist legislators advocated for workers' rights, especially during strikes, and were the first New York legislators ever to propose a bill legalizing the dissemination of printed information describing birth control methods. They also sponsored legislation banning landlords from raising rents in the first year after a tenant moved into an apartment and requiring thirty days' notice for all rent increases. Feigenbaum proposed that the city build public housing for low-income New Yorkers and charge for rent only what it cost to maintain the buildings. Waldman advocated what he called a "social security" system of government-financed old-age pensions and unemployment insurance. He also asked the legislature to set up a state-run system of universities that would cost nothing to attend. None of these bills even made it out of committee.[33]

By the time the city's socialist assemblymen ran for reelection in 1919, the political situation had changed dramatically. The bloody aftermath of the Russian Revolution of 1917 made socialists' calls for the toppling of the capitalist order terrifying to many Americans. The moderate socialists elected to the assembly became suspect in large part because of the tactics of their radical anarchist brethren. In April 1919, Italian American anarchists sent bombs through the mail to three dozen notable American government officials and business leaders. Many of the targets were New Yorkers, including J. P. Morgan Jr., John D. Rockefeller Jr., Mayor John Hylan, Police Commissioner Richard Enright, and Commissioner of Immigration Frederic Howe.

The first of the booby-trapped parcels to be opened, addressed to former U.S. senator Thomas Hardwick of Georgia, blew off his housekeeper's hands. Luckily, nearly half the remaining bombs were being held in a New York post office because of insufficient postage, and after the Hardwick explosion, investigators quickly recovered most of the rest before they could be delivered. Refusing to be deterred, the anarchists planted still more bombs two months later. One, intended for Attorney General A. Mitchell Palmer, exploded at the front door of his home near Dupont Circle on the second of June, blowing to bits the anarchist who was transporting it and damaging homes all up and down the block. The residences of public officials in Cleveland, Pittsburgh, Boston, Paterson, and New York were bombed the same day.[34]

Thus began the Red Scare of 1919–20. The Justice Department intensified its surveillance not just of anarchists but of more moderate socialists and labor leaders all over the United States. Palmer put twenty-four-year-old J. Edgar Hoover in charge of the raids. One did not have to do or say anything illegal to be arrested by Hoover's men. For immigrants, mere membership in a suspected radical organization could lead to arrest and deportation. Even taking free night classes sponsored by a communist- or socialist-affiliated group became grounds for deportation. Among those deported during the Red Scare were Goldman and Berkman, who, after their release from prison in 1919, were banished to the Soviet Union along with several hundred other radicals on a military transport ship that the press dubbed the "Red Ark." Hoover went personally to Ellis Island to see Goldman off.

The American Civil Liberties Union protested the illegal and unconstitutional tactics employed by Hoover, yet most Americans supported these so-called Palmer Raids. Thousands of immigrants had been arrested and hundreds deported by June 1920, when a federal judge in Boston ruled that membership in a radical organization alone was not grounds for the detention or deportation of immigrants. This decision, for all intents and purposes, brought the Palmer Raids to an end.[35]

Immigrants like Goldman and Berkman could be summarily deported primarily because they had chosen not to become citizens and therefore lacked the constitutional protections that citizenship confers. Citizenship did shield most immigrant socialists from summary arrest and deportation, but it could not protect the socialist assemblymen from their fellow legislators. Despite the air of suspicion that hung over socialists at the height of the Red Scare, five New York assembly districts had once again, in November 1919, elected socialists to represent them in Albany. On the first day of the legislative session that began the following January, however, assembly speaker Thaddeus Sweet called the five socialists (veterans Waldman, Claessens, and Orr, as well as newcomers Samuel DeWitt and Charles Solomon) to the well of the chamber and announced that he would not allow them to take their seats. Socialists were bound by oath to follow "instructions" from foreign leaders, he said, and were therefore ineligible to serve the interests of the people of New York and the United States in the legislature. The assembly voted to suspend the socialists from office pending a hearing that would be followed by a vote of expulsion.

In the hearings, which dominated the legislature's proceedings from January 20 to the first of April, those in favor of expulsion cited speeches made by Claessens in which, complaining about election fraud employed against socialist candidates, he condemned the "American Republic" as "one huge institution based upon fraud." Those supporting expulsion also focused attention on the clause in the Socialist Party constitution that forbade its members to "vote to appropriate moneys for military or naval purposes," calling it incompatible with the legislators' responsibility to maintain the state militia. The accused responded that they were democratic socialists whose rhetoric was meant to inspire Americans to use ballots, not bullets, to effect political change. But the legislators, Republicans in particular, insisted that the socialists should not be seated. "We must expel these Socialists," exclaimed Brooklyn assemblyman Frederick Wells at the climax of the debate. "If we do not, our children and our grandchildren will be washing the blood off the doorsteps." On the first of April, the assembly voted by overwhelming majorities to expel all five.[36]

The expulsions made headlines nationwide, and while nationally most Americans supported the legislature's decision, New Yorkers were more ambivalent. Charles Evans Hughes called the decision "a calamity," adding, "Those who make their patriotism a vehicle for intolerance are very dangerous." The Democratic World, no friend of socialism, called the proceedings "a legislative lynching" and proclaimed, "If the people of New York are to retain their free institutions, if they are not to be Russianized by their stupid politicians, their first concern must be the restoration of representative government which was overthrown yesterday in Albany by the Assembly." Yet many New Yorkers considered the legislature completely justified in its actions. The Times applauded the decision, calling it "a courageous act" of "self-defense" against an organization whose purpose is "to overthrow the American Government and institutions by violence."[37]

The ousted assemblymen all declared their intention to run in the special election called for September to fill their vacant seats. To try to insure their defeat, Republicans and Democrats combined forces to run a single candidate against each socialist. Nonetheless, all five socialists won landslide victories, capturing far higher proportions of the vote than they had just ten months earlier. When they returned to Albany, the sitting legislators tried to save face by voting to seat two of them, DeWitt and Orr. DeWitt was a World War I veteran, and neither he nor Orr had made the kinds of inflammatory public criticisms of the United States that the others had. But when their socialist colleagues were expelled a second time, DeWitt and Orr resigned in protest. The major parties, anxious to avoid such clashes in the future, used a combination of gerrymandering and "fusion" tickets (in which the Democrats and Republicans agreed on a candidate they could both support) to make it more difficult for the socialists to carry future elections.[38]

Anarchist bombings, the Red Scare, and the controversy over the election of socialists to the New York State Assembly played a major role in Congress's decision to enact the most sweeping immigration restrictions in American history. Calls for Congress to take action intensified after the deadliest terror attack on American soil to that date struck New York in mid-September, 1920. At noon on Thursday the sixteenth, a huge bomb exploded outside the headquarters of J. P. Morgan & Co. at 23 Wall Street, across from the New York Stock Exchange. The timer-detonated bomb, which was concealed in a horse-drawn wagon parked outside Morgan's offices, consisted of approximately one hundred pounds of dynamite and five hundred pounds of cast-iron ball projectiles. The blast killed thirty-eight and injured hundreds. The pockmarks caused by the spray of the iron balls are still visible today in the walls of the Morgan building. No one was ever arrested or indicted for the bombing, which appears to have been the work of Italian immigrant anarchists from Massachusetts. It was the deadliest civilian terror attack in the United States until the Oklahoma City bombing of 1995.[39]

Immediately after the Wall Street attack, calls for immigration restriction grew louder. "We think the bars ought to be down now," argued the *Chicago Tribune* in an editorial titled "Immigration, Invasion, Revolution," published thirteen days after the bombing. "If America does not propose to commit suicide," it should not "offer itself as an asylum for every form of political and social disease in revolutionary Europe ... Immigration of this character is invasion, and invasion means conquest. For America, shut the gates."[40]

Adding to the urgency was the realization that after a six-year lull, the number of immigrants entering the United States was suddenly surging. "Ellis Island Faces Influx of Millions," blared a headline in the *New York Times,* while

Italian immigrant anarchists were most likely responsible for this bombing on Wall Street in 1920 that killed thirty-eight and wounded hundreds. Such incidents paved the way for the immigration restrictions put in place in 1921 and 1924.

the *Los Angeles Times* reported that "the destitute and the diseased are clamoring for admission in numbers not before equaled." Worst of all, the "'economic parasites' now arriving in floods" came not to work, according to the *Washington Post,* but "to escape work" in "the greatest influx of foreigners the United States has ever known." Many Americans had thought that immigration would remain low after the war as a result of the literacy test enacted by Congress in 1917, but that had "proved insufficient," as the "chaos at Ellis Island" in late September and early October made clear. The Italians, Greeks, and Syrians who dominated the new flood of immigrants were "lazy and lousy" and would remain "aliens to the end." As a result, most Americans came to agree with the *Post* that "preventing further pollution of American blood" ought to be the number one priority of Congress.[41]

Members of Congress considered all sorts of proposed remedies to the "immigration emergency." Some suggested temporarily halting all immigration— for six months, a year, or, as the House Immigration Committee eventually recommended, two years. Others wanted to set quotas on the number of immigrants admitted from each foreign nation, while still others suggested adopting quotas for each "ethnic group" instead. In the end, the House approved a bill banning immigration for fourteen months, but the Senate considered that too harsh and instead opted for quotas. The number of immigrants allowed into the United States from any given country over the next year under the Emergency Quota Act of 1921 would be equal to 3 percent of the total foreign-born from that country already in the United States as of 1910, the last year for which census figures were available. Congress eventually extended these quotas for two additional years.[42]

Commissioner General of Immigration William Husband called the 1921 act "one of the most radical and far-reaching events in the annals of immigration legislation," an assessment that was not much of an exaggeration. Immigrants had been able to come to the United States in unlimited numbers until 1882, when most Chinese immigration was outlawed. Japan had agreed to halt almost all of its emigration to the United States under American pressure in the winter of 1907–8. Congress had banned immigration from the rest of Asia (including what we today call the Middle East) in 1917. But now Americans would pick and choose which countries should supply the most and least immigrants and set a numerical limit on overall immigration, policies even the Know Nothings had never proposed.[43]

The practical effect of the Emergency Quota Act was to cut immigration from southern and eastern Europe by about 80 percent from prewar levels while leaving immigration from England, Ireland, Germany, and Scandinavia largely untouched. Italy, for example, had on average sent 220,000 immigrants per year to the United States in the decade leading up to World War I, but the new law would permit only 42,000. Russia would be allowed 34,000 per year. As a result of the new law, immigration fell from about 800,000 for the twelve months ending June 30, 1921, to 300,000 a year later.

The Emergency Quota Act divided each nation's immigration quota into monthly allocations, and the efforts made to snare the coveted slots would seem farcical had the stakes not been so high. Just before midnight on the last day of each month, a dozen or more ships would position themselves just outside the Narrows, the spot where the southwest tip of Brooklyn comes closest to the eastern edge of Staten Island. Immigration officials had designated this waterway the official entry point to New York Harbor and declared that the order in which the ships crossed this imaginary line would determine the order in which their immigrant passengers would be counted toward meeting each month's quotas. Those who arrived too late were to be returned to Europe at the shipping line's expense. The steamship companies eventually began to coordinate with American consulates to try to insure that the number of passengers the companies accepted did not exceed the monthly quotas, but this was not always feasible. A consulate might assure a steamship company that it could safely bring five hundred British immigrants to New York in a given month, but if five hundred British subjects entered the United States from Canada while the company's ship was at sea, then the passengers on the ship would be turned away.[44]

For British immigrants, such a setback might be relatively brief. The British quota was so high compared to the number of Britons who sought to emigrate that immigrants turned away one month would almost certainly be admitted soon after. In many months the British quota actually went unfilled. But for immigrants from eastern Europe, finding a way into the United States could be a matter of life and death. In 1919 and the first half of 1920, pogroms once again swept Ukraine; thousands were killed. "Jews drowned in pools of blood," recalled one immigrant who lived through the attacks. Even the Jewish section of the Anbinders' tiny hometown of Holoskov, previously spared by anti-Semitic vigilantes, came under attack in June 1919 in a murderous slaughter that left ninety-five dead. "Almost the whole town was plundered," reported Jewish investigators. "The population is fleeing in all directions." My great-grandfather Froim Leib Anbinder must have been frantic with worry when he got word of the pogrom, wondering if his wife and five children had survived. News of the attack must have compounded the guilt he felt at not having been able to save enough from his work as a presser to bring his family over before the war had made emigration all but impossible.[45]

Froim Leib's wife, Beyle, and their children, including my grandfather Tulea, survived the pogrom and were among the thousands of Jews fleeing in all directions in its aftermath. Beyle and her children traveled 120 miles southwest to Kishinev in what was then Romania but is now Moldova. They were lucky to have left. Those who remained behind suffered through one of the worst famines the world has ever known. Terrible food shortages resulting in part from drought and in part from ongoing fighting in the Russian Civil War began in 1919, peaked in 1921, and continued until 1923. "People swelled with hunger and died amidst terrible suffering," recalled Bertha Fox, who managed to make it from Ukraine to the United States in 1922. "Even if one could get a piece of bread for a high price, the dough had been mixed with sawdust," a common practice during the famine to make the meager supply of flour go further. By 1921, Chaim Kusnetz's family of six was subsisting on a pint of milk and a half pound of such bread per day. He finally made it to America in 1923. Even the most conservative estimates place the death toll at more than 1 million.[46]

The war, the pogroms, the famine, and the quota law all impacted Beyle and her children as they tried to reunite with Froim Leib in America. Somehow they made it from Kishinev to Antwerp. Froim Leib must have finally sent them money, or perhaps Beyle's parents, who remained in Holoskov, assisted them. In any event, they bought tickets for the steamship *Lapland* in July 1921,

RESTRICTION

only to be denied passage at the last second (they were placed on the manifest but their names were subsequently crossed off), perhaps because they were deemed too sickly to travel. At last in early September they managed to sail to New York aboard the *Finland,* but the family was detained at Ellis Island because they were deemed likely to become public charges. Again their detention probably resulted from illness, as four of Beyle's five children were sent to the Ellis Island hospital. They must have been seriously ill, too, because it took six weeks for the first of them, sixteen-year-old Feyge (whom I knew as my great-aunt Florence), to be released. Four days later Tulea was discharged, then a week later seventeen-year-old Ruchel. Finally, on November 30, the baby of the family, Sonia, was released as well. She was so small and sickly that the family lied about her age at Ellis Island, saying she was nine when she was actually eleven or twelve. They at last reunited with Froim Leib after eleven long years.[47]

Even though the 1921 Quota Act had reduced Italian immigration by 85 percent from prewar levels and that from Russia by 87 percent, most Americans believed that there were still too many southern and eastern Europeans arriving on their shores. In 1924, congressional Republicans proposed a bill to reduce immigration even further, from 350,000 to 150,000 per year, with the vast majority of the reduction coming from the quotas for southern and eastern Europeans. The new quotas would be determined, explained the bill's sponsors, Senator David Reed of Pennsylvania and Representative Albert Johnson of Washington, in proportion to the "national origins" of the entire American population. So if the Census Bureau determined that 4 percent of Americans as of 1920 were of Italian origin (either Italian immigrants or native-born descendants of Italians), Italy would be assigned 4 percent of the 150,000 immigration slots. Until the Census Bureau could complete such a study, the bill would put in place temporary quotas that would cut by an additional 90 percent the already severely reduced quotas set in 1921 for Italy, Russia, and other southern and eastern European nations. The bill exempted immigrants from North and South America from the quotas, but it banned the immigration of Asians completely. The nations of Africa each got a token quota of one hundred immigrants.[48]

Congressmen representing New York and other northeastern cities bitterly condemned the Reed-Johnson bill. "The mathematics of the bill disclose the intentional discrimination against the Jews and the Italians," charged Republican congressman Fiorello La Guardia. The bill had been crafted "to favor the so-called Nordic races," agreed New York's Democratic representatives. "You know that during the war we had the fancy to denounce Germany for advancing the idea of the 'superman' and 'supernation,'" Congressman James Gallivan of Boston reminded his colleagues during the floor debate in the House. "Now that doctrine of superiority which was originally sponsored in this country by the Ku Klux Klan seems to have found an expression in this proposed legislation." The debate was so contentious that at one point Gallivan and a proponent of the bill had to be separated to prevent a fistfight.[49]

There were some aspects of the bill that its opponents did find praiseworthy. Under the Reed-Johnson proposal, most immigrant processing would take place at consulates in the immigrants' countries of origin, so that aspiring Americans would know before boarding a ship whether they had satisfied the United States' legal requirements for immigration and secured a quota slot. Immigrants would no longer have to invest their life savings on the trip to America only to be barred at Ellis Island. The bill also exempted from the quotas the wives and minor children of American citizens, so that men like Froim Leib would not have to worry that they would be separated forever from the families they had left behind. For those who fell under the quota system, preference would be given to the parents of American citizens, eighteen- to twenty-year-old children of citizens, and agricultural workers and their families. But in the eyes of the New York congressional delegation, none of these facts compensated for the bill's objectionable features. "If our forefathers could see what their sons are doing now," Congressman Samuel Dickstein told a meeting in New York organized to protest the bill, "they would be ashamed of themselves."[50]

The bill's supporters, ranging from Gompers's American Federation of Labor to the American Legion and the Ku Klux Klan, saw no reason to feel ashamed. "It is true that 75 per cent. of our immigration will hereafter come from Northwestern Europe," admitted Reed, "but it is fair that it should do so, because 75 per cent. of us who are now here owe our origin to immigrants from these same countries . . . The racial composition of America at the present time thus is made permanent." Reed called the bill the most important to be considered by Congress in a half century. "Its adoption means that [the] America of our grandchildren will be a vastly better place to live in. It will mean a more homogeneous nation, more self-reliant, more independent and more closely knit by common purpose and common ideas." The bill passed both houses of Congress by huge bipartisan majorities, and on May 26, 1924, President Calvin Coolidge signed it into law.[51]

The National Origins Act is one of the most momentous laws enacted in all of American history. With relatively few exceptions, Americans had welcomed immigrants to their shores for more than three hundred years before Congress decided to "shut the gates" in 1924. Now the United States turned away from its historic role as an asylum for the world's huddled masses. The successive imposition of restrictions on the Chinese, Japanese, and other Asians had signaled the beginnings of this change, but the speed with which Americans suddenly embraced the seismic shift in policy surprised American and international observers alike.

THE IMPACT OF IMMIGRATION RESTRICTION, 1914–1965

	IMMIGRANTS ADMITTED IN YEAR ENDING JUNE 30, 1914	IMMIGRANTS ADMITTED IN 1922 UNDER THE EMERGENCY QUOTA ACT	IMMIGRANT QUOTA, 1929–1965
Germany	35,734	19,053	25,957
Great Britain	48,729	42,670	65,721
Ireland*	24,688	Counted under Great Britain	17,853
Italy	283,738	42,057	5,802
Russia	255,660	43,284	2,784
Greece	35,832	3,457	307

Source: *Annual Report of the Commissioner General of Immigration to the Secretary of Labor, Fiscal Year Ended June 30, 1922* (Washington, D.C., 1922), 5; *Annual Report of the Commissioner General of Immigration to the Secretary of Labor, Fiscal Year Ended June 30, 1924* (Washington, D.C., 1924), 4, 6–7; *Statistical Abstracts of the United States, 1929* (Washington, D.C., 1929), 102, 105.

For New York and New Yorkers, the sudden curtailment of immigration was especially consequential because the law targeted the city's biggest immigrant communities. Italian immigration was cut from prewar levels by 98 percent, Russia's by 99 percent. The dynamism of New York's economy relied in large measure on these newcomers. For centuries, many of the immigrants coming to America had settled initially in New York City before eventually moving on to other locales. There was no reason to believe that the city's immigrants in 1924 would not one day relocate as well, but who would replace them? Over the course of the next forty years, until Congress repealed the National Origins Act in 1965, immigrants would play a diminishing role in the story of New York.

* The Ireland figure for 1914 includes all of Ireland. The Ireland quota for 1929–1965 is for the Free State of Ireland. The remainder falls under the Great Britain quota.

20

REFUGE

THE IMPACT OF IMMIGRATION RESTRICTION on New York City was profound. "The one great element that has changed the east side has been the stoppage of immigration," wrote William Feigenbaum, a socialist who had once represented the Lower East Side in the state legislature, in the *Times* in 1927. "Ceaseless immigration," he said, was what gave the district "its character." But East Broadway, which once had "swarmed with large families," was now "a wilderness of warehouses, fur shops and stores . . . Teeming streets are being depopulated, life is leaving the once vivid neighborhood, and old men and women very often have all the room for themselves that not so long ago the elders had to share with countless children." A few years later, the city's leading Italian-language daily, *Il Progresso Italo-Americano,* came to a similar conclusion concerning Manhattan's Italian immigrant neighborhoods. "Many apartment houses are vacant," the paper reported, "while in 1920 one could not find a room here for an arm and a leg."

Most of the depopulation of these enclaves resulted from immigrants moving to other boroughs rather than from a decrease in the city's overall immigrant population. Many Jews, now able to afford better Brooklyn neighborhoods than Brownsville and East New York, were moving to Bensonhurst, Coney Island, and Flatbush, noted Feigenbaum, "or even to Queens." By 1932, Jews (not all of them immigrants) constituted a majority of the inhabitants in Brownsville, Coney Island, East Flatbush, Far Rockaway, Kensington, Midwood, and Sea Gate in Brooklyn; Hunts Point, Morrisania, Highbridge, and Fordham Heights in the Bronx; and the Upper West Side of Manhattan. Italian Americans (again, not all immigrants) not only dominated East Harlem and the area now known as SoHo but also made up the majority of the population in parts of the Bath Beach, Bedford-Stuyvesant, Bensonhurst, Borough Park, Bushwick, Dyker Heights, Fort Greene, Gravesend, and Red Hook neighborhoods of Brooklyn, and the Baychester, Belmont, Gun Hill Road, and Williamsbridge sections of the Bronx. Previously, immigrants moving out of Manhattan for the backyard gardens and roomier apartments of the outer boroughs had been replaced by thousands of new arrivals fresh from Ellis Island. Now, the incoming greenhorns numbered only in the hundreds, and Manhattan's Jewish and Italian districts were becoming far less crowded.[1]

There were still *some* Italian and eastern European immigrants settling in the once congested neighborhoods. Several thousand newcomers could enter the country legally each year, and many of them moved in with friends, relatives, or landsmen in New York City. But far outnumbering these legal newcomers were the tens of thousands who immigrated illegally after the discriminatory quotas first took effect in 1921. "Big Ring Smuggles Aliens and Liquor," shouted a page-one headline in the *Times* in 1922, noting that smugglers who had begun sneaking alcohol into the United States after the beginning of Prohibition in 1919 used the same land, sea, and even air routes to bring in illegal immigrants once the quota law took effect.

Experts disagreed about the scope of illegal immigration. Already by 1922, the commissioner general of immigration conceded that it had reached "alarming proportions." The Department of Labor, under whose aegis immigration fell, estimated that in 1927 there were 1 million illegal immigrants living in the United States, but the *Times* put the true figure at 2 million. Between 100,000 and 300,000 new undocumented aliens were said to be arriving annually. "The bootlegging of aliens," noted Commissioner General of Immigration Harry Hull in 1927, "has grown to be an industry second in importance only to the bootlegging of liquor."[2]

Then as now, the cheapest and easiest way to move illegally to the United States was to obtain a legitimate tourist or student visa and remain in the country when it expired. Many illegal immigrants from northern and western Europe employed this tactic, but few ragged refugees from eastern Europe or impoverished Italians from Calabria or Sicily could succeed at this ruse. Nonetheless, tens of thousands of undocumented aliens entered the United States in this manner in the 1920s. New York State alone was said to be home to eighty thousand of these visa overstayers.

The most expensive way to enter the United States illegally, in contrast, was with a forged visa. While officials at each American consulate knew how many visas they could issue each year, inspectors at Ellis Island had no master list. As a result, a lucrative market developed for fake visas. They could be bought in Poland during the 1920s for $500. One could also buy a real visa. The American vice consul in Warsaw sold a stack of blank visas to a gang of immigrant smugglers for $1,200, which the crooks quickly resold at a hefty profit. When the American official refused to supply the gang with more, they blackmailed him by threatening to expose the initial sale.

Smugglers developed another means of getting legitimate visas. They solicited residents of countries with large quotas such as Germany to obtain real visas, which the gangs then purchased and resold. Germans with Jewish-sounding names were especially sought after for this scam. The authorities eventually caught on and began to question immigrants more carefully at Ellis Island to be sure they were actually the people named on their visas. Despite coaching from the visa sellers, many of these fraudulent immigrants were detected and sent back to Europe.

Most immigrants could not afford forged entry documents. They preferred to legally enter a country bordering on the United States and then somehow complete the journey illicitly. The majority of British and eastern European Jews who sought to enter the United States in this manner did so through Canada. For anywhere from $25 to $100, aspiring immigrants could find a boatman willing to transport them from Windsor, Ontario, across the Detroit River to Michigan in a skiff. Taxi drivers from Montreal all the way to Vancouver also did a thriving side business smuggling immigrants across the border. They openly solicited customers at the docks where immigrants landed. Taxicab drivers in Winnipeg did the same at the city's main train station.[3]

One fairly typical eastern European Jew who illicitly crossed the Canadian border on her way to New York was Minnie Yezernitzsky. Born in 1912 in the small town of Ruzhany in modern-day Belarus, Minnie later recalled that every young Jew in town sought to emigrate upon finishing high school. Her older sisters had gone directly to New York, but with the restrictions put in place in 1921 and 1924, Minnie and her high school classmates could not legally join them. Some Ruzhany emigrants decided to try Palestine; one was future Israeli prime minister Yitzhak Shamir, three years Minnie's junior. Others went to Argentina, and still others to Cuba. But hoping to be as close to her sisters as possible, Minnie decided to go to Canada, and eventually moved in with a cousin in Montreal. "I was eighteen," she later recalled, "and full of life."

Minnie's cousin took her to a dress factory where the boss asked ominously if she would "do anything to earn a few dollars." Minnie was horrified to have to work on the Sabbath, but she adjusted and eventually became an expert sewing machine operator. Paid by the piece, she was soon earning $15 to $17 a week. Minnie "dressed quite well," she recalled, had a boyfriend, went dancing on Saturday nights, and had lots of friends who came from Ruzhany or its environs. "Still," she said, "I was drawn to be with my sisters." Learning this, one of her brothers-in-law in New York insisted that Minnie "sneak across the border to America." Her New York relatives would pay whatever it cost.

For $200 (the equivalent of about $3,000 today), a man agreed to smuggle Minnie into the country and arrange her transportation to New York. Minnie could not bring anything with her, as it might arouse suspicion should they be stopped, but her cousin agreed to ship her clothes and other possessions to her. One morning, she recounted, "the man led me to the border, and there, next to a forest, stood a car with New York license plates and two Christian men." After waiting in the woods for what seemed like an eternity, they set off for New York. Two policemen stopped them along the way, but after checking the driver's license and questioning them briefly, they allowed Minnie and her escorts to proceed. Finally, at 6:00 a.m., they reached Brooklyn. When her sister opened her apartment door, Minnie "burst out crying hysterically," she said, "seeing my eldest sister whom I did not remember at all except from pictures."[4]

The cheapest way to cross the border from Canada illicitly was by ferry. With fifteen thousand men and women taking ferries daily from Windsor to their workplaces in Detroit's factories, immigration inspectors could not possibly stop and interrogate each passenger. Border patrolmen scanned the crowds rushing down the gangplanks, looking for men and women who seemed out of place. But as the *Times* noted in 1927, "an American suit of clothes and hair-cut to match" made it virtually impossible to detect the illegal immigrants among the throng of morning commuters.[5]

Unlike those from northern and eastern Europe, citizens of Mediterranean countries who wanted to enter the United States illegally did so primarily via Cuba. These were typically Italians, but large numbers from Greece and Syria (which then comprised modern-day Lebanon as well as Syria) also attempted to enter the United States illicitly. As was the case in Canada, smugglers in Havana brazenly advertised their services and fees. These immigrants might pay $100 to be transported to the vicinity of the Florida Keys, the *Times* reported, "and there may be another $50 for the sponge fisherman who relays the cargo to shore."

If smugglers landed too many immigrants in Florida at once, they might arouse suspicion. When several dozen disoriented Italians, Greeks, and Syrians suddenly began wandering around sleepy Fort Myers in the summer of 1927, for example, locals notified the police, who quickly arrested the gate-crashers. Other smugglers took their human cargo to Bimini, a Bahamian island fifty miles east of Miami, where the immigrants secured passage to Florida's Atlantic coastline. According to the *Times*, it was not uncommon for smugglers to abandon their passengers on a deserted island or even throw them overboard to avoid being caught red-handed if they feared the authorities were about to intercept them.

Another popular method for sneaking immigrants into the United States from Cuba was to bribe sailors to transport them on commercial passenger ships. Smugglers might take the would-be immigrants to Nassau, where the criminals would use a combination of cash and liquor (which the crewmen could sell for a hefty profit at an American port) to entice the seamen to take charge of some illegal immigrants. One smuggler told an undercover American investigator that when these ships docked in Miami or New York, "many times the stowaways are marched off right under [the immigration officer's] very nose by being dressed like dock workers, stewards, baggage handlers, engine-room crew, sailors," and so forth.[6]

With the press harping incessantly on the problem of illegal immigration after the National Origins Act went into effect in 1924, the federal government tried to step up both prevention and prosecution. The task was truly daunting. When the National Origins Act became law, the United States Border Patrol had only 472 agents to guard more than 7,500 miles of border with Canada and Mexico and 5,000 miles of coastline. (Today there are more than twenty thousand Border Patrol officers.) By 1926, the Border Patrol had increased its force to 632, still wholly inadequate, the commissioner general of immigration admitted, but the parsimonious Republican congresses of the twenties refused to appropriate enough money to vastly increase the Border Patrol's size. In 1932 there were still fewer than one thousand officers guarding the borders. Nonetheless, the apprehension of illegal immigrants in the United States rose from just a few thousand in the fiscal year ending June 30, 1925, to twelve thousand two years later and eighteen thousand the year after that. Arrests soon leveled off at about twenty thousand per year.[7]

While these figures may seem impressive, authorities lacked both the manpower and the will to organize and carry out the kinds of proactive raids on the residences and workplaces of suspected illegal immigrants that we associate with immigration enforcement today. Apart from ferry terminal and border station arrests, most immigrants who were caught after successfully crossing the border or coming ashore were apprehended as a result of sheer luck rather than an effective enforcement strategy.

Take, for example, the case that received the most publicity in the early years of restriction. On Sunday July 13, 1924, Anthony Camardo of Sheepshead Bay, Brooklyn, steered his forty-two-foot sloop, the *Bessie B.*, toward the docks at Rockaway Point, the western tip of a peninsula that juts into lower New York Bay about a half mile southeast of Brooklyn's south shore. The officers on a nearby police launch, tasked with intercepting rumrunners landing cargoes of illicit booze, found it strange that Camardo had the *Bessie B.*'s hatches shut tight despite the hot summer weather. They decided to take a closer look. As the policemen boarded the sloop, the half-dozen taxis inexplicably waiting by the piers suddenly sped away. The officers descended into the hold and pulled back a tarp, expecting to uncover cases of liquor. Instead, they found thirty-one frightened and bewildered Italian illegal immigrants.

It turned out that while Camardo was fishing that afternoon, smugglers in a rowboat had approached the *Bessie B.* and offered the Brooklynite $75 if he would motor over to a three-masted schooner farther out in the bay, hide its thirty-one passengers in his sloop, and land them at Rockaway Point, where they would be picked up by a fleet of taxis. The schooner had carried the immigrants all the way from Palermo in a voyage that had taken nearly four weeks.

At the court hearing, the port's commissioner of immigration, Henry Curran, urged the judge to sentence the immigrants to twenty years' hard labor before they were deported, to deter others from sneaking into the country. But the magistrate ruled that he had no power to assess any punishment other than deportation. No wonder so many people, from all over the world, were willing to pay smugglers for the chance to start a new life in New York.[8]

Most cases of illegal immigration came to the attention of the authorities in New York only because other New Yorkers informed on them. More often than not, these tips arrived at Curran's office on Ellis Island as anonymous letters. "There is an alien who ran off with my wife last week," began one missive reprinted in the *Times*. "They are living at _____. I don't want my wife back but the alien is here without any right." Another letter writer felt compelled to report an illegal immigrant because the foreigner had a job while the informant was unemployed, and "I need the job." In one unusual case, a mother in Italy informed on her own child. "My son is in New York — he sneaked in. Please send him back because I need him to support me."[9]

Minnie Yezernitzsky was one of the illegal immigrants caught as a result of an informant's tip. Upon her arrival in New York from Montreal, she found work in a Manhattan dress factory along Sixth Avenue in the Garment District, where clothing manufacturers had begun moving their operations in Manhattan during the 1920s. She became an activist within the International Ladies' Garment Workers' Union, something her boss had to tolerate both because it was a union shop and because she was one of his best dressmakers. Though Minnie was voluble and outgoing, in the spring of 1936 she fell in love with Chaim Kusnetz, a quiet, devout metalworker who wooed her by writing Yiddish poems about his devotion to her. A year later, by which point Minnie had been living in New York for four or five years, her boss asked her and all his other employees for their full names and addresses as part of the registration process for the new Social Security system. When Minnie asked her boss not to submit her name, he realized she was in the country illegally; he then gleefully reported her to the authorities. A few days later, a detective appeared at Minnie's workplace, arrested her, and took her to Ellis Island, where illegal immigrants were detained pending deportation. "They asked me questions, took fingerprints and photographs — just as they would of a real criminal," she recalled. "I had no food at all and didn't sleep all night. I could not stop crying."

The next day Minnie was released on $500 bond put up by her brother-in-law. He hired a lawyer, who told Minnie that the only way she could avoid deportation was to marry Chaim, who had become an American citizen. She did so a few days later, just before her hearing at Ellis Island. There, she had to use her correspondence with Chaim — even the poems — to prove that her marriage was not a sham. When questioned about how she had entered the United States, she followed the instructions of her attorney and testified untruthfully that she did not know until she was arrested at her workplace that she had entered the United States illegally. Three months later, Minnie had to return to Canada, pick up a visa, and answer hours of questions about her marriage, just as if she had never been in the United States. But by virtue of her marriage and authorized reentry into the country, she became a legal immigrant.[10]

Most "smuggled aliens" (the term then used for illegal immigrants) could not count on having a citizen ready to marry them. As a result, a market developed in New York for forged documents that might convince the authorities that an illegal immigrant had actually entered the country lawfully. One criminal ring peddling such papers extended its reach into federal offices in Washington and at Ellis Island. Its members bribed employees at the New York facility to go into the island's old ledger books and add the names of illegal immigrants to archived ship manifests so that the immigrants, if detained, could refer the authorities to the doctored manifests to "prove" that they had entered the country legally. Bozo Galantich, for example, who had crossed over from Canada by shinnying across the girders of the Niagara Falls Bridge in 1927, paid to have an Ellis Island employee add his name to the manifest of a ship that arrived in New York in 1931. A former Brooklyn congressman, Michael J. Hogan, was convicted in 1935 of soliciting $300 bribes from three different Italian illegal immigrants. In return for the payments, he promised to use his connections in Washington to obtain documents indicating that they had entered the United States lawfully. Prosecutors alleged in 1935 that a single New York ring specializing in forging evidence of lawful admission for illegal immigrants had taken in more than $1 million in its ten years of operation.[11]

Those who objected to the presence of so many smuggled aliens demanded that Congress require all non-citizens to register with the government. Immigrants would have to come forward, prove their legal status, and receive an identification card with their photo and fingerprints, which they would be required to present whenever their right to be in the country was questioned. As

early as 1924, the *Herald Tribune* had argued that this was the only way to ferret out the thousands of illegal immigrants pouring into the United States each
year. New York congressmen such as Fiorello La Guardia, Emanuel Celler, and
Samuel Dickstein, who represented heavily immigrant constituencies, objected
to the registry idea and other immigrant identification proposals. Fingerprint-
ing would subject immigrants to unnecessary humiliation, they claimed, because criminals were the only other Americans who were routinely fingerprinted. Furthermore, such programs would inevitably lead to discrimination,
the congressmen argued, since law enforcement officials in New York would be
much more likely to ask Jews and Italians for proof of legal status than other
city residents.[12]

Americans put so much effort into ferreting out Jewish and Italian illegal immigrants in large part because they did not consider them capable of being "true
Americans." Some Jewish and Italian Americans thought they could prove that
they were true Americans by embracing the most American of all pastimes:
baseball. Aficionados of the game prided themselves on the idea that baseball
was a genuine meritocracy. "The Mick, the Sheeny, the Wop, the Dutch, and the
Chink, the Cuban, the Indian, the Jap or the so-called Anglo-Saxon — his nationality is never a matter of moment if he can pitch, or hit, or field," the *Sport-
ing News* declared in 1923.[13]

Even before the arrival of many Italian and Jewish immigrants to New York,
baseball managers there considered the ethnicity of their players in formulat-
ing game plans. "You want two or three quick-thinking sons of Celt to keep the
Germans and others moving," said New York Giants manager Bill Joyce in 1896.
"Now you take a German, you can tell him what to do and he will do it. Take an
Irishman and tell him what to do, and he is liable to give you an argument. He
has his own ideas. So I have figured it out this way. Get an Irishman to do the
scheming. Let him tell the Germans what to do and then you will have a great
combination."[14]

In the 1920s, as Americans became determined to stanch the flow of Jews
and Italians into the country, baseball team owners became equally determined to increase attendance by adding Jews and Italians to their rosters. The
Brooklyn Robins — later renamed the Dodgers — were the first team to sign
a gifted Jewish player when they added Moe Berg to their lineup in 1923. The
New York–born son of Jewish immigrants from Ukraine, Berg spent only one
season in Brooklyn, but he had a fifteen-year major league career before becoming a spy for the Office of Strategic Services during World War II. A student at Princeton prior to signing with Brooklyn, the multilingual Berg once
skipped spring training and the first month of the regular season to finish the

courses he had begun that winter at the Sorbonne. Another year, he refused to report to his team until he completed his final exams at Columbia Law School. Among his other idiosyncrasies was his obsessive refusal to let anyone so much as touch one of the ten newspapers he bought each day until he had read every word. Casey Stengel, who saw quite a few ballplayers in his five decades in the game, called Berg "the strangest man ever to play baseball."[15]

The Dodgers' Manhattan rivals, the Giants, became better known for their Jewish players. "The stories of [Giants manager] John McGraw's efforts to develop a Jewish star are legion," wrote the editors of *The American Hebrew* in 1937. In 1923, the same year Berg made his debut in Brooklyn, McGraw signed Mose Solomon. At the press conference announcing Solomon's acquisition, McGraw made no effort to conceal the reason for elevating him directly from a Class C minor league team in Hutchinson, Kansas, to the major leagues. "We appreciate that many of the fans in New York are Jews," he told the reporters, "and we have been trying to land a prospect of Jewish blood." Solomon ultimately played in just two games during his season as a Giant.[16]

A few years later, on opening day 1928, McGraw sent a relative unknown named Andy Cohen onto the field to play second base. Cohen delivered a three-hit, two-run, two-RBI performance which so impressed fans that they stormed the field to carry him on their shoulders after the final out was recorded. It was, McGraw said, "the greatest ovation . . . given any player in all my life." A *Times* profile called Cohen "The Baseball Star Whose Name Is an Asset." During the offseason, Cohen parlayed his fame into a vaudeville act, performing Jewish and Irish ethnic humor with Giants teammate Shanty Hogan.[17]

The Yankees became known for their Italian ballplayers. The Bronx Bombers were also the only New York team whose "ethnic" players were true baseball stars. In 1925 the team paid $50,000 for the rights to a young San Franciscan named Tony Lazzeri, son of Italian immigrants, who had attracted national attention by hitting sixty home runs for the Salt Lake City Bees. Even the signing of unknown sandlot players with virtually no chance of ever making the majors made headlines in the 1920s if they were Italian Americans. The number of Italian Americans in baseball soon grew rapidly. "The Irish are good ball players with their alertness and avidity of mind, but they are being challenged right under their noses," observed the *Sporting News* in 1931. "The Italians have found baseball and they like it."[18]

Of course, it was another child of Italian immigrants, Joe DiMaggio, who became the Yankees' most famous Italian American ballplayer. Yet when DiMaggio made his Yankees debut in 1936, his Italian heritage was rarely mentioned in the press, an indication of how far New York's major immigrant groups had come in gaining acceptance (in baseball, at least) over the dozen years since the passage of the National Origins Act in 1924.[19]

The restrictions imposed on some groups by the 1924 statute gave other New Yorkers new opportunities. The city's African American population, for example, grew dramatically during and after World War I as hundreds of thousands of southern blacks moved to New York, Chicago, and other northern cities, both to escape violence and discrimination in the South and to fill a labor shortage caused by the war. As a result of this "Great Migration," the city's African American population increased 60 percent from 1910 to 1920 and 100 percent from 1920 to 1930, to a total of 328,000.

Many of these migrants were attracted to New York by the prospect of landing jobs that would have gone to immigrants before restriction. "Most Negroes who have got work in this city have been taken on largely because the white employer could not [g]et anybody else," reported the Newark correspondent of the African American *Chicago Defender* in November 1924 of a phenomenon that was also taking place just across the Hudson in New York. "Forced to admit Negroes because of a Republican administration which closed the flood gates of European immigration, employers have now become accustomed to the former cotton picker and he is making his way in grand style." African Americans were being offered "skilled work" and "other fairly responsible positions" they could not attain before, the *Defender* reported. Why? "Blood calls to blood. In most cases the white worker is the one chosen. The Democratic policy is to put foreigners on American jobs by permitting them to enter into the country in great numbers and gobble up the work. The Republican policy is to protect the American laborer, white and black."[20]

African Americans saw immigration restriction as a golden opportunity. "Our people are vitally interested in who gets the work in this country," recognized the *Defender*, and "it has been their salvation in this city to find a federal government which held the foreigners off and gave him a chance. That was his only opportunity to make good." The Great Migration might have been far smaller, and the racial composition of New York and other northern cities might today be far different, had it not been for the immigration restrictions of the 1920s.[21]

Harlem filled during the 1920s not only with native-born African Americans but with foreign-born people of color as well. By 1930, 55,000 Caribbean immigrants had settled in New York City (a figure that does not include Puerto Ricans, who by this point were American citizens). Barbados was the source of many of these newcomers, though others came from Jamaica, Trinidad and To-

bago, and other British possessions. They primarily entered the United States
under the generous British immigration quota. Most of these foreign-born
African Americans in this period lived in Harlem; they composed about 25
percent of that area's black population in 1925 (and one in six black residents
citywide). The Bedford-Stuyvesant neighborhood in Brooklyn contained the
second-largest concentration of Caribbean immigrants in the city. As an African American scholar aptly put it in 1939, New York had become the "new
world mecca of the negro peoples."[22]

Like their native-born Harlem neighbors, most Caribbean immigrants
worked as laborers, janitors, busboys, elevator operators, cooks, and dishwashers. Caribbean women toiled primarily as domestic servants. These immigrant
workers, however, became especially well known for refusing to display the
subservience usually demanded of African Americans by white New Yorkers.
West Indians were "notably lacking in the Southern Negro's diplomacy" and
made "lots of noise about their rights," complained the *Saturday Evening Post* in
1925. The Pullman Railcar Company, a major employer of African Americans,
had a policy of not hiring black immigrants precisely because of their refusal to
meekly accept insults from passengers. "The outstanding contribution of West
Indians to American Negro life," wrote one of the newcomers in 1925, "is the in-
sistent assertion of their manhood in an environment that demands too much
servility and unprotesting acquiescence from men of African blood."[23]

The personification of this "New Negro" mindset was a New Yorker named
Marcus Garvey. Garvey was a journalist from Jamaica who believed that Africans and their descendants in the Americas had become too dependent
on whites as a result of the European colonization of the African continent.
Through an organization he created in Jamaica, the United Negro Improvement Association, Garvey sought to rally blacks to return to Africa and retake
their homeland from European colonizers so they could shape their own destinies, free from racism and white domination. To those who called this a pipe
dream, Garvey replied that no army on earth could stop Africans and their descendants in other parts of the world — 400 million people all told — if they devoted themselves to African liberation and self-determination. They should establish themselves "as a mighty race and nation, nevermore to be disrespected
by men." By the early 1920s, the UNIA had about seventy thousand dues-pay-
ing members (including thousands in New York), and there were hundreds of
thousands more who sympathized with its goals. These fellow travelers might
not want to return to Africa themselves, but they found Garvey's notions of
self-reliance and autonomy thrilling.

Many Americans saw Garvey's movement as alarming, all the more so since
it was led by an immigrant agitator. Federal authorities hoped to find some

means of undermining his popularity, and in 1922 they indicted him for mail fraud for supposedly misrepresenting the prospects of the black-owned steam-ship company that he helped start. Found guilty, he began a five-year prison term in 1925 but was released and deported to Jamaica in 1927. Although the UNIA never recovered, Garvey profoundly influenced such future black nationalist leaders as Malcolm X and Louis Farrakhan.[24]

There were many Italian immigrants in Harlem who wished that the Back to Africa movement would succeed because they often had to compete with African Americans for the same jobs, and central Harlem's growing black population threatened to spill over into Italian-dominated East Harlem. Violent conflict between the groups actually predated the Great Migration. In 1903, striking Italian construction workers became enraged when employers recruited African Americans to replace them. "The niggers won't stay here — we'll scare them off," declared one Italian American, and sure enough, a mob of men and women managed to drive the African Americans away.[25]

African Americans were appalled that New Yorkers referred to them using the same hated slurs employed by white southerners. Even more galling was the fact that immigrants who spoke little English nonetheless knew and used the n-word. "One of the first epithets that many European immigrants learned when they got off the boat was the term 'nigger,'" Ralph Ellison observed years later. "It made them feel instantly American." Italian radicals who hoped to organize the entire American "proletariat," regardless of race, into one big union lamented that to so many white Americans, including Italian immigrants, "race hatred is a national duty."[26]

These animosities bubbled to the surface more frequently during and after World War I, as the African American population of Harlem skyrocketed. A fight between African American and Italian American boys over a ball game escalated into an adult riot near the corner of Second Avenue and 126th Street in October 1916. Initially, the two sides threw bricks at each other, but they eventually began firing at each other with pistols, and two Italian Americans were wounded. The *Times* reported that "there had long been ill-feeling" between the two groups.[27]

Even more tension developed between Italians and their other new East Harlem neighbors — recent arrivals from Puerto Rico. Puerto Ricans were not technically immigrants after 1898, when the United States annexed the island after taking it from Spain during the Spanish-American War. And very few Puerto Ricans initially took advantage of their new status as Americans to migrate to the United States. Only 1,500 lived in the continental United States in 1910, 554 of them in New York City. But the Puerto Rican–born population of the city multiplied over the next several decades — to 7,000 in 1920, 45,000 in

1930, and 61,000 in 1940. More than 80 percent of Puerto Ricans living in the continental United States that year resided in New York City.[28]

Puerto Ricans came to New York for the same reasons that others immigrated to the city. Like the Irish in the nineteenth century, most Puerto Ricans were terribly poor, and because they were subjects of a foreign colonial power, the island's residents believed that prospects for improving their economic status were dismal. Like Italian immigrants, Puerto Ricans often ventured to New York not expecting to stay there permanently. Bernardo Vega recalled in his memoirs that on the ship bringing him to New York, he and his fellow Puerto Rican passengers agreed that after a few years they would "return home with pots of money. Everyone's mind was on that farm they'd be buying or the business they'd set up in town." And like both the Irish and the Italians, many Puerto Ricans migrated to New York because they had heard that no one went hungry there. "I came to New York because the food situation was very bad in Puerto Rico and there was no work," one migrant told a New York newspaper in 1947. "I don't like it here but I hate it there. Here at least I can live."[29]

Others left Puerto Rico to avoid having to follow the dictates of overbearing parents. Homero Rosado of Ponce wanted a university education, but his father declared that only Rosado's sisters could go to college; Homero must work to support the family. Determined to get a university degree, Rosado defied his father and in 1930, at age seventeen, he slipped away to San Juan, borrowed $25, and used the money to buy a one-way ticket on the weekly steamer to New York. Ten years later he had not yet made it to college and was working as a handyman. Elisa Baeza, as the eldest daughter among nine children, likewise chafed at her parents' demand that she care for her younger siblings. At age seventeen, she accepted a cousin's invitation to come live with her in New York.[30]

Antonio Rivera Hernández also rebelled against parental dictates. When he was a boy, he later recalled, "we had no money," and there were many mouths to feed. Rivera Hernández dreamed of being a lawyer, but his parents decided that he should become a teacher in rural Puerto Rico instead and sent him to get a degree in education. After a year he dropped out, and "to keep me from a life of decadence," he explained, "my father gave me the passage to New York City." There, Rivera Hernández got a job as a dental technician, later worked for the post office, and eventually became one of the first Puerto Rican insurance agents employed by the John Hancock Life Insurance Company.[31]

Such white-collar work was the exception rather than the rule for Puerto Rican New Yorkers, especially in the period before World War II. The typical Puerto Rican migrant worked as a day laborer on a construction site. Puerto Ricans also washed and pressed clothes in the city's laundries; worked as porters at New York's train stations, docks, bus terminals, and hotels; served as janitors in office buildings, as apartment building handymen ("supers" in New York parlance), and as short-order cooks and dishwashers. Puerto Rican women primarily found employment in the garment industry, working in sweatshops if they were single and as finishers or seamstresses at home if they were married. Other Puerto Rican women toiled as hotel maids, housekeepers, waitresses, salesclerks, and factory operatives. Studies of the city economy indicated that much of New York's light industry would have left New York in the 1940s and 1950s had it not been for the influx of Puerto Ricans who took jobs being vacated by Jewish and Italian immigrants as they became more prosperous and moved to Brooklyn or the Bronx.[32]

Violence often flared between the Puerto Ricans and their Harlem neighbors. "Relations among the different nationalities were fraught with tension," recalled Vega years later. "Women would often clash while shopping, and at times the fights in the neighborhood bars would become serious." Sometimes the quarrels involved rival neighborhood businesses. Jewish storekeepers in Harlem, for example, resented competition from the Puerto Ricans' small corner groceries known as *bodegas*. "The newcomers have opened their own stores and patronize no others," reported the *Times*. On July 28, 1926, Vega recounted, word spread to the Puerto Ricans trying to escape the summer heat in Central Park that "mobs armed with clubs had begun to attack Puerto Ricans with a fury." Vega rushed back to El Barrio to find that "several stores owned by Puerto Ricans had been attacked. The sidewalks in front of the *bodegas* were covered with shattered glass, rice, beans, plantains, and tropical vegetables . . . Terror gripped El Barrio." The attack "had left more than fifty people wounded, some critically."[33]

Puerto Ricans quickly demonstrated to their neighbors that they would not tolerate such treatment. A few days after the attack, hearing rumors that the perpetrators were thugs hired by Harlem's Jewish shopkeepers, the leaders of the Puerto Rican community in Harlem called Carlos Tapia, who ran a Puerto Rican longshoreman's boardinghouse in Red Hook, Brooklyn. Tapia brought thirty-five Puerto Rican stevedores — and probably some of the enforcers from his illegal "numbers" (private lottery) operation as well — to Harlem and, as he put it, "disrupted" business at the candy stores, tailor shops, delis, and other businesses run by those who supposedly had orchestrated the original violence. "We made sure the victims knew the reason for our attack." No mass assault on the neighborhood's bodegas ever took place again.[34]

Eventually their neighbors acquiesced to Puerto Rican dominance of the territory bounded by Fifth Avenue on the west, Park Avenue (and later Third Avenue) on the east, 116th Street to the north, and 103rd Street to the south.

"Our countrymen made it clear that we were in charge in that part of town," noted Vega. Poet Jack Agüeros agreed that 103rd Street was where El Barrio ended and "America began." An American-born child of Puerto Rican immigrants growing up in East Harlem in the late forties, Agüeros knew that crossing any of these boundaries was perilous. If "we decided to go swimming to Jefferson Park pool" on First Avenue, he wrote in 1971 for a collection called *The Immigrant Experience: The Anguish of Becoming American,* "we knew we risked a fight and a beating from the Italians. And when we went to La Milagrosa Church" on Seventh Avenue at 114th Street, which the Catholic archdiocese of New York designated in 1926 as the parish for the city's Hispanic population, "we knew we risked a fight and a beating from the blacks." If they ventured south of 103rd Street, they "risked dirty looks, disapproving looks, and questions from the police, like, 'What are you doing in this neighborhood?' and 'Why don't you kids go back where you belong?'"[35]

Sometimes parents, ignorant of the dangers involved for teenagers in crossing these boundaries, inadvertently sent their sons into harm's way. In his autobiography *Down These Mean Streets,* Piri Thomas (the New York–born son of a Puerto Rican mother and a Cuban-born father) recounted how, after his baby brother died, his parents moved the family "to Italian turf" on 114th Street east of Third Avenue. There he became the target of the neighborhood's Italian bully Rocky, who called him a "dirty fuckin' spic" and humiliated Piri at every turn. One day, Piri's mother sent him "to the Italian market on 115th Street and First Avenue, deep in Italian country. Man, that was stompin' territory. But I went." Piri decided that if he encountered Rocky and his gang, he was going to fight back. Sure enough, as he was hurrying around the corner at First Avenue and 114th Street on his way home from the market, he and Rocky crossed paths. The ensuing fight landed Piri in the hospital for several days, but he won the respect of both Rocky and his own father, who told him he was now *"un hombre."* Despite his injuries, Piri "felt proud as hell." But the family moved back to El Barrio.[36]

This drawing of ethnic boundary lines was not a specifically anti–Puerto Rican sentiment. Irish Americans had resented the influx of Italians into "their" neighborhoods in the late nineteenth century just as much as Italian Americans disdained the flow of Puerto Ricans into theirs. Puerto Ricans "are not like us," one Italian East Harlemite explained to educator Leonard Covello in 1938. "We're American. We eat meat at least three times a week. What do they eat? Beans! So they work for beans. That's why we have trouble here." Worse yet, "the Porto Ricans are all Negroes, lazy and never working," one Italian immigrant complained to a sociologist. "The men spend all their time drinking and smoking and gambling." Italian immigrants found Puerto Rican women just as objectionable. They "are awful dirty people, the women are all bad." The Irish had said the exact same things about the Italians only a few years earlier.[37]

Native-born Americans did not view the Puerto Ricans any more favorably than did the Italians. "Puerto Ricans were not born to be New Yorkers," insisted the authors of a guidebook to the city. "They are mostly crude farmers, subject to congenital tropical diseases, physically unfitted for the northern climate, unskilled, uneducated, non-English-speaking, and almost impossible to assimilate and condition for healthful and useful existence in an active city of stone and steel." Others saw little difference between the Puerto Ricans and the southern and eastern European immigrants. The "verminous, crime-ridden slum called East Harlem," *Time* reported menacingly in 1946, overflows with "hordes of Italians, Puerto Ricans, Jews and Negroes." The promiscuous mixing of races and ethnic groups in East Harlem particularly alarmed outside observers. "Negroes, whites and every intermediate shade of human being were living not only under the same roof but by the dozen in the same rooms," exclaimed *Scribner's Commentator* in 1940.[38]

Other reporting on El Barrio echoed that on nineteenth-century Five Points. "Few have running water," *Scribner's* reporter Charles Hewitt observed of the neighborhood's residents, "but most are not even conscious of that lack; for it is unknown in Porto Rico." Sanitary conditions could also be alarming. "In an average home on 112th street," Hewitt wrote, "I found nearly 80 persons using a single outdoor privy." The tenements in Spanish Harlem became just as torridly hot in the summer as those in other parts of town. Like tenement dwellers in other sections of Manhattan a generation earlier, Puerto Ricans resorted to sleeping on fire escapes and rooftops or even in Central Park to escape the oppressive heat. Spanish Harlem was also said to contribute a disproportionate amount of disease, crime, and pauperism to the city. These "crowded and filthy conditions," Hewitt insisted, "do not belong to this century."[39]

Such reports were more than nativist hyperbole. Vega agreed that over the course of the 1920s and 1930s, living conditions in Spanish Harlem "grew worse and worse. Once a building was occupied by our countrymen, no more maintenance was done on it. Garbage collection also became inadequate, and the whole neighborhood gave the impression of being totally neglected." All the habitable spaces in the area's tenements, including the "cellars and basements, were packed with people. Men, women, and children shared what little room they had with rats, cockroaches, and garbage."[40]

These problems — for Puerto Ricans and all of New York's immigrants — grew far worse with the onset of the Great Depression that began after the stock market crash of October 1929. The severity of the Depression is incomprehensible today. The unemployment rate reached 16 percent in 1931, peaked at 25 percent in 1933, and was still at 20 percent in 1935. New York, with a relatively diversified economy and lacking much heavy industry, was not as hard-hit as cities like Pittsburgh, Detroit, and Cleveland. But the garment industry was devastated as Americans stopped buying new clothes, and another of New York's biggest employment sectors, construction, also saw massive layoffs. Even in 1940, when the unemployment rate for New York's garment workers had fallen to "only" 14 percent, 31 percent of New York's construction workers still lacked jobs.[41]

The Great Depression also had a major impact on immigration. The number of immigrants entering the United States decreased dramatically, from about 150,000 (the quota limit) in 1929 to 62,000 in 1931 and only 12,000 in 1933. Immigration would not reach pre-Depression levels again until 1950. Furthermore, many immigrants left the United States to return to their native lands. While immigrants generally believed that the United States was the best place to strike it rich, many decided that it was far easier to be poor in their homeland, where housing and food were far less expensive than in New York. The Great Depression thus became the only period in American history when more immigrants left the country than entered it. From 1930 to 1934, about 20 percent of New York City's Puerto Rican–born residents returned to the Caribbean. Even the "old" immigrants joined the exodus. Angela and Malachy McCourt were among the many Irish who decided to depart New York for their native land, in their case bringing their four American-born sons with them. The miserable poverty they suffered in Limerick was probably far worse than anything they would have experienced in New York, but the ordeal did at least inspire their eldest son, Frank, to write one of the most moving memoirs ever published by a New Yorker, or any American, *Angela's Ashes*.[42]

Immigration to the United States has always declined during economic downturns. It still does today. But the low level of immigration to the United States in the thirties — a rate not seen since the 1820s — was not merely the result of slackening demand. Hundreds of thousands of would-be immigrants applied for visas, only to have American consular officials turn down almost all of them on the grounds that immigrants without substantial savings were likely to become public charges because there were no jobs to be had. Even a letter from a relative in New York stating that the applicant would be welcome to work in the family business would not satisfy America's gatekeepers. To be sure, immigration during the Depression would have fallen even without such onerous restrictions. But it was policy, not a lack of interest in coming to America, that drove immigration to such unprecedentedly low levels.[43]

For immigrants already in New York when the stock market crashed, the Great Depression was devastating. Hundreds of thousands lost their jobs. Even worse, hundreds of thousands lost their savings, and not just because they drained their bank accounts while seeking new jobs. The savings institution most popular with the city's Jewish immigrants, the Bank of the United States, with sixty branches and 400,000 customers, went out of business in December 1930. In an era before federal deposit insurance, these immigrants lost almost everything they had. Even decades later, Irving Howe remembered the "terrible day in the early thirties we heard that the Bank of the United States — Jewish-owned! — had failed, and I sat in our apartment listening to my aunt and grandmother wailing over the loss of the few hundred dollars they had scraped together." While the closing of the Bank of the United States affected more New York immigrants than any other single failure, a number of the small banks that catered to New York's Italian immigrants went bankrupt as well, wiping out the emergency funds many families had set aside for just such a crisis.[44]

The government stepped in to ease the suffering where it could. In New York, neighborhood "relief" stations initially doled out this aid, which typically took the form of "tickets" New Yorkers could exchange at local businesses for food, fuel, or clothing. Immigrants — both citizens and aliens — qualified for this assistance, and it helped hundreds of thousands avoid hunger. But immigrants believed that they were not all being treated equally in the distribution of this aid. "We receive persistent and detailed complaints from destitute *hispanos*," noted the city's Spanish-language daily *La Prensa*, "who, after speaking to relief station officials, either don't receive any aid at all or are given some indefinite date — which never actually arrives." Relief options multiplied when Franklin Roosevelt became president in 1933 and instituted his New Deal. He pumped far more federal dollars into local home relief programs. But other immigrants of color who lived among the city's native-born African Americans in Harlem just west of the Puerto Rican enclave also complained bitterly of being discriminated against in the dispersal of relief, resentment that helped fuel the Harlem riots of March 1935.[45]

Many Americans today mistakenly believe that immigrants did not become eligible for welfare until the Great Society programs of the 1960s. In fact, New York's immigrants qualified for and took government benefits many decades earlier. And even before these programs were initiated, "Boss" Tweed and his successors had assisted indigent immigrants with government jobs as well as food and fuel bought with taxpayer dollars diverted to Tammany Hall. Even the *Wall Street Journal*, never a fan of government handouts to the poor, has recognized that modern Asian and Latino immigrants do not get significantly more government assistance than did European immigrants seventy-five or one hundred years ago. "Folklore Says Great-Grandpa Didn't Take Handouts," read its descriptive subheading over a 1995 story acknowledging this fact. "Actually, He

Took Plenty." The newspapers of the period document European immigrant community leaders demanding their fair share of relief benefits and even the occasional Republican complaint that immigrants who had not become citizens were getting too much assistance.[46]

The most important additional relief measure initiated by Roosevelt that helped immigrants was his massive public works program. In recent years, Americans have been told by their leaders that government must economize during economic downturns. Roosevelt, in contrast, took advantage of record low interest rates to carry out hundreds of big-ticket projects that Americans knew they needed but had not been able to muster the collective will to undertake. The infrastructure projects built in New York City with New Deal financing created the modern city we know today. They include the Triborough (now RFK) Bridge connecting the Bronx, Queens, and Manhattan (1933–1936); Manhattan's Henry Hudson Parkway (1934–1937); the Lincoln Tunnel, connecting Manhattan to New Jersey (1934–1937); Manhattan's Sixth Avenue subway line (1934–1940); the East River (now FDR) Drive (1935–1937); the Queens-Midtown Tunnel (1936–1940); La Guardia Airport (1937–1939); the Belt Parkway, the Cross Island Parkway, and Southern State Parkway on Long Island (1938–1940); as well as the Brooklyn-Battery Tunnel (1940–1950). These projects employed tens of thousands of New Yorkers who would otherwise have remained unemployed. Another seventy thousand New Yorkers were put to work building or improving city parks. By the winter of 1936, the New Deal's Works Progress Administration had hired 248,474 New Yorkers, ranging from skilled Irish sandhogs and welders to Italian stonemasons and laborers. Their work left New Yorkers with the modern transportation infrastructure that it still relies on now more than ever, given how difficult it is to get such massive projects built (or even adequately maintained) today. These positions paid far less than the same jobs in the private sector, in order to give workers an incentive to find non-government employment as the Depression eased. "Their standard of living is considerably lowered," noted a government report, referring specifically to New York's immigrants. Yet thanks to public works projects and other types of relief, "they are not subjected to hunger."[47]

Despite the terrible stresses of the Great Depression, Americans in some ways became more forgiving of the undocumented aliens already in their midst. In 1929 Congress in essence granted amnesty to immigrants who had arrived illegally before July 1, 1921, or who had arrived legally but then overstayed their visas. By 1934, the government had extended partial amnesty to the huge numbers of undocumented aliens who had arrived in the United States from July 1921 through June 1924. They could not become citizens, reported the *Times,* but would now be free from the threat of deportation. In 1935 the De-

"Sandhogs" working seventy feet below the riverbed of the East River on the Queens-Midtown Tunnel in 1939. Jobs on infrastructure projects like this one helped many New York immigrants survive the Great Depression.

partment of Labor (led by New Yorker Frances Perkins) began allowing illegal immigrants whose deportations would break up families to go to Canada and reenter the United States legally as permanent residents. This was the provision that had enabled Minnie Kusnetz to escape deportation. Finally, in 1940, Congress authorized the suspension of orders of deportation when removal from the country would cause "serious economic detriment" to an immigrant's immediate family.[48]

There were limits to this forgiveness. The government allowed only undocumented Europeans to adjust their status by reentering the United States from Canada. The many undocumented Asians were still subject to deportation. So too were Mexicans, even those who had entered the country legally (and in some cases become American citizens). Thousands of non-citizens were deported without cause, and thousands of citizens of Mexican descent were coerced to accept "voluntary repatriation." In many of these cases, Mexican Americans were so severely discriminated against in the distribution of Depression-era unemployment benefits that they elected to board free buses and trains provided by state and local governments to take them back to Mexico rather than face the humiliation of being denied jobs and government relief because, they were told, there was only enough for "real" Americans.[49]

Some in Congress wanted to go even further. In 1935, Representative Martin Dies of Texas proposed a bill that would mandate the deportation of all the nation's illegal immigrants, whose numbers, Dies estimated, had grown to 3.5 million. The Dies proposal would also have given 4 million legally admitted aliens who had not yet undergone naturalization twelve months to, in Dies's words, "become citizens or go home," even though an immigrant who had not already been in the United States for four years could not become a citizen in a year's time.

The Dies bill and others like it never became law. Deportations actually declined sharply once Franklin Roosevelt became president, so much so that the government stopped publishing the numbers. The Great Depression certainly was a terrible time to be a Mexican immigrant in the United States, but the Mexican population of New York City at this point was negligible. With a mayor (La Guardia) very sympathetic to immigrants in City Hall, another New Yorker famous for defending immigrants' rights (Dickstein) chairing the House Immigration Committee, and still another New Yorker sympathetic to immigrants' needs (Perkins) heading the Department of Labor, New York's undocumented aliens must have felt a little less vulnerable than they had previously.[50]

Another reason why New York's immigrants could feel more secure was that their increasing political clout made it harder for officeholders to ignore or neglect them. The city's two biggest immigrant groups, Jews and Italians, took enormous pride in La Guardia's election as mayor in 1933. But more important to solving the problems in the immigrants' day-to-day lives were their local representatives. Gone were the days when Tammany could safely nominate Irish Americans for high office and expect the new immigrants to vote the straight party ticket. In the year when New Yorkers first elected Roosevelt president, they sent to Congress such American-born sons of Jewish immigrants as Sol Bloom, Emanuel Celler, Samuel Dickstein, and William Sirovich. Italian immigrants, typically perceived as less politically active than Jewish newcomers, managed to control only East Harlem's congressional seat. It was filled from 1923 to 1951 by La Guardia, James Lanzetta, and Vito Marcantonio. All three were popular with their Puerto Rican as well as Italian constituents. Marcantonio also won the admiration of African American voters, proposing civil rights bills in Congress that would have outlawed poll taxes and made lynching a crime punishable in federal courts. Puerto Ricans demonstrated nascent political clout in the New Deal era too, electing Oscar García Rivera to the state legislature several times beginning in 1937. García Rivera, who had arrived in New York in 1925, put himself through law school at St. John's University with income from a post office job and used his legal practice as a springboard into politics.[51]

Not everything these politicians did was popular with their immigrant constituents. In 1934 La Guardia declared war on the city's pushcarts, condemning them as unsightly, unsanitary, and a major cause of traffic congestion. La Guardia also viewed pushcart-lined streets as an embarrassment in much the same way that other children of immigrants found their parents' Old World customs mortifying. The mayor proposed that the city move the pushcart peddlers into city-financed indoor markets.

La Guardia was roundly booed by the peddlers when he appeared at the opening of the city's first such market, in East Harlem, running from 111th to 116th Street underneath the gloomy stone viaduct that carried the New York Central (now Metro North) Railroad tracks above Park Avenue. But La Guardia was unapologetic. "Today you have graduated from pushcart peddlers into merchants," he boasted. And apart from the peddlers themselves, many immigrants applauded the demise of the pushcarts, especially those that sold food. Pushcarts are "very unsanitary," complained a group of East Harlem mothers. "The streets are full of flies and at night when they leave, there are about thirty ashcans on the sidewalks full of garbage." Believing that the local high school principal, Leonard Covello, had political influence, they asked him "to try to do something to have these pushcarts taken away from our streets and make it a better and safer place to live in." La Guardia banned carts from selling all food, even New Yorkers' beloved hot dogs. While a *Times* editorial admitted that the removal of the pushcarts was beneficial overall, the editors nonetheless acknowledged some sadness in having to bid "farewell to another bit of old New York."[52]

A more consequential change for immigrants advanced by La Guardia and other New Dealers was public housing. Twenty years earlier, immigrant socialists had proposed to alleviate the high rents New Yorkers had to pay, even for decrepit tenement apartments, by demanding that the government build housing and rent it at cost. Most Americans considered such ideas radical insanity in the 1910s, but twenty years and hundreds of rent strikes later, New Yorkers were willing to give public housing a try.

The first project involved a renovation, not new construction. The New York City Housing Authority used a federal loan to buy the fifteen dilapidated, Astor-owned five-story tenements on the south side of East 3rd Street between Avenue A and First Avenue and on the west side of Avenue A between 2nd and 3rd streets on the Lower East Side. Using federally financed public works employees, the city tore down every third building to reduce congestion and to enable additional windows to be cut on the sides of the buildings. The interiors got new oak floors and brass light fixtures. Rent ranged from $15 to $19 per month, depending on the occupants' income. The manager of "First Houses," as the complex was christened, received 3,800 applications for the 122 apartments. She screened out New Yorkers who earned too much to qualify and those who earned too little, choosing in particular those who were steadily employed but living in tenements with insufficient ventilation and sanitation. One First Houses resident had lived so long in a tenement with windowless interior rooms that until she moved into her new apartment, she told the manager, "I never knew what color my furniture was." It was the first municipally built, owned, and managed housing project in the United States.[53]

Critics were skeptical that the success of First Houses could be replicated on a large enough scale to improve the lives of the hundreds of thousands of New Yorkers who still lived in dark, dirty, outmoded tenements, but La Guardia and his housing commissioner, Langdon Post, were determined to try. Post told the press in 1935 that he hoped to create new housing for 500,000 families over the next ten years. That was a pipe dream — it would have cost billions. But with the financial backing of the new Federal Housing Authority, La Guardia and Post did manage to construct fifteen thousand apartments by 1945. Some replaced the worst barracks-style tenements in East Harlem and the Lower East Side. Others were built in the Bronx, Brooklyn, and Queens.

Today we tend to think of big-city public housing as crime-and-drug-ridden towers of failure. But those problems would only develop a generation later, as the economically stable initial tenants were replaced with the urban poor. Following the lead of social critic Jane Jacobs, many assume that the scale of the public housing complexes doomed them to failure, but the fact that middle-class New Yorkers lived (and continue to live) in buildings of similar scale suggests that poverty, rather than architecture, lies at the root of public housing's woes in cities like New York. During the 1930s and 1940s, when thousands of immigrants and their American-born children moved into New York's first public housing projects, they were grateful for the vastly improved living conditions and reasonable rents such housing offered.[54]

One defining feature of New York during the Great Depression was huge public works projects in housing and transportation. Another was ethnic conflict. Animosity between the city's religious, ethnic, and racial groups was as old, of course, as the city itself. But the economic hardships of the Great Depression made New Yorkers especially anxious and likely to blame others for their problems. Jews blamed anti-Semitism for their inability to find jobs during the Depression. Many Christians blamed the entire economic catastrophe on supposed Jewish control of Wall Street and the slowness of the recovery on Jews who administered the New Deal. Puerto Rican and African American New Yorkers blamed white racism for their persistent poverty.

Those anxieties were heightened still further by the chaotic international situation of the 1930s. Japan aggressively colonized Korea and parts of China. The Spanish Civil War provoked passionate debate among the various large immigrant communities in New York, as most Catholics supported the insurgents under General Francisco Franco while the left advocated the Republican cause. The rise to power of Hitler in Germany and Mussolini in Italy also divided immigrant New Yorkers. German and Italian Americans tended to take pride in the prosperity and respect their homelands enjoyed under these authoritarian leaders, while those on the left were aghast at the suppression their ideological brethren suffered under these fascist regimes. The governments of Franco, Mussolini, and Hitler were all unabashedly anti-Semitic, something that made New York's Jews especially uneasy because so many of them still had relatives in Europe.

While the situation overseas made New York's Jews nervous, the appalling increase in American anti-Semitism during these same years worried them even more. Some of the nation's most outspoken anti-Semites, like Henry Ford and Charles Lindbergh, were midwesterners whose influence in New York seemed minimal. New York's Jews felt much more threatened by two groups that did flourish in the city: the German American Bund and the Christian Front.

The Bund, established in 1936, was essentially the American affiliate of Hitler's Nazi Party, complete with swastikas, Hitler salutes, and storm troopers. Most of its members were German immigrants or their children. (Only those who could prove German heritage were permitted to join.) Its leader was Fritz Kuhn, a chemist who had fought in the German army in World War I and who immigrated to the United States in 1928 and had become a citizen in 1934. Kuhn ran the Bund from its national headquarters at 178 East 85th Street in Yorkville, a predominantly German neighborhood on the Upper East Side of Manhattan. In fact, the Bund had far more members in New York City than in any other place in America. The height of the Bund's notoriety came with its rally for "true Americanism" staged at Madison Square Garden on February 20, 1939. Nearly twenty thousand attendees cheered as Kuhn, standing beneath a giant portrait of George Washington (whom American Nazis called "the first fascist"), denounced "Frank D. Rosenfeld" and his "Jew Deal."[55]

Some Jews called for La Guardia to ban Bund rallies, arguing that its calls to "kill the Jews" were incitements to violence. Others, recalling the suppression of Jewish socialists during the Palmer Raids, felt that much as they despised the American Nazis, the First Amendment protected their hate speech. Judge Nathan Perlman, a Polish Jewish immigrant and former congressman, found what he considered a middle ground. Using his contacts in law enforcement, he arranged a meeting with the notorious Jewish gangster Meyer Lansky, also a Polish Jewish immigrant. Perlman offered to pay Lansky if the gangster would use his thugs to "disrupt" local Bund meetings, using as much violence as they found appropriate, as long as no one was killed.

Lansky agreed but refused to take any money. "I was a Jew and felt for those Jews in Europe who were suffering," he explained years later to an Israeli interviewer. "They were my brothers." Lansky fondly recounted one of his raids on a Bund rally in Yorkville. "The stage was decorated with a swastika and a picture of Hitler." Several hundred Bund followers were in attendance when the meeting began and "the speakers started ranting. There were only fifteen of us, but we went into action . . . Most of the Nazis panicked and ran out. We chased them and beat them up . . . We wanted to show them that Jews would not always sit back and accept insults."[56]

Menacing as the American Nazis of the 1930s may seem today, New York Jews saw the Christian Front, an organization inspired by the weekly radio broadcasts of Father Charles Coughlin, a Catholic priest from Michigan, as even more of an immediate threat. Unlike the Bund, which had a relatively limited following, Coughlin's syndicated radio show was wildly popular and drew an especially large audience of Irish Catholics. At the start of the New Deal, Coughlin supported Roosevelt and his relief programs. By 1936, however, he had become disillusioned with FDR, convinced that because of the influence of Jewish bankers, Jewish labor leaders, and Jewish communists, the president was not doing enough to aid those in need. When Coughlin spoke at a rally in a Philadelphia stadium in 1936, the *Times* noted ominously, "the men and women in the stands . . . thrust their hands upward and forward in what closely resembled the Nazi salute." In 1938 Coughlin called for his followers to form a "Christian front" against a predicted communist takeover of America, and soon Christian Front clubs began appearing wherever in the Northeast and Midwest there were large Irish Catholic populations. Coughlin's anti-Semitism became so virulent (and his defense of Hitler's policies toward Germany's Jews so strident) that several radio stations, including his New York outlet, refused to continue airing his broadcasts. This censorship, however, served only to convince his devoted followers that Jews now controlled the media.[57]

Members of the Christian Front began to appear all over New York selling Coughlin's magazine, *Social Justice,* and loudly condemning the influence of Jews in America. New York's Jews were appalled. It was one thing to rant from the traditional soapbox forums in Times Square or on Park Row across from

City Hall, but Christian Front street speakers were spewing their hate in Jewish neighborhoods like the Upper West Side of Manhattan and Flatbush in Brooklyn. Worse still, their harangues seemed to lead directly to anti-Semitic vandalism and violence. In Washington Heights, the south Bronx, and Brooklyn, Jews were assaulted on the streets by teenagers shouting anti-Semitic slurs. Synagogues and Jewish businesses all over the city were vandalized. "This is not the usual 'polite anti-Semitism' to which we have become more or less accustomed in the United States," observed a prominent New York Methodist. "It is a militant, hate-breeding" organization. And because "its membership is about 90 per cent Catholic, the Christian Front well merits the title of 'Catholic Klan.'"[58]

What New York's Jews found most appalling about the Christian Front was that the New York police seemed unwilling to stop the anti-Semitic crime that grew along with it. "We are tired of approaching a police captain, hat in hand, saying 'Please Captain McCarthy (or O'Brien) . . . My boy was hit because he is a Jew. Will you send a cop?' And we are damned sick and tired of . . . hearing the usual answer: 'Ah, the boys are just playing.'" In several well-publicized cases, the police did nothing when Christian Front speakers shouted insults at Jews, but when Jews responded with their own invective, *they* were hauled off to jail on charges of disturbing the peace. La Guardia staunchly defended the police in public, but privately asked his subordinates to determine how many New York policemen belonged to the Christian Front. In an anonymous survey conducted as part of the investigation, four hundred officers admitted that they were or had been members, and many others probably hid their affiliation. The head of the Front in Brooklyn testified in court that five hundred police officers had applied to join the organization in that borough alone. FBI director J. Edgar Hoover claimed to have a list of 1,500 policemen citywide who had applied for Christian Front membership.[59]

Perhaps because of lobbying by Jews and other New Yorkers, or perhaps because Europe appeared to be descending imminently into war, the police finally began to arrest some members of the Christian Front and its offshoots like the Christian Mobilizers, whose hatemongering seemed to invite violence. In September 1939, Ralph Ninfo, the twenty-nine-year-old son of Councilman Salvatore Ninfo, was sentenced to seventy-five days' hard labor at the city's Rikers Island jail for disorderly conduct after telling a crowd at the corner of Broadway and 72nd Street that he would "like to see every Jew in the United States hanged." Ninfo's soapbox partner, found guilty of the same charge, had told the gathered crowd that he "wished to see Jewish blood flow all over America."[60]

Many New York Christians, including many Catholics, came to the defense of the city's Jewish population. Residents in several boroughs formed interfaith groups to protect Jews from those who, as one put it, "had been terrorizing the

Bronx by nightly street meetings, petitions and literature." Some Irish Catholics themselves recognized the irony involved in this Irish-led religious harassment. In passing judgment on Florence Nash, a child of Irish immigrants arrested for haranguing Jews as they passed her on the street while she sold *Social Justice,* magistrate Michael Ford reminded her that her parents "undoubtedly came to this country, as my parents did, to escape the persecution of the English government . . . The persecution you have perpetrated could be perpetrated also against your own race."[61]

The Christian Front's public activities subsided somewhat in January 1940, when J. Edgar Hoover announced the arrest and indictment of eighteen members, including Brooklyn leader John F. Cassidy, on charges of conspiring to overthrow the government. Hoover alleged that the group intended to seize "the reins of government in this country as Hitler did in Germany" and bring about the complete "eradication of the Jews in the United States" as well. At the time of their arrest, these Christian Front members were found to possess a large collection of weapons, five thousand rounds of ammunition, and more than a dozen half-completed bombs. The conspirators, Hoover alleged, planned to use the bombs to blow up the offices of the communist *Daily Worker,* the Yiddish-language socialist daily *Forward,* and various Jewish congressmen. Some of the arrested were Irish and German immigrants, the remainder mostly American-born men of Irish and German ancestry. As soon as the arrests were announced, Coughlin disavowed the Christian Front and its followers. At their trial a few months later, the defendants' attorney managed to impugn the reliability of the FBI's paid informants. Cassidy testified convincingly that they had not intended to overthrow the government but were arming themselves to resist the *communists'* inevitable attempt to seize the reins of power. One of the defendants committed suicide during the trial, but the jury found Cassidy and eight others not guilty.* It deadlocked eleven to one in favor of acquittal for the remaining five, and the government never retried them.[62]

By this point Jewish immigration was growing once again, despite the restrictions, driven primarily by refugees from Hitler's Germany. When Hitler first came to power, most fleeing Jews chose to settle in other parts of Europe. With Hitler menacing the entire continent by the end of 1938, however, the mass of refugees now sought admission to the United States. Yet despite calls from

---

* Despite his acquittal, Cassidy did suffer a punishment of sorts. Just before his arrest, Cassidy passed the bar exam after five years of trying. But the state nonetheless refused to admit him to the bar on the grounds that despite his acquittal, the evidence at trial had shown that he had a propensity to "take the law into [his] own hands." He became a field accountant for construction projects. More than fifty years later, Cassidy's son-in-law appealed the decision, and in 1995, at age eighty-five, Cassidy was admitted to the bar.

American Jews and humanitarian groups, the Roosevelt administration accepted hardly any more German refugees than could be allowed into the country under Germany's normal immigration quota. By June 1939, 309,000 Jews in areas under German control had applied for one of that year's thirty thousand or so quota slots.* Some suggested "mortgaging" Germany's future quota slots so that more refugees could be admitted immediately, but that would have required an act of Congress that never materialized. A bill proposed by one of New York's U.S. senators, Robert Wagner (himself an immigrant from Germany), to allow twenty thousand German Jewish children under the age of fourteen to enter the country as refugees over two years above and beyond the German quota, also failed to muster support. The wife of Roosevelt's commissioner of immigration, James Houghteling, explained that her husband opposed Wagner's plan because "20,000 children would all too soon grow up to be 20,000 ugly adults." Roosevelt could have used his substantial political capital to try to push for these bills or some other kind of legislation that would have allowed more refugees to enter the United States, but he demurred. Instead FDR tried to persuade Latin American nations to admit the refugees. They were no more willing to take the Jews than the rest of the world.[63]

The climax of the refugee crisis came with the ill-fated voyage of the *St. Louis,* a ship that left Hamburg in May 1939 carrying more than 937 Jewish refugees who had permission to settle in Cuba or at least stay there temporarily. As the ship crossed the Atlantic, however, the Cuban government bowed to internal anti-Semitism and announced that it would admit no more Jewish refugees, not even those who had valid American visas that would allow them to enter the United States later that year. Threatened by the Cuban navy, the ship sailed to the southeast coast of Florida, its German captain hoping that some nation would agree to accept his passengers. "The refugees could even see the shimmering towers of Miami rising from the sea," reported the *Times,* "but for them they were only the battlements of another forbidden city." Finally, with no North or South American country willing to take the *St. Louis's* passengers, the ship returned to Europe. Belgium, France, Great Britain, and the Netherlands had agreed to divide the refugees among them. But they were not safe from Hitler on the Continent. Of the 620 *St. Louis* passengers forced to resettle there, 254 were killed during the war, primarily in the Nazi death camps at Auschwitz and Sobibor. "The cruise of the St. Louis," the *Times* ruefully concluded, "cries to high heaven of man's inhumanity to man."[64]

---

* The German quota was in flux in these years as Hitler took over more territory. The quota of 25,957 increased to 27,360 once Germany annexed Austria, and to 30,234 when it occupied Czechoslovakia.

Jewish refugees on the *St. Louis*, 1939. No country would take them in, and the ship was eventually forced to return with them to Europe. Although the United States took in more refugees during World War II than any other nation, New York's Jews were shocked that the Roosevelt administration would not provide a safe haven for more Jews fleeing Nazi Germany.

While it is easy to condemn Roosevelt or Congress for not taking in more refugees from Hitler's Europe, the United States *did* admit far more of these refugees than any other nation. Of the 523,000 Jews who lived in Germany when Hitler came to power, about 282,000 had managed to flee by the time World War II began in September 1939, and about 95,000 of those refugees were admitted into the United States. In fact, about half the passengers on the *St. Louis* eventually did succeed in immigrating to the United States, either during or after the war. In addition to the Germans, thousands of refugees relocated to New York from Russia, France, and other war-torn nations. In all, the United States took in somewhere between 200,000 and 250,000 refugees, of whom perhaps two-thirds were Jews.[65]

Louis and Paula Kissinger and their two teenage sons were typical of Jewish refugees who settled in New York. Louis had been a schoolteacher in Fürth, a small town in northern Bavaria just outside Nuremberg. Though the Kissingers were Orthodox Jews, they considered themselves thoroughly and devoutly German. They were dismayed, therefore, when just weeks after Hitler's rise to power in 1933, all the Jewish doctors in town were fired from their posts at the local hospital and all the Jewish civil servants, including Louis Kissinger, lost their jobs too. Later that spring, the town's largest Jewish-owned store was ordered closed, while the Nazis organized a boycott of all the town's other Jewish businesses. Jews were also banned from the town beach. Then in 1934, a cap was placed on the number of Jews who could attend the public schools, and in 1936, Jews were banned from attending them altogether. Kissinger supported his family by starting a private Jewish school that same year. His sons, one of them recalled years later, were "often . . . chased through the streets, and beaten up" for no other reason than that they were Jewish.

Despite all this, Louis Kissinger thought the family should stay in Germany. Surely Germans would come to their senses and the madness would pass. But Paula Kissinger had seen enough. Her brother-in-law had already been sent to Dachau. She refused to watch her teenage sons suffer the same fate. Paula contacted a first cousin who had been born in Brooklyn and now lived in Larchmont, in affluent Westchester County, just north of New York City. Paula's cousin provided the affidavit of support that enabled the Kissingers to snare four of the prized German quota slots. In August 1938 they crossed the English Channel and on the thirtieth boarded the *Île de France* for New York. And not a moment too soon. *Kristallnacht* came in November; the Nazis seized Jewish businesses and property a few weeks after that. Before long, the concentration camps turned into death camps. Three of Louis's sisters and their husbands, along with most of their children, were among the several dozen family members killed by the Nazis by the time the war was over.[66]

Those tragic events, however, lay in the future. When the Kissingers arrived in New York in September 1938, the city was well prepared to meet, greet, and integrate them and their fellow refugees. Officials knew which refugees would be arriving on each ship and worked in conjunction with dozens of volunteer groups to help settle them. Because the majority of the refugees were Jewish, the Hebrew Immigrant Aid Society was by far the busiest of the relief organizations. It lodged the newcomers who did not go immediately to live with friends or relatives, offered a three-day crash course in English and American civics, and provided a free job placement service.

The biggest and most important institution helping the city's refugees adjust to their new lives in America was the New York City public school system. Back before immigration restriction, the city's schools had offered English and civics courses to the newcomers. When immigration was reduced to a trickle, the city largely eliminated these classes. Now, the school system shifted its night school program into high gear again. "As never before in its history," reported the *Times* in January 1939, "the evening division of the New York City school system is crowded to capacity with serious-minded students — persecuted ref-

ugees from central Europe — eager to absorb the language, traditions and literature of their newly adopted land." Five thousand refugees had already enrolled
in such classes, according to the *Times*, and many more were on waiting lists for
their chance to take them.

The refugees' teachers faced a far different task than they had before World
War I. Back then, many of the immigrants in night school had received very
little formal education before coming to America. In 1939, though, the students
were "in large measure . . . professional men." Twenty-five percent of the night
students already had college degrees. Female refugees were less likely than
men to enroll in these classes, unless they came to America without male family members. The *Times* told of one class composed of twenty Czech women,
"some with husbands or fathers left behind in concentration camps." These refugees often attended class with their children, who "help their parents decipher
the English words."[67]

Unlike the Italian farm laborer and Jewish peddler, who had known what
kind of work awaited them in the United States, the new refugees had no idea
what jobs they would find. "The change these people had to undergo can
hardly be overestimated," wrote a social scientist who interviewed several hundred refugees just after World War II ended. Putting food on the table was their
immediate priority, and the language barrier and American skepticism toward
their qualifications made it extremely difficult for them to resume their former
occupations. The refugees simply had to take whatever work they could get.
"Here was the former factory owner who now peddled cakes and candies, or
the manager of a department store who worked as a laborer in a cemetery." A
former steel exporter peddled pencils. A professor of classics worked as a dishwasher. In some cases, housewives who had until recently employed domestic
servants now found themselves scrubbing the floors and toilets of others.[68]

Not every refugee had to change careers. German doctors could continue to
practice their profession. So could most scientists. Enrico Fermi, who left Italy for the United States in 1938 a few months after winning the Nobel Prize in
physics because he feared for the safety of his Jewish wife, Laura, had no shortage of job offers before he accepted a position at Columbia. Fordham University snagged its own Nobel physicist, Victor Francis Hess, who left Austria in
1938 because he too had a Jewish wife. New York University also got a Nobel
laureate, German pharmacologist Otto Loewi. A fourth Nobel refugee, Norwegian novelist Sigrid Undset, settled in Brooklyn Heights.[69]

The New York arts world also benefited tremendously from the influx of refugees. In the sphere of music, those who relocated to New York included com-
posers Kurt Weill and Béla Bartók, pianist Vladimir Horowitz, and conductor
Arturo Toscanini. Artists were particularly drawn to New York City. Salvador

Dalí, Marcel Duchamp, and Piet Mondrian, among many others, made New York their new home. They helped New York become the capital of the international art world in the postwar years. The American government purposefully adopted a visa policy that favored them. After Germany invaded France in 1940, FDR directed his Advisory Committee on Refugees to draw up a list of Europeans "of superior intellectual attainment" who might be in danger of persecution and offer them visas without their even having to ask. Approximately 3,400 visas were issued under this initiative — about a third of which were used.[70]

Even many unknown refugees managed to thrive in New York. Those with an entrepreneurial bent seemed especially able to replicate their commercial success in America. Heinrich Spitzer, who owned his own "knit goods" business in Germany, took a job as a stock clerk upon arrival in New York to "learn American methods." Once he had collected enough intelligence, he went into business for himself. By the end of 1939, he had a dozen employees. A German manufacturer who had operated a multimillion-dollar dress business in Europe lost almost everything to the Nazis but managed to smuggle out some of his wife's jewelry. He pawned it and used the proceeds to start manufacturing dresses in Brooklyn. Soon he had thirty-five workers on his payroll. But such stories were the exception rather than the rule. Only 39 percent of refugees who had been business owners and managers in Europe were able to resume such work within five years of their arrival in the United States. Those most likely to recommence their former occupations were professionals (doctors, scientists, and so on) and skilled craftsmen. Two-thirds of them found similar work within five years of settling in the United States.[71]

One of the refugees who could not manage to find steady employment was Louis Kissinger. Upon their arrival in New York, he and his family had found an apartment in Washington Heights, in northwest Manhattan, just a few blocks north of where the George Washington Bridge disgorged its traffic from New Jersey. Washington Heights was a favorite destination of German Jewish refugees, so much so that they sometimes referred to it as the "Fourth Reich of Germany." Perhaps because Louis was surrounded by so many German-speakers, he found it very difficult to learn English, even though the family decided to speak only English at home to help him master the language. Feelings of inadequacy sent Louis spiraling into depression, so that even when a friend offered to take him on as a bookkeeper, he was not able to work regularly. Paula became the family's primary breadwinner, first as a servant and then as a caterer.[72]

At the beginning of 1940, the family decided that while Paula was getting her business off the ground, their eldest son, Heinz, would work full-time to supplement the family's meager income. He had been attending George Washington High School along with his brother since their arrival in New York, and it was in order to fit in at school that Heinz decided to Americanize his name to Henry. He now switched to the night session to accommodate his work schedule. Henry took a menial job at a shaving brush factory on West 15th Street owned by the husband of Paula Kissinger's cousin, the one who had sponsored the Kissingers' immigration to America. Henry's assignment at the factory was to dip badger bristles into acid to bleach them and then squeeze as much acid as possible out of the bristles before others attached them to the shaving brush handles. Almost sixteen when he began the job, Henry worked from 8:00 to 5:00 and was paid $11 a week. After work, he would take the subway home, eat a quick dinner, and then rush off to three hours of night school so he could get his diploma. Despite the exhausting hours, Heinz earned excellent grades in everything but math, aided by the fact that he had studied English in Germany. A year after his arrival, he was essentially fluent, though unlike most immigrants his age (and even his own brother), he never learned to speak without an accent. Henry continued to work at the brush factory — albeit with a promotion to a much higher-paid position in the shipping department — even after he graduated from George Washington in 1941 and enrolled at City College to study accounting. He lived at home and registered for classes that met at night so he could continue to help support his family.[73]

By this point, the war in Europe was monopolizing the attention of New Yorkers and virtually all Americans. Many, like La Guardia and Roosevelt, believed that American entry into the war on the side of Great Britain and France was inevitable. Others, in particular German and Irish Americans, thought the United States should stay out of the conflict. They argued that the nation's ethnic mix made it impossible to enter a war that pitted the homelands of half the nation's immigrants against the other half. Pointing to the fighting between Catholics and Jews and the boycotts of Jewish businesses that were being led by an offshoot of the Front, the Christian Mobilizers, municipal judge Herbert O'Brien told the Senate Foreign Relations Committee in February 1941 that a virtual state of "civil war" already existed in the city. "New York City is a veritable powder keg," testified Queens Democratic leader William Goodwin, a Coughlin follower, before the same committee, "and our entry into this war might touch it off."[74]

The Japanese attack on Pearl Harbor in December 1941 and the decisions of both Hitler and Mussolini to declare war on the United States four days later rendered such arguments moot, as Roosevelt had no choice but to enter the conflict both in Europe and in the Pacific. That all three nations had chosen preemptive war against the United States disarmed Roosevelt's isolationist foes and also helped unite Americans, even the nation's immigrants, in support of the war effort. "Now we know where we stand," declared Italian American grocer Al Cazazza after the Axis powers suddenly forced the United States into the conflict. "We are all together, this unites us all."[75]

Not quite all. One of the first things Americans did after their entry into the war was to take steps to remove from their midst immigrants who they believed were likely to sympathize with, or even aid, the nations against which the United States was fighting. "For the time being New York has a concentration camp of its own," reported the *Times* as Ellis Island was converted into a detention facility for those deemed a threat to national security. On the very day the Japanese attacked Pearl Harbor, the FBI began rounding up many of the 2,500 or so Japanese-born New Yorkers to bring them to Ellis Island for internment. By December 11, 413 German-born Americans had been taken there as well. Italians who authorities believed might aid America's wartime enemies were interned there too. Most internees were aliens, but some, like Fritz Kuhn, leader of the Bund, were naturalized American citizens. Each detainee received a hearing at which he or she could present witnesses and be represented by a lawyer. Many of the detainees were able to convince the authorities that they posed no threat. One was Metropolitan Opera star Ezio Pinza, who was held at Ellis Island for three months. Those detainees the tribunal judged to be a danger to national security, however, were shipped to detention camps such as the Crystal City Internment Camp near San Antonio or Fort Lincoln Internment Camp on the outskirts of Bismarck, North Dakota. Kuhn and William Bishop, an illegal immigrant from Austria who was one of the defendants in the Christian Front sedition case, were among the New Yorkers sent to these camps.[76]

Despite the hysteria that resulted in the detention of many immigrants on dubious grounds, New York *was* crawling with immigrant spies. Machinist Rene Froehlich, who had immigrated from Germany as an eleven-year-old in 1923, was drafted into the army in 1941 and conveyed information to the Germans on American troop and ship movements that came across his desk in his capacity as an army typist on Governors Island in New York Harbor. A German immigrant from Queens, Herman Lang, attempted to transmit to the German government top-secret aerial bomb site information stolen from his workplace in Manhattan. Kurt Ludwig, born in Ohio but raised in Germany, recruited German Americans in Queens to help him with his espionage. In 1941 he hired Lucy Boehlmer, an eighteen-year-old blonde who had immigrated to New York from her native Stuttgart in 1929, to coax sensitive information from soldiers on Long Island. The press referred to Boehlmer as the "Maspeth Mata Hari." For every spy the FBI caught, many more were undoubtedly never detected.[77]

Also undetected was the U-boat that ventured into New York Harbor in January 1942. From where it surfaced off Rockaway Beach, the sailors on board

could clearly see the Parachute Jump and the Wonder Wheel at the Coney Island amusement park. Had the German spies in New York been able to coordinate their efforts with the German U-boats, which returned nine months later
and laid mines in the harbor, they could have wreaked real havoc throughout
the city.[78]

While the FBI rounded up suspected spies, the military recruited soldiers.
Immigrants had constituted a substantial portion of the army and navy in
World War I and the Civil War, but the foreign-born played a relatively minor
role in fighting World War II. Because of immigration restrictions, New York's
foreign-born population had grown fairly old: the average age of a New York
immigrant in 1940 was forty-eight, compared to just thirty-one for natives. The
foreign-born still made up 29 percent of the city's population, but they constituted only 5 percent of men aged eighteen to thirty-five. By the end of the
war in 1945, 891,000 of New York's 7.5 million inhabitants had either enlisted
or been drafted into the military, but only a small number of them were immigrants. The press and Hollywood might boast that the American army was
a true "melting pot," but the Irish, Italians, Jews, and Poles who fought side by
side were almost always the children or grandchildren of immigrants rather
than adopted Americans themselves.[79]

Of the New York immigrants who did fight in the war, many had only recently left Europe as refugees. Perhaps the most famous New York refugee
turned soldier was Hitler's own nephew, English-born William Patrick Hitler.
The younger Hitler was something of a louse himself. After growing up in England, he went to Germany in the mid-1930s hoping to cash in on his name. He
apparently even attempted to blackmail his uncle when he did not succeed. He
fled Germany in 1938 and moved to Queens, where he tried to support himself
by giving anti-Nazi lectures organized by publisher William Randolph Hearst.
Despite the navy's misgivings about his loyalty to the United States, the American Hitler was allowed to enlist in 1944 because the propaganda value of his
service was too good to pass up.[80]

While most everything William Patrick Hitler did seemed to be driven by
mercenary motivations, New York's Jewish refugees had far loftier reasons to
fight. "I, who have been robbed of all I possessed and driven out of my homeland," wrote one Jewish refugee soldier, "have so much more reason for wanting to get a whack at Hitler than has the average American citizen who has not
yet suffered from him." Despite such inducements to fight, most immigrant
soldiers (and most native-born, too) were draftees rather than volunteers. One
was my grandfather Tulea Anbinder. He was sent not to the front lines but to
Fort Wayne, where he treated the dental woes of the army's recruits, many of
whom had had little or no dental care before entering the service.[81]

Henry Kissinger was also drafted. In early 1943, the nineteen-year-old was sent to basic training in Spartanburg, South Carolina. When he completed his three-month boot camp, the army made him an American citizen as well. Soon Kissinger's younger brother Walter was drafted too. Henry's letter of advice to him conveys a sense of what Henry's first six months in the army had been like. Keep "your eyes and ears open and your mouth closed," he wrote to Walter. "Always stand in the middle because details are always picked from the end. Always remain inconspicuous because as long as they don't know you, they can't pick on you . . . Don't become too friendly with the scum you invariably meet there. Don't gamble! There are always a few professional crooks in the crowd and they skin you alive . . . Don't go to a whore-house. I like a woman, as you do. But I wouldn't think of touching those filthy, syphilis-infected camp followers."[82]

The war was a huge boon to the New York economy. The garment industry, which had languished for years, was now awash in orders for military uniforms. Other kinds of manufacturing benefited as well. New York was a major transshipment point for men and matériel, and by the end of the war, the city could boast the world's largest warehouse, which sat among hundreds of other supply sheds and administrative buildings at the Brooklyn Army Base in Sunset Park. Hundreds of thousands of soldiers and sailors also shipped out from the city's piers, using its hotels and restaurants before doing so.

Another large employer in the city during the war was the navy. Today, Americans do not associate New York with the navy, but back then New York was a true navy town in large part because of the vast Brooklyn Navy Yard. The war made the Navy Yard an even more massive presence in the city's economy. By 1944, seventy thousand New Yorkers worked in what was probably the world's biggest shipyard. By the end of the war, the Navy Yard had built five aircraft carriers and three battleships, including the *Missouri,* the ship on whose decks the Japanese government signed the instrument of surrender that for all intents and purposes ended the war. Because of security concerns, relatively few immigrants were permitted to work at the Navy Yard or the Brooklyn Army Base during the war, but they employed thousands of immigrants' children. With so many men off fighting, wages in New York rose sharply in the early 1940s as companies became desperate to attract workers, and as a result, these defense jobs often paid far more than any of these "second-generation" Americans had earned before. They brought this pay home to their families, and in that manner the war helped boost the standard of living of immigrant New Yorkers as well.[83]

A New York military operation that did employ immigrants at its highest levels was the Manhattan Project, the program to design and construct the first atomic bomb. It was called the Manhattan Project because it originated in the Manhattan physics laboratories of Columbia University. It was there in Pupin Hall on West 120th Street just east of Broadway that physicists produced the manmade uranium fission chain reactions that led to the making of the first atomic bomb. Among the immigrant physicists who worked on the project in its New York phase were Fermi, Isidor Rabi (born in the part of Austria-Hungary that is now Poland), Leo Szilard (Hungary), and Walter Zinn (Canada). Lacking the necessary space to advance the project toward the construction of a nuclear weapon, the Manhattan Project was moved to the University of Chicago (where the scientists worked under the football field) as well as to laboratories in Tennessee, New Mexico, and Washington State.[84]

As the Manhattan Project was entering its final phases, the Kissinger brothers were sent to the front lines, Walter in the Pacific and Henry with the Eighty-fourth Infantry Division in Europe. Henry hoped he would be part of the assault on Germany so he could have the satisfaction of helping to defeat the Nazis, who had treated him so mercilessly and forced him to flee his homeland. In November 1944 he got his wish. "I am back where I wanted to be," he wrote to his parents at the end of the month. "I think of the cruelty and barbarism those people out there in the ruins showed when they were on top. And then I feel proud and happy to be able to enter here as a free American soldier."[85]

Given his fluency in German, Kissinger was at this point reassigned to counterintelligence. His job was to interview German civilians in towns his unit occupied, determine which if any of them might pose a threat to American troops, and oversee the evacuation of those considered "unreliable." That winter, Kissinger and his unit faced grave danger during the German counteroffensive known as the Battle of the Bulge. But once it was repulsed, he resumed his counterintelligence efforts, earning a Bronze Star in April 1945 for his work in discovering and breaking up a Gestapo sleeper cell left behind by the fleeing Germans in Hanover.

Later that month Kissinger had the grim task of helping to liberate the Nazi concentration camp at Ahlem just outside of Hanover. "As our jeep travelled down the street," Kissinger wrote soon afterward, "skeletons in striped suits lined the road . . . Cloth seemed to fall from the bodies" of the survivors, and each head "was held up by a stick that once might have been a throat. Poles hang from the sides where arms should be, poles are the legs." Kissinger crisscrossed the camp, telling each prisoner, "You are free." But he took no pleasure in the job. "What kind of freedom can I offer? I see my friend enter one of the huts and come out with tears in his eyes: 'Don't go in there. We had to kick them to tell the dead from the living.'" Kissinger wished the sights he had seen at Ahlem could be preserved in concrete "for future generation[s] to look upon and take stock."[86]

Kissinger spent two more years in Germany as part of the American occupation. At first he continued his intelligence-gathering work, but later he was assigned to teach incoming officers intelligence techniques and German history as the army attempted to prevent both a resurgence of pro-Nazi sentiment and a rise in pro-communist feelings that might aid the United States' new rival, the Soviet Union. Finally, in the late spring of 1947, four years after he first entered the army, Kissinger returned home to Washington Heights.

For the 98 percent of New York soldiers who managed to make it home, the war often profoundly changed their lives. The experience the immigrants' American-born sons gained in the army and navy, and the G.I. Bill benefits they would receive, filled the city's Italian and Jewish newcomers with pride. They believed that their children would now be much more likely to achieve the American dream. For the city's many Puerto Rican soldiers, who had been given more responsibility and treated with more dignity in the army than they had been accustomed to in New York, the war inspired in them a determination to demand more rights and respect once they returned to the city.

The war also altered Henry Kissinger's life. Had it not been for the war, he would likely have finished his degree in accounting at City College and been satisfied to keep the books of Washington Heights' German American merchants and manufacturers. But his success in the army, the mentoring and encouragement he received from his commanders, and in particular his stint teaching intelligence officers prompted him to aspire to loftier goals. "I shall write, I may lecture later on . . . I have extreme confidence." That confidence, shared by millions of New Yorkers, would shape the city, its immigrants, and the entire era that followed the war.[87]

TOP TEN SOURCES OF NEW YORK'S IMMIGRANTS, 1960

Italy	280,786
USSR	204,578
Poland	168,824
Germany	152,192
Ireland	114,008
Austria	84,301
Great Britain	61,018
Hungary	45,567
Greece	28,845
Canada	28,150
Total foreign-born	**1,463,821**
Total population	**7,781,984**

Note: The Census Bureau specified the birthplace of only "white" immigrants in 1960. Immigrants born in Northern Ireland are listed under Ireland.

Source: Ira Rosenwaike, *Population History of New York City* (Syracuse, 1972), 205.

21

RENAISSANCE

THROUGH MUCH OF THE PAST, Rome was considered "the capital of the world." Others awarded that designation to Paris. Ernest Hemingway set a short story of that name in Madrid. But in the years immediately after World War II, there was near universal agreement that New York had achieved that status. The war helped Wall Street displace London as the headquarters of international finance and likewise enabled New York to overtake Paris to become the world capital of fashion and the arts. The United Nations decided in December 1946 to place its headquarters not along the Seine, the Thames, the Tiber, or the Rhine, or even on the banks of the Schuylkill (as the *Times* predicted a day before the decision was announced), but alongside New York's East River. Compared to the great cities of Europe, Sergeant Milton Lehman of New York observed in *Stars and Stripes* as he prepared to return home in 1945, "New York is still the promised land."[1]

Because of the restrictions put in place in 1924, however, New York in 1945 was not the promised land for many new immigrants. Congress did pass a Displaced Persons Act in 1948 that allowed 200,000 refugees to be admitted to the United States over a two-year period. But the act was not quite as generous as it seemed: it allowed refugees in only on the condition that the countries from which they came would forfeit a future immigration slot for each one. The United States cut the immigration quotas of nations with refugees in half until the "borrowed" quota slots had been "repaid." Because the United States admitted approximately forty thousand Italian refugees, for example, and Italy had an annual immigration quota of about five thousand, Italy lost half of those five thousand slots for each of the next sixteen years. Had the immigration laws remained unchanged, Latvia would have lost half its tiny annual immigration quota of 286 until the year 2274.[2]

Consequently, the immigrant population of New York continued to decline.

There were still 2,017,000 immigrants living in the city in 1950 — more than the *entire* population of every other American city except Chicago and Philadelphia. But the average age of a New York immigrant was now fifty-two. As these immigrants aged and died, the immigrant population of the city dwindled to 1.9 million in 1960 and 1.4 million in 1970. Having accounted for 41 percent of the population as late as 1910, immigrants made up just 18 percent of New York's residents in 1970. The rest of the world might continue to think of New York as a city of immigrants, but longtime New Yorkers could feel the difference.[3]

The immigrant population declined so rapidly in part because Congress closed some loopholes that had allowed significant numbers of Caribbean immigrants to enter the country in the decades after it restricted immigration in 1924. The McCarran-Walter Act of 1952 ended the ability of such immigrants to enter in virtually unlimited numbers under the quotas of their European colonizers. Up until this point, Jamaica, Barbados, and other islands in the British West Indies had each sent several thousand immigrants to New York annually. Henceforth they would be limited to one hundred per year. The islands' tiny quotas did not change when they began to gain their independence. In 1963, Jamaican prime minister Alexander Bustamante called his nation's minuscule immigration quota "an insult to ourselves and our country."[4]

Immigration was so sparse in the postwar years that in 1954 the government closed Ellis Island. When Americans heard the words "Ellis Island" in that era, they conjured images of a detention center rather than an immigration depot. Even after World War II ended, detention continued to be its main function. Immigration officials held incoming immigrants suspected of communist sympathies at Ellis Island, and non-citizens already in the New York area suspected of communist allegiance were held there as well, pending judicial hearings. In a single twelve-month period from 1953 to 1954 at the height of Senator Joseph McCarthy's anticommunist crusade, the government detained some 38,000 people at Ellis Island. One suspected communist was held there for four years. But as McCarthy's reputation began to decline in the wake of the Army-McCarthy hearings in the spring of 1954, President Dwight Eisenhower decided that he could help rein in the witch hunts by closing Ellis Island and other detention centers, which were becoming an international embarrassment. Henceforth all but a handful of alien "subversives" would remain free, pending their hearings.[5]

"If all the stories of all the people who stopped briefly or for a longer time on Ellis Island could be written down," mused the *Times*' editors as the famous immigration station shut down, "they would be the human story of perhaps the greatest migration in history." In its sixty-two years of operation, the editorial noted, "immigration slowly rose to majestic tides, and then, under pressure of wars, new laws and economic recessions, declined." Not only had Ellis Island's millions of immigrants made countless concrete contributions to American society, but in addition, "they make part of what is now the American temperament—a livelier and richer national personality than could have existed without them. Perhaps some day a monument to them will go up on Ellis Island," the editors suggested, because "the memory of this episode in our national history should never be allowed to fade."[6]

One group of newcomers—though technically not immigrants—did continue to arrive in New York in record numbers in this period: Puerto Ricans. There was good reason for the government not to consider Puerto Ricans immigrants. The citizens of many independent North and South American nations (such as Mexico and the Dominican Republic) could immigrate to the United States in unlimited numbers, but only if they qualified for admission. The Border Patrol and the Immigration and Naturalization Service turned away thousands each year because they were judged to be communists, prostitutes, mentally deficient, or (most often) likely to become a public charge. Puerto Ricans, by contrast could come and go as they pleased, no matter their financial status, political beliefs, or medical conditions. When ships or—increasingly after World War II—airplanes from Puerto Rico arrived in New York, their passengers underwent no more screening than travelers arriving from Boston or Chicago.

And arrive they did. From 1940 to 1950 the number of Puerto Rican natives living in New York City tripled, from 61,000 to 187,000. Jobs were plentiful during the war, when even work as a janitor, cook, or domestic paid 250 percent more than the same position in San Juan. With New York's economy booming in the 1950s while Puerto Rico's remained stagnant, the flow of "Boriqueños" to the city increased still further. New York was virtually the only place in the continental United States where Puerto Ricans were willing to settle. In 1950, 83 percent of all natives of Puerto Rico living on the mainland resided in New York City. By 1960, when New York's Puerto Rico–born population peaked at 430,000, they outnumbered every New York immigrant group except for eastern European Jews. Puerto Rican migration to New York would continue, albeit at lower levels, in subsequent decades.[7]

Illegal immigrants from other nations saw the ubiquity of New York's Puerto Ricans—and the fact that their skin color varied tremendously—as an opportunity. When the authorities arrested undocumented aliens from places as diverse as Barbados, Argentina, and Pakistan, the detainees would invariably claim to be natives of Puerto Rico, something that was difficult for authorities to disprove. Undocumented aliens could buy fake Puerto Rican birth certificates in Harlem for as little as $30 in the 1930s.[8]

By the late fifties and early sixties, Americans increasingly came to believe that the United States' restrictive immigration laws should be liberalized. Two factors contributed to this national change of heart. First, as the millions of children of the southern and eastern European immigrants came of age and gained political clout, they found it unfair that Irish Americans could bring as many family members to the United States as they wished but Italian Americans and Polish Americans could not. Second, in a period of the Cold War when the United States, the Soviet Union, and China were competing to win allies in Asia, Africa, and South America, the Russians and the Chinese repeatedly pointed to Americans' discriminatory immigration quotas as proof that the United States did not practice the egalitarian principles that its leaders preached.

In 1962 Senator Philip Hart of Michigan complained that the United States' immigration laws were "grist for the propaganda mills of Moscow and Peiping." One of New York's senators, Jacob Javits, agreed that the immigration statutes were "creating ill-will abroad, furnishing a target for Communist propaganda and making our effort to win over the uncommitted nations more difficult." Descendants of immigrants from southern and eastern Europe were especially vocal. A Jewish leader called the National Origins Act the "most racist law in American history," while the American Committee on Italian Migration argued that the quota system "adds another argument to the Communists' constant barrage of criticism of the restrictions in American immigration laws." When Massachusetts senator John F. Kennedy ran for president in 1960, he made eliminating the "unjust" quota system a constant refrain of his campaign.[9]

Once Kennedy entered the White House, however, the Bay of Pigs, the Cuban Missile Crisis, and other foreign policy matters dominated his attention. Only in July 1963, under pressure from liberals in both parties, did Kennedy return to the immigration issue. In a message to Congress, he proposed that the annual cap on immigration be raised from 157,000 to 165,000 and that the quotas that favored the nations of northwest Europe be phased out over a five-year period, to be replaced by a system that set no limits on immigration from any given country except for the stipulation that no single nation could receive more than 10 percent of any year's immigration visas. Immigration from the Americas would remain unlimited.[10]

With Kennedy's assassination a few months later, the push for immigration reform was again sidetracked. But JFK's successor, Lyndon Johnson, eventually made immigration reform one of the must-pass pieces of his Great Society legislative agenda. In order to get Democratic Senate opponents from the South (in particular Senator James Eastland of Mississippi and Senator Sam Ervin of North Carolina) to accept a plan that would make the United States less "Anglo-Saxon," the bill's sponsors — Hart in the Senate and Emanuel Celler of Brooklyn in the House — had to agree to amendments that, for the first time, would also set numerical limits on immigration from the Americas, something opposed by southwestern agricultural interests that relied on the seasonal migration of cheap Mexican labor to harvest their crops.

As finally approved by Congress in September 1965, the Hart-Celler Act removed all individual country quotas and replaced them with an overall annual limit of 120,000 immigrants from the "Western Hemisphere" (the Americas) and 170,000 from the "Eastern Hemisphere" (the rest of the world). No country in the Eastern Hemisphere could claim more than 10 percent of that hemisphere's quota slots in any given year, but in a concession to southwestern farmers, there was no such limitation on immigrants from the Americas.* While immigrants with highly sought-after job skills had received priority under the existing quota system, under the new law immigrants reuniting with family members already legally residing in the United States would be allotted 84 percent of the quota slots. Another 10 percent would go to immigrants with desirable occupational skills, and the remaining 6 percent to refugees, in particular those fleeing "any Communist or Communist-dominated country." In addition, continuing in slightly revised form a provision contained in the 1924 quota act, Hart-Celler exempted from quota limitations the parents, spouses, and unmarried minor children of citizens and legal aliens, enabling them to join their loved ones in the United States in unlimited numbers. The act would take effect on June 30, 1968.[11]

Johnson hailed Hart-Celler as "one of the most important acts" of his administration, "for it does repair a very deep and painful flaw in the fabric of

---

* In 1976 Congress replaced the hemispheric limits of 120,000 and 170,000 with an overall worldwide cap of 290,000, with no more than 20,000 immigration slots to be given to any one nation. This change, which for the first time placed a limit on Mexican immigration, had two unintended consequences. First, it encouraged Mexicans, who in the past had moved frequently in and out of the United States, to stay permanently for fear of not being able to gain readmission. Second, by suddenly limiting a century-old tradition of Mexican labor migration into the United States on which millions of Mexican families had become dependent, it led to the widespread illegal immigration from Mexico that would become a major American political issue beginning in the 1980s.

American justice. It corrects a cruel and enduring wrong in the conduct of the American Nation . . . It will strengthen us in a hundred unseen ways." Yet the law's supporters insisted that Americans would barely notice its impact. "This bill that we will sign today is not a revolutionary bill," said Johnson at the signing ceremony held at the base of the Statue of Liberty. "It does not affect the lives of millions." Senator Edward Kennedy, one of the act's co-sponsors, agreed. "Our cities will not be flooded with a million immigrants annually . . . The present level of immigration remains substantially the same . . . The ethnic mix of this country will not be upset."[12]

While Johnson and Kennedy were right to call the Hart-Celler law one of the most momentous legislative accomplishments of the 1960s, their predictions about its impact could not have been more inaccurate. They underestimated the consequences of the law because they overestimated Europeans' interest in continuing to immigrate to the United States, underestimated the desire of Asians and Latinos to become Americans, and grossly underestimated how many parents, children, and spouses of those new immigrants would come to the United States. With Europe finally achieving prosperity after decades of re-construction following World War II, very few residents of western Europe ap-plied to immigrate to America. Their places within the Eastern Hemisphere quota were quickly filled by Asians and southern and eastern Europeans who had aspired to come to the United States for decades. These newcomers spon-sored quota-exempt relatives at a far higher rate than had the English, Ger-mans, and Irish who dominated immigration before 1965, pushing the number of quota-exempt immigrants to record levels. These newcomers could in turn sponsor still more quota-exempt immigrants.

Overzealous anticommunism drove immigration higher still after 1965. Congress voted several times to expand the number of refugees who could come to the United States fleeing communism, increasing the number of immigrants from Cuba, China, and Southeast Asia, to name only a few ex-amples. Persecuted Christians also received exemptions from the numerical limits, as did those who claimed to have been punished for violating China's one-child policy. Once someone had an asylum application approved, he or she could bring spouses, parents, and unlimited numbers of children to the United States, just like regular immigrants. Within ten years of the implemen-tation of the Hart-Celler Act, the United States was admitting one quota-ex-empt immigrant for every one of the 290,000 quota immigrants. By 1982, the number of quota-exempt immigrants exceeded 290,000, and in subsequent years the gap between quota-exempt and quota immigrants continued to widen.[13]

As a comparison of the top ten immigration sources from 1960 and 1980 shows, American immigration changed profoundly under the Hart-Celler Act. By the latter year, Asia had replaced Europe as the main source of America's immigrants. The Caribbean had become a much bigger contributor of immigrants as well. And the total number of immigrants arriving in the United States had doubled.

TOP TEN SOURCES OF IMMIGRANTS ADMITTED TO THE UNITED STATES, 1960 AND 1980

1960		1980	
SOURCE OF IMMIGRANTS	NUMBER OF IMMIGRANTS	SOURCE OF IMMIGRANTS	NUMBER OF IMMIGRANTS
Canada	44,668	Mexico	56,680
Mexico	32,708	Vietnam	43,483
Germany	29,452	Philippines	42,316
United Kingdom	20,875	Korea	32,320
Italy	13,369	China	27,651
Netherlands	8,654	India	22,607
Cuba	8,126	Jamaica	18,970
Portugal	6,766	Dominican Republic	17,245
Ireland	6,010	United Kingdom	15,485
Japan	5,699	Cuba	15,045
TOTAL	265,398	TOTAL	530,639

Source: *Annual Report of the Immigration and Naturalization Service, 1960* (Washington, D.C., [1960]), 19; *1980 Statistical Yearbook of the Immigration and Naturalization Service* (Washington, D.C., [1980]), 15–17. Totals are for fiscal year, not calendar year. Not all immigrants counted in these figures actually arrived in the United States in the year stated. Some had originally arrived on tourist or student visas or by other means but had their status adjusted to "immigrant" in the year stated.

The impact of Hart-Celler was equally profound in New York City, though that impact is hard to measure with precision because it is not possible to know exactly how many immigrants move to New York in any given year. But we can get a sense of the transformation by comparing the change in each immigrant group's population in the first dozen years after the law went into effect in 1968.

NEW YORK IMMIGRANT GROUPS WHOSE POPULATION
INCREASED MOST FROM 1960 TO 1980

SOURCE OF IMMIGRANTS	POPULATION INCREASE IN N.Y. FROM 1960 TO 1980	TOTAL N.Y. POPULATION, 1980	POPULATION RANK AMONG N.Y. IMMIGRANTS, 1980
Dominican Republic	111,000	121,000	2
China	64,000	85,000	4
Jamaica	61,000	93,000	3
Haiti	47,000	50,000	8
Colombia	36,000	41,000	12
Ecuador	36,000	39,000	14
Guyana	22,000	32,000	16
India	20,000	22,000	21
Korea	20,000	20,000	23
Cuba	20,000	50,000	9
Philippines	17,000	21,000	22

Source: United States Bureau of the Census, *Census of Population: 1960,* vol. 1, *Characteristics of the Population,* pt. 34, *New York* (Washington, D.C., 1963), 434; *The Newest New Yorkers: Characteristics of the City's Foreign-Born Population* (New York, 2013), 16 (for 1980 figures). Jamaica and Guyana figures for 1960 are my own estimates because some Jamaican-born New Yorkers in that year were counted as natives of the short-lived West Indies Federation, while natives of Guyana were not separately enumerated in the 1960 census.

The biggest difference between New York and the rest of the United States in 1980 was that the city lacked a large Mexican population. Vietnamese immigrants for the most part avoided New York as well, settling mainly in California, Texas, and the Washington, D.C., area.[14]

Hart-Celler also changed immigrant New York because it prevented any one or two groups from dominating the city's population of newcomers. On the eve of the Civil War, more than 80 percent of New York's immigrants came from just two places — Ireland and the German states. Those two groups dwarfed New York's other immigrant groups for several generations. Later on, Italians and eastern European Jews far outnumbered all other immigrants arriving in the city. Hart-Celler led to a diversification of immigration to the United States.[15] Nonetheless, three immigrant groups concentrated in New York to such an extent that only a dozen years after Hart-Celler became law, they had grown significantly larger than the rest: Dominicans, Chinese, and West Indians.

Dominicans, in theory, could have come to the United States in large numbers before Hart-Celler. Like Mexicans, Dominicans were exempt from quota limitations under the National Origins Act, though many would have been turned away as likely to become public charges. But the main obstacle to emigration for Dominicans was political. Rafael Trujillo, the brutal dictator who ruled the Dominican Republic from 1930 to 1961, frowned upon emigration and suppressed it by severely restricting Dominicans' ability to obtain passports. When Trujillo was assassinated in 1961, these international travel restrictions were lifted, and thousands of Dominicans rushed to leave the country. At least 75 percent of them settled in New York City.

There were long-standing ties between the United States and the Dominican Republic. President Ulysses S. Grant had attempted to purchase the Dominican Republic in 1870, and even though the treaty of annexation failed to win ratification in the Senate, American planters remained heavily invested in Dominican sugar and tobacco production. Dominicans' exposure to Americans increased exponentially in 1916, when the United States began an eight-year-long occupation of the entire island of Hispaniola (which includes both the Dominican Republic and Haiti). The government justified this incursion on the grounds that Germany might make it a U-boat staging ground if the United States did not occupy it first.

In April 1965 the United States again invaded the Dominican Republic, this time in order to forestall the installation of a left-wing government that the CIA believed would become a "communist dictatorship" controlled by Cuba's Fidel Castro. With the help of U.S. Marines, the Dominican army quickly suppressed the country's left-wing political parties and leaders, and American troops departed a year later. Yet the occupation had left an indelible impression. To one of the many "Yankee Go Home" signs scrawled on the walls of the capital, Santo Domingo, one Dominican added "y llévame contigo!" — and take me with you! It cannot be a coincidence that the year the marines left the Dominican Republic, Dominican immigration was 50 percent higher than in any previous year on record.[16]

Some of these emigrants were well-to-do and middle-class Dominicans who feared that the newly installed, American-backed right-wing government would punish them, as Trujillo would have, for their leftist politics. Others were rushing to make it to America before the Hart-Celler Act took effect in 1968, since that law would, for the first time, impose numerical restrictions on Dominican immigration to the United States. And poor Dominicans decided to leave their country in the hope of finding a better and more prosperous life in New York. They became adept at sidestepping the "likely to become a public charge" restriction by passing pooled money from person to person as each went for his or her visa interview. Many others made it to New York by over-staying tourist or student visas. Others traveled to Puerto Rico and concealed themselves among the Boriqueños boarding planes or ships bound for New York. And, of course, large numbers of Dominicans could settle in New York because they were the relatives of those who had already moved legally to the United States.[17]

Initially, there was no one part of New York where Dominicans concentrated. A story about them in the *Times* in 1971 listed Corona in Queens, the Upper West Side of Manhattan, the East Bronx, and south Brooklyn as the areas where most Dominicans were settling. Dominican immigrants soon did begin to cluster, however, in Henry Kissinger's old neighborhood of far northern Manhattan, Washington Heights. "The Dominicans are coming here in massive numbers," observed the president of the Hispanic-American Alliance of Washington Heights in 1976, at a time when Cubans and Puerto Ricans still far outnumbered Dominicans in that neighborhood. A decade later, Dominicans were the dominant Latino population in that part of Manhattan. By 1990 they outnumbered every other group — Latino or not — making up 40 percent of the neighborhood's population. In that year there were more than twice as many Dominican immigrants living in Manhattan (93,000) as there were immigrants from any other country in the world (China was second, with 39,000), and 225,000 Dominican immigrants in the city as a whole.[18]

Dominicans came to New York expecting to earn more money than in the Caribbean, but they often found that the jobs available to them paid poorly. Even in the late 1990s, Dominican immigrants lagged behind most other foreign-born groups in per capita income. "It's painful," noted a Dominican immigrant, "that you have been let go by your own country and come to a new place dreaming of a better life and that does not happen."[19]

Like most New Yorkers, about half of all Dominicans in the last decades of the twentieth century worked in the service sector. For Dominican men, this often meant driving taxis, primarily the "livery cabs" that predominate in immigrant neighborhoods. Passengers cannot legally hail these taxis on the street, and in that era they could be summoned only by telephone. Most Dominican livery cab drivers grouped themselves into cooperatives, each one owned by anywhere from ten to sixty *socios,* or partners. The *socios* almost always drove cabs, but the cooperative would hire additional drivers to work during peak demand or at hours that the *socios* did not want to work. The taxis were dispatched from the cooperative's base (*la base*), typically located in a commercial space or an apartment on the ground floor of a tenement in a Dominican neighborhood. Driving a livery cab was dangerous work. In the early 1990s, at the peak of the crack epidemic, dozens of drivers were killed annually during robberies. Nonetheless, Dominicans drove the vast majority of the city's forty thousand or so livery cabs operating at that time.[20]

While many Dominican men in the service sector found jobs in transportation, Dominican women worked disproportionately in beauty salons. The owners of these shops — invariably women — worked in them too, and each one typically employed four to six additional Dominican women to help run the salon. At first these were concentrated in the Dominican neighborhoods of northern Manhattan and the west Bronx ("a salon on nearly every block," noted a sociologist), but eventually Dominican beauty salons spread in large numbers to Harlem as well as certain parts of Queens and Brooklyn. The *Times* reported in 1999 that in central Harlem, "hair salons that are owned and operated by Dominicans are everywhere." These shops thrived by underpricing their non-Dominican competition. "A wash-and-set at a Dominican salon might cost as little as $10 or $15," noted the same *Times* story, "while an African-American salon on average charges twice that or more." By the end of the century, Dominican women were as well known in certain parts of New York for their beauty parlors as were Korean women for running nail salons and South Asian men for driving yellow taxis.[21]

The two other employment sectors in which Dominicans were disproportionately represented were manufacturing and trade. In 1980, 49 percent of employed Dominicans worked in manufacturing — garment sweatshops in particular, but really in every facet of manufacturing that went on in the city. Yet apart from the garment industry, manufacturing was a dying field in New York. From 1980 to 2000, two-thirds of the city's manufacturing jobs disappeared. By the latter year, only 12 percent of Dominicans worked in that once thriving sector.[22]

In trade (19 percent of Dominican employment as of 2000), Dominicans became known throughout the city for running bodegas, the tiny grocery stores that proliferated in the city's Latino neighborhoods. Typically the bodega owner (known as a *bodeguero,* and almost always a man) got his start by combining savings with loans from family, friends, or wealthy Dominicans in order to purchase an existing store. Because there were so many bodegas in Latino neighborhoods, competition was fierce and business was often slow. Many bodegas had no employees other than the owner. He would find a trusted friend to mind the store if he had to leave it during business hours, which were typically from 8:30 or 9:00 in the morning until 10:00, 11:00, or even midnight, seven days a week. "I'm like a slave in this place," complained one *bodeguero.* Successful bodega proprietors did not typically stay in the business for life. Their dream was either to sell at a handsome profit and return to the Dominican Republic or, if an owner was really ambitious, to use the windfall from the sale of a thriving bodega to purchase an independent supermarket, another field dominated by Dominicans in late twentieth-century New York.[23]

Often forgotten amidst the thousands of *bodegueros* and livery cab drivers were the substantial number of middle-class Dominicans who relocated to New York. Many lawyers, doctors, and businessmen joined the migrant flow. Perhaps the best known was Oscar de la Renta. Born in 1932 the youngest of seven children and the only son, de la Renta grew up in comfortable circumstances in Santo Domingo. His father wanted him to join the family insurance business, but Oscar, who later recalled that even as a boy he usually got what he wanted, chose instead to study art in Madrid. Though he received a sizable allowance from his parents, de la Renta sketched clothing for newspapers and fashion designers to earn extra money. One such drawing, of his own design, caught the eye of Francesca Lodge, wife of the American ambassador in Ma-

Dominican immigrant Oscar de la Renta burst onto the American fashion scene in the 1960s. With a talent for self-promotion, de la Renta soon became as famous as the starlets and first ladies who wore his clothes.

drid, in 1956. She commissioned the dress for the coming-out party she had planned for her daughter. A photo of the Lodges' daughter in the dress made the cover of *Life* magazine and launched de la Renta's career in fashion design. He apprenticed for two years at a couture house in Paris, but then at age thirty-one decided to move to New York to "get into ready-to-wear," he explained at the time, "because that's where the money is." Showered with job offers, he initially took a position with Elizabeth Arden, but after two and a half years, he struck out on his own.[24]

De la Renta's timing could not have been better. American department stores had traditionally stripped out the labels from all the clothing they sold and put in their own. American fashion designers were largely anonymous. That changed in the late 1960s, allowing designers to become celebrities in their own right, and none became more famous than Oscar de la Renta. Socialites, first ladies, and movie stars all demanded to wear his clothing. "His clothes give you such a wonderful feeling," explained one of his famous customers. "His evening things make you feel like you're walking on air." Soon he became as famous as the celebrities he dressed, and the press eagerly reported on his fabulous parties and jet-setting lifestyle, which included frequent visits to his two vacation homes in the Dominican Republic. In 1980 a *New York Times Magazine* cover story profiling his glamorous life was titled "Living Well Is Still the Best Revenge." He died in 2014, but his fashion empire remains nearly as strong as ever.[25]

The growth of New York's Dominican community over the last third of the twentieth century was extraordinary. From an almost insignificant population in 1960, Dominicans vaulted to ninth place among New York's immigrant groups in 1970 and second place (behind only Italy) in 1980. By 1990, the 225,000 Dominican immigrants in New York were not just the largest foreign-born group in the city but nearly twice as large as their nearest rival. They would remain the biggest immigrant population in the city for the next quarter century, growing another 64 percent to 369,000 by the year 2000. "In the Dominican Republic I was happy," admitted one immigrant who arrived at about that time, "but I had no future. In New York I have a lot of problems, but I have opportunity."[26]

If current demographic trends continue, the Chinese will, before long, displace the Dominicans as New York's biggest immigrant group. New York had a Chinese enclave well before the first Latino and West Indian neighborhoods developed in the 1920s. The city's first Chinatown emerged around 1880 as Chinese immigrants living in the western United States were driven out of their communities by violence and intimidation. Shunned in most other parts of the city, New York's early Chinese residents created a residential enclave on Mott Street below Canal. By 1900 it included neighboring Pell and Doyers streets. The city's Chinese immigrants were almost all men, and a preponderance of them worked in the laundry business, which the Chinese entered as increasingly middle-class Irish American women abandoned that trade. Many other Chinese immigrants worked as cigar makers, while the enclave's most well-to-do inhabitants were merchants specializing in exports to and imports from China. Most of these immigrants came from one part of China — the counties surrounding the Pearl River delta in the southern province then known as Canton (today Guangdong).[27]

The Chinese Exclusion Act of 1882 devastated New York's Chinese community, because with virtually no Chinese women in the United States, the enclave seemed destined for eventual extinction. But that did not happen. Like other restricted immigrant groups, the Chinese resorted to illegal immigration, sneaking across the Canadian and Mexican borders or stowing away on ships, strategies made more difficult after 1892, when Congress mandated that Chinese Americans carry government-issued photo identification proving that they had entered the United States legally. The Chinese adapted, however, relying less on illicit border crossings and more on fraudulent legal entry into the United States. The Exclusion Act offered exceptions for merchants and the children of American-born Chinese Americans. Thousands of would-be Chinese immigrants persuaded or paid legal Chinese American merchants to claim the newcomers as their business partners. Even more got Chinese Americans to swear falsely that new immigrants were their children — known in the Chinese American community as "paper sons." As a result, the Chinese population of New York actually *rose* after the passage of the Exclusion Act, from about one thousand in 1880 to six thousand in 1900 (though many of these Chinese New Yorkers were legal immigrants who moved to New York from the West, fleeing anti-Chinese violence in the 1880s). The Chinese-born population of the city reached nearly seven thousand in 1930. The Chinese Exclusion Act was repealed in 1943, but China received an annual immigration quota of only 105 slots. Nonetheless, the return of legal immigration facilitated a revival in illegal immigration as well, so that by 1960, more than 21,000 Chinese immigrants lived in New York.[28]

Because the Hart-Celler Act gave preference to immigrants who were joining family members already in the United States, most of the Chinese who arrived in New York in the years immediately after its passage continued to come from Guangdong. Yet because of Chinese emigration restrictions and the fact that the United States did not normalize diplomatic relations with the People's Republic of China until 1979, many more of these emigrants came from Hong

THE GUANGDONG AND FUJIAN PROVINCES OF CHINA

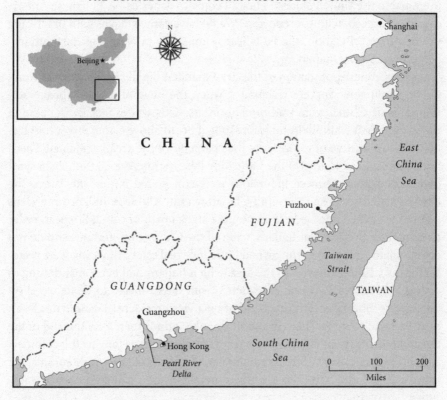

Kong, then still controlled by Great Britain. Many others came from Taiwan. Finally, with the improvement of relations with China and the easing of emigration restrictions by the Chinese government, New York's Chinese population became more varied, though South China still predominated.[29]

In the 1990s, however, the background of New York's Chinese immigrants began to change radically. Large numbers of immigrants, most of them illegal, were starting to arrive from Fujian, the coastal province immediately northeast of Guangdong. Even though Fuzhou, the capital of Fujian province, is just five hundred miles from Guangzhou, the capital of Guangdong, this influx of Fujianese represented a seismic cultural shift for New York's Chinese community. Not only do the two groups eat totally different foods, but often they cannot even speak to each other; the Fujianese speak their own dialect and cannot understand the Cantonese dialects.

So many young Fujianese men came to America that in some towns in China there seemed to be hardly any remaining. "In Fuzhou, not much gentlemen," one female immigrant told the *Times* in 2001, explaining why she too had immigrated to the United States. "They all come to America." A Fujianese American priest agreed, telling a reporter, "We do have some villages with practically no men there." By 2000, the Fujianese immigrants in New York far outnumbered those from Guangdong.[30]

As the Chinese population of the city expanded rapidly in the wake of Hart-Celler, some New Yorkers resented it when the new immigrants began settling outside Chinatown's traditional borders. This was especially the case in the 1970s, when Chinese immigrants spilled north above Canal Street into Little Italy. "We just want to preserve the character of the area," explained Theodore Tarantini, a founder of the Little Italy Restoration Association. Even symbolic acts against Chinese incursions were considered important. When the city translated street signs around Chinatown into Chinese, Italian Americans painted over the Chinese lettering on the signs north of Canal Street in order to demarcate the line that Italians believed the Chinese immigrants should not cross. Italian Americans who owned Little Italy real estate, however, were grateful for the Chinese interest in the area, which Italians had been abandoning in droves for decades. "My main business is with the Chinese," Little Italy real estate investor John Zaccaro (husband of 1984 vice presidential candidate Geraldine Ferraro) told the *Times* in 1980. "Thank God for them." By the end of the twentieth century, an entente of sorts was worked out: as long as the commercial spaces on Mulberry Street remained in the hands of Italian restaurants, the transition of Little Italy into a Chinese neighborhood could go ahead peacefully.[31]

By that point, Chinatown was growing far more rapidly to the east than to the north. The Fujianese enclave centered on East Broadway on the Lower East Side had grown far larger than the Guangdong stronghold centered on Mott Street. The Fujianese also dominated the Chinatowns that had blossomed in Flushing, Queens (where they displaced the Taiwanese), and Sunset Park, Brooklyn. The advent of the Fujianese immigration had important implications for the size of New York's Chinese population as well, for while a majority of Cantonese immigrants settled in California, most Fujianese immigrants chose New York as their American home.[32]

The Chinese came to the United States for the same reasons as most other immigrants — to better their own financial situation and to secure improved opportunities for their children. In the United States "there is hope," said one Chinese immigrant in the 1990s. "I was seeking a better life." Even though Americans saw Chinese immigrants struggling to survive, often paid well below minimum wage if they were undocumented, the Chinese viewed things differently. As an attorney who represented Chinese clients seeking asylum observed, "Everyone sends money home no matter how little they're earning so it seems like the streets here are paved with gold." Sometimes the choice to emigrate was not an individual one. "It's a family or clan decision," a source familiar with Chinese immigrant smuggling told a reporter in 1999. "We'll invest in you, you'll help us get there." Most Chinese who considered relocating to the United States had trouble imagining a reason *not* to make the move. "I can't think of a single bad thing about America," one Fujianese remarked. "Life's just better there."[33]

It is hard to determine how many Chinese immigrants came to the United States in the last decades of the twentieth century. Legal immigration averaged 35,000 a year in the 1980s and 42,000 annually in the 1990s, and perhaps a third of these newcomers settled, at least initially, in New York. But by the end of the 1980s, huge numbers of Chinese immigrants began entering the United States illegally, and it is very difficult to estimate the size of this clandestine flow. There may have been one smuggled immigrant for every legal one. In the first half of the 1990s, the *Times* estimated, 100,000 undocumented Chinese entered the United States each year — outpacing legal immigration by more than two to one. Large numbers of Chinese illegal immigrants, however, eventually became legal. As we shall see, many won asylum; many more qualified for the periodic amnesty programs that Congress enacted in the late twentieth century. Others married citizens and became legal residents in that manner.[34]

The legal and illegal immigration worlds often overlapped. Take the case of a relatively early Fujianese immigrant to New York, Cheng Chui Ping. Around 1964, when Ping was fifteen, her father, a sailor, entered the United States illegally by jumping ship in an American port. He worked for more than a decade as a dishwasher in New York's Chinatown, sending money back to his family three or four times a year, until he was deported in 1977. Meanwhile, soon after Ping got married in 1969, she and her husband, Cheung Yick Tak, managed to escape the People's Republic of China and settle in Hong Kong. Despite their good fortune, Ping's husband left for New York too, using the same method to enter the United States as his father-in-law. Yick Tak managed to stay in New York only two years before authorities sent him back to Hong Kong.

When Yick Tak reunited with Ping, he found that in his absence she had fared much better in Hong Kong than he had in New York. Ping had opened a variety store in Hong Kong's Fujianese enclave, and the business thrived. She was a savvy businesswoman and very good with numbers. In 1979 Ping opened a clothing factory across the bay from Hong Kong on the Chinese mainland. By that point, she had given birth to two daughters.

Despite her mercantile success, Ping was not satisfied. In June 1981 she walked into the U.S. consulate in Hong Kong and applied for an immigration visa. When the consular official interviewing her asked what she would do in America, she said she would work as a domestic servant. Why, the official responded, would she want to trade her life as a businesswoman in Hong Kong for that of a domestic in America? "It is for the sake of my children's future that I am willing to be a servant," she replied. That response satisfied the American, and a few months later she received her visa. She flew to New York via Anchorage in November, leaving her two daughters behind with Yick Tak. A year later, the three of them joined Ping in New York (under the provision allowing immediate family members to join immigrants without numerical limitation). They opened a tiny twelve-foot-wide shop at 145B Hester Street, just east of the Bowery, which was very much like the one she had run in Hong Kong, carrying items sought after by the city's quickly expanding Fujianese immigrant community. "Sister Ping" became a fixture in the community, renowned in particular for helping her fellow Fujianese when they needed a loan or a job.

For the Chinese who came to New York illegally, the beginning of the trip was typically the same — a bus out of Fujian, sneaking across the border into Hong Kong, and then a flight to some other transit point, typically Bangkok. There the immigrants waited weeks, and sometimes months, while their smugglers, known in Chinese as "snakeheads," procured travel documents for their customers. The best documents were real, acquired through bribery at an embassy. Next best was a slightly altered legitimate document, perhaps a Taiwanese passport with a genuine U.S. tourist visa in which the original owner's photo had been carefully removed and replaced with the likeness of an illegal immigrant. About half of the illicit immigrants would then fly to the United States, often taking circuitous routes to help avoid suspicion, because Bangkok had become well known as a jumping-off point for illegal immigrants.[35]

Another 40 percent of Chinese illegal immigrants flew most of the way to the United States but then completed their journey over land. Some flew to Mexico, but many others arrived in Guatemala and had to be smuggled into Mexico before making the attempt to enter the United States. Most then crossed the border on foot, but some were brought into the United States hidden in trucks, buses, or false-bottomed compartments in cars and vans. The head or "big" snakehead typically had "little snakeheads" (often family members) supervise the immigrants on each leg of their journey. One might meet the immigrants in Hong Kong, others would pick them up at the airports in Bangkok and Guatemala City, and yet another would meet them at JFK or LAX or, if they crossed the border by land, at a prearranged location just inside the country. However they made it into the United States, the immigrants would next be brought to what they and their smugglers referred to as a "safe house" in New York.[36]

"Safe house" was really a misnomer. The purpose of the "safe house" was not to keep the immigrants safe from the immigration enforcement authorities, but to keep the newcomers from escaping into America without paying the balance they owed to the snakehead. In the early 1980s, the typical price an immigrant had to pay to be smuggled to New York was $18,000, but it reached $25,000 in 1989, $30,000 in 1993, and $40,000 by 1998. The immigrant usually provided about a quarter of this fee up front and had to supply the balance on arrival in New York. The immigrants did not carry such a sum on their perilous journey and instead relied on family members (typically in China) to pay the snakehead the remainder. The debt collectors who ran the safe houses, invariably located in windowless basements, made life for the newcomers as unpleasant as possible so that their family members in China would pay the balance due to the snakehead quickly and fully.

"The place I was kept was hell," recalled a forty-year-old man from Fuzhou of his safe house experience. "We were starving all the time. The air was awful." Immigrants whose families paid quickly were allowed to leave before conditions became unbearable. But for the significant minority of immigrants whose families were slow to pay, the safe houses were truly hellish, as was the case for the man from Fuzhou. "They yelled at or beat us whenever they wished," he said, especially when the immigrants were on the phone with their relatives beseeching them to pay the snakehead. "Often, people were beaten until they were bloody." The debt collectors often sexually abused female immigrants whose families did not pay promptly, even raping them if they did not receive payment by the end of the grace period. If after several weeks a female immigrant's family had not paid her debt, she might be "sold" to a brothel and forced to repay her debt that way.[37]

Given the outrageous interest rates they might charge an immigrant's family, Chinese loan sharks were not the source of the cash most illegal immigrants used to pay for their passage to the United States. The majority of smuggled Chinese actually came from middle-class backgrounds, or at least had family members who did, and the money to finance the journey was usually borrowed from those family members. "You borrow $1,500 from one person, another $3,000 from another person," one immigrant explained. An immigrant sometimes relied on a wide network of extended family members to meet the snakehead's price. Indeed, one of the reasons so many Chinese immigrants came from Fujian was not because that Chinese province was so poor but because it was so prosperous: its residents could afford the huge snakehead fees. The Fujian economy was so dynamic that the province attracted migrants from other parts of China, such as Sichuan, who knew they could find jobs there that paid better than in their native regions. "The Sichuanese coming here is the same as us Fujianese going to America," noted one Fuzhou resident. "The Sichuanese are doing the bad jobs that nobody else wants to do here, just like we do in your country."[38]

Having assumed such crushing debt and knowing how shameful it would be if they did not quickly repay the family members who had risked their savings to finance their move to New York, the smuggled immigrants worked extraordinarily hard and practiced incredible frugality so every possible penny could be sent back to China to pay down their debts. The illegal immigrants worked overwhelmingly in one of two kinds of places — either Chinese restaurants or garment factories. A survey in the 1990s found that 80 percent of smuggled Chinese men and 90 percent of women worked in one of these two fields. This was the case even though in China the majority of these immigrants had been employed in the professions, owned a business, or held a clerical position.[39]

Chinese restaurant workers typically labored twelve hours a day, six days a week, with Mondays the usual day off. But often the newest immigrants took part-time jobs on their day off — slipping take-out menus under doors in apartment buildings or manning the kitchen's skeleton crew on Mondays — in order to bring in more cash and pay their debts off faster. Very few of the immigrants had food industry experience. They started off as kitchen helpers, doing anything the cooks needed done — prepping the food, taking out garbage, or cleaning the cookware and dishes. After months or years in that position, an immigrant could become a line cook, an important promotion because it paid nearly 40 percent more, on average, than the entry-level position ($1,600 per month versus $1,150 for a kitchen helper in 1993). If an immigrant learned a little English, he might become a deliveryman, a job that typically paid a little more than a kitchen helper but not as much as a cook, though it did offer a break from the monotony of the kitchen. "The boss and the pots and pans and the other workers," said a former farmer from Fujian province who had become a Chinese restaurant cook, when asked about his life in America. "That's it." Other illegal immigrants echoed the same sentiment: "Work. That's all we do."

Waiters had the highest-paying jobs in Chinese restaurants, but that position required more English than most smuggled immigrants were able to master. Younger immigrants from urban parts of China seemed most adept at picking up enough English to win these coveted jobs. In New York's Chinatowns, the newcomers could enroll in "Practical English for Chinese Restaurants," a crash course designed to give them the language skills they needed to work at the front of a restaurant. In 2001 a reporter for the *Times* came across a twenty-four-year-old woman from Fujian who was taking one of these classes. The journalist found her practicing her pronunciation of phrases like "smoking area," "your food will be with you soon," and "it's nice to see you again." Once

Many Chinese immigrant men found their first jobs in New York in the kitchens of Chinese restaurants, even though almost none of them had worked in this field in China.

they gained some experience, many waiters and cooks moved out of the city to staff Chinese restaurants in strip malls all across America, where they hoped to find better pay, cheaper living expenses, and less demanding bosses. Once they paid off their smuggling debts, many of these same cooks and waiters bought an existing restaurant or started one of their own. When they did, they sought their workers from among New York's newest Chinese immigrants.[40]

The arrival of so many Chinese women in New York revitalized the city's garment manufacturing sector, which had been flagging since the 1960s as the immigrant workforce shrank. By 1981, there were about five hundred garment factories operating in Manhattan's Chinatown, employing nearly twenty thousand workers. These jobs had not changed much over the course of the century. The work was still subdivided among many workers, each given a specific task, with pay depending on the complexity of the job. Unlike in the sweatshops of the past, women were doing almost all the work in the garment industry by the 1980s. Other than pressing, still considered a man's job, all the other tasks were performed by women. Older women did most of the "finishing" that had once been assigned to children.

Not only were the tasks largely unchanged, but conditions in garment facto-

When Chinese immigrant women arrived in New York in the 1980s and 1990s, their first job was often in a garment factory, either in lower Manhattan or in a Chinese enclave in Brooklyn or Queens.

ries were essentially the same as well, modern labor laws notwithstanding. Inspectors commonly found fire exits padlocked, just like at the Triangle Waist company. Immigrant women still worked terribly long hours, in crowded, dusty, often stifling conditions. "In the summertime, the temperature inside is so hot. There is no ventilation at all," said one Chinese garment worker. And the pay was still incredibly low. It was not legal to pay workers by the piece unless they were guaranteed minimum wage. Furthermore, those who worked more than a certain number of hours per day or per week had to be paid a higher "overtime" wage, but both these rules were largely ignored, especially when the employer assumed that his workers were illegal immigrants. "I can't do nothing," a Latino sweatshop worker complained in 1995, echoing a sentiment expressed by many Chinese garment workers as well. "If I claim the overtime, they will fire me." As a result, a Chinese American reporter who went undercover to work in a Sunset Park garment factory in 1995 was paid just $54 for eighty-four hours of work, when the legal minimum (at the minimum wage of $4.25 for the first forty hours and time and a half for every hour thereafter) was $450. In order to continue satisfying their employers' seemingly insatiable demands for productivity, Chinese immigrant women who gave birth to children after arriving in New York often sent the babies to China to be raised by their grandparents so the immigrants could keep their jobs and finish paying off their debts. The children would be brought back to New York when they were old enough to attend public school full-time.[41]

Despite periodic press coverage throughout the 1980s and 1990 of conditions "that rival the most sordid garment factories described and photographed by [Jacob] Riis," garment factory conditions over the course of these decades actually grew worse rather than better. With so many new immigrants pouring into the city, including thousands of undocumented aliens, employers could always find another desperate newcomer willing to work for starvation wages. "In the past, the conditions were not nearly as bad as they are now," said Ying Ye Deng Chan, a fifty-six-year-old Chinese naturalized immigrant, in 1995. During her twelve years doing garment work in New York, she said, "things have gotten much, much worse."[42]

Working conditions also deteriorated in these years because the push for clothing "made in the USA" led the city's garment industry to expand rapidly while city and state budget crises resulted in slashed inspection staffs. In 1995 there were two thousand garment factories openly operating in the city with at least fifty thousand employees, and another two thousand or so illicit sweatshops that may have employed another thirty thousand to forty thousand more. That was at least double the number of shops and workers in the city a decade earlier. By the 1990s, the industry had expanded beyond Chinatown and the Garment District surrounding Manhattan's Seventh Avenue. In the middle of the decade, hundreds of sweatshops could be found in Sunset Park and Williamsburg in Brooklyn, in Corona and Long Island City in Queens, and in the south Bronx.[43]

Illegal home work revived in this period as well. When clothing contractors got big short-term orders that could not be completed in their existing workspace, they had workers do the sewing in their apartments so the order could be completed on time. Pieceworkers could likewise earn extra money and pay off their smuggling debts faster by taking extra sewing home, even though to do so was against the law. "Especially in the Bronx, you'll see a lot of home work," a state labor inspector told a reporter in 1990. "Whole Vietnamese and Cambodian families stay home and make bows and hair bands — the ones sold at newsstands . . . It's cash all the way down the line: ten cents apiece, dollar a dozen, for cutting the ribbon, tying it up, gluing the clip into it . . . If you have four or five family members making hair bands ten to twelve hours a day, seven days a week, you scrape by."[44]

Immigrants who worked incredibly hard to pay off their debts as quickly as possible also went to extraordinary lengths to cut their housing costs to the

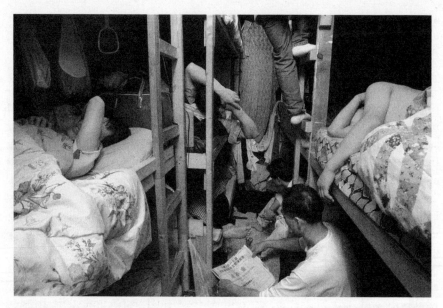

Owing tens of thousands of dollars to the "snakeheads" who smuggled them into the United States, Chinese immigrants who entered the United States illegally often cut their housing costs to the bone by living in bunkhouses like this one, in which a dozen or more men might sleep in a single twelve-by-twelve-foot room.

bare minimum. Newly arrived Chinese immigrant men typically lived in tiny bunk rooms that looked like something right out of Riis's *How the Other Half Lives*. By lining the walls of a one-room, twelve-by-twelve-foot "studio" apartment with triple-tiered bunk beds, a Chinese landlord could charge $650 per month in rent (to be split by the occupants of the twelve beds) rather than the $500 per month he might get to rent the room empty to a single tenant. The immigrants found this system appealing because they could each pay just $54 a month rent, allowing them to send almost every bit of their pay back to China. The most enterprising immigrants might cut their costs even further by subletting their bunks to other immigrants during the hours of the day when they were at work. African, Mexican, and other New York immigrants also employed this system of sharing bunks to maximize their ability to save and thereby send more money back to their homeland.[45]

Despite such living and working conditions, the Chinese did not usually regret their decision to come to America. They felt a deep sense of familial obligation and believed they could better fulfill it in the United States than in China. "I like what I am doing now," said a nineteen-year-old Fujianese garment worker in the mid-1990s. "All I hope for is to repay the smuggling debts as soon as possible and then send money home to help my family enjoy a comfortable life. It's no big deal that I myself have to endure some hardship here. If a person's bitterness can bring happiness to so many people, it's worth it."

The Chinese also relished the elevated status that accrued to themselves and their families from their immigration to New York. Because of the remittances he had sent, explained a thirty-six-year-old smuggled Fujianese immigrant, "my family became rich. My parents are happy because they are respected by others" now. A twenty-one-year-old from the same Fujianese city cited his own success at *fanshen* — changing his social status — as a reason he did not regret his decision to emigrate. After all, he pointed out, "there are so many opportunities to make money here."[46]

No Chinese immigrant was more attuned to the opportunities to make money in New York than Sister Ping. Like all of New York's Chinese immigrants, she chafed at the exorbitant fees that the Bank of China charged to remit money to loved ones back home. The bank profited further when it exchanged the immigrants' hard-earned dollars for Chinese yuan, something that annoyed the immigrants even more because those yuan became less valuable by the day compared to the dollars the immigrants had brought to the bank. Sister Ping decided to offer her own money transfer service, which would charge less than the Bank of China *and* deliver dollars rather than yuan to the immigrants' relatives. She was soon moving millions of dollars in remittances from New York to Fujian and payments to snakeheads from Fujian to New York.[47]

Sister Ping also became an immigrant smuggler. As described in Patrick Radden Keefe's *The Snakehead*, by 1984 she was charging $18,000 to smuggle Fujianese who could not get visas into the United States. Her business was a family affair. Her sister Susan sneaked the immigrants into Hong Kong, cleaned them up and provided clothes and luggage so they could pass as tourists, and sent them on to Guatemala City, where her brother awaited them. He would move them to Mexico, where Sister Ping often personally oversaw the final leg of the journey, loading the immigrants into a secret compartment in a van and then meeting them on the other side of the border. Then she might fly with them from Los Angeles to New York. Later on, Sister Ping let underlings take these risks while she stayed in New York, tallying up her profits. For several million dollars, she bought the entire building at 47 East Broadway, right across the street from the Bank of China's headquarters, where she moved her store and opened a restaurant as well. The line often snaking out the door of the shop consisted of customers waiting their turn to send money to China.

It did not take long for federal authorities to catch wind of Sister Ping's immigrant smuggling operation, but when agents of the Immigration and Naturalization Service discovered its complexity and scope — with operations in

Guatemala, Mexico, Thailand, Hong Kong, and China — they realized that they lacked the budget to investigate and prosecute her. They approached the FBI in 1985, but it had no interest in devoting manpower and money to the international investigation of a crime whose maximum penalty was six months in prison. The U.S. attorney's office also declined to take the case. The INS agent in charge of the investigation decided to pay a visit to Sister Ping to at least let her know they were on to her, but she was clearly well versed in the likelihood of prosecution. "You don't have the time to get me," she coolly told the agent. "Or the resources."[48]

In the end, the authorities did get Sister Ping, but only because one of her smuggling operations failed so spectacularly and publicly that authorities were forced to act. Her downfall began in, of all places, Tiananmen Square. In the wake of the massacre of antigovernment protesters that took place there in 1989, President George H. W. Bush issued an executive order in April 1990 declaring that no Chinese citizen who had arrived in the United States, even illegally, before the Tiananmen Square massacre could be deported back to China. The order also stated that "enhanced consideration" should be given to any Chinese seeking asylum who expressed a fear of persecution if they were returned to China because of "that country's policy of forced abortion or coerced sterilization." As a result of Bush's order, the success rate for the Chinese in asylum cases quickly shot up from about 30 percent to 85 percent. And even if such an application failed, one could remain in the United States as long as one could provide evidence (not hard to obtain in Chinatown) that one had entered the United States before the Tiananmen Massacre.

Bush's executive order caused a sensation in Fujian province. "Everybody went crazy," recalled a Chinese journalist covering Fuzhou. "The area was in a frenzy. Farmers put down their tools, students discarded their books, workers quit their jobs, and everybody was talking about nothing but going to America." Sister Ping and other snakeheads were inundated with requests from Fujianese seeking to be smuggled to New York.[49]

There was only one problem. American authorities had begun cracking down on illegal Chinese immigration routed through the Bangkok airport, sending agents there to check documents before would-be immigrants could reach the United States. Sister Ping and other snakeheads now had hundreds of customers stranded in Thailand who needed to be moved. Seeking a new way to get their customers to America, and requiring the ability to send hundreds at a time rather than a dozen, the snakeheads decided to follow the lead of Taiwanese immigrant traffickers and smuggle their customers into the United States by ship. Sister Ping took on a variety of partners in the enterprise, including one who had successfully landed illegal immigrants in Boston from an oceangoing vessel, using fishing boats to ferry the passengers ashore. It would have made the most sense to transport these immigrants to the West Coast of the United States, "only" an eight-thousand-mile journey from Thailand. But since some ships sent by their competitors had recently been intercepted by authorities in the Pacific, Ping's associates decided that their vessel would take the seventeen-thousand-mile route westward across the Indian Ocean, south around the tip of Africa, and then northward through the South and North Atlantic directly to New York.

The ship leased by the smugglers, the *Najd II,* left southern Thailand in July 1992 with approximately three hundred emigrants. The ship had tiny staterooms with two beds per room, better than the steerage of old. But there was no running water; the passengers were given a couple of small bottles of water per day to drink and one with which to wash themselves. It soon became clear to the immigrants that the *Najd II* was a broken-down rust bucket on its last legs. Even if it had moved at the snail-like pace of ten nautical miles per hour, it would have been able to make it to New York in two months, but in that amount of time it got only as far as Mauritius, a thousand miles off the east coast of Africa and only a quarter of the way to the United States. The authorities in Mauritius, hearing rumors of the ship's illicit enterprise, refused to let it land, so it limped northward, away from its proper course, toward Kenya. By this point, passengers were getting half rations of water. The authorities in Mombasa banned the ship from landing too, but it anchored in a mangrove swamp anyway. It was in no condition to complete its journey.[50]

By this point the ship's supplies were running out, so the three hundred emigrants lowered whatever cash they had with them down to boats piloted by Kenyans who sold them food. When their cash ran out, the passengers began sneaking into Mombasa, where they sought help at a Chinese restaurant. The owner let the passengers call their relatives, who wired them money directly to the restaurant. Sister Ping dispatched a courier with $1,000 for each of her twenty customers aboard the ship to help sustain them while she and her partners devised a new means of conveying them to New York. The more prosperous passengers took rooms at a hotel while they waited for their new ship to arrive. When the hotel's Indian restaurant went out of business, some of the *Najd II*'s enterprising passengers took over the space and opened a Chinese restaurant, which quickly became a success.

Sister Ping's partners decided that rather than lease another ship, they would buy one. After all, they expected to be making quite a few smuggling trips over the coming years. By the time they found one they could afford (a cargo ship they aptly renamed the *Golden Venture*), hired a crew, sailed it from Thailand to Mombasa with nearly one hundred additional immigrants, and readied it for the long voyage to New York, it was April. But only two hundred of the original three hundred passengers from the *Nadj II* boarded the *Golden Venture* for the final leg of their journey. Some had gone back to China. Others had found alternate transportation to the United States. A few even stayed in Mombasa to run the Chinese restaurant they had opened. But when Sister Ping's twenty passengers were ferried to the ship and saw they would have to sleep on plywood boards on the floor of a dank and bare cargo hold rather than in beds, most of them refused to go aboard. The *Golden Venture* left with only two of them, infuriating Sister Ping.[51]

By this point, the story of the three hundred illegal would-be immigrants stranded in Mombasa had made international news. The *South China Post* even reported the name of the emigrants' new ship and the smugglers' plan to take it to New York. But such was the state of immigration enforcement in those days that the United States made no effort to intercept the vessel. As the *Golden Venture* neared New York at the beginning of June, a full year after the original passengers had left Thailand, the snakeheads on board received instructions to proceed to the Massachusetts coast instead. When they got there, however, none of the promised fishing boats appeared to ferry the passengers to shore. A shootout between rival Chinatown gangs that took place across the Hudson from New York City in Teaneck, New Jersey, had left dead or under arrest most of the leaders of the gang Sister Ping had hired to offload the *Golden Venture*'s passengers. This gang had so dominated the East Coast offloading of Chinese illegal immigrants that no trustworthy substitutes could be found to do the job. With the *Golden Venture* passengers on starvation rations and rail thin by this point, the snakeheads on board gave the crewman steering the vessel orders to head to New York. (The captain had been locked in his cabin when he said he wanted to proceed to the Azores to get more supplies.) Eleven months and more than seventeen thousand miles after leaving Thailand, the snakeheads had decided that the ordeal had to end, one way or another. The passengers, who by this point had been subsisting for months on peanuts and rice boiled in rusty water, felt the same way.[52]

One of the more audacious snakeheads proposed sailing right up the East River and offloading the passengers at one of the abandoned piers on the outskirts of Chinatown. But eventually they decided to run the ship aground on Rockaway Beach, just a half a mile from where Anthony Camardo had been caught trying to land his boatload of smuggled Sicilians seventy years earlier. At about 1:30 a.m. on Sunday morning June 6, the helmsman aimed the ship straight toward the beachfront promenade at Jacob Riis Park and set the motor to full throttle. The snakeheads told the immigrants to brace themselves.

About two hundred yards from shore, there was a loud thud as the ship sud-

The *Golden Venture* with the one hundred passengers who refused to jump into the water still on board. That a ship of this size brought three times this number of immigrants to New York in a barren cargo hold is hard to fathom.

denly ran aground on a sandbar. The passengers were ordered to leap over-board and swim to shore. "We were told as long as we set foot on American soil, we would be able to stay in this country," one of the passengers later re-counted. In the pandemonium that followed, about two hundred passengers jumped into the water. A storm had just passed through, and the sea was rough and choppy with high swells. The shock of the fifty-degree water stunned many of the immigrants. Others were overwhelmed by the waves or pulled away from the beach by the riptide. Of the ten who drowned or died of heart attacks in the water, one was an immigrant for whom Sister Ping was responsible. The rest of the passengers who jumped into the ocean eventually dragged themselves onto the beach or were rescued by policemen who happened upon the scene and the Coast Guardsmen they called for help. As the immigrants came ashore, they vomited seawater and shivered uncontrollably; many were slightly purple from being in the cold water for so long. Others rolled in the sand in a kind of mad delirium. After daybreak, the Coast Guard boarded the ship, stepping carefully to avoid the small piles of feces all over the deck, and rescued the one hundred or so passengers who remained on board.[53]

The *Golden Venture* passengers, who had waited so long to experience the wonders of America, must have been sorely disappointed at their reception. President Bill Clinton vowed to use the incident to show the nations of the world that America would not "lose control of our borders." Even before Clin-

With smuggled immigrants literally washing up on the city's shoreline in 1993, New Yorkers could no longer ignore the issue of illegal immigration or its consequences.

ton made this statement, the head of the INS office in New York decided to make an example of them in the hopes that doing so would deter further illegal immigration. Rather than release the immigrants while their asylum applications were pending, the standard procedure, he threw them all in jail. They were initially detained in New Jersey, but most were eventually moved to York, Pennsylvania. More than fifty of them spent three and a half years behind bars. The case of the *Golden Venture,* according to the *Times,* had "set off a national argument about illegal immigration."[54]

When we discuss immigration, we inevitably make analogies to water. We talk about the "flow" of immigration, the "flood" of undocumented aliens, and so forth. The analogy is apt, for just as it is virtually impossible to redirect the flow of a river — water goes where it wants to go — it is likewise almost impossible to stem the flow of people into a nation whose borders are so vast and whose citizens refuse to be subjected to constant identity checks. The stories of the *Golden Venture*'s passengers after they were washed ashore in Queens bear this out. Of the 260 or so who made it to the beach alive in 1993, about 220 were still living in the United States a dozen years later. Fifty disappeared into American society, either slipping away from the authorities at Riis Park or failing to appear in court after judges granted them bail. Another fifty won their asylum cases. After embarrassing news stories about the fifty-five who still languished in the York detention center more than three years after their arrival, President Clinton summarily released them as well — an act that did not make them legal but did allow them to stay in the United States. One hundred and ten of their compatriots at York had been deported, but by

2006, at least sixty of them had sneaked back in, including one who had been forced to undergo a sterilization operation upon his return to China because he had fathered three children before he boarded the *Golden Venture*. Some still worked in Chinese restaurant kitchens, while others by that point owned their own businesses.[55]

After the *Golden Venture* ran aground, Sister Ping initially remained in New York, operating her restaurant and other enterprises, legal and illegal, from 47 East Broadway. She was lucky that she had let her business partners buy and operate the *Golden Venture*. But as it became clear that many of those already arrested associates were spilling their guts to the authorities in the hopes of receiving reduced sentences, she decided in September 1994 to flee to Hong Kong. Knowing so many passport forgers, Sister Ping continued to move easily around the world, overseeing her snakehead operations. Meanwhile, twenty-two others had either pleaded guilty or been convicted of crimes connected to the *Golden Venture*'s voyage. The last, labeled the "mastermind" of the ship's journey by the press, was arrested in Thailand while polishing his Mercedes-Benz.

The FBI eventually managed to track down Sister Ping by following her children, and in April 2000, American agents helped the Hong Kong police arrest her to face a U.S. indictment for alien smuggling, hostage taking (holding immigrants in safe houses until they paid their fees), trafficking in ransom proceeds, and two counts of money laundering. She managed to drag out the fight over her extradition to the United States for three years, and by the time the case went to trial in 2005, New York's tabloid press had concluded that *she* was the true mastermind behind the *Golden Venture,* or as a *Daily News* headline put it, "EVIL INCARNATE." The jury convicted her on three of the five counts, and the judge, apparently agreeing with the *Daily News'* assessment, sentenced her to the maximum penalty allowed, thirty-five years. Yet when she died of pancreatic cancer in a Texas prison in April 2014, the reaction in New York suggested that the Chinese, even many of her own brutalized customers, did not view her as evil at all. One called her "a modern day Robin Hood." To Chinese immigrants, Sister Ping had offered them what Americans selfishly withheld — the opportunity to escape China, move to New York, and pursue the American dream.[56]

The third-largest immigrant group in New York in the decades after the implementation of the Hart-Celler Act was from Jamaica. Yet Jamaicans are most appropriately considered not on their own but as part of the non-Hispanic Caribbean immigrant population commonly known as "West Indians." If grouped together, the newcomers from Jamaica, Haiti, Trinidad and Tobago, Guyana, and Barbados (along with the small immigrant contingents from the other Caribbean islands) have since 1980 constituted the largest immigrant group in New York. Even if one leaves aside French-speaking Haiti and considers only the anglophone Caribbean, those small countries rank as the number-one source of immigrants in New York.[57]

The reasons why so many West Indians immigrated to New York will sound familiar by this point. The United States occupied Haiti from 1915 to 1934, creating economic and transportation linkages between the two countries that encouraged immigration. The remaining West Indian nations were British colonies until about the time of the Hart-Celler Act, and the adjustment to postcolonial status left them with unemployment rates of 15 percent in the best of times and 25 percent during economic downturns. For those under age twenty-four, unemployment rarely dipped below 40 percent and reached as high as 50 percent in 1980. In that year, the per capita gross domestic product of Jamaica was barely one-tenth that of the United States. Things were even worse in Haiti, the poorest nation in the Americas. "You cannot make a living in Haiti" and "You cannot move up in Haiti" were among the islanders' most commonly repeated laments.[58]

The people of the West Indies had traditions of out-migration that predated the Hart-Celler Act. Many of them had moved to Harlem during the 1910s and 1920s. When the immigration restrictions of 1924 put a stop to that, the West Indians migrated to Great Britain instead. But in 1961, the British in their own outburst of nativism decided to ban migration from the United Kingdom's Caribbean possessions to the British Isles, beginning July 1, 1962. After a few years of pent-up emigration demand, the Hart-Celler Act made it possible for the West Indies' would-be migrants to come to the United States once again. From 1965 to 1980, 76,000 Jamaicans, 44,000 Haitians, 34,000 Trinidadians, 29,000 Guyanese, and 15,000 Barbadians settled in New York City. Many of those who remained hoped to join their friends or family members in New York soon. A poll conducted in Jamaica in the late seventies found that 60 percent of all residents would move to the United States if they could. By the end of the millennium, about a third of New York's African American populace was foreign-born, and four non-Hispanic Caribbean nations (Jamaica, Guyana, Haiti, and Trinidad and Tobago) held spots on the top ten list of the largest immigrant groups in New York.[59]

Before 1970, New York's West Indian immigrants tended to live, as they had for decades, in Harlem and the Bedford-Stuyvesant neighborhood in central Brooklyn among native-born African Americans. But as the flow grew, they started creating new, more distinctly West Indian enclaves in the Crown

THE PRINCIPAL SOURCES OF NEW YORK'S CARIBBEAN IMMIGRANTS

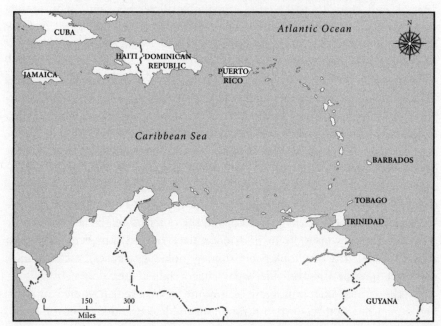

Heights, Flatbush, and East Flatbush sections of Brooklyn. By the mid-1980s, West Indian immigrants had become so numerous that they were able to create additional enclaves at the north-central edge of the Bronx near the Westchester County line and in the distinctly middle-class southeast Queens neighborhoods of Cambria Heights, Laurelton, Queens Village, and Springfield Gardens. Yet East Flatbush, with a population that was 46 percent foreign-born in 1990, remained the city's most West Indian neighborhood.[60]

One reason why West Indians preferred these new neighborhoods to their old ones was that they could make them feel distinctly Caribbean. "It's like our own little village here," one Guyanese immigrant said of his Flatbush home. "It's an old Caribbean tradition of families living close together." An East Flatbush bank manager from Trinidad felt the same way. "I feel like I'm at home," she told a *Times* reporter in 1987 in explaining why she would never move out of Brooklyn. "You get the music. You get the food. You get everything."[61]

West Indians also chose these sections of Brooklyn because they offered them the best chance to own their own home, virtually an obsession with anglophone Caribbean immigrants. "Their first dollar of savings goes into buying homes," observed Major Owens, the area's congressman, in 1988. A prominent

West Indian attorney in Brooklyn insisted that his countrymen settled in these neighborhoods specifically because "owning a house is very important to Caribbeans, and Brooklyn had a large supply of available housing." Because they worked so hard to become homeowners, Owens predicted that soon "the new black middle class from Crown Heights to Flatbush would be predominantly of West Indian descent."[62]

West Indian immigrants worked in an unusually wide variety of occupations to save the money necessary to purchase homes of their own. The biggest employment category in 1979 for men was "machine operator" (which included factory work, welding, and auto mechanics), but "biggest" meant only 5 percent, reflecting the huge variety of work West Indians did. They were disproportionately represented in several other jobs, including security guard, janitor, nurse's aide, and driver. West Indians became especially well known for this last occupation. Many of them drove unlicensed "gypsy cabs" and jitney vans. The latter picked up customers at bus stops in the outer boroughs in between the appearance of city buses. In the mid-1990s, they charged $1.00 versus the $1.50 it cost to ride a city bus, took paper money (unlike city buses), made change, and sometimes dropped off elderly passengers right at their doorsteps.[63]

Unlike in most other immigrant communities, West Indian women outnumbered men nearly three to two throughout the late twentieth century, something that had been the case ever since 1900. In the first decades of the century, it was the demand for English-speaking West Indian domestic servants that had drawn so many Caribbean women to New York. West Indian women continued to fill large numbers of these jobs after 1965, though increasingly they got work as nannies rather than cleaning women. (In 1980, one in eleven West Indian women in New York worked as a live-in nanny.) But far more West Indian women found jobs in nursing. In 1979, 21,000 out of 64,000 West Indian women working in New York were employed as nurses or nurses' aides. Another 11,000 worked as secretaries and office clerks, and 7,000 had household jobs as cleaners or nannies. Hart-Celler was in part responsible for the large number of West Indian nurses, as the law gave those who had experience in occupational fields with large numbers of vacancies, such as nursing, priority in receiving immigration visas. But many other West Indians got their nursing training only after they arrived in the United States. West Indians worked disproportionately in hospitals and nursing homes, even in non-nursing positions, indicative of the key role networking played in helping them find jobs.[64]

Beulah Reid from Trinidad exemplified all of these trends, as well as the tremendous West Indian work ethic. In her twenties, Reid worked in San Juan, Trinidad, at the Glamour Girl lingerie factory, dreaming amid the piles of nighties and negligees of owning her own home. A former co-worker at Glamour Girl talked Reid into joining her in New York. Reid arrived there at age thirty in 1971, leaving behind her husband and two children. When she reached New York, Reid initially stayed with a great-uncle in Brooklyn, but soon moved to a furnished room with a shared bathroom and kitchen that cost her $18 a week. Through another immigrant friend, Reid found a job as a live-in housekeeper in Saddle River, New Jersey. She took the position, even though it paid only $60 a week, because her employers agreed to sponsor her for permanent residence under a provision that allowed those who worked in hard-to-fill occupations the right to receive permanent residence status in two years. On weekends, Reid returned to Brooklyn and stayed in her furnished room. Once she had fulfilled her two-year commitment, she moved back to Brooklyn and waited for her permanent residency permit (or "green card") to come through.

At that point, Reid began seeking work at an employment agency for domestics in Harlem, arriving there from Brooklyn each morning at 8:00 a.m. hoping to land a job for the day. When she did, she was paid $12 for a half day of work and $25 for a full day. "I wouldn't say it was hard," Reid told a reporter years later. "Money was small, but the rent was cheap. And I knew it was a sacrifice I was making for one day to have my family with me and life would be better. So I went along with it." With the help of another Trinidadian immigrant friend, Reid landed a steadier job as a clerk for Bankers Trust once her green card came through. Her husband and teenage son, able to gain legal admission to the United States as Reid's immediate relatives, soon joined her, while her daughter stayed in Trinidad with Reid's mother. They too joined Reid a few years later, and she soon had a third child.

Though many New Yorkers would have considered the Bankers Trust job a reason to relax, especially after she had received a few pay raises, Reid did not view things that way. Like so many West Indian immigrants, she would not rest until she owned her own home. So Reid went to night school to earn a general equivalency high school diploma so she could qualify for better-paying positions at the bank, moving from $98 a week when she started to $600 a week eventually. Still not satisfied, she took nursing classes so she could become a certified nurse's aide and worked at that job on Saturdays and Sundays when the bank was closed. In the meantime, she separated from her husband.

In 1987 Reid finally achieved her dream and bought a house on a leafy block in East Flatbush. It was not detached, as she had hoped, but it was hers. Eighty percent of the $35,000 down payment came from her own savings, and the remaining $7,000 was provided by Reid's son, who gave her money he had been saving to buy his first car. Still she did not slow down. She continued to work both jobs, and when she lost the bank position in 1991, she became a licensed day care provider on weekdays while working as a home health aide on weekends. "I can't tell you when I last didn't work seven days a week," the sixty-two-year-old grandmother of four told the *Times* in 2003, thirty-two years after her arrival in New York. While Beulah Reid's work ethic was extraordinary, among West Indian immigrants it was not at all that unusual. "God Bless America," declared Cambria Heights restaurant owner Shubert Denis shortly after the turn of the twenty-first century in a typical assessment. "This is the only country — I believe — that gives immigrants a chance."[65]

While West Indian New Yorkers could overcome economic adversity through hard work and perseverance, they were often surprised at the way the color of their skin shaped their lives in New York. "When you get to America, you have to start thinking about race," complained a Jamaican computer programmer in the early 1990s. "In Manhattan you walk into a store; you'll find that people will be following you around. Things like that you have never been accustomed to." He hated that when he entered a subway car, the white women would clutch their handbags in fear. "That has been, to me, my worst problem to overcome since I have been here." Other West Indian immigrants (and many dark-skinned Dominicans, too) resented how palpable it was that "some neighborhoods are not yet ready for black people. And," said one, "I don't want to be a hero."[66]

In fact, many of the highest-profile cases of racial violence in New York in the late twentieth century involved not native-born African Americans but West Indian immigrants. Late on a Friday night in December 1986, for example, a twenty-three-year-old Trinidadian immigrant named Michael Griffith drove with some friends from his Bedford-Stuyvesant home to south Queens to pick up pay he was owed from his job as a construction worker. When Griffith's friend's car broke down, Griffith and two others walked south on Cross Bay Boulevard to seek assistance. They crossed under the Belt Parkway and went into the New Park Pizzeria, where they asked to use the phone. They were told no but decided nonetheless to order a pizza.

What Griffith and his friends apparently did not realize was that when they passed under the Belt Parkway, then had crossed one of the city's many invisible ethnic and racial borderlines and entered Howard Beach, a virtually all-white neighborhood of large detached houses and front lawns that one could have mistaken for suburbia were it not next to JFK Airport. When Griffith and his friends left the pizzeria, around 12:45 a.m., they were accosted by a mob of white teenagers who had been drinking behind the restaurant. "Niggers, you don't belong here," shouted the baseball-bat-wielding teens as they attacked the three black men. Griffith and his friends ran, but the white thugs chased after them. They caught Griffith a second time when he came to a fence separating the neighborhood from the parkway. To escape his attackers, Griffith squeezed through a hole and darted onto the highway, where he was struck and killed by a car. The incident, though not the first of its kind, sparked heated debate about the extent of racism in the city and what New Yorkers — both black and white — could or should do about it. African American political activism resulting from the Howard Beach attack helped bring about the election of the city's first black mayor, David Dinkins, a few years later.[67]

Despite what had happened in Howard Beach, Dinkins liked to refer to New York as a "gorgeous mosaic" composed of peoples from all over the globe. That view was put to the test five years after Howard Beach when, on Monday August 19, 1991, rioting broke out in Crown Heights after a car in the entourage of the leader of the Lubavitch Hasidic Jewish sect, whose members had started settling in Crown Heights in large numbers, jumped the sidewalk and killed Gavin Cato, the seven-year-old son of Guyanese immigrants. That night, after rumors of lenient treatment for the Jewish driver spread through the neighborhood, black rioters shouting "Let's get the Jew" attacked Yankel Rosenbaum, a twenty-nine-year-old Australian university lecturer living in Crown Heights for the summer while conducting archival research in Manhattan. One member of the mob, sixteen-year-old Lemrick Nelson, the New York–born son of Trinidadian immigrants, stabbed Rosenbaum. Although hospital staff initially announced that Rosenbaum would recover, he died the next morning.

The Crown Heights rioting went on for three days, with black rioters breaking the windows of the neighborhood's Jewish residents and attacking the press and police. "It's pandemonium," exclaimed one frightened Jewish resident by phone to a reporter as rocks were hitting her windows. Jews claimed that the rioting was nothing less than a pogrom. African Americans insisted that Jewish neighborhood patrols had been mistreating the neighborhood's black residents for years, that Jewish landlords gouged West Indian residents, and that Jews received preferential treatment from the police. "MOSAIC CRUMBLES," blared the headline of one New York tabloid in a none-too-subtle dig at the mayor. The belief of white New Yorkers that Dinkins had not done enough to quickly quell the violence helped lead to his defeat in the mayoral election two years later by Republican Rudolph Giuliani, who ran a law-and-order campaign that won the support of hundreds of thousands of white Democrats.[68]

Police treatment of black men in New York gained international attention on a Saturday night in the summer of 1997. On August 9, employees at Club Rendez-Vous in East Flatbush called the police to break up a fight among the patrons. When the officers tried to intervene, someone "sucker punched" Officer Justin Volpe in the face. Believing incorrectly (as Volpe himself later admitted) that his assailant had been thirty-year-old Abner Louima, a Haitian immigrant, the police arrested Louima and beat him savagely on the way to the Seventieth Precinct station house. There, with the assistance of at least one other officer, the enraged Volpe dragged Louima to a bathroom, where he brutally sodomized him with the handle of a toilet plunger and then bragged about it to the rest of the precinct.

Still bleeding profusely the next morning, Louima was taken by ambulance to Coney Island Hospital, where the police officers who brought him in blamed Louima's injuries on a "homosexual" encounter. Hospital staff knew better and urged Louima's family to file a complaint with the police department's internal affairs bureau. Volpe was arrested a few days later. Midway through his trial in 1999, Volpe changed his plea to guilty and was sentenced to thirty years in prison. Charles Schwarz, the officer who held Louima down while Volpe brutalized the Haitian, served five years in prison. Louima, meanwhile, required two months in the hospital and three major operations to his colon and bladder to repair the damage done by his attackers.[69]

The incidents involving Michael Griffith in Howard Beach, Gavin Cato in Crown Heights, and Abner Louima in East Flatbush might have made West Indians think twice about their decision to immigrate to New York. But while these newcomers hated the way race defined so many aspects of their lives in New York, few West Indians seemed to regret having come to the United States. These events did prompt West Indians, feeling that their voices were not being adequately heard in city government, to try to establish and wield political clout independently of native-born African Americans. The most notable manifestation of this desire for recognition was the 2000 Democratic primary for Congress in central Brooklyn, where longtime incumbent Major Owens was challenged for his seat by a West Indian immigrant, Una Clarke. Owens defeated Clarke, but her bid for the seat put African Americans on notice that the immigrants would henceforth demand to play a greater role in the city's political life. (Clarke's daughter Yvette, however, did win the congressional seat in 2006 after Owens decided to retire.)[70]

The three groups discussed in this chapter thus far — Dominicans, Chinese, and West Indians — accounted for more than 40 percent of the city's immigrants in the year 2000. But while these groups had steadily maintained their place atop New York's immigrant hierarchy, some significant changes had taken place in the city's overall immigrant population.

ORIGINS OF NEW YORK CITY'S MOST NUMEROUS IMMIGRANT GROUPS, 1980 AND 2000

1980		2000	
COUNTRY OF BIRTH	POPULATION 1980	COUNTRY OF BIRTH	POPULATION 2000
1. Italy	156,000	1. Dominican Republic	369,000
2. Dominican Republic	121,000	2. China	262,000
3. Jamaica	93,000	3. Jamaica	179,000
4. China	85,000	4. Guyana	131,000
5. Russia/USSR	78,000	5. Mexico	123,000
6. Poland	77,000	6. Ecuador	115,000
7. Germany	61,000	7. Haiti	96,000
8. Haiti	50,000	8. Trinidad & Tobago	89,000
9. Cuba	50,000	9. Colombia	84,000
10. Ireland	42,000	10. Russia/USSR	81,000
TOTAL FOREIGN-BORN	**1,670,000**	**TOTAL FOREIGN-BORN**	**2,871,000**

Source: *The Newest New Yorkers: Characteristics of the City's Foreign-Born Population* (New York, 2013), 16.

Although the prominence of the Dominicans, Chinese, and West Indians remained steady from 1980 to 2000, almost everything else in New York's immigrant population had changed. The Italians, Germans, and Irish, still a major presence in 1980, had fallen to eleventh, twenty-second, and twenty-eighth, respectively. Just as important was the quiet rise of the non-Caribbean Hispanics. Colombians, Ecuadoreans, and Mexicans all made the top ten list in the year 2000. Especially notable was the meteoric rise of the city's Mexican population from thirty-sixth place in 1980 to fifth two decades later. The increase in non-Caribbean Hispanics was especially notable because it took place almost entirely outside the city's public consciousness. The press barely took note of the huge rise in New York's Mexican, Colombian, and Ecuadorean population, while continuing to run story after story on other groups of far lesser numerical significance. Scholarly interest has mirrored that of the public. More books have been published about New York's Korean immigrants, for example, than about its Mexicans, Ecuadoreans, and Colombians combined.

One reason why certain New York immigrant groups got so much attention at the close of the century was that these populations, while less numerous than non-Caribbean Hispanics, played a much more visible role in the daily lives of well-to-do New Yorkers. Thousands of non-Caribbean Hispanic immigrants might provide the bulk of the day labor on Manhattan construction sites that native-born New Yorkers walked past every day, but they had very little direct contact with these immigrants. Yet these same native-born New Yorkers might have interacted daily with an Indian taxi driver or a Korean greengrocer.

Today we tend to think of South Korea as an economic powerhouse churning out popular cars and flat-screen televisions, as well as a wide range of industrial products. But in 1970, all of that was still in the future. South Korean politics was fraught with violence and instability. The possibility of another war with the North seemed very real. South Korea was also terribly crowded: it was the third-most densely populated country in the world (among nations with a population above 10 million). Furthermore, the presence of the U.S. military on the Korean peninsula for decades before the enactment of Hart-Celler had given Koreans a familiarity with Americans that made it much easier for them to imagine moving to the United States. For all these reasons, hundreds of thousands of South Koreans poured into the United States in the first two decades after Hart-Celler became law. New York was not the favorite destination of these immigrants; far more settled in Los Angeles. But those Koreans who did choose New York found homes overwhelmingly in Queens, especially in Flushing, but also in Jackson Heights, Corona, and Elmhurst.[71]

The Koreans who came to New York were decidedly middle class. In the 1980s, 67 percent of their heads of household had college degrees, and all but a tiny handful had held white-collar jobs before emigrating. The immigrants were Koreans who lived comfortably in their homeland but felt that the Korean economy limited their opportunities. Despite their high levels of educational achievement, few Korean immigrants in New York worked in the fields in which they had been trained in Korea. An exception was Hwang Jin Hwan, a pharmacist who arrived in New York in 1972. He earned a pharmacy degree in New York, which enabled him to get jobs working the graveyard shift in hospital pharmacies in Harlem and Queens that native-born pharmacists did not want.[72]

The most common occupational choice for Korean immigrants was to open a small neighborhood greengrocery. Korean immigrants in the late twentieth century were six times more likely to own their own businesses than other New Yorkers. As of 1999, they operated more small businesses than any other immigrant group in the New York metropolitan area. Many Koreans came to

New York with the savings necessary to open these stores. Others scrimped and saved for several years until they could purchase a greengrocery of their own. "You don't need much money to get started with a fruit and vegetable store," an auto mechanic from Korea turned greengrocer in New York told the *Times* in 1976. "You work hard, your family works, and that is it. You can make it." Many Koreans saw these groceries as a temporary necessity, a way to earn a living while they learned enough English to resume their former careers. "We study English and then maybe go back to our professions," explained another immigrant, perhaps a bit overoptimistically. By the mid-1990s, there were 2,500 Korean-owned greengroceries all across New York. New Yorkers loved them because their produce was far nicer than that found in supermarkets, and they were open late, often twenty-four hours a day.[73]

In 1990, Korean greengrocers found themselves at the center of a controversy that gained international attention. Black New Yorkers had complained for years that Korean grocers spied on them as they shopped, unfairly suspecting them of shoplifting more than white customers. African Americans also undoubtedly resented that Korean immigrants seemed to wield more economic power in their neighborhoods than they did. These tensions came to a head in January 1990 at the Family Red Apple grocery at 1823 Church Avenue in Flatbush when Gieslaine Felissaint, a forty-six-year-old Haitian-born home health aide, went to the cashier to pay for her purchases. What happened next became the subject of a trial for assault, a $6 million civil suit, and a vitriolic sixteen-month boycott of the grocery.

According to Felissaint, she took some plantains and peppers to the cashier, but seeing a long line, put them back and began to leave the store. A store employee demanded to look inside her bag, and when she refused to open it, Felissaint later testified in Creole, she was slapped, punched, and kicked to the floor. She identified Pong Ok Jang, brother of the store's owner, as her main assailant, and he was subsequently charged by the Brooklyn district attorney with misdemeanor assault. Jang's account differed in almost every detail. He testified that Felissaint made it to the cash register with her produce but when asked for three dollars gave the cashier only two. When she was asked for a third dollar, she threw the peppers into the cashier's face, called her a "Chinese, Korean motherfucker," and began knocking the counter displays to the floor, at which point the store's employees grabbed her in an attempt to stop her and escort her out of the store, which is when she fell to the floor and demanded an ambulance.

Supporters of Felissaint organized a boycott of Family Red Apple that was joined (and eventually dominated) by a well-known Brooklyn black nationalist, Sonny Carson. "Black power, black power. Let's kick their ass," he shouted outside the store during one "Day of Outrage." The boycotters picketed in front of the store, often threatening those who tried to enter and ignoring a judge's order that they stay at least fifty feet away from the entrance. The market, which had once taken in several thousand dollars a day, was now grossing less than a hundred. Even when a jury acquitted Jang of assault twelve months after the incident, the boycott continued unabated, as the protesters attributed the verdict to a racist justice system. The demonstrations ended only when, after sixteen months of anemic sales, the family sold the store. In the wake of the boycotts, Korean immigrants began accelerating a trend that had already begun before the Red Apple incident — diversifying their retail operations by opening fewer greengroceries in impoverished neighborhoods and instead starting businesses such as dry cleaners, fish markets, and nail salons in neighborhoods with more affluent customers.[74]

By the late 1980s, another immigrant employment niche that had become very visible to native-born New Yorkers was the South Asian taxi driver. Initially, most of these immigrant taxi drivers were from India, especially the northwest Indian state of Punjab, where most of the inhabitants are Sikhs. "In the last decade," the *Times* reported in 1998, "the turban has become the symbol of the New York City taxicab driver, just as a Brooklyn accent was four decades ago." The city's earlier wave of Indian immigrants, dominated by physicians and engineers, found it frustrating that the New Yorkers who had once associated India with their emergency room doctors now thought of Indians as the drivers who did not know their way around the city.[75]

At the dawn of the new century, however, even though New Yorkers still tended to think of their taxi drivers as "Indian," a significant change had taken place. Other South Asians — Muslims — had far surpassed Punjabis and other Indians in the taxi industry. In the early years of the twenty-first century, Bangladeshi immigrants had become the number-one source of New York taxi drivers, constituting 18 percent of the total. Pakistanis, also Muslims, ranked second at 15 percent. Indians were now third, making up 10 percent of the hack fleet. Taxi driving was the dominant occupation of the city's Muslim South Asian population. In 1991, when New York had a total Pakistani population of fewer than fifteen thousand, fully eight thousand of those immigrants drove cabs.[76]

In fact, without many New Yorkers even noticing, Muslim immigrants had become the fastest-growing immigrant group in the city in the last decade of the twentieth century. New York's Muslim South Asian population increased by more than 300 percent from 1990 to 2000. The city's immigrant populations from Egypt and Nigeria, which included many Muslims, were growing tremendously fast as well. But when two jet airliners came soaring out of the city's clear blue skies on the morning of September 11, 2001, and were crashed into the Twin Towers of the World Trade Center by Islamist terrorists, New Yorkers would suddenly become very conscious of the large Muslim population in their midst. Everyone who looked foreign, and even vaguely Middle Eastern, became suspect in the eyes of millions of New Yorkers and Americans in general. Calls to cut off Muslim immigration and even to deport Muslims came from all over America, even from some New Yorkers. How the city and its immigrants handled the devastation resulting from the 9/11 attacks would test New Yorkers' dedication to the ideals of their city of dreams.[77]

22

TODAY

THE TERRORIST ATTACKS of September 11, 2001, killed 2,600 people in New York. One-fifth of them were immigrants. Not one of the nineteen killers was an immigrant. Most had entered the country on tourist or business visas, and one had a student visa. Yet many Americans were quick to blame the United States' supposedly lax immigration policies for the attacks.

Afterward, many immigrants in New York faced hostility that they had never previously experienced. "Before 9/11, it was beautiful," recalled a Muslim taxi driver from Bangladesh shortly after the tragedy. "We enjoyed our job. We made some money. I would help my parents financially. I couldn't complain. Everything was fine. Now the job, people in the street, customers, neighbors — all the people have changed." Not only adults but even children had to face this sudden animosity. "You are from a terrorist country," an American-born third-grader, the child of Pakistani immigrant parents, was told by an elementary school classmate in the Midwood section of Brooklyn. A female Muslim high school student, also in Brooklyn, resented the sudden "hatred against us."

Immigrants who thought that their native-born neighbors had seen them as fellow New Yorkers were shocked to discover how conditional that acceptance really was. "For 11 years, I've been thinking I'm American," remarked an Algerian-born taxi driver, but the backlash against Muslim foreigners taught him otherwise. Muslim immigrants were not the only ones who suffered. A passenger on a Greyhound bus cursed at and assaulted a Pakistani Sikh from Queens, mistaking him for a Muslim. Such incidents were common.[1]

Animosity from an angry and nervous public turned out to be the least of the Muslim immigrants' post-9/11 concerns. In June 2002 the federal government announced that all male non-citizens aged sixteen and older who had been born in twenty-five predominantly Muslim countries would have to report to an Immigration and Naturalization Service office to be fingerprinted, photographed, and questioned. Of the 84,000 who came forward nationwide, 14,000 were detained. What was especially frightening about the process was that the detainees could be held indefinitely without being charged, and the government insisted it had no responsibility even to inform the detainees' family members that their loved ones were incarcerated. They just disappeared.

Some resurfaced months later in Lahore or Dhaka, deported for having been in the country illegally, usually having overstayed a tourist or student visa. Others were held for years while authorities attempted to determine if they had ties to terrorist organizations. In New York, Bangladeshis, Egyptians, and especially Pakistanis (then the city's largest Muslim group) were affected by the crackdown. To make matters worse, the New York Police Department began a program of "covert" but heavy-handed surveillance of all Muslim New Yorkers. No probable cause to suspect an immigrant of terrorist activities was necessary to tap Muslims' phones, photograph their movements, monitor their financial transactions, or question their neighbors about their activities.[2]

The cumulative effect of the hostility, detentions, and surveillance was devastating to the residents of Little Pakistan in the Midwood section of Brooklyn and to other Muslim communities as well. Thousands of the detainees were deported, even though their wives and American-born children were allowed to remain in New York. Thousands more left of their own accord, some returning to Pakistan, while many more moved to Canada. Even legal immigrants were leaving, noted a Pakistani shopkeeper. "People are scared of what's going on and they feel it's safer to move somewhere else." The departures had a huge impact on those who remained behind. Dozens of Pakistani businesses in Midwood closed. With so many of their customers gone, they no longer made enough money to cover the rent. The Makki Mosque on Coney Island Avenue had once been so crowded that some worshippers had to pray outside on the sidewalk. "Now the rooms are empty inside," a taxi driver reported sadly.[3]

Even for Muslims whose incomes did not depend on other Muslim New Yorkers, life became filled with humiliation and fear. "It completely messed with the psyche of the community," said one Muslim a decade later. South Asian Muslims who had become citizens began carrying their passports with them because it made things easier when they were inevitably stopped and questioned. Pakistani men who used to congregate to watch cricket on television stopped doing so because *any* gathering of Muslim men seemed to result in visits from the police or FBI and increased surveillance thereafter. Inasmuch as none of the 9/11 terrorists was from Pakistan or Bangladesh, the two largest sources of Muslim immigrants in New York, newcomers from these countries did not understand why they were being subjected to such withering scrutiny.

Some non-Muslim Brooklynites eventually began to speak out on behalf of their beleaguered neighbors. "People are suffering," Brooklyn's Roman Catholic bishop, Nicholas DiMarzio, complained to the press in 2004. "Some of it is the unintended consequences of 9/11, but we have to do something about it. It's immoral. It's just wrong." Navila Ali, a twenty-year-old Bangladeshi immigrant and the oldest of three children, had lived in New York since age eight. She became the de facto head of her family when her father was suddenly deported. "I've been here 12 years, and I always thought in my soul and heart, I'm American," she told the *Times*. Up until 9/11, she had felt safer in New York than in South Asia. "But I don't feel that way anymore."[4]

Every time there was another terror attack—from the failed efforts of the "shoe bomber" in December 2001 to the carnage in San Bernardino in December 2015—anti-Muslim vitriol resurfaced, taking a cumulative toll on the city's Muslim immigrants. "When I'm on the train, people don't want to sit beside me," lamented an immigrant from Egypt in 2015. "I'd like to talk but it's easier to be silent. It's sad." Even the uniformed employees of the city were not immune from such treatment. "It's not uncommon to hear 'Muslim, go back to your country,'" reported a Bangladesh-born subway station agent that same year. "We get that all the time."[5]

Muslims were not the only New York immigrants hurt by 9/11 and its aftermath. The city's Chinese immigrants suffered as well, primarily because of the proximity of Manhattan's Chinatown to ground zero. Manhattan below Canal Street was closed to vehicular traffic for weeks after the attack, crippling Chinatown's already reeling garment industry (which was suffering from, of all things, competition from China). Even after the police once again allowed traffic downtown, some business was permanently lost. Without jobs, thousands fewer women came to Manhattan's Chinatown each day from Flushing and Sunset Park, which hurt Manhattan's Chinese merchants. Mei Wah Trinh, a fruit and vegetable vendor on Canal Street, told the *Times* that she no longer saw half her regular customers, who were primarily garment workers. "Sometimes they walk by and I call out to them, but they say they have no more work." Chinatown's restaurants and gift shops lost millions in sales as well.[6]

The aftermath of 9/11 prompted some of New York's immigrants to move. For some, this merely meant relocating to another borough. Manhattan's Chinese population fell by 16 percent from 2000 to 2010, and Flushing received a good deal of this Chinese influx. "After 9/11 . . . everybody moved to Queens," one Chinese American there noted ten months after the attack. "There's a lot of crazy stuff happening in Manhattan, so Flushing is growing." But the Chinese population of Brooklyn expanded even faster, especially in southwest Brooklyn neighborhoods like Sunset Park, Bensonhurst, and Dyker Park. Other Chinese immigrants left New York City altogether, buying existing Chinese restaurants or opening new ones in small towns that did not yet have any. "Every state has a Chinese restaurant," one Fujianese immigrant who was leaving New York for Hiawassee, Georgia, sixteen months after 9/11 told a reporter. "Americans depend on us to eat."[7]

The Chinese were not the only New York immigrants to leave the city in the wake of 9/11. Many Dominicans, New York's largest immigrant group, moved away as well. Some went only as far as Yonkers (just north of the New York City line) or Union City, New Jersey, but large numbers chose to relocate to places like Reading, Pennsylvania, where they opened bodegas in low-income neighborhoods. "We saw a spike after Sept. 11," said a resident of Reading. "Ask them why they come here, they say, 'We wanted to get away.'" Dominicans liked these smaller towns because for the price of a mortgage down payment alone in the Bronx, the immigrants could own a house in these exurbs free and clear.[8]

After a disaster, a city's inhabitants can feel as if they will never truly recover —that the veil of sadness will never lift. But most people, like the cities they live in, do eventually heal. New York had rebounded after a quarter of the city burned to the ground in 1776. The city's German immigrant community eventually recovered after more than one thousand of its members, mostly children, died in 1904 when the *General Slocum,* a steamship chartered for an end-of-the-school-year excursion, caught fire and became a floating inferno in the East River. The pall cast over New York by the events of 9/11 eventually lifted as well.[9]

One of the ways that recovery became manifest was in the rebound in New York's immigrant communities. By 2004, the city's economy —dealt a staggering blow by the terrorist attack —was booming again. In that year the Department of Buildings granted more residential construction permits than in any year since 1972. New construction was especially brisk in Queens, the borough where the most new immigrants were settling.[10]

Queens was far from the only beneficiary of the revival. Manhattan's Chinatown was once again full of tourists. Its sidewalk stands overflowing with fish, exotic vegetables, and medicinal herbs were thronged with customers. The city's Muslim communities also experienced a remarkable rebound. Little Pakistan regained its former vitality as the siege mentality there eventually waned, and Coney Island Avenue once again filled with Pakistani shoppers. In 2005, more Muslim immigrants were granted legal permanent residence in the United States than in any other year since the mid-eighties. The ongoing anti-Muslim climate in the country, exacerbated by the war in Iraq, did not deter many Muslim immigrants. "I got freedom," Nur Fatima happily exclaimed in 2006, describing why she had come to New York from Pakistan. "Freedom of everything." In America, Fatima was able to stop wearing a hijab and take a job as a security guard, both of which would have been impossible, she said, in her homeland. "This is a second birth for me."[11]

While the Pakistani community merely regained its former size in the decade after 9/11, the predominantly Muslim Bangladeshi population *grew* by 76 percent over the same time span, quietly surpassing Colombians, Trinidadians, and even Koreans and Indians to become the eighth-largest immigrant group in the city by 2014. (It had been forty-second largest in 1990.) Bangladeshis created big, tight-knit enclaves in the Parkchester and Westchester Square neighborhoods in the Bronx, the Kensington–Ocean Parkway section of Brooklyn, and the Briarwood, Jamaica, and Jamaica Hills neighborhoods of Queens. "I feel like I'm living in my own country," bragged Ansar Lovlu, a Bangladeshi resident of Brooklyn and editor of one of several Bengali-language newspapers published in the city. "You don't have to learn English to live here. That's a great thing!"[12]

Today, 3.2 million of New York's 8.5 million residents, 37 percent of the total, are immigrants.* That's the same proportion of foreign-born who lived in the city in 1900, immediately after it annexed Brooklyn, Queens, and Staten Island, but less than the 41 percent who were immigrants in 1920, and far below the post-Revolutionary high of 51 percent reached in 1855. Thanks largely to the Hart-Celler Act's requirement that immigrant visas be doled out to a wide variety of nations from different hemispheres, New York's immigrants today are more diverse than ever before. Some 910,000 New Yorkers were born in Asia, 860,000 hail from Caribbean islands, 750,000 come from Central and South America, 470,000 are from Europe, and 145,000 are from Africa.

---

* To describe New York "today," I rely on data published from 2010 onward. As specified in the endnotes, some of my statistics on New York today come from the 2010 census, some from the New York City Department of Planning report *The Newest New Yorkers* (2013 ed.), and some from the Census Bureau's 2014 American Community Survey, the most recent census data available when this book went to press in early 2016.

TOP SOURCES OF NEW YORK'S IMMIGRANT POPULATION, 2014

COUNTRY OF BIRTH	NUMBER	TREND, 2010–2014
Dominican Republic	402,000	rising
China	389,000	rising sharply
Mexico	187,000	stable
Jamaica	175,000	rising
Guyana	143,000	rising
Ecuador	138,000	stable
Haiti	88,000	falling
Bangladesh	88,000	rising sharply
India	81,000	rising
Trinidad and Tobago	78,000	falling
Colombia	68,000	falling sharply
Ukraine	67,000	rising sharply
Russia	65,000	falling sharply
Korea	62,000	falling sharply
Philippines	57,000	rising sharply
Poland	49,000	falling sharply
Italy	48,000	stable
Pakistan	45,000	rising
United Kingdom	32,000	falling
El Salvador	29,000	falling sharply
TOTAL FOREIGN-BORN	**3,160,000**	

Source: U.S. Census, American Community Survey, 2014, accessed via socialexplorer.com. A "sharp" increase or decrease in population denotes a change of 10 percent or more from 2010 to 2014.

As always, New York's immigrants today are not dispersed uniformly across the five boroughs. The city's two biggest immigrant groups, for example, Dominicans and Chinese, rarely live in the same areas. There are now more Dominicans in the Bronx than in any other borough, yet almost no Chinese settle there. Dominicans dominate upper Manhattan, where there are few Chinese, while the Chinese predominate in lower Manhattan. The Chinese in the outer boroughs live primarily in Queens and south Brooklyn, areas largely avoided by Dominicans. There are several neighborhoods in Queens and Brooklyn that

THE PROPORTION OF IMMIGRANTS IN THE POPULATION OF NEW YORK CITY'S NEIGHBORHOODS, 2010

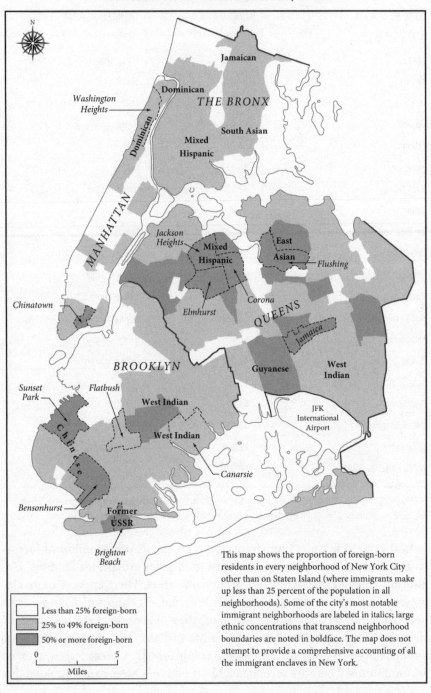

This map shows the proportion of foreign-born residents in every neighborhood of New York City other than on Staten Island (where immigrants make up less than 25 percent of the population in all neighborhoods). Some of the city's most notable immigrant neighborhoods are labeled in italics; large ethnic concentrations that transcend neighborhood boundaries are noted in boldface. The map does not attempt to provide a comprehensive accounting of all the immigrant enclaves in New York.

Less than 25% foreign-born
25% to 49% foreign-born
50% or more foreign-born

0   5
Miles

are fairly evenly divided between Asians and Hispanics, but those Hispanics are overwhelmingly Mexicans, Ecuadoreans, and Colombians. Morningside Heights in Manhattan, home to Columbia University, is the only neighborhood in all of New York where the city's number-one and number-two immigrant groups actually rank first and second in immigrant population.[13]

While the locations in northern Manhattan and the Bronx where Dominicans concentrate have remained relatively stable for several decades, the list of New York's Chinese neighborhoods is expanding rapidly. Twenty years ago, there were really just four Chinese neighborhoods in New York: Manhattan's largely Cantonese Chinatown, located where Five Points had once sat; the newer Fujianese Chinatown on the Lower East Side, centered on East Broadway; Flushing in Queens; and Sunset Park in Brooklyn. But like so many immigrant groups before them, the Chinese are leaving their original settlements for neighborhoods in the outer boroughs. They are now the largest immigrant group in Bath Beach, Bay Ridge, Bensonhurst (which has the largest Chinese population of any neighborhood in the city), Borough Park, Dyker Heights, Homecrest, Madison, and Sunset Park in Brooklyn, as well as in Bayside, Elmhurst, Flushing, Forest Hills, Murray Hill, and Rego Park in Queens.[14]

Why have the Chinese been spreading out so dramatically, after remaining concentrated in a small number of tight-knit communities for more than a century? In part, they have simply run out of room in their traditional enclaves. But gentrification has also priced many Chinese immigrants out of lower Manhattan. Landlords who once turned a blind eye to the illegal subdividing of apartments into overcrowded bunk rooms now call in building inspectors to issue citations to such tenants so they can evict them and bring in more affluent renters or convert their apartments into condominiums.

Another factor drawing immigrants out of Manhattan's congested Chinese neighborhoods is that, like other New Yorkers who marry and have children, they want more space and better schools. "For the kids and their education, we want less Chinese, so they can join society," one Chinese immigrant told the *Times* in 2015 of her decision to move to Homecrest in south Brooklyn. After ten years in Manhattan's Chinatown, Lucy Lee relocated to Bensonhurst for similar reasons. "In Chinatown, you can speak your own language and get around all right," she said in 2005. She eventually moved to Bensonhurst, however, because "this is a better lifestyle and you can — what's that word? — assimilate."[15]

Mexicans — the third-largest immigrant group in the city — have now surpassed the Chinese to become the group that lives in the most crowded conditions. Today, one is much more likely to find Mexicans rather than Chinese crowded into an illegally subdivided bunk room. "David and His 26 Roommates," an investigative report that appeared in *New York* magazine in 2005, detailed how landlords, building superintendents, and immigrant middlemen who recruit tenants all share in the profits generated by illicitly cramming immigrants into dank and dangerous lodging spaces. The number of apartment units in New York officially designated as overcrowded increased nearly 20 percent from 2005 to 2015. An immigrant is the head of household in 70 percent of those overcrowded dwellings.[16]

Mexicans continue to be the city's underappreciated immigrant group, perhaps because they are numerous everywhere but dominant almost nowhere. While Dominicans, Chinese, and even Jamaicans are each the largest immigrant group in a dozen or more New York neighborhoods, Mexicans are the most populous in only two — East Harlem in Manhattan and Corona in Queens. Mexicans are almost always the second-biggest immigrant group in Dominican neighborhoods in the Bronx and Manhattan, and are found in significant numbers virtually everywhere except southern Queens. Mexican immigrants are especially prevalent in day labor, construction, and behind-the-scenes service jobs such as food and janitorial work.

New York's Mexicans come disproportionately from a single Mexican state — Puebla — in south-central Mexico, southeast of Mexico City. "Anywhere that hard work needs doing, you'll find these immigrants from the state of Puebla," notes Miami-based Univision journalist Jorge Ramos. "They are helping New York City remain the capital of the world." Like the Italians before them, many Mexican immigrants originally intended to stay in New York only long enough to help their families pay off debts, buy a business, or build a house back in Puebla. But having paid so much to smugglers to get into the United States, they are reluctant to go back to Mexico, knowing they might not be able to return should their financial situation require it. When the Great Recession set in, however, and the demand for workers plummeted in the fields that Mexicans dominate, they abruptly stopped coming to New York. After rising sharply from 1990 to 2010, the number of Mexican immigrants in the city remained virtually unchanged from 2010 to 2014.[17]

Another large and often overlooked Latino immigrant group in New York is Ecuadoreans. They have held steady in sixth place among New York's immigrant groups since 2000. Residentially, Ecuadoreans concentrate much more so than Mexicans, living primarily in Corona, Elmhurst, Jackson Heights, Ridgewood, and Sunnyside in Queens, but also in significant numbers in the Bronx. Ecuadoreans do much the same work as Mexicans. Among the undocumented, who by one estimate make up 70 percent of the Ecuadorean population in New York, three-quarters of the men are employed in restaurants, supermarkets, day labor, or construction.[18]

Day labor is often Ecuadoreans' first work experience in New York. "At one time or another you find yourself on the corner" where laborers gather to seek work, noted an Ecuadorean immigrant named Victor. "But usually it's just your first job." Undocumented day laborers are typically paid $70 a day for construction work, and a little less for other jobs such as hauling debris or cleaning swimming pools. For newly arrived immigrants, securing work as a day laborer can be daunting. Victor did not initially know how to stand out among the crowds of young men hoping to be hired, but eventually he learned the importance of getting out onto the street before dawn and not standing on a corner with too many other laborers. A huge throng, he discovered, "intimidates those who are looking for workers. They like to talk with fewer guys to set the price and day's plan." Beyond the difficulty of getting hired in the first place, another reason why immigrants sought to avoid day labor if they could was that at the end of the day, the strangers who had hired them often did not pay them. "Sometimes you have to wait a number of days to get paid . . . That scares you."[19]

Male immigrants are not the only ones who gather on the street looking for work. There are several locations around the city where immigrant women congregate hoping to be hired, typically by housewives to clean their homes for a day, but sometimes for garment work as well. An investigative report in the *Times* in 2005 found large numbers of Ecuadorean women, along with some Mexicans and Poles, on the streets seeking day labor. One Ecuadorean explained that she had come to New York to earn money for a heart operation needed by her son, whom she had left with family in Ecuador along with his two siblings. "The little I make here I send to him," she said. "Many times I just want to go to be with him, but I don't have the money to do so. It gives me a desperate feeling."[20]

Ecuadoreans, Mexicans, and Chinese are all especially numerous in Queens. Today, not only is Queens home to more immigrants (1.1 million) than any other New York City borough, but also it is the place where immigrants constitute the largest proportion of the population (48 percent). One Queens neighborhood, Elmhurst, is home to immigrants from more than 120 different countries. If one measures diversity by variety of birthplaces, it is probably the most diverse neighborhood in the world. Seventy-one percent of Elmhurst's inhabitants are foreign-born, the highest proportion of any neighborhood in the city. Nonetheless, nearly half of Elmhurst's immigrants come from just three countries: China, Ecuador, and Mexico.[21]

Each part of Queens has its own distinct ethnic characteristics. Northwest Queens, for example, is largely non-Dominican Hispanic. Northeast Queens is East Asian, with the Chinese and Koreans predominating, especially in Flushing, Bayside, and Murray Hill. On many of the streets radiating east and west off Main Street in Flushing just south of Roosevelt Avenue, 85 percent of the residents are immigrants, the highest proportion found in any locale in the city. Three-quarters of these immigrants are Chinese. Southern Queens, in contrast, is mostly West Indian, with Guyanese, Jamaicans, and Haitians most numerous in the southeast, while Guyanese and Trinidadians are preponderant in the southwest.[22]

The Guyanese, the second-largest immigrant group in Queens (and fifth largest in the city), are another population that gets very little attention from the press or academics. Most New Yorkers probably cannot locate Guyana on a map. (It is on the northern coast of South America just east of Venezuela.) If Guyana rings a bell at all, it is because in 1978, just a dozen years after the nation gained its independence from Great Britain, cult leader Jim Jones led nearly one thousand of his followers in mass suicide by directing them to drink poisoned Kool-Aid after they killed a U.S. congressman who had come to investigate their commune. Before that incident, Guyana (formerly British Guyana) was best known as a huge producer of sugarcane. The sugar was cultivated by African slaves until the British outlawed slavery in the 1830s, after which Guyana's plantation owners began importing laborers from India to work in the cane fields too. As a result, a third of Guyana's population is descended from African slaves and about half are ethnic Indians.

Black Guyanese immigrants tend to settle in central Brooklyn's West Indian neighborhoods with the Jamaicans, Haitians, and Trinidadians. The Indo-Guyanese, however, primarily lay down roots in Queens, where most of New York's South Asians live. The Indo-Guyanese often live in the same neighborhoods as the South Asian Indians, yet relations between the two groups are sometimes strained. The natives of India seek to distinguish themselves from the Indo-Guyanese. The two groups eat different foods and have few common cultural traits other than, in some cases, their religion, which does not bridge the significant gap between them. "We look like Indian," explained one Guyanese New Yorker, "but we're not Indian." A few years ago, a Queens Indian organization held a beauty pageant that was won by a Guyanese immigrant. When the organizers found out where she was born, they refused to give her the grand prize —a free trip to India.[23]

Brooklyn, the borough of hipsters, is also becoming much more diverse. As recently as 1980, one could accurately sum up the population of Brooklyn as Italians, Jews, West Indians, and African Americans. Today, the Italian Americans from southwest Brooklyn neighborhoods like Bensonhurst, Canarsie, and Dyker Heights have mostly moved out or died off, replaced primarily by Chinese newcomers. There are also rapidly expanding enclaves of Arabs in Bay

Ridge, Bangladeshis in Kensington, Burmese in Sheepshead Bay, and Mexicans in Sunset Park, while Uzbeks are spreading out all across south Brooklyn (and in Rego Park, Queens, as well). Central Brooklyn, in contrast, remains the home of West Indians; they account for three-quarters of its 250,000 immigrants. The West Indian–born population of central Brooklyn is declining, however. Jamaican immigration remains robust, but these new arrivals now often settle in the north Bronx, while the number of Haitians and Trinidadians immigrating to New York is dwindling.[24]

There is still a significant Jewish immigrant population in Brooklyn, but it is smaller than and different from the foreign-born Brooklyn Jewish population of the past. In the 1970s and 1980s, the United States took in a large number of Jewish refugees from the Soviet Union. They settled overwhelmingly in the Brighton Beach neighborhood of south Brooklyn, but also to some extent in Midwood, Sheepshead Bay, and Homecrest. These aging immigrants are now being augmented by new arrivals — not as uniformly Jewish — from Ukraine and Russia. The residents of the twelve or so blocks between Brighton Beach Avenue and the Brighton Beach Boardwalk are 80 percent foreign-born, the second-highest concentration of immigrants in any of the city's census tracts.[25]

The Bronx has experienced faster growth in its immigrant population since 9/11 than Manhattan, Brooklyn, or even Queens. In the decade after 9/11, the foreign-born population of the Bronx increased 22 percent, four times the rate of growth in Queens and ten times that of Manhattan and Brooklyn. Many of these new immigrants are Dominicans relocating from Washington Heights to the west Bronx. But some of the city's most quickly growing immigrant groups are also establishing enclaves in the borough. Bangladeshis have expanded the size of their communities in Parkchester and Westchester Square. Jamaicans have increased their dominance of the north Bronx to include the neighborhoods of Baychester, Co-op City, Eastchester, Edenwald, Wakefield, Williamsbridge, and Woodlawn. The Bronx is also home to the city's largest African immigrant population. Newcomers from Ghana are the fifth-largest immigrant group in Bronx County, behind only Dominicans, Mexicans, Jamaicans, and Ecuadoreans. The West Africans live primarily in two enclaves — Bedford Park and Soundview — but are a growing presence in Concourse Village as well. Nigerians are the second-largest African group in the city, but they divide themselves fairly evenly between the Bronx and Brooklyn. Meanwhile, the Little Italy centered on Arthur Avenue has become a Little Albania.[26]

Staten Island has the smallest number of immigrants of the five boroughs, and the percentage of its residents who are foreign-born (21 percent as of 2010) is also the smallest. Nonetheless, in proportional terms, its immigrant population is growing faster than that of any other borough, and it too has recently developed significant new immigrant enclaves. There is a sizable Sri Lankan community in Tompkinsville in the northeast part of the island, across the bay from Brooklyn. Large numbers of West Africans (Liberians in particular) live in northern Staten Island as well as in the Park Hill neighborhood. On the southern end of the island, Italians are still the number-one immigrant group, though Russians and Ukrainians are gaining on them quickly. Mexicans are actually the largest immigrant group on Staten Island, something that became well known in 2010 when a series of attacks on Mexican immigrants there by native-born residents drew attention to its Mexican community.[27]

The story of immigrant New Yorkers changes constantly on its surface, yet not at all at its heart. On the surface, contemporary immigrants seem totally different. They come from nations unlike the homelands of previous waves of immigrants. Some practice religions that are unfamiliar to most native New Yorkers. They appear to make no effort to learn English. They seem to live wholly cut off from mainstream American society and, unlike previous generations, retain many ties to their homelands. Consequently, they don't seem to assimilate like yesteryear's immigrants. Many believe that immigrants sap our economic vitality. Even worse, as one well-known New Yorker famously said in 2015, "they're bringing drugs. They're bringing crime. They're rapists." But perhaps worst of all, we are told, they don't share our values and therefore can't ever become "real Americans."[28]

Yet today's immigrants at their core are no different from previous generations of newcomers. From the colonial period to the present, *every* generation of Americans has viewed the newest group to arrive as completely unlike previous immigrants. The Dutch felt that way about the Lutherans and Quakers. The English belittled the Germans and mistrusted the Irish. The children of the German and Irish immigrants disdained the Italians and eastern European Jews. Those groups thought that Puerto Ricans were ruining the city, and so on. That every one of these groups has become an accepted part of the city's fabric suggests that today's new groups will one day be viewed that way too.

Every group of immigrants coming to New York has gone to great lengths to bring its Old World culture and traditions with it to America. The Dutch, English, Scots, Irish, Germans, Italians, east European Jews, and all the rest who arrived as adults socialized in New York almost exclusively with other immigrants from their homelands — often only with those from the particular part of the old country that they came from. They ate much the same food as they had "back home" (albeit typically adding more meat), followed the news from their birthplaces more closely than American current events, sang the same songs and played the same games they always had, and worried that American values would ruin their children. When pundits complain that today's immigrants don't assimilate like those from the past, they are harking back to a golden era that never actually existed.[29]

In fact, today's immigrants are more likely to be conversant with American history and politics than those of previous eras. To become an American citizen today, an immigrant must pass an English exam and a civics test that most native-born Americans would fail if they had to take it. From 1820 to 1920, in contrast, when the immigrant ancestors of most of today's native-born Americans arrived in the United States, an immigrant could become a citizen without knowing a single word of English or answering a single question about American history or government. Furthermore, Italian, Jewish, and German immigrants in the past were just as isolated in their ethnic enclaves as today's immigrants — probably even more so. Today, for example, New York's Dominicans are avid followers of America's "national pastime," baseball, bringing them into one part of mainstream American culture far more quickly than previous generations of newcomers. Nonetheless, most adult immigrants have never assimilated enough to make their native-born critics happy and probably never will.[30]

Do today's immigrants pose a new danger that those of the past did not — a threat to America's national security? Security concerns involving immigrants are also nothing new. For several centuries of American history, the Irish were perceived as a national security threat every bit as frightening as that posed by al-Qaeda or the Islamic State today. Colonial New Yorkers lived in perpetual fear that Catholic immigrants would join forces with England's Catholic foes to overthrow British rule. In the eighteenth century, when New Yorkers caught rebellious slaves setting fires that threatened to destroy the entire city, their knee-jerk reaction was to execute some Catholic immigrants along with the slaves, since they found it hard to imagine that Catholics were not somehow involved in the plot.

In the nineteenth century, mayoral candidate Samuel F. B. Morse insisted that among the thousands of incoming Catholic immigrants were what we would today call sleeper cells, which would, when the signal came, rise up to take control of the United States. That fantasy never came to pass, but decades later, many New Yorkers doubted that Irish Catholic immigrants could be trusted to support the Union during the Civil War — doubts borne out by the chaos and carnage of the draft riots. Decades later, many New Yorkers still associated the Irish with "rum, Romanism, and rebellion."

By the last decades of the nineteenth century, Americans began to fear foreign-born socialists more than Catholics. German firebrands like Johann Most who advocated violence as propaganda terrified many Americans, but Italian and eastern European Jewish radicals eventually inspired even more dread, especially in the wake of the anarchist bombing campaign that killed dozens in both the United States and Europe. Yet prior to the 2016 election campaign, no prominent member of any American political party — not even the Know Nothings — ever proposed banning an entire ethnic or religious group from immigrating to the United States because of the sins of a few of the group's members. (Most Chinese immigration was banned in the 1880s, but not because the Chinese were deemed a threat to national security.) Then and now, most Americans believe that we should search out and punish those who break our laws (or conspire to do so) rather than stigmatize entire ethnicities and religions.

Anti-immigrant sentiment in the general public waxes and wanes, but even when nativism has grown strong, even when it becomes a central feature of a presidential campaign, it is far less virulent than in the past. Entire political parties once made anti-immigrant sentiment their defining feature. That nativist parties no longer exist indicates that, overall, Americans are more accepting of immigrants than they ever have been. In the nineteenth and early twentieth centuries, a rise in anti-immigrant feeling typically led to proposals to reduce the number of immigrants allowed into the United States or to take away some of their rights, such as the right to vote. That such calls are very rarely heard nowadays reflects a virtual consensus that legal immigration is unobjectionable, another major change from the past.

Many Americans do object to immigration primarily on economic grounds. Indeed, the impact of immigrants on our taxes, unemployment rate, and overall economic performance is one of the most complicated — and controversial — questions economists debate today. There are a few things, however, that we can say about this issue with some certainty. Most New Yorkers who own businesses benefit from having more potential customers arriving in the city to buy their goods and services. The employees of those businesses benefit from immigration too, because immigrant customers generate the sales that support their jobs. Immigrants are also beneficial to anyone who owns real estate; they increase demand for rental properties and boost the sale price for those who are selling. New Yorkers who want their homes cleaned cheaply, their renovation projects done inexpensively, or their elderly kin cared for at a moderate price gain from the presence of immigrants as well.

Perhaps most important for the city as a whole, immigrants revitalize poor neighborhoods. The local economy would have been devastated when nearly a million native-born New Yorkers moved out of the city in the 1970s had not almost as many immigrants arrived to take their place. The majority of the new residents who eventually took up residence in the boarded-up and dilapidated buildings of the south Bronx and central Brooklyn in the 1970s were immigrants. They helped turn those neighborhoods around. Without them, huge swaths of Brooklyn and the Bronx today might resemble Detroit, where the job market and real estate prices have both collapsed. In 2008, immigrants accounted for 32 percent of all economic activity in the city. Neighborhoods where immigrants cluster also have significantly less crime than neighborhoods that lack many foreign-born residents.[31]

Immigrants may, however, suppress the incomes of certain American-born workers. A native New Yorker who wants to work in construction, house cleaning, or the restaurant industry certainly has a lot more competition because of immigration; illegal immigration in particular drives down wages in those fields. Teenagers may also find it harder to get work, because immigrants willing to commit to full-time employment are much more attractive to employers in fields like fast food than teens who work only part-time.

One of the fiercest debates among economists concerns whether or not immigrants fill jobs that natives are no longer willing to do. History teaches us that there is no such thing as a job natives won't do. In the past, when immigrants were in short supply, crops got harvested, homes got cleaned, and restaurants were staffed, but employers had to pay more to get the work done. It may not be a coincidence that median wages for black men grew steadily in the 1950s and 1960s but stagnated in the two decades afterward, once significant numbers of immigrants again began arriving in the United States. But economists vehemently disagree about the extent to which competition from immigrants hurts native-born Americans on the bottom rungs of the economic ladder. (There is no doubt that immigration helps the economies of the countries where New York's immigrants were born. Immigrants sent $9 billion in remittances back to their homelands from New York City in 2012, a staggering sum.)[32]

Unlike in the past, when the United States was on the gold standard, Americans today do not object to the amount of money immigrants send abroad. Americans' biggest complaint by far concerning immigrants is that there is too much illegal immigration and that the government does not do enough to curtail it. Of the 11 million or so illegal immigrants living in the United States today, about 500,000 of them reside in New York City. Most Americans believe that illegal immigrants should "get in line" and immigrate legally, just like their own ancestors did. There are several fallacies, however, that underpin this viewpoint. First, for most of American history, there was no immigration "line." Every immigrant who wanted to come to the United States could do so without any wait at all. The immigration of Asians was eventually limited quite severely, but otherwise, even after Americans began imposing various medical and financial restrictions, 98 to 99 percent of Europeans and North Americans who wanted to come to the United States could do so without standing in any line. Waiting in a line began only in 1921, and even then, close relatives of those already in the United States were allowed to skip the line altogether. Consequently, *very* few Americans have ancestors who waited in an immigration line.[33]

The second fallacy is the belief that a line exists in which most of today's illegal immigrants could have waited. This is simply not true. The vast majority of visas given to immigrants today are reserved for family members of those already legally in the United States, and almost all of the remainder are awarded to those with highly sought-after job skills (nurses, software engineers, even university professors). If you do not have such a skill or a close relative already lawfully in the United States who can sponsor you, there is *no way to immigrate legally* — no line to get in at all.* A poor Mexican or Ecuadorean without American relatives thus does not have the same opportunity to immigrate that a poor Irishman or German or Italian or eastern European Jew once had. Americans are certainly within their rights to decide that they no longer want to give other people the same opportunities that their own ancestors had. But Americans ought to acknowledge as much rather than perpetuate the myth that their forebears followed the same rules that today's illegal immigrants flout.[34]

What about the argument that today's immigrants do not share American values? A poll taken in 2015, for example, found that 56 percent of Americans view the values of Islam as incompatible with those of Americans. Yet every argument typically put forward as to why Muslims can't make good Americans — that they won't accept religious pluralism; that they have no experience with democracy and will subvert its principles; that they are prone to violence; that they follow the dictates of foreign religious leaders; that they segregate themselves so thoroughly from the rest of American society that they can never assimilate; and that the tenets of their religion are incompatible with the principles that make America great — was once made against Irish Catholic immigrants. Today, few would argue that Irish Catholics do not make good American citizens.[35]

Some might imagine that with an increase in Muslim immigration coming at the same time that groups like al-Qaeda, the Islamic State, and terrorists inspired by them are targeting the United States, Americans will never accept

---

* Some visas are reserved each year for people from countries that have very few immigrants already living in the United States. These are known as "diversity visas." But only a tiny handful of the world's emigrants are eligible for these, and the odds of winning one in the annual drawing are hardly better than the odds of winning the Powerball. Would-be immigrants from countries that have already sent large numbers of immigrants to the United States are ineligible for diversity visas.

Muslim immigrants the way they eventually accepted Catholics and Jews. Yet the story of New York's immigrants shows that yesterday's un-American religion is today's mainstream one. In the seventeenth century, Lutherans, Quakers, and Huguenots were considered radicals and a threat to the safety of the city. Before long, those groups were welcome and Catholics were considered a menace. Then radical Jews and Italians. And now radical Muslims. There is no reason to believe that Muslims will not one day be as much an accepted part of American society as Jews and Italians and Irish Catholics are now.

What does the future hold for New York and its immigrants? Historians are leery of writing about the present, much less the future, but a couple of predictions seem fairly safe. First, the Chinese will soon pass Dominicans as the largest immigrant group in New York. Second, immigrants will increasingly bypass New York City and move directly to its suburbs. This trend started several decades ago and shows no signs of abating. Third, the newest immigrants will begin to take over the ethnic business niches of older immigrant groups. Italian-run pizza shops now seem to be the exception rather than the rule in New York City. Greek diners are also becoming a thing of the past. They are being bought by Koreans, in part because Koreans are abandoning the greengrocer trade in droves, though it is not yet clear which new immigrant group will assume control of that field. It is also likely that New York's post-1965 immigrant groups will become more politically active. It took Italians several generations before they began to wield political clout fully commensurate with their numbers, and New York's Asian and Latino residents are finally beginning to do so too. In 2009 New Yorkers elected their first Asian American to citywide office, and before long a Latino or an Asian American is bound to become mayor.[36]

It is also a safe bet that immigrants' children will fare even better economically than their parents, as has been the case in New York for generations. They will get more education, find better jobs, become more financially stable, and integrate more thoroughly into American society than their mothers and fathers.[37]

One final prediction: immigrants from all over the world will continue to make New York their destination. For so many of the world's immigrants, New York continues to epitomize their dreams — more so than any other city on the planet. Its freedom, vitality, opportunities, cosmopolitanism, and renown as a mecca for those with outsized ambitions have attracted more immigrants than any other city for centuries.

Life magazine acknowledged the city's hypnotic hold on dreamers the world over more than one hundred years ago, in words that ring as true today as when they were written in 1909: "New York is the metropolis of America, the mouth of the republic, the tongue of the nation, the eye of the continent, a pocket edition of Babel, a digest of the United States, with fewer Americans and more Americanism than any spot between Calais, Me., and the Kingdom of Heaven." To people all over the globe, "New York is the promised land, looking green, fat, luscious and joyous from the outside deserts; the promised land flowing with milk and honey . . . where the flesh pots smell savory, where the labels are better than the bottles, where the bricks are gold and the goods are green . . . Every race on earth claims New York," because it epitomizes all they dream of achieving. To generations past, present, and future, "New York is It. No man will ever see its finish."[38]

APPENDIX

ACKNOWLEDGMENTS

NOTES

SELECT BIBLIOGRAPHY

ILLUSTRATION CREDITS

INDEX

APPENDIX

POPULATION OF MAJOR IMMIGRANT GROUPS IN NEW YORK, 1850–2014

	1850	1860	1870	1880	1890	1900	1910	1920	1930
EUROPE									
Austria	109	1,692	2,737	4,743	27,193	90,477	190,246	126,739	127,169
England & Wales	23,671	27,977	32,588	30,593	36,872	70,522	80,262	73,123	80,140
France	4,990	8,074	8,265	9,910	10,535	14,755	18,293	23,085	23,400
Germany	56,141	118,292	151,216	163,482	210,723	324,224	278,137	194,155	237,588
Greece		19	43	69	263	1,309	8,038	21,455	27,182
Hungary			521	4,101	12,222	31,516	76,627	64,393	59,883
Ireland	133,730	203,740	201,990	198,595	190,418	275,102	252,672	203,450	220,631
Italy	708	1,464	2,794	12,223	39,951	145,433	340,770	390,832	440,250
Poland		1,566	2,393	9,020	6,759	37,873	*see note*	145,679	238,339
Romania						10,499	33,586	38,139	46,750
Russian Empire/USSR/ former USSR		467	1,151	4,551	48,790	180,432	484,193	479,800	442,432
Scotland	7,660	9,204	7,562	8,683	11,242	19,836	23,123	21,545	38,535
Sweden		606	1,558	3,194	7,069	28,320	34,952	33,703	37,267
United Kingdom									

	1940	1950	1960	1970	1980	1990	2000	2014
EUROPE								
Austria	145,106	124,256	84,301	48,024	26,160	12,072	6,700	4,980
England & Wales	64,411	53,614		30,511	22,790			
France	19,696	20,461	18,877	15,514	12,999	11,609	12,386	19,259
Germany	224,749	185,467	152,192	98,336	60,760	38,259	27,708	18,591
Greece	28,593	29,815	28,845	35,000	41,760	31,894	29,805	18,922
Hungary	62,588	51,968	45,567	31,717	22,660	14,631	11,144	5,984
Ireland	181,826	144,808	114,008	75,382	42,763	31,252	22,604	11,994
Italy	409,489	344,115	280,786	212,160	156,280	98,868	72,481	47,800
Poland	194,163	179,878	168,824	119,604	77,160	61,265	65,999	49,102
Romania	40,655	29,409	24,754	21,165	17,560	17,585	19,280	14,744
Russian Empire/USSR/ former USSR	395,696	314,603	204,578	117,363	78,340	80,815	151,135	131,358
Scotland	33,292	26,405		11,683	6,408			
Sweden	28,881	20,424	11,677	6,140		1,961	2,421	
United Kingdom			61,018			28,740	28,996	31,600

POPULATION OF MAJOR IMMIGRANT GROUPS IN NEW YORK, 1850–2014

	1850	1860	1870	1880	1890	1900	1910	1920	1930
THE AMERICAS									
Canada		3,899	4,501	7,147	8,398	21,926	27,180	25,582	40,118
Colombia									
Cuba			1,294			2,011			
Dominican Republic									
Ecuador									
El Salvador									
Guyana									
Haiti									
Honduras									
Jamaica									
Mexico		54	64	132	155	282	426	2,572	4,292
Peru									
Trinidad & Tobago									
ASIA									
Bangladesh									
China		51	175	787	2,048	6,080	3,936	4,001	6,629
India			23	89	120	250	238	413	630
Korea									
Pakistan									
Philippines									
AFRICA									
Ghana									
Nigeria									
TOTAL	235,733	383,717	419,094	478,670	639,943	1,270,080	1,944,357	2,028,160	2,358,686

Note: Blank cells in this chart indicate either that no immigrant population from that nation was reported in a given year or, more commonly, that the immigrants from that place were subsumed under a census category such as "Asia," "Other Europe," "South America," etc. The blank cell for Poland in 1910 results from the Census Bureau decision to include the population of Poland within the figures for Austria, Ger-

	1940	1950	1960	1970	1980	1990	2000	2014
THE AMERICAS								
Canada	40,345	35,860	28,150	20,545	15,320	13,818	17,318	21,133
Colombia			5,306	22,581	41,020	65,731	84,404	67,558
Cuba			25,959	63,043	49,720	41,039	26,030	14,026
Dominican Republic			8,182	51,231	120,600	225,017	369,186	401,595
Ecuador			2,970	16,075	39,000	60,451	114,944	137,597
El Salvador			292	793		18,453	26,802	28,939
Guyana					31,960	76,150	130,647	142,981
Haiti				20,245	50,160	71,892	95,580	88,467
Honduras			2,243	4,672	9,520	17,890	32,358	33,188
Jamaica				40,672	93,100	116,128	178,922	175,136
Mexico	2,973	3,300		3,541	7,380	32,689	122,550	187,156
Peru			1,454	3,814		19,818	27,278	28,931
Trinidad & Tobago				13,773	39,160	56,478	88,794	78,349
ASIA								
Bangladesh					1,280	8,695	42,865	88,135
China			21,529	37,348	85,100	160,399	261,551	388,593
India			1,554	5,032	21,500	40,419	68,263	80,917
Korea			602	2,665	20,380	56,949	70,990	62,457
Pakistan			315	932	4,440	14,911	39,165	45,304
Philippines			4,399	8,275	21,260	36,463	49,644	56,540
AFRICA								
Ghana						5,634	14,915	26,528
Nigeria						5,676	15,689	20,341
TOTAL	2,080,020	1,788,625	1,463,821	1,437,058	1,670,199	2,082,931	2,871,032	3,160,471

many, and Russia owing to the military occupation of Poland by those nations. Population of "Ireland" includes the entire island of Ireland except for 1960, 1990, 2000, and 2014, when components of the United Kingdom population were not specified. "China" includes Hong Kong and Taiwan. The Census Bureau published data only on New York's "white" immigrants in 1940, 1950, and 1960.

Sources: J.D.B. DeBow, *Statistical View of the United States* (Washington, D.C., 1854), 399; Joseph Kennedy, *Population of the United States in 1860* (Washington, D.C., 1864), 609; *The Statistics of the Population of the United States* (Washington, D.C., 1872), 388–91; *Compendium of the Tenth Census* (Washington, D.C., 1882), 546–51; *Report on the Population of the United States at the Eleventh Census: 1890* (Washington, D.C., 1895), 670–73; *Twelfth Census of the United States Taken in the Year 1900: Population*, pt. 1 (Washington, D.C., 1906), 950–53; *Thirteenth Census of the United States Taken in the Year 1910*, vol. 1, *Population* (Washington, D.C., 1913), 856–57; *Fourteenth Census of the United States Taken in the Year 1920*, vol. 2, *Population* (Washington, D.C., 1922), 729–31; *Fifteenth Census of the United States: 1930*, vol. 2, *Population* (Washington, D.C., 1933), 248–50; *Sixteenth Census of the United States: 1940*, vol. 2, *Population*, pt. 5, *New York–Oregon* (Washington, D.C., 1943), 159; *Census of Population: 1950*, vol. 2, *Characteristics of the Population*, pt. 32, *New York* (Washington, D.C., 1952), 99; *1970 Census of Population: Detailed Characteristics, New York* (Washington, D.C., 1972), 720; *1980 Census of Population: General Social and Economic Characteristics, New York* (Washington, D.C., 1982), sec. 1, 931–35; *1990 Census of Population: Social and Economic Characteristics, New York* (Washington, D.C., 1992), sec. 1, 789; Ira Rosenwaike, *Population History of New York City* (Syracuse, 1972), 205–6; New York Department of City Planning, *The Newest New Yorkers: Characteristics of the City's Foreign-Born Population*, 2013 ed. (New York, 2013), 17; "Place of Birth for the Foreign-Born Population," American Community Survey, 2014 (One-Year Estimates), United States Census Bureau, accessed via Social Explorer.

ACKNOWLEDGMENTS

In a very real sense, the origins of *City of Dreams* can be traced to a chance meeting in the spring of 1993. I was in Anaheim at the annual convention of the Organization of American Historians, which had just awarded a prize to my first book, a study of the anti-immigrant Know Nothing Party of the 1850s. My conference badge had a ribbon on it that said PRIZE WINNER, so as I roamed the convention hall where publishers displayed their latest history books, I attracted far more attention from the editors in attendance than was normal for a thirty-year-old assistant professor from the University of Wyoming.

One of the editors who congratulated me on my prize, Bruce Nichols of the Free Press, looked no older than me. "What are you going to be working on next?" he asked. "A history of Five Points, a forgotten New York neighborhood that was the most famous immigrant slum in nineteenth-century America," I replied. "That's not the kind of book we could publish," he said. "Do you have something planned after that?" Yes, I said. "I want to write the history of immigrant life in New York City, from the first Dutch settlers all the way to the present." Bruce's eyes lit up. "*That's* the book I want to publish," he said. "Make sure you get back in touch with me when you're ready to work on that."

As it turned out, Bruce did publish *Five Points*, which came out in 2001. By then, I had left Wyoming for Washington, D.C., and before long Bruce left the Free Press. But we stayed in touch, and Bruce's unbridled enthusiasm for *City of Dreams* kept me going as the years passed and I wondered if I had been crazy to take on so vast a project. Once the manuscript started coming together, Bruce offered expert advice on additions, deletions, and every other part of the writing and revision process. His talents made *City of Dreams* a far better book than I could have written alone.

By the time the manuscript made its way to Bruce, I had racked up a long list of debts. My agent Jill Grinberg spent years working with me as I shaped and reshaped my proposal. I especially value how she constantly reminded me that I should never waver from my vision of what *City of Dreams* should be. Likewise, over countless lunches for more than a decade, my good friend Marianne Szegedy-Maszak helped me through the ups and downs of the writing life as we worked to complete our respective book projects.

I had an army of research assistants aid me in pulling together the material for *City of Dreams*. They included Stacy Bondurant, Caitlyn Borghi, Lindsay Chervinsky, Madeline Crispell, Connie Golding, Bill Horne, Nick Juravich, Jon Keljik, Alsion Nordin, Maggie Pszonak, Tamar Rabinowitz, Lisa Randall, Michael Salgarolo, Zach Sanders, Ashley Somawang, and Whitney Tarella. I must particularly commend the unparalleled efforts of Hope McCaffrey and Katie Carper, who even agreed to continue working on the project after they graduated when I could find no one else with their extraordinary combination of talents.

I am also indebted to the many historians (and a few friends) who offered advice or read portions of the manuscript: Steve Barlas, Ron Bayor, Ed Berkowitz, Mary Elizabeth Brown, Nancy Foner, Joyce Goodfriend, Walter Kamphoefner, Kevin Kenny, Alan Kraut, Karen Ward Mahar, Denis Maika, Bernadette McCauley, Deirdre Moloney, Daniel Nagel, Johann Neem, Leila Nowroozi, Mae Ngai, Phil Ranlet, Dan Schwartz, Adam I. P. Smith, Marian Smith, Dave Stebenne, Richard Stott, and Andrew Zimmerman. They saved me from countless factual and interpretive errors.

Once the project reached the home stretch, I was lucky to have a fabulous team help me to the finish line. They included the ever-patient Ben Hyman at Houghton Mifflin Harcourt and my fabulous copyeditor Amanda Heller. Chris Robinson wove his usual magic creating the perfect maps for *City of Dreams*. I am particularly grateful to Gina Broze, my amazingly resourceful photo researcher.

Finally, I am most indebted to the members of my family, who with grace and good humor adjusted to my inability to focus on pretty much anything other than this book as the project entered its final, frantic year. My parents were unstintingly supportive as always, and my father offered his typically perceptive advice about every chapter. My eldest children, Jacob and Dina, having been through all this before, were far more patient with me than I deserved. So too were my wife, Lisa, and my younger children, Maya and Celia, who adjusted as I devoted nearly every waking minute to the book in the summer and fall of 2015. It is to them, with all my love, that I dedicate *City of Dreams*.

NOTES

Prologue

1. "The New Year Welcomed," *Times,* January 1, 1892, 2. In the notes that follow, all cited newspapers were published in New York unless otherwise noted. I have provided page numbers for newspaper and magazine articles published before 1990 but not for those that appeared thereafter. Because most people access old newspapers online these days, page numbers might seem unnecessary. But these papers are typically scanned from decaying microfilm copies, and as a result, optical scanning often fails to properly read not only the text but also sometimes even the article titles. Consequently, I have provided titles and page numbers to make it easy for readers to find my original sources. By the 1990s, when I began collecting newspaper articles for this book, newspaper content was being uploaded online digitally, so knowing page numbers became less important for finding an article if one knew the title. In fact, because newspapers began producing so many different editions, the number on the page in the edition I consulted might not be the one provided in the online version. For the *New York Times,* the newspaper cited most often in these notes, the page number given for an article at nytimes.com sometimes differs from that given at timesmachine.nytimes.com, and often varies from that given at proquest.com, the most-used source in academia for searching major American newspapers of the past. So I have opted not to provide page numbers for newspaper articles published in 1990 or later. One may also find slight variations between the newspaper dates given in these notes and those found for the same article at a newspaper's website because in some cases newspaper websites give as the date of an article the date it was first posted online rather than the date it appeared in print. Whenever I was aware of such discrepancies, I have provided the date an article appeared in print. Finally, the websites of major magazines such as newyorker.com do not typically provide the page numbers on which the print versions of their articles originally appeared, so in those instances as well I have not given page numbers. But in all such cases, these articles can easily be accessed online with the information provided in the notes.

2. Entries for Moore family, manifest of the *Nevada,* January 2, 1892, "New York Passenger Lists," Record Group 36, National Archives, accessed via ancestry.com; birth dates for the Moore children are from Cork baptismal records found at familysearch.org. Mary

was born December 10, 1870; Cornelius, May 28, 1872; Anne, May 30, 1874; Anthony, December 5, 1876; and Philip, December 17, 1879. Unless otherwise specified, all ship manifest citations are drawn from the collections of the National Archives and were accessed via ancestry.com.

3. "Sunk by the *Nevada*," *Times*, May 7, 1884, 1; "The *Nevada*'s Disaster," *Times*, May 8, 1884, 8; *Nevada* data from norwayheritage.com; number of passengers on previous *Nevada* voyages from "New York Passenger Lists."

4. Manifest of the *Nevada*, January 2, 1892, ancestry.com.

5. Even on a normal day, immigrants waiting on their ships to land could distinctly hear the sounds on Manhattan Island. See Jocelyn Cohen and Daniel Soyer, eds., *My Future Is in America: Autobiographies of Eastern European Jewish Immigrants* (New York, 2006), 141.

6. John B. Weber, *The Autobiography of John B. Weber* (Buffalo, 1924), 13–29, 87–96; "Platt's Man Chosen," *Times*, March 13, 1890, 1.

7. "Unfit for Their Work," *Times*, January 14, 1890, 3; "Biglin Gets a Scoring," *Times*, April 12, 1890, 8.

8. Weber, *Autobiography*, 89; "Farewell Castle Garden," *Times*, April 19, 1890, 5.

9. "The Weather Report," *Tribune*, January 2, 1892, 5.

10. Guion Line dock location from 1890 New York City Directory, accessed via ancestry .com.

11. "An Irish Lass's New Year's Gift," *Tribune*, January 2, 1892, 3; "Landed on Ellis Island," *Times*, January 2, 1892, 2; "First Immigrant on Ellis Island," *Herald*, January 2, 1892, 2; "Ellis Island Opened," *Press*, January 2, 1892, 10; "Annie's Golden Greeting," *World*, January 2, 1892, 12; "The New Immigrant Depot," *Irish World*, January 9, 1892, 8.

12. "Annie's Golden Greeting," *World*, January 2, 1892, 12 ("little"); "The New Immigrant Depot," *Irish World*, January 9, 1892, 8 (other quotations).

13. "Reports from the Nation," *Times*, May 16, 1965, sec. 4, 4; "About New York," *Times*, June 21, 1977, 25.

14. Alex Haley, *Roots* (Garden City, N.Y., 1976); Matthew Jacobson, *Roots Too: White Ethnic Revival in Post–Civil Rights America* (Cambridge, Mass., 2006), 1–388.

15. "Mrs. O'Connell Killed," *Clovis (N.M.) News Journal*, August 30, 1923, 1; http://www .honoringourancestors.com/wrong-annie/index.html.

16. "Historical Focus at Ellis Island" *Oswego (N.Y.) Palladium Times*, June 10, 1988, 3 (Associated Press report on Middleton being honored at Ellis Island); "Statues with Limitations," *Times*, May 23, 1993.

17. "First Through Gates of Ellis I., She Was Lost. Now She's Found," *Times*, September 14, 2006 (Smolenyak quotation); Jesse Green, "Immigrant Number One," *New York*, May 9, 2010.

18. Death certificates of Winifred Schayer, August 10, 1905; Walter Schayer, May 14, 1909; Edward Raymond Schayer, March 17, 1912; Harry Philip Schayer, October 4, 1919, New York County death records, New York Municipal Archives. Annie had lost another child earlier in her marriage, a fact recorded in the 1900 census, though the child's name is not listed. See entry for Annie Schayer, dwelling 8, enumeration district 22, New York County, manuscript population schedules, 1900 U.S. census, National Ar-

chives, accessed via ancestry.com. Unless otherwise specified, all census information refers to New York County (Manhattan), is drawn from the manuscript U.S. census population schedules, is in the collections of the National Archives, and was accessed via ancestry.com. New York State census population schedules were also accessed via ancestry.com unless otherwise noted.

19. "First Through Gates of Ellis I., She Was Lost. Now She's Found," *Times,* September 14, 2006; New York City Almshouse Admission Card for Julia Moore, January 6, 1909, death certificates of Matthew Moore, August 28, 1907, and Julia Moore, April 20, 1927 ("senile"), accessed via ancestry.com.

20. Green, "Immigrant Number One."

21. New York Telephone Company, Manhattan telephone directory for winter–spring 1944, 929. The value of the inheritance was calculated at http://www.measuringworth.com, a site created by economic historians.

22. Green, "Immigrant Number One."

23. Konrad Bercovici, *Around the World in New York* (New York, 1924), 3.

1. Settlement

1. Russell Shorto, *The Island at the Center of the World: The Epic Story of Dutch Manhattan and the Forgotten Colony That Shaped America* (New York, 2004), 73–74, 153 (*wilden*). Historians debate the name of the Indian tribe or subtribe that "sold" Manhattan to Minuit; I have relied on Reginald Bolton, *New York City in Indian Possession,* 2nd ed. (New York, 1975), 14–15; but also see Paul Otto, *The Dutch-Munsee Encounter in America: The Struggle for Sovereignty in the Hudson Valley* (New York, 2006), 4–20.

2. C. A. Weslager, *A Man and His Ship: Peter Minuit and the Kalmar Nyckel* (Wilmington, Del., 1989), 14; Bertrand van Ruymbeke, "The Walloon and Huguenot Elements in New Netherland and Seventeenth-Century New York: Identity, History, and Memory," in *Revisiting New Netherland: Perspectives on Early Dutch America,* ed. Joyce D. Goodfriend (Boston, 2005), 41–47; James Williams, "Peter Minuit," in *American National Biography Online* (New York, 2000); Bernard Bailyn, *The Barbarous Years: The Peopling of British North America; The Conflict of Civilizations, 1600–1675* (New York, 2012), 197–200.

3. Williams, "Minuit"; Shorto, *Island,* 48.

4. Williams, "Minuit"; A. J. F. van Laer, *Documents Relating to New Netherland, 1624–1626, in the Henry E. Huntington Library* (San Marino, Calif., 1924), 44 (quotation), 89–90.

5. Shorto, *Island,* 47–49; Van Laer, *Documents Relating to New Netherland,* 176 (quotation), 240. Letter writers in the seventeenth and eighteenth centuries were very erratic with capitalization; they especially liked to capitalize words in the middle of sentences. To make their thoughts easier to follow, I have silently changed to lowercase capitalized words in quotations dating prior to 1815 that are not typically capitalized today.

6. Shorto, *Island,* 49, 59; Henri van der Zee and Barbara van der Zee, *A Sweet and Alien Land: The Story of Dutch New York* (New York, 1978), 2.

7. Van der Zee and Van der Zee, *Sweet and Alien Land,* 2 ("inhabited"); Van Laer, *Documents Relating to New Netherland,* 51–52 ("contracts"). (These Dutch authors translate the instructions slightly differently.)

8. Peter Francis Jr., "The Beads That Did Not Buy Manhattan Island," *New York History* 67 (1986): 5–22; Paul Otto, "Real Estate or Political Sovereignty? The Dutch, Munsees, and the Purchase of Manhattan Island," in *Opening Statements: Law, Jurisprudence, and the Legacy of Dutch New York,* ed., Albert Rosenblatt and Julia Rosenblatt (Albany, 2013), 67–79; Shorto, *Island,* 55, 58; Peter Schagen to the States General, received November 7, 1626, http://www.newnetherlandinstitute.org/history-and-heritage/additional -resources/dutch-treats/peter-schagen-letter/ ("purchased"); Richard Howe, "Notes on the Manhattan Purchase," http://www.gothamcenter.org/blotter/?p=776; Mrs. Schuyler van Rensselaer, *History of the City of New York in the Seventeenth Century,* 2 vols. (New York, 1909), 1:49 ("pier").

9. *Papers Relating to the First Settlement of New York by the Dutch* (Edinburgh, 1888), 40; Shorto, *Island,* 59–60; Richard Howe, "Hovels or Holes? Notes on the First Dutch Houses on Manhattan," http://www.gothamcenter.org/blotter/?p=855 ("hovels").

10. Jaap Jacobs, *The Colony of New Netherland: A Dutch Settlement in Seventeenth-Century America* (Ithaca, 2009), 149 (quotations); Shorto, *Island,* 65–66; Weslager, *Man and His Ship,* 63–66.

11. Alb. Joachimi and Govert Brasser to the States General, April 10, 1632, in *Documents Relative to the Colonial History of the State of New-York Procured in Holland, England and France,* ed. E. B. O'Callahan, 11 vols. (Albany, 1853–1861), 1:48 (quotation); Van der Zee and Van der Zee, *Sweet and Alien Land,* 28; Shorto, *Island,* 65–75.

12. I. N. Phelps Stokes, *The Iconography of Manhattan Island, 1498–1909,* 6 vols. (New York, 1915–1928), 4:72; Shorto, *Island,* 74–75.

13. Van der Zee and Van der Zee, *Sweet and Alien Land,* 79–82; Shorto, *Island,* 114–17; Weslager, *Man and His Ship,* 84–156.

14. Van der Zee and Van der Zee, *Sweet and Alien Land,* 21; Simon Schama, *The Embarrassment of Riches: An Interpretation of Dutch Culture in the Golden Age* (Berkeley, 1988), 289–372.

15. Van der Zee and Van der Zee, *Sweet and Alien Land,* 19–20; Shorto, *Island,* 25–27.

16. Shorto, *Island,* 34; Van der Zee and Van der Zee, *Sweet and Alien Land,* 5.

17. Van der Zee and Van der Zee, *Sweet and Alien Land,* 5–8; Oliver Rink, *Holland on the Hudson: An Economic and Social History of Dutch New York* (Ithaca, 1986), 61–62.

18. Rink, *Holland on the Hudson,* 90–91; C. R. Boxer, *The Dutch in Brazil, 1624–1654* (1957; repr., Hamden, Conn., 1973), 21–23; Van Cleaf Bachman, *Peltries or Plantations: The Economic Policies of the Dutch West India Company in New Netherland, 1623–1639* (Baltimore, 1969), 44–73.

19. Shorto, *Island,* 40, 44; Van der Zee and Van der Zee, *Sweet and Alien Land,* 10–11 ("yacht").

20. Shorto, *Island,* 47–49; Van der Zee and Van der Zee, *Sweet and Alien Land,* 11.

21. E. B. O'Callaghan, ed., *The Documentary History of the State of New-York,* 4 vols. (Albany, 1850–51), 4:81 ("bubbling"); Shorto, *Island,* 42–43, 60; Jacobs, *Colony,* 8 ("chestnuts"); Adriaen van der Donck, *A Description of New Netherland* (Lincoln, Neb., 2008), 60 ("spoon").

22. Shorto, *Island,* 42–43 ("fear"), 54 ("chiefs"); J. Franklin Jameson, ed., *Narratives of New Netherland, 1609–1644* (New York, 1909), 105–6, 126, 217 (remaining quotations).

23. Stokes, *Iconography*, 4:55–56; Shorto, *Island*, 41; Abbot Emerson Smith, *Colonists in Bondage: White Servitude and Convict Labor in America, 1607–1776* (Chapel Hill, 1947), 16–19, 230.

24. "Letter from the Directors at Amsterdam to Petrus Stuyvesant," in *Correspondence, 1647–1653, New Netherlands Documents Series*, ed. Charles T. Gehring, vol. 9 (Syracuse, 2000), 90 ("lords"); Jacobs, *Colony*, 51–54.

25. Kenneth Morgan, *Slavery and Servitude in Colonial North America: A Short History* (New York, 2000), 8; Ernst van den Boogaart, "The Servant Migration to New Netherland, 1624–1664," in *Colonialism and Migration: Indentured Labor Before and After Slavery*, ed. P. C. Emmer (Dordrecht, 1986), 62–65; Aaron Fogleman, "From Slaves, Convicts, and Servants to Free Passengers: The Transformation of Immigration in the Era of the American Revolution," *Journal of American History* 85 (1998): 46, 68–69.

26. Jacobs, *Colony*, 53–55; "From Bronck to the Bronx, a Name and a Swedish Heritage to Celebrate," *Times*, August 19, 2014.

27. Jacobs, *Colony*, 34–35.

28. Jaap Jacobs, "Soldiers of the Company: The Military Personnel of the West India Company in Nieu Nederlandt," in *Jacob Leisler's Atlantic World in the Later Seventeenth Century: Essays on Religion, Militia, Trade, and Networks*, ed. Hermann Wellenreuther (Berlin, 2009), 11–32; Jacobs, *Colony*, 37–39, 41.

29. Jacobs, *Colony*, 41, 47 (quotation); J. H. Innes, *New Amsterdam and Its People: Studies, Social and Topographical, of the Town Under Dutch and Early English Rule* (New York, 1902), 237–44; Shorto, *Island*, 106; Willem Frijhoff, "Govert Loockermans," unpublished essay available at http://www.newnetherlandinstitute.org/files/4914/1079/7337/Loockermans_narrative_and_genealogy_final_revision_3.pdf.

30. Jacobs, *Colony*, 36; Van der Zee and Van der Zee, *Sweet and Alien Land*, 23–25; *OED Online* (December 2012), s.v. "steerage."

31. Van der Zee and Van der Zee, *Sweet and Alien Land*, 23–24; Schama, *Embarrassment of Riches*, 169 (salmon).

32. Shorto, *Island*, 53–54.

33. Van der Zee and Van der Zee, *Sweet and Alien Land*, 14–15; Jacobs, *Colony*, 213–16; *Papers Relating to the First Settlement of New York by the Dutch*, 33–34; Shorto, *Island*, 82–83; Rink, *Holland on the Hudson*, 87; Richard Howe, "Hovels or Holes? Notes on the First Dutch Houses on Manhattan," http://www.gothamcenter.org/blotter/?p=855.

34. *Papers Relating to the First Settlement of New York by the Dutch*, 34 ("men work"); Jacobs, *Colony*, 42–43 ("slave master").

35. Van der Zee and Van der Zee, *Sweet and Alien Land*, 13, 49; Jacobs, *Colony*, 119, 124–27; Eric Sanderson, *Mannahatta: A Natural History of New York City* (New York, 2009), 126–27.

36. Van der Zee and Van der Zee, *Sweet and Alien Land*, 13; Jacobs, *Colony*, 122; Jameson, *Narratives of New Netherland*, 130 (quotation).

37. Jacobs, *Colony*, 130–31, 184.

38. Ibid., 44, 132–36, 220; Innes, *New Amsterdam and Its People*, 75–78, 237; Van der Zee and Van der Zee, *Sweet and Alien Land*, 100, 354.

39. Rink, *Holland on the Hudson*, 88 (quotation); Jacobs, *Colony*, 112.

40. Jameson, *Narratives of New Netherland*, 83–84; Rink, *Holland on the Hudson*, 87; Shorto, *Island*, 55, 76; Jacobs, *Colony*, 109–11.

41. Rink, *Holland on the Hudson*, 128–29; Van der Zee and Van der Zee, *Sweet and Alien Land*, 77.

42. Rink, *Holland on the Hudson*, 135–37; Shorto, *Island*, 89, 105–6.

43. Shorto, *Island*, 105–6; Elizabeth Sutton, *Capitalism and Cartography in the Dutch Golden Age* (Chicago, 2015), 112–22.

44. Otto, *Dutch-Munsee Encounter*, 113–17; Van der Zee and Van der Zee, *Sweet and Alien Land*, 102–3, 106, 110; Shorto, *Island*, 117–19.

45. Otto, *Dutch-Munsee Encounter*, 117–20; Shorto, *Island*, 124 ("hacked"); Van der Zee and Van der Zee, *Sweet and Alien Land*, 119 (other quotations); Donna Merwick, *The Shame and the Sorrow: Dutch-Amerindian Encounters in New Netherland* (Philadelphia, 2006), 135–79.

46. Otto, *Dutch-Munsee Encounter*, 121–26; Louis Wright, *The Colonial Civilisation of North America, 1607–1763* (London, 1949), 135–36 (quotation); Shorto, *Island*, 127, 140–41; Van der Zee and Van der Zee, *Sweet and Alien Land*, 124–27.

47. Alan Simpson, *Puritanism in Old and New England* (Chicago, 1955), 1–60; Edmund Morgan, *Visible Saints: The History of a Puritan Idea* (1963; repr., Ithaca, 1965), 1–112.

48. Eve LaPlante, *American Jezebel: The Uncommon Life of Anne Hutchinson, the Woman Who Defied the Puritans* (New York, 2004), 19–207; Timothy Hall, *Anne Hutchinson: Puritan Prophet* (Boston, 2010), 1–139.

49. M. J. Lewis, "Anne Hutchinson," in *Portraits of American Women: From Settlement to the Present*, ed. G. J. Barker-Benfield and Catherine Clinton (New York, 1998), 45–50.

50. Van der Zee and Van der Zee, *Sweet and Alien Land*, 135–37; LaPlante, *American Jezebel*, 231–39.

51. Jaap Jacobs, "Like Father, Like Son? The Early Years of Petrus Stuyvesant," in Goodfriend, *Revisiting New Netherland*, 229–36; Van der Zee and Van der Zee, *Sweet and Alien Land*, 150–52.

52. Van der Zee and Van der Zee, *Sweet and Alien Land*, 151–52; Shorto, *Island*, 149–50.

53. Van der Zee and Van der Zee, *Sweet and Alien Land*, 157–59.

54. Shorto, *Island*, 169–70 ("chained"), 178 ("pieces"); Van der Zee and Van der Zee, *Sweet and Alien Land*, 170–71 ("slackness").

55. Van der Zee and Van der Zee, *Sweet and Alien Land*, 355.

56. Shorto, *Island*, 62 ("breeches"), 83–86 ("touching"); Van der Zee and Van der Zee, *Sweet and Alien Land*, 352–53, 356–57.

57. Van der Zee and Van der Zee, *Sweet and Alien Land*, 171; Shorto, *Island*, 184–85.

58. Shorto, *Island*, 171, 201–3, 227–28 ("heaven"); Van der Zee and Van der Zee, *Sweet and Alien Land*, 168, 194, 201; Jacobs, *Colony*, 50 ("farmers"); Sutton, *Capitalism and Cartography*, 100–112, 122–28.

59. Shorto, *Island*, 229–30, 243, 257–58, 265 ("absolute"), 268, 271; Van der Zee and Van der Zee, *Sweet and Alien Land*, 160 ("haughty"), 175, 231, 242–44; Dennis Maika, "Securing the Burgher Right in New Amsterdam: The Struggle for Municipal Citizenship in the Seventeenth-Century Atlantic World," in Goodfriend, *Revisiting New Netherland*,

114–16; Joep de Koning, "From Van der Donck to Visscher: A 1648 View of New Amsterdam," *Mercator's World* 5 (July–August 2000): 28–33; Sutton, *Capitalism and Cartography*, 100–112, 122–28.

60. Jameson, *Narratives of New Netherland*, 259 ("eighteen"); Thelma Wills Foote, *Black and White Manhattan: The History of Racial Formation in Colonial New York City* (New York, 2004), 41 ("Babel"); Van der Zee and Van der Zee, *Sweet and Alien Land*, 97; John O. Evjen, *Scandinavian Immigrants in New York, 1630–1674* (1916; repr., Baltimore, 1972), passim; Shorto, *Island*, 271–72.

61. Rink, *Holland on the Hudson*, 145; Jameson, *Narratives of New Netherland*, 272 (quotation); Shorto, *Island*, 159; Innes, *New Amsterdam and Its People*, 192.

62. Rink, *Holland on the Hudson*, 169, 234; Paul Finkelman, "'A Land That Needs People for Its Increase': How the Jews Won the Right to Remain in New Netherland," in *New Essays in American Jewish History*, ed. Pamela Nadell, Jonathan Sarna, and Lance Sussman (Cincinnati, 2010), 24–26; Jacobs, *Colony*, 198–200; Leo Hershkowitz, "New Amsterdam's Twenty-Three Jews — Myth or Reality?" in *Hebrew and the Bible in America: The First Two Centuries*, ed. Shalom Goldman (Hanover, N.H., 1993), 172–73; Howard Rock, *Haven of Liberty: New York Jews in the New World, 1654–1865* (New York, 2012), 11–12; Boxer, *Dutch in Brazil*, 238–41.

63. Finkelman, "Land That Needs People," 27–28 (Stuyvesant quotations), 41; Rink, *Holland on the Hudson*, 169, 234; Van der Zee and Van der Zee, *Sweet and Alien Land*, 291; Jameson, *Narratives of New Netherland*, 392–93 (other quotations).

64. Jacobs, *Colony*, 199–200 ("gladly" and "sums"); Van der Zee and Van der Zee, *Sweet and Alien Land*, 292; Finkelman, "Land That Needs People," 42–43 (other quotations).

65. Jacobs, *Colony*, 201; Van der Zee and Van der Zee, *Sweet and Alien Land*, 292; Shorto, *Island*, 275; Innes, *New Amsterdam and Its People*, 86–87; "Resolution to Exempt Jews from Military Service," August 28, 1655, in *Council Minutes, 1655–1656*, ed. Charles T. Gehring, vol. 6 of *New Netherlands Document Series* (Syracuse, 1995), 81; Rock, *Haven*, 16 (quotation).

66. Jacobs, *Colony*, 201–2; Van der Zee and Van der Zee, *Sweet and Alien Land*, 292–93 (quotation); Rock, *Haven*, 18–20; Leo Hershkowitz, "Asser Levy and the Inventories of Early New York Jews," *American Jewish History* 80 (1991): 24–29.

67. Peter Christoph, "Lutherans and the Law in New Netherland: The Politics of Religion," in Rosenblatt and Rosenblatt, *Opening Statements*, 139–44; Jacobs, *Colony*, 161–62; Shorto, *Island*, 275 (quotation).

68. Van der Zee and Van der Zee, *Sweet and Alien Land*, 297–98 ("pleased"); Jameson, *Narratives of New Netherland*, 394; Jacobs, *Colony*, 164–67 ("winking").

69. Jacobs, *Colony*, 167 ("latrine"); Van der Zee and Van der Zee, *Sweet and Alien Land*, 293–94 (other quotations).

70. Charles Gehring, "Prosecution or Persecution: The 1657 Flushing Incident," in Rosenblatt and Rosenblatt, *Opening Statements*, 117–24; Van der Zee and Van der Zee, *Sweet and Alien Land*, 294–95 (quotations).

71. Shorto, *Island*, 275–76 (quotations); Kenneth Jackson and David Dunbar, eds., *Empire City: New York Through the Centuries* (New York, 2002), 33–35; Dennis Maika, "Com-

memoration and Context: The Flushing Remonstrance Then and Now," *New York History* 89 (2008): 28–42; Evan Haefeli, *New Netherland and the Dutch Origins of American Religious Liberty* (Philadelphia, 2012), 156–71.

72. WIC Directors to Stuyvesant, April 16, 1663, in *Documents Relating to the History of the Early Colonial Settlements, Principally on Long Island,* ed. B. Fernow (Albany, 1883), 526 (quotations), vol. 14 of *Documents Relating to the Colonial History of the State of New York,* 15 vols. (Albany, 1853–1887); Finkelman, "Land that Needs People," 40; Van der Zee and Van der Zee, *Sweet and Alien Land,* 295–96; Shorto, *Island,* 275–76; Jacobs, *Colony,* 169–70.

73. Jacobs, *Colony,* 203–5; Van der Zee and Van der Zee, *Sweet and Alien Land,* 253–54; Maika, "Securing the Burgher Right," 119–20; Graham Hodges, *Root and Branch: African Americans in New York and East Jersey, 1613–1863* (Chapel Hill, 1999), 13–14, 31.

74. E. B. O'Callaghan, comp., *Laws and Ordinances of New Netherland, 1638–1674* (Albany, 1868), 12; Hodges, *Root and Branch,* 12; E. B. O'Callaghan, ed., *Calendar of Historical Manuscripts in the Office of the Secretary of State, Albany, N.Y.* (Albany, 1865), 195; Peter R. Christoph, "The Freedmen of New Amsterdam," in *A Beautiful and Fruitful Place: Selected Rensselaerswijck Seminar Papers,* ed. Nancy A. M. Zeller (Albany, 1991), 157–70; Joyce Goodfriend, "Merging the Two Streams of Migration to New Netherland," *New York History* 92 (2011): 133–49; Joyce Goodfriend, "Slavery in Colonial New York City," *Urban History* 35 (2008): 485–96.

75. Shorto, *Island,* 84.

76. Ibid. ("ropes"); Hodges, *Root and Branch,* 13–14; Joyce Goodfriend, *Before the Melting Pot: Society and Culture in Colonial New York City, 1664–1730* (Princeton, 1992), 116.

77. Rink, *Holland on the Hudson,* 163; Maika, "Securing the Burgher Right," 104; Hodges, *Root and Branch,* 7–8, 13–14, 31; E. B. O'Callaghan, *Voyages of the Slavers St. John and Arms of Amsterdam, 1659, 1663; Together with Additional Papers Illustrative of the Slave Trade Under the Dutch* (Albany, 1867), xxv. Estimates of New Amsterdam's population in 1664 vary from a low of 1,500 to a high of 2,000, making it impossible to determine precisely the proportion of the population that was enslaved.

78. Shorto, *Island,* 247, 265; Van der Zee and Van der Zee, *Sweet and Alien Land,* 225–50 (quotation, 230).

79. Blake A. Bell, "The New Englanders Who Signed Thomas Pell's 1654 Agreement Acquiring Much of Today's Bronx and Lower Westchester Counties from Native Americans," *Bronx County Historical Society Journal* 46 (Spring–Fall 2009): 25–28; Van der Zee and Van der Zee, *Sweet and Alien Land,* 312–15, 413.

80. Van der Zee and Van der Zee, *Sweet and Alien Land,* 317–19, 383, 428, 443–45; Shorto, *Island,* 292.

81. Shorto, *Island,* 296–305 (quotations); Van der Zee and Van der Zee, *Sweet and Alien Land,* 455–63.

82. Shorto, *Island,* 304–5 ("immunities"); text of the Articles of Capitulation in *Collections of the New-York Historical Society for the Year 1869* (New York, 1870), 335.

83. Hershkowitz, "Asser Levy," 24–29; Jacobs, *Colony,* 55–56; Goodfriend, *Before the Melting Pot,* 116.

84. Shorto, *Island,* 306; Van der Zee and Van der Zee, *Sweet and Alien Land,* 480; Edwin

Burrows and Mike Wallace, *Gotham: A History of New York City to 1898* (New York, 1999), 133.

2. Rebellion

1. Donald Shomette and Robert Haslach, *Raid on America: The Dutch Naval Campaign of 1672–1674* (Columbia, S.C., 1988), 75, 157.

2. Joyce Goodfriend, "Looking Backward, Looking Forward: The Dutch Restoration of 1673–74 and the Narratives of Seventeenth-Century New York History," *De Halve Maen* 84 (Spring 2011): 3–6; Henri van der Zee and Barbara van der Zee, *A Sweet and Alien Land: The Story of Dutch New York* (New York, 1978), 482–85 (quotation); Russell Shorto, *The Island at the Center of the World: The Epic Story of Dutch Manhattan and the Forgotten Colony That Shaped America* (New York, 2004), 308; Edwin Burrows and Mike Wallace, *Gotham: A History of New York City to 1898* (New York, 1999), 82–83.

3. Paul Nelson, "Francis Lovelace," in *Oxford Dictionary of National Biography*, online ed. (New York, 2008); Burrows and Wallace, *Gotham*, 83 (quotations); Van der Zee and Van der Zee, *Sweet and Alien Land*, 491–92; I. N. Phelps Stokes, *The Iconography of Manhattan Island, 1498–1909*, 6 vols. (New York, 1915–1928), 4:303. Because the Dutch and the English did not use the same calendar, the date when New York was returned to English control is sometimes given as October 31 (by the English) and sometimes as November 10 (by the Dutch).

4. Burrows and Wallace, *Gotham,* 84.

5. Joyce Goodfriend, *Before the Melting Pot: Society and Culture in Colonial New York City, 1664–1730* (Princeton, 1992), 13, 16, 52–54 ("knack" and "conquered"), 61; Joyce Goodfriend, "Foreigners in a Dutch Colonial City," *New York History* 90 (Fall 2009): 241–69; Ira Rosenwaike, *Population History of New York City* (Syracuse, 1972), 7; Shorto, *Island*, 310 ("chiefest").

6. Goodfriend, *Before the Melting Pot,* 42–44, 136.

7. Ibid., 46, 109, 136, 213–15 ("gable"); "Travelling in America," *Blackwood's Edinburgh Magazine* 18 (October 1825): 429 ("muches"); Charles Wolley, *A Two Years' Journal in New York* (1701; repr., Cleveland, 1902), 71 ("flying").

8. Goodfriend, *Before the Melting Pot,* 94, 104, 106, 189, 196.

9. Stuart Prall, *The Bloodless Revolution: England, 1688* (Garden City, N.Y., 1972), 3–89; Burrows and Wallace, *Gotham,* 94; Joyce Goodfriend, "The Limits of Religious Pluralism in Eighteenth-Century New York City," in *Amsterdam–New York: Transatlantic Relations and Urban Identities Since 1653,* ed. George Harinck and Hans Krabbendam (Amsterdam, 2005), 67–86.

10. Prall, *Bloodless Revolution,* 89–277.

11. Thomas Archdeacon, *New York City, 1664–1710: Conquest and Change* (Ithaca, 1976), 105–7; Samuel Crompton, "Dongan, Thomas," in *American National Biography Online* (New York, 2000); Michael Hall, Lawrence Leder, and Michael Kammen, eds., *The Glorious Revolution in America: Documents on the Colonial Crisis of 1689* (Chapel Hill, 1964), 99–100, 109 (quotation), 111.

12. Bernard Bailyn, *The Barbarous Years: The Peopling of British North America; The Con-*

flict of Civilizations, 1600–1675 (New York, 2012), 266; David Voorhees, "The 'Fervent Zeale' of Jacob Leisler," *William and Mary Quarterly,* 3rd ser., 51 (1994): 447–55; David Voorhees, "Leisler's Pre-1689 Biography and Family Background," in *A Beautiful and Fruitful Place: Selected Rensselaerwijck Papers,* ed. Elisabeth Funk and Martha Shattuck, vol. 2 (Albany, 2011), 47–54.

13. Voorhees, "Fervent Zeale," 455–59.

14. Ibid., 449, 465–67 (quotations); Goodfriend, *Before the Melting Pot,* 47–50; Joyce Goodfriend, "The Huguenots in Colonial New York City: A Demographic Profile," in *Memory and Identity: Minority Survival Among the Huguenots in France and the Atlantic Diaspora,* ed. Bertrand Van Ruymbeke and Randy Sparks (Columbia, S.C., 2003), 241–54; David Voorhees, "Jacob Leisler and the Huguenot Network in the English Atlantic World," in *From Strangers to Citizens: The Integration of Immigrant Communities in Britain, Ireland and Colonial America, 1550–1750,* ed. Randolph Vigne and Charles Littleton (Brighton, UK, 2001), 323–25; Neil Kamil, *Fortress of the Soul: Violence, Metaphysics, and Material Life in the Huguenots' New World, 1517–1751* (Baltimore, 2005), 803.

15. New York Militia to William and Mary, June 1689, and Leisler to William and Mary, in *Documents Relative to the Colonial History of the State of New-York, Procured in Holland, England and France,* ed. E. B. O'Callaghan, 11 vols. (Albany, 1853–1861), 3:584, 615; Randall Balmer, "Traitors and Papists: The Religious Dimensions of Leisler's Rebellion," *New York History* 70 (1989): 353; John Murrin, "English Rights as Ethnic Aggression: The English Conquest, the Charter of Liberties of 1683, and Leisler's Rebellion in New York," in *Authority and Resistance in Early New York,* ed. William Pencak and Conrad Wright (New York, 1988), 56–94.

16. Leisler to Major Nathan Gold, June 2 [12?], 1689, in *The Documentary History of the State of New-York,* ed. E. B. O'Callaghan, 4 vols. (Albany, 1849–1851), 2:14 ("raigns"); Hall, Leder, and Kammen, *Glorious Revolution,* 109, 111; Archdeacon, *New York City,* 112; Burrows and Wallace, *Gotham,* 97; Voorhees, "Fervent Zeale," 471–72 ("Germanian"); William III to Nicholson, July 30, 1689, in *Ecclesiastical Records, State of New York,* ed. Hugh Hastings, 7 vols. (Albany, 1901), 2:970.

17. Burrows and Wallace, *Gotham,* 98 (quotations); Archdeacon, *New York City,* 112–17; Balmer, "Traitors and Papists," 353.

18. Burrows and Wallace, *Gotham,* 99 (all but final quotation); Archdeacon, *New York City,* 116–19; David Lovejoy, *The Glorious Revolution in America* (New York, 1972), 274–75 (final quotation).

19. O'Callaghan, *Documentary History,* 2:345 (quotation); Archdeacon, *New York City,* 119–20; Adelaide Skeel and David Barclay, "Major Patrick MacGregorie," *Historical Papers* (Historical Society of Newburgh Bay and the Highlands) 7 (1900): 61.

20. Archdeacon, *New York City,* 120–21 (quotation); Hall, Leder, and Kammen, *Glorious Revolution,* 115–16.

21. O'Callaghan, *Documentary History,* 2:379 ("for King"); Reverend Samuel Miller quoted in William Dunlap, *History of the New Netherlands, Province of New York, and State of New York,* 2 vols. (New York, 1839–40), 1:209 ("martyr").

22. Hall, Leder, and Kammen, *Glorious Revolution,* 120–21; Burrows and Wallace, *Gotham,* 112; Balmer, "Traitors and Papists," 362, 367.

3. Anglicization

1. Padraig Lenihan, *Consolidating Conquest: Ireland, 1603–1727* (New York, 2008), 23–86; Edwin Burrows and Mike Wallace, *Gotham: A History of New York City to 1898* (New York, 1999), 102; William Berrian, *An Historical Sketch of Trinity Church, New York* (New York, 1847), 11–14; Joyce Goodfriend, *Before the Melting Pot: Society and Culture in Colonial New York City, 1664–1730* (Princeton, 1992), 56, 84, 187 (weights and measures), 190 (schools); Joyce Goodfriend, "The Limits of Religious Pluralism in Eighteenth-Century New York City," in *Amsterdam–New York: Transatlantic Relations and Urban Identities Since 1653,* ed. George Harinck and Hans Krabbendam (Amsterdam, 2005), 67–86; David Narrett, "From Mutual Will to Male Prerogative: The Dutch Family and Anglicization in Colonial New York," in *A Beautiful and Fruitful Place: Selected Rensselaerwijck Papers,* ed. Elisabeth Funk and Martha Shattuck, vol. 2 (Albany, 2011), 83–87; Marilyn F. Symmes, *Impressions of New York: Prints from the New-York Historical Society* (New York, 2005), 28–29.

2. *Collections of the New-York Historical Society for the Year 1909* (New York, 1910), 119, 190 (Crudge); Goodfriend, *Before the Melting Pot,* 137–39 (other quotations).

3. Goodfriend, *Before the Melting Pot,* 55–56, 135, 137–38.

4. Ibid., 58, 138; Bernard Bailyn, *Voyagers to the West: A Passage in the Peopling of America on the Eve of the Revolution* (New York, 1986), 271–85.

5. Goodfriend, *Before the Melting Pot,* 59, 142–44 ("indigent"); Joyce Goodfriend, "A New Look at Presbyterian Origins in New York City," *American Presbyterians* 67 (Fall 1989): 199–207; Burrows and Wallace, *Gotham,* 132; Stephen M. Millett, *The Scottish Settlers of America: The Seventeenth and Eighteenth Centuries* (Columbus, Ohio, 1996), 183–86; Ned Landsman, *Scotland and Its First American Colony, 1683–1765* (Princeton, 1985), 214–15; Mary Lou Lustig, *Robert Hunter, 1666–1734: New York's Augustan Statesman* (Syracuse, 1983), 144–45 ("majority").

6. Burrows and Wallace, *Gotham,* 130–31; Goodfriend, *Before the Melting Pot,* 145 (quotation), 148; Kerby Miller, *Emigrants and Exiles: Ireland and the Irish Exodus to North America* (New York, 1985), 137–54.

7. Goodfriend, *Before the Melting Pot,* 144–45, 148.

8. Jared Sparks, *The Works of Benjamin Franklin,* 10 vols. (Boston, 1840), 1:562; Miller, *Emigrants,* 139 (ballad); Burrows and Wallace, *Gotham,* 131; Goodfriend, *Before the Melting Pot,* 135, 148 (ads).

9. Goodfriend, *Before the Melting Pot,* 146 (quotation), 149; Ann Maury, *Memoirs of a Huguenot Family* (New York, 1872), 296, 298.

10. Goodfriend, *Before the Melting Pot,* 140–41; Burrows and Wallace, *Gotham,* 120–23.

11. Stuart Prall, *The Bloodless Revolution: England, 1688* (Garden City, N.Y., 1972), 281–83, 298–300; E. B. O'Callaghan, ed., *The Documentary History of the State of New-York,* 4 vols. (Albany, 1849–1851), 1:186 (Dongan).

12. Goodfriend, *Before the Melting Pot,* 46, 84, 134–35, 151; Burrows and Wallace, *Gotham,* 104; instructions to Governor Hunter in *Documents Relative to the Colonial History of the State of New-York, Procured in Holland, England and France,* ed. E. B. O'Callaghan, 11 vols. (Albany, 1853–1861), 5:132 (quotation).

13. Burrows and Wallace, *Gotham*, 104–5, 115, 133–35; Goodfriend, *Before the Melting Pot*, 207.

14. Wayne Andrews, ed., "A Glance at New York in 1697: The Travel Diary of Dr. Benjamin Bullivant," *New-York Historical Society Quarterly* 40 (1956): 66; John Miller, *A Description of the Province and City of New York* (London, 1843), 14–15, 28; William Byrd to his brother Daniel, March 8, 1685, in *Virginia Historical Register and Literary Advertiser* 2 (1849): 208.

15. James Murray to Reverend Baptist Boyd, November 7, 1737, in *John Crimmins, Irish-American Historical Miscellany* (New York, 1905), 61–64.

16. Fletcher quoted in Simon Middleton, *From Privileges to Rights: Work and Politics in Colonial New York City* (Philadelphia, 2006), 135; William Smith, *The History of the Province of New-York, from the First Discovery to the Year 1732* (London, 1757), 211.

17. Goodfriend, *Before the Melting Pot*, 19, 156–57; Leigh Shaw-Taylor et al., "The Occupational Structure of England c. 1710 to c. 1871: Work in Progress," working paper of the University of Cambridge Geography Department's "Occupational Structure of Britain" project, 2010.

18. Goodfriend, *Before the Melting Pot*, 65–67, 156–57, 169.

19. Nan Rothschild, *New York City Neighborhoods: The 18th Century* (San Diego, 1990), 95–96; Bruce Wilkenfeld, "New York City Neighborhoods, 1730," *New York History* 57 (1976): 180; Goodfriend, *Before the Melting Pot*, 151; Burrows and Wallace, *Gotham*, 134–35.

20. Goodfriend, *Before the Melting Pot*, 77–78, 155, 198–99 (quotations), 204–5; Burrows and Wallace, *Gotham*, 135–36.

21. Ira Rosenwaike, *Population History of New York City* (Syracuse, 1972), 8, 14; Gary Nash, "The New York Census of 1737: A Critical Note on the Integration of Statistical and Literary Sources," *William and Mary Quarterly*, 3rd ser., 36 (1979): 428–35; Goodfriend, *Before the Melting Pot*, 134; Bailyn, *Voyagers to the West*, 25–62, 99.

22. Goodfriend, *Before the Melting Pot*, 133–34; I. N. Phelps Stokes, *The Iconography of Manhattan Island, 1498–1909*, 6 vols. (New York, 1915–1928), 4:435–37.

23. Burrows and Wallace, *Gotham*, 151 ("many children"); Goodfriend, *Before the Melting Pot*, 53, 153–54 (other quotations).

24. William Andrews, *The Bradford Map* (New York, 1893), 19, 27–39; William Andrews, *James Lyne's Survey* (New York, 1900), 3–13; "James Lyne's Survey," *Times*, September 1, 1900, book review sec., 14; Burrows and Wallace, *Gotham*, 109–10 (quotation).

25. Burrows and Wallace, *Gotham*, 110–11; for Hurricane Sandy flooding, see http://www.nytimes.com/newsgraphics/2012/1120-sandy/survey-of-the-flooding-in-new-york-after-the-hurricane.html. For the original shoreline and wetlands of Manhattan, I consulted Egbert Viele, *Sanitary & Topographical Map of the City and Island of New York* (New York, 1865); and Eric Sanderson, *Mannahatta: A Natural History of New York City* (New York, 2009), 84–85, 97.

26. Charles E. Clark, "William Bradford," in *American National Biography Online* (New York, 2000).

27. Henry Jones Jr., *The Palatine Families of New York: A Study of the German Immigrants Who Arrived in Colonial New York in 1710*, 2 vols. (Universal City, Calif., 1985), 2:1124;

Burrows and Wallace, *Gotham*, 129–30; Philip Otterness, *Becoming German: The 1709 Palatine Migration to New York* (Ithaca, 2004), 9–41; John Lynn, *The Wars of Louis XIV, 1667–1714* (New York, 1999), 197, 293–94 ("desolation"), 339.

28. Otterness, *Becoming German*, 78–84, 89–112, 137, 204; Charles Clark, "John Peter Zenger," in *American National Biography Online*.

29. Jones, *Palatine Families*, 2:1124; Clark, "Zenger"; Lewis Morris Jr. to the Lords of Trade, July 19, 1729, in O'Callaghan, *Documents Relative to the Colonial History of the State of New-York*, 5:887 (quotation); Robert Cray, "William Cosby," in *American National Biography Online*; Stanley Katz, *Newcastle's New York: Anglo-American Politics, 1732–1753* (Cambridge, Mass., 1968), 61–68; Eugene Sheridan, *Lewis Morris, 1671–1746: A Study in Early American Politics* (Syracuse, 1981), 148–52.

30. Morris to the Lords of Trade, December 15, 1733, in *The Papers of Lewis Morris*, ed. Eugene Sheridan, 3 vols. (Newark, 1991–1993), 2:73; Clark, "Zenger"; Cray, "Cosby"; Thomas L. Purvis, "James Alexander," in *American National Biography Online*.

31. "Goshen, August 21, 1734," *New-York Weekly Journal*, October 7, 1734, 1.

32. Katz, *Newcastle's New York*, 80–81; Gary Nash, *The Urban Crucible: Social Change, Political Consciousness, and the Origins of the American Revolution* (Cambridge, Mass., 1979), 143 (quotations).

33. William Putnam, *John Peter Zenger and the Fundamental Freedom* (Jefferson, N.C., 1997), 60–61, 68, 74–75, 79 (quotations); Clark, "Zenger."

34. Putnam, *Zenger*, 65, 82–84.

35. Ibid., 85–89; *The Trial of John Peter Zenger* (London, 1765), 13–14 (quotation).

36. *Trial of John Peter Zenger*, 14, 28, 43–44, 46–48.

37. William Dunlap, *History of the New Netherlands, Province of New York, and State of New York*, 2 vols. (New York, 1839), 1:302 (quotation); Paul Finkelman, ed., *A Brief Narrative of the Case and Tryal of John Peter Zenger, Printer of the* New York Weekly Journal (Boston, 2010), 31–40.

38. William Smith [Jr.], *The History of the Late Province of New-York, from Its Discovery, to the Appointment of Governor Colden, in 1762*, 2 vols. (New York, 1829), 2:38–39.

39. Jill Lepore, *New York Burning: Liberty, Slavery, and Conspiracy in Eighteenth-Century Manhattan* (New York, 2005), 40–50 ("rising," 49–50); Daniel Horsmanden, *The New York Conspiracy, or A History of the Negro Plot* (New York, 1810), 174–75 ("church-out"); Burrows and Wallace, *Gotham*, 163 (slave's complaint about not being able to spend nights with his wife); Graham Hodges, *Root and Branch: African Americans in New York and East Jersey, 1613–1863* (Chapel Hill, 1999), 65–68.

40. Lepore, *New York Burning*, 120, 176–82 ("master-piece"); Hodges, *Root and Branch*, 93–95; Horsmanden, *New York Conspiracy*, 313–18 ("popish plot," 314); Thelma Foote, *Black and White Manhattan: The History of Racial Formation in Colonial New York City* (New York, 2004), 132–39; *A List of White Persons Taken into Custody on Account of the Conspiracy, 1741*, broadside, New-York Historical Society.

41. *A List of Negroes Committed on Account of the Conspiracy*, broadside, New-York Historical Society; Lepore, *New York Burning*, xii, 108–10, 136–38, 192–97; Horsmanden, *New York Conspiracy*, 291, 313–18 (quotations).

42. Lepore, *New York Burning*, 202–4.

4. Americanization

1. Seymour Schwartz, *Cadwallader Colden: A Biography* (Amherst, N.Y., 2013), 9–21, 28–31; Mary Lou Lustig, *Robert Hunter, 1666–1734: New York's Augustan Statesman* (Syracuse, 1983), 146; Edwin Purple, *Genealogical Notes of the Colden Family in America* (New York, 1873), 12.

2. George Kubler, *Historical Treatises, Abstracts & Papers on Stereotyping* (New York, 1936), 159–69; Cadwallader Colden, *The History of the Five Indian Nations Depending on the Province of New-York in America* (New York, 1727); William Carter, "Anglicizing the League: The Writing of Cadwallader Colden's History of the Five Indian Nations," in *Anglicizing America: Empire, Revolution, Republic,* ed. Ignacio Gallup-Diaz, Andrew Shankman, and David Silverman (Philadelphia, 2015), 84; John Duffy, *The Sanitarians: A History of American Public Health* (Urbana, 1990), 21–22; Saul Jarcho, "Cadwallader Colden as a Student of Infectious Disease," *Bulletin of the History of Medicine* 29 (1955): 101–6; Brooke Hindle, *The Pursuit of Science in Revolutionary America, 1735–1789* (Chapel Hill, 1956), 38–48; Brooke Hindle, "Cadwallader Colden's Extension of Newtonian Principles," *William and Mary Quarterly,* 3rd ser., 13 (1956): 459–75; Roy Lokken, "Cadwallader Colden's Attempt to Advance Natural Philosophy Beyond the Eighteenth-Century Mechanistic Paradigm," *Proceedings of the American Philosophical Society* 122 (1978): 365–76; H. W. Rickett and Elizabeth Hall, eds., *Botanic Manuscript of Jane Colden, 1724–1766* (New York: 1963); Bonnie Shapiro, "Jane Colden," in *American National Biography Online* (New York, 2000); Asa Gray, *Selections from the Scientific Correspondence of Cadwallader Colden* (New Haven, 1843), 3–51; Alfred Hoermann, *Cadwallader Colden: A Figure of the American Enlightenment* (Westport, Conn., 2002), xii ("genius"); Raymond Stearns, *Science in the British Colonies of America* (Urbana, 1970): 559–75 ("next to Franklin," 559).

3. Colden to Mr. Jordan, March 26, 1717, in "The Letters and Papers of Cadwallader Colden," vol. 1, "1711–1729," in *Collections of the New-York Historical Society for the Year 1917* (New York, 1918), 39.

4. Livingston Rutherfurd, *John Peter Zenger: His Press, His Trial, and a Bibliography of Zenger Imprints* (New York, 1904), 6, 23, 29.

5. Schwartz, *Colden,* 127–56.

6. Thomas Carney and Susan Kolb, "The Legacy of 'Forsey v. Cunningham': Safeguarding the Integrity of the Right to Trial by Jury," *Historian* 69 (2007): 664–65.

7. Thomas Truxes, "Waddell Cunningham," in *Oxford Dictionary of National Biography,* online ed. (Oxford, January 2008); Thomas Truxes, ed., *Letterbook of Greg and Cunningham, 1756–57: Merchants of New York and Belfast* (New York, 2001), 43–45.

8. Thomas Truxes, *Defying Empire: Trading with the Enemy in Colonial New York* (New Haven, 2008), 9–18, 39–41, 43, 46, 48, 54, 156–71, 177; Truxes, *Letterbook,* 46–49, 50, 55, 88, 110 (quotations).

9. Herbert Johnson, "George Harison's Protest: New Light on Forsey versus Cunningham," *New York History* 50 (1969): 64; Carney and Kolb, "Forsey v. Cunningham," 665–88; Truxes, *Letterboook,* 12n, 51; *The Report of an Action of Assault, Battery, and Wound-*

ing, Tried in the Supreme Court of Judicature for the Province of New-York . . . Between Thomas Forsey, Plaintiff, and Waddel[l] Cunningham, Defendant (New York, 1764), 1–2.

10. Carney and Kolb, "Forsey v. Cunningham," 668–76, 678–79, 680–81, 685–86.

11. Ibid., 683–86.

12. F. Engelman, "Cadwallader Colden and the New York Stamp Act Riots," *William and Mary Quarterly*, 3rd ser., 10 (1953): 565–66 ("destroy"), 577; E. B. O'Callaghan, ed., *Documents Relative to the Colonial History of the State of New-York, Procured in Holland, England and France*, 11 vols. (Albany, 1853–1861), 7:761 (other quotations).

13. Robert Livingston to Robert Livingston, November 2, 1765, *American Monthly Magazine* 2 (January 1893): 63 ("every man"); Engelman, "Colden and the New York Stamp Act Riots," 561, 570–75 (all other quotations); Edmund Morgan and Helen Morgan, *The Stamp Act Crisis: Prologue to Revolution*, repr. ed. (Chapel Hill, 1995), 206; Richard Ketchum, *Divided Loyalties: How the American Revolution Came to New York* (New York, 2002), 138–42.

14. Engelman, "Colden and the New York Stamp Act Riots," 561, 576–78.

15. Ibid. (quotation, 577); Ketchum, *Divided Loyalties*, 146–48, 168–73, 209; Carney and Kolb, "Forsey v. Cunningham," 686–87.

16. Colden to H. S. Conway, March 28, 1766, in *Collections of the New-York Historical Society for the Year 1877* (New York, 1878), 107.

17. Ketchum, *Divided Loyalties*, 176–209; Colden to the Earl of Hillsborough, October 4, 1769, in O'Callaghan, *Documents Relative to the Colonial History of the State of New-York*, 8:189.

18. Joseph Tiedemann, *Reluctant Revolutionaries: New York City and the Road to Independence* (Ithaca, 1997), 115–16 ("dismal"); John Maunsell to Major Gates, May 15, 1767, in I. N. Phelps Stokes, *The Iconography of Manhattan Island, 1498–1909*, 6 vols. (1915–1928; repr., New York, 1967), 4:775 ("embarrassed"); Paul Nelson, "Sir Henry Moore," in *American National Biography Online* (New York, 2000); Ketchum, *Divided Loyalties*, 209 (other quotations); Truxes, *Letterbook*, 8.

19. Ketchum, *Divided Loyalties*, 209–11; O'Callaghan, *Documents Relative to the Colonial History of the State of New-York*, 8:189 (quotation).

20. Colden to Hillsborough, December 16, 1769, and January 6, 1770, Hillsborough to Colden, January 18 and February 17, 1770, in O'Callaghan, *Documents Relative to the Colonial History of the State of New-York*, 8:193–94, 198–202, 205–6.

21. William MacDougall, *American Revolutionary: A Biography of General Alexander McDougall* (Westport, Conn., 1977), 24–26, 159–63; Roger Champagne, *Alexander McDougall and the American Revolution in New York* (Schenectady, 1975), 18–20. I have modernized McDougall's idiosyncratic punctuation to make his meaning clear.

22. MacDougall, *American Revolutionary*, 25; Frank Moore, *Diary of the American Revolution from Newspapers and Original Documents*, 2 vols. (New York, 1860), 1:55–56.

23. MacDougall, *American Revolutionary*, 29; Champagne, *McDougall*, 20–22; Ketchum, *Divided Loyalties*, 219; Colden to Hillsborough, February 21, 1770, in O'Callaghan, *Documents Relative to the Colonial History of the State of New-York*, 8:208.

24. J. P. MacLean, *An Historical Account of the Settlements of Scotch Highlanders in Amer-*

ica Prior to the Peace of 1783 (Cleveland, 1900), 176–87 ("Mohocks," 181); Ian Graham, *Colonists from Scotland: Emigration to North America, 1707–1783* (1956; repr., Cleveland, 2006), 77–80; MacDougall, *American Revolutionary*, 3–4.

25. Colden to William Smith, January 15, 1759, in vol. 2 of William Dunlap, *History of the New Netherlands, Province of New York, and State of New York, to the Adoption of the Federal Constitution*, 2 vols. (New York, 1840), appendix, lvi–lvii (quotation); Graham, *Colonists from Scotland*, 77–80.

26. MacDougall, *American Revolutionary*, 10–12; Champagne, *McDougall*, 6–7.

27. MacDougall, *American Revolutionary*, 12–15 (quotation, 14); Champagne, *McDougall*, 7–8.

28. MacDougall, *American Revolutionary*, 15–21; Champagne, *McDougall*, 8–10; entry of November 12, 1767, Alexander McDougall Waste Book, McDougall Papers, New-York Historical Society ("wench"); James Thacher, *A Military Journal During the American Revolutionary War* (Boston, 1823), 388–89 (other quotations).

29. MacDougall, *American Revolutionary*, 15–21; Champagne, *McDougall*, 8–10.

30. "To the Betrayed Inhabitants of the City and Colony of New York," in *The Documentary History of the State of New-York*, ed. E. B. O'Callaghan, 4 vols. (Albany, 1849–1851), 3:317–21.

31. Tiedemann, *Reluctant Revolutionaries*, 144–47; Maud Goodwin et al., eds., *Historic New York, Being the Second Series of the Half Moon Papers* (New York, 1899), 268; Gustave Straubenmuller, *A Home Geography of New York City* (Boston, 1905), 173–74; Jesse Lemisch, *Jack Tar vs. John Bull: The Role of New York's Seamen in Precipitating the Revolution* (New York, 1997), 130–33.

32. Colden to the Earl of Hillsborough, February 21, 1770, in O'Callaghan, *Documents Relative to the Colonial History of the State of New-York*, 8:208 ("consist"); Franklin to McDougall, March 18, 1770, in MacDougall, *American Revolutionary*, 38; Ketchum, *Divided Loyalties*, 165 ("shaking").

33. Tiedemann, *Reluctant Revolutionaries*, 148–49 ("piece of wood"); Lemisch, *Jack Tar*, 136–40; letter from New York dated January 22, 1770, in *The London Magazine, or Gentleman's Monthly Intelligencer* 39 (March 1770): 166 (other quotations); Lee Boyer, "Lobster Backs, Liberty Boys, and Laborers in the Streets: New York's Golden Hill and Nassau Street Riots," *New York Historical Society Quarterly* 57 (1973): 281–308; Straubenmuller, *Home Geography*, 175; Colden to Hillsborough, February 21, 1770, in O'Callaghan, *Documents Relative to the Colonial History of the State of New-York*, 8:208.

34. Ketchum, *Divided Loyalties*, 229; MacDougall, *American Revolutionary*, 29 (quotations); Tiedemann, *Reluctant Revolutionaries*, 148–49.

35. MacDougall, *American Revolutionary*, 34 (quotations); John Miller, *Origins of the American Revolution* (1943; repr., Stanford, 1959), 305–6; Ketchum, *Divided Loyalties*, 220.

36. Ketchum, *Divided Loyalties*, 221–22 (quotation); Champagne, *McDougall*, 31–34 (quotation), 42, 230; MacDougall, *American Revolutionary*, 36–37.

37. Virginia Harrington, *The New York Merchant on the Eve of the Revolution* (1935; repr., Gloucester, Mass., 1964), 342–43.

5. Revolution

1. "Extract of a Letter," *New-York Journal,* April 21, 1774, 3; I. N. Phelps Stokes, *The Iconography of Manhattan Island, 1498–1909,* 6 vols. (1915–1928; repr., New York, 1967), 4:850; Paul Nelson, *William Tryon and the Course of Empire: A Life in British Imperial Service* (Chapel Hill, 1990), 117 (quotation).

2. Nelson, *William Tryon,* 118–22; Richard Ketchum, *Divided Loyalties: How the American Revolution Came to New York* (New York, 2002), 243–47.

3. "Extract of a Letter," *New-York Journal,* April 21, 1774, 3; Ketchum, *Divided Loyalties,* 247–51; Colden to the Earl of Dartmouth, September 7, 1774, in *Documents Relative to the Colonial History of the State of New-York, Procured in Holland, England and France,* ed. E. B. O'Callaghan, 11 vols. (Albany, 1853–1861), 8:488.

4. Kerby Miller, *Emigrants and Exiles: Ireland and the Irish Exodus to North America* (New York, 1985), 155; Bernard Bailyn, *Voyagers to the West: A Passage in the Peopling of America on the Eve of the Revolution* (New York, 1986), 98–103; Peter Lindert and Jeffrey Williamson, "American Inequality and Living Standards up to 1870," paper delivered at American Historical Association Meeting, Washington, D.C., January 2, 2014; Catherine Crary, "The Humble Immigrant and the American Dream: Some Case Histories," *Mississippi Valley Historical Review* 46 (1959): 46–66; David Doyle, *Ireland, Irishmen, and Revolutionary America, 1760–1820* (Dublin, 1981), 72–74; Aaron Fogleman, "Migrations to the Thirteen British North American Colonies, 1700–1775: New Estimates," *Journal of Interdisciplinary History* 22 (1992): 698; "London, June 2," *New-York Gazette,* August 21, 1775, 1; Edwin Burrows and Mike Wallace, *Gotham: A History of New York City to 1898* (New York, 1999), 194–95; Ira Rosenwaike, *Population History of New York City* (Syracuse, 1972), 8, 14.

5. Ron Chernow, *Alexander Hamilton* (New York, 2004), 10–22, 40 (quotations, 11, 20). Hamilton's date of birth is not certain. Some sources place it in January 1755, while in others it is said to be 1757. I found Chernow's reasoning for choosing the earlier year persuasive and have utilized that date in my sketch of Hamilton's early life.

6. Ibid., 17, 20–28 (quotations, 17, 20); Broadus Mitchell, *Alexander Hamilton: Youth to Maturity, 1755–1788* (New York, 1957), 12–20.

7. Mitchell, *Hamilton,* 20–26 (quotation); Chernow, *Hamilton,* 29–34.

8. Gertrude Atherton, ed., *A Few of Hamilton's Letters: Including His Description of the Great West Indian Hurricane of 1772* (New York, 1903), 261–67.

9. John C. Hamilton, *Life of Alexander Hamilton,* 2 vols. (New York, 1840), 1:7.

10. Chernow, *Hamilton,* 37–40, 46–50; Mitchell, *Hamilton,* 22, 34–35.

11. Chernow, *Hamilton,* 47, 54–55 (quotation); Roger Champagne, *Alexander McDougall and the American Revolution in New York* (Schenectady, 1975), 32.

12. *The Papers of Alexander Hamilton,* ed. Harold Syrett, 27 vols. (New York, 1961–1987), 1:45–78, 81–165 (quotation, 122).

13. Stokes, *Iconography,* 4:881–84 (quotation).

14. Champagne, *McDougall,* 91, 100; Chernow, *Hamilton,* 72.

15. Paul Nelson, "Charles Lee," in *American National Biography Online* (New York, 2000);

"Charles Lee," in *Appleton's Cyclopedia of American Biography*, ed. James Wilson and Charles Fiske, 7 vols., rev. ed. (New York, 1898–1900), 3:657–61; John Alden, *General Charles Lee: Traitor or Patriot?* (Baton Rouge, 1951), 40, 77–78, 169.

16. Alden, *Lee*, 98–102; Thomas Balch, ed., *Papers Relating Chiefly to the Maryland Line During the Revolution* (Philadelphia, 1857), 40 (quotation).

17. *The Remembrancer, or Impartial Repository of Public Events, Part II, for the Year 1776* (London, 1776), 85 (quotation); Peter Elting to Captain Richard Varick, July 30, 1776, in *New York City During the American Revolution* (New York, 1861), 103; Henry Onderdonk Jr., *Revolutionary Incidents of Suffolk and Kings Counties* (New York, 1849), 116.

18. Chernow, *Hamilton*, 78–84; Champagne, *McDougall*, 111–18; Schwartz, *Colden*, 156.

19. Doyle, *Ireland, Irishmen, and Revolutionary America*, 110 (first two quotations); "Extracts from the Letter-Book of Captain Johann Heinrichs of the Hessian Jäger Corps, 1778–1780," *Pennsylvania Magazine of History and Biography* 22 (1898): 137–39.

20. Maya Jasanoff, *Liberty's Exiles: American Loyalists in the Revolutionary World* (New York, 2011), 33; R. Vail, "The Loyalist Declaration of Dependence of November 28, 1776," *New-York Historical Society Quarterly* 31 (1947): 68–71; Philip Ranlet, *The New York Loyalists* (Knoxville, 1986), 113–17; Ruma Chopra, *Unnatural Rebellion: Loyalists in New York City During the Revolution* (Charlottesville, 2012), 66–67; Burrows and Wallace, *Gotham*, 220; E. Alfred Jones, "Letter of David Colden, Loyalist, 1783," *American Historical Review* 25 (1919): 79–86; Catherine Crary, "The Tory and the Spy: The Double Life of James Rivington," *William and Mary Quarterly*, 3rd ser., 19 (1959): 61–72; Alfred Lorenz, *Hugh Gaine: A Colonial Printer-Editor's Odyssey to Loyalism* (Carbondale, Ill., 1972), 1–130.

21. Benjamin Carp, "The Night the Yankees Burned Broadway: The New York City Fire of 1776," *Early American Studies* 4 (2006): 471–511; Laurens Schwartz, *Jews and the American Revolution: Haym Salomon and Others* (Jefferson, N.C., 1987), 5–12; Edgar McManus, "Haym Salomon," in *American National Biography Online*; Charles Russell, *Haym Salomon and the Revolution* (New York, 1930), 81–85.

22. Burrows and Wallace, *Gotham*, 242, 250; "Recollections of General [Jeremiah] Johnston, Part 2," *Journal of Long Island History* 13 (1976): 24 (quotations); Edwin Burrows, *Forgotten Patriots: The Untold Story of American Prisoners During the American Revolution* (New York, 2008), 12–14, 52–54, 62–64, 75–76, 107–11, 199, 203, 316.

23. Schwartz, *Jews*, 12–13, 25–27.

24. Carol Humphrey, "James Rivington," in *American National Biography Online* ("Judas"); *Papers of Hamilton*, 1:176 ("detestable"); Chopra, *Unnatural Rebellion*, 41–42.

25. McManus, "Salomon"; Russell, *Salomon*, 86–108, 128–281; Schwartz, *Jews*, 33–92.

26. Thomas Wertenbaker, *Father Knickerbocker Rebels: New York City During the Revolution* (New York, 1948), 253 (quotation); Burrows and Wallace, *Gotham*, 245, 259; Jasanoff, *Liberty's Exiles*, 85–93.

27. Crary, "Rivington," 61–62 (quotation), 69–71; Chopra, *Unnatural Rebellion*, 221.

28. Lorenz, *Gaine*, 134–35; Paul Nelson, "Cadwallader David Colden," and Steven Bullock, "Cadwallader Colden II," in *American National Biography Online*; Judith Van Buskirk,

Generous Enemies: Patriots and Loyalists in Revolutionary New York (Philadelphia, 2002), 183–95.

29. Chernow, *Hamilton*, 168–290.

6. Republic

1. *Genealogical Record of the Saint Nicholas Society of the City of New York* (New York, 1905), passim, http://www.saintnicholassociety.org/history.htm.

2. William Duer, *New York as It Was, During the Latter Part of the Last Century* (New York, 1849), 3 (quotation); Craig Hanyan, "William Alexander Duer," in *American National Biography Online* (New York, 2000).

3. Duer, *New York as It Was*, 6–8 (quotations); Benjamin Carp, "The Night the Yankees Burned Broadway: The New York City Fire of 1776," *Early American Studies* 4 (2006): 477.

4. Jonathan Bean, "William Duer," in *American National Biography Online*; Robert Jones, *"The King of the Alley": William Duer, Politician, Entrepreneur, and Speculator, 1768–1799* (Philadelphia, 1992), 1–2 (quotation).

5. Duer, *New York as It Was*, 12 (quotations); Eric Homberger, *The Historical Atlas of New York City*, rev. ed. (New York, 2005), 50 (palisade); ship types and ports of origin taken from "Bradford's Marine List," which appeared in almost every issue of the *New-York Journal and State Gazette* in 1784.

6. Duer, *New York as It Was*, 11–15 (quotations); Robert Augustyn, *Manhattan in Maps, 1527–1995* (New York, 1997), 83.

7. We do not know the precise population of New York City in 1783, but it was estimated to be 23,000 in 1786, and was surely significantly lower than that when the British evacuated along with nearly all of their loyalist supporters in November 1783. Ira Rosenwaike, *Population History of New York City* (Syracuse, 1972), 16–19.

8. Kerby Miller, *Emigrants and Exiles: Ireland and the Irish Exodus to North America* (New York, 1985), 169; Mary Black, *New York City's Gracie Mansion: A History of the Mayor's House* (New York, 1984), 18–47; Ellen Stern, *Gracie Mansion: A Celebration of New York City's Mayoral Residence* (New York, 2005), 16–26.

9. Peter Kenny et al., *Duncan Phyfe: Master Cabinetmaker in New York* (New York, 2011), 23–36 ("rage"); Walter Dyer, "Duncan Phyfe Furniture," *House Beautiful* 37 (March 1915): 120–21 (other quotations).

10. Kenneth Porter, *John Jacob Astor, Business Man*, 2 vols. (1931; repr., New York, 1966), 1:3–6; Alexander Emmerich, *John Jacob Astor and the First Great American Fortune* (Jefferson, N.C., 2013), 19–21.

11. Porter, *Astor*, 1:6–10; Emmerich, *Astor*, 21–27.

12. Porter, *Astor*, 1:10–12, 351–52; Emmerich, *Astor*, 33–37.

13. Emmerich, *Astor*, 37–49; "Jacob Astor," *New-York Packet*, May 22, 1786, 3 (quotation).

14. Porter, *Astor*, 1:27–38 (quotation, 31); Emmerich, *Astor*, 49–54.

15. Porter, *Astor*, 1:38–41, 129–243; John Haeger, *John Jacob Astor: Business and Finance in the Early Republic* (Detroit, 1991), 148 (quotation); Jones, *"King of the Alley,"* 175–78, 185–207.

16. Porter, *Astor*, 1:75–109, 2:910–52, 1121 (quotation); Emmerich, *Astor*, 60–105; "The Wealthiest Americans Ever," *Times*, July 15, 2007.

17. Charles Carey Jr., "William Colgate," in *American National Biography Online*; Shields Hardin, *The Colgate Story* (New York, 1959), 19–30, 47–62; W. W. Everts, *William Colgate: The Christian Layman* (Philadelphia, 1881), 57–71.

18. Miller, *Emigrants and Exiles*, 170, 172.

19. Kerby Miller et al., eds., *Irish Immigrants in the Land of Canaan: Letters and Memoirs from Colonial and Revolutionary America, 1675–1815* (New York, 2003), 418; Leo Ryan, *Old St. Peter's: The Mother Church of Catholic New York (1785–1935)* (New York, 1935), 36–57.

20. Miller, *Emigrants and Exiles*, 181, 187.

21. Donald Roper, "Thomas Addis Emmet," in *American National Biography Online* (quotation); David Wilson, *United Irishmen, United States: Immigrant Radicals in the Early Republic* (Ithaca, 1998), 1–2, 29–31; Miller, *Irish Immigrants*, 608–11.

22. *The Public Statutes at Large of the United States of America*, 18 vols. (Boston, 1845–1878), 1:566–69, 570–72 ("dangerous"), 596–97 (other quotations); Wilson, *United Irishmen*, 48 ("wild"); John Miller, *Crisis in Freedom: The Alien and Sedition Acts* (Boston, 1951), 97–102.

23. Roper, "Emmet"; King to Henry Jackson, August 23, 1799, and Emmet to King, April 9, 1807, in William MacNeven, *Pieces of Irish History* (New York, 1807), 235–48 ("malcontents," 237); Emil J. Hafner, "William James MacNeven," and Michael Durey, "William Sampson," in *American National Biography Online*; Victor Greene, *American Immigrant Leaders, 1800–1910: Marginality and Identity* (Baltimore, 1987), 25–27; Miller, *Irish Immigrants*, 611–18.

24. G. Edward White, *The Marshall Court and Cultural Change, 1815–35* (New York, 1988), 204–14; Roper, "Emmet"; Hafner, "MacNeven"; Miller, *Irish Immigrants*, 618–19.

25. Bernard M'Kenna to Father Henry Conwell, September 15, 1811, in Miller, *Irish Immigrants*, 419–24.

26. Miller, *Emigrants and Exiles*, 169, 177.

27. See http://www.census.gov/population/www/documentation/twps0027/tab05.txt; and Emmet and MacNeven's tract *Emigration to America: Hints to Emigrants from Europe* (London, 1817), 28 (number of immigrants and proportion that were Irish).

28. Timothy Dwight, *Travels in New-England and New-York*, 4 vols. (New Haven, 1822), 3:469 ("Swedes"); [James Fenimore Cooper], *Notions of the Americans*, new ed., 2 vols. (Philadelphia, 1835), 1:135–36 ("christendom"); Francis Lieber, *The Stranger in America, or Letters to a Gentleman in Germany* (Philadelphia, 1835), 127; Rosenwaike, *Population*, 35, 39, 42, 50–51, 65, 163.

29. Miller, *Emigrants and Exiles*, 194–96; House of Commons, *Poor Inquiry* (Ireland), *Appendix F, Containing Baronial Examinations Relative to Con Acre Quarter or Score Ground, Small Tenantry, Consolidation of Farms and Dislodged Tenantry, Emigration* (London, 1836), 134 (fare); Aristide Zolberg, *A Nation by Design: Immigration Policy in the Fashioning of America* (New York, 2006), 110–13; *Public Statutes at Large*, 3:488–89; H. J. M. Johnston, *British Emigration Policy, 1815–1830: "Shovelling Out Paupers"* (Oxford, 1972), 25–26.

30. For the impact of the Canadian legislation of 1847, see Colonial Land and Emigration

Commission, *Twelfth General Report of the Colonial Land and Emigration Commissioners, 1852* (London, 1852), 13–14; Jonathan Keljik, "Canadians' Consternation: Irish Immigration, Competition, and Canada's Relationship to the United States and the British Empire in the 1840s," *49th Parallel: An Interdisciplinary Journal of North American Studies* 27 (Winter 2012): 9–11 (e-journal available at http://www.49thparallel.bham .ac.uk/back/issue27/Keljik.pdf).

31. Susan B. Carter et al., eds., *Historical Statistics of the United States*, 2 vols. (New York, 2006), 1:560; Miller, *Emigrants and Exiles*, 198, 271; Tyler Anbinder, *Five Points: The Nineteenth-Century New York City Neighborhood That Invented Tap Dance, Stole Elections, and Became the World's Most Notorious Slum* (New York, 2001), 44–45.

32. Miller, *Irish Immigrants*, 636.

33. Ibid., 608; Roper, "Emmet"; Hafner, "MacNeven"; Richard Purcell, "The Irish Emigrant Society of New York," *Studies: An Irish Quarterly Review* 27 (1938): 583–99; I. N. Phelps Stokes, *The Iconography of Manhattan Island, 1498–1909*, 6 vols. (New York, 1915–1928), 5:1596; Emmet and MacNeven, *Emigration to America*, 8–9.

34. Thomas Addis Emmet to Jane Emmet, March 2, 1818, Whitlock Family Papers, New-York Historical Society, reproduced at http://blog.nyhistory.org/however-be-you -scotch-or-irish-thomas-addis-emmets-letter-to-his-daughter-jane/.

35. Ronald Bayor and Timothy Meagher, eds., *The New York Irish* (Baltimore, 1996), 23; Robert Ernst, *Immigrant Life in New York City, 1825–1863* (1949; repr., Syracuse, 1994), 302–3; Stokes, *Iconography*, 5:1590; Diane Haberstroh and Laura DeGrazia, eds., *Voices of the Irish Immigrant: Information Wanted Ads in "The Truth Teller," New York City, 1825–1844* (New York, 2005).

36. Elizabeth Blackmar, *Manhattan for Rent, 1785–1850* (Ithaca, 1990), 103–4, 169, 177–79, 243; Anbinder, *Five Points*, 15–18; John H. Griscom, *The Sanitary Condition of the Laboring Population of New York* (New York, 1845), 6–11.

37. Anbinder, *Five Points*, 19–20.

38. "For the New York Evening Post," *Evening Post*, September 21, 1826, 2; "The Five Points," *Sun*, May 27, 1834, 2 ("afternoon"); "A Visit to the Five Points," *Sun*, May 29, 1834, 2 ("wretchedness").

39. John Palmer, *Journal of Travels in the United States of North America and in Lower Canada, Performed in the Year 1817* (London, 1818), 6; C. H. Wilson, *The Wanderer in America* (Thirsk, UK, 1822), 18–19; Stokes, *Iconography*, 5:1597, 1649 (quotation); Charles Dickens, *American Notes* (1842; repr., London, 1985), 78–79; Paul Gilje, *The Road to Mobocracy: Popular Disorder in New York City, 1763–1834* (Chapel Hill, 1988), 228–32; "The Croton Water and the Streets," *Tribune*, September 17, 1842, 2; Catherine McNeur, *Taming Manhattan: Environmental Battles in the Antebellum City* (Cambridge, Mass., 2014), 23–41; "Mayor's Office, 10 a.m.," *Evening Post*, May 17, 1849, 2; "The Great War on the New York Piggeries," *Frank Leslie's Illustrated Newspaper* (August 13, 1859): 159.

40. Tyler Anbinder, "From Famine to Five Points: Lord Lansdowne's Irish Tenants Encounter North America's Most Notorious Slum," *American Historical Review* 107 (2002): 381–85.

41. "A Few Weeks in New York by a Returned Emigrant," *New Monthly Magazine and Lit-*

erary Journal 48, pt. 3 ([September] 1836): 358–59 (quotations); "No Irish Need Apply," *Herald*, July 12, 1830, 2; Rebecca Fried, "No Irish Need Deny: Evidence for the Historicity of NINA Restrictions in Advertisements and Signs," *Journal of Social History* 49 (Summer 2016), http://jsh.oxfordjournals.org/content/early/2015/07/03/jsh.shv066.full .pdf?keytype=ref&ijkey=F7EKls4zO9IUtsl ("advance access" version).

42. Gilje, *Road to Mobocracy,* 129–37.

43. Anbinder, *Five Points,* 27–29; "There Are Rumors of Bloody Wars in the Sixth Ward," *Evening Post,* April 9, 1834, 2 (*"damned Irishmen"*); Allan Nevins, ed., *The Diary of Philip Hone, 1828–1851* (New York, 1936), 123 ("barbarity"); Gilje, *Road to Mobocracy,* 140–41.

44. Anbinder, *Five Points,* 29–31; "The O'Connell Guards," *Courier and Enquirer,* quoted in *Evening Post,* June 25, 1835, 2; "A Riot," *Sun,* June 22, 1835, 2.

45. Leo Hershkowitz, "The Native American Democratic Association in New York City, 1835–1836," *New-York Historical Society Quarterly* 46 (1962): 41–59; Louis Scisco, *Political Nativism in New York State* (New York, 1901), 26–29 (quotation); Tyler Anbinder, *Nativism and Slavery: The Northern Know Nothings and the Politics of the 1850s* (New York, 1992), 10.

46. *Historical Statistics of the United States,* 1:560; William Adams, *Ireland and the Irish Emigration to the New World: From 1815 to the Famine* (1932; repr., Baltimore, 1980), 158–60, 203–6.

47. Rosenwaike, *Population,* 16–19, 39–42; *Census of the State of New-York for 1845* (Albany, 1846), charts 29–1 to 29–5.

7. Famine

1. Kerby Miller, *Emigrants and Exiles: Ireland and the Irish Exodus to North America* (New York, 1985), 281 (quotations); George Nichols, *A History of the Irish Poor Law* (London, 1856), 310–11.

2. "The Scarcity," *British Magazine and Monthly Register of Religious and Ecclesiastical Information* 31 (January 1, 1847): 108 ("demoniac"); John Mitchel, *The Crusade of the Period: And the Last Conquest of Ireland (Perhaps)* (New York, 1878), 247.

3. Diary of Archdeacon John O'Sullivan of Kenmare, quoted in Tyler Anbinder, *Five Points: The Nineteenth-Century New York City Neighborhood That Invented Tap Dance, Stole Elections, and Became the World's Most Notorious Slum* (New York, 2001), 56; House of Commons, "Correspondence from January to March 1847, Relating to the Measures Adopted for the Relief of Distress in Ireland. Board of Works Series [Second Part]," Command Paper 797 (1847), 182 ("dozens").

4. Peter Gray, *The Irish Famine* (London, 1995), 48–69, 94; James Donnelly Jr., "'Irish Property Must Pay for Irish Poverty': British Public Opinion and the Great Irish Famine," in *"Fearful Realities": New Perspectives on the Famine,* ed. Chris Monash and Richard Hayes (Dublin, 1996), 60–76.

5. "Ireland," *Times* (London), April 9, 1844, 6, March 24, 1847, 6, and December 11, 1848, 6 (inability of the poorest Irish to emigrate); Gerard Moran, *Sending Out Ireland's Poor:*

Assisted Emigration to North America in the Nineteenth Century (Dublin, 2004), 36–58; Miller, *Emigrants and Exiles,* 296; "Condition and Care of Emigrants On Board Ship," *Times,* October 15, 1851, 4.

6. House of Commons, "Twelfth General Report of the Colonial Land and Emigration Commissioners," Command Paper 1499 (1852), 13–14; "Twelfth General Report," *Justice of the Peace and County, Borough, Poor Law Union, and Parish Law Recorder* 16 (July 3, 1852): 420; Michael and Mary Rush to "Dear Father and Mother," September 6, 1846, in *Irish University Press Series of British Parliamentary Papers,* "Colonies: Canada" series, 33 vols. (Shannon, 1969), 17:100–101 (quotations); Miller, *Emigrants and Exiles,* 298.

7. "The Flight of a Quarter of a Million Inhabitants," *Times* (London), December 26, 1848, 4.

8. Miller, *Emigrants and Exiles,* 291, 299 ("before long"); "Ireland," *Times* (London), March 22, 1850, 6; "Ireland," *Times* (London), March 11, 1851, 4 ("glowing"); "Ireland," *Times* (London), September 29, 1851, 1; Susan B. Carter et al., eds., *Historical Statistics of the United States,* 2 vols. (New York, 2006), 1:560; *Annual Reports of the Commissioners of Emigration of the State of New York, from the Organization of the Commission, May 5, 1847, to 1860* (New York, 1861), 288. For immigration to New York before 1847, one must consult *Passengers Arriving in the United States: Letter from the Secretary of State Transmitting Statements of the Number and Designation of Passengers Arriving in the United States,* 28th Cong., 2nd sess., House of Representatives, Doc. no. 13 (1844); *Passengers from Foreign Countries: Letter from the Secretary of State Transmitting Statements of the Number of Passengers who Arrived in the United States,* 29th Cong., 1st sess., House of Representatives, Doc. no. 216 (1846); *Passengers Arriving in the United States: Letter from the Secretary of State Transmitting Statements of the Number and Designation of Passengers Arriving in the United States,* 29th Cong., 2nd sess., House of Representatives, Doc. no. 98 (1847); *Passengers Arriving in the United States: Letter from the Secretary of State Transmitting Statements of the Number and Designation of Passengers Arriving in the United States,* 30th Cong., 1st sess., House of Representatives, Ex. Doc. no. 47 (1848).

9. Robert Hill, "From Famine to Fraud: The Truth About Ireland's Best-Selling Famine Diary," *Matrix* 38 (1992): 5–12.

10. "The Depopulation of Ireland," *Illustrated London News* 18 (May 10, 1851): 386–88; House of Commons, "Second Report from the Select Committee on Emigrant Ships, Together with the Proceedings of the Committee, Minutes of Evidence, Appendix and Index," Sessional Paper 349 (1854), vi–vii ("cattle"), 75, 92 (other quotations), 105, 108, 128, 158; Terry Coleman, *Passage to America: A History of Emigrants from Great Britain and Ireland to America in the Mid-Nineteenth Century* (1972; repr., London, 1992), 57, 72–77; David Hollett, *Passage to the New World: Packet Ships and the Irish Famine Emigrants, 1845–1851* (Abergavenny, 1995), 43–53; Friedrich Kapp, *Immigration and the Commissioners of Emigration of the State of New York* (New York, 1870), 61–84.

11. Coleman, *Passage to America,* 72–77, 88–90; Hollett, *Passage to the New World,* 76–98.

12. *Annual Reports of the Commissioners of Emigration of the State of New York,* 343; *Passengers Arriving in the United States: Letter from the Secretary of State,* Ex. Doc. no. 47

(1848); *Passengers Arriving in the United States: Letter of the Secretary of State Communicating the Number and Designation of Passengers Arriving in the United States,* 30th Cong., 2nd sess., House of Representatives, Ex. Doc. no. 10 (1848).

13. William Smith, *An Emigrant's Narrative, or A Voice from the Steerage* (New York, 1850), 6; Miller, *Emigrants and Exiles,* 254, 257, 260 (quotation); Coleman, *Passage to America,* 17–20; "The Tide of Emigration to the United States and to the Colonies," *Illustrated London News* 17 (July 6, 1850): 21–22; Martin Weitz to his father, brother, sister-in-law, and children, July 16, 1854, in Walter Kamphoefner, *News from the Land of Freedom: German Immigrants Write Home* (Ithaca, 1991), 339.

14. *Annual Reports of the Commissioners of Emigration of the State of New York,* 343; Coleman, *Passage to America,* 90, 139; Miller, *Emigrants and Exiles,* 257; Robert Albion, *Square-Riggers on Schedule: The New York Sailing Packets to England, France, and the Cotton Ports* (Princeton, 1938), 317–23.

15. John Raithby, ed., *The Statutes of the United Kingdom of Great Britain and Ireland,* 63 vols. (London, 1807–1869), 2:55–63 (1803 Passengers Act), 7:9–10 (1817 Passengers Act), 16:499–510 (1842 Passengers Act); *The Statutes of the United Kingdom of Great Britain and Ireland, 59 George III, 1819* (London, 1819), 663 (1819 Passengers Act); Thomas Granger et al., comps., *A Collection of Statutes Connected with the General Administration of the Law,* 3rd ed., 10 vols. (London, 1836), 9:306–11 (1835 Passengers Act); Lewis Hertslet, comp., *A Complete Collection of the Treaties and Conventions and Reciprocal Regulations at Present Subsisting Between Great Britain and Foreign Powers,* 31 vols. (London, 1840–1925), 8:277–83, 288–91 (1848 Passengers Act), 366–407 (1849 Passengers Act), 9:306–9 (1851 Passengers Act), 316, 350–81 (1852 Passengers Act), 10:348 (1855 Passengers Act).

16. "Second Report from the Select Committee on Emigrant Ships," 53; House of Commons, "First Report from the Select Committee on Emigrant Ships, with the Minutes of Evidence Taken Before Them," Command Paper 163 (1854), 57–59, 125; Edward Laxton, *The Famine Ships: The Irish Exodus to America* (New York, 1997), 116 (quotations).

17. "First Report from the Select Committee on Emigrant Ships," 22, 39, 124; "Second Report from the Select Committee on Emigrant Ships," viii, 81–82, 151, 154, 211; "A Steerage Emigrant's Journal from Bristol to New York," *Chambers's Edinburgh Journal,* new ser., 10 (October 21, 1848): 265; Stephen De Vere to T. F. Elliott, November 30, 1847, in House of Commons, "First Report from the Select Committee of the House of Lords, on Colonization from Ireland; Together with the Minutes of Evidence," Sessional Paper 415 (1848), 45; "Condition and Care of Emigrants On Board Ship," 4; Hertslet, *Complete Collection,* 9:361.

18. Mary McNeill, *Vere Foster* (Tuscaloosa, 1971), 13–27, 43–46, 60–100, 225–41; House of Commons, "Emigrant Ship 'Washington.' Copy of a Letter from Lord Hobart to the Colonial Land and Emigration Commissioners," Sessional Paper 198 (1851), 3–7 (quotation, 4); Coleman, *Passage to America,* 104.

19. Letter of Vere Foster, December 1, 1850, in "Emigrant Ship 'Washington,'" 2; Johann Bauer to his "parents & brothers and sisters," May 11, 1854, in Kamphoefner, *News from the Land of Freedom,* 153.

20. *OED Online* (New York, 2013), s.v. "steerage"; "Second Report from the Select Commit-

tee on Emigrant Ships," 93–94 (quotation); Coleman, *Passage to America,* 111–12; Miller, *Emigrants and Exiles,* 255, 258.

21. "First Report from the Select Committee on Emigrant Ships," 176; Miller, *Emigrants and Exiles,* 255; Coleman, *Passage to America,* 111–12 (quotation).

22. Hertslet, *Complete Collection,* 9:356–57.

23. Miller, *Emigrants and Exiles,* 259 (quotations); Coleman, *Passage to America,* 119–27; Angela Heck to "Dearest Relations," July 1, 1854, in Kamphoefner, *News from the Land of Freedom,* 371.

24. "Second Report from the Select Committee on Emigrant Ships," 53–55 (quotations); Coleman, *Passage to America,* 119–27.

25. Thomas Addis Emmet, *Incidents of My Life* (New York, 1911), 140 (quotation); Smith, *Emigrant's Narrative,* 19; John Heagerty, *Four Centuries of Medical History in Canada,* 2 vols. (Toronto, 1928), 1:121.

26. Sherwin Nuland, "Hate in the Time of Cholera," *New Republic* (May 26, 1997): 34; *Encyclopædia Britannica Online,* s.v. "typhus"; Heagerty, *Four Centuries,* 1:118–30 ("teeming," 121); Smith, *Emigrant's Narrative,* 18–30; Coleman, *Passage to America,* 128 ("dieing"), 151, 170–74; Miller, *Emigrants and Exiles,* 255, 292; Nickolaus Heck to "Dearest Relations," July 1, 1854, in Kamphoefner, *News from the Land of Freedom,* 373.

27. "Things in Ireland," *Tribune,* May 19, 1849, 1; "The Cholera," *Herald,* July 27, 1849, 2; Charles Rosenberg, *The Cholera Years: The United States in 1832, 1849, and 1866* (Chicago, 1962), 104–14; *The Diary of Philip Hone, 1828–1851,* ed. Allan Nevins (New York, 1936), 879, 881, 883–84; Robert Ernst, *Immigrant Life in New York City, 1825–1863* (1949; repr., Syracuse, 1994), 238.

28. Marguerite Corporaal, "Rites of Passage: The Coffin Ship as a Site of Immigrants' Identity Formation in Irish and Irish American Fiction, 1855–85," *Atlantic Studies* 8 (2011): 343–59; Raymond Cohn, "Mortality on Immigrant Voyages to New York, 1836–1853," *Journal of Economic History* 44 (1984): 297.

29. *Annual Reports of the Commissioners of Emigration of the State of New York,* 10; "First Report from the Select Committee on Emigrant Ships," 13, 19, 125; untitled editorial and "The Public Health," *Times* (London), September 17, 1847, 4–5 ("Black Hole"); De Vere to Elliott, November 30, 1847, in "First Report of the Select Committee on Colonization from Ireland," 45–50.

30. Coleman, *Passage to America,* 146–54; untitled editorial, *Times* (London), September 17, 1847, 4 (quotation); Miller, *Emigrants and Exiles,* 292; Hollett, *Passage to the New World,* 168–80.

31. Untitled editorial, *Times* (London), September 17, 1847, 4. Estimate of the proportion of New York's Irish immigrants who came to North America via Canada based on the "test books" of New York's Emigrant Savings Bank, held in the New York Public Library (and available on ancestry.com). The test books record the port arrival in North America for each depositor. Among the six thousand Irish-born depositors who opened accounts from 1850 to 1858 (the bank's first eight years of operation) and listed their arrival port, only 8 percent reported having landed at Canadian ports. See https://dataverse.harvard.edu/dataverse/anbinder.

32. Smith, *Emigrant's Narrative,* 23; Coleman, *Passage to America,* 169–70; Miller, *Emi-*

grants and Exiles, 262; Maria Diedrich, *Love Across Color Lines: Ottilie Assing and Frederick Douglass* (New York, 1999), 95–96 ("enchanting").

33. "Steerage Emigrant's Journal from Bristol to New York," 266 (first quotation); Smith, *Emigrant's Narrative,* 27; "The Quarantine Stations," *Harper's Weekly* (May 23, 1857): 324; *Annual Reports of the Commissioners of Emigration of the State of New York,* 9–10, 42–43, 58–59, 74, 134, 153; John Fahey, "James Irwin: Irish Emigrant Agent, New York City, 1846–1858," *New York History* 92 (2012): 228–31, 236–37. In the winter, when few Europeans emigrated, ships had few passengers, and contagious disease aboard these vessels was uncommon, ships did not typically stop to have their passengers examined by a doctor. See *Report of Select Committee Appointed by the Legislature of New-York to Examine into Frauds Upon Emigrants* (Albany, 1847), testimony, 42.

34. Miller, *Emigrants and Exiles,* 263 (Hogan); "Emigrants and Emigrant Life," *Harper's Weekly* (June 26, 1858): 405 ("scoundrels").

35. *Report of Select Committee Appointed by the Legislature of New-York to Examine into Frauds Upon Emigrants,* 2–3, and testimony, 8, 16–17, 29 (all but last quotation); An Act for the Protection of Emigrants Arriving in the State of New-York, chap. 219, *Laws of the State of New-York Passed at the Seventy-First Session of the Legislature* (Albany, 1848), 328–33; Vere Foster, *Work and Wages, or The Penny Emigrant's Guide to the United States and Canada,* 5th ed. (London, n.d.), 10 ("extortionate").

36. *Illustrated London News* (March 9, 1850): 166; Richard Purcell, "The Irish Emigrant Society of New York," *Studies: An Irish Quarterly Review* 27 (1938): 594–96; Ernst, *Immigrant Life,* 32–35; H. Wilson, comp., *Trow's New York City Directory for the Year Ending May 1, 1856* (New York, 1855), 420 and appendix, 48–49.

37. Packet line docking locations from *Trow's New York City Directory for the Year Ending May 1, 1856,* appendix, 31.

38. Coleman, *Passage to America,* 242–43; Ernst, *Immigrant Life,* 31; Bruce Seymour, *Lola Montez: A Life* (New Haven, 1996), 297.

39. "Castle Garden: How Emigrants Are Treated on Landing," *Times,* August 4, 1855, 1.

40. Ibid.; Ernst, *Immigrant Life,* 31–32; "Emigration — from First to Last — Scenes at Castle Garden," *Frank Leslie's Illustrated Newspaper* (January 20, 1866): 281; "Castle Garden Labor Exchange," *Harper's Weekly* (August 15, 1868): 516, 518.

41. "Castle Garden: How Emigrants Are Treated on Landing," 1.

8. Irish Metropolis

1. Kerby Miller, *Emigrants and Exiles: Ireland and the Irish Exodus to North America* (New York, 1985), 295–97, 580.

2. "Factious First Warders," *Herald,* June 24, 1876, 3 (quotation). Irish proportion of the New York population in 1860 is based on ancestry.com's transcription of the 1860 manuscript census. See "All New York City Residents, 1860 Census" at https://dataverse .harvard.edu/dataverse/anbinder.

3. Location of Irish enclaves based on the residence of depositors who opened the first eighteen thousand accounts at New York's Emigrant Savings Bank (available at https:// dataverse.harvard.edu/dataverse/anbinder), supplemented with John Ridge, "Irish

County Colonies in New York City (Part I)," *New York Irish History* 25 (2011): 58–68, and "Irish County Colonies in New York City (Part II)," *New York Irish History* 26 (2012): 47–55.

4. "How New-Yorkers Live," *Times*, June 20, 1859, 8; [George G. Foster], *New York in Slices: By an Experienced Carver* (New York, 1849), 23 ("rubbish-heap"); *Report of the Select Committee Appointed to Investigate the Health Department of the City of New York* (Albany, 1859), 13–14; John H. Griscom, *The Sanitary Condition of the Laboring Population of New York* (1845; repr., New York, 1970), 8 ("atmosphere").

5. "The Abodes of the Poor," *Times*, July 1, 1859, 2; "Dwellings for the Poor," *Morning Courier and New-York Enquirer*, January 13, 1847, 2; *The Eleventh Annual Report of the New York Association for Improving the Condition of the Poor* (New York, 1854), 23 ("worn out"); "Backgrounds of Civilization — Realities of the Five Points," *New York Illustrated News* (February 25, 1860): 232–33.

6. Districts 3–6, Ward Six, 1855 New York State census, Old Records Division, New York County Clerk's Office, available at familysearch.org (household size and building material for Five Points tenements); "All New York City Residents, 1860 Census" (Wards One and Four for household size); "Report of the Select Committee Appointed to Examine into the Condition of Tenant Houses in New-York and Brooklyn," in *Documents of the Assembly of the State of New-York*, 80th Session, 1857 (Albany, 1857), doc. 205, 17–18; Richard Plunz, *A History of Housing in New York City: Dwelling Type and Social Change in the American Metropolis* (New York, 1990), 13.

7. Tyler Anbinder, *Five Points: The Nineteenth-Century New York City Neighborhood That Invented Tap Dance, Stole Elections, and Became the World's Most Notorious Slum* (New York, 2001), 77–78.

8. "Tenement Houses in New-York," *Times*, March 28, 1856, 1 ("sluggish"); "Dwellings for the Poor," *Times*, April 7, 1856, 3 ("surprise"); "Our City's Condition," *Times*, June 12, 1865, 1 ("liquid ooze"); Griscom, *Sanitary Condition*, 7 ("plaster" and "smeared").

9. Owen Kildare, *My Mamie Rose: The Story of My Regeneration* (New York, 1903), 15; "Among the Tenement Houses During the Heated Term," *Harper's Weekly* 23 (August 9, 1879): 629; "Midsummer Nights Among City Tenements," *Harper's Weekly* 27 (June 30, 1883): 401, 410; "The Recent 'Hot Term,'" *Frank Leslie's Illustrated Newspaper* (August 12, 1882): 390 (quotations), 392–93.

10. Robert De Forest and Lawrence Veiller, eds., *The Tenement House Problem*, 2 vols. (1903; repr., New York, 1970), 1:390–94; Kildare, *My Mamie Rose*, 19.

11. "Condition of Tenant Houses in New-York and Brooklyn," 18–19 (quotation); *Report of the Select Committee Appointed to Investigate the Health Department*, 66, 111; Lawrence Veiller, "Back to Back Tenements," in De Forest and Veiller, *Tenement House Problem*, 1:293.

12. "How New-Yorkers Live," *Times*, June 20, 1859, 8 ("filthy"); "The Abodes of the Poor," *Times*, July 1, 1859, 2; "Night and Morning," *Times*, May 21, 1871, 8; Samuel Prime, *Life in New York* (New York, 1847), 179–80 ("battle"); "The Dens of Death," *Tribune*, June 5, 1850, 5–6; "The Dens of Death," *Tribune*, June 13, 1850, 1 ("Without air"); Griscom, *Sanitary Condition*, 10.

13. "Walks Among the New-York Poor," *Times*, April 19, 1853, 2; "Tenement Houses," *Times*,

March 14, 1856 ("filthy"), 2; "Tenant Houses," *Times*, March 31, 1856, 1; "Condition of the City," *Times*, June 2, 1857, 5 ("infected").

14. "A Large House," *Evening Post*, August 20, 1850, 2 ("praiseworthy" and "well worthy"); "New-York City; Legislative Committee on Tenement Houses," *Times*, March 17, 1856, 8 ("wretched-looking"); "Condition of the City," *Times*, June 2, 1857, 5 ("very filthy"); "The Citizens' Association," *Frank Leslie's Illustrated Newspaper* (July 1, 1865): 231–33 ("scores").

15. "New-York City; Legislative Committee on Tenement Houses," *Times*, March 17, 1856, 8 ("fetid vapor"); "Condition of the City," *Times*, June 2, 1857, 5 ("most sickening"); "The Abodes of the Poor," *Times*, July 1, 1859, 2; "A Nuisance Removed," *Times*, December 8, 1872, 4; "Tenement Life in New York," *Harper's Weekly* (March 29, 1879): 245 ("Divill"); "Extending the Charity," *Tribune*, January 12, 1894, 7; *Report of the Tenement House Committee as Authorized by Chapter 479 of the Laws of 1894* (Albany, 1895), 142–44.

16. "The Dens of Death," *Tribune*, June 5, 1850, 5–6; *Sixteenth Annual Report of the New York Association for the Improvement of the Condition of the Poor* (New York, 1859), 37; *Thirteenth Annual Report of the Children's Aid Society* (New York, 1866): 28; "Our City's Condition," *Times*, June 12, 1865, 1. The figures on inhabitants per apartment were derived by surveying the Perris insurance maps and New York City Department of Housing "block and lot" records to identify buildings most likely to have the neighborhood's standard two-room apartments, and then determining the number of residents by consulting the 1855 New York State manuscript census in conjunction with the city directories. For the most densely populated neighborhoods in the world today, I consulted "List of City Districts by Population Density," http://en.wikipedia.org/w/index.php?title=List_of_city_districts_by_population_density&oldid=652400162, and "Dharavi in Mumbai Is No Longer Asia's Largest Slum," *Times of India*, July 6, 2011.

17. I define "men" as males aged sixteen or older. All percentages rounded to the nearest whole number except those under 1, which are rounded to the nearest tenth of a percent. The occupational categories are made up of the following vocations: Professionals include physicians, clergymen, lawyers, and architects. Business owners include clothiers, dry goods dealers, food and liquor dealers, grocers, hotel and boardinghouse keepers, manufacturers, merchants, "proprietors," restaurateurs, and shopkeepers. Lower-status white-collar workers were overwhelmingly clerks, but this category also includes a few salesmen, government workers, actors, and teachers. The skilled worker category is composed of assayers, bakers, blacksmiths, bleachers, boilermakers, brass workers, brewers and distillers, bricklayers, burnishers, butchers, cabinetmakers, carpenters, carvers, caulkers, chandlers, coach and wagon makers, confectioners, coopers, coppersmiths, dyers, factory workers, furriers, glassmakers, glaziers, guilders, gunsmiths, hatters, ironworkers, jewelers, leather workers, locksmiths, masons, mechanics, musical instrument, oil, paint, and paper makers, painters, plasterers, plumbers, polishers, potters, precious metal workers, precision instrument makers, printers, refiners, roofers, sail makers and riggers, sawyers, shipbuilders, shoemakers, stonecutters, tailors, textile workers, tobacco workers, turners, upholsterers, varnishers, and weavers. Unskilled workers are defined as cartmen, chimney sweeps, hostlers and grooms, laborers, policemen (so classified because people from any occupational category took these jobs when

offered), porters, sailors, waiters, and watchmen. Finally, "other/difficult to classify" includes adult students, authors, drovers, expressmen, farmers, financiers, fishermen, florists, gamblers, gardeners, gentlemen, hunters, peddlers, ragpickers, railroad conductors, scavengers, speculators, superintendents, and undertakers. The data, in Excel format, is available as "1860 New York City 1% Census Sample," in "City of Dreams Replication Data" at https://dataverse.harvard.edu/dataverse/anbinder.

18. Anbinder, *Five Points*, 120; Miller, *Emigrants and Exiles*, 267 (quotation).

19. "The Anarchy of Labor," *Tribune*, July 9, 1845, 2; "Labor Movements," *Tribune*, May 8, 1850, 4; "Labor Movements," *Tribune*, May 13, 1850, 6; "The Laborers' Demand," *Tribune*, May 14, 1850, 4 ("energetic"); John Maguire, *The Irish in America* (London, 1868), 232–33 ("idleness"); Richard Stott, *Workers in the Metropolis: Class, Ethnicity, and Youth in Antebellum New York City* (Ithaca, 1990), 119; Anbinder, *Five Points*, 121; Robert Ernst, *Immigrant Life in New York City, 1825–1863* (1949; repr., Syracuse, 1994), 216 (nativity of laborers).

20. [James Blum], *Three Years Among the Working-Classes in the United States During the War* (London, 1865), 11 ("Hurry up"); John White, *Sketches from America* (London, 1870), 370; Stott, *Workers in the Metropolis*, 128, 131–32, 140; Miller, *Emigrants and Exiles*, 326.

21. Walter Kamphoefner et al., eds., *News from the Land of Freedom: German Immigrants Write Home* (Ithaca, 1993), 538 (quotation); test book entries for accounts 10266, 12129, 15694 (Tucker), 954, 8009, 49326 (Carson), 5414, 7915, 26724 (Coghlan), 7859, 14941, 22248 (Campbell), Emigrant Industrial Savings Bank Papers, New York Public Library, accessed via ancestry.com.

22. Vere Foster, *Work and Wages, or The Penny Emigrant's Guide to the United States* (London, n.d.), 3; *The Eighteenth Annual Report of the New York Association for Improving the Condition of the Poor* (New York, 1861), 21–23; "The Anarchy of Labor," *Tribune*, July 9, 1845, 2; Edith Abbott, "Wages of Unskilled Labor in the United States, 1850–1900," *Journal of Political Economy* 13 (June 1905): 363. My analysis of the trades in which the Irish were commonly employed comes from "1860 New York City 1% Census Sample" and Ernst, *Immigrant Life*, 214–17.

23. Accounts 1464, 5554, 11056 (Hughes) and 9439, 17313, 24550 (Ahern), Emigrant Bank Papers.

24. "The Street-Venders of New York," *Scribner's Monthly* 1 (December 1870): 115; Anbinder, *Five Points*, 119 ("Fresh"); Annie Polland and Daniel Soyer, *Emerging Metropolis: New York Jews in the Age of Immigration, 1840–1920* (New York, 2012), 23. Proportion of Donegal peddlers is from the Emigrant Savings Bank records. There were 245 distinct male Irish-born peddlers among the customers who opened the first eighteen thousand accounts at the bank, and of these, forty-six (19 percent) were born in Donegal. Donegal natives made up only 3 percent of the bank's Irish-born customers. My data on the sixteen thousand individuals who opened the bank's first eighteen thousand accounts can be found in Excel format at https://dataverse.harvard.edu/dataverse/anbinder.

25. *The Life and Adventures of Henry Smith, the Celebrated Razor Strop Man* (Boston, 1848), v–vi, 7–42; "Street-Venders of New York," 122–23.

26. Accounts 10919, 13701 (Torpey), 4072, 9137, 14324 (Healy), 2618, 2767, 7104 (Higgins), Emigrant Bank Papers.

27. Accounts 17126, 24549, 37904 (Deasey), 8154, 33955, 48908 (Sullivan), 11650, 36079, 42928 (Harrington), Emigrant Bank Papers.

28. G[eorge] G. Foster, *New York by Gas-Light* (New York, 1850), 60–61 (quotation); "Condition of Tenant Houses in New-York and Brooklyn," 25–26; *Monthly Record of the Five Points House of Industry* 1 (January 1858): 224–25; "The Background of Our Civilization — No. 3: At the Five Points," *New York Illustrated News* (February 25, 1860): 229, 232.

29. Stott, *Workers in the Metropolis*, 218–19; Matthew Breen, *Thirty Years of New York Politics Up-to-Date* (New York, 1899), 251–52, 255; Maguire, *Irish in America*, 287 (quotation); Charles Stelzle, *A Son of the Bowery: The Life Story of an East Side American* (New York, 1926), 47.

30. Edward Spann, *The New Metropolis: New York City, 1840–1857* (New York, 1981), 348 ("scarcely"); Charles Loring Brace, *The Dangerous Classes of New York and Twenty Years' Work Among Them* (New York, 1872), 64–65; Jon Kingsdale, "The 'Poor Man's Club': Social Functions of the Urban Working-Class Saloon," *American Quarterly* 25 (1973): 476–80; Madelon Powers, *Faces Along the Bar: Lore and Order in the Workingman's Saloon, 1870–1920* (Chicago, 1998), 11–206.

31. Stelzle, *Son of the Bowery*, 48; "Boss Government," *The Nation* (November 4, 1875): 288; Susan Curtis, *A Consuming Faith: The Social Gospel and Modern American Culture* (Baltimore, 1991), 254–56.

32. Edward Levine, *The Irish and Irish Politicians: A Study of Cultural and Social Alienation* (Notre Dame, 1966), 117; Breen, *Thirty Years*, 231–33, 251–55. For an example of an impoverished famine immigrant who managed to open a saloon before the start of the Civil War, see Tyler Anbinder, "Lord Palmerston and the Irish Famine Emigration," *Historical Journal* 44 (2001): 441–43. Number and proportion of Irish immigrant saloonkeepers is based on "1860 New York City 1% Census Sample."

33. According to the 1860 census, 35 percent of Irish-born women were employed, compared to 18 percent of other immigrant women and 16 percent of native-born women. See "1860 New York City 1% Census Sample."

34. Ibid.

35. Ibid. This chart includes the occupations of women aged sixteen or higher. The occupations making up each category are as follows: The servant category includes cooks, domestics, houseworkers, and servants. Needle trades include carpet sewer, dressmaker, fur seamstress, fur sewer, hoopskirt maker, milliner, seamstress, shirt cutter, tailor, tailoress, vest maker, and "works in carpet factory." The washing category includes ironer and washer. The business owner category includes boardinghouse proprietor, clothier, clothing store proprietor, fancy store operator, grocer, junk store proprietor, liquor dealer, porterhouse keeper, saloonkeeper, and storekeeper. Other/difficult to categorize includes crockery seller, dealer in soapstone, flower maker, fruit seller, glass peddler, huckster, market woman, nun, teacher, tobacco factory worker, and waitress.

36. Margaret Lynch-Brennan, *The Irish Bridget: Irish Immigrant Women in Domestic Service in America, 1840–1930* (Syracuse, 2009), 86, 99–100; "Gavazzi-ism: The Poor Irish

Servant Maids," *Irish-American*, May 28, 1853, 2 (including quotation from *Sun*); "'No Irish Need Apply,'" *Irish-American*, May 16, 1857, 2; "Wanted — A Cook, Washer and Ironer," *Herald*, May 13, 1853, 5; Ernst, *Immigrant Life*, 67; Howard Gitelman, "No Irish Need Apply: Patterns of and Response to Ethnic Discrimination in the Labor Market," *Labor History* 14 (1973): 56–68. Cf. Richard Jensen, "'No Irish Need Apply': A Myth of Victimization," *Journal of Social History* 36 (2002): 405–29; and Rebecca Fried, "No Irish Need Deny: Evidence for the Historicity of NINA Restrictions in Advertisements and Signs," *Journal of Social History* 49 (Summer 2016), http://jsh.oxfordjournals.org /content/early/2015/07/03/jsh.shv066.full.pdf?keytype=ref&ijkey=F7EKls4zO9IUtsl ("advance access" version).

37. "Labor in New-York: Its Circumstances, Conditions and Rewards," *Tribune*, November 6, 1845, 2 (quotation); Hasia Diner, *Erin's Daughters in America: Irish Immigrant Women in the Nineteenth Century* (Baltimore, 1983), 80–94; Lynch-Brennan, *Irish Bridget*, 90– 95, 100–106, 109–14; Faye Dudden, *Serving Women: Household Service in Nineteenth-Century America* (Middletown, Conn., 1983), 194–209.

38. [William Bobo], *Glimpses of New-York City, by a South Carolinian* (Charleston, 1852), 187 (first two quotations); "Labor in New-York: Its Circumstances, Conditions and Rewards," *Tribune*, November 6, 1845, 2 (final quotation); Anbinder, *Five Points*, 126–27; Lynch-Brennan, *Irish Bridget*, 127–38.

39. Lynch-Brennan, *Irish Bridget*, 114–17; "Labor in New-York: Its Circumstances, Conditions and Rewards," *Tribune*, November 6, 1845, 2.

40. Lynch-Brennan, *Irish Bridget*, 91–92; "Irish Remittances to Friends in Ireland," *Frank Leslie's Illustrated Newspaper* (March 13, 1880): 27; Maguire, *Irish in America*, 315 (quotations), 317–18.

41. *Eighteenth General Report of Emigration Commissioners, 1858* (London, 1858), 101. The report states that from 1848 through 1857, emigrants sent £9.95 million to Great Britain. Remittance figures for 1858 through 1860 and the British estimate that 90 percent of American remittances to Great Britain went to Ireland are from Robert Doan, "Green Gold to the Emerald Shores: Irish Immigration to the United States and Transatlantic Monetary Aid, 1854–1923" (Ph.D. diss., Temple University, 1999), 280–81. The modern value of those remittances was determined using the calculators at https://www.mea suringworth.com.

42. "A Movement for the Shirt-Sewers," *Tribune*, March 27, 1851, 4; "Labor and the Laborers," *Tribune*, June 8, 1853, 5–6 ("serf" and "wretchedness"); "The Industrial Classes of New York," *Herald*, June 11, 1853, 4; "The Case of Margaret Byrne," *Times*, March 1, 1855, 4; Wirt Sikes, "Among the Poor Girls," *Putnam's Magazine*, new ser., 1 (April 1868): 433–36; Anbinder, *Five Points*, 122–26. For the proportion of needlewomen who were immigrants, see "1860 New York City 1% Census Sample."

43. Accounts 315, 2541, 28606, 13655–7, 30883, 32947, and 103191, Emigrant Bank Papers; entry for Mary Mulvey, family 1130, district 1, Ward Seven, 1850 census. On teaching as a means of socioeconomic mobility, see Janet Nolan, *Servants of the Poor: Teachers and Mobility in Ireland and Irish America* (Notre Dame, 2004). Literacy rates are based on test book entries of all accounts opened by Irish immigrants in 1860, the year the bank

began asking for depositors' signatures. The literacy rate of Emigrant Bank customers who came to the United States before the famine was identical to that of famine immigrants.

44. Test books and deposit ledgers for accounts 23603 and 6524 (the latter for Sullivan's daughter Mary Sullivan Shea), Emigrant Bank Papers; "Backgrounds of Civilization — Realities of the Five Points," *New York Illustrated News* (February 18, 1860): 216; "The Abodes of the Poor," *Times,* July 1, 1859, 2; Samuel Halliday, *The Lost and Found, or Life Among the Poor* (New York, 1859), 207–8 (quotations); entry for Sandy Sullivan, family 1136, district 2, Ward Six, 1860 census; *Nineteenth Annual Report of the New York Association for Improving the Condition of the Poor* (New York, 1862), 22.

45. Solon Robinson, *Hot Corn: Life Scenes in New York Illustrated* (New York, 1854), 44; *The Diary of George Templeton Strong,* ed. Allan Nevins, 4 vols. (New York, 1952), 2:149; "C.L.B." [Charles Loring Brace], "Walks Among the New-York Poor," *Times,* March 12, 1853, 3; Foster, *New York by Gas-Light,* 115–19; Anbinder, *Five Points,* 129–33.

46. Miller, *Emigrants and Exiles,* 315–16, 318–19 (all quotations); Jay Dolan, *The Immigrant Church: New York's Irish and German Catholics, 1815–1865* (1975; repr., Notre Dame, 1983), 39–40.

47. *Census of the State of New-York for 1855* (Albany, 1857), 208; Michael Coogan to the Editor, July 16, 1853, *Irish-American,* July 30, 1853, 4 ("good beef"); Peter Welsh to Patrick Prendergast, June 1, 1863, in *Irish Green and Union Blue: The Civil War Letters of Peter Welsh,* ed. Lawrence Kohl (New York, 1986), 100–102.

48. Eliza Quinn to her parents, January 22, 1848, in House of Commons, "Third Report from the Select Committee of the House of Lords on Colonization from Ireland," Sessional Paper 86 (1849), 128; Pat McGowan to his parents, December 21, 1847, BR146/10/13, Broadlands Papers, University of Southampton.

9. Kleindeutschland

1. *Annual Reports of the Commissioners of Emigration of the State of New York, from the Organization of the Commission,* May 5, 1847, to 1860 (New York, 1861), 288; Susan B. Carter et al., eds., *Historical Statistics of the United States,* 2 vols. (New York, 2006), 1:560–61. For the percentage of German immigrants who landed in New York, see *Passengers Arriving in the United States: Letter from the Secretary of State Transmitting Statements of the Number and Designation of Passengers Arriving in the United States,* 29th Cong., 2nd sess., House of Representatives, Doc. no. 98 (1847), and 30th Cong., 1st sess., House of Representatives, Ex. Doc. no. 47 (1848); *Passengers Arriving in the United States: Letter of the Secretary of State Communicating the Number and Designation of Passengers Arriving in the United States,* 30th Cong., 2nd sess., House of Representatives, Ex. Doc. no. 10 (1848); *Passengers Arriving in the United States: Letter from the Secretary of State Transmitting a Statement of the Number and Designation of Persons Arriving in the United States,* for 31st Cong., 1st sess., Ex. Doc. no. 7 (1849), 31st Cong., 2nd sess., Ex. Doc. no. 16 (1851), and 32nd Cong., 1st sess., House of Representatives, Ex. Doc. no. 100 (1852); *Passengers Arriving in the United States: Letter from the Secretary of State Transmitting Tabular Statements Showing the Number, &c., of Passengers Who*

Arrived in the United States During the Last Year, 32nd Cong., 2nd sess., Ex. Doc. no. 45 (1853), 33rd Cong., 2nd sess., Ex. Doc. no. 77 (1855), and 34th Cong., 1st sess., Ex. Doc. no. 29 (1856).

2. Joseph Kennedy, *Population of the United States in 1860, Compiled from the Original Returns of the Eighth Census* (Washington, D.C., 1864), 609–23; Stanley Nadel, *Little Germany: Ethnicity, Religion, and Class in New York City, 1845–80* (Chicago, 1990), 1. On Moritz Weil, see Merton Wilner, *Niagara Frontier: A Narrative and Documentary History,* 4 vols. (Chicago, 1931), 4:542–43; S. Falk, "A History of the Israelites in Buffalo," *Publications of the Buffalo Historical Society* 1 (1879): 292–96; entry for Moritz Weil, family 1628, Ward Four, Buffalo, Erie County, N.Y., 1850 census; entries for Moritz Weil and his father, Aaron Weil, *Buffalo City Directory for 1853* (Buffalo, 1853), 372.

3. Nadel, *Little Germany,* 17; Mack Walker, *Germany and the Emigration, 1816–1885* (Cambridge, Mass., 1964), 154, 157–58, 166.

4. Nadel, *Little Germany,* 18; Heinrich Bürgers to Karl Marx, August 30, 1847, in vol. 2, pt. 3 of *Marx-Engels Gesamtausgabe* (Berlin, 1972–), 352 (quotation).

5. *The Reminiscences of Carl Schurz,* 2 vols. (New York, 1907), 1:398–406.

6. Kennedy, *Population of the United States in 1860,* 608–15; Nadel, *Little Germany,* 18.

7. C. Stürenburg, *Klein-Deutschland: Bilder aus dem New Yorker Alltagsleben* (New York, 1886), 185; *Census of the State of New-York for 1855* (Albany, 1857), 105–18.

8. "New-York City: Germans in America," *Times,* June 27, 1855, 1; Robert Ernst, *Immigrant Life in New York City, 1825–1863* (1949; repr., Syracuse, 1994), 42 ("Bowery"); Nadel, *Little Germany,* 29, 32, 34, 36; Charles Stelzle, *A Son of the Bowery: The Life Story of an East Side American* (New York, 1926), 17–19; Walter Kamphoefner et al., eds., *News from the Land of Freedom: German Immigrants Write Home* (Ithaca, 1993), 538–39 ("Stuttgart").

9. Nadel, *Little Germany,* 37–39 (quotation); concentration of different German groups based on my transcriptions of every inhabitant of Wards Ten, Eleven, Thirteen, and Fifteen recorded in the population schedules of the 1860 census. See "All New York City Residents, 1860 Census" at https://dataverse.harvard.edu/dataverse/anbinder.

10. The types of tenements found in Little Germany can be determined through an analysis of the fire insurance maps of the period. The mixture of wood and brick tenements in the southeastern portion of the district can be found in plates 26, 29, and 30 of William Perris, *Maps of the City of New-York,* 3rd ed., 6 vols. (New York, 1857–1859). For the dominance of brick tenements in the northern portion of Kleindeutschland, see plates 35–37, 39–40, and 43. All these maps are available at digitalcollections.nypl.org.

11. "New-York City: Legislative Committee on Tenement Houses," *Times,* March 17, 1856, 8; "The Tenement Committee," *Times,* July 7, 1856, 4 (bedbug quotations); "Dwellings for the Poor," *Times,* April 7, 1856, 3 (other quotations); "Condition of the City," *Times,* June 2, 1857, 5.

12. Samuel Gompers, *Seventy Years of Life and Labor: An Autobiography,* 2 vols. (New York, 1925), 1:24.

13. "Walks Among the New-York Poor," *Times,* January 22, 1853, 2; "The Tenement Committee," *Times,* July 7, 1856, 4 ("refreshing"); "Condition of the City," *Times,* June 2, 1857, 5 (first two quotations).

14. "The Tenement Committee," *Times,* July 7, 1856, 4; population density calculated ac-

cording to population figures from *Population of the United States in 1860* (Washington, D.C., 1864), 337. Square mileage I calculated myself using the ward boundaries and Google Maps.

15. Gender ratio based on "1850 New York City 1% Census Sample" and "1860 New York City 1% Census Sample"; German occupations based on occupations listed on ship manifests for 18,203 German immigrants who landed in New York from 1846 to 1854. Of the 6,400 adult men in that group who stated that they intended to settle in New York, only about 11 percent listed farm work as their previous occupation. and only 3 percent stated that they were laborers. The vast majority listed artisanal trades. The data, in Excel format and labeled "Famine-Era New York Passenger Manifest Sample," can be found at https://dataverse.harvard.edu/dataverse/anbinder. The number of German Jews in New York in 1860 is typically given as 40,000, an estimate based on a report stating that 4.6 percent of weddings in New York City in 1865 were Jewish. Multiplying the 813,000 New Yorkers by 4.6 percent brings one almost to 40,000. I have used a lower estimate because, since a disproportionate number of immigrants were young adults, reliance on wedding data probably overstates Jews' representation in the city's overall population. See Jacob Marcus, *To Count a People: American Jewish Population Data, 1585–1984* (Lanham, Md., 1990), 149; Hyman Grinstein, *The Rise of the Jewish Community of New York, 1654–1860* (Philadelphia, 1945), 471, n. 14.

16. According to the 1860 census, there were approximately 33,000 German artisans out of a male adult population of 61,000, versus 22,000 American-born artisans out of 76,000 adult males and 27,000 Irish-born tradesmen out of 78,000 adult males. See "1860 New York City 1% Census Sample"; Ernst, *Immigrant Life*, 214–17 (proportion of Germans in specific trades); and Nadel, *Little Germany*, 64 (German laborers in other cities). In 1860, 1 percent of New York's German-born men were professionals, 14 percent were business owners, 10 percent worked as clerks or in other lower-status white-collar jobs, 58 percent were skilled workers, 11 percent held unskilled positions, and 6 percent held other kinds of jobs or were difficult to classify.

17. Kamphoefner, *News from the Land of Freedom*, 373 (quotations); Nadel, *Little Germany*, 68.

18. Annie Polland and Daniel Soyer, *Emerging Metropolis: New York Jews in the Age of Immigration, 1840–1920* (New York, 2012), 23; Lynn Downey, *Levi Strauss & Co.* (Charleston, 2007), 9–15.

19. Nick Salvatore, "Samuel Gompers," in *American National Biography Online* (New York, 2000); Gompers, *Seventy Years*, 1:2, 6, 17–22; entry for Samuel Gomperts, manifest of the *London*, July 30, 1863, "New York Passenger Lists." On the prevalence of smoking, see I. N. Phelps Stokes, *The Iconography of Manhattan Island, 1498–1909*, 6 vols. (New York, 1915–1928), 5:1717, 1760.

20. Salvatore, "Gompers"; Nadel, *Little Germany*, 72 ("To the West"); Gompers, *Seventy Years*, 1:19, 44–45 (all other quotations);.

21. Nadel, *Little Germany*, 39–40 (quotation), 66–67; "1860 New York City 1% Census Sample." Ethnicity of grocers based on an examination of surnames in *Doggett's New York City Street Directory for 1851* (New York, 1851), supplemented by information from the 1855 New York State census population schedules. I found twenty-four Five Points

grocers who were obviously Irish American, forty-four with German surnames, and twenty-nine whose last names did not clearly indicate an ethnicity.

22. Nadel, *Little Germany,* 84.

23. Richard Lieberman, *Steinway & Sons* (New Haven, 1995), 9–12.

24. Ibid., 13.

25. Entries for Steinweg family, manifest of the *Helena Sloman,* June 29, 1850, "New York Passenger Lists"; Lieberman, *Steinway,* 15–33, 53, 73–86 ("into trouble," 16); Nadel, *Little Germany,* 70 ("cannot advise"); D. W. Fostle, *The Steinway Saga: An American Dynasty* (New York, 1995), 14–15 ("into trouble"); entry for Henry Steinway, family 338, district 6, Ward Fourteen, 1855 New York State census.

26. Anna Maria Klinger to her "parents and brothers and sisters," March 18, 1849, in Kamphoefner, *News from the Land of Freedom,* 536–37.

27. Emile Dupré to his mother, November 21, 1860, in *Germans in the Civil War: The Letters They Wrote Home,* ed. Walter Kamphoefner and Wolfgang Helbich (Chapel Hill, 2006), 42 ("block"); Silke Wehner, "German Domestic Servants in America, 1850–1914: A New Look at German Immigrant Women's Experiences," in *People in Transit: German Migrations in Comparative Perspective, 1820–1930,* ed. Dirk Hoerder and Jörg Nagler (New York, 1995), 273–75 (other quotations).

28. Kamphoefner, *News from the Land of Freedom,* 534–36, 539, 541–42.

29. Joseph Rubin and Charles Brown, eds., *Walt Whitman of the New York Aurora* (State College, Pa., 1950), 18; Junius H. Browne, *The Great Metropolis: A Mirror of New-York* (Hartford, 1869), 129–30; [William M. Bobo], *Glimpses of New-York City, by a South Carolinian* (Charleston, 1852), 162; Tyler Anbinder, *Five Points: The Nineteenth-Century New York City Neighborhood That Invented Tap Dance, Stole Elections, and Became the World's Most Notorious Slum* (New York, 2001), 176–77.

30. Charles H. Haswell, *Reminiscences of an Octogenarian, 1816–1860* (New York, 1897), 360 (quotation); Browne, *Great Metropolis,* 165–66; Alvin F. Harlow, *Old Bowery Days: The Chronicles of a Famous Street* (New York, 1931), 175, 381, 415–16, 535; Anbinder, *Five Points,* 177.

31. Marriage Register, 1854–1859, Church of the Transfiguration, 29 Mott Street, New York; Gompers, *Seventy Years,* 1:34–35 ("stripper"); Nadel, *Little Germany,* 51.

32. Nadel, *Little Germany,* 109–20; "New-York City: Germans in America," *Times,* June 27, 1855, 1; "Turn Vereins in America," *Harper's Weekly* (September 20, 1890): 734–35.

33. Ira Rosenwaike, *Population History of New York City* (Syracuse, 1972), 42; http://people.hofstra.edu/geotrans/eng/gallery/Map_World%20Largest%20Cities%201850.pdf.

34. Alexander Marjoribanks, *Travels in South and North America* (London, 1853), 305–6 ("extraordinary"); Jeremiah O'Donovan, *A Brief Account of the Author's Interview with His Countrymen, and of the Parts of the Emerald Isle Whence They Emigrated* (Pittsburgh, 1864), 93 ("heterogeneous"); *Annual Reports of the Commissioners of Emigration,* 340. My estimate that 70 percent of immigrants planning to settle in New York State intended to live in New York City is based on a sample of more than ten thousand immigrants who stated their intended place of settlement when they arrived in the port of New York from 1846 to 1854. The data, in Excel format and labeled "Famine-Era New York Passenger Manifest Sample," can be found at https://dataverse.harvard.edu/data

verse/anbinder. For an explanation of the methodology used to collect and interpret these data, see Tyler Anbinder and Hope McCaffrey, "Which Irish Men and Women Immigrated to the United States During the Great Famine Migration of 1846–54?," *Irish Historical Studies* 39 (2015): 637–42.

35. "Wanted! A New Declaration of Independence," *Evening Express*, March 30, 1855, 1. Proportion of voting-age New Yorkers (twenty-one or older) who were foreign-born is from "1860 New York City 1% Census Sample."

10. Politics

1. Tyler Anbinder, *Five Points: The Nineteenth-Century New York City Neighborhood That Invented Tap Dance, Stole Elections, and Became the World's Most Notorious Slum* (New York, 2001), 7–13, 26–32; Paul Weinbaum, *Mobs and Demagogues: The New York Response to Collective Violence in the Early Nineteenth Century* (Ann Arbor, 1979), chaps. 1–2; Paul Gilje, *The Road to Mobocracy: Popular Disorder in New York City, 1763–1834* (Chapel Hill, 1987), 121–72.

2. "The Proposed State School Law," *Freeman's Journal*, October 27, 1849, 2 (quotation); I. N. Phelps Stokes, *The Iconography of Manhattan Island, 1498–1909*, 6 vols. (New York, 1915–1928), 5:1762, 1767; Tyler Anbinder, *Nativism and Slavery: The Northern Know Nothings and the Politics of the 1850s* (New York, 1992), 10–11.

3. Edwin Burrows and Mike Wallace, *Gotham: A History of New York City to 1898* (New York, 1999), 630–31; "Public Schools," *Herald*, April 11, 1842, 2; "Alderman Jones on the School Question," *Tribune*, April 12, 1842, 2; Anbinder, *Five Points*, 154–55; Robert Wister, "John Hughes," in *American National Biography Online* (New York, 2000); Richard Shaw, *Dagger John: The Unquiet Life and Times of Archbishop John Hughes of New York* (New York, 1977), 13–26, 139–75.

4. Joseph Rubin and Charles Brown, eds., *Walt Whitman of the New York Aurora* (State College, Pa., 1950), 58–59, 67–68 (quotations); Joann Krieg, *Whitman and the Irish* (Iowa City, 2000), chap. 3; Jerome Mushkat, *Tammany: The Evolution of a Political Machine* (Syracuse, 1971), 1–2, 8–26 (origins of Tammany Hall as synonymous with New York Democratic Party).

5. "The Terrible Election Riot in the Sixth Ward," *Herald*, April 14, 1842, 2; Anbinder, *Five Points*, 155–56.

6. Rubin and Brown, *Walt Whitman of the Aurora*, 77 (Whitman quotations), 78, 80; "Election Riots," *Tribune*, April 12, 1842, 2; "Election Riots," *Tribune*, April 13, 1842, 2; "The Terrible Election Riot in the Sixth Ward," *Herald*, April 14, 1842, 2 (other quotations); Anbinder, *Five Points*, 156–57.

7. Lewis Dow Scisco, *Political Nativism in New York State* (New York, 1901), 45–47; Eugene Exman, *The Brothers Harper* (New York, 1965), 183–210.

8. J. Frank Kernan, *Reminiscences of the Old Fire Laddies* (New York, 1885), 23–24, 501; Anbinder, *Five Points*, 146.

9. William M. Ivins, *Machine Politics and Money in Elections in New York City* (1887; repr., New York, 1970), 13–14, 25; *Manual of the Corporation of the City of New York for 1856*

(New York, 1856), 225; "The Process of Electing Mr. Wood," *Tribune*, October 20, 1856, 4; Anbinder, *Five Points*, 146–47.

10. Anbinder, *Five Points*, 147; Ivins, *Machine Politics*, 9–11; Matthew Breen, *Thirty Years of New York Politics Up-to-Date* (New York, 1899), 39–43.

11. Anbinder, *Five Points*, 150.

12. Kernan, *Reminiscences*, 49–50 (quotations); Anbinder, *Five Points*, 150–51.

13. Kernan, *Reminiscences*, 48–50.

14. Anbinder, *Five Points*, 151–54.

15. "At a Meeting of the German Democratic Republican Citizens of the First Ward," *Herald*, November 4, 1850, 1; "The German Vote," *Herald*, October 21, 1852, 2; "Political Notices," *Times*, October 28, 1852, 5; "The Irish Vote," *Herald*, October 29, 1852, 4; "The Germans and Education," *Times*, June 29, 1855, 4 (quotation).

16. "Torchlight Procession," *Evening Post*, October 26, 1852, 2; "The Irish Vote," *Herald*, October 29, 1852, 4; "A German Republican Procession Atrociously Assaulted," *Herald*, October 9, 1856, 4.

17. Anbinder, *Nativism and Slavery*, 76–78; William Gienapp, *Origins of the Republican Party, 1852–1856* (New York, 1987), 148; John Krout, "The Maine Law in New York Politics," *New York History* 17 (1936): 260–72.

18. David Potter, *The Impending Crisis, 1848–1861* (New York, 1976), 145–76; Michael Holt, *The Rise and Fall of the American Whig Party* (New York, 1999), 804–35.

19. Anbinder, *Nativism and Slavery*, ix, 92; "The Know-Nothings," *Tribune*, November 16, 1853, 4.

20. "Wanted! A New Declaration of Independence," *Evening Express*, March 30, 1855, 1; untitled article, *Tribune*, December 1, 1855, 4.

21. Benjamin Klebaner, "The Myth of Foreign Pauper Dumping in the United States," *Social Science Review* 35 (1961): 302–9; Kerby Miller, *Emigrants and Exiles: Ireland and the Irish Exodus to North America* (New York, 1985), 295–96; Wolfgang Helbich and Walter Kamphoefner, "'The Hour of Your Liberation Is Getting Closer and Closer,'" *Studia Migracyjne-Przeglad Polonijny* 35, no. 3 (2009): 46–47; Mack Walker, *Germany and the Emigration, 1816–1885* (Cambridge, Mass., 1964), 85–87, 146, 172–73; Gerhard Bassler, "The 'Inundation' of British North America with 'the Refuse of Foreign Pauperism': Assisted Emigration from Southern Germany in the Mid-Nineteenth Century," *German Canadian Yearbook* 4 (1978): 93–113; Günter Moltmann, "Die Transportation von Sträflingen im Rahmen der deutschen Amerikaauswanderung des 19 Jahrhunderts," in *Deutsche Amerikaauswanderung im 19 Jahrhundert*, ed. Günter Moltmann (Stuttgart, 1976), 147–97.

22. Anbinder, *Nativism and Slavery*, 113–14; "Mr. Coogan and the Irish Cause," *Irish-American*, October 6, 1854, 2.

23. "What Causes Election Riots," *Evening Express*, August 10, 1855, 1; "The Know-Nothings," *Tribune*, June 15, 1854, 4; Anbinder, *Nativism and Slavery*, 117–18.

24. "The Papal Hierarchy in America," *Mirror*, November 2, 1855, 2; Anbinder, *Nativism and Slavery*, 104–5, 114, 117–20.

25. "Religion and Party," *Evening Express*, September 10, 1855, 1.

26. "Protestant Religion in Newark," *The Citizen* (September 16, 1854): 584; "The Cartmen's Society," *Times*, July 10, 1854, 6.

27. Anbinder, *Nativism and Slavery*, 103–26.

28. "German Anti-Maine Law Demonstration," *Times*, March 25, 1854, 8 ("dark aims"); "Germans!" *Herald*, November 7, 1854, 4; "Scenes of Election Night," *Times*, November 8, 1854, 5 ("meddles"); "The Germans on K.N.'s and the Maine Law," *Times*, May 25, 1855, 3 ("if we must").

29. "The Know Nothings and the Southern Democratic Members of Congress," *Herald*, January 8, 1855, 4; "Scenes of Election Night," *Times*, November 8, 1854, 5 (German grocer).

30. "Meeting of the German Democrats," *Herald*, February 24, 1854, 8.

31. Ibid., (quotations); "German Meeting on the Nebraska Bill," *Tribune*, February 24, 1854, 5; *Trow's New York City Directory for 1855–56* (New York, 1855), 696 (Richter).

32. "The Nebraska Question," *Herald*, March 4, 1854, 8 (quotations); "Grand German Demonstration," *Times*, March 4, 1854, 8. On the relationship between the Forty-eighters and the abolition movement, see Mischa Honeck, *We Are the Revolutionists: German-Speaking Immigrants and the American Abolitionists After 1848* (Athens, Ga., 2011); and Daniel Nagel, *Von Republikanischen Deutschen zu Deutsch-Amerikanischen Republikanern: Ein Beitrag zum Identitätswandel der Deutschen Achtundvierziger in den Vereinigten Staaten 1850–1861* (St. Ingbert, 2012).

33. "New-York City: The Latest Returns," *Times*, November 11, 1854, 1; "Still Another Party! The German Democrats in the Field," *Times*, September 24, 1855, 1 (quotation).

34. "From a German to the Germans," *Times*, July 23, 1856, 1 ("honor"); "Great German Fremont Meeting," *Times*, August 22, 1856, 1 ("We have not"); "Tremendous Gathering of the Germans in Favor of John Chas. Fremont for President," *Herald*, August 22, 1856, 1; "The German Vote," *Times*, August 25, 1856, 4; "Great German Fremont Meeting," *Herald*, October 8, 1856, 8; "German Republican Meeting," *Tribune*, October 8, 1856, 5; untitled news story, *Times*, October 9, 1856, 4 ("with the Republicans").

35. "The Foreign Vote," *Times*, November 7, 1856, 4 (quotation); "The German Vote and the Presidential Election," *Times*, November 25, 1856, 3 (six thousand Germans). Comparison of the 1856 voting results in Kleindeutschland with those of the previous four years suggests that few Germans had changed their allegiance since 1852.

36. "German Republicans," *Times*, November 5, 1855, 4 (offices that did not involve liquor); "Slidell, Belmont, and Buchanan," *Times*, June 12, 1856, 2; "The Germans," *Times*, October 22, 1856, 4; "The German Vote and the Presidential Election," *Times*, November 25, 1856, 3 (quotation).

37. Paul Weinbaum, "Temperance, Politics, and the New York City Riots of 1857," *New York Historical Society Quarterly* 59 (1975): 246–50; Anbinder, *Five Points*, 278–80.

38. Anbinder, *Five Points*, 280–92.

39. "Renewal of the Riots in the Seventeenth Ward," *Tribune*, July 14, 1857, 5 ("shot down"); "The Second Avenue Riot," *Tribune*, July 14, 1857, 6; "The Seventeenth Ward Riots," *Tribune*, July 15, 1857, 4–5 (other quotations); Weinbaum, "Temperance," 258–63; "Another Terrible Riot in Second Avenue," *Herald*, July 13, 1857, 1; "Accounts by Other Re-

porters," *Herald,* July 14, 1857, 1; "The City Riots," *Herald,* July 15, 1857, 1; Anbinder, *Nativism and Slavery,* 254–57.

40. "The State Elections," *Irish-American,* October 29, 1853, 2; "The Slavery Question," *Irish-American,* January 21, 1854, 2; "Northern Abolitionists," *Irish-American,* January 31, 1857, 2.

41. "Negro Subordination," *Day Book,* November 11, 1857, 2; "The Abolitionists at Syracuse," *Irish-American,* May 17, 1851, 2; "Mrs. Stowe in Cork," *Irish-American,* June 11, 1853, 2.

42. "Kansas and Senator Douglas," *Irish-American,* January 9, 1858, 2 (quotation); "Slavery," *Irish-American,* October 30, 1858, 2; Anbinder, *Five Points,* 306–7.

43. Anbinder, *Five Points,* 292–95; "Politics," *Leader,* November 6, 1858, 4 ("too Irish"); "The County Nominations," *Irish-American,* October 23, 1858, 2; "Unworthy Prejudice," *Irish-American,* November 6, 1858, 2; "For Governor of the Almshouse," *Times,* November 29, 1858, 1 (almshouse candidates); "The Charter Election," *Tribune,* December 8, 1858, 4.

44. "The Ivy Green," *Leader,* March 12, 1859, 4; Anbinder, *Five Points,* 235–36.

45. "The Importance of the Issue," *Freeman's Journal,* October 6, 1860, 4; untitled news story, *Tribune,* November 1, 1860, 4; "Workmen Not Slaves," *Tribune,* November 3, 1860, 5 (origins of German circular); "Tailors!" and "IRISH AND GERMAN LABORERS!" *Herald,* November 6, 1860, 5; "Citizen Cuffee" and "Adopted Citizens, Be Warned," *Daily News,* November 6, 1860, 4.

46. "The Election," *Tribune,* November 8, 1860, 5.

11. War

1. Service record of Felix Brannigan, Company A, Seventy-fourth New York Infantry Regiment, National Archives; entry for Felix Brannigan, manifest of the *Lord Ashburton,* September 28, 1855, "New York Passenger Lists." Brannigan must have been vain about his age, because with each census he appears in, he subtracted a few more years from his birth date. By 1880, he was listing himself as eleven years younger than he would have been according to the age given on the ship manifest. See entries for Brannigan, dwelling 371, Ward Seven, District of Columbia, 1870 census population schedules, and dwelling 33, enumeration district 40, District of Columbia, 1880 census.

2. Felix Brannigan to [his sister], July 16, 1862, Felix Brannigan Papers, Library of Congress.

3. Among the works that quote Brannigan's infamous two sentences are Benjamin Quarles, *The Negro in the Civil War* (1953; repr., Boston, 1989), 31; James McPherson, *The Struggle for Equality: Abolitionists and the Negro in the Civil War and Reconstruction* (1964; repr., Princeton, 1992), 193; Randall Jimmerson, *The Private Civil War: Popular Thought During the Sectional Conflict* (Baton Rouge, 1988), 93; Philip Paludan, *A People's Contest: The Union and the Civil War* (Lawrence, Kans., 1996), 209; Gerald Astor, *The Right to Fight: A History of African Americans in the Military* (New York, 1998), 22; Adele Alexander, *Homelands and Waterways: The American Journey of the Bond Family, 1846–1926* (New York, 1999), 48; Gail Buckley, *American Patriots: The Story of Blacks in the Military from the Revolution to Desert Storm* (New York, 2001), 103; Har-

old Holzer, ed., *State of the Union: New York and the Civil War* (New York, 2002), 36; John David Smith, *Black Soldiers in Blue: African American Troops in the Civil War Era* (Chapel Hill, 2003), 6; James Horton and Lois Horton, *Slavery and the Making of America* (New York, 2005), 185; Jabari Asim, *The N Word: Who Can Say It, Who Shouldn't, and Why* (New York, 2007), 88; James Oakes, *The Radical and the Republican: Frederick Douglass, Abraham Lincoln, and the Triumph of Antislavery Politics* (New York, 2007), 203; Thomas Krannawitter, *Vindicating Lincoln: Defending the Politics of Our Greatest President* (Lanham, Md., 2008), 31; Alan Guelzo, *Fateful Lightning: A New History of the Civil War and Reconstruction* (New York, 2012), 183; John David Smith, *Lincoln and the U.S. Colored Troops* (Carbondale, 2013), 30; David Williams, *I Freed Myself: African American Self-Emancipation in the Civil War Era* (New York, 2014), 127; Bob Luke and John David Smith, *Soldiering for Freedom: How the Union Army Recruited, Trained, and Deployed the U.S. Colored Troops* (Baltimore, 2014), 9.

4. Adrian Cook, *The Armies of the Streets: The New York City Draft Riots of 1863* (Lexington, Ky., 1974), 193–95, 213–18. Historians generally cite a higher death toll than the one hundred or so confirmed deaths, asserting that many dead rioters must have been spirited away and buried secretly so their friends would not have to face the supposed shame of admitting that loved ones were among the rioters shot down by the authorities. But given that there is no reliable contemporary evidence to support assertions that the death toll was many times the official count, I have relied on the confirmed fatality figures.

5. Brannigan's service record; index of the naturalization certificate of Felix Brannigan, New York County Superior Court, June 19, 1868, U.S. Naturalization Records Indexes, accessed via ancestry.com; entry for Brannigan, dwelling 371, Ward Seven, District of Columbia, 1870 census, and dwelling 33, enumeration district 40, District of Columbia, 1880 census; *The Papers of Ulysses S. Grant*, ed. John Simon, 32 vols. (Carbondale, 1967–2012), 23:392, 25:310; "Washington," *Times*, March 10, 1875, 1.

6. For prosecutions of voting rights violations in Brannigan's office during his four years in Mississippi, see cases 1302–45, 1354–56, Civil and Criminal Execution Docket, United States District Court for the Southern District of Mississippi, Record Group 118, National Archives Southeast Region Research Center, Atlanta.

7. Felix Brannigan to [his sister?], July 16, 1862, Brannigan Papers.

8. Julius and Lisette Wesslau to his parents, December 26, 1860, in *Germans in the Civil War: The Letters They Wrote Home*, ed. Walter Kamphoefner and Wolfgang Helbich (Chapel Hill, 2006), 59–60.

9. "The Calculations of South Carolina" (Spencer) and "Interesting Home News," *Times*, December 14, 1860, 1, 4; "New Military Organization for the Protection of Municipal Rights and the South," *Herald*, December 14, 1860, 2; "The Kerrigan Conspiracy," *Tribune*, December 17, 1860, 8 ("military organization"); *Charleston Mercury*, December 21, 1861, quoted in Philip Foner, *Business and Slavery: The New York Merchants and the Irrepressible Conflict* (Chapel Hill, 1941), 294.

10. "The Irish and Disunion," *Times*, December 17, 1860, 4.

11. *The Diary of George Templeton Strong*, ed. Allan Nevins and Milton Thomas, 4 vols.

(New York, 1952), 3:127; Emile Dupré to his parents, April 26, 1861, in Kamphoefner and Helbich, *Germans in the Civil War,* 44.

12. *The Union Army: A History of Military Affairs in the Loyal States, 1861–65,* 8 vols. (Madison, 1908), 2:67, 77, 79.

13. Entry for Michael Corcoran, family 1883, Ward Fourteen, 1850 census; entry for Michael Corcoan, dwelling 137, district 2, Ward Fourteen, 1855 New York State census; entry for Michael Corcoran, *Trow's New York City Directory for the Year Ending May 1, 1856* (New York, 1855), 185; "Sketch of General Corcoran," *Irish-American,* January 2, 1864, 2; "Obituary," *Herald,* December 24, 1863, 8; "Gen. Michael Corcoran," *Tribune,* December 24, 1863, 1; test book entry for account 14,761, Emigrant Savings Bank Papers, New York Public Library.

14. "The Sixty-Ninth Regiment," *Irish-American,* September 3, 1859, 2; "Sketch of General Corcoran," *Irish-American,* January 2, 1864, 2 (quotations).

15. "Our Irish Soldiers," *Harper's Weekly* (October 20, 1860): 658; "The Sixty-Ninth Regiment and Lord Renfrew," *Tribune,* October 27, 1860, 8; "The Court-Martial of Col. Corcoran," *Times,* November 17, 1860, 8; "General City News: Presentations to Col. Corcoran," *Times,* March 6, 1861, 8; "Military Intelligence," *Herald,* December 21, 1860, 8; "Colonel M. Corcoran," *Irish-American,* January 19, 1861, 3.

16. "The Sixty-Ninth Regiment," *Irish-American,* April 27, 1861, 2 ("volunteers"); "The 69th Regiment," *Irish-American,* May 11, 1861, 2; "Local Military Movements," *Times,* June 8, 1861, 9; "The Regiments at the Capital," *Times,* July 1, 1861, 2; Susannah Bruce, *The Harp and the Eagle: Irish-American Volunteers and the Union Army, 1861–1865* (New York, 2006), 55–58, 62–63, 68; "The 'Irish Rifles,' 37th Regiment N.Y. Volunteers," *Irish-American,* August 10, 1861, 2; "The 37th New York 'Irish Rifles,'" *Irish-American,* August 30, 1862, 4; Michael Cavanagh, *Memoirs of Gen. Thomas Francis Meagher* (Worcester, Mass., 1892), 371 (Corcoran quotation); Paul Wylie, *The Irish General: Thomas Francis Meagher* (Norman, 2007), 19–120.

17. *Union Army,* 2:53–54, 64, 70, 78–79; "Military Movements in New York: The DeKalb Regiment," *Herald,* June 20, 1861, 5; Ella Lonn, *Foreigners in the Union Army and Navy* (Baton Rouge, 1951), 94–97.

18. William Burton, *Melting Pot Soldiers: The Union's Ethnic Regiments* (1988; repr., New York, 1998), 84–85; Ezra Warner, *Generals in Blue: Lives of the Union Commanders* (Baton Rouge, 1964), 37; Carl Schurz, *The Reminiscences of Carl Schurz,* 3 vols. (London, 1909), 1:186, 197; István Vida, *Hungarian Émigrés in the American Civil War: A History and Biographical Dictionary* (Jefferson, N.C., 2012), 83–88; passport application of Julius Stahel, December 5, 1899, U.S. Passport Applications, 1795–1925, National Archives, accessed via ancestry.com; Carl Wittke, *Refugees of Revolution: The German Forty-Eighters in America* (Philadelphia, 1952), 22 (Struve), 85 (Stahel), 233 (Blenker); "Baden: Defeat of the Republicans," *Tribune,* May 15, 1848, 2; "State of Europe," *Tribune,* October 19, 1848, 1; "The Germans and Freedom," *Times,* July 25, 1856, 3; "City Items," *Tribune,* April 3, 1860, 7.

19. Warner, *Generals in Blue,* 530–31, 545–46; entry for Max Weber, *Trow's New York City Directory for the Year Ending May 1, 1856,* 864; Wittke, *Refugees,* 65–66; Larry Tagg, *The*

Generals of Gettysburg: The Leaders of America's Greatest Battle (Cambridge, Mass., 2003), 127–29, 131–32; "De Kalb Regiment," *Times*, May 26, 1861, 8; Lonn, *Foreigners*, 217–18; "Gen. Baron Von Steinwehr," *Times*, February 26, 1877, 5; "Departure of the Seventh Steuben Volunteers," *Tribune*, May 25, 1861, 8; entry for Bendix, family 37, district 2, Ward Nineteen, 1855 New York State census; "Death of Gen. John E. Bendix," *Times*, October 9, 1877, 4; "Foreign Officers," *Times*, August 17, 1861, 9.

20. Terry Johnston Jr., ed., *"Him on One Side and Me on the Other": The Civil War Letters of Alexander Campbell, 79th New York Infantry Regiment, and James Campbell, 1st South Carolina Battalion* (Columbia, S.C., 1999), 1–8; Michael Bacarella, *Lincoln's Foreign Legion: The 39th New York Infantry, The Garibaldi Guard* (Shippensburg, Pa., 1996), 21–31.

21. Bacarella, *Lincoln's Foreign Legion*, 21–31, 231–96; "Local Military Matters," *Tribune*, May 29, 1861, 8; Lonn, *Foreigners*, 230–31; Frank Alduino and David Coles, "'Ye Come from Many a Far Off Clime; and Speak in Many a Tongue': The Garibaldi Guard and Italian-American Service in the Civil War," *Italian Americana* 22 (2004): 47–63.

22. "The City Military Excitement," *Times*, April 20, 1861, 1 (quotation); James McPherson, *Battle Cry of Freedom: The Civil War Era* (New York, 1988), 322, 332–35, 339; E. Merton Coulter, *The Confederate States of America, 1861–1865* (Baton Rouge, 1950), 14–15; William T. Sherman, *Memoirs of Gen. William T. Sherman, by Himself*, 2 vols. (1875; repr., New York, 1891), 1:180.

23. Testimony of General Tyler in *Report of the Joint Committee on the Conduct of the War: Part II — Bull Run — Ball's Bluff* (Washington, D.C., 1863), 201 ("Victory"); Ted Ballard, *Staff Ride Guide for the Battle of First Bull Run* (Washington, D.C., 2007), 15; McPherson, *Battle Cry*, 340–41; Bruce, *Harp and the Eagle*, 68, 75; William Todd, *The Seventy-Ninth Highlanders: New York Volunteers in the War of Rebellion, 1861–1865* (Albany, 1886), 34.

24. William C. Lusk, *War Letters of William Thompson Lusk* (New York, 1911), 58–59 ("Up"); Alexander Campbell to Jane Campbell, July 28, 1861, in Johnston, *"Him on One Side,"* 33–34 ("licked"); "The Seventy-Ninth at Bull Run," *Tribune*, July 29, 1861, 6 (other quotations); Todd, *Seventy-Ninth Highlanders*, 37–43; Ethan Rafuse, *A Single Grand Victory: The First Campaign and Battle of Manassas* (Wilmington, Del., 2002), 175–78; Ballard, *Bull Run*, 20–29.

25. *World* quoted in "Thomas Francis Meagher," *Irish-American*, August 17, 1861, 1; Captain James Kelly to Colonel W. T. Sherman, July 24, 1861, and Sherman to Captain W. A. Baird, July 25, 1861, in *War of the Rebellion: A Compilation of the Official Records of the Union and Confederate Armies*, ser. 1, 53 vols. (Washington, D.C., 1880), 2:369–72; "The War for the Union: Desperate Fighting at Bull's Run," *Irish-American*, July 27, 1861, 2; "Letters from the 69th Regt.," *Irish-American*, August 3, 1861, 4 (descriptions of Meagher).

26. Rafuse, *Single Grand Victory*, 179–81; Ballard, *Bull Run*, 29–31; William Davis, *Battle at Bull Run: A History of the First Major Campaign of the Civil War* (Baton Rouge, 1977), 217–19; David Detzer, *Donnybrook: The Battle of Bull Run, 1861* (New York, 2004), 384–85; Brigadier General Irvin McDowell to Lieutenant Colonel Townsend, July 21, 1861, in *War of the Rebellion*, ser. 1, 2:316.

27. Alexander Campbell to Jane Campbell, July 28, 1861, in Johnston, *"Him on One Side,"* 34.

28. Blenker to McDowell, August 4, 1861, and Beauregard to General S. Cooper, August 26, 1861, in *War of the Rebellion,* ser. 1, 2:427, 497; JoAnna McDonald, *"We Shall Meet Again": The First Battle of Manassas* (New York, 1999), 185–96; Detzer, *Donnybrook,* 418–19; Burton, *Melting Pot Soldiers,* 86.

29. Julius Wesslau to [?], July 23, 1861, in Kamphoefner and Helbich, *Germans in the Civil War,* 61; *Union Army,* 2:82–83, 89–91, 92–93; Walter Kamphoefner et al., eds., *News from the Land of Freedom: German Immigrants Write Home* (Ithaca, 1993), 374; *The Memoirs of Wladimir Krzyzanowski,* ed. James Pula (San Francisco, 1978), 42–45; "Death of Gen. Krzyzanowski," *Times,* February 1, 1887, 8.

30. *Union Army,* 2:79, 96–97, 105, 114–15; "The Tammany Regiment," *Irish-American,* November 9, 1861, 3; "Our Soldiers," *Irish-American,* June 14, 1862, 2 ("mainly Irish"); "What Has Become of the Irish Brigade?" *Irish-American,* October 11, 1862, 2 (Excelsior Brigade "almost exclusively" Irish).

31. "The Midnight March Across the Potomac: Letter from the Quartermaster of the Sixty-Ninth Regiment," *Herald,* June 2, 1861, 5; entry for Joseph Tully, family 1808, division 1, Ward Nineteen, 1860 census.

32. [Charles Halpine], *The Life and Adventures, Songs, Services, and Speeches of Private Miles O'Reilly* (New York, 1864), 159–60; Christian Samito, *Becoming American Under Fire: Irish Americans, African Americans, and the Politics of Citizenship During the Civil War Era* (Ithaca, 2009), 32 (Meagher). For Halpine's career, see William Hanchett, *IRISH: Charles G. Halpine in Civil War America* (Syracuse, 1970).

33. Cavanagh, *Memoirs of Meagher,* 369, 376, 417 (Meagher and Confederate quotations); Peter Welsh to Patrick Prendergast, June 1, 1863, in *Irish Green and Union Blue: The Civil War Letters of Peter Welsh,* ed. Lawrence Kohl (New York, 1986), 103 ("school"); "Col. Corcoran in Washington," *Times,* August 19, 1862, 8; John Hassard, *Life of the Most Reverend John Hughes* (New York, 1866), 481–82.

34. Peter Welsh to Patrick Prendergast, June 1, 1863, in Kohl, *Irish Green and Union Blue,* 100–102; Lieutenant P. S. Devitt to the Editor, "Irishmen in the American Army," *Irish-American,* November 29, 1862, 4; James McPherson, *For Cause and Comrades: Why Men Fought in the Civil War* (New York, 1997), 113–14.

35. Alexander Dupré to his parents, May 16, June 6, August 15, 1861, and Emile Dupré to his sister Lina, October 5, 1861, in Kamphoefner and Helbich, *Germans in the Civil War,* 45–47; Robert Sneden, *Eye of the Storm: A Civil War Odyssey,* ed. Charles Bryan Jr. and Nelson Lankford (New York, 2000), xiii.

36. Sneden, *Eye of the Storm,* 3–4.

37. McPherson, *Battle Cry of Freedom,* 423–27; Stephen Sears, *To the Gates of Richmond: The Peninsula Campaign* (New York, 1992), 3–39.

38. McPherson, *Battle Cry of Freedom,* 427; Brannigan to [his sister], May 4 [*sic*], 1862, Brannigan Papers.

39. Brigadier General Joseph Hooker to Captain Chauncey McKeever, May 10, 1862, in *War of the Rebellion,* ser. 1, vol. 11, pt. 1, 467; Sneden, *Eye of the Storm,* 3, 10, 35–36, 68.

40. Sneden diary entry, June 29, 1862, in *Eye of the Storm,* 75–76.

41. Sneden diary entry, July 1, 1862, ibid., 93–95; Sears, *To the Gates*, 181–336 ("murder," 335); David Conyngham, *The Irish Brigade and Its Campaigns, with Some Account of the Corcoran Legion* (Glasgow, 1866), 24–29.

42. Sneden diary entry, July 1, 1862, in *Eye of the Storm*, 96–98 ("disfigured"); "The Irish Brigade" and "The Battles Before Richmond: Official List of Killed and Wounded," *Irish-American*, July 19, 1862, 2–3; Conyngham, *Irish Brigade*, 106 ("dying"); General George Sykes to Captain Frederick Locke, July 7, 1862, in *War of the Rebellion*, ser. 1, vol. 11, pt. 2, 352 (singling out Bendix for his "coolness, courage, and valor"); Sears, *To the Gates*, 335; *The American Civil War Research Database* (Alexandria, Va., 2014), http://asp6new.alexanderstreet.com.proxygw.wrlc.org/cwdb/cwdb.object.details.aspx?handle=battleregiments&id=3131&pagePos=1&sortorder=killed (accessed June 10, 2014).

43. Julius Wesslau to [his parents], July 23, 1861, in Kamphoefner and Helbich, *Germans in the Civil War*, 62.

44. Edwin Burrows and Mike Wallace, *Gotham: A History of New York City to 1898* (New York, 1999), 873; "How the Town Goes On," *Daily News*, March 26, 1861, 4.

45. Julius Wesslau to his parents, May 14, 1862, in Kamphoefner and Helbich, *Germans in the Civil War*, 62; William Dodge to William Kinney, March 9, 1863, quoted in Thomas Kessner, *Capital City: New York City and the Men Behind America's Rise to Economic Dominance, 1860–1900* (New York, 2003), 41; Burrows and Wallace, *Gotham*, 873–77; *The Twenty-Second Annual Report of the New York Association for Improving the Condition of the Poor* (New York, 1865), 24.

46. "The Monster Festival," *Times*, August 30, 1861, 5; Ronald Bayor and Timothy Meagher, eds., *The New York Irish* (Baltimore, 1996), 196–97.

47. Bayor and Meagher, *New York Irish*, 197 (quotation); "The Distressed Families of Soldiers," *Tribune*, December 20, 1861, 5.

48. Kohl, *Irish Green and Union Blue*, xvii–xviii, 114, 156–57.

49. Alexander Campbell to Jane Campbell, June 16 and 25, 1862, James Campbell to Alexander Campbell, "June 1862," in Johnston, *"Him on One Side,"* 97–102; Patrick Brennan, *Secessionville: Assault on Charleston* (Campbell, Calif., 1996), 195–285.

50. Alexander Campbell to Jane Campbell, July 25 and September 4, 1862, in Johnston, *"Him on One Side,"* 106–7, 114–15.

51. Alexander Campbell to Jane Campbell, March 8, 1863, ibid., 132.

52. Johnston, *"Him on One Side,"* 120–42.

53. Ibid., 165–67; entries for Alexander and Jane Campbell, family 710, division 3, Ward Twenty, 1860 census; family 1265, Middletown, Middlesex County, Conn., 1870 census; family 136, enumeration district 284, Middletown, Middlesex County, Conn., 1900 census.

54. James McPherson, *Crossroads of Freedom: Antietam* (New York, 2002), 41–116; Heinrich Müller to his parents, July 25, 1865, in Kamphoefner and Helbich, *Germans in the Civil War*, 249.

55. Meagher to Captain Hancock, September 30, 1862, in *War of the Rebellion*, ser. 1, vol. 19, pt. 1, 294; "Antietam — The Dead of the Brigade," *Irish-American*, October 18, 1862, 2; Bruce, *Harp and the Eagle*, 118–20 ("to be shot"); Conyngham, *Irish Brigade*, 145–51; Stephen Sears, *Landscape Turned Red: The Battle of Antietam* (New Haven, 1983), 238–39,

242–46; John Priest, *Antietam: The Soldiers' Battle* (Shippensburg, Pa., 1989), 142–44, 158–64, 180–93.

56. Alphons Richter to his parents and sisters, October 11, 1862, and Julius and Lisette Wesslau to his parents, October 26, 1862, in Kamphoefner and Helbich, *Germans in the Civil War*, 64, 100; Angela Heck to her sister, brother-in-law, and "all at home," October 26, 1862, in Kamphoefner, *News from the Land of Freedom*, 374.

57. "Casualties in the Irish Brigade," *Irish-American*, September 27, 1862, 2; "What Has Become of the Irish Brigade?" *Irish-American*, October 11, 1862, 2 ("singling out"); "The Dead of the Brigade," *Irish-American*, October 18, 1862, 2; "The Irish Brigade and Its Losses," *Irish-American*, November 1, 1862, 2; Bruce, *Harp and the Eagle*, 148; Harold Hammond, ed., *Diary of a Union Lady, 1861–1865* (New York, 1962), 183 (Daly).

58. McPherson, *Battle Cry*, 569–72; William Corby, *Memoirs of Chaplain Life* (Chicago, 1893), 132; Conyngham, *Irish Brigade*, 168 ("wholesale"); "The Irish Brigade at Fredericksburg," *Irish-American*, January 10, 1863, 2 ("shroud"); Colonel George von Schack to Lieutenant D. K. Cross, December 15, 1862, General Thomas Meagher to [Lieutenant John Blake?], December 20, 1862, Lieutenant Colonel Robert Bentley to Blake, December 21, 1862, Captain Patrick Condon to Blake, December 24, 1862, Captain James Saunders to [Blake?], December 22, 1862, and Patrick Kelly to Captain William Hart, December 20, 1862, in *War of the Rebellion*, ser. 1, 21:236, 240–52; Francis O'Reilly, *The Fredericksburg Campaign: Winter War on the Rappahannock* (Baton Rouge, 2003), 305–17; George Rable, *Fredericksburg! Fredericksburg!* (Chapel Hill, 2002), 230–33; Craig Warren, "'Oh, God, What a Pity!': The Irish Brigade at Fredericksburg and the Creation of a Myth," *Civil War History* 47 (2001): 194–95, 202.

59. Daniel Callaghan, *Thomas Francis Meagher and the Irish Brigade in the Civil War* (Jefferson, N.C., 2006), 137 ("reckless"); Corby, *Memoirs*, 132 ("disgraced"); William Fox, *Regimental Losses in the Civil War, 1861–1865* (Albany, 1889), 36–37; "A Visit to the Irish Brigade," *Irish-American*, December 27, 1862, 1 ("sad Christmas").

12. Uprising

1. Alphons Richter, diary entry, September 6, 1862, in *Germans in the Civil War: The Letters They Wrote Home*, ed. Walter Kamphoefner and Wolfgang Helbich (Chapel Hill, 2006), 99; Valentin Bechler to his wife, November 11, 1862, in Robert Goodell and P. A. M. Taylor, "A German Immigrant in the Union Army: Selected Letters of Valentin Bechler," *Journal of American Studies* 4 (1971): 161 ("keep quiet").

2. James McPherson, *For Cause and Comrades: Why Men Fought in the Civil War* (New York, 1977), 122; Peter Welsh to his wife, February 3, 1863, and undated fragment, ca. February 1863, in *Irish Green and Union Blue: The Civil War Letters of Peter Welsh*, ed. Lawrence Kohl (New York, 1986), 62, 66; Chandra Manning, *What This Cruel War Was Over: Soldiers, Slavery, and the Civil War* (New York, 2007), 81–94; Jonathan White, *Emancipation, the Union Army, and the Reelection of Abraham Lincoln* (Baton Rouge, 2014), 40, 63.

3. "Eine Emancipations-Proklamation des Präsidenten," *Staats-Zeitung*, September 25, 1862 ("terrible"); "Sixty Days Ago," *Tribune*, September 23, 1862, 4; "The President's

Proclamation," *Times*, September 23, 1862, 4. I am grateful to Daniel Nagel of the University of Mannheim for locating and translating the passage from the *Staats-Zeitung*.

4. Hughes to Seward in John Hassard, *Life of the Most Reverend John Hughes* (New York, 1866), 437 ("time enough"); "Archbishop Hughes on Slavery and the War," *Herald*, October 8, 1861, 6 (other Hughes quotations); "The Position of the Union," *Irish-American*, December 14, 1861, 2 ("inkling"); "Have We a War Policy?" *Irish-American* October 11, 1862, 2; "Register and Vote," *Irish-American*, November 1, 1862, 2 ("treason"); Florence Gibson, *The Attitudes of the New York Irish Toward State and National Affairs, 1848–1892* (New York, 1951), 135–41.

5. "The War in America," *Irish-American*, October 12, 1861, 1.

6. "A New Role for Irish-Americans," *Irish-American*, January 17, 1863, 2.

7. Emerson Fite, *Social and Industrial Conditions in the North During the Civil War* (1910; repr., Williamstown, Mass., 1976), 189; Sterling Spero and Abram Harris, *The Black Worker: A Study of the Negro and the Labor Movement* (New York, 1931), 17; Edwin Burrows and Mike Wallace, *Gotham: A History of New York City to 1898* (New York, 1999), 884; Ronald Bayor and Timothy Meagher, eds., *The New York Irish* (Baltimore, 1996), 203–4 (quotation); Edward Spann, *Gotham at War: New York City, 1860–1865* (Wilmington, Del., 2002), 96. For another erroneous claim that black strikebreakers had taken Irish jobs on the New York docks, this time in 1862, see Williston Lofton, "Northern Labor and the Negro," *Journal of Negro History* 34 (1949): 261. The source cited by Lofton actually describes an Irish-led anti-black riot in Cincinnati. The source that Spero and Harris cite ("A Struggle Between the Races," *Fincher's Trades Review*, July 11, 1863, 22) describes a longshoremen's strike in Buffalo, not New York City. Albon P. Man in "Labor Competition and the New York Draft Riots of 1863," *Journal of Negro History* 36 (1951): 386, 398–400, is properly skeptical of claims that African Americans served as strikebreakers in New York in the weeks before the draft riots.

8. That African Americans were not used as strikebreakers in the June 1863 longshoremen's walkout is corroborated in "Strike Among the 'Longshoremen," *Tribune*, June 9, 1863, 8; Ibid., 2; "Meeting of the Master Stevedores," *Tribune*, June 10, 1863, 1; "The 'Longshoremen's Strike — Extraordinary Proceedings; Three Thousand Men Refusing to Work; Soldiers Loading Government Vessels," *Evening Post*, June 13, 1863, 3; "City Intelligence: The 'Longshoremen's Strike; Deserters Loading Government Vessels," *Herald*, June 14, 1863, 8; "Local Intelligence: The Labor Difficulty," *Times*, June 14, 1863, 6; "City Intelligence: The Longshoremen's Strike," *Evening Post*, June 15, 1863, 4; "The Stevedores' Strike," *Tribune*, June 15, 1863, 2; "The 'Longshoremen's Strike," *Herald*, June 16, 1863, 7; "Our Convalescent Soldiers," *Tribune*, June 18, 1863, 3; "One Thousand 'Longshoremen Resumed Work," *Tribune*, June 20, 1863, 3.

9. "Learn Trades or Starve!" *African Repository* 29 (May 1853): 136; "The National Freedman's Relief Association and the Contrabands," *Tribune*, December 1, 1862, 8; Karl Wesslau to his parents, New York, July 28, 1863, in Kamphoefner and Helbich, *Germans in the Civil War*, 65.

10. Bayor and Meagher, *New York Irish*, 203.

11. *The Dred Scott Decision: Opinion of Chief Justice Taney, with an Introduction by Dr.*

J. H. Van Evrie (New York, 1860), 19; *The Complete Lincoln-Douglas Debates of 1858*, ed. Paul Angle (Chicago, 1958), 266–67. Van Evrie was publisher of the antiwar, antiemancipation *Day Book*.

12. James McPherson, *Battle Cry of Freedom: The Civil War Era* (New York, 1988), 638–40.

13. Ibid., 639–41; Ernest Furgurson, *Chancellorsville 1863: The Souls of the Brave* (New York, 1992), 172–95; Stephen Sears, *Chancellorsville* (Boston, 1996), 260–81, 487–88; Christian Keller, *Chancellorsville and the Germans: Nativism, Ethnicity, and Civil War Memory* (New York, 2007), 46–91, 146–67; *The Memoirs of Wladimir Krzyzanowski*, ed. James Pula (San Francisco, 1978), 48 ("lost his head"); Bruce Sutherland, "Pittsburgh Volunteers with Sickles' Excelsior Brigade: Part 3, Fredericksburg and Chancellorsville," *Western Pennsylvania Historical Magazine* 45 (1962): 258–59.

14. Entry for Eugene Jacobson, dwelling 116, enumeration district 12, Denver, Arapahoe County, Colorado, 1880 census; entry for Gottlieb Luty, dwelling 640, Ward Six, Allegheny City, Allegheny County, Pa., 1870 census; entries for Joseph Gion, dwelling 84, West Pittsburgh, Allegheny County, Pa., 1870 census, and dwelling 38, Chartiers, Allegheny County, Pa., 1880 census; Theophilus Rodenbough, *Uncle Sam's Medal of Honor* (New York, 1886), 29–30 (quotation).

15. Sears, *Chancellorsville*, 293–96 ("Old Jack's," 293); Furgurson, *Chancellorsville*, 201–3; [William Parker Snow], *Southern Generals: Who They Are, and What They Have Done* (New York, 1865), 193 (remaining quotations).

16. Rodenbough, *Uncle Sam's Medal of Honor*, 30–32. It is possible, perhaps even likely, that the party of Confederates Luty and Brannigan saw being shot at was not the one in which Jackson was mortally wounded. Luty believed that he had left the Union lines around midnight, but Jackson was shot several hours earlier, around 9:30. Luty also recollected that General Berry had been killed while he and Brannigan were gone, but in fact the general was shot at 7:30 the following morning. Despite these possible embellishments, the valor of these men in voluntarily undertaking such a dangerous assignment cannot be questioned. Edward Gould, *Major-General Hiram G. Berry* (Rockland, Me., 1899), 266–67.

17. Rodenbough, *Uncle Sam's Medal of Honor*, 31 (quotation); J. W. Jones, *The Story of American Heroism: Thrilling Narratives of Personal Adventures During the Great Civil War as Told by the Medal Winners and Roll of Honor Men* (Springfield, Ohio, 1897), 249–52; Furgurson, *Chancellorsville*, 203–11; Sears, *Chancellorsville*, 297–307.

18. Sears, *Chancellorsville*, 297–307, 492; Susannah Bruce, *The Harp and the Eagle: Irish-American Volunteers and the Union Army, 1861–1865* (New York, 2006), 156.

19. James Geary, *We Need Men: The Union Draft in the Civil War* (DeKalb, Ill., 1991), 49–86; "City Intelligence: The Quota of This City," *Evening Post*, July 10, 1863, 2; Daniel Callaghan, *Thomas Francis Meagher and the Irish Brigade in the Civil War* (Jefferson, N.C., 2006), 165.

20. "The Commencement," *Herald*, July 14, 1863, 1; Abraham Lincoln, "Opinion on the Draft" [September 1863?], in *The Collected Works of Abraham Lincoln*, ed. Roy P. Basler, 9 vols. (New Brunswick, N.J., 1953–1955), 6:447–48; Tyler Anbinder, "Which Poor Man's Fight? Immigrants and the Conscription of 1863," *Civil War History* 52 (2006): 354; Pe-

ter Welsh to his wife, July 22, 1863, in Kohl, *Irish Green and Union Blue,* 113 ("No conscription"). Although Lincoln's memorandum was never published, other Republicans echoed his sentiments in public. See, for example, "The National Militia Act," *Tribune,* March 23, 1863, 4; "The Conscription," *Tribune,* July 18, 1863, 4; "The Exemption," *Tribune,* July 20, 1863, 4; "The $300 Exemption," *Times,* July 15, 1863, 4; "Misapprehensions About the Draft," *Times,* July 19, 1863, 5; "Letter from a Poor Man," *Times,* September 16, 1863, 8; "The Merits of the Draft Question," *Herald,* July 19, 1863, 4.

21. Anbinder, "Which Poor Man's Fight?," 354–55; Julius and Lisette Wesslau to his parents, October 26, 1862, in Kamphoefner and Helbich, *Germans in the Civil War,* 63; Geary, *We Need Men,* 140–50; Carl Sandburg, "Lincoln and Conscription," *Journal of the Illinois State Historical Society* 32 (1939): 5–19.

22. "The Draft," *Herald,* July 12, 1863, 8; "The Commencement," *Herald,* July 14, 1863, 1 (quotations).

23. "The Mob in New-York," *Times,* July 14, 1863, 1 (quotations); "The Draft," *Herald,* July 14, 1863, 1; "Fires During the Riots," *Times,* October 21, 1863, 2.

24. "The Mob in New-York," *Times,* July 14, 1863, 1; David Barnes, *The Draft Riots in New York* (New York, 1863), 14–16; "Fires During the Riots," *Times,* October 21, 1863, 2; George Opdyke, *Official Documents, Addresses, Etc., of George Opdyke* (New York, 1866), 271; "Epitome of the Week," *Frank Leslie's Illustrated Newspaper* (September 26, 1863): 3; Iver Bernstein, *The New York City Draft Riots: Their Significance for American Society and Politics in the Age of the Civil War* (New York, 1990), 37–38. Bernstein confuses Opdyke's armory, which the rioters burned on Monday, with the Union Steam Works a block away, where the munitions had been moved and which the rioters attacked on Tuesday once they learned that the guns and ammunition were there.

25. "The Riots Resumed To-day," *Evening Post,* July 14, 1863, 3 ("showed"); Barnes, *Draft Riots,* 14–15 (other quotations), 38–40, 42–44; William Seraile, *Angels of Mercy: White Women and the History of New York's Colored Orphan Asylum* (New York, 2011), 70–71.

26. Adrian Cook, *The Armies of the Streets: The New York City Draft Riots of 1863* (Lexington, Ky., 1974), 82 ("Kill"); Bernstein, *New York City Draft Riots,* 47–48; Barnes, *Draft Riots,* 115.

27. Barnet Schecter, *The Devil's Own Work: The Civil War Draft Riots and the Fight to Reconstruct America* (New York, 2005), 163; "Miscellaneous Movements," *Times,* July 15, 1863, 1; "The Raging Riot — Its Character, and the True Attitude Toward It," *Times,* July 15, 1863, 4 ("infuriate"); "The Riot Continued," *Tribune,* July 15, 1863, 1, 8; "The Conscription," *Herald,* July 15, 1863, 1, 5; Charles Loring Brace, "The Poor and the Rich: A Lesson from the July Riots," *Times,* October 18, 1863, 5 ("$300 man"); Emile Dupré to his mother, July 17, 1863, and Marie Wesslau to her parents, July 28, 1863, in Kamphoefner and Helbich, *Germans in the Civil War,* 55, 66.

28. Report of Lieutenant Thomas Wood, July 20, 1863, in Joel Headley, *The Great Riots of New York, 1712 to 1873* (New York, 1873), 346; "The Affair at Broome and Pitt Streets," *Herald,* July 15, 1863, 1; "The Marines Fire upon the Crowd," *Times,* July 15, 1863, 1; Cook, *Armies of the Streets,* 213–16. One might wonder how historians know that the claims of contemporaries that Irish immigrants dominated the mobs of rioters are accurate.

Irish-born men aged sixteen to forty (the most likely ages for rioters) made up 30 percent of the city's male population in 1860. In contrast, 64 percent of the rioters (killed or arrested) whose birthplaces could be identified were born in Ireland. One might argue that the arrest figures are unreliable as they may reflect prejudicial and selective policing rather than the true composition of the rioting mobs. But even if one looks only at those killed during the riots, exclusive of policemen and soldiers, the preponderance of Irish surnames is unmistakable. Cook, *Armies of the Streets*, 196–97, 213–18; proportion of male New Yorkers aged sixteen to forty born in Ireland is based on the author's database containing the name, age, and birthplace of the more than 800,000 New Yorkers listed in the 1860 census. This can be found, in Excel format, at https://dataverse .harvard.edu/dataverse/anbinder.

29. Headley, *Great Riots*, 196–97, 355; Schecter, *Devil's Own Work*, 176–77; Barnes, *Draft Riots*, 15–16; "The Scenes in Second and Third Avenues," *Herald*, July 15, 1863, 5.

30. Barnes, *Draft Riots*, 113 ("revolting atrocities"); "The Scenes in Second and Third Avenues," *Herald*, July 15, 1863, 5 (all other quotations); "The Killing of Col. O'Brien," *Tribune*, July 20, 1863, 3; "The Late Col. O'Brien," *Herald*, January 30, 1864, 6; "Local Intelligence: The Murder of Col. O'Brien," *Times*, July 4, 1867, 2; Cook, *Armies of the Streets*, 118–19.

31. Headley, *Great Riots*, 204 ("very wild"), 223–25 ("Parisian"), 342; Barnes, *Draft Riots*, 17–19; Schecter, *Devil's Own Work*, 179–81; *World* quoted in Steven Jaffe, *New York at War: Four Centuries of Combat, Fear, and Intrigue in Gotham* (New York, 2012), 166 ("Pools"), 181 ("wild howlings"); "Barricades on the First-Avenue" and "The Riot in Second-Avenue," *Times*, July 15, 1863, 1.

32. "Scenes in the Negro Quarters," *Herald*, July 15, 1863, 1; Cook, *Armies of the Streets*, 134–36 (Derrickson quotations); test book entries for William Cruise, accounts 13497 and 31218, Emigrant Savings Bank Papers, New York Public Library, accessed via ancestry.com.

33. "Scenes in the Negro Quarters," *Herald*, July 15, 1863, 1 ("all gone"); "Exodus of Blacks from the Five Points," *Herald*, July 17, 1863, 1; Bernstein, *New York City Draft Riots*, 282; Barnes, *Draft Riots*, 115–16; Schecter, *Devil's Own Work*, 222 ("overrun").

34. Cook, *Armies of the Streets*, 140–43 ("all you damned"); Bernstein, *New York City Draft Riots*, 28–29; "A Morning Riot in Thirty-Second Street," *Times*, July 16, 1863, 1; Barnes, *Draft Riots*, 114; Martin Pasternak, *Rise Now and Fly to Arms: The Life of Henry Highland Garnet* (New York, 1995), 113 ("demon"); "Attack upon Negroes in the Thirteenth Ward," *Herald*, July 16, 1863, 8. Some press reports place the third lynching on West 36th Street, while others say West 32nd.

35. Reports of Lieutenant B. Franklin Ryer and Captain Richard Shelley, in Headley, *Great Riots*, 231–32, 347–50, 356; "Another Day of Rioting," *Times*, July 16, 1863, 1; "The Riot," *Tribune*, July 16, 1863, 1; "General T. P. Mott Dead," *Herald*, November 24, 1894, 10; Frederick Phisterer, comp., *New York in the War of the Rebellion, 1861–1865*, 3rd ed., 6 vols. (Albany, 1912), 3:987–88, 1565–68 (Mott), 1606–7 (Ryer).

36. "An Evening Riot in the First-Avenue," *Times*, July 16, 1863, 1; "Bloody Riot in First Avenue," *Herald*, July 16, 1863, 5; [Ellen Leonard], "Three Days of Terror," *Harper's New*

Monthly Magazine 34 (January 1867): 229 (quotations); Schecter, *Devil's Own Work*, 218–20; Cook, *Armies of the Streets*, 152–55; "Gen. Edward Jardine Dead," *Times*, July, 17, 1893, 5; Phisterer, *New York in the War*, 3:1831–43 (Jardine).

37. See, for example, Bernstein, *New York City Draft Riots*, 39; Wallace and Burrows, *Gotham*, 895; Bruce, *Harp and the Eagle*, 180.

38. "Riot Subsiding," *Times*, July 17, 1863, 1; "The Riot," *Tribune*, July 17, 1863, 1; Schecter, *Devil's Own Work*, 222; Barnes, *Draft Riots*, 157. The Twenty-sixth Michigan Infantry arrived in the city on Wednesday night into Thursday morning as well, on its way home on furlough, and assisted in the pacification actions, but these troops had spent their entire nine months of service guarding Alexandria, Virginia, and had no battle experience. One and perhaps two additional units appeared in New York on Wednesday night and Thursday morning. The press reported the arrival of the artillery of the Eighth New York Infantry Regiment, and readers may have supposed that these soldiers were part of the German regiment of that designation which had left the city in 1861 after the attack on Fort Sumter. In fact, that unit had disbanded earlier in 1863, and the soldiers who arrived in New York at the conclusion of the riots with that designation were part of a newly created militia organization mustered into service in Harrisburg in June as part of the reaction to Lee's invasion of the North. The final unit supposed to have arrived in New York at the end of the rioting was the 162nd New York Infantry Regiment, which was composed primarily of New York City policemen. The main body of this unit, however, was stationed at Port Hudson, Louisiana, at the time of the riots, so the newspaper that reported its presence probably meant to refer to the 152nd. The following week, after the riots were over, several New England units (such as the Sixteenth Vermont Infantry) that were heading home from Gettysburg did stop in New York City, a choice undoubtedly dictated by a desire to overawe the rioters, but these units that had seen action in Gettysburg did not play any role in suppressing the unrest.

39. Joseph Choate to his wife, July 16, 1863, in Edward Martin, *The Life of Joseph Hodges Choate as Gathered Chiefly from His Letters*, 2 vols. (New York, 1921), 1:257; "Riot Subsiding," *Times*, July 17, 1863, 1; Schecter, *Devil's Own Work*, 225–29.

40. Report of Captain H. R. Putnam in Headley, *Great Riots*, 334–36 ("fiends"); "Quiet Restored," *Times*, July 18, 1863, 1; "The Riot," *Tribune*, July 18, 1863, 1, 8; Schecter, *Devil's Own Work*, 229–31.

41. "The Draft and the Riots," *Irish-American*, July 25, 1863, 2 ("saturnalia"); Cook, *Armies of the Streets*, 194–95; *The Diary of George Templeton Strong*, ed. Allan Nevins and Milton Thomas, 4 vols. (New York, 1952), 4:25. The figures for the mortality rate of Civil War gunshot victims in the Union army are from William Fox, *Regimental Losses in the American Civil War, 1861–1865* (Albany, 1889), 24. Seventy-one percent of Civil War gunshot victims survived their wounds. Of those who did not, 61 percent died on the battlefield and the remainder succumbed to their injuries later.

42. Cook, *Armies of the Streets*, 213–32; Barnes, *Draft Riots*, 113–16.

43. "Fires During the Riots," *Times*, October 21, 1863, 2; *Diary of Strong*, 3:342. The most complete published list of criminal acts during the riots, taken from police records, is in Barnes, *Draft Riots*, 32–105.

44. "The Insurrection," *Tribune*, July 18, 1863, 4 ("atrocities"); "The Irish," *Tribune*, July 20,

1863, 4; "The Effect of the Late Riots," *Harper's Weekly* (August 8, 1863): 498; *Diary of Strong,* 3:343, 352.

45. "The Draft and the Riots" and "More Assaults on 'the Irish,'" *Irish-American,* July 25, 1863, 2; Peter Welsh to his wife, July 17 and August 2, 1863, in Kohl, *Irish Green and Union Blue,* 110, 115.

46. Karl Wesslau to his parents, July 28, 1863, in Kamphoefner and Helbich, *Germans in the Civil War,* 65–66.

47. "The Insurrection," *Tribune,* July 18, 1863, 4 ("Fernando"); Harold Hammond, ed., *Diary of a Union Lady, 1861–1865* (New York, 1962), 251.

48. Letter to the editor, *Times,* July 15, 1863, 4; "What Caused the Mob," *Tribune,* July 17, 1863, 4; Charles Loring Brace, "The Poor and the Rich: A Lesson from the July Riots," *Times,* October 18, 1863, 5; Hammond, *Diary of a Union Lady,* 248.

49. Anbinder, "Which Poor Man's Fight?," 352–53; Emile Dupré to his mother, July 28, 1864, Emilie Wesslau to her parents, July 28, 1863, Karl Wesslau to his parents, December 14, 1864, and Heinrich Müller to his parents, July 25, 1865, in Kamphoefner and Helbich, *Germans in the Civil War,* 57, 66, 69 ("move"), 249 ("get me").

50. Anbinder, "Which Poor Man's Fight?," 349–50; Tyler Anbinder, *Five Points: The Nineteenth-Century New York City Neighborhood That Invented Tap Dance, Stole Elections, and Became the World's Most Notorious Slum* (New York, 2001), 317–18; Bayor and Meagher, *The New York Irish,* 207; Burrows and Wallace, *Gotham,* 896.

51. Karl Wesslau to his parents, December 14, 1864, in Kamphoefner and Helbich, *Germans in the Civil War,* 69; Bayor and Meagher, *New York Irish,* 207; Bruce, *Harp and the Eagle,* 199 (quotation).

52. Entry for Joseph Pulitzer, manifest of the *Garland,* August 31, 1864, Boston Passenger and Crew Lists, National Archives, accessed via ancestry.com; service record of Joseph Pouletzes, Company L, First New York (Lincoln) Cavalry, *The American Civil War Research Database* (Alexandria, Va., 2014); James Morris, *Pulitzer: A Life in Politics, Print, and Power* (New York, 2010), 9–23; István Vida, *Hungarian Émigrés in the American Civil War: A Historical and Biographical Dictionary* (Jefferson, N.C., 2012), 179–81.

53. Karl Wesslau to his parents, July 28, 1863, and May 28, 1864, in Kamphoefner and Helbich, *Germans in the Civil War,* 65, 67; *The Twenty-Second Annual Report of the New York Association for Improving the Condition of the Poor* (New York, 1865), 24; Edward Young, *Special Report on Immigration* (Washington, D.C., 1872), xxi.

54. Robert Sneden, *Eye of the Storm: A Civil War Odyssey,* ed. Charles Bryan and Nelson Lankford (New York, 2000), 147–49, 190, 214.

55. "David Goodman Croly," *Real Estate Record and Builders Guide* 43 (May 4, 1889): 613–14 ("conscious"); entry for David Croly, family 1853, Ward Five, 1850 census; *Memories of Jane Cunningham Croly* (New York, 1904), 6; "Women's Work on Newspapers," *Washington Post,* February 20, 1887, 6.

56. "Death of David G. Croly," *Boston Herald,* April 30, 1889, 8; "David Goodman Croly," *Real Estate Record and Builders Guide* 43 (May 4, 1889): 613, and (May 18, 1889): supp. pp. 3–11; *Memories of Jane Cunningham Croly,* 11 ("volcanic"), 208 ("magnetism").

57. *Miscegenation: The Theory of the Blending of the Races, Applied to the American White Man and Negro* (New York, 1864), i–ii, 55–60, 65 (quotation); David Levy, *Herbert Croly*

of the New Republic: The Life and Thought of an American Progressive (Princeton, 1985), 13–14.

58. Sidney Kaplan, "The Miscegenation Issue in the Election of 1864," *Journal of Negro History* 34 (1949): 277, 286–313, 319, 324; *Congressional Globe,* 38th Cong., 1st sess. (1864), 133, 1074–80, 1620, 2048, 2979; Samuel Cox, *Eight Years in Congress from 1857–1865* (New York, 1865), 352–70; "The Beastly Doctrine of Miscegenation and Its High Priests," *Richmond Whig,* April 8, 1864, 4; "'Miscegenation' at the North," *Charleston Mercury,* April 12, 1864, 1; "Practical Miscegenation in New York," *Augusta (Ga.) Constitutionalist,* April 17, 1864, 1; "Miscegenation," *Houston Telegraph,* June 24, 1864, 2.

59. "The Victory: Lincoln Re-Elected," *Tribune,* November 9, 1864, 1; Kaplan, "Miscegenation Issue," 326–38.

60. Captain August Horstmann to his parents, July 16, 1864, in Kamphoefner and Helbich, *Germans in the Civil War,* 128; Peter Welsh to Patrick Prendergast, June 1, 1863, in Kohl, *Irish Green and Union Blue,* 100–102; Manning, *What This Cruel War Was Over,* 149–50 ("cessation"), 183–86; McPherson, *For Cause and Comrades,* 176–78; White, *Emancipation,* 106–11.

61. Sneden, *Eye of the Storm,* 257–305; Karl Wesslau to his parents, June 13, 1865, in Kamphoefner and Helbich, *Germans in the Civil War,* 70.

62. "Virginia! Richmond and Petersburg Taken!" *Tribune,* April 4, 1863, 1; "The Rejoicings Last Night," *Herald,* April 4, 1865, 5; "The End of the War," *Irish-American,* April 8, 1865, 2; "Virginia! Lee Surrenders! The Rebellion Ended!" *Tribune,* April 10, 1865, 1; Marie Wesslau to her parents, New York, June 13, 1865, and Julius Wesslau to his parents, June 21, 1865, in Kamphoefner and Helbich, *Germans in the Civil War,* 71–72.

13. Transition

1. James McPherson, *Battle Cry of Freedom: The Civil War Era* (New York, 1988), 859.

2. *Annual Report of the Commissioners of Emigration of the State of New York for 1885* (n.p., 1886), 61–63; *Annual Report of the Commissioner General of Immigration to the Secretary of the Treasury for the Fiscal Year Ending June 30, 1896* (Washington, D.C., 1896), 9 (1895 figure is for the fiscal year that ran from July 1, 1895, to June 30, 1896).

3. Manifest of the *Nevada,* January 2, 1892, "New York Passenger Lists."

4. *Annual Report of the Chamber of Commerce of the State of New York for the Year 1859–'60* (New York, 1860), 278; Frederich Kapp, *Immigration, and the Commissioners of Emigration of the State of New York* (New York, 1870), 38, 241.

5. "Machine Politics," *Portland (Me.) Daily Advertiser,* August 30, 1850, 2; "Machine Politics," *Albany Evening Journal,* September 17, 1858, 2; "The Post-Office," *Tribune,* October 26, 1858, 4; "The Charter Election," *Commercial Advertiser,* December 3, 1858, 2; "Our City Politics," *Tribune,* April 21, 1859, 4 (quotation); "The Tammany, Mozart, and Other Machines — A Grand Smash Imminent," *Herald,* October 28, 1863, 6.

6. Entry for William Tweed, family 128, district 1, Ward Seven, 1850 census, and family 210, district 1, Ward Seven, 1855 New York State census; Leo Hershkowitz, *Tweed's New York: Another Look* (Garden City, N.Y., 1977), 5–7, 85, 148–49; "What Comes of Having a Bad Memory," *Times,* August 22, 1871, 4 (bankruptcy).

7. Alexander Callow Jr., *The Tweed Ring* (New York, 1966), 11; Tyler Anbinder, "William Magear Tweed," in *American National Biography Online* (New York, 2000).

8. "City Politics," *Herald*, September 3, 1867, 10 ("Tweed Ring"), September 23, 1867, 8, March 10, 1868, 4 ("all the offices"); "The Way They Do It," *Tribune*, October 18, 1869, 4; "Probably," *Harper's Weekly* (April 11, 1868): 227; "King Tweed and His Subjects," *Times*, September 28, 1870, 4. The first reference I have found to "Boss Tweed" is in "Rush for the Spoils," *Herald*, May 3, 1870, 6.

9. "Senator Tweed's Betrayal of the Democratic Party," *World*, March 28, 1870, 4; "Why Attack Mr. Tweed?" *Times*, September 29, 1870, 4.

10. Thomas Lowry, *Tarnished Eagles: The Courts-Martial of Fifty Union Colonels and Lieutenant Colonels* (Mechanicsburg, Pa., 1997), 47–51; "The City Judiciary Election: Its Hopeless and Hopeful Aspects," *Times*, November 7, 1863, 4; John Davenport, *The Election and Naturalization Frauds in New York City, 1860–1870*, 2nd ed. (New York, 1894), 49–56.

11. *Report of the Special Committee of the Board of Aldermen Appointed to Investigate the "Ring Frauds"* (New York, 1878), 133–37; William M. Ivins, *Machine Politics and Money in Elections in New York City* (1887; repr., New York, 1970), 25.

12. *Report of the Select Committee on Alleged New York Election Frauds* (Washington, D.C., 1869), 38–50; Tyler Anbinder, *Five Points: The Nineteenth-Century New York City Neighborhood That Invented Tap Dance, Stole Elections, and Became the World's Most Notorious Slum* (New York, 2001), 321–27. Once he entered politics, Cuddy began to declare himself American-born to census enumerators, but he was a native of Ireland, like his older and younger siblings William, Robert, and Cornelius, who continued to report themselves as Irish-born throughout their lives. See entries for the Cuddy family on the manifest of the ship *Hibernia*, February 28, 1842, "New York Passenger Lists," and family 1713, Ward Six, 1850 census.

13. Entries for Michael Norton, family 304, district 6, Ward Five, 1855 New York census; family 34, district 4, Ward Eight, 1860 census; S. R. Harlow and S. C. Hutchins, *Life Sketches of the State Officers, Senators, and Members of the Assembly of the State of New York in 1868* (Albany, 1868), 123–25 (quotation); "Michael Norton Dead," *Times*, April 24, 1889, 2.

14. Untitled article, *Tribune*, October 10, 1868, 4 ("mill"); "How Naturalized Citizens Are Made: Shameless Conduct of Tammany Hall Judges," *Tribune*, October 14, 1868, 2 ("train"); "The Naturalization Frauds," *Tribune*, October 24, 1868, 4; "Naturalization in New York," *Herald*, October 19, 1868, 10; "The Work of Naturalization," *Tribune*, October 24, 1868, 4; "Naturalization" and "The Alleged Naturalization Frauds in Our Courts," *Times*, October 17, 1868, 4, 5; "Naturalization," *Times*, October 24, 1868, 5; entry for Benjamin Rosenberg, family 862, district 3, Ward Seventeen, 1860 census; Davenport, *Election and Naturalization Frauds*, 123, 141; Anbinder, *Five Points*, 323–24.

15. William Tweed to H. L. Davis, October 24, 1846, H. L. Davis Papers, New-York Historical Society (vote for Harper); Tyler Anbinder, "'Boss' Tweed: Nativist," *Journal of the Early Republic* 15 (1995): 109–16.

16. "Board of Supervisors: Full Report of the County Substitute and Relief Committee," *Herald*, October 27, 1863, 10; "New York Quota Full," *Herald*, May 21, 1864, 4; "Cost of

the War," *Times*, July 1, 1865, 3; Ronald Bayor and Timothy Meagher, eds., *The New York Irish* (Baltimore, 1996), 207; "The 'Tweed Association,'" *Irish-American*, September 2, 1871, 5; John Pratt, "Boss Tweed's Public Welfare Program," *New-York Historical Society Quarterly* 45 (1961): 396–411; untitled article, *The Nation* 6 (May 7, 1868): 363; Dexter A. Hawkins, *Sectarian Appropriations of Public Money and Public Property in the City of New York* (New York, 1872), 4; Eugene Lawrence, "The Romish Victory over the Common Schools," *Harper's Weekly* (December 14, 1872): 974.

17. *The Diary of George Templeton Strong*, ed. Allan Nevins and Milton Thomas, 4 vols. (New York, 1952), 4:236, 352.

18. Albert Paine, *Thomas Nast: His Period and His Pictures* (1904; repr., New York, 1980), 1–15; Fiona Halloran, *Thomas Nast: The Father of Modern Political Cartoons* (Chapel Hill, 2012), 1–18; entry for Nast, family 416, Ward Ten, 1850 census.

19. "Frank Leslie," *Frank Leslie's Illustrated Newspaper* (January 24, 1880): 382; entry for Leslie, family 1032, Williamsburg, Kings County (Brooklyn), 1850 census; Joshua Brown, *Beyond the Lines: Pictorial Reporting, Everyday Life, and the Crisis of Gilded Age America* (Berkeley, 2002), 17–22.

20. Paine, *Nast*, 16–82.

21. "Christmas Eve, 1862," *Harper's Weekly* (January 3, 1863): 8–9, 14; Paine, *Nast*, 86 ("only a picture"); "Caricature in America," *All the Year Round* (September 28, 1878): 299 ("think Thomas Nast").

22. "Santa Claus in Camp" and "Santa Claus Among Our Soldiers," *Harper's Weekly* (January 3, 1863): 1, 6; Thomas Nast, *Thomas Nast's Christmas Drawings for the Human Race* (New York, 1890); William Waits, *The Modern Christmas in America: A Cultural History of Gift Giving* (New York, 1993), 128–29; Penne Restad, *Christmas in America: A History* (New York, 1995), 146–47; Stephen Nissenbaum, *The Battle for Christmas* (New York, 1996), 86–88.

23. "This Is a White Man's Government," *Harper's Weekly* (September 5, 1868): 568; Halloran, *Nast*, 107–11.

24. "The Government of the City of New York," *Harper's Weekly* (February 9, 1867): 88; "Excommunication of Modern Civilization," *Harper's Weekly* (December 25, 1869): 824; "Shadows of Forthcoming Events," *Harper's Weekly* (January 22, 1870): 56–57; "The Greek Slave" and "Senator Tweed in a New Role," *Harper's Weekly* (April 16, 1870): 248–49; "New York Excelsior," *Harper's Weekly* (June 4, 1870): 356.

25. "The Orangemen: History and Progress of the Organization," *Morning Telegraph*, July 9, 1871, 1; Tony Gray, *The Orange Order* (London, 1972), 57–87.

26. "History of the Orange Riots in New-York," *Times*, July 12, 1871, 1; "Grand Orange and Protestant Parade," *Herald*, July 12, 1868, 1; "Riot on the Boulevard" and "Riot in the Bowery," *Herald*, July 13, 1869, 5, 7; "Riot at Elm Park," *Evening Post*, July 13, 1870, 6; "Orangeism on Its Native Soil," *Herald*, July 30, 1871, 6; Michael Gordon, *The Orange Riots: Irish Political Violence in New York City, 1870 and 1871* (Ithaca, 1993), 27, 36. The Battle of the Boyne actually took place on July 1, 1690, according to the Julian calendar, which translates to July 11 in the current Gregorian calendar. Why the Battle of the Boyne is commemorated on July 12 is not clear.

27. "Terrible Riot," *Tribune*, July 13, 1870, 1; Gordon, *Orange Riots*, 33 ("Croppies").

28. "Terrible Riot," *Tribune*, July 13, 1870, 1; "Orange and Green," *Herald*, July 11, 1871, 10 (rumor of gunfire); Gordon, *Orange Riots*, 40.

29. "Terrible Riot," *Tribune*, July 13, 1870, 1; "A Bloody Faction Fight," *Herald*, July 13, 1870, 7; "Bloody Riot," *Times*, July 13, 1870, 1 (quotation).

30. "Terrible Riot," *Tribune*, July 13, 1870, 1 ("Stones" and "extermination"); "Bloody Riot," *Times*, July 13, 1870, 1; Gordon, *Orange Riots*, 39–40 ("Men").

31. Gordon, *Orange Riots*, 41, 221–23.

32. *Diary of George Templeton Strong*, 4:295; "Edith O'Gorman on the Elm Park Riot," *Times*, July 16, 1870, 3.

33. "The Twelfth of July: What It Means in America," *Irish-American*, July 23, 1870, 4; "Orange Riot in New York," *Pilot* (Boston), July 23, 1870, 4; "Orange and Green," *Herald*, July 11, 1871, 10 ("Americans forget"); "Orangeism," *Irish-American*, July 29, 1871, 5; "What an 'Ancient Hibernian' Thinks," *Herald*, July 11, 1871, 10 ("outrages"); "Another County Heard From: What a County Down Man Thinks," *Herald*, July 10, 1871, 8; "Another County Heard From: The Voice of Limerick," *Herald*, July 10, 1871, 8; "The 'Twelfth of July,'" *Irish-American*, July 1, 1871, 4; "The 12th of July Parade," *Irish-American*, July 8, 1871, 4; Gordon, *Orange Riots*, 47–48.

34. Christening of Thomas Nast, September 27, 1840, Saint Mary's Catholic Church, Landau, Bavaria, in "Germany: Births and Baptisms," accessed via familysearch.org; "The Promised Land," *Harper's Weekly* (October 1, 1870): 625; "America (?) Sympathizes with the Pope," *Harper's Weekly* (January 21, 1871): 61; "Church & State: Europe [and the] United States," *Harper's Weekly* (February 19, 1870): 121; "Church and State," *Harper's Weekly* (February 25, 1871): 172; Halloran, *Nast*, 33–38.

35. "Ribbonmen vs. Orangemen," *Tribune*, July 1, 1871, 8; "A Riot Impending," *Tribune*, July 10, 1871, 1; "The Orange Procession an Insult," *Herald*, July 11, 1871, 4; "The People's Opinion on the Orange Parade," *Times*, July 10, 1871, 5.

36. "Surrender to the Mob: The Orangemen's Parade Forbidden," *Tribune*, July 11, 1871, 1; letter signed "A Sixty-Year-Old American Citizen," in "Protests from the People," *Tribune*, July 12, 1871, 8 (quotation); "Terrorism Rampant; The City Authorities Overawed by the Roman Catholics; Superintendent Kelso Forbids the Orange Parade," *Times*, July 11, 1871, 1; Gordon, *Orange Riots*, 49–50, 59–61.

37. "Tammany's Surrender," *Tribune*, July 12, 1871, 1, 8; "A Big Back Down," *Times*, July 12, 1871, 1; Gordon, *Orange Riots*, 85–91 (quotation, 86).

38. "A Terrible Day" and "A Fatal Riot," *Times*, July 13, 1871, 1, 4; "The Recent Riot," *Times*, July 14, 1871, 1; "Minor Topics," *Times*, July 15, 1871, 4 (Nast); Gordon, *Orange Riots*, 89–90, 97–98, 104–5 (quotation), 110–14. For the rental of hotel rooms to view a riot, see Anbinder, *Five Points*, 288.

39. Gordon, *Orange Riots*, 116–17, 120 ("two Irish"), 123, 126 ("indiscriminate"); "EXCELSIOR!" *Herald*, July 13, 1871, 3-5 ("leaving," 3); "Firing on the Mob," *Times*, July 13, 1871, 5 ("quickstep").

40. "The Dead and Wounded," *Times*, July 13, 1871, 5; "The Hibernian Mob," *Sun*, July 13, 1871, 1; "After the Battle," *Herald*, July 13, 1871, 5; "The Massacre: Another Account," *Irish World* [Boston], July 22, 1871, 5; Gordon, *Orange Riots*, 126, 129–30, 224–37.

41. "Excelsior! Law Triumphs — Order Reigns," *Herald*, July 13, 1871, 3; "Yesterday's Dis-

turbances," *Times,* July 13, 1871, 4; "Spirit of the Mob," *Tribune,* July 14, 1871, 1; "Bravo! Bravo!" *Harper's Weekly* (July 29, 1871): 689.

42. "We Demand Justice," *Irish-American,* July 22, 1871, 4 ("demand"); "Can You Wait?" *Irish-American,* July 29, 1871, 4 ("Murder"); "'The Irish!'" *Irish-American,* August 12, 1871, 4 ("gorilla faces").

43. "Can You Wait?" *Irish-American,* July 29, 1871, 4.

44. "The Tammany Riot," *Tribune,* July 13, 1871, 4 ("frightful"); "Tammany Sentenced," *Tribune,* July 14, 1871, 8; "Irish Character and the Late Riot," *Times,* July 16, 1871, 4; "The Tammany Riot," *Harper's Weekly* (July 29, 1871): 693.

45. Gordon, *Orange Riots,* 188 (quotation); "The Power Behind the Throne," *Harper's Weekly* (October 29, 1870): 697; "Our Modern Falstaff Reviewing His Army," *Harper's Weekly* (November 5, 1870): 713; "Tweedledee and Sweedledum," *Harper's Weekly* (January 14, 1871): 40; "Under the Thumb," *Harper's Weekly* (June 10, 1871): 536; "On to Washington," *Harper's Weekly* (June 17, 1871): 552; "Some Are Born Great, Some Achieve Greatness," *Harper's Weekly* (July 1, 1871): 608; "The Glorious Fourth" and "Three Blind Mice," *Harper's Weekly* (July 22, 1871): 668, 680 (despite its date, this issue of *Harper's* was prepared before the 1871 riots). On the Chinese, see "Throwing Down the Ladder by Which They Rose," *Harper's Weekly* (July 23, 1870): 480; "The New Comet," *Harper's Weekly* (August 6, 1870): 505; "The Chinese Question," *Harper's Weekly* (February 18, 1871): 149. On papal infallibility, see "I Am Now Infallible," *Harper's Weekly* (July 30, 1870): 496; "The Luther of the Nineteenth Century" and "A Midsummer Night's Dream," *Harper's Weekly* (July 15, 1871): 648, 656.

46. "Something That Will Not Blow Over" and "The New Horse Plague," *Harper's Weekly* (July 29, 1871): 696–97, 704; "Shakespeare on the Late Riot" and "How We Go Up," *Harper's Weekly* (August 5, 1871): 716, 728; "Not a Bailable Case," *Harper's Weekly* (August 12, 1871): 752; "Who Stole the People's Money?" *Harper's Weekly* (August 19, 1871): 764; "The President of the United States and His Cabinet for 1872" and "Thomas Nast," *Harper's Weekly* (August 26, 1871): 788, 803–5 ("his part"); "The Rich Growing Richer, the Poor Growing Poorer" and "The Usual Irish Way of Doing Things," *Harper's Weekly* (September 2, 1871): 812, 824; "Wholesale and Retail," *Harper's Weekly* (September 16, 1871): 865; "A Group of Vultures Waiting for the Storm to 'Blow Over,' — 'Let Us Prey'" and "What the German Democrats Have Done About It," *Harper's Weekly* (September 23, 1871): 889, 896; "Too Thin!" "The Only Way to Get Our Tammany Rulers on the Square," "The American River Ganges," and "Which Nobody Can Deny," *Harper's Weekly* (September 30, 1871): 905, 914, 916, 920. Nast's national following is evident in "Nast, the Artist," *Cincinnati Gazette,* August 21, 1871, 1; "Nast the Artist," *Providence Evening Press,* September 1, 1871, 1; "Thomas Nast," *Philadelphia Inquirer,* November 10, 1871, 4; "Nast," *San Francisco Bulletin,* December 21, 1871, 2.

47. Kenneth Ackerman, *Boss Tweed: The Rise and Fall of the Corrupt Pol Who Conceived the Soul of Modern New York* (New York, 2005), 127–28, 148–50; "The Ring and the City Armories" and "More Ring Villainy," *Times,* July 8, 1871, 4–5; "Louis John Jennings," *Times,* February 10, 1893, 5; "Who Killed the Ring?" *Daily Graphic,* August 2, 1875, 3; entries for Matthew J. O'Rourke, dwelling 221, Ward Fourteen, 1855 New York State census; dwelling 275, electoral district 13, Ward Twenty, 1870 census (second enumeration);

dwelling 61, enumeration district 84, Kings County (Brooklyn), 1880 census; and family 204, enumeration district 54, Kings County, 1900 census.

48. Ackerman, *Boss Tweed*, 123–63; David Morphet, *Louis Jennings MP: Editor of the New York Times and Tory Democrat* (London, 2001), 113–14; Callow, *Tweed Ring*, 198–206; entry for James O'Brien, dwelling 432, district 2, Ward Twenty-one, 1855 New York census; "Died," *Evening Post,* May 7, 1883 (death notice for O'Brien's father with his Irish place of birth); "James O'Brien Dead," *Tribune*, March 6, 1907, 7; "Tweed's Arch Foe, James O'Brien, Dead," *Times,* March 6, 1907, 9; "Obituary: James Watson," *Herald,* January 31, 1871, 5; "The County Court-House," *Harper's Weekly* (September 9, 1871): 836, 839. Very little about O'Brien's early life in either the *Times* or *Tribune* obituary is accurate.

49. Entry for John Foord, dwelling 187, enumeration district 44, Kings County (Brooklyn), 1880 census; Jennings quoted in "Boss Tweed and His Men," *Napier (N.Z.) Daily Telegraph,* June 25, 1887, 2; Ackerman, *Boss Tweed*, 131, 160, 164–65.

50. Charles Wingate, "An Episode in Municipal Government," *North American Review* 121 (July 1875): 150–52; Paine, *Nast,* 179–82 ("bars," 182).

51. "The Secret Accounts," *Times,* July 22, 24, 26, 1871, 1; "The Master Thief," "Tweed's Guilt," and "Proofs of Tweed's Guilt," *Times,* October 26, 1871, 4, 5, 9–10; "Tweed's Dilemma" and "The Arrest of Tweed," *Times,* October 27, 1871, 1; "Tweed's Jury" and "Tweed's Temporary Escape," *Times,* February 1, 1873, 1, 4; "Justice At Last," *Times,* November 20, 1873, 1; "Tweed's Sentence Void," *Tribune,* June 16, 1875, 1; "Tweed's Release," *Tribune,* June 23, 1875, 1; "Tweed a Fugitive," *Tribune,* December 6, 1875, 1; "A Verdict Against Tweed," *Times,* March 9, 1876, 1; Paine, *Nast,* 336–37; Anbinder, "Tweed"; Ackerman, *Boss Tweed,* 167–344.

52. "Who Killed the Ring?" *The Nation* (November 23, 1871): 334-35; "Who Killed the Ring?" *Evening Post,* November 23, 1871, 2; untitled editorial, *Hartford Courant,* November 4, 1871, 2; "Thomas Nast," *Philadelphia Inquirer,* November 10, 1871, 4.

53. Gordon, *Orange Riots,* 188 ("nativist"); "Belmont versus Tweed," *Herald,* August 22, 1869, 6; "More of the Belmont-Tweed Imbroglio," *Herald,* September 8, 1869, 6; Irving Katz, *August Belmont: A Political Biography* (New York, 1968), 187–93; "Political: The German Democracies' Repudiation of Tammany," *Tribune,* August 29, 1871, 4; "What the German Democrats Have Done About It," *Harper's Weekly* (September 23, 1871): 896; "Honor to Whom Honor," *Tribune,* November 10, 1871, 4; "Who Killed the Ring?" *The Nation* (November 23, 1871): 6–7; "Ottendorfer and O'Brien," *Commercial Advertiser,* November 20, 1871, 2; Stanley Nadel, *Little Germany: Ethnicity, Religion, and Class in New York City, 1845–80* (Urbana, 1990), 150–52; "A House Divided," *Harper's Weekly* (October 14, 1871): 963; entry for John Kelly, dwelling 151, enumeration district 477, 1880 census. For continued support for Tweed among Irish Americans, see "William M. Tweed," *Irish-American,* September 23, 1871, 4; "The 'City Frauds,'" *Irish-American,* November 4, 1871, 4; and Kerby Miller, *Emigrants and Exiles: Ireland and the Irish Exodus to North America* (New York, 1985), 330–31.

54. "Some Useful Lessons" and "The City Vote," *Times,* November 7, 1872, 4 (quotations), 8.

55. "Discontented Democrats," *Herald,* June 15, 1873, 7.

56. Untitled article, *The Nation* 6 (May 7, 1868): 363; Eugene Lawrence, "The Romish Victory over the Common Schools," *Harper's Weekly* (December 14, 1872): 974; [John Gil-

mary Shea], "The Anti-Catholic Issue in the Late Election," *American Catholic Quarterly Review* 6 (1881): 38 ("shame"); Edmund Dunne, *Our Public Schools: Are They Free or Are They Not?* (New York, 1875), 14; "The Pastoral Letter of the Third Plenary Council of Baltimore," *American Catholic Quarterly Review* 10 (1885): 13 ("institutions"); Donald C. Shearer, *Pontificia Americana* (Washington, D.C., 1933): 367-71; Lloyd Jorgenson, *The State and the Non-Public School, 1825-1925* (Columbia, Mo., 1987), 111-45.

57. Thomas Nast, "Our Common Schools As They Are and As They May Be," *Harper's Weekly* (February 26, 1870): 140-42; Eugene Lawrence, "The Priests and the Children," *Harper's Weekly* (September 30, 1871): 915 ("ceaseless," "succession"); Eugene Lawrence, "The Pope and the Teacher," *Harper's Weekly* (November 4, 1871): 1042 ("multitude," "bulwark"); Eugene Lawrence, "Compulsory Education in New York," *Harper's Weekly* (January 16, 1875): 49, 58; "Reading of the Bible: The Opposition of the Roman Catholics," *Times*, July 25, 1873, 2; "The School Question," *Times*, October 2, 1873, 5; "The School Question," *Times*, April 1, 1875, 5; "Local Miscellany: The School Question," *Times*, April 4, 1875, 12; "The Catholic Attack on the Schools," *Times*, April 5, 1875, 4; "Catholic and Public Schools," *Times*, April 7, 1875, 12; "Shall We Have Catholic Public Schools," *Times*, April 10, 1875, 6; Ward McAfee, *Religion, Race, and Reconstruction: The Public School in the Politics of the 1870s* (Albany, 1998), 27-78.

58. "The American River Ganges," *Harper's Weekly* (September 30, 1871): 916; "Church — State — School: The Irrepressible Conflict," *Tribune*, December 18, 1875, 5.

59. "Local Miscellany: Conclave of Catholic Pastors," *Tribune*, May 14, 1870, 2; "The Public Schools and the Priesthood: Dr. McGlynn and Farrell," *Tribune*, May 21, 1870, 4; "Catholics and the School Question," *Pilot* (Boston), September 4, 1875, 4; "Grant on the School Question," *Irish-American*, October 9, 1875, 4; "Grant's Position Defined," *Irish-American*, December 18, 1875, 3; "The Danger to the Schools," *Tribune*, December 11, 1875, 6; Tyler Anbinder, "Ulysses S. Grant, Nativist," *Civil War History* 43 (1997): 129-39; Marie Klinkhamer, "The Blaine Amendment of 1875: Private Motives for Political Action," *Catholic Historical Review* 42 (1956): 15-49; Stephen Green, "The Blaine Amendment Reconsidered," *American Journal of Legal History* 36 (1992): 38-69.

60. Entry for William R. Grace, family 74, Ward Three, Kings County (Brooklyn), 1865 New York State census, and family 519, enumeration district 290, Great Neck, Queens County, 1880 census; "Sketches of the Candidates," *Herald*, October 19, 1880, 3; "William R. Grace's Career," *Times*, March 22, 1904, 9.

61. "The Democratic Factions," *Times*, October 16 and 19, 1880, 2; "The Mayoralty," *Times*, October 19, 1880, 4; "The Mayoralty," *Herald*, October 19, 1880, 6; "The Nomination for Mayor," *Tribune*, October 19, 1880, 4; "Dividing Public Offices" and "Roman Catholicism in Politics," *Times*, October 20, 1880, 4, 8; "Public Schools in Peril," *Times*, October 30, 1880, 1 ("dictates"); "Result of the City Vote," *Times*, November 4, 1880, 8; "The Mayoralty: Mr. Grace's Letter of Acceptance" and "The Mayoralty Canvass," *Irish-American*, November 6, 1880, 1, 4 ("bigotry"); "The City Elections" and "A Foiled Attack," *Irish-American*, November 13, 1880, 4; "The City Vote," *Times*, November 6, 1878, 1-2; "Analyzing the City Vote," *Times*, November 7, 1880, 7; Marquis James, *Merchant Adventurer: The Story of W. R. Grace* (Wilmington, Del., 1993), 153-59.

62. James, *Grace*, 162–77; Lawrence Clayton, *Grace: W. R. Grace & Co., The Formative Years: 1850–1930* (Ottawa, Ill., 1985), 84–99.

63. "Unusual Burden for Early Olympian," *Times*, July 26, 2012 (quotations); Britt Peterson, "The Irish Whales: America's Gluttonous, English-Hating, Gold-Medal-Winning Olympic Heroes of the Early 20th Century," *Slate*, July 26, 2012.

64. "Martin Sheridan Is Dead," *Times*, March 28, 1918, 12 (quotation); "To No Earthly King: The United States Flag-Bearing Incident at the 1908 Olympic Games Opening Ceremony," *Journal of Olympic History* (September 1999): 21–28; "The Marathon's Random Route to Its Length," *Times*, April 20, 2012; "The United States," *Times (London)*, November 19, 1908, 7.

65. Alan Katchen, *Abel Kiviat, National Champion: Twentieth-Century Track & Field and the Melting Pot* (Syracuse, 2009), 5, 31–32, 51, 339 ("greatest race"); Ralph Wilcox, "Irish Americans in Sports: The Nineteenth Century," in *Making the Irish American: History and Heritage of the Irish in the United States*, ed. Joseph Lee and Marion R. Casey (New York, 2006), 451.

66. The occupational data in these paragraphs and the ones that follow are based on data from Steven Ruggles, J. Trent Alexander, Katie Genadek, Ronald Goeken, Matthew B. Schroeder, and Matthew Sobek, *Integrated Public Use Microdata Series: Version 5.0* (Minneapolis, 2010), accessed at usa.ipums.org. I cleaned up the IPUMS data and assigned an occupational category to each occupation. My versions of these data, and a list of the occupations that make up each occupational category, are available as "1860 New York City 1% Census Sample," "1880 New York City 1% Census Sample," and "1900 New York City 5% Census Sample," in "Replication Data for *City of Dreams*" at https://dataverse.harvard.edu/dataverse/anbinder.

67. For the birthplaces of New York's German immigrants in the late nineteenth century, see Nadel, *Little Germany*, 19–26.

68. In 1880, one in three Irish-born adult women worked for pay, compared to one in five German immigrant women. In 1860, one in six German-born women worked for pay, compared to one in three Irish immigrant women.

69. Janet Nolan, *Servants of the Poor: Teachers and Mobility in Ireland and Irish America* (Notre Dame, 2004), 1–4.

70. Test book entry for John Bergen, account 4534, Emigrant Savings Bank Papers, New York Public Library; entries for McGuire family, family 140, division 2, Ward Twenty-two, 1860 census, and family 154, enumeration district 233, 1880 census; entry for the Pulleyn family, family 84, enumeration district 236, 1900 census; family 205, enumeration district 591, Ward Twelve, 1910 census; family 141, enumeration district 819, assembly district 11, 1920 census; family 332, enumeration district 552, 1930 census; "John J. Pulleyn, Banker, 86, Dead: Former Head of the Emigrant Industrial Savings Served in Port Authority Post," *Times*, April 4, 1947, 23; Tyler Anbinder, "Moving Beyond 'Rags to Riches': New York's Irish Famine Immigrants and Their Surprising Savings Accounts," *Journal of American History* 99 (2012): 764.

71. Test book entry for Joseph Kingsley, account 12901, Emigrant Savings Bank Papers; entries for Joseph Kingsley, passenger manifest, *Devonshire*, November 25, 1852, "New

York Passenger Lists"; family 270, district 2, Ward Six, 1860 census; family 115, enumeration district 243, Ward Nineteen, Baltimore, Baltimore County, Md., 1900 census; family 50, enumeration district 276, District of Columbia, 1920 census; family 25, enumeration district 747, borough of Osborne, Ohio Township, Allegheny County, Pa., 1930 census; "Norfolk Southern Votes: Major Kingsley Succeeds L. A. Beck in Presidency," *Times*, May 16, 1947, 34.

14. Liberty

1. Edward Berenson, *The Statue of Liberty: A Transatlantic Story* (New Haven, 2012), 8–11; Yasmin Khan, *Enlightening the World: The Creation of the Statue of Liberty* (Ithaca, 2010), 11–26, 33–41.
2. Berenson, *Statue*, 30–56, Khan, *Enlightening the World*, 47–81, 102–3, 135.
3. Berenson, *Statue*, 73–83; "The French Statue," *Times*, September 29, 1876, 4.
4. "The Bedloe's Island Statue," *Times*, September 25, 1876, 8; "The Statue of Liberty," *Times*, February 6, 1877, 2 (quotation); Berenson, *Statue*, 85–86.
5. "The Statue of Liberty," *Times*, December 28, 1881, 5; "A Gift Statue," *Times*, December 26, 1883, 4; "Pedestal Loan Exhibition," *Tribune*, December 4, 1883, 2; Maureen C. O'Brien, *In Support of Liberty: European Paintings at the 1883 Pedestal Fund Art Loan Exhibition* (Southampton, N.Y., 1986), 17–21.
6. "Emma Lazarus," *Times*, November 20, 1887, 16; "Newport's Summer Residents," *Tribune*, May 18, 1878, 2; Esther Schor, *Emma Lazarus* (New York, 2006), 3–56.
7. Constance Cary Harrison, "She Gave an Impulse to Higher Things," *American Hebrew* 33 (December 9, 1887): 69 (an issue devoted almost entirely to reminiscences of Lazarus).
8. "Among the Russian Jews," *Times*, March 26, 1882, 12; Schor, *Lazarus*, 121–27, 133–36, 147–50, 175, 241.
9. Schor, *Lazarus*, 155–74.
10. Ibid., 185–89; A. Dunning Rea, "Mrs. Burton Harrison (1843–1920)," in *Encyclopedia Virginia*, http://www.EncyclopediaVirginia.org/Harrison_Burton_Mrs_1843–1920.
11. Harrison, "She Gave an Impulse to Higher Things," 69.
12. Emma Lazarus, *The Poems of Emma Lazarus*, 2 vols. (Boston, 1888), 1:202–3; "Admiring Objects of Art," *Times*, December 4, 1883, 2; Schor, *Lazarus*, 190.
13. Berenson, *Statue*, 77–86.
14. James Morris, *Pulitzer: A Life in Politics, Print, and Power* (New York, 2010), 29–206; Denis Brian, *Pulitzer: A Life* (New York, 2001), 8–66.
15. Morris, *Pulitzer*, 236 ("more sentiment"); "An Appeal," *World*, March 16, 1885, 4 (other quotations).
16. "The Money Kings and the Statue of Liberty," *World*, April 12, 1885, 1; "One Hundred Thousand Dollars!" *World*, August 11, 1885, 1; "The New York World," *New Haven Register*, August 12, 1885, 2; Morris, *Pulitzer*, 237; Oscar Handlin, *Statue of Liberty* (New York, 1971), 54.
17. "Up With the Pedestal," *World*, April 1, 1885, 5; "Pennies for the Pedestal," *World*, April 3, 1885, 5; Schor, *Lazarus*, 213–39.
18. "Emma Lazarus," *Times*, November 20, 1887, 16; "Miss Emma Lazarus Dead," *Herald*,

November 20, 1887, 11; "Funeral of Miss Emma Lazarus," *Tribune*, November 22, 1887, 10; "A View of Miss Lazarus," *Evening Post*, November 21, 1887, reprinted in *Jewish Messenger*, November 25, 1887, 5; [Josephine Lazarus], "Emma Lazarus," *The Century* 36 (October 1888): 875–84; Lazarus, *Poems*, 1:202–3.

19. "France's Gift Accepted" and "The Unveiling of the Statue," *Times*, October 29, 1886, 1–4; "Welcome to the Land of Freedom," *Frank Leslie's Illustrated Newspaper* (July 2, 1887): 324–25, 327.

20. M. E. Ravage, *An American in the Making: The Life Story of an Immigrant* (New York, 1917), 4 (quotation); *Thirtieth Annual Report of the Corporation of the Chamber of Commerce of the State of New York, for the Year 1887–'88*, 2 vols. (New York, 1888) 2:191; Susan Carter et al., eds., *Historical Statistics of the United States*, 2 vols. (New York, 2006), 1:561–62; Simon Kuznets, "Immigration of Russian Jews to the United States: Background and Structure," *Perspectives in American History* 9 (1975): 39.

21. Carter, *Historical Statistics of the United States*, 1:561–62; *Fourteenth Census of the United States Taken in the Year 1920*, 13 vols. (Washington, D.C., 1921–1923), 2:688, 729–31; Christopher Sterba, *Good Americans: Italian and Jewish Immigrants During the First World War* (New York, 2003), 19.

22. John Klier, "Pale of Settlement," in *The YIVO Encyclopedia of Jews in Eastern Europe*, ed. Gershon Hundert, 2 vols. (New Haven, 2008), 2:1311–14; *Oxford English Dictionary Online* (New York, 2014), s.v. "pale," n. 1.

23. "Shtetl," in *YIVO Encyclopedia*, 2:1732–39; Jeffrey Shandler, *Shtetl: A Vernacular Intellectual History* (New Brunswick, N.J., 2014), 7–49; Yohanan Petrovsky-Shtern, *The Golden Age Shtetl: A New History of Jewish Life in East Europe* (Princeton, 2014), 1–28; Kuznets, "Immigration of Russian Jews," 71; Yaffa Eliach, *There Once Was a World: A 900-Year Chronicle of the Shtetl of Eishyshok* (Boston, 1998), 270–99.

24. *Emigration Conditions in Europe*, vol. 4 of *Reports of the Immigration Commission, Presented by Mr. Dillingham* (Washington, D.C., 1911), 272–80; David Vital, *A People Apart: The Jews in Europe, 1789–1939* (New York, 1999), 294–95; Isidore Singer, ed., *The Jewish Encyclopedia*, 12 vols. (New York, 1901–1906), 10:526–27; Irving Howe, *World of Our Fathers* (New York, 1976), 5; John Klier, *Russians, Jews, and the Pogroms of 1881–1882* (New York, 2011), 207–33; Petrovsky-Shtern, *Golden Age Shtetl*, 15.

25. I. Michael Aronson, *Troubled Waters: The Origins of the 1881 Anti-Jewish Pogroms in Russia* (Pittsburgh, 1990), 49–56, 61; Vital, *People Apart*, 284 (quotation); Klier, *Russians, Jews, and the Pogroms*, 26–43.

26. Vital, *People Apart*, 283–84 ("heaps"); Klier, *Russians, Jews, and the Pogroms*, 44–47, 384–414; Hans Rogger, *Jewish Policies and Right-Wing Politics in Imperial Russia* (London, 1986), 56–112; "The Diary of Dr. George M. Price," *Publications of the American Jewish Historical Society* 40, pt. 2 (1950): 174–75 ("very anxious").

27. Aronson, *Troubled Waters*, 205–6 (quotation); Klier, *Russians, Jews, and the Pogroms*, 207–33; Michael Aronson, "The Attitudes of Russian Officials in the 1880s Toward Jewish Assimilation and Emigration," *Slavic Review* 34 (1975): 1–3; Vital, *People Apart*, 293; Abraham Cahan, *The Education of Abraham Cahan*, trans. Leon Stein et al. (Philadelphia, 1969), 195; "Russian Atrocities!" *Jewish Messenger*, October 7, 1881, 4; "The Russian Jews," *Jewish Messenger*, June 30, 1882, 5.

28. "Refugee Russian Jews," *Herald*, November 18, 1881, 8; "Jewish Immigration: Possible Arrival of Many Hebrews from the Empire of the Czar," *Herald*, December 3, 1881, 2; "What Can Be Done for the Russian Jews," *Jewish Messenger*, December 9, 1881, 4; "The Exodus of Russian Jews to the United States," *Frank Leslie's Illustrated Newspaper* (March 4, 1882): 23; "In Defence of the Russian Jews," *Jewish Messenger*, April 28, 1882, 5; "And Still They Come: The Battery Deluged with Vagrant Russian Jews," *Truth*, June 8, 1882, 3; "More Russian Jews," *Herald*, July 8, 1882, 9; "The Flight of the Russian Jews to This Country," *Frank Leslie's Illustrated Newspaper* (July 8, 1882): 307; "Russian Jews in Castle Garden," *Frank Leslie's Illustrated Newspaper* (August 5, 1882): 373, 375; *Historical Statistics of the United States*, 1:560–62; *Thirtieth Annual Report of the Chamber of Commerce*, 2:192; "Moscow," "Population and Migration," and "Saint Petersburg," in *YIVO Encyclopedia*, 2:1203, 1427, 1652.

29. "Moscow," 2:1203; Mary Antin, *From Plotzk to Boston* (Boston, 1899), 11; "Indigent Russian Jews Detained at the Barge Office," *Frank Leslie's Illustrated Newspaper* (September 26, 1891): 113; "The Emigration of Russian Jews to the United States" and "The Jewish Immigration," *Frank Leslie's Illustrated Newspaper* (December 12, 1891): 327, 333, 335; entry for Berke Gutkin, passenger 529, manifest of the *Normannia*, November 16, 1891, "New York Passenger Lists"; entries for Barnet Gutkin, family 38, enumeration district 1649, assembly district 35, Bronx County, 1910 census, and family 319, enumeration district 380, assembly district 7, Bronx County, 1920 census; Vital, *People Apart*, 310; *Historical Statistics of the United States*, 1:561.

30. Victor Bérard, *The Russian Empire and Czarism* (London, 1905), 134 ("*Balout*"); testimony of Major W. E. Evans-Gordon, in *Report of the Royal Commission on Alien Immigration, with Minutes of Evidence and Appendix*, 27 vols. (London, 1903), 1:456, 459 (other quotations).

31. Irving Howe and Eliezer Greenberg, *Voices from the Yiddish: Essays, Memoirs, Diaries* (Ann Arbor, 1972), 37; Howe, *World of Our Fathers*, 14 (quotation); *Emigration Conditions in Europe*, 272.

32. Eliach, *There Once Was a World*, 547 ("beautiful"); Zoza Szajkowski, "How the Mass Migration to America Began," *Jewish Social Studies* 4 (1942): 301 (other quotations).

33. Ravage, *American in the Making*, 5; Antin, *From Plotzk to Boston*, 11–12.

34. *Trow's New York City Directory for the Year Ending May 1, 1873* (New York, 1872), 876; entry for Isidor Munstuk, dwelling 9, enumeration district 147, 1880 census; his birthplace is in the marriage record of his daughter Sara Munstuk to Albert Wolff, June 27, 1891, New York City Marriage Records, familysearch.org.

35. *Historical Statistics of the United States*, 1:561–62; Gerald Sorin, *A Time for Building: The Third Migration, 1880–1920*, vol. 3 of *The Jewish People in America*, 5 vols. (Baltimore, 1992), 34 (quotation).

36. Shlomo Lambroza, "The Pogroms of 1903–1906," in *Pogroms: Anti-Jewish Violence in Modern Russian History*, ed. John Klier and Shlomo Lambroza (New York, 1992), 195–207, 210–11; Vital, *People Apart*, 509–11; "Cause of the Massacres," *Times*, May 19, 1903, 2 (quotation); entry for Mendel Dandishensky, manifest of the *Patria*, July 30, 1896, "New York Passenger Lists."

37. Lambroza, "Pogroms," 225–27; Gerald Surh, "Ekaterinoslav City in 1905: Workers, Jews, and Violence," *International Labor and Working Class History* 64 (2003): 139–66.

38. Lambroza, "Pogroms," 225 (quotation), 232–34; Robert Weinberg, "The Pogrom of 1905 in Odessa: A Case Study," in Klier and Lambroza, *Pogroms,* 248–81; "From Kishineff to Bialystok: A Table of Pogroms from 1903 to 1906," in *The American Jewish Year Book, 5667: September 20, 1906, to September 8, 1907* (Philadelphia, 1906), 40, 56, 62; Rebecca Kobrin, "The 1905 Revolution Abroad: Mass Migration, Russian Jewish Liberalism, and American Jewry, 1903–1914," in *The Revolution of 1905 and Russia's Jews,* ed. Stefani Hoffman and Ezra Mendelsohn (Philadelphia, 2008), 227–29, 232.

39. *My Future Is in America: Autobiographies of Eastern European Jewish Immigrants,* ed. Jocelyn Cohen and Daniel Soyer (New York, 2006), 135.

40. Ravage, *American in the Making,* 3–4; Hasia Diner, *Hungering for America: Italian, Irish, and Jewish Foodways in the Age of Migration* (Cambridge, Mass., 2001), 160–63; Howe, *World of Our Fathers,* 57, 60 ("Those days"); Cohen and Soyer, *My Future Is in America,* 21 ("I want"), 189, 192.

41. Emma Goldman, *Living My Life,* 2 vols. (New York, 1931), 1:12–13.

42. Sorin, *Time for Building,* 34–36 ("terrifying"); Cohen and Soyer, *My Future Is in America,* 184, 207 ("Pogroms"); Israel Kasovich, *The Days of Our Years: Personal and General Reminiscences (1859–1929)* (New York, 1929), 163–67; diary of Rabbi Baruch Rozenblum of Brest, entries of April and May 1882, accessed at brest-belarus.org/bc/Rozenblum Diary/Pogroms1b.i.html. Although the pogroms Rozenblum describes in his diary took place hundreds of miles from his home in Brest (in modern-day Belarus), he noted that they had caused his Jewish neighbors to begin emigrating.

43. *Historical Statistics of the United States,* 1:562; entry for Froim Leib Anbinder, manifest of the *Campania,* April 2, 1910, "New York Passenger Lists"; Kuznets, "Immigration of Russian Jews," 39.

44. *Annuario Statistico della Emigrazione Italiana dal 1876 al 1925* (Rome, 1926), 88; Leonard Covello, *The Heart Is the Teacher* (New York, 1958), 39; Bolton King and Thomas Okey, *Italy To-Day* (London, 1901), 167; Pascal D'Angelo, *Son of Italy* (1924; repr., Toronto, 2003), 48; Jerre Mangione and Ben Morreale, *La Storia: Five Centuries of the Italian American Experience* (New York, 1992), 51; Samuel Baily, *Immigrants in the Lands of Promise: Italians in Buenos Aires and New York City, 1870–1914* (Ithaca, 1999), 33–34, 41; Robert Lumley and Jonathan Morris, eds., *The New History of the Italian South: The Mezzogiorno Revisited* (Exeter, UK, 1997), 42–58.

45. Ignazio Silone, *Fontamara,* trans. Harvey Fergusson II (1930; repr., New York, 1960), 4 ("inflexible"); D'Angelo, *Son of Italy,* 7–9; Antonio Mangano, "The Effect of Emigration upon Italy: Toritti and San Demetrio," *Charities and the Commons* 20 (1908): 174–75 ("abominable"); Walter Weyl, "Italy's Exhausting Emigration," *The American Review of Reviews* 39 (1909): 178 ("abject").

46. Michael La Sorte, *La Merica: Images of Italian Greenhorn Experience* (Philadelphia, 1985), 4 ("thief"); Mangione and Morreale, *La Storia,* 89 ("stealing").

47. *Emigration Conditions in Europe,* 153–55, 158–64; Mangione and Morreale, *La Storia,* 63, 73, 78; Villari quoted in King and Okey, *Italy To-Day,* 138; Leonard Moss, "The Passing

of Traditional Peasant Society in the South," in *Modern Italy: A Topical History Since 1861*, ed. Edward Tannebaum and Emiliana Noether (New York, 1974), 148–54.

48. Mangione and Morreale, *La Storia*, 73; Pier Luigi Ballini, *La Questione Elettorale nella Storia d'Italia: Da Crispi a Giolitti (1893–1913)* (Rome, 2007), 3–195, 673–85; Adolfo Rossi, *Un Italiano in America* (Milan, 1899), 4 (quotation), 105–6, 156–63.

49. *Annuario Statistico della Emigrazione Italiana*, 88; Baily, *Immigrants in the Lands of Promise*, 58–61.

50. *Annuario Statistico della Emigrazione Italiana*, 88, 94, 103, 108, 111, 126, 132, 135, 138; Peter Coan, *Ellis Island Interviews: In Their Own Words* (New York, 1997), 52 (quotation).

51. Francesco Ventresca, *Personal Reminiscences of a Naturalized American* (New York, 1937), 16–17; Covello, *Heart Is the Teacher*, 4–5; Edward Corsi, *In the Shadow of Liberty: The Chronicle of Ellis Island* (New York, 1935), 20; Mark Choate, *Emigrant Nation: The Making of Italy Abroad* (Cambridge, Mass., 2008), 157; Mangione and Morreale, *La Storia*, 88–89 (quotation); Ravage, *American in the Making*, 3–15.

52. *Emigration Conditions in Europe*, 228–35; Mangione and Morreale, *La Storia*, 89, 101; Dino Cinel, *The National Integration of Italian Return Migration, 1870–1929* (New York, 1991), 96–111.

53. D'Angelo, *Son of Italy*, 49–52; La Sorte, *La Merica*, 5 ("ground"); Mangione and Morreale, *La Storia*, 92–94, 101; Weyl, "Italy's Exhausting Emigration," 178 ("abysmal"); Coan, *Ellis Island Interviews*, 65.

54. Norman Douglas, *Old Calabria* (Boston, 1915), 209; *Emigration Conditions in Europe*, 222–26; Choate, *Emigrant Nation*, 97 ("salute"); Mangano, "Effect of Emigration upon Italy," 177; Weyl, "Italy's Exhausting Emigration," 180 (other quotations).

55. Mangione and Morreale, *La Storia*, 78; Choate, *Emigrant Nation*, 97 ("abandoned"), 190; Giustino Fortunato, *Pagine e Ricordi Parlamentari*, 2 vols. (Rome, 1947), 2:35 ("Oh God"; thanks to Taylor Papallo for translation assistance); "Volcano Victims May Number 500," *Times*, April 10, 1906, 1; Charles Banks and Opie Read, *The History of the San Francisco Disaster and Mount Vesuvius Horror* (n.p., 1906), 337–51; "Scenes in Doomed Vesuvian Towns," *Times*, April 22, 1906, 11; "Italy Shaken," *Times*, December 29, 1908, 1; "Dead in Quake May Be 100,000," *Times*, December 30, 1908, 1–2; "150,000 Dead," *Times*, December 31, 1908, 1–2; "To Rebuild Messina" and "Four Days Among the Ruins," *Times*, January 5, 1909, 1–2; "Ruined Cities First Pictured," *Times*, January 10, 1909, pt. 3, 1–2; "Within the Dead Cities of Italy," *Times*, January 31, 1909, magazine sec., 1.

56. King and Okey, *Italy To-Day*, 131 ("terrible"); Weyl, "Italy's Exhausting Emigration," 178 ("emigration of hunger"); Mangione and Morreale, *La Storia*, 79 ("that's why"); Diner, *Hungering for America*, 29–47.

57. Choate, *Emigrant Nation*, 25–26; Baily, *Immigrants in the Lands of Promise*, 24–27; Ercole Sori, *L'Emigrazione Italiana dall'Unita alla Seconda Guerra Mondiale* (Bologna, 1979), 25; *Annuario Statistico della Emigrazione Italiana*, 123, 126, 132, 135, 138. These province-by-province emigration figures are somewhat misleading because a "bird of passage" who made four trips to the United States before finally settling permanently in America is counted four times in the Italian emigration figures.

58. Howe, *World of Our Fathers*, 35–36 (quotation); Baily, *Immigrants in the Lands of Promise*, 32.

59. D'Angelo, *Son of Italy*, 55; Ravage, *American in the Making*, 10, 55; Broughton Brandenburg, *Imported Americans: The Story of the Experiences of a Disguised American and His Wife Studying the Immigration Question* (New York, 1903), 127.

60. D'Angelo, *Son of Italy*, 55; Ventresca, *Personal Reminiscences*, 20; Covello, *Heart Is the Teacher*, 19; Coan, *Ellis Island Interviews*, 38–39.

61. *Emigration Conditions in Europe*, 251, 254; Rose Cohen, *Out of the Shadow* (New York, 1918), 13–18, 47–56; Morris Raphael Cohen, *A Dreamer's Journey: The Autobiography of Morris Raphael Cohen* (Boston, 1949), 59–60; Cahan, *Education of Abraham Cahan*, 187, 199.

62. Szajkowski, "How the Mass Migration to America Began," 295–97, 301–4; "Brody," in *YIVO Encyclopedia of Jews in Eastern Europe*, 1:246–47; Antin, *From Plotzk to Boston*, 41–43.

63. Howe, *World of Our Fathers*, 28, 39; Moses Rischin, *The Promised City: New York's Jews, 1870–1914* (Cambridge, Mass., 1962), 33; Mangione and Morreale, *La Storia*, 102.

64. Edward Steiner, *From Alien to Citizen: The Story of My Life in America* (New York, 1914), 30–32; Brandenburg, *Imported Americans*, 162–70; Mangione and Morreale, *La Storia*, 101–2; Howe, *World of Our Fathers*, 38; Baily, *Immigrants in the Lands of Promise*, 52.

65. Barbara Lüthi, "Germs of Anarchy, Crime, Disease, and Degeneracy: Jewish Migration to the United States and the Medicalization of European Borders Around 1900," in *Points of Passage: Jewish Migrants from Eastern Europe in Scandinavia, Germany, and Britain, 1880–1914*, ed. Tobias Brinkmann (New York, 2013), 35–39; Howe, *World of Our Fathers*, 37; Mangione and Morreale, *La Storia*, 102; Choate, *Emigrant Nation*, 98; D'Angelo, *Son of Italy*, 56; Brandenburg, *Imported Americans*, 131; William Richardson, ed., *Supplement to the Revised Statutes of the United States*, vol. 1, 1874–1891, 2nd ed., rev. (Washington, D.C., 1891), 934–37; William McKinney, comp., *The Federal Statutes Annotated: Supplement, 1909* (Northport, N.Y., 1909), 160–79; Anne-Emanualle Birn, "Six Seconds Per Eyelid: The Medical Inspection of Immigrants at Ellis Island," *Dynamis* 17 (1997): 312.

66. Emma Beckerman, *Not So Long Ago: A Recollection* (New York, 1980), 8 ("horror"); D'Angelo, *Son of Italy*, 56; Cohen, *Dreamer's Journey*, 61 ("huddled"); Kasovich, *Days of Our Years*, 172; *Steerage Conditions*, vol. 37 of *Reports of the Immigration Commission, Presented by Mr. Dillingham* (Washington, D.C., 1911), 6–7, 23 (remaining quotations); Brandenburg, *Imported Americans*, 174–204; Henry Fairchild, *Immigration: A World Movement and Its American Significance* (New York, 1913), 174–82.

67. Coan, *Ellis Island Interviews*, 54 ("Nine"); Kasovich, *Days of Our Years*, 172–73 ("Hundreds"); Brandenburg, *Imported Americans*, 36; La Sorte, *La Merica*, 25.

68. *Steerage Conditions*, 22–23 (quotations); "Women in Steerage Grossly Ill Used," *Times*, December 14, 1909, 3.

69. Cohen, *Out of the Shadow*, 60; Cohen, *Dreamer's Journey*, 61 (all but final quotation); Edward Steiner, *On the Trail of the Immigrant* (New York, 1906), 36 ("miserable").

70. H. Phelps Whitmarsh, "The Steerage of To-Day: A Personal Experience," *Century Magazine* 55 (February 1898): 537 (quotations); Maria Parrino, ed., *Italian-American Autobiographies* (Providence, 1993), 107; interview of Louise Nagy, September 16, 1985, *Ellis*

Island Oral History Project, ser. AKRF, no. 33, in *North American Immigrant Letters, Diaries, and Oral Histories* (Alexandria, Va., 2003); Brandenburg, *Imported Americans*, 164.

71. *Steerage Conditions*, 10–13, 24–42; Drew Keeling, "The Improvement of Travel Conditions for Migrants Crossing the North Atlantic, 1900–1914," in Brinkmann, *Points of Passage*, 107–29; Howe, *World of Our Fathers*, 41; Mangione and Morreale, *La Storia*, 104; Baily, *Immigrants in the Lands of Promise*, 52–53.

72. Anna Walther, *A Pilgrimage with a Milliner's Needle* (New York, 1917), 197; Goldie Stone, *My Caravan of Years: An Autobiography* (New York, 1945), 252; Coan, *Ellis Island Interviews*, 49, 54, 155 (Edelman), 207; Lily Daché, *Talking Through My Hats* (New York, 1946), 12.

73. D'Angelo, *Son of Italy*, 58; Louis Adamic, *Laughing in the Jungle: The Autobiography of an Immigrant in America* (1932; repr., New York, 1969), 40; Coan, *Ellis Island Interviews*, 49, 54, 56, 316.

74. Rose Pesotta, *Bread Upon the Waters* (New York, 1944), 11; Goldman, *Living My Life*, 1:11; Brandenburg, *Imported Americans*, 205; Frederic Haskin, *The Immigrant: An Asset and a Liability* (New York, 1913), 74.

75. "In Memory of Emma Lazarus," *Times*, May 6, 1903, 9.

15. Ellis Island

1. Peter Coan, *Ellis Island Interviews: In Their Own Words* (New York, 1997), 54; Kyra Goritzina, *Service Entrance: Memoirs of a Park Avenue Cook* (New York, 1939), 13; Jerre Mangione and Ben Morreale, *La Storia: Five Centuries of the Italian American Experience* (New York, 1992), 112 ("Tears").

2. Pascal D'Angelo, *Son of Italy* (1924; repr., Toronto, 2003), 58; Stephen Graham, *With Poor Immigrants to America* (New York, 1914), 41 (quotation).

3. William Richardson, ed., *Supplement to the Revised Statutes of the United States, 1874–1891, Forty-Third to Fifty-First Congress, Inclusive*, 2nd ed., 2 vols. (Washington, D.C., 1891–1901), 1:86–88 (Page Act), 370–71 (1882 Immigration Act), 342, 458–61 (Chinese Exclusion Act and amendments made in 1884), 479–80, 541–42, 633 (contract labor law of 1885 and amendments made in 1887 and 1888); Keith Fitzgerald, *The Face of the Nation: Immigration, the State, and National Identity* (Stanford, 1996), 120; *Reports of the Industrial Commission on Immigration* (Washington, D.C., 1901), vol. 15 of *Reports of the Industrial Commission*, 19 vols. (Washington, D.C., 1900–1902), 647–59.

4. "The Investigation Over," *Times*, September 1, 1887, 8 ("snare"); "Unfit for Their Work," *Times*, January 14, 1890, 3; "Biglin Gets a Scoring," *Times*, April 12, 1890, 8; *Report of the Select Committee of the House of Representatives to Inquire into the Alleged Violation of the Laws Prohibiting the Importation of Contract Laborers, Paupers, Convicts, and Other Classes* (Washington, D.C., 1889), 2 (other quotations).

5. John Weber, *Autobiography of John B. Weber* (Buffalo, 1924), 88–89 ("affrighted"); Vincent Cannato, *American Passage: The History of Ellis Island* (New York, 2009), 45 (other quotations).

6. "In Favor of Ellis Island," *Times*, March 25, 1890, 5; "Examining the Islands: Congress-

men Looking for a Place to Land Immigrants," *Tribune*, March 25, 1890, 5; "Ellis Island Selected," *Times*, April 6, 1890, 5; "On Ellis Island," *Times*, April 16, 1890, 8; "Farewell Castle Garden," *Times*, April 19, 1890, 5; "Barge Office Doors Open," *Times*, April 20, 1890, 16; "Uncle Sam's New Hotel," *Tribune*, June 29, 1890, 16.

7. Ronald Bayor, *Encountering Ellis Island: How European Immigrants Entered America* (Baltimore, 2014), 32; Cannato, *American Passage*, 19–29; Ann Novotny, *Strangers at the Door: Ellis Island, Castle Garden, and the Great Migration to America* (Riverside, Conn., 1971), 63–69.

8. Richardson, *Supplement to the Revised Statutes*, 1:934–37.

9. "An Enormous Building," *Times*, July 28, 1891, 8; "New Immigration Depot," *Tribune*, December 27, 1891, 13.

10. "Fire on Ellis Island," *Times*, June 15, 1897, 1 (quotation); "Caring for Immigrants," *Times*, June 16, 1897, 1.

11. Marian Smith [chief historian, Historical Research Branch, U.S. Citizenship and Immigration Services], "Where Are the Castle Garden Records?" unpublished manuscript in possession of the author.

12. "Caring for Immigrants," *Times*, June 16, 1897, 1; "Ellis Island" and "Immigrants on the Piers," *Times*, June 17, 1897, 6, 12; Victor Safford, *Immigration Problems: Personal Experiences of an Official* (New York, 1925), 199–200; Novotny, *Strangers*, 134–35; "New Immigrant Station, *Tribune*, October 14, 1900, pt. 2, 3; "New Immigration Station," *Times*, December 3, 1900, 5; "Again at Ellis Island," *Tribune*, December 17, 1900, 3; "Art Awards at Paris," *Times*, August 28, 1900, 2.

13. Edward Corsi, *In the Shadow of Liberty: The Chronicle of Ellis Island* (New York, 1935), 5; Graham, *With Poor Immigrants*, 41 (quotation).

14. Bayor, *Encountering Ellis Island*, 27–30; Broughton Brandenburg, *Imported Americans: The Story of the Experiences of a Disguised American and His Wife Studying the Immigration Question* (New York, 1904), 212 (quotation); Alfred Reed, "Going Through Ellis Island," *Popular Science Monthly* 82 (January 1913): 11.

15. Brandenburg, *Imported Americans*, 213–16; Bayor, *Encountering Ellis Island*, 31.

16. Bayor, *Encountering Ellis Island*, 39; Louis Adamic, *Laughing in the Jungle: The Autobiography of an Immigrant in America* (1932; repr., New York, 1969), 41.

17. Brandenburg, *Imported Americans*, 216; Alfred Reed, "The Medical Side of Immigration," *Popular Science Monthly* 80 (April 1912): 386; E. H. Mullan, "The Medical Inspection of Immigrants at Ellis Island," *Medical Record: A Weekly Journal of Medicine and Surgery* 84 (December 27, 1913): 1167–68; E. H. Mullan, "Mental Examination of Immigrants: Administration and Line Inspection at Ellis Island," *Public Health Reports* 32 (May 18, 1917): 733–36 (Mullan quotations); Safford, *Immigration Problems*, 238–57; Bayor, *Encountering Ellis Island*, 45–46.

18. Mullan, "Medical Inspection," 1168 ("eye man"); Bayor, *Encountering Ellis Island*, 47–48; Howard Markel, *When Germs Travel: Six Major Epidemics That Have Invaded America and the Fears They Have Unleashed* (New York, 2004), 101 ("struck"); Anne-Emanuelle Birn, "Six Seconds Per Eyelid: The Medical Inspection of Immigrants at Ellis Island, 1892–1914," *Dynamis* 17 (1997): 290–93; Arthur Henry, "Among the Immigrants," *Scribner's Magazine* 29 (March 1901): 302.

19. Birn, "Six Seconds Per Eyelid," 292; Fiorello La Guardia, *The Making of an Insurgent, An Autobiography, 1882–1919* (Philadelphia, 1948), 64–65.

20. Mullan, "Mental Examination," 736; Coan, *Ellis Island Interviews*, 124; Geddes to Marquess Curzon, received January 29, 1923, House of Commons, *Accounts and Papers* (London, 1923), 25:279, accessed at http://freepages.genealogy.rootsweb.ancestry.com/~quarantine/british3.htm.

21. Bayor, *Encountering Ellis Island*, 48–49 ("bashful"); Amy Fairchild, *Science at the Borders: Immigrant Medical Inspection and the Shaping of the Modern Industrial Labor Force* (Baltimore, 2003), 64 (Jones).

22. Mullan, "Mental Examination," 735–36, 738, 740, 746; John Richardson, *Howard Andrew Knox: Pioneer of Intelligence Testing at Ellis Island* (New York, 2011), 69–141; Reed, "Medical Side," 389; *Annual Report of the Commissioner General of Immigration to the Secretary of Labor, Fiscal Year Ended June 30, 1915* (Washington, D.C., 1915), 126.

23. *Immigration Legislation*, vol. 39 of *Reports of the Immigration Commission Presented by Mr. Dillingham* (Washington, D.C., 1911), 51–65, 102–21; Cannato, *American Passage*, 195.

24. James Richardson, *A Compilation of the Messages and Papers of the Presidents*, 11 vols. (n.p., 1908), 11:1211 (final quotation); *Addresses and Presidential Messages of Theodore Roosevelt, 1902–1904* (New York, 1904), 265 ("race suicide"), 301–2 (all other Roosevelt quotations); "Topics of the *Times*," *Times*, February 26, 1903, 8; "President Starts Ellis Island Inquiry," *Times*, September 17, 1903, 1; "Probing Ellis Island," *Times*, October 6, 1903, 16; "Immigration Reforms Will Be Approved," *Times*, December 4, 1903, 2; *Annual Report of the Commissioner General of Immigration* (1915), 126.

25. Howard Grose, *Aliens or Americans?* (New York, 1906), 123 ("new immigration"); "Sketches of Business Men in New-York City," *Times*, September 3, 1893, 16; entry for Lazarus Straus and family, dwelling 405, Talbatton, Talbot County, Ga., 1860 census; Oscar Straus, *Under Four Administrations: From Cleveland to Taft* (Boston, 1922), 4–37; Naomi Cohen, *A Dual Heritage: The Public Career of Oscar S. Straus* (Philadelphia, 1969), 5–13.

26. "Sketches of Business Men in New-York City," *Times*, September 3, 1893, 16; Oscar Straus, *The Origin of Republican Form of Government in the United States* (New York, 1885); Oscar Straus, *Roger Williams: The Pioneer of Religious Liberty* (New York, 1894); Oscar Straus, *The American Spirit* (New York, 1913); "Oscar S. Straus Dies from Heart Attack," *Times*, May 4, 1926, 7; Straus, *Under Four Administrations*, 210 (quotation).

27. Straus, *Under Four Administrations*, 216–17; Cannato, *American Passage*, 172–74.

28. "Fitchie's Successor Chosen," *Tribune*, April 2, 1902, 2; "Four Years of Progress at Ellis Island," *Times*, February 12, 1905, magazine sec., 5; "W. Williams Named," *Tribune*, May 19, 1909, 3; "Williams Regains Immigration Office," *Times*, May 19, 1909, 2; "Back to Ellis Island," *Tribune*, May 29, 1909, 7; "Williams in Charge at Ellis Island," *Times*, May 29, 1909, 6; Cannato, *American Passage*, 162–68 (quotation, 163); Robert Watchorn, *The Autobiography of Robert Watchorn* (Oklahoma City, 1959), 8–35, 143–53.

29. "Put Up the Bars on Immigrants," *Times*, June 5, 1909, 5 ("low-grade"); "New Bars for 'Undesirables' at Ellis Island," *Times*, July 18, 1909, magazine sec., 11 ("low vitality");

William Williams, "The Sifting of Immigrants," *Journal of Social Science* 44 (September 1906): 42 ("standing").

30. Cannato, *American Passage,* 184, 195–96; Bayor, *Encountering Ellis Island,* 61; Deirdre Moloney, *National Insecurities: Immigrants and U.S. Deportation Policy Since 1882* (Chapel Hill, 2012), 82–87; *Annual Report of the Commissioner General of Immigration* (1915), 126. Women and children were half as likely as men to be turned away at Ellis Island. See Mark Choate, *Emigrant Nation: The Making of Italy Abroad* (Cambridge, Mass., 2008), 99.

31. Cannato, *American Passage,* 197–98 ("nonsense," "outrage," "knife"); "Jews Complain of Deportation," *Times,* November 14, 1909, 10; Max Kohler, "The Immigration Question, with Particular Reference to the Jews of America," *Thirty-Seventh Annual Report of the Union of American Hebrew Congregations* (March 1911): 6593 (Kohler); Irving Howe, *World of Our Fathers* (New York, 1976), 56 ("Haman"); "Newspaper Criticism," folders 5–9, box 2, William Williams Papers, Manuscripts and Archives Division, New York Public Library.

32. Cannato, *American Passage,* 197–98 ("stench"); "Our Shores Barred to Foreign Outcasts," *Times,* July 10, 1909, 14.

33. Cannato, *American Passage,* 180.

34. Ernest Abbott, "America's Welcome to the Immigrant," *The Outlook* 72 (October 4, 1902): 259, 262; Linda Miller, *The New York Charities Directory,* 28th ed. (New York, 1919), 35, 100, 123, 137, 145, 149, 170, 178, 198, 207, 224, 241, 256, 272–73, 286, 289, 301, 320–21; Ivan Cizmić, "The Experience of South Slav Immigrants on Ellis Island and the Establishment of the Slavonic Immigrant Society in New York," in *In the Shadow of the Statue of Liberty: Immigrants, Workers, and Citizens in the American Republic, 1880–1920,* ed. Marianne Debouzy (Urbana, 1992), 67–82; Bayor, *Encountering Ellis Island,* 93–94.

35. John Carr, *Guide to the United States for the Jewish Immigrant: A Nearly Literal Translation of the Second Yiddish Edition* (New York, 1912), 9–10 (quotations); Annie Polland and Daniel Soyer, *Emerging Metropolis: New York Jews in the Age of Immigration, 1840–1920* (New York, 2012), 153–54; Howe, *World of Our Fathers,* 47–48.

36. Bayor, *Encountering Ellis Island,* 94–95; "The Nation's Immigration Policy," *Times,* January 19, 1911, 8 (success rate of appeals).

37. Bayor, *Encountering Ellis Island,* 34; Coan, *Ellis Island Interviews,* 124; Brandenburg, *Imported Americans,* 217; Adamic, *Laughing,* 41–45.

38. Coan, *Ellis Island Interviews,* 124 (quotation); Marie Jastrow, *A Time to Remember: Growing Up in New York Before the Great War* (New York, 1979), 46.

39. Adamic, *Laughing,* 41–45.

40. D'Angelo, *Son of Italy,* 58–61; Safford, *Immigration Problems,* 83–84; Brandenburg, *Imported Americans,* 220; *Annual Report of the Commissioner of Immigration to the Secretary of Commerce and Labor for the Fiscal Year Ended June 30, 1911* (Washington, D.C., 1911), 9; Howe, *World of Our Fathers,* 45; Bayor, *Encountering Ellis Island,* 50.

41. "Immigration Bill Vetoed," *Tribune,* March 3, 1897, 3; "Mr. Cleveland's Immigration Veto," *Times,* March 4, 1897, 6; "Immigration Bill Veto at Last Minute," *Times,* February

15, 1913, 1; "President Vetoes Immigration Bill," *Tribune*, February 15, 1913, 1; "The Immigration Veto," *Tribune*, February 15, 1913, 8; "House Upholds Taft on Literacy Test," *Times*, February 20, 1913, 5; "Dillingham Argues for Literacy Test," *Times*, February 14, 1914, 2 (quotation); "The President and the Literacy Test," *Tribune*, January 3, 1915, 10; "Why Taft Opposed the Literacy Test," *Times*, January 17, 1915, sec. 3, 2; "Monster Protest on Literacy Test," *Times*, January 26, 1915, 4; "Immigration Veto Sent to Congress," *Times*, January 29, 1915, 4; "The Immigration Bill Veto," *Times*, January 29, 1915, 8; "House Upholds Veto of the Alien Bill," *Times*, February 5, 1915, 1; "President Vetoes Immigration Bill," *Times*, January 30, 1917, 1; "The Immigration Bill Veto," *Times*, January 31, 1917, 10; "Immigration Bill Enacted Over Veto," *Times*, February 6, 1917, 12; "The Immigration Law," *Times*, February 7, 1917, 12; "Immigration in Congress," *Immigration Journal* 1 (1916): 1–6; *Message from the President of the United States Vetoing H. R. 6060, An Act to Regulate the Immigration of Aliens to and the Residence of Aliens in the United States* (Washington, D.C., 1915); *Statutes of the United States of America, Passed at the Second Session of the Sixty-Fourth Congress, 1916–1917*, 2 pts. (Washington, D.C. 1917), pt. 1, 874–98.

42. *Annual Report of the Commissioner General of Immigration to the Secretary of Labor, Fiscal Year Ended June 30, 1920* (Washington, D.C., 1920), 13, 198; Brandenburg, *Imported Americans*, 50–51; Bayor, *Encountering Ellis Island*, 51; "Shortcomings of the Literacy Test," *Times*, October 28, 1917, sec. 8, 2.

43. H. G. Wells, *The Future in America: A Search After Realities* (London, 1906), 63–64; Bayor, *Encountering Ellis Island*, 77; "Italians Show Their Vengeance," *Times*, May 21, 1894, 2.

44. Bayor, *Encountering Ellis Island*, 20; Leonard Covello, *The Heart Is the Teacher* (New York, 1958), 29–31.

45. Brandenburg, *Imported Americans*, 220 (quotation); Covello, *Heart Is the Teacher*, 19–20; Bayor, *Encountering Ellis Island*, 50, 78.

46. Jastrow, *Time to Remember*, 44–46; Marie Ganz, *Rebels: Into Anarchy — And Out Again* (New York, 1920), 2; Coan, *Ellis Island Interviews*, 226, 248; David Brownstone, Douglass Brownstone, and Irene Franck, *Island of Hope, Island of Tears* (New York, 1979), 207; Bayor, *Encountering Ellis Island*, 79–80, 93–94.

47. D'Angelo, *Son of Italy*, 77 ("wonderful"); Bruce Stave, John Sutherland, and Aldo Salerno, *From the Old Country: An Oral History of European Migration to America* (New York, 1994), 41–44 ("bewildered"), 47–50; Coan, *Ellis Island Interviews*, 109, 181 ("overwhelming"); Corsi, *In the Shadow*, 22–23.

48. Coan, *Ellis Island Interviews*, 162 (quotation); D'Angelo, *Son of Italy*, 58.

16. The Lower East Side

1. Konrad Bercovici, *Around the World in New York* (New York, 1924), 4, 20–21; Linda Jacobs, *Strangers in the West: The Syrian Colony of New York City: 1880–1900* (New York, 2015), 27–137.

2. "Resolved," *Jewish Messenger*, May 21, 1880, 3; "For Dr. Dwyer's Family," *Times*, July 1, 1888, 3; "Over on the East Side," *Times*, August 27, 1895, 13; Moses Rischin, "Toward the

Onomastics of the Great New York Ghetto: How the Lower East Side Got Its Name,"
in *Remembering the Lower East Side: American Jewish Reflections,* ed. Hasia Diner
(Bloomington, Ind., 2000), 13–27; Moses Rischin, *The Promised City: New York's Jews,
1870–1914* (Cambridge, Mass., 1962), 80 (for the Lower East Side's boundaries; others set
its northern border at Houston Street).

3. "Where Dwell the Victims of the 'Sweater,'" *Herald,* August 21, 1892, 8; Jacob Riis,
How the Other Half Lives: Studies Among the Tenements of New York (New York, 1890),
105.

4. David Blaustein, "The Different Peoples of the Lower East Side," in *Seventeenth Annual
Report of the University Settlement Society of New York* (New York, 1904), 8; Annie Polland and Daniel Soyer, *Emerging Metropolis: New York Jews in the Age of Immigration,
1840–1920* (New York, 2012), 112; Rischin, *Promised City,* 79–80.

5. Characterization of the origins of the Lower East Side's inhabitants based on the population schedules of the federal censuses of 1900 and 1920. For 1900, see enumeration
districts 33, 64–88, 112–14, 129–38, 165–93, 220–46, 273–98, 319–46, and 367–95, 1900
census; for 1920, see assembly district 1, enumeration districts 1–36, assembly district
2, enumeration districts 107–66, assembly district 3, enumeration districts 314–95, assembly district 6, enumeration districts 462–519, and assembly district 8, enumeration
districts 586–657, 1920 census. The easiest way to check the accuracy of Blaustein's characterization of the Lower East Side's Jewish "colonies" is to compare it to the block-by-
block tally of the nativity of each "head of household" in Manhattan in 1900 published
in *First Report of the Tenement House Department of the City of New York,* 2 vols. (New
York, 1903), 2:31–103.

6. Proportion of women based on a 1 percent sample of New York City's population as
recorded in the 1920 U.S. census prepared by Steven Ruggles, J. Trent Alexander, Katie
Genadek, Ronald Goeken, Matthew B. Schroeder, and Matthew Sobek, *Integrated Public Use Microdata Series: Version 5.0* (Minneapolis, 2010), and available as "1920 New
York City 1% Census Sample" at https://dataverse.harvard.edu/dataverse/anbinder. Cf.
Polland and Soyer, *Emerging Metropolis,* 112; David Vital, *A People Apart: The Jews in
Europe, 1789–1939* (New York, 1999), 307. The census does not list the religion of each
inhabitant. In order to try to identify the city's east European Jews, I looked at all immigrants born in Russia, Poland, "Russian Poland," "Austrian Poland," Romania,
Bessarabia, and Galicia. This method leads to the inclusion of some non-Jews as well,
but perusing the immigrants' surnames and given names indicates that fewer than 10
percent of New York's immigrants born in these places were non-Jews. (The non-Jews
can usually be identified because their surnames and given names differ significantly
from the Jews'.) All subsequently cited employment figures referring to east European
Jews are based on census data for immigrants born in these places.

7. Abraham Cahan, *Yekl: A Tale of the New York Ghetto* (New York, 1896), 28 (final quotation); Arnold Bennett, "Your United States," *Harper's Monthly Magazine* 125 (1912): 820
(all other quotations); William Elsing, "Life in New York Tenement-Houses," *Scribner's*
11 (June 1892): 715.

8. "Where Dwell the Victims of the 'Sweater,'" *Herald,* August 21, 1892, 8; *Report of the Tenement House Committee as Authorized by Chapter 479 of the Laws of 1894* (Albany, 1895),

11, 257, 267; *Report of the New York City Commission on Congestion of Population* (New York, 1911), 6–7, 86, 110, 114; Edward Pratt, *Industrial Causes of Congestion of Population in New York City* (New York, 1911), 29–36; "The New-York Tenements," *Times,* March 24, 1895, 30; "Life on the East Side," *Times,* April 3, 1898, 18; "New York's Population More than 4,000,000," *Times,* December 25, 1904, 7; "New Census of City," *Times,* October 10, 1909, part three, 5; "Social Map of the Lower East Side," *Times,* April 3, 1910, magazine sec., 2 (contains a block-by-block listing of population density); "Many New Yorkers Live 1,000 to an Acre," *Tribune,* March 10, 1912, part II, 2; "Manhattan's Population Density, Past and Present" and "Everybody Inhale: How Many People Can Manhattan Hold?" *Times,* March 4, 2012; Irving Howe, *World of Our Fathers* (New York, 1976), 143–44; Jason Barr and Teddy Ort, "Population Density Across the City: The Case of 1900 Manhattan," working paper, Department of Economics, Rutgers University, Newark, April 2014. These sources often list contradictory figures for the population density of the Lower East Side and its component districts, often in the very same year. The figures cited in the text are those that seem the most reliable. For the most densely populated places in the world as of 2015, I consulted "List of City Districts by Population Density," http://en.wikipedia.org/w/index.php?title=List_of_city_districts_by_population _density&oldid=652400162, and "Dharavi in Mumbai Is No Longer Asia's Largest Slum," *Times of India,* July 6, 2011.

9. *Reports of the Industrial Commission on Immigration* (Washington, D.C., 1901), vol. 15 of *Reports of the Industrial Commission,* 19 vols. (Washington, D.C., 1900–1902), 481–84; Nellie Bly, "In the Biggest New York Tenement," *World,* August 5, 1894, 1; "New-York Tenements: Evolution of Some and Present Condition of Others," *Tribune,* December 22, 1902, 5; Rischin, *Promised City,* 87; Robert de Forest and Lawrence Veiller, eds., *The Tenement House Problem,* 2 vols. (New York, 1903), 1:415.

10. Entries for Isidor Munstuk in *Trow's New York City Directory* for 1873–1882; entry for Isidor Munstuk, dwelling 9, enumeration district 147, 1880 census.

11. Lawrence Veiller, *Tenement House Reform in New York, 1834–1900* (New York, 1900), 26–28; Jane Addams, "The Housing Problem in Chicago," *Annals of the American Academy of Political and Social Science* 20 (July 1902): 105; Jacob Riis, *The Battle with the Slum* (New York, 1902), 76–112.

12. "Prize Tenements," *Times,* March 16, 1879, 6; Allan Forman, "Some Adopted Americans," *American Magazine* 9 (November 1888): 51–52 ("great"); *Reports of the Industrial Commission on Immigration,* 487 ("Hebrew").

13. Riis, *How the Other Half Lives,* 105.

14. Dwellings 12 and 15, enumeration district 144, assembly district 2, 1920 census; *Atlas of the Borough of Manhattan, City of New York* (New York, 1916), plate 17 (for the dimensions of Max Dandeshane's tenement building, from which we can deduce the size of his apartment); entry for Max Dandeshane, dwelling 33, enumeration district 232, 1900 census.

15. "Tenement Evils as Seen by the Tenants," in de Forest and Veiller, *Tenement House Problem,* 1:386 (quotations), 413; Robert de Forest, "Tenement House Regulation — The Reasons for It — Its Proper Limitations," *Annals of the American Academy of Political and Social Science* 20 (July 1902): 93; Mary Sayles, "Housing Conditions in Jersey City,"

Annals of the American Academy of Political and Social Science 20 (July 1902): 139; Elsing, "Life in New York Tenement-Houses," 699.

16. "Tenement Evils as Seen by the Tenants," 1:387–88, 413 (quotations); *First Report of the Tenement House Department,* 1:134; "Tenement House Reform," *Times,* February 27, 1901, 8; Tyler Anbinder, *Five Points: The Nineteenth-Century New York City Neighborhood That Invented Tap Dance, Stole Elections, and Became the World's Most Notorious Slum* (New York, 2001), 348.

17. "A Night on New York's East Side," *Charities* 14 (1905): 965–66; "The Recent Hot Term," *Frank Leslie's Illustrated Newspaper* (August 12, 1882): 390, 392–93; "A Summer Resort on the Roof," *Harper's Weekly* 29 (August 1, 1885): 491, 496; "New York City," *Frank Leslie's Illustrated Newspaper* (July 23, 1887): 373; "Sleep on Hot Nights," *Tribune,* August 9, 1903, illus. supp. sec., 5; "Roof Sleeping Now Popular in New York," *Times,* July 5, 1908, 11; Forman, "Some Adopted Americans," 52; Polland and Soyer, *Emerging Metropolis,* 115.

18. "Heat's Holocaust in the Five Boroughs," *Times,* July 2, 1901, 1; "Six Score Stricken in Deadly Heat Wave," *Times,* July 11, 1903, 1; "How to Get Sleep on Hot Summer Nights," *Times,* June 26, 1910, magazine sec., 6; "Hot Wave Is Broken," *Times,* August 2, 1915, 4.

19. "Panic in a Flat-House," *Tribune,* November 17, 1891, 1; "Two Women Die in Flames: Another Fatal Tenement-House Fire," *Tribune,* April 29, 1892, 1; "Fatal Tenement-House Fire," *Times,* February 4, 1893, 9 (Cohens); "Flames Shot Up Airshaft," *Times,* November 22, 1893, 9; "Three Perish in a Midnight Fire," *Times,* January 6, 1900, 1; "Crowded Tenement Afire," *Times,* November 7, 1900, 14; "Wild Panic at a Tenement Fire," *Times,* January 4, 1901, 14; "Four Perish in a Tenement Fire," *Times,* January 9, 1901, 1; "Five Lives Lost in an East Side Fire," *Times,* August 20, 1902, 14; "Eighteen Suffocated at Fire," *Tribune,* November 1, 1903, 1; "14 Lives Are Lost in Tenement Fire," *Times,* September 5, 1904, 1; "Rabbi Dead, 5 Missing in Midnight Fire," *Times,* December 3, 1912, 5; "Missing in Tenement Fire," *Times,* November 30, 1914, 4.

20. "Daring Rescue by Strangers: Mrs. Goldstein Taken Across an Airshaft," *Times,* January 21, 1894, 5; "Mother and Baby Saved by a Boy," *Times,* December 8, 1910, 3; "Children Saved from Fire," *Times,* February 27, 1911, 6; "Thrilling Rescues at Tenement House Fire," *Tribune,* October 14, 1911, 1.

21. *Report of the Tenement House Committee,* 13; de Forest and Veiller, *Tenement House Problem,* 1:387.

22. Proportion of tenements that were barracks-style and dumbbell-style in 1916 based on a sample of about half the Lower East Side's residential blocks in *Atlas of the Borough of Manhattan,* which differentiates barracks-style from dumbbell tenements on its fire insurance maps. My sample included all the 148 residential blocks on plates 13, 16–19, 24–25, and 28. The remaining 112 residential blocks of the Lower East Side, on plates 7, 12, 14, 15, 23, 26, 27, 29, and 30, were not sampled. On those 148 blocks, I found 2,708 barracks-style tenements, 931 dumbbell tenements, 300 "new law" tenements (whose design followed the guidelines of the 1901 Tenement Act), and 166 buildings that appear to have been primarily commercial rather than residential.

23. Riis, *How the Other Half Lives,* 108; "Where Dwell the Victims of the 'Sweater,'" *Herald,* August 21, 1892, 8; Howe, *World of Our Fathers,* 139.

24. Burton Hendrick, "The Jewish Invasion of America," *McClure's* 40 (March 1913): 126–27; Howe, *World of Our Fathers,* 59, 82; Polland and Soyer, *Emerging Metropolis,* 13; *My Future Is in America: Autobiographies of Eastern European Jewish Immigrants,* ed. Jocelyn Cohen and Daniel Soyer (New York, 2006), 144–45 (quotation).

25. *My Future Is in America,* 141–42.

26. Morris Raphael Cohen, *A Dreamer's Journey: The Autobiography of Morris Raphael Cohen* (Boston, 1949), 66; M. E. Ravage, *An American in the Making: The Life Story of an Immigrant* (New York, 1917), 78; *My Future Is in America,* 24 ("Warsaw"); Howe, *World of Our Fathers,* 71–72, 75 (other quotations).

27. Entry for Froim Leib Anbinder, manifest of the *Campania,* April 2, 1910, "New York Passenger Lists"; entry for Froim L. Anbinder, election district 52, assembly district 22, Kings County (Brooklyn), 1925 New York State census; Riis, *How the Other Half Lives,* 128–29.

28. *My Future Is in America,* 140-41, 144 (Domnitz quotations); Rischin, *Promised City,* 105, 183; Polland and Soyer, *Emerging Metropolis,* 118; *The Jewish Landsmanschaften of New York* (New York, 1938), 27–32, 150, 378–97; Daniel Soyer, *Jewish Immigrant Associations and American Identity in New York, 1880–1939* (Cambridge, Mass., 1997), 49–112; Hutchins Hapgood, *The Spirit of the Ghetto* (1901, repr., Cambridge, Mass., 1967), 12; *The Jewish Communal Register of New York City, 1917–1918* (New York, 1918), 735–864.

29. Louis Waldman, *Labor Lawyer* (New York, 1944), 21; *My Future Is in America,* 144 (Domnitz); Elizabeth Ewen, *Immigrant Women in the Land of Dollars: Life and Culture on the Lower East Side, 1890–1925* (New York, 1985), 68–71; Polland and Soyer, *Emerging Metropolis,* 116.

30. Bertha Smith, "The Way of the Pushcart Man," *The Craftsman: An Illustrated Monthly Magazine for the Simplification of Life* [ed. Gustav Stickley], 9 (October 1905): 223 (quotation); *Reports of the Industrial Commission on Immigration,* 319–21; Laura Hapke, *Sweatshop: The History of an American Idea* (New Brunswick, N.J., 2004), 17–66; Daniel Bender, *Sweated Work, Weak Bodies: Anti-Sweatshop Campaigns and the Language of Labor* (New Brunswick, N.J., 2004), 46–48.

31. *Reports of the Industrial Commission on Immigration,* 319–21.

32. Riis, *How the Other Half Lives,* 128–31; *Reports of the Industrial Commission on Immigration,* 319–21; Howe, *World of Our Fathers,* 81, 156–57; *Men's Ready-Made Clothing* (Washington, D.C., 1911), vol. 2 of *Report on Condition of Woman and Child Wage-Earners in the United States,* 19 vols. (Washington, D.C., 1910–1913), 446–76, 730–35; Jesse Pope, *The Clothing Industry in New York* (Columbia, Mo., 1905), 32, 66–67, 79, 256–60; *Seventh Annual Report of the Factory Inspectors of the State of New York* (Albany, 1893), 12–13, 26 ("fire-escapes"); *Report of the Committee of Manufactures on the Sweating System* (Washington, D.C., 1893), 207–10; Rose Cohen, *Out of the Shadow* (New York, 1918), 85 ("hands off"). Pay could vary tremendously depending on the quality of the item being manufactured and whether the work was done in "high" season, when labor was in short supply, or in the "slack" season, when there was little garment work to be found.

33. "Not the Hebrews of Fiction," *Times,* September 13, 1894, 2.

34. *Men's Ready-Made Clothing,* 446–76, 730–35; Pope, *Clothing Industry,* 32, 66–67, 79, 256–60; *Seventh Annual Report of the Factory Inspectors of the State of New York,* 12–13,

26 (quotation); Cohen, *Out of the Shadow*, 83; *Report of the Committee of Manufactures on the Sweating System*, 207–10; *Report of the Tenement House Committee*, 250; "Sweatshop Girl Tailors," *Tribune*, June 10, 1897, 5; *Oxford English Dictionary Online* (March 2015), s.v. "sweater," "sweating," and "sweated."

35. Pope, *Clothing Industry*, 67, 259; *Reports of the Industrial Commission on Immigration*, 369–70; Charles Collin, ed., *The Revised Statutes of the State of New York: Fifth and Sixth Supplemental Volumes*, 9th ed. (New York, 1892), chap. 655, 3634–36; "Where Dwell the Victims of the 'Sweater,'" *Herald*, August 21, 1892, 8. *The Oxford English Dictionary* dates the first use of the term "sweatshop" to 1892; I found it used in the *Irish-American* as early as 1890. See *OED Online*, s.v. "sweatshop"; "Current Events," *Irish-American*, June 28, 1890, 5; Hapke, *Sweatshop*, 17–19.

36. "Not the Hebrews of Fiction," *Times*, September 13, 1894, 2.

37. Ibid.; "The Relation of Tuberculosis to the Tenement House Problem," in de Forest and Veiller, *Tenement House Problem*, 1:461–70; "Consumption," in *The Jewish Encyclopedia*, 12 vols. (1901; new ed., New York, 1925), 4:245–47; Rischin, *Promised City*, 87 ("hotbeds"); Cohen, *Out of the Shadow*, 81 ("millions"); Alan Kraut, *Silent Travelers: Germs, Genes, and the Immigrant Menace* (New York, 1994), 177; Howe, *World of Our Fathers*, 81.

38. Employment figures adapted from the 5 percent sample of 1900 U.S. census found in Ruggles, *Integrated Public Use Microdata Series*, available as "1900 New York City 5% Census Sample" at https://dataverse.harvard.edu/dataverse/anbinder. The figures for the Lower East Side were derived by creating subsamples that included only blocks located within the boundaries of the Lower East Side as defined at the beginning of this chapter. This subsample can be found on my Dataverse page as "1900 Lower East Side 5% Census Sample."

My figures for Jews in the garment industry differ from those of other scholars who utilized different samples. Pope, *Clothing Industry*, 106–8, cites a lower percentage of Jews working in the garment industry, but his sample included the American-born children of east European Jews, and these children were much less likely to work in the garment industry than their parents. Others claim that 60 percent of Lower East Side Jews worked in the garment industry, but this figure is based on a survey of inhabitants of only three of the five wards that made up the Lower East Side. More important, the age of the average respondent to that survey was over fifty, far older than the typical east European immigrant, suggesting that the survey sample was not representative of the entire Lower East Side population. See Howe, *World of Our Fathers*, 80, 154; Polland and Soyer, *Emerging Metropolis*, 118; Lloyd Gartner, "The Jews of the New York's East Side, 1890–1893: Two Surveys by the Baron de Hirsch Fund," *American Jewish Historical Quarterly* 53 (1964): 264–72.

39. "1900 New York City 5% Census Sample"; "1900 Lower East Side 5% Census Sample"; Sophie Ruskay, *Horsecars and Cobblestones* (New York, 1948), 56.

40. *Immigrants in Cities*, 2 vols. (Washington, D.C., 1911), 1:198, 2:291, 546, vols. 26 and 27 of *Reports of the Immigration Commission, Presented by Mr. Dillingham*, 42 vols. (Washington, D.C., 1911); "Working Girls in Cities," *Times*, September 30, 1889, 5; Polland and Soyer, *Emerging Metropolis*, 123; Susan Glenn, *Daughters of the Shtetl: Life and Labor*

in the Immigrant Generation (Ithaca, 1990), 73–74 (quotation); Harry Roskolenko, *The Time That Was Then: The Lower East Side, 1900–1914, An Intimate Chronicle* (New York, 1971), 41–48. Glenn's contention that 56 percent of Russian Jewish immigrant households took in boarders is based on a sample of only 296 households. A bigger survey in the same congressional study put the number at 48 percent.

41. Pope, *Clothing Industry*, 106–7; Rischin, *Promised City*, 58; entries for Froim L. Anbinder, election district 52, assembly district 22, Kings County (Brooklyn), 1925 New York State census, 91, and dwelling 114, district 534, Kings County, 1930 census; entry for Tulea Anbinder, household 66, enumeration district 24–139, Kings County, 1940 census.

42. "1900 New York City 5% Census Sample"; Polland and Soyer, *Emerging Metropolis*, 124; Howe, *World of Our Fathers*, 77–80; Rischin, *Promised City*, 55.

43. Minnie Goldstein, "Success or Failure?" in *My Future Is in America*, 24–25, 28.

44. E. Idell Zeisloft, *The New Metropolis, 1600–1900: Memorable Events of Three Centuries* (New York, 1899), 531.

45. Daniel Soyer, ed., *A Coat of Many Colors: Immigration, Globalism, and Reform in New York City's Garment Industry* (New York, 2005), 105–8 ("soul"); Howe, *World of Our Fathers*, 80 (other quotations); Irving Howe and Kenneth Libo, *How We Lived: A Documentary History of Immigrant Jews in America, 1880–1930* (New York, 1979), 68–69; *Directory of Directors in the City of New York, 1911–1912* (New York, 1911), 43; entries for Isaac A. Benequit, family 398, enumeration district 1550, assembly district 34, Bronx County, 1910 census; dwelling 48, enumeration district 95, assembly district 2, Bronx County, 1920 census; election district 54, assembly district 16, Kings County (Brooklyn), 1925 New York State census; dwelling 135, enumeration district 1370, Kings County, 1930 census.

46. Smith, "Way of the Pushcart Man," 228.

47. *Eighteenth Annual Report of the Bureau of Labor Statistics of the State of New York for the Year 1900* (Albany, 1901), 292; Roskolenko, *Time That Was Then*, 93; Riis, *How the Other Half Lives*, 115–16.

48. Bercovici, *Around the World*, 76–77 ("Babel"); *Report of the Bureau of Labor Statistics for the Year 1900*, 292; Roskolenko, *Time That Was Then*, 106.

49. Smith, "Way of the Pushcart Man," 223 (quotation); Hasia Diner, *Roads Taken: The Great Jewish Migrations to the New World and the Peddlers Who Forged the Way* (New Haven, 2015), 155–99; Howe, *World of Our Fathers*, 140, 166; "1900 New York City 5% Census Sample"; "1920 New York City 1% Census Sample."

50. "1900 New York City 5% Census Sample"; "1920 New York City 1% Census Sample." For similar findings using a different methodological approach, see Thomas Kessner, *The Golden Door: Italian and Jewish Immigrant Mobility in New York City, 1880–1915* (New York, 1977), 104–60.

51. Maurice Fishberg, *The Jews: A Study of Race and Environment* (New York, 1911), 368; Polland and Soyer, *Emerging Metropolis*, 130–31; Bercovici, *Around the World in New York*, 216 (quotation); Jeffrey Gurock, *When Harlem Was Jewish, 1870–1930* (New York, 1979), 27–85; entry for Jacob Munstuk, block A, election district 16, and entry for Isidor Munstuk, block B, election district 40, 1905 New York State census.

52. Polland and Soyer, *Emerging Metropolis*, 7, 132–33; entries for Jacob and Matie Mun-

stuk, enumeration district 1404, Bronx County, 1910 census; block 1, election district 36, Bronx County, 1915 New York State census; and dwelling 51, family 315, enumeration district 1501, 1920 census; Steven Lowenstein, *Frankfurt on the Hudson: The German-Jewish Community of Washington Heights, 1933–1983* (Detroit, 1989), 22–46; entries for Barnet Gutkin in *Trow's General Directory of the Boroughs of Manhattan and Bronx, City of New York, for the Year Ending August 1, 1913* (New York, 1912), 628; *Trow's General Directory of the Boroughs of Manhattan and Bronx, City of New York, for the Year Ending August 1, 1914* (New York, 1913), 512; *Polk and Trow's General Directory of New York City for 1915* (New York, 1915), 847.

53. Isa Kapp, "By the Waters of the Grand Concourse," in *Commentary on the American Scene: Portraits of Jewish Life in America,* ed. Elliot Cohen (New York, 1953), 269–80; "Looking Back at the Grand Concourse's First Century," *Times,* March 18, 2009; "Grand, Wasn't It?" *Times,* August 20, 2009; Constance Rosenblum, *Boulevard of Dreams: Heady Times, Heartbreak, and Hope Along the Grand Concourse in the Bronx* (New York, 2009), 15–124; Ruth Gay, *Unfinished People: Eastern European Jews Encounter America* (New York, 1996), 50, 65–66; Polland and Soyer, *Emerging Metropolis,* 134 ("daughter").

54. Rischin, *Promised City,* 92–93; Howe, *World of Our Fathers,* 131–32 (quotations); entry for Max Dandeshane, dwelling 20, enumeration district 800, Ward Twenty-six, Kings County (Brooklyn), 1910 census; Hugo Ullitz, *Atlas of the Borough of Brooklyn,* 4 vols. (Brooklyn, 1905), 4, plate 2.

55. Deborah Dash Moore, "On the Fringes of the City: Jewish Neighborhoods in Three Boroughs," in *The Landscape of Modernity: Essays on New York City, 1900–1940,* ed. David Ward and Olivier Zunz (New York, 1992), 257; Polland and Soyer, *Emerging Metropolis,* 131–32 (quotation); Alter Landesman, *Brownsville: The Birth, Development, and Passing of a Jewish Community in New York* (New York, 1971), 17–98.

56. Howe, *World of Our Fathers,* 131; entries for Max Dandeshane, dwelling 20, enumeration district 800, Ward Twenty-six, Kings County (Brooklyn), 1910 census, and dwelling 92, enumeration district 74, assembly district 2, Kings County, 1920 census; entries for Froim Leib Anbinder, enumeration district 52, assembly district 22, Kings County, 1925 New York census, 91, and dwelling 114, enumeration district 534, Kings County, 1930 census; Ralph Foster Weld, *Brooklyn Is America* (New York, 1950), 112; Kenneth Jackson, ed., *The Neighborhoods of Brooklyn* (New Haven, 1998), 40–43, 109–12, 116–20, 157–60.

57. Jane Ziegelman, *97 Orchard: An Edible History of Five Immigrant Families in One New York Tenement* (New York, 2010), 87–88; Virginia Marquardt, ed., *Survivor from a Dead Age: The Memoirs of Louis Lozowick* (Washington, D.C., 1997), 20.

58. Hasia Diner, *Hungering for America: Italian, Irish, and Jewish Foodways in the Age of Migration* (Cambridge, Mass., 2001), 186; Samuel Golden, "Some Days Are More Important: A Memoir of Immigrant New York, 1903–1913," in *Jewish Settlement and Community in the Western Modern World,* ed. Ronald Dotterer, Deborah Dash Moore, and Steven M. Cohen (Selinsgrove, Pa., 1991), 171.

59. Riis, *How the Other Half Lives,* 128; John Cooper, *Eat and Be Satisfied: A Social History of Jewish Food* (Northvale, N.J., 1993), 149; Ziegelman, *97 Orchard,* 150–51.

60. Diner, *Hungering for America,* 200; Jenna Weissman Joselit, *The Wonders of America: Reinventing Jewish Culture, 1880–1950* (New York, 1994), 203; Ruth Glazer, "The Jewish

Delicatessen," in Cohen, *Commentary on the American Scene,* 191–204; Howe, *World of Our Fathers,* 127 (quotation); David Sax, *Save the Deli: In Search of Perfect Pastrami, Crusty Rye, and the Heart of the Jewish Delicatessen* (Boston, 2009), 25; Ted Merwin, *Pastrami on Rye: An Overstuffed History of the Jewish Deli* (New York, 2015), 17–38.

61. Alfred Kazin, *A Walker in the City* (New York, 1951), 34.

62. Joselit, *Wonders of America,* 209; Ratner's menu at http://menus.nypl.org/menu_pages/53932.

63. Jacob Marcus, *To Count a People: American Jewish Population Data, 1585–1984* (Lanham, Md., 1990), 150–51; Moore, "On the Fringes," 268; Polland and Soyer, *Emerging Metropolis,* 7; Hasia Diner, *Lower East Side Memories: A Jewish Place in America* (Princeton, 2000), 17–126; Enrico Sartorio, *Social and Religious Life of Italians in America* (Boston, 1918), 19 ("to America").

17. Little Italys

1. Ship manifest entries for Angelo and Pasquale D'Angelo, *Celtic,* April 7, 1910, "New York Passenger Lists"; Pascal D'Angelo, *Son of Italy* (1924; repr., Toronto, 2003), 71, 74, 94, 105–7.

2. D'Angelo, *Son of Italy,* 107–9.

3. Ibid., 129, 134, 144, 148, 151, 153, 157, 160 (quotations); "Brooklyn's Library-Made Poet," *Bulletin of the Brooklyn Public Library,* 4th ser., 1 (November 1922): 137.

4. Carl Van Doren, "The Roving Critic," *The Nation* 114 (January 25, 1922): 98–99; "Editorial Paragraphs" and "*The Nation's* Poetry Prize," *The Nation* 114 (February 8, 1922): 137, 163; Carl Van Doren, intro. to *Son of Italy* (1924 ed.), x–xi (quotations).

5. "A Neighbor of Old Ovid Sings for the Heathen," *San Diego Evening Tribune,* February 4, 1922, 12; Pascal D'Angelo, "Songs of Light, Parts I and II," *Bookman* 55 (March 1922): 55; "Songs of Light III," *Bookman* 55 (May 1922): 228; "Sudden Gold," *Bookman* 56 (October 1922): 141; "Dawn," *Bookman* 59 (June 1924): 496; "Life in Life," *Bookman* 59 (August 1924): 662; "The Last Shore," *Bookman* 60 (September 1924): 30; "Accident in the Coal Dump," *Bookman* 60 (November 1924): 369; "A Poet from the Slums," *Literary Digest* 73 (April 8, 1922): 34–35, 40; "Laborer Poet Writes amid Hardships," *Boston Herald,* April 30, 1922, E1; Pascal D'Angelo, "To Some Modern Poets," *Century Magazine* 104 (June 1922): 176; Pascal D'Angelo, "Song of Night," *Century Magazine* 105 (March 1923): 662; Pascal D'Angelo, "Midday" and "Song of Light," *Current Opinion* 72 (June 1922): 820; Pascal D'Angelo, "Night Scene" and "To a Warrior," *Liberator* 5 (July 1922): 23, 27; "Current Magazines," *Times,* June 25, 1922, magazine sec., 13; Thomas Moult, comp., *The Best Poems of 1922* (New York, 1923), 60–61; "The Pick and Shovel Poet," *Brooklyn Daily Eagle,* March 25, 1923, magazine sec., 4; Pascal D'Angelo, "Osoona," *Literary Review* (June 30, 1923): 797; D'Angelo, *Son of Italy,* 168 (quotations).

6. "Pick and Shovel Poet Lives on Dime a Day," *Brooklyn Daily Eagle,* February 4, 1923, B3; "The Pick and Shovel Poet," *Brooklyn Daily Eagle,* March 25, 1923, magazine sec., 4 ("clean and strong"); "Pascal D'Angelo," *Boston Herald,* December 6, 1924, 13 ("fame"); "A Pick and Shovel Man," *Herald Tribune,* December 21, 1924, book review sec., 3; "Poet of Section Gang," *Springfield (Mass.) Republican,* December 29, 1924, 6; "Poet of the

Pick and Shovel," *Times*, January 4, 1925, book review sec., 18; "Pascal D'Angelo, 'Poet of Pick and Shovel,' Has Published Autobiography," *Brooklyn Daily Eagle*, January 4, 1925, 7; "Pick and Shovel Poet Tells His Homely Story," *San Francisco Chronicle*, January 11, 1925, arts sec., 4; "Literature," *New Orleans Times-Picayune*, March 1, 1925, supp., 6; "Triumph of D'Angelo, Pick and Shovel Poet," *Literary Digest* 84 (March 7, 1925): 44–50.

7. "Pick and Shovel Poet Lives on Dime a Day," *Brooklyn Daily Eagle*, February 4, 1923, B3 ("shabby" and "pay more"); "The Pick and Shovel Poet," *Brooklyn Daily Eagle*, March 25, 1923, magazine sec., 4 ("his heart").

8. Pascal D'Angelo, "Omnis Sum," reprinted in *Son of Italy*, 110.

9. "Pick and Shovel Poet's Kin Seek Funeral Fund," *Herald Tribune*, March 17, 1932, 12 (quotations); "Honored Burial Guaranteed for Destitute Poet," *Brooklyn Daily Eagle*, March 18, 1932, "Home Talk" sec., 1; "Pascal D'Angelo Funeral Held in Brooklyn Church," *Herald Tribune*, March 20, 1932, 22; "Verses, Dictionary Poet's Only Estate," *Brooklyn Daily Eagle*, March 27, 1932, 12.

10. "Monument Planned for D'Angelo Grave," *Brooklyn Daily Eagle*, August 21, 1932, 16; "Pascal D'Angelo," *Saturday Review of Literature* 8 (March 26, 1932): 620; Bruce Catton, "Why Poets Starve," *Riverside (Calif.) Daily Press*, April 1, 1932, 12; D'Angelo, *Son of Italy* (1924 ed.), xi ("precious").

11. "The Italians at Castle Garden," *Herald*, December 12, 1872, 7; Ira Rosenwaike, *Population History of New York City* (Syracuse, 1972), 67, 95; *Fifteenth Census of the United States: 1930*, vol. 2, *Population* (Washington, D.C., 1933), 233 (Italian-born population of United States in 1900 and 1930).

12. George Manson, "The 'Foreign Element' in New York City: V — The Italians," *Harper's Weekly* (October 18, 1890): 817; "Shot Down by His Wife," *Times*, October 21, 1886, 8; "Battle with Italians," *Times*, July 18, 1887, 8; "Little Italy in New-York," *Times*, May 31, 1896, 32; William Shedd, *Italian Population in New York* (New York, [1934]), 9.

13. Viola Roseboro, "The Italians of New York," *Cosmopolitan* 4 (January 1888): 397; "Flashes from the Slums," *Sun*, February 12, 1888, 10; "New York's 'Little Italy,'" *Frank Leslie's Illustrated Newspaper* (August 11, 1888): 415; Allan Forman, "Some Adopted Americans," *American Magazine* 9 (November 1888): 46–47; Jacob Riis, *How the Other Half Lives: Studies Among the Tenements of New York* (New York, 1890), 55.

14. Jacob Riis, *The Battle with the Slum* (New York, 1902), 39–40; Charlotte Adams, "Italian Life in New York," *Harper's Monthly Magazine* 62 (April 1881): 681; Manson, "'Foreign Element,'" 818.

15. "Report of Tenement-House Commission," February 17, 1885, in *Documents of the Senate of the State of New York. One Hundred and Eighth Session, 1885*, vol. 5 (Albany, 1885), doc. 36, 233–35; Tyler Anbinder, *Five Points: The Nineteenth-Century New York City Neighborhood That Invented Tap Dance, Stole Elections, and Became the World's Most Notorious Slum* (New York, 2001), 358–59.

16. "Flashes from the Slums," *Sun*, February 12, 1888, 10.

17. Louise Odencrantz, *Italian Women in Industry: A Study of Conditions in New York City* (New York, 1919), 31; *Report of the New York City Commission on Congestion of Population* (New York, 1911), 137; *Atlas of the Borough of Manhattan, City of New York* (New

York, 1916), plates 20, 22, 31; Elizabeth Watson, "Home Work in the Tenements," *The Survey* 25 (1910–11): 777 (quotation).

18. *Immigrants in Cities: A Study of the Population of Selected Districts in New York, Chicago, Philadelphia, Boston, Cleveland, Buffalo, and Milwaukee,* 2 vols., vol. 1 (Washington, D.C., 1911), 199, vol. 26 of *Reports of the Immigration Commission,* 42 vols. (Washington, D.C., 1911); Jacob Riis, *A Ten Years' War: An Account of the Battle with the Slum in New York* (Boston, 1900), 53–54; Lillian Betts, "The Italian in New York," *University Settlement Studies* 1 (1905–6), 90–91; Donna Gabaccia, *From Sicily to Elizabeth Street: Housing and Social Change Among Italian Immigrants, 1880–1930* (Albany, 1984), 66–77.

19. Images 04071, 04072, 04081, 04112, 04123, 04124, 04125, 04126 (quotation from caption), 04132, 04133 (Ceru family), 04139, 04140, 04141, 04143, 04147, 04148, 04151, 04208, 04304 (214 Elizabeth Street), and 04319, National Child Labor Committee Collection, Prints and Photographs Division, Library of Congress, available at http://www.loc.gov/pictures/collection/nclc/.

20. *Report of the New York City Commission on Congestion,* 178; "Social Geography of the East Side," *Times,* April 3, 1910, magazine sec., 1–2.

21. George Bromley and Walter Bromley, *Atlas of the City of New York, Borough of Manhattan,* 4 vols., vol. 3 (Philadelphia, 1898–99), plates 37, 40; George Bromley and Walter Bromley, *Atlas of the City of New York, Borough of Manhattan* (Philadelphia, 1911), plate 33; "'Little Italy' Breeds Grip," *Times,* December 25, 1898, 2 ("the streets"); Watson, "Home Work in the Tenements," 780 ("pin"); "Tenement House Evils," *Times,* November 24, 1894, 9 ("worst"); Robert Orsi, *The Madonna of 115th Street: Faith and Community in Italian Harlem, 1880–1950* (New Haven, 1985), 29–31; Gerald Meyer, "Italian Harlem: Portrait of a Community," in *The Italians of New York: Five Centuries of Struggle and Achievement,* ed. Philip Cannistraro (New York, 1999), 57–67.

22. Gerald Meyer, *Vito Marcantonio: Radical Politician, 1902–1954* (Albany, 1989), 114; Simone Cinotto, *The Italian American Table: Food, Family, and Community in New York City* (Urbana, 2013), 94 (quotations).

23. Leonard Covello, *The Heart Is the Teacher* (New York, 1958), 21.

24. Phyllis Williams, *South Italian Folkways in Europe and America* (New Haven, 1938), 45; Edward Corsi, *In the Shadow of Liberty* (New York, 1935), 23.

25. Betts, "Italian in New York," 90–91 ("never crossed"); Jennifer Guglielmo, *Living the Revolution: Italian Women's Resistance and Radicalism in New York City, 1880–1945* (Chapel Hill, 2010), 121 ("didn't need"); Enrico Sartorio, *Social and Religious Life of Italians in America* (Boston, 1918), 19 ("down to America").

26. D'Angelo, *Son of Italy,* 62; "Social Geography of the East Side," *Times,* April 3, 1910, magazine sec., 1; Cinotto, *Italian American Table,* 86–87; Covello, *Heart,* 22; Edward Alsworth Ross, "Italians in America," *Century Magazine* 88 (1914): 444.

27. *Immigration in Cities,* 1:275; Samuel Baily, *Immigrants in the Lands of Promise: Italians in Buenos Aires and New York City, 1870–1914* (Ithaca, 1999), 132, 134; Williams, *South Italian Folkways,* 46.

28. D'Angelo, *Son of Italy,* 71; "Italians in New-York," *Tribune,* June 2, 1895, 26 (quotation); Roseboro, "Italians of New York," 399.

29. Manson, "'Foreign Element,'" 817 (quotation); Roseboro, "Italians of New York," 400–

402; "Shocking Plight of Italian Poor in New York City," *Herald*, September 18, 1892, 11; "Antonio Shows His Colors," *Times*, August 1, 1888, 8; Edwin Fenton, *Immigrants and Unions, A Case Study: Italians and American Labor, 1870–1920* (New York, 1975), 95–135; Gunther Peck, *Reinventing Free Labor: Padrones and Immigrant Workers in the North American West, 1880–1930* (New York, 2000); Humbert Nelli, "The Italian Padrone System in the United States," *Labor History* 5 (1964): 153–67; "Poor Sons of Sunny Italy," *Times*, July 27, 1888, 8; "Two Italians in One Trap," *Times*, August 7, 1888, 8.

30. S. Merlino, "Italian Immigrants and Their Enslavement," *Forum* 15 (1893): 188.

31. *John Swinton's Paper*, January 20, 1884, 1; Adolfo Rossi, *Un Italiano in America* (Milan, 1899), 54.

32. Dino Cinel, *The National Integration of Italian Return Migration, 1870–1929* (New York, 1991), 97–111; *Annual Report of the Commissioner General of Immigration to the Secretary of Labor and Commerce for the Year Ended June 30, 1911* (Washington, D.C., 1912), 88–105.

33. "1920 New York City 1% Census Sample," https://dataverse.harvard.edu/dataverse/anbinder.

34. "Italian Life in New York," *Harper's New Monthly Magazine* 62 (April 1881): 677; Konrad Bercovici, *Around the World in New York* (New York, 1924), 125, 127–28.

35. "1920 New York City 1% Census Sample"; Odencrantz, *Italian Women in Industry*, 31–53; Cinotto, *Italian American Table*, 29; Guglielmo, *Living the Revolution*, 76 (quotation).

36. Elizabeth Ewen, *Immigrant Women in the Land of Dollars: Life and Culture on the Lower East Side, 1890–1925* (New York, 1985), 246–47.

37. "1900 New York City 5% Census Sample"; "1920 New York City 1% Census Sample"; Harry Roskolenko, *The Time That Was Then: The Lower East Side, 1900–1914, an Intimate Chronicle* (New York, 1971), 69.

38. Odencrantz, *Italian Women in Industry*, 180–83; Ewen, *Immigrant Women*, 122.

39. Watson, "Home Work in the Tenements," 778–80 ("Everybody"); Sarah Stein, *Plumes: Ostrich Feathers, Jews, and a Lost World of Global Commerce* (New Haven, 2008), 120–26.

40. Ewen, *Immigrant Women*, 122–23; Miriam Cohen, *Workshop to Office: Two Generations of Italian Women in New York City, 1900–1950* (Ithaca, 1992), 47–49 ("no time").

41. Mary Van Kleeck, "Child Labor in New York City Tenements," *Charities and the Commons* 19 (1908): 1405–15 (quotation, 1407); Mary Van Kleeck, *Artificial Flower Makers* (New York, 1913), 90–117.

42. Hine's captions for images 04072 and 04146, National Child Labor Committee Collection, Prints and Photographs Division, Library of Congress; entry for Angelo Malatesta, family 243, enumeration district 38, Bridgeport, Fairfield County, Conn., 1910 census; entry for Agostina Malatesta, enumeration district 68, Bridgeport, Fairfield County, Conn., 1920 census; manifest entry for Agostina Dondera, *Ems*, November 23, 1892, "New York Passenger Lists."

43. Anbinder, *Five Points*, 377.

44. "The Suffering Italians," *Times*, December 14, 1872, 8; "Only Birds of Passage," *Times*, July 28, 1888, 8; "Birds of Passage," *Times*, March 9, 1906, 8, and March 11, 1906, 8; Guglielmo, *Living the Revolution*, 14; Baily, *Immigrants in the Lands of Promise*, 118; Cinel,

National Integration of Italian Return Migration, 122–49. Conversion rate of the Italian lira to the U.S. dollar in 1914 is based on Board of Governors of the Federal Reserve System, *Banking and Monetary Statistics* (Washington, D.C., 1943), 673. Conversion of 1914 dollars to 2015 dollars from https://www.measuringworth.com.

45. "Tiny Places of Worship: The Humble Synagogues of the Poorer East Side," *Tribune,* February 16, 1896, 25.

46. Bishop Thomas A. Becker to Archbishop James Gibbons, December 17, 1884, box 1, Records of the St. Raphael Society, Center for Migration Studies, New York ("Ignorance"); Bernard Lynch, "The Italians in New York," *Catholic World* 47 (April 1888): 68–70 ("elementary truths"); Bishop Thomas Becker and Archbishop James Gibbons to Reverend Simeoni, in Stephen M. DiGiovanni, *Archbishop Corrigan and the Italian Immigrants* (Huntington, Ind., 1994), 29 ("listless ignorance").

47. DiGiovanni, *Archbishop Corrigan and the Italian Immigrants,* 60 ("farewell"); Lynch, "Italians in New York," 72 ("humiliation").

48. Mary Elizabeth Brown, *Churches, Communities, and Children: Italian Immigrants in the Archdiocese of New York, 1880–1945* (New York, 1995), 48–59, 62–70, 181–88; Mary Elizabeth Brown, "Italian Immigrant Catholic Clergy and an Exception to the Rule: The Reverend Antonio Demo, Our Lady of Pompei, Greenwich Village, 1899–1933," *Church History* 62 (1983): 43; Mary Elizabeth Brown, "The Making of Italian-American Catholics: Jesuit Work on the Lower East Side, New York, 1890's–1950's," *Catholic Historical Review* 73 (1987): 199–202; Anbinder, *Five Points,* 380–88; "Thousands Do Homage to Our Lady of Mount Carmel," *Times,* July 17, 1904, 7; Orsi, *Madonna of 115th Street,* 54.

49. Leonard Covello, *The Social Background of the Italo-American School Child* (Totowa, N.J., 1972), 330–45 ("sandwich," 339); Covello, *Heart,* 31 ("understand").

50. Mark Wyman, *Round-Trip to America: The Immigrants Return to Europe, 1880–1930* (Ithaca, 1993), 9–12; Cinel, *National Integration of Italian Return Migration,* 97–111.

51. *Thirteenth Census of the United States Taken in the Year 1910,* vol. 1, *Population* (Washington, D.C., 1913), 856; *Fourteenth Census of the United States Taken in the Year 1920,* vol. 2, *Population* (Washington, D.C., 1922), 730; *Fifteenth Census of the United States: 1930,* vol. 2, *Population* (Washington, D.C., 1933), 249; Shedd, *Italian Population,* 6–13; Frank Cavaioli, "Returning to Corona's Little Italy," *Italian Americana* 15 (1997): 32–33; entry for Angelo Malatesta, family 243, enumeration district 38, Bridgeport, Fairfield County, Conn., 1910 census; entry for Agostina Malatesta, family 160, enumeration district 68, Bridgeport, Fairfield County, Conn., 1920 census.

18. Reform

1. "Want Riis Honored: Rockaway Park Residents Urge Change in Park's Name," *Times,* June 7, 1914, sec. 8, 1; Nicholas Bloom and Matthew Lasner, eds., *Affordable Housing in New York: The People, Places, and Policies That Transformed a City* (Princeton, 2015), 128–31.

2. Jacob A. Riis, *The Making of an American* (New York, 1901), 1–41 ("kissed," 32–33, "green," 39); Tom Buk-Swienty, *The Other Half: The Life of Jacob Riis and the World of Immigrant America,* trans. Annette Buk-Swienty (New York, 2008), 19–44, 49–56.

3. Riis, *Making of an American,* 44–69 (quotations, 66–67); Buk-Swienty, *Other Half,* 57–63.

4. Riis, *Making of an American,* 70–100 ("meat-bones," 66, and "nastiness," 69); Buk-Swienty, *Other Half,* 63–78, 85–90 ("terrible").

5. Riis, *Making of an American,* 102–25; Buk-Swienty, *Other Half,* 80–85, 91–101.

6. Riis, *Making of an American,* 126–174; Buk-Swienty, *Other Half,* 104–24. The modern value of his $3,000 windfall was calculated at http://www.measuringworth.com/uscompare/.

7. Buk-Swienty, *Other Half,* 133–76; Riis, *Making of an American,* 175–233, 235 (quotation); Bonnie Yochelson and Daniel Czitrom, *Rediscovering Jacob Riis: Exposure Journalism and Photography in Turn-of-the-Century New York* (New York, 2007), 8–10, 20–24; *Report of the Tenement House Committee as Authorized by Chapter 479 of the Laws of 1894* (Albany, 1895), 142–45. Riis wrote, "My scrap-book from the year 1883 to 1896 is one running comment on the Bend." Riis, *Making of an American,* 275. This scrapbook is in the Riis Collection, Manuscript Division, Library of Congress.

8. James Lane, *Jacob A. Riis and the American City* (Port Washington, N.Y., 1974), 29–44; Yochelson and Czitrom, *Rediscovering Jacob Riis,* 109–15.

9. Riis, *Making of an American,* 266–67.

10. Ibid., 267–73 (quotations, 268, 273). For the dating of Riis's first tenement photographs to 1887, I have relied on Maren Stange, *Symbols of Ideal Life: Social Documentary Photography in America, 1890–1950* (New York, 1989), chap. 1.

11. Riis, *Making of an American,* 273–97 (quotations, 297).

12. Ibid., 297–303; Jacob Riis, "How the Other Half Lives: Studies Among the Tenements," *Scribner's Magazine* 6 (December 1889): 643–62.

13. Riis, *Making of an American,* 309.

14. Riis, *How the Other Half Lives: Studies Among the Tenements of New York* (New York, 1890), 273.

15. Ibid., 268–70.

16. James Russell Lowell to Riis, November 21, 1890, in Riis, *Making of an American,* 308; quotations from "In the World of Literature," *Press,* November 23, 1890 ("thrilling" and "harrowing"); untitled review, *The True Nationalist,* November 29, 1890 ("startling"); "Literary Brevities," *Chicago Times,* December 20, 1890 ("shuddering"); "How the Other Half Lives," *Boston Times,* November 30, 1890 ("saddening"); "How the Other Half Lives," *The Critic,* December 27, 1890 ("literally"); and "How the Other Half Lives," *The Independent,* January 1, 1891 ("unerring"), all in Riis scrapbook.

17. *Chicago Tribune,* December 13, 1890, in Riis scrapbook; Riis, *Making of an American,* 328; James Hijiya, "Four Ways of Looking at a Philanthropist: A Study of Robert Weeks de Forest," *Proceedings of the American Philosophical Association* 124 (1980): 404–18.

18. Lawrence Veiller, *The Tenement House Reform in New York, 1834–1900* (New York, 1900), 31–36; I. N. Phelps Stokes, *The Iconography of Manhattan Island, 1498–1909,* 6 vols. (New York, 1915–1928), 5:2018; "Mulberry Bend Park," *Times,* October 7, 1892, 10; "Mulberry Bend as a Park," *Times,* January 21, 1893, 9; "For the Mulberry Bend Park," *Times,* January 28, 1893, 10; "All Saddled on the City," *Times,* May 20, 1893, 9; "Condition of Mulberry Bend," *Times,* December 7, 1894, 2; "Pay for Mulberry Bend Park," *Times,*

January 22, 1895, 9; "Bought a House for $1.50," *Times,* June 7, 1895, 7; "Rapid Transit and Parks," *Times,* June 20, 1895, 3; "Complaint Against Mulberry Bend," *Times,* December 21, 1895, 14; "Rear Tenements Must Go," *Times,* June 23, 1896, 9; "Mulberry Park Opened," *Times,* June 16, 1897, 7; Jacob Riis, *The Battle with the Slum* (New York, 1902), 264, 268–70; Riis, *Making of an American,* 183; Jacob Riis, "The Clearing of Mulberry Bend: The Story of the Rise and Fall of a Typical New York Slum," *Review of Reviews* 12 (August 1895): 172.

19. William Fryer, ed., *The Tenement House Law of the City of New York* (New York, 1901), 20–42; Andrew Dolkart, *Biography of a Tenement House in New York City: An Architectural History of 97 Orchard Street,* 2nd ed. (Chicago, 2012), 65–85; Roy Lubove, *The Progressives and the Slums: Tenement House Reform in New York City, 1890–1917* (Pittsburgh, 1962), 117–84; "Tenement House Reform," *Times,* February 27, 1901, 8; "Moderate Tenement House Reform," *Tribune,* April 10, 1901, 6; "The Tenement Houses," *Times,* April 11, 1901, 8; "Tenement House Bill a Law," *Tribune,* April 13, 1901, 2; "Tenement Houses," *Tribune,* April 28, 1901, supp., 8–9; "The New Tenement House Law," *Tribune,* June 29, 1901, 6; "The New Tenement Houses," *Times,* July 14, 1901, 8; "Will Fight to Repeal Tenement House Law," *Times,* October 13, 1901, 24; "The Work of the City's Tenement House Department," *Times,* July 20, 1902, 24; "Tenement House Reform," *Times,* November 2, 1902, 6; "The Tenement Houses," *Times,* February 24, 1903, 8; "City to Oppose Tenement Law Plans," *Times,* March 6, 1903, 3 (number of windowless rooms); "Tenement House Reform," *Times,* March 7, 1903, 8; "The New Tenement House Bill," *Tribune,* March 11, 1903, 8; "Tenement Reform Has Come to Stay," *Tribune,* March 28, 1903, 8; "Tenement House Litigation," *Tribune,* November 10, 1903, 8.

20. Lubove, *Progressives and the Slums,* 265–66; Burton Hendrick, "A Great Municipal Reform," *Atlantic Monthly* 92 (November 1903): 665–73.

21. Yochelson and Czitrom, *Rediscovering Jacob Riis,* 119; "Why Jacob A. Riis Doesn't Want to Be Mayor of New York," *Times,* August 27, 1905, magazine sec., 2; "A Memorial to Jacob A. Riis," *Outlook* 111 (December 22, 1915): 926 (quotation).

22. Tyler Anbinder, *Five Points: The Nineteenth-Century New York City Neighborhood That Invented Tap Dance, Stole Elections, and Became the World's Most Notorious Slum* (New York, 2001), 243–56.

23. "The University Settlement Idea," *Tribune,* December 21, 1891, 6; "College Settlements," *Times,* December 18, 1892, 16; "College Settlement Work," *Times,* October 1, 1893, 18 (quotations); "Work of the College Settlement," *Times,* March 15, 1894, 9; "What the University Settlement Does for the Immigrant," *Tribune,* December 21, 1919, magazine sec., 6.

24. Helen Rand Thayer, "Blazing the Settlement Trail," *Smith Alumnae Quarterly* 2 (April 1911): 130–37; "An East-Sider by Choice," *The Outlook* 72 (October 4, 1902): 315–17; "College Settlement's Quarter-Century Duel with Vice," *Tribune,* January 11, 1914, pt. 5, 4; Moses Rischin, *The Promised City: New York's Jews, 1870–1914* (Cambridge, Mass., 1962), 206; Emily Dinwiddie, comp., *New York Charities Directory,* 13th ed. (New York, 1903), 255–64; Lina Miller, *The New York Charities Directory,* 29th ed. (New York, 1920), xxxix–xl.

25. Beatrice Siegel, *Lillian Wald of Henry Street* (New York, 1983), 1–8; Marjorie Feld, *Lillian Wald: A Biography* (Chapel Hill, 2008), 22, 31. Biographies of Wald all give her birth date as March 10, 1867, but it appears that once she became an adult, Wald subtracted three years from her age. When she was a child, in 1870 and again in 1880, her parents told census takers that "Lillie" was born in 1864. Some biographers also state that her father was a "German Jew," but in her passport application, Wald wrote that her father was born in Warsaw, and Max's Civil War draft registration confirms that he was born in Poland. See entry for family of Max D. Wald, family 339, Ward One, Dayton, Montgomery County, Ohio, 1870 census; family 2, enumeration district 79, Rochester, Monroe County, N.Y., 1880 census; passport application of Lillian Wald, received at U.S. Department of State March 24, 1919, U.S. Passport Applications, 1795–1925, Record Group 59, National Archives; Civil War draft registration of Max D. Wald, June 1863, in "Consolidated List of All Persons . . . Subject to Military Duty," First Congressional District of Ohio, 624, Record Group 110, National Archives.
26. Siegel, *Lillian Wald,* 15–16.
27. Ibid., 22–23; Lillian Wald, *The House on Henry Street* (New York, 1915), 4–6.
28. Wald, *House on Henry Street,* 6–8 (quotation); Feld, *Lillian Wald,* 6, 23–24, 30–32, 41–44; Annie Polland and Daniel Soyer, *Emerging Metropolis: New York Jews in the Age of Immigration, 1840–1920* (New York, 2012), 144.
29. Wald, *House on Henry Street,* 8–13; Siegel, *Lillian Wald,* 31–40; "Work in the Nurses' Settlement," *Tribune,* February 24, 1897, 5.
30. Siegel, *Lillian Wald,* 33–38 (Wald quotations); "Where Dwell the Victims of the 'Sweater,'" *Herald,* August 21, 1892, 8; Naomi Cohen, *Jacob H. Schiff: A Study in American Jewish Leadership* (Hanover, N.H., 1999), 92–95.
31. Irving Howe, *World of Our Fathers* (New York, 1976), 93; Doris Groshen Daniels, "Lillian Wald," in *American National Biography Online* (New York, 2000) (number of nurses in 1913).
32. Rischin, *Promised City,* 207–8.
33. Feld, *Lillian Wald,* 86–89, 91–122; Siegel, *Lillian Wald,* 70–77, 99–102, 115–49.
34. Arieh Sclar, "A Sport at Which Jews Excel: Jewish Basketball in American Society, 1900–1951" (Ph.D. diss., State University of New York at Stony Brook, 2008), 38, 58 ("no superior"); Peter Levine, *Ellis Island to Ebbets Field: Sport and the American Jewish Experience* (New York, 1992), 17 ("young god"), 27.
35. Levine, *Ellis Island to Ebbets Field,* 17, 27 ("appeals"); Sclar, "A Sport at Which Jews Excel," 58 ("good deal").
36. Robert Peterson, *Cages to Jump Shots: Pro Basketball's Early Years* (Lincoln, Neb., 1990), 4, 9 (quotations); Levine, *Ellis Island to Ebbets Field,* 53.
37. Sclar, "A Sport at Which Jews Excel," 67–68, 95 (quotations); "Yale Five Upset by City College," *Times,* December 24, 1916, 14.
38. Sophie Ruskay, *Horsecars and Cobblestones* (New York, 1948), 62–63 ("talk religion"); Jane Robbins, "The First Year at the College Settlement," *The Survey* 27 (February 24, 1912): 1801 ("Irish"); "Charity Workers Answer Priest," *Times,* April 14, 1908, 5; "Jews Support Father Curry," *Times,* September 15, 1908, 6 ("atheists").

39. "Lillian Wald Dies," *Times*, September 2, 1940, 15; Feld, *Lillian Wald*, 178–79 (Goldmark).
40. Ronald Bayor and Timothy Meagher, eds., *The New York Irish* (Baltimore, 1996), 165–66; Bernadette McCauley, *Who Shall Take Care of Our Sick? Roman Catholic Sisters and the Development of Catholic Hospitals in New York City* (Baltimore, 2005), 16–49.
41. Mary Louise Sullivan, *Mother Cabrini: "Italian Immigrant of the Century"* (New York, 1992), 13–209, 262–86; Stephen DiGiovanni, "Mother Cabrini: Early Years in New York," *Catholic Historical Review* 77 (1991): 56–77.
42. Arthur Aufses Jr. and Barbara Niss, *This House of Noble Deeds: The Mount Sinai Hospital, 1852–2002* (New York, 2002), 1–4; *The Story of the First Fifty Years of the Mount Sinai Hospital, 1852–1902* (New York, 1944), 1–17; Joseph Hirsh and Beka Doherty, *The First Hundred Years of the Mount Sinai Hospital of New York, 1852–1952* (New York, 1952), 3–24; Tina Levitan, *Islands of Compassion: A History of the Jewish Hospitals of New York* (New York, 1964), 23–150; Dorothy Levenson, *Montefiore: The Hospital as Social Instrument, 1884–1984* (New York, 1984), 3–33; Polland and Soyer, *Emerging Metropolis*, 152–53; Rischin, *Promised City*, 106; *The Medical Directory of the City of New York* (New York, 1895), 325–40.
43. Samuel Gompers, *Seventy Years of Life and Labor: An Autobiography*, 2 vols. (New York, 1925), 1:63–163; Nick Salvatore, "Samuel Gompers," in *American National Biography Online* (New York, 2000).
44. "Tenement Cigar-Making," *Times*, January 30, 1884, 3; "Tenement Cigar Bill Signed," *Tribune*, May 13, 1884, 1; "Unjust to the Workingmen," *Times*, October 9, 1884, 8; "Tenement House Cigars: Unconstitutional to Prohibit Their Manufacture," *Times*, January 21, 1885, 3; Gompers, *Seventy Years*, 1:183–98; Theodore Roosevelt, *Theodore Roosevelt: An Autobiography* (1913; repr., New York, 1922), 81 (quotation).
45. Gompers, *Seventy Years*, 1:164–287; Salvatore, "Samuel Gompers" (quotation).
46. Tom Goyens, *Beer and Revolution: The German Anarchist Movement in New York City, 1880–1914* (Urbana, 2007), 86–109; Frederic Trautmann, *The Voice of Terror: A Biography of Johann Most* (Westport, Conn., 1980), 3–111.
47. Emma Goldman, *Living My Life*, 2 vols. (New York, 1931), 1:3–25 (quotation, 6); Vivian Gornick, *Emma Goldman: Revolution as a Way of Life* (New Haven, 2011), 6–25; Alice Wexler, *Emma Goldman: An Intimate Life* (New York, 1984), 3–54.
48. Goldman, *Living My Life*, 1:26–78 (quotation, 36); Gornick, *Emma Goldman*, 49–51; Paul Avrich and Karen Avrich, *Sasha and Emma: The Anarchist Odyssey of Alexander Berkman and Emma Goldman* (Cambridge, Mass., 2012), 27–50; Candace Falk, *Love, Anarchy, and Emma Goldman: A Biography* (New Brunswick, 1984), 1–66; "Nellie Bly Again: She Interviews Emma Goldman," *World*, September 17, 1893, 1, 3; Helen Minkin, *Storm in My Heart: Memories from the Widow of Johann Most* (Oakland, 2015), 25–43.
49. Alexander Berkman, *Prison Memoirs of an Anarchist* (New York, 1912), 33–35 (quotation); Avrich and Avrich, *Sasha and Emma*, 51–97; "Anarchy's Den," *World*, July 28, 1892, in *Emma Goldman: A Documentary History of the American Years*, ed. Candace Falk, 3 vols. (Urbana, 2003–), 1:111–15; Paul Kahan, *The Homestead Strike: Labor, Violence, and American Industry* (New York, 2014), 5–21, 42–100; Paul Krause, *The Battle for Homestead, 1880–1892: Politics, Culture, Steel* (Pittsburgh, 1992), 3–46.

50. Goldman, *Living My Life*, 1:122–23 ("worst enemy"); "Howls for Emma Goldman," *Times*, August 20, 1894, 2; Gornick, *Emma Goldman*, 38–41.

51. Caroline Milbank, *New York Fashion: The Evolution of American Style* (New York, 1989), 50–52; "Liberating Clothing Made in Confinement," *Times*, March 22, 2011.

52. "40,000 Called Out in Women's Strike," *Times*, November 23, 1909, 16; "Waist Strike On; 18,000 Women Out," *Times*, November 24, 1909, 18; "Waist Strike Grows," *Times*, November 25, 1909, 20; "40,000 Strikers Out Now," *Times*, November 26, 1909, 5; Polland and Soyer, *Emerging Metropolis*, 189 ("working girl"); Rischin, *Promised City*, 247 ("traitor"); Melvyn Dubofsky, *When Workers Organize: New York City in the Progressive Era* (Amherst, 1968), 49–58.

53. "40,000 Strikers Out Now," *Times*, November 26, 1909, 5 (quotation); "Girl Strikers Riot," *Times*, November 27, 1909, 3; "Girl Strikers Go to City Hall," *Times*, December 4, 1909, 20; "Police Mishandle Girl Strike Pickets," *Times*, December 10, 1909, 13; "To Arbitrate the Waist Strike," *Times*, December 11, 1909, 3; "Reject Union Plea," *Tribune*, December 12, 1909, 12; "Miss Morgan Aids Girl Waist Strikers," *Times*, December 14, 1909, 1; "Critical Time for Shirtwaist Strike," *Times*, December 15, 1909, 8; "Girl Strikers Tell the Rich Their Woes," *Times*, December 16, 1909, 3; "Hope to End Strike by New Year," *Times*, December 24, 1909, 3; "Facing Starvation to Keep Up the Strike," *Times*, December 25, 1909, 2; "Strike to Go On," *Tribune*, December 28, 1909, 8; "Strikers Vote Down New Peace Plan," *Times*, December 31, 1909, 2; "Settling the Waist Strike," *Times*, January 16, 1910, 16; "To End General Strike," *Tribune*, February 7, 1910, 4; "Mrs. Belmont to Buy Only Union Waists," *Times*, February 8, 1910, 5; "Shirtwaist Shops After the Strike," *The Survey* 25 (October 1, 1910): 7–8; Annelise Orleck, *Common Sense and Little Fire: Women and Working-Class Politics in the United States, 1900–1965* (Chapel Hill, 1995), 57–63; Polland and Soyer, *Emerging Metropolis*, 189; Rischin, *Promised City*, 247.

54. "20,000 Cloak Makers Cheer for a Strike," *Times*, June 30, 1910, 11 ("blot"); "Big Cloak Strike Brings Out 50,000," *Times*, July 8, 1910, 1 ("war"); "Cloak Strike Settled," *Tribune*, September 3, 1910, 1; "Cloak Strike Ends," *Times*, September 3, 1910, 1; "'The Union Spectre,'" *Times*, December 17, 1911, 14; Polland and Soyer, *Emerging Metropolis*, 189–90.

55. Leon Stein, *The Triangle Fire* (1962; repr., Ithaca, 2011), 13, 26–27, 30–33; David Von Drehle, *Triangle: The Fire That Changed America* (New York, 2003), 104–8, 116–20; *Preliminary Report of the Factory Investigating Commission, 1912*, 3 vols. (Albany, 1912), 2:580.

56. Arthur McFarlane, "Fire and the Skyscraper: The Problem of Protecting Workers in New York's Tower Factories," *McClure's Magazine* 37 (September 1911): 467–80; Stein, *Triangle Fire*, 38–39, 47–50, 53–56; Von Drehle, *Triangle*, 116–38.

57. "More Than 140 Die" and "Incidents of the Fire," *Tribune*, March 26, 1911, 1, 3; "141 Men and Girls Die in Waist Factory Fire," *Times*, March 26, 1911, 1–5; "Triangle Survivors Slid Down Cables," *Times*, December 13, 1911, 20; Stein, *Triangle Fire*, 16–20 (quotation, 18), 59–60, 62–65; Von Drehle, *Triangle*, 148–60.

58. McFarlane, "Fire and the Skyscraper," 478–80; Stein, *Triangle Fire*, 18–21 ("Thud"); Von Drehle, *Triangle*, 147–48, 167; Lowell Limpus, *History of the New York Fire Department* (New York, 1940), 307 ("hail"); "The Worthless Fire Escape and the Death Trap Below

It," clipping from unidentified New York newspaper, Kheel Center for Labor-Management Documentation & Archives, School of Industrial Labor Relations, Cornell University.

59. "141 Men and Girls Die in Waist Factory Fire," *Times*, March 26, 1911, 1–2; Stein, *Triangle Fire*, 73, 226–31; Von Drehle, *Triangle*, 271–83. The best source for information on the victims of the fire is the website of Cornell University's Kheel Center for Labor-Management Documentation & Archives, http://trianglefire.ilr.cornell.edu/victimsWitnesses/victimsList.html, which has been updated with recent genealogical findings. For the origins of this list, see "100 Years Later, the Roll of the Dead in a Factory Fire Is Complete," *Times*, February 20, 2011; entries for Max Blanck, family 377, enumeration district 339, 1900 census, and family 160, enumeration district 733, 1910 census.

60. "141 Men and Girls Die in Waist Factory Fire," *Times*, March 26, 1911, 1–2 ("sobbing"); "The Calamity," *Times*, March 26, 1911, 14 ("appalling"); Polland and Soyer, *Emerging Metropolis*, 195 ("daze"); Rischin, *Promised City*, 253 ("taste of food"); Stein, *Triangle Fire*, 20.

61. "Sweeping Investigations to Fix Blame for Fire," *Evening Telegram*, March 27, 1911, 2; "Locked in Factory, the Survivors Say" and "Greed the Trouble, Clergymen Assert," *Times*, March 27, 1911, 1, 5; "Blame Shifted on All Sides for Fire Horror," *Times*, March 28, 1911, 1; "Fix the Fire Blame, Orders the Court," *Times*, April 1, 1911, 3; "Coroner Seeks to Fix Fire Blame," *Times*, April 11, 1911, 6; "Indict Owners of Burned Factory," *Times*, April 12, 1911, 1 ("mute"); "Charge Girls' Death to Factory Owners," *Times*, April 18, 1911, 20; Stein, *Triangle Fire*, 158, 198–203.

62. "Triangle Waist Men Put on Trial," *Times*, December 5, 1911, 16; "Door Was Locked at Factory Fire," *Times*, December 9, 1911, 3; "Exits Shut Tight at Triangle Fire," *Times*, December 14, 1911, 3; "Deny Locked Doors, but Girls Insist," *Times*, December 19, 1911, 8; "Triangle Witnesses Deny Locked Doors," *Times*, December 20, 1911, 11; "Say Triangle Exits Were Never Locked," *Times*, December 21, 1911, 20; "Triangle Witnesses Got Increased Pay," *Times*, December 22, 1911, 7; "Triangle Owner Tells of the Fire" and "Somebody Surely Is Lying," *Times*, December 23, 1911, 6, 8; "Triangle Fire Case to Jury Today," *Times*, December 27, 1911, 6; "Triangle Owners Acquitted by Jury," *Times*, December 28, 1911, 1; "Regrets Voting for Triangle Acquittal," *Times*, December 29, 1911, 8; "The Failure of Justice," *Tribune*, December 28, 1911, 6.

63. "Settle Triangle Fire Suits," *Times*, March 12, 1914, 1; Von Drehle, *Triangle*, 264 (quotation).

64. Von Drehle, *Triangle*, 214–15; Rischin, *Promised City*, 254; Polland and Soyer, *Emerging Metropolis*, 197; "Max Blanck Arraigned," *Times*, September 20, 1913, 20; "Fines Blanck for Locks," *Times*, September 27, 1913, 9; "12 Burn to Death in Factory," *Times*, November 7, 1915, 1; George Price, "Fire! The Warning from Williamsburg," *The Survey* 35 (November 20, 1915): 181–82.

65. Walter Tittle, "The Leader of Tammany Hall," *World's Work* 54 (1927): 658.

66. "His Real Name Solomon: 'Silver-Dollar' Smith Is Not a Smith At All," *Times*, October 23, 1889, 5; "'Silver Dollar' in a Row," *Times*, December 5, 1894, 6; "Charles J. Smith Dies," *Times*, December 23, 1899, 14; "'Silver Dollar' Smith Dead," *Tribune*, December 23, 1899, 6; "'Silver Dollar' Smith Dead," *Washington Post*, December 23, 1899, 3; "Fu-

neral of Charles Smith," *Times,* December 25, 1899, 10; James Ford, *Forty-Odd Years in the Literary Shop* (New York, 1921), 170–72 ("fool"); Polland and Soyer, *Emerging Metropolis,* 180–81.

67. Entry for Michael A. Rofrano, family 6, enumeration district 43, assembly district 1, 1920 census; James Barrett and David Roediger, "The Irish and the 'Americanization' of the 'New Immigrants' in the Streets and in the Churches of the Urban United States, 1900–1930," *Journal of American Ethnic History* 24 (Summer 2005): 12; Paul Moses, *An Unlikely Union: The Love-Hate Story of New York's Irish and Italians* (New York, 2015), 211–14; "Sulzer Defies Foley Henchmen in District Riot," *Times,* November 2, 1913, 1, 5; "Rofrano on Stand Blames Tammany," *Times,* June 30, 1914, 4; "An Undesirable," *Times,* July 1, 1914, 10; "Rofrano, 'With a Punch,'" *Times,* July 9, 1914, 18; "Rofrano Indicted, Police Hunt Him," *Times,* September 15, 1915, 1; "Rofrano Gives Up," *Times,* May 16, 1916, 1; "Rofrano Hid in City for Eight Months," *Times,* May 19, 1916, 7; "Swears Rofrano, as 'King,' Made Him Murder Gaimari," *Times,* October 18, 1916, 1; "Rofrano Freed, Throng Cheers," *Times,* November 13, 1916, 1.

68. "An Easy-Going Campaign," *Times,* October 28, 1892, 5; "Edwin Einstein Resigns," *Times,* January 7, 1895, 9; "Hebrews Want Representation," *Times,* July 9, 1895, 8; "Edwin Einstein Dead," *Times,* January 25, 1905, 9; Polland and Soyer, *Emerging Metropolis,* 178; Ehud Manor, *Forward: The Jewish Daily Forward (Forverts) Newspaper: Immigrants, Socialism and Jewish Politics in New York, 1890–1917* (Portland, Ore., 2009), 42 ("rich").

69. Gordon Goldberg, *Meyer London: A Biography of the Socialist New York Congressman, 1871–1926* (Jefferson, N.C., 2013), 5–6, 17; entry for Meyer London, family 51, enumeration district 3, 1920 census; "East Side Gets a Voice," *Kansas City Star,* November 16, 1914, 9 ("It is bad"); Harry Roskolenko, *The Time That Was Then: The Lower East Side, 1900–1914, An Intimate Chronicle* (New York, 1971), 199 ("fiery").

70. Goldberg, *Meyer London,* 44–63 ("air," 59).

71. August Claessens and William Feigenbaum, *The Socialists in the New York Assembly: The Work of Ten Socialist Members During the Legislative Session of 1918* (New York, 1918), 45–66 (quotation, 55).

72. Goldberg, *Meyer London,* 44–63; Arthur Gorenstein, "A Portrait of Ethnic Politics: The Socialists and the 1908 and 1910 Congressional Elections on the East Side," *Publications of the American Jewish Historical Society* 50 (1961): 204 ("victims"); Polland and Soyer, *Emerging Metropolis,* 190; Louis Waldman, *Labor Lawyer* (New York, 1944), 79–88.

73. "Socialist's Victory Sets a City Record," *Times,* November 5, 1914, 6; "East Side Gets a Voice," *Kansas City Star,* November 16, 1914, 9; "Mr. London of New York," *Cleveland Plain Dealer,* November 17, 1914, 8; "Introducing Meyer London, Congressman," *Kalamazoo Gazette,* November 15, 1914, 17; "New York Socialist Elected to Congress," *Washington Bee,* November 21, 1914, 2 (quotation); "Girl Must Have Union Card to Wed, Is Plan of Socialist Congressman," *Washington Post,* November 8, 1914, 10; Goldberg, *Meyer London,* 67–73.

74. "Introducing Meyer London, Congressman," *Kalamazoo Gazette,* November 15, 1914, 17.

75. "The Campaign: Why We Should Vote the Socialist Ticket," *The Fur-Worker,* October 1, 1917, 7 ("madness").

19. Restriction

1. Arthur Henry, "Among the Immigrants," *Scribner's Magazine* 29 (March 1901): 302; Alfred Reed, "The Medical Side of Immigration," *Popular Science Monthly* 80 (April 1912): 386; Alfred Reed, "Going Through Ellis Island," *Popular Science Monthly* 82 (January 1913): 6–9 (quotations); E. H. Mullan, "The Medical Inspection of Immigrants at Ellis Island," *Medical Record: A Weekly Journal of Medicine and Surgery* 84 (December 27, 1913): 1167–68; E. H. Mullan, "Mental Examination of Immigrants: Administration and Line Inspection at Ellis Island," *Public Health Reports* 32 (May 18, 1917): 733–36.

2. Reed, "Going Through Ellis Island," 6–9.

3. J.F.F. to the Editor, "Romance vs. Reality," *Times*, May 23, 1899, 6.

4. Edward Alsworth Ross, "Italians in America," *Century Magazine* 88 (1914): 440–41, 444; "New Bars for 'Undesirables' at Ellis Island," *Times*, July 18, 1909, magazine sec., 11; *Immigrants in Cities*, 2 vols. (Washington, D.C., 1911), 1:155–56, vols. 26 and 27 of *Reports of the Immigration Commission, Presented by Mr. Dillingham*, 42 vols. (Washington, D.C., 1911).

5. [James] Appleton Morgan, "What Shall We Do with the 'Dago'?," *Popular Science Monthly* 38 (1890–91): 177; "I Live on Charity," *Times*, June 19, 1896, 9; George Kibbe Turner, "The Daughters of the Poor: A Plain Story of the Development of New York City as a Leading Center of the White Slave Trade of the World, Under Tammany Hall," *McClure's Magazine* 34 (1909): 58.

6. Gino Speranza to the Editor, *Times*, April 18, 1903, 8 ("nonsense"); "The 'Black Hand,'" *Times*, April 5, 1908, 10 ("yellow press"); "The Vendetta in New-York," *Times*, April 23, 1883, 5; "A Mafia in New York," *Times*, August 5, 1900, 5; "True Story of the Origin of the Black Hand," *Times*, January 8, 1905, magazine sec., 7; "Seeing Manhattan: The Land of the 'Black Hand,'" *Times*, July 2, 1905, magazine sec., 7; "Black Hand Scare Fun for This Girl," *Times*, September 26, 1905, 9; "Black Hand Letters a Joke," *Times*, November 10, 1905, 18; "Is 'the Black Hand' a Myth or a Terrible Reality," *Times*, March 3, 1907, magazine sec., 10; "Black Hand Steals Four-Year-Old Girl," *Times*, September 2, 1907, 16; Gaetano D'Amato, "The 'Black Hand' Myth," *North American Review* 187 (1908): 543–49; "The Mafia," *Times*, April 2, 1909, 8; "Two Pictures of the Mafia and Black Hand," *Times*, July 18, 1909, magazine sec., 3; "The Mafia in New York," *Times*, August 17, 1909, 25; "Black Hand Letter to Mrs. Havemeyer Came Apparently from Small Boys," *Times*, February 25, 1910, 1; "Caruso Pays Up to Black Hand," *Times*, March 26, 1910, 4; "Black Hand Manacled At Last," *Times*, April 3, 1910, magazine sec., 6.

7. "Declares Mafia Cry Is a Police Fiction," *Times*, April 26, 1903, 10.

8. Entries for Prospero and Giuseppe Petrosino, manifest of the *Denmark*, November 8, 1872, "New York Passenger Lists"; naturalization certificate of Joseph Petrosino, October 17, 1881, Superior Court, New York County, accessed via ancestry.com; "Petrosino a Terror to Criminal Bands," *Times*, March 14, 1909, 2; "Perils of Petrosino," *Herald*, July 5, 1914, magazine sec., 1–2 (quotation), and August 9, 1914, magazine sec., 4; "Detective in a Derby Hat," *Times*, March 12, 1944, magazine sec., 17, 30; "Exhibit Shows Off Mementos of a Legendary NYC Lawman, Lt. Joseph Petrosino," *Daily News*, November 8, 2009.

9. "Blames Immigration for the Black Hand," *Times,* January 6, 1908, 14.

10. "Bingham's Secret Service Started," *Herald,* February 20, 1909, 6; "Perils of Petrosino," *Herald,* July 5, 1914, magazine sec., 2; "100-Year-Old Murder of Anti-Mafia Officer Joseph Petrosino Solved by Italian Police," *The Independent* (UK), June 24, 2014.

11. Theodore Bingham, "Foreign Criminals in New York," *North American Review* 188 (1908): 384; "Reply to Mr. Bingham," *Tribune,* September 15, 1908, 9; "The Jews and Gen. Bingham," *Times,* September 16, 1908, 8; "Wrong About Jews, Bingham Admits," *Times,* September 17, 1908, 16; Jenna Weissman Joselit, "An Answer to Commissioner Bingham: A Case Study of New York Jews and Crime, 1907," *Yivo Annual of Jewish Social Science* 18 (1983): 121–31, 134–36; *Immigration and Crime* (Washington, D.C., 1911), 1, vol. 36 of *Reports of the Immigration Commission, Presented by Mr. Dillingham,* 42 vols. (Washington, D.C., 1911); Ross, "Italians in America," 440–43.

12. Richard Jensen, *The Battle Against Anarchist Terrorism: An International History, 1878–1934* (New York, 2014), 131–258; "I.W.W. Pickets Pen Rockefellers," *Times,* May 4, 1914, 1; "Marie Ganz Gets Sixty Days," *Times,* May 7, 1914, 7; "I.W.W. Bomb Meant for Rockefeller Kills Four of Its Makers," *Times,* July 5, 1914, 1–2; "Berkman Reveals Anarchists' Plot," *Times,* February 16, 1915, 6; Marie Ganz, *Rebels: Into Anarchy—And Out Again* (New York, 1920), 154–89, 228–39; Thai Jones, *More Powerful Than Dynamite: Radicals, Plutocrats, Progressives, and New York's Year of Anarchy* (New York, 2012), 205–54; Kenyon Zimmer, *Immigrants Against the State: Yiddish and Italian Anarchism in America* (Urbana, 2015), 41–42.

13. Arthur Link, *Wilson: The Struggle for Neutrality, 1914–1915* (Princeton, 1960), 31, 65–66.

14. "Reserves Throng to Answer Calls," *Times,* August 4, 1914, 7; "Reservists Flock to the Consulates," *Times,* August 5, 1914, 6.

15. Ross Wilson, *New York and the First World War: Shaping an American City* (Burlington, Vt., 2014), 53–78.

16. "President Urges Temperate Speech," *Times,* August 19, 1914, 4 (Wilson quotation); "Another War Play Presented," *Tribune,* April 20, 1915, 7; "Loyal to America, War on the Hyphen," *Times,* October 6, 1915, 4; "War on the Hyphen Is Popular At Once," *Times,* October 8, 1915, 3; "Wilson on Trail of Hyphenate," *Tribune,* October 27, 1915, 3; *Irish World* quoted in Thomas Henderson, *Tammany Hall and the New Immigrants: The Progressive Years* (New York, 1976), 173 ("anti-hyphen wave").

17. Percy Andreae, "On Preparedness," *The Way-Bill* 7 (June 1916): 4; "Says Hyphen Helps His Americanism," *Tribune,* March 19, 1915, 6 ("devotion"); "No Room for the Hyphen," *Times,* June 14, 1916, 12; "Rabbi Wise Assails the Hyphen Voter," *Times,* November 6, 1916, 4.

18. Henderson, *Tammany Hall and the New Immigrants,* 171.

19. "Hughes Rejects All Hyphenism; Americanism Above All, Says Wilson," *Times,* June 14, 1916, 1 ("undiluted"); "The President and the Hyphen," *Literary Digest* 53 (October 14, 1916): 935 ("mortified"); "Both Candidates Got Hyphen Vote," *Times,* November 9, 1916, 6; "How the Hyphen Voted," *Literary Digest* 53 (November 25, 1916): 1394–95.

20. "Munitions Explosions Shake New York," *Times,* July 30, 1916, 1–2 (quotation); "Munition Explosions Cause Loss of $20,000,000," "Millions of Persons Heard and Felt

Shock," "Ellis Island Like War-Swept Town," and "The Responsibility," *Times*, July 31, 1916, 1–2, 8.

21. "Railroad Heads to Be Arrested for Explosion," *Times*, August 1, 1916, 1; "Black Tom Verdict In," *Times*, August 23, 1916, 5; Steven Jaffe, *New York at War: Four Centuries of Combat, Fear, and Intrigue in Gotham* (New York, 2012), 196–98; Chad Millman, *The Detonators: The Secret Plot to Destroy America and an Epic Hunt for Justice* (New York, 2006), 3–98; Jules Witcover, *Sabotage at Black Tom: Imperial Germany's Secret War in America, 1914–1917* (Chapel Hill, 1989), 3–25, 152–70, 257–312.

22. Alexander Trachtenberg, ed., *The American Socialists and the War: A Documentary History of the Attitude of the Socialist Party Toward War and Militarism Since the Outbreak of the Great War* (New York, 1917), 3 (quotation); Wilson, *New York and the First World War*, 141–49.

23. "Proclamation of War with Germany, April 6, 1917," in Naval War College, *International Law Documents: Neutrality, Breaking of Diplomatic Relations, War, with Notes, 1917* (Washington, D.C., 1918), 227–28 ("write"); Jaffe, *New York at War*, 204; "What Papers May Print Told by Burleson," *Tribune*, October 10, 1917, 1 ("Wall Street").

24. Jaffe, *New York at War*, 206–8.

25. American Civil Liberties Union, *War-Time Prosecutions and Mob Violence* (New York, 1918), 5, 9; "Masked Patriots Beat Pro-German," *Times*, January 7, 1918, 1; "The Vigilantes Make a Nation-Wide Search for Enemies Within," *Tribune*, January 13, 1918, sec. 5, 4; "Denounce Socialists: Gotham Aldermen Called Traitors," *Los Angeles Times*, February 27, 1918, 11; "Lynched German Begged to Have Body Buried in Flag," *Tribune*, April 11, 1918, 16; "Compel Priest to Ring Bell and Kiss Flag," *Times*, July 20, 1918, 4; "1,000 Disloyal Teachers Here Says Moffett," *Tribune*, November 28, 1917, 8.

26. Wilson, *New York and the First World War*, 185–87; Erik Kirschbaum, *Burning Beethoven: The Eradication of German Culture in the United States During World War I* (New York, 2014), 119–37.

27. "Anarchists Demand Strike to End War," *Times*, May 19, 1917, 11; "Plotters Here Against Draft Under Watch," *Times*, May 30, 1917, 1; "Meeting of Reds Traps Slackers," *Times*, June 12, 1917, 1; "Emma Goldman and A. Berkman Behind the Bars," *Times*, June 16, 1917, 1, 18; "Anarchists Deny Urging Violence," *Times*, July 4, 1917, 5; "Convict Berkman and Miss Goldman," *Times*, July 10, 1917, 1; "Highest U.S. Court Grants Bail to Reds," *Times*, July 20, 1917, 13; "O'Leary Indicted on Sedition Charge," *Times*, November 24, 1917, 3; "Affirms Sentence on Emma Goldman," *Times*, January 15, 1918, 10; Paul Avrich and Karen Avrich, *Sasha and Emma: The Anarchist Odyssey of Alexander Berkman and Emma Goldman* (Cambridge, Mass., 2012), 272–88.

28. Richard Slotkin, *Lost Battalions: The Great War and the Crisis of American Nationality* (New York, 2005), 3, 109 (quotation); Christopher Sterba, *Good Americans: Italian and Jewish Immigrants During the First World War* (New York, 2003), 71.

29. David Hochstein, "Abstract of WWI Military Service Record," accessed via ancestry.com; *History of the Seventy-Seventh Division* (New York, 1919), 8; *77th Division: Summary of Operations in the World War* (Washington, D.C., 1944), 21, 104; "Hochstein Killed by a Shell During Drive on Argonne," *Tribune*, January 29, 1919, 8; "David Hoch-

stein," *Tribune,* April 4, 1919, 14; http://data.newsday.com/long-island/data/history/world-war-i-deaths/.

30. "This Is Ed Sullivan Speaking," *Chicago Tribune,* September 12, 1953, 19 (quotation); Edward Lengel, *To Conquer Hell: The Meuse-Argonne, 1918; The Epic Battle That Ended the First World War* (New York, 2008), 270–74.

31. Jacob Marcus, *The Jew in the American World: A Source Book* (Detroit, 1996), 308 (Krotoshinsky quotations); Abraham Krotoshinsky, answers to "War Record of American Jews" questionnaire, Office of Jewish War Records, accessed via ancestry.com; "Krotoshinsky Was Formerly a Barber" and "New York Chaplain Cited for Bravery," *Times,* December 19, 1918, 24; "Why Not Give Him a Job," *Washington Post,* November 28, 1927, 6; "About New York," *Times,* February 2, 1940, 20; "Krotoshinsky, 60, World War I Hero," *Times,* November 5, 1953, 31 ("hero"); Sterba, *Good Americans,* 181 ("remember").

32. Charles Minder, *This Man's War: The Day-by-Day Record of an American Private on the Western Front* (New York, 1931), 140.

33. "10,000 Socialists Shout for Peace," *Times,* September 24, 1917, 6; "Mayoralty Vote by Assembly District" and "Hillquit Says Result Is Big Party Victory," *Times,* November 7, 1917, 1, 4; "Elected Socialist Officials Take Office," *Call,* January 3, 1918, 2; "Brooklyn Veterans Will Be Missed This Winter," *Brooklyn Daily Eagle,* December 23, 1917, local sec., 3; "August Claessens, 69, Dies," *Brooklyn Daily Eagle,* December 10, 1954, 13; "Elmer Rosenberg," *Times,* April 12, 1951, 33; "William Karlin, 62, a Labor Attorney," *Times,* December 7, 1944, 25; Louis Waldman, *Labor Lawyer* (New York, 1944), 11–62; "W. Feigenbaum, Newsman, Politico," *Brooklyn Daily Eagle,* April 24, 1949, 40; "Joseph A. Whitehorn," in *The New York Red Book* (Albany, 1917), 196; "Two Socialists Are Sent to Assembly from Kings County," *Brooklyn Daily Eagle,* November 9, 1916, 1 (Whitehorn); "A. I. Shiplacoff, 56, Labor Leader, Dies," *Times,* February 8, 1934, 19; "Samuel Orr" and "Charles Garfinkel," in *The New York Red Book* (Albany, 1918), 150, 164; World War I draft registration card for Samuel Orr, June 8, 1917, accessed via ancestry.com; "Mrs. Byrne Fasts in Workhouse Cell," *Times,* January 25, 1917, 20 (birth control); Robert Fogelson, *The Great Rent Wars: New York, 1917–1929* (New Haven, 2013), 132.

34. "Red Bombs Palmer's House," *Washington Post,* June 3, 1919, 1; Richard Powers, *Not Without Honor: The History of American Anticommunism* (1995; repr., New Haven, 1998), 22–23.

35. "Clean Up the Reds!" *Washington Post,* June 4, 1919, 6; Vincent Cannato, *American Passage: The History of Ellis Island* (New York, 2009), 320–25; Powers, *Not Without Honor,* 23–34; "Red Ark with 250 All Ready to Sail," *Times,* December, 20, 1919, 1.

36. "Evidence Against Socialists Admitted in Face of Bitter Protests by Counsel," *Times,* January 23, 1920, 1–2 ("fraud," "military"); *New York Red Book* [for 1920], 20–22; Louis Waldman, *Albany: The Crisis in Government; The History of the Suspension, Trial and Expulsion from the New York State Legislature in 1920 of Five Socialist Assemblymen by Their Political Opponents* (New York, 1920), 1–233 ("blood," 227); "Oust 5 Socialists," *Times,* April 2, 1920, 1.

37. "Albany," *The Socialist Review* 8 (May 1920): 354 ("calamity"); "Hughes Upholds Socialists' Rights," *Times,* January 10, 1920, 1, 3; Waldman, *Albany,* 232 ("lynching"); "Expul-

sion of the Socialists," *Times*, April 2, 1920, 14 ("courageous"); "The Expulsion," *Tribune*, April 2, 1920, 12.

38. "Ousted Socialists Make Fight Today," *Times*, September 16, 1920, 3; "Ousted Socialists All Win at Polls," *Times*, September 17, 1920, 13; "Assembly Ousts 3 Socialists," *Tribune*, September 22, 1920, 1–2; "Assembly Again Expels Three Socialists," *Times*, September 22, 1920, 1; "Seated Socialists Formally Resign," *Times*, September 24, 1920, 8; "The Disqualified Socialists," *Times*, September 23, 1920, 9; "Revolutionary Socialists," *Times*, September 27, 1920, 12; "Assembly Refuses to Oust Socialists," *Times*, April 5, 1921, 21; "Socialists Elected, Aldermen Concede," *Times*, November 2, 1921, 3.

39. "Wall Street Explosion Kills 30," *Times*, September 17, 1920, 1–3; Beverly Gage, *The Day Wall Street Exploded: A Story of America in Its First Age of Terror* (New York, 2009), 245–46, 325–30.

40. "Immigration, Invasion, Revolution," *Chicago Tribune*, September 29, 1920, 8.

41. "Ellis Island Faces Influx of Millions," *Times*, October 8, 1920, 21; "Immigrant Tide Mounts," *Los Angeles Times*, October 3, 1920, 11; "Aliens Becoming a Menace," *Washington Post*, September 25, 1920, 6; "Immigrant Tide Greatest Known," *Times*, October 3, 1920, sec. 10, 13 ("ever known," Greeks and Syrians); "Dangers of Immigration," *Chicago Tribune*, October 6, 1920, 8 ("insufficient"); "Chaos at Ellis Island," *Times*, September 25, 1920, 9; "Pollution of Americanism," *Washington Post*, September 26, 1920, 16 ("lazy," "aliens," "pollution").

42. "The Immigration Emergency," *Tribune*, December 11, 1920, 8; "Immigration Solutions," *Tribune*, December 29, 1920, 8; "Jews Oppose Bill to Halt Aliens a Year," *Tribune*, January 5, 1921, 19; "The Johnson Bill," *Washington Post*, January 15, 1921, 6; "Year's Ban on Aliens," *Los Angeles Times*, December 14, 1920, 11; "Senate Limits Immigration to 355,461 in a Year," *Times*, February 20, 1921, 1; "A 3 Per Cent Immigration Bar," *Tribune*, February 21, 1921, 6; "Immigration Bill Passed," *Times*, February 27, 1921, 4; "Wilson Kills 4 Bills in Last Day in Office," *Times*, March 5, 1921, 8; "Immigration Bill Passed by House," *Times*, April 23, 1921, 2; "Immigration Bill Passed by Senate," *Times*, May 4, 1921, 1–2; "Immigration Bill Passed," *Times*, May 14, 1921, 8; "Immigration Act Now Law," *Times*, May 20, 1921, 14; "Prepare to Enforce Immigration Law," *Times*, May 21, 1921, 6; "An Immigration Policy," *Times*, May 24, 1921, 14; "To Restrict Immigration Two More Years," *Times*, May 12, 1922, 40; *Annual Report of the Commissioner General of Immigration to the Secretary of Labor, Fiscal Year Ended June 30, 1921* (Washington, D.C., 1921), 16, 18 (quotas for each nation).

43. *Annual Report of the Commissioner General of Immigration, 1921*, 16.

44. Cannato, *American Passage*, 331; "Controlling Immigration at the Source," *Times*, August 3, 1924, 14.

45. "The Murder of a Race," *The Nation* 114 (March 8, 1922): 295–300; Jocelyn Cohen and Daniel Soyer, eds., *My Future Is in America: Autobiographies of Eastern European Jewish Immigrants* (New York, 2006), 207 ("drowned"); Elias Heifetz, *The Slaughter of the Jews in the Ukraine in 1919* (New York, 1921), 408 ("fleeing"); Kelly Scott Johnson, "Sholem Schwarzbard: Biography of a Jewish Assassin" (Ph.D. diss., Harvard University, 2012), 109.

46. *My Future Is in America*, 225 (quotations), 251–52; H. H. Fisher, *The Famine in Soviet*

Russia, 1919–1923: The Operations of the American Relief Administration (Stanford, 1927), 246–66; Richard Pipes, *Russia Under the Bolshevik Regime, 1919–1924* (New York, 1994), 410–19.

47. Entries for the Anbinder family on the manifests of the *Lapland*, August 4, 1921, and the *Finland*, September 15, 1921, "New York Passenger Lists," and "Record of Aliens Held for Special Inquiry" from the *Finland*, September 25, 1921, accessed via ancestry.com.

48. "Greater Cut Is Planned in Immigration," *Tribune*, January 27, 1924, sec. 2, 1; "Immigration Bill Taken Up in House," *Times*, April 6, 1924, 10; "America of the Melting Pot Comes to End," *Times*, April 27, 1924, sec. 9, 3.

49. "Speakers Attack Alien Quota Bill," *Times*, March 3, 1924, 12 ("mathematics"); "20 New York Congressmen Hit Alien Bill," *Tribune*, February 25, 1924, 1 ("to favor"); "Immigration Bill Starts Fist Fight," *Times*, April 9, 1924, 25 (Gallivan quotations).

50. "Speakers Attack Alien Quota Bill," *Times*, March 3, 1924, 12 (quotation); Mae Ngai, *Impossible Subjects: Illegal Aliens and the Making of Modern America* (Princeton, 2004), 21–55.

51. "Legion and Labor Would Bar Aliens," *Times*, March 24, 1924, 2; "Preserving the American Race," *Times*, April 5, 1924, 14; "America of the Melting Pot Comes to End," *Times*, April 27, 1924, sec. 9, 3 (quotations); "Huge Votes for Exclusion," *Times*, May 16, 1924, 1–2; "The New Immigration Restrictions," *Times*, May 28, 1924, 22.

20. Refuge

1. "Drama of Life Changes on the East Side," *Times*, February 20, 1927, 9, 23; Simone Cinotto, *The Italian American Table: Food, Family, and Community in New York City* (Urbana, 2013), 76 ("vacant"); "Unique Settlement Ready for Brooklyn Red Hook District," *Herald Tribune*, May 13, 1928, sec. 2, 9; William Shedd, *Italian Population in New York* (New York, [1934]), 13–14; Beth Wenger, *New York Jews and the Great Depression: Uncertain Promise* (New Haven, 1996), 82.

2. "Big Ring Smuggles Aliens and Liquor," *Times*, September 26, 1922, 1; "Bootlegged Immigrants," *Times*, May 5, 1924, 14; "Smuggling Aliens into the U.S.A.," *Washington Post*, September 14, 1924, magazine sec., 3; "2,000,000 Aliens Are Here Without the Right to Stay," *Times*, July 26, 1925, sec. 7, 16; "Alien 'Gate Crashers' Still Pour in Over Our Frontiers," *Times*, June 19, 1927, sec. 8, 9; *Annual Report of the Commissioner General of Immigration to the Secretary of Labor: Fiscal Year Ending June 30, 1922* (Washington, D.C., 1922), 15; *Annual Report of the Commissioner General of Immigration to the Secretary of Labor: Fiscal Year Ending June 30, 1927* (Washington, D.C., 1927), 15; *Annual Report of the Commissioner General of Immigration to the Secretary of Labor: Fiscal Year Ending June 30, 1932* (Washington, D.C., 1932), 45 (smuggling by air).

3. "Illegal Residents Live Lives of Fear," *Times*, November 11, 1934, sec. 8, 2 (visa overstays); Libby Garland, *After They Closed the Gates: Jewish Illegal Immigration to the United States, 1921–1965* (Chicago, 2014), 94, 103, 119, 143; "Nine Indicted Here as Fake Visa Ring," *Times*, March 5, 1930, 19; *Annual Report of the Commissioner General of Immigration to the Secretary of Labor: Fiscal Year Ending June 30, 1924* (Washington, D.C., 1924), 13–15.

4. Minnie Kusnetz, "I Haven't Lost Anything by Coming to America," in *My Future Is in*

America: Autobiographies of Eastern European Jewish Immigrants, ed. Jocelyn Cohen and Daniel Soyer (New York, 2006), 288–302 (quotations, 292, 297, 302).

5. "Alien 'Gate Crashers' Still Pour in over Our Frontiers," *Times,* June 19, 1927, sec. 8, 9; *Annual Report of the Commissioner General of Immigration to the Secretary of Labor: Fiscal Year Ending June 30, 1923* (Washington, D.C., 1923), 23–27.

6. "Alien 'Gate Crashers' Still Pour in over Our Frontiers," *Times,* June 19, 1927, sec. 8, 9 ("fisherman"); "Hold Smuggled Aliens," *Times,* July 10, 1927, sec. 2, 9; Garland, *After They Closed the Gates,* 94, 104, 111, 114, 139 ("many"); *Annual Report of the Commissioner General of Immigration, 1923,* 20–23.

7. *Annual Report of the Commissioner General of Immigration to the Secretary of Labor: Fiscal Year Ending June 30, 1926* (Washington, D.C., 1926), 16, 20; *Annual Report of the Commissioner General of Immigration to the Secretary of Labor: Fiscal Year Ending June 30, 1928* (Washington, D.C., 1928), 23; *Annual Report of the Commissioner General of Immigration, 1932,* 44; "Illegal Residents Live Lives of Fear," *Times,* November 11, 1934, sec. 8, 2.

8. "Seize Sloop Hiding Smuggled Italians," *Times,* July 14, 1924, 1; "Schooner Brought Smuggled Aliens," *Times,* July 15, 1924, 15; "Asks Heavy Penalty on Smuggled Aliens," *Times,* August 22, 1924, 15; "Bootlegged Aliens Unpunished," *Herald Tribune,* October 2, 1924, 12; "Smuggled Aliens," *Herald Tribune,* October 5, 1924, sec. 2, 6.

9. "Illegal Residents Live Lives of Fear," *Times,* November 11, 1934, sec. 8, 2.

10. Cohen and Soyer, *My Future Is in America,* 233–82, 303–10 (quotation, 307–8); file of Minnie Kusnetz, file 55943/704, entry 9, Record Group 85, National Archives.

11. "$1,000,000 Mulcted from Aliens Here," *Times,* April 10, 1935, 4; "Exposer of Racket Dies in a Mystery," *Times,* June 6, 1935, 1–2; "Alien Frauds Laid to Ex-Official," *Times,* June 26, 1935, 3; "Alien Frauds Laid to Ex-Federal Aide," *Times,* October 9, 1935, 19; "Hogan Convicted of Taking Bribes," *Times,* October 16, 1935, 19; Garland, *After They Closed the Gates,* 108.

12. "Dealing with Smuggled Aliens," *Herald Tribune,* August 27, 1924, 10; "Denies Alien Card Reflects on Races," *Times,* June 26, 1928, 9; "The Registration of Aliens," *Times,* June 21, 1931, sec. 3, 2; Garland, *After They Closed the Gates,* 166.

13. Peter Levine, *Ellis Island to Ebbets Field: Sport and the American Jewish Experience* (New York, 1993), 3.

14. David L. Fleitz, *The Irish in Baseball: An Early History* (Jefferson, N.C., 2009), 90.

15. Nicholas Dawidoff, *The Catcher Was a Spy: The Mysterious Life of Moe Berg* (New York, 2011), 19, 37–38 (quotation); Alan Patterson, "The Eastern European Jewish Immigrant Experience with Baseball in the Late Nineteenth and Early Twentieth Century," *Modern Judaism* 28 (February 2008), 95–96.

16. Levine, *Ellis Island to Ebbets Field,* 122 ("legion"); "Giants Purchase a Jewish Slugger," *Lewiston [Maine] Evening Journal,* September 13, 1923, 5; Robert Weintraub, "Mose Solomon: The Hunt for the Hebrew Ruth," in *Jewish Jocks: An Unorthodox Hall of Fame,* ed. Franklin Foer and Marc Tracy (New York, 2012), 30–32 ("appreciate").

17. William M. Simons, "The Golem, the Rabbi, and 'That Long-Sought Hebrew Star': Jews in 1920s Baseball," in *The Cooperstown Symposium on Baseball and American Culture,*

2009–2010, ed. William M. Simons (Jefferson, N.C., 2011), 58; Levine, *Ellis Island to Ebbets Field*, 111 ("greatest"); "Cohen Leads Giants to Opening Victory," *Times*, April 12, 1928, 20; "Topics of the *Times*," *Times*, April 13, 1928, 24; "Andy Cohen Keeps His Name," *Times*, July 22, 1928, sec. 7, 16 ("Asset"); "Ball Players Enter Vaudeville," *Times*, October 5, 1928, 25.

18. "M'Graw Turns Down Roush-Kelly Deal," *Times*, December 23, 1925, 15; "Yankees Sign Joe Freschi as 'Little Italy' Rejoices," *Washington Post*, July 30, 1927, 13; Lawrence Baldassaro, *Beyond DiMaggio: Italian Americans in Baseball* (Lincoln, Neb., 2011), 18, 59, 98, 117 (quotation).

19. Tom Clavin, *The DiMaggios: Three Brothers, Their Passion for Baseball, Their Pursuit of the American Dream* (New York, 2013), 10; "Peppino, the Fence-Buster," *Times*, May 23, 1936, 20; "Joe DiMaggio: Baseball's Most Sensational Big-League Star Starts What Should Be His Best Year So Far," *Life* (May 1, 1939): 69.

20. Isabel Wilkerson, *The Warmth of Other Suns: The Epic Story of America's Great Migration* (New York, 2010); Philip Kasinitz, *Caribbean New York: Black Immigrants and the Politics of Race* (Ithaca, 1992), 41; "Embargo on Immigration Helped Labor: Act Shut Out Foreign Cheap Workers," *Chicago Defender*, November 1, 1924, 2.

21. "Embargo on Immigration Helped Labor: Act Shut Out Foreign Cheap Workers," *Chicago Defender*, November 1, 1924, 2, Nicholas Lemann, *The Promised Land: The Great Black Migration and How It Changed America* (New York, 1991), 40.

22. Kasinitz, *Caribbean New York*, 23–25, 41–44 (quotation, 43). The proportion of black immigrants from Barbados is based on the 1930 census. Most census takers in New York merely listed the birthplace of black immigrants as the "West Indies," but some recorded the specific Caribbean island. More of these listings specify Barbados than any other Caribbean island. See Integrated Public Use Microdata Series (IPUMS) 1% Sample of the 1930 U.S. Census, available as "1930 New York City 1% Census Sample," in "*City of Dreams* Replication Data," https://dataverse.harvard.edu/dataverse/anbinder.

23. Kasinitz, *Caribbean New York*, 47 ("rights"); W. A. Domingo, "The Tropics in New York," *Survey Graphic* 6 (1925): 650 ("manhood").

24. William Mugleston, "Marcus Garvey," in *American National Biography Online* (New York, 2000); entry for Marcus Garvey, dwelling 22, enumeration district 1409, assembly district 21, 1920 census; Bob Blaisdell, ed., *Selected Writings and Speeches of Marcus Garvey* (Mineola, N.Y., 2004), 110 (quotation); Judith Stein, *The World of Marcus Garvey: Race and Class in Modern Society* (Baton Rouge, 1986), 24–107, 128–52, 186–208.

25. "Riot Among Pavers," *Times*, June 19, 1904, 10; "Bullets and Bricks Fly in Race Riot," *Times*, July 8, 1907, 2; Jennifer Guglielmo, *Living the Revolution: Italian Women's Resistance and Radicalism in New York City, 1880–1945* (Chapel Hill, 2010), 107 (quotation).

26. *The Collected Essays of Ralph Ellison*, ed. John Callahan (New York, 2003), 587; Guglielmo, *Living the Revolution*, 107 ("duty").

27. "Race Riot in Harlem," *Times*, October 9, 1916, 12 (quotation); "Negro City in Harlem Is Race Capital," *Times*, March 1, 1925, sec. 8, 6.

28. "Puerto Ricans in Continental United States," Census Bureau "Special Report" issued in conjunction with the 1950 census, available at http://www2.census.gov/prod2/decen

nial/documents/41601756v4p3ch11.pdf; Ira Rosenwaike, *Population History of New York City* (Syracuse, 1972), 139 (1930 figures).

29. Virginia Sánchez Korrol, *From Colonia to Community: The History of Puerto Ricans in New York City*, rev. ed. (Berkeley, 1994), 17–28, 44 ("can live"); Claudio Remeseira, ed., *Hispanic New York: A Sourcebook* (New York, 2010), 73 ("pots").

30. Sánchez Korrol, *From Colonia to Community*, 40, 43; entry for Homero Rosado, household 8, enumeration district 31–1495A, assembly district 17, 1940 census; Félix Matos-Rodríguez and Pedro Hernández, *Pioneros: Puerto Ricans in New York City, 1896–1948* (Charleston, 2001), 106.

31. Sánchez Korrol, *From Colonia to Community*, 41.

32. Ibid., 33, 36; Lawrence Chenault, *The Puerto Rican Migrant in New York City* (New York, 1938), 71–75.

33. "Trio Held as Police Block Harlem Riot," *Times*, July 27, 1926, 21; "Ask Police Protection," *Times*, July 30, 1926, 29 ("newcomers"); César Andreu Iglesias, ed., *Memoirs of Bernardo Vega: A Contribution to the History of the Puerto Rican Community in New York* (New York, 1984), 142–43, 151.

34. Ramon Colon, *Carlos Tapia: A Puerto Rican Hero in New York* (New York, 1976), 76–77 (quotations); entry for Carlos Tapia, dwelling 25, enumeration district 957, Kings County (Brooklyn), 1930 census; Lorrin Thomas, *Puerto Rican Citizen: History and Political Identity in Twentieth-Century New York City* (Chicago, 2010), 42–43; Sánchez Korrol, *From Colonia to Community*, 150–51.

35. Vega quoted in Remeseira, *Hispanic New York*, 98–99; Jack Agüeros, "Halfway to Dick and Jane: A Puerto Rican Pilgrimage," in *The Immigrant Experience: The Anguish of Becoming American*, ed. Thomas Wheeler (New York, 1971), 94.

36. Piri Thomas, *Down These Mean Streets* (New York, 1967), 24–38 (quotations); "Piri Thomas, Spanish Harlem Author, Dies at 83," *Times*, October 19, 2011.

37. Cinotto, *The Italian American Table*, 83 ("lazy," "gambling," "awful"); Leonard Covello, *The Heart Is the Teacher* (New York, 1958), 223 (all other quotations).

38. Jack Lait and Lee Mortimer, *New York: Confidential! The Lowdown on Its Bright Life* (New York, 1948), 109; "Veto Vito?" *Time*, November 4, 1946, 24; Charles Hewitt Jr., "Welcome Paupers and Crime: Porto Rico's Shocking Gift to the United States," *Scribner's Commentator 7*, no. 5 (March 1940): 13–14.

39. Hewitt, "Welcome Paupers and Crime," 13–14 (quotations); Sánchez Korrol, *From Colonia to Community*, 150; Thomas, *Puerto Rican Citizen*, 134–38.

40. *Memoirs of Bernardo Vega*, 155.

41. David Kennedy, *Freedom from Fear: The American People in Depression and War, 1929–1945* (New York, 1999), 86–88; Beth Wenger, *New York Jews and the Great Depression: Uncertain Promise* (New Haven, 1996), 18; Ronald Bayor, *Neighbors in Conflict: The Irish, Germans, Jews, and Italians of New York City, 1929–1941*, 2nd ed. (Urbana, 1988), 12–13.

42. Susan Carter et al., eds., *Historical Statistics of the United States*, 2 vols. (New York, 2006), 1:562; Sánchez Korrol, *From Colonia to Community*, 32; "Aliens Quit U.S. Faster Than They Are Entering," *Herald Tribune*, July 11, 1935, 17; "Ellis Island Faces a Different Task," November 12, 1933, sec. 8, 2; "Why the Emigrant Leaves Our Shores," *Times*, April

1, 1934, sec. 9, 2; "From the East Side," *Times*, July 27, 1935, 12; Frank McCourt, *Angela's Ashes* (New York, 1996).

43. Thomas, *Puerto Rican Citizen*, 92; *Annual Report of the Commissioner General of Immigration, 1932*, 1–14.

44. "Bank of U.S. Closes Doors," *Times*, December 12, 1930, 1–2; Wenger, *New York Jews and the Great Depression*, 10–14 (quotation); "Broderick Closes the Berardini Bank," *Times*, November 1, 1931, 21.

45. Thomas, *Puerto Rican Citizen*, 93, 107 (quotation); Cheryl Greenberg, *Or Does It Explode: Black Harlem in the Great Depression* (New York, 1991), 140–63.

46. Kennedy, *Freedom from Fear*, 144–45, 171–88; "Book Tells Needy Where to Get Help," *Times*, November 26, 1933, sec. 2, 2; "Muddled Masses: The Growing Backlash Against Immigration Includes Many Myths," *Wall Street Journal*, April 26, 1995; "Aliens Within Our Gates," *Times*, January 31, 1934, 16; "N. Y. Supporting Army of Aliens on Relief Roll," *Chicago Tribune*, March 13, 1935, 5; "Aliens Relief Jobs Continued by WPA," *Times*, June 21, 1936, 6; "Relief Preference to Aliens Denied," *Times*, September 17, 1936, 25.

47. "Half Relief Funds to Be Spent Direct," *Times*, June 12, 1935, 13; "Ground Is Broken on East Side Drive," *Times*, August 29, 1935, 23; "East River Drive Open," *Times*, October 31, 1936, 18; "New Section Ready on East Side Drive," *Times*, June 24, 1937, 27; "Roosevelt 'Built' East Drive Link," *Times*, June 30, 1937, 12; "City Clears Way for Highway Route to Ring Manhattan," *Times*, December 11, 1937, 1; "City Votes $16,000,000 to Build Brooklyn-Queens Belt Parkway," *Times*, October 14, 1938, 1, 6; "Belt Road to Open to Traffic Today," *Times*, June 29, 1940, 12; Mason Williams, *City of Ambition: FDR, La Guardia, and the Making of Modern New York* (New York, 2013), 135–84; Barbara Blumberg, *The New Deal and the Unemployed: The View from New York City* (Lewisburg, Pa., 1979), 124–44; Wenger, *New York Jews and the Great Depression*, 17 (quotation).

48. "Illegal Residents Live Lives of Fear," *Times*, November 11, 1934, sec. 8, 2; "How Grandma Got Legal," *Los Angeles Times*, May 16, 2006 (quotation); Mae Ngai, *Impossible Subjects: Aliens and the Making of Modern America* (Princeton, 2004), 82–89.

49. "Colorado Aliens Face Deportation," *Times*, March 31, 1935, sec. 4, 6; Roger Daniels, *Guarding the Golden Door: American Immigration Policy and Immigrants Since 1882* (New York, 2004), 63–65; Ngai, *Impossible Subjects*, 75.

50. "Aliens Are People Too," *Times*, January 21, 1935, 14; "Aliens Within Our Gates," *Times*, January 24, 1935, 18; "The Persecution of Aliens," *Chicago Tribune*, March 31, 1935, 14; "Bill to Deport Aliens, Create Jobs Pushed," *Herald Tribune*, June 23, 1935, 17 (quotation); "Bill to Deport 6 Million Aliens Given Impetus," *Washington Post*, June 23, 1935, 1; "Condemns Moves to Harass Aliens," *Times*, June 30, 1935, sec. 4, 10; "Deporting of Aliens Is Voted by V.F.W.," *Times*, July 1, 1935, 3.

51. Bayor, *Neighbors in Conflict*, 30–40; "House Likely to Be Democratic by Big Margin," *Times*, November 9, 1932, 6; Gerald Meyer, *Vito Marcantonio: Radical Politician, 1902–1954* (Albany, 1989), 22–44, 112–72; Peter Jackson, "Vito Marcantonio and Ethnic Politics in New York," *Ethnic and Racial Studies* 6 (1983): 50–64; Thomas, *Puerto Rican Citizen*, 102. On García Rivera, see Oscar García Rivera Papers, Archives of the Puerto Rican Diaspora, Hunter College, New York.

52. "Peddlers Protest New Market Plan," *Times*, July 6, 1934, 36; "La Guardia to Ban Sale of Dry Goods Outdoors," *Times*, July 15, 1934, 5; "Pushcarts Losing Ground," *Times*, August 25, 1935, sec. 4, 10; "Mayor Orders Curb on Pushcart Permits," *Times*, November 13, 1934, 4; "Market in Harlem Opened by Mayor," *Times*, May 5, 1936, 24; "More Pushcarts to Vanish," *Times*, September 20, 1936, sec. 4, 10; "Pushcart Sales of Hot Dog Barred," *Times*, May 12, 1937, 25; "Farewell to Pushcarts," *Times*, July 23, 1937, 18 ("farewell"); Cinotto, *Italian American Table*, 97–98 (other quotations); Suzanne Wasserman, "The Good Old Days of Poverty: Merchants and the Battle Over Pushcart Peddling on the Lower East Side," *Business and Economic History* 27 (1998): 330–38.

53. "Astor Would Sell Tenements to City," *Times*, March 15, 1934, 3; "Astor Tenements Ordered Vacated," *Times*, March 30, 1934, 23; "City Housing Starts with Sale by Astor," *Herald Tribune*, December 8, 1934, 1; "120 'First Families' Get New Homes," *Times*, December 1, 1935, sec. 4, 10; "First Houses Open," *Times*, December 4, 1935, 1; "In the Beginning, New York Created First Houses," *Times*, September 24, 1995 (quotation); Nicholas Dagen Bloom, *Public Housing That Worked: New York in the Twentieth Century* (Philadelphia, 2006), 13–44, 270.

54. "First Houses," *Times*, December 4, 1935, 22; "Vast Housing Plan Envisaged for City," *Times*, December 8, 1935, sec. 4, 10; "First Houses Assailed," *Times*, December 19, 1935, 8; Bloom, *Public Housing That Worked*, 1–10.

55. Mexico border entry card for Fritz Kuhn, Laredo, Texas, May 19, 1928, accessed via ancestry.com; Ira Katznelson, *Fear Itself: The New Deal and the Origins of Our Time* (New York, 2013), 57 (quotations); German American Bund file, Federal Bureau of Investigation, accessed at https://vault.fbi.gov/german-american-bund/german-american -federation-bund-part-11-of-10/view; "Nazis Hail George Washington as First Fascist," *Life*, March 7, 1938, 17; Sander Diamond, *The Nazi Movement in the United States, 1924–1941* (Ithaca, 1974), 202–337.

56. Robert Rockaway, *But — He Was Good to His Mother: The Lives and Crimes of Jewish Gangsters* (Jerusalem, 1993), 225–28.

57. "Jews Assail Coughlin," *Times*, August 18, 1936, 11; "Coughlin Repeats Roosevelt Attack," *Times*, September 27, 1936, 28 ("thrust"); "WMCA Contradicts Coughlin on Jews," *Times*, November 21, 1938, 7; "In Defense of Restraint," *Herald Tribune*, November 28, 1938, 14; "Coughlin Defends Address on Jews," *Times*, November 28, 1938, 1; "The Silencing of Father Coughlin," *Herald Tribune*, November 30, 1938, 18; "Coughlin Tells Need for 'Christian Front,'" *Times*, August 21, 1939, 6; "Coughlin Supports Christian Front," *Times*, January 22, 1940, 1; Alan Brinkley, *Voices of Protest: Huey Long, Father Coughlin, and the Great Depression* (New York, 1982), 269–73; Donald Warren, *Radio Priest: Charles Coughlin, the Father of Hate Radio* (New York, 1996), 129–87.

58. "Coughlin Denounced by Methodist Group," *Times*, May 1, 1940, 9 ("'polite'"); Bayor, *Neighbors in Conflict*, 155–63.

59. Bayor, *Neighbors in Conflict*, 156 ("tired"); Thomas Kessner, *Fiorello H. La Guardia and the Making of Modern New York* (New York, 1989), 520–24; "Swears 500 Police Favored 'Front,'" *Times*, May 24, 1940, 12; Stephen Norwood, "Marauding Youth and the Christian Front: Antisemitic Violence in Boston and New York During World War II," *American Jewish History* 91 (2003): 242.

60. "Crowd Battles Police in Bronx," *Times*, August 14, 1939, 16; "Five Held in Bronx Row," *Times*, August 15, 1939, 4; "Ninfo Son, on Fast, Jailed for 75 Days," *Times*, September 26, 1939, 21 (quotations).

61. "Inter-Faith Group Is Formed in Bronx," *Times*, October 23, 1939, 14 ("terrorizing"); "Court Scores Woman for Attack on Jews," *Times*, August 16, 1939, 17 ("persecution").

62. "18 Seized in Plot to Overthrow U.S." *Times*, January 15, 1940, 1, 3; "F.B.I. Arrests 18 Here for Plot to 'Seize U.S., Set Up a Dictator,'" *Herald Tribune*, January 15, 1940, 1 (quotations), 3; "Cassidy's Letters Read at Plot Trial," *Times*, May 1, 1940, 11; "Cassidy Defends Anti-Red Activity," *Times*, May 23, 1940, 14; "Nine Acquitted of Sedition Plot," *Times*, June 25, 1940, 1, 24; Warren, *Radio Priest*, 188–98; "Banning of J. F. Cassidy from State Bar Sought," *Herald Tribune*, January 28, 1942, 34; "John F. Cassidy in Army," *Times*, March 28, 1942, 8; "J. F. Cassidy Barred from Practicing Law," *Times*, November 15, 1944, 29 (quotation in footnote); "Lawyer's Fifty Year Journey to the Bar," *Times*, May 31, 1995.

63. "German-Jewish Refugees, 1933–1939," online *Holocaust Encyclopedia* of the United States Holocaust Memorial Museum (accessed December 2015); Richard Breitman and Allan Lichtman, *FDR and the Jews* (Cambridge, Mass., 2013), 67–135; "Roosevelt Finds Quotas Limit Aid," *Times*, November 18, 1938, 2; David Large, *And the World Closed Its Doors: The Story of One Family Abandoned to the Holocaust* (New York, 2003), 139–40 ("ugly adults"); "21 Jewish Refugees Face Return to Reich," *Times*, October 30, 1938, 17; "Forbidden to Land Anywhere, 37 Refugees Try New York," *Times*, January 12, 1939, 1; "Stranded Jewish Refugees Offer Puzzle in New York," *Los Angeles Times*, January 12, 1939, 2; "Salvador Bars Refugees," *Times*, July 31, 1939, 7.

64. "700 Jewish Refugees Await Fate Off Cuba," *Times*, May 28, 1939, 15; "Cuba Orders Liner and Refugees to Go," *Times*, June 2, 1939, 1; "907 Refugees Quit Cuba on Liner," *Times*, June 3, 1939, 1; "The Promised Land," *Washington Post*, June 3, 1939, 10; "Refugee Ship Idles Off Florida Coast," *Times*, June 5, 1939, 1; "Cuba Recloses Door to Refugees," *Times*, June 7, 1939, 1; "Refugee Ship," *Times*, June 8, 1939, 24 ("shimmering"); "Man's Inhumanity," *Times*, June 9, 1939, 20; "Netherlands to Take 194 of Liner's Refugees; Belgium and France May Admit Rest of 900," *Times*, June 13, 1939, 1; "907 Refugees End Voyage in Antwerp," *Times*, June 18, 1939, 1; "500 Refugees on Way to Temporary Homes," *Times*, June 20, 1939, 6; Breitman and Lichtman, *FDR and the Jews*, 135–41; Sarah Ogilvie and Scott Miller, *Refuge Denied: The* St. Louis *Passengers and the Holocaust* (Madison, 2006), 174–75.

65. "German-Jewish Refugees, 1933–1939"; Ogilvie and Miller, *Refuge Denied*, 174–75; Maurice Davie, *Refugees in America: Report of the Committee for the Study of Recent Immigration from Europe* (New York, 1947), 21–37.

66. Niall Ferguson, *Kissinger, 1923–1968: The Idealist* (New York, 2015), 35 (quotation), 62–81.

67. "Many Refugees in Schools Here," *Times*, January 8, 1939, sec. 2, 9 (quotations); "Volunteer Group to Aid Refugees," *Times*, November 26, 1939, sec. 2, 6; "3,400 Refugees Seeking Places in Melting Pot," *Herald Tribune*, December 7, 1939, 25; "Survey Reveals High Caliber of Nazi Refugees," *Herald Tribune*, December 8, 1939, 9.

68. Davie, *Refugees in America*, 120–23.

69. Ibid., 432.

70. Serge Guilbaut, *How New York Stole the Idea of Modern Art: Abstract Expressionism,*

Freedom, and the Cold War (Chicago, 1983), 17–194; Davie, *Refugees in America*, 324–33; Daniels, *Guarding the Golden Door*, 84 (quotation).

71. "3,400 Refugees Seeking Places in Melting Pot," *Herald Tribune*, December 7, 1939, 25 (quotations); Davie, *Refugees in America*, 132.

72. Ferguson, *Kissinger*, 102–3; Ernest Stock, "Washington Heights' 'Fourth Reich,'" in *Commentary on the American Scene: Portraits of Jewish Life in America*, ed. Elliot Cohen (New York, 1953), 224–42.

73. Ferguson, *Kissinger*, 102–3; Walter Isaacson, *Kissinger: A Biography* (New York, 1992), 37–38.

74. "New Yorkers Say Civil Uprising Will Come Here If We Enter War," *Times*, February 8, 1941, 1.

75. Philip Cannistraro, ed., *The Italians of New York: Five Centuries of Struggle and Achievement* (New York, 1990), 140.

76. "Harbor Camp for Enemy Aliens," *Times*, January 25, 1942, magazine sec., 29 (quotation); Steven Jaffe, *New York at War: Four Centuries of Combat, Fear, and Intrigue in Gotham* (New York, 2012), 238; Vincent Cannato, *American Passage: The History of Ellis Island* (New York, 2009), 350–55; "Ezio Pinza Seized as Enemy Alien," *Times*, March 13, 1942, 1; "Ezio Pinza Freed After 11 Weeks on Ellis Island," *Times*, June 5, 1942, 19; Ezio Pinza, *Ezio Pinza: An Autobiography* (New York, 1958), 202–28; "When Being Italian Was a Crime," *Village Voice*, April 11, 2000.

77. Jaffe, *New York at War*, 237; entry for Rene Froehlich, dwelling 121, enumeration district 1749, Kings County (Brooklyn), 1930 census; "Girl, 2 Boys Admit Aiding 'Master Spy,'" *Times*, September 4, 1941, 12; "$60,000 Holds Queens Girl, 2 Youths as Spies," *Brooklyn Eagle*, September 4, 1941, 3 ("Maspeth Mata Hari"); "FBI Nabs 2d Woman as Spy," *Brooklyn Eagle*, September 5, 1941, 1, 21; "Selectee Is Seized as a German Spy," *Times*, September 24, 1941, 6; "Mechanic Denies Bombsite Sale," *Times*, November 1, 1941, 17; "33 in Spy Ring Get Heavy Sentences," *Times*, January 3, 1942, 1.

78. Jaffe, *New York at War*, 240–41; "Tanker Torpedoed 60 Miles Off Long Island," *Times*, January 15, 1942, 1.

79. *Sixteenth Census of the United States: 1940*, vol. 2, *Characteristics of the Population*, pt. 5, *New York–Oregon* (Washington, D.C., 1943), 159 (total foreign-born in 1940); Integrated Public Use Microdata Series (IPUMS) 1% sample of New York City's population from the 1940 U.S. Census, available in "*City of Dreams* Replication Data" at https://dataverse.harvard.edu/dataverse/anbinder; Jaffe, *New York at War*, 254; "Maquis Now Convinced U.S. Is a Melting Pot," *Times*, September 3, 1944, 12; "Our All-American Army," *Chicago Tribune*, February 7, 1945, 12.

80. Jaffe, *New York at War*, 236; Ron Rosenbaum, *Explaining Hitler: The Search for the Origins of His Evil*, updated ed. (Boston, 2014), 33–36.

81. Ferguson, *Kissinger*, 115.

82. Ibid., 116.

83. Jaffe, *New York at War*, 245, 250–51; Richard Goldstein, *Helluva Town: The Story of New York City During World War II* (New York, 2010), 64–71.

84. Jaffe, *New York at War*, 251; Richard Rhodes, *The Making of the Atomic Bomb* (New York, 1986), 268–81, 401; "Why They Called It the Manhattan Project," *Times*, October

30, 2007; "Columbia's Historic Atom Smasher Is Now Destined for the Junk Heap," *Times*, December 20, 2007.

85. Ferguson, *Kissinger*, 138.

86. Ibid., 167–68.

87. Ibid., 203.

21. Renaissance

1. "U.N. Body to Renew Site Debate Today," *Times*, December 11, 1946, 1; "Rockefeller Site Accepted by U.N. Committee," *Times*, December 13, 1946, 1; Charlene Mires, *Capital of the World: The Race to Host the United Nations* (New York, 2013), 145–228; Annie Polland and Daniel Soyer, *Emerging Metropolis: New York Jews in the Age of Immigration, 1840–1920* (New York, 2012), xi (quotation).

2. Haim Genizi, *America's Fair Share: The Admission and Resettlement of Displaced Persons, 1945–1952* (Detroit, 1993), 66–128; Roger Daniels, *Guarding the Golden Door: American Immigration Policy and Immigrants Since 1882* (New York, 2004), 106–9; "U.S. Immigration Laws," *Times*, December 2, 1956, sec. 4, 7.

3. New York City Department of City Planning, *The Newest New Yorkers: Characteristics of the City's Foreign-Born Population* (New York, 2013), 10. Average age of immigrants based on a 1 percent sample of New York City's population as recorded in the U.S. census of 1950 prepared by Steven Ruggles, J. Trent Alexander, Katie Genadek, Ronald Goeken, Matthew B. Schroeder, and Matthew Sobek, *Integrated Public Use Microdata Series: Version 5.0* (Minneapolis, 2010), and available as "1950 New York City 1% Census Sample" at https://dataverse.harvard.edu/dataverse/anbinder.

4. Daniels, *Guarding the Golden Door*, 119–20; "Jamaica's Leader Urges U.S. to End Immigration Curbs," *Times*, June 12, 1963, 5 (quotation); "Refugee Needs Speed Changes in the Laws," *Times*, December 2, 1956, sec. 4, 7.

5. "Ellis Island to Go as Alien Station," *Times*, June 3, 1954, 55; "Alien, Long Held, Freed," *Times*, August 12, 1954, 10; "Ellis Island Ends Alien Processing," *Times*, November 13, 1954, 20; Vincent Cannato, *American Passage: The History of Ellis Island* (New York, 2009), 371–76.

6. "Last Man Off Ellis Island," *Times*, November 14, 1954, sec. 4, 8.

7. "Officials Worried by Influx of Migrant Puerto Ricans," *Times*, August 2, 1947, 1, 15; "Puerto Ricans in Continental United States," Census Bureau "Special Report" issued in conjunction with the 1950 census, available at http://www2.census.gov/prod2/decennial/documents/41601756v4p3ch11.pdf; Ira Rosenwaike, *Population History of New York City* (Syracuse, 1972), 139 (1960 figure); Virginia Sánchez Korrol, *From Colonia to Community: The History of Puerto Ricans in New York City* (Berkeley, 1983), 38 (250 percent), 212–18; "Rising Hispanic Migration Heightens City Tensions," *Times*, April 4, 1966, 1, 16.

8. Vivek Bald, *Bengali Harlem and the Lost Histories of South Asian America* (Cambridge, Mass., 2013), 160.

9. "Red Gains Linked to U.S. Alien Laws," *Times*, March 18, 1957, 56 ("adds"); "Senator Pledges HIAS a Bill to Rectify Alien Laws," *Times*, March 12, 1962, 4 (Hart); "Kennedy Gets Plea on Immigration Law," *Times*, April 15, 1962, 3 ("most racist"); "6 Senators

Offer Immigration Bill," *Times*, July 3, 1963, 24 (Javits); John F. Kennedy to the Editor, *Times*, March 10, 1959, 34; "Text of Kennedy's Address Before Throng at Labor Day Rally in Detroit," *Times*, September 6, 1960, 38; "Two Candidates Agree on Need to Liberalize Immigration Law," *Times*, October 24, 1960, 19.

10. "President Urges Repeal of Quotas for Immigration," *Times*, July 24, 1963, 1, 13; "A New Immigration Law," *Times*, July 25, 1963, 17; John F. Kennedy, "A Nation of Immigrants," *Times*, August 4, 1963, magazine sec., 6–7, 56; Daniels, *Guarding the Golden Door*, 129–32.

11. Immigration and Nationality Act of 1965, 79 Stat. 911; Daniels, *Guarding the Golden Door*, 133–37.

12. Lyndon Johnson, "Remarks at the Signing of the Immigration Bill, Liberty Island, New York," *Public Papers of the Presidents*, accessed at http://www.presidency.ucsb.edu/ws/index.php?pid=27292 (Johnson quotations); "Johnson Signs New Immigration Bill," *Times*, October 4, 1965, 1; Bill Ong Hing, *Defining America Through Immigration Policy* (Philadelphia, 2004), 95 ("upset").

13. "U.S. to Admit Cubans Castro Frees," *Times*, October 4, 1965, 1; Daniels, *Guarding the Golden Door*, 190–218; *1987 Statistical Yearbook of the Immigration and Naturalization Service* (Washington, D.C., 1988), 8 (table 4).

14. "'65 Law Changes Ethnic Patterns of Immigration," and "Immigration Shifts," *Times*, August 31, 1970, 1, 37; "Shifting Patterns of Immigration Add New Flavor to the City's Melting Pot," *Times*, September 25, 1972, 39; "Census Finds That New York's Pot Is Still Melting," *Times*, April 25, 1982, 38; "Major Changes in Immigration to City Seen," *Times*, January 24, 1985, B4.

15. "The New New Yorkers," *Times*, November 3, 1985, magazine sec., 24–28, 95–97; "No. 7 Line — The Orient Express," *Times*, November 20, 1988, magazine sec., 26ff.

16. Christian Krohn-Hansen, *Making New York Dominican: Small Business, Politics, and Everyday Life* (Philadelphia, 2013), 32–33; Jesse Hoffnung-Garskof, *A Tale of Two Cities: Santo Domingo and New York After 1950* (Princeton, 2008), 68–89, 95 ("contigo"); Ramona Hernández and Francisco Rivera-Batiz, *Dominicans in the United States: A Socioeconomic Profile, 2000* (New York, 2003), 20; David Coleman, "Lyndon Johnson and the Dominican Intervention of 1965," National Security Archive Electronic Briefing Book, http://nsarchive.gwu.edu/NSAEBB/NSAEBB513/; "Job-Hunting Dominicans Devise Methods to Enter the U.S. Illegally," *Times*, June 1, 1970, 18 (yearly Dominican immigration figures).

17. Hoffnung-Garskof, *Tale of Two Cities*, 90–93; Krohn-Hansen, *Making New York Dominican*, 33–34; "Dominicans Crowd 3 Roads Leading Out of Poverty," *Times*, May 15, 1970, 3; "Job-Hunting Dominicans Devise Methods to Enter the U.S. Illegally," *Times*, June 1, 1970, 18; "Illegal Status of Dominicans Shaping Their Lives in the City," *Times*, November 9, 1971, 49, 52; Frank Graziano, *Undocumented Dominican Migration* (Austin, 2013), 86–119.

18. "Illegal Status of Dominicans Shaping Their Lives in the City," *Times*, November 9, 1971, 49, 52; "Spanish Influx Felt in Washington Heights," *Times*, August 12, 1976, 27 (quotation); "Dominican Immigration Alters Hispanic New York," *Times*, September 1, 1992; "Unmasking Roots of Washington Heights Violence," *Times*, October 17, 1993 (40

percent); "Dominicans In, Irish Out in Northern Manhattan," *Times,* October 5, 1997; Glen Hendricks, *The Dominican Diaspora: From the Dominican Republic to New York City — Villagers in Transition* (New York, 1974), 80; Krohn-Hansen, *Making New York Dominican,* 37–49; foreign-born by county for every census year since 1870 available at http://dsl.richmond.edu/panorama/foreignborn/#decade=1990&county=G3600610.

19. "Already Struggling, Dominicans Sink Deeper into Poverty, Study Finds," *Times,* November 10, 1997.

20. Hernández and Rivera-Batiz, *Dominicans in the United States,* 43; Krohn-Hansen, *Making New York Dominican,* 69–87.

21. Krohn-Hansen, *Making New York Dominican,* 87–90; Ginetta Candelario, *Black Behind the Ears: Dominican Racial Identity from Museums to Beauty Shops* (Durham, N.C., 2007), 153, 177–222 ("every block," 187); "Flak in the Great Hair War: African-Americans vs. Dominicans," *Times,* October 13, 1999 (other quotations).

22. Ramona Hernández, "On Dominicans in New York City's Garment Industry," in *A Coat of Many Colors: Immigration, Globalization, and Reform in New York City's Garment Industry,* ed. Daniel Soyer (New York, 2005), 169–91; Roger Waldinger, *Through the Eye of the Needle: Immigrants and Enterprise in New York's Garment Trades* (New York, 1986), 105–22.

23. Krohn-Hansen, *Making New York Dominican,* 93–133 ("slave," 115); "Bodegas Find Prosperity amid Change," *Times,* November 19, 1986, C8; "The Legacy of the Dominican Bodega," *El Diario/La Prensa,* July 31, 2015, translated at http://voicesofny.org/2015/07/the-legacy-of-the-dominican-bodega/.

24. "Oscar de la Renta, Who Clothed Stars and Became One, Dies at 82," *Times,* October 20, 2014; Sarah Mower, *Oscar: The Style, Inspiration, and Life of Oscar de la Renta* (New York, 2002), 8–69; "Diana Vreeland, Editor, Dies," *Times,* August 23, 1989, A1 (quotation); "Coty's Winnie Given to Oscar," *Times,* June 30, 1967, 32.

25. "Oscar de la Renta," *Times,* October 20, 2014; Mower, *Oscar,* 67 ("air"); "Living Well Is Still the Best Revenge," *Times,* December 21, 1980, magazine sec., 5.

26. *Newest New Yorkers,* 16; David Brotherton and Luis Barrios, *Banished to the Homeland: Dominican Deportees and Their Stories* (New York, 2011), 163-291; "Flood of Dominicans Lets Some Enter U.S. by Fraud," *Times,* February 19, 1997; "Finally, Back to the Island for a Summer at Home," *Times,* August 22, 2005 (quotation).

27. John Kuo Wei Tchen, *New York Before Chinatown: Orientalism and the Shaping of American Culture, 1776–1882* (Baltimore, 1999), 167–291; Arthur Bonner, *Alas! What Brought Thee Hither? The Chinese in New York, 1800–1950* (Madison, N.J., 1997), 1–86, 159–80; Tyler Anbinder, *Five Points: The Nineteenth-Century New York City Neighborhood That Invented Tap Dance, Stole Elections, and Became the World's Most Notorious Slum* (New York, 2001), 396–423; Renqiu Yu, *To Save China, To Save Ourselves: The Chinese Hand Laundry Alliance of New York* (Philadelphia, 1992), 8–9; Mary Ting Yi Lui, *The Chinatown Trunk Mystery: Murder, Miscegenation, and Other Dangerous Encounters in Turn-of-the-Century New York City* (Princeton, 2005), 1–80, 143–74.

28. Peter Kwong, *Chinatown, N.Y.: Labor and Politics, 1930–1950,* rev. ed. (New York, 2001), 26–156; Erika Lee, *At America's Gates: Chinese Immigration During the Exclusion Era* (Chapel Hill, 2003), 111–243; Peter Kwong, *The New Chinatown,* rev. ed. (New York,

1996), 14–16; Heather Lee, "A Life Cooking for Others: The Work and Migration Experiences of a Chinese Restaurant Worker in New York City, 1920–1946," in *Eating Asian American: A Food Studies Reader*, ed. Roger Ji-Song Ku et al. (New York, 2013), 53–77.

29. "New Money, People and Ideas Alter Chinatown of Tradition," *Times*, December 28, 1981; "The New Blood in Chinatown," *Times*, June 22, 1997; "Within Chinatown, a Slice of Another China," *Times*, July 22, 2001; Kwong, *The New Chinatown*, 175; Min Zhou, *Chinatown: The Socioeconomic Potential of an Urban Enclave* (Philadelphia, 1992), 42–45; Hsiang-Shui Chen, *Chinatown No More: Taiwan Immigrants in Contemporary New York* (Ithaca, 1992), 51–90; Bernard Wong, "The Chinese: New Immigrants in New York's Chinatown," in *New Immigrants in New York*, ed. Nancy Foner (New York, 1987), 245.

30. "The New Blood in Chinatown," *Times*, June 22, 1997; "Within Chinatown, a Slice of Another China," *Times*, July 22, 2001; "For Immigrant Family, No Easy Journeys," *Times*, January 4, 2003; "A Long and Costly Journey," *Bergen Record*, July 9, 1998 ("no men"); Ko-Lin Chin, *Smuggled Chinese: Clandestine Immigration to the United States* (Philadelphia, 1999), 3, 20, 111–13; Marlowe Hood, "Sourcing the Problem: Why Fuzhou?" in *Human Smuggling: Chinese Migrant Trafficking and the Challenge to America's Immigration Tradition*, ed. Paul Smith (Washington, D.C., 1997), 169–95.

31. "Little Italy Is Restive as Chinatown Expands," *Times*, April 26, 1974, 39 ("preserve"); "Chinatown Leaps the 'Wall' and Moves into Little Italy," *Times*, July 13, 1980, 6 ("Thank God"); Peter Jackson, "Ethnic Turf: Competition on the Canal Street Divide," *New York Affairs* 7 (1983): 149–58; Philip Napoli, "Little Italy: Resisting the Asian Invasion, 1965–1995," in *Race and Ethnicity in New York City*, ed. Jerome Krase and Ray Hutchison (Boston, 2004), 245–63.

32. "Within Chinatown, a Slice of Another China," *Times*, July 22, 2001; Chin, *Smuggled Chinese*, 20, 111.

33. "A Long and Costly Journey," *Bergen Record*, July 9, 1998 ("hope" and "gold"); "Human Cargo Big Business," *Sun Media Newspapers*, September 20, 1999 ("clan"); "It's the 'Rich' Chinese Who Flee to U.S.," *Seattle Post-Intelligencer*, February 10, 2000 ("single").

34. *2000 Statistical Yearbook of the Immigration and Naturalization Service* (Washington, D.C., 2002), 21; "The Golden Venture, Plus 100,000," *Times*, June 9, 1993.

35. Patrick Radden Keefe, *The Snakehead: An Epic Tale of the Chinatown Underworld and the American Dream* (New York, 2009), 24–37 (quotation, 35).

36. Chin, *Smuggled Chinese*, 49–61, 79–93, 175–79; "Arrests Made in Smuggling of Immigrants," *Times*, December 11, 1998.

37. Chin, *Smuggled Chinese*, 97–110, 177 (quotations, 106); "A Long and Costly Journey," *Bergen Record*, July 9, 1998; "Voyage to Life of Shattered Dreams: At Cost of $30,000, Woman Goes from Poverty in China to Prostitution in Chinatown," *Times*, July 23, 1993.

38. "Bus Crash in the Bronx Ends a Man's Fight for His Family," *Times*, March 21, 2011 ("borrow"); "It's the 'Rich' Chinese Who Flee to U.S.," *Seattle Post-Intelligencer*, February 10, 2000 ("bad jobs"); "Immigrant Dream of Plenty Turns to Misery and Regret," *Times*, June 8, 1993.

39. Chin, *Smuggled Chinese,* 175, 181.

40. Gwen Kinkead, *Chinatown: Portrait of a Closed Society* (New York, 1992), 21–22; Chin, *Smuggled Chinese,* 113–16, 182; "Within Chinatown, a Slice of Another China," *Times,* July 22, 2001 ("boss" and "smoking"); "Bus Crash in the Bronx Ends a Man's Fight for His Family," *Times,* March 21, 2011 ("all we do"); Lauren Hilgers, "The Kitchen Network: America's Underground Chinese Restaurant Workers," *New Yorker,* October 13, 2014.

41. Margaret Chin, *Sewing Women: Immigrants and the New York City Garment Industry* (New York, 2005), 56–137; Xiaolan Bao, *Holding Up More Than Half the Sky: Chinese Women Garment Workers in New York City, 1948–92* (Urbana, 2001), 15–70, 110–42, 213–44; "New York Is Fighting Spread of Sweatshops," *Times,* November 16, 1987, A1; "Despite Tough Laws, Sweatshops Flourish," *Times,* February 6, 1995 (quotations); "65 Cents an Hour," *Times,* March 12, 1995; "Reaping Abuse for What They Sew," *Washington Post,* February 16, 1997; Jan Lin, *Reconstructing Chinatown: Ethnic Enclave, Global Change* (Minneapolis, 1998), 62–68; "Women Keep Garment Jobs by Sending Babies to China," *Times,* September 14, 1999; "Chinese-American Children Sent to Live with Kin Abroad Face a Tough Return," *Times,* July 24, 2009.

42. "Thriving Sweatshops Feed on Immigrants' Desire for Work," *Times,* March 25, 1986, B2; "Garment Sweatshops Are Spreading," September 6, 1987, 38; "Investigators Find Sweatshops Are in the Resurgence," *Times,* September 4, 1988, 26; "Despite Tough Laws, Sweatshops Flourish," *Times,* February 6, 1995 ("sordid"); "Sweatshop Job Abuse Worsening," *Times,* September 13, 1995 ("worse"); Kinkead, *Chinatown,* 27–33.

43. "New Money, People and Ideas Alter Chinatown of Tradition," *Times,* December 28, 1981; "Despite Tough Laws, Sweatshops Flourish," *Times,* February 6, 1995; "Sweatshop Job Abuse Worsening," *Times,* September 13, 1995.

44. "New York Is Fighting Spread of Sweatshops," *Times,* November 16, 1987, B4; Kinkead, *Chinatown,* 31 (quotation).

45. "For Poor, Life 'Trapped in a Cage,'" *Times,* October 6, 1996; "Snakeheads That Bite and Hang On," *Times,* April 14, 2005; Kinkead, *Chinatown,* 17–19.

46. Chin, *Smuggled Chinese,* 129, 176.

47. Keefe, *Snakehead,* 42–47.

48. Ibid., 42–56 (quotation, 56).

49. Ibid., 97–101 (quotations, 100–101).

50. Ibid., 109–32; "Snakeheads Take the Stand," *Newsday,* May 24, 2005.

51. Keefe, *Snakehead,* 128–42.

52. Ibid., 146–74; "Immigrants Escape in High Seas Drama," *South China Morning Post,* April 4, 1993; "A Long and Costly Journey," *Bergen Record,* July 9, 1998.

53. "7 Die as Crowded Immigrant Ship Grounds Off Queens," *Times,* June 7, 1993; "Chinese Immigrants Tell of Darwinian Voyage," *Times,* June 12, 1993 (quotation); Keefe, *Snakehead,* 1–19, 172–76.

54. "President Chooses an Expert to Halt Smuggling of Aliens," *Times,* June 19, 1993 ("lose control"); "U.S. Decides to Free Golden Venture Immigrants," *Times,* February 15, 1997; "Chinese Deportee Is Again Caught Trying to Enter U.S.," *Times,* June 4, 1998; "Making It Ashore, but Still Chasing U.S. Dream," *Times,* April 9, 2006 ("argument").

55. "Dozens of Chinese from 1993 Voyage Still in Jail," *Times,* February 3, 1997; "Making It Ashore, but Still Chasing U.S. Dream," *Times,* April 9, 2006.

56. Keefe, *Snakehead,* 219–22, 291–321 ("incarnate," 309); "Mastermind of Golden Venture Smuggling Ship Gets 20 Years," *Times,* December 2, 1998; "Trial Starts with Details of Immigrant Smuggling," *Times,* May 17, 2005; "Ringleader Gets 35-Year Term in Smuggling of Immigrants," *Times,* March 17, 2006; "A Smuggler of Immigrants Dies in Prison, but Is Praised in Chinatown," *Times,* April 27, 2014 ("Robin Hood"); Patrick Radden Keefe, "Requiem for a Snakehead," *New Yorker,* May 5, 2014.

57. Nancy Foner, "West Indian Migration to New York: An Overview," in *Islands in the City: West Indian Migration to New York,* ed. Nancy Foner (Berkeley, 2001), 1.

58. Michel Laguerre, *American Odyssey: Haitians in New York City* (Ithaca, 1984), 23–24; Philip Kasinitz, *Caribbean New York: Black Immigrants and the Politics of Race* (Ithaca, 1992), 28–29; Susan Buchanan Stafford, "The Haitians: The Cultural Meaning of Race and Ethnicity," in Foner, *New Immigrants in New York,* 134 (quotations); "Haiti Has No Bootstraps," *Times,* February 14, 1982, sec. 4, 19.

59. Milton Vickerman, "Jamaicans: Balancing Race and Ethnicity," in *New Immigrants in New York,* ed. Nancy Foner, rev. ed. (New York, 2001), 202; Kasinitz, *Caribbean New York,* 26, 54; "Race Trouble in Britain," *Times,* August 23, 1961, 32; "British Tories Urge Immigration Curbs," *Times,* October 12, 1961, 14; "Britain to Curb Migrant Influx," *Times,* November 11, 1961, 4; "Immigrants Jam Ports in Britain," *Times,* July 1, 1962, 11; "British Put Curb on Immigration," *Times,* July 2, 1962, 23; Foner, "West Indian Migration to New York," 1, 4.

60. Kasinitz, *Caribbean New York,* 39, 55–61, 64–67; Kyle Crowder and Lucky Tedrow, "West Indians and the Residential Landscape of New York," in Foner, *Islands in the City,* 106; Laguerre, *American Odyssey,* 50, 55.

61. Vickerman, "Jamaicans," 201; Peter Blauner, "Islands in the City," *New York,* April 21, 1986, 66 ("village"); "Spirit of Trade Winds and Palm Trees in Brooklyn," *Times,* September 20, 1987, 76 ("home").

62. Blauner, "Islands in the City," 68–69 ("supply"); "Caribbean Verve Brightens New York," *Times,* June 3, 1988, B1, B5 (Owens).

63. Kasinitz, *Caribbean New York,* 104–6; "Man with a Van," *Times,* August 10, 1997; "Dream On," *Wall Street Journal,* July 21, 1997.

64. Kasinitz, *Caribbean New York,* 104–6; Suzanne Model, "Where New York's West Indians Work," in Foner, *Islands in the City,* 72; Vickerman, "Jamaicans," 204, 217; Tamara Mose Brown, *Raising Brooklyn: Nannies, Childcare, and Caribbeans Creating Community* (New York, 2011), 27, 37–70.

65. "In Brooklyn Woman's Path, a Story of Caribbean Striving," *Times,* June 28, 2003 (other quotations); "Business Booms for Afro-Caribbeans," *Newsday,* February 25, 2003 ("God Bless").

66. Foner, "West Indian Migration to New York," 11 ("hero"); Milton Vickerman, "Tweaking a Monolith: The West Indian Immigrant Encounter with 'Blackness,'" in Foner, *Islands in the City,* 245 (other quotations); "Dominicans Face Assimilation in Black and White," *Washington Post,* May 14, 1999; Stafford, "Haitians," 147.

67. "Black Man Dies After Beating by Whites in Queens," *Times,* December 21, 1986, 1 (quotation); "Area Is an Insular Community," *Times,* December 21, 1986, 44; "Police Search Queens for Attackers," *Times,* December 22, 1986, B2; "Koch Comment on 'Deep South' Angers Mayors," *Times,* December 25, 1986, 36; Charles Hynes and Bob Drury, *Incident at Howard Beach: The Case for Murder* (New York, 1990), 11–25, 37–38.

68. "Fatal Crash Starts Melee with Police in Brooklyn," *Times,* August 20, 1991; "Hasid Dies in Stabbing," *Times,* August 21, 1991 ("pandemonium"); "Clashes Persist in Crown Heights," *Times,* August 22, 1991; "Jews Saying Restraint on Brooklyn Was a Mistake," *Times,* August 31, 1991; "Penalty in Crown Heights Case Means a Little More Jail Time," *Times,* August 21, 2003; Edward Shapiro, *Crown Heights: Blacks, Jews, and the 1991 Brooklyn Riot* (Waltham, Mass., 2006), 1–29, 36–62 (other quotations, 6, 62).

69. "Officers Investigated in a Suspect's Injuries," *Times,* August 13, 1997; "Family Describes a Readily Friendly Man," *Times,* August 13, 1997; "The Frightful Whisperings from a Coney Island Hospital Bed," *Daily News,* August 13, 1997; "Officer Charged in Man's Torture," *Times,* August 14, 1997; "They Saw Louima's Terror," *Daily News,* September 5, 1997; Marie Brenner, "Incident in the 70th Precinct," *Vanity Fair* (December 1997); "In Surprise, Witness Says Officer Bragged About Louima Torture," *Times,* May 20, 1999; "Officer, Seeking Some Mercy, Admits to Louima's Torture," *Times,* May 26, 1999; "Volpe Sentenced to a 30-Year Term," *Times,* December 14, 1999; "On Eve of Trial, Ex-Officer Agrees to Perjury Term in Louima Case," *Times,* September 22, 2002; "The Abner Louima Case, 10 Years Later," *Times* "City Room" blog, August 9, 2007.

70. Vickerman, "Jamaicans," 215; Evrick Brown, "The Caribbean Nation-State in Brooklyn Politics: An Examination of the Una Clarke–Major Owens Congressional Race," in Krase and Hutchison, *Race and Ethnicity in New York City,* 221–44. For the increasing political involvement of Latino immigrants in this period, see Michael Jones-Correa, *Between Two Nations: The Political Predicament of Latinos in New York City* (Ithaca, 1998), 69–106.

71. Illsoo Kim, *New Urban Immigrants: The Korean Community in New York* (Princeton, 1981), 24–97; Pyong Gap Min, *Changes and Conflicts: Korean Immigrant Families in New York* (Needham Heights, Mass., 1998), 9–13.

72. Illsoo Kim, "The Koreans: Small Business in an Urban Frontier," in Foner, *New Immigrants* (1987), 222–23; Kim, *New Urban Immigrants,* 40; Joanne Petty, interview with the author, December 10, 2015, Arlington, Va.

73. Kim, "Koreans," 225; Pyong Gap Min, *Ethnic Solidarity for Economic Survival: Korean Greengrocers in New York City* (New York, 2008), 28–36; "The Korean Greengrocer: Produce Is More Varied," *Times,* February 18, 1976, 36 (quotations); "For City's Korean Greengrocers, Culture Often Clashes with the Law," *Times,* August 11, 1984, 25; "Korean Entrepreneurs Find Their Dream Is Tarnishing," *Times,* December 27, 1990; "A Korean Family's Dream, a Community's Struggle," *Times,* March 13, 1996.

74. Min, *Ethnic Solidarity,* 78–96; Claire Kim, *Bitter Fruit: The Politics of Black-Korean Conflict in New York City* (New Haven, 2000), 109–87; "Black-Korean Who-Pushed-Whom Festers," *Times,* May 7, 1990; Jonathan Rieder, "Trouble in Store," *New Republic,* July 2, 1990 (quotations); "Woman Who Touched Off Boycott Describes Attack,"

Times, January 5, 1991; "Jury Acquits Korean Cited by Boycotters," *Times*, January 31, 1991; "Owner Sells Grocery That Was Boycotted," *Times*, May 29, 1991; "The Storefront Ethic Is in Their Blood," *Times*, December 17, 2000; "The Korean Grocer Disappears," *Daily News*, January 13, 2011.

75. "Why Your Cabby Can't Find Grand Central," *Times*, January 23, 1986, A1; "The Spoilers: India's Elite Felt Smug and Exalted. Then Came the Taxi Drivers from Punjab," *Times*, April 19, 1998; "Cabby Who Fled India Finds New Struggle," *Times*, June 9, 1998 (quotation); Graham Hodges, *Taxi! A Social History of the New York City Cabdriver* (Baltimore, 2007), 159–61; Diditi Mitra, "Punjabi American Taxi Drivers: The New White Working Class?" *Journal of Asian American Studies* 11 (2008): 303–36; Diditi Mitra, "Social Capital Investment and Immigrant Economic Trajectories: A Case Study of Punjabi American Taxi Drivers in New York City," *International Migration* 50 (2012): 67–84.

76. Aminah Mohammad-Arif, *Salaam America: South Asian Muslims in New York* (London, 2002), 32–52; "King of the Pakistani Cabbies," *Times*, November 12, 1995; "Study of Taxi Drivers Finds More Immigrants at Wheel," *Times*, July 7, 2004.

77. *The Newest New Yorkers, 2000: Immigrant New York in the New Millennium* (New York, 2004), 13.

22. Today

1. "Giving Voice to the Immigrant Victims of 9/11," *Daily News*, September 11, 2011; Monisha Das Gupta, "Of Hardship and Hostility: The Impact of 9/11 on New York City Taxi Drivers," in *Wounded City: The Social Impact of 9/11 on New York City*, ed. Nancy Foner (New York, 2005), 208–10, 213–28 ("beautiful," 208); Aminah Mohammad-Arif, *Salaam America: South Asian Muslims in New York* (London, 2002), 268–80; Anny Bakalian and Medhi Bozorgmehr, *Backlash 9/11: Middle Eastern and Muslim Americans Respond* (Berkeley, 2009), 1–37; "The 2 Worlds of Muslim American Teenagers," *Times*, October 7, 2001 ("hatred"); "New York Taxi Drivers Need Disaster Relief," *Times*, March 2, 2002; "More Insulted and Attacked After Sept. 11," *Times*, March 11, 2002; "Going By 'Joe,' Not 'Yussef,'" but Still Feeling Like an Outcast," *Times*, September 11, 2002; "New York's Pakistani Areas Live with a Lingering Fear," *Wall Street Journal*, November 13, 2002 ("terrorist"); "Muslims Face Deportation, but Say U.S. Is Their Home," *Times*, June 13, 2003 ("11 years"); "From Immigrants, Stories of Scrutiny, and Struggle," *Times*, July 20, 2004 (bus).

2. "U.S. Makes It Easier to Detain Foreigners," *Times*, November 28, 2001; "Fearful, Angry, or Confused, Muslim Immigrants Register," *Times*, April 25, 2003; "Between Two Worlds in Brooklyn: To Lead the Faithful in a Faith Under Fire," *Times*, March 6, 2006; Migration Policy Institute, "DHS Announces End to Controversial Post-9/11 Immigrant Registration and Tracking Program," May 17, 2011, http://www.migrationpolicy.org/article/dhs-announces-end-controversial-post-911-immigrant-registration-and-tracking-program; "A Post-9/11 Registration Effort Ends, but Not Its Effects," *Times*, May 30, 2011; "In Brooklyn, 9/11 Damage Continues," *Times*, June 7, 2003; "The Pursuit of Immigrants in America After Sept. 11," *Times*, June 8, 2003.

3. "Some Mideast Immigrants, Shaken, Ponder Leaving U.S.," *Times*, November 23, 2001;

"In Brooklyn, 9/11 Damage Continues," *Times*, June 7, 2003 (quotations); "From Immigrants, Stories of Scrutiny, and Struggle," *Times*, July 20, 2004.

4. "New York's Arab Enclave Trips Radar Post-9/11," *Los Angeles Times*, July 1, 2002 (passports); "In Brooklyn, 9/11 Damage Continues," *Times*, June 7, 2003; "New York Drops Unit That Spied on Muslims," *Times*, April 15, 2014 ("psyche"); "From Immigrants, Stories of Scrutiny, and Struggle," *Times*, July 20, 2004 (other quotations); "I'm a Muslim, Not a Terrorist: So Why Did the NYPD Spy on Me for Years?" *Washington Post*, February 7, 2016.

5. "'Do You Know Me? Do You Know My Heart?'" *Times*, December 10, 2015.

6. "The Immigrants: Testing the System of Relief," *Times*, October 5, 2001; "Battered by Sept. 11, Chinatown Economy Remains Crippled," *Times*, November 21, 2001 (quotation); "In Chinatown, a Taste of Revival," *Times*, November 28, 2001; "Downtown Is Slower to Embrace Optimism," *Times*, December 23, 2001; Margaret Chin, "Moving On: Chinese Garment Workers After 9/11," in Foner, *Wounded City*, 188–90, 195–200. For the decline of the garment industry, see "Manhattan's Chinatown Pressured to Sell Out," *Washington Post*, May 21, 2005; and Daniel Soyer, ed., *A Coat of Many Colors: Immigration, Globalization, and Reform in New York City's Garment Industry* (New York, 2005), 22.

7. Min Zhou, "Chinese: Diverse Origins and Destinies," in *One Out of Three: Immigrant New York in the Twenty-First Century*, ed. Nancy Foner (New York, 2013), 127–38; "For Immigrants, Changes in Store," *Washington Post*, July 29, 2002 ("After 9/11"); New York City Department of City Planning, *The Newest New Yorkers, 2000* (New York, 2004), 58–79; New York City Department of City Planning, *The Newest New Yorkers: Characteristics of the City's Foreign-Born Population* (New York, 2013), 36–43, 44–57; Tarry Hum, *Making a Global Immigrant Neighborhood: Brooklyn's Sunset Park* (Philadelphia, 2014), 55, 63, 67–69; "For Immigrant Family, No Easy Journeys," *Times*, January 4, 2003 ("Every state").

8. "Leaving New York, with Bodega in Tow," *Times*, October 29, 2006.

9. Edward O'Donnell, *Ship Ablaze: The Tragedy of the Steamboat* General Slocum (New York, 2003), 71–285.

10. "Housing Boom Echoes in All Corners of the City," *Times*, August 4, 2005.

11. "The Coney Island of Their Mind," *Times*, June 19, 2005; "More Muslims Arrive in U.S., After 9/11 Dip," *Times*, September 10, 2006 (quotation); "Sara Hylton's Images Depict Little Pakistan's Quiet Conflicts," *Times*, December 4, 2015.

12. "More Muslims Arrive in U.S., After 9/11 Dip," *Times*, September 10, 2006; "In Race for an Assembly Seat, a Challenger Courts the Bangladeshi Vote," *Times*, August 18, 2010; "Take the A Train to Little Guyana," *Times*, June 8, 2013 (quotation); "Westchester Square, the Bronx," *Times*, November 26, 2013. Bangladeshis' Bronx enclave also identified in the Census Bureau's American Community Survey data for 2010–2014, accessed via socialexplorer.com.

13. *Newest New Yorkers* (2013 ed.), 30–61; "Then as Now: New York's Shifting Ethnic Mosaic," *Times*, January 23, 2011.

14. *Newest New Yorkers* (2013 ed.), 40–41, 56–57; "A New Generation Moves On, but Not Too Far," *Times*, August 17, 2008.

15. "Chinatown Gentrifies, and Evicts," *Times,* August 23, 2002; "Manhattan's Chinatown Pressured to Sell Out," *Washington Post,* May 21, 2005; "Housing Boom Echoes in All Corners of the City," *Times,* August 4, 2005 ("assimilate"); "Canal Street, Is That Really You?" *Times,* December 5, 2010; "With an Influx of Newcomers, Little Chinatowns Dot a Changing Brooklyn," *Times,* April 15, 2015 ("join").

16. Robert Courtney Smith, "Mexicans: Civic Engagement, Education, and Progress Achieved and Inhibited," in Foner, *One Out of Three,* 246–53, 259–61; "David and His 26 Roommates," *New York,* May 16, 2005; "Rise in Overcrowded New York City Apartments Shows Need for More Housing," *Daily News,* October 5, 2015.

17. Robert Courtney Smith, *Mexican New York: Transnational Lives of New Immigrants* (Berkeley, 2006), 19–23; "Mexicans from Puebla Create Mini-Version of Their Home State in New York," *Newsday,* September 9, 2001; "Coming to America: Rural Mexicans Flock to New York," *Sun,* September 8, 2003; "Celebrating Mexican Life in New York," *Times,* December 8, 2004; "Study Paints Clearer Picture of Mexicans in City," *Times,* March 3, 2005; "Mass Migration Has Left Many Towns in Mexico Half-Empty, but Much Wealthier," *The Atlantic* (April 2007); "A Mexican Baby Boom in New York," *Times,* June 4, 2007; "In the Shadows, Day Laborers Left Homeless as Work Vanishes," *Times,* January 2, 2010; Jorge Ramos, "Puebla York," August 11, 2015, fusion.net; Gabriel Thompson, *There's No José Here: Following the Lives of Hidden Mexican Immigrants* (New York, 2007), 1–117. Reduction in Mexican immigration since 2010 based on a comparison of the 2010 and 2014 Mexican immigrant population figures in U.S. Census Bureau, Foreign-Born Population, American Community Survey.

18. *Newest New Yorkers* (2013 ed.), 56; Jason Pribilsky, *La Chulla Vida: Gender, Migration, and the Family in Andean Ecuador and New York City* (Syracuse, 2007), 160–74, 177 (70 percent undocumented).

19. Pribilsky, *La Chulla Vida,* 184–86 (quotations); Ann Miles, *From Cuenca to Queens: An Anthropological Story of Transnational Migration* (Austin, 2004), 1–114; "For Day Laborers, an Intersection of Fear," *Times,* November 16, 2008; "Killing Haunts Ecuadoreans' Rise in New York," *Times,* December 15, 2008.

20. "Invisible to Most, Women Line Up for Day Labor," *Times,* August 15, 2005.

21. *Newest New Yorkers* (2013 ed.), 55–56; "Exploring the Challenges of Immigration," *USA Today,* October 13, 1997; "The Pot Finally Melts: New York Becomes 'Most Diverse City in World History,'" *Newsday,* March 18, 2001; "Queens One of 'Most Diverse Places on Earth,' New Figures Show," *Daily News,* July 12, 2009; "Most Diverse Place in America? It's Not Where You Think," June 12, 2015, http://www.cnn.com/2015/06/12/us/most-diverse-place-in-america/.

22. *Newest New Yorkers* (2013 ed.), 56–57; U.S. Census Bureau, Foreign-Born Population, American Community Survey, 2010–2014, prepared by Social Explorer; "In Little Argentina, Transplants Watch as Their Homeland Unravels," *Times,* December 30, 2001.

23. "Indian, Twice Removed: Guyanese Immigrants Cautious About Being Labeled," *Times,* December 17, 2004 (quotation); "From Asia to the Caribbean to New York, Appetite Intact," *Times,* April 20, 2007; "Terror Arrests Puzzle Many in Guyanese Enclave in Queens," *Times,* June 5, 2007; "India in Queens, with a Caribbean Accent," *Times,* May 24, 2009; "Little Guyana, An Indo-Guyanese Enclave in Queens," *Washington*

Post, October 9, 2014; Joseph Berger, *The World in a City: Traveling the Globe Through the Neighborhoods of New York* (New York, 2007), 181–89.

24. *Newest New Yorkers* (2013 ed.), 37–41.

25. Ibid.; "Take the A Train to Little Guyana," *Times,* June 8, 2013; Hum, *Making a Global Immigrant Neighborhood,* 62–66; Judith De Sena and Timothy Shortell, *The World in Brooklyn: Gentrification, Immigration, and Ethnic Politics in a Global City* (Lanham, Md., 2012), 7–45; "Fearing for Many at Home, City's Burmese Unite to Aid Cyclone Victims," *Times,* May 11, 2008; Fran Markowitz, *A Community in Spite of Itself: Soviet Jewish Émigrés in New York* (Washington, D.C., 1993), 53–87, 265–67; Annelise Orleck, "Soviet Jews: The Continuing Russification of Jewish New York," in Foner, *One Out of Three,* 90–116; Berger, *World in a City,* 74–86, 143–52; U.S. Census Bureau, Foreign-Born Population, American Community Survey, 2010–2014.

26. *Newest New Yorkers* (2013 ed.), 34, 202–5; U.S. Census Bureau, Foreign-Born Population, American Community Survey, 2010–2014; David Badillo, "New Immigrants in the Bronx: Redefining a Cityscape," *Bronx County Historical Society Journal* 44 (2007): 19–37; "American Dream Is a Ghana Home," *Times,* August 21, 2002; "With Fanfare, Shanti People from Ghana Install Their New York Chief," *Times,* June 4, 2012; Berger, *World in a City,* 160–66; Paul Stoller, *Money Has No Smell: The Africanization of New York City* (Chicago, 2002), 11–175; "Albanian? Now *That's* Italian," *Times,* June 6, 2004.

27. Bernadette Ludwig, "Liberians: Struggles for Refugee Families," in Foner, *One Out of Three,* 200–210; "From a Staten Island Haven, Liberians Reveal Scars of War," *Times,* September 18, 2007; "Seaside Views, Sri Lankan Tastes," *Times,* January 24, 2010; "Staten Island Neighborhood Reels After Wave of Attacks on Mexicans," *Times,* July 31, 2010; "Mexican Youth Is Attacked on Staten Island," *Times,* August 2, 2010; "An African Pageant Reflects the Changing Face of Staten Island," *Times,* August 5, 2011; "Take the A Train to Little Guyana," *Times,* June 8, 2013; "On Staten Island, Savoring Flavors of Sri Lanka," *Times,* July 15, 2015; Naomi Fertitta, *New York: The Big City and Its Little Neighborhoods* (New York, 2009), 150–57.

28. "Donald Trump's False Comments Connecting Mexican Immigrants and Crime," *Washington Post,* July 8, 2015.

29. For contrasting views, see "From Many, One Nation: America Must Again Assimilate Its Immigrants," *Washington Post,* February 9, 1997; "Latino Immigrants' Children Found Grasping English," *Times,* November 30, 2007; "The Right Road to America?" *Washington Post,* December 16, 2007; "Where Education and Assimilation Collide," *Times,* March 15, 2009; "Hispanics, the New Italians," *Times,* April 20, 2013; "When Assimilation Stalls," *Times,* April 27, 2013; "America's Assimilating Hispanics: The Evidence Shows They Are Following the Path of Earlier Immigrants," *Wall Street Journal,* June 18, 2013; "Newest Immigrants Assimilating as Fast as Previous Ones, Report Says," *Times,* September 21, 2015.

30. The most thorough study of immigrant assimilation today is Mary Waters and Marisa Gerstein Pineau, eds., *The Integration of Immigrants into American Society* (Washington, D.C., 2015), 1–372, while the best comparison of assimilation past and present is Nancy Foner, *From Ellis Island to JFK: New York's Two Great Waves of Immigration* (New Haven, 2000), 169–87.

31. "The Role of Immigrants in the New York City Economy," New York State Comptroller's Office Report 17–2010 (January 2010): 4 (32 percent of economic activity); "Open Doors Don't Invite Criminals," *Times*, March 11, 2006; Louis Winnick, *New People in Old Neighborhoods: The Role of New Immigrants in Rejuvenating New York's Communities* (New York, 1990), 123–91.

32. The various sides of the debate on immigrants and the economy are laid out, without the academic jargon, in "Liberals Duck Immigration Debate," *Times*, September 7, 1995; "Immigration and Poverty," *Newsweek*, July 15, 1996; "Errors About Immigrants: The Government Spends Much More on the Native Born," *Washington Post*, June 19, 1997; Katherine Reynolds Lewis, "Do Immigrants Really Take Jobs That Americans Won't Do?" Newhouse News Service, January 21, 2004; "15 Years on the Bottom Rung," *Times*, May 26, 2005; "Yes, Immigration May Lift Wages," *Times*, November 3, 2005; "The Manicure Menace," *Times*, May 30, 2006; "The Worker Next Door," *Times*, June 3, 2006; "Immigration Math: It's a Long Story," *Times*, June 18, 2006; "Here Illegally, Working Hard and Paying Taxes," *Times*, June 19, 2006; "The Immigration Equation," *Times*, July 9, 2006; Daniel Griswold, "As Immigrants Move In, Americans Move Up," *Cato Institute Free Trade Bulletin*, no. 38 (July 2009); Nathan Marwell, "Wage Disparities and Industry Segregation: A Look at Black-White Income Inequality from 1950–2000," *Profitwise News and Views* (July 2009): 10; "The Role of Immigrants in the New York City Economy"; "Study Belies Image of Immigrants in the Work Force," *Times*, April 15, 2010; "How Immigrants Create More Jobs," *Times*, October 30, 2010; "The Anti-Immigration Crusader," *Times*, April 17, 2011; "The Next Immigration Challenge," *Times*, January 11, 2012; "Immigration and American Jobs," *Times*, October 19, 2012; "Do Illegal Immigrants Actually Hurt the U.S. Economy?" *Times*, February 12, 2013. The World Bank used money transfer records to estimate that American immigrants remitted $123,273,000,000 in 2012. We also know that 7.5 percent of all American immigrants lived in New York City in that year. My estimate of $9 billion is 7.5 percent of the World Bank's figure. See http://www.pewsocialtrends.org/2014/02/20/remittance-map/.

33. For the number of illegal immigrants, see *Newest New Yorkers* (2013 ed.), 186.

34. "How Long Is the Immigration 'Line'?" *Washington Post*, January 31, 2013; "Five Myths About the Immigration 'Line,'" *Washington Post*, February 1, 2013.

35. Public Religion Research Institute, *Anxiety, Nostalgia, and Mistrust: Findings from the 2015 American Values Survey* (Washington, D.C., 2015), 4.

36. *Newest New Yorkers* (2013 ed.), 174; "Asylum Fraud in Chinatown: An Industry of Lies," *Times*, February 22, 2014; "America's Melting Pot Spreads to the 'Burbs," *Christian Science Monitor*, August 10, 1999; "Newer Immigrants Taking Over Diners," *Times*, March 16, 2008; "A New York Staple for Decades, Korean Grocers Are Dwindling," *Times*, June 2, 2011; Laura Vanderkam, "Where Did the Korean Greengrocers Go?" *City Journal* (Winter 2011); "Immigrants Rally in City, Seeking Rights," *Times*, October 5, 2003; "Korean New Yorkers Hope for Council Seat in Queens, Their First," *Times*, May 6, 2009; "A New Comptroller, Cheered by Asian-Americans Declaring a New Era," *Times*, January 1, 2010; "With an Influx of Newcomers, Little Chinatowns Dot a Changing Brooklyn," *Times*, April 15, 2015.

37. Philip Kasinitz, John Mollenkoph, Mary Waters, and Jennifer Holdaway, *Inheriting the City: The Children of Immigrants Come of Age* (New York, 2008), 1–24, 342–70; "Closer Scrutiny as Chinese Seek to Give Birth in the United States," *Times*, August 25, 2015; "Immigrants' Children Find Better Lives, Study Shows," *Times*, May 18, 2008.

38. Joseph Smith, "Little Old New York," *Life* 53 (March 4, 1909): 298.

SELECT BIBLIOGRAPHY

This bibliography represents only a tiny fraction of the scholarship consulted in the writing of this book. Those who seek a lengthier list of articles and book on immigrants in New York, particularly more work by social scientists covering the period since 1980, can consult my unabridged bibliography at https://dataverse.harvard.edu/dataverse/anbinder.

Abdelhady, Dalia. *The Lebanese Diaspora: The Arab Immigrant Experience in Montreal, New York, and Paris*. New York, 2011.

Abreu, Christina. *Rhythms of Race: Cuban Musicians and the Making of Latino New York City and Miami, 1940–1960*. Chapel Hill, 2015.

Ahmed, Yasmine. *The New York Egyptians: Voyages and Dreams*. New York, 2010.

Almeida, Linda Dowling. *Irish Immigrants in New York City, 1945–1995*. Bloomington, 2001.

Anbinder, Tyler. *Five Points: The Nineteenth-Century New York City Neighborhood That Invented Tap Dance, Stole Elections, and Became the World's Most Notorious Slum*. New York, 2001.

————. "Moving Beyond 'Rags to Riches': New York's Irish Famine Immigrants and Their Surprising Savings Accounts." *Journal of American History* 99 (2012): 741–70.

Baily, Samuel. *Immigrants in the Land of Promise: Italians in Buenos Aires and New York City, 1870–1914*. Ithaca, 1999.

Bald, Vivek. *Bengali Harlem and the Lost Histories of South Asian America*. Cambridge, Mass., 2012.

Basinski, Sean. "Hot Dogs, Hipsters, and Xenophobia: Immigrant Street Food Vendors in New York." *Social Research* 81 (2014): 397–408.

Bayor, Ronald. *Neighbors in Conflict: The Irish, Germans, Jews, and Italians of New York City, 1929–1941*. Baltimore, 1978.

Bayor, Ronald, and Timothy Meagher, eds. *The New York Irish*. Baltimore, 1996.

Benson, Kathleen, and Philip Kayal, eds. *A Community of Many Worlds: Arab Americans in New York City*. New York, 2002.

Binder, Frederick, and David Reimers. *All the Nations Under Heaven: An Ethnic and Racial History of New York City*. New York, 1995.

Biney, Moses. *From Africa to America: Religion and Adaptation Among Ghanaian Immigrants in New York.* New York, 2011.

Bishop, Jacqueline. *My Mother Who Is Me: Life Stories from Jamaican Women in New York.* Trenton, 2006.

Bogen, Elizabeth. *Immigration in New York.* New York, 1987.

Bonner, Arthur. *Alas! What Brought Thee Hither? The Chinese in New York, 1800–1950.* Cranbury, N.J., 1997.

Brotherton, David, and Luis Barrios. *Banished to the Homeland: Dominican Deportees and Their Stories of Exile.* New York, 2011.

Brown, Mary Elizabeth. *Churches, Communities, and Children: Italian Immigrants in the Archdiocese of New York, 1880–1945.* New York, 1995.

Brown, Tammy. *City of Islands: Caribbean Intellectuals in New York.* Jackson, Miss., 2015.

Brumberg, Stephen. *Going to America, Going to School: The Jewish Immigrant Public School Encounter in Turn-of-the-Century New York City.* New York, 1986.

Buff, Rachel. *Immigration and the Political Economy of Home: West Indian Brooklyn and American Indian Minneapolis.* Berkeley, 2001.

Buk-Swienty, Tom. *The Other Half: The Life of Jacob Riis and the World of Immigrant America.* Translated by Annette Buk-Swienty. New York, 2008.

Cannato, Vincent. *American Passage: The History of Ellis Island.* New York, 2009.

Chen, Hsiang-Shui. *Chinatown No More: Taiwan Immigrants in Contemporary New York.* Ithaca, 1992.

Chen, Michelle. "A Cultural Crossroads at the 'Bloody Angle': The Chinatown Tongs and the Development of New York City's Chinese American Community." *Journal of Urban History* 40 (2014): 357–79.

Chin, Ko-Lin. *Chinatown Gangs: Extortion, Enterprise, and Ethnicity.* New York, 2000.

———. *Smuggled Chinese: Clandestine Immigration to the United States.* Philadelphia, 1999.

Chin, Margaret. *Sewing Women: Immigrants and the New York City Garment Industry.* New York, 2005.

Cinotto, Simone. *The Italian American Table: Food, Family, and Community in New York City.* Urbana, 2013.

Cohen, Miriam. *Workshop to Office: Two Generations of Italian Women in New York City, 1900–1950.* Ithaca, 1993.

Corcoran, Mary. *Irish Illegals: Transients Between Two Societies.* Westport, Conn., 1993.

Cordero-Guzmán, Hector, Robert Smith, and Ramón Grosfoguel, eds. *Migration, Transnationalization, and Race in a Changing New York.* Philadelphia, 2001.

DeSena, Judith, and Timothy Shortell, eds. *The World in Brooklyn: Gentrification, Immigration, and Ethnic Politics in a Global City.* Lanham, Md., 2012.

Diner, Hasia. *Hungering for America: Italian, Irish, and Jewish Foodways in the Age of Migration.* Cambridge, Mass., 2003.

———. *Lower East Side Memories: A Place in America.* Princeton, 2000.

———, ed. *Remembering the Lower East Side: American Jewish Reflections.* Bloomington, 2000.

Dolan, Jay. *The Immigrant Church: New York's Irish and German Catholics, 1815–1865.* Baltimore, 1975.

Dolkart, Andrew. *Biography of a Tenement House in New York City: An Architectural History of 97 Orchard Street.* 2nd ed. Chicago, 2012.

Duany, Jorge. *Quisqueya on the Hudson: The Transnational Identity of Dominicans in Washington Heights.* New York, 1994.

Ernst, Robert. *Immigrant Life in New York City, 1825–1860.* New York, 1948.

Ewen, Elizabeth. *Immigrant Women in the Land of Dollars: Life and Culture on the Lower East Side, 1890–1925.* New York, 1985.

Fisher, Maxine. *The Indians of New York City: A Study of Immigrants from India.* Columbia, Mo., 1980.

Fitzgerald, Maureen. *Habits of Compassion: Irish Catholic Nuns and the Origins of New York's Welfare System, 1830–1920.* Urbana, 2006.

Foner, Nancy. *From Ellis Island to JFK: New York's Two Great Waves of Immigration.* New Haven, 2000.

———, ed. *Islands in the City: West Indian Migration to New York.* Berkeley, 2001.

———, ed. *New Immigrants in New York.* New York, 1987; rev. ed., 2001.

———, ed. *One Out of Three: Immigrant New York in the Twenty-First Century.* New York, 2013.

Friedman-Kasaba, Kathie. *Memories of Migration: Gender, Ethnicity, and Work in the Lives of Jewish and Italian Women in New York, 1870–1924.* Albany, 1996.

Gabaccia, Donna. *From Sicily to Elizabeth Street: Housing and Social Change Among Italian Immigrants, 1880–1930.* Albany, 1984.

Gafic, Zijah. *Muslims of New York.* Sarajevo, 2008.

Gálvez, Alyshia. *Guadalupe in New York: Devotion and the Struggle for Citizenship Rights Among Mexican Immigrants.* New York, 2010.

Garland, Libby. *After They Closed the Gates: Jewish Illegal Immigration to the United States, 1921–1965.* Chicago, 2014.

Gay, Ruth. *Unfinished People: Eastern European Jews Encounter America.* New York, 1996.

Glazer, Nathan, and Daniel Patrick Moynihan. *Beyond the Melting Pot: The Negroes, Puerto Ricans, Jews, Italians, and Irish of New York City.* Cambridge, Mass., 1963.

Glenn, Susan. *Daughters of the Shtetl: Life and Labor in the Immigrant Generation.* Ithaca, 1990.

Golway, Terry. *Machine Made: Tammany Hall and the Creation of Modern American Politics.* New York, 2014.

Goodfriend, Joyce. *Before the Melting Pot: Society and Culture in Colonial New York City, 1664–1730.* Princeton, 1992.

———. "Foreigners in a Dutch Colonial City." *New York History* 90 (2009): 241–69.

Gordon, Michael. *The Orange Riots: Irish Political Violence in New York City, 1870 and 1871.* Ithaca, 1993.

Goyens, Tom. *Beer and Revolution: The German Anarchist Movement in New York City, 1880–1914.* Urbana, 2007.

Guglielmo, Jennifer. *Living the Revolution: Italian Women's Resistance and Radicalism in New York City, 1880–1945.* Chapel Hill, 2010.

Haslip-Viera, Gabriel, et al., eds. *Boricuas in Gotham: Puerto Ricans in the Making of Modern New York City.* Princeton, 2004.

Haslip-Viera, Gabriel, and Sherrie Baver. *Latinos in New York: Communities in Transition.* Notre Dame, 1996.

Hauser, Brooke. *The New Kids: Big Dreams and Brave Journeys at a High School for Immigrant Teens.* New York, 2011.

Henderson, Thomas. *Tammany Hall and the New Immigrants: The Progressive Years.* New York, 1976.

Hoffnung-Garskof, Jesse. *A Tale of Two Cities: Santo Domingo and New York After 1950.* Princeton, 2008.

Hosler, Akkiko. *Japanese Immigrant Entrepreneurs in New York City: A New Wave of Ethnic Business.* New York, 1998.

Howe, Irving. *World of Our Fathers.* New York, 1976.

Hum, Tarry. *Making a Global Immigrant Neighborhood: Brooklyn's Sunset Park.* Philadelphia, 2014.

Jacobs, Jaap. *The Colony of New Netherland: A Dutch Settlement in Seventeenth-Century America.* Ithaca, 2009.

Jacobs, Linda. *Strangers in the West: The Syrian Colony of New York City, 1880–1900.* New York, 2015.

Jones-Correa, Michael. *Between Two Nations: The Political Predicament of Latinos in New York City.* Ithaca, 1998.

Karpathakis, Anna. "Home Society Politics and Immigrant Political Incorporation: The Case of Greek Immigrants in New York City." *International Migration Review* 33 (1999): 55–78.

————. "'Whose Church Is It Anyway?' Greek Immigrants of Astoria, New York, and Their Church." *Journal of the Hellenic Diaspora* 20 (1994): 97–122.

Kasinitz, Philip. *Caribbean New York: Black Immigrants and the Politics of Race.* Ithaca, 1992.

Katz, Daniel. *All Together Different: Yiddish Socialists, Garment Workers, and the Labor Roots of Multiculturalism.* New York, 2011.

Keefe, Patrick Radden. *The Snakehead: An Epic Tale of the Chinatown Underworld and the American Dream.* New York, 2009.

Kelly, Mary. *The Shamrock and the Lily: The New York Irish and the Creation of a Transatlantic Identity, 1845–1921.* New York, 2005.

Kessner, Thomas. *The Golden Door: Italian and Jewish Mobility in New York City, 1880–1915.* New York, 1977.

Khandelwal, Madhulika. *Becoming American, Being Indian: An Immigrant Community in New York City.* Ithaca, 2002.

Kim, Claire. *Bitter Fruit: The Politics of Black-Korean Conflict in New York City.* New Haven, 2000.

Kim, Illsoo. *New Urban Immigrants: The Korean Community in New York.* Princeton, 1981.

Kinkead, Gwen. *Chinatown: A Portrait of a Closed Society.* New York, 1992.

Kosak, Hadassa. *Cultures of Opposition: Jewish Immigrant Workers, New York City, 1881–1905.* Albany, 2000.

Krohn-Hansen, Christian. *Making New York Dominican: Small Business, Politics, and Everyday Life.* Philadelphia, 2013.

Kwong, Peter. *Chinatown, New York: Labor and Politics, 1930–1950.* New York, 1979; rev. ed., 2001.

_____. *Forbidden Workers: Illegal Chinese Immigrants and American Labor.* New York, 1997.

_____. *The New Chinatown.* New York, 1987.

Laguerre, Michel. *American Odyssey: Haitians in New York City.* Ithaca, 1984.

_____. *Ethnicity as Dependence: The Haitian Community in New York City.* New York, 1978.

Landesman, Alter. *Brownsville: The Birth, Development, and Passing of a Jewish Community in New York.* New York, 1971.

Laó-Montes, Agustín, and Arlene Dávila, eds. *Mambo Montage: The Latinization of New York.* New York, 2001.

Lee, Sonia. *Building a Latino Civil Rights Movement: Puerto Ricans, African Americans, and the Pursuit of Racial Justice in New York City.* Chapel Hill, 2014.

Lemekh, Halyna. *Ukrainian Immigrants in New York: Collision of Two Worlds.* El Paso, 2010.

Lessinger, Johanna. *From the Ganges to the Hudson: Indian Immigrants in New York City.* Boston, 1995.

Lin, Jan. *Reconstructing Chinatown: Ethnic Enclaves and Global Change.* Minneapolis, 1998.

Lowenstein, Steven. *Frankfurt on the Hudson: The German-Jewish Community of Washington Heights, 1933–1983.* Detroit, 1989.

Lui, Mary. *The Chinatown Trunk Mystery: Murder, Miscegenation, and Other Dangerous Encounters in Turn-of-the-Century New York City.* Princeton, 2005.

Maffi, Mario. *Gateway to the Promised Land: Ethnic Cultures on New York's Lower East Side.* New York, 1995.

Maira, Sunaina. *Desis in the House: Indian American Youth Culture in New York City.* Philadelphia, 2002.

Margolis, Maxine. *An Invisible Minority: Brazilians in New York City.* Boston, 1998.

_____. *Little Brazil: An Ethnography of Brazilian Immigrants in New York City.* Princeton, 1994.

Markel, Howard. *Quarantine! East European Jewish Immigrants and the New York City Epidemics of 1892.* Baltimore, 1997.

Markowitz, Fran. *A Community in Spite of Itself: Soviet Jewish Émigrés in New York City.* Washington, D.C., 1993.

McCauley, Bernadette. *Who Shall Take Care of Our Sick?: Roman Catholic Sisters and the Development of Catholic Hospitals in New York City.* Baltimore, 2005.

Michels, Tony. *A Fire in Their Hearts: Yiddish Socialists in New York.* Cambridge, Mass., 2005.

Miles, Ann. *From Cuenca to Queens: An Anthropological Story of Transnational Migration.* Austin, 2004.

Mills, C. Wright, Rose Kahn Goldsen, and Clarence Senior. *The Puerto Rican Journey: New York's Newest Migrants.* New York, 1950.

Min, Pyong. *Changes and Conflicts: Korean Immigrant Families in New York.* Boston, 1998.

_____. *Ethnic Solidarity for Economic Survival: Korean Greengrocers in New York City.* New York, 2008.

Mohammed-Arif, Aminah. *Salaam America: South Asian Muslims in New York.* New York, 2002.

Moses, Paul. *An Unlikely Union: The Love-Hate Story of New York's Irish and Italians.* New York, 2015.

Nadel, Stanley. *Little Germany: Ethnicity, Religion, and Class in New York City: 1845–80.* Urbana, 1990.

New York City Department of City Planning. *The Newest New Yorkers.* New York, 1997, 1999, 2004, 2013.

Orsi, Robert. *The Madonna of 115th Street: Faith and Community in Italian Harlem, 1880–1950.* New Haven, 1985.

Papademetriou, Demetrios, and Nicholas DiMarzio. *Undocumented Aliens in the New York Metropolitan Area.* New York, 1986.

Park, Kyeyoung. *The Korean American Dream: Immigrants and Small Business in New York City.* Ithaca, 1997.

Pencak, William, Selma Berrol, and Randall M. Miller. *Immigration to New York.* Philadelphia, 1991.

Poros, Maritsa. *Modern Migrations: Gujarati Indian Networks in New York and London.* Stanford, 2010.

Pozzetta, George. "The Mulberry District of New York City: The Years Before World War One." In *Little Italies in North America,* edited by Robert Harney and J. Vincenza Scarpaci, 7–40. Toronto, 1981.

Pribilsky, Jason. *La Chulla Vida: Gender, Migration, and the Family in Andean Ecuador and New York City.* Syracuse, 2007.

Qutub, Ishaq. *The Immigrant Arab Community in New York City.* East Lansing, Mich., 1962.

Reid, Ira. *The Negro Immigrant: His Background, Characteristics, and Social Adjustment, 1899–1937.* New York, 1939.

Ricourt, Milagros. *Dominicans in New York City: Power from the Margins.* New York, 2002.

Ricourt, Milagros, and Ruby Danta. *Hispanas de Queens: Latino Panethnicity in a New York City Neighborhood.* Ithaca, 2003.

Rischin, Moses. *The Promised City: New York's Jews, 1870–1914.* Cambridge, Mass., 1962.

Rock, Howard, Annie Polland, Daniel Soyer, and Jeffrey Gurock. *City of Promises: A History of the Jews of New York.* 3 vols. General ed., Deborah Dash Moore. New York, 2012.

Rosenbaum, Emily, and Samantha Friedman. *The Housing Divide: How Generations of Immigrants Fare in New York's Housing Market.* New York, 2007.

Sánchez Korrol, Virginia. *From Colonia to Community: The History of the Puerto Ricans in New York City, 1917–1948.* Berkeley, 1994.

Sawada, Mitziko. *Tokyo Life, New York Dreams: Urban Japanese Visions of America, 1890–1924.* Berkeley, 1996.

Seligman, Scott. *The First Chinese American: The Remarkable Life of Wong Chin Foo.* Hong Kong, 2013.

Shapiro, Edward. *Crown Heights: Blacks, Jews, and the 1991 Brooklyn Riot.* Waltham, Mass., 2006.

Shokeid, Moshe. *Children of Circumstances: Israeli Emigrants in New York.* Ithaca, 1988.

Shorto, Russell. *The Island at the Center of the World: The Epic Story of Dutch Manhattan, the Forgotten Colony That Shaped America.* New York, 2004.

Smith, Robert. *Mexican New York: Transnational Lives of New Immigrants.* Berkeley, 2006.

Soyer, Daniel, ed. *A Coat of Many Colors: Immigration, Globalization, and Reform in New York City's Garment Industry.* New York, 2005.

Staub, Shalom. *Yemenis in New York City: The Folklore of Ethnicity.* Philadelphia, 1989.

Stein, Leon. *The Triangle Fire.* New York, 1962.

Stoller, Paul. *Money Has No Smell: The Africanization of New York City.* Chicago, 2002.

Tang, Eric. *Unsettled: Cambodian Refugees in the New York City Hyperghetto.* Philadelphia, 2015.

Tchen, John. *New York Before Chinatown: Orientalism and the Shaping of American Culture, 1776–1882.* Baltimore, 1999.

Thomas, Lorrin. *Puerto Rican Citizen: History and Political Identity in Twentieth-Century New York City.* Chicago, 2010.

Tomasi, Silvano. *Piety and Power: The Role of the Italian Parishes in the New York Metropolitan Area, 1880–1930.* New York, 1975.

Tuchman, Gaye, and Harry Gene Levine. "New York Jews and Chinese Food: The Social Construction of an Ethnic Pattern." *Journal of Contemporary Ethnography* 22 (1993): 382–407.

van der Zee, Henri, and Barbara van der Zee. *A Sweet and Alien Land: The Story of Dutch New York.* New York, 1978.

Viladrich, Anahí. *More Than Two to Tango: Argentine Tango Immigrants in New York City.* Tucson, 2013.

Waldinger, Roger. *Still the Promised City? African-Americans and New Immigrants in Postindustrial New York.* Cambridge, Mass., 1996.

_____. *Through the Eye of the Needle: Immigrants and Enterprise in New York's Garment Trades.* New York, 1986.

Waters, Mary. *Black Identities: West Indian Immigrant Dreams and American Realities.* New York, 1999.

Watkins-Owens, Irma. *Blood Relations: Caribbean Immigrants and the Harlem Community, 1900–1930.* Bloomington, 1996.

Weinberg, Sydney. *World of Our Mothers: The Lives of Jewish Immigrant Women.* Chapel Hill, 1988.

Winnick, Louis. *New People in Old Neighborhoods: The Role of New Immigrants in Rejuvenating New York's Communities.* New York, 1990.

Yee, Shirley. *An Immigrant Neighborhood: Interethnic and Interracial Encounters in New York Before 1930.* Philadelphia, 2011.

Yochelson, Bonnie, and Daniel Czitrom. *Rediscovering Jacob Riis: Exposure Journalism and Photography in Turn-of-the-Century New York.* New York, 2007.

Zhao, Linda. *Financing Illegal Migration: Chinese Underground Banks and Human Smuggling in New York City.* New York, 2013.

Zhou, Min. *Chinatown: The Socioeconomic Potential of an Urban Enclave.* Philadelphia, 1992.

Ziegelman, Jane. *97 Orchard: An Edible History of Five Immigrant Families in One New York Tenement.* New York, 2010.

ILLUSTRATION CREDITS

Page xii: SS *Nevada,* photo courtesy of the Mormon Migration website, BYU Harold B. Lee Library.

Page xvi: Original Ellis Island immigration station, collection of Maggie Blanck.

Page xviii: Statue of Annie Moore in Cobh, Ireland. © Olaf Protze, Lightrocket/Getty Images. Sculpture by Jeanne Rynhart.

Page xxi: Annie Moore, courtesy of her descendants Pat Somerstein and Michael Shulman.

Page xxiii: Photo of young immigrants (possibly Annie Moore and her brothers), from the collection of Colonel John B. Weber, Bob Hope Memorial Research Library, Ellis Island, National Museum of Immigration.

Page 12: Image of a pinnace from Nicolaes Witsen, *Aeloude en Hedendaegsche Scheeps-bouw en Bestier* (Amsterdam, 1671), digital image courtesy of the Getty's Open Content Program.

Page 15: New Amsterdam, ca. 1660 (map), Chris Robinson.

Page 26: Detail from Nicolaes Visscher, *Novi Belgii Novaeque Angliae,* Geography and Map Division, Library of Congress (http://hdl.loc.gov/loc.gmd/g3715.ct000001).

Page 33: Unidentified artist, *Peter Stuyvesant,* Collection of the New-York Historical Society, Gift of Robert Van Rensselaer Stuyvesant (1909.2).

Page 37: *The City of New Orange,* 1673, Miriam and Ira D. Wallach Division of Art, Prints and Photographs, Print Collection, The New York Public Library Digital Collections (1650610).

Page 48: *A South Prospect of Ye Flourishing City of New York in the Province of New York in America,* Miriam and Ira D. Wallach Division of Art, Prints and Photographs, Print Collection, The New York Public Library, Astor, Lenox and Tilden Foundations (ps_prn_cd40_576).

Page 57: *A Plan of the City of New York from an Actual Survey,* Miriam and Ira D. Wallach Division of Art, Prints and Photographs, The New York Public Library Digital Collections (54912).

Page 59: The Relationship Between the Expansion of Manhattan Island and the Flooding Resulting from Hurricane Sandy, 2012 (map), Chris Robinson.

Page 70 *Left:* Wollaston, John (ca. 1710–ca. 1767). *Cadwallader Colden,* 1749–52. Oil on canvas, 30 x 25 in. (76.2 x 63.5 cm). Bequest of Grace Wilkes, 1922 (22.45.6). © The Metropolitan Museum of Art/ Art Resource, NY. *Right:* Wollaston, John (ca. 1710–ca. 1767). *Mrs. Cadwallader Colden,* 1749–52. Oil on canvas, 30 x 25 in. (76.2 x 63.5 cm). Bequest of Grace Wilkes, 1922 (22.45.7). © The Metropolitan Museum of Art/Art Resource, NY.

Page 72: BELUM.U23, *Captain Waddell Cunningham,* 1730–97 (c. 1786), Robert Home 1752–1834. © National Museums Northern Ireland, Collection Ulster Museum.

Page 81: John Ramage, *Alexander McDougall,* Collection of the New-York Historical Society, Purchase, the Louis Durr Fund (1953.318).

Page 96: *Representation du Feu Terrible a Nouvelle Yorck,* Miriam and Ira D. Wallach Division of Art, Prints and Photographs, Print Collection, The New York Public Library Digital Collections (psnypl_pm_972).

Page 100: Charles Willson Peale, *Alexander Hamilton,* Art Properties, Avery Architecture & Fine Arts Library, Columbia University.

Page 102: Judge William Alexander Duer, Prints and Photographs Division, Library of Congress (LC-USZ62-109849).

Page 103: New York Under British Occupation, 1776–1783 (map), Chris Robinson.

Page 105: Robertson, Archibald (1765–1835). Attributed to Archibald Robertson, *Collect Pond, New York City,* 1798. Watercolor and black chalk on off-white laid paper, 17-3/4 x 23-1/16 in. (45.1 x 58.7 cm). The Edward W. C. Arnold Collection of New York Prints, Maps, and Pictures, Bequest of Edward W. C. Arnold, 1954 (54.90.168). Photo by Geoffrey Clements. © The Metropolitan Museum of Art/Art Resource, NY.

Page 108: John Wesley Jarvis, *John Jacob Astor,* c. 1825, National Portrait Gallery, Smithsonian Institution, Gift of Susan Mary Alsop/Art Resource, NY.

Page 114: Thomas Addis Emmet, engraving after a portrait by Louis François Aubry, in Richard Mad-den, *The United Irishmen: Their Lives and Times,* 2 vols. (London, 1843), 2: opp. p. 126, collection of the author.

Page 119: Five Points, Collection of the New-York Historical Society (33648).

Page 121: George Catlin, *Five Points,* 1827, oil on canvas, private collection.

Page 125: New York's Largest Immigrant Enclaves, 1845 (map), Chris Robinson.

Page 126: *Bird's Eye View of New-York & Brooklyn: Drawn from Nature & on Stone by J. Bachman[n]* (New York, 1851), Prints and Photographs Division, Library of Congress (LC-DIG-pga-03106).

Page 130: "Boy and Girl at Cahera," *Illustrated London News* (February 20, 1847): 116, Hulton Archive/ Getty Images.

Page 134: "The Departure," *Illustrated London News* (July 6, 1850): 20, collection of the author.

Page 136: Cutaway view of an immigrant sailing ship, *Die Gartenlaube* 38 (1854): 450–51, The Technoseum, Mannheim, Germany.

Page 138: "Emigration Vessel — Between Decks," *Illustrated London News* (May 10, 1851): 387, collection of the author.

Page 139: "The Steerage of the Steamer 'Waesland' Engulfed in a Tremendous Wave," *Frank Leslie's Illustrated Newspaper* (December 24, 1881), vol. LIII, no. 1,369: 273. University of Washington Libraries, Special Collections (UW37266).

Page 143: "Attack on the Quarantine Establishment," *Harper's Weekly* (September 11, 1858): 581, courtesy of HarpWeek/TextBASE, Inc.

Page 145: "Runners of the Olden Time," *Harper's Weekly* (June 26, 1858): 405, courtesy of HarpWeek/Text-BASE, Inc.

Page 146: "Medical Inspection at Castle Garden," *Frank Leslie's Illustrated Newspaper* (January 20, 1866): 280–81, from the Lincoln Financial Foundation Collection, courtesy of the Indiana State Museum and Allen County Public Library.

Page 147: "Emigrant Depot, Castle Garden," *Harper's Weekly* (September 2, 1865): 552–53, courtesy of HarpWeek/TextBASE, Inc.

Page 150: The Nativity of Adult New Yorkers by Ward, 1860 (map), Chris Robinson.

Page 152: Gustavus Pach, *View in the Five Points,* 1875, Miriam and Ira D. Wallach Division of Art, Prints and Photographs, Photography Collection, The New York Public Library Digital Collections (G91F179_046F).

Page 153: Floor Plans of Typical New York Tenement Buildings, Chris Robinson.

Page 155: "New York City: The Recent Heated Term," *Frank Leslie's Illustrated Newspaper* (August 12, 1883): 392–93, collection of the author.

Page 157: Gotham Court, *Frank Leslie's Illustrated Newspaper* (July 1, 1865): 222–23, from the Lincoln Financial Foundation Collection, courtesy of the Indiana State Museum and Allen County Public Library.

Page 163: "The Voting-Place, No. 488 Pearl Street," *Harper's Weekly* (November 13, 1858): 724, courtesy of HarpWeek/TextBASE, Inc.

Page 166: New York street with signs advertising servants, Brown Brothers.

Page 175: The Principal Sources of New York's Mid-Nineteenth-Century German Immigrants (map), Chris Robinson.

Page 176: New York's Kleindeutschland, 1860 (map), Chris Robinson.

Page 183: William Steinway, courtesy of Henry Z. Steinway Archive.

Page 191: "Interior of a Polling-Booth," *Frank Leslie's Illustrated Newspaper* (November 17, 1860): 406–7, from the Lincoln Financial Foundation Collection, courtesy of the Indiana State Museum and Allen County Public Library.

Page 203: "View from the 'Dead Rabbit' Barricade," *Frank Leslie's Illustrated Newspaper* (July 18, 1857): 108, University of Washington Libraries. Photo courtesy of the author.

Page 206: "Lincoln Rally," *Harper's Weekly* (October 13, 1860): 648–49, courtesy of HarpWeek/TextBASE, Inc.

Page 214: "Officers of the 69th New York State Militia," Prints and Photographs Division, Library of Congress (LC-DIG-ppmsca-34210).

Page 216: Julius Stahel, Prints and Photographs Division, Library of Congress (LC-DIG-cwpb-05218).

Page 217: "Garibaldi Guard!," Art Resource, NY.

Page 219: "Gallant Charge of the Sixty-Ninth Regiment," *Harper's Weekly* (August 10, 1861): 508, courtesy of HarpWeek/TextBASE, Inc.

Page 226: Robert Knox Sneden, *Malvern Hill*, Virginia Historical Society.

Page 232: "Wounded Soldiers in Hospital," Mathew Brady Photographs of Civil War–Era Personalities and Scenes, Record Group 111, National Archives (524777).

Page 244: "The Riots in New York: Destruction of the Coloured Orphan Asylum," *Illustrated London News* (August 15, 1863): 168, Art and Picture Collection, The New York Public Library Digital Collections (812649).

Page 245: "The Riots in New York: The Mob Lynching a Negro in Clarkson-Street," *Illustrated London News* (August 8, 1863): 129, The New York Public Library Digital Collections (809576).

Page 247: "The Draft Riots in New York: The Battle in Second Avenue," Art and Picture Collection, The New York Public Library Digital Collections (809554).

Page 251: "The Riots in New York: Conflict Between the Military and the Rioters in First Avenue," *Illustrated London News* (Aug. 15, 1863): 168, Art and Picture Collection, The New York Public Library Digital Collections (809571).

Page 256: "Enlisting Irish and German Emigrants on the Battery at New York," *Illustrated London News* (September 17, 1864): 288, from the Lincoln Financial Foundation Collection, courtesy of the Indiana State Museum and Allen County Public Library.

Page 258: Robert Knox Sneden, *Andersonville*, Virginia Historical Society.

Page 265: William Tweed, Prints and Photographs Division, Library of Congress (LC-USZ62-22467).

Page 267: Judge John McCunn, Prints and Photographs Division, Library of Congress (LC-DIG-cw-pbh-02239).

Page 268: Thomas Nast, "That's What's the Matter," *Harper's Weekly* (October 7, 1871): 944, courtesy of HarpWeek/TextBASE, Inc.

Page 269: "The Naturalization of Foreigners in New York City," *Frank Leslie's Illustrated Newspaper* (November 13, 1869): 141, Prints and Photographs Division, Library of Congress (LC-USZ62-121666).

Page 272: Thomas Nast's depiction of his first meeting with Frank Leslie, in Albert Bigelow Paine, *Thomas Nast: His Period and His Pictures* (New York: The Macmillan Company, 1904), 18, courtesy of FCIT/ClipArt ETC (http://etc.usf.edu/clipart/67300/67372/67372_leslie_f.htm).

Page 273: Thomas Nast, "Christmas Eve," *Harper's Weekly* (January 3, 1863): 8–9, courtesy of HarpWeek/TextBASE, Inc.

Page 274: Thomas Nast, "This Is a White Man's Government," *Harper's Weekly* (September 5, 1868): 568, courtesy of HarpWeek/TextBASE, Inc.

Page 280: "New York City—The Orange Riot of July 12th—View on Eighth Avenue Looking from Twenty-Fifth Street Toward the Grand Opera House," *Frank Leslie's Illustrated Newspaper* (July 29, 1871): 328–29, Prints and Photographs Division, Library of Congress (LC-USZ62-120337).

Page 283 *Top left:* Thomas Nast, "Under the Thumb," *Harper's Weekly* (June 10, 1871): 536, courtesy of HarpWeek/TextBASE, Inc. *Top right:* Thomas Nast, "The Brains," *Harper's Weekly* (October 21, 1871): 992, courtesy of HarpWeek/TextBASE, Inc. *Bottom left:* Thomas Nast, "The Greek Slave," *Harper's Weekly* (April 16, 1870): 248, courtesy of HarpWeek/TextBASE, Inc. *Bottom right:* Thomas Nast, "The Unconditional Surrender, July 11th," *Harper's Weekly* (July 29, 1871): 696–97, courtesy of HarpWeek/TextBASE, Inc.

Page 286: "A House Divided Against Itself Shall Not Stand," *Harper's Weekly* (October 14, 1871): 963, courtesy of HarpWeek/TextBASE, Inc.

Page 288: Thomas Nast, "The American River Ganges," *Harper's Weekly* (September 21, 1871): 916, courtesy of HarpWeek/TextBASE, Inc.

Page 290: "A Refutation of Darwinism," *Harper's Weekly* (October 13, 1883): 655, courtesy of HarpWeek/TextBASE, Inc.

Page 292: "McGrath," Prints and Photographs Division, Bain Collection, Library of Congress (LC-DIG-ggbain-09314).

Page 298: "Colossal Hand and Torch 'Liberty,'" Prints and Photographs Division, Library of Congress (LC-DIG-ppmsca-02957).

Page 301 *Left:* Emma Lazarus, Bettmann/Getty Images (515417238). *Right:* "Joseph Pulitzer at the Age of Thirty-Four," in Alleyne Ireland, *Joseph Pulitzer: Reminiscences of a Secretary* (New York, 1914), 42–43, State Historical Society of Missouri (SHS 008722).

Page 303: "New York — Welcome to the Land of Freedom," *Frank Leslie's Illustrated Newspaper* (July 2, 1887): 324–25, Prints and Photographs Division, Library of Congress (LC-USZ62-113735).

Page 305: "In einer polnischen Judenstadt," akg-images/Alamy (B5MT99).

Page 308: "Newly Arrived Jewish Exiles from Russia Leaving Castle Garden for the Emigrants' Quarters on Ward's Island," *Frank Leslie's Illustrated Newspaper* (March 4, 1882), vol. LIV, no. 1,380: 21, University of Washington Libraries, Special Collections (UW37268).

Page 311: "Grausam hingeschlachtete jüdische Kinder in Jekaterinoslaw," William A. Rosenthall Judaica Collection, Postcard Portfolio 18, cofc-war-postcard18-019. The College of Charleston Libraries.

Page 314: Anbinder family photo, courtesy of the author.

Page 318: Italians going to the Emigrant Assistance Office in Chiasso, Switzerland, courtesy of the Fondazione Paolo Cresci per la Storia dell'Emigrazione Italiana, Lucca, Italy.

Page 334: "Immigrant Landing Station, N.Y.," Prints and Photographs Division, Library of Congress (LC-USZ62-37784).

Page 338: "U.S. Inspectors Examining Eyes of Immigrants, Ellis Island," Prints and Photographs Division, Library of Congress (LC-USZ62-7386).

Page 343: Oscar Straus, courtesy of Straus Historical Society, Inc., Smithtown, NY.

Page 347: Lewis Hine, "Climbing into the Promised Land, Ellis Island, 1908," gelatin silver photograph, 13-5/16 x 11 in. (33.8 x 27.9 cm), Brooklyn Museum, Gift of Walter and Naomi Rosenblum (84.237.1).

Page 348: "The Pens at Ellis Island, Registry Room," Miriam and Ira D. Wallach Division of Art, Prints and Photographs, Photography Collection, The New York Public Library Digital Collections (416750).

Page 349: "Immigrant Inspection at Ellis Island," Ellis Island historic photographs photo gallery, Ellis Island, Part of Statue of Liberty National Monument (https://www.nps.gov/media/photo/view .htm?id=BCD9B1E1-155D-451F-6751F04A0F5D2B58).

Page 355: Select Manhattan Immigrant Enclaves, 1900 (map), Chris Robinson.

Page 357: The Central and Southern Portions of the Lower East Side, 1910 (map), Chris Robinson.

Page 359: *Street Scenes, Hester Street, Jewish Quarter,* 1898, Byron Company Collection, Museum of the City of New York (93.1.1.15379).

Page 360: Jessie Tarbox Beals, "Family in Room in Tenement House," Museum of the City of New York (90.13.3.125).

Page 362: *Reports of the Industrial Commission on Immigration, Including Testimony, with Review and Digest, and Special Reports* (Washington, DC, 1901), 482–83, Harvard University.

Page 364 *Left:* Jacob Riis, "Bath-tub in Airshaft," Museum of the City of New York (90.13.4.49). *Right:* "Airshaft of a Dumbbell Tenement, New York City," Records of the Public Housing Administration, Record Group 196, National Archives (535468).

Page 367: Jacob Riis, "Knee-Pants at Forty-Five Cents a Dozen," Keystone/Hulton Archive/Getty Images (3331510).

Page 370: Lewis Hine, "Woman Carrying Heavy Bundle of Clothing to Be Finished at Home," Prints and Photographs Division, Library of Congress (LC-USZ62-04159).

Page 373: Lewis Hine, "Group of Sweatshop Workers," Prints and Photographs Division, Library of Congress (LC-DIG-nclc-04454).

Page 377: "Street Vendors, 1898, Hester St.," Museum of the City of New York (93.1.1.18132).

Page 384: Jacob Riis, "Lodgers in a Crowded Bayard Street Tenement — 'Five Cents a Spot,'" Hulton Archive/Getty Images (3238344).

Page 387 *Left:* "A Poet from the Slums," *Literary Digest* (April 8, 1922): 35, Robarts Library, University of Toronto. *Right:* "Pascal D'Angelo with a Pick on Railroad Tracks," *Literary Digest* 84 (March 7, 1925): 44, University of Washington Libraries, Special Collections (UW37267).

Page 392: Jacob Riis, "Bandit's Roost," Museum of the City of New York (90.13.4.104).

Page 393: Lewis Hine, "High Up on the Roof of a Rickety Tenement," Prints and Photographs Division, Library of Congress (LC-DIG-nclc-04304).

Page 395: "Little Italy, First Avenue," Prints and Photographs Division, Library of Congress (LC-DIG-ggbain-03087).

Page 397: Lewis Hine, "Group of Italian Street Laborers," Miriam and Ira D. Wallach Division of Art, Prints and Photographs, Photography Collection, The New York Public Library Digital Collections (464269).

Page 400: "Mulberry St.," Prints and Photographs Division, Library of Congress (LC-DIG-det-4a08193).

Page 403: Lewis Hine, "6 Cents a Gross," Prints and Photographs Division, Library of Congress (LC-DIG-nclc-04072).

Page 404: "Newsboys Selling *Atlantis*," *Atlantis Newspaper* PG128, Box Number 24, Record Number 1063, Historical Society of Pennsylvania (1063).

Page 413: Jacob and Elisabeth Riis, Maple Grove Cemetery Archives, Kew Gardens, NY.

Page 420: Lillian Wald, courtesy of Medical Center Archives of New York–Presbyterian/Weill Cornell.

Page 422: "A Visiting Nurse Climbing over the Roof of a Tenement," MPI/Archive Photos/Getty Images (3090426).

Page 429: Emma Goldman, International Institute of Social History, Amsterdam (BG A5/477).

Page 432: Garment workers on strike, Brown Brothers.

Page 436: Triangle fire, Kheel Center for Labor-Management Documentation & Archives, School of Industrial and Labor Relations, Cornell University (5780-087pb1f5c).

Page 437: Bodies of Triangle fire victims, Kheel Center for Labor-Management Documentation & Archives, School of Industrial and Labor Relations, Cornell University (5780-087pb1f5ap).

Page 438: Daisy Lopez Fitze, Kheel Center for Labor-Management Documentation and Archives, School of Industrial and Labor Relations, Cornell University (5780pb39f2of).

Page 450: "The Fool Pied Piper," *Puck*, June 2, 1909, Prints and Photographs Division, Library of Congress (LC-DIG-ppmsca-26380).

Page 453: "Chinese Day in the Fourth Liberty Loan Campaign," Unofficial Collection of World War I Photographs, Record Group 165, National Archives (533667).

Page 455: Damage caused by the sabotage at the Black Tom Island depot, Associated Press/AP Images.

Page 464: Wall Street bombing of 1920, *New York Daily News*/Getty Images (491368951).

Page 489: "Construction Workers, or Sandhogs, Working Nearly Seventy Feet below the East River, New York," Three Lions/Hulton Archive/Getty Images (3301808).

Page 498: Passengers on the deck of the *St. Louis*, Planet News Archive/Getty Images (138599712).

Page 520: Oscar de la Renta, *New York Times*, September 29, 1967, Arthur Brower/*The New York Times*/Redux Pictures.

Page 523: The Guangdong and Fujian Provinces of China (map), Chris Robinson.

Page 529: New York City Chinatown restaurant kitchen, 1980, photograph by Harvey Wang.

Page 530: New York City Chinatown garment factory, 1980, photograph by Harvey Wang.

Page 532: Chinese immigrant bunk room, *New York Times*, October 6, 1996, Fred R. Conrad/*The New York Times*/Redux Pictures.

Page 537: *Golden Venture* freighter, Charles A. Arrigo for *New York Daily News*. © Daily News, L.P. (New York). Used with permission.

Page 538: "SAVED," *New York Daily News* Archive/Getty Images (97295702).

Page 541: The Principal Sources of New York's Caribbean Immigrants (map), Chris Robinson.

Page 558: The Proportion of Immigrants in the Population of New York City's Neighborhoods, 2010 (map), Chris Robinson.

INDEX

Page numbers in *italics* indicate illustrations, maps, and tables.

Pope, Jesse, 374
Popular Science Monthly/anti-immigrant articles, 445–46, 448
population (New York)
  in 1700s, 39, 56
  in 1783, 106, 597n7
  in 1820/1830, 116
  in 1845, 106, 127, 186
  in 1855, 128, 186
  in 1860, 186–87
  in 1950/average age, 510
  in 2010/immigrant percentage, 556
  changes 1980–2000 and, 546–47, *547*
  comparison to Philadelphia/Boston, 115–16
  English (1600s), 38–39
  following World War II, 509–11
  growth (1783–1845), 106
  increases by groups (1960–1980), *516*
  Irish/German immigrants (late 1840s–early 1850s) and, 186
  nativity/adults by ward (1860), *150*
  See also ethnic enclaves/New York; immigrants/New York
Post, Langdon, 492
potato blight
  cause/effects, 127
  locations affected, 127
  See also Irish potato famine
Premero, Jan, 31–32
Prensa, La (newspaper), 487
Prime, Samuel, Reverend, 156
privateering description, 71–72
Progresso Italo-Americano, Il (newspaper), 470
Prohibition, 471
Protestantism
  King James Bible and, 190
  New York/Leisler's Rebellion and, 40–46
  school question/religion, 190–91, 192, 198, 287–89, *288*
public housing "First Houses," 491–92
Puck, 450
Puerto Rican immigrants
  airplanes use, 511
  bodegas, 483

conflicts with Jews, 483
conflicts with neighbors/discrimination, 483, 484–85
employment, 482–83
New York locations/Spanish Harlem, 483–84, 485
numbers following World War II, 511
political power, 490
population numbers, 481–82, 511
reasons for coming to New York, 482
World War II soldiers and, 507
Pulitzer, Joseph, xvi–xvii, 256–57, 301–2, *301*, 361
Pullman Railcar Company, 480
Puritans
  beliefs, 20, 21, 40
  discrimination/violence and, 30
  Massachusetts Bay Colony, 20–21
  New York City and, 40
pushcarts
  peddlers and, 376–77, *377*
  restrictions/bans on, 491

Quakers
  beliefs, 29–30
  Flushing Remonstrance/significance, 30
  New Amsterdam/discrimination and, 29–31
  Pennsylvania and, 58–59
  Puritans discrimination/violence against, 30
Queens and immigrants today, 561–62
Quinn, Eliza, 171

Rabi, Isidor, 506
Raets, Gerdruudt, 2
Ramos, Jorge, 560
Ravage, Marcus, 321, 368
Raymond, Henry, 284
Red Scare (1919–1920), 461–63
Redactor Espagnol, El (newspaper), 118
Reed, Alfred C.
  anti-immigrant views, 445–46
  inspection of immigrants, 336, 445
Reed, David, 467, 468
Reed-Johnson bill. *See* Natural Origins Act (1924)